LAWYERS AND THE LEGAL PROFESSION: CASES AND MATERIALS

Fourth Edition

LAWYERS AND THE LEGAL PROFESSION: CASES AND MATERIALS

Fourth Edition

Roy D. Simon
Howard Lichtenstein Distinguished Professor of Legal Ethics
Hofstra University School of Law

Carol A. Needham
Professor of Law
Saint Louis University School of Law

Burnele V. Powell
Miles and Ann Loadhold Professor of Law
University of South Carolina School of Law

Carolina Academic Press
Durham, North Carolina

Library of Congress Cataloging-in-Publication Data

Simon, Roy D.
Lawyers and the legal profession / Roy D. Simon, Carol A. Needham, Burnele V. Powell. --4th ed.
p. cm.
Includes bibliographical references and index.
ISBN 978-0-8205-6115-8 (hard cover)
1. Legal ethics--United States--Cases. 2. Practice of law--United States--Cases. I. Needham, Carol A. II. Powell, Burnele V. (Burnele Venable), 1947- III. Title.
KF306.S58 2008
340.023'73-dc22
2008034801

Carolina Academic Press, LLC
700 Kent Street
Durham, North Carolina 27701
Telephone (919) 489-7486
Fax (919) 493-5668
www.cap-press.com

Printed in the United States of America
2024 Printing

DEDICATION

This book is dedicated to the memory of my father:
Roy D. Simon
1910-1984
He taught ethics by example throughout his life, —R.D.S.

This book is dedicated to my husband Tom Timmermann
and our daughter Genevieve Emily Needham Timmermann, —C.A.N.

This book is dedicated to Professor James E. Jones, Jr., Professor of Law Emeritus
and Professor of Industrial Relations Emeritus at the University of Wisconsin,
whose ethic of candor has made honesty a necessity and rationality an obligation
for all around him, —B.V.P.

PREFACE TO THE FOURTH EDITION

Woody Allen once said that he had very bad interpersonal relationships with machines. Many law students seem to have bad interpersonal relationships with textbooks. We want to change that. We want this book to be easy to get along with, so we have employed several features to make this book user friendly. For example:

We give you the black letter law. Learning the law ought to be the easiest part of law school, so we start many chapters by telling you the law in plain English. For key topics like confidentiality, conflicts of interest, and communicating with adverse parties, we have created outlines that summarize the law as clearly and concisely as possible. For other topics, we have written short introductory essays about the law. This way, you can quickly grasp the basic concepts and be ready to spend class time discussing more sophisticated and more interesting issues. After all, you ought to spend most of your class time debating what the law *ought* to be, not what the law is.

We put you on the cutting edge. This book thrusts you into the middle of the debate over issues that have not been uniformly decided — the ones that lawyers and the legal profession are struggling with right now. Some of the chapters in this fourth edition are entirely new, including those on the unauthorized practice of law and multijurisdictional practice; every chapter has been revised and updated. We include some classic cases to provide historical perspective or to illustrate timeless concepts, but our main effort is to involve you in the debate over the issues that trouble lawyers today, and that will still be engaging lawyers when you begin practicing law in the next year or two.

We read the book with you. We wish we could sit next to you when you read this book so that we could tap you on the shoulder every so often and say, "Wait a second — try to form your own opinion of the issue before you read what the court says," or "Can what the court just said be right?" or "Stay awake — here comes the important part of the case." We can't do that in person, but we do the next best thing — we interrupt cases and articles with "Authors' Comments" that prod you to think out issues for yourself before you read on, or that highlight important parts of a case, or that summarize the relevant law before the court applies it. The key to being a good lawyer isn't just understanding what you read — most lawyers can do that pretty well. Rather, the key is being able to think out issues independently and creatively on your own. Our Authors' Comments will help you do that. Please read them carefully and give them some real thought.

We involve you as a participant, not just an observer. If this book were a video game, you could participate in the reading by clicking a mouse or using the game controller. For this book, your controller is your pen. We often ask you to pause and write down your thoughts about an issue before you read the rest of an opinion, or to circle "yes" or "no" in response to our questions, or to list a few arguments of your own. We give you space to do that right in the book so you can have your answers in front of you during class discussion. You also have a chance to choose options for subjects such as mandatory pro bono. Use your pen as often as you can in this book — we want you to be an active creator, not just a passive sponge.

We put you in a lawyer's role. Thinking about lawyers when you're at home with your feet up on the desk is pretty easy, but acting like a lawyer in the face of a challenging opponent, judge, client, or bar committee is hard. In other words, practicing law is a lot harder than talking about law. There are times in a career in the law in which *The Emperor's New Clothes* may come to mind as you courageously stand your ground, even though others are pushing hard to get you to bend your professional judgment. With this book you have a chance to get into a lawyer's role now, particularly in deciding what you'd do as a member of a law firm's conflicts committee or when you encounter a situation like one of the secrecy scenarios. So far in law school, you've been learning to "think like a lawyer" about cases, statutes, and legal problems. In this course, we want you to learn to think like a lawyer about your law practice, your clients, and your profession.

We make cases easy to read. We edit cases tightly so that they focus on the precise issues we are discussing. We often summarize the facts, and we typically edit out discussions about procedure and peripheral issues. We eliminate most citations so that opinions flow more smoothly. We include citations only if a case is integral to the court's opinion, or if the court includes an explanatory parenthetical, or if a cited case is reprinted elsewhere in this book. We delete footnotes unless they say something important or amusing. Finally, we've tried to choose cases that tell interesting stories.

We don't overload you with note cases. Our notes and questions are designed to get you to think about what you've read and to stimulate interesting class discussions, not to give you new information, so we seldom brief cases in the notes. This book is designed to provoke debate, not to serve as a treatise or research source.

We don't take ourselves too seriously. Law school (and law school textbooks) ought to be fun. You're spending three years in law school, so you may as well enjoy it as much as you can. To help you enjoy this book we use a conversational style and we use some humor here and there. Our observations might not make you roll on the floor in hysterics — I mean, we're not exactly Letterman, Stewart, and O'Brien — but you might find yourself smiling once in a while, even when you are studying serious topics.

We've spent a lot of time working on this book so that it is as clear, provocative, and fun as we could make it. We hope you enjoy reading it, and we'd love to hear your reactions. If you want to comment on the book, please e-mail us at Roy.Simon@Hofstra.edu, Needhamc@slu.edu, powellbv@law.sc.edu, or call Carol at (314) 977-7104 or drop Roy a line at Hofstra Law School, California Avenue, Hempstead, NY 11550. We look forward to hearing from you. Thanks!

Roy D. Simon

Carol A. Needham

Burnele V. Powell

November 2008

ACKNOWLEDGMENTS

Professor Murray L. Schwartz of UCLA School of Law was a pioneer in the field of modern legal ethics. He wrote the First and Second Editions of this book. His excellent materials provided a solid base for this new edition. We are grateful that we have the opportunity to carry on his work for another generation of law students.

Literally hundreds of law students at Hofstra University, Saint Louis University, and the University of South Carolina tested drafts of this textbook in our classes on legal ethics. Our students showed us what worked in the classroom and what did not. We appreciate their patience and their thoughtful comments as this book evolved. In addition, Nancy Rapoport of the University of Nevada, Las Vegas, Lisa Lerman of Catholic University in Washington, D.C. and Lance Tibbles of Capital University in Columbus, Ohio tested earlier drafts of these materials in their professional responsibility courses and gave us useful feedback. Their insights and suggestions have been most helpful.

For this new edition, much of the substantive and technical editing was coordinated by University of South Carolina Senior Researcher for Faculty Support Greg Flowers, his research assistant Patricia McWilliams and law student Jenna Stephens. Invaluable assistance with research, editing, and diligent proofreading was provided by Stephen Schaeffer, Steve Chapman, Lisa Luetkemeyer, Andrew Schultz, and Jaime Miller, hard-working law students at Saint Louis University and Levi Rosenthal, Evan Kusnitz, Brian Kramer, and Michael Licare, equally hard-working law students at Hofstra. Their enthusiasm for the project and creative suggestions have added substantially to the book you have in your hands. The work of our administrative assistants, Toni Dean, Mary Dougherty, and Joanne Masci is also reflected in every page of this book. Their work at every stage of the publication process was essential.

Our families have our appreciation for their magnificent support and encouragement without which no book is possible. We are delighted to salute them here: Carol's husband Tom Timmermann and daughter Genevieve Emily Needham Timmermann; Roy's wife Karen and children Joshua, Nicole, Daniel, and Rebecca and Rebecca's husband Sam; Burnele's wife and daughter, Brenda and Berkeley, all are owed a great debt for their patience. We thank them from the bottom of our hearts for giving us the time to write this book.

The many copyright holders who gave permission to use their work in this book are generally acknowledged where their work appears. We are delighted to have the opportunity to include their work in this book. We particularly appreciate permission from Lawrence J. Fox, partner at Drinker Biddle & Reath LLP and one of the most creative minds in professional responsibility, to use his stories in this edition of the book. Finally, we thank in advance all of you who will be kind enough to call, write, or e-mail us to comment on this book.

TABLE OF CONTENTS

Chapter 1
CREATING AND MAINTAINING A PROFESSION

Few tasks are as daunting for those of us who teach legal ethics — or, perhaps your law school calls it *professional responsibility* or *the law of lawyering,* or simply *lawyering,* the title doesn't matter — as answering the challenge to sum up in a few pages what a casebook (and by extension a course) is all about. Fortunately for the editors of this casebook, this is the fourth edition. That means that we now have more than simply a history to fall back on; we have what by now qualifies as a tradition. In 1979, when Professor Murray Schwartz wrote in the preface to the first edition of this book that one of its central themes would be the values and the behavior required of members of the legal profession, it is that tradition to which he was alluding. He wanted openly to assess "the conflict between, on the one hand, the behavior necessary for realization of the lawyer's personal values, and, on the other, the behavior necessary for realization of the values implicit in and dictated by the role of lawyer." He was challenging users of this book not simply to read it, but to come to appreciate an underlying set of ideals, much in the way that a master in the martial arts seeks to impart not just the mechanics, but an appreciation for the underlying values of an ancient, honorable, and honored tradition. In that tradition, therefore, we are urging you to look back with appreciation for the work of the generation of teachers cited throughout these pages — Schwartz, Freedman, Hazard, Wolfram, Rhode, to name a few — while simultaneously looking forward to the time when it will be your responsibility to assume the mantel of teacher of legal ethics to the next generation of lawyers. Put another way, we see you as part of the vanguard for the standards and values of the legal profession and intend over the following pages to equip you, no matter how you might ultimately use your legal education, to meet the challenges that might confront you in the realm of legal ethics.

And no, that warrior image is not simply for effect. Indeed, we very much want you to keep in mind the metaphor of the public champion. You are probably saying to yourself, "Sure, but the lawyer as the last samurai — or one of Korea's Hwarang warriors — doesn't that stretch the imagination?" But has it occurred to you that lawyers are called *esquire* for a reason? The symbol of the profession — Recall your chess set? — is a horse, representing the knights whose code of honor and fealty to the King eventually transformed the Middle Ages and helped to lay the foundation for the notions of limited sovereignty, constitutional rule, and individual freedom, to which much of the world is heir to today. So, perhaps, it is not so far-fetched to think of lawyers, like the clergy and military — bishops and rooks, if you prefer — as sharing a tradition that marks them as something well beyond simply paid partisans and pettifoggers.

Indeed, it is that tradition — one which links lawyers to lawyers down the generations and which ties every lawyer to some law professor, mentor, friend, colleague, or other lawyer — that this book and ultimately this course is about. Through a series of comments, summaries, cases, notes, and questions, this book invites you to become part of the continuing dialogue about the issues that are central to the legal profession (and our society generally): What does it mean to be a professional? What does it mean to be a lawyer? And how does one practice law at the highest level?

This is a large order, one that involves nothing less than an exploration of the moral, ethical, jurisprudential, political, and socio-economic implications of lawyers in our society. Still, for all of their intractable nature, the questions at the core of this book persist because every serious effort to resolve them provides a meaningful step forward in the progress of the profession and the society it serves. Here is how one writer summed up some recent scholarship about the competing concerns:

> Hart and Hogg describe how the original professions of law, church, and the military provided young aristocrats with a socially acceptable way of making a

> living. These were high-status individuals; the term *professional* was synonymous with *upper class*. In time, a newer set of occupational professions developed, such as medicine, pharmacy, and accountancy. In response . . . the original professions fought to defend their status by encouraging principles that have come to define all other professions. These principles include a disdain for competition, self-promotion, advertising, and bald profiteering; a belief in the principle of payment for work — rather than working for pay; and a belief in the superiority of the motive of service.[1]

Consider, then, your own views about Hart and Hogg's variation on what we have referred to above as *the central issues of the profession*. Let's, for a moment, step away from lawyers and try a bit of deconstruction. Take their first point: "The term *professional* was synonymous with *upper class*. In time, a newer set of occupational professions developed, such as medicine, pharmacy, and accountancy." Implicit in that assertion is our question: What does it mean to be a professional?

Think about the variety of people who today consider themselves professionals. Could horrormeister Wes Craven's film, *Red Eye*, be any scarier than in the scene in which Cillian Murphy, a contract-killer, turns to Rachel McAdams, a hotel customer service representative, and says, "Look, we're both *professionals* and we know how this is done"?

Seriously, though, these days it seems that anybody with a white-collar job and a five-figure salary is referred to as a professional — and they are constantly in the news. In a June 25, 2006 commentary for the *New York Times*, for example, Daniel Akst, a frequent contributor to the business page, inveighed against what he saw as the disproportionate treatment suffered by two of the nation's most high-profile corporate leaders, Harry C. Stonecipher, who had only recently ended his tenure as chief executive of Boeing, and Robert L. Nardelli, then-chief executive at Home Depot.

Akst's complaint was that after turning around operations at Boeing, by spearheading Boeing's return to the commercial airline market with production of the *787 Dreamliner* and ushering in a new set of standards of conduct at Boeing, Stonecipher had been ousted by Boeing's Board of Directors. The ouster came less than 15 months after Stonecipher had, himself, been brought in by Boeing to replace a CEO who had resigned after being implicated in a procurement scandal.

Understating the situation, Akst suggested that Boeing's Board of Directors had "reacted unfavorably" to events surrounding Mrs. Stonecipher's filing for divorce — events including the discovery of explicit e-mails between Stonecipher and his paramour, another Boeing executive. True, there was no consensual relationship agreement — sometimes known as a love contract — in place. But Stonecipher did not supervise the unidentified 48-year-old woman, who for more than 20 years had worked at jobs that were several levels below him in the organization. Nor did he give her preferential treatment, or sexually harass her. Furthermore, the relationship was consensual and to all appearances sincere — not one for which Boeing believed disciplining was required. Nor did Boeing lose money during Stonecipher's tenure; its stock price had, in fact, increased over the period.

Some saw Stonecipher's big mistake as letting those e-mails get out. But a different view was expressed by Charles M. Elson, director of a corporate governance program at the University of Delaware, who observed in the *Washington Post*: "In this environment, office romances have serious legal complications today that they didn't have 20 years ago. . . . It's not the relationship, it's the judgment that got you into the relationship that can get you into trouble."[2]

---

[1] SUZANNE C. LOWE, MARKETPLACE MASTERS: HOW PROFESSIONAL SERVICE FIRMS COMPETE TO WIN 8 (2004) (citing Hart and Hogg at footnote 7).

[2] Renae Merle, *Boeing CEO Resigns Over Affair With Subordinate*, WASHINGTON POST, March 8, 2005,

What most exercised Akst, however, was that, although Stonecipher was ousted by Boeing, Robert L. Nardelli, who had presided over a five-year economic decline at Home Depot during much of the same period, had been rewarded for his stint. Boeing ousted Stonecipher, but the Home Depot Board rewarded Robert Nardelli with compensation valued at $245 million.[3]

NOTES AND QUESTIONS

1. What does it mean to be a professional? Are corporate CEOs professionals? How about businessmen and women, generally? What about public school teachers, lobbyists, and journalists? Why (or why not)?

2. Assume that you were a member of the Boards of Directors of both Boeing and Home Depot. Would you have voted to oust Stonecipher? Would you vote to oust Nardelli? Has either (or both) acted unprofessionally? How so?

3. Akst contended that what really got Stonecipher into trouble was, essentially, that he was driven by lust rather than money. As he put it, "It's bizarre, if not entirely surprising, that this kind of indiscretion will get you into more trouble than taking your shareholders to the cleaners financially." Who decides what should drive a corporate leader? Who should decide? Does the general good of the society have anything to do with it? Should it?

Consider Hart and Hogg's second observation: "In response . . . the original professions fought to defend their status by encouraging principles that have come to define all other professions." The implicit assertion is that the professional ideal evolved, at least in part, as a means of differentiating, for example, what lawyers do (and cannot do) from the conduct of others in the society and especially in the marketplace. More directly, the question is: What does it mean to be a lawyer?

Suppose that Able Attorney, an attorney whose firm's practice concentrates on white-collar crime defense, comes to you seeking legal advice. Able Attorney tells you that he represents the CEO of a nationally known high-volume home-building and supply corporation, which he fictitiously calls Build-a-Box Corp. Based on your regular reading of the business pages, you immediately suspect that the ultimate client is Robert Nardelli, of Home Depot, but you do not comment at this point.

Able Attorney explains that he needs your advice about some legal advice that he gave to the CEO. First, however, he tells you that you should know that Build-a-Box is contemplating a major expansion. World-wide, it will open twelve superstores a year over the next several years. Hundreds of millions of dollars a year will be needed to finance the initiative, code-named 0-to-60 (an inside joke referencing the high-performance Ferrari 599's ability to go from zero to sixty miles per hour in under four seconds). The critical point, though, is that five business days from now "Billions Bank" is scheduled to sign an agreement with Build-a-Box committing it to provide lead financing for the project in the amount of one billion dollars.

Able Attorney then tells you that the CEO recently received an inquiry from The Back Bay Alumnae Association, giving him a heads-up that they are considering honoring him next year as an "Alumni of Achievement" for the Bachelor of Science degree Build-a-Box's website shows him as having earned in 1990. As the CEO

---

available at http://www.washingtonpost.com/wp-dyn/articles/A13173-2005Mar7.html (last visited Nov. 5, 2008).

[3] For more regarding this scandal, see Howard Kurtz, *A Costly Affair*, WASHINGTON POST, March 10, 2005, *available at* http://www.washingtonpost.com/wp-dyn/articles/A23268-2005Mar10.html (last visited Nov. 5, 2008).

explained it, however, "It was now his belief that what he actually received was a PhD diploma, not a BS degree, as the website incorrectly states."[4]

The CEO went on to explain that the website clearly misstates his academic record, and for that he takes full responsibility. But the story gets worse: since he did not keep copies of his transcript and Back Bay's records for that era were destroyed by a computer hacker several years ago, it is his understanding that neither he nor the online Back Bay College, can now document that even the PhD diploma, which is awarded for completing a three-year program in philosophy and ethics, was actually awarded.

What concerns Able Attorney is that he advised the CEO that, since it was arguable that he had merely committed an innocent mistake, his best course of action was to do nothing until he could find a convenient time, perhaps a couple of weeks after the closing, when he could advise the Board of Directors of Build-a-Box about the situation. As Able Attorney explained to the CEO, "Such a delay would not needlessly disrupt the launch of 0-to-60 or upset the markets, and it would provide time for Build-a-Box to organize a public relations strategy to deal with any ensuing fallout."

NOTES AND QUESTIONS

1. What does it mean to be a lawyer? What advice would you have given the CEO?

2. Under the circumstances, was it unethical for an attorney to tell a client to do nothing, when the attorney knew that other people were depending on his client's reputation and commitment to honesty, good faith actions, and the highest degree of integrity?

3. Assume that you told Able Attorney that he should reconsider his opinion and advise the Build-a-Box Board of Directors immediately that the website "misstates" the CEO's academic record. Remember, you suspect that client to be Nardelli of Home Depot, but you do not know for sure. If Able Attorney refuses to tell the Board, should you advise either the Build-a-Box Board or Billions Bank about the "misstatement"? Why? Why not?

4. Are you beginning to experience moral qualms about your decision? Consider whether any of the three possible philosophical approaches to the broad question of what it means to be a lawyer captures your sense.

a. Richard Wasserstrom, *Lawyers as Professionals: Some Moral Issues*, 5 HUMAN RIGHTS 1 (1975), urges:

> . . . Conventional wisdom has it that where the attorney-client relationship exists, the point of view of the attorney is properly different — and appreciably so — from that which would be appropriate in the absence of the attorney-client relationship. For where the attorney-client relationship exists, it is often appropriate and many times even obligatory for the attorney to do things that, all other things being equal, an ordinary person need not, and should not do. What is characteristic of this role of a lawyer is the lawyer's required indifference to a wide variety of ends and consequences that in other contexts would be of undeniable moral significance. Once a lawyer represents a client, the lawyer has a duty to make his or her expertise fully available in the realization of the end sought by the client, irrespective, for the most part, of the moral worth to which the end will be put or the character of the client who seeks to utilize it. Provided that the end sought is not illegal, the lawyer is, in essence, an amoral technician whose peculiar skills and knowledge in respect to the law are available to those with whom the relationship of client is established.

b. Gerald J. Postema, *Self-Image, Integrity, and Professional Responsibility,*

[4] For the historical facts on which this hypothetical is, in part, based, see *RadioShack CEO Lied on Resume*, USA TODAY, February 16, 2006, *available at* http://www.usatoday.com/money/companies/management/2006-02-16-lying-exec_x.htm (last visited March 22, 2008).

in THE GOOD LAWYER 306–10 (David Luban ed., 1984) suggests that the available perspectives are several, including (1) viewing law as an amoral enterprise that is exempt from moral judgment; (2) viewing law as an amoral enterprise which, by definition, permits lawyers to participate so long as, but only so long as, they are willing to sacrifice their morals; and (3) viewing law as an activity that must be subjected to an "integration strategy," pursuant to which the essential moral imperatives of the legal profession and one's own essential moral imperatives are balanced in an overall conception of self, which essentially involves understanding of the constant need for change, an appreciation of what is possible to change, and a willingness to withdraw from the profession in the face of irresolvable conflict.

c. Burnele V. Powell, *Risking the Terrible Question of Religion in the Life of the Lawyer*, 66 FORDHAM L. REV. 1321 (1998), suggests another possibility: viewing opportunities to work through ostensible conflicts between one's moral and professional obligations — below expressed as those of religion and law — not as unexpected and undesired obstacles to be overcome, but as part of each individual's existential process of defining themselves.

> [Thus,] although there cannot be a reconciling of the obligations that flow from these two paradigms, we can pay respectful homage to both. To start with, we can note that there will likely be only rare instances of conflict between the obligations of the lawyer who would have religion play a significant role in influencing his or her life and the obligations of any other lawyer. To the extent that our laws are not completely lacking moral content, religiously oriented lawyers and nonreligious lawyers alike, should be able to find large areas of common ground. As for the limited set of instances that the terrible question reveals to be problematic, there can be no choice for the religiously committed lawyer other than to choose withdrawal from the legal representation, if not from the legal profession. Although the professional sacrifice would be great, the moral loss in not doing so under the appropriate circumstance must be counted greater. Furthermore, if the cost of being a lawyer for whom religion makes a difference is not a significant cost, then the commitments we make in proclaiming ourselves to be religious lawyers surely cannot be seen as something of value. Moreover, the real concern of the religious lawyer must not be with the loss of the right to engage in a particular representation or even loss of the license to practice law. If commitment to have religion in one's life as a lawyer does not risk being costly, then to that extent, we are devaluing religion itself.

For the time being, let's assume that if one of the above perspectives (or some variation of one of them) doesn't sufficiently describe your own perspective, there is still plenty of time for your views to evolve. That is, in part, what this course is about; we are carving out space for a discussion about what it means to be part of the legal profession. At this stage, it is more important that you begin that discussion than that you achieve a resolution. Indeed, it is probable that you will be unable to fully establish your moral grounding, at least until you have had an opportunity to consider the substantive and procedural obligations that the rules of the legal profession generally impose on lawyers.

This brings us to that third recurring question: How does one practice law at the highest level? Hart and Hogg suggest that the answer lies in principles that have emerged over time to distinguish *professionals* from individuals who might be said, simply, to be engaged in the buying and selling of goods, the delivery of social services, or the handling of financial transactions. "These principles," you will recall, "include a disdain for competition, self-promotion, advertising, and bald profiteering; a belief in the principle of payment for work — rather than working for pay; and a belief in the superiority of the motive of service."

As evolved by lawyers (but taking nothing away from the independent course of development of the clergy and the military), the formal articulation of these principles in the United States did not take place until 1887, when Alabama adopted principles articulated by two distinguished lawyers. The first was Baltimore attorney David Hoffman, who in 1836 was the first to publish a book of ethical legal principles, FIFTY RESOLUTIONS IN REGARD TO PROFESSIONAL DEPORTMENT, which he had originally outlined in a series of speeches. The second was one of Hoffman's contemporaries, George Sharswood of Philadelphia, who in 1854, published materials from his own lectures, under the title *An Essay on Professional Ethics*. Hoffman's and Sharswood's principles proved so influential that they were embraced by the Bar of Alabama as part of that state's creation of the nation's first mandatory code of professional conduct. The American Bar Association later followed suit, instituting the Canons of Professional Ethics in 1908. The Alabama and ABA codes, therefore, served as inspirations for similar adoptions in other jurisdictions.

Today, every state has a code of professional conduct that defines what is required of lawyers practicing in that jurisdiction. Through the elaboration provided by judicial opinions, informal advisories, scholarly commentaries, and observed patterns of practice, this body of standards and interpretations is frequently referred to as *the law of lawyering*, and it describes the generally accepted — although not necessarily officially codified — conduct of lawyers in the various jurisdictions.

Still, it is the formal codification of the standards of professional responsibility that counts most. Such codes are commonly the product of a two-stage process. At the national level, the American Bar Association (ABA), the world's largest voluntary professional-membership organization, works through its sections, committees, and other entities to identify issues of compelling national concern to the profession. When a matter is deemed of sufficient urgency (e.g., involving broad-ranging moral, political, jurisprudential, ethical, or economic concerns), it is likely to generate a request that the President of the ABA launch a reform effort. In many instances, a nationally-drawn blue ribbon commission (or at the very least an internally constituted ABA taskforce) results and is charged with examining the problem. And as was recently the case with the Joyce Foundation's support of the Joint Commission to Evaluate the Model Code of Judicial Conduct's[5] review of the judicial standards of conduct, such commissions will receive funding from both the ABA and charitable foundations with interest in public policy. If successfully concluded, commission reports (but not the commentaries accompanying the black letter law) will be laid before the ABA House of Delegates for adoption as ABA policy.

Note, however, that ABA policies have no legal effect; they have only persuasive force. After they have been included as part of the ABA's Model Rules, however, they serve as suggestions to the jurisdictions (and, indeed, deliberative bodies worldwide) considering similar concerns. Thus, to the extent that ABA Model Rules prove persuasive, they have a chance to be adopted, in whole or in part, first as the recommendations of independently functioning commissions appointed by the state bars or the state supreme courts in the several jurisdictions, and then ultimately as mandatory rules promulgated by the highest courts of each jurisdiction. By this process of extended, multilevel, multijurisdictional debate, the rules governing lawyers and judges emerge.

---

[5] "In 1922, the ABA appointed a commission on judicial ethics, chaired by Chief Justice William Howard Taft, to draft a code of judicial conduct. . . . In 1969, the ABA again began a comprehensive process to review, evaluate and update the judicial ethics canons. The resulting Model Code of Judicial Conduct, adopted by the ABA in 1972, changed the style and form of the rules, providing 7 canons in place of the original 36 canons, and cleaning up [*Sic*] much of the hortatory language while maintaining the substance of the canons." *ABA Joint Commission to Examine the Model Code of Judicial Conduct*, http://www.abanet.org/judicialethics/about/background.html (last visited Nov. 5, 2008).

For our immediate purposes, though, what should be underscored is that the judicial interpretations and academic commentaries that result from the Model Rules and their progeny will form the heart of our discussion about professionals, lawyers, and the practice of law.

Chapter 2

THE GATES TO THE PROFESSION — THE KEYS TO THE OFFICE

A. BECOMING AND BEING A LAWYER

The current bar admission process is fairly uniform from state to state, but that is only part of the process. Most states have three separate criteria for admission — three "gates," if you please, through which you must pass. The three gates are:

1. *Graduation from law school.* Except in a few states, you cannot be admitted to the bar unless you have graduated from an accredited law school.
2. *Bar exam.* In every state, you have to take and pass the bar examination. Wisconsin has a special arrangement for graduates of Wisconsin law schools, which we will discuss later in this Chapter. In most states, you also have to pass the Multistate Professional Responsibility Exam, known as the MPRE.
3. *Character and fitness test.* In addition, you have to be approved by the Character and Fitness Committee, which evaluates moral character.

We will not here elaborate on the fact that graduation from law school — accredited or otherwise — is an important first step to becoming licensed in virtually all jurisdictions; we defer that discussion until we focus on legal education in Chapter 3, Admission to the Bar. Instead, we begin our discussion with the licensing requirements. Even so, we note that becoming licensed to practice law is only the formal, publicly declared step. In addition, a new lawyer must become competent in handling the matters that are placed in her care — what we treat here as qualifying to hold the keys to the office where those representations take place. In this chapter, therefore, we undertake a two-part discussion. In Section 1, we look at the gates and gatekeepers (*viz.*, curriculum requirements, the bar exam and the MPRE, and character and fitness committees). In Section 2, we consider the competency obligation — what it takes to become licensed as a lawyer and eligible to practice law.

First things first, then: Let's consider what will, some summer soon, be the focus of activity for many of you.

1. The Gates: Bar Examinations, The Multistate, and The MPRE

a. ***The typical bar exam.*** Do you dread the bar exam? Remember that serious preparation makes taking the bar exam a lot less anxiety-ridden. Pass rates on the bar exam are quite high in most states, and courses designed to prepare you for the bar exam are generally effective. If you pay attention in law school and attend a bar exam course (and study hard), you should pass. The MPRE has an even higher pass rate than the bar exam, so as long as you prepare seriously, you should pass that on the first try too. So relax for a few minutes while we talk about the bar exam, its purposes, and its limitations.

The bar exam is designed to screen out people who are not qualified, in terms of knowledge or communicative ability or time management (or some combination), to practice law. The typical state bar exam lasts two full days and is divided into two parts: an essay section about the law of the state giving the test, and a multiple-choice section called the "Multistate" exam. New York, for example, gives essay questions on such things as civil procedure, corporations, criminal law, evidence, family law, taxation, remedies, torts, wills, and the UCC.

b. ***Is the Multistate Bar Exam a good idea?*** Here's what Justice Henderson of the Supreme Court of South Dakota had to say in *Petition of Draeger*, 463 N.W.2d 346

(S.D. 1990). There, the court granted a reinstatement petition from a lawyer who had been suspended for three years for shoplifting, but added the condition that Draeger retake the South Dakota Bar Examination, including the Multistate exam and the MPRE. In dissent, Justice Henderson agreed that Draeger should have to retake the MPRE, but argued against requiring him to take the Multistate Bar Exam. Specifically, Justice Henderson criticized the Multistate Exam as one that requires the person tested to choose the "best of the worst answers," and an unfair test of knowledge. Justice Henderson went on to say:

> . . . this type of test is tricky and therefore breeds fear. . . . It is academic baloney at its zenith.
>
> Unfortunately, this test fails many deserving young people who have given seven years of their lives to become lawyers. . . . Easy it is for those who create the examination; mechanical it is for those who grade it; anguish it is for those who are forced to take it.

Do you agree? Why or why not?

c. ***The MPRE.*** The MPRE, which is required in all but three states (Maryland, Washington, and Wisconsin), is another test without any essay questions. It consists only of fifty multiple-choice questions about professional ethics under the ABA's Model Code of Professional Responsibility and Model Rules of Professional Conduct. (There are also a few questions about the ABA's Code of Judicial Conduct.) The purpose of the test is to ensure basic familiarity with these ethics codes. Unlike the bar exam, the MPRE can be taken while you are still in law school — it is given in March, August, and November each year. You should take it as early in law school as you can so that it won't distract you from studying for the bar exam, and so you can take it again if you fail.

Some students want their textbook and course in Professional Responsibility to prepare them for the MPRE. The authors have a brief comment on this. This book won't hurt you when you prepare for the MPRE, but it's not designed to focus on helping you pass that test — the way the one-day commercial courses are. You don't need your professor or this textbook to prepare you for the MPRE. You need your professor and this book to prepare you for forty years of law practice after you are admitted to the bar. If your professor or this book concentrated mainly on pounding the text of the ABA Model Rules and the ABA Model Code into your head, you'd fall asleep in class after about two weeks (maybe sooner). Besides, regulation of the legal profession is a dynamic process. The places where the lines are drawn can and do change over time. Wording in the relevant rule can be amended, for example, or the U.S. Supreme Court can issue an opinion which completely changes the analysis of a particular issue. The "right answer" on a test given five years ago might not be the right answer to the same question today. But, the competing policy considerations do tend to remain the same. Rather than memorizing the words of today's ethics rules, our purpose is to equip you to think about lawyers and the legal profession as part of the continuing debate about changing regulations that will engage you throughout your professional life.

d. ***"Performance" tests.*** Over 30 states — including Alaska, California, and Colorado — have adopted a "performance" component on their bar exams. California, for example, includes in its bar exam two drafting assignments based on a simulated file that includes memos, letters, police reports, newspaper articles, etc. Applicants have three hours to draft such things as a deposition outline, a statute, a closing argument, and an investigation plan. Colorado gives applicants two half-hour questions on such things as comparing two rules of evidence or identifying issues to research and documents to request based on a short client statement. Alaska gives applicants a set of cases and statutes — only some of which are relevant — and asks them to answer particular questions based on a given set of facts.

The format of the "performance" questions in these states differs substantially from the format of the traditional bar exam, but the skills they test are not very different from the skills tested by the usual bar exam questions — legal analysis and writing ability. So far, no state has instituted an oral or "live" performance component to test litigation skills. No state requires a student to take a simulated deposition or present a closing argument, for example. Nor does any state test an applicant's ability to draft legal documents, such as a sales contract or closing documents for a real estate transaction. Nor does any state test an applicant's ability to negotiate a settlement or a transaction. Why do you think the states don't test live courtroom skills, drafting skills, or negotiation skills? Should states begin to test these things as part of the bar examination?

Do you think the bar exam should have a performance component? What should a performance component test? What are the arguments for and against a performance component? Should an applicant actually have to pass the performance component to pass the bar exam, or should the grade on the performance component just be one factor in the overall grade? And how should the performance exam be graded? Who should grade it — lawyers? Judges? Law professors?

If there is a performance component, should it be administered at about the same time as the regular bar exam, or should it be administered after lawyers have been in practice for six months or a year or more? Lawyers who pass the regular bar exam could be granted a limited license, but lawyers who want to appear in court or be "first chair" in negotiations or in transaction closings would have to pass the "skills" or "performance" bar exam. If the performance/skills exam is a "second stage" exam given months or years after the bar exam, should it be a single exam covering all kinds of skills, or several separate exams, each of which covers certain specific skills? Should a lawyer have to show competence in all of the different skills, or only in those areas where the lawyer is practicing?

e. ***Should the bar exam be abolished?*** Now for a more radical question: should we abolish the bar exam? Once students have graduated from law school after three years of rigorous courses, examinations, and papers, is it fair to force them to take a mammoth do-or-die test? Wisconsin is apparently the only state that doesn't think so. If you graduate from one of Wisconsin's two law schools — University of Wisconsin or Marquette — then you don't have to take the bar exam to become licensed as a lawyer in that state.

Does the bar exam work? Does it screen out unqualified candidates? Or does it just test your memory, or your endurance, or your ability to take tests?

Suppose your state's highest court has appointed you to a committee to decide whether to (a) abolish the bar exam, (b) revise the bar exam, or (c) continue the bar exam pretty much as it is. What are the arguments in favor of each of these options? Whether or not you want to abolish the regular bar exam, do you want to abolish the MPRE? Why or why not?

f. ***People with learning disabilities.*** The Americans with Disabilities Act, 42 U.S.C. §§ 12101–12213, provides that a person with a disability which substantially affects a major life activity, such as working, is entitled to a "reasonable accommodation." Several courts have held that people with learning disabilities are entitled to reasonable accommodations when taking the bar exam. For example, in *Bartlett v. New York State Board of Law Examiners*, 970 F. Supp. 1094, 1147 (S.D.N.Y. 1997), the court held that a woman with learning disabilities affecting her reading speed and comprehension was entitled to reasonable accommodations on the bar exam, including (a) "double time" to take the exam; (b) the use of a computer to write answers to the essay questions; (c) permission to circle multiple choice answers in the examination booklet rather than being required to fill in little circles on an answer sheet; and (d) a large print version of the exam. The Board of Law Examiners' appeal to the Second Circuit for reconsideration was denied, *Bartlett*, 2 F. Supp. 2d 388 (S.D.N.Y. 1997), but on appeal the decision was affirmed in part and vacated in part, 156 F. 3d 321 (2d Cir. 1998), then vacated and remanded, 527 U.S. 1031 (1999).

What do you think of this ruling? Do you think a person with serious reading problems has the ability to become a lawyer? The court noted that the plaintiff, Ms. Bartlett, had earned not only a law degree but also a Ph.D. in Educational Administration. If she could earn those degrees, can she be a capable lawyer? Or will allowing extra time and other accommodations for people with learning disabilities eventually lower the standards for bar admission and threaten the quality of the profession? If you think Ms. Bartlett can be a capable lawyer, how will she cope with crisis situations in which she must read and analyze cases and documents quickly, under time pressure? If you think she cannot be a capable lawyer, do you think Congress should change the Americans with Disabilities Act (or that the Second Circuit interpret the Act) to provide that bar candidates with learning disabilities are not entitled to more time or other special accommodations on the bar exam?

g. ***Character and fitness tests.*** We'll consider this aspect of the licensing process in more detail in the chapter on Bar Admission. At this point you simply need to know that applicants for admission must provide answers to a series of pointed questions intended to ferret out applicants who have engaged in activities which might call into question the applicant's trustworthiness or ability to comply with legal requirements. To understand the scope and dimension of the character and fitness considerations in attorney licensing, consider this bar applicant's situation described by Randall Samborn in *Morally Fit*, THE NATIONAL LAW JOURNAL (November 27, 1989).

The article reported the Iowa Supreme Court's consideration of whether a state senator who had pled guilty to disorderly conduct after being charged with *fellating* with an exotic dancer at a bachelor party, should be allowed to take the state's bar exam. The Board of Law Examiners said no, intending that the candidate should have to wait four years before taking the exam. But the Iowa Supreme Court saw it differently (6-3), saying that in light of the candidate's clean record in the interim, he "should not be permanently judged" and excluded as a result of admittedly intemperate conduct that had occurred three years earlier at a bachelor party.

Two dissenting justices thought that the candidate's parallel (but unrelated) involvement in a paternity action, taken together with his explanation for his debauchery ("extreme intoxication") was evidence that something more than a single instance of "intemperance and misconduct" was presented.

NOTES AND QUESTIONS

1. ***Thumbs Up or Thumbs Down?*** If you were on the Iowa Supreme Court, would you give a thumbs up or thumbs down to the state senator? If you vote yes (i.e., that he does possess the requisite moral character), why did you vote that way? Because his misconduct wasn't so bad? Because it was an isolated incident? Because his public service makes up for his misconduct? Because he's been a good boy since this incident happened a few years ago? Some other reason? If you're not sure whether or not you would approve of his character and fitness, what additional information would you like to have about him to help you decide?

2. ***Morality Police?*** Should character and fitness committees function as morality police? Whose business is it whether an aspiring lawyer went to a bachelor party and got a little carried away? Is it the public's business? Is it the state's business? What does sexual morality have to do with the practice of law?

3. ***Gender Gap?*** When you initially thought about the state senator's case, did you expect class discussion to divide along gender lines, with women thinking that the senator did not have the requisite moral character to sit for the bar exam and men thinking that he did? (If so, do men and women have different values about sexual conduct, or are men more afraid that their own past conduct would flunk the character and fitness test, or is there some other reason that men and women disagree on this issue?) Or do you expect the class to divide along other lines, with some men and women on one side of the issue and other men and women on the other side of the

issue? For example, do you expect people to divide along religious lines, age lines, racial lines, or urban-rural lines? Or do you expect almost everyone to agree on one side of the issue or the other? (Which side?)

4. ***Miscreants, Misanthropes, and Iconoclasts.*** We will revisit these themes later when we discuss wife battering, child abuse, and sex with clients. For the moment, if you think that Senator Sturgeon should have been denied admission to the bar for lack of moral character, what other categories of actions do you think should also prevent applicants from becoming licensed as lawyers? The point of asking these questions is to get you thinking about exactly what is special about lawyers, and what their qualifications should be.

5. ***Would You Let a Murderer Become a Lawyer?*** In the 1960s, James Hamm was an aspiring minister in Kansas who was happily married. In the early 1970s he drifted to Arizona and became a street person, a drug addict, and a drug dealer. In 1974, during a drug deal that went sour, Mr. Hamm shot and killed a man by putting two bullets in his head. Hamm pleaded guilty to first degree murder and was sentenced to prison for twenty-five years to life. While in prison, he was a model inmate. He took self-improvement courses, remarried, and earned a B.A. from Northern Arizona University. In 1992, after seventeen years behind bars, Hamm won parole. Soon afterwards he applied to law school at Arizona State University ("ASU") and was admitted.

In 1997, Hamm graduated from ASU Law School, and in 1998 he formally asked the Arizona Board of Executive Clemency to release him from parole. The Board held a hearing at which the murder victim's sister testified. She said that if Hamm was permanently released from parole "it will be as if this crime never happened." But two ASU law professors testified in Hamm's favor, one calling him "a leader among law students." In addition, the judge who sentenced Hamm to prison in 1974 wrote a letter to the Clemency Board saying the time was ripe for Hamm to be discharged from parole and "permitted to pursue the formal requirements of entering into the legal profession."

Hamm also applied for admission to the Arizona Bar. This outraged many people. One ASU alumnus wrote a letter to the editor saying he was ashamed to be an alumnus of a school that "lobbies to eliminate capital punishment, while admitting convicted murderers to law school." Another man wrote a letter saying that the legal profession was already subject to enough ridicule and contempt without admitting a convicted murderer to practice. The letter continued:

> It seems that certain doors should be permanently and irrevocably closed because of certain acts. For example, a convicted embezzler should be prohibited from becoming a banker. A convicted child molester should be prevented from becoming a teacher or a pediatrician. Likewise, a convicted murderer should be precluded from engaging in a profession that the public and the State Bar rules of ethics expect to embody the law. . . .
>
> . . . The State Bar should slam the door on Mr. Hamm's application just as surely as a murderer slams the door on his victim's future.

But others were more supportive. An ACLU lawyer said that refusing to admit Hamm to the Bar would be "to deny that anyone can change. . . . It is to say that a society can never, ever, forgive. I know of no code of honor that is that unforgiving."

What do you think? Assume that Mr. Hamm really is rehabilitated — that he is a model citizen and has the intellectual ability to become a lawyer. If you were a member of the Arizona State Bar's Committee on Character and Fitness, would you recommend to the Arizona Supreme Court that James Hamm's application to become a lawyer be approved? Or would you recommend that the application be denied? Why? Do you believe it is impossible for a convicted murderer to be completely rehabilitated, or do you believe that a convicted murderer should be denied admission to the bar forever even if he is completely rehabilitated?

2. Practicing Law Professionally

Once lawyers are in practice, the incentives for quality and integrity radically change. No longer are incentives designed and given out by professors, deans, and peers. There are no more grades for writing good papers or exams. Instead, incentives and penalties are the province of a wide variety of people with whom lawyers come into contact: (a) employers; (b) co-workers; (c) secretaries, paralegals, and clerical employees; (d) judges; (e) fellow lawyers; (f) clients; (g) juries; (h) the press; (i) disciplinary authorities; (j) the bar association; (k) legal malpractice insurers; (l) client protection funds; (m) prosecutors; and (n) government agencies.

The rewards for quality and integrity are obvious — higher pay, greater responsibility, more interesting cases, more people working for you, faster promotions, more "clout," more referrals and recommendations from clients and other lawyers, favorable press coverage, victories in court, higher self-esteem, and greater job satisfaction. Unfortunately, these rewards are not confined to those who exhibit quality and integrity. Sometimes, lousy lawyers or shady lawyers make a lot of money, win a lot of cases, get lots of referrals, etc. In a free market society, are there ways to prevent incompetence and dishonesty from being rewarded? How?

Now we look at the other side of the equation — after entry into the kingdom — where we ask what it takes to maintain the most important keys in the realm as a practicing lawyer. On this side, our concerns are with identifying, avoiding, and penalizing incompetence and dishonesty.

B. THE RULES GOVERNING COMPETENCE

Model Rule 1.1, the first rule in the ABA Model Rules, requires lawyers to be competent. Missouri's competence rule is identical. It provides:

Missouri Rule 4-1.1. Competence

> A lawyer shall provide competent representation to a client. Competent representation requires the legal knowledge, skill, thoroughness and preparation reasonably necessary for the representation.

The old Model Code of Professional Responsibility did not expressly mandate competent representation, but it sought the same end by providing, in DR 6-101(A), that a lawyer was prohibited from accepting or continuing to handle any matter "which he knows or should know that he is not competent to handle," and that a lawyer was required to undertake "preparation adequate in the circumstances" for each case the lawyer handled.

What does it mean to be "competent"? New Hampshire's version of Rule 1.1 puts some flesh on the skeleton in a fashion that probably expresses the definition of competence in most states. New Hampshire's Rule 1.1(b)–(c) provides as follows:

Rule 1.1. Competence

(b) Legal competence requires at a minimum:

  (1) specific knowledge about the fields of law in which the lawyer practices;
  (2) performance of the techniques of practice with skill;
  (3) identification of areas beyond the lawyer's competence and bringing those areas to the client's attention;
  (4) proper preparation; and
  (5) attention to details and schedules necessary to assure that the matter undertaken is completed with no avoidable harm to the client's interest.

(c) In the performance of client service, a lawyer shall at a minimum:

(1) gather sufficient facts regarding the client's problem from the client, and from other relevant sources;
(2) formulate the material issues raised, determine applicable law and identify alternative legal responses;
(3) develop a strategy, in collaboration with the client, for solving the legal problems of the client; and
(4) undertake actions on the client's behalf in a timely and effective manner including, where appropriate, associating with another lawyer who possesses the skill and knowledge required to assure competent representation.

New Hampshire's list may strike you as obvious, but fulfilling these demands is anything but easy. If you think that it is, take the time to peruse your state's bar journal reports on lawyers who have been disciplined. Note, particularly, how many attorneys who have been practicing law for more than seven years are reported there.

But even if you find yourself surprised by the demographics of the lawyer disciplinary process, one thing that will not surprise you — assuming that previously you have given it any thought at all — is the number of people it takes to keep our profession on track. The fact is that, just as the old African proverb suggests that "it takes a village to raise a child," it should not be surprising that it takes a lot of people — indeed, a society — to maintain a profession. Let's take a look at the roles of some of those actors:

a. ***Clients.*** How can clients express anger, dissatisfaction, or lack of confidence in a lawyer who fails to perform competently and honestly? Here's a list in order of increasing seriousness:

   - *Don't recommend the lawyer.* Clients can continue to use the lawyer on the pending matter but refuse to recommend the lawyer to others.
   - *Don't use lawyer again.* Clients can continue to use the lawyer on the pending matter but go to another lawyer next time they have legal problems, rather than using the same lawyer again.
   - *Fire the lawyer.* Clients can fire the lawyer in midstream, hiring a new lawyer to complete the pending matter.
   - *Actively bad-mouth the lawyer.* Angry clients can actively spread their negative views about the lawyer.
   - *Report the lawyer to the disciplinary authorities.* Clients can report the lawyer to the disciplinary authorities for investigation and possible action.
   - *Sue the bastard.* Clients can sue the lawyer for legal malpractice, breach of fiduciary duties, misrepresentation, fraud, or other sins.

b. ***Employers, co-workers, and support staff.*** Employers can withhold raises, delay or deny promotion, give out boring work, or fire incompetent or dishonest lawyers. Co-workers can ask not to work with dishonest or incompetent lawyers. If the co-workers are partners, they can also boot a dishonest or incompetent lawyer out of the partnership (or leave the partnership themselves) to avoid the risk of *vicarious liability*. Secretaries, paralegals, and other support staff can give them low priority. It's hard for a lawyer to look good and work efficiently if the clerical staff take a long time to finish the lawyer's work.

c. ***Judges.*** Judges can criticize the work of incompetent or dishonest lawyers in written opinions as well as on the record in open court, impose sanctions on them, or report them to disciplinary authorities. Judges can also require more elaborate or more formal submissions from untrustworthy lawyers. For example, lawyers with good reputations can often obtain a continuance or a favorable discovery ruling simply on their word, without submitting formal evidence about their schedules or the efforts they made to locate documents. Lawyers who have bad reputations can be required by judges to submit affidavits or documentation to obtain the same things. Judges may also put incompetent or untrustworthy lawyers on tight litigation schedules and call frequent status conferences to make sure the lawyer is following the schedule.

d. ***The press.*** The press can run stories about dishonest or incompetent lawyers. This happens more and more often. The general press is far more interested in lawyers than it used to be, partly because of shows like *Law and Order*, *Boston Legal*, and *Shark*, and movies and books like *The Firm*, and *Presumed Innocent*. Beyond that, the legal press is much larger than it was even ten years ago. There are now three national newspapers and many monthly lawyers' magazines, including the *National Law Journal*, the *American Lawyer*, the *Legal Times*, and *Lawyers Weekly U.S.A.* On top of that are daily legal newspapers in Chicago, New York, Los Angeles, and many other communities.

e. ***Other attorneys.*** Other attorneys have many weapons that they can use against incompetent or dishonest attorneys. They can give bad recommendations and refuse to refer business. In litigation, they can refuse to grant extensions or other favors. In transactions, other attorneys may refuse to believe anything that is not documented, and may insist that all agreements be in writing.

f. ***Juries.*** If a lawyer was really incompetent or dishonest, a jury hearing a suit against the lawyer can sock the lawyer with enormous damages, including punitive damages and damages for the client's emotional distress.

g. ***Disciplinary authorities.*** Disciplinary authorities can impose a wide range of sanctions on errant lawyers. The sanctions include (from most serious to least serious):

1. *Disbarment.* A disbarred lawyer cannot practice law and cannot obtain readmission to the bar without making a motion to the state's highest court showing that the lawyer is sorry for what happened, has reformed and is now of good moral character. In many states, a lawyer who is disbarred cannot seek reinstatement for at least five years. Many disbarred lawyers are never reinstated, or are not reinstated for many years. In some states, disbarred lawyers cannot even serve as paralegals.
2. *Suspension.* A suspended lawyer cannot practice law for a specified period of time. This time period can be as short as a week or as long as several years. Suspended lawyers cannot resume practice without submitting evidence of good moral character.
3. *Interim suspension.* Some states give their disciplinary authorities power to suspend a lawyer immediately, on an interim basis, if the lawyer appears to pose an immediate danger to clients. Lawyers with alcohol or drug problems are typical targets of such suspensions. The interim suspension is followed by a full investigation and hearing into the lawyer's conduct.
4. *Probation.* A recent trend is to put errant lawyers on probation. If the lawyer violates another rule during the probation period, then the lawyer will face severe sanctions.
5. *Monetary fines.* Some states have given their disciplinary authorities the power to impose fines on lawyers. These fines are usually in addition to other sanctions.
6. *Public reprimand.* The next step down from a suspension is a public reprimand, which some states call public censure. Whatever it is called, the reprimand is published in the bar journal or in a published opinion. Other lawyers and sometimes a lawyer's clients are likely to hear about a public reprimand.
7. *Community service.* Occasionally, disciplinary authorities will require a lawyer to engage in community service (i.e., to perform a certain amount of pro bono work). This sanction is of recent origin and is relatively rare.
8. *Continuing legal education.* With increasing frequency, disciplinary authorities provide that a lawyer must take and pass a law school legal ethics course or CLE courses on legal ethics as a condition of readmission to the bar. Sometimes, disciplined lawyers are also required to re-take and pass

the Multistate Professional Responsibility Exam as well.

9. *Private reprimand.* Less serious violations of the rules are likely to be punished by a private reprimand, also called a private censure or an admonishment. This penalty is akin to a misdemeanor conviction with a sentence of probation. As long as the lawyer stays out of trouble, it has little practical consequence — but if the lawyer gets in trouble again, the bar will come down hard on her.
10. *Warning.* If a lawyer comes close to violating the rules but does not actually do so, then the disciplinary authorities may issue a warning. (Sometimes, a warning is given when a lawyer violates a rule because of negligence or ignorance, or when the disciplinary authorities adopt a new interpretation of a rule that could not have been readily foreseen.) Later violations will be punished more severely.

h. ***Client Protection Funds.*** Client protection funds are funds that reimburse clients whose attorneys have stolen from them. These funds raise money in four ways — by soliciting donations from lawyers, by sharing in bar association dues, by obtaining legislative appropriations, and by suing the lawyers who stole the money. Every state now has such a fund.

i. ***Prosecutors.*** Far more often than in the past, lawyers are facing criminal prosecution. These prosecutions are reserved for serious offenses, but the efforts to uncover these serious offenses are increasing.

j. ***Government agencies.*** Administrative agencies like the FDIC have been suing lawyers (and other professionals) with a vengeance in recent years, obtaining literally hundreds of millions of dollars in damages from lawyers to recover losses in the savings and loan debacle. When financial institutions fail, lawyers are now considered primary targets because of their deep pockets and their involvement in the affairs of their clients. Moreover, when government agencies conclude that lawyers who practice before them have been dishonest, the agencies often bar the lawyers from practicing before them in the future. This "micro-disbarment" is a harsh penalty because a regulatory lawyer who cannot appear before the regulators is almost powerless and is branded with a scarlet letter.

k. ***Malpractice insurers.*** Malpractice insurers who encounter incompetent lawyers can raise premiums, impose conditions on insurance, or refuse to renew a policy. If the insurer discovers that the lawyer was dishonest on the application for insurance or in making a claim, or if the insurer concludes that a lawyer has been sued as a result of fraud or dishonesty rather than negligence, the insurer may deny coverage and refuse to defend. (Most legal malpractice insurance policies do not cover intentional wrongs, and fraud is an intentional wrong.)

   If malpractice insurance is canceled, a lawyer need not stop practicing. Although an increasing number of states require lawyers to disclose to their clients and/or to the licensing authority information regarding their malpractice insurance coverage (including Illinois, Michigan, North Carolina, Ohio, and Pennsylvania) only Oregon requires insurance coverage. Most states permit lawyers to practice without malpractice insurance coverage (and, though estimates vary, perhaps 20% of lawyers do so). But practicing without insurance is very risky, and defending a claim without insurance is both risky and expensive. An uninsured lawyer who is hit with a malpractice or fraud claim must pay for his own defense (unless he wants to represent himself and have a fool for a client). The lawyer must also pay the settlement or judgment out of his own pocket. If the case goes to trial and results in a large judgment, an uninsured lawyer may lose all of his personal assets.

You now have a broad outline of the outside forces that influence lawyers. With that background, over the succeeding chapters we will examine some particular issues in maintaining and improving quality and integrity in the legal profession.

Chapter 3
ADMISSION TO THE BAR

The goal of the bar admission process is to ensure a bar of high quality and impeccable integrity. Does the bar administration process achieve this result? If not, what should be changed?

You are probably familiar with the main hurdles you must overcome in order to become a lawyer. The bar admission process is fairly uniform from state to state. Most states have five separate criteria for admission — you must (1) graduate from an ABA-accredited law school, (2) pass the Multistate Professional Responsibility Exam (the "MPRE"), (3) pass the state's bar exam, (4) satisfy the Character and Fitness Committee, and (5) take the oath of office. Some states add additional requirements, and some provide alternative ways of becoming a lawyer, but the overwhelming majority of lawyers follow the conventional path just described. This chapter will examine that conventional path.

A. LAW SCHOOL GRADUATION AND SPECIFIC CURRICULUM REQUIREMENTS

Does your state require you to take certain courses in law school in order to qualify to take the bar exam? Until 1992, South Carolina Supreme Court Rule 5 required bar applicants to take specified law school courses, including business law, civil procedure, commercial law, constitutional law, contracts, criminal law, domestic relations, equity, evidence, property, taxation, and torts. Wisconsin still requires bar applicants to take specific courses, and requires them to achieve a particular G.P.A. (Of course, Wisconsin is also the only state with the diploma privilege, allowing those who graduate from one of Wisconsin's two law schools to skip the Wisconsin bar exam altogether.) Is state control of the law school curriculum a good idea? Why or why not?

What is the ideal law school curriculum? If you were on a bar association committee charged with designing a required curriculum for all bar applicants, what would the curriculum contain? Would students have any options (e.g., "You can either take Corporations or Securities Law") or distributional requirements (e.g., "You must take at least one upper-level course in business, litigation, and skills") or would the curriculum be the same for all students?

Even in the states that do not directly require bar applicants to take certain courses, the bar exam is a powerful influence on the courses law schools offer and the courses law students choose to take in law school. Is this a positive effect or a negative effect of the bar exam? If there were no bar exam, how do you think the law school curriculum would change? How do you think student course selections would change? What courses would you have taken or not taken if there were no bar exam and/or no MPRE? Would these changes be for the better or for the worse?

To ask a more explosive question, should the states abandon the requirement that you graduate from an accredited law school? Abraham Lincoln didn't go to law school (or take a bar exam, for that matter). Lincoln just "read law" and worked with other lawyers until he knew enough to hang up his shingle. Why should you have to go to law school? If you know enough to pass the bar exam, why should you have to spend three years and tens of thousands of dollars going to law school?

Seven states already agree that three years of law school are not essential to become a lawyer. In California, Vermont, Virginia, and Washington State, you can serve as an apprentice in a law office for a period of time rather than attending law school. In Maine, New York, and Wyoming, you can be admitted to the bar if you have a combination of work in the law and attendance at an accredited law school. All seven states impose some structure on the apprenticeship program — you can't just answer the phone and file loose-leaf services for a few years and then take the bar exam — but at least you don't have to go to law school. Very few people skip law school, and those who do usually have trouble passing the bar exam, but it is an option in these seven states. Is it a good option?

If you were on a state bar committee studying your state's bar admission process, would you recommend that your state allow people to take the bar exam without going to law school? If so, what would applicants have to do instead of law school to qualify to sit for the bar exam? Could they just study law on their own (for example, by taking the bar review course)? Or would they have to work in a law office? Would the lawyer running the office have to meet certain standards? For example, must the lawyer running the office have a certain number of years of experience, or be recommended by other lawyers or judges, or have a general practice? What are the advantages and disadvantages of allowing people to take the bar exam without graduating from law school?

B. THE BAR EXAMINATION AND THE MPRE

Performance tests. In 1997, the National Conference of Bar Examiners ("NCBE") — the same people who compose and administer the MPRE — began administering a Multistate Performance Test, or "MPT." Today, 32 states include the MPT component on their bar exams. The NCBE's website describes the MPT as follows[1]:

> The Multistate Performance Test is designed to test an applicant's ability to use fundamental lawyering skills in a realistic situation. Each test evaluates an applicant's ability to complete a task which a beginning lawyer should be able to accomplish.
>
> The materials for each MPT include a File and a Library. The File consists of source documents containing all the facts of the case. The specific assignment the applicant is to complete is described in a memorandum from a supervising attorney. The File might also include, for example, transcripts of interviews, depositions, hearings or trials, pleadings, correspondence, client documents, contracts, newspaper articles, medical records, police reports, and lawyer's notes. Relevant as well as irrelevant facts are included. Facts are sometimes ambiguous, incomplete, or even conflicting. As in practice, a client's or supervising attorney's version of events may be incomplete or unreliable. Applicants are expected to recognize when facts are inconsistent or missing and are expected to identify sources of additional facts.
>
> The Library consists of cases, statutes, regulations and rules, some of which may not be relevant to the assigned lawyering task. The applicant is expected to extract from the Library the legal principles necessary to analyze the problem and perform the task. The MPT is not a test of substantive law, and problems may arise in a variety of fields. Library materials provide sufficient substantive information to complete the task.
>
> The MPT requires applicants to (1) sort detailed factual materials and separate relevant from irrelevant facts; (2) analyze statutory, case, and administrative materials for relevant principles of law; (3) apply the relevant law to the relevant facts in a manner likely to resolve a client's problem; (4) identify and resolve ethical dilemmas, when present; (5) communicate effectively in writing; (6) complete a lawyering task within time constraints.
>
> These skills will be tested by requiring applicants to perform one of a variety of lawyering tasks. Although it is not feasible to list all possibilities, examples of tasks applicants might be instructed to complete include writing the following: a memorandum to a supervising attorney; a letter to a client; a persuasive memorandum or brief; a statement of facts; a contract provision; a will; a

[1] *See* www.ncbex.org/multistate-tests/mpt/mpt-faqs/description1/ (last visited Nov. 5, 2008).

counseling plan; a proposal for settlement or agreement; a discovery plan; a witness examination plan; a closing argument.

C. CHARACTER AND FITNESS: MISCONDUCT BEFORE LAW SCHOOL

Who decides whether you have the proper character and fitness to practice law? In most states, the state's highest court appoints a Character and Fitness Committee that collects reams of data from bar applicants, checks numerous references, and interviews each candidate individually. If the Character and Fitness Committee recommends that the applicant be admitted, the courts usually go along with the recommendation and administer the oath of office to the applicant. If the Character and Fitness Committee recommends against admission, the applicant can appeal the negative recommendation. The initial appeal is typically to a review panel of the Character and Fitness Committee. Later appeals are usually to the state's appellate courts, usually ending in the state's highest court. Federal courts do not get involved in state bar admission matters unless the case raises federal issues, such as due process, equal protection, or violations of federal statutes.

Why would the Character and Fitness Committee recommend against your admission to the bar? There are lots of reasons — as many reasons as there are character flaws (and prejudices against certain character traits). One of the most common reasons for denial of admission to the bar is lack of candor on the bar application. Applicants who fail to disclose some past sin (even a minor one) or who misrepresent some part of their past are usually summoned to a hearing and asked to explain the situation. If the Character and Fitness Committee believes that an omission or misrepresentation was deliberate, the Committee is likely to recommend against admission. The "Watergate principle" kicks in: a cover-up is even worse than the original sin. Nixon could probably have remained in office if he had openly and candidly acknowledged what happened right after the Watergate break-in. Instead, he sat in the Oval Office talking about how much it would cost to pay for the silence of people who could implicate the White House. (By the way, after Nixon resigned the Presidency, he was disbarred in New York for his dishonesty.)

The authors, therefore, have one strong bit of advice for you: *Tell the truth, the whole truth, and nothing but the truth on your bar application.* List every employer — even the ones who fired you and said they'd torpedo your bar application. List every arrest, conviction, parking ticket, and college disciplinary charge against you. List everything the bar asks you about. It's a lot easier to explain why you did something wrong a few years ago than it is to explain why you are lying today. If the Character and Fitness Committee concludes that you are a liar today, you'll never get a law license. Wouldn't you feel like a fool if you went to law school for three years, paid an arm and a leg in tuition, worked your tail off, passed the bar exam and the MPRE, and then couldn't get admitted to the bar?

Many people who have encounters with the justice system decide to attend law school and become lawyers. Some of these encounters with the justice system involve civil suits, such as divorce proceedings, debt collection proceedings, or personal injury suits arising out of auto accidents. Other encounters involve charges or convictions arising out of speeding tickets, reckless driving charges, or more serious criminal wrongdoing. Some encounters implicate codes of morality but not criminal conduct. Should the following categories of people pass the character and fitness standards necessary to be admitted to the bar?

- People who have been convicted of fraud
- People who have been convicted of murder
- Unmarried people who are living together
- Married people who commit adultery

- Men (married or unmarried) who patronize prostitutes
- U.S.-based supporters of al-Qaeda
- People who defaulted on their student loans, or declared personal bankruptcy to avoid paying them
- Alcoholics
- People who've been arrested for drunk driving
- Rehabilitated drug addicts
- Former radicals, killers, etc., who have reformed and are now leading ordinary, straight lives

D. CHARACTER AND FITNESS: MISCONDUCT DURING LAW SCHOOL

One of the reasons the Character and Fitness Committee may reject your admission to the bar may be in your past and therefore beyond your control. But one area that is still very much in your control is your conduct in law school. An especially sensitive area concerns positions of trust, especially positions as an officer of the Student Bar Association or any other club or organization in which you are entrusted with funds or submit applications for reimbursements for expenditures.

IN RE MUSTAFA

631 A.2d 45 (D.C. 1993)

SULLIVAN, ASSOCIATE JUDGE.

John W. Mustafa II, passed the July 1991 Bar examination and is an applicant for admission to the Bar of the District of Columbia. . . .

I.

In his third year of law school at the University of California at Los Angeles, Mustafa and Larry Brennan served as co-chief justices of the law school's moot court program, and shared access to and control over the program's checking account. [The account held student-paid dues of $25.00 each to cover moot court expenses not paid by the University.] Over a five-month period, between October 1990 and February 1991, Mustafa wrote thirteen checks totaling $4,331, approximately $3,510 of which he converted to his personal use.[2] On at least seven occasions, he wrote checks to reimburse himself for expenditures which had been, or would be, reimbursed by the university's accounting department. At other times, he failed to make any notation about the use of the money or falsified the purpose of the checks.[3]

Mustafa admitted to Brennan on June 14, 1991, that he had taken $1,000 from the fund to pay his sister's bail and that he would repay the money from a loan he had arranged from his then-prospective employer. Several days later, Brennan discovered that less than $800 remained in the account, rather than the $1,300 he had expected. Brennan closed the account. On June 25th, Mustafa presented Brennan with a cashier's check for $2,200. On June 28th, Brennan disclosed Mustafa's misconduct to the law

[2] Mustafa explained that he used the funds principally to pay his rent and other bills, to pay a $1,000 bail for his sister, to lend another sister $750 so she could leave an abusive husband, and to pay expenses for a law student to compete in a Chicago moot court competition. Mustafa also assumed responsibility for approximately $811 which he claimed were legitimate moot court program expenses for which he could provide no documentation.

[3] In particular, on November 28, 1990, he wrote a check to himself for $1,500, stating falsely on the check stub that it was for air fare to a competition in New York. Mustafa returned this amount to the fund via a personal check on January 2, 1991. Again, on February 28, 1991, he wrote a check for $1,500, indicating on the stub that the check was for $75.00 for Girl Scout cookies.

school dean; on the same day, Mustafa disclosed his misconduct to a law school professor and to the Committee. After an investigation, the university was satisfied that Mustafa had made full restitution and disposed of the matter by issuing a letter of censure to be placed in his confidential student discipline file for four years. As required by the university, Mustafa disclosed his misconduct to the law firm at which he is presently employed as a law clerk.

AUTHORS' COMMENT:
If you were a member of the Character and Fitness Committee, would you recommend that Mr. Mustafa be admitted to the Bar? Whatever your answer, what is your standard for granting or denying admission? What qualities must an applicant demonstrate to gain admission to the Bar, in your view?

II.

Following a hearing, the Committee found that Mustafa always intended to repay the sums taken from the fund, principally because he repaid $1,500 on January 2, 1991, kept an accurate mental record of how much he had taken from the fund, and made full restitution before there was any threatened action by the law school. The Committee was also impressed by Mustafa's honesty and forthrightness before the Committee and during the law school investigation. Moreover, Mustafa's references from two law school professors, three former members of the moot court program board, a former employer, and three partners and two associates from the law firm where Mustafa is employed, were, to the Committee, powerful testimony of his current good character. The Committee unanimously recommended that Mustafa be admitted to the Bar.

In order to gain admission to the Bar, an applicant must demonstrate "by clear and convincing evidence, that the applicant possessed good moral character and general fitness to practice law in the District of Columbia" at the time of the applicant's admission. This court will "accept findings of fact made by the Committee unless they are unsupported by substantial evidence of record," will "make due allowance for the Committee's opportunity to observe and evaluate the demeanor of the applicant where relevant," and will "afford the Committee's recommendations some deference. . . . "

Mustafa candidly acknowledges that he, like few others in his position, was placed in a position of trust in handling others' money and that he "failed that test." As the Committee recognized, Mustafa's conduct, while it did not result in a criminal conviction, . . . "could be considered criminal in nature and would almost invariably have resulted in the disbarment of an attorney admitted to practice." There is no doubt that an attorney who mismanages the funds of a client will ordinarily face disbarment. Similarly, an attorney convicted of a crime involving moral turpitude faces automatic disbarment. A disbarred attorney would be ineligible to apply for reinstatement for five years. D.C. Bar R. XI, § 16(e). While we do not hold as a matter of law that an applicant for admission to the Bar, like a disbarred attorney, must necessarily wait a minimum of five years from the date of proven misconduct[4] before applying for admission to the Bar, we conclude that on the record here, particularly the relatively short period of time that has elapsed since the date of his misconduct, Mustafa has failed to establish that he

[4] [F]or a number of reasons, including the total time required for investigating and conducting criminal and/or disbarment proceedings, a disbarred attorney may be ineligible for reinstatement to the bar for much longer than five years after his or her misconduct. The process of reinstatement is also time consuming, usually taking over a year.

has the good moral character required for admission to the Bar.

In reaching this conclusion, we are mindful of Mustafa's outstanding law school record[5] and his appropriate conduct since the embezzlement: he cooperated with the university and the Committee; he has married; and he has volunteered in several community projects since coming to the District of Columbia. "It is by no means our purpose to discourage the applicant" from continuing his positive personal and professional development. Indeed, on the record here, it appears likely that Mustafa will be able to establish the requisite good moral character at some future time. At present, however, "[o]ur consideration of the entire record leaves us unpersuaded that [Mustafa] now possesses 'those qualities of truth-speaking, of a high sense of honor, of granite discretion, of the strictest observation of fiduciary responsibility, that have . . . been compendiously described as [the] moral character' necessary for the practice of law." (quoting *Schware v. Board of Bar Examiners*, 353 U.S. 232 (1957) (Frankfurter, J., concurring)). In sum, Mustafa has not demonstrated his present fitness for the privilege of membership in the District of Columbia Bar.

Accordingly we deny Mustafa's application for admission to the Bar of the District of Columbia.

So Ordered.

NOTES AND QUESTIONS

1. ***Fair or Unfair?*** Was the court fair or unfair to deny Mustafa immediate admission to the District of Columbia Bar? What factors influence you most strongly one way or the other?

2. ***Postscript: What Happened to Mustafa?*** We don't know if Mustafa was ever admitted to practice in the District of Columbia, but we do know that he was eventually admitted to practice in California. In 2001, however, about ten years after the law school incidents, Mustafa was charged with serious professional misconduct in California. Mustafa stipulated to various kinds of misconduct, including fraud, repeatedly failing to return repeated phone calls from clients, commingling personal and business funds in his client trust account, writing checks for personal expenses against his client trust account, and failing to cooperate in the State Bar's investigation of his misconduct. The California Supreme Court then suspended Mustafa for two years, placed him on five years probation, ordered him to make restitution, ordered him to take the MPRE again, and imposed other sanctions. In LISA LERMAN & PHILIP SCHRAG, ETHICAL PROBLEMS IN THE PRACTICE OF LAW 61 (2005), the authors report that the California State Bar filed additional charges against Mustafa in 2002, while he was still suspended from practice. Mustafa did not respond to these charges but instead resigned from the Bar.

E. CHARACTER AND FITNESS: LYING ON THE BAR APPLICATION

Whatever the facts of an applicant's background, one sure way to make the situation worse is to lie on the bar application. Here's a case about a man who did just that in Florida.

---

[5] Mustafa was a staff member and editor of the law review; he was one of two co-chief justices of the moot court program; was named one of twelve outstanding advocates during his second year of law school; and was one of three graduating law students selected by the law school Dean, Susan Westerberg Prager, to attend an annual donors' dinner. He also participated in several other law school activities.

FLORIDA BOARD OF BAR EXAMINERS v. M.B.S.

955 So. 2d 504 (2007)

[A law school graduate that the court identifies only as "M.B.S." applied for admission to the Florida Bar in March 2003. The investigation into M.B.S.'s background uncovered information that reflected adversely upon his character and fitness. After an investigative hearing before the Florida Board of Bar Examiners (the "Board") in September 2004, the Board served four "specifications" (meaning charges) on M.B.S.

Specification 1 alleged M.B.S. had engaged in "illegal, irresponsible, or improper behavior" and had "demonstrated a lack of respect for the law and/or the rights of others." The specification detailed nine instances of various conduct by M.B.S. from January 1990 through March 2002 for which he was arrested, charged, or sentenced for various criminal offenses. For example, in 1990 he was charged with the unauthorized use of a Florida driver's license after he used a false driver's license to gain entry to a nightclub, and later in 1990 he pled no contest to a charge of possession of cannabis. That same month, M.B.S. tried to sell two tablets of Valium (a controlled substance) to an undercover police officer in a bar. M.B.S. pled guilty, was placed on probation for two years, and was ordered to perform twenty-five hours of community service. In 1992, M.B.S. used a credit card from a stolen briefcase to purchase gold, and later attempted to purchase another $1200 worth of gold from the same store, but was arrested after the salesperson called the police. He pled guilty to two counts of fraudulent use of a credit card, two counts of grand theft, and other charges. M.B.S. was sentenced to three years of probation. The theft led to the revocation of M.B.S.'s earlier probation for the Valium charge. He served three months in jail after his probation was revoked, and was placed on three years' probation to run concurrently with the probation for the theft of the briefcase. In 2001, while in law school, M.B.S. was arrested for driving over 100 miles per hour in a 55-mile-per-hour zone and swerving around other cars from lane to lane. He was found guilty of reckless driving and sentenced to fifty hours of community service. In March 2002, while a third year law student, M.B.S. got into a fight in a nightclub. Police officers were forced to use mace to subdue him. He was arrested and charged with disorderly conduct.]

Specification 2 alleged that M.B.S. had "submitted false information on his law school application." He falsely claimed that his college attendance had not been interrupted for any reason when it had been interrupted at least twice. He stated he was a campaign advisor and event organizer for "quite a few well-known Congressman [sic], Governors as well as local representatives" for the Vermont Republican Party in the early 1990s, which was totally false. He claimed he had performed volunteer work, helping "at-risk" youth and participating in a community-policing project, but that information was a blatant lie. He provided false information about six of the eight prior jobs he listed, inventing some of them. He submitted false information concerning the arrests, charges, and criminal convictions, including failing to update his application when there were new occurrences.

Specification 3 alleged that M.B.S. had "submitted false information to the Florida Supreme Court on an application to participate in a law school practice program" (i.e., a clinic) by checking the blank in front of the statement: "There is nothing in my background which reflects adversely on my character" and misrepresenting facts for submission to this Court.

Specification 4 alleged M.B.S. submitted false information on his Application for Admission to The Florida Bar regarding his history of arrests and convictions. For example, M.B.S. denied ever serving time in jail, which was untrue.

A formal hearing on the specifications was held on May 20, 2005. The Board found that all of the specifications had been proven and were disqualifying. However, the Board found that M.B.S. had "proven his rehabilitation by clear and convincing evidence." The Board summarized the evidence this way:

The record establishes that M.B.S. suffered from alcoholism and a debilitating Obsessive-Compulsive Disorder (hereinafter "OCD"). M.B.S. first started exhibiting symptoms of OCD in 1986. M.B.S. describes how the OCD manifested itself in his Chronological Medical History. M.B.S. provides an extensive description of all of the attempts to treat his OCD, both by way of counseling and medication. *Id.* Ultimately, M.B.S. started self-medicating by drinking alcohol. M.B.S.'s use of alcohol increased to the point that he became alcohol dependent.

M.B.S. joined Alcoholics Anonymous in January 2004. M.B.S. also executed a Florida Lawyers Assistance, Inc. contract on August 23, 2004. M.B.S.'s sobriety date is April 12, 2004. Therefore, M.B.S. appeared at the formal hearing with 13 months of sobriety. As things stand now, were M.B.S. to be admitted conditionally with a three year period of probation as recommended by the Board, M.B.S. would have over five years of sobriety at the end of the conditional admission period, assuming he maintains his sobriety.

In addition to the steps taken by M.B.S. to address his substance addiction and his OCD, M.B.S. documented at the formal hearing an extraordinary amount of community service.

Sharon Bourassa, the director of special projects and litigation for Legal Aid in Broward County, Florida, testified by telephone. Ms. Bourassa has known M.B.S. for two years. M.B.S. works in her unit under her supervision, and she knows M.B.S. both professionally and personally.

M.B.S. interviews clients for Legal Aid, many of them former inmates and individuals on welfare. In addition, M.B.S. has done research for Ms. Bourassa in a class-action case that will have significant impact concerning the support services available to the poor. . . .

Ms. Bourassa does not consider M.B.S. an intern anymore because of the work he has done and the amount of time he spends in the office. M.B.S. has taken a lot of responsibility in the office, freeing up Ms. Bourassa and others to work. . . . If Ms. Bourassa did not have M.B.S. working in her office, it would have a significant adverse impact on their ability to serve the clients they have.

M.B.S. frequently advocates for the cases of certain clients to be taken. Ms. Bourassa thinks M.B.S. will be very successful in criminal defense because he can really relate to the clients.

M.B.S. takes a very good holistic approach to helping the office's inmate clients. Ms. Bourassa testified that many of these clients would have recidivism problems if they did not work to address all of the issues in the inmate's life. Ms. Bourassa described M.B.S.'s involvement in Alcoholics Anonymous as "very zealous." . . .

Ms. Bourassa described M.B.S. as a person with a very good heart. She used the analogy of watching him turn into a butterfly from being a caterpillar over the past two years. She has worked in this area for 23 years, but this is only the third time she has agreed to testify on someone's behalf.

Ms. Bourassa described M.B.S. as a person of honesty and integrity. Ms. Bourassa was asked specifically about M.B.S.'s truthfulness, in light of the lack of candor described in the Specifications that M.B.S. admitted. Ms. Bourassa testified that as dishonest as M.B.S. was during his alcoholism, he has now become almost overly honest in recovery.

Ms. Bourassa testified that if she had an opening right now, she would hire M.B.S., especially to work with inmates. Ms. Bourassa has a close working relationship with the public defender's office, and she intends to get M.B.S. a job in that office if he is admitted to the Bar.

Nikki Elliott has worked in the legal field for 18 years, and has been a paralegal in the Broward County Legal Aid office for four years, and has worked closely with M.B.S. for the past two years. Ms. Elliot described M.B.S. as very caring, considerate, honest, loyal, dedicated, motivated, and hard-working.

. . . Ms. Elliott testified that M.B.S. works harder than some of their paid employees. . . .

Ms. Elliott also described how M.B.S. went beyond what would normally be expected to help other clients of their office, such as getting an ex-offender into culinary school, and giving a client one of M.B.S.'s suits so the client could wear it to a job interview. Ms. Elliott testified they have never had a volunteer like M.B.S.

Jeremy Garron is an inactive attorney in New Jersey who now works moving furniture in Florida. Mr. Garron did not stop practicing law in New Jersey because of any disciplinary action against him, but rather to try to deal with his alcoholism. Mr. Garron is a member of Alcoholics Anonymous . . .

Mr. Garron has seen M.B.S. change from the person who was hostile to someone who is genuinely involved with the Alcoholics Anonymous program.

Mr. Garron knows that M.B.S. attends Alcoholics Anonymous meetings every day, sometimes two to three meetings a day. . . .

Robert Farrell worked for Farrell Advertising for 39 years, and was the vice president of sales for different companies. Mr. Farrell is a member of Alcoholics Anonymous. Mr. Farrell has known M.B.S. for 16 months. Mr. Farrell and M.B.S. have slowly become friends, and they share the same sponsor in Alcoholics Anonymous.

Mr. Farrell and M.B.S. call each other all the time and have a strong bond of friendship. In spite of M.B.S.'s relative young age, he has been able to help a lot of older people in Alcoholics Anonymous. Mr. Farrell estimated that 90 per cent of the time M.B.S. spends in the program is geared toward helping other people. M.B.S. has started to sponsor someone else in the program. . . .

M.B.S. also testified at the formal hearing about his recovery from alcoholism and his community service. With regard to his service to Alcoholics Anonymous, M.B.S. has been secretary to one group, and is currently the treasurer of another group. M.B.S. has chaired multiple meetings.

M.B.S. also described how his involvement with Alcoholics Anonymous has helped him turn his life around. M.B.S. is in the process of being confirmed into the Catholic Church, and feels that his religion has helped his recovery because it gives him a much more concrete higher power that he recognizes is in control.

M.B.S. considers his work at Legal Aid as part of his recovery. M.B.S. does not attend a lot of Alcoholics Anonymous meetings because he feels like drinking, but because he can help other people, and by helping them, he is helping himself.

M.B.S. is heavily involved in a broad re-entry coalition, which attracted him through his work at Legal Aid. The list of community service organizations in which M.B.S. is involved includes The Dependency Division of the Seventeenth Judicial Circuit, Legal Aid of Broward County, Family, Inc., The Round Table Meetings of the Broward County Health and Rehabilitative Service Providers, The Broward County Re-entry Coalition for Ex-Offenders, Women in Distress, The Consortium of Faith-Based Organizations/Community-Based Organizations, The South Florida Human Rights Council, Neighbors for Neighbors Rescue and Relief for Hurricanes Frances and Jeanne, judicial campaigns, Public Awareness Committee, Re-entry Summit Convention, making a presentation at Broward Success Institute, Operation Election Protection, American

Civil Liberties Union, Elijah's Fathering Ministry, meeting regarding North Broward Hospital District Policies, making a presentation at Broward Correctional Institute, Job Fair at Sheridan Tech, Trial Assistance, South Florida Human Rights Council Education Committee Meeting, T.J. Reddick Bar Association, and a meeting with State Attorney Michael J. Satz to discuss ways to reduce recidivism.

As this list would indicate, M.B.S. has, over the past two years, been committed on a full-time basis to performing community service. He is able to do this in part because of gifts and/or loans from his parents and a Social Security disability he has been receiving for his OCD.

M.B.S. testified that he now follows three rules: "if it is not mine, I don't take it; if it is not true, I don't say it; if it doesn't feel right, I don't do it."

In addition to the evidence described above, M.B.S. introduced into evidence some 72 exhibits, most being character letters. These exhibits also provided some documentary evidence of the extensive community service in which M.B.S. has engaged.

AUTHORS' COMMENT:

That's the basic record. If you were on the Florida Board of Bar Examiners, would you recommend that M.B.S. be admitted to the Florida Bar, or not? Why? Here is how the Board viewed the record:

The Board acknowledges the extensive misconduct described in the Specifications, and the serious questions this conduct raises in determining whether M.B.S. should be admitted to the Bar. It should be noted that the last time M.B.S. engaged in conduct that was disqualifying was in March 2003 (over two years prior to the formal hearing) when he provided some information on his Florida Bar Application that was false, misleading, or lacking in candor. Since that time, through two appearances before the Board for his investigative and formal hearings, M.B.S. has displayed absolute candor.

The Board was impressed with the extent of rehabilitation established by M.B.S. at his formal hearing. This was proven through documentary evidence, testimony of character witnesses, and the testimony of M.B.S. himself. The Board also acknowledges the high regard in which M.B.S. is held by those who testified on his behalf. The extent of M.B.S.'s involvement in the community is among the most impressive seen by the Board from an applicant attempting to establish rehabilitation.

The Board had the opportunity to observe the demeanor of M.B.S., and to evaluate his credibility. The Board was convinced that M.B.S. was credible, and the Board was further impressed with M.B.S.'s changed attitude about how he conducts himself.

The Board recognized that M.B.S. had presented "a classic case of extensive and serious disqualifying conduct that needed to be weighed against an impressive showing of rehabilitation." M.B.S. had "a very heavy burden to establish his rehabilitation considering the pervasive and serious nature of the disqualifying conduct found proven in the Specifications." The Board quoted the New Jersey Supreme Court as saying: "An applicant's attitude and behavior subsequent to disqualifying misconduct must demonstrate a reformation of character so convincingly that it is proper to allow admission to a profession whose members must stand free from all suspicion."

The Board ultimately concluded that M.B.S. has undergone this reformation of character, and that he clearly and convincingly established that fact at the formal hearing. The Board therefore recommended that M.B.S. be granted a conditional admission for three years (essentially a three year probationary period of admission), which would provide "a further safeguard and check to ensure M.B.S. conducts himself properly as a member of the Bar." The next step in the bar admission process was for the Florida Supreme Court to confirm or reject the Board's recommendation. The Supreme Court initially rejected the Board's recommendation of conditional admission and denied M.B.S.'s application for admission, but M.B.S. moved for rehearing. We now reprint extensive excerpts from the Florida Supreme Court's opinion upon rehearing.]

PER CURIAM.

[T]he Board recommended that M.B.S. be conditionally admitted to The Florida Bar and serve a three-year probationary period with specified conditions. M.B.S. agreed to these conditions.

Because the Board's findings concerning M.B.S.'s rehabilitation were conclusory and the initial conduct so clearly disqualifying and egregious, the Court reviewed the entire record. . . .

The Board provided the additional factual detail which the Court had requested on the disqualifying conduct, but also addressed in more detail the rehabilitation evidence upon which it based its recommendation for conditional admission. The Board outlined alcoholism and an obsessive-compulsive disorder (OCD)[2]. The Board concluded that M.B.S. exhibited symptoms of OCD and ultimately began self-medicating with alcohol, which led to alcohol dependence. . . .

According to the Board, M.B.S. documented an extraordinary amount of community service. The director of special projects and litigation for Legal Aid in Broward County, Florida, Sharon Bourassa, testified on M.B.S.'s behalf by telephone. . . . Bourassa testified that if she had an opening, she would hire M.B.S., especially to work with inmates. A paralegal in the same office also testified on M.B.S.'s behalf and testified to M.B.S.'s hard work and caring and considerate attitude in dealing with clients. . . .

Analysis

. . . The egregiousness of the disqualifying conduct at issue here, including M.B.S.'s deplorable lack of truthfulness, the minimal rehabilitation in scope and depth, and the lack of any logical relationship between the misconduct and the evidence of rehabilitation compelled the Court to review the factual underpinnings of the Board's recommendation in this case. Our review raised more than serious doubts as to M.B.S.'s character and fitness. . . . M.B.S.'s conduct, until very recently, has been the antithesis of that which this Court requires for members of our profession to protect the public. He has a demonstrated thirteen-year history of lying (as recently as March 2003), stealing, breaking the law (as recently as March 2002), abusing alcohol (including as recently as April 2004), and violence (three bar fights, the last in March 2002). . . .

---

[2] [According to the American Psychiatric Association's Diagnostic and Statistical Manual of Mental Disorders, 4th Ed., the essential features of Obesessive-Compulsive Disorder are recurrent obsessions (persistant ideas) or compulsions (repetitivc behaviors) that are severe enough to be time consuming or cause marked distress or significant impairment. — Eds.]

AUTHORS' COMMENT:

After all of that history of crime and violence, what part of M.B.S.'s record do you suppose is most disturbing to the court? It's the part that is most relevant to you as a law student because it's the part you can still avoid or remedy. Read on.

Most disturbing is the shocking lack of honesty and candor M.B.S. exhibited on his law school application to obtain admission, his application to be submitted to this Court to participate in a law school practice program, and his application for admission to the Bar, all of which were submitted under oath. He clearly lied at each step of the process in very significant ways. Truthfulness and candor are the most important qualifications for Bar membership. M.B.S. lied in June 1999, when he completed his application for admission to law school, inventing fictitious jobs, employers, and volunteer activities, to improve his chances of admission. When he was asked why he had lied, he said: "I thought that if I had told the truth about all my past history, I wouldn't have gotten into law school. And I really wanted to go to law school." He lied again in April 2001, on his application submitted to this Court for participation in a law school practice program, when he swore there was nothing in his background that might reflect adversely on his character. When asked about this lie, M.B.S. said: "I was — I rationalized that question because of the way that it was worded. . . . Obviously if it had said have you ever been arrested, I would have had to answer differently or I would have been untruthful." He lied again in March 2003 on his Bar application. He misrepresented or slanted the facts concerning his arrests, particularly the theft of the briefcase. He also denied ever serving time and failed to disclose that he was intoxicated at the time of his arrest in 1994.

The Court is not persuaded that M.B.S.'s alcoholism adequately excuses, explains, or really addresses M.B.S.'s lack of candor and honesty or that there is even a nexus between alcohol and the most significant aspects of his egregious conduct. It is one thing to deny that one has a problem with alcohol or to try to hide one's consumption. It is another to fabricate jobs, employers, and volunteer activities to improve one's chances of admission to law school or to blatantly lie to this Court and on the Bar application.

"[T]he requirement of proof of rehabilitation is firm and fixed. This is not a mere pro forma requirement, but one requiring meaningful substance." Here . . . we find the proof of rehabilitation presented by the respondent lacks meaningful substance. The conditional admission process is intended to apply to persons who have an established history of conduct related to conditions clearly subject to rehabilitation who can enter a plan for some period of time after admission. Such a course of action can only be considered after rehabilitation has been established; the plan is to continue the process. Further, there must be a clear nexus between the disqualifying conduct and the condition subject to rehabilitation and the future plan. Conditional admission is not intended to replace the need for a clear and convincing record of rehabilitation. Further, disqualifying conduct extending over a long period of time will require a longer period of rehabilitation to satisfy the Court that the applicant can maintain the high standards of the profession and the professionalism necessary after gaining admission. Finally, the more serious the disqualifying conduct, the greater the burden of proof of rehabilitation. An applicant who engages in serious criminal conduct and breach of trust just days before entering law school and who thereafter demonstrates a further lack of candor must demonstrate behavior and character of the highest level subsequent to the disqualifying conduct to clearly and convincingly establish that admission is proper to a profession that requires its members to be absolutely above and beyond suspicion.

When the nature and quantity of M.B.S.'s egregious behavior over thirteen years is weighed against the two-year period of sobriety and recovery activities and volunteer work shown here, the misconduct still vastly overwhelms and outweighs the rehabilitation. M.B.S.'s rehabilitation evidence will need to be of the highest order over a longer period than has been shown to overcome his past misdeeds.

The nature and timing of M.B.S.'s metamorphosis and rehabilitation are additional reasons for the Court's caution. M.B.S. exhibited some of the most egregiously disqualifying conduct — lying to gain entry to law school, lying to this Court to be certified to participate in the law school practice program under chapter 11 of the Rules Regulating the Florida Bar, and lying to the Board on his Bar application — very recently. He only began attending AA meetings in January 2004, and only attained sobriety in April 2004. He entered into a contract with FLA, Inc. on August 23, 2004. A few weeks later, in September 2004, he participated in an investigative hearing before the Board. After numerous years of abusing alcohol, breaking the law, and lying, he suggests that he has turned his life around only a few months before investigative and formal hearings before the Board. He claims to have suddenly gained control over his OCD and alcoholism, after years of being totally unable to overcome the problems presented by either. The Court requires more convincing evidence that this is truly a turning point in M.B.S.'s life and not just another deception and deliberate ploy to gain admission. There is no evidence that M.B.S. was even under the influence of alcohol when he perjured himself on multiple occasions.

The sincerity and depth of M.B.S.'s newfound candor and honesty are another concern. His lies on his application to this Court for participation in a law school practice program are a good example. He checked the option that said there was nothing in his background to reflect adversely on his character. The choice he did not check read: "There is something in my background which might reflect adversely on my character." (Emphasis removed.) M.B.S.'s explanation that he lied because of the way the form was worded is a self-serving rationalization that is diametrically opposed to that level of openness and candor which is a necessary prerequisite for admission to a profession that has honesty as its bedrock.

M.B.S.'s testimony convinces the Court that he has failed to accept full responsibility for his actions, especially his lack of candor, by attempting to transfer some of the blame to his alcoholism, his parents (for enabling him over the years), and the wording of one of the forms upon which he lied. M.B.S. attributed much of his misconduct to what he referred to as "character defects" and testified that some of these defects disappeared when he stopped drinking. Yet, there was nothing to suggest that M.B.S. was intoxicated when he made false statements under oath or that he was unaware of the truth. Such quibbling is inconsistent with a firm conviction that M.B.S. fully comprehends and intends to correct the error of his ways. Yet, he believes he is fit to assume the significant responsibility of serving the people of this state as an attorney.[2]

The fact that M.B.S. was thirty-four years old at the time of the formal hearing before the Board, but was still financially dependent, at least in part, on his parents is further cause for caution. "Merely showing that an individual is now living as and doing those things he or she should have done throughout life, although necessary to prove rehabilitation, does not prove that the individual has undertaken a useful and constructive place in society." . . .

While it is to be hoped that M.B.S.'s proclaimed turnaround lasts, it is the Court's obligation to protect the public and the profession by ensuring the fitness of every lawyer admitted to the Bar. Requiring M.B.S. to clearly and convincingly establish a

[2] Another example of M.B.S.'s tenuous grasp of the concept of complete candor is provided by the discrepancies in M.B.S.'s statements concerning his conversion to another faith. He offered two different stories concerning who gave him a rosary and confused significant terms, although he claimed to have studied the materials concerning his new faith thoroughly.

longer record of success before allowing his admission best fulfills that obligation. The process and intent of conditional admission must not degenerate into a process that simply ushers undesirable candidates into The Florida Bar and foists them upon Florida's citizens.

Conclusion

With all of the many reasons for caution discussed above, the Court disapproves the Board's recommendation that M.B.S. be admitted. M.B.S.'s application for admission is denied at this time for the standard period of two years. If and when M.B.S. reapplies for admission, he must satisfy the concerns we express and must present objectively verifiable evidence of his continuing, uninterrupted sobriety during the interim period, as well as other suitable evidence of rehabilitation.

It is so ordered.

ANSTEAD, J., dissenting.

I would accept the Board's recommendation. . . .

[W]e need only to consider the short shrift the majority gives to the evidence of rehabilitation presented at the evidentiary hearing before the Board, compared to the extensive and comprehensive review of the evidence and findings by the Board. In a single brief paragraph, the majority first asserts that the Board found that evidence of "an extraordinary amount of community service" was presented at the hearing; the majority then, in effect, directly refutes this statement by characterizing the evidence presented as consisting only of the brief testimony of a legal aid attorney and paralegal. In the balance of the opinion the majority essentially substitutes its view of the credibility and weight of the evidence and rejects the Board's firsthand assessment.

[A]gain in stark contrast to the majority's exclusive focus on the applicant's misconduct, we must consider the Board's conscientious attempt to carry out its responsibilities to evaluate *both* the extensive evidence of prior misconduct and the extensive evidence of rehabilitation:

Because I conclude the Board has correctly and conscientiously carried out its responsibilities I would approve the Board's findings and recommendation.

NOTES AND QUESTIONS

1. ***What was the Worst Thing M.B.S. did?*** Of all of the many problems in M.B.S.'s background, which ones did you consider the worst? In other words, what is the minimum combination of bad acts for which you would have denied M.B.S. admission to the Florida Bar? Or would you have agreed with the dissent and granted M.B.S. conditional admission to the Bar?

2. ***A Bar Examiner's View.*** In 2004, the South Texas Law Review held a Symposium entitled "The Ethics of Law Students." One of the speakers at the Symposium was Julia E. Vaughan, who has been the Executive Director of the Texas Board of Law Examiners since March 2000 and was a Member of that Board from 1995 through 2000. The published version of her talk gives excellent advice to law students.

JULIA E. VAUGHAN, ADDRESSING LAW STUDENT DISHONESTY: THE VIEW OF ONE BAR ADMISSIONS OFFICIAL

45 S. Tex. L. Rev. 1009 (2004)*

. . . Bar admission authorities tend to focus on truthfulness in law school applications and the aspiring attorney's conduct during law school simply because the vast majority of applicants are in law school at the time they apply for bar admission. Under bar admission rules . . . requiring an appraisal of an aspiring attorney's present character, the focus is properly on what he or she has been doing recently. In a purely temporal sense the law schools are the best source of current information.

. . . As an integral part of every Texas law school's orientation, an official representative of the Texas Board of Law Examiners is invited to address entering students concerning licensing requirements, including the investigation and assessment of present character and fitness. At this time, recently admitted students . . . are notified of the opportunity for voluntary full disclosure of misrepresentations on their law school applications to reduce or eliminate concerns of present dishonesty. Our experience has been that, following this explanation, law school admissions authorities report a number of recently admitted students accept the invitation for voluntary full disclosure and offer amendments to correct misrepresentations on their law school applications. . . .

[F]ew instances of adverse admission decisions or negative character and fitness determinations by licensing authorities appear to have resulted from isolated incidents of minor academic or criminal misconduct occurring prior to a student's application for law school. However, inquiries and investigations into academic and criminal misconduct are of equal dignity in a broad sense because severity, recency or pattern of misconduct can only be evaluated in the context of the individual's record of recent conduct in its entirety.

Bar admission authorities have access to official criminal history reports to verify applicant self-reports. Law schools may be less able to verify, but that should not hinder schools from making reasonable inquiry. Simply stated, the willingness of an aspiring law student to conceal or misrepresent any misconduct, whether academic or nonacademic, in connection with a recent application to gain admission to law school points to a much more serious problem than the often minor underlying misconduct that has been omitted from the application. A recent decision to be dishonest on a law school application virtually always carries more weight than the more remote misconduct in deciding on present character and fitness. Thus, it is imperative for an applicant to proactively set the record straight with the law school and bar admission authorities. . . .

[A] hyper-competitive environment exists both for the aspiring law student and for law schools aspiring to improve their overall ranking in U.S. News and World Report's annual publication comparing each law school to the country's most elite institutions. Apparently the competition among certain law schools for elite students mirrors the competition among certain students for acceptance to elite law schools. A vital step toward the continued integrity of the academy, the students and the legal profession, is for law schools to actively oppose any trend to condone concealing, manipulating or misreporting by aspiring students eager to achieve a competitive advantage over their peers just as strongly as they would seek to reverse any trend by peer institutions to conceal, manipulate or misreport statistical information about the institution to achieve a competitive advantage in national rankings.

. . . In Texas, and virtually all other jurisdictions, a decision on character and fitness will view the aspiring attorney's honesty as a paramount consideration. Honesty in the law school application process is a vital part of the functional assessment of the aspiring attorney's present character and fitness.

F. SHOULD LAWYERS EDUCATED OUTSIDE THE U.S. BE ADMITTED IN THE UNITED STATES?

Should lawyers who are educated and licensed outside the U.S. be admitted to practice law in the United States? That question is arising with increasing frequency in the global economy, especially given the turmoil and class unrest in many countries around the world. The following case sets forth a fairly typical scenario, and in the process analyzes the role of the law school curriculum and the bar examination in determining whether a person has the necessary qualifications to sit for the bar exam.

OSAKWE v. BOARD OF BAR EXAMINERS

448 Mass. 85 (2006)

CORDY, J.

The respondent, Board of Bar Examiners (board), denied the application of the petitioner, Gregory C. Osakwe, to sit for the Massachusetts bar examination. . . .

1. *Background.* Osakwe graduated from the University of Nigeria with a bachelor of laws (LL.B.) degree in 1990. He then attended the Nigerian Law School in Abuja, where he passed the Nigerian bar examination and was called to the bar of the Federal Republic of Nigeria in December, 1990. Osakwe later moved to Trinidad and Tobago. In 1996, he earned a legal education certificate from the Hugh Wooding Law School and was admitted to practice in the Republic of Trinidad and Tobago. Osakwe then moved to Connecticut, where he earned a master of laws (LL.M.) degree from the University of Connecticut School of Law in May, 2001. Subsequently, Osakwe was permitted to sit for and passed the New York bar examination. He was admitted to practice in New York in February, 2003. In June of that same year, he was admitted to practice before the United States District Court for the District of Connecticut. Osakwe presently practices Federal immigration law in Connecticut and New York.

In June, 2004, Osakwe applied for admission to the Massachusetts bar. . . . In a reply letter, the board informed Osakwe that, in its estimation, he lacked the requisite academic qualifications to sit for the examination. . . .

2. *Qualifications for taking the bar examination.* . . . The educational requirements to sit for the examination include. . . . an ABA-accredited law school. . . .

Osakwe seeks to sit for the examination under the exception to the J.D. requirement for foreign-trained lawyers . . . In general, the board "may" permit "[g]raduates of the common-law faculties of law schools in foreign countries (other than Canada) whose jurisprudence rests upon the common-law tradition" to sit for the examination. . . .

"[T]here is clearly a direct rational connection between the requirement of graduation from an accredited law school and an applicant's fitness to practice law. The ABA standards relating to the accreditation of law schools provide assurance that applicants to the bar 'have experienced a generally uniform level of appropriate legal education.' " Thus, when we review the credentials of those educated abroad, the ABA standards provide a touchstone for the analysis. "[T]here must be a recognizable and significant resemblance between a foreign applicant's complete legal education and the legal education that generally is provided to a recipient of a juris doctor degree in a law school approved by the ABA."

One might argue that we should dispense with a rigorous application of the educational requirement for those with significant education and experience in foreign common-law jurisdictions. This would allow more candidates to sit for the bar examination and would make the results of that examination our primary mode of assessing an applicant's qualifications. . . .

The argument to dispense with a rigorous application of the educational requirement, however, does not fully capture the different purposes served by the bar examination and the educational requirement. The examination's main purpose is to subject all candidates to a uniform objective evaluation. It also provides evidence that, faced with novel factual situations, candidates can apply legal principles quickly and correctly. This is, we think, a necessary but not a sufficient qualification for the practice of law in this Commonwealth. The bar examination is not simply a summary examination of topics covered in law school; nor is law school simply a prolonged preparation for the examination. The bar examination alone cannot substitute for the intellectual development and professional acculturation that form the basis of the legal education requirement. Nor can the bar examination we administer, as rigorous and thorough as it may be, cover any of its topics with the depth and subtlety required in accredited law schools.

AUTHORS' COMMENT:

Given the criteria set out by the Massachusetts Supreme Court for being eligible to take the Massachusetts bar exam, would you allow Mr. Osakwe to sit for the bar exam? Why or why not?

3. *Analysis*. . . . "Our requirement of an equivalent legal education is not to test the intellectual capabilities of an attorney who has graduated from a foreign institution, but to examine the applicant's familiarity with the fundamentals of American law. We do so because there is a strong public interest in ensuring that the license to practice law in this Commonwealth be granted to applicants only on a reasonable showing that they have demonstrated that familiarity." Our analysis of Osakwe's application thus will consider whether he has gained from education and experience the requisite familiarity with the fundamentals of American law. The rule and the board guidelines . . . suggest that we think about this "familiarity with the fundamentals of American law" in two ways. First, there is an evaluation of exposure to the common-law tradition — its topical division of the law, its principles of reasoning, and its basic rules. We shall refer to this portion of the analysis as the "general" evaluation. . . . [T]he board will look to see if an applicant has studied in the common-law faculty of a school in a country "whose jurisprudence rests upon the common-law tradition." Then there is an evaluation of exposure to American law — the "particular" evaluation. . . . [T]he board generally will require such courses to be not in the basic common-law topics, but in particularly American subjects, for example, American constitutional law, Federal courts and jurisprudence, and the Uniform Commercial Code. The board also considers other evidence of familiarity with American law, including a review of courses completed for credit in obtaining an LL.M. degree from an American law school, admission to practice in other United States jurisdictions, and the length and nature of practice or teaching in other United States jurisdictions.

[I]n *Wei Jia* [*v. Board of Bar Examiners*, 427 Mass. 777 (1998)] . . . , we evaluated the credentials of an applicant who first trained in a Chinese law school. He then received advanced degrees from Tulane Law School and was admitted to the bar in both Louisiana and New York. . . . Wei Jia's courses at Tulane focused almost exclusively on international business transactions, and included only one of the basic J.D. courses, contracts. In rejecting Wei Jia's petition, we observed:

> If greater similarities existed between the law of the People's Republic of China and our law; if the former were based on the English common-law

> system, which it is not; if the petitioner, as a graduate student at Tulane, had taken for credit and passed more of the courses required of a juris doctor degree, which he has not; if the petitioner had engaged in the practice of law in Louisiana or New York for some substantial period of time, which he has not, this would be a different case.

Osakwe presents one particular example of the "different case". . . .

Nigeria, like Massachusetts, has a legal system derived from the English common-law tradition. Students who train in Nigerian law schools are educated in that tradition. A review of Osakwe's transcripts reveals that he has taken a wide array of courses, many of them offered as part of the core curriculum at ABA-approved law schools. His transcript from the University of Nigeria shows courses in property, torts, contracts, evidence, constitutional law, land law, equity, jurisprudence, company law, international law, and commercial law. His transcript from the Nigerian Law School shows further courses in civil procedure, criminal procedure, company law, evidence, and the completion of a general paper on law and ethics. . . .

This is not to say that Osakwe's education was the same as that of lawyers with an American J.D., in that his common-law courses in Nigeria would not have delved into the particular way that the tradition has developed here. We are, however, satisfied that Osakwe's education has given him sufficient exposure to the common-law tradition to satisfy the "general" portion of our analysis.

Osakwe has also shown that he has sufficient education in and exposure to American law to satisfy our "particular" analysis. . . . Osakwe's LL.M. training at the University of Connecticut School of Law . . . shows graded course work in American civil procedure, American criminal procedure, immigration law, Federal taxation, torts, and United States law and legal institutions. . . . Whatever deficiencies there may have been in Osakwe's exposure to American law in particular were, we think, cured by his LL.M. program . . . .

Additionally, we find Osakwe's admission and practice in other American jurisdictions to be relevant to the particular analysis and helpful (although not conclusive) to his claim. [T]he record evidence here shows that Osakwe was not only admitted to the New York bar and the Federal bar in the District of Connecticut, but that he also has actively practiced law in those courts for the past three years.

Our evaluation of Osakwe's educational qualifications has revealed that he has sufficient general exposure to the common-law tradition and specific knowledge of American law. . . . We refer Osakwe's application to the board with instructions that he be allowed to sit for the bar examination.

So ordered.

NOTES AND QUESTIONS

1. ***Common Law Countries.*** Many lawyers from around the world would like to become lawyers in the United States. In *Osakwe*, the Massachusetts Supreme Court said that the Board of Law Examiners will look to see if an applicant has studied law in a country "whose jurisprudence rests upon the common-law tradition." Did you know that the jurisprudence of Nigeria rests on the common-law tradition? Did you know that the jurisprudence of China does not? If studying law in a common-law jurisdiction is an essential (albeit not sufficient) prerequisite to sitting for the bar exam in a particular state, which countries does that rule out? Do people from those countries have to start law school all over again in the United States if they want to sit for the bar?

2. ***How much Competition do Foreign Lawyers Pose?*** If many states follow the lead of Massachusetts in *Osakwe* and allow foreign-educated lawyers to sit for the bar exam, how much competition is that likely to pose for you over the coming decades?

Will foreign lawyers take jobs away from you and your classmates (and American lawyers generally)? Or will foreign lawyers perhaps bring clients into the American legal system who are currently unserved, increasing the prosperity and engagement of those clients in America and effectively creating new potential clients for American lawyers? In any event, apart from any effect foreign lawyers may have on the incomes of American lawyers, will the proliferation of foreign-educated lawyers be a positive development or a negative one for the American economy, the American legal profession, or American clients?

3. ***Partnerships with Foreign Lawyers.*** Rule 5.4 of the ABA Model Rules of Professional Conduct prohibits a lawyer from sharing legal fees with a nonlawyer or from forming a partnership with a nonlawyer if any of the activities of the partnership constitute the practice of law. Should foreign lawyers be considered nonlawyers for purposes of this rule? If so, forming a multinational law firm will be very difficult. If foreign lawyers are not considered nonlawyers, then should all foreign lawyers be considered lawyers for purposes of Rule 5.4, or should foreign lawyers be considered lawyers only if their education meets some (or all) of the tests applied in *Osakwe* for purposes of determining whether a foreign lawyer should be permitted to sit for an American bar exam?

Chapter 4

THE UNAUTHORIZED PRACTICE OF LAW BY NON-LAWYERS

Lawyers have a legal monopoly on the giving of legal advice and the provision of legal services. That gives lawyers the opportunity to do interesting and lucrative work that non-lawyers are not permitted to do. A non-lawyer who gives unauthorized legal advice is engaged in the unauthorized practice of law, which is prohibited in every state and is a crime (usually a misdemeanor) in many states. Moreover, in every jurisdiction, a lawyer who assists a non-lawyer in the unauthorized practice of law is violating the rules of professional conduct.

Unfortunately, even after you get your law license you will be admitted to practice in only one jurisdiction, and you will ordinarily be permitted to practice law only in the jurisdiction where you are licensed. (A few of you will take two bar exams during the summer after graduation and become licensed in two states, but because most states give the bar exam at around the same time of year, becoming licensed in three states during the summer after you graduate is almost impossible.) If you engage in the practice of law in a jurisdiction where you are not licensed, then — unless that "foreign" jurisdiction's rules permit you to do so — you are engaged in the unauthorized practice of law just as any other non-lawyer would be in that jurisdiction.

These two ideas — that non-lawyers are prohibited from practicing law at all, and that lawyers may not practice law where they are not licensed — are the subject of this chapter and the next chapter.

A. THE DEBATE OVER RESTRICTIONS ON THE PRACTICE OF LAW

Every jurisdiction in the U.S. requires that a person be licensed as an attorney before that person performs certain activities. A person who is not licensed as a lawyer in any state and who engages in certain actions is said to be engaged in the unauthorized practice of law, or "UPL." Penalties for violating a state's prohibition on unauthorized practice of law include: (a) injunctions against continuing the offending activity, (b) disgorgement of any fees that have been collected, (c) refusal to enforce fee contracts for fees that have not yet been collected, and (d) misdemeanor criminal charges. In some states, the legislature has adopted statutes setting penalties for those who engage in the unauthorized practice of law.

In addition, a jurisdiction's professional responsibility rules typically provide that lawyers licensed in that state can neither commit UPL elsewhere, nor assist a non-lawyer in committing UPL. Courts have consistently claimed inherent power to control the gates to the practice of law. When a person becomes licensed as a member of the bar in a state, that person is admitted to practice before the courts in that jurisdiction. The courts, not the governor or the legislature, admit you to practice law. Even if you are not a litigator and never appear before the courts again after you take the attorney's oath of office, the courts have authority to control your behavior through rules of professional conduct and to discipline you for violating those rules. Judicial opinions enforce and sometimes expand the provisions prohibiting UPL.

Some people criticize the broad restrictions against the unauthorized practice of law. In economic terms, UPL restrictions limit legal services on the supply side — they limit the pool of suppliers of legal services to those who have been admitted to the bar (i.e., licensed to practice) in a given jurisdiction. Critics say that UPL restrictions increase costs to consumers of legal services (i.e., clients), who must seek representation from an artificially limited monopoly of providers. Critics also argue that the methods we use to ascertain minimum competence (passing a bar exam and, in most states, graduating from a law school that meets certain standards) do not accurately measure whether a person is competent to deliver a specific legal service. For example, someone who has never graduated from college (let alone law school) could have a sophisticated working knowledge of basic consumer bankruptcy law and might be able to provide competent assistance to a client in filing for personal bankruptcy. In contrast, a lawyer who has for fifteen years exclusively practiced in an area unrelated to bankruptcy (such as residential real estate) might not provide competent bankruptcy advice even though the lawyer graduated at the top of his class from a well-regarded law school and easily passed the bar exam.

Defenders of the current system have both positive and negative reasons for continuing and even expanding existing UPL restrictions. On the positive side, defenders say that when a person has been admitted as a member of the bar, that person has demonstrated the ability to successfully engage in legal reasoning. On the negative side, defenders of UPL restrictions warn that people who deliver legal services without the proper training and without qualifying for a law license can significantly harm their clients, who may not discover the deficiencies until it is too late to correct them. (When do you think a client will discover a problem with a will that was supposed to leave the client's valuable stamp collection to his beloved nephew Timothy? When the client is six feet under! — a little too late to fix the error.) Thus, there are good reasons for imposing some conditions on entry into the profession rather than having complete ease of entry and then weeding out those who prove to be unfit after they have harmed a client.

Critics have proposed at least three alternatives to the current system. One alternative is that anyone should be permitted to practice law as long as the person does not misrepresent his or her credentials (e.g., you cannot call yourself a "lawyer" if you do not have a law license or say you graduated from law school if you did not). The market will then favor those who offer the best value for the money (the same way the market operates for cars, carpets, and carpenters), and the market will drive incompetent or dishonest practitioners out of business. A second alternative is that the non-lawyers should be permitted to practice law to serve poor people who otherwise would have no lawyers at all. A third alternative is that government agencies or private organizations should license non-lawyers in special fields (e.g., personal bankruptcy, or residential real estate closings). These alternative systems could be combined with each other. For example, the government could allow a non-lawyer to serve poor clients only in narrow fields (e.g., landlord-tenant law or consumer rights) and only if the non-lawyer has demonstrated competence in those fields (e.g., through an examination or apprenticeship).

Which side of the debate do you think has the stronger argument? Do you oppose or defend the current system? Could providers of legal services provide the same quality legal advice to clients even if they did not attend law school, pass the bar exam, and pass the character investigation?

Traditionally the courts have exercised the power to define unauthorized practice. But do legislatures share this power? What if a legislature decided to pass a law allowing non-lawyers to engage in activities that the courts have traditionally defined as unauthorized practice? Do legislatures have the power to authorize what would otherwise be unauthorized practice? An excerpt from Q. Johnstone & D. Hopson, Lawyers and Their Work 165–71 (1967), a classic book in this field, tells the tale of the struggle between the legislature, the courts, and the people of Arizona when the Arizona legislature decided to loosen restrictions on the practice of law.

> If the courts do not wish to follow a statute or administrative regulation pertaining to unauthorized practice, the common judicial view is that they need not do so, for courts are supreme in this field. Despite their inherent powers over unauthorized practice, it is possible for courts to have these powers clipped by constitutional amendment. In 1962, this happened in Arizona. The Supreme Court of that state in 1961 handed down a sweeping decision prohibiting title

companies and real estate brokers from preparing legal instruments and giving legal advice. [*See State Bar of Arizona v. Arizona Land Title & Trust Co.*, 90 Ariz. 76, 366 P.2d 1 (1961).] Under an Arizona initiative procedure, the brokers then had a constitutional amendment put on the ballot giving licensed real estate brokers and salesmen extensive rights to draft legal instruments in connection with their work. A bitter campaign over the issue then ensued, and at election time, the amendment carried by a four to one margin in a popular vote. The amendment provides:

> *Art. 26, Section 1.* Any person holding a valid license as a real estate broker or a real estate salesman regularly issued by the Arizona State Real Estate Department when acting in such capacity as broker or salesman for the parties, or agent for one of the parties to a sale, exchange, or trade, or the renting and leasing of property, shall have the right to draft or fill out and complete, without charge, any and all instruments incident thereto, including, but not limited to, preliminary purchase agreements and earnest money receipts, deeds, mortgages, leases, assignments, releases, contracts for sale of realty, and bills of sale.

If a referendum on this amendment were held where you live, how would you vote?

B. DEFINING "THE PRACTICE OF LAW"

A key issue in any analysis of UPL is the standard that will be applied to determine whether a particular activity is or is not "the practice of law." Exactly what is prohibited? Everyone agrees that representing another person in court is the practice of law. However, many state and federal agencies will allow a non-lawyer to represent someone at an administrative proceeding, such as an unemployment hearing or a social security hearing. Should that be allowed?

Outside of court, unauthorized practice doctrine becomes more complex. One reason is that persons in many other professions perform activities that seem quite similar to giving legal advice. Accountants, for example, advise clients about tax laws and represent taxpayers before the IRS. Life insurance agents advise people about the tax implications of naming beneficiaries and other estate planning issues. Sports agents negotiate contracts on behalf of baseball players, and talent agents represent singers in negotiations with Sony and MTV. Insurance adjusters evaluate claims and negotiate settlements on behalf of insurance companies, while real estate agents help people draft contracts to buy homes and advise sellers about disclosure requirements. Are all of these activities "the practice of law"? Are any of them?

1. Judicially Recognized Tests

How should we define the practice of law? What tests should we use to determine whether someone is engaged in the unauthorized practice of law? In Q. Johnstone & D. Hopson, Lawyers and Their Work, the authors categorize the various tests courts have applied from time to time to determine whether a particular activity is the practice of law. Here are three of the more commonly applied tests:

(1) *The incidental test.* By this test, a layman may perform whatever legal services are incidental or ancillary to established practices in his business.

(2) *The simple-complex test.* If difficult and complex legal tasks are involved, only a lawyer may do them; simple legal tasks, on the other hand, may be performed by laymen.

(3) *The legal skill and knowledge test.* If no more than ordinary business intelligence is required, a layman may act; but the activity is the practice of law if the skill that is needed is peculiar to one trained and experienced in the law.

NOTES AND QUESTIONS

How would the following fact patterns be sorted out by a court applying the tests just described by Professor Johnstone? If you were a judge, which of the activities below would you consider to be the unauthorized practice of law?

- **a.** Alex Ackerman, not licensed as a lawyer in any state, tells people who visit his website that he is willing to write a will and set up a trust for them at no charge, as long as they leave 10% of their property to any university they choose. Ackerman is not affiliated with any university and will not personally profit in any way from writing wills.
- **b.** Bernice Bently, not licensed as a lawyer in any state, opens a storefront office offering her assistance with tax questions. She keeps racks of federal and state tax return forms on hand and charges only $50 to help people choose the right forms and fill them out correctly. For example, Bently recently explained to a farmer the difference between dividends and interest income and helped a waitress figure out whether her IRA contribution was deductible or non-deductible.
- **c.** Cora Cole, who is not licensed to practice law in any state, runs a small candy store and drafts legal papers on the side. For example, a mechanic told Cole he had been sued for $750 in small claims court after his tree fell on a neighbor's car during a windstorm. Cole wrote up an answer denying liability and sold the mechanic a $25 book explaining the procedures in small claims court. Another client, a railroad conductor, paid Cole $100 to draft a simple will, which Cole did by filling in the blanks on a form will on a CD-ROM program called Quicken Family Lawyer.
- **d.** Dori Darwin, not licensed as a lawyer in any state, mediated a dispute between a restaurant owner and a former chef and wrote up the contract under which they agreed to settle their lawsuit.
- **e.** Edward Exec, the Vice-President of Purchasing at the Furnwell Furnace Corporation ("Furnwell"), is not licensed to practice law in any state. Furnwell has been sued in small claims court for $400 by a local coffee vendor who claims Furnwell did not pay his bill for coffee services. It would cost Furnwell at least $500 to hire an outside lawyer to study the file and show up in court. Furnwell therefore sent Edward Exec to explain to the court why Furnwell did not pay the coffee vendor's bill and to seek dismissal of the suit because the coffee vendor did not attach any invoices or other documentation.
- **f.** Fred Furnwell, Jr., the Chief Engineer at Furnwell Furnace Corporation, graduated from law school but went straight into the family furnace business without taking the bar exam. Furnwell Furnace was recently sued for $600,000 by a woman whose Furnwell furnace exploded in her basement, causing major damage to her home. The company asked Fred to draft papers and appear in court to defend Furnwell Furnace Corporation.
- **g.** Average Guy, who attended two years of college but is not a lawyer, was recently sued for $200,000 by a neighbor who slipped on some ice on Guy's front steps while attending a Superbowl party at Guy's house. The neighbor claims serious injuries. If he wins his lawsuit then Guy will have to declare bankruptcy. Guy thinks the neighbor either was at fault or is faking his injuries. To save on legal fees, Guy has decided to defend the lawsuit himself.

2. Tests in Statutes and Rules

In 2004, the ABA Standing Committee on Client Protection conducted a survey on unlicensed practice of law. It asked all states and the District of Columbia whether their jurisdiction defined the "practice of law." Twenty-eight of the thirty six jurisdictions that responded had defined the "practice of law" by statute, rule, advisory opinion, or case law.[1]

An example of the terms in a statute defining the practice of law is Title 15, Chapter 19, Article 3 in the Code of Georgia:

> *Section 5-19-50* The practice of law in this state is defined as: (1) Representing litigants in court and preparing pleadings and other papers incident to any action or special proceedings in any court or other judicial body; (2) Conveyancing; (3) The preparation of legal instruments or all kinds whereby a legal right is secured; (4) The rendering of opinions as to the validity or invalidity of titles to real or personal property; (5) The giving of any legal advice; and (6) Any action taken for others in any matter connected with the law.

Another approach taken in states such as Washington is to provide much more guidance about permitted activities. After articulating the definition in part (a) of its General Rule 24, the rest of the Washington rule details actions which are specifically permitted:

> (a) *General Definition:* The practice of law is the application of legal principles and judgment with regard to the circumstances or objectives of another entity or person(s) which require the knowledge and skill of a person trained in the law. This includes but is not limited to:
>
> (1) Giving advice or counsel to others as to their legal rights or the legal rights or responsibilities of others for fees or other consideration.
>
> (2) Selection, drafting, or completion of legal documents or agreements which affect the legal rights of an entity or person(s).
>
> (3) Representation of another entity or person(s) in a court, or in a formal administrative adjudicative proceeding or other formal dispute resolution process or in an administrative adjudicative proceeding in which legal pleadings are filed or a record is established as the basis for judicial review.
>
> (4) Negotiation of legal rights or responsibilities on behalf of another entity or person(s).
>
> (b) *Exceptions and Exclusions:* Whether or not they constitute the practice of law, the following are permitted:
>
> (1) Practicing law authorized by a limited license to practice pursuant to Admission to Practice Rules 8 (special admission for: a particular purpose or action; indigent representation; educational purposes; emeritus membership; house counsel), 9 (legal interns), 12 (limited practice for closing officers), or 14 (limited practice for foreign law consultants).
>
> (2) Serving as a courthouse facilitator pursuant to court rule.
>
> (3) Acting as a lay representative authorized by administrative agencies or tribunals.
>
> (4) Serving in a neutral capacity as a mediator, arbitrator, conciliator, or facilitator.

---

[1] These jurisdictions are: Alabama, Alaska, Arizona, Colorado, Connecticut, District of Columbia, Florida, Indiana, Kentucky, Louisiana, Maine, Maryland, Michigan, Minnesota, Mississippi, Missouri, Nebraska, New Mexico, North Carolina, Oklahoma, Oregon, Pennsylvania, South Carolina, Utah, Virginia, Washington, West Virginia, and Wyoming.

(5) Participation in labor negotiations, arbitrations or conciliations arising under collective bargaining rights or agreements.

(6) Providing assistance to another to complete a form provided by a court for protection under RCW chapters 10.14 (harassment) or 26.50 (domestic violence prevention) when no fee is charged to do so.

(7) Acting as a legislative lobbyist.

(8) Sale of legal forms in any format.

(9) Activities which are preempted by Federal law.

(10) Serving in a neutral capacity as a clerk or court employee providing information to the public pursuant to Supreme Court Order.

(11) Such other activities that the Supreme Court has determined by published opinion do not constitute the unlicensed or unauthorized practice of law or that have been permitted under a regulatory system established by the Supreme Court.

(c) *Non-lawyer Assistants:* Nothing in this rule shall affect the ability of non-lawyer assistants to act under the supervision of a lawyer in compliance with Rule 5.3 of the Rules of Professional Conduct.

(d) *General Information:* Nothing in this rule shall affect the ability of a person or entity to provide information of a general nature about the law and legal procedures to members of the public.

(e) *Governmental agencies:* Nothing in this rule shall affect the ability of a governmental agency to carry out responsibilities provided by law.

(f) *Professional Standards:* Nothing in this rule shall be taken to define or affect standards for civil liability or professional responsibility.

NOTES AND QUESTIONS

1. ***Changed Results?*** How would your analysis of the permissibility of the actions of Ackerman, Bently, Cole, Darwin, Exec, Furnwell, or Guy (described earlier in this section) change if the jurisdiction adopted a statute modeled on the language in Georgia's Code or on Washington's Rule 24?

2. ***Goldilocks and UPL.*** Are the Georgia or Washington definitions of the practice of law too broad? Too narrow? Just right? What changes would you make if you were drafting new language for your own jurisdiction?

C. JUDICIAL APPLICATION OF UPL STANDARDS

In the following case, the Florida Supreme Court opinion applied Florida's standard for defining the practice of law. As you read it, consider whether you agree with the Florida standard and with the result in the case. Would you allow the activity at issue here or not?

THE FLORIDA BAR v. MIRAVALLE

761 So. 2d 1049 (2000)

HARDING, C.J.

Candice L. Miravalle, individually, (Miravalle) and Express Legal Services, Inc., a Florida corporation (respondents), petition this Court to review a referee's report recommending that respondents be enjoined from engaging in the unlicensed practice of law. . . .

Miravalle is the owner and operator of Express Legal Services, Inc., a business in Melbourne, Brevard County, Florida. At no time during these events was Miravalle a member of The Florida Bar. In December 1995, Miravalle prepared a marital settlement agreement and final judgment of dissolution of marriage for Peter and Holly Berkowitz. In August 1996, Miravalle prepared a motion to reopen a bankruptcy case, a motion seeking cancellation and discharge of a judgment, a motion to declare that a judgment was not a lien on homestead property and to quiet title, and orders relating thereto, for Frances Totten. In September 1997, Miravalle prepared a motion to reopen a bankruptcy case and a notice of service for Joseph Delphino. None of the above-mentioned documents were forms approved by the Supreme Court of Florida. [Under Florida's court rules, non-attorneys are permitted to fill out forms that are approved by the Florida Supreme Court, but are not permitted to fill out unapproved forms.]

In her responses to the Bar's interrogatories, respondent Miravalle admitted that she: (a) engaged in oral communications to obtain information to prepare these documents; (b) took information from other documents in order to prepare these documents; (c) engaged in legal research with regard to these documents; and (d) drafted and typed these documents.

Respondents ran newspaper advertisements during 1997, 1998, and 1999 containing the question, "Are you ignoring your legal needs because you can't afford an attorney?" These advertisements contained respondents' business name and listed legal areas in which Express Legal Services offered assistance. The referee found that there were no genuine issues of material fact [and] concluded that respondents were engaged in the unlicensed practice of law because they were not simply operating a secretarial or typing service, but instead were rendering personal services which could reasonably cause members of the public to rely on them to properly prepare legal documents. Further, the referee found that respondents' use of their business name and advertisements constitutes the unlicensed practice of law because the business name and advertisements suggested to the public that respondents were authorized to provide legal services when, by law, respondents were only authorized to provide secretarial or typing services. . . .

[T]he referee's report recommends that we ratify and adopt the summary judgment order entered against respondents, enjoin respondents from engaging in the practice of law, and tax costs against respondents. Respondents petition this Court for review, objecting to the referee's report and claiming that the referee erred in granting the Bar's motion for summary judgment. Respondents argue their conduct does not constitute the practice of law. Alternatively, respondents argue that even if their conduct constitutes the practice of law under current case law, this Court should reconsider its prior holdings and find that paralegals and other non-lawyers must be allowed to perform legal services. Respondents argue that to hold otherwise would violate their constitutional right to contract and also deprive them of equal protection of the laws.

AUTHORS' COMMENT:

Putting aside the constitutional arguments for a moment, what do you think? Should Ms. Miravalle be permitted to (a) talk to clients to obtain the information necessary to prepare legal documents; (b) take information from other documents in order to prepare the legal documents; (c) engage in legal research regarding the legal documents; and (d) draft and type the legal documents? If not, why not? If so, should the courts regulate her conduct in any way?

Analysis

. . . Both [the Bar and respondents] agree that Miravalle engaged in oral communications, took information from other documents, and conducted legal research for the purpose of preparing these documents. Finally, respondents do not contest that they used the word "legal" in their business name and advertisements; nor do they contest the authenticity of the advertisements offered into evidence by the Bar. Therefore, there is no genuine issue of material fact and the issue facing this Court is whether these acts constitute the unlicensed practice of law.

The referee concluded that respondents' preparation of legal documents for their customers constitutes the unlicensed practice of law. We agree. This Court has repeatedly held that the preparation of legal documents by a non-lawyer for another person to a greater extent than typing or writing information provided by the customer on a form constitutes the unlicensed practice of law. This Court has also specifically held that a non-lawyer who orally takes information from an individual to complete a form when the form has not been approved by this Court is engaged in the unlicensed practice of law.[1] Thus, we find as a matter of law that respondents engaged in the unlicensed practice of law by engaging in oral communication, taking information from written documents, and conducting legal research for the purpose of preparing legal documents not approved by this Court.

We also agree with the referee that respondents' use of their business name and the manner in which they advertise their services constitute the unlicensed practice of law. In *Florida Bar v. Davide*, 702 So. 2d 184 (Fla. 1997), this Court held that it constituted the unlicensed practice of law for a non-lawyer to use "Florida Law Center, Inc." as a company name because "the use of the name is misleading and gives the public the expectation that Florida Law Center, Inc., has expertise in the field of law." We further held in *Davide* that it constitutes the unlicensed practice of law for a non-lawyer to advertise that his or her company specializes in legal areas and to use advertisements that describe legal procedures. In the instant case, respondents use the business name "Express Legal Services, Inc." In their advertisements, they ask the question, "Are you ignoring your legal needs because you can't afford an attorney?" Under this question is a list of legal fields, such as bankruptcy, adoption, eviction and divorce, in which respondents offer assistance. Thus, we conclude that respondents' use of the name "Express Legal Services, Inc." and the manner in which they advertise their services constitute the unlicensed practice of law under *Davide*.

We also conclude that respondents' challenges concerning the constitutionality of prohibiting nonattorneys from offering legal services are without merit. In the past, we have said that regulating the practice of law among non-lawyers does not violate non-lawyers' constitutional rights. In *The Florida Bar v. Schramek*, 616 So. 2d 979 (Fla. 1993), this Court found no merit to the non-lawyer's allegation that the regulation of non-lawyers unconstitutionally deprived him of his right to engage in business. In so holding, this Court stated that "prohibiting the unlicensed practice of law is 'not done to aid or protect the members of the legal profession either in creating or maintaining a monopoly or closed shop. It is done to protect the public from being advised and represented in legal matters by unqualified persons.'" [*S*]*ee also Florida Bar v.*

---

[1] A non-lawyer may take information orally pursuant to Rule Regulating The Florida Bar 10 2.1(a), which provides:

> [I]t shall not constitute the unlicensed practice of law for a non-lawyer to engage in limited oral communications to assist a person in the completion of blanks on a legal form approved by the Supreme Court of Florida. Oral communications by non-lawyers are restricted to those communications reasonably necessary to elicit factual information to complete the blanks on the form and inform the person how to file the form.

Respondents clearly exceeded the conduct allowed to be performed by non-lawyers under this rule.

Furman, 376 So. 2d 378, 381 (Fla.1979) (adopting referee's report in UPL case where referee stated "[t]he fact she is an expert stenographer does not give her any legal right to engage in divorce and adoption practice anymore than a nurse has the right to set up an office for performing tonsillectomy or appendectomy operations or a dental assistant to do extractions or fill teeth"). Because the regulation of the unlicensed practice of law serves the critical role of protecting the public from unqualified individuals who are attempting to perform legal services, non-lawyers do not have a constitutional right to practice law by drafting legal documents or giving legal advice.

Conclusion

Accordingly, we approve the report of the referee and adopt the order granting the Bar's motion for summary judgment. Respondents Candice L. Miravalle, individually, Express Legal Services, Inc., a Florida Corporation, and any employees or persons acting in concert with respondents are permanently and perpetually enjoined from engaging in the unlicensed practice of law in the State of Florida. Judgment is entered for The Florida Bar. . . .

NOTES AND QUESTIONS

1. ***Approved Forms.*** In Florida and a number of other states, the bar has organized efforts to help people through the process of representing themselves *pro se*. In Florida, for example, forms that have been approved by the courts for simple divorces, child support, visitation, step-parent adoption, landlord-tenant matters, and other relatively straightforward situations in which people commonly attempt to represent themselves *pro se* are available to the public, usually from the clerk of the court.

In the landlord-tenant area, for example, the Florida Supreme Court has approved forms for various notices: a complaint for eviction for failure to pay rent, a complaint for eviction other than for failure to pay rent, a summons for an eviction claim, a summons for a damages claim, a final judgment for damages, a final judgment for eviction, and a writ of possession.

In one of the first cases discussing the use of these forms, the Florida Supreme Court held that a non-lawyer property manager may fill out the official forms needed to file for eviction, and doing so will not violate the unauthorized practice laws.

2. ***Helping People Fill Out Forms.*** How much should the state allow non-lawyers to help people fill out the court-approved forms? Do you see any problems with allowing the employees in the clerk's office at a court to talk with people and help them fill out the court-approved forms? What if a barely literate *pro se* litigant brings along a friend who could read the words on the form to her? How about a friend who has been through his own divorce, and could help the litigant choose the right forms for his situation, which would avoid some mistakes?

Would you allow a retired schoolteacher to talk with *pro se* litigants and help them find the right form for their situations? Would you allow the retired teacher to answer people's questions about how to decide what assets to include in a bankruptcy petition? Would the retired teacher run afoul of the UPL restrictions if she handed out business cards that read:

> "I can help you with your divorce, eviction or bankruptcy. I'm not a lawyer, but I've helped many friends with these and similar situations."
>
> Iimma Smarty
> 207 True Street

Should we say that simply filling in the form for someone else who supplies the information is permitted, but only a lawyer is allowed to *select* the form for another person?

3. ***Computer Programs.*** Computer programs that will help people create legal documents or write letters to resolve legal disputes are widely available. With the right program a person can draft trusts, wills, powers of attorney, sales contracts, simple complaints, and many other common legal documents. When the user finishes answering the questions posed by the program, he can print out a finished document that is tailored to reflect the information he has given regarding his situation. Many of these programs include help and advice if the user is unsure of an answer or puzzled about something. The courts long ago held that writing books and broadcasting written information about the law is protected by the First Amendment and cannot be prosecuted as the unauthorized practice of law.

To the man on the street, it must be perplexing to try to figure out precisely what the lawyer is doing that is so much more valuable than the result the client can get by buying a $50 computer program and filing out his own divorce paperwork, or buying a "will kit" from a non-lawyer. Can you explain to prospective clients why they should hire lawyers at considerable expense to draft the documents that the computer program could draft for a fraction of the expense? Do all clients need the greater degree of sophistication lawyers bring to bear in the analysis of legal issues?

The documents prepared by computer software may not be tailored to address the idiosyncrasies of every situation, but they are a fraction of the cost of having documents drafted by a real lawyer. For less than $100, you can buy a disk with dozens of forms and use the disk again and again if new problems arise. Of course, unless you obtain the updates, the program will not reflect later changes in the relevant statutes, regulations, I.R.S. letter rulings or judicial opinions. What if the user does not realize that his situation contains quirks beyond those contemplated by those who wrote the program?

4. ***Quicken Family Lawyer Does Dallas.*** Quicken Family Lawyer, formerly sold by Parsons Technology, Inc., is a collection of computer software that prompts users to answer a series of questions posed by the computer. Based on the answers, the program produces a variety of legal documents tailored to the user's particular situation. A U.S. District Court in Texas concluded that the sale and distribution of Quicken Family Lawyer constituted "the practice of law" within the meaning of Texas Government Code § 81.01 (1998), and enjoined Parsons from selling and distributing Quicken Family Lawyer within Texas. *Unauthorized Practice of Law Committee v. Parsons Technology, Inc.*, 1999 U.S. Dist. LEXIS 813, 1999 WL 47235 (N.D. Tex. 1999). Parsons appealed, but before the appeal was decided, the Texas Legislature amended section 81.01 to add language providing that "the 'practice of law' does not include the design, creation, publication, distribution, display, or sale . . . [of] computer software, or similar products if the products clearly and conspicuously state that the products are not a substitute for the advice of an attorney." In light of the new legislation, the appellate court vacated the lower court's injunction and judgment. *The Unauthorized Practice of Law Committee v. Parsons Technology, Inc.*, 179 F.3d 956 (5th Cir. 1999).

5. ***Restrictions on Suspended or Disbarred Attorneys.*** What difference would it make if the person accused of UPL was once licensed as a lawyer? For example, what if a disbarred lawyer prepared forms for clients filing for personal bankruptcy, advised them on which forms were the right ones to file, and discussed with them what information to include? If the goal is client protection, couldn't we argue that at least this person had some legal training and experience?

As you might predict, courts do not look favorably upon disbarred lawyers performing these activities. In *Iowa Supreme Court Commission on Unauthorized Practice of Law v. Sturgeon*, 635 N.W.2d 679 (Iowa 2001), a disbarred lawyer who had engaged in precisely the activities just listed in this note was held to have engaged in UPL.

Would it change the analysis if the lawyer was disbarred for an act completely unrelated to his or her professional life? For example, what if a lawyer was disbarred after a felony conviction for driving under the influence and causing a fatal auto accident? Do you think the lawyer is still as capable of competent legal analysis as he was before the accident? What theory of client protection could justify saying that he can no longer practice at all? If the facts of the felony conviction are precisely the same, but the defendant was a law student rather than a lawyer at the time of the conviction, should he be refused admission to the bar?

6. ***Supervising Disbarred Attorneys.*** Note that a lawyer can run afoul of his jurisdiction's UPL rule simply by helping a non-lawyer to practice. Any lawyer who employs a disbarred lawyer as an assistant or as a paralegal should carefully monitor the actual work that person performs. Judging from the numerous court decisions on this point, a surprising number of lawyers employ disbarred lawyers whom they allow to directly advise clients and generally practice without supervision. As you might predict, courts considering these cases hold the ostensibly supervising attorney accountable.

7. ***No Fees Necessary.*** So far, most of the materials in this chapter have concerned the unauthorized practice of law by non-lawyers who have charged for their services. But whether a person is engaged in the unauthorized practice of law does not depend on whether the person charges a fee. Even if the person is just helping out a friend, he or she can be guilty of the unauthorized practice of law. This is an important concept for law students because friends and family members often ask law students for help or advice on legal problems. (I often get questions from law students about whether they can help a friend negotiate a new lease or help a relative file some court papers. The answer is "no.") Being charged with the unauthorized practice of law would be a bad way to start your career. And even if you are never charged with UPL, the application to the bar may ask you whether you have ever engaged in the practice of law. You don't want to put yourself in a position where the truth will hurt you because lying on the bar application is not an option.

Few people are actually prosecuted for the crime of unauthorized practice, but generosity and good intentions may end up hurting the people that non-lawyers try to help. Just look at the next case, where friends of an elderly women having surgery bought her a will kit, discussed the terms of the will, and typed up the woman's handwritten instructions without change. The court voided the parts of the will that left money to the helpful friends. Was this fair?

MARKS v. ESTATE OF MARKS

957 P.2d 235 (Wash. Ct. of Appeals 1998)

KURTZ, J.

. . . Diana Crichton Marks was a professor at Whitworth College until her retirement in 1990. She was a devout Christian who taught Sunday School for several churches. In the mid 1980s, she began attending the Christian Life Center (now Christian Life Church). After joining the church, Ms. Marks was asked to teach Sunday School. Sometime in 1986–87, she was asked if she would take the pulpit on an interim basis. Eventually, she took over on a full-time basis and was ordained by the church. This ministry was very important in Ms. Marks' life, and her life revolved around the church.

In 1989, Hartwell Marks, Ms. Marks' brother, and his family moved into Ms. Marks' home after he lost his home due to financial problems. Mr. Marks had not been gainfully employed for several years while he unsuccessfully attempted to develop an exercise bicycle. It was understood that Mr. Marks and his family would stay for approximately six weeks while they looked for a new place to live.

Mr. Marks and his family remained in Ms. Marks' home for three years, until Ms. Marks asked them to leave. Mr. Marks claims that he left his sister's home on good terms; other witnesses indicate that when Ms. Marks asked Mr. Marks to leave, he became extremely angry. After Mr. Marks left his sister's home, they did not visit, see, speak or write to each other, even after Mr. Marks had a stroke, and even though they both lived in Spokane less than six miles apart. Mr. Marks never returned to the Christian Life Church. Ms. Marks did not advise her brother of her medical condition prior to her death.

In September 1994, Ms. Marks was admitted to Sacred Heart Medical Center in Spokane complaining of fatigue and swelling in her lower extremities. Soon thereafter, she was referred to an experimental cancer program at the University of Washington. Because the treatment, after initial surgery, would be on an outpatient basis, Ms. Marks made arrangements with her friends, Eldon and Judith Blanford, to stay in their home near Seattle. Ms. Blanford, who was in Spokane visiting an ill relative, offered to assist Ms. Marks by accompanying her on the flight to Seattle.

The evening before her surgery scheduled September 14, Ms. Marks discussed her situation with Ms. Blanford. Reportedly, she stated that she was not afraid to die, but she said, "I'm afraid of all the things I have to do before I die," specifically referring to having to make a will. Ms. Blanford offered to contact her attorney in the morning.

On the day of the surgery, Ms. Blanford called her own attorney, who said he could not prepare a will right away, but he suggested Ms. Blanford purchase a will kit at a stationery store. Ms. Marks agreed Ms. Blanford should purchase the kit. Ms. Blanford went to the Office Depot near her home and selected the kit. Ms. Marks paid Ms. Blanford for the kit. Ms. Marks read the instructions and began to talk about what she wanted various people to receive. Ms. Blanford wrote the bequests as Ms. Marks talked. Ms. Marks then asked Ms. Blanford to call her investment counselor to obtain the information concerning all her investments.

The day after Ms. Marks' surgery, Ms. Blanford retyped the language from the will kit onto her home computer because she was unable to feed the forms through her word processing program. She filled in the information as related by Ms. Marks and gave her a draft. Ms. Marks did not make any substantive changes to the draft, but corrected some typographical errors. Over the next couple days, Ms. Marks reviewed at least two more drafts, correcting typographical errors. When Kemsley Marks, her sister, arrived from Texas, they discussed at length the bequests under the will.

AUTHORS' COMMENT:

Did Ms. Blanford engage in the unauthorized practice of law? If so, the will (or parts of it) may be void. Before you read on, reread the last three paragraphs (beginning "The evening before her surgery . . ."). Exactly what did Ms. Blanford do to help Ms. Marks prepare her will? Did these activities constitute the practice of law?

On September 20, 1994, Ms. Marks signed her Last Will and Testament before Denise Andres, an acquaintance of the Blanfords, and Ms. Andres' pastor, Rick B. Danner, Sr. The will was also witnessed by a hospital notary, Pamela Brown. During the time Ms. Marks was preparing her will, she was visited by several people, including William and Diana Lee and Gail and Larry Wolf.

Ms. Marks discussed the will with the Wolfs and rather than expressing any uncertainty, she stated she had prepared the will because "there were some members of the family who could possibly make trouble." When speaking to William and Diana Lee, she explained her testamentary plan — "her moneys," the money she made in her lifetime — would go to the "kingdom, the Lord's work." She also advised the Lees that certain family members might not be happy with her decision. The Lees observed that despite being weak, Ms. Marks remained strong-willed and resolute. She steadfastly refused physical therapy, despite persistent urgings of a physical therapist and the Lees themselves.

The will provided that Ms. Marks' home in Spokane and 50 percent of the residuary of her estate would go to her sister, Kemsley Mudie Marks. Ms. Marks left to her brother, Charles Harrison Marks, Jr., several investment accounts and stocks. She left to her developmentally disabled niece, Susan Lee Marks, her rare coin collection for purposes of Susan's long-term care. She left Hartwell Lee Marks, Hartwell Marks' son and her nephew, her car and a life insurance policy worth approximately $48,000. Ms. Marks gave Hartwell Marks a small investment portfolio and forgave him a $3,000 loan he had not repaid. Ms. Marks stated that Mr. Marks had received more than $100,000 in "documented loans" from their deceased sister, which reduced the value of the inheritance they shared after their sister's death. Mr. Marks admits all of these statements are true, except he claims that the $100,000 plus was an "investment" and not a loan. Ms. Marks left Judy Potter, her personal secretary, some Monsanto stocks. Ms. Blanford received some diamonds. Ms. Marks left Bonnie June Harding, a long-time friend, $20,000.

The Christian Life Center was the church Ms. Marks pastored. From her estate, Ms. Marks left her church $100,000. Personal Freedom in Christ Ministries, the Blanfords' religious organization, was given $100,000. This ministry is administered on a day-to-day basis by the Blanfords. Ms. Marks was a founder of the corporation and served on its Board of Directors. Additionally, Ms. Marks gave Faith Family Church $25,000 to be used for the purpose of providing the salaries of Jim Buehl and his wife, the church's pastors. Ms. Marks had met the Buehls several times, had ministered at the church on a few occasions, was aware that the church was unable to pay the Buehls' salaries, and was also aware that the Buehls were in financial need. Finally, Ms. Marks made a specific bequest to the Mission's Fund of the Christian Life Center, the financial arm of the Christian Life Church charged with missionary work.

[Ms. Marks died sometime between September 20th and October 11th.] The September 20, 1994, will of Diana Crichton Marks, which is the subject of this action, was admitted to probate on October 11, 1994. On November 23, 1994, Hartwell Marks filed a petition, amended September 25, 1995, contesting the validity of the will and seeking an order appointing him substitute personal representative of his sister's estate. . . . By the time the case reached trial, the trial court was faced with two issues: (1) whether Ms. Marks' will was the product of fraud and undue influence, and (2) whether Eldon and Judith Blanford and Kemsley Marks engaged in the unauthorized practice of law.

The matter was tried to the court over four days, with the court considering the testimony of 19 witnesses and many exhibits. The trial court ruled that the September 20, 1994, will was not a product of undue influence or fraud and was valid. Nevertheless, the court found that Eldon and Judith Blanford had unwittingly engaged in the unauthorized practice of law while assisting Ms. Marks in the preparation of her will and, as a matter of public policy, Judith Blanford must be divested of her bequest, and the Personal Freedom in Christ Ministries, of which the Blanfords are the principal administrators, must be divested of its bequest. . . .

The unauthorized practice of law is generally acknowledged to include "not only the doing or performing of services in the courts of justice, throughout the various stages thereof, but in a larger sense includes legal advice and counsel and the preparation of legal instruments by which legal rights and obligations are established." The selection and completion of preprinted form legal documents is also deemed the "practice of law."

Here, the court found the Blanfords' activities in selecting a will kit, discussing the distribution of assets and whether it was fair, obtaining the inventory of investments, typing the will, and arranging for the signing and witnessing of the will constituted the unauthorized practice of law.

The rules regulating the conduct of lawyers are applicable to lay people who engage in the practice of law. The Rules of Professional Conduct govern the conduct of lawyers and in part prohibit a lawyer from preparing an instrument giving the lawyer or a person related to the lawyer as parent, child, sibling, or spouse any substantial gift from a client, including a testamentary gift, except where the client is related to the donee.

RULES OF PROFESSIONAL CONDUCT 1.8(c). Because a lawyer preparing Ms. Marks' will could not have designated himself or herself a beneficiary, the Blanfords are also precluded from doing so. The trial court voided the gifts to the Blanfords and their religious organization. . . . In construing a will, the paramount duty of the court is to give effect to the testator's intent. Because the trial court found no evidence warranting avoidance of the entire will, and recognizing its duty to honor Ms. Marks' intent, the court only voided the portions relating to the Blanfords. The court correctly invalidated only the portions of the will relating to the bequests to the Blanfords and their personal religious organization. . . . [We affirm.]

NOTES AND QUESTIONS

1. ***Do You Agree?*** Do you agree with the court that the Blanfords engaged in the unauthorized practice of law? Why or why not? If you agree that they engaged in the practice of law, would you change your mind if the Blanfords (a) had not purchased the will kit, or (b) had not discussed the terms of the will with Ms. Marks, or (c) had not typed up the form according to Ms. Marks' handwritten instructions? If you do not agree that they engaged in the practice of law, how were their activities different from the activities of a lawyer who chooses an appropriate form, discusses how the client would like to fill out the form, and has a secretary type up the form?

2. ***What Should the Blanfords Have Done?*** This was not a case where unsavory people used improper means to persuade an elderly person to leave them a lot of money in a will. The trial court expressly found that the will "was not a product of undue influence or fraud and was valid." Instead, this is a case where an elderly woman wanted to write a will and asked a friend to call a lawyer. The lawyer was too busy to draft a will so the lawyer suggested that the elderly woman buy a will kit. (A will kit is basically some forms and instructions for making a valid will, which is pretty easy to do.) The elderly woman thought this was a good idea but obviously could not leave her hospital bed to buy the will kit, so she asked her friend to buy it for her. The friend went to Office Depot and bought a will kit.

When the elderly woman got the will kit, she naturally discussed the terms of her will with her friend. When the elderly woman decided what she wanted to do with her worldly assets, she filled in the form with a pen and asked her friend to type it up. Where did the friend go wrong? What should the friend have done to protect the elderly woman's assets as she wished and to protect her own right to receive a $100,000 bequest under the will? In other words, what could the Blanfords have done to avoid the unauthorized practice of law?

Chapter 5
THE UNAUTHORIZED PRACTICE OF LAW BY LAWYERS

Within the next year or two, someone will say to you, "Congratulations! You have passed the MPRE, graduated from law school, passed the bar exam, been approved by the character and fitness committee, and taken the oath of office as an attorney and counselor at law. You are now a lawyer." That's a great accomplishment. But here's a travel advisory: be careful how you practice law in any state that has not admitted you to practice. You are an "out-of-state lawyer" in every jurisdiction except the one that granted you your law license, and out-of-state lawyers may or may not be welcome. Out-of-state lawyers who practice law may be engaging in the unauthorized practice of law ("UPL"), which is a crime in some states. Therefore, practicing law beyond the borders of your home jurisdiction — so-called "multijurisdictional practice" — may be risky.

In the previous chapter, we discussed the unauthorized practice of law by nonlawyers. In this chapter, we discuss the unauthorized practice of law by lawyers. More specifically, we discuss the law, the risks, and some possible approaches to the "multijurisdictional" practice of law by lawyers — the practice of law by lawyers in jurisdictions where they have not been admitted to practice.

A. THE TRADITIONAL APPROACH TO OUT-OF-STATE LAWYERS

In recent years, many United States jurisdictions have significantly changed their treatment of out-of-state lawyers. In a majority of states, lawyers who are in good standing in another state (and not disbarred or suspended in any jurisdiction) may practice law within certain limits on a "temporary" basis. But things were not always this way. The traditional approach was much more stringent, at least on paper.

For many decades, the basic rule regarding out-of-state practice was that an out-of-state lawyer who provided legal services in any jurisdiction other than the one in which he was licensed was technically guilty of the unauthorized practice of law. This was true even though the out-of-state lawyer was a member of the bar in good standing in his "home" jurisdiction (the state in which he was licensed). However, because the traditional rule was harsh and often impractical, the courts created numerous exceptions. For example:

- *pro hac vice admission*, which is available in every state and federal court, allows an out-of-state lawyer to ask a court to grant the out-of-state lawyer official permission to appear in a case pending before that court.
- *associating with local counsel*, pursuant to which a lawyer admitted elsewhere is permitted to work with a locally admitted lawyer on a representation, when the representation is related to litigation or to a transaction (although the out-of-state lawyer would not be permitted to appear in a court in the *foreign state* without first being admitted *pro hac vice*).
- *in-house counsel rules*, pursuant to which in-house lawyers are permitted to give legal advice to their employers in about half of the jurisdictions in the U.S., typically after they have moved to an office in the new state, but usually subject to the proviso that the foreign lawyer not represent their employer in court nor represent or advise any clients other than the employer.

However, significant gaps in the law remained, especially regarding the limits of *pro hac vice* admission. For example, under the traditional approach, a lawyer could not depose witnesses in any state other than the one in which the lawyer was admitted *pro hac vice*. If a lawsuit involved parties and witnesses from several states (as is often the case), *pro hac vice* admission conferred no benefits on a lawyer outside the borders of that state granting *pro hac vice* status. Moreover, *pro hac vice* admission was not available for transactional (non-courtroom) practice. Thus, an out-of-state lawyer who negotiated a loan agreement or handled the sale of a business in a state where the lawyer was not admitted was (in theory, at least) committing the unauthorized practice of law. Because courts are authorized to admit out-of-state lawyers only for litigation matters, courts have no power to admit a lawyer for a particular transaction.

Despite these gaps, lawyers who engaged in these activities (taking a deposition, negotiating a loan agreement, handling the sale of a business) under the traditional UPL rules did not expect to be prosecuted for unauthorized practice of law or to suffer any other penalty, even though their activities technically violated the UPL restrictions in states where they were not licensed. Practicing law away from home still entailed some risk because courts occasionally refused to enforce a fee agreement by an out-of-state lawyer who had committed unauthorized practice of law, but, by and large, the states abided by the aspiration expressed in EC 3-9 in the ABA Model Code of Professional Responsibility:

> . . . In furtherance of the public interest, the legal profession should discourage regulation that unreasonably imposes territorial limitations upon the right of a lawyer to handle the legal affairs of a client or upon the opportunity of a client to obtain the services of a lawyer of the client's choice in all matters practice. . . .

EC 3-9 thus raised an important theme in the rules governing lawyers: client choice. Just as the law gives clients the right to fire an attorney at any time and for (almost) any reason in order to choose a different attorney more to the client's liking, so the law should give clients the right to hire an attorney of their choice at the outset. In deciding a motion to disqualify an attorney based on a conflict of interest, a court will typically balance the policies served by the conflict rules against the client's right to choice of counsel, weighing that right heavily. EC 3-9 cautions the states not to "unreasonably" impose territorial restrictions on a client's right to choose an attorney. What does that mean? What is an "unreasonable" territorial restriction on a client's right to choice of counsel? The rest of this chapter is aimed at discussing that question.

NOTES AND QUESTIONS

1. ***Reasonable or Unreasonable?*** The following scenarios present fairly typical situations that confront attorneys, clients, and the legal profession in a national, highly mobile economy like ours where clients frequently cross state borders or conduct business across state lines. With respect to each scenario, would a state be acting reasonably or unreasonably if it adopted or enforced a rule prohibiting the out-of-state lawyer from serving his or her client? (Assume that all of the lawyers are in good standing in their home states and have not been suspended or disbarred in any jurisdiction.)

A. Alicia Aguirre is a "deal" lawyer (a transactional lawyer) in South Bend, Indiana (home of Notre Dame). Her clients, most of whom are small businesses, often do business with companies in the Chicago area (in Illinois). One of Alicia's clients, Carl Sandburg LLC, is going to Chicago next week to negotiate a major contract with Big Shoulders, Inc. Sandburg wants Alicia to go with him to Chicago to sit in on the negotiations. Should the rules allow Alicia to accompany Sandburg to Chicago?

B. Bart Branson is a litigator in Birmingham, Alabama, specializing in construction litigation. A Texas company, Loan Star Lending Corporation, recently retained Bart to represent it in filing suit against an Arizona-based construction company that botched a major expansion project at Loan Star's corporate headquarters in Dallas.

(1) Bart plans to go to Texas to meet with Loan Star executives at their Dallas headquarters and then to conduct a reasonable inquiry into the facts so

that he can fully comply with the Texas version of Rule 11 before he files suit in a Texas state court. Should the rules allow him to meet with his clients and to conduct the investigation in Texas before he files suit?

(2) Once suit is filed, Bart will seek admission *pro hac vice* in the Texas court. Assuming he is admitted *pro hac vice*, he will need to interview and depose various witnesses in Arizona in connection with the litigation. Should the rules permit him to travel to Arizona to interview witnesses? What about to depose witnesses? Should the rules require Bart to associate with local counsel for either purpose?

C. Cindy Crawford is a patent lawyer in Philadelphia. One of her best clients is an inventor named Ben Franklin. Ben's offices are in Philadelphia but he lives across the river in New Jersey and spends a lot of time working at home. He has asked Cindy to come to his home in New Jersey to discuss (a) the patent application for a new invention he has been working on in his basement workshop, and (b) a consulting contract with an engineer he would like to hire. Patent applications are exclusively a matter of federal law, but the consulting contract is entirely a matter of state law. Should the rules permit Cindy to go to her client's home in New Jersey to discuss these legal matters?

D. Diane Denakos is an employment lawyer in Atlanta. Her largest client is Spy vs. Spy, Inc., which designs and installs surveillance systems (like cameras and recording equipment) that businesses use to keep an eye on their employees and factories. Spy vs. Spy has offices in Tennessee, Georgia, Florida, and Missouri. The company has asked her to visit every one of the company's offices in the next three months to make sure that every office is in compliance with state and federal laws prohibiting employment discrimination. Should the rules permit her to do so?

E. Elvis Expresley is an entertainment lawyer in New York. He represents a New York City recording company named Off the Record that negotiates concert deals with indie bands. A few years ago, Elvis helped to incorporate an affiliated company named On the Record, a Nashville, Tennessee company that negotiates recording contracts with country music artists. Both Off the Record and On the Record are controlled by Sam Phillips. Late last year, On the Record got into a dispute with a band named Graceland over alleged underpayment of royalties. The recording contract provides for mandatory arbitration and contains a choice-of-law clause specifying Tennessee law. Consequently, each party is preparing for an arbitration to be held in Nashville. Elvis has had numerous telephone calls and has exchanged many emails with the lawyer for Graceland, and has traveled three times to Tennessee to attempt to negotiate a settlement before the arbitration proceeding formally begins. If the settlement negotiations fail, Elvis will be lead counsel at the arbitration proceeding. Should the rules permit Elvis' prior activities and future plans? If not, what should be the penalty for violating the rules against unauthorized practice?

B. THE TRADITIONAL APPROACH IS ENFORCED AND EXPANDED

In January 1998, the California Supreme Court decided *Birbrower, Montalbano, Condon & Frank, P.C. v. Superior Court*, 17 Cal. 4th 119, 949 P.2d 1 (1998), a case that applied the traditional UPL rules with a vengeance and got everyone's attention. Lawyers had always known that being physically present in jurisdictions where they were not licensed to practice carried risks, but the California Supreme Court suggested in *Birbrower* that a lawyer could be guilty of the unauthorized practice of law by communicating with clients by phone, fax, or email. This case shocked many lawyers and sparked a debate within the legal profession (led by the ABA) that eventually resulted in changes that relaxed the traditional rules. But, like a tall building at sunset, the *Birbrower* case continues to cast a long, long shadow over the UPL landscape.

BIRBROWER, MONTALBANO, CONDON & FRANK, P.C. v. SUPERIOR COURT

949 P.2d 1 (1998)

CHIN, J.

Business and Professions Code section 6125 states: "No person shall practice law in California unless the person is an active member of the State Bar." We must decide whether an out-of-state law firm, not licensed to practice law in this state, violated section 6125 when it performed legal services in California for a California-based client under a fee agreement stipulating that California law would govern all matters in the representation.

Although we are aware of the interstate nature of modern law practice and mindful of the reality that large firms often conduct activities and serve clients in several states, we do not believe these facts excuse law firms from complying with section 6125. Contrary to the Court of Appeal, however, we do not believe the Legislature intended section 6125 to apply to those services an out-of-state firm renders in its home state. We therefore conclude that, to the extent defendant law firm Birbrower, Montalbano, Condon & Frank, P.C. (Birbrower), practiced law in California without a license, it engaged in the unauthorized practice of law in this state. We also conclude that Birbrower's fee agreement with real party in interest ESQ Business Services, Inc. (ESQ), is invalid to the extent it authorizes payment for the substantial legal services Birbrower performed in California. If, however, Birbrower can show it generated fees under its agreement for limited services it performed in New York, and it earned those fees under the otherwise invalid fee agreement, it may, on remand, present to the trial court evidence justifying its recovery of fees for those New York services. Conversely, ESQ will have an opportunity to produce contrary evidence. Accordingly, we affirm the Court of Appeal judgment in part and reverse it in part, remanding for further proceedings consistent with this opinion.

I. Background

The facts with respect to the unauthorized practice of law question are essentially undisputed. Birbrower is a professional law corporation incorporated in New York, with its principal place of business in New York. During 1992 and 1993, Birbrower attorneys, defendants Kevin F. Hobbs and Thomas A. Condon (Hobbs and Condon), performed substantial work in California relating to the law firm's representation of ESQ. Neither Hobbs nor Condon has ever been licensed to practice law in California. None of Birbrower's attorneys was licensed to practice law in California during Birbrower's ESQ representation.

ESQ is a California corporation with its principal place of business in Santa Clara County. In July 1992, the parties negotiated and executed the fee agreement in New York, providing that Birbrower would perform legal services for ESQ, including "All matters pertaining to the investigation of and prosecution of all claims and causes of action against TANDEM COMPUTERS INCORPORATED [Tandem]." The "claims and causes of action" against Tandem, a Delaware corporation with its principal place of business in Santa Clara County, California, related to a software development and marketing contract between Tandem and ESQ dated March 16, 1990 (Tandem Agreement). The Tandem Agreement stated that "The internal laws of the State of California (irrespective of its choice of law principles) shall govern the validity of this Agreement, the construction of its terms, and the interpretation and enforcement of the rights and duties of the parties hereto." Birbrower asserts, and ESQ disputes, that ESQ knew Birbrower was not licensed to practice law in California.

While representing ESQ, Hobbs and Condon traveled to California on several occasions. In August 1992, they met in California with ESQ and its accountants. During these meetings, Hobbs and Condon discussed various matters related to ESQ's dispute with Tandem and strategy for resolving the dispute. They made recommendations and gave advice. During this California trip, Hobbs and Condon also met with Tandem representatives on four or five occasions during a two-day period. At the meetings, Hobbs and Condon spoke on ESQ's behalf. Hobbs demanded that Tandem pay ESQ $15 million. Condon told Tandem he believed that damages would exceed $15 million if the parties litigated the dispute.

Around March or April 1993, Hobbs, Condon, and another Birbrower attorney visited California to interview potential arbitrators and to meet again with ESQ and its accountants. Birbrower had previously filed a demand for arbitration against Tandem with the San Francisco offices of the American Arbitration Association (AAA). In August 1993, Hobbs returned to California to assist ESQ in settling the Tandem matter. While in California, Hobbs met with ESQ and its accountants to discuss a proposed settlement agreement Tandem authored. Hobbs also met with Tandem representatives to discuss possible changes in the proposed agreement. Hobbs gave ESQ legal advice during this trip, including his opinion that ESQ should not settle with Tandem on the terms proposed.

ESQ eventually settled the Tandem dispute, and the matter never went to arbitration. But before the settlement, ESQ and Birbrower modified the contingency fee agreement. The modification changed the fee arrangement from contingency to fixed fee, providing that ESQ would pay Birbrower over $1 million. The original contingency fee arrangement had called for Birbrower to receive "one-third (1/3) of all sums received for the benefit of the Clients . . . whether obtained through settlement, motion practice, hearing, arbitration, or trial by way of judgment, award, settlement, or otherwise. . . ."

In January 1994, ESQ sued Birbrower for legal malpractice and related claims in Santa Clara County Superior Court. Birbrower removed the matter to federal court and filed a counterclaim, which included a claim for attorney fees for the work it performed in both California and New York. The matter was then remanded to the superior court. There ESQ moved for summary judgment and/or adjudication on the first through fourth causes of action of Birbrower's counterclaim, which asserted ESQ and its representatives breached the fee agreement. ESQ argued that by practicing law without a license in California and by failing to associate legal counsel while doing so, Birbrower violated section 6125, rendering the fee agreement unenforceable. Based on these undisputed facts, the Santa Clara Superior Court granted ESQ's motion for summary adjudication of the first through fourth causes of action in Birbrower's counterclaim. The court also granted summary adjudication in favor of ESQ's third and fourth causes of action in its second amended complaint, seeking declaratory relief as to the validity of the fee agreement and its modification. The court concluded that: (1) Birbrower was "not admitted to the practice of law in California"; (2) Birbrower "did not associate California counsel";[3] (3) Birbrower "provided legal services in this state"; and (4) "The law is clear that no one may recover compensation for services as an attorney in this state unless he or she was a member of the state bar at the time those services were performed."

Although the trial court's order stated that the fee agreements were unenforceable, at the hearing on the summary adjudication motion, the trial court also observed: "It seems to me that those are some of the issues that this Court has to struggle with, and then it becomes a question of if they aren't allowed to collect their attorney's fees here, I don't think that puts the attorneys in a position from being precluded from collecting all of their attorney's fees, only those fees probably that were generated by virtue of

[3] Contrary to the trial court's implied assumption, no statutory exception to section 6125 allows out-of-state attorneys to practice law in California as long as they associate local counsel in good standing with the State Bar.

work that they performed in California and not that work that was performed in New York." . . .

Birbrower petitioned the Court of Appeal for a writ of mandate directing the trial court to vacate the summary adjudication order. The Court of Appeal denied Birbrower's petition and affirmed the trial court's order, holding that Birbrower violated section 6125. The Court of Appeal also concluded that Birbrower's violation barred the firm from recovering its legal fees under the written fee agreement, including fees generated in New York by the attorneys when they were physically present in New York, because the agreement included payment for California or "local" services for a California client in California. The Court of Appeal agreed with the trial court, however, in deciding that Birbrower could pursue its remaining claims against ESQ, including its equitable claim for recovery of its fees in quantum meruit.

We granted review to determine whether Birbrower's actions and services performed while representing ESQ in California constituted the unauthorized practice of law under section 6125 and, if so, whether a section 6125 violation rendered the fee agreement wholly unenforceable.

II. Discussion

A. *The Unauthorized Practice of Law*

The California Legislature enacted section 6125 in 1927 as part of the State Bar Act (the Act), a comprehensive scheme regulating the practice of law in the state. Since the Act's passage, the general rule has been that, although persons may represent themselves and their own interests regardless of State Bar membership, no one but an active member of the State Bar may practice law for another person in California. The prohibition against unauthorized law practice is within the state's police power and is designed to ensure that those performing legal services do so competently.

A violation of section 6125 is a misdemeanor. Moreover, "No one may recover compensation for services as an attorney at law in this state unless [the person] was at the time the services were performed a member of The State Bar."

Although the Act did not define the term "practice law," case law explained it as "the doing and performing services in a court of justice in any matter depending therein throughout its various stages and in conformity with the adopted rules of procedure." (*People v. Merchants Protective Corp.* (1922) 189 Cal. 531, 535, 209 P. 363 (Merchants).) Merchants included in its definition legal advice and legal instrument and contract preparation, whether or not these subjects were rendered in the course of litigation. . . .

In addition to not defining the term "practice law," the Act also did not define the meaning of "in California." In today's legal practice, questions often arise concerning whether the phrase refers to the nature of the legal services, or restricts the Act's application to those out-of-state attorneys who are physically present in the state.

Section 6125 has generated numerous opinions on the meaning of "practice law" but none on the meaning of "in California." In our view, the practice of law "in California" entails sufficient contact with the California client to render the nature of the legal service a clear legal representation. In addition to a quantitative analysis, we must consider the nature of the unlicensed lawyer's activities in the state. Mere fortuitous or attenuated contacts will not sustain a finding that the unlicensed lawyer practiced law "in California." The primary inquiry is whether the unlicensed lawyer engaged in sufficient activities in the state, or created a continuing relationship with the California client that included legal duties and obligations.

Our definition does not necessarily depend on or require the unlicensed lawyer's physical presence in the state. Physical presence here is one factor we may consider in deciding whether the unlicensed lawyer has violated section 6125, but it is by no means exclusive. For example, one may practice law in the state in violation of section 6125 although not physically present here by advising a California client on California law in connection with a California legal dispute by telephone, fax, computer, or other modern technological means. Conversely, although we decline to provide a comprehensive list of what activities constitute sufficient contact with the state, we do reject the notion that a person automatically practices law "in California" whenever that person practices California law anywhere, or "virtually" enters the state by telephone, fax, e-mail, or satellite. . . . We must decide each case on its individual facts.

AUTHORS' COMMENT:

Is the California Supreme Court saying that you can be found guilty of unlawfully practicing law "in California" — a misdemeanor — without ever setting foot in California? Suppose you are a lawyer licensed in New York (or any place other than California.) One day you are sitting in your office, which is not in California, and a client calls you (or emails you) from California asking for your legal advice. If you respond, would the *Birbrower* court think you were violating § 6125? Does it depend on the amount of time you spend responding? Or on whether you have only one phone call with your client, as opposed to many phone calls? Does it matter whether you are advising about litigation or a transaction? Does it matter whether the client is a California citizen, or whether the question requires advice on California law, or whether the litigation or transaction is happening (or will eventually happen) in California rather than some other state? Think about these questions as you read on.

This interpretation acknowledges the tension that exists between interjurisdictional practice and the need to have a state-regulated bar. As stated in the American Bar Association Model Code of Professional Responsibility, Ethical Consideration EC 3-9, "Regulation of the practice of law is accomplished principally by the respective states. Authority to engage in the practice of law conferred in any jurisdiction is not per se a grant of the right to practice elsewhere, and it is improper for a lawyer to engage in practice where he is not permitted by law or by court order to do so. However, the demands of business and the mobility of our society pose distinct problems in the regulation of the practice of law by the states. In furtherance of the public interest, the legal profession should discourage regulation that unreasonably imposes territorial limitations upon the right of a lawyer to handle the legal affairs of his client or upon the opportunity of a client to obtain the services of a lawyer of his choice in all matters including the presentation of a contested matter in a tribunal before which the lawyer is not permanently admitted to practice." . . .

If we were to carry the dissent's narrow interpretation of the term "practice law" to its logical conclusion, we would effectively limit section 6125's application to those cases in which nonlicensed out-of-state lawyers appeared in a California courtroom without permission. . . . Indeed, the dissent's definition of "practice law" . . . substantially undermines the Legislature's intent to protect the public from those giving unauthorized legal advice and counsel.

Exceptions to section 6125 do exist, but are generally limited to allowing out-of-state attorneys to make brief appearances before a state court or tribunal. They are narrowly drawn and strictly interpreted. For example, an out-of-state attorney not licensed to practice in California may be permitted, by consent of a trial judge, to appear in California in a particular pending action.

In addition, with the permission of the California court in which a particular cause is pending, out-of-state counsel may appear before a court as counsel pro hac vice. A court will approve a pro hac vice application only if the out-of-state attorney is a member in good standing of another state bar and is eligible to practice in any United States court or the highest court in another jurisdiction. The out-of-state attorney must also associate an active member of the California Bar as attorney of record and is subject to the Rules of Professional Conduct of the State Bar.

The Act does not regulate practice before United States courts. Thus, an out-of-state attorney engaged to render services in bankruptcy proceedings was entitled to collect his fee. . . .

B. The Present Case

The undisputed facts here show that . . . Birbrower engaged in unauthorized law practice in California on more than a limited basis, and no firm attorney engaged in that practice was an active member of the California State Bar. . . . As the Court of Appeal concluded, ". . . the Birbrower firm's in-state activities clearly constituted the [unauthorized] practice of law" in California.

Birbrower contends, however, that section 6125 is not meant to apply to any out-of-state attorneys. Instead, it argues that the statute is intended solely to prevent nonattorneys from practicing law. This contention is without merit because it contravenes the plain language of the statute. Section 6125 clearly states that no person shall practice law in California unless that person is a member of the State Bar. The statute does not differentiate between attorneys or nonattorneys, nor does it excuse a person who is a member of another state bar. . . .

Birbrower next argues that we do not further the statute's intent and purpose — to protect California citizens from incompetent attorneys — by enforcing it against out-of-state attorneys. Birbrower argues that because out-of-state attorneys have been licensed to practice in other jurisdictions, they have already demonstrated sufficient competence to protect California clients. But Birbrower's argument overlooks the obvious fact that other states' laws may differ substantially from California law. Competence in one jurisdiction does not necessarily guarantee competence in another. By applying section 6125 to out-of-state attorneys who engage in the extensive practice of law in California without becoming licensed in our state, we serve the statute's goal of assuring the competence of all attorneys practicing law in this state.

California is not alone in regulating who practices law in its jurisdiction. Many states have substantially similar statutes that serve to protect their citizens from unlicensed attorneys who engage in unauthorized legal practice. Like section 6125, these other state statutes protect local citizens "against the dangers of legal representation and advice given by persons not trained, examined and licensed for such work, whether they be laymen or lawyers from other jurisdictions. Whether an attorney is duly admitted in another state and is, in fact, competent to practice in California is irrelevant in the face of section 6125's language and purpose. Moreover, . . . a decision to except out-of-state attorneys licensed in their own jurisdictions from section 6125 is more appropriately left to the California Legislature.

Assuming that section 6125 does apply to out-of-state attorneys not licensed here, Birbrower alternatively asks us to create an exception to section 6125 for work incidental to private arbitration or other alternative dispute resolution proceedings. Birbrower points to fundamental differences between private arbitration and legal proceedings, including procedural differences relating to discovery, rules of evidence, compulsory process, cross-examination of witnesses, and other areas. . . .

We decline Birbrower's invitation to craft an arbitration exception to section 6125's prohibition of the unlicensed practice of law in this state. Any exception for arbitration is best left to the Legislature, which has the authority to determine qualifications for admission to the State Bar and to decide what constitutes the practice of law. . . .

Finally, Birbrower urges us to adopt an exception to section 6125 based on the unique circumstances of this case. Birbrower notes that "Multistate relationships are a common part of today's society and are to be dealt with in commonsense fashion." In many situations, strict adherence to rules prohibiting the unauthorized practice of law by out-of-state attorneys would be " 'grossly impractical and inefficient.' "

Although, as discussed, we recognize the need to acknowledge and, in certain cases, accommodate the multistate nature of law practice, the facts here show that Birbrower's extensive activities within California amounted to considerably more than any of our state's recognized exceptions to section 6125 would allow. Accordingly, we reject Birbrower's suggestion that we except the firm from section 6125's rule under the circumstances here.

C. Compensation for Legal Services

. . . It is a general rule that an attorney is barred from recovering compensation for services rendered in another state where the attorney was not admitted to the bar. The general rule, however, has some recognized exceptions.

Initially, Birbrower seeks enforcement of the entire fee agreement, relying first on the federal court exception discussed *ante*. This exception does not apply in this case; none of Birbrower's activities related to federal court practice.

A second exception on which Birbrower relies to enforce its entire fee agreement relates to "Services not involving courtroom appearance." California has implicitly rejected this broad exception through its comprehensive definition of what it means to "practice law." Thus, the exception Birbrower seeks for all services performed outside the courtroom in our state is too broad under section 6125.

Some jurisdictions have adopted a third exception to the general rule of nonrecovery for in-state services, if an out-of-state attorney "makes a full disclosure to his client of his lack of local license and does not conceal or misrepresent the true facts." . . . Recognizing these exceptions would contravene not only the plain language of section 6125 but the underlying policy of assuring the competence of those practicing law in California.

Therefore, as the Court of Appeal held, none of the exceptions to the general rule prohibiting recovery of fees generated by the unauthorized practice of law applies to Birbrower's activities in California. Because Birbrower practiced substantial law in this state in violation of section 6125, it cannot receive compensation under the fee agreement for any of the services it performed in California. Enforcing the fee agreement in its entirety would include payment for the unauthorized practice of law in California and would allow Birbrower to enforce an illegal contract.

Birbrower asserts that even if we agree with the Court of Appeal and find that none of the above exceptions allowing fees for unauthorized California services applies to the firm, it should be permitted to recover fees for those limited services it performed exclusively in New York under the agreement. In short, Birbrower seeks to recover under its contract for those services it performed for ESQ in New York that did not involve the practice of law in California, including fee contract negotiations and some corporate case research. . . .

We agree with Birbrower that it may be able to recover fees under the fee agreement for the limited legal services it performed for ESQ in New York to the extent they did not constitute practicing law in California, even though those services were performed for a California client. Because section 6125 applies to the practice of law in California, it does not, in general, regulate law practice in other states. Thus, although the general rule against compensation to out-of-state attorneys precludes Birbrower's recovery under the fee agreement for its actions in California, the severability doctrine may allow it to receive its New York fees generated under the fee agreement. . . .

Therefore, we conclude the Court of Appeal erred in determining that the fee agreement between the parties was entirely unenforceable because Birbrower violated section 6125's prohibition against the unauthorized practice of law in California. Birbrower's statutory violation may require exclusion of the portion of the fee attributable to the substantial illegal services, but that violation does not necessarily entirely preclude its recovery under the fee agreement for the limited services it performed outside California. . . .

III. Disposition

We conclude that Birbrower violated section 6125 by practicing law in California. To the extent the fee agreement allows payment for those illegal local services, it is void, and Birbrower is not entitled to recover fees under the agreement for those services. The fee agreement is enforceable, however, to the extent it is possible to sever the portions of the consideration attributable to Birbrower's services illegally rendered in California from those attributable to Birbrower's New York services. . . .

AUTHORS' COMMENT:

Judge Chin's majority opinion was joined by four other justices. Would you have joined? Why or why not? If you were going to dissent, which parts of the majority opinion would you attack? How?

Kennard, J., dissenting.

In California, it is a misdemeanor to practice law when one is not a member of the State Bar. In this case, New York lawyers who were not members of the California Bar traveled to this state on several occasions, attempting to resolve a contract dispute between their clients and another corporation through negotiation and private arbitration. Their clients included a New York corporation and a sister corporation incorporated in California; the lawyers had in previous years represented the principal owners of these corporations. The majority holds that the New York lawyers' activities in California constituted the unauthorized practice of law. I disagree.

The majority focuses its attention on the question of whether the New York lawyers had engaged in the practice of law in California, giving scant consideration to a decisive preliminary inquiry: whether, through their activities here, the New York lawyers had engaged in the practice of law at all. In my view, the record does not show that they did. In reaching a contrary conclusion, the majority relies on an overbroad definition of the term "practice of law." I would adhere to this court's decision in *Baron v. City of Los Angeles* (1970) 2 Cal. 3d 535, more narrowly defining the practice of law as the representation of another in a judicial proceeding or an activity requiring the application of that degree of legal knowledge and technique possessed only by a trained legal mind. Under this definition, this case presents a triable issue of material fact as to whether the New York lawyers' California activities constituted the practice of law.

II

Business and Professions Code section 6125 states: "No person shall practice law in California unless the person is an active member of the State Bar." The Legislature, however, has not defined what constitutes the practice of law. . . .

The majority's overbroad definition would affect a host of common commercial activities. On point here are comments that Professor Deborah Rhode made in a 1981 article published in the Stanford Law Review: "For many individuals, most obviously accountants, bankers, real estate brokers, and insurance agents, it would be impossible to give intelligent counsel without reference to legal concerns that such statutes reserve as the exclusive province of lawyers. As one [American Bar Association] official active in unauthorized practice areas recently acknowledged, there is growing recognition that " 'all kinds of other professional people are practicing the law almost out of necessity.' " Moreover, since most legislation does not exempt gratuitous activity, much advice commonly imparted by friends, employers, political organizers, and newspaper commentators constitutes unauthorized practice. For example, although the organized bar has not yet evinced any inclination to drag [nationally syndicated advice columnist] Ann Landers through the courts, she is plainly fair game under extant statutes [proscribing the unauthorized practice of law]." (Rhode, *Policing the Professional Monopoly: A Constitutional and Empirical Analysis of Unauthorized Practice Prohibitions*, 34 Stan. L. Rev. 1, 47, fns. omitted.)

Unlike the majority, I would for the reasons given above adhere to the more narrowly drawn definition of the practice of law that this court articulated in *Baron:* the representation of another in a judicial proceeding or an activity requiring the application of that degree of legal knowledge and technique possessed only by a trained legal mind. Applying that definition here, I conclude that the trial court should not have granted summary adjudication for plaintiffs based on the Birbrower lawyers' California activities. . . .

AUTHORS' COMMENT:

Do you like the dissent's definition of the unauthorized practice of law — "the representation of another in a judicial proceeding or an activity requiring the application of that degree of legal knowledge and technique possessed only by a trained legal mind"? How does it differ from the majority's definition? Under either definition, do you think the Birbrower lawyers were practicing law "in" California when they helped their client prepare for an arbitration proceeding to resolve a contract dispute?

III

As I mentioned earlier, Birbrower's clients had a software development and marketing agreement with Tandem. The agreement provided that its validity, interpretation, and enforcement were to be governed by California law. It also contained an arbitration provision. After a dispute arose pertaining to Tandem's performance under the agreement, Birbrower initiated an arbitration on behalf of its clients by filing a claim with the American Arbitration Association in San Francisco, and held meetings in California to prepare for an arbitration hearing. Because the dispute with Tandem was settled, the arbitration hearing was never held. . . .

Representing another in an arbitration proceeding does not invariably present difficult or doubtful legal questions that require a trained legal mind for their resolution. Under California law, arbitrators are "not ordinarily constrained to decide according to the rule of law. . . ."

[U]nder this court's decisions, arbitration proceedings are not governed or constrained by the rule of law; therefore, representation of another in an arbitration proceeding, including the activities necessary to prepare for the arbitration hearing, does not necessarily require a trained legal mind.

Commonly used arbitration rules further demonstrate that legal training is not essential to represent another in an arbitration proceeding. Here, for example, Birbrower's clients agreed to resolve any dispute arising under their contract with Tandem using the American Arbitration Association's rules, which allow any party to be "represented by counsel or other authorized representative." Rules of other arbitration organizations also allow for representation by nonattorneys. . . .

The American Arbitration Association and other major arbitration associations thus recognize that nonattorneys are often better suited than attorneys to represent parties in arbitration. The history of arbitration also reflects this reality, for in its beginnings arbitration was a dispute-resolution mechanism principally used in a few specific trades (such as construction, textiles, ship chartering, and international sales of goods) to resolve disputes among businesses that turned on factual issues uniquely within the expertise of members of the trade. In fact, "rules of a few trade associations forbid representation by counsel in arbitration proceedings, because of their belief that it would complicate what might otherwise be simple proceedings." The majority gives no adequate justification for its decision to deprive parties of their freedom of contract and to make it a crime for anyone but California lawyers to represent others in arbitrations in California. . . .

In this case, plaintiffs have not identified any specific California activities by the New York lawyers of the Birbrower firm that meet the narrow definition of the term "practice of law". . . . Accordingly, I would reverse the judgment of the Court of Appeal and direct it to remand the matter to the trial court with directions to vacate its order granting plaintiff's motion for summary adjudication and to enter a new order denying that motion.

NOTES AND QUESTIONS

1. ***Which Side Is Right?*** Did the Birbrower firm engage in the unauthorized practice of law in California or not? Does your answer depend on how you define the practice of law? Do you think the "practice of law" ought to be defined broadly, as in the majority opinion, or narrowly, as in the dissenting opinion?

2. ***Telephone, Fax, and E-mail.*** For practicing lawyers, the scariest part of the *Birbrower* opinion was the passage suggesting that a lawyer could be found guilty of practicing law in California just by talking with a California client on the phone or sending a few faxes or e-mails. The court said: "[O]ne may practice law in the state in violation of section 6125 although not physically present here by advising a California client on California law in connection with a California legal dispute by telephone, fax, computer, or other modern technological means."

How would the *Birbrower* court's expansive view of the unauthorized practice of law affect the legal profession and the public? Would lawyers be restricted to advising clients only in the states where they were licensed? What would this mean for clients living near a state border, or for corporations that engage in business in numerous states? Would multi-state corporations have to hire a different lawyer in each state? Think about the implications of the California Supreme Court's view that a lawyer may violate a state's unauthorized practice law even if the lawyer never sets foot inside that state. What will this mean for the kind of practice you want do after you finish law school?

3. ***Florida's Proposed Rule.*** In 1998, the Florida Bar circulated a proposed new Rule 3-1.3 that was even more sweeping than the *Birbrower* decision. Proposed Rule 3-1.3 provided as follows:

Lawyers Admitted in Jurisdictions Other than Florida

> The Supreme Court of Florida has the authority to regulate conduct that constitutes the practice of law in Florida. In the exercise of this authority for the

> protection of the public, the court has determined that lawyers, whether or not admitted to practice law in Florida, who solicit or advertise for legal employment in Florida or who target solicitations or advertisements for legal employment at Florida residents are engaging in the practice of law. Consequently, lawyers who engage in such activity must do so only in accordance with the applicable provisions of these Rules Regulating The Florida Bar, as well as other applicable law.

Will such a rule protect the public against bad lawyers, or deprive the public of the choice of good lawyers? If you were commenting on Florida's proposed rule, what would you say? (The Florida Supreme Court ultimately rejected the proposed rule, explaining that an out-of-state lawyer soliciting business in Florida without a Florida law license was engaged in the unauthorized practice of law!)

4. ***Pre-2002 Version of ABA Model Rule 5.5.*** The wording of Model Rule 5.5 before it was amended in 2002 is still in effect in many jurisdictions, including Michigan. The wording is short and simple:

> A lawyer shall not:
>
> (a) practice law in a jurisdiction where doing so violates the regulation of the profession in that jurisdiction; or
>
> (b) assist a person who is not a member of the bar in the performance of an activity that constitutes the unauthorized practice of law.

After the court's decision in *Birbrower*, then, a lawyer licensed in Illinois or Virginia (but not in California) who advised a California client on California law in California ran the risk not only of violating California's UPL ban, but also of violating the UPL prohibition in Illinois or Virginia, the state in which he or she was licensed to practice. That is, when an Illinois or Virginia lawyer violated California's statutory prohibition on the unauthorized practice of law, the lawyer was simultaneously violating Rule 5.5(a)'s mandate that a lawyer shall not "practice law in a jurisdiction where doing so violates the regulation of the profession in that jurisdiction."

C. BROADER PERMISSION TO ENGAGE IN MULTIJURISDITIONAL PRACTICE

Should a law license be more like a driver's license? Once you have a valid driver's license in one state, you may legally drive all across the United States. You don't need to get a new driver's license in each state you travel through, and you don't need to register with the state or even give notice that you are present in the state. Even if you move to a new state permanently, you often don't need to get a new driver's license until your old driver's license expires. Should a law license be more like that? Once you are licensed to practice law in one state, should you be free to move about the country?

In light of the complexity of assessing the competing policy factors regarding multijurisdictional practice, in the fall of 2000, the president of the ABA appointed a new ABA Commission on Multijurisdictional Practice. This blue-ribbon group was charged with formulating language that would take into account the concerns voiced by disciplinary counsel, bar admissions personnel, clients who retain counsel, lawyers across the spectrum of private practice, international trade negotiators (who count legal services as one of the many goods and services which are exchanged across national boundaries), lawyers working in government, bar associations, in-house counsel, and private citizens. The MJP Commission received written comments and heard testimony from hundreds of organizations and individuals.

At the ABA's August 2002 Annual Meeting, all of the MJP Commission's recommendations were approved by the ABA's House of Delegates by a substantial margin. Twenty-eight states moved quickly to adopt new amendments (or substantially similar language) to their versions of Model Rule 5.5. The amended rules expand the scope of practice permitted for out-of-state lawyers advising clients in those jurisdictions. In addition to the states that have already adopted new language, state bar associations and other organizations in many of the remaining states have approved amendments to their professional responsibility rules permitting some form of multijurisdictional practice, and the proposals are moving through the process for consideration by the courts in those states. Some states have adopted regulations that track the exact language of ABA Model Rule 5.5, while others have enacted rules with modified language. Updates posted on the website of the ABA's Center for Professional Responsibility reflect state-by-state developments regarding multijurisdictional practice. How does amended ABA Model Rule 5.5 work? It is worth taking time to engage in a section-by-section analysis. We'll refer to the wording of Rule 5.5 in Delaware, which is identical to that of the Model Rule.

The first section of the 2002 language for Rule 5.5 retains the prohibition from the earlier version of the rule:

> (a) A lawyer shall not practice law in a jurisdiction in violation of the regulation of the legal profession in that jurisdiction, or assist another in doing so.

The next section of the amended version of Rule 5.5 makes it clear that a lawyer not admitted in the state is not allowed to open an office to work in that state on a long-term basis. And, an out-of-state lawyer is also not allowed to advertise, distribute business cards, or otherwise try to get the business of potential clients in that state. Thus, the amended version of Delaware's Rule 5.5(b) provides:

> (b) A lawyer who is not admitted to practice in this jurisdiction shall not:
>
> (1) except as authorized by these Rules or other law, establish an office or other systematic and continuous presence in this jurisdiction for the practice of law; or
>
> (2) hold out to the public or otherwise represent that the lawyer is admitted to practice law in this jurisdiction.

Amended Rule 5.5(c) permits lawyers who are not disbarred or suspended from practice in any jurisdiction to provide legal services "on a temporary basis" in the host jurisdiction in certain circumstances. Rule 5.5 (c)(1) codifies the judicially created exception to the old rule for work performed in association with locally admitted co-counsel, and Rule 5.5 (c)(2) somewhat enlarges the long-standing *pro hac vice* exception, by permitting legal services prior to obtaining the *pro hac vice* admission. No big deal there. Rule 5.5 (c)(3) now provides express permission to engage in arbitration, mediation, and other ADR methods, which came as a welcome relief after *Birbrower*, where the unauthorized practice of law in large part consisted of activities focused on preparing for an arbitration. But Rule 5.5 (c)(4) announces a sweeping change:

> (c) A lawyer admitted in another United States jurisdiction, and not disbarred or suspended from practice in any jurisdiction, may provide legal services on a temporary basis in this jurisdiction that:
>
> (1) are undertaken in association with a lawyer who is admitted to practice in this jurisdiction and who actively participates in the matter;
>
> (2) are in or reasonably related to a pending or potential proceeding before a tribunal in this or another jurisdiction, if the lawyer, or a person the lawyer is assisting, is authorized by law or order to appear in such proceeding or reasonably expects to be so authorized;
>
> (3) are in or reasonably related to a pending or potential arbitration, mediation, or other alternative dispute resolution proceeding in this or another jurisdiction, if the services arise out of or are reasonably related to the lawyer's practice in a jurisdiction in which the lawyer is admitted to practice and are not services for which the forum requires pro hac vice admission; or

(4) are not within paragraphs (c)(2) or (c)(3) and arise out of or are reasonably related to the lawyer's practice in a jurisdiction in which the lawyer is admitted to practice. [Emphasis added.]

Under 5.5(c)(4), the out-of-state lawyer in good standing will have considerable freedom to practice law while temporarily in another U.S. jurisdiction. The MJP Commission rejected proposals to limit such lawyers to representations which have a connection to the state in which the lawyer is licensed (the lawyer's home state) or to work only for clients with ties to that home state. On the other hand, the Commission also rejected a proposal that would have removed the requirement that the work in the host state must be only temporary.

The new language does open some new areas for disagreement. One can easily imagine some skirmishes over the precise amount of time a lawyer can spend in a state before she will no longer be considered to be practicing on a temporary basis. Some states might declare that after a lawyer has been present in the state a certain number of days his presence is no longer temporary. Others might distinguish between out-of-state clients and host state clients, and allow the out-of-state lawyer to represent his out-of-state clients for a longer period than they will allow him to give legal advice to host state clients.

The final provision omits the requirement that the services be provided only on a temporary basis, although comment 17 notes that a lawyer who establishes an office to serve his employer may be required by the host state to register, participate in mandatory continuing legal education and/or pay into client protection funds. Rule 5.5(d)(1) allows lawyers employed by corporations, other entities, or the government to provide legal services other than court appearances. Rule 5.5(d)(2) authorizes legal services when allowed under federal law (including a statute, court rule, executive regulation or judicial precedent).

(d) A lawyer admitted in another United States jurisdiction, and not disbarred or suspended from practice in any jurisdiction, may provide legal services in this jurisdiction that:

(1) are provided to the lawyer's employer or its organizational affiliates and are not services for which the forum requires pro hac vice admission; or

(2) are services that the lawyer is authorized to provide by federal law or other law of this jurisdiction.

NOTES AND QUESTIONS

How would you analyze the following fact patterns under the 2002 version of Rule 5.5? (Assume that all of the lawyers in the fact patterns are in good standing in their home states and have not been suspended or disbarred in any jurisdiction.)

A. David Duncan, who is licensed only in California, asks Helen Hillstrom, licensed in North Dakota, to appear with Duncan on a case being litigated in North Dakota federal court. Hillstrom agrees to file in the North Dakota federal court the motions and briefs written by Duncan, but does not want to do any other work on the matter. May Duncan appear in court in North Dakota? Is Hillstrom's limited involvement permissible?

B. Fred Frank, who is licensed only in Kansas, travels to Delaware to assist lawyers licensed in Delaware in a trial scheduled to start a year from now. Once underway, the trial is expected to take eight months. The company Frank is representing in the litigation has been a client of his for ten years. Frank does not plan to appear in court or to take any depositions in the case, and therefore will not be seeking admission *pro hac vice*. Instead, Frank will be conducting legal research, drafting documents, interviewing witnesses, working on jury instructions, preparing complex exhibits, and orchestrating the work of the expert witnesses. What do you think of these plans?

(1) One way to handle the logistics is to set up office space in Delaware and have Frank plan to move to Delaware and work there for the next eighteen months. Is this permitted?

(2) An alternative is to have Frank remain in Kansas as much as possible, doing research, drafting and similar tasks in Kansas, and traveling to Delaware only when it is absolutely necessary. Is Frank permitted to do this?

(3) Would it change your analysis if the client is a new client for Frank, and the work involves federal regulations that Frank has made the focus of his practice in Kansas?

(4) Greg Gadgett, licensed in Kansas but not in Delaware, will be supervising the work Frank does in Delaware. Gadgett anticipates that in a few weeks he will be admitted *pro hac vice* in Delaware. Assuming that Gadgett is indeed admitted *pro hac vice*, can he properly supervise Frank's work in Delaware?

(5) Are the Delaware lawyers permitted to work with the Kansas lawyers as co-counsel?

C. Timothy L. Wright, who is licensed only in Missouri, is an environmental law expert who works in Missouri as in-house counsel for a major consumer products retailer. Wright is asked by his employer to evaluate the company's potential environmental liability in connection with its operations at plants located in 15 different states.

(1) Can Wright travel to each of the states, spending about three weeks in each state, and giving legal advice to the plant managers in those states?

(2) Is Wright exposed to UPL prosecution if he instead remains in Missouri and has documents sent to him there and participates in out-of-state meetings only by conference call, but gives the same legal advice to the out-of-state plant managers?

(3) Would it make a difference in either case if Wright gave legal advice only to company officials in the Missouri headquarters rather than to the plant managers scattered around the country?

(4) Would it make a difference if the plant managers sent the relevant documents to the non-lawyer executives at the company's Missouri headquarters, and those executives passed along the documents to Wright, rather than have the plant managers send documents to Wright directly?

(5) May Wright represent an additional wholly-owned subsidiary of the company, which will require him to spend about two weeks every month in Colorado on an on-going basis?

(6) May Wright continue to advise the corporation, including the two subsidiaries, in this manner if he leaves his job as in-house counsel and opens his own private law firm as a solo practitioner in Missouri?

(7) May Wright continue to advise the corporation, including the two subsidiaries, if he leaves his job as in-house counsel to join a large "national" firm that has offices in several states, including Colorado, and includes partners or associates who are admitted in those states?

D. THE BIG PICTURE REGARDING MULTIJURISDICTIONAL PRACTICE

Before we close this chapter, let's think about the big picture. In any given state, the lawyers who usually speak with the loudest voices are the lawyers who are licensed in that state. These lawyers decide whether to pursue the process of amending the rules in effect in that state. When that state adopts the 2002 changes to Rule 5.5, are in-state lawyers able to do anything more in their own states than they were before the changes? No. The change in State X benefits out-of-state lawyers who can now ethically come into

State X to practice temporarily, not the in-state lawyers in State X who already have the right to practice there. What are the implications?

1. ***Requiring Similar Treatment for Host State Lawyers.*** In some states, there is some attraction to opening the door only to lawyers licensed in those states in which "our" lawyers can obtain reciprocal treatment. How would that work if the potential host jurisdiction allowed out-of-state lawyers to perform legal services in more situations than does the home state?

For example, suppose the potential host jurisdiction follows the language of Model Rule 5.5(c)(4) and permits services provided on a temporary basis which arise out of or are reasonably related to the lawyer's practice in a jurisdiction in which the lawyer is admitted. But suppose the home state requires that the work be done only for an existing client when the transaction originates in or is otherwise related to a jurisdiction in which the lawyer is admitted. In this situation, it can be argued that the home state is not allowing the lawyers licensed in the host jurisdiction the same scope of activities, so the host state lawyers are not receiving parallel treatment in the other state.

In a related issue, how will we evaluate the situation of lawyers licensed in three or four states? Will the host jurisdiction allow them to provide legal services as long as at least one of the states in which the lawyer is licensed would give a similar scope of activities to the host jurisdiction's lawyers? Or only if all of the states do so?

2. ***Effect on Local Bar Organizations, Pro Bono and Mentoring.*** Is something lost when outsiders who are not licensed in a state provide legal services to the citizens of that state? If lucrative legal work in Ohio is scooped up by securities lawyers licensed in New York, who will provide pro bono services to the clients in Ohio?

Is there a problem in transmitting the values of the profession, when the lawyers working in a city no longer see the same persons in the courthouse? What about the situation of transactional lawyers who no longer see local attorneys representing the other parties in the transactions they are working on? And will the lawyers whose work occasionally takes them out of state be able to mentor law students there?

Who will spend the time it takes to keep local bar organizations going? Cynics may say that the out-of-state lawyers aren't likely candidates. On the other hand, isn't it possible that an out-of-state lawyer might become involved in local pro bono work and bar activities as a way of burnishing her image and making contacts that may eventually generate referrals? But is it likely that an out-of-state lawyer will be able to do this when she practices in six or seven different states?

3. ***Possible Effects on Fees.*** If the out-of-state lawyers are coming from major metropolitan legal markets elsewhere, isn't it possible that their fees will be too high for the local market? Conversely, if the out-of-state lawyers have figured out ways to be more efficient, and are able to do competent legal work for lower legal fees, wouldn't that be advantageous for the local clients?

4. ***Possible Effects on Clients.*** Yes, there are synergies and lower costs possible when providers conduct a volume business. But — to analogize to the retail business — is something lost when Wal-Mart and Home Depot take away the business that used to go to the locally owned stores? If so, what? And what benefits do the local residents get in return for giving up the benefits of locally owned stores?

Is something similarly destroyed when out-of-state lawyers take away the legal business that used to go to the locally licensed lawyers? What, precisely, is lost? Or, has this already happened? Do clients already seek out lawyers who focus their practice in certain areas regardless of where those lawyers are licensed? Will adopting the language of Model Rule 5.5 accelerate that process, slow it down, or have no effect? Why?

Chapter 6
INTRODUCTION TO SECRECY

The bedrock of the attorney-client relationship is the client's trust of the attorney. If the client does not trust the attorney, the attorney-client relationship is in serious trouble. The client's trust of the attorney rests on two things: (1) *secrecy*, and (2) *loyalty*. What do these terms mean? What is secrecy? What is loyalty?

Secrecy. Secrecy refers to a lawyer's ethical obligation not to use or reveal information relating to the representation of a client. The information may come directly from a client, or from documents or third parties (e.g., witnesses or co-workers), or from the lawyer's own head. Communications by a client to a lawyer in confidence for the purpose of seeking legal advice are protected by the attorney-client privilege, which prevents anyone from compelling either the attorney or the client to reveal confidential communications between them absent a waiver or exception. Information gathered by a lawyer from sources other than the client is not protected by the attorney-client privilege but is protected by the ethical duty of confidentiality, which prohibits a lawyer from using or revealing information relating to the representation of a client absent the client's consent or some other exception. Information created by the lawyer (e.g., interview notes, memos to the file) is protected by the work product doctrine, which is codified in Rule 26 of the Federal Rules of Civil Procedure, as well as in state statutes or court rules in some jurisdictions. For convenience, we lump all three of these sources — the attorney-client privilege, the ethical duty of confidentiality, and the work product doctrine — under the single heading of secrecy.

Loyalty. Clients must also be able to trust you to work only for their interests, and never against their interests. They expect you to be completely loyal to them — not to stab them in the back or to line your own pocket (or enrich your family and friends) at the client's expense. Clients expect you not to abandon them or turn against them when a richer or more glamorous client comes along. Clients should be able to trust you to avoid all conflicts of interest, or at least to tell them when a conflict of loyalties has arisen or might arise. We will discuss this aspect of trust under the heading of "loyalty." This section of the book focuses on secrecy. Later chapters will focus on loyalty (i.e., avoiding conflicts of interest).

A. AN OUTLINE ON SECRECY

To help you master the fundamentals of the rules of secrecy, here is an outline addressing the three main branches in secrecy — the attorney-client privilege, the ethical duty of confidentiality, and the work-product doctrine. Each branch has a separate analysis. Be careful not to confuse them. The better you understand the basic concepts in this outline, the more time you can spend on more interesting and sophisticated issues that build on these fundamental concepts.

Secrecy (also broadly referred to as "confidentiality") has three main branches:

- *Ethics.* Under the rules of legal ethics, you generally cannot *voluntarily* tell other people anything about your client without your client's express or implied consent, or some other exception.
- *Evidence.* Under the rules of evidence, you generally cannot be *compelled* to reveal communications with your client.
- *Procedure.* Under the rules of civil and criminal procedure, you generally cannot be compelled to reveal written material created in anticipation of litigation or for trial. Courts give especially strong protection to a lawyer's mental impressions, opinions, and conclusions as a lawyer.

Now we'll describe each branch in greater detail.

1. The Duty of Confidentiality

a. The secrecy obligation — grounded on the ethics rules — is defined and governed by the *Rules of Professional Conduct.* The rules of professional conduct vary from state to state, but for now we will focus on the ABA Model Rules of Professional Conduct (the "Model Rules") rather than on state variations. Under Model Rule 1.6, you have a professional duty not to voluntarily reveal to others any "information relating to the representation" unless the rules of ethics carve out a specific exception. This general rule describes *the ethical obligation of confidentiality.*

b. The ethical obligation of confidentiality prevents you from revealing information voluntarily, but it does not protect your client when statutes, court rules, or court orders require you to disclose information. Thus, the ethical obligation of confidentiality requires you to claim the attorney-client privilege whenever it arguably applies. But the ethical obligation of confidentiality alone, without the attorney-client privilege, will not entitle you to withhold testimony if you are called as a witness at a trial or deposition. If you are subpoenaed before a court or other tribunal to testify about a client, a court may require you to testify fully unless the information is protected by the attorney-client privilege. It will not help to say, "I have an ethical duty not to tell you any information relating to my representation of my client."

c. The ethical obligation of confidentially is limited in two ways:

   i. You cannot refuse to testify or provide interrogatory answers unless your testimony is expressly protected by the *attorney-client privilege* (which is part of the law of *evidence*).

   ii. You cannot refuse to produce documents or disclose your opinions unless the information is protected by the attorney-client privilege or by the *work-product doctrine* (which is codified in the rules of civil and criminal procedure).

2. The Attorney-Client Privilege

a. Under the rules of evidence, you generally cannot be *compelled* to reveal confidential communications with your client. The communications include both what you said to your client and what your client said to you, and they include both oral and written communications.

b. You can refuse to produce documents or to disclose your opinions in testimony if the documents or your testimony is expressly protected by the *attorney-client privilege,* which is part of the law of *evidence.*

3. Work-Product Protection

a. Under Rule 26(b)(3) of the Federal Rules of Civil Procedure, you generally cannot be *compelled* to reveal written material created in anticipation of litigation or for trial.

b. Rule 26(b)(3) provides especially strong protection for your mental impressions, opinions, and conclusions as a lawyer.

c. You can refuse to produce documents in discovery or refuse to disclose your opinions when they are protected by the work-product doctrine.

d. The Federal Rules of Criminal Procedure also protect some forms of work product, however, battles over work product arise less frequently in criminal cases.

4. Quick Summary

The ethical duty of confidentiality, rooted in the rules of ethics, prevents lawyers from volunteering what they know about a client or a client's matter, regardless of the source. The attorney-client privilege, rooted in the rules of evidence, prevents lawyers from being compelled to tell what they discussed (orally or in writing) with their clients. The work product doctrine, rooted in the rules of civil procedure, generally prevents lawyers from being compelled to reveal information they created for purposes of litigation. (All of these rules have exceptions, which we will cover in detail later.)

5. Who is a "Client"?

One more preliminary question has to be answered before we can explore secrecy in detail. Rule 1.6 (like many other rules) creates duties only to a person who is a "client" (meaning a current client). If a person is not your client and never was your client, then you do not owe that person a duty of confidentiality under Rule 1.6. Likewise, the attorney-client privilege and the work product doctrine depend on whether you have a client, and who that client is. Whether a person is considered a "client" depends on the circumstances.

a. The main test is whether the person *reasonably believes* she is your client.
    i. The first question is whether a person *believes* he or she is your client.
    ii. If so, the second question is whether that belief is *reasonable* in light of all the circumstances.

b. In most situations, it will be clear whether a person is or is not a current client. For example, a person who hires you to represent her in a personal injury suit or a real estate closing is your current client until the matter concludes or the client fires you. It does not matter whether the legal problem involves drafting a document (such as a will), structuring a transaction (such as negotiating an employment contract), or resolving a dispute (such as pending or threatened litigation or arbitration). If the person hires you for a specific purpose, then you are her lawyer and she is your client.

c. In many situations, however, it may not be clear whether or not you represent a particular person. In fact, you may genuinely believe that the person is *not* your client. We will explore these situations in depth later on, but for now here are a few examples that can lead to a finding of an attorney-client relationship even when you do not think the person is your client:
    i. If you represent a corporation in a lawsuit but you deal day in and day out with the corporation's officers, some of the officers may think that you represent them as individuals in addition to representing the company.
    ii. If you represent a trade association (like an association of sporting good retailers) but you solicit and receive confidential information from trade association members, those members may consider you their lawyer.
    iii. If a person tells you confidential information about her legal problems in hopes that you will accept her case, but you do not clearly reject the case, the person may consider you her lawyer until you tell her otherwise.
    iv. Similarly, if you think your work for a particular client is completed but you fail to tell the client that the attorney-client relationship is over, the person may reasonably believe she is still your client and you are still her lawyer.

It is premature to catalog and explore all of the situations in which the existence of an attorney-client relationship may be ambiguous, but keep in mind, whether a person is a client is judged initially from the client's perspective. Care is required, therefore, to assure that an attorney-client relationship does not arise by implication of law because you have failed to make clear that you do not have an attorney-client relationship.

d. Remember, too, once a person has become a client, the protection of Rule 1.6 lasts forever:

   i. The death of a client does not extinguish your duty of confidentiality.
   ii. The termination of the attorney-client relationship does not extinguish your duty of confidentiality.
   iii. However, after an attorney-client relationship ends, you may — pursuant to Rule 1.9(c) — reveal information that has become "generally known."

e. *Other sources of authority:* Rule 1.6 is not the only source of confidentiality duties. Even if a person is not your "client," you may have an obligation to keep information confidential, because of the requirements of other laws, especially agency law or contract law. As with Rule 1.6, breach of these duties of confidentiality may subject you to a lawsuit, judicial or disciplinary sanctions, or other penalties. For example:

   i. In business negotiations, an agreement between the parties may require you, as a matter of contract law, to keep secret all information that you learn about the opposing side during the negotiations.
   ii. In litigation, a protective order issued by the court or stipulated to by the parties may obligate you to keep secret certain information that you obtain through discovery.
   iii. In litigation, fiduciary duties may prohibit you from revealing information you learn about a co-defendant as part of a joint defense arrangement.
   iv. While serving as executor of an estate, you may owe duties of confidentiality to the beneficiaries of the estate even though they are not clients.
   v. When an opposing lawyer or opposing party presses the wrong buttons or has the wrong information, she may inadvertently send you confidential information by post, fax, voice-mail, e-mail, or even in person. You may owe duties of confidentiality to the sender even though the sender is not your client.

Now that we have given you an overview of the ethical duty of confidentiality, the evidentiary law of the attorney-client privilege, and the procedural doctrine of work product, and have briefly explored the meaning of the vital word "client," we are ready to study confidentiality, attorney-client privilege, and work product in greater depth.

B. THE DUTY OF CONFIDENTIALITY

The key point to remember about secrecy is that you learn many things when you are a practicing attorney that you are not free to tell anyone outside your law firm except your client. The scope of the obligation to remain silent is articulated in Model Rule 1.6 and its counterparts adopted in each state. As a general rule, once a lawyer has learned information in the course of representing a client, the lawyer is not free to reveal that information to others unless an exception to the duty of confidentiality applies. This means, for example, that if you are the lawyer writing a prenuptial agreement for a Hollywood star, the duty of confidentiality prevents you from telling anyone not working at your law firm about his investment in a Peruvian gold mine, the value of the antiques in his New York co-op or any other information you learn in the course of your work on the prenuptial agreement.

1. ABA Model Rule 1.6

Secrecy raises difficult issues. To a large extent, these issues are governed by rules of professional conduct. In the ABA Model Rules of Professional Conduct, the main rule governing confidentiality is Rule 1.6. Take a few minutes to read carefully the black letter text of ABA Model Rule 1.6. (In New York, the only state that still bases its ethics rules on the old ABA Model Code of Professional Responsibility, the main rule governing confidentiality is DR 4-101. Take a minute to read that rule, too.)

a. ABA Model Rule 1.6(a) does not formally define confidential information, but it does define the scope of what is protected by the ethical duty of confidentiality. A lawyer has a duty not to reveal "*information relating to the representation of a client*" unless an exception applies.
b. DR 4-101(A) of the old ABA Model Code of Professional Responsibility defines the scope of protected information much more specifically, dividing protected information into two categories, "confidences" and "secrets." DR 4-101(A) provides:

> "Confidence" refers to information protected by the attorney-client privilege under applicable law, and "secret" refers to other information gained in the professional relationship that the client has requested be held inviolate or the disclosure of which would be embarrassing or would be likely to be detrimental to the client.

What do you think of ABA Model Rule 1.6? Does it define the scope of confidential information correctly? How does Rule 1.6 relate to the attorney-client privilege and the work-product doctrine? And since Rule 1.6 governs only "information," what are the rules regarding physical evidence, such as guns, documents, and dead bodies?

2. State Variations

Each state is free to adopt, modify, or reject the ABA Model Rules. Regarding confidentiality, most states have adopted ABA Model Rule 1.6 with some modifications. Consequently, the rules governing confidentiality differ from state to state, sometimes radically. Yet despite these differences among the states, our outline is a good start because ABA Model Rule 1.6 frames the main issues that each state has to address in its own secrecy rule. Keep in mind, though, that if you practice in more than one state — for example, by litigating in the courts of other states or by becoming licensed in another state — the secrecy rules may differ as you move from state to state.

C. THE RULES OF EVIDENCE: THE ATTORNEY-CLIENT PRIVILEGE

This section examines the attorney-client privilege. In federal courts and in most states, the attorney-client privilege is a creature of common law, not statute. It is much stronger than the ethical rule of confidentiality, but also much narrower — it covers much less information.

1. The attorney-client privilege applies only when "5 C's" are present.

   a. Client
   b. Communicates
   c. Confidentially with
   d. Counsel (i.e., a lawyer acting as a lawyer)
   e. To obtain Counsel (i.e., to obtain legal advice).

2. If all five of these elements are present, then the attorney-client privilege applies. Once the privilege attaches, then no one — not even a court — can compel the lawyer or client to reveal the privileged information unless an exception applies or the privilege is waived.

3. But if one or more of these five elements is missing, then the attorney-client privilege does not apply. The attorney-client privilege applies only if all five elements are present. Every element is essential.

4. When a lawyer represents a corporation, the lawyer's communications to or from all corporate officers, directors, or employees — no matter how low or high the person's rank — are protected by the attorney-client privilege in federal courts and most state courts, so long as the five C's are present. (However, some states narrow the privilege in the corporate setting.)

5. However, there are some situations in which the attorney-client privilege either does not apply from the beginning or is considered waived. Here are the most prominent examples:

a. *Waiver:* If the client waives the privilege as to a given subject, then the privilege no longer exists for information on that subject.

  i. For example, if the client (or the lawyer) intentionally reveals privileged information by deliberately turning over privileged documents during discovery, or by deciding not to object to a question seeking privileged information at the client's deposition, then the privilege is waived.

  ii. Moreover, the client cannot selectively waive the privilege — the client cannot reveal a little bit of privileged information on a given subject or topic and then claim the attorney-client privilege as to the rest of the information about the same subject or topic.

    (1) Selective waiver would unfairly allow the client to use privileged information favorable to his case and then withhold privileged information unfavorable to his case. This kind of partial or selective waiver is not permitted.

    (2) With respect to any given subject, the attorney-client privilege is an all-or-nothing affair; once it is waived as to any part of a subject, it is usually waived as to every part of the subject.

  iii. Waiver can also be accidental rather than deliberate. For example, a lawyer or client may accidentally turn over privileged documents in response to a discovery request in litigation. Most courts will apply a multi-factored test to determine whether the privilege has been waived. Typically, the most important factor is whether the party claiming the privilege took reasonably adequate steps to protect privileged documents against disclosure.

  iv. When a client is a corporation, a change in the management team, such as that following a hostile takeover or the appointment of a trustee in bankruptcy, will result in a change in the persons who can waive the privilege on behalf of the entity.

b. *Crime-fraud exception:* If the client uses the lawyer's services to commit a crime or fraud, then the client's communications with the lawyer are not privileged, even if the lawyer did not know the client was engaging in a crime or fraud at the time the communications were made. The crime-fraud exception depends on the client's *intent* to commit a crime or fraud, not on the attorney's *knowledge* of that intent. (But the crime-fraud exception does not destroy the privilege when a lawyer is hired to defend a client against accusations of a *past* crime or fraud. It applies only when the client was already planning or engaged in a crime or fraud at the time the client used the lawyer's services.)

c. *Joint clients exception:* If two clients hire the same lawyer, and they later get into a dispute with each other, then they do not have an attorney-client privilege vis-à-vis each other. For example:

i. Suppose two clients are sued for negligently putting up stands that collapsed during a rock concert, and both clients hire the same lawyer to defend them. In a joint interview with the lawyer, the clients admit negligence. If the clients later cross-claim against each other, neither client can claim the attorney-client privilege against the other regarding communications with the joint lawyer. And once the privilege is waived with respect to the other client (perhaps because one client introduces privileged communications into evidence against the other), then the privilege is waived as to everyone in the world.

ii. But as long as the two joint clients do not blame each other, they can continue to claim the attorney-client privilege against their adversaries, and against anyone else in the world who tries to breach the privilege. Unless they lose the privilege by getting into a dispute with each other, they will not lose the privilege if either gets into a dispute with anyone else.

d. *"Advice of counsel" defense.* A client also waives the attorney-client privilege if he defends a lawsuit by claiming that he acted based on "advice of counsel."

i. Because "scienter" (knowledgeable intent) is an element of some crimes — especially white collar crimes like securities law violations — defendants sometimes say they didn't know it was wrong because their lawyers said it was okay.

ii. When a client puts the advice of a lawyer into issue, the client waives the attorney-client privilege relating to that advice.

e. *Lawyer's self-defense exception.* A lawyer has the right to disclose confidential information (including information protected by the attorney-client privilege) in self-defense. The corollary is that the client waives the attorney-client privilege by attacking the lawyer.

i. By suing a lawyer for malpractice, for example, a client waives the attorney-client privilege for all communications with the defendant lawyer.

ii. Without this waiver, the lawyer would be defenseless. Also, the ethical right to disclose in self-defense would be meaningless without a parallel exception to the attorney-client privilege.

D. THE RULES OF PROCEDURE: THE WORK-PRODUCT DOCTRINE

When attorneys conduct legal research or take notes of witness interviews or write memos about legal strategies, the written product is called "work-product" and is protected against disclosure by various rules of procedure, in both civil and criminal matters. We will not study work-product in detail because it is typically studied in the first year Civil Procedure course, but you need to be aware of the scope of work-product protection in order to represen t your clients competently. If you inadvertently waive work-product protection, that might be malpractice, and might seriously harm your client.

1. *Civil cases:* Based on the United States Supreme Court's classic opinion in *Hickman v. Taylor*, 329 U.S. 495 (1947), the Federal Rules of Civil Procedure, and analogous state rules of civil procedure, protect an attorney's "work-product" relating to litigation. Work product is divided into two categories: (1) ordinary work product, and (2) opinion work product.

a. *Ordinary work product:* Under Fed. R. Civ. P. 26(b)(3), work-product includes information recorded by an attorney (or by the attorney's client, or by the attorney's agents) in anticipation of (i.e., "because of") litigation or in preparation for trial. Work by a party or by an attorney's investigators, paralegals, and consulting experts in anticipation of litigation or for trial is considered work-product and has the same protection as if it were prepared by the attorney personally.

i. For example, if an attorney for a tugboat company sends a paralegal to interview witnesses to an accident that is likely to give rise to a lawsuit, the paralegal's report to the attorney is work-product.

ii. In contrast, accident records kept by the tugboat captain in the "ordinary course of business" or for purposes of reporting to the government probably will not qualify as work product.

iii. Rule 26(b)(3) allows a party to obtain discovery of ordinary work product materials only upon a two-pronged showing that:

(1) the party seeking discovery has "substantial need" of the materials in the preparation of her case, and

(2) the party is unable without "undue hardship" to obtain the "substantial equivalent" of the work product materials by other means.

b. *Opinion work product:* Opinion work product consists of the mental impressions, conclusions, opinions, or legal theories of an attorney or other representative of a party concerning litigation. For example, if an attorney interviews a witness and writes notes such as, "This witness has doubtful credibility" or "We can use this witness to develop a theory of recklessness rather than mere negligence," those notes constitute opinion work product. Opinion work product is virtually immune from discovery.

i. Rule 26(b)(3) (just quoted above) provides that even when a party makes the required showing of substantial need for the work product materials and inability to obtain the substantial equivalent without undue hardship, "the court shall protect against disclosure of the mental impressions, conclusions, opinions, or legal theories" recorded by the party's attorney or other representative concerning the litigation. In other words, a court will not order a party to produce opinion work product even when the party seeking discovery has made the showing necessary to obtain ordinary work product protection.

ii. However, the ironclad protection afforded opinion work product is subject to waiver just as materials protected by the attorney-client privilege are subject to waiver. For example, if a lawyer shows opinion work product materials to a witness to refresh the witness's memory while the witness is preparing to testify at a deposition, the work product protection may be waived and a court will have discretion to order their disclosure. See Fed. R. Evid. 612.

c. *Experts.* When experts generate reports, opinions, or other work product materials, the level of protection provided by the Federal Rules of Civil Procedure depends on whether the expert is considered a "trial expert" or merely a "consulting expert."

i. Trial experts. With respect to an expert whose opinion may be presented at trial, Rule 26(a)(2)(B) requires a party to send a report to opposing counsel stating (among other things) the expert's opinions, the basis for those opinions, and the data or other information the expert considered in forming those opinions. In addition, Rule 26(b)(4)(A) allows any party to depose a trial expert — and during the deposition the expert must generally answer questions about communications with the lawyer that would merit work product protection for a consulting expert.

ii. Consulting experts. When an expert is merely a consulting expert who has been retained or employed in anticipation of litigation or for trial but is not expected to be called as a witness at trial, Fed. R. Civ. P. 26(b)(4) allows discovery only upon a showing of "exceptional circumstances under which it is impracticable for the party seeking discovery to obtain facts or opinions on the same subject by other means."

iii. However, once a lawyer designates an expert as a "trial expert" (i.e., an expert expected to testify at trial), then work-product protection is waived and everything written or said by that expert in forming her opinion may be discovered by the other side.

d. *Tangible things vs. oral communications:* The work-product doctrine generally protects only tangible things, not oral communications. However, the work product doctrine also generally protects the oral equivalent of tangible work product. For example, if the work product doctrine protects notes made by the other side's consulting expert, then you are not allowed to ask the consulting expert to answer the question, "What did you write in your notes?"

e. *Witness statements:* In some jurisdictions, the work-product doctrine protects witness statements. But there's a big difference between a signed witness statement and your own notes of what a witness said. In virtually all jurisdictions, if you make notes about what a witness told the lawyer and never show the notes to the witness, then your notes are protected as work-product.

f. In sum, work-product protection for ordinary work product in civil cases is weaker than the attorney-client privilege because it is subject to much broader exceptions, but work-product protection for opinion work product is virtually absolute.

2. *Criminal cases:* Work-product protection also extends to lawyers in criminal cases.

a. *General rule:* Fed. R. Crim. P. 16(b) provides that except as to scientific and medical reports, the general rule allowing criminal discovery "does not authorize the discovery or inspection of reports, memoranda, or other internal defense documents made by the defendant, or his attorneys or agents in connection with the investigation or defense of the case, or of statements made by the defendant . . . ."

b. Fed. R. Crim. P. 16(a) grants reciprocal protection to the government for "internal government documents made by the attorney for the government or other government agents in connection with the investigation or prosecution of the case. . . . "

c. In addition, because the lawyer is the client's agent, the Fifth Amendment privilege against self-incrimination would probably prohibit the state from compelling a lawyer to turn over work-product notes that would incriminate her client.

d. However, work-product protection is less important in criminal cases because prosecutors and defense lawyers in criminal cases have very limited rights of discovery compared to civil cases.

E. PHYSICAL EVIDENCE: DOCUMENTS AND THINGS

So far, we have mainly focused on *information*. Different secrecy rules may apply to *physical evidence* — to documents and things. The rules depend first and foremost on whether we are talking about a civil case or a criminal case.

1. *Civil cases.* In civil matters, a lawyer or party has no general obligation to turn over evidence to anyone unless the evidence falls into the narrow automatic disclosure provisions of Fed. R. Civ. P. 26(a)(1) or unless a party or government agency has made a formal request. Such formal requests may take three forms:

a. *Civil investigative demands.* Many federal government agencies have the power to issue civil investigative demands (CID's) to obtain documents or other physical evidence. CID's are the civil equivalent of a criminal grand jury subpoena. They are typically served as an investigative tool before litigation is filed. (State agencies have similar powers in civil investigations.)
b. *Subpoenas.* Once federal litigation is pending, all parties to the litigation have power under Fed. R. Civ. P. 45 to serve subpoenas on any third party seeking documents or things. (State discovery rules contain similar subpoena powers.)
c. *Discovery requests.* All parties to pending federal litigation have power under Fed. R. Civ. P. 34 to request documents and things. (State discovery rules are typically modeled on Fed. R. Civ. P. 34.)

However, a CID, subpoena, or discovery request does not obligate you to turn over documents protected by the attorney-client privilege. The basic federal rule on the scope of discovery, Fed. R. Civ. P. 26(b), limits discovery to matters which are "not privileged." Nor does a demand require you to turn over documents protected as work product, unless the requesting party meets the showing required under Fed. R. Civ. P. 26(b)(3) ("substantial need" and unable to obtain the "substantial equivalent" in any other way without "undue hardship").

Accordingly, to satisfy your ethical duty of confidentiality, you are obligated to assert the attorney-client privilege or work product protection whenever either would arguably protect against disclosure. Your client may decide to waive the protection. However, he or she may properly do so only after you have explained the advantages and disadvantages of this course of action.

2. *Criminal cases.* In criminal cases, substantive state or federal law may require lawyers to turn over physical evidence. The demand may be in response to a subpoena. For example, if your client hands you a smoking gun and says, "Here's the murder weapon," you are ordinarily required to turn it over to the police or the prosecutor without awaiting a request. In other situations, you may hold evidence until you receive a formal request. Duties to turn over physical evidence stem from four different sources:

a. *Statutes.* Even without being subpoenaed, various state and federal statutes — often called obstruction of justice statutes — require people (including lawyers) to turn over to the police or prosecutors any physical evidence of crimes in their possession.
b. *Subpoenas.* Subpoenas may require lawyers to turn over physical evidence that they would not otherwise be required to turn over.
c. *Ethics.* Rule 3.4(a) prohibits a lawyer from "unlawfully" destroying, altering, or concealing evidence with material value. Rule 3.4(a) thus requires lawyers to follow state and federal statutes and to respond to judicial subpoenas. (But Rule 3.4(a) is only a rule of preservation; it doesn't obligate a lawyer to turn over evidence unless failing to do so would constitute unlawfully "concealing" it.)
d. *Discovery requests.* Fed. R. Crim. P. 16(a) allows a federal criminal defendant to request that the government produce documents and tangible things. If the defendant serves such a request, then the government may serve a similar request on the defendant. Fed. R. Crim. P. 26.2 provides a method for discovery of witness statements. (Some states have similar discovery rules.)

However, even when you are required to turn over evidence, the attorney-client privilege generally prohibits you from telling authorities information about the evidence. Thus, even if you have a duty to hand over physical evidence, you do not have a duty to talk about what the evidence shows or how and when you obtained it. Unless an exception to the attorney-client privilege applies, the only thing you have to tell authorities is where the evidence was originally located and whether you altered it after you received it.

That completes a working outline of the basic concepts of secrecy. It shows you the three major categories of protection for information relating to a client: (1) the ethical obligation of confidentiality, which is found in the Rules of Professional Conduct, particularly in Rule 1.6; (2) the attorney-client privilege, which is part of the law of evidence; and (3) the work-product doctrine, which is part of the rules of civil and criminal procedure.

F. A SECRECY SCENARIO

How do the rules of secrecy apply to a typical attorney-client relationship? It may be harder to apply these rules than you think. Here's a scenario that takes you through the stages of a lawyer-client relationship, from the first telephone call to the end of the trial and the client's subsequent malpractice suit against the lawyer. Each stage of the facts is followed by italicized questions.

As you read, write down your answers to the italicized questions. If you have trouble answering the questions, go back and consult the outline. Here's the scenario:

A potential new client named George Raymond is coming in for an interview. You don't know Mr. Raymond. He called last week when you were out of the office, and your secretary wrote down the following phone message: "Mr. Raymond saw your ad in the Yellow Pages. He was in an auto accident after a party last month. He says the accident was partly his fault, but he was hurt and wants to sue the other driver, who was more at fault."

Question 1. Is the phone message protected by Rule 1.6? Is the phone message protected by the attorney-client privilege? Is the phone message protected by the work-product doctrine? Does it matter that the secretary is not a lawyer?

Your secretary told Mr. Raymond to come in for an interview. Shortly before the interview, you received a letter from Mr. Raymond. The letter said:

George Raymond
97 Appalachia Drive
Wood Mill, New York

Dear Counsel:

Before we meet, I want you to know that I am a recovering alcoholic. Two months ago I joined Alcoholics Anonymous and for six weeks I did not have a single drink. Then I went to a party and got drunk. On the way home I sped through a yellow light and hit a car that turned right on red without stopping. I should have slowed down, but the other car should have stopped at the red light. That's the basic situation. See you soon.

Sincerely,

George Raymond

Question 2. Is Mr. Raymond's letter protected by Rule 1.6? Is it protected by the attorney-client privilege? Is it protected by the work-product doctrine?

The next day, Mr. Raymond came in for the interview and told you the following story:

I drank in college, but nothing unusual. Then, during the recession, I lost my job and began drinking heavily. A few months ago I realized I had a problem and got help. I joined Alcoholics Anonymous. I didn't have a drink for six weeks. Then my college roommate, Don Grimm, threw a party for a bunch of friends. I was only going to have one beer but I kept having "one more." I think I drank five or six beers altogether. When it was time to go home, I told my friends I shouldn't drive, but they said it was too far out of the way to take me and I was sober enough to drive myself. So, that's what I did.

On the way home, I gunned the engine to get through a yellow light. I saw a car coming from the right, but I thought it would stop. Instead, the car turned right on red without stopping. Or maybe the light turned green for the other car while I was going across the intersection. Whatever happened, I crashed into the other car. I was knocked out and didn't wake up until I was in the hospital. I had a concussion and some broken bones. The hospital took a blood sample that showed my alcohol content to be just under the legal limit, but this was two hours after the accident. At the time of the accident, I was probably over the legal limit.

While I was in the hospital, I asked about the other driver. The nurse, Joy Lutero, told me the other driver was an old man and he had been hurt badly. He was in serious condition and was also in the hospital. I told the nurse it was my fault and started crying. She said not to worry about it now, but I felt terrible and guilt-ridden, so I wrote a letter to the other driver to tell him how sorry I was. I told him all about getting drunk at the party and everything. But before I mailed the letter, I saw your ad in the Yellow Pages. I decided to talk to you before I did anything. Now, I realize it was mostly the other driver's fault and I want to sue him. I'm also worried I may get prosecuted for drunk driving. Can you help me?

Question 3. Is your conversation with Mr. Raymond protected by Rule 1.6? Is it protected by the attorney-client privilege? Is it protected by the work-product doctrine?

Mr. Raymond then handed you the original letter that he had written to the other driver but had never mailed. It was basically a confession, in great detail. You read the letter and put it in your file with your notes of your interview with Mr. Raymond.

Question 4. Is the draft letter by Mr. Raymond protected by Rule 1.6? Is it protected by the attorney-client privilege? Is it protected by the work-product doctrine? Are your interview notes protected? (Caution: These questions about the draft letter are not easy.)

At the end of the conversation, you agreed to represent Mr. Raymond in bringing a civil case against the other driver for personal injury, but you told Mr. Raymond that you don't handle criminal matters, and you could not defend him if he got prosecuted for driving while intoxicated. Mr. Raymond signed a retainer agreeing to pay you a 25% contingent fee out of any monetary recovery in his civil case before trial (plus expenses), and 33% of any recovery at or after trial (plus expenses). He also gave you the names and phone numbers of some witnesses, including the nurse he talked to in the hospital (Joy Lutero) and the friend who threw the party (Don Grimm).

Question 5. Is your interview with Mr. Raymond protected even though you turned down the criminal part of the case? In other words, is only the civil part of the conversation protected, or is the criminal part also protected by the rules of secrecy? If you had turned down the entire case, would the attorney-client privilege or the ethical obligation of confidentiality apply?

The next day you called Don Grimm, the friend who threw the party. You told Don that you were representing George Raymond and that you wanted to know what happened on the night of the accident. Don confirmed that Mr. Raymond got drunk, but said that he told Mr. Raymond to stay overnight because he was in no condition to drive home. Then Grimm said, "By the way, can I be sued for serving beer to someone who had an accident on the way home? I knew that he was drunk already when I served the last couple of rounds, but I forgot that he had to drive home." You again told Grimm that you represent George Raymond and therefore could not answer Grimm's question.

Question 6. Is your conversation with Don Grimm covered by the attorney-client privilege? Is it protected by Rule 1.6? Are your notes of the conversation protected by the work-product doctrine? If you need expert advice from another partner at your firm to help you answer these questions, may you discuss the situation with your partner? If you are a sole practitioner, or if no other lawyer in your firm can help you answer your questions, may you reveal confidential information to a lawyer outside of your firm to make sure you are complying with the Rules of Professional Conduct?

Next, you telephoned Joy Lutero, the nurse who took care of Mr. Raymond in the hospital. She said,

> When I first talked to Mr. Raymond, he told me he was practically passing out when he was driving home. A few days later, he showed me the letter that he wrote to the old man that he hit. I told Mr. Raymond that if the letter was true, he'd better talk to a lawyer. But I also talked to the old man, who was in the hospital at the same time. The old man said he was not supposed to be driving at night because his vision is bad. He also said that he had some special night vision glasses, but he wasn't wearing them so he didn't see your client's car coming and didn't stop at the intersection before he turned right, even though he knew he had the red light.

You took notes of your conversation with Ms. Lutero. Then, to preserve the helpful parts of her recollection, you drafted a statement for her to sign. The statement contained the part saying that the old man did not have his special glasses on, that he knew the light was red, and that he did not stop at the red light — all the parts of the nurse's story that are good for your client's case. (Obviously, there are hearsay problems with the statement, but you'll worry about that later. For now, your goal is to make it difficult for the nurse to change her story later on.) The nurse signed the statement and you put it in your file. She did not ask for a copy and you did not give her one.

Question 7. Is your conversation with Joy Lutero covered by the attorney-client privilege? Is it protected by Rule 1.6? Are your notes of the conversation protected by the work-product doctrine? Is her signed statement discoverable by the opposing party?

After a few more witness interviews, you filed a complaint on Mr. Raymond's behalf in state court. Eventually, pursuant to the rules of civil procedure, the other side filed a set of interrogatories (written questions) and document requests. These read as follows:

DEFENDANT'S FIRST SET OF INTERROGATORIES AND DOCUMENT REQUESTS

1. State the names, addresses, and telephone numbers of any person who saw the plaintiff drinking before the accident.
2. What color was the light when the plaintiff entered the intersection immediately before the accident?
3. Produce all documents containing information relating to the accident or the party before the accident.

Question 8. Could you answer these interrogatories and produce the requested documents on your client's behalf without violating the ethical obligation of confidentiality, the attorney-client privilege, or the work-product doctrine? Is your client required to answer the interrogatories despite the ethical obligation of confidentiality and the attorney-client privilege?

A few weeks later, the defendant's lawyer took Mr. Raymond's deposition. Here are some of the questions the defendant's lawyer asked the plaintiff:

> Were you at a party before the accident?
>
> Did you drink anything?

What did you drink?

As you approached the intersection, what color was the light?

What color was the light when you entered the intersection?

Did you look up at the light as you entered the intersection?

In the hospital, did you speak to anyone about the accident?

Did you write anything down about the accident?

Did you write anything to the defendant?

When did you first talk to a lawyer about the accident?

Did you call other lawyers before hiring your current lawyer?

Did any other lawyers refuse to take your case?

If so, what reasons did they give for not taking your case?

Did you show your attorney any documents?

Was anyone else present when you interviewed with your current attorney?

If so, who?

What did you tell your attorney about the accident?

What is your fee agreement with your attorney?

What have you told your friends about the accident?

Have you told anyone about conversations with your attorney?

Question 9. Should you object to any of these questions on grounds of attorney-client privilege, Rule 1.6, or work-product? Is your client required to answer them if the ethical obligation of confidentiality or the attorney-client privilege applies?

After George Raymond's deposition (but before the old man's deposition), the opposing attorney met with you to discuss settlement. The opposing attorney said that the jury would favor a frail old man over a young, wild client like Mr. Raymond. You said "I know all about the old man. He wasn't even supposed to be driving at night because his vision is bad. And he wasn't wearing his special night vision glasses, so he didn't see my client's car coming and didn't stop at the intersection before he turned right."

Question 10. Did you have authority to reveal this information? Under what theory? Did revealing this information waive the attorney-client privilege or the ethical obligation of confidentiality?

Eventually, the case went to trial. During trial, the old man testified. At one point, he said that his driver's license allowed him to drive at night as long as he wore "night vision" glasses. You are looking at a copy of his driver's license. The driver's license is not restricted to daytime driving and says nothing about night vision glasses. You know that the witness is confusing his driver's license with the terms of his auto insurance policy, which you obtained through discovery. (The auto insurance policy requires him to wear night vision glasses when driving after dark.)

Question 11. In your closing argument, can you argue to the jury that the old man's driver's license requires him to wear special glasses when driving at night? Can you argue that the old man himself <u>says</u> that he must wear special glasses when driving at night? Can you be silent on that issue? Or do you have to tell the court or jury that the old man is confused?

The jury came in with a verdict in favor of the old man and against George Raymond. You filed post-trial motions seeking judgment notwithstanding the verdict, a reduction in the amount of the damages, and, in the alternative, a new trial. While writing these motions, you learned that the medical records you submitted to prove George Raymond's injuries were false. (You suspect that Raymond paid someone to alter them.)

Question 12. If Raymond refuses to correct the records, may you disclose to the court that the records are false? <u>Must</u> you disclose that the records were false?

The judge denied your post-trial motions, so you lost the case. A few months later, George Raymond sued you for legal malpractice. He alleged that you failed to interview certain witnesses, failed to obtain certain crucial information from him, and made other serious mistakes.

Worse, a federal grand jury is reportedly investigating your law practice. Newspaper reports say that the grand jury is looking for evidence that a group of personal injury lawyers, including yourself, routinely falsified evidence by using phony photographs and false accident reconstruction reports.

In addition, the State Bar Disciplinary Authority has formally charged you with improper conduct, including falsifying evidence in George Raymond's case and coercing the nurse (Joy Lutero) into signing a false statement.

Question 13. May you respond to any of these charges? Are there any restrictions on what you may say? Do you still have any obligation to protect the client's secrets?

A few months later, George Raymond unexpectedly died. His widow came to ask you what really happened with the accident. She is the executor of his estate and is gathering everything that belongs to Mr. Raymond. She wants to see your complete files on the case, including your work-product and the notes of your interviews with your client. A day later, the police came around with some questions about your conversations with your client, and they brandished a subpoena commanding you to produce the files.

Question 14. Assuming that none of this information has been disclosed before (even at trial) and that the attorney-client privilege has not been waived, may you disclose this information to the widow? (This is a hard question.) Do you have to produce your files to the police in response to the subpoena?

At the grand jury investigation, the prosecutor asks you some questions about George Raymond's drunk driving. The answers to the questions would reveal both privileged information and information protected by Rule 1.6.

Question 15. Do you have to claim the attorney-client privilege? Do you have to assert the ethical obligation of confidentiality? If the elements of the attorney-client privilege are still in place, can the court properly order you to testify anyway? If the information is protected only by Rule 1.6 (and not by the attorney-client privilege), can the court properly order you to testify?

You claimed the attorney-client privilege, but the court ruled against you and held that the information was not privileged. You appealed but the court's ruling was upheld on appeal.

Question 16. Must you now answer the prosecutor's questions, or may you continue to claim the attorney-client privilege or the ethical obligation of confidentiality?

That's the end of the scenario. Was it easy or hard to answer the questions? Either way, go back and reread the outline and see if your answers were correct.

Chapter 7
THE ATTORNEY-CLIENT PRIVILEGE

The attorney-client privilege and the ethical duty of confidentiality are the most basic building blocks of a successful attorney-client relationship. The privilege prevents outsiders from *compelling* the attorney or client to reveal their communications and the ethical duty of confidentiality prevents the attorney from *volunteering* the information to outsiders without the client's consent.

A. A QUICK LOOK AT THE FUNDAMENTALS

This section quickly reviews and expands on some fundamentals of the attorney-client privilege.

What are the elements of the attorney-client privilege?

The attorney-client privilege takes effect when five conditions ("the 5 C's") are present: a Communication from a Client to Counsel in Confidence for the purpose of seeking legal Counsel. Once those conditions are in place, the privilege "attaches." Conversely, if any of the 5 C's are missing, the attorney-client privilege does not attach. For example, if the client brings a friend into the lawyer's office for the initial client interview, then no privilege will attach for that conversation because a "stranger" to the attorney-client relationship is present, destroying the element of confidentiality.

Who is a "stranger" to the attorney-client relationship?

A "stranger" is someone who is neither the lawyer nor the client nor one of their agents. The lawyer's agents include the lawyer's secretary, paralegal, and others who assist the lawyer in providing legal services. A client's agents include people like a foreign language interpreter, a sign language interpreter for a deaf client, or others necessary to enable the client to communicate with the lawyer.

Can a court order disclosure of privileged information?

When the five conditions (the 5 C's) are present, the attorney-client privilege is virtually absolute. A court has no power to order disclosure of privileged communications unless the party seeking disclosure can establish a *waiver* or *exception*. In other words, a party seeking to overcome the attorney-client privilege must show either that the party claiming the privilege has waived the privilege or that some exception permits disclosure.

What's covered by the privilege?

Virtually everything that the client communicates to the lawyer, whether orally or in writing, will be protected by the attorney-client privilege. Reciprocally, the lawyer's communications *to* the client are protected by the attorney-client privilege. Why? Because the lawyer's advice to the client nearly always directly or indirectly reflects the client's communications to the lawyer. If you knew what the lawyer told the client, you could figure out a lot about what the client told the lawyer.

What about documents?

If a client communicates with her lawyer in writing — by letter, memo, e-mail, fax, or any other written method of communication — the communication is privileged as long as it is made in confidence for the purpose of seeking legal advice. However, a client cannot turn existing, non-privileged documents into privileged communications simply by handing them to the lawyer. Unless the document was *created* as a confidential communication between the client and counsel, it does not become privileged simply because the client later gives it to a lawyer. If that could be done, clients would be able to defeat every discovery request just by shipping truckloads of documents to their lawyers. (On the other hand, if a corporation has a folder of privileged documents — for example, a folder of correspondence between corporate executives and outside counsel, or between corporate executives and in-house counsel — the privilege is not lost or diminished if those documents are given to the lawyer.)

Who controls the privilege? Who can waive it?

Once established, the privilege belongs to the client, not the attorney. Thus, in theory, only the client can claim — or waive — the privilege. But the lawyer is the "agent" of the client for most purposes, and the lawyer therefore has authority to assert the privilege on the client's behalf. Moreover, because a lawyer must zealously represent a client (loyalty) and must diligently protect the client's confidential information, the lawyer is ethically *obligated* to claim the privilege when it applies and to avoid any actions or omissions that will waive the privilege unintentionally. However, because the lawyer is the client's authorized agent, the client suffers if the lawyer blunders. Thus, if a lawyer fails to claim the attorney-client privilege when it applies (for example, if the lawyer carelessly turns over privileged documents to the other side during discovery, or fails to object to a deposition question that asks the client to divulge privileged information, and the client answers the question), then the court will typically find that the client has waived the privilege. (The client may then sue the lawyer for legal malpractice or breach of fiduciary duty, but the privileged cat is out of the privilege bag.)

What destroys the privilege or prevents it from arising?

A client can destroy (waive) the privilege by disclosing privileged communications to outsiders. Furthermore, if the client communicates confidentially with counsel for the purpose of committing a crime or fraud, then the privilege does not attach — there is no privilege for communications intended to facilitate a crime or fraud. This is called the "crime-fraud exception." The crime-fraud exception reflects public policy that a privilege should not survive if it is abused. The crime-fraud exception also reflects a literal interpretation of the elements of the attorney-client privilege: if a client communicates with counsel in confidence for the purpose of committing a fraud, then those communications are not really for the purpose of obtaining legal advice.

Now let's take a closer look at the important distinction between *communications* (which are privileged) and *facts* (which are not privileged). In later chapters, we'll look at the exceptions to the attorney-client privilege.

Can facts be privileged?

The privilege protects only *communications*, not facts. A client cannot hide facts by telling them to an attorney. Let's illustrate the distinction between communications and facts.

- Suppose a man is indicted for beating his girlfriend. The client says to his lawyer, in confidence and for the purpose of seeking legal advice, "I hit my girlfriend because I was angry. Is uncontrollable anger a defense?" That communication is privileged even though the client has confessed to committing a crime in the recent past.

- Now suppose the client is testifying at trial and the prosecutor asks, "Did you tell your lawyer that you hit your girlfriend because you were angry?" The defense attorney must jump up and shout "Objection! That question calls for information protected by the attorney-client privilege! You have no right to inquire into confidential communications between a lawyer and a client." The objection will be sustained. The privilege applies because the question seeks information about a *communication* with the lawyer.

- But suppose instead that the prosecutor asks the client, "Did you hit your girlfriend because you were angry?" Now the defense attorney has no ground for objection. The attorney-client privilege does not apply because the question calls only for a *fact*, not for a communication. That *fact* does not become privileged just because the client communicated this fact to his lawyer. Just as a client cannot hide a smoking gun (or a smoking gun document) by handing it over to the lawyer, so the client cannot hide facts by telling them to the lawyer. (Don't carry the physical evidence analogy too far. The law obligates lawyers to turn over material physical evidence to the prosecutor, but the law does not obligate lawyers to turn over facts to the prosecutor. Why do you suppose that is so? What's the difference between facts and physical evidence?)

In short, the only thing that's privileged is the content of the conversation or other communications between the attorney and the client. What the client *knew* or *did* before talking to the attorney or after talking to the attorney is not privileged. What the client *said* or *wrote* to the attorney is privileged.

A more subtle application of the distinction between facts and communications arises if the *lawyer* is called to testify.

- If the lawyer is asked, "What did your client say to you about hitting his girlfriend?" then the lawyer must claim the attorney-client privilege, because the question explicitly seeks information about a communication.
- But suppose the lawyer is asked, "Did your client hit his girlfriend?" Does this question ask about a fact or about a communication? At first blush, it seems to ask about a fact. May the lawyer properly claim the attorney-client privilege? Yes, because the question *implicitly* asks about the client's communications with the lawyer. The lawyer has no personal knowledge about whether the client hit his girlfriend, so the question is really whether the client *told* the lawyer that he hit his girlfriend. The privilege therefore applies, and the lawyer can (and therefore must) claim the attorney-client privilege. (If the lawyer had actually been present when the client hit the girlfriend, then the lawyer would probably be disqualified either because the lawyer would be a material witness or because the lawyer would have a conflict between his own interests and his client's interests. We will cover conflicts of interest and the lawyer-witness rule later.)

Would the privilege also apply to information that the lawyer learned from a *witness* who saw the client hit the girlfriend? Should it apply? Does the ethical obligation of confidentiality apply to information the lawyer learned from the witness rather than from the client?

B. A TEST ON THE ATTORNEY-CLIENT PRIVILEGE

Now it's time to test your command of the attorney-client privilege.

Suppose client Tony Piccolo has been involved in an accident and goes to Lawyer for legal advice. Lawyer assures Client Piccolo that everything Piccolo says is confidential and will not be disclosed. Piccolo then tells Lawyer fully and frankly about the accident, including the information that (a) a man named Thomas witnessed the incident and (b) Thomas said to Piccolo, "You ran the red light."

Lawyer now contacts Witness Thomas, who says to Lawyer, "Your client ran the red light." May Lawyer, Client Piccolo, or Witness Thomas properly invoke the attorney-client privilege as to any of the following questions?

A. Insurance adjuster calls Lawyer before suit is filed. Adjuster asks, "I know you've talked to Witness Thomas. What did Thomas tell you about who ran the red light?"

B. In depositions, Opposing Party asks Client:

1. "What did witness Thomas say to you at the accident scene?" and
2. "What did you tell your lawyer about your conversation with witness Thomas at the accident scene?" and
3. "Did you see the color of the light right before the accident?"

C. Opposing party also deposes witness Thomas and asks him:

1. "What did you tell Lawyer about the accident?"
2. "What did you tell Client Piccolo about the accident?"

D. A breathalyzer test indicated that Piccolo's blood alcohol level was above the legal limit at the time of the accident. The District Attorney, therefore, opens a criminal manslaughter investigation into the accident. As part of this investigation, the District

Attorney calls Client Piccolo to testify before the grand jury. The District Attorney asks Piccolo:

1. "What did you tell your Lawyer about the accident?"
2. "What did you see at the scene of the accident?"
3. "What did Witness Thomas say to you at the accident scene?"

E. During a confidential meeting with Lawyer to prepare for Client Piccolo's upcoming testimony before the grand jury, Piccolo hands Lawyer a letter, saying, "I have written a letter to you to tell you some of the things Witness Thomas said to me and others at the scene of the accident. As you can see, Thomas used a lot of racial and ethnic slurs. Make sure the District Attorney knows these facts. The grand jurors will never believe Thomas when they find out he's a racist and a bigot." Lawyer did not give the letter to the District Attorney but (without revealing the source) told the District Attorney the facts about Thomas's racist and bigoted remarks. The grand jury did not indict Piccolo. After getting the good news that he was not indicted, Piccolo said to Lawyer, "I made up that whole thing about Thomas being a racist. He never said any of those things, but I figured if the District Attorney and the grand jurors thought the only eyewitness was a racist and a bigot, they would not indict me."

1. Is the letter from Piccolo to Lawyer privileged?
2. Is the conversation between Piccolo and Lawyer, before Piccolo's grand jury testimony, protected by the attorney-client privilege?
3. Is the conversation between Lawyer and the District Attorney privileged?
4. Is the conversation between Piccolo and Lawyer, after Piccolo's grand jury testimony, protected by the attorney-client privilege?

Are you confident of your answers? You should be. The questions are pretty basic (except the questions about the phony charges of racism against Thomas). If you are not sure of any of your answers, review the outline in the previous chapter and the review in this chapter. You need a solid grasp of the fundamentals before moving on to more complex issues.

Chapter 8
CLIENT IDENTITY AND THE ATTORNEY-CLIENT PRIVILEGE

A. INTRODUCTION

Prosecutors and civil plaintiffs want to get as much information as they can about defendants and potential defendants. They want to pierce the attorney-client privilege when they can. Therefore, the battle in the courtroom often concerns whether the attorney-client privilege applies at all. Because the attorney-client privilege is so old and so well-established, no one makes a broadside attack on the attorney-client privilege. No one says, "Your honor, I move that this court suspend operation of the attorney-client privilege in this case so we can get at the truth. I move that we not let the defendant and his attorney hide behind the privilege." No court would listen to such an argument.

Since frontal attacks on the privilege aren't possible, litigants chip around the edges, seeking information that is on the fringe of protected communications or just outside the scope of protection. Some people consider these attacks on the attorney-client privilege to be the only way to learn essential facts and get at "the truth." Others view these attacks as a cancer that will eventually eat away at the entire privilege and destroy the adversary system of justice.

In this section, we will look at battles over the applicability of the privilege when an attorney invokes the privilege to protect a client's name, to protect a client's whereabouts, or to protect a deceased client. These are border skirmishes in the constant struggle to establish the boundaries of the attorney-client privilege. But they are hard fought skirmishes because so much is at stake. Defenders of the attorney-client privilege view these attacks as the first warnings of an all-out government assault on the sanctity of the attorney-client relationship. Prosecutors and others seeking privileged information view the attorney-client privilege as a kind of Iron Curtain behind which sinister clients and their attorneys can conspire without fear of being discovered. Which view is correct? Does it depend on the circumstances? What circumstances?

B. CLIENT IDENTITY

What if a prosecutor or civil plaintiff can't even find out the *name* of a potential defendant? Can the potential defendant's attorney keep the client's identity secret? Ordinarily, the identity of a client is not protected by the privilege. Indeed, DR 7-106 (B)(2) of the old ABA Model Code of Professional Responsibility states: "In presenting a matter to a tribunal, a lawyer shall disclose . . . (2) Unless privileged or irrelevant, the identities of the clients he represents and of the persons who employed him." But DR 7-106(B)(2) implies by using the phrase "[u]nless privileged," the identity of a client may be privileged in rare circumstances. Specifically, the client's identity is privileged if the client's communication of his own name meets the five conditions (the 5 C's) necessary to trigger the protection of the privilege. The majority opinion in the next case finds these rare circumstances — and provokes a strong dissent. Would you join the majority, or would you join the dissent?

DEAN v. DEAN

607 So. 2d 494 (Fla. App. 4th Dist. 1992)

Farmer, J.

The issue raised here is whether the attorney-client privilege can be used to prevent the disclosure of the identity of a person who had previously consulted an attorney regarding the return of stolen property belonging to one of the parties in a civil case. As we explain along the way, under the circumstances of this case the privilege bars such disclosure.

The facts are unusual, to say the least. During the pendency of the Deans' dissolution of marriage case, the husband's place of business was allegedly burgled, resulting in the loss of two duffel bags containing various personal items belonging to husband's daughter, and from $35,000 to $40,000 in cash. Sometime after the theft, an unidentified person telephoned [attorney] Krischer at his office. He related the conversation as follows:

> I received a telephone call from an individual who knew that I was an attorney; knew I was an attorney that was involved in the Baltes[1] matter and the individual asked me for advice with regard to returning property. I advised this person on the telephone that the experience that I have had in the State Attorney's office was that the best avenue was to turn the property over to an attorney and let the attorney bring it to the State Attorney's office or to the law enforcement.

At another point, Krischer added:

> Obviously I have been through this before and I knew all the questions to ask this person and I got all the responses back which indicates to me this person knew I was a lawyer, was asking for legal advice and did not want their identity revealed.

Krischer met twice and had one telephone conversation with this person. Nearly six weeks after the second meeting, the two duffel bags containing only the daughter's personal property were delivered to Krischer's office by someone who told his receptionist that he "would know what they are." No cash was included with the returned items. Krischer then delivered the bags to the police, telling them that they "may have some connection with" husband.

In a twist of irony, these events came to light through Krischer's former secretary, who had also by then become a client of husband's lawyer. Soon after, husband's lawyer served Krischer with a subpoena for a deposition, seeking the identity of Krischer's contact. Krischer asserted the privilege at the deposition. Husband then moved to compel the testimony. After a hearing, the trial court granted the motion, saying in part:

> The purpose of the attorney-client privilege is to encourage the free and full disclosure by clients of information to attorneys so that adequate legal representation can be supplied. It is not however the purpose of the attorney-client privilege to act as a vehicle by which individuals can use an attorney to insulate themselves from disclosure relative to activities which do not involve legal representation. In this case, Mr. Krischer did not appear in court or render any legal opinions; rather he merely advised the person to use an attorney as a conduit and then acted in that capacity to deliver stolen goods to the police. He did nothing and gave no opinions that could not have been done or given by any member of the public.

There are other factors which weigh against the existence of an attorney-client relationship. Mr. Krischer testified that when he is hired by a new client it is his office procedure to create a three by five card with the name and address of the client; and to enter the name of the client in his computer system. None of these office procedures

---

[1] This refers to a widely publicized case in which a hit-and-run driver consulted Krischer for advice and, afterwards, Krischer asserted the attorney-client privilege when asked to disclose the name of the driver. The fact that the person consulting Krischer in this case referred to the widely publicized case when Krischer kept the identity of his contact confidential might reasonably be taken as evidencing the contact's strong interest in confidentialiaty.

were followed with reference to this individual. Mr. Krischer also testified that he did not receive a fee for his services in this matter and that he does not expect to receive a fee in the future. While these facts certainly do not preclude the existence of an attorney-client relationship, I find them to be more consistent with Mr. Krischer having acted as a conduit than as an attorney in this matter.

The [trial] court concluded that there was no attorney-client relationship, and thus no privilege, and ordered Krischer to answer the questions as to the identity of his contact. [Krischer appealed to this court.]

The attorney-client privilege, though dating back to Elizabethan England, did not become developed in its present form until the nineteenth century. It rests on the theory that:

"In order to promote freedom of consultation of legal advisers by clients, the apprehension of compelled disclosure by the legal advisers must be removed; hence the law must prohibit the disclosure except on the client's consent." 8 Wigmore at § 2291. One of the most eloquent formulations of the rationale for the privilege is thus:

> Every man can ascertain the law by consulting a lawyer. But . . . [t]he communication must be privileged to the utmost extent, or it will not be made. Thus it will be one consequence of [the failure to accord the privilege], that the law will be in no way open to the community at large: to them it will be a sealed book.

8 Wigmore at § 2291. By the early eighteen hundreds, it was generally understood that the privilege did not depend on the existence of a formal proceeding or even an incipient controversy; rather it was accepted that all "communications made in seeking legal advice for any purpose were within the principle of the privilege." As Wigmore describes this development, the privilege was in time extended:

> to include communications made, first during any other litigation; next, in contemplation of litigation; next, during a controversy but not yet looking to litigation; and, lastly, in any consultation for legal advice, wholly irrespective of litigation or even of controversy.

In the words of the treatise, "it has never since been doubted to be the law."

In short, since its modern development, the privilege is founded wholly on subjective considerations: "in order to promote freedom of consultation of legal advisers by clients, the apprehension of compelled disclosure by the legal advisers must be removed. . . ." 8 Wigmore at § 2291. Or, as it was stated more recently:

> The [privilege] rests on the need for the advocate and counselor to know all that relates to the client's reasons for seeking representation if the professional mission is to be carried out.

Trammel v. United States, 445 U.S. 40, 51 (1980). Hence, it logically follows that the privilege does not turn on the client actually hiring or engaging the attorney; it is enough if the client merely consulted the attorney about a legal question "with the view to employing [the attorney] professionally . . . although the attorney is not subsequently employed."

What thus originally began as the product of prudential rules devised by common law judges in recognition of these ideas has now become codified by statute,[3] as well as

[3] See Section 90.502, Florida Statutes (1991), which provides in relevant part:

(2) A client has a privilege to refuse to disclose, and to prevent any other person from disclosing, the contents of confidential communications when such other person learned of the communications because they were made in the rendition of legal services to the client.

disciplinary rules governing the conduct of lawyers. . . . Under FEC [Florida Evidence Code] section 90.502(1)(b), a "client" is defined as any person "who consults a lawyer with the purpose of obtaining legal services or who is rendered legal services by a lawyer." We construe this language as continuing the common law focus on subjective considerations, viz., on the person seeking consultation with a lawyer, rather than on what the lawyer does.

AUTHORS' COMMENT:

Under the standard just stated, did Krischer have an attorney-client relationship with Dean?

It is thus necessary in this case that we focus not on what Krischer did but on what the client intended. Krischer testified that his contact sought legal advice from him — which is, he contends, paradigmatically a legal service — and hence became his client for the purpose of invoking the privilege. We agree.

Krischer's testimony makes plain the intent of his client.

Q. Is it true that the employment by you, by person "x" was predicated on the fact that you would keep person "x's" identity confidential?

A. Yes, that was the condition of the employment.

Q. Was your employment also a condition that you were person "x's" lawyer for all purposes?

A. Correct. The individual called — I can expedite this if I can state a couple of things, judge. I had obviously been through this previously in another case. I was well aware of what was needed to be established in order to protect this client. I inquired of this client if that individual knew I was an attorney. That individual indicated that they did. I inquired if they were seeking legal advice. They indicated that they did. They discussed a legal problem with me. I gave them legal advice.

A condition precedent to this person discussing the legal problem with me was that I not divulge their identity. This person came to me with knowledge of my previous actions in a previous case and felt that I could be trusted, and on that condition precedent I listened to the problem, gave advise [sic] and rendered legal services.

The trial judge obviously accepted this testimony as truthful, but said that he must look beyond Krischer's "conclusion in this regard to the underlying facts." In effect, the [trial] court decided that the issue should turn on what the undisclosed person sought to accomplish with the legal advice obtained or on what Krischer did in consequence of the contact.

. . . .

[W]e conclude that the trial court has misinterpreted the privilege and the policies underlying it. It is indisputable that his contact . . . consulted Krischer as an attorney. It is indisputable that the client sought legal advice about a specific matter. It is indisputable that the specific matter concerned a crime that had already been committed, not a planned or future act which might be a crime. And it is indisputable that the client insisted on confidence.

[I]t has long been understood that the representation of a client in a court or legal proceeding is not indispensable for the invocation of the privilege. That Krischer's client sought him out for purely legal advice was enough. Legal advice, after all, is by itself a legal service. It is not necessary to the existence of the privilege that the lawyer render some additional service connected with the legal advice. Nor, as we know, is it even necessary that the lawyer appear in court or contemplate some pending or future legal proceeding.

And even if it were, the engagement of an attorney to effect the return of stolen property should certainly qualify. Surely there is a public purpose served by getting stolen property in the hands of the police authorities, even if the identity of the thief is not thereby revealed. Here the consultation resulted in exactly that. Krischer advised his client to turn over the property to the state attorney or the police. A lawyer's advice can be expected to result in the return of the property if the confidentiality of the consultation is insured.

At the same time, even if the person who returns the property is the thief, there is an equal privilege against self incrimination as well as a right to the effective assistance of counsel in defending against the criminal charge. That the criminal charge is not yet pending when the thief seeks to return previously stolen property after consultation with a lawyer is, as we have seen, irrelevant to the privilege. Thus, the mere fact that the consulted attorney acts as a "conduit" for the return of stolen property does not support the conclusion that the attorney has engaged in unprotected consultation with the person seeking the advice. A legal service has been rendered just as surely as when the lawyer represents the accused thief in a criminal trial.

We need not be long detained by Krischer's failure to follow his usual procedures for enrolling new clients, or that he did not expect to receive a fee for his services. These facts dwell on Krischer's actions, not on his client's purpose in contacting him. The failure of Krischer to memorialize his dealings with this client is not surprising in view of the obvious need for confidentiality in the matter, coupled with the limited amount of time and work necessary for Krischer to render his services to the client. Payment of a fee has never been indispensable to the relationship or the existence of the privilege.

We find that the trial court departed from the essential requirements of law in compelling disclosure of Krischer's client. We grant certiorari, quash the order requiring Krischer to reveal the identity of his client, and dismiss the subpoena.

AUTHORS' COMMENT:

Do you agree with the opinion, or would you dissent? What are the best arguments against the majority opinion? Suppose you were a law clerk and the judge said to you, "Judge Farmer has just sent me a proposed majority opinion holding that there was an attorney-client privilege here. That's ridiculous! I'm going to dissent. Find me a way to affirm the trial court's holding that there was no privilege." The actual dissent in this case follows. Before you read it, think about what arguments you yourself could develop for a dissent.

GLICKSTEIN, C.J., dissenting.

The attorney in this case described his participation as a "conduit," who had been contacted by an unnamed party, to deliver stolen property to the police, and who subsequently delivered the property to the police. The attorney's participation was concluded when the stolen property was turned over to the police. The attorney was not paid a fee for his participation, and he did not expect to be paid a fee. Furthermore, standard office procedures regarding new clients were not followed in this matter.

In my view, the evidence in this case clearly shows that the unnamed party intended for the attorney to act merely as an agent or conduit for the delivery of property which was completely unrelated to legal representation. The evidence also shows that the attorney in this case was not acting in his professional capacity. For these reasons, I believe the attorney-client privilege does not apply to these circumstances.

NOTES AND QUESTIONS

1. ***Which Side Are You on?*** Now that you've read the entire case, would you join the majority or the dissent? Why? Which arguments are most persuasive to you? What are the strongest counterarguments? Would you add anything? What?

2. ***Request for Confidentiality.*** Suppose Krischer's client had not specifically requested that his identity be kept confidential. Would that have made a difference? Should it? Aren't clients entitled to assume that their identity will be kept secret if the revelation of their identity would subject them to criminal charges, even if they don't expressly request confidentiality?

3. ***A Saga of Client Identity in New York.*** Florida isn't the only state where courts are struggling with the issue of confidentiality for client identification. Consider the following hypothetical, based on a situation that developed in New York:

> Suppose that you, an attorney, received a telephone call from Mr. Michael Gilberg, asking that you advise him about what to do as a result of the following developments.
>
> Gilberg tells you that this morning he received a subpoena to appear before Judge Harold L. Wood, who is presiding in a wrongful-death action, captioned *D'Alessio v. John Doe*. Ms. Grace D'Alessio is the daughter of Vincent Fiorito, whose body was found dead 23 months ago laying in the street in front of his house. The coroner ruled that Fiorito's death was due to massive head and chest-cavity injures, which most certainly caused immediate death. The cause of death was officially said to have been caused by a hit-and-run driver. There were no witnesses to Fiorito's death and no one has reported involvement in an automobile accident. The statute of limitations for wrongful death lawsuits expires in thirty days.
>
> Judge Wood issued the subpoena after being told by D'Alessio's lawyer, Howard Rudnick, that Gilberg had approached him and said: "I am willing to help you out with your wrongful-death case by revealing the name of my client, who was your unknown driver, if first you are successful in persuading Judge Wood to convince the District Attorney to drop all criminal charges related to my client and the death of Vincent Fiorito."
>
> Gilberg strenuously denies that he had any such conversation with Rudnick. Nevertheless, Judge Wood ordered Gilberg to appear in his courtroom at 9:00 a.m. sharp Monday morning and to be ready to testify as to the name of his client.
>
> Gilberg said that he told the judge that, even if it were true that he had a client related to Fiorito's death, he could not reveal the client's name because of his duty under M.R. 1.6 to maintain the confidences and secrets of his client.
>
> Judge Wood responded, however, that Gilberg had yet to establish that he had an attorney-client relationship with anybody. Moreover, "the law can hardly allow a lawyer to conceal a client's identity, just because the client is afraid to let the civil or criminal law processes run their course."

4. ***What to Do?*** If you were in Mr. Gilberg's shoes and were faced with a choice between revealing your client's identity and going to jail for contempt, what would you choose? Why?

5. ***No Eyewitnesses.*** Despite an extensive investigation, the police never found any eyewitnesses to Mr. Fiorito's death. Does this make a difference to you? Should the scope of the attorney-client privilege depend on whether there are other sources of information besides the attorney? To ask this question another way, is the attorney-client privilege outweighed here by the public's need to know?

6. ***Criminal vs. Civil Charges.*** Mr. Fiorito's death triggered both a criminal investigation by the District Attorney and plans for a civil suit for damages by Mr. Fiorito's daughter. Should one of these carry more weight than the other in deciding the scope of the attorney-client privilege, or are the civil and criminal matters of equal weight? In other words, does public policy more strongly argue for invading the attorney-client privilege to obtain information for a criminal case than for a civil case? Why or why not?

7. ***What Happened?*** Gilberg had guts. He filed a motion for a protective order, but the court accused him of "a continuing attempt to delay" the case and again ordered him to appear for a deposition. Gilberg did appear for his deposition, but he objected to every question and would not reveal his client's name. Eventually, he appealed the lower court ruling that his client's identity was not privileged. How do you think such an appeal should come out? Here is a very brief excerpt from the appellate opinion.

D'ALESSIO v. GILBERG

205 A.D.2d 8, 1994 N.Y. App. Div. LEXIS 9522 (2d Dep't. 1994)

Charles B. Lawrence, J.

The issue to be decided in this case is whether an attorney can be compelled to reveal the name of an individual who consulted him regarding that individual's possible past commission of a crime. We conclude that under the circumstances of this case, where the crime, if any, has already been committed, there is no possibility of further criminal acts occurring if the individual is not identified, and the disclosure sought would expose the client to possible criminal prosecution, that the client's name is privileged information that the attorney cannot be compelled to reveal. . . .

By decision and order dated September 24, 1992, the Supreme Court granted the petitioner's motion and directed the attorney to appear for an examination before trial. The [trial] court concluded, in pertinent part, that the privilege was not applicable under the circumstances because the information sought to be revealed was the client's identity and because the purpose of the privilege would not be served by shielding an individual from the possibility of civil and criminal liability. . . .

AUTHORS' COMMENT:

Would the purpose of the privilege be served by shielding Gilberg's client from possible civil and criminal liability? If so, how? If not, should Gilberg be forced to reveal the identity of his client?

. . . So strong is the State's regard for the confidentiality of attorney-client communications that an attorney exposes himself to possible disciplinary charges if he fails to keep confidential a communication from his client without the client's consent (see, Code of Professional Responsibility DR 4-101). However, since the privilege serves to shield evidence from discovery, and thereby potentially thwart the fact-finding process, it is to be strictly construed in keeping with its purpose. . . .

[I]t has generally been held that the client's name, in and of itself, is not privileged, as it is considered to be neither confidential nor a communication. However, such "nonevidentiary information" may qualify as privileged "where disclosure might be inappropriate because inconsistent with the trust and duty assumed by an attorney". . . . Under the circumstances of this case we conclude that the client's identity does constitute a confidential communication, and therefore cannot be revealed by the attorney without the client's consent. . . .

[T]he client consulted the attorney in connection with his or her involvement in a fatal hit-and-run accident. Disclosure of his identity would reveal his possible involvement in a crime in connection with that accident, which is the precise situation for which he sought legal advice. Under these circumstances his or her identity constitutes a confidential communication, the disclosure of which is prohibited by the dictates of the attorney-client privilege. . . .

"To be sure the exercise of the privilege may at times result in concealing the truth and allowing the guilty to escape. That is an evil, however, which is considered to be outweighed by the benefit which results to the administration of justice generally." We conclude that the identity of the individual who allegedly was driving the vehicle which struck and killed Vincent Fiorito is privileged insofar as it was communicated confidentially to that individual's attorney, and therefore the Supreme Court erred in directing that attorney to reveal that information. . . .

NOTES AND QUESTIONS

1. ***Do You Agree?*** Would you have joined the appellate opinion in *Gilberg*? Why or why not? Can you think of any interests that would outweigh the privilege for client identity in circumstances such as these? For example, would it matter to you if a lawyer for a hit-and-run driver admitted that his client was an alcoholic who was drunk at the time of the accident and was continuing to drink and drive, even though his license had been repeatedly suspended?

2. ***No Guts, No Glory.*** Michael Gilberg's story shows that you can be a hero just for adhering to your obligation to assert the attorney-client privilege when you think it applies. Would you have the courage that Gilberg showed? Would you have the courage that Linda Backiel shows in the next article of this Chapter?

3. ***Client Whereabouts.*** So far, we've been discussing client identity. What if everyone knows *who* your client is, but no one knows *where* your client is? Are you obligated to reveal your client's whereabouts? Can a court compel you to reveal your client's whereabouts? Let's consider a situation that happened a few years ago in Philadelphia. A lawyer named Linda Backiel was representing a political radical who was free on bail. The client jumped bail, and authorities believed Backiel knew where her client was. Could she reveal the client's whereabouts if she wanted to do so? If she did not want to reveal her client's whereabouts, could the court compel her to reveal the client's whereabouts, or could she claim the attorney-client privilege?

Let's bring it closer to home. Suppose your client jumped bail, and the court ordered you either to tell where the client was or go to jail. Would you tell, or would you go to jail? Would you sit for weeks in a jail populated by people accused of serious crimes so that you could protect the attorney-client privilege? Now read Linda Backiel's story. Would you follow in her footsteps? Is she a role model or a fool, a hero or a villain?

MONROE FREEDMAN, WHEN KEEPING SECRETS BECOMES A CRIME

THE CONNECTICUT LAW TRIBUNE, January 21, 1991*

Linda Backiel Esq. spent the holiday season in prison outside Philadelphia. She was sent there by Senior U.S. District Judge Charles Weiner on Dec. 10, 1990, and could remain incarcerated until June.

The lawyer's offense: She would not testify about her client in the secrecy of a grand jury.

Because she has been imprisoned for criminal contempt of court, Backiel (pronounced Back-EEL) could get out of prison at any time simply by agreeing to give testimony against her client. I don't know Backiel personally, but I did testify before Judge Weiner as an expert witness on her behalf (on a pro bono basis) about the ethics rules governing the situation.

Under oath, Backiel told the judge at the December hearing that she would never violate her client's trust and confidence. Her conviction was convincing.

But the prosecutor, Assistant U.S. Attorney Ronald Levine, was unconvinced. Indeed, his response to Backiel's assertion of will was chilling: had she ever been in prison?, he asked. Levine allowed the question and the negative response to hang in the air. His message was clear: The 45-year-old Backiel — who, at 5-foot-3 and 100 pounds, could be described as frail — might think she is a person of principle, but prison is tougher than she knows. The government will break Backiel and her principles. . . . .

Between Two Masters

One doesn't have to be sympathetic to Backiel's politics to see the danger to all criminal-defense lawyers — and to the criminal-justice system — created by the government practices endorsed by Judge Weiner.

The harm grows out of a legal whipsaw. Backiel's ethical responsibilities are governed by Pennsylvania's Rules of Professional Conduct, which are closely patterned on the American Bar Association's Model Rules of Professional Conduct. Rule 1.6(a) provides in part: "A lawyer *shall not* reveal information relating to representation of a client unless the client consents after consultation." (Emphasis added.)

The phrase "relating to representation" is intended to be read literally. Thus, the lawyer's obligation to withhold information about a client goes far beyond the more limited attorney-client evidentiary privilege. The lawyer has a duty to protect a client's "secrets" — which means any information that would be harmful or even embarrassing to the client if revealed — and not just material that falls within the technical boundaries of the privilege.

The text of Rule 1.6 allows no exception where the lawyer is ordered by a court to reveal the information. The ABA's official comment on Rule 1.6 does hint at an exception — "The lawyer must comply with the final orders of a court . . . requiring the lawyer to give information about the client" — but the introductory scope note to the rules says the comments are only "guides," while the text of each rule is "authoritative."

Thus, there is no assurance that the comment will be read to modify Rule 1.6. The rule appears to leave the lawyer whipsawed. If a court orders a lawyer to reveal a client's confidences or secrets, the lawyer risks contempt of court if she refuses. But if she complies with the order, disciplinary action looms, along with impairment of the lawyer-client relationship and the client's effective assistance of counsel.

One might hope that a bar disciplinary committee, faced with an attorney who

* Monroe Freedman, when this article was published, was the Howard Lichtenstein Distinguished Professor of Legal Ethics at Hofstra University Law School. Reprinted with permission of *Legal Times*,

revealed client information to a grand jury, would not read Rule 1.6 literally. One might hope that such a committee would, instead, create an exception for a lawyer subject to a court order — even though that exception would violate the rule's scope note.

But Linda Backiel cannot predict that the rules will be bent in her favor. As far as she knows, she is caught: Rule 1.6 commands that she "shall not" reveal information "relating to" her representation of her client — period.

Even if the comment to Rule 1.6 is read to create an unexpressed exception, it requires that she make "every effort practicable" to avoid disclosure and not answer until compelled by "final orders." Backiel contemplates another try before Judge Weiner, and perhaps an appeal. She is still working on making every effort practicable.

The Glory of the Profession

The importance of this case is much larger than the rights of Backiel and her client. The government's increasing practice of subpoenaing lawyers to testify against their clients has sent shock waves through the criminal-justice system in recent years. In 1987, then-U.S. Attorney William Weld (now the new governor of Massachusetts) said he was issuing 50 such subpoenas per year — and that was in only one of the nation's 94 federal districts. The National Association of Criminal Defense Lawyers estimates that the federal government issues at least several hundred grand-jury subpoenas each year seeking to compel lawyers to testify about their clients.

Generally, the government is after attorney-fee information because prosecutors are "pushing forfeiture," according to a NACDL spokesman, or trying to make out a racketeering or tax case. Not only criminal-defense lawyers are at risk; attorneys who handle commercial transactions can easily be drawn into grand-jury proceedings against a client when the case involves money trails. What's most unusual about the Backiel case is that the prosecution is after information that goes directly to the substance of the client's alleged crime.

Surely the most serious kind of conflict of interest is created when a lawyer's representation of a client is limited by the lawyer's understandable concern to avoid her own imprisonment and the stigma of contempt of court. Justice William Brennan Jr. once called the relationship of trust between lawyer and client the "cornerstone of the adversary system and effective assistance of counsel." And a century ago, Justice David Brewer — upholding the disbarment of a lawyer who had violated his client's confidences — observed that fidelity to that trust is "the glory of our profession."

As any defense lawyer will confirm, the relationship of trust and confidence is extremely difficult to establish and maintain. An accused who is under the threat of imprisonment is typically suspicious of any officer of the court, including defense counsel. A defense lawyer known to have testified secretly before a grand jury about any client will suffer a devastating blow to her ability to render effective assistance to any client thereafter. If her livelihood doesn't dry up, her clientele will certainly clam up. . . .

NOTES AND QUESTIONS

1. ***The Glory of the Profession?*** Do you agree that keeping a client's confidences secret against all pressure is "the glory of the profession"? Or do you think lawyers ought to be permitted to reveal client confidences when necessary to catch a bail jumper, especially one awaiting trial on charges of attempting to dynamite the United States Capitol building?

2. ***Balancing Test?*** Is the attorney-client privilege a balancing test that should weigh the public's need for information against the policies underlying the privilege? Or is the attorney-client privilege absolute, applying even if the public has urgent need for the information and it is impossible to learn the information from anyone but the attorney? Or is the attorney-client privilege almost absolute, with narrow exceptions?

Chapter 9

THE ATTORNEY-CLIENT PRIVILEGE AND PHYSICAL EVIDENCE

So far we've only talked about the attorney-client privilege with regard to information. What about physical evidence, things that you can see and touch? Are they covered under the attorney-client privilege?

A. THE CATEGORIES OF PHYSICAL EVIDENCE

Let's start by identifying five basic categories of physical evidence:

1. Evidence given to you by a client. What should you do when a client hands you relevant physical evidence, such as a drawing, a gun, a document, a pair of bloodstained shoes — anything you can physically hold or touch? Which of the following options may or must you choose:

- Preserve it in your office?
- Examine it and give it back to the client?
- Refuse to touch it or look at it at all?
- Turn it over to the police or prosecutor?
- Send it to an expert to have it tested?
- Destroy it?

That's a wide range of options. In this chapter we will discuss various situations to give you a better idea about what your options are and what lawyers are permitted or required to do. Is the physical evidence itself protected by the attorney-client privilege? If your client tells you where he got the evidence, or tells you something about the evidence, are those remarks privileged?

2. Evidence given to you by a third party. What if a witness, a friend of your client, or anyone else who is not your client, gives you or shows you an item of evidence? Which options apply now?

3. Evidence that you find on your own. What should you do if you search the scene of a crime and find a gun, or a body, or a victim's wallet? Leave it where it is? Take it to the police? Photograph it? Look at it and put it back? Throw it in the river?

4. Evidence that you only see but do not touch. What if you see physical evidence but do not touch it or take possession of it? Is your observation privileged? Should you do anything with the evidence, or tell anyone about it, or should you just leave it where you found it? Suppose your client gives you a guided tour of the murder scene, complete with an explanatory narrative. Are your client's remarks privileged?

5. Evidence that you only hear about but do not see or touch. What if your client or someone else tells you the location of physical evidence? Do you have to go look at it? Should you? Does the attorney-client privilege protect your client's instructions about where to find the evidence? What if your client gives you a map showing where the bodies are buried (or where the stolen money is buried, or where he hid the murder weapon)? Is that map privileged?

Overriding all of these questions about specific categories of physical evidence is one larger question: What can you (or must you) tell the authorities? If you learn the location of physical evidence, or find out who has control of it, or observe it without touching it at the scene of a crime, must you tell the police or prosecutors? If you turn over physical evidence to the police, may you tell them (or must you tell them) who gave it to you, or where it came from, or anything else about the evidence or its source?

Courts have puzzled over these questions for many years. There are some reasonably fixed rules by now, but each situation is unique, and physical evidence still presents some knotty problems for courts. Here is a classic case that paints a graphic picture and is still cited as good law on physical evidence. As you read it, consider how you would articulate the competing policies at stake here. What is the main policy supporting a requirement that the defense lawyer (or his investigator) disclose the location where the wallet was found if the lawyer learned of the location in a privileged communication with a client? What is the main policy against requiring such disclosure? How would you balance those policies?

B. HANDLING PHYSICAL EVIDENCE

PEOPLE v. MEREDITH

631 P.2d 46 (Cal. 1981)

TOBRINER, J.

Defendants Frank Earl Scott and Michael Meredith appeal from convictions for the first degree murder and first degree robbery of David Wade. Meredith's conviction rests on eyewitness testimony that he shot and killed Wade. Scott's conviction, however, depends on the theory that Scott conspired with Meredith and a third defendant, Jacqueline Otis, to bring about the killing and robbery. To support the theory of conspiracy the prosecution sought to show the place where the victim's wallet was found, and, in the course of the case this piece of evidence became crucial. The admissibility of that evidence comprises the principal issue on this appeal.

At trial the prosecution called Steven Frick, who testified that he observed the victim's partially burnt wallet in a trash can behind Scott's residence. Scott's trial counsel then adduced that Frick served as a defense investigator. Scott himself had told his former counsel that he had taken the victim's wallet, divided the money with Meredith, attempted to burn the wallet, and finally put it in the trash can. At counsel's request, Frick then retrieved the wallet from the trash can. Counsel examined the wallet and then turned it over to the police.

The defense acknowledges that the wallet itself was properly admitted into evidence. The prosecution in turn acknowledges that the attorney-client privilege protected the conversations between Scott, his former counsel, and counsel's investigator. Indeed the prosecution did not attempt to introduce those conversations at trial. The issue before us, consequently, focuses upon a narrow point: whether under the circumstances of this case Frick's observation of the location of the wallet, the product of a privileged communication, finds protection under the attorney-client privilege.

This issue, one of first impression in California, presents the court with competing policy considerations. On the one hand, to deny protection to observations arising from confidential communications might chill free and open communication between attorney and client and might also inhibit counsel's investigation of his client's case. On the other hand, we cannot extend the attorney-client privilege so far that it renders evidence immune from discovery and admission merely because the defense seizes it first.

Balancing these considerations, we conclude that an observation by defense counsel or his investigator, which is the product of a privileged communication, may not be admitted unless the defense by altering or removing physical evidence has precluded the prosecution from making that same observation. In the present case the defense investigator, by removing the wallet, frustrated any possibility that the police might later discover it in the trash can. The conduct of the defense thus precluded the prosecution from ascertaining the crucial fact of the location of the wallet. Under these circumstances, the prosecution was entitled to present evidence to show the location of the wallet in the trash can; the trial court did not err in admitting the investigator's testimony. . . .

We first summarize the evidence other than that relating to the discovery and location of the victim's wallet. . . . On the night of April 3, 1976, Wade (the victim) and

Jacqueline Otis, a friend of the defendants, entered a club known as Rich Jimmy's. Defendant Scott remained outside by a shoeshine stand. A few minutes later codefendant Meredith arrived outside the club. He told Scott he planned to rob Wade, and asked Scott to go into the club, find Jacqueline Otis, and ask her to get Wade to go out to Wade's car parked outside the club.

In the meantime, Wade and Otis had left the club and walked to a liquor store to get some beer. Returning from the store, they left the beer in a bag by Wade's car and reentered the club. Scott then entered the club also and, according to the testimony of Laurie Ann Sam (a friend of Scott's who was already in the club), Scott asked Otis to get Wade to go back out to his car so Meredith could knock him in the head.

When Wade and Otis did go out to the car, Meredith attacked Wade from behind. After a brief struggle, two shots were fired; Wade fell, and Meredith, witnessed by Scott and Sam, ran from the scene. Scott went over to the body and, assuming Wade was dead, picked up the bag containing the beer and hid it behind a fence. Scott later returned, retrieved the bag, and took it home where Otis and Meredith joined him.

We now recount the evidence relating to Wade's wallet, basing our account primarily on the testimony of James Schenk, Scott's first appointed attorney. Schenk visited Scott in jail more than a month after the crime occurred and solicited information about the murder, stressing that he had to be fully acquainted with the facts to avoid being sandbagged by the prosecution during the trial. In response, Scott gave Schenk the same information that he had related earlier to the police. In addition, however, Scott told Schenk something Scott had not revealed to the police: that he had seen a wallet, as well as the paper bag, on the ground near Wade. Scott said that he picked up the wallet, put it in the paper bag, and placed both behind a parking lot fence. He also said that he later retrieved the bag, took it home, found $100 in the wallet and divided it with Meredith, and then tried to burn the wallet in his kitchen sink. He took the partially burned wallet, Scott told Schenk, placed it in a plastic bag, and threw it in a burn barrel behind his house.

Schenk, without further consulting Scott, retained Investigator Stephen Frick and sent Frick to find the wallet. Frick found it in the location described by Scott and brought it to Schenk. After examining the wallet and determining that it contained credit cards with Wade's name, Schenk turned the wallet and its contents over to Detective Payne, investigating officer in the case. Schenk told Payne only that, to the best of his knowledge, the wallet had belonged to Wade.

The prosecution subpoenaed Attorney Schenk and Investigator Frick to testify at the preliminary hearing. When questioned at that hearing, Schenk said that he received the wallet from Frick but refused to answer further questions on the ground that he learned about the wallet through a privileged communication. Eventually, however, the magistrate threatened Schenk with contempt if he did not respond yes or no when asked whether his contact with his client led to disclosure of the wallet's location. Schenk then replied yes, and revealed on further questioning that this contact was the sole source of his information as to the wallet's location.

At the preliminary hearing Frick, the investigator who found the wallet, was then questioned by the district attorney. Over objections by counsel, Frick testified that he found the wallet in a garbage can behind Scott's residence.

Prior to trial, a third attorney, Hamilton Hintz, was appointed for Scott. Hintz unsuccessfully sought an in limine ruling that the wallet of the murder victim was inadmissible and that the attorney-client privilege precluded the admission of testimony concerning the wallet by Schenk or Frick.

At trial Frick, called by the prosecution, identified the wallet and testified that he found it in a garbage can behind Scott's residence. On cross-examination by Hintz, Scott's counsel, Frick further testified that he was an investigator hired by Scott's first attorney, Schenk, and that he had searched the garbage can at Schenk's request. Hintz later called Schenk as a witness: Schenk testified that he told Frick to search for the wallet immediately after Schenk finished talking to Scott. Schenk also stated that Frick brought him the wallet on the following day; after examining its contents Schenk delivered the wallet to the police. Scott then took the stand and testified to the information about the wallet that he had disclosed to Schenk. The jury found both Scott and Meredith guilty of first degree murder and first degree robbery. . . .

Defendant Scott concedes, and we agree, that the wallet itself was admissible in evidence. Scott maintains, however, that Evidence Code section 954 bars the testimony of the investigator concerning the location of the wallet. We consider, first, whether the California attorney-client privilege codified in that section extends to observations which are the product of privileged communications. We then discuss whether that privileged status is lost when defense conduct may have frustrated prosecution discovery. Section 954 provides: "[T]he client . . . has a privilege to refuse to disclose, and to prevent another from disclosing, a confidential communication between client and lawyer. . . . " Under that section one who seeks to assert the privilege must establish that a confidential communication occurred during the course of the attorney-client relationship.

AUTHORS' COMMENT:

Section 954 of the California Evidence Code generally accords with definitions of the attorney-client privilege in other jurisdictions. Therefore, other jurisdictions would most likely agree with the holding in this case unless they weighed the competing policy considerations differently. This is not just a California case.

Scott's statements to Schenk regarding the location of the wallet clearly fulfilled the statutory requirements. Moreover, the privilege did not dissolve when Schenk disclosed the substance of that communication to his investigator, Frick. Under Evidence Code section 912, subdivision (d), a disclosure which is reasonably necessary to accomplish the purpose for which the attorney has been consulted does not constitute a waiver of the privilege. If Frick was to perform the investigative services for which Schenk had retained him, it was reasonably necessary, that Schenk transmit to Frick the information regarding the wallet. Thus, Schenk's disclosure to Frick did not waive the statutory privilege.

The statutes codifying the attorney-client privilege do not, however, indicate whether that privilege protects facts viewed and observed as a direct result of confidential communication. To resolve that issue, we turn first to the policies which underlie the attorney-client privilege, and then to the cases which apply those policies to observations arising from a protected communication.

The fundamental purpose of the attorney-client privilege is, of course, to encourage full and open communication between client and attorney. Adequate legal representation in the ascertainment and enforcement of rights or the prosecution or defense of litigation compels a full disclosure of the facts by the client to his attorney. . . . Given the privilege, a client may make such a disclosure without fear that his attorney may be forced to reveal the information confided to him.

In the criminal context, as we have recently observed, these policies assume particular significance: As a practical matter, if the client knows that damaging information could more readily be obtained from the attorney following disclosure than from himself in the absence of disclosure, the client would be reluctant to confide in his lawyer and it would be difficult to obtain fully informed legal advice. . . . Thus, if an accused is to derive the full benefits of his right to counsel, he must have the assurance of confidentiality and privacy of communication with his attorney.

Judicial decisions have recognized that the implementation of these important policies may require that the privilege extend not only to the initial communication between client and attorney but also to any information which the attorney or his investigator may subsequently acquire as a direct result of that communication. In a venerable decision involving facts analogous to those in the instant case, the Supreme Court of West Virginia held that the trial court erred in admitting an attorney's testimony as to the location of a pistol which he had discovered as the result of a privileged communication from his client. That the attorney had observed the pistol, the court pointed out, did not nullify the privilege:

> All that the said attorney knew about this pistol, or where it was to be found, he knew only from the communications which had been made to him by his client confidentially and professionally, as counsel in this case. And it ought therefore, to have been entirely excluded from the jury. It may be, that in this particular case this evidence tended to the promotion of right and justice, but . . . "[t]ruth like all other good things may be loved unwisely, may be pursued too keenly, may cost too much."

State of West Virginia v. Douglass (1882) 20 W. Va. 770, 783 (citation omitted). This unbearable cost, the Douglass court concluded, could not be entirely avoided by attempting to admit testimony regarding observations or discoveries made as the result of a privileged communication, while excluding the communication itself. Such a procedure, Douglass held, was practically as mischievous in all its tendencies and consequences, as if it has required [the attorney] to state everything, which his client had confidentially told him about this pistol. It would be a slight safeguard indeed, to confidential communications made to counsel, if he was thus compelled substantially, to give them to a jury, although he was required not to state them in the words of his client.

More recent decisions reach similar conclusions. In Washington *ex rel.* Sowers v. Olwell 394 P.2d 681 (1964), the court reviewed contempt charges against an attorney who refused to produce a knife he obtained from his client. The court first observed that "[t]o be protected as a privileged communication . . . the securing of the knife- . . . must have been the direct result of information given to Mr. Olwell by his client." The court concluded that defense counsel, after examining the physical evidence, should deliver it to the prosecution, but should not reveal the source of the evidence; "[b]y thus allowing the prosecution to recover such evidence, the public interest is served, and by refusing the prosecution an opportunity to disclose the source of the evidence, the client's privilege is preserved and a balance reached between these conflicting interests."

Finally, we note the decisions of the New York courts in New York v. Belge 372 N.Y.S.2d 798 (1975), *aff'd*, New York v. Belge 376 N.Y.S.2d 771 (1975). Defendant, charged with one murder, revealed to counsel that he had committed three others. Counsel, following defendant's directions, located one of the bodies. Counsel did not reveal the location of the body until trial, 10 months later, when he exposed the other murders to support an insanity defense.

Counsel was then indicted for violating two sections of the New York Public Health Law for failing to report the existence of the body to proper authorities in order that they could give it a decent burial. The trial court dismissed the indictment; the appellate division affirmed, holding that the attorney-client privilege shielded counsel from prosecution for actions which would otherwise violate the Public Health Law.

The foregoing decisions demonstrate that the attorney-client privilege is not strictly limited to communications, but extends to protect observations made as a consequence of protected communications. We turn therefore to the question whether that privilege encompasses a case in which the defense, by removing or altering evidence, interferes with the prosecution's opportunity to discover that evidence.

When defense counsel alters or removes physical evidence, he necessarily deprives the prosecution of the opportunity to observe that evidence in its original condition or location. As amicus Appellate Committee of the California District Attorney Association points out, to bar admission of testimony concerning the original condition and location of the evidence in such a case permits the defense in effect to destroy critical information; it is as if, he explains, the wallet in this case bore a tag bearing the words located in the trash can by Scott's residence, and the defense, by taking the wallet, destroyed this tag. To extend the attorney-client privilege to a case in which the defense removed evidence might encourage defense counsel to race the police to seize critical evidence.

We therefore conclude that courts must craft an exception to the protection extended by the attorney-client privilege in cases in which counsel has removed or altered evidence. Indeed, at oral argument, defense counsel acknowledged that such an exception might be necessary in a case in which the police would have inevitably discovered the evidence in its original location if counsel had not removed it. Counsel argued, however, that the attorney-client privilege should protect observations of evidence, despite subsequent defense removal, unless the prosecution could prove that the police probably would have eventually discovered the evidence in the original site.

AUTHORS' COMMENT:

Do you support defense counsel's proposal that the attorney-client privilege should protect observations of evidence, even if defense counsel has later removed the evidence, unless the prosecution can prove that the police probably would have eventually discovered the evidence in the original site? Why or why not?

We have seriously considered counsel's proposal, but have concluded that a test based upon the probability of eventual discovery is unworkably speculative. Evidence turns up not only because the police deliberately search for it, but also because it comes to the attention of policemen or bystanders engaged in other business. In the present case, for example, the wallet might have been found by the trash collector. Moreover, once physical evidence (the wallet) is turned over to the police, they will obviously stop looking for it; to ask where, how long, and how carefully they would have looked is obviously to compel speculation as to theoretical future conduct of the police.

We therefore conclude that whenever defense counsel removes or alters evidence, the statutory privilege does not bar revelation of the original location or condition of the evidence in question. We thus view the defense decision to remove evidence as a tactical choice. If defense counsel leaves the evidence where he discovers it, his observations derived from privileged communications are insulated from revelation. If, however, counsel chooses to remove evidence to examine or test it, the original location and condition of that evidence loses the protection of the privilege. Applying this analysis to the present case, we hold that the trial court did not err in admitting the investigator's testimony concerning the location of the wallet.

NOTES AND QUESTIONS

1. ***Delivering Evidence to the Prosecution.*** Defense lawyers in criminal cases are prohibited from hiding physical evidence in their offices. If a defense lawyer actually takes possession of physical evidence, he or she must turn it over to the prosecution. Courts widely agree on this principle. *See, e.g., California v. Superior Court (Fairbank)*, 237 Cal. Rptr. 158, 159 (1987) (defense counsel may not retain physical evidence pertaining to the crime charged); *Commonwealth v. Stenhach*, 514 A.2d 114, 119 (1986), (appeal denied) 534 A.2d 769 (1987) (overwhelming majority of states hold that physical evidence of a crime in the possession of a criminal defense attorney is not subject to a privilege but must be delivered to the prosecution); *Hitch v. Pima County Superior Court*, 708 P.2d 72, 78 (1985) (if the attorney has reasonable grounds to believe that the evidence might be destroyed he may turn the physical evidence over to the prosecution). Many other cases also support this proposition so don't ever let a client talk you into hiding evidence in your office. It's unethical and illegal.

2. ***Basic Principles.*** Virtually every court agrees with the basic principle that a lawyer for a criminal defendant must give the authorities physical evidence that the lawyer receives from the client if the evidence is material to the case. The courts have difficulty, however, in determining exactly what the prosecution can say to the jury about the source of the evidence.

Obviously, it would destroy the defendant's case if the prosecutor could stand before the jury and say, "We will now offer into evidence the stolen wallet. Guess where we got it? From the defendant's lawyer!" The defendant says he doesn't know anything about this wallet, but somehow it ended up in the hands of his lawyer. What is the jury going to think? They are going to think, Hmmm, the defendant's lawyer must have gotten the wallet from the defendant. How did the defendant get it? He stole it! He's guilty! So we can't let the prosecutor say he got the wallet from the defendant or the defendant's lawyer, because that would do too much damage to the attorney-client privilege.

On the other hand, the evidence probably won't be admissible unless the prosecution can lay some foundation about how it got the evidence. It can't just say, "Here's a wallet," or "Here are some bullets." It has to connect these things to the defendant. It has to establish a chain of custody, a chain that links the physical evidence to the original source, to prove that it's what it's supposed to be, and not some phony stuff that the police stored in an evidence locker until they needed it for a case. We don't want the police dripping blood on a shirt the day before trial and saying, "This came from the defendant."

To lay a foundation, the prosecution has to say, "These are the clothes that the accused was wearing when witnesses saw him on the night of the crime, and they have bloodstains on them that match the blood of the victim." But how can the prosecutor do that without getting the defendant's lawyer to testify or stipulate? Maybe the prosecutor can't. But if the defense lawyer does stipulate that the bloodstained clothes are the ones the defendant was wearing on the night of the alleged crime, doesn't that stipulation violate the attorney-client privilege? Maybe it does. That's the riddle. Courts still don't know exactly how to handle this situation. What would you suggest?

3. ***Are Ethics Rules Relevant?*** Do the rules of legal ethics have anything to do with the lawyer's obligations to turn over physical evidence? Rule 3.4(a) provides (with emphasis added) as follows:

> A lawyer shall not:
>
> (a) unlawfully obstruct another party's access to evidence or unlawfully alter, destroy, or conceal a document or other material having potential evidentiary value. A lawyer shall not counsel or assist another person to do any such act.

What does it mean to unlawfully obstruct another party's access to evidence or unlawfully alter, destroy, or conceal material having potential evidentiary value? The answer depends on whether the lawyer is subject to state or federal law, and whether the materials have been subpoenaed.

4. ***State Law.*** Under state law in most states, destroying physical evidence is a crime even before a subpoena is issued. Many states prohibit the destruction of evidence if, believing that an official proceeding or investigation is pending or about to be instituted, a person acts with purpose to impair its verity or availability in such proceeding or investigation.

5. ***Federal Law.*** Under federal law, intentional destruction of documents or other evidence after a subpoena for them has been issued is an obstruction of justice or a criminal contempt. *See* 18 U.S.C. § 1503 (obstruction of judicial proceedings), § 1505 (administrative and legislative proceedings), and § 401(3) (criminal contempt). But destruction of evidence before a subpoena is issued is a federal crime only if: (a) the documents are relevant to a pending grand jury or criminal investigation; and (b) the destruction was done with a corrupt or evil intent.

6. ***Should we Change Rule 3.4?*** Rule 3.4 only prohibits a lawyer from advising a client to alter, conceal, or destroy documents or other evidence unlawfully. Does that rule go far enough? Should we change the rule to prohibit a lawyer from advising the client to destroy relevant evidence at any time, even if the evidence is relevant only to threatened or possible future proceedings? Should we amend Rule 3.4(a) to provide:

> In representing a client, the lawyer shall not advise or assist in the destruction of documents, records, or other real evidence when the lawyer knows or reasonably should know that they are relevant to any foreseeable, planned or pending action.

Is the adversary system imperiled because the existing rule allows those possessing evidence to destroy it? If there were a broader prohibition, would lawyers get around it by advising clients that they (the clients) have a legal right to destroy documents? Does Rule 3.4(a) in its current form go far enough?

7. ***White Collar Crimes.*** Lawyers who deal with white-collar clients are unlikely to encounter stolen wallets, sawed-off shotguns, and paper bags full of cash. Yet they frequently encounter similar questions, in civil suits more often than in criminal cases. Let's look at a few white collar situations that you may one day encounter in practice.

> A. Suppose a manager at a corporate client hears a rumor that the EPA is looking into the company's dumping practices for toxic waste. The CEO asks you to review the company's files and to destroy any documents that may look incriminating. Should you comply? Should the answer turn on whether it would be a crime to destroy the documents? Should it depend on whether you think the documents are definitely relevant, probably relevant, probably irrelevant, or definitely irrelevant to the rumored EPA investigation? (Is relevance relevant to this inquiry?) What do you think the rules of ethics ought to be in this situation?
>
> B. Suppose the CEO of the same client simply asks you to *identify* any incriminating documents in the client's files. Should you do so, knowing that the CEO may then destroy the documents to save his own skin?
>
> C. Suppose the CEO is more subtle, and simply asks you to explain what *kinds* of documents might be viewed as establishing a violation of law? Again, you suspect that the CEO will destroy the documents if he knows what to look for. Should you give him the requested advice?
>
> D. Suppose the CEO proposes to introduce a regular annual review of the files, in which your job as the company's lawyer will be to identify (and perhaps destroy) possible incriminating documents. Should you help the company implement the plan? Why or why not?

8. ***Practical Considerations.*** Even if it is legal to destroy documents, it may be a bad idea to do so as a practical matter. Consider this advice from Note, *Legal Ethics and the Destruction of Evidence*, 88 YALE L.J. 1665, 1675 (1979):

> The destruction of a document to prevent its use at trial precludes that party from later introducing secondary evidence to prove the document's contents, but does not bar the opposing party from doing so. Moreover, the intentional destruction of a document to prevent its use at trial, even when not illegal, creates an adverse inference that a party's whole case is weak. Finally, any questions asked of a client under oath concerning the destruction must be answered honestly to avoid outright perjury. It is possible that the answers will be as damaging as the actual contents of the destroyed documents.

9. ***The Famous Kodak Case.*** Document concealment by a major Wall Street law firm became a legendary scandal. In a huge civil antitrust action, *Berkey Photo, Inc. v. Eastman Kodak Corp.*, 74 F.R.D. 613 (S.D.N.Y. 1977) (resulting in a plaintiff's verdict of over $100 million), lawyers for the plaintiff sought routine discovery of notes and letters of an economist who was serving as an expert witness for Kodak. A team of thirty lawyers at Donavan Leisure was handling Kodak's defense. Mahlon Perkins, Jr., the Donovan partner working with the expert witness, almost casually stated, in response to an exchange during the expert's deposition, that certain documents (which were relatively inconsequential) "had not been retained." The assertion was repeated in a subsequent affidavit.

During the expert's testimony at the subsequent trial, however, the question of the missing documents recurred, and a copy of a supposedly missing document was produced. Judge Marvin Frankel, who was presiding over the trial, asked for a detailed affidavit explaining why the missing document had not been produced earlier. It then transpired that the missing documents and others had not been destroyed but were sitting in a suitcase in a closet in attorney Perkins' office.

The false statements under oath led to a contempt-of-court conviction for Perkins and his resignation from the firm. The disclosure also contributed to a huge jury verdict against Kodak in the antitrust suit ($113 million after trebling, subsequently reversed on appeal and then settled for $6,750,000). The scandal also led to the discharge of Donovan Leisure as Kodak's antitrust counsel and damage to several other careers. Judge Frankel remarked that "this course of self-help, mistake, and/or extreme carelessness . . . reflects a kind of single-minded interest in winning, winning, winning. . . . " Perkins, described by colleagues as a quiet, dignified, scholarly man, was a graduate of the Harvard law school, a scholar at Oxford, and active in community organizations.

Perkins' lawyer in the contempt proceedings was Harold Tyler, a former federal judge and U.S. Deputy Attorney General. At Perkins's sentencing, Tyler commented that "there, possibly but for the grace of God, go I, because of the pressures which come upon men and women who practice law in big cases." For a fascinating report of the full story, see Stewart, *Kodak and Donovan Leisure — The Untold Story*, AM. LAW. 24 (1983).

C. THE CONSEQUENCES OF DESTROYING EVIDENCE

1. The Tort of Spoliation

Completely apart from any ethical considerations, destroying evidence may subject a client to civil liability. The tort is known as "spoliation of evidence" and is among the newest of torts under the common law. There are two varieties — intentional spoliation and negligent spoliation.

In *County of Solano v. Delancy*, 264 Cal. Rptr. 721 (Cal. App. 1st Dist. 1989), the court described the elements of a cause of action for *intentional* spoliation of evidence:

> (1) pending or probable litigation involving plaintiff; (2) knowledge by the defendant of the existence or likelihood of the litigation; (3) intentional "acts of spoliation" on the part of the defendant designed to disrupt the plaintiff's case; (4) disruption of plaintiff's case; and (5) damages proximately caused by the acts of the defendant.

In another case, *Continental Insurance Co. v. Herman*, 576 So. 2d 313 (Fla. App. 1991), the court listed the elements of a cause of action for *negligent* destruction of evidence as:

> (1) existence of a potential civil action, (2) a legal or contractual duty to preserve evidence which is relevant to the potential civil action, (3) destruction of the evidence, (4) significant impairment in the ability to prove the lawsuit, (5) a causal relationship between the evidence destruction and the inability to prove the lawsuit, and (6) damages.

During the 1980s and into the 1990s, the clear trend was for more jurisdictions to recognize the tort in some form. Thus, if your client won a suit after intentionally or negligently destroying key evidence, the client could still face a new and separate tort suit for spoliation of evidence. In recent years, however, most courts have pulled back from imposing tort liability for destroying evidence.

In the late 1990s, however, in *Cedars-Sinai Medical Center v. Superior Court*, 18 Cal. 4th 1, 954 P.2d 511 (1998), the California Supreme Court disapproved *County of Solano v. Delancy* and declined to adopt a tort for intentional spoliation of evidence by a party to the underlying cause of action if the spoliation victim knew of or should have known of the spoliation before the decision on the merits of the underlying action. The court said:

> No one doubts that the intentional destruction of evidence should be condemned. Destroying evidence can destroy fairness and justice, for it increases the risk of an erroneous decision on the merits of the underlying cause of action. Destroying evidence can also increase the costs of litigation as parties attempt to reconstruct the destroyed evidence or to develop other evidence, which may be less accessible, less persuasive, or both.
>
> That alone, however, is not enough to justify creating tort liability for such conduct. We must also determine whether a tort remedy for the intentional first party spoliation of evidence would ultimately create social benefits exceeding those created by existing remedies for such conduct, and outweighing any costs and burdens it would impose. Three concerns in particular stand out here: the conflict between a tort remedy for intentional first party spoliation and the policy against creating derivative tort remedies for litigation related misconduct; the strength of existing nontort remedies for spoliation; and the uncertainty of the fact of harm in spoliation cases.

Weighing all of those considerations, the California Supreme Court held that there is "no tort remedy for the intentional spoliation of evidence by a party to the cause of action to which the spoliated evidence is relevant" where the spoliation victim "knows or should have known of the alleged spoliation before the trial or other decision on the merits of the underlying action."

A year later, in *Temple Community Hosp. v. Superior Court*, 20 Cal. 4th 464, 976 P.2d 223 (1999), the California Supreme Court considered a related issue not resolved in *Cedars-Sinai* — "whether a tort cause of action will lie against a person who is not a party in a lawsuit but who intentionally destroys or suppresses evidence that would be relevant in the lawsuit." Based on many of the considerations in *Cedars-Sinai*, the court declined to recognize a tort cause of action for intentional spoliation by a third party. "The doubtful benefit of the proposed tort remedy is outweighed by the prospect of a spiral of litigation giving rise to verdicts based upon speculation," the court reasoned. "In addition, it would be anomalous for a nonparty to be liable in damages, including punitive damages, for conduct that would not give rise to tort liability if committed by a party. We conclude that no tort cause of action will lie for intentional third party spoliation of evidence."

In 2004, the New York Court of Appeals followed California's lead and declined to create or recognize a cause of action for negligent spoliation of evidence and impairment of a claim or defense. "The burden of forcing a party to preserve when it has no notice of an impending lawsuit, and the difficulty of assessing damages," the court said, "militate against establishing a cause of action for spoliation . . . where there was no duty, court order, contract or special relationship." *MetLife Auto & Home v. Joe Basil Chevrolet, Inc.*, 1 N.Y.3d 478, 807 N.E.2d 865 (2004).

2. Litigation Sanctions for Destroying Evidence

Even where courts do not recognize an independent tort for destroying relevant evidence, courts may impose sanctions on the destroying party, such as (a) dismissing the answer, (b) precluding the defendant from introducing any evidence about the condition of the destroyed evidence, (c) ordering the destroying party to pay monetary sanctions to the opposing party, or (d) entering a default judgment against the party which destroyed the documents.

Sanctions for withholding or destroying evidence can have significant repercussions for you and your clients. Just consider the disastrous results for Morgan Stanley in *Coleman (Parent) Holdings, Inc. v. Morgan Stanley & Co.*, No. CA 03-5045 AI, (Fla. Palm Beach County Ct. Mar. 23, 2005) (order on CPH's renewed motion for entry of default judgment) (*available* thru *Morgan Stanley To Pay $1.4 Billion For Fraudulent Practices*, 2-8 Mealey's Litig. Rep. Disc. 6 (2005)) (LEXIS). During discovery, Coleman asked Morgan Stanley for thousands of computer tapes. Morgan Stanley's lawyers told the court that the tapes had been overwritten and could no longer be produced. In fact, back-up tapes did exist and many of them had been uploaded into a searchable archive. The court found that Morgan Stanley had deliberately violated a series of discovery orders and had lied to the court.

As a sanction, the court imposed an "adverse inference" jury instruction (meaning the jury could assume that the destroyed tapes would have been damaging to Morgan Stanley). The court also awarded a partial default judgment in Coleman's favor and instructed the jurors that they could take Morgan Stanley's document destruction into consideration as they decided whether an award of punitive damages was appropriate. The jury awarded a total of $1.45 billion to plaintiff, $604 million in compensatory damages and $850 million in punitive damages.

The next case gives you an idea of how courts assess whether sanctions should be imposed when lawyers for a company argue that the destruction of the evidence was the result of the routine operation of a company's normal document retention program.

MOSAID TECHNOLOGIES INC. v. SAMSUNG ELECTRONICS CO.

348 F. Supp. 2d 332 (D.N.J. 2004)

MARTINI, J.

This matter is before the Court on defendants Samsung Electronics Co., et al.'s ("Samsung's") appeal of Magistrate Judge Hedges' July 7, 2004 and September 1, 2004 Orders. Samsung appealed four different sanctions. Previously, this Court affirmed two of the four sanctions . . . The remaining two sanctions — a spoliation inference jury instruction concerning Samsung's destruction of e-mails and monetary sanctions constituting attorneys' fees and costs associated with MOSAID's motion for sanctions and attempts to obtain discovery — will now be addressed. . . .

Samsung also came up short in its obligation to preserve and produce e-discovery materials. More specifically, after the inception of this litigation in September 2001,

Samsung never placed a "litigation hold" or "off switch" on its document retention policy concerning e-mail. Unchecked, Samsung's automatic computer e-mail policy allowed e-mails to be deleted, or at least to become inaccessible, on a rolling basis. As a result, Samsung failed to produce a single technical e-mail in this highly technical patent litigation because none had been preserved. For Samsung's complete and utter failure to produce e-mails responsive to MOSAID's document requests, MOSAID sought sanctions before Magistrate Judge Hedges. . . .

On July 7, 2004, Magistrate Judge Hedges issued his first opinion and order concerning the spoliation inference. After finding Samsung's reasons for failing to produce any technical e-mails to be unconvincing, he granted MOSAID's request for the spoliation inference. . . . . He also granted MOSAID's request for reasonable attorneys' fees and costs associated with the motion for sanctions and MOSAID's attempts to secure discovery. On September 1, 2004, Magistrate Judge Hedges issued his second opinion and order concerning the spoliation inference. . . . Magistrate Judge Hedges found that the following instruction was . . . appropriately tailored to redress Samsung's conduct:

> You have heard that defendants failed to produce virtually all technical and other e-mails in this case. Plaintiff has argued that these e-mails were in defendants' control and would have proven facts relevant to the issues in this case.
>
> If you find that defendants could have produced these e-mails, and that the evidence was within their control, and that the e-mails would have been relevant in deciding disputed facts in this case, you are permitted, but not required, to infer that the evidence would have been unfavorable to defendants.
>
> In deciding whether to draw this inference you may consider whether these e-mails would merely have duplicated other evidence already before you. You may also consider whether you are satisfied that defendants' failure to produce this information was reasonable. Again, any inference you decide to draw should be based on all the facts and circumstances of this case.

Regarding the monetary sanctions, Magistrate Judge Hedges awarded MOSAID a total of $566,839.97 in fees and costs.

Samsung timely appealed those orders. On appeal, Samsung contends that the spoliation inference is an extreme sanction that was wrongly imposed given the facts of this case. According to Samsung, the Magistrate Judge gave short shrift to the following "critical" facts: MOSAID's document requests did not specifically and explicitly state that they sought e-mails and MOSAID never raised the topic of e-mails at any discovery conference prior to the close of fact discovery; MOSAID never complained about Samsung's failure to produce e-mails until after the close of fact discovery; and MOSAID represented to the Court at a January 2003 hearing that it did not need e-mails. Samsung also contends that the spoliation inference jury instruction chosen by the Magistrate Judge is contrary to established Third Circuit law because it would permit an adverse inference to be drawn for negligent destruction of e-mails. And finally, Samsung maintains that any part of the attorneys' fees and costs awarded for its failure to preserve e-mails should be vacated because there was no need for Samsung to retain any e-mails.

AUTHORS' COMMENT:

Do any of Samsung's arguments persuade you that the sanctions against Samsung for failure to preserve and produce e-mails were wrongly imposed? If so, which arguments are strongest? If not, what is wrong with Samsung's arguments?

Discussion

Spoliation is "the destruction or significant alteration of evidence, or the failure to preserve property for another's use as evidence in pending or reasonably foreseeable litigation." Evidence of spoliation may give rise to sanctions. Potential sanctions for spoliation include: dismissal of a claim or granting judgment in favor of a prejudiced party; suppression of evidence; an adverse inference, referred to as the spoliation inference; fines; and attorneys' fees and costs. This Court has the authority to impose spoliation sanctions pursuant to the Federal Rules of Civil Procedure and this Court's inherent authority.

Sanctions are appropriate when there is evidence that a party's spoliation of evidence threatens the integrity of this Court. Spoliation sanctions serve a remedial function by leveling the playing field or restoring the prejudiced party to the position it would have been without spoliation. They also serve a punitive function, by punishing the spoliator for its actions, and a deterrent function, by sending a clear message to other potential litigants that this type of behavior will not be tolerated and will be dealt with appropriately if need be.

[Dismissal of the lawsuit or suppression of evidence are drastic sanctions. The Magistrate Judge did not impose those sanctions.] A far lesser sanction is the spoliation inference, . . . an adverse inference that permits a jury to infer that "destroyed evidence might or would have been unfavorable to the position of the offending party." This inference is predicated upon the common sense observation that when a party destroys evidence that is relevant to a claim or defense in a case, the party did so out of the well-founded fear that the contents would harm him.

In order for the spoliation inference to apply, four essential factors must be satisfied. First, "it is essential that the evidence in question be within the party's control." Second, "it must appear that there has been actual suppression or withholding of the evidence." Third, the evidence destroyed or withheld was relevant to claims or defenses. And fourth, it was reasonably foreseeable that the evidence would later be discoverable. "While a litigant is under no duty to keep or retain every document in its possession, even in advance of litigation, it is under a duty to preserve what it knows, or reasonably should know, will likely be requested in reasonably foreseeable litigation."

In this case, Samsung's deleted or inaccessible e-mails easily satisfy factors one, three and four. The e-mails of Samsung's employees were clearly within Samsung's control since the inception of this litigation. That evidence was relevant to claims or defenses in this case. MOSAID has submitted an affidavit by a former Samsung memory designer that testifies to the extensive use of e-mail within Samsung and the subject matter that is oftentimes discussed in those e-mails. Magistrate Judge Hedges found that based on that evidence, MOSAID had made a prima facie showing of relevance, and this Court agrees.

It was also reasonably foreseeable that technical e-mails would later be sought in discovery. Samsung's argument that MOSAID did not specifically request e-mails in its discovery requests is inapt. The duty to preserve exists as of the time the party knows or reasonably should know litigation is foreseeable. At the latest, in this case, that time was September 2001, the time when MOSAID filed and served the complaint. Samsung had notice that this litigation had begun and therefore had an affirmative obligation to preserve potentially relevant evidence, including technical e-mails.

Samsung's argument that MOSAID failed to request e-mails is also wrong. As Magistrate Judge Hedges found, MOSAID's discovery requests encompassed e-mails. Although MOSAID did not use the word "e-mail" in its discovery requests, it broadly defined the word "document" to include, without limitation, "typed . . . matter," "other data compilations," "letters," "correspondence," "notes to the files," "interoffice communications," "statements," and so on. Samsung offers no good faith explanation why its e-mails did not fall within the scope of the word "document" as defined by MOSAID. After all, "e-mail" is short for "electronic mail," which any reasonable litigant would understand qualifies as a "letter," "correspondence," "communication," etc. Indeed, Samsung, in its arguments why the spoliation inference should not be imposed, has referred to e-mail as "e-mail correspondence" and "e-mail communications." In addition, Samsung knew that e-mails were discoverable having asked for them in its own discovery requests.

As for Samsung's argument that MOSAID should have complained earlier than it did about Samsung's failure to produce e-mails, the Court will not permit Samsung to shift the blame for its discovery practices. As documented in the Court's October 1, 2004 Opinion, Samsung's document production was highly deficient. Not having received Samsung's complete non-e-mail production until at least September 17, 2004, MOSAID's motion for sanctions was timely. Accordingly, Samsung had a duty to preserve and produce technical e-mails in this case.[8] . . .

AUTHORS' COMMENT:

At this point the court discussed the degree of culpability required to establish the non-producing party's "actual suppression" of the evidence, which is the second factor necessary to justify the "spoliation inference." Some courts have interpreted "actual suppression" to mean that the evidence must be "*intentionally* or *knowingly* destroyed or withheld, as opposed to lost, accidentally destroyed or otherwise properly accounted for," while other courts have taken "a more flexible approach." Which standard best serves the purpose of imposing sanctions for spoliation of evidence? Is it fair for a court to instruct the jury on a "spoliation inference" if the non-producing party did not intentionally or knowingly destroy the missing evidence but was merely negligent? And what was Samsung's level of culpability here? The court now resolves that issue.

Primarily, the spoliation inference serves a remedial function — leveling the playing field after a party has destroyed or withheld relevant evidence. As long as there is some showing that the evidence is relevant, . . . the offending party's culpability is largely irrelevant as it cannot be denied that the opposing party has been prejudiced. Contrary to Samsung's contention, negligent destruction of relevant evidence can be sufficient to

---

[8] Samsung's argument that MOSAID represented to the Court that it did not need e-mail mischaracterizes what MOSAID said. MOSAID, in what appears to be a reasonable attempt to expedite discovery, represented that if it received certain final documentation, it would not continue to seek e-mails concerning that final documentation. Significantly, rather than supporting Samsung's argument, MOSAID's representation to the Court demonstrates that it was in fact seeking discovery of e-mails.

give rise to the spoliation inference. If a party has notice that evidence is relevant to an action, and either proceeds to destroy that evidence or allows it to be destroyed by failing to take reasonable precautions, common sense dictates that the party is more likely to have been threatened by that evidence. By allowing the spoliation inference in such circumstances, the Court protects the integrity of its proceedings and the administration of justice.

In this case, Samsung's actions warrant the sanction of a spoliation inference. Samsung knew it had a duty to preserve potentially discoverable evidence. Samsung knew that e-mails were potentially relevant to this litigation. Indeed, Samsung itself asked for e-mails in its discovery requests. Samsung also knew how to institute a "litigation hold" and stop the spoliation of e-mails, having done so in one of its divisions in another litigation beginning in 2002. And yet, Samsung failed to institute a "litigation hold" when this litigation began. Further, Samsung did not put a "litigation hold" in place after it received MOSAID's discovery requests. As Magistrate Judge Hedges found, any reasonable litigant would have interpreted MOSAID's discovery requests to include e-mails. But Samsung willfully blinded itself, taking the position that MOSAID's document requests did not seek e-mails and therefore Samsung had no obligation to prevent their continued destruction while this litigation continued. In short, Samsung's actions go far beyond mere negligence, demonstrating knowing and intentional conduct that led to the nonproduction of all technical e-mails.

Moreover, the Court is neither impressed nor moved by Samsung's belated efforts to retrieve e-mails that were allegedly retained by a "litigation hold" imposed for a different lawsuit. The volume of potentially relevant evidence — "approximately 15–20 Gigabytes of e-mail and attachment data from the local folders for approximately 200 DRAM Design engineers" — is staggering and serves to put into focus the extent of Samsung's spoliation. Amazingly, Samsung did not undertake efforts to preserve and collect potentially relevant e-mails until after Magistrate Judge Hedges issued his September 1, 2004 Order. In other words, Samsung waited approximately three years after the beginning of this litigation, over a year after the close of fact discovery and approximately seven months after MOSAID filed its sanctions motion before it actually expended any effort to comply with an obligation that existed, at the latest, in September 2001. Given these circumstances, the sanctions imposed by Magistrate Judge Hedges are appropriate and fair.

More specifically, the Court approves and hereby adopts Magistrate Judge Hedges proposed spoliation inference jury instruction. As discussed above, it accurately reflects the law in this circuit and . . . will be given as part of the jury charge. Further, with regard to the monetary sanctions imposed, the Court has reviewed the Magistrate Judge's findings and concludes that they are supported by the evidence. Although Samsung contends that monetary sanctions should not be imposed for its complete spoliation of technical e-mails, relying on the same arguments it proffered to reverse the spoliation inference, this Court finds that they are an appropriate, additional sanction that is necessary to compensate MOSAID for the time and effort it was forced to expend in an effort to obtain discovery it was entitled to.

Conclusion

The duty to preserve potentially relevant evidence is an affirmative obligation that a party may not shirk. When the duty to preserve is triggered, it cannot be a defense to a spoliation claim that the party inadvertently failed to place a "litigation hold" or "off switch" on its document retention policy to stop the destruction of that evidence. As discoverable information becomes progressively digital, e-discovery, including e-mails and other electronic documents, plays a larger, more crucial role in litigation. In this district, in October 2003, Local Civil Rule 26.1 was amended to include a section concerning discovery of digital information. Among other things, that rule requires counsel to investigate how a client's computers store digital information, to review with the client potentially discoverable evidence, and to raise the topic of e-discovery at the Rule 26(f) conference, including preservation and production of digital information. Unless and until parties agree not to pursue e-discovery, the parties have an obligat ion to preserve potentially relevant digital information. Parties who fail to comply with that obligation do so at the risk of facing spoliation sanctions.

Although Rule 26.1(d) was not in effect at the start of this litigation, Samsung was aware that it had a duty to preserve potentially discoverable evidence. It knew that its technical e-mails were potentially relevant to the claims and defenses existing in this lawsuit. And Samsung chose to do nothing about the spoliation of those e-mails. As a result, MOSAID has suffered prejudice from the nonproduction of countless e-mails because its ability to prove infringement, and other issues, has been potentially hindered.

In light of the above, the Court affirms the spoliation inference jury instruction and monetary sanctions imposed by Magistrate Judge Hedges. These are the least burdensome sanctions the Court can impose while still attempting to level what has become an uneven playing field.

NOTES AND QUESTIONS

1. ***Amended Federal Rules of Civil Procedure.*** The *Mosaid* opinion was issued in 2004. About two years after the opinion, effective December 1, 2006, the Federal Rules of Civil Procedure were amended to address the subject of electronic discovery more specifically. Rule 16, which governs scheduling orders, now addresses disclosure or discovery of electronically stored information. Rule 26, the general rule governing discovery, replaces the old phrase "data compilations" with the new phrase "electronically stored information" and adds a new Rule 26(b)(2)(B), which provides:

> A party need not provide discovery of electronically stored information from sources that the party identifies as not reasonably accessible because of undue burden or cost. On motion to compel discovery or for a protective order, the party from whom discovery is sought must show that the information is not reasonably accessible because of undue burden or cost. If that showing is made, the court may nonetheless order discovery from such sources if the requesting party shows good cause . . .

Perhaps most relevant to the *Mosaid* opinion, a new Rule 37(f) has been added to the rule governing sanctions for improper conduct during discovery. Rule 37(f), entitled "Electronically Stored Information," provides as follows:

> Absent exceptional circumstances, a court may not impose sanctions under these rules on a party for failing to provide electronically stored information lost as a result of the routine, good-faith operation of an electronic information system.

If Rule 37(f) had applied when *Mosaid* was decided, would you have imposed sanctions on Samsung for failing to preserve and produce the missing e-mails?

2. ***Shredding Party.*** Your client, Azul Restaurant, owned by Amid Azul, has received a demand letter from a disgruntled supplier, Fred's Fish. Azul's chef recently refused to take delivery of certain specially-ordered goods from Fred's Fish, and Azul has not yet paid for fish that were delivered months ago. Fred's letter threatens to file a breach of contract complaint if Azul does not resolve the problem to the supplier's satisfaction within thirty days. Mr. Azul gave you a copy of the letter and asked what the repercussions will be if he holds a "shredding party" at which he and his secretary destroy records of shipments from Fred's Fish and delete all internal e-mails relating to the contract with Fred's Fish. What is your advice?

3. ***Discipline, Too.*** Litigation sanctions imposed by the court hearing a case are not the only dangers facing attorneys whose clients destroy evidence. Remember that a lawyer who "unlawfully alters, destroys or conceals a document or other material with

potential evidentiary value" (or "counsels or assists" someone else — such as a client — to engage in any of those actions) will also be subject to discipline for violating ABA Model Rule 3.4 (a).

4. ***Solving Problems.*** Apply the *Mosaid* case to the three problems in Section F of this Chapter. Does it help you solve them, or is the *Mosaid* case wholly distinguishable and inapplicable?

D. STANDARDS FOR CRIMINAL JUSTICE

The ABA has adopted highly influential Standards for Criminal Justice that include rules governing physical evidence. Standard 4-4.6 provides:

> (a) Defense counsel who receives a physical item under circumstances implicating a client in criminal conduct should disclose the location of or should deliver that item to law enforcement authorities only: (1) if required by law or court order, or (2) as provided in paragraph (d).
>
> (b) Unless required to disclose, defense counsel shall return the item to the source from whom defense counsel received it, except as provided in paragraphs (c) and (d). In returning the item to the source, defense counsel should advise the source of the legal consequences pertaining to possession or destruction of the item. Defense counsel should also prepare a written record of these events for his or her file, but should not give the source a copy of such record.
>
> (c) Defense counsel may receive the item for a reasonable period of time during which defense counsel: (1) intends to return it to the owner; (2) reasonably fears that return of the item to the source will result in destruction of the item; (3) reasonably fears that return of the item to the source will result in physical harm to anyone; (4) intends to test, examine, inspect, or use the item in any way as part of defense counsel's representation of the client; or (5) cannot return it to the source. If defense counsel tests or examines the item, he or she should thereafter return it to the source unless there is reason to believe that the evidence might be altered or destroyed or used to harm another or return is otherwise impossible. If defense counsel retains the item, he or she should retain it in his or her law office in a manner that does not impede the lawful ability of law enforcement to obtain the item.
>
> (d) If the item received is contraband, i.e., an item, possession of which is in and of itself a crime, such as narcotics, defense counsel may suggest that the client destroy it where there is no pending case or investigation relating to this evidence and where such destruction is clearly not in violation of any criminal statute. If such destruction is not permitted by law or if in defense counsel's judgment he or she cannot retain the item, whether or not it is contraband, in a way that does not pose an unreasonable risk of physical harm to anyone, defense counsel should disclose the location of or should deliver the item to law enforcement authorities.
>
> (e) If defense counsel discloses the location of or delivers the item to law enforcement authorities under paragraphs (a) or (d), or to a third party under paragraph (c)(1), he or she should do so in the way best designed to protect the client's interests.

NOTES AND QUESTIONS

1. ***How Does Standard 4-4.6 Apply to the Problems at the End of this Chapter?***

2. ***Practical Advice to Defense Counsel.*** Professor Norman Lefstein, a well-known former public defender who helped write Standard 4-4.6, gives the following practical advice: "Defense attorneys should be encouraged to search for physical evidence, either personally or through their investigators, only when there is a genuine belief that the evidence is likely to be helpful to the client's defense." Do you agree? Why or why not?

3. ***Anonymous Disclosures.*** Professor Lefstein would also prohibit an attorney from anonymously disclosing physical evidence to law enforcement authorities. Would you prohibit that? What if the anonymous disclosure would not immediately be traceable to a client? For example, suppose you are defending a client on murder charges, and the client says, "I did it, but I'm not guilty, I'm insane. I've killed other people, too. I can't help it. I try not to kill, but I can't stop myself." You ask for evidence about the other people, and the client tells you where the bodies are. You go with the client into a remote area near an abandoned mineshaft, and the client points to the decaying bodies of two teenagers shoved inside a collapsed wooden shed. You don't touch the bodies, but now you know where they are. You know that the parents of the dead teenagers are in a state of panic and dread because they don't know whether their children are alive or dead. You ask your client for permission to reveal the location of the bodies, but your client refuses.

May you ethically make an anonymous call to the police telling them where the bodies are? An anonymous call will not link the bodies to your client; it will just enable the police to identify the bodies, notify the grieving parents, and begin an investigation. Are you in favor of allowing such an anonymous call?

You can test your view while reading the following macabre scenario that illustrates the agony of keeping information confidential. How would you have felt if you had been one of the lawyers for the defendant in the bone-chilling true story below, based on a 1984 book, *Privileged Information*, by R. Alibrandi and Frank Armani? (Frank Armani was one of the defense lawyers in the story.) Keep in mind that although the courts speak in terms of the attorney-client privilege, they are really addressing the ethical obligation of confidentiality.

E. THE GRISLY CASE OF THE BURIED BODIES

In mid-August 1973, a man named Robert Garrow was charged with murder. Law enforcement authorities also concluded that Garrow had committed several other known murders and rapes, and suspected him of murdering two young women who were missing, but had insufficient evidence to charge him with those crimes.

Frank Armani, a Syracuse, New York sole practitioner who had previously represented Garrow in both civil and criminal matters, was appointed by the court to defend Garrow. A second lawyer named Belge was appointed as Armani's co-counsel. Armani and Belge advised Garrow that his only defense to the murder charge was insanity. They also advised him that he should tell them everything about himself, including any killings and rapes with which he had not been formally charged, so that they could develop evidence to back up the insanity plea.

In a momentous revelation, Garrow told the lawyers that he had murdered and dismembered the two missing girls. Garrow also told the lawyers where he had hidden the girls' mutilated bodies. On August 31, 1973, the lawyers found the bodies in the locations Garrow had described. The lawyers said nothing about their findings, even though the parents of one of the murdered girls met with Armani and pleaded with him to disclose whatever he knew about the missing girls. (After that meeting, Armani was so shaken and so afraid that he would reveal his client's secret that he refused to meet with the other girl's parents.) The bodies were not discovered until December 1973.

On direct examination at his trial in June 1974, Garrow admitted that he had committed three murders (including the murders of the two missing girls) and seven rapes in addition to the murder for which he was being tried. At the close of that day's proceedings, Belge held a press conference and revealed that he and Armani had known of the other murders and of the whereabouts of the two bodies since August 1973, but that their obligations to their client had prevented them from revealing that information, despite the pain this had caused themselves and others.

Garrow's defense of insanity was rejected and he was convicted of murder. Subsequently, Belge was indicted for violation of the New York Public Health Law, which requires anyone knowing of the death of a person without medical attendance to report it to the proper authorities. The County Court granted Belge's motion to dismiss the indictment, holding that the client's privilege against self-incrimination protected him from compulsory disclosure of the other murders, and that the lawyer-client privilege prohibited the lawyer from disclosing what his client had told him. The court stated:

> The effectiveness of counsel is only as great as the confidentiality of its client-attorney relationship. If the lawyer cannot get all the facts about the case, he can only give his client half of a defense. This, of necessity, involves the client telling his attorney everything remotely connected with the crime.

People v. Belge, 372 N.Y.S.2d 798, 801, 1975 N.Y. Misc. LEXIS 2874 (1975). The appellate court affirmed the dismissal of the indictment with a Memorandum Opinion:

> We affirm the Order of the Trial Court which properly dismissed the indictments laid against defendant for alleged violations of section 4200 (duty of a decent burial) and section 4143 (requirement to report death occurring without medical attendance) of the Public Health Law. We believe that the attorney-client privilege attached insofar as the communications were to advance a client's interests, and that the privilege effectively shielded the defendant-attorney from his actions which would otherwise have violated the Public Health Law.
>
> In view of the fact that the claim of absolute privilege was proffered, we note that the privilege is not all-encompassing and that in a given case there may be conflicting considerations. We believe that an attorney must protect his client's interests, but also must observe basic human standards of decency, having due regard to the need that the legal system accord justice to the interests of society and its individual members.
>
> We write to emphasize our serious concern regarding the consequences which emanate from a claim of an absolute attorney-client privilege. Because the only question presented, briefed and argued on this appeal was a legal one with respect to the sufficiency of the indictments, we limit our determination to that issue and do not reach the ethical questions underlying this case.

People v. Belge, 50 A.D.2d 1088, 376 N.Y.S.2d 771, 771–72, 1975 N.Y. App. Div. LEXIS 12121 (1975).

NOTES AND QUESTIONS

1. *Privilege vs. Confidentiality.* The opinions in *Belge* speak in terms of the attorney-client privilege. Is this accurate? Did anyone subpoena the defense lawyers to testify? No. The question is whether the lawyers could voluntarily have revealed the information about the other murders, without awaiting a court subpoena and a final order to testify. The *communications* in *Belge* were covered by the attorney-client privilege because the client (Garrow) communicated confidentially with counsel about the other murders for the purpose of obtaining counsel (the "5 Cs"), but Garrow's lawyers never *invoked* the attorney-client privilege, because they were never called to *testify*. The courts in *Belge* are really addressing the ethical obligation of confidentiality, not the attorney-client privilege.

The attorney-client privilege is formally invoked only when a court tries to compel a lawyer to reveal client information. The ethical obligation of confidentiality, in contrast, applies at all times. No court sought to compel Armani to reveal what he knew about the other murders. Rather, Armani had to struggle with whether to reveal the information voluntarily to the parents of the dead girls before trial. (At trial, he revealed the information voluntarily, as part of his client's insanity defense.)

Of course, there is a close relationship between the ethical obligation of confidentiality and the attorney-client privilege. A lawyer has an ethical obligation to claim the attorney-client privilege where applicable, and to keep secret all communications protected by the attorney-client privilege so that the privilege will not accidentally be waived. (Remember that the privilege protects communications — "My client told me X" — not the facts contained in those communications.) Thus, the ethical obligation of confidentiality prohibited Armani from voluntarily revealing communications protected by the attorney-client privilege and the information Armani learned from those communications.

Even if the communications about the dead bodies had not been privileged — for example, if the information about the dead bodies had come from a non-client, such as a local farmer — the ethical obligation of confidentiality would still have prohibited Armani from voluntarily revealing the information without his client's consent. That's another key difference between the attorney-client privilege and the ethical obligation of confidentiality. The ethical obligation applies to communications from any source, and to the information contained in those communications, whereas the privilege applies only to communications from a client.

2. ***Secrecy and Morality.*** Do you agree that the lawyers in *Belge* did nothing wrong by failing to reveal the whereabouts of the dead girls until after their client had testified at trial? If you disagree, is your disagreement based on a different reading of the rules of professional conduct, or on your moral sense of right and wrong? What should be the relationship between secrecy and morality? Phrased differently, what should be the role of your personal moral beliefs when you implement (or violate) the rules of legal ethics?

3. ***What to Tell the Client?*** Suppose Garrow had handed the lawyers a blood-stained knife and said, "Take this and don't let the police have it. It's covered by the privilege you told me about, isn't it?" Is Garrow right? Do the confidentiality rules permit lawyers to withhold physical evidence from the police? Do they require lawyers to do so? What would be the best rule?

4. ***What is "Consent"?*** Suppose that soon after the lawyers in *Belge* discovered the bodies, Garrow agreed that the lawyers could bolster his insanity defense by having Garrow testify about his other crimes, including the location of the bodies of the two missing girls. Could the lawyers still have remained silent about the bodies until the time of trial? Would Garrow's agreement to reveal the information at trial amount to "consent" to reveal it to the parents in advance of trial?

5. ***Danger to Others.*** Suppose a search party was engaging in a very hazardous search for the victims in *Belge*, at substantial peril to the searchers. (For example, suppose the bodies were buried high on a mountain and the search was being conducted during a winter storm.) Would that have made a difference in the lawyers' professional obligations to remain silent?

Or, consider a different kind of danger to others. Suppose another person was being prosecuted for committing one of the other murders (the ones Garrow was not charged with) and the prosecution's evidence made conviction of that person likely. If the lawyers learned from Garrow that he was the murderer, could they disclose what he had told them? Suppose someone else was convicted and Garrow told the lawyers after the conviction that he (Garrow) was the murderer?

6. ***Tapes and Photographs.*** Armani and Belge made tape recordings of their interviews with Garrow, and took photographs of the scene of the crime. The police did not have the tapes or photos. Could Armani and Belge properly destroy those tapes and photographs? Once created, are the tapes and photographs tangible evidence that must be preserved and perhaps handed over to the authorities? The answer is no. Physical evidence refers to things used in the commission of the crime, not the lawyer's records of the crime. Photographs and tapes made by a lawyer are equivalent to a lawyer's notes, and are considered work-product. They are not covered by the attorney-client

privilege (though tapes of confidential conversations with a client would be covered by the attorney-client privilege as well as work product), but they are not "physical evidence" and need not be turned over to the police.

7. ***What is "Information Relating to the Representation"?*** After Garrow's conviction, he escaped from state custody. One of his trial attorneys (who no longer represented him) advised authorities about Garrow's preferred method of hiding and likely whereabouts, basing that advice upon his interviews with Garrow during the previous representation. Did that advice violate the lawyer's ethical obligation of confidentiality? Why or why not? If not, should it?

F. THREE PROBLEMS TO CONSIDER

Problem 1

Ron Green was accused of murdering his wife, who was found stabbed to death in their home. The police thoroughly searched the home and the abandoned farm house where a trail of blood led to the defendant, but were unable to find the murder weapon. Before a scheduled appointment with the state's medical expert who would conduct a psychiatric examination in connection with Green's diminished capacity defense, Green told his lawyers that he had hidden the knife in a pile of automotive parts under the basement steps of his house, which the police had missed. Green's lawyers did not take possession of the knife, but they are afraid that not telling the police the location of the knife is concealment and obstruction of the investigation. They are worried that they have an ethical obligation to disclose the location of the knife to the prosecution. Given the extensive search of the house that has already occurred, Green's lawyers think it is highly unlikely that the police will conduct a second search of the house. His lawyers also think that if Green tells the police where to find the knife, the jury will find him to be more credible.

a. Are Green's lawyers obstructing the investigation if they do not tell the police the location of the knife?
b. What options do they have?
c. Which course of action would you choose and why?
d. Is it proper for Green's lawyers to take into account the effect telling or failing to tell will have on their reputation with the prosecutor or the court?

Problem 2

An investigator for Geoff Melnick, the lawyer defending Douglas Doley in a capital case, discovered during trial that the defendant had written a letter to his brother which contained threats against others (presumably including the murder victim). The investigator obtained the letter from the defendant's mother and gave it to lawyer Melnick. When the lawyer saw that the letter contained threats against others, he asked the State Bar Advisory Committee whether he had an obligation to report the threats. After being told that he should report, Melnick read the letter to the judge presiding over the trial. The judge called the police and Melnick told a detective "the salient facts in the letter so that the detective could understand the nature, severity and breadth of the threats contained in the letter." The court granted Melnick's motion to withdraw as defense counsel.

Subsequently, Melnick resisted a grand jury subpoena directing him to appear and bring with him any letters or writings purportedly authored by the defendant which "led to or served as a basis for [the defendant's] trial counsel requesting leave to withdraw as trial counsel." When Melnick's motions to quash were denied, he was held in civil contempt for refusing to comply with the subpoena.

The court of appeals affirmed the order requiring that Melnick give the document to the grand jury. The issue is now on appeal to the highest court in the state, and you are a law clerk for one of the justices.

a. How would you analyze the issues in your bench memo for the judge?
b. What difference would it make if the case were decided under the Model Code of Professional Conduct rather than the Model Rules?

Problem 3

Six months before his trial for murdering his wife, Boyd gave his attorney a note that he said was a suicide note written by his late wife. The note was addressed to their daughter and read:

> Dear Suzanne,
>
> I am sorry I ruined your wedding. Your dad told me about your concerns of interfering in Jenalu's and the possibility that I might ruin hers. I won't be there, so put your mind at ease. You will understand after the wedding is done. I love you all. Mom

a. Is this note information relating to the representation of a client that is protected under the Duty of Confidentiality?
b. Should the note be produced in response to the court's reciprocal discovery order, or can it be withheld on attorney-client privilege grounds?

Chapter 10

EXCEPTIONS TO THE ETHICAL DUTY OF CONFIDENTIALITY

We have studied the general principles of secrecy, including the details of the scope and strength of the ethical duty of confidentiality, the attorney-client privilege, and the work product doctrine. In this chapter we will study exceptions to the ethical duty of confidentiality. These exceptions are vitally important. Rules that prohibit disclosure deprive society of information — information that might help solve crimes, resolve disputes, or increase the fairness of transactions. The stronger the secrecy rules are (i.e., the harder they are to overcome), the more information is kept from courts, business partners, and society in general. The weaker the secrecy rules are, the less is kept private from others. We therefore need to craft exceptions that strike a balance between the interests of clients and the interests of society (i.e., the public), taking into account all of the competing interests and concerns.

In every U.S. jurisdiction, the rule of confidentiality has two components: (1) a basic definition of what is covered by the mantle of secrecy (i.e., what a lawyer must keep secret absent an exception), and (2) a list of exceptions that permit or require a lawyer to disclose otherwise protected information. Given this dichotomy, there is no need to speak of a "waiver" of the ethical obligation of confidentiality. A given piece of information either may (or must) be disclosed or it must not be disclosed. But clients are always free to disclose confidential information themselves, or to give informed consent to their lawyer's disclosure of the confidential information.

As we have already seen, the scope of the information protected by the basic definition of ABA Model Rule 1.6 is enormous — under Rule 1.6, a lawyer is prohibited from revealing any information "relating to the representation of a client" unless an exception applies. This is even broader than DR 4-101(A) in the old ABA Model Code, which protected all "confidences" and "secrets," meaning all information protected by the attorney-client privilege, as well as all other information gained in the professional relationship that the client instructed the lawyer to keep secret or the disclosure of which would be embarrassing or detrimental to the client.

Because the basic definition of protected information is very broad in every jurisdiction, the real questions in determining the strength of the duty of confidentiality are:

- What are the exceptions to the ethical duty of confidentiality? In other words, when do the rules permit (or require) disclosure of protected information?
- What is the scope of each exception? What does each one encompass and exclude?

Parallel questions surround the attorney-client privilege. The basic definition of the attorney-client privilege has been well established for centuries, but the means of waiving the attorney-client privilege and the exceptions to the attorney-client privilege are still evolving.

In this chapter, we will review and discuss the exceptions to the ethical duty of confidentiality. Later, in a separate chapter, we will turn to waivers and exceptions under the attorney-client privilege.

A. EXCEPTIONS TO THE DUTY OF CONFIDENTIALITY

There are thirteen exceptions to the attorney's duty of confidentiality. Nine of them are found in the language of Model Rule 1.6. The other four are found in Rules 1.9, 1.13, 3.3(a), and 3.3 (b). Here is the list, followed by a discussion of each of the exceptions in more detail.

1. Obtaining client's informed consent;
2. Having implied authority;
3. Preventing reasonably certain death or substantial bodily harm;
4. Preventing a *client* from committing a crime or fraud reasonably certain to substantially injure another's financial interests or property when the client has used (or is using) the lawyer's services to further the crime or fraud;
5. Preventing, mitigating or rectifying substantial injury to financial interests or property that is reasonably certain to result at some point in the future (or has already resulted) from client's crime or fraud *if* the client has used lawyer's services to further the crime or fraud;
6. Obtaining legal advice about a lawyer's own compliance with the rules of professional conduct;
7. Defending against allegations related to a representation or bringing a claim against a client;
8. Complying with other law;
9. Complying with a court order;
10. Dealing with information that has become generally known after the representation has ended;
11. Dealing with false evidence that has been offered to a tribunal;
12. Acting when the lawyer knows of criminal or fraudulent conduct related to a proceeding before a tribunal; and
13. Dealing with a clear violation of law to prevent substantial injury to the organization (when the client is an organization).

The first nine exceptions listed above are contained in ABA Model Rule 1.6, which is one of the most important rules of professional responsibility. We are not permitted to reprint ABA Model Rules without copyright permission, but fortunately Delaware has adopted ABA Model Rule 1.6 verbatim. Thus, Delaware Rule 1.6 provides as follows:

DELAWARE RULE 1.6 CONFIDENTIALITY OF INFORMATION

(a) A lawyer shall not reveal information relating to the representation of a client unless the client gives informed consent, the disclosure is impliedly authorized in order to carry out the representation or the disclosure is permitted by paragraph (b).

(b) A lawyer may reveal information relating to the representation of a client to the extent the lawyer reasonably believes necessary:

(1) to prevent reasonably certain death or substantial bodily harm;

(2) to prevent the client from committing a crime or fraud that is reasonably certain to result in substantial injury to the financial interests or property of another and in furtherance of which the client has used or is using the lawyer's services;

(3) to prevent, mitigate or rectify substantial injury to the financial interests or property of another that is reasonably certain to result or has resulted from the client's commission of a crime or fraud in furtherance of which the client has used the lawyer's services;

(4) to secure legal advice about the lawyer's compliance with these Rules;

(5) to establish a claim or defense on behalf of the lawyer in a controversy between the lawyer and the client, to establish a defense to a criminal charge or civil claim against the lawyer based upon conduct in which the client was involved, or to respond to allegations in any proceeding concerning the lawyer's representation of the client; or

(6) to comply with other law or a court order.

We will not try to cover all of the exceptions to Rule 1.6 in depth. Instead, we will say something about each exception, then look at the key exceptions in more detail.

1. ***Client gives informed consent under Rule 1.6(a).*** In every jurisdiction, a lawyer may reveal information covered by the ethical obligation of confidentiality if the client consents after full disclosure. This means the lawyer must explain to the client exactly what the lawyer intends to disclose and how the disclosure is likely to affect the client.

For example, suppose a lawyer represents a manufacturer that sells machines to factory owners. One factory owner who bought machines has now filed a civil suit alleging that the manufacturer (your client) breached a contract to supply machines to make squirt guns. Specifically, the buyer alleges that the machines don't do what was promised. Your client initially denied the allegations and said the machines work fine but the buyer just doesn't know how to use them. Recently, however, your client changed his story. He now tells you that the machines don't do what was promised because the buyer changed the specifications for the machines at the last minute. The client also appears to be a bit apologetic, saying "You may want to relay to the customer that those last-minute changes confused us, but we can fix the machines quickly."

You do not have implied authority to concede that the machines aren't working right because that admission would probably harm your client. (As we explain below, you never have implied authority to disclose information that would harm your client. You may have express authority under another exception, but implied authority does not exist unless disclosure would help your client.) You, therefore, cannot disclose the problem to the buyer unless you get your client's informed consent. To do that, you need to explain to your client the content of the proposed disclosure and the advantages and disadvantages of making the disclosure. For example, you have to explain whether the attorney-client privilege will be waived, or whether any other negative consequences will result, if you disclose that the machines have a problem but can easily be fixed. You should also explain what will happen if you do *not* make the disclosure. Here, the buyer may later find out the same information in a deposition, after the litigation has grown more hostile and more expensive. Telling the client about these consequences isn't just necessary to get truly "informed consent," it's also good counseling.

2. ***Implied authority — Rule 1.6(a).*** A lawyer may reveal information covered by the ethical duty of confidentiality if the lawyer is "impliedly authorized" to do so. (The old ABA Model Code does not expressly mention implied authority, see DR 4-101.) A lawyer has implied authority under Rule 1.6(a) only if (1) the disclosures are required by the rules of procedure, or (2) the disclosures will help the client, not hurt the client. A lawyer *never* has implied authority to disclose information harmful to the client. Informed consent or express authority from another exception is needed to disclose information harmful to your client. Moreover, you *never* have implied authority to override a client's express instructions not to disclose. As Comment 5 to ABA Model Rule 1.6 states: "*Except to the extent that the client's instructions or special circumstances limit that authority*, a lawyer is impliedly authorized to make disclosures about a client when appropriate in carrying out the representation."

The most common example of implied authority is that a lawyer generally is impliedly authorized to reveal facts that will help the client in negotiations. If a lawyer is negotiating about an auto accident and the client has told the lawyer that the client had a green light, the lawyer may tell the opposing lawyer that the client had a green light, because that will help achieve the client's goals.

A lawyer also generally has implied authority to turn over documents responsive to a legitimate request for production of documents in pending litigation. However, if disclosing certain documents would be harmful to the client, then the lawyer should consult with the client before producing them. The client might prefer to settle (or even default or dismiss the suit) rather than produce damaging documents.

3. ***To prevent reasonably certain death or substantial bodily harm — Rule 1.6(b)(1).*** The duty to keep information relating to the representation of a client confidential is one of a lawyer's most fundamental duties, and the drafters of the rules did not lightly include exceptions. As originally adopted in 1983, Rule 1.6(b)(1) permitted

a lawyer to reveal information protected by Rule 1.6 only to the extent the lawyer reasonably believed necessary to "prevent the *client* from committing a *criminal* act that the lawyer believes is likely to result in *imminent* death or substantial bodily harm." (Emphasis added.) Many people thought this formulation was too restrictive, and in 2002 the ABA amended the rule to eliminate the three italicized requirements (client, criminal, imminent). The current rule requires only that the disclosure be designed to prevent reasonably certain death or substantial bodily harm. The act that causes harm no longer needs to be an act of the client. It can be an act by anyone. The act no longer needs to be a criminal act. It can be any type of act (e.g., violation of an environmental law) as long as the act is reasonably certain to kill or seriously injure someone. And the harm no longer needs to be imminent as long as it is reasonably certain. However, the disclosure may still be no broader than the lawyer reasonably believes necessary to prevent the future harm.

For example, suppose a lawyer is representing a defendant who is charged with plotting terrorist acts, and the lawyer learns from her client, while investigating an important defense witness, that the witness, Mr. Gray, is plotting a truck bomb attack on a government building during working hours. Furthermore, she learns that the witness has masterminded three other bombings of federal buildings in the past two years, and is funded by a foreign terrorist organization. What, if anything, would the lawyer be permitted to disclose? Under the language of Model Rule 1.6(b)(1), the lawyer may disclose only the information necessary to prevent the truck bombing now being planned. The lawyer may not disclose the witness's past crimes or his source of funding, because that information is not necessary to prevent a future death or to prevent the occurrence of substantial bodily injury. Model Rule 1.6(b)(1) does not authorize the disclosure of past crimes, no matter how violent. And note that Model Rule 1.6(b)(1) never mandates disclosure. Under Model Rule 1.6, disclosure always remains in the discretion of the lawyer, even when the disclosure will prevent certain death.

4. ***To prevent the client from committing a crime or fraud that is reasonably certain to result in substantial injury to the financial interests or property of another and in furtherance of which the client has used or is using the lawyer's services — Rule 1.6(b)(2).*** As just discussed, Rule 1.6(b)(1) applies whenever death or serious bodily harm is reasonably certain to result from any source or cause — client or nonclient, criminal or noncriminal — but it does not allow disclosure in situations that involve only financial or property harm. Rule 1.6(b)(2) was added in 2003 to fill that gap, but it was a highly controversial addition to the rules, and passed the ABA House of Delegates by a narrow margin.

Moreover, the exception itself is narrow. Rule 1.6(b)(2) applies only when the *client* is *using (or has used) the lawyer's services* to commit a future *crime or fraud* that will almost *certainly* harm someone else's *property* substantially or cost someone a lot of *money*. It does not give a lawyer authority to report the client's intended misconduct that does *not* rise to the level of crime or fraud, or to reveal a client's crime or fraud that *might* injure another person's property or finances but is not reasonably certain to do so, or to reveal a client's intention to commit a crime or fraud which will be accomplished without using the lawyer's services, or to reveal a client's intention to commit a crime or fraud that will cause only minor injury to money or property, or to reveal information protected by Rule 1.6(a) (i.e., related to the representation of a client) about a *nonclient's* intention to commit a crime or fraud that will injure another person's property or finances. Like every exception to confidentiality, Rule 1.6(b)(2) gives authority to disclose only when every element of the rule is met.

5. ***To prevent, mitigate or rectify substantial injury to the financial interests or property of another that is reasonably certain to result or has resulted from the client's commission of a crime or fraud in furtherance of which the client has used the lawyer's services — Rule 1.6 (b)(3).*** This exception was also added to the ABA Model Rules in August of 2003, and also by a narrow margin. It overlaps Rule 1.6(b)(2)

with respect to preventing a client from using the lawyer' services to commit a crime or fraud that is reasonably certain to injure another's financial or property interests, but it goes much further. Even if the client has already committed the crime or fraud, and even if the harm has already occurred, Rule 1.6(b)(3) authorizes a lawyer to disclose the information necessary to mitigate or rectify the harm. Indeed, even if the client has already committed the crime or fraud but the harm has not yet occurred, the lawyer may reveal information necessary to prevent the harm. Thus, this exception would come into play if the client had used an opinion letter or a contract written by the lawyer to accomplish a fraud. If the lawyer's services were not used by the client to further the client's crime or fraud, then this exception to the duty of confidentiality does not apply. When the exception does not apply, the lawyer cannot disclose information to people defrauded by the client, the prosecutor, the local investigative journalist or anyone else.

6. ***To secure legal advice about the lawyer's compliance with these Rules — Rule 1.6 (b)(4).*** Lawyers sometimes need to consult other lawyers to determine whether their own conduct complies with applicable standards. But until 2002, Model Rule 1.6 did not contain an explicit exception permitting an attorney to consult another lawyer. Of course, lawyers were permitted to do so with a client's informed consent, but obtaining consent was often impractical, either because the client was the source of the problem (e.g., the lawyer needed advice about what the rules required if the client was engaged in an ongoing fraud), or because the lawyer wanted legal advice about the rules before talking to the client about a particular problem (e.g., a possible conflict of interest, or the lawyer's desire to withdraw from a matter because of client misconduct).

Before the 2002 amendments, many lawyers sought ethics advice from other lawyers without client consent based on hoped-for interpretations of Rule 1.6. These situations were often grounded in necessity, the common practice of using hypotheticals, and the custom of the profession. Still, lawyers often had an uneasy feeling. Model Rule 1.6 now includes an explicit exception allowing lawyers to secure legal advice about whether they are complying with the ethics rules.

7. ***Lawyer's claim or self-defense — Rule 1.6(b)(5).*** Rule 1.6(b)(5), the so-called "self-defense" exception to the duty of confidentiality, permits a lawyer to reveal information relating to representation of a client to the extent the lawyer reasonably believes "necessary," in any of three situations:

- *to establish a claim or defense on behalf of the lawyer in a controversy between the lawyer and the client:* This category would include bringing a lawsuit against a client to collect unpaid legal fees, or defending against a client's suit accusing the lawyer of legal malpractice.
- *to establish a defense to a criminal charge or civil claim against the lawyer based upon conduct in which the client was involved:* This category would include situations such as a criminal indictment accusing the lawyer of conspiring with the client to commit a crime, or a civil complaint accusing the lawyer of committing securities law violations while preparing SEC filings for the client.
- *to respond to allegations in any proceeding concerning the lawyer's representation of the client:* This category permits a lawyer to respond to allegations in any kind of legal proceeding, be it a grand jury proceeding, a civil trial, a disciplinary proceeding, or any other type of legal proceeding. It applies even if the lawyer is not a party to the proceeding. Moreover, a lawyer need not wait for formal charges to be filed against him before disclosing the information necessary to defend himself. Under Rule 1.6, the lawyer may disclose as soon as he feels threatened by the likelihood that charges will be filed against him — see Rule 1.6, Comment 10.

In all instances of self-defense, the disclosure must be no broader than necessary for the lawyer to prevail in a dispute with the client or to successfully defend against civil or criminal charges or against allegations made in some other type of formal legal proceeding.

8. ***Other law — Rule 1.6(b)(6)*** also permits a lawyer to reveal confidential information to comply with other law. Other law might include Securities and Exchange Commission rules requiring a lawyer to disclose evidence of fraud to the SEC, or a statute requiring a person to report bank-currency transactions exceeding a specific dollar amount. The "other law" exception does not necessarily override the ethical duty of confidentiality. In fact, the clarity of the asserted law's intent affects whether a lawyer has a duty to consult with the client about the disclosure. Comment 12 to Rule 1.6 of the Indiana Rules of Professional Conduct, which is identical to Comment 12 to ABA Model Rule 1.6, explains it this way:

> [12] Other law may require that a lawyer disclose information about a client. Whether such a law supersedes Rule 1.6 is a question of law. . . . When disclosure of information appears to be required by other law, the lawyer must discuss the matter with the client. . . . If, however, the other law supersedes this Rule and requires disclosure, paragraph (b)(6) permits the lawyer to make such disclosures as are necessary to comply with the law.

Thus, when a lawyer perceives that a statute, court rule, or some other source of law outside the rules of professional conduct requires disclosure of information covered by Rule 1.6, the lawyer must confer with the client about the legal requirement of disclosure, the implications of disclosure, and how to make the disclosure in compliance with the law. Note that both the text and Comment to Rule 1.6(b)(6) authorize disclosure only where other law *requires* such disclosure, not merely where such disclosure is *permitted* by law. The text of Rule 1.6(b)(6) authorizes disclosure only to comply with other law, and Comment 12 says that if other law requires disclosure, then paragraph (b)(6) permits disclosures necessary to comply with the law. For example, if a statute has been enacted requiring U.S. residents, including lawyers, to report information relating to past bombings of federal buildings, the statute would constitute "other law." Thus, it would impact the lawyer's handling of the information about Mr. Gray, which we discussed earlier.

9. ***Court order — Rule 1.6(b)(6).*** Rule 1.6(b)(6) permits (but, curiously, does not require) a lawyer to reveal confidential information to comply with a court order. For example, a court might order a lawyer to testify or to turn over certain documents after the court has ruled that the documents are not covered by the attorney-client privilege. The lawyer has the right to appeal the disclosure order before complying, but if the order is upheld on appeal, or if the lawyer does not appeal, the lawyer "may" reveal the information necessary to comply with the court order even though the information would otherwise be protected under Rule 1.6(a). (Of course, if the lawyer decides not to reveal the information called for by the court order, the lawyer may be punished for contempt of court, but the lawyer would not be violating Rule 1.6(b)(6) because Rule 1.6 merely permits disclosure, never mandates it.)

Conversely, if a lawyer is called as a witness to give testimony concerning a client, then (unless the client has given the lawyer informed consent to waive the privilege) Rule 1.6(a) requires the lawyer to remain silent unless and until a court orders the lawyer to disclose, thus providing grounds for the exception in Rule 1.6(b)(6).

That completes the catalog of exceptions to the ethical duty of confidentiality articulated in Rule 1.6, but it does not complete the catalog of situations in which a lawyer may disclose information "relating to the representation of a client." In addition to the exceptions within Rule 1.6 itself, three other Model Rules trump Rule 1.6, adding four more distinct exceptions:

10. ***Information that became generally known after a representation ended — Rule 1.9(c).*** When a lawyer and client have ended their attorney-client relationship, Rule 1.9(c) provides that the former client's confidential information continues to be protected by Rule 1.6 *unless* the information has become "generally known." Thus, if information that was once protected by Rule 1.6 becomes generally known, an attorney may freely disclose the information. (Some would argue, based on custom and policy,

that the generally known exception also applies to current clients as well, and is thus another exception to the duty of confidentiality, but the text of Rule 1.6 does not expressly contain any exception for information that is generally known.)

11. *False evidence offered to a tribunal — Rule 3.3(a)(3).* Model Rule 1.6 never mandates disclosure, but Model Rule 3.3 sometimes does. Rule 3.3 prohibits a lawyer from offering evidence that the lawyer "knows" to be false. Rule 3.3 (a) (3) also discusses what a lawyer must do if the lawyer finds out, after the fact, that a client or a witness called by the lawyer (not by another party) has testified falsely, or that an exhibit offered into evidence by the lawyer is false, and efforts to remedy the problem without disclosure to the court have failed or would be futile. Under Rule 3.3(a)(3), the lawyer must take reasonable remedial measures, including, if necessary, disclosure to the tribunal. Thus, if a lawyer learns that the client (or any other witness called by the lawyer) has committed perjury, Rule 3.3 (a) requires the lawyer to disclose the perjury to the tribunal unless the lawyer can correct the problem in some other manner. Rule 3.3(c) makes clear that the duty to disclose perjury under Rule 3.3 applies *even if* compliance requires disclosure of information otherwise protected by Rule 1.6. (We later devote an entire chapter to the complex problem of perjury as part of the materials about the adversary system.)

12. *Criminal or fraudulent conduct related to proceedings before a tribunal — Rule 3.3 (b).* If a lawyer representing a client in an adjudicative proceeding who knows that any person (client, opposing party, or otherwise) intends to engage, is engaging, or has engaged in criminal or fraudulent conduct relating to the proceeding, shall take reasonable remedial measures, including, if necessary, disclosure to the tribunal. Rule 3.3(b) in its present form was added to the Model Rules in 2002 as part of the sweeping Ethics 2000 changes. Rule 3.3(b) complements paragraph (a) by providing that if a lawyer (i) represents a client in an adjudicative proceeding and (ii) knows that a person intends to engage, is engaging or has engaged in criminal or fraudulent conduct related to the proceeding, then the lawyer "shall take reasonable remedial measures, *including, if necessary, disclosure to the tribunal.* (Emphasis added.)

Thus, where other remedial measures have failed or would be futile, Rule 3.3(b) *requires* disclosure to the tribunal whenever a lawyer learns that *any* "person" — client, friendly witness, or hostile witness, another lawyer, a juror, or a complete stranger — *intends* to commit a fraud or crime relating to the proceeding (e.g., bribing a juror, intimidating a witness, or falsifying evidence), or is currently engaging in such misconduct, or has already engaged in such conduct. In other words, Rule 3.3(b) covers past, present, and future crimes or frauds by any person in connection with the proceeding. Rule 3.3(b) thus overlaps Rule 3.3(a)(3) as to *past* perjury, but adds obligations to remedy present or future perjury as well as other crimes and frauds that can damage the integrity of a trial, hearing, or other adjudicative proceeding in which the lawyer represents a client.

Sometimes a lawyer can effectively remedy these wrongs (especially intended wrongs that have not yet been committed) by methods short of disclosing information protected by Rule 1.6. But to make sure we understand that a lawyer has to abide by Rule 3.3(b) even if the wrongdoing can only be remedied by violating Rule 1.6, Model Rule 3.3(c) provides that the duties stated in paragraphs (a) and (b) apply *even if* compliance requires disclosure of information otherwise protected by Rule 1.6.

13. *When the client is an organization, a clear violation of law may be revealed to prevent substantial injury to the organization — Rule 1.13.* The ABA amended Rule 1.13(b) in August of 2003 in the wake of the scandals at Enron, WorldCom, Adelphia, and other large corporations. Basically, Rule 1.13(b)(b) provides that when a lawyer for an organization knows that a corporate officer or employee is engaged in illegal conduct that reasonably might be imputed to the organization and is likely to result in substantial injury to the organization, the lawyer must take steps to put a stop to the wrongful conduct. Ordinarily, this requires the lawyer to report up the ladder within the organization, all the way to the organization's highest authority if the situation is serious enough. Before the 2003 amendments, if a lawyer climbed all the way up the ladder, but still could not stop the wrongful conduct, Rule 1.13 gave the lawyer the right to resign (i.e., withdraw) but not to report the misconduct outside the organization. The 2003 amendment changed Rule 1.13 (c) to give a lawyer permission to report the wrongdoing to authorities outside the organization (such as the Securities and Exchange Commission or the District Attorney) *whether or not Rule 1.6 permits such disclosure*, but only if, and to the extent the lawyer reasonably believes necessary, to prevent substantial injury to the organization. Note that the lawyer is allowed but not required to "report out." The discretion to report out exists only, to the extent the lawyer reasonably believes necessary, to prevent substantial injury to the organization. Rule 1.13 is one of the most complex rules in the Model Rules, and we will study it in depth later.

That ends our brief catalogue of the thirteen exceptions to the ethical obligation of confidentiality. Now let's apply them to some situations.

B. ANOTHER SECRECY SCENARIO: "IS IT IN THE GENES"?

You should now have enough information from this book and from the relevant ABA Model Rules and other ethics rules to answer questions based on a scenario about confidential information and its exceptions. Here is the scenario and the questions:

Basic background: You are representing a client, Bree O'Dell, a talented biologist who has been offered a new job as Vice President for Product Development at Bios-Fear, a Boston-based company that genetically engineers crops like corn and switch grass to make them more efficient as fuels. (The company's advertising slogans are "Get more miles to the bushel" and "Grow out of your oil addiction!") Dr. O'Dell is a prize catch for Bios-Fear because she has an M.B.A. from Wharton, plus high-level business experience as an executive at Geneering (an innovative biotech company with steadily growing profits), plus a Ph.D. in Molecular Biology from MIT, which is a unique combination. She probably has the best resume you've ever seen as an employment lawyer. Most people don't hire a lawyer to negotiate an employment contract, but this contract will be well into six figures (they're talking in the $500,000 range), with a lot of benefits, so it's worth Dr. O'Dell's money to hire you to negotiate the package. (You are charging her your usual hourly rate, which is $350 per hour.)

Yesterday you met with Dr. O'Dell for a couple of hours to find out all about what she wants, doesn't want, and doesn't care about. For example, Dr. O'Dell told you that she wants the company to give her an interest-free mortgage on the new home she plans to buy. (She's already picked out a four bedroom colonial in Newton.) She has two kids in college right now (one at Cornell and the other at N.Y.U.) and she can't afford a bank mortgage on such a big house. She also needs family health coverage because her husband lost his job (and his benefits) as an executive at Computer Associates after the government investigations revealed wrongdoing there. (Her husband wasn't indicted, but some of the improper practices took place on his watch.) She also wants at least a $1.2 million budget for a new research lab to pursue her own particular interests in biotechnology research.

She told you her bottom line on salary is $400,000. She'd like to earn north of $500,000, partly for the prestige, but she's thrilled to be offered a position that combines her three great loves — biology, business, and the Boston Red Sox. She would, therefore, be willing to accept a salary of as little as $400,000 (plus benefits, of course). Finally, she said she wanted the company to lease a car for her but didn't care what kind. "I'm not a car buff," she said. "I could get around in a 1972 Datsun with the floor boards missing if I had to — I did it in college."

This afternoon, you're meeting with Bios-Fear's General Counsel to hammer out the details of Dr. O'Dell's contract.

Question 1. Initial Meeting with O'Dell

When you meet with Bios-Fear's General Counsel, may you disclose any of the following information absent express consent from your client?

(1) *Dr. O'Dell wants the company to give her an interest-free mortgage*
(2) *She has already picked out a four bedroom house in Newton (a tony suburb close to Boston).*
(3) *She has two kids in college and can't really afford a commercial mortgage on a big house now.*
(4) *She needs family health coverage because her husband lost his job as an executive at Computer Associates.*
(5) *She wants at least a $1.2 million budget for her own science laboratory.*
(6) *She'd like to earn at least $500,000 at Bios-Fear.*
(7) *The minimum salary she'll accept is $400,000.*
(8) *She's thrilled to be offered a position that combines her two great loves, biology and business.*
(9) *She wants a company car.*
(10) *She doesn't care what kind of car the company gives her.*
(11) *She's a big Boston Red Sox fan.*

Question 2. O'Dell's Consent

A) *If you think you are not permitted to reveal any of the items in Question 1 without express client consent, may you reveal them if you obtain Dr. O'Dell's informed consent?*
B) *What would you have to tell the client to obtain her informed consent?*

Additional background: Your meeting with Bios-Fear's General Counsel went well. You reached a tentative agreement on most of the terms and are now translating the basic terms into specific contract language. During one of your many phone calls and meetings with Dr. O'Dell regarding the specific terms, she mentions to you that at her current science lab, which is studying immunization against anthrax, the lab lost track of a container filled with a relatively pure strain of anthrax. This just happened a few weeks ago and has not yet been reported to any government or law enforcement agency because her current employer (Geneering) is still hoping to find the missing anthrax and doesn't want to spook the stock market or the public unnecessarily. However, a regulation jointly promulgated by the Environmental Protection Agency ("EPA") and the Food and Drug Administration ("FDA") requires any person with knowledge of missing anthrax to report that knowledge to the EPA or the FDA immediately.

Question 3. The Lost Anthrax

A) *May (or must) you disclose that Geneering (or Dr. O'Dell's lab there) has lost track of a container of anthrax?*
B) *If you are not sure what to do, may you ask another lawyer in your firm what you may or must do to comply with your ethical obligations or other law?*
C) *If no lawyer in your firm is an ethics expert, may you call an ethics expert from outside the firm to advise you?*

Additional background: When you Google Dr. O'Dell to help you learn more about her extraordinary credentials, you cannot find any reference to her Ph.D. at MIT. In a rather tense meeting, she admits to you that she did not actually receive a Ph.D. from MIT, but has an "ABD" degree ("all but dissertation"). "Please don't tell anyone," she pleads with you, "My research track record is extraordinary, and it doesn't make any difference what my education was. What matters is my ability, and I've proven that."

Question 4. No Ph.D.

A) *May (or must) you reveal to anyone that Dr. O'Dell never actually received a Ph.D. from MIT?*

B) *If so, who?*

Additional background: Assume now that you did not learn about Dr. O'Dell's lack of a Ph.D. until after all of the terms of the employment contract were agreed upon and executed, and Dr. O'Dell had been working at Bios-Fear for about six months. You also learned, after your attorney-client relationship with her ended, that Dr. O'Dell was fired from her job at Geneering for improper scientific research practices before she began negotiating with Bios-Fear. You have finished all of your legal work for Dr. O'Dell and she is now a former client.

Question 5. After your Representation is Complete

A) *May (or must) you reveal to anyone that Dr. O'Dell never actually received a Ph.D. from MIT, or that she was fired from her job at Geneering?*

B) *If so, who?*

Additional background: Suppose you did not tell anyone about any of the negative things you found out about Dr. O'Dell, but out of curiosity you spent a lot of time on-line finding out more about the talented Dr. O'Dell. Then an investigative reporter for *Newsweek* found out the truth about Dr. O'Dell (not from you) and wrote about the true story in a major piece in *Newsweek*. The press is excited but skeptical about the *Newsweek* story, so some reporters come to you for additional information.

Question 6. The Newsweek Story

A) *May you confirm to the press which details of the Newsweek story are true?*

B) *May you tell reporters additional facts that you learned from Dr. O'Dell when she was your client?*

C) *May you reveal new information that you have found through your own investigation and through hours of Internet surfing?*

Additional background: Because Bios-Fear was impressed with your skill and professionalism when you represented Dr. O'Dell in the employment contract negotiations, Bios-Fear hired you to represent the company in various employment law matters. One of your assignments is to develop a policy for retaining employment records of current and former employees. During your work on this project, one of the employees tells you that he is going to destroy or alter all of Dr. O'Dell's employment records at Bios-Fear so that the company "doesn't look stupid" when people find out that the company fell hook, line, and sinker for her claim to have a Ph.D. from MIT and for her other lies and deceptions. You counsel this employee not to destroy the records, but he says he is going to do it "for the good of the company."

Question 7. Your Representation of Bios-Fear

A) *May (or must) you reveal to the employee's supervisors, or to Bios-Fear's Board of Directors, that the employee plans to alter or destroy Dr. O'Dell's employment records?*

B) *May (or must) you reveal that information to the District Attorney, the stockholders of Bios-Fear, or anyone else outside the company?*

Additional background: Regrettably, Dr. O'Dell did not pay the full amount of your bill when you represented her in negotiating her employment contract. After sending her numerous reminder letters, and after she declined to participate in a fee arbitration proceeding (which some jurisdictions require lawyers to offer before filing a suit against a client for fees), you file a suit against Dr. O'Dell for the balance due on your legal fee bill.

Question 8. The Fee Dispute

A) May you reveal any confidential information in your Complaint seeking legal fees? If so, what information may you reveal?

B) Do you have to ask the court for permission to file the Complaint under seal?

Additional background: Dr. O'Dell was forced out of her job by Bios-Fear soon after the *Newsweek* story broke. She has now sued you for legal malpractice, alleging that the employment contract you negotiated did not have enough job security and did not provide sufficient severance pay or continuation of benefits in the event she was fired.

Question 9. O'Dell's Malpractice Suit

A) May you reveal any confidential information to defend yourself against the legal malpractice charges?

B) Is there any confidential information that you may not reveal in order to defend yourself?

Additional background: The anthrax container from Dr. O'Dell's lab at Geneering was eventually found in the hands of an Idaho-based anti-government militia named McVeigh's Posse. When the FBI asked Dr. O'Dell who else knew about the missing anthrax before the government found out about it, she named you. Consequently, you have been called to testify before a federal grand jury looking into the entire matter. You are not yet a grand jury target, however (meaning that the prosecutor is not directly investigating possible wrongdoing by you).

Question 10. The Grand Jury I

When you testify before the grand jury, may you reveal confidential information about Dr. O'Dell?

Additional background: After the grand jury investigated the anthrax incident for awhile, you were notified that you were now a target of the investigation. (That's probably the scariest thing that can happen to a lawyer.) You are once again summoned to testify before the grand jury. Grand jury work is not something employment lawyers should dabble in, and you don't want a fool for a client, so you of course hire a lawyer to defend you.

Question 11. The Grand Jury II

May you reveal confidential information about Dr. O'Dell to your lawyer for purposes of obtaining the best possible legal defense?

Additional background: The grand jury decides not to indict you for anything but does indict Dr. O'Dell for obstruction of justice based on her failure to disclose the missing anthrax. Dr. O'Dell hires the famous and feared criminal defense lawyer Connie Jochran to defend her. The case soon goes to trial. During a break in the trial, Ms. Jochran overhears Dr. O'Dell say to her brother-in-law, "Offer the tall juror with the moustache $20,000 to hold out for an acquittal," and she hands him a stack of $100 bills. The brother-in-law stashes the bills in his coat pocket and says, "Consider it done."

Question 12. Attempted Bribery

May (or must) Ms. Jochran disclose to the court that Dr. O'Dell and her bother-in-law are planning to bribe a juror?

Additional background: During Dr. O'Dell's testimony at the anthrax trial, she falsely testifies that she promptly ordered her subordinates to report the anthrax incident as soon as she learned about it and that they told her they had done so. Ms. Jochran at first thought this was true, but later in the trial came to know that it was false.

Question 13. O'Dell's Testimony

May (or must) Ms. Jochran reveal to the court that Dr. O'Dell has testified falsely?

Chapter 11
EXCEPTIONS TO THE ATTORNEY-CLIENT PRIVILEGE

A. COMPARISON WITH EXCEPTIONS TO CONFIDENTIALITY

In an earlier chapter, we identified thirteen separate and distinct exceptions to the ethical duty of confidentiality; nine from Rule 1.6 itself; one from Rule 1.9(c) (pertaining only to former clients); one from Rule 1.13 (pertaining to wrongdoing within an organization); and two from Rule 3.3 (pertaining to perjury or other wrongs in a trial, arbitration, or some other adjudicative proceeding). Those exceptions permit a lawyer to volunteer information that would otherwise be protected by Rule 1.6.

Some of those exceptions also apply to the attorney-client privilege, but others do not. Of course, a client may give informed consent to a lawyer to waive the attorney-client privilege, but a lawyer has no implied authority to do so without the client's consent. Thus, a lawyer has an ethical duty under Rule 1.6 to preserve the attorney-client privilege and to assert the attorney-client privilege whenever it applies.

In the same spirit, when a client has not given informed consent to waive the privilege, a lawyer has no right to reveal information protected by the attorney-client privilege unless one of the thirteen exceptions to the ethical duty of confidentiality applies. Even if the client has expressly or impliedly waived the attorney-client privilege, a lawyer may not voluntarily disclose information that was once protected by the attorney-client privilege *unless* an exception to the ethical duty of confidentiality applies. This is completely logical. The ethical duty of confidentiality is much broader than the attorney-client privilege. The ethical duty of confidentiality protects "information relating to the representation" even if it is not privileged; whether the privilege for a given communication was waived, is subject to an exception, or never existed at all, a lawyer may not voluntarily reveal that communication if it constitutes information relating to the representation of a client. Thus, the ethical duty of confidentiality functions as an "outer fence" to protect a client's confidential information and prevent it from escaping the lawyer's lips (or pen) even when the very same information has already escaped the "inner fence" of the attorney-client privilege through waiver or an exception.

But the ethical duty of confidentiality is a relatively weak fence and may be overcome by court order. If a court, a grand jury, an administrative agency, or an opposing lawyer seeks to compel a lawyer to reveal information that is protected only by the ethical duty of confidentiality (but not by the attorney-client privilege), the lawyer may not claim the attorney-client privilege. The lawyer may not say, "I object to that question or document request because it calls for communications protected by the attorney-client privilege." Thus, if the privilege has been waived, whether intentionally or unintentionally, the ethical duty of confidentiality still prohibits the lawyer from revealing the formerly-privileged communication without compulsion (i.e., prohibits the lawyer from *volunteering* disclosure of the information), but the ethical duty cannot protect a communication against *compelled* disclosure (i.e., disclosure ordered by a court).

Moreover, even if a client has not expressly waived the privilege, a court may nevertheless compel disclosure if the disclosure fits one of the three exceptions to the attorney-client privilege. As mentioned earlier in the book, these exceptions include (a) the testamentary exception, (b) the crime-fraud exception, and (c) the deceased client exception (which, as we have seen, many courts do not recognize). The latter two exceptions (crime-fraud and deceased client) reflect the view that the values underlying the attorney-client privilege are outweighed by other public policy concerns.

To sum up, the attorney-client privilege protects confidential communications between client and counsel where the communications are made for the purpose of providing the client with legal counsel (i.e., legal advice). If any of those five elements is missing, the attorney-client privilege never attaches. Even if the privilege does attach, the client may expressly waive the privilege by deliberately disclosing privileged communications or by knowingly permitting her attorney or another person to do so. A client may also impliedly waive the privilege by acting inconsistently with the purpose of the privilege, which is to encourage full and frank communication between client and counsel. Even if the client has not expressly or impliedly waived the privilege, in a few situations, the courts will sweep aside the protection of the attorney-client privilege in favor of an exception. Always keep in mind that exceptions and waivers in the attorney-client privilege context do *not* give an attorney the right to disclose the information voluntarily. Rather, they *permit* an attorney to disclose information when a court, a prosecutor, or an opposing party succeeds in compelling disclosure.

B. A BRIEF CATALOGUE OF WAIVERS AND EXCEPTIONS TO THE ATTORNEY-CLIENT PRIVILEGE

That brings us to the heart of this chapter — the circumstances under which a client will be deemed to have waived the privilege and the circumstances in which courts will apply an exception to the privilege even if the client has not waived it. The following are brief descriptions of three major exceptions and four major sources of waiver that apply in the context of the attorney-client privilege.

1. ***Testamentary exception.*** When competing claimants are asserting claims under the will of a decedent, a court may compel the lawyer who drafted the will to testify to information shedding light on the testator's intent. ("The testator, Mr. Lear, told me that his youngest daughter, Cordelia, did not love him as much as her older sisters loved him, so he was leaving his entire estate to the two older daughters, Regan and Goneril.") The theory is that testators, if they had a choice, would want to waive the privilege in order to make sure that their intentions are honored.

2. ***The crime-fraud exception.*** This exception applies when the client has used the lawyer's services to commit a crime or fraud. Society does not want a client to be able to use the privilege as a shield when the client has abused the privilege by tricking the lawyer into helping the client commit a crime. Note that the client nearly always opposes application of the crime-fraud exception because the attorney's testimony is likely to be powerful evidence against the client in a criminal prosecution or in a civil suit for fraud. (We could also characterize the crime-fraud exception as a waiver by conduct — the client has waived the privilege by engaging in conduct inconsistent with its purposes — but courts and commentators almost universally refer to it as the crime-fraud "exception.")

3. ***Deceased client exception.*** This relatively new exception is not well-defined and is far from widespread. It applies when a client has died and society's need for privileged information outweighs the likely harm to the deceased client. Many courts do not recognize this privilege.

4. ***Waiver by disclosure.*** A client may waive the attorney-client privilege by turning over privileged documents to another party in litigation, by mistakenly e-mailing or faxing privileged documents to another person or by revealing privileged communications to another person. The intentional disclosure of privileged information nearly always waives the privilege. The unintentional disclosure of privileged communications may or may not waive the privilege, depending on various factors such as the time pressures the client was under and the precautions the client took to prevent the inadvertent disclosure.

5. ***Waiver by failure to object.*** A client may be deemed to have waived the attorney-client privilege if her lawyer fails to object to a question that calls for privileged

information. Once the testimony has been given in answer to the question, the information is no longer protected.

6. ***Waiver by attacking a lawyer's work.*** This exception parallels the well-known exception that a client claiming damages from an injury waives the physician-patient privilege if the client puts her physical condition in issue. Similarly, a client who sues her lawyer (or former lawyer) for legal malpractice waives the right to claim the attorney-client privilege for communications relevant to the malpractice claim.

7. ***Waiver by putting the advice of counsel in issue.*** A client may waive the attorney-client privilege if the client defends against criminal charges by claiming that she relied on the advice of her counsel that the conduct in question was legal. This is in essence the defensive counterpart to waiver by attacking the lawyer's work; rather than attacking the advice as wrong, the client here simply says that she had no criminal intent because she believed her conduct to be legal, based on counsel's advice.

Chapter 12

DEAD MAN TALKING: THE ATTORNEY-CLIENT PRIVILEGE AFTER A CLIENT DIES

Should the attorney-client privilege survive after a client dies? Or does the privilege follow the client to the grave, there to remain forever? This chapter will present three variations on that theme.

A. ATTORNEYS AS VOLUNTARY WITNESSES

We have portrayed the attorney-client privilege as close to absolute. Should a court override the attorney-client privilege on public policy grounds (a/k/a "interest of justice" grounds) if there is a compelling need for the privileged matter at trial? For example, suppose one man is in prison for a murder that another man committed, and the real killer confidentially confesses to his attorneys that he committed the crime. May the attorneys for the guilty man (the one who confessed but is not in prison) come forward and reveal that their client is really the guilty one? You might say, "No, lawyers can't turn against their clients. They have to keep silent because lawyers can't reveal a confidential confession that would send their own client to jail." However, what if the guilty client is *dead*? In that situation, is there an adequate public interest in creating an exception to the attorney-client privilege so that justice can be done?

The next case addresses that scenario. Before reading it, consider which result is supported by better policy arguments. Should the court admit the testimony of the former attorneys for the dead man, even if it is privileged, on the grounds that the evidence is not otherwise available and it is necessary to reach a just result? Or should the attorney-client privilege be eternally inviolate if the client is no longer alive to waive it?

STATE v. MACUMBER

544 P.2d 1084 (Ariz. 1976)

Hays, J.

William Wayne Macumber was found guilty of two counts of first degree murder. He was sentenced to serve two concurrent terms of life imprisonment, and now appeals. . . .

At trial, it was alleged that another individual had confessed to the crime for which Macumber was being tried. This confession had been made to two attorneys who were willing to testify at the trial of the appellant, the person said to have confessed having died. The court refused the evidence finding, *sua sponte*, that it was privileged.

ARS § 13-1802 provides that an attorney shall not be examined as to any communication made to him by his client without the consent of his client. The privilege is that of the client and only he or someone authorized by law to do so on his behalf may claim it. However, in the absence of the privileged individual, the privilege may be asserted by another including the trial court itself.

The privilege does not terminate with death. It has been commonly suspended only in cases where the communication would be logically thought to further the interests of the deceased such as a will, or where a person normally able by statute to invoke the privilege for another does so to exclude evidence in a prosecution for a crime against that person.

The attorney-client privilege is statutory and an attorney is not allowed to waive the privilege under the circumstances of this case. The legislature has presumably weighed the possibility of hampering justice by originally providing for the privilege. . . .

AUTHORS' COMMENT:

Are you convinced that there should not be a public interest exception even when disclosure will not harm the client and there is no other way of obtaining the evidence? What is the best argument you can make in dissent? Compare with the opinion that follows.

HOLOHAN, J. concurring.

. . . I cannot agree with the decision of the majority to refuse to admit evidence of the confession by a third person that he killed the same individuals that the defendant is charged with murdering.

The nature of the defense evidence was contained in an offer of proof. Essentially, the evidence was expected to show that a third person, now deceased, had admitted in 1968 to two attorneys that he had committed the dual murders with which the defendant was charged. . . .

When the attorneys learned that the defendant was being charged with the murders which their former client claimed to have committed, they sought and received an informal opinion from the Committee on Ethics of the State Bar which advised the attorneys that the privilege of attorney-client did not apply to prevent them from disclosing the information to the defense, prosecution, and court. The attorneys, upon receiving the advice of the Ethics Committee, disclosed their information to the defense and prosecution, but the trial judge ruled the information privileged and not admissible. . . . .

[T]he attorney-client privilege has been held to survive the death of the client. Whether the rule should be followed in a case such as this or an exception created would require an extended discussion not called for in a specially concurring opinion. The real problem is whether the privilege can survive the constitutional test of due process.

It is basic that an accused has the right to present a defense to a criminal charge, and, to accomplish this right, the accused has the right to compel the attendance of witnesses and the right to present their testimony. Even a claim of privilege may have to give way when faced with the necessity by the accused to present a defense. The problem of balancing competing interests, privilege versus a proper defense, is a difficult one, but the balance always weighs in favor of achieving a fair determination of the cause.

A state's rules of evidence cannot deny an accused person's right to present a proper defense. In the case at issue the interest to be protected by the privilege would seem to be at an end because of the client's death.

When the client died there was no chance of prosecution for other crimes, and any privilege is merely a matter of property interest. Opposed to the property interest of the deceased client is the vital interest of the accused in this case in defending himself against the charge of first degree murder. When the interests are weighed, I believe that the constitutional right of the accused to present a defense should prevail over the property interest of a deceased client in keeping his disclosures private. I would allow the defendant to offer the testimony of the attorneys concerning the confession of their deceased client.

NOTES AND QUESTIONS

1. ***Choose Sides.*** Do you agree with the majority in *Macumber* or with Judge Holohan's opinion? Or would you write a separate opinion?

2. ***Wrong Message?*** Does this case send the wrong message about the attorney-client privilege? In the *Restatement of the Law Governing Lawyers*, the Chief Reporter originally cited *Macumber* in the notes explaining the scope of the privilege. When the notes were revised, the Chief Reporter deleted it because many people worried that it sent the "wrong message" about the privilege. What is the "message" of the *Macumber* case? Is it a message to lawyers, to judges, to law students, or to the general public? Is it the right message or the wrong message?

B. IS THE ATTORNEY-CLIENT PRIVILEGE SUBJECT TO A BALANCING TEST?

If you went to a lawyer to discuss your legal problems, would you care whether the attorney-client privilege would survive after you died? Suppose you asked your attorney whether the attorney-client privilege would continue after your death and your attorney said, "Generally, the attorney-client privilege will protect your confidential communications with me after you die. But there are some exceptions. For example, if there is a contest over your will, the so-called 'testamentary exception' would permit your attorney to testify about your intent in writing the will even if the attorney's testimony about your intent revealed privileged information. Or, if a prosecutor subpoenaed me to testify and to turn over my notes because the prosecutor needed to know what you told me, the court would balance the competing interests and might order me to turn over my notes and to testify even though the notes and testimony would reveal your privileged communications."

If that were the law — if you knew that your attorney's notes could be turned over after you died — would you be candid with your attorney? Would you be as candid with your attorney as you would be if a prosecutor could never get your privileged information after your death, even if the prosecutor had no other way to obtain the same evidence? That question, which grew out of one of Kenneth Starr's investigations during his years as Independent Counsel, is at the root of the next case.

SWIDLER & BERLIN v. UNITED STATES

524 U.S. 399 (1998)

REHNQUIST, C. J., delivered the opinion of the Court, in which STEVENS, KENNEDY, SOUTER, GINSBURG, and BREYER, JJ., joined.

Petitioner, an attorney, made notes of an initial interview with a client shortly before the client's death. The Government, represented by the Office of Independent Counsel, now seeks his notes for use in a criminal investigation. We hold that the notes are protected by the attorney-client privilege.

This dispute arises out of an investigation conducted by the Office of the Independent Counsel into whether various individuals made false statements, obstructed justice, or committed other crimes during investigations of the 1993 dismissal of employees from the White House Travel Office. Vincent W. Foster, Jr. was Deputy White House Counsel when the firings occurred. In July, 1993, Foster met with petitioner James Hamilton, an attorney at petitioner Swidler & Berlin, to seek legal representation concerning possible congressional or other investigations of the firings. During a 2-hour meeting, Hamilton took three pages of handwritten notes. One of the first entries in the notes is the word "Privileged." Nine days later, Foster committed suicide.

In December 1995, a federal grand jury, at the request of the Independent Counsel, issued subpoenas to petitioners Hamilton and Swidler & Berlin for, inter alia, Hamilton's handwritten notes of his meeting with Foster. Petitioners filed a motion to quash, arguing that the notes were protected by the attorney client privilege and by the work product privilege. The District Court, after examining the notes in camera, concluded they were protected from disclosure by both doctrines and denied enforcement of the subpoenas.

The Court of Appeals for the District of Columbia Circuit reversed. *In re Sealed Case*, 124 F.3d 230 (1997). While recognizing that most courts assume the privilege survives death, the Court of Appeals noted that holdings actually manifesting the posthumous force of the privilege are rare. Instead, most judicial references to the privilege's posthumous application occur in the context of a well recognized exception allowing disclosure for disputes among the client's heirs. It further noted that most commentators support some measure of posthumous curtailment of the privilege. The Court of Appeals thought that the risk of posthumous revelation, when confined to the criminal context, would have little to no chilling effect on client communication, but that the costs of protecting communications after death were high. It therefore concluded that the privilege was not absolute in such circumstances, and that instead, a balancing test should apply. It thus held that there is a posthumous exception to the privilege for communications whose relative importance to particular criminal litigation is substantial. While acknowledging that uncertain privileges are disfavored, *Jaffee v. Redmond*, 518 U.S. 1, 17–18 (1996), the Court of Appeals determined that the uncertainty introduced by its balancing test was insignificant in light of existing exceptions to the privilege. The Court of Appeals also held that the notes were not protected by the work product privilege.

The dissenting judge would have affirmed the District Court's judgment that the attorney client privilege protected the notes. He concluded that the common-law rule was that the privilege survived death. He found no persuasive reason to depart from this accepted rule, particularly given the importance of the privilege to full and frank client communication.

Petitioners sought review in this Court on both the attorney client privilege and the work product privilege.[1] We granted certiorari, and we now reverse.

The attorney client privilege is one of the oldest recognized privileges for confidential communications. *Upjohn Co. v. United States*, 449 U.S. 383, 389 (1981); *Hunt v. Blackburn*, 128 U.S. 464, 470 (1888). The privilege is intended to encourage "full and frank communication between attorneys and their clients and thereby promote broader public interests in the observance of law and the administration of justice." *Upjohn*. The issue presented here is the scope of that privilege; more particularly, the extent to which the privilege survives the death of the client. Our interpretation of the privilege's scope is guided by "the principles of the common law . . . as interpreted by the courts . . . in the light of reason and experience." Fed. Rule Evid. 501; *Funk v. United States*, 290 U.S. 371 (1933).

The Independent Counsel argues that the attorney-client privilege should not prevent disclosure of confidential communications where the client has died and the information is relevant to a criminal proceeding. There is some authority for this position. One state appellate court, *Cohen v. Jenkintown Cab Co.*, 238 Pa. Super. 456, 357 A. 2d 689 (1976), and the Court of Appeals below have held the privilege may be subject to posthumous exceptions in certain circumstances. In *Cohen*, a civil case, the

[1] Because we sustain the claim of attorney-client privilege, we do not reach the claim of work product privilege.

court recognized that the privilege generally survives death, but concluded that it could make an exception where the interest of justice was compelling and the interest of the client in preserving the confidence was insignificant.

But other than these two decisions, cases addressing the existence of the privilege after death — most involving the testamentary exception — uniformly presume the privilege survives, even if they do not so hold. *See, e.g., Mayberry v. Indiana*, 670 N. E. 2d 1262 (Ind. 1996); *Morris v. Cain*, 39 La. Ann. 712, 1 So. 797 (1887); *People v. Modzelewski*, 611 N. Y. S. 2d 22, 203 A. 2d 594 (1994). Several State Supreme Court decisions expressly hold that the attorney-client privilege extends beyond the death of the client, even in the criminal context. See *In re John Doe Grand Jury Investigation*, 408 Mass. 480, 481–483, 562 N.E.2d 69, 70 (1990); *State v. Doster*, 276 S.C. 647, 650–651, 284 S.E.2d 218, 219 (1981); *State v. Macumber*, 112 Ariz. 569, 571, 544 P.2d 1084, 1086 (1976). In *John Doe Grand Jury Investigation*, for example, the Massachusetts Supreme Court concluded that survival of the privilege was "the clear implication" of its early pronouncements that communications subject to the privilege could not be disclosed at any time. The court further noted that survival of the privilege was "necessarily implied" by cases allowing waiver of the privilege in testamentary disputes.

Such testamentary exception cases consistently presume the privilege survives. *See, e.g., United States v. Osborn*, 561 F.2d 1334, 1340 (CA9 1977); *DeLoach v. Myers*, 215 Ga. 255, 259–260, 109 S. E. 2d 777, 780–781 (1959); *Doyle v. Reeves*, 112 Conn. 521, 152 A. 882 (1931); *Russell v. Jackson*, 9 Hare. 387, 68 Eng. Rep. 558 (V.C. 1851). They view testamentary disclosure of communications as an exception to the privilege: "The general rule with respect to confidential communications . . . is that such communications are privileged during the testator's lifetime and, also, after the testator's death unless sought to be disclosed in litigation between the testator's heirs." The rationale for such disclosure is that it furthers the client's intent.[2]

Indeed, in *Glover v. Patten*, 165 U.S. 394, 406–408 (1897), this Court, in recognizing the testamentary exception, expressly assumed that the privilege continues after the individual's death. The Court explained that testamentary disclosure was permissible because the privilege, which normally protects the client's interests, could be impliedly waived in order to fulfill the client's testamentary intent.

The great body of this caselaw supports, either by holding or considered dicta, the position that the privilege does survive in a case such as the present one. Given the language of Rule 501, at the very least the burden is on the Independent Counsel to show that "reason and experience" require a departure from this rule.

The Independent Counsel contends that the testamentary exception supports the posthumous termination of the privilege because in practice most cases have refused to apply the privilege posthumously. He further argues that the exception reflects a policy judgment that the interest in settling estates outweighs any posthumous interest in confidentiality. He then reasons by analogy that in criminal proceedings, the interest in determining whether a crime has been committed should trump client confidentiality, particularly since the financial interests of the estate are not at stake.

---

[2] About half the States have codified the testamentary exception by providing that a personal representative of the deceased can waive the privilege when heirs or devisees claim through the deceased client (as opposed to parties claiming against the estate, for whom the privilege is not waived). *See, e.g.*, Ala. Rule Evid. 502 (1996); Ark. Code Ann. § 16-41-101, Rule 502 (Supp. 1997); Neb. Rev. Stat. § 27 503, Rule 503 (1995). These statutes do not address expressly the continuation of the privilege outside the context of testamentary disputes, although many allow the attorney to assert the privilege on behalf of the client apparently without temporal limit. *See, e.g.*, Ark. Code Ann. § 16-41-101, Rule 502(c) (Supp. 1997). They thus do not refute or affirm the general presumption in the case law that the privilege survives. California's statute is exceptional in that it apparently allows the attorney to assert the privilege only so long as a holder of the privilege (the estate's personal representative) exists, suggesting the privilege terminates when the estate is wound up. *See* Cal. Code Evid. Ann. §§ 954, 957 (West 1995). But no other State has followed California's lead in this regard.

But the Independent Counsel's interpretation simply does not square with the caselaw's implicit acceptance of the privilege's survival and with the treatment of testamentary disclosure as an "exception" or an implied "waiver." And the premise of his analogy is incorrect, since cases consistently recognize that the rationale for the testamentary exception is that it furthers the client's intent. There is no reason to suppose as a general matter that grand jury testimony about confidential communications furthers the client's intent.

Commentators on the law also recognize that the general rule is that the attorney-client privilege continues after death. *See, e.g.*, 8 Wigmore, Evidence § 2323 (McNaughton rev. 1961); Frankel, *The Attorney-Client Privilege After the Death of the Client*, 6 Geo. J. Legal Ethics 45, 78–79 (1992); 1 J. Strong, McCormick on Evidence § 94, p. 348 (4th ed. 1992). Undoubtedly, as the Independent Counsel emphasizes, various commentators have criticized this rule, urging that the privilege should be abrogated after the client's death where extreme injustice would result, as long as disclosure would not seriously undermine the privilege by deterring client communication. *See, e.g.*, C. Mueller & L. Kirkpatrick, 2 Federal Evidence § 199, at 380–381 (2d ed. 1994); Restatement (Third) of the Law Governing Lawyers § 127, Comment d (Proposed Final Draft No. 1, Mar. 29, 1996). But even these critics clearly recognize that established law supports the continuation of the privilege and that a contrary rule would be a modification of the common law.

Despite the scholarly criticism, we think there are weighty reasons that counsel in favor of posthumous application. Knowing that communications will remain confidential even after death encourages the client to communicate fully and frankly with counsel. While the fear of disclosure, and the consequent withholding of information from counsel, may be reduced if disclosure is limited to posthumous disclosure in a criminal context, it seems unreasonable to assume that it vanishes altogether. Clients may be concerned about reputation, civil liability, or possible harm to friends or family. Posthumous disclosure of such communications may be as feared as disclosure during the client's lifetime.

The Independent Counsel suggests, however, that his proposed exception would have little to no effect on the client's willingness to confide in his attorney. He reasons that only clients intending to perjure themselves will be chilled by a rule of disclosure after death, as opposed to truthful clients or those asserting their Fifth Amendment privilege. This is because for the latter group, communications disclosed by the attorney after the client's death purportedly will reveal only information that the client himself would have revealed if alive.

AUTHORS' COMMENT:

Do you agree that "only clients intending to perjure themselves will be chilled by a rule of disclosure after death"? Why or why not? Why might a client want to keep information secret after death even if the client is telling the truth to his attorney? Think of an example of something a client might tell an attorney that the client would never want revealed even after death.

The Independent Counsel assumes, incorrectly we believe, that the privilege is analogous to the Fifth Amendment's protection against self-incrimination. But as suggested above, the privilege serves much broader purposes. Clients consult attorneys for a wide variety of reasons, only one of which involves possible criminal liability. Many attorneys act as counselors on personal and family matters, where, in the course of obtaining the desired advice, confidences about family members or financial problems must be revealed in order to assure sound legal advice. The same is true of owners of small businesses who may regularly consult their attorneys about a variety of problems arising in the course of the business. These confidences may not come close to any sort of admission of criminal wrongdoing, but nonetheless be matters which the client would not wish divulged.

The contention that the attorney is being required to disclose only what the client could have been required to disclose is at odds with the basis for the privilege even during the client's lifetime. In related cases, we have said that the loss of evidence admittedly caused by the privilege is justified in part by the fact that without the privilege, the client may not have made such communications in the first place. *See Jaffe*, 518 U.S., at 12; *Fisher v. United States*, 425 U.S. 391, 403 (1976). This is true of disclosure before and after the client's death. Without assurance of the privilege's posthumous application, the client may very well not have made disclosures to his attorney at all, so the loss of evidence is more apparent than real. In the case at hand, it seems quite plausible that Foster, perhaps already contemplating suicide, may not have sought legal advice from Hamilton if he had not been assured the conversation was privileged.

The Independent Counsel additionally suggests that his proposed exception would have minimal impact if confined to criminal cases, or, as the Court of Appeals suggests, if it is limited to information of substantial importance to a particular criminal case.[3] However, there is no case authority for the proposition that the privilege applies differently in criminal and civil cases, and only one commentator ventures such a suggestion, see Mueller & Kirkpatrick, supra, at 380–381. In any event, a client may not know at the time he discloses information to his attorney whether it will later be relevant to a civil or a criminal matter, let alone whether it will be of substantial importance. Balancing ex post the importance of the information against client interests, even limited to criminal cases, introduces substantial uncertainty into the privilege's application. For just that reason, we have rejected the use of a balancing test in defining the contours of the privilege.

In a similar vein, the Independent Counsel argues that existing exceptions to the privilege, such as the crime-fraud exception and the testamentary exception, make the impact of one more exception marginal. However, these exceptions do not demonstrate that the impact of a posthumous exception would be insignificant, and there is little empirical evidence on this point.[4] The established exceptions are consistent with the purposes of the privilege, while a posthumous exception in criminal cases appears at odds with the goals of encouraging full and frank communication and of protecting the client's interests. A "no harm in one more exception" rationale could contribute to the

---

[3] Petitioner, while opposing wholesale abrogation of the privilege in criminal cases, concedes that exceptional circumstances implicating a criminal defendant's constitutional rights might warrant breaching the privilege. We do not, however, need to reach this issue, since such exceptional circumstances clearly are not presented here.

[4] Empirical evidence on the privilege is limited. Three studies do not reach firm conclusions on whether limiting the privilege would discourage full and frank communication. Alexander, *The Corporate Attorney Client Privilege: A Study of the Participants*, 63 St. John's L. Rev. 191 (1989); Zacharias, *Rethinking Confidentiality*, 74 Iowa L. Rev. 352 (1989); Comment, *Functional Overlap Between the Lawyer and Other Professionals: Its Implications for the Privileged Communications Doctrine*, 71 Yale L.J. 1226 (1962). These articles note that clients are often uninformed or mistaken about the privilege, but suggest that a substantial number of clients and attorneys think the privilege encourages candor. Two of the articles conclude that a substantial number of clients and attorneys think the privilege enhances open communication, and that the absence of a privilege would be detrimental to such communication. The third article suggests instead that while the privilege is perceived as important to open communication, limited exceptions to the privilege might not discourage such communication. Similarly, relatively few court decisions discuss the impact of the privilege's application after death. This may reflect the general assumption that the privilege survives — if attorneys were required as a matter of practice to testify or provide notes in criminal proceedings, cases discussing that practice would surely exist.

general erosion of the privilege, without reference to common law principles or "reason and experience."

Finally, the Independent Counsel, relying on cases such as *United States v. Nixon*, 418 U.S. 683, 710 (1974), and *Branzburg v. Hayes*, 408 U.S. 665 (1972), urges that privileges be strictly construed because they are inconsistent with the paramount judicial goal of truth seeking. But both *Nixon* and *Branzburg* dealt with the creation of privileges not recognized by the common law, whereas here we deal with one of the oldest recognized privileges in the law. And we are asked, not simply to "construe" the privilege, but to narrow it, contrary to the weight of the existing body of caselaw.

It has been generally, if not universally, accepted, for well over a century, that the attorney-client privilege survives the death of the client in a case such as this. While the arguments against the survival of the privilege are by no means frivolous, they are based in large part on speculation — thoughtful speculation, but speculation nonetheless — as to whether posthumous termination of the privilege would diminish a client's willingness to confide in an attorney. In an area where empirical information would be useful, it is scant and inconclusive.

Rule 501's direction to look to "the principles of the common law as they may be interpreted by the courts of the United States in the light of reason and experience" does not mandate that a rule, once established, should endure for all time. But here the Independent Counsel has simply not made a sufficient showing to overturn the common law rule embodied in the prevailing caselaw. Interpreted in the light of reason and experience, that body of law requires that the attorney client privilege prevent disclosure of the notes at issue in this case. The judgment of the Court of Appeals is

Reversed.

AUTHORS' COMMENT:

What should the dissenters argue? What are the weaknesses in the majority opinion? Before you read what Justice O'Connor and the other two dissenters think, write down one or two colorable arguments that could be made against the majority opinion (whether you personally agree with the arguments or not).

JUSTICE O'CONNOR, with whom JUSTICE SCALIA and JUSTICE THOMAS join, dissenting.

Although the attorney-client privilege ordinarily will survive the death of the client, I do not agree with the Court that it inevitably precludes disclosure of a deceased client's communications in criminal proceedings. In my view, a criminal defendant's right to exculpatory evidence or a compelling law enforcement need for information may, where the testimony is not available from other sources, override a client's posthumous interest in confidentiality.

We have long recognized that "the fundamental basis upon which all rules of evidence must rest — if they are to rest upon reason — is their adaptation to the successful development of the truth." *Funk v. United States*, 290 U.S. 371, 381 (1933). In light of the heavy burden that they place on the search for truth, "evidentiary privileges in litigation are not favored, and even those rooted in the Constitution must give way in proper circumstances," *Herbert v. Lando*, 441 U.S. 153, 175 (1979). Consequently, we construe the scope of privileges narrowly. We are reluctant to recognize a privilege or read an existing one expansively unless to do so will serve a "public good transcending the normally predominant principle of utilizing all rational means for ascertaining truth." *Trammel v. United States*, 445 U.S. 40, 50 (1980) (internal quotation marks omitted).

The attorney-client privilege promotes trust in the representational relationship, thereby facilitating the provision of legal services and ultimately the administration of justice. The systemic benefits of the privilege are commonly understood to outweigh the harm caused by excluding critical evidence. A privilege should operate, however, only where "necessary to achieve its purpose," and an invocation of the attorney-client privilege should not go unexamined "when it is shown that the interests of the administration of justice can only be frustrated by [its] exercise," *Cohen v. Jenkintown Cab Co.*, 238 Pa. Super. 456, 464, 357 A. 2d 689, 693–694 (1976).

I agree that a deceased client may retain a personal, reputational, and economic interest in confidentiality. But, after death, the potential that disclosure will harm the client's interests has been greatly diminished, and the risk that the client will be held criminally liable has abated altogether. Thus, some commentators suggest that terminating the privilege upon the client's death "could not to any substantial degree lessen the encouragement for free disclosure which is [its] purpose." 1 J. Strong, McCormick on Evidence § 94, p. 350 (4th ed. 1992); *see also* Restatement (Third) of the Law Governing Lawyers § 127, Comment d (Proposed Final Draft No. 1, Mar. 29, 1996). This diminished risk is coupled with a heightened urgency for discovery of a deceased client's communications in the criminal context. The privilege does not "protect" disclosure of the underlying facts by those who communicated with the attorney," *Upjohn*, and were the client living, prosecutors could grant immunity and compel the relevant testimony. After a client's death, however, if the privilege precludes an attorney from testifying in the client's stead, a complete "loss of crucial information" will often result, *see* 24 C. Wright & K. Graham, Federal Practice and Procedure § 5498, p. 484 (1986).

As the Court of Appeals observed, the costs of recognizing an absolute posthumous privilege can be inordinately high. Extreme injustice may occur, for example, where a criminal defendant seeks disclosure of a deceased client's confession to the offense. In my view, the paramount value that our criminal justice system places on protecting an innocent defendant should outweigh a deceased client's interest in preserving confidences. Indeed, even petitioner acknowledges that an exception may be appropriate where the constitutional rights of a criminal defendant are at stake. An exception may likewise be warranted in the face of a compelling law enforcement need for the information. "Our historic commitment to the rule of law . . . is nowhere more profoundly manifest than in our view that the twofold aim of criminal justice is that guilt shall not escape or innocence suffer." *Nixon* (internal quotation marks omitted). Given that the complete exclusion of relevant evidence from a criminal trial or investigation may distort the record, mislead the factfinder, and undermine the central truth-seeking function of the courts, I do not believe that the attorney-client privilege should act as an absolute bar to the disclosure of a deceased client's communications. When the privilege is asserted in the criminal context, and a showing is made that the communications at issue contain necessary factual information not otherwise available, courts should be permitted to assess whether interests in fairness and accuracy outweigh the justifications for the privilege.

A number of exceptions to the privilege already qualify its protections, and an attorney "who tells his client that the expected communications are absolutely and forever privileged is oversimplifying a bit." In the situation where the posthumous privilege most frequently arises — a dispute between heirs over the decedent's will — the privilege is widely recognized to give way to the interest in settling the estate. This testamentary exception, moreover, may be invoked in some cases where the decedent would not have chosen to waive the privilege. For example, "a decedent might want to provide for an illegitimate child but at the same time much prefer that the relationship go undisclosed." Among the Court's rationales for a broad construction of the posthumous privilege is its assertion that "many attorneys act as counselors on personal and family matters, where, in the course of obtaining the desired advice, confidences about family members or financial problems must be revealed . . . which the client would not wish divulged." That reasoning, however, would apply in the testamentary context with equal force. Nor are other existing exceptions to the privilege — for example, the crime-fraud exception or the exceptions for claims relating to attorney competence or compensation — necessarily consistent with "encouraging full and frank communication" or "protecting the client's interests." Rather, those exceptions reflect the understanding that, in certain circumstances, the privilege "ceases to operate" as a safeguard on "the proper functioning of our adversary system." *See United States v. Zolin*, 491 U.S. 554, 562–563 (1989).

Finally, the common law authority for the proposition that the privilege remains absolute after the client's death is not a monolithic body of precedent. Indeed, the Court acknowledges that most cases merely "presume the privilege survives," and it relies on the case law's "implicit acceptance" of a continuous privilege. Opinions squarely addressing the posthumous force of the privilege "are relatively rare." *See* 124 F.3d at 232. And even in those decisions expressly holding that the privilege continues after the death of the client, courts do not typically engage in detailed reasoning, but rather conclude that the cases construing the testamentary exception imply survival of the privilege. *See, e.g., Glover*; *see also* WRIGHT & GRAHAM ("Those who favor an eternal duration for the privilege seldom do much by way of justifying this in terms of policy").

Moreover, as the Court concedes, there is some authority for the proposition that a deceased client's communications may be revealed, even in circumstances outside of the testamentary context. California's Evidence Code, for example, provides that the attorney-client privilege continues only until the deceased client's estate is finally distributed, noting that there is little reason to preserve secrecy at the expense of excluding relevant evidence after the estate is wound up and the representative is discharged. And a state appellate court has admitted an attorney's testimony concerning a deceased client's communications after "balancing the necessity for revealing the substance of the [attorney-client conversation] against the unlikelihood of any cognizable injury to the rights, interests, estate or memory of [the client]." The American Law Institute, moreover, has recently recommended withholding the privilege when the communication "bears on a litigated issue of pivotal significance" and has suggested that courts "balance the interest in confidentiality against any exceptional need for the communication." RESTATEMENT (THIRD) OF THE LAW GOVERNING LAWYERS § 127, at 431, Comment d; *see also* 2 C. Mueller & L. Kirkpatrick, FEDERAL EVIDENCE, § 199, p. 380 (2d ed. 1994) ("If a deceased client has confessed to criminal acts that are later charged to another, surely the latter's need for evidence sometimes outweighs the interest in preserving the confidences").

Where the exoneration of an innocent criminal defendant or a compelling law enforcement interest is at stake, the harm of precluding critical evidence that is unavailable by any other means outweighs the potential disincentive to forthright communication. In my view, the cost of silence warrants a narrow exception to the rule that the attorney-client privilege survives the death of the client. Moreover, although I disagree with the Court of Appeals' notion that the context of an initial client interview affects the applicability of the work product doctrine, I do not believe that the doctrine applies where the material concerns a client who is no longer a potential party to adversarial litigation.

Accordingly, I would affirm the judgment of the Court of Appeals. Although the District Court examined the documents in camera, it has not had an opportunity to balance these competing considerations and decide whether the privilege should be trumped in the particular circumstances of this case. Thus, I agree with the Court of Appeals' decision to remand for a determination whether any portion of the notes must be disclosed. With respect, I dissent.

NOTES AND QUESTIONS

1. ***How Do You Vote?*** Would you line up with the majority or the dissenters? Or would you concur separately?

2. ***Is the Privilege Really So Certain?*** In his brief to the Supreme Court, Kenneth Starr pointed out that the attorney-client privilege is already subject to a number of exceptions that make the privilege at least somewhat uncertain, so one more exception wouldn't make much difference to clients. Is he right?

3. ***Do Clients Really Care What Happens After They Die?*** You're in law school, so for most of you and your classmates thoughts of death may seem to be a long ways off. If you go to an attorney to look over a lease or help you with a personal injury suit, you probably don't care whether your conversation may become available to prosecutors after you die. But what about old people, or middle-aged people, or terminally ill people? Would their conversations have been chilled if the Supreme Court had gone the other way in *Swidler & Berlin*? Or are criminal investigations sufficiently rare that most people do not care whether or not their communications with an attorney are protected after death?

4. ***Empirical Evidence.*** The Supreme Court lamented the lack of empirical evidence about whether the attorney-client privilege actually encourages clients to be more candid with their lawyers. "In an area where empirical information would be useful, it is scant and inconclusive," Justice Rehnquist wrote. The problem, of course, is that the privilege itself gets in the way of doing empirical research about it. Attorneys aren't allowed to reveal privileged information and clients don't want to reveal privileged information. Could you design an empirical study to test whether the attorney-client privilege really increases "a client's willingness to confide in an attorney"? In the space below, write down two questions you could put on a survey to find out how well the attorney-client privilege is working:

5. ***How To Preserve The Privilege.*** Near the beginning of Justice Rehnquist's opinion, he observed: "One of the first entries in the notes is the word 'Privileged.'" That is important practical advice. When you take notes of a conversation with a client, one of the first things you should write down should be the word "privileged" (or "privileged & confidential" or "attorney-client privileged" or "attorney work product"). Write it at the top of the page. Write a similar phrase at the top of letters to clients, memos to the file, etc. These words cannot guarantee protection against disclosure, but they clarify your intentions and improve the chances that the privilege will apply.

C. A BALANCING TEST FOR DISCLOSING PRIVILEGED COMMUNICATIONS?

Swidler & Berlin held that under the Federal Rules of Evidence, the attorney-client privilege survives death. This is also the rule in virtually every state, even though the states are not bound by federal court decisions regarding the Federal Rules of Evidence.

The rule that the attorney-client privilege survives death is a policy-based rule, not a text-based rule. It is based mainly on the premise that revealing privileged information after a client's death might harm the reputation of the client or the client's surviving loved ones. But what if the party seeking the privileged information can show that the deceased client's reputation and loved ones will *not* be harmed by disclosure? In that situation, should a court have discretion to order disclosure of the privileged communications? Should the court be required to *order* disclosure? Should other factors or conditions be relevant to a court's decision whether to order disclosure?

In 2003, in *In re Investigation of the Death of Miller* (which is the next case), the North Carolina Supreme Court addressed these questions. As you read *Death of Miller*, consider the differences between the attorney-client privilege and the work product doctrine. Under Fed. R. Civ. P. Rule 26(b)(3) (which codifies work product doctrine), a party seeking discovery of work product materials must show both that: (1) it "has substantial need of the materials in the preparation of the party's case", and (2) it is "unable without undue hardship to obtain the substantial equivalent of the materials by other means." Should this work product test also be used to decide whether to order disclosure of communications protected by the attorney-client privilege after a client has died? How does the work product test differ from the disclosure test articulated by the *Miller* court?

Also, consider again (as you did when reading *Swidler & Berlin*) whether it would be appropriate to use a balancing test in the context of the attorney-client privilege. *Swidler & Berlin* rejected a balancing test, but was that the right call? Even if it was the right call under the facts of that case, would a balancing test nevertheless be appropriate under the facts of *Death of Miller*? After all, balancing tests are used in many areas of law, including highly sensitive areas such as equal protection and the First Amendment. Why not attorney-client privilege?

IN RE INVESTIGATION OF THE DEATH OF MILLER

584 S.E.2d 772 (N.C. 2003)

LAKE, CHIEF JUSTICE.

This case involves the attorney-client privilege and raises the primary question of whether, in the context of a pretrial criminal investigation, there can be a viable basis for the application of an interest of justice balancing test or an exception to the privilege which would allow a trial court to compel disclosure of confidential communications where the client is deceased, an issue of first impression for this Court.

On 2 December 2000, Eric D. Miller (Dr. Miller) died at Rex Hospital in Raleigh, North Carolina, as a result of arsenic poisoning. Investigation by law enforcement officials established the following: Dr. Miller was a post-doctoral research scientist and was married to Ann Rene Miller (Mrs. Miller). On the evening of 15 November 2000, Dr. Miller went bowling at AMF Bowling Center in Raleigh, North Carolina, with several of Mrs. Miller's co-workers. While at the bowling alley, Dr. Miller partially consumed a cup of beer given to him by Mrs. Miller's co-worker Derril H. Willard (Mr. Willard). Dr. Miller commented to those present that the beer had a bad or funny taste.

On 16 November 2000, Dr. Miller was hospitalized at Rex Hospital in Raleigh with symptoms later determined to be consistent with arsenic poisoning. Five days later, Dr. Miller was transferred to North Carolina Memorial Hospital in Chapel Hill, North Carolina, where he remained until discharge on 24 November 2000. Dr. Miller was physically unable to return to work and remained at home under the care of Mrs. Miller and his parents. Dr. Miller slowly regained his physical strength until the morning of 1 December 2000, when he became violently ill and was again hospitalized. On 2 December 2000, Dr. Miller died from arsenic poisoning. Within one week of Dr. Miller's death, law enforcement officials interviewed all of the persons present at the bowling alley the night Dr. Miller consumed the suspect beer, with the exception of Mr. Willard. The police were unable to interview Mr. Willard. Mrs. Miller was interviewed on the day of her husband's death and stated that she had no idea why anyone would have poisoned Dr. Miller. Shortly after the autopsy was completed on Dr. Miller's body, it was cremated at the direction of Mrs. Miller. All of the investigators' subsequent requests to interview Mrs. Miller were rejected.

During the course of the investigation, law enforcement officials concluded that Mrs. Miller was involved in a relationship with her co-worker, Mr. Willard. Investigators subpoenaed telephone records for Mrs. Miller's home, office, and cellular phones for a period of time before the initial hospitalization of Dr. Miller until the day he died. An analysis of telephone records showed several calls between Mr. Willard and Mrs. Miller, with a total of 576 total minutes of conversation. The evidence also showed an increase in the frequency and duration of these telephone calls immediately before and after the incident which occurred at the bowling alley. In addition, numerous e-mail messages between Mrs. Miller and Mr. Willard were found on Mrs. Miller's computer. During interviews with Yvette B. Willard (Mrs. Willard), the wife of Mr. Willard, investigators learned that Mr. Willard had acknowledged his romantic involvement with Mrs. Miller.

Shortly after Dr. Miller's death, Mr. Willard sought legal counsel from criminal defense attorney Richard T. Gammon (respondent), who, according to an affidavit of Mrs. Willard, advised Mr. Willard that he could be charged with the attempted murder of Dr. Miller. Within days after his meeting with respondent, Mr. Willard committed suicide. Mr. Willard left a will naming Mrs. Willard as the executrix of his estate.

On 20 February 2002, the State filed a Petition in the Nature of a Special Proceeding in Superior Court, Wake County, requesting that the trial court conduct a hearing and, if needed, an *in camera* examination to determine whether the attorney-client privilege should be waived or whether compelled disclosure of communications between respondent and Mr. Willard was warranted for the proper administration of justice . . .

On 7 March 2002, after a hearing, the trial court entered an order granting the State's petition and requiring respondent to provide the trial court with a sealed affidavit containing information relevant to the murder investigation into the death of Dr. Miller that was obtained from his attorney-client relationship with Mr. Willard. The order provided that the trial court would conduct an *in camera* review of the information contained in respondent's affidavit to determine if the interest of justice required disclosure of the information to the State. . . .

AUTHORS' COMMENT:

To make sense of this case, you have to imagine what is in that sealed envelope. What do you think the prosecutor would like to find in that envelope? Why do you suppose Mr. Willard went to talk with an attorney? Can you think of a motive for Mr. Willard to commit suicide?

In essence, this case presents the question of whether, during a criminal investigation, there can be a legal basis for the application of an interest of justice balancing test or an exception to the attorney-client privilege which would allow a trial court to compel the disclosure of confidential attorney-client communications when the client is deceased. The State asserts basically two propositions in support of disclosure: (1) that a deceased client's personal representative may waive the confidentiality of the communications, and (2) that in the interest of justice a trial court has the inherent authority to hear the State's petition and to apply a balancing test to determine by *in camera* review whether any disclosure should be made. . . .

[*1. May a deceased client's personal representative waive the attorney-client privilege?*]

Turning now to the State's first contention, the State asserts that Mrs. Willard, as executrix of Mr. Willard's estate, effectively waived any attorney-client privilege that may have existed by submitting an affidavit purporting to waive the privilege on Mr. Willard's behalf. The State specifically argues that, as executrix of Mr. Willard's estate, Mrs. Willard was empowered to waive the privilege pursuant to two sections of the North Carolina General Statutes . . . . The trial court held that the estate of Mr. Willard waived the attorney-client privilege based upon the fact that Mr. Willard did not specifically take actions to preclude his estate from waiving the privilege upon his death. [After analyzing the pertinent North Carolina statutes and cases and applying the doctrine of *expressio unius est exclusio alterius*, the Court concluded that because Mr. Willard's will did not expressly grant the executrix the power to waive his attorney-client privilege, Mrs. Willard does not have the power to waive Mr. Willard's attorney-client privilege. In a footnote, the Court noted that many jurisdictions have enacted provisions empowering a personal representative to claim and exercise (and by necessary inference also waive) the decedent's attorney-client privilege, but the North Carolina General Assembly has not enacted any such provision.]

[*2. Does a trial court have inherent authority to apply a balancing test?*]

In its second basic contention, the State asserts that the trial court properly accepted the premise of a balancing test. The State argues that the information sought from respondent is not available from any other source, that the relief granted the State is narrow in that an *in camera* review by the trial court must occur before the State has access to any of the information, and that disclosure under such circumstances and procedure will cause no substantial harm to the attorney-client privilege and all that such privilege embodies.

After weighing the State's arguments for the public's interest in justice in the instant case against respondent's arguments for the public's interest in protecting the privilege, and before conducting an *in camera* review, the trial court concluded:

> [T]he State's and the public's interest in determining the identity of the person or persons responsible for the death of Eric Miller outweigh the public interest in protecting . . . the attorney-client privilege.

The public's interest in protecting the attorney-client privilege is no trivial consideration, as this protection for confidential communications is one of the oldest and most revered in law. The privilege has its foundation in the common law and can be traced back to the sixteenth century. The attorney-client privilege is well-grounded in the jurisprudence of this State. [W]hen the relationship of attorney and client exists all confidential communications made by the client to his attorney on the faith of such relationship are privileged and may not be disclosed.

There are exceptions to this general rule of application to all communications between a client and his attorney; however, the facts of this case do not fall under any one of the well-established exceptions. *See, e.g., State v. McIntosh*, 336 N.C. 517 (1994) (where uncontroverted evidence showed the defendant consulted with his attorney solely to facilitate his surrender, such communication relating to the surrender was not privileged); *State v. Taylor*, 327 N.C. 147 (1990) (when a client alleges ineffective assistance of counsel, the client waives the attorney-client privilege as to the matters relevant to the allegation); *State v. Brown*, 327 N.C. 1, 21 (1990) (communications are not privileged when made in the presence of a third person not acting as an agent of either party); *In re Will of Kemp*, 236 N.C. at 684 (the privilege is not applicable when an attorney testifies regarding the testator's intent to settle a dispute over an estate).

The rationale for having the attorney-client privilege is based upon the belief that only full and frank communications between attorney and client allow the attorney to provide the best counsel to his client. *Upjohn Co. v. United States*, 449 U.S. 383, 389 (1981). The privilege "rests on the theory that encouraging clients to make the fullest disclosure to their attorneys enables the latter to act more effectively, justly and expeditiously — benefits out-weighing the risks of truth-finding posed by barring full disclosure in court."

In considering whether an attorney can be compelled to disclose confidential attorney-client communications, it is noteworthy that unlike other profession-related, privileged communications, the attorney-client privilege has not been statutorily codified. [The Court noted that the North Carolina Legislature had expressly established a physician-patient privilege, a psychologist-patient privilege, a school counselor privilege, a marital and family therapy privilege, a social worker privilege, a professional counselor privilege, and an optometrist-patient privilege, and had provided that confidential information obtained in such relationships could be disclosed only on the authorization of the privilege holder (or, if the holder was deceased, then by the holder's executor, administrator or next of kin). The same statutes gave judges power to compel disclosure if disclosure is necessary to a proper administration of justice. Yet the Legislature had made other statutory privileges (such as the clergyman privilege or the marital therapist privilege), in essence absolute by not including any provision for a judge to compel disclosure if necessary to a proper administration of justice. Because the Legislature has not enacted statutory provisions governing the attorney-client privilege, the Court said it must look solely to the common law for its proper application.]

With regard to case law, the State asserts that the rationale in *Cohen v. Jenkintown Cab Co.*, 238 Pa. Super. 456, 357 A.2d 689 (1976), supports the application of a balancing test in the case *sub judice*. In *Cohen*, the court concluded that the interests of justice required disclosure of a deceased client's communications with his attorney. The court balanced the necessity of revealing the confidential communications against the possibility of harm to the client's estate, reputation, or rights and interests. The rationale supporting the decision in *Cohen* was that the attorney-client privilege exists to aid in the administration of justice, and when this goal is frustrated by its application, the trial court can compel disclosure.

In response to the State's argument, respondent asserts that the United States Supreme Court's decision in *Swidler* is virtually indistinguishable from the instant case. The Court in *Swidler* explicitly rejected the balancing test as applied to the attorney-client privilege in *Cohen*. In *Swidler*, Vincent W. Foster, Jr. was the Deputy White House Counsel when the Office of Independent Counsel investigated whether various crimes were committed during the 1993 dismissal of several employees from the White House Travel Office. In July 1993, Foster met with an attorney at the firm of Swidler & Berlin for legal representation in regard to possible investigations which might be conducted into the employee firings. Nine days after Foster met with his attorney, he committed suicide.

In 1995, a federal grand jury issued subpoenas in order to obtain the handwritten notes made by Foster's attorney during the July 1993 meeting. The federal district court reviewed the handwritten notes *in camera* and concluded that they were protected from disclosure by the attorney-client privilege and the work-product privilege. The Court of Appeals for the District of Columbia Circuit reversed, concluding that an exception to the attorney-client privilege applied. The Court of Appeals applied a balancing test and determined that the uncertainty introduced by its balancing test was insignificant in light of existing exceptions to the privilege. The United States Supreme Court reversed the Court of Appeals, refusing to permit disclosure of the confidential communications between Foster and his attorney.

The United States Supreme Court reasoned that when a client communicates with his attorney, he may not then be aware of the possibility that his statements might later become part of a civil or criminal matter. The Court also recognized the dangers associated with invoking exceptions to the attorney-client privilege:

> Knowing that communications will remain confidential even after death encourages the client to communicate fully and frankly with counsel. While the fear of disclosure, and the consequent withholding of information from counsel, may be reduced if disclosure is limited to posthumous disclosure in a criminal

> context, it seems unreasonable to assume that it vanishes altogether. Clients may be concerned about reputation, civil liability, or possible harm to friends or family. Posthumous disclosure of such communications may be as feared as disclosure during the client's lifetime.

Moreover, the Court expressly rejected the application of a balancing test to the attorney-client privilege when the client has died and the privileged information at issue is pursued to further a criminal investigation:

> Balancing *ex post* the importance of the information against client interests, even limited to criminal cases, introduces substantial uncertainty into the privilege's application.

In the instant case, as in *Swidler*, the client sought legal advice from an attorney just days before he committed suicide. The facts as reflected in the record support the assumption that Mr. Willard was well aware of the criminal investigation and discussed the circumstances surrounding the death of Dr. Miller with respondent and with Mrs. Willard. It is apparent that Mr. Willard attempted to keep the information he communicated to respondent private. Unlike his co-workers, Mr. Willard refused to speak with law enforcement officials regarding the death of Dr. Miller, and most notably, he chose to commit suicide before he was questioned or otherwise pressured to reveal whether he was involved in the death of Dr. Miller.

In assessing the adoption of a balancing test, as proposed by the State, we are cognizant of both the principal justification for such tests and the concerns for its application. Balancing tests provide trial courts with the flexibility to respond to unique circumstances and unanticipated situations. Bright-line rules, on the other hand, limit future judicial discretion and provide trial courts, and litigants, with predictability and consistency. A strict balancing test involving the attorney-client privilege, in the context of the present case after the client's death, subjects the client's reasonable expectation of nondisclosure to a process without parameters or standards, with an end result no more predictable in any case than a public opinion poll, the weather over time, or any athletic contest. Such a test, regardless of how well intentioned and conducted it may be, or how exigent the circumstances, would likely have, in the immediate future and over time, a corrosive effect on the privilege's traditionally stable application and the corresponding expectations of clients. Moreover, the proposed factors to be balanced are not capable of precise discernment or application in this case, or any case, and seem to add little to an assessment of whether the privilege should be waived.

The practical consequences of a balancing test include the difficulty of demonstrating equality of treatment, the decline of judicial predictability, and the facilitation of judicial arbitrariness. These concerns are further well expressed as follows: Simply stated, the balancing test (1) does not ensure, even in theory, that like cases will be treated alike, and (2) so muddies the areas of the law it comes to dominate that those governed by it are left without clear guidance about what behavior is permitted and what is not. In light of these considerations, it appears that the application of a balancing test exception, even under such conditions as proposed by the State in the instant case, would invite procedures and applications so lacking in standards, direction and scope that the privilege in practice would be lost to the exception.

The attorney-client privilege is unique among all privileged communications. In practice, communications between attorney and client can encompass *all* subjects which may be discussed in any other privileged relationship and indeed all subjects within the human experience. As such, it is the privilege most beneficial to the public, both in facilitating competent legal advice and ultimately in furthering the ends of justice. We therefore conclude that the balancing test as proposed by the State is not appropriate and should not be applied under the circumstances of the instant case.

The next step in our inquiry is to further examine the evidence or facts revealed in the record and determine whether any other reason or basis for exception to the privilege exists which would warrant disclosure of the information respondent possesses.

We recognize first in this regard that the primary goal of our adversarial system of justice is to ascertain the truth in any legal proceeding. This proposition has been well stated as follows:

> The pertinent general principle, responding to the deepest needs of society, is that society is entitled to every man's evidence. As the underlying aim of judicial inquiry is ascertainable truth, everything rationally related to ascertaining the truth is presumptively admissible. Limitations are properly placed upon the operation of this general principle only to the very limited extent that permitting a refusal to testify or excluding relevant evidence has a public good transcending the normally predominant principle of utilizing all rational means for ascertaining truth.

. . . While the attorney-client privilege is an essential component in our system of justice, many ethical and moral dilemmas exist as a result of this limitation on finding the truth. For example, one critic of the privilege has opined:

> Confidentiality rules invite attorneys to withhold information that could prevent harm to third parties in the course of representing their clients. The rules promote a culture of winning at any cost short of dishonesty while avoiding consideration of others.

It is further well established that the attorney-client privilege is not absolute. When certain extraordinary circumstances are present, the need for disclosure of attorney-client communications will trump the confidential nature of the privilege.

With these principles in mind, we turn to the resolution of the primary issue presented in this case.

It is universally accepted and well founded in the law of this State that not all communications between an attorney and a client are privileged. This Court has recognized a five-part test to determine whether the attorney-client privilege applies to a particular communication:

> (1) the relation of attorney and client existed at the time the communication was made, (2) the communication was made in confidence, (3) the communication relates to a matter about which the attorney is being professionally consulted, (4) the communication was made in the course of giving or seeking legal advice for a proper purpose although litigation need not be contemplated and (5) the client has not waived the privilege.

McIntosh, 336 N.C. at 523–24. If any one of these five elements is not present in any portion of an attorney-client communication, that portion of the communication is not privileged. For example, pursuant to the second prong of this test, if it appears that a communication was not regarded as confidential or that the communication was made for the purpose of being conveyed by the attorney to others, the communication is not privileged. In addition, the fourth prong of this test makes it clear that the attorney-client privilege cannot serve as a shield for fraud or as a tool to aid in the commission of future criminal activities; if a communication is not "made in the course of seeking or giving legal advice for a proper purpose," it is not protected.

In the usual instance, it is impossible to determine whether a particular communication meets the elements of the test set forth in *McIntosh*, particularly the third and fourth prongs, without first knowing the substance of that communication. Thus, an *in camera* review of the content of an attorney-client communication may be necessary before a trial court is able to determine whether that communication is privileged:

> The burden is always on the party asserting the privilege to demonstrate each of its essential elements. This burden may not be met by mere conclusory

> or ipse dixit assertions, or by a blanket refusal to testify. Rather, sufficient evidence must be adduced, usually by means of an affidavit or affidavits, to establish the privilege with respect to each disputed item.

More than a century ago, this Court held that the responsibility of determining whether the attorney-client privilege applies belongs to the trial court, not to the attorney asserting the privilege. Thus, a trial court is not required to rely solely on an attorney's assertion that a particular communication falls within the scope of the attorney-client privilege. In cases where the party seeking the information has, in good faith, come forward with a nonfrivolous assertion that the privilege does not apply, the trial court may conduct an *in camera* inquiry of the substance of the communication. . . .

We therefore conclude that, in the instant case, the trial court's decision to conduct an *in camera* review of the communications between respondent and Mr. Willard was procedurally correct. The trial court did not err in ordering respondent to provide the trial court with a sealed affidavit containing the communications which transpired between Mr. Willard and respondent, for the purpose of determining whether the attorney-client privilege applies to any portion of the communication. . . .

Turning now more specifically to the five-part *McIntosh* test, we note that the unique facts of the instant case, as reflected in the record, raise concerns, particularly regarding the application of the third and fourth prongs of the *McIntosh* test. As to the third prong, the communications must relate to a matter about which the attorney is being professionally consulted, and considering also the first prong of the test in this regard, it is clear that only those communications which are between the attorney and the client and which are part of the client's actual purpose for the legal consultation are privileged. While communications made by a client to an attorney which pertain to the culpability or interests of the client are privileged and ordinarily remain privileged after the client's death, communications between an attorney and a client that relate to or concern the interests, rights, activities, motives, liabilities, or plans of some third party, the disclosure of which would not tend to harm the client, do not logically fall within North Carolina's definition of attorney-client privileged information. With regard to the fourth prong of the *McIntosh* test, the communications must relate to communications between the attorney and the client for a proper purpose. While communications concerning the client's own criminal culpability and his defense is certainly privileged, it is difficult to fathom how any communications relating to a third party's criminal activity, concealment thereof or obstruction of justice could fall within such category, when disclosure thereof would not tend to harm the client. The concept of proper purpose relates not only to whether the communications involve the client's future illegal activity, obstruction of justice or activity directly or indirectly aiding a third party in some illegal activity, but it also relates only to communications that would properly benefit the client as opposed to a third party.

The author of one leading treatise on the law of evidence explained that the attorney-client privilege should be asserted only by the person whose interest the particular rule of privilege is intended to safeguard. *McCormick on Evidence* § 92, at 368. This interpretation of the privilege is consistent with the privilege's underlying purpose:

> While once it was conceived that the privilege was set up to protect the lawyer's honor, we know that today it is agreed that the basic policy of the rule is that of encouraging clients to lay the facts fully before their counsel. They will be encouraged by a privilege which they themselves have the power to invoke. *To extend any benefit or advantage to someone as attorney, or as party to a suit, or to people generally, will be to suppress relevant evidence without promoting the purpose of the privilege.*

Id. at 369 (emphasis added). . . . Although an attorney may assert the privilege when necessary to protect the interests of the client, the privilege belongs solely to the client.

The law of privileged communications between attorney and client is that the privilege is that of the client. *He alone is the one for whose protection the rule is enforced.*

. . . [W]e believe that communications between attorney and client regarding any criminal activity of a third party, which do not tend to harm the interests of the client, do not satisfy the third and fourth prongs of the *McIntosh* test, and such communications are therefore not privileged. Accordingly, we hold that when a trial court, after conducting an *in camera* review as described below, determines that some or all of the communications between a client and an attorney do not relate to a matter that affected the client at the time the statements were made, about which the attorney was professionally consulted within the parameters of the *McIntosh* test, such communications are not privileged and may be disclosed.

With regard to the instant case, in determining whether Mr. Willard's statements to respondent should be disclosed, the trial court should consider the circumstances surrounding Mr. Willard at the time he communicated with counsel. In applying the *McIntosh* factors, the trial court should be mindful that the statements were made by Mr. Willard when he presumably knew he was a suspect in a criminal investigation. In this context, it is conceivable that statements by Mr. Willard which implicated a third party may have also implicated him in a crime. If so, those statements, if then revealed, would have subjected him to criminal liability. Therefore, at the time Mr. Willard made the statements, anything he said relating his collaborative involvement with a third party in the death of Dr. Miller was covered by the attorney-client privilege. . . . .

We further conclude that in considering, by *in camera* review, whether communications asserted to be privileged should be disclosed, a trial court should additionally apply the maxim *cessante ratione legis, cessat ipsa lex.* When the underlying justification for the rule of law, or in this case the privilege, is not furthered by its continued application, the rule or privilege should cease to apply. It is contrary to the spirit of the common law itself to apply a rule founded on a particular reason to a law when that reason utterly fails. The application of this maxim was further well stated by the United States Supreme Court as follows:

> If the reasons on which a law rests are overborne by opposing reasons, which in the progress of society gain a controlling force, the old law, though still good as an abstract principle, and good in its application to some circumstances, must cease to apply as a controlling principle to the new circumstances.

In this regard, and specifically with respect to the attorney-client privilege, the United States Supreme Court has stated that since the privilege has the effect of withholding relevant information from the factfinder, it applies only where necessary to achieve its purpose.' Thus, we further consider at this point in our analysis whether nondisclosure in the present case furthers the purpose for which the privilege exists.

When a client retains an attorney for legal advice in regard to an ongoing criminal investigation, the client's desire to keep the communication confidential is premised upon three possible consequences in the event of disclosure: (1) that disclosure might subject the client to criminal liability; (2) that disclosure might subject the client, or the client's estate, to civil liability; and (3) that disclosure might harm the client's loved ones or his reputation. Therefore, in determining whether the reasons for the privilege still exist after the client is deceased, the trial court should consider the *Swidler* factors.

AUTHORS' COMMENT:

This case concerns a client who is dead, but what if a client is alive? Are the three *Swidler* factors still the only factors that a court ought to consider in deciding whether an attorney-client communication is privileged?

In the instant case, the trial court should consider whether these possible consequences would apply to, or would have any negative or harmful effect on, Mr. Willard's rights and interests if the State was permitted to obtain the information communicated between Mr. Willard and respondent. In the event the trial court, upon *in camera* review, should conclude that any of these consequences still apply to any portion of the communications, they should remain undisclosed. If, on the other hand, the trial court should determine that the communications asserted to be privileged would have no negative impact on Mr. Willard's interests, the purpose for the privilege no longer exists. When application of the privilege will no longer safeguard the client's interests, no reason exists in support of perpetual nondisclosure.

We acknowledge that, while some risk of withholding information might remain if an attorney were permitted, even under this very narrow premise, to disclose privileged information after a client has died, the instant case presents unique circumstances in which there may be little or no risk of harm to the client. It is indeed a rare case where the full application of the above rationale would apply; therefore, trial courts should carefully analyze each individual factual situation on a case-by-case basis when determining whether to permit disclosure of information asserted to be privileged. In this regard, we emphasize that in approving *in camera* review pursuant to the narrow principles herein set forth, we are in no way sanctioning or suggesting any general application of special proceedings or grand jury investigations by prosecutors in the nature of fishing expeditions or otherwise which would tend to diminish in any way the great value to the public of the attorney-client privilege by its proper application through the judicial process.

In summary then, we hold that when a client is deceased, upon a nonfrivolous assertion that the privilege does not apply, with a proper, good-faith showing by the party seeking disclosure of communications, the trial court may conduct an *in camera* review of the substance of the communications. To the extent any portion of the communications between the attorney and the deceased client relate solely to a third party, such communications are not within the purview of the attorney-client privilege. If the trial court finds that some or all of the communications are outside the scope of the attorney-client privilege, the trial court may compel the attorney to provide the substance of the communications to the State for its use in the criminal investigation, consistent with the procedural formalities set forth below. To the extent the communications relate to a third party but also affect the client's own rights or interests and thus remain privileged, such communications may be revealed only upon a clear and convincing showing that their disclosure does not expose the client's estate to civil liability and that such disclosure would not likely result in additional harm to loved ones or reputation. We do not reach the issue of whether any such information so provided by any attorney would be admissible in any future criminal prosecution. In the event a subsequent criminal prosecution ensues, the trial court would apply the rules of evidence to this information in the event it is tendered in evidence and determine then whether it is admissible against a defendant.

Upon *in camera* review, in the event the trial court concludes that any portion of the communications made between the client and the attorney is either not subject to the attorney-client privilege, or though privileged no longer serves the purpose of the privilege and may be disclosed, the attorney's affidavit and the information contained therein must nevertheless remain sealed and preserved in the records of the trial court for appellate review in the event of an immediate appeal. The trial court's determination of the applicability of the privilege or disclosure affects a substantial right and is therefore immediately appealable. . . . Consequently, the trial court should carefully guard the contents of any materials it receives from the *in camera* review, even if it concludes that the information is not protected by the attorney-client privilege, so long as the party objecting to disclosure gives notice of immediate appeal. . . . .

Based upon the foregoing, the decision of the trial court is affirmed in part, reversed in part, and remanded for further proceedings consistent with this opinion.

Affirmed in part, reversed in part, and remanded.

NOTES AND QUESTIONS

1. ***Three Categories of Information.*** In its summary near the end of the case, the *Miller* Court essentially divides attorney-client communications between deceased clients and their attorneys into three categories:

- *Communications between the attorney and the deceased client that relate solely to a third party.* Such communications are not protected by the attorney-client privilege, and the trial court may compel the attorney to provide the substance of the communications to the State for its use in the criminal investigation.
- *Communications that relate to a third party but also affect the client's own rights or interests.* These communications remain privileged, but the court may order them revealed upon a clear and convincing showing that their disclosure does not expose the client's estate to civil liability and that such disclosure would not likely result in additional harm to loved ones or reputation.
- *Communications that relate solely to the client's own interests.* These communications, which the Court does not expressly mention in the summary, presumably remain privileged forever, and the court cannot order their disclosure.

Do these categories make sense to you?

2. ***Wanted Dead or Alive.*** The prosecution and defense in a criminal case, and the plaintiff and defendant in a civil case, are going to want attorney-client communications that they think will help their side, whether the client is dead or alive. Is there any reason that the categories set out in *Death of Miller* should not apply to clients who are alive? Does the Court do enough to limit its holding to deceased clients? Suppose the client made the communication twenty years ago; should it still be protected just because the client is still alive, even if the disclosure will not subject the client to the threat of criminal or civil litigation, or harm to loved ones or reputation?

3. ***In Business Since 1577.*** The attorney-client privilege is an old, old privilege. One of the cases cited in *Death of Miller* is *Berd v. Lovelace*, a case published in 1577. The full text of the report of that case provides as follows:

> *A solicitor served with process to testify, ordered not to be examined.* Thomas Hawtry, gentlemen, was served with a subpoena to testify his knowledge touching the cause in variance; and made oath that he hath been, and yet is a solicitor in this suit, and hath received several fees of the defendant; which being informed to the Master of the Rolls, it is ordered that the said Thomas Hawtry shall not be compelled to be deposed, touching the same, and that he shall be in no danger of any contempt, touching the not executing of the said process; Berd, plaintant; Lovelace, defendant (Anno 19 Eliz. [1576–77]).

In your own words, explain what happened in *Berd v. Lovelace*. Were the policies clear enough more than 400 years ago to decide that case so easily? What are those policies?

Under *Death of Miller*, would the result of the case have changed if the defendant (Lovelace) had died before Hawtry was called as a witness?

4. ***In Camera Inspection.*** Is the *Miller* court correct that it is often difficult to ascertain whether an attorney-client communication is privileged unless the court takes a look at the communication *in camera*? Suppose you are a judge and a defense attorney claims that a certain conversation with her client is privileged. Without knowing what was communicated, can you determine whether: "(a) the communication relates to a matter about which the attorney is being professionally consulted," or "(b) the communication was made in the course of giving or seeking legal advice for a proper purpose"?

5. ***Draft a Dissent.*** The opinion in *Investigation of Death of Miller* was unanimous. But there certainly are some plausible grounds for a dissent. Assume you are clerking for a Justice of the North Carolina Supreme Court who says, "I'm going to dissent. Draft a dissent for me." What would be the main points in your draft dissent?

Chapter 13

CORPORATIONS, CORRUPTION, AND CONFIDENTIALITY

In many areas of the law, corporations are treated differently from "two-legged" individuals. In civil procedure, for example, an individual always has only one "domicile" for purposes of diversity jurisdiction, but a corporation may have two domiciles (both its place of incorporation and its principal place of business). In tax law, corporate taxes are treated differently from individual taxes. And in the world of legal ethics, corporations are subject to special rules regarding the attorney-client privilege and the ethical duty of confidentiality. This chapter explains and discusses those special rules.

The most difficult problems of secrecy arise when a corporation, as an entity, is suspected or accused of corruption or other crimes, or when individual officers, directors, or employees within a corporation appear to be engaging in criminal or fraudulent activity. In both settings, a corporation typically undertakes an internal investigation to discover and root out any wrongful activity. That raises two questions: (1) What is the scope of the attorney-client privilege for a corporation? and (2) What are the exceptions to the duty of confidentiality when the client is a corporation? This chapter will address both questions.

A. THE ATTORNEY-CLIENT PRIVILEGE FOR ORGANIZATIONS

So far in our study of the attorney-client privilege, we have been concentrating on the attorney-client privilege for individuals. What about organizations? Can corporate clients, partnerships, and other organizations claim the protection of the attorney-client privilege? Or is the attorney-client privilege restricted to individuals, just as the Fifth Amendment privilege against self-incrimination is restricted to individuals?

The answer is that the attorney-client privilege *does* extend to corporations — but it may not protect corporations as fully as it protects individuals. In this chapter, we will see how the privilege applies to organizations, especially corporations.

To say that a corporation has an attorney-client privilege, however, brings up an immediate problem: who is the client? In other words, who can claim the corporation's attorney-client privilege? A corporation itself is not a natural person; it is a legal fiction, a juridical entity, a creature of the state. It is not created via human biology but rather is created via government bureaucracy. Stripped of its tangible assets and its "human capital" (officers, employees, directors), a corporation is a mere piece of paper, a certificate of incorporation issued by the Secretary of State's office. But the corporation acts and communicates through people. The corporate certificate can't talk. When a lawyer communicates with a corporation, the lawyer communicates with people — with officers, directors, or employees.

The key question is: Can an attorney who represents a corporation claim the attorney-client privilege for communications with all officers, directors, and employees, or just with some of them? And, if only with some, which ones?

We can safely assume that a lawyer's conversation with the President or CEO of a corporation is privileged, because the President or CEO seems to speak for the corporation and embody its interests. What about the custodian? If the lawyer talks to a custodian while investigating a tort claim against the corporation, is that conversation privileged? If so, who can waive the attorney-client privilege on behalf of the corporation? Who owns the privilege? Before tackling these questions, let us set out a scenario that raises these and other related questions.

B. A SECRECY SCENARIO: LET THERE BE LUX?

Imagine that you represent Lux Corporation, which specializes in making and installing lighting fixtures in office buildings. Lux leases the factory at which it assembles the lighting fixtures, and it buys light bulbs and metal fixture parts from other companies, so the company does not own much. Its main assets are receivables (money already owed for goods sold) and work in progress (meaning fixtures that will soon be sold).

For the past three years, you have been the principal outside counsel to Lux, handling a variety of general corporate matters. The key event happened exactly one year ago, when you acted as counsel for the client in negotiating a loan from Metro Bank and drafting the loan documents. Under the terms of the loan documents, Metro Bank gave Lux a $5 million unsecured loan to expand Lux's offices and increase Lux's working capital. The loan was for a three-year term. During the three years, Lux only had to pay interest, on a monthly basis. At the end of three years, Lux had to pay back the $5 million principal amount. At the loan closing, as counsel for Lux, you issued a formal opinion to the bank in the customary form. Your letter stated:

> It is my opinion, based on due diligence, that: (i) Lux Corporation (hereinafter "the client") has been duly organized and is in good standing as a foreign corporation in every state where the nature of its business requires such qualification; (ii) the loan transaction has been duly authorized by all necessary corporate action and the loan documents have been properly executed on behalf of the client by its duly authorized officers; (iii) all obligations cited in the loan documents are enforceable against the client in accordance with their terms (subject only to the application and effect of bankruptcy and insolvency laws and the like); and (iv) all installation contracts are enforceable obligations under applicable law against the client's customers.

At the loan closing, Metro Bank relied not only on your opinion but also on the client's audited financial statements which were accompanied by an unqualified opinion in the usual form from the client's independent auditors. The audited financial statements showed the client was a financially sound enterprise, with a net worth in excess of $15 million, and with no outstanding indebtedness other than to trade creditors. Lux's treasurer signed, executed and submitted to Metro Bank a certificate accompanying the audited financial statements warranting that, at the date of the loan closing, there had been "no material adverse change in the financial condition of Lux Corporation," and that the audited financial statements accurately reflected its financial condition at the date of the loan closing. Metro Bank thereupon closed the loan and advanced the full $5 million loan proceeds to your client.

Unknown to you, however, and also unknown to the accounting firm, Lux's chief executive officer and treasurer have for the past three years been engaged in a fraud, manufacturing millions of dollars worth of false lighting installation contracts. In many cases, the fraud was relatively easy to carry off because Lux actually did some work in the building in question. The fraud essentially consisted of altering the original contracts, or forging change orders, in a way that inflated the contract amount. As a result, the client's audited financial statements for the past three years (including the statements on which Metro Bank relied in closing the loan) were materially misleading. In fact, the company's net worth is not in excess of $15 million (as indicated in the audited financial statements) but rather is less than the $5 million borrowed from Metro Bank.

A couple of months ago, you developed a strong gut instinct that something was amiss at Lux. When you visited Lux's offices to work on some contract and employment matters, you took the liberty to review a number of lighting contracts and question some of the mid-level managers, factory supervisors, and assembly line workers at Lux about the amount of work the company has been doing, how long it takes the company to fill a contract for 1,000 lighting fixtures, how much overtime the workers had been putting in, and other questions designed to figure out whether Lux's audited financial statements were honest and accurate.

When you gathered enough information to press the CEO and the treasurer about the true state of the company's financial condition, they both confessed the fraud to you. They have not told the independent auditors or anybody else, but they have earnestly represented to you that they stopped creating bogus contracts and will be scrupulously honest — "as honest as Abraham Lincoln," they said — in the future. However, they are unwilling to issue corrected financial statements, which of course would disclose the prior fraud to Metro Bank. In addition, they have told you that they are planning to retain a new law firm, Morganthau & Giuliani, as Lux's main outside counsel and do not intend to disclose the prior fraud to the new firm. Moreover, the CEO and treasurer expressly instructed you not to answer any questions from Morganthau & Giuliani about Lux or any work you have done for Lux. Finally, they asked you and your firm to continue handling a few projects for Lux because your firm's total resignation (withdrawal) would "send bad signals to the business community."

You expect that Lux will use Morganthau & Giuliani (its new firm) for future assignments involving the false financial statements — assignments you could not ethically handle because you know Lux's true financial situation. These assignments may include new loan transactions, but they may also consist of ongoing dealings with Metro Bank — the kinds of routine issues that come up when maintaining a line of credit. Further reliance by Metro Bank on the fraudulent financial statements would also necessarily entail reliance on your opinion vouching for the principal assets reflected in those financial statements.

The CEO and the treasurer have told you they will do everything within their power to strengthen the company financially during the two years remaining before the $5 million debt to the bank matures. They have also told you that, despite a serious threat of bankruptcy, Lux ultimately will survive and thrive because it is slowly developing a good volume of honest business. You believe that they are sincere about their determination to succeed and their prediction that the company will survive. However, the CEO and treasurer have also agreed that even if Lux survives, there's "no way, no how" that Lux will be in a position to repay the full $5 million loan to Metro Bank when the principal comes due in two years. The CEO and the treasurer have asked you to remain publicly and officially as counsel to the company, because your experience puts you in a good position to assist the company's survival efforts in ways that would not directly implicate the opinion you issued a year ago endorsing the company's false financial statements.

This scenario raises many questions about your options and obligations under the Rules of Professional Conduct and other law. In particular:

1. May you (or must you) reveal the fraud to anyone inside Lux? If so, who?

2. May you (or must you) reveal the fraud to anyone *outside* Lux? If so, who?

3. May you (or must you) continue doing legal work for Lux? Are there any limitations on the kinds of assignments you are permitted to handle?

4. If you are subpoenaed to testify before a grand jury, or to give a deposition in a civil fraud suit against Lux, will your conversations with the CEO, treasurer, and others at Lux be protected by the attorney-client privilege? Is the answer the same for: (a) conversations leading up to the Metro Bank loan a year ago; (b) your investigative conversations with various Lux mid-level managers, factory supervisors, and assembly line workers; and (c) your conversations with the CEO and treasurer about the fraud?

Keep all of these questions in mind as you read the materials in this chapter.

C. THE ATTORNEY-CLIENT PRIVILEGE FOR CORPORATIONS IN THE COURTS

An early effort to define the scope of the attorney-client privilege for corporations came in a case still cited frequently, *City of Philadelphia v. Westinghouse Elec. Corp.*, 210 F. Supp. 483 (E.D. Pa. 1962), *aff'd mem.*, 312 F.2d 686 (3d Cir. 1963). That case laid the foundation for the so-called "control group test" as "a limitation on the privilege" for corporations. Under the control group test, the attorney-client privilege protects corporations only if the person communicating with the lawyer is a member of the "control group" — the elite group of corporate officers and employees who actually control the corporation and make its policies. More colloquially, we can call the control group "the brains of the outfit."

Today, however, the control group test is on the wane. The federal courts and many states have abandoned it in favor of a far more expansive privilege for corporations. The next opinion, the *Upjohn* case, is the foundation of the prevailing current approach to the attorney-client privilege, and the binding authority on the attorney-client privilege in federal courts.

1. The Attorney-Client Privilege in Federal Courts

Before reading *Upjohn*, remember the "five C's" of the attorney-client privilege: (1) a Communication (2) between a Client (3) and the client's Counsel (4) in Confidence, (5) for the purpose of giving or receiving legal Counsel.

Keep in mind also that in the federal courts questions of privilege are governed by Rule 501 of the Federal Rules of Evidence, which tells federal courts to apply the common law "in light of reason and experience." Is Justice Rehnquist's opinion for the Court persuasive to you in terms of "reason"? Why or why not?

UPJOHN CO. v. UNITED STATES

449 U.S. 383 (1981)

JUSTICE REHNQUIST delivered the opinion of the court.

We granted certiorari in this case to address important questions concerning the scope of the attorney-client privilege in the corporate context. . . .

[Upjohn is a pharmaceutical company. Upjohn's General Counsel, Thomas, learned that one of Upjohn's foreign managers had apparently given bribes or kickbacks to foreign government officials to get the foreign governments to buy products from Upjohn. Upjohn launched a major investigation. Upjohn's General Counsel sent a questionnaire to all foreign managers seeking detailed information concerning improper payments, and (together with outside counsel) the General Counsel interviewed questionnaire recipients and other Upjohn officers and employees.]

[When Upjohn finished investigating, it sent a report to the Internal Revenue Service (IRS) disclosing some questionable payments. The IRS then began investigating the tax consequences of the questionable payments. (For example, the IRS might disallow some previously claimed deductions, or might assess fraud penalties.) As part of this investigation, the IRS issued a civil summons (basically equivalent to a subpoena) demanding that Upjohn produce the questionnaire responses and the memoranda and notes of interviews. Upjohn refused on the grounds of the attorney-client privilege and the work-product doctrine. A federal district court rejected Upjohn's claims. The Court of Appeals affirmed, holding that under the so-called "control group test," the attorney-client privilege did not apply to communications with lower-level managers. The Supreme Court had to decide whether the privilege covered all corporate employees, or only to those in the control group, or to something in between.]

Federal Rule of Evidence 501 provides that "the privilege of a witness . . . shall be governed by the principles of the common law as they may be interpreted by the courts of the United States in light of reason and experience." The attorney-client privilege is the oldest of the privileges for confidential communications known to the common law. Its purpose is to encourage full and frank communication between attorneys and their clients and thereby promote broader public interests in the observance of law and administration of justice. The privilege recognizes that sound legal advice or advocacy serves public ends and that such advice or advocacy depends upon the lawyer being fully informed by the client. . . . Admittedly complications in the application of the privilege arise when the client is a corporation, which in theory is an artificial creature of the law, and not an individual; but this Court has assumed that the privilege applies when the client is a corporation, and the Government does not contest the general proposition.

The Court of Appeals, however, considered the application of the privilege in the corporate context to present a "different problem," since the client was an inanimate entity and "only the senior management, guiding and integrating the several operations, . . . can be said to possess an identity analogous to the corporation as a whole." The first case to articulate the so-called "control group test" adopted by the court below, *Philadelphia v. Westinghouse Electric Corp.*, 210 F. Supp. 483, 485 (ED Pa. 1962), reflected a similar conceptual approach:

> "Keeping in mind that the question is, Is it the corporation which is seeking the lawyer's advice when the asserted privileged communication is made?, the most satisfactory solution, I think, is that if the employee making the communication, of whatever rank he may be, is in a position to control or even to take a substantial part in a decision about any action which the corporation may take upon the advice of the attorney, . . . then, in effect, *he is (or personifies) the corporation* when he makes his disclosure to the lawyer and the privilege would apply." (Emphasis supplied.)

Such a view, we think, overlooks the fact that the privilege exists to protect not only the giving of professional advice to those who can act on it but also the giving of information to the lawyer to enable him to give sound and informed advice. The first step in the resolution of any legal problem is ascertaining the factual background and sifting through the facts with an eye to the legally relevant. . . .

In the case of the individual client the provider of information and the person who acts on the lawyer's advice are one and the same. In the corporate context, however, it will frequently be employees beyond the control group as defined by the court below — "officers and agents . . . responsible for directing [the company's] actions in response to legal advice" — who will possess the information needed by the corporation's lawyers. Middle-level-and indeed lower-level-employees can, by actions within the scope of their employment, embroil the corporation in serious legal difficulties, and it is only natural that these employees would have the relevant information needed by corporate counsel if he is adequately to advise the client with respect to such actual or potential difficulties. . . .

The control group test adopted by the court below thus frustrates the very purpose of the privilege by discouraging the communication of relevant information by employees of the client to attorneys seeking to render legal advice to the client corporation. The attorney's advice will also frequently be more significant to noncontrol group members than to those who officially sanction the advice, and the control group test makes it more difficult to convey full and frank legal advice to the employees who will put into effect the client corporation's policy. *See, e.g., Duplan Corp. v. Deering Milliken, Inc.*, 397 F. Supp. 1146, 1164 (SC 1974) ("After the lawyer forms his or her opinion, it is of no immediate benefit to the Chairman of the Board or the President. It must be given to the corporate personnel who will apply it").

The narrow scope given the attorney-client privilege by the court below not only makes it difficult for corporate attorneys to formulate sound advice when their client is faced with a specific legal problem but also threatens to limit the valuable efforts of corporate counsel to ensure their client's compliance with the law. In light of the vast and complicated array of regulatory legislation confronting the modern corporation, corporations, unlike most individuals, "constantly go to lawyers to find out how to obey the law," particularly since compliance with the law in this area is hardly an instinctive matter . . . . [I]f the purpose of the attorney-client privilege is to be served, the attorney and client must be able to predict with some degree of certainty whether particular discussions will be protected. An uncertain privilege, or one which purports to be certain but results in widely varying applications by the courts, is little better than no privilege at all. The very terms of the test adopted by the court below suggest the unpredictability of its application. The test restricts the availability of the privilege to those officers who play a "substantial role" in deciding and directing a corporation's legal response. Disparate decisions in cases applying this test illustrate its unpredictability.

AUTHORS' COMMENT:

Do you agree that an uncertain attorney-client privilege for corporations is "little better than no privilege at all"? Would a corporation's lawyers investigate thoroughly even if there were no privilege? Why or why not? If they would investigate even without a privilege, does it really make much difference whether the privilege is narrow or broad? Continue reading.

The communications at issue were made by Upjohn employees to counsel for Upjohn acting as such, at the direction of corporate superiors in order to secure legal advice from counsel. As the Magistrate found, "Mr. Thomas consulted with the Chairman of the Board and outside counsel and thereafter conducted a factual investigation to determine the nature and extent of the questionable payments *and to be in a position to give legal advice to the company with respect to the payments*." (Emphasis supplied.) Information, not available from upper-echelon management, was needed to supply a basis for legal advice concerning compliance with securities and tax laws, foreign laws, currency regulations, duties to shareholders, and potential litigation in each of these areas. The communications concerned matters within the scope of the employees' corporate duties, and the employees themselves were sufficiently aware that they were being questioned in order that the corporation could obtain legal advice. The questionnaire identified Thomas as "the company's General Counsel" and referred in its opening sentence to the possible illegality of payments such as the ones on which information was sought. A statement of policy accompanying the questionnaire clearly indicated the legal implications of the investigation. The policy statement was issued "in order that there be no uncertainty in the future as to the policy with respect to the practices which are the subject of this investigation." It began "Upjohn will comply with all laws and regulations," and stated that commissions or payments "will not be used as a subterfuge for bribes or illegal payments" and that all payments must be "proper and legal." Any future agreements with foreign distributors or agents were to be approved "by a company attorney" and any question concerning the policy were to be referred "to the company's General Counsel." This statement was issued to Upjohn employees worldwide, so that even those interviewees not receiving a questionnaire were aware of the legal implications of the interviews. Pursuant to explicit instructions from the Chairman of the Board, the communications were considered "highly confidential" when made, and have been kept confidential by the company. Consistent with the underlying purposes of the attorney-client privilege, these communications must be protected against compelled disclosure.

The Court of Appeals declined to extend the attorney-client privilege beyond the limits of the control group test for fear that doing so would entail severe burdens on discovery and create a broad "zone of silence" over corporate affairs. Application of the attorney-client privilege to communications such as those involved here, however, puts the adversary in no worse position than if the communications had never taken place. The privilege only protects disclosure of communications; it does not protect disclosure of the underlying facts by those who communicated with the attorney:

> "[T]he protection of the privilege extends only to *communications* and not to facts. A fact is one thing and a communication concerning that fact is an entirely different thing. The client cannot be compelled to answer the question, 'What did you say or write to the attorney?' but may not refuse to disclose any relevant fact within his knowledge merely because he incorporated a statement of such fact into his communication to his attorney." *Philadelphia v. Westinghouse Electric Corp.*, 205 F. Supp. 830, 831 (ED Pa. 1962).

. . . Here the Government was free to question the employees who communicated with Thomas and outside counsel. Upjohn has provided the IRS with a list of such employees and the IRS has already interviewed some 25 of them. While it would probably be more convenient for the Government to secure the results of petitioner's internal investigation by simply subpoenaing the questionnaires and notes taken by petitioner's attorneys, such considerations of convenience do not overcome the policies served by the attorney-client privilege. As Justice Jackson noted in his concurring opinion in *Hickman v. Taylor*, 329 U.S., at 516: "Discovery was hardly intended to enable a learned profession to perform its functions . . . on wits borrowed from the adversary."

Needless to say, we decide only the case before us, and do not undertake to draft a set of rules which should govern challenges to investigatory subpoenas. Any such approach would violate the spirit of Federal Rule of Evidence 501. See S. Rep. No. 93-1277, p. 13 (1974) ("the recognition of a privilege based on a confidential relationship . . . should be determined on a case-by-case basis"). . . .

NOTES AND QUESTIONS

1. *A General Rule?* Chief Justice Burger concurred in the judgment but argued that the Court should go further in "articulating a standard that will . . . afford guidance to corporations, counsel advising them, and federal courts." He suggested the following formulation:

> [A]s a general rule, a communication is privileged at least when, as here, an employee or former employee speaks at the direction of the management with an attorney regarding conduct or proposed conduct within the scope of employment. The attorney must be one authorized by the management to inquire into the subject and must be seeking information to assist counsel in performing any of the following functions: (a) evaluating whether the employee's conduct has bound or would bind the corporation; (b) assessing the legal consequences, if any, of that conduct; or (c) formulating appropriate legal responses to actions that have been or may be taken by others with regard to that conduct.

2. *Former Employees.* Chief Justice Burger's formulation protects communications with former employees. Do you agree that an attorney's communications with former employees should be privileged? Courts are split on this issue. What are your arguments for and against extending the privilege to former employees?

3. ***Work-product Protection.*** The *Upjohn* Court also held that the work-product privilege was applicable to IRS summonses. To the extent that the notes and memoranda sought by the Government were not communications protected by the attorney-client privilege, they involved attorneys' mental processes in evaluating such communications. Under Rule 26 of the Federal Rules of Civil Procedure and *Hickman v. Taylor*, 329 U.S. 495 (1947), such work-product cannot be disclosed simply on a showing of need or inability to obtain the equivalent. Since the Government had not made the requisite showing of substantial need, the documents did not need to be produced.

4. ***Do Corporations Need Absolute Protection?*** The premise of *Upjohn* is that corporations and their officers and employees would behave differently if the privilege were narrow or uncertain. But some commentators argue that corporations would behave the same even if the privilege were not absolute. For example, Professor Stephen Saltzburg, author of a well-known evidence treatise, argues: "The premise of the nonabsolute character of the work-product doctrine is that lawyers who need information to provide legal advice will seek it from knowledgeable witnesses, even without an absolute privilege protecting their work." Do you agree with Professor Saltzburg? Or do you think corporate lawyers would avoid seeking information if their investigations might not be privileged?

5. ***Does Scope of Authority Matter?*** Suppose one of Upjohn's truck drivers has a traffic accident while operating a company truck. Without any direction from a top-level official of the company, he goes to the General Counsel and tells him that he consumed several drinks at an office party before setting out. Should the privilege apply to this communication even though it was not made "at the direction of corporate superiors in order to secure legal advice from counsel"?

Suppose the same truck driver by chance sees an outside supplier hand a stack of $20 bills to a Purchasing Manager at Upjohn. The truck driver has no responsibilities relating to purchasing. He confides his suspicions to the General Counsel. Is the privilege inapplicable because the communication does not relate to the employee's duties for the corporation? Does the majority opinion in *Upjohn* answer this question? Does Chief Justice Burger's formulation of the privilege answer it?

6. ***Fifth Amendment Privilege.*** The attorney-client privilege is very different from the privilege against self-incrimination, so be careful not to confuse them. Corporations do *not* have a Fifth Amendment privilege against self-incrimination. To illustrate, suppose an officer of Ripoff Corporation is subpoenaed to testify before a grand jury. The officer is as pure and innocent as Snow White, but she knows that the corporation (through various other officers) has been engaged in a massive fraud. The officer realizes that her testimony will result in criminal charges against the corporation, though not against her personally, since she was not involved in the fraud. The officer may want to "take the Fifth" — to refuse to testify on grounds that the testimony may incriminate the corporation — but the courts will not permit this. Courts will not permit anyone to assert the Fifth Amendment on behalf of a corporation. Only if the individual *personally* fears criminal prosecution can she claim the privilege against self-incrimination.

Now let's contrast the Fifth Amendment scenario to the attorney-client privilege scenario. Suppose the same corporate officer appears before the grand jury and is asked, "What did you tell the corporation's lawyer when you were investigating the fraud?" May she claim the corporation's attorney-client privilege even though she cannot claim the Fifth Amendment privilege? Yes, she may claim the attorney-client privilege on behalf of the corporation. Similarly, if the corporation's lawyer is subpoenaed to testify before the grand jury, the lawyer can invoke the attorney-client privilege on behalf of her corporate client. The attorney-client privilege is distinct, separate, and independent of the Fifth Amendment privilege against self-incrimination.

7. ***Waiver of the Attorney-Client Privilege.*** How does a corporation waive its attorney-client privilege? Does it have to sign a document saying, "We hereby knowingly

and intelligently waive our otherwise inviolable attorney-client privilege?," or at least utter words to that effect? No. Waiving the privilege does not require official words or actions intended to waive the privilege. Because it is a "privilege," we only take it away when the holder of the privilege abuses it or acts inconsistently with it. A concise explanation of the law of waiver is found in the following footnote from *X Corp. v. Doe*, 805 F. Supp. 1298 (E.D. Va. 1992):

> Waiver, which may be express or implied, occurs where a disclosure is "inconsistent with maintaining the confidential nature of the attorney-client relationship." For example, if a client communicates with his attorney with the intent or understanding that the attorney will reveal the content of the communication to others, the privilege is waived. Moreover, voluntary disclosure by the client to a third party waives the privilege as to both the specific communication and all other communications relating to the same subject matter. Inadvertent disclosure to third parties may also waive the privilege if the disclosure occurs "under circumstances of such extreme or gross negligence as to warrant deeming the act of disclosure to be intentional." *See Federal Deposit Ins. Corp. v. Marine Midland Realty Credit Corp.*, 138 F.R.D. 479, 482 (E.D. Va. 1991) (on the facts presented, the failure to take reasonable precautions to avoid the inadvertent disclosure of three letters resulted in waiver of the privilege as to those letters).

2. The Attorney-Client Privilege in State Courts

The *Upjohn* opinion articulates federal law regarding the attorney-client privilege for corporations. But it is by no means universally accepted in the state courts, where each state remains free to accept or reject the *Upjohn* approach. *Upjohn* was decided under the Federal Rules of Evidence, which do not apply in state courts unless the state has adopted them. *Upjohn* is therefore not binding on state courts.

Although many states have decided to follow *Upjohn*, some state courts have openly expressed disagreement with it. Illinois, for example, continues to follow the "control group" test that the *Upjohn* Court rejected. Arizona has taken a more subtle and flexible approach that it calls a "functional" approach. Other states have their own variations. Remember that whenever you are litigating on behalf of or against a corporation in a state court you will need to research the law of the attorney-client privilege in that state to determine its scope.

Moreover, even if you never plan to litigate in your life but intend only to work on transactions and office practice matters, you need to know the scope of the attorney-client privilege so that you can properly advise your clients (corporate or otherwise) about how to structure communications within the corporation in a way that will preserve the attorney-client privilege under the relevant state's law. When communications fall outside the protection of the privilege, they may be subject to discovery or subpoena in the event of litigation or an investigation.

SAMARITAN FOUNDATION v. GOODFARB

862 P.2d 870 (Ariz. 1993)

MARTONE, J.

. . . A child's heart stopped during surgery at the Phoenix Children's Hospital in the Good Samaritan Regional Medical Center in 1988. A Good Samaritan lawyer investigated the incident and directed a nurse paralegal to interview three nurses and a scrub technician who were present during the surgery. Each of these Samaritan employees signed a form agreeing to accept legal representation from Samaritan's legal department. The paralegal summarized the interviews in memoranda that she then submitted to corporate counsel.

The child and her parents brought an action against Phoenix Children's Hospital and the physicians who participated in the surgery, alleging that the cardiac arrest and resulting impairment were caused by the defendants' medical negligence. When deposed two years later, the four Samaritan employees were unable to remember what happened in the operating room. Having learned of the existence of the interview summaries through discovery, plaintiffs sought their production. Samaritan, a non-party, and Phoenix Children's Hospital resisted, arguing that the interview summaries were protected by the attorney-client privilege and the work-product doctrine. The trial court ordered production of the summaries for in camera review. It said it would strike out attorney work-product and then release to the plaintiffs those portions of the summaries that would otherwise constitute witness statements. In short, the trial judge treated the documents as though they were not within the corporate attorney-client privilege, but were within the work-product doctrine.

Samaritan and Children's Hospital filed petitions for special action in the court of appeals arguing, among other things, that under the rule of Upjohn Co. v. United States, the employee communications summarized in the memoranda were within Samaritan's attorney-client privilege. The court of appeals accepted jurisdiction but denied relief. . . .

II. Analysis. . . .

B. The Problem of the Corporate Client

When a client is a person, things are relatively simple. That person's communications are client communications. But when the client is a corporation, things become complex. The corporation is a fictional entity which has independent status under the law. But it can only act through its agents. Thus, the client, the corporate entity, and its agents, who are the only ones who can communicate, are separated. Client communications cannot be identified simply as those of particular agents, as in the control group test, because although an agent can make statements on behalf of the corporate client, he or she can also make statements as an individual. But how do we determine which communications made by the corporation's agent are those of the corporate client and not merely those of the individual speaker?

We are not the first to acknowledge the complexity of the issue and to seek some unifying answer. Two competing theories have emerged. Illinois adopted the control group test in *Consolidation Coal Co. v. Bucyrus-Erie Co.*, 89 Ill. 2d 103 (1982). If otherwise privileged, it protects communications by decisionmakers or those who substantially influence corporate decisions. . . . [T]he control group test is underinclusive. . . .

A second major test, the subject matter test, takes a broader approach to deal with the underinclusiveness of the control group test. . . . Under it, an employee, within or without the control group, can make a privileged communication to corporate counsel if it is made at the direction of his superiors and if the subject matter upon which advice is sought is the employee's performance of his duties. The vice of the subject matter test as it has evolved is its overinclusiveness. It will capture statements by employees who, because of their duties, are witnesses to the conduct of others.

How do we avoid the underinclusiveness of the control group test, and at the same time avoid the overinclusiveness of a broad interpretation of the subject matter test? . . .

AUTHORS' COMMENT:

The court has just asked a difficult but vital question. The control group test is too narrow because it fails to extend the privilege to some people who are speaking for the corporation, while the subject matter test, as articulated in *Upjohn*, is too broad because it extends the privilege to people who are merely witnesses and are not speaking for the corporation. Can you suggest a middle ground? Let's see how the court wrestles with this problem.

C. The Privilege for Communications in the Course of Seeking Legal Advice

Client communications tend to fall into two categories: those initiated by the employee seeking legal advice and those made in response to an overture initiated by someone else in the corporation. It is universally accepted that communications directly initiated by an employee to corporate counsel seeking legal advice on behalf of the corporation are privileged. We agree that these kinds of communications by a corporate employee, regardless of position within the corporate hierarchy, are privileged. When a corporate employee or agent communicates with corporate counsel to secure or evaluate legal advice for the corporation, that agent or employee is, by definition, acting on behalf of the corporation and not in an individual capacity. These kinds of communications are at the heart of the attorney-client relationship. And it is plain that these communications can occur at any level of the chain of command. At one end of the spectrum is the chief executive officer seeking advice from corporate counsel on the antitrust implications of corporate behavior, even if the behavior is not his. At the other end, the driver of a corporate truck may run into corporate counsel's office seeking advice about an accident. In either case, the privilege applies because the employee is seeking legal advice concerning that employee's duties (the chief executive officer) or behavior (the driver) on behalf of the corporation. As to these kinds of legal communications, including the communication of facts, we hold that all communications made in confidence to counsel in which the communicating employee is directly seeking legal advice are privileged.

D. The Privilege for Factual Communications Made by Employees in Response to Overtures by Someone Else in the Corporation

The real debate concerning the proper scope of the corporation's attorney-client privilege is its applicability to factual communications made in response to an overture initiated by someone else in the corporation. Unless there is some self-limiting feature, the breadth of corporate activity could transform what would be witness communications in any other context into client communications. In such an event, the costs of the privilege are potentially much greater when asserted by a corporation over the statements of its agents than when asserted by an individual over his or her own statements. But there is no countervailing benefit. The rationale of the privilege is that by assuring the individual client that his or her communications cannot be disclosed without consent, it encourages the client to be candid. But this only works if the communicator controls the privilege. In the corporate context, the privilege belongs to the corporation and not the person making the communication.[4]

If an employee has exposed the corporation to liability, it seems less problematic to legitimize the corporation's control over the privileged nature of the employee's

---

[4] Indeed, one commentator has suggested a theory of corporate attorney-client privilege that applies only to the communications of persons "who have the authority to control the subsequent use and distribution of the communications." Stephen A. Saltzburg, *Corporate and Related Attorney-Client Privilege Claims: A Suggested Approach*, 12 Hofstra L. Rev. 279, 306 (1984). By vesting so much authority in the communicator, this approach, too, has the potential to be widely over and underinclusive.

communications. After all, it is the action of this employee that is being imputed to the corporation. It is this employee's statements that are directly admissible against the corporation under Rule 801(d)(2)(D), Ariz. R. Evid. This employee's statements are also the most important in enabling corporate counsel to assess the corporation's legal exposure and formulate a legal response. And none of this has anything at all to do with whether the employee is a member of a control group. We must, therefore, always look at the relationship between the communicator and the incident giving rise to the legal matter, the nature of the communication and its context.

If the employee is not the one whose conduct gives rise to potential corporate liability, then it is fair to characterize the employee as a "witness" rather than as a client. The vice of the control group test is that it includes in the privilege the factual statements of control group employees even if they were mere witnesses to the events in question, while at the same time it fails to take into account the need to promote institutional candor with respect to factual communications of non-control group employees whose conduct has exposed the corporation to possible adverse legal consequences. The test is both overinclusive and underinclusive. We, therefore, reject the control group test as unsatisfactory on its own terms.

Over and above its inadequacy as a theory to deal with the complex problems of the attorney-client privilege in the corporate context, there are other reasons to avoid the control group test. Our world is growing smaller. Corporate activity is increasingly global and almost always national. Although its outer limits are unclear, Upjohn at a minimum rejects the control group test as a rule of federal common law. We should minimize disparities between federal and state law when it comes to privilege. When clients seek legal advice, they do not expect that the privilege will exist for purposes of some claims but not others. . . .

But what of Upjohn? . . . Samaritan argues that Upjohn adopted a broad version of the subject matter test, which includes within the privilege communications by all employees who speak at the direction of their corporate superiors to the corporation's lawyer regarding matters within the scope of their corporate duties in order to facilitate the formulation of legal advice for the corporation. . . . .

We are of the view that a broad interpretation of the subject matter test, requiring only that the communication concerns factual information gained in the course of performing the speaker's corporate duties, is inadequate. The employee's connection to the liability-causing event is too attenuated to fit the classical model of what it means to be a client. Such a broad standard would only exclude from the privilege factual communications of employees whose knowledge was truly fortuitous. For example, under a broad formulation, the statement of a corporate officer who glances out the window and happens to see the corporation's truck negligently collide with another vehicle would not be privileged. However, the statement of a corporate employee who is present in the truck by virtue of his or her corporate duties but was not driving the truck or otherwise involved in causing the accident would be privileged. This is the construction urged by Samaritan and the various amici. We believe, however, that the latter person also should be considered a mere witness for purposes of the privilege. Although the employee's presence, and hence the employee's knowledge, is a function of his or her corporate employment, the employee bears no other connection to the incident. The employee did not cause it. His actions did not subject the corporation to possible liability. When this employee speaks, it is not about his or her own actions, but the actions of someone else — the driver.

We, therefore, reject a broad version of the subject matter test. We believe it is subject to a narrower interpretation, one more consistent with the concerns we have expressed. Many of the most often cited authorities suggest that we require that the employee's communication relate to the employee's own activities that are within the scope of his or her employment and are being attributed to the corporation. . . .

> [A]n uncertain privilege is tantamount to no privilege at all. Unless the privilege is known to exist at the time the communication is made, it will not promote candor. Thus, an uncertain privilege has the potential of achieving the worst possible result: it could harm the truth seeking process without a corresponding increase in candor. Balancing competing interests is appropriate when formulating the extent of the privilege, but balancing on a case by case basis defeats the purpose of the privilege. We conclude that a narrow but absolute privilege is preferable to a broad but amorphous one. . . .

We therefore hold that, where someone other than the employee initiates the communication, a factual communication by a corporate employee to corporate counsel is within the corporation's privilege if it concerns the employee's own conduct within the scope of his or her employment and is made to assist the lawyer in assessing or responding to the legal consequences of that conduct for the corporate client. This excludes from the privilege communications from those who, but for their status as officers, agents or employees, are witnesses.

We believe that this is the appropriate place to draw the line. It has all the advantages of a narrow reading of Upjohn (rough comparability with federal common law) without the attendant disadvantages of a broad reading of Upjohn (fails to limit the scope of the privilege to its purpose). Thus, litigants may not be faced with drastically different privileges in a single proceeding. . . .

AUTHORS' COMMENT:

The court now has to decide how to apply its new modified subject matter test, or "functional" test, to the facts of the Samaritan case. Would you hold that the communications at issue are privileged or not privileged under the functional test?

III. Resolution

Applying our test to the facts of this case, we conclude that the statements made by the nurses and scrub technician to Samaritan's counsel are not within Samaritan's attorney-client privilege. These employees were not seeking legal advice in confidence. The initial overture was made by others in the corporation. Although the employees were present during the operation, their actions did not subject Samaritan to potential liability. Their statements primarily concerned the events going on around them and the actions of the physicians whose alleged negligence caused the injuries. These statements were not gathered to assist Samaritan in assessing or responding to the legal consequences of the speaker's conduct, but to the consequences for the corporation of the physician's conduct. Thus, these Samaritan employees were witnesses to the event, and their statements are not within the attorney-client privilege. . . .

IV. Conclusion

We reject the control group test because it is inadequate to deal with the complexity of the attorney-client privilege in the corporate setting. It is both overinclusive and underinclusive. Because we reject the control group test, we also reject a qualified privilege for non-control group employees. We reject an expansive subject matter test for corporate employee communications. Instead, we adopt a functional approach and hold that where an employee is not seeking legal advice in confidence, his or her communications to corporate counsel are within the corporation's privilege if they concern the employee's own conduct within the scope of his or her employment and are made to assist the lawyer in assessing or responding to the legal consequences of that conduct for the corporation. This approach more closely approximates the nature and scope of the attorney-client privilege where the client is an individual. The employee communications here were not of this sort. Thus, they were not within the corporation's attorney-client privilege.

We affirm the order of the trial court but vacate that part of the opinion of the court of appeals that relates to the corporate attorney-client privilege.

NOTES AND QUESTIONS

1. ***Do You Agree?*** Do you agree with the Arizona Supreme Court? Why or why not? What are the most compelling arguments in favor of the opinion? What are the strongest counterarguments you can develop? Would you add anything?

2. ***Will Corporations Stop Investigating?*** Because of the broad impact of an opinion defining the attorney-client privilege for corporations, the *Samaritan* case attracted enormous attention. Dozens of amici, from McDonnell-Douglas to the Arizona Chamber of Commerce to the First Interstate Bank of Arizona, filed briefs in the Arizona Supreme Court. Amici argued that if the court rejected *Upjohn*'s broad approach to the attorney-client privilege for corporate investigations, then corporations would severely curtail their investigations. The Arizona Supreme Court rejected that argument, stating:

> We are not persuaded by the amici that, without a broader privilege, corporations will forego prompt post-accident investigations. By not extending the privilege, we place the corporate client on a par with the individual client asserting a privilege as to his or her own communications. This is the purpose of our functional approach. It is, in any event, in the interest of the corporation to be informed, and in most cases it will conclude that ignorance is too high a price to pay to avoid taking witness statements that are potentially discoverable. After all, even those statements have the more qualified protection afforded by the work-product doctrine. We are not persuaded that a corporation will intentionally put itself in the position of being the last to know the facts when it is facing potential liability for the acts of its agents. Finally, under the privilege as we have defined it, the kind of communications most likely to be characterized as client statements will be privileged.

Amici also argued that, without a broader privilege, corporations will cease policing their own activities to ensure that they comply with the law. We do not agree. Corporations comply with the law because they wish to avoid liability.

Do you agree with the court or do you agree with amici? Why?

D. DISCLOSURE OF A CORPORATION'S CONFIDENTIAL INFORMATION

Earlier, we studied ABA Model Rule 1.6, entitled "Confidentiality of Information," which sets forth the general rule of confidentiality and sets out a number of exceptions. The general rule of confidentiality stated in Rule 1.6(a) and the exceptions stated in Rule 1.6(b) apply to corporations and other organizations just as they do to individuals. However, ABA Model Rule 1.13, states an additional exception to the duty of confidentiality. This exception, articulated in Rule 1.13(c), was the subject of a long battle within the legal profession and was not added to the ABA Model Rules until 2003, when the legal profession was feeling intense pressure to combat and prevent the kinds of massive corporate frauds that brought down Enron, WorldCom, Adelphia, Global Crossing, and several other large companies.

Much of the pressure on the legal profession came from the federal Securities and Exchange Commission (the "SEC" or the "Commission"), which adopted regulations in 2003 to comply with the new Sarbanes-Oxley Act of 2002. The provision of the

Sarbanes-Oxley Act that most directly affected the legal profession was § 307, now codified at 15 U.S.C. § 7245. It provides as follows:

§ 7245. Rules of professional responsibility for attorneys

[T]he Commission shall issue rules, in the public interest and for the protection of investors, setting forth minimum standards of professional conduct for attorneys appearing and practicing before the Commission in any way in the representation of issuers, including a rule—

(1) requiring an attorney to report evidence of a material violation of securities law or breach of fiduciary duty or similar violation by the company or any agent thereof, to the chief legal counsel or the chief executive officer of the company (or the equivalent thereof); and

(2) if the counsel or officer does not appropriately respond to the evidence (adopting, as necessary, appropriate remedial measures or sanctions with respect to the violation), requiring the attorney to report the evidence to the audit committee of the board of directors of the issuer or to another committee of the board of directors comprised solely of directors not employed directly or indirectly by the issuer, or to the board of directors.

In keeping with the mandate of § 7245, the SEC issued regulations "setting forth minimum standards of professional conduct for attorneys" who appear and practice before the SEC. Those regulations, which are codified at 17 C.F.R. Part 205, are too detailed and complex to cover in an introductory course on professional responsibility, but lawyers who represent corporations regulated by the SEC must become familiar with the SEC's Sarbanes-Oxley regulations.

In this section, we will limit our focus to ABA Model Rule 1.13. Our aim is to help you understand Rule 1.13 and to develop a systematic approach to analyzing problems that arise under Rule 1.13. Before we begin, we will set out a few basic principles about corporate governance:

- Shareholders are technically considered the owners of the corporation, but typically are not involved in the day-to-day operations of the company. Rather, the shareholders vote their shares to elect members of the Board of Directors. (The members of the Board of Directors are called "Directors.")
- The day-to-day decisions of a corporation are typically made by the executives (i.e., officers, such as the Chief Executive Officer, treasurer, president, and vice-presidents) and by the corporation's other employees.
- The Board of Directors hires and fires the executives who run the corporation, including the Chief Executive Officer. The Board of Directors (often referred to as "the Board") is the highest authority in a corporation.

1. Who is Your Client?

When addressing secrecy questions, the first question to ask is: Who is your client? Model Rule 1.13(a) answers this question by saying: "A lawyer employed or retained by an organization represents the organization acting through its duly authorized constituents." Thus, when you represent a corporation, you do not ordinarily represent the individuals who run the corporation unless you have expressly agreed to do so. You represent only the corporate entity itself, not the officers, directors, or employees of the corporation. This has enormous implications for the attorney-client privilege and the ethical duty of confidentiality. You owe a duty of confidentiality under Model Rule 1.6 only to your client, not to anyone else. You can invoke the attorney-client privilege only on behalf of your client, but not on behalf of anyone else.

2. Objecting Within the Organizational Client ("Reporting Up")

The lawyer working for a client is required to "abide by the client's decisions concerning the objectives of the representation." Model Rule 1.2 (a). When the lawyer is representing an entity, such as a corporation, a partnership, a union or other organization, the constituents or members of the organization are the ones who have the power to make the key decisions regarding the goals of the representation. Since the lawyer is the agent for the client, ordinarily the lawyer is supposed to accept the decisions made by the constituents of the client, even when the lawyer disagrees with those decisions, or doubts their "utility or prudence." Generally speaking, "Decisions concerning policy and operations, including ones entailing serious risk, are not as such in the lawyer's province." See Comment 2 to Model Rule 1.13. Stated bluntly, ordinarily the lawyer's job is to give legal advice, not to make business decisions.

However, there are limits to the lawyer's acquiescence. In certain circumstances, lawyers who are concerned about misconduct within an organization must keep pursuing the issue by "climbing the ladder" of the organization's hierarchy. The purpose of going up the ladder is to explain the lawyer's view of the apparent misconduct to the higher-ups in the chain of command.

For example, Lawyer represents RxCo, Inc., a company that sells kidney dialysis equipment. One of RxCo's engineers told Lawyer that the machines RxCo has been receiving from a particular foreign supplier, Foreign Med, Inc., do not clear the blood sufficiently to meet applicable federal laws. Lawyer knows that it is illegal for Foreign Med to sell defective machines to hospitals in the U.S. and that RxCo has delivered twenty of the machines to hospitals and dialysis clinics during the past three months. RxCo has thirty additional defective machines scheduled to be shipped in the next few weeks. May Lawyer disclose what he knows to the hospitals and clinics that have bought the machines, or to the FDA, or to anyone else?

No, not at this point. At this early stage of the lawyer's inquiry, it would be a violation of his duty of confidentiality for Lawyer to communicate the illegal activity to anyone outside RxCo. It doesn't matter whether the communication is by fax, phone, or otherwise. Lawyer would be subject to discipline if he notified the hospitals which received the machines or the Food and Drug Administration at this point.

However, there are actions that Lawyer can and must take. If necessary — meaning if Lawyer does not receive a satisfactory response on the way up the corporate ladder — Lawyer must go all the way up the ladder to the highest authority able to direct the action of the organization. When the client is a corporation, like RxCo, this will ordinarily be the board of directors. (In a partnership, the "highest authority" would be the general partner or general partners. The governance structure in partnerships is often not as clear as it is in corporations.) As you might imagine, going to the highest authority takes a lot of courage, especially if the managers, executives, and board members you need to persuade are (a) downplaying the significance of the issues being brought to their attention and/or are (b) unwilling to implement the changes being suggested.

Before the 2003 amendments to the ABA Model Rules of Professional Conduct, if remonstrating with the client (i.e., trying vigorously to talk the client into complying with the law) did not produce the change thought was necessary, Rule 1.13 provided only limited options. If not convinced that the action was illegal, then the first alternative was for Lawyer to drop the issue altogether. (For example, perhaps the earlier test results for the dialysis machines were ambiguous, or perhaps the law was unclear, or perhaps further testing of the dialysis machines might reveal that they actually performed properly.) Or Lawyer might still think the test results were accurate but become convinced that the initial reading of the regulations governing the dialysis machines was wrong, and that the machines met all legal requirements even based on present test results.

However, if the lawyer remained convinced that the client was engaged in illegal conduct, the second alternative was to withdraw from the representation — to stop representing the client. But for an in-house lawyer, this meant quitting their job. (You might attempt to withdraw solely from work on the kidney dialysis machines, but if you try to do that, the corporation may fire you.) If you have enough savings on hand to support yourself and your family for a year or two, that will increase your freedom to act on your independent professional judgment, but few people are in that financial situation. If you are working at a law firm, even one which has many other clients, the decision to withdraw will not mean quitting your job, but withdrawal can still be a difficult step that may cause your billable hours (or your likelihood of becoming a partner) to drop precipitously.

One thing to remember as you navigate these situations is that you are accountable for the decisions you make. It is easier to find a new job than it is to spend several years mired in civil litigation, disciplinary charges, or even criminal charges in connection with a client's activities, especially when you knew the conduct was wrong when you participated in it. As with other ethical dilemmas that pit morals against money, if you end up getting suspended or disbarred, you will really have money problems.

Even if you decide to withdraw, there is the question of *how* to withdraw. Most often, lawyers who withdraw do so quietly, with no public fanfare. But a third option, at least under the pre-2003 version of the Model Rules (which is still in effect in many states), is to make what is called a "noisy withdrawal." This term means that when the lawyer withdraws she simultaneously (and as noticeably as possible) disavows or disaffirms previous legal work for a client. A noisy withdrawal is, thus, a kind of whistleblowing by dramatic conduct. Lawyer does not actually reveal the facts or give information about what RxCo did. Instead, Lawyer would say to victims, "You can no longer rely on my earlier opinion that the client's activities were legal and proper. Forget I ever said the deal was legitimate or that the machines complied with FDA requirements."

A lawyer making a noisy withdrawal doesn't explain what the client is doing wrong, but the disaffirmance of his earlier opinions is a strong signal (at least for those sophisticated enough to understand it) that major problems have arisen at RxCo — problems that caused Lawyer to walk away.

Lawyer also has another option — an option every person (lawyers and nonlawyers alike) always has available when it comes to the law. Lawyer can engage in civil disobedience and go public — that is, he can find a way to leak an important document to someone outside the organization in order to get the word out about the wrongdoing. Be warned, though that civil disobedience is not for the faint of heart. From Gandhi to Thoreau to King, its adherents have advanced it as a way to guarantee punishment. The philosophical claim is that when power is used to perpetuate injustice, the only course available to one of conscience is to openly break the rules and demand that the threatened punishment be imposed and, as a result, exposed to public scrutiny. Thus, the lawyer who decides to leak information out of a sense that conscience and the public interest require that radical step should understand that it is not permitted under the rules of professional conduct and will, almost certainly, lead to disciplinary sanctions and serious social penalties. At the very least, you should expect to be frozen out of professional interactions and to face difficulty finding a new job as a lawyer.

In states that have adopted the language of the 2003 amendments, lawyers have an additional option — you may (but do not have to) tell someone outside the organization. This could include the Securities and Exchange Commission, the FDA, or the hospitals and clinics that have purchased the defective kidney dialysis equipment sold by your client. It is important enough to say it again: Under the 2003 version of ABA Model Rule 1.13, if the lawyer has gone all the way up the ladder to the top authority within the organization and is still not satisfied that the issue has been correctly resolved, a lawyer is allowed to disclose otherwise confidential information relating to the representation, whether or not Rule 1.6 permits such disclosure. The lawyer's ability to disclose under Rule 1.13 (c) expressly trumps the duty of confidentiality in Rule 1.6! In other words, even if Rule 1.6 would prohibit disclosure, Rule 1.13(c) may permit disclosure. Rule 1.13(c) has, in effect, created a new exception to the Rule 1.6 duty of confidentiality.

3. Types of Legal Practice

The situation in which disclosure is allowed is more likely to arise in transactional practice than in a litigation setting. Lawyers advising clients on transactions often work with clients regarding their current and future conduct: advising them on requirements under banking regulations, preparing for meetings with regulatory agencies, restructuring payment terms for debt, or interpreting IRS opinion letters, for example. Litigators, in contrast, are often taking a retrospective look at events. Litigators are historians. They find out what happened in the past. Transactional lawyers are creators and problem solvers. They change the path of the future.

Lawyers doing transactional work also provide their clients with documents which their clients use in the client's dealings with third parties. For example, transactional lawyers may write legal opinion letters for the client to show a bank or to show a prospective purchaser of a subsidiary, or they may write offering circulars for clients issuing securities to show to potential investors. Lawyers engaged in transactional work are likely to work on multiple transactions for a client and to get to know quite a bit of information about how the client's business operates. In addition, it is not uncommon for an employee to mention a situation that has troubled him once he has worked with the lawyer on other matters, even if the lawyer has not been officially asked to work on that matter by the senior executives.

4. When Is a Lawyer Permitted to Disclose Outside the Entity ("Reporting Out")?

Under Rule 1.13(b), a lawyer who discovers wrongdoing within an organizational client is required to "proceed as is reasonably necessary in the best interest of the organization." Accordingly, if a lawyer representing an entity (e.g., a corporation, a partnership, a union, or other organization) knows that an officer, employee, or other person associated with the organization is (1) engaging in illegal conduct; (2) intending to engage in illegal conduct; or (3) refusing to act as required by law, *and* if the violation is "likely to result in substantial injury to the organization," then the lawyer must take whatever steps are "reasonably necessary" to serve the corporation's best interests under the circumstances.

Analytically, then, the first requirement is that the lawyer "knows" that the illegal conduct is planned or on-going. Model Rule 1.0(f) says that "knows" "denotes actual knowledge of the fact in question." But it also says that knowledge "may be inferred from circumstances." Thus, "knows" means a greater degree of certainty than simply having a "reasonable belief," but knowledge does not mean absolute certainty.

If the lawyer "knows" of the illegal conduct, then the lawyer must also determine whether or not the illegal conduct is "likely to result in substantial injury to the organization." If so, the lawyer's duties to climb the ladder presumptively kick in, unless the lawyer reasonably believes that climbing the ladder is not necessarily in the best interest of the organization.

Climbing the ladder means to seek a remedy by going progressively higher within the chain of command in the organization — all the way to the highest authority that can act on behalf of the organization, if necessary. If that does not cure the wrongdoing, then in the limited circumstances delineated in Model Rule 1.13 (c), the lawyer may "report out" — that is, he may reveal information related to the representation whether or not Rule 1.6 permits such disclosure — to those outside the organization.

Reporting outside the organization is a radical step, and marked a radical departure from the ABA's past stance on the question. The circumstances described by Rule 1.13(c), therefore, are very demanding — more demanding than the circumstances that trigger the lawyer's obligation under Rule 1.13(b) to go up the ladder and "report up." Under Rule 1.13(c), disclosure is allowed only if the organization's highest authority either insists upon or fails to address in a timely and appropriate manner an action, or a refusal to act that is clearly a violation of law. The lawyer must determine whether the questionable action or refusing to act of the person associated with the organization is a *clear* violation of law. Next, the lawyer will need to determine whether the persons heading the organization are correcting the illegal action or refusal to act. If the correction has not occurred in a reasonable time, and the wrongful conduct is "reasonably certain" to result in substantial injury to the organization (not just "likely" to result in substantial injury as in Rule 1.13(b)), then the lawyer may at last disclose. Finally, the extent of the permitted disclosure is limited to disclosures the lawyer reasonably believes necessary to prevent substantial injury to the organization.

5. "Noisy Withdrawal"

If a jurisdiction has not adopted the 2003 version of Model Rule 1.13 (c) which grants permission to report out, then the most the lawyer can do is engage in a "noisy withdrawal." A lawyer ending a client representation in this way would "explicitly disaffirm the work product prepared by the lawyer in the course of the representation," which may alert others that there was some problem with the information supporting that work product.

E. ANOTHER SECRECY SCENARIO: THE COMPUTER GLITCH

You've been out of law school for a few years and you're beginning to develop a successful practice. One day an important new client comes to you, a growing computer software company named Compu-Soft that is listed on the NASDAQ stock exchange. The company is planning to produce a software program called "Bat-Man" that will make notebook computer batteries last twice as long, and another program called Wapple that will enable Windows-based computers to run the Mac operating system. The company has hired some talented software engineers. Now the company needs your help negotiating contracts to supply leading electronics chains (like Comp-USA and Best Buy) and to license the software to computer manufacturers (like Dell, H-P, and Lenovo).

You successfully negotiate several contracts to purchase and promote the software as soon as it is ready, which Compu-Soft's CEO promises will be within six to eight months. You write up and sign various warranties and disclosure documents, and you accompany the CEO, Jean Roloff, to some of the company's presentations to purchasing managers and computer makers. Roloff is charismatic and persuasive — a born salesman — and seals the deal on lots of licenses and distribution agreements based on your disclosure documents and his charm and vision.

Eight months later, however, Compu-Soft still doesn't have any products ready to ship. Some of the stores and computer makers ask you to find out when the company will begin producing the product. You call your client and the CEO, Roloff, tells you that the software is "about to ship" and that investors should be patient because Compu-Soft is "about to take off." Soon after, Roloff calls to tell you the good news that he has shipped Version 1.0 of the Bat-Man software. Roloff sends out a press release, and Compu-Soft's stock price shoots up.

You soon receive several calls from stores that purchased the software complaining that the software frequently doesn't work. You call Roloff and he tells you that there are a few bugs in the program but that Version 1.1 will soon be out and tests have proved that in fact it works. Roloff then issues another press release announcing an "upgrade" of the product, and share prices climb again.

This set of events repeats itself another two or three times, first with higher versions of Bat-Man and then with a couple of versions of Wapple. Stores call Compu-Soft to complain about delays and to ask when the new software will ship. After Compu-Soft finally ships the software, stores call to report numerous customer complaints. Each time Roloff claims to have fixed the problem and comes out with an even better product than originally promised. But the stores, computer makers, and investment analysts are clearly running out of patience, and some customers are complaining that Bat-Man not only doesn't work but has actually damaged other software already installed on their computers (word processing programs, spreadsheets, etc.). Some of the remaining customers threaten to sue Compu-Soft in a class action for consequential damages. You again press Roloff about whether he is solving the problems with the software, and he assures you that he is. He even says he has fired the Chief Engineer and hired a new one, "a bright young engineer who used to work for IBM and Google."

Soon afterwards, several suits are filed against Compu-Soft for fraud and breach of warranty. One of them alleges that Compu-Soft knew that Bat-Man could not work. Another suit, this one by an investor, alleges securities fraud for failing to disclose problems with the first two versions of the product. You contact the fired engineer, Fred Klapson, to get more of the story.

Fred Klapson is very negative. He says he told Roloff from the start that the product couldn't do what Roloff was promising, and that version 1.0 was not ready to ship when Roloff insisted on shipping the product. Nor did any of the later versions truly cure the problems. Instead, the "upgraded" versions were trial-and-error programs that just substituted one set of problems for another. Roloff insisted on shipping them because shipping out an upgrade was the only way to keep investors, computer makers, and stores interested in the product. The "upgraded" versions were never successfully tested, and some of the upgrades were in fact versions that had been developed at the same time as Version 1.0 and had never worked properly even in the lab.

You call Roloff and confront him with this damning information. Roloff is indignant. "That so-called engineer Fred Klapson was a fraud. He promised the world and couldn't deliver. He kept telling me that the product was improved and ready to ship but each time the same problems recurred. Now I've hired a real engineer, someone who used to work at IBM, and she says she can get the job done." You talk to the new engineer and she says she can "turn things around in short order."

This time, you monitor the situation more closely. When it comes time for Compu-Soft to file its annual Form 10-K with the Securities and Exchange Commission, you talk to the Chief Engineer personally to find out the status of the product. (By now, share prices have fallen because analysts have gotten wise to the repeated problems with the product.) The Chief Engineer (who was hired away from IBM at a fabulous salary and continues to earn huge bonus checks and stock options) insists that the company is on the verge of a "major breakthrough." Roloff insists that the Form 10-K says that "minor problems" have been resolved, that a breakthrough product is "around the corner," and that demand is expected to be at least 50% greater than originally planned because of sharply increasing demand for notebook computers.

However, you are cautious and you talk to several lower-level engineers. They laugh at the idea of an imminent breakthrough and tell you that the Bat-Man product is still "vaporware — it doesn't exist." You confront Roloff with this and he says the lower-level people "don't see the whole picture" and "don't have the training to second-guess the Chief Engineer." However, while searching the file cabinets for information needed to prepare the SEC filings, you find memos to Roloff from the new Chief Engineer in which the new Chief Engineer confirms that Bat-Man is vaporware. The Chief Engineer is skeptical that Roloff's original goal of doubling battery life can ever be achieved until new technologies are developed, which Compu-Soft does not have the resources to do.

Now you are seriously worried. The memos are "smoking guns," and they convince you that Roloff is lying and the Chief Engineer is lying, too. Can you tell anyone? Must you tell anyone? What should you do?

You have a big problem. If you tell when you shouldn't, you may be liable for malpractice, breach of fiduciary duties, and a disciplinary violation. But if you don't tell when you should, you may be liable for big bucks to an array of customers, investors, and maybe even government regulators. You consult the head of your firm's ethics committee and she says, "Research the problem immediately, and let me know what you find." She gives you a quick list of questions to research:

- How sure do you have to be before you tell? How much factual investigation do you have to do before you decide whether or not to tell? What if your client won't cooperate in the investigation? Do you have to warn the client why you are investigating?
- If you think or know that your client is engaged in a crime or fraud, can you tell anyone? Must you tell anyone? Can you (or your law firm) be held liable if you fail to tell?
- If you investigate and conclude that you may tell or must tell, who can you tell? When? How much can (or must) you reveal?
- Do you have to warn or advise your client before you can actually blow the whistle?
- If you do not reveal the information outside the company but are subpoenaed to testify before a grand jury, at trial, or in a civil deposition, will the attorney-client privilege protect your conversations with Roloff, the various engineers, or others at Compu-Soft?
- May you and the firm continue representing Compu-Soft in this matter? In any matter? Do you need anyone's permission to withdraw?

Based on the materials you have studied so far, you should be able to give your law firm's ethics committee some plausible advice.

Chapter 14
PRINCIPLES OF THE ADVERSARY SYSTEM

As a lawyer, you must follow the rules of professional conduct in the jurisdictions where you are licensed to practice. These rules are often referred to as rules of "ethics," but that is misleading. They are rules of "conduct" — rules that tell you what you must do (and must not do) as a lawyer. As you will see throughout this book, many of these rules of professional conduct are far from intuitive. In fact, they are often counterintuitive.

Before you begin studying any specific rules, you should realize that all of the rules are part of a system — the adversary system. Just as fish swim in water and humans breathe air, lawyers operate in the adversary system. What is the adversary system? What are the principles of the adversary system?

The most fundamental principle is expressed in Canon 7 of the old ABA Model Code of Professional Responsibility, which says: "A Lawyer Should Represent a Client Zealously Within the Bounds of the Law." That means a lawyer should take all legal measures to help the client achieve the client's legitimate objectives in a matter — but a lawyer may not take any illegal measures to assist a client, or advise a client to use illegal methods. The lawyer must stay within the bounds of the law.

Applying that principle is not easy. In this chapter we will ask whether the adversary system is working well, or whether we should reform it. Would a less adversarial system be better? What would be the costs and benefits of having a system that is less adversarial?

We begin by asking a question that you may already have been asked: "How can you defend a person who is guilty?" Examining this question will take us to the guts of the adversary system.

A. DEFENDING THE GUILTY

John Peter Zenger, a printer and writer, is justly remembered as one of our country's most inspiring founders. In 1733, he began publishing a weekly series of attacks on William Cosby, the new Colonial Governor of the New York Provinces who had just arrived from England. No one could have foreseen the perturbations that Zenger's attacks would cause. They would ripple through the Colonies, convulse in the American Revolution, inspire the First Amendment, and eventually connect national democratic movements from the 1789 storming of the Bastille to the 1989 demonstrations in Tiananmen Square. As Gouverneur Morris called it when the First Congress debated the Bill of Rights, it was truly "the morning star of that liberty which subsequently revolutionized America."

Zenger's demand was a modest one. He wanted freedom to publish his political views, and the political views of others. More specifically, he wanted freedom to publish those views even when he knew (and presumably intended) that they would undermine Governor Cosby's leadership by holding him up to public ridicule and inciting disbelief and distrust of the governing authorities. Thus, when Zenger agreed to publish the words of rabble-rousing Rip Van Dam, Zenger was indicted for the crime of seditious libel, for the law of libel at that time did not distinguish between destroying a man's reputation by spreading false information and diminishing a Governor's reputation by declaring the truth.

The facts leading to the charge of seditious libel against Zenger were shocking: In a brazen effort to increase his personal wealth, Governor Cosby demanded that Rip Van Dam remit to the Governor half the salary that Van Dam had been paid for serving as Acting Governor in the year before Cosby became Governor. Van Dam responded with characteristic feistiness, stating that he would be delighted to remit half his salary if Governor Cosby would first turn over to him any payments the Governor had received in kickbacks since taking office as Governor. Governor Cosby, no shrinking violet himself, countered by suing Van Dam for the claimed share of his salary. But the Governor didn't stop there. Apparently fearing that he could not obtain justice in the usual public courts, Governor Cosby filed suit in the Supreme Court, claiming that a breach of the King's administrative rules had occurred, and that Van Dam therefore owed him the claimed sums. Conveniently, three of Cosby's own subordinates would hear the case. The surprise was not that the Court ultimately ruled 2-1 for the Governor, but that the verdict was not unanimous. Chief Justice Lewis Morris dissented.

Indeed, Chief Justice Morris's dissent displayed such temerity that Governor Cosby could not be content with simply raking in his winnings. He sent a letter to Chief Justice Morris demanding that he explain his dissent. Chief Justice Morris willingly complied, but not in a private letter as Cosby expected. Rather, Morris explained himself in the most public manner possible — by publishing his dissent in John Peter Zenger's weekly newspaper, *The New-York Weekly Journal.*

Governor Cosby responded to Chief Justice Morris's affront by prosecuting Zenger, as publisher, for the crime of seditious libel. By now, though, what had begun as stubborn expressions of political pique by political rivals had become a matter of state. The very legitimacy of English law was at stake. Chief Justice Morris's dissent implied that Governor Cosby's right to Van Dam's salary rested solely on the Governor's ability to manipulate the courts into lending an aura of legitimacy to a naked money grab. And if the legitimacy of the Crown's representative in the colony was at risk, Cosby argued, it shouldn't matter whether what was published was true. The issue was not whether Governor Cosby had sought to claim part of his predecessor's salary as his own; or had failed properly to maintain records of his work performance; or had abused his authority by having the case assigned to a court of partisan underlings.[1] What was in dispute was not the truth of what was said, but rather whether the King's subjects should be allowed to publish such truths to the world.

Governor Cosby did what he could to stack the odds against Zenger. Foreshadowing the style used in 2007 by Pakistan's then-President Pervez Musharraf, Governor Cosby removed Chief Justice Morris from the Supreme Court and replaced him with a handpicked political lackey (James DeLancey). Chief Justice DeLancey soon issued a ruling defining libel as anything "scandalous," even if it was true.[2] And in another maneuver of raw power, Governor Cosby had Zenger's initial defense lawyers disbarred.

At that point, a lawyer named Andrew Hamilton rose to Zenger's defense. Andrew Hamilton (who was the uncle of Founding Father Alexander Hamilton) could easily have been sent over by Hollywood central casting. Hamilton was a former Attorney General of Pennsylvania who had gone on to become among the most successful trial lawyers in the Colonies. He was also a man of style and broad learning, with many talents, including architecture, a field in which he left an indelible mark as the architect of Philadelphia's famed Independence Hall.

It was Hamilton's "unheard of defense that the articles complained of told the truth!"[3] The key to the success of this defense was the jury. The case would be tried directly to a jury, and Hamilton knew that he could win the case if he could convince the jury how

---

[1] Zenger printed the allegedly seditious articles following a legal dispute between two public officials, William Cosby and Rip Van Dam. Cosby was appointed governor of New York in 1731, but did not officially take office until 1732. During the interim, Van Dam, the current governor, continued to discharge his official responsibilities, and collect a salary. Cosby, believing that he was entitled to the salary collected by Van Dam during this period, sued the lame duck governor for restitution. The New York Supreme Court decided in favor of Van Dam. *See Legal Encyclopedia: Peter, John Zenger, available at* http://www.answers.com/topic/john-peter-zenger (site last visited Nov. 5, 2008).

[2] Samuel Eliot Morison & Henry Steele Commager, I The Growth of the American Republic, 122 (1962).

[3] *Id.*

much was at stake. At the end of Zenger's trial, Hamilton earned a place in the pantheon of great lawyers with this stirring closing argument:

> It is natural, it is a privilege, I will go farther, it is a right, which all free men claim, that they are entitled to complain when they are hurt. They have a right publicly to remonstrate against the abuses of power in the strongest terms, to put their neighbors upon their guard against the craft or open violence of men in authority, and to assert with courage the sense they have of the blessings of liberty, the value they put upon it, and their resolution at all hazards to preserve it as one of the greatest blessings heaven can bestow. . . .
>
> The loss of liberty, to a generous mind, is worse than death. And yet we know that there have been those in all ages who for the sake of preferment, or some imaginary honor, have freely lent a helping hand to oppress, nay to destroy, their country. . . . This is what every man who values freedom ought to consider. . . .
>
> Power may justly be compared to a great river. While kept within its due bounds it is both beautiful and useful. But when it overflows its banks, it is then too impetuous to be stemmed; it bears down all before it, and brings destruction and desolation wherever it comes. If, then, this is the nature of power, let us at least do our duty, and like wise men who value freedom use our utmost care to support liberty, the only bulwark against lawless power, which in all ages has sacrificed to its wild lust and boundless ambition the blood of the best men that ever lived. . . .
>
> But to conclude: The question before the Court and you, Gentlemen of the jury, is not of small or private concern. It is not the cause of one poor printer, nor of New York alone, which you are now trying. No! It may in its consequence affect every free man that lives under a British government on the main of America. It is the best cause. It is the cause of liberty. And I make no doubt but your upright conduct this day will not only entitle you to the love and esteem of your fellow citizens, but every man who prefers freedom to a life of slavery will bless and honor you as men who have baffled the attempt of tyranny, and by an impartial and uncorrupt verdict have laid a noble foundation for securing to ourselves, our posterity, and our neighbors, that to which nature and the laws of our country have given us a right to liberty of both exposing and opposing arbitrary power . . . by speaking and writing truth.[4]

The jury took less than an hour to find John Peter Zenger not guilty of seditious libel. This was the result of great lawyering against great odds. It was a momentous victory for Zenger, and for the people. Zenger walked out of court a free man and immediately returned to publishing attacks on the Governor. The Colonies were set on a constitutional path that forbade government from abridging the right to freedom of speech; and the victory "marked the rise of a lawyer class. . . . The increase of commerce brought more litigation, and the need for skilled lawyers; and in one colony after another the men of best repute who had defended clients in the courts formed a bar, with rules of entry

---

[4] *See* for a fuller account, Doug Linder, *The Trial of John Peter Zenger: An Account* (2001), *available at* http://www.law.umkc.edu/faculty/projects/ftrials/zenger/zenger.html (This site was last visited August 14, 2008).

and of conduct that had the force of law."[5] With the help of lawyers, America was on the road to independence and enduring liberty.

NOTES AND QUESTIONS

1. ***What Can We Learn from John Peter Zenger and Andrew Hamilton?*** The stirring story of Andrew Hamilton, John Peter Zenger, and the birth of a free press should fill us with pride in the legal profession. Without a brilliant and courageous lawyer at his side, Zenger would have been carted off to prison and freedom of expression would have suffered a serious, perhaps fatal, blow. Then and now, people view Hamilton as a hero for standing up to an arrogant and oppressive government. However, should Hamilton have defended Zenger? Zenger was guilty of violating the law of libel as the courts had articulated it, and Hamilton knew it. How could Hamilton defend someone who was guilty? Perhaps you will argue that Zenger was guilty only in a technical sense because eventually (many years later) the law would recognize truth as an absolute defense to libel charges. Or perhaps you believe that appealing to the emotions of the jurors to free a guilty man was justified because the entire prosecution had been riddled with official corruption and abuse of power. But whatever justification you might perceive, Zenger's conduct as a publisher met the definition of seditious libel. Is a lawyer ever justified in defending someone who is guilty? When? Why?

Should lawyers who defend the guilty today be regarded as heroes, or as villains? What would happen to our free society if prosecutors had unfettered power to enforce the laws that corrupt governors railroaded through the legislature? Could we retain our liberties? The decline of freedom might not happen overnight — our system of checks and balances, our federalist system of overlapping state and federal authority, and our vigilant and aggressive bar would impede any effort to take away our fundamental freedoms — but we did not always have those freedoms, and nothing guarantees that we always will have them. What role do lawyers play in ensuring those freedoms? If we made a rule that lawyers were not allowed to defend people they knew to be guilty, could other freedoms survive?

If you are beginning to view lawyers as heroes (or at least as valuable bulwarks of freedom rather than as troublemakers), does the public share your view? Do you think most members of the general public understand or appreciate the role of lawyers, and view them as indispensable protectors of a free society, even when they defend the "guilty"?

2. ***"How Can You Defend a Person Who is Guilty?"*** Every law student and every lawyer is confronted from time to time with the question: "How can you defend someone who is guilty?" You need to be ready to answer that question. If you do not have a ready answer, you will discredit yourself and the legal profession. If you can't explain why lawyers "defend the guilty," many people will assume there is no explanation. Worse, they may assume that lawyers defend the guilty for only one reason: money. (We will address the justifications for defending the guilty later in this book.)

3. ***Are Transactions and Civil Matters Different?*** Maybe you don't plan to take criminal cases. But are civil matters and transactions so different? Consider these questions:

> (A) How can you defend a driver in a negligence suit if you think the driver was drunk when he ran over a little girl walking home from school? And what if the driver is an alcoholic and likely to drink and drive again?
>
> (B) How can you advise a client to take a tax deduction that the IRS is likely to disallow if it audits the return?

---

[5] MORISON & COMMAGER, *supra* note 1, at 122–23.

(C) How can you demand a high selling price in negotiations to sell a business when your client's business probably isn't worth half of what you are asking?

(D) How can you continue to represent a large corporate client if you find out that the client has used your services in the past to commit a massive fraud?

Those questions are just as important as the questions about defending the guilty. Even in civil litigation, and even in non-litigation matters, you'll be asked, expected, and often obligated to develop and argue for positions you don't agree with. Will you be able to do it? Do you want to do it?

All of these questions go to the heart of the adversary system, the system of justice we use in America. If you don't believe in the adversary system, you can't understand your role as a lawyer. If you can't understand your role, you can't play it well, and therefore can't serve your clients well. If you don't serve your clients well, who are you serving? Yourself? The public interest? Society? Let's talk about your role as a lawyer in the adversary system, starting with the principles that undergird the adversary system.

B. THE LAWYER'S PROFESSIONAL ROLE

To ask the question, "What is your role as a lawyer?", is easier said than done. The problem is that any satisfactory answer to the question depends on the answer to two underlying questions: "Whose interests do you, the lawyer, serve?" and "What values are you trying to achieve?"

The role assigned to lawyers in the American adversary system is essentially a utilitarian role — it seeks the greatest good for the greatest number. Our system does not give lawyers complete freedom to design their own roles, but rather defines particular roles — prosecutor, zealous defense lawyer, business advisor, etc. — in certain ways. In other words, the roles we play in carrying out obligations are imposed on us by the society in which we operate. The purpose of this chapter is to describe and question these roles.

In theory, we can think of at least four different roles that lawyers could theoretically play when resolving a dispute, facilitating a transaction, or providing general advice and counseling: (1) serve only the client; (2) serve only the state; (3) serve all parties equally; and (4) serve the public interest. Let us consider how a lawyer might best serve each of these four proposed interests.

1. Serve the Client

To return to Canon 7 of the old ABA Model Code of Professional Responsibility: "A Lawyer Should Represent a Client Zealously Within the Bounds of the Law." A lawyer should try to maximize the results for the client — to get as much of what the client wants as it is possible to get — using legal means.

The word "represent" is key. We stand, essentially, in the shoes of our clients. We "represent" our clients and their interests, not our own interests. Our role is to do for our clients what they could legitimately do for themselves if they had legal training and skill.

DR 7-101(A) expanded on this idea by saying: "A lawyer shall not intentionally: (1) Fail to seek the lawful objects of the client through reasonably available means permitted by law and the Disciplinary Rules. . . ." In other words, if you can think of a legitimate way to achieve your client's objectives, then you must do it. If you can legally get your client off on a criminal charge, you must do it. If you can legally get your client more money in a civil suit for damages, you must do it. If you can legally reduce your client's risks in a contract, you must do it. The client is the boss. The client tells you what he wants, and your job is to get as much of it as possible using reasonably available legal and ethical means.

2. Serve the State

An alternative conception of the lawyer's role was followed in the old Soviet Union. The lawyer's goal was to serve the interests of the state. A lawyer was an agent of the government, not of the client. Should we transplant that idea to America? Suppose you agree to defend a client in a criminal case, and after some investigation you determine that the client "did it" — that the client is "guilty." Should you refuse to represent the client any further? Should you inform on the client? Should you change sides and assist the state in prosecuting your client?

What would happen to attorney-client communications if a lawyer's main role was to advance the interests of the state? Imagine a typical conversation:

> *Lawyer:* You've been charged with murder one. Tell me everything so I can use all of my legal skills to analyze the facts and apply the law.
>
> *Client:* OK. Me and my pal Ziggy was at the bar when Jack walked in. I says, "Where's my money for that stash of weed?" Jack says, "I ain't payin' for it. It was lousy stuff." So I shot him.
>
> *Lawyer:* Well, I can't defend you. I only defend innocent people, not people who are guilty. In fact, I'm going to the prosecutor with what you just said and testify against you. I taped our conversation so I can prove what you said.

Does that scenario sound outlandish? We hope so. But keep it in mind when you are tempted to work against the interests of a client instead of serving the client's interests. Think about how our system would work if you were an agent of the state instead of an agent of the client. Would your clients trust you? Would they confide in you? Would they level with you?

3. Serve All Parties Equally

Another conception of the lawyer's role is to serve all parties equally, trying to achieve the best resolution of the dispute in light of the law and the facts. In that role, you would listen carefully to your client and to the opposing parties, then advocate for the best resolution of the dispute. You would not give any special weight to the interests of your own client. Instead, you would try to bring about the fairest or most moral or just solution to the dispute as you saw it, regardless of what your own client wanted.

This is a wonderful role — but it is a role that is already taken. It is the judge's role. Why would a client pay his own lawyer to play a role that the public provides at virtually no cost, complete with a courtroom and bailiff?

Moreover, a lawyer taking on the role of a judge might not produce a better or fairer result than an actual judge would produce. A real judge is constrained by established rules of evidence, procedure, and substantive precedent. A lawyer playing the judge's role would not necessarily be so constrained. Rather, the lawyer would apply her own ideas about evidence, procedure, precedent, fairness, and morality. And unless the lawyers for all parties agreed on the "best" result, they would still need to go to a judge to resolve their differences. We can imagine, in theory, a system where the lawyers for the disputing parties advocate for their differing ideas of fairness, rather than advocating for the best results for their own individual clients. But it is hard to see how such a system would work in practice.

4. Serve the Public Interest

A fourth conception of a lawyer's role is to serve the public interest. If you played that role, you would recommend that the client follow the course of action most likely to serve the public interest rather than the client's narrow, self-centered interests. For example, if the state sued your client for violating environmental laws by discharging toxic waste from the client's outdated factory, you would focus not on the technicalities of the law (did your client really violate the law?), but rather on the best outcome for the public (which might be environmental cleanup, new technology to reduce the pollution, or even shutting down the client's factory). Or, if your client were charged with child abuse, you would decide whether to fight the charges or to recommend that the client get treatment, plead guilty, or even lose custody of the child to a foster parent.

The problem with this public interest role is: Who defines the "public interest?" Is the public interest whatever the lawyer personally thinks is best for society? Is it what the polls indicate that a majority of the public believes? Is it what a "public interest" organization (like the Sierra Club or the Children's Defense Fund) believes? And, how is the public interest defined geographically? Is it local, statewide, or national?

The danger is that each lawyer would define the public interest according to her own personal beliefs. Each person would do what is right in her own eyes. The result would be a legal system in which a client could obtain zealous representation only when a lawyer agreed with the client on what was in the public interest. Representing clients would then become merely a vehicle for lawyers to represent their own personal interests. That might be a good way to run a legal system in Plato's Republic, where lawyers would be anointed philosopher-kings and would be given a broad mandate to define and advance the public interest. But it is inconsistent with America's rugged individualism, where clients deserve the right to have a lawyer who speaks for them, fights for them, and enforces the constitutional right to be presumed innocent until proven guilty beyond a reasonable doubt in accordance with due process of law.

Unless we want to amend the Constitution to get rid of the Bill of Rights, a client needs a lawyer who will battle to enforce the client's own individual rights no matter what the lawyer personally believes. The Constitution doesn't confer rights only upon people approved by lawyers — it confers rights on everyone. If we admit (as we do) that individuals lack the legal knowledge and skill to enforce their rights on their own without a lawyer's help, and if we take individual rights seriously (including the right to effective assistance of counsel), then logic compels us to believe in an adversary system where a lawyer's role is to represent a client zealously within the bounds of the law.

The purpose of this book is to decide what the rules of professional conduct should be in the context of an adversary system — a system where a lawyer is commanded to take all reasonable and legitimate steps to advance the interest of the client.

C. THE LAWYER'S CONSCIENCE

A recurring question involves whether the adversary system leaves any room for lawyers to exercise their own conscience. We'll examine this broad question by asking a more specific question: If you think your client is guilty, do you have to argue to the jury that your client is *not* guilty?

Suppose you had been appointed by the court to defend Kenneth Glenn Hinson, facing a mandatory life sentence because of South Carolina's "Two Strikes and You're Out" law. Before Hinson became your client, he was convicted of raping a teenage girl in 1991. He therefore already has one strike before you begin representing him.

This time Hinson is charged with kidnapping two teenage girls in the trailer park where they all lived. (The girls lived within two hundred yards of Hinson's trailer.) The prosecution charges that Hinson surreptitiously stole into the trailer where the 17-year-old girls lived. Hinson took the first girl to a large underground bunker that he admits building about two months earlier. He then returned and kidnapped the other girl. He bound both girls with duct tape, sexually abused them, and left them to die in the windowless underground dungeon with no air supply. But, after the girls had been imprisoned for about 24 hours, they escaped and alerted the police. The police began a massive search, and soon found and arrested Hinson, who was hiding in the woods behind his trailer. The police showed Hinson duct tape, sex toys, and marijuana that had been found in the bunker. Hinson admitted that these things were all his, but he denied kidnapping or sexually assaulting the girls.

You were appointed to defend Hinson. After interviewing Hinson, you think he's guilty. You don't know for sure, but you think so because he admits to having sex with the girls, building the bunker, fleeing the police, and possessing marijuana. His implausible story about what he claims "really happened" strikes you as a web of lies. Do you have to argue to the jury that Hinson is not guilty? Do you have to argue to the jury that his story about what happened is true? In short, do you have to make an argument that you think is false?

NOTES AND QUESTIONS

1. ***Are Lawyers Immoral?*** The question "How can you represent a guilty person?" is really two separate questions. The first question is *institutional*: Does our system of justice require that lawyers furnish zealous representation even to defend the guilty? The second question is *individual*: Is an individual lawyer morally accountable for the results of a trial — for helping a "guilty" person go free?

"Moral accountability," in turn, is a complex idea that often blends three distinct moral standards:

a. The lawyer's own personal moral standard;
b. The community's moral standard; and
c. A general or "universal" moral standard, not confined to any particular community.

Which of these three distinct moral standards do you think a lawyer should follow?

2. ***Is it Immoral to Help the Guilty?*** One attitude, which finds support from thinkers such as Jeremy Bentham, is that assisting a thief, a rapist, or a murderer to evade the toils of the law is disreputable, if not immoral. Bentham's view was popular for many years. In fact, the zealous advocacy model of lawyer behavior was not generally accepted before the twentieth century. The first prominent American lawyer to publish rules of legal ethics, David Hoffman (1774–1854), thought that lawyers should not exert themselves too hard for "guilty" clients. In Hoffman's pioneering book RESOLUTIONS IN REGARD TO PROFESSIONAL DEPORTMENT (1836), one of the first American books on legal ethics, Hoffman said:

> Persons of atrocious character, who have violated the laws of God and man, are entitled to no such special exertions from any member of our pure and honourable profession; and indeed, to no intervention beyond securing them a fair and dispassionate investigation of the *facts* of their cause, and the due application of the law. . . .[6]

Hoffman believed that the guilty are entitled to a defense, but that such a defense is proper only when handled dispassionately and without resort to "the artifices of eloquence." Hoffman's view is no longer the accepted norm of professional behavior. Should it be?

3. ***Boswell's View.*** Boswell, the great biographer of Samuel Johnson, asked Johnson, "But what do you think of supporting a cause which you know to be bad?" Dr. Johnson replied, "Sir, you do not know it to be good or bad till the Judge determines it." In other words, Dr. Johnson is saying, we cannot ask whether we should defend the "guilty" because until a case ends we do not know who is guilty and who is not. Is Johnson right? Are lawyers unable to distinguish guilty clients from innocent ones until a judge makes an official pronouncement? If lawyers can tell who is guilty and who is not, why do we need a judge and jury? If lawyers cannot tell, how can they decide who to defend

---

[6] DAVID HOFFMAN, RESOLUTIONS IN REGARD TO PROFESSIONAL DEPORTMENT (1836).

zealously, on the one hand, and who to defend without any "special exertions" (to quote Hoffman), on the other hand? Is it not the lawyer's job to make judgments about a client's guilt or innocence?

4. ***Factual Guilt vs. Legal Guilt.*** Johnson's quip points out the theoretical difficulty of deciding that a client is "guilty" before a jury decides the client is guilty. To say that a defendant is "guilty" may refer to two very different things: *factual* guilt ("the defendant did it") and *legal* guilt ("the government proved it"). In both senses, calling a client "guilty" before the jury renders its verdict is problematic.

The problem with factual guilt is: How can a lawyer ever "know" for certain that a client is guilty? A client may appear to be guilty, or even confess, and still not actually be guilty. Unless the client admits to facts making up every element of an offense, under circumstances that make the confession reliable, how can a lawyer claim to "know" that the client is *factually* guilty? The great trial lawyer Edward Bennett Williams (founder of Williams & Connolly in Washington, D.C.) reportedly said, "I never know whether a client is guilty." But many lawyers, even after giving a client the benefit of every doubt, cannot agree with Williams. These lawyers "know" — with whatever certainty that anything in human affairs can be reliably "known" — that some of their clients are factually guilty. They know that a client is guilty because the client confesses to the lawyer, or cannot credibly explain solid evidence of guilt.

But how can a client be called "guilty" in the sense of *legal* guilt unless the prosecution — after the evidence is filtered and tested through the rules of evidence, cross-examination, and the rigorous procedures of a fair trial — persuades a jury that the accused is guilty "beyond a reasonable doubt"? If we genuinely accept the presumption of innocence (and shouldn't we?), then it is an oxymoron to say that a lawyer got a "guilty" person off. A person is presumed innocent until proven guilty, and if the jury finds a defendant not guilty, then the person was never guilty, period.

Of course, if the jury convicts the lawyer's client, the lawyer faces two new dilemmas. First, what should the lawyer do at sentencing? Should the lawyer try to persuade the judge to give the guilty person a light sentence? Second, should the lawyer urge the client to appeal, and then work hard to get the conviction overturned? (Newspapers often report that some vicious killer has just been set free and perhaps has killed again after a successful appeal, or after getting sentenced to probation instead of prison.) Should lawyers try to get people off who have already been found guilty? These may be harder questions, because now the lawyer knows factually and legally that the client really is guilty. For now, we'll leave these questions aside and focus on trial conduct.

5. ***The Lawyer's Role.*** The second aspect of Dr. Johnson's famous quip is institutional: it is not the lawyer's role to determine guilt or innocence. That is the role of the judge or jury. As Baron Bramwell put it, "A client is entitled to say to his counsel, 'I want your advocacy, not your judgment; [for judgment] I prefer that of the Court.' " This argument has particular force for English barristers, who even today may not refuse any client unless they lack the time or competence to handle the case properly. This is called the "taxicab rule" or "cab rank rule" — a barrister *must* defend any client who asks for the barrister's services, just as a taxicab driver must take the next passenger in line.

The result of the taxicab rule is a separation between the client's criminal behavior and the barrister's legitimate advocacy. The English system reinforces that separation by leaving the messy details of interviewing clients and witnesses to solicitors, who are free to pick and choose among clients, and may therefore ethically reject (or accept) clients they believe are factually guilty.

American lawyers are different. First, American lawyers combine the functions of the English solicitor and barrister, because American lawyers typically handle both the investigation and the trial. American lawyers thus come face to face with the truth, which may be ugly. Second, American lawyers do not follow the taxicab rule. American lawyers never have to accept paying clients that they don't want. (Court appointments are another story, because MRPC 6.2 says that a lawyer "shall not seek to avoid appointment by a tribunal to represent a person except for good cause. . . ." In the court-appointed situation, American lawyers are thus like English barristers — they have to take every appointed client that comes along.) In the private sector, American lawyers don't have to take a case unless they *want* the case.

Are American lawyers more morally accountable than English barristers when they defend "guilty" clients? After all, they could have rejected these clients, or perhaps withdrawn from their cases upon determining factual guilt. Are American lawyers morally accountable if they do it for the money? What about appointed counsel, who have no choice? What about public defenders, who get paid very little and who often see the job of defender as heroic, defending the oppressed and the underclass against the onslaught of social injustice, police abuse, and the state's vast investigative and prosecutorial resources? If a person who is acquitted of murder kills again, who is to blame? The lawyer? The jury? The prosecutor? The system? Society? The murderer? All of the above?

6. *The Adversary System and the Truth.* One way of justifying a lawyer's vigorous defense of every client is to argue that the adversary process is the best available means for determining the truth. The adversary system produces a kind of "free market" model, similar to Holmes' "marketplace of ideas." Each side offers the jury (or judge) a competing version of the truth, and the jury chooses the one that sounds best.

Even if you agree with that idea, there are two problems. First, how can advocacy of something that the lawyer knows is untruthful serve the ends of truth? How can a lawyer claim to be helping the search for truth by making a guilty client appear not guilty — by making a truthful prosecution witness seem like a liar, or by making a defendant's unlikely story seem likely? If the version of the facts being argued by the defense is not true, how can the adversary system foster truth?

Second, the "marketplace of ideas" analogy doesn't really work, because juries produce only verdicts, not narratives. The jury does not produce an account of what really happened — it simply renders a verdict of guilty or not guilty on each count. The jury may find the prosecutor's version of the truth much more believable than the defendant's version and yet return a verdict of not guilty, because the jury cannot accept the prosecutor's version unless the prosecutor has proven beyond a reasonable doubt that the defendant is guilty. Thus, the jury may be persuaded that the defendant is guilty by a preponderance of the evidence, or even by clear and convincing evidence, but the defendant will still go free because our system prohibits criminal conviction absent proof of guilt beyond a reasonable doubt. Thus, the criminal justice system does not produce truth, it produces verdicts. The truth may never be known.

Because of the problems in arguing that the adversary system is the best way of finding the truth, the argument in favor of the adversary system is usually phrased as a systemic one. A careful exploration of the problem is found in Mitchell, *The Ethics of the Criminal Defense Attorney — New Answers to Old Questions*, 32 Stan. L. Rev. 293, 298 (1980). Mitchell says the function of a defense attorney is "making the screens work," just as window screens let in fresh air and keep out bugs. The "screens" are the rules of evidence and the right to due process of law (including the right to confront and cross-examine witnesses, the right to effective assistance of counsel, the right to subpoena witnesses, and the standard of guilt beyond a reasonable doubt). By providing a vigorous defense for the accused and forcing the prosecution to follow all of the rules and prove guilt beyond a reasonable doubt, the defense attorney makes the police, prosecutor, judge, and jury more fully aware of their roles within the criminal justice system and more likely to perform them competently and within their proper limits. Thus, the defense lawyer prods the system to work better, and the "screening" of innocent and guilty persons by the justice system gradually becomes more thorough and accurate.

Another way of putting it is that the State, to protect the people, has designed a system that takes the risk that some guilty defendants will go free in order to minimize convictions of innocent persons. The lawyer is assigned a role in that system and may properly conclude that the ethics of functioning in that assigned role outweigh any immoral consequences stemming from a *particular* instance of advocacy. The system is *designed* to let some guilty people go free so that fewer innocent people will be imprisoned. Helping some guilty clients "walk" is the price society pays to make sure innocent clients retain their liberty.

7. ***Individual Dignity.*** Another justification for defending the guilty is that defending the guilty upholds and protects individual dignity. The American experience since the Declaration of Independence is the pursuit of ideals such as "liberty" and "equality." These ideals are the essence of individual dignity in America. That is what Andrew Hamilton and his client, John Peter Zenger, were fighting for. Important aspects of these ideals are embodied in the Bill of Rights. The Sixth Amendment right to the effective assistance of counsel is among those remarkable rights that make America great, and it applies to all defendants, not just those that defense lawyers (or prosecutors) consider innocent. To uphold the Sixth Amendment right to effective assistance of counsel — without which government could run roughshod over the people — lawyers have a duty to defend the accused, including those who are guilty.

Monroe Freedman, a champion of individual liberty and zealous advocacy, argues: "The concept of a right to counsel is one of the most significant manifestations of our regard for the dignity of the individual." Because a free society so greatly respects the dignity of the individual, the right to counsel is accorded even to a person "known by the state to have committed a heinous offense." MONROE FREEDMAN, LAWYERS' ETHICS IN AN ADVERSARY SYSTEM 2, 4 (1975). Is Professor Freedman right? Does society show regard for the dignity of the individual by furnishing counsel even for the guilty?

Related to this concern for individual dignity is Mitchell's reason for choosing to defend the guilty: to help ensure that the criminal justice process teaches its participants, particularly the accused, the right lessons. By defending the guilty, the defense lawyer hopes to teach the judge and jury that the accused has human worth and deserves a measure of respect, and to teach the accused that "the indigent defendant is not alone and worthless without money." Is Mitchell right? Or are some criminal defendants worthless and undeserving of any respect?

8. ***Horrible Prisons.*** Even if you accept the general proposition that a lawyer morally *may* defend the guilty, why *should* a lawyer do so? Perhaps the high costs of inflicting punishment justify defending the guilty. The costs include a criminal justice system that is based on power and fear, that is often corrupt, that costs a fortune to operate, and that produces intolerable and often unconstitutional prisons.

What if the defendant is not only factually guilty, but will endanger society if acquitted? Even Mitchell is morally troubled about that. As a practical matter, though, Mitchell thinks that this morally troublesome situation rarely arises, because dangerousness and guilt are difficult to determine. But what if a defendant is both factually guilty and dangerous? What if a defendant has raped before and says he can't stop himself from raping again? Should you defend him? Zealously? Why or why not?

9. ***Civil Cases.*** Do the arguments that justify zealous representation of a guilty criminal defendant also justify zealous representation of a civil plaintiff or defendant known by the attorney to be wrong? For example, the argument about horrible prisons doesn't apply in the context of civil cases, where losers don't go to prison. What are the arguments for defending the "guilty" (i.e., those who are at fault) in civil cases? Is moral accountability the same for the civil litigator as for the criminal defense lawyer?

D. SHOULD WE REFORM THE ADVERSARY SYSTEM?

Let's get a reaction to the adversary system from a highly respected former federal judge from the Southern District of New York, the late Marvin Frankel, who saw trials day in and day out for many years. What does this judge think of the accuracy of the adversary system? Does he think the system needs to be redesigned to get at the truth more often?

MARVIN E. FRANKEL, THE SEARCH FOR TRUTH: AN UMPIREAL VIEW

123 U. Pa. L. Rev. 1031, 1036–37 (1975)*

We proclaim to each other and to the world that the clash of adversaries is a powerful means for hammering out the truth. Sometimes, less guardedly, we say it is "best calculated to getting out all the facts. . . ." That the adversary technique is useful within limits none will doubt. That it is "best" we should all doubt if we were able to be objective about the question. Despite our untested statements of self-congratulation, we know that others searching after facts — in history, geography, medicine, whatever — do not emulate our adversary system. We know that most countries of the world seek justice by different routes. What is much more to the point, we know that many of the rules and devices of adversary litigation as we conduct it are not geared for, but are often aptly suited to defeat, the development of the truth.

We are unlikely ever to know how effectively the adversary technique would work toward truth if that were the objective of the contestants. Employed by interested parties, the process often achieves truth only as a convenience, a by-product, or an accidental approximation. The business of the advocate, simply stated, is to win if possible without violating the law. (The phrase "if possible" is meant to modify what precedes it, but the danger of slippage is well known.) His is not the search for truth as such. To put that thought more exactly, the truth and victory are mutually incompatible for some considerable percentage of the attorneys trying cases at any given time.

Certainly, if one may speak the unspeakable, most defendants who go to trial in criminal cases are not desirous that the whole truth about the matters in controversy be exposed to scrutiny. This is not to question the presumption of innocence or the prosecution's burden of proof beyond a reasonable doubt. In any particular case, because we are unwilling to incur more than a minimal risk of convicting the innocent, these bedrock principles must prevail. The statistical fact remains that the preponderant majority of those brought to trial did substantially what they are charged with. While we undoubtedly convict some innocent people, a truth horrifying to confront, we also acquit a far larger number who are guilty, a fact we bear with much more equanimity.

One reason we bear it so well is our awareness that in the last analysis truth is not the only goal. An exceedingly able criminal defense lawyer who regularly serves in our court makes a special point of this. I have heard him at once defy and cajole juries with the reminder that the question is not at all "guilt or innocence," but only whether guilt has been shown beyond a reasonable doubt. Whether that is always an astute tactic may be debated. Its doctrinal soundness is clear.

NOTES AND QUESTIONS

Trash Talk. Judge Frankel says the adversary system isn't very accurate. Does that mean we need to redesign the system? Is the system we have now a silly one? Is it a system in which a bunch of liars and actors try to fool twelve people chosen for their ignorance? (A cynical saying goes, "How would you like to be tried in front of twelve

---

people too dumb to get out of jury duty?") Would you reform the system to get at the truth in a better way? Before you jump on the bandwagon with Judge Frankel, let's hear from Professor Monroe Freedman, a staunch believer in the adversary system, and one of its most eloquent defenders.

MONROE H. FREEDMAN, JUDGE FRANKEL'S SEARCH FOR TRUTH

123 U. Pa. L. Rev. 1060–66 (1975)*

The theme of Judge Marvin E. Frankel's Cardozo Lecture [parts of which we just read] is that the adversary system rates truth too low among the values that institutions of justice are meant to serve. Accordingly, Judge Frankel takes up the challenging task of proposing how that system might be modified to raise the truth-seeking function to its rightful status in our hierarchy of values. His proposals, delivered with characteristic intellect, grace, and wit, are radical and, I believe, radically wrong.

Judge Frankel directs his criticism at the adversary system itself and at the lawyer as committed adversary. Challenging the idea that the adversary system is the best method for determining the truth, Judge Frankel asserts that "we know that others searching after facts — in history, geography, medicine, whatever — do not emulate our adversary system." I would question the accuracy of that proposition, at least in the breadth in which it is stated. Moreover, I think that to the extent that other disciplines do not follow a form of adversarial process, they suffer for it. Assume, for example, a historian bent upon determining whether Edward de Vere wrote the plays attributed to William Shakespeare, or whether Richard III ordered the murder of the princes in the Tower, or even whether it was militarily justifiable for the United States to devastate Nagasaki with an atomic bomb. Obviously, the historian's inquiry would not be conducted in a courtroom, but the conscientious historian's search for truth would necessarily involve a careful evaluation of evidence marshalled by other historians strongly committed to sharply differing views on those issues. In short, the process of historical research and judgment on disputed issues of history is — indeed, must be — essentially adversarial. In medicine, of course, there is typically less partisanship than in historical research because there is less room for the play of political persuasion, and less room for personal interest and bias than in the typical automobile negligence case. Nevertheless, anyone about to make an important medical decision for oneself or one's family would be well advised to get a second opinion. And if the first opinion has come from a doctor who is generally inclined to perform radical surgery, the second opinion might well be solicited from a doctor who is generally skeptical about the desirability of surgery. According to one study, about nineteen percent of surgical operations are unnecessary. A bit more adversariness in the decision-making process might well have saved a gall bladder here or a uterus there.

Moreover . . . it is well established in our law that the extent of due process — meaning adversary procedures — properly varies depending upon the matter at stake in litigation. In medical research, the situation is similar, and recent instances of dishonesty at the Sloan-Kettering Institute and at Harvard illustrate the increasing importance of adversariness in medical research. Prior to World War II, apparently, the material rewards of biological research were small, "scientific chicanery" was extremely limited, and adversariness was of minimal concern, but the stakes have risen since then. Now that publication of discoveries has become essential to professional advancement and to obtaining large grants of money, rigorous verification, as through replication by a skeptical colleague, has become a common requirement.

NOTES AND QUESTIONS

Churchill's Caution. Maybe the adversary system doesn't work as well as we want it to, but when you study the adversary system, you should always keep in mind the famous words of Sir Winston Churchill: "It has been said that democracy is the worst form of government except all the others that have been tried." The adversary system may be a deeply flawed system, but it's better than any other system yet devised by mankind. In either case, the adversary system is the only system we have in America for the trial of criminal cases. Such a system works only if everybody plays their role, and does not play anyone else's role.

Large parts of this book are devoted to helping you understand the lawyer's role, and its limits. In this chapter, we've defined the lawyer's role when appointed or hired to defend a client who is factually guilty of the act charged. That role is to use every legitimate means approved by the client to defeat the prosecution's case.

E. IS THE ADVERSARY SYSTEM A BATTLE BETWEEN EQUALS?

Is the adversary system a battle between equals? Phrased more broadly, is the adversary system fair? That's a huge question. We confine our discussion to one main aspect: financial resources. Specifically, consider these two questions:

1. In criminal cases, is the adversary system fair to a defendant who is too poor to afford a lawyer?
2. In criminal cases, is the adversary system fair to the prosecutor (i.e., the people) when a defendant is very wealthy?

We cannot possibly hope to answer these questions definitively. They go to the heart of the many philosophical questions about the adversary system. But in the words of John F. Kennedy at his inauguration, "Let us begin."

One way to begin is to compare the defense resources available to a typical poor person with the defense resources available to a wealthy celebrity defendant like O.J. Simpson.

1. Resources Available to a Poor Defendant

Let's assume that a poor person has no money to hire a private lawyer. Fortunately, every poor person charged with a serious crime will still have a lawyer, because the Supreme Court's landmark decision in *Gideon v. Wainwright*, 372 U.S. 335 (1963), and its progeny established that the Sixth Amendment gives poor people a constitutional right to be represented by counsel at the state's expense at a criminal trial.

Of course, friends and relatives may chip in to raise money to hire a private lawyer, and some lawyers do criminal defense work pro bono — but most poor defendants in criminal cases are represented either by public defenders or court-appointed lawyers. (A public defender is a full-time criminal defense lawyer on the public payroll who does nothing but represent indigent criminal defendants. A court-appointed lawyer is a private lawyer appointed by the court for a particular case and paid out of the public treasury at a rate set by statute or court rule.)

Attorneys, of course, can't do everything themselves. They typically need a long list of other people to defend a criminal case, whether the case is a death-penalty case or a routine burglary case. For example, attorneys usually need investigators to find out the facts, paralegals to help organize files, and court reporters to make transcripts. Sometimes criminal defense lawyers also need expert witnesses such as psychiatrists, DNA experts, or ballistics experts. The public is constitutionally required to pay for some of these people but not all of them, and the public is certainly not required to hire the top people in a field and pay top dollar for their services.

2. Resources Available to a Wealthy Defendant

Now let's consider what it's like to be a wealthy defendant. We'll use the famous example of the trial of O.J. Simpson. When O.J. Simpson got divorced in 1992, court records indicate that his net worth was $10.8 million, and that he was earning between $730,000 and $1 million each year from his endorsements and his broadcasting work. He probably had even more money by the time he was charged with murder in June of 1994. In short, he had enough money to pay for a first-class defense. And he did. Here are some of the people and types of people he hired to defend him against charges of murder:

- A team of at least nine highly regarded lawyers, including Howard Weizmann, Robert Shapiro, Alan Dershowitz, Johnnie Cochran, F. Lee Bailey, Gerald Uelmen, Robert Kardashian, LeRoy Taft, and Sara L. Caplan;
- Two lawyers who are experts on the use of DNA evidence, Barry Scheck and Peter Neufeld. (Scheck, of course, became an important part of the defense team at trial, conducting some devastating cross-examinations and making some of the closing arguments.);
- Autopsy experts to refute prosecution theories of how and when Nicole Simpson was killed, blood stain experts to deal with blood on the gloves, car seats, driveways, etc., and experts on techniques of police investigation to look for mistakes in the LAPD's work;
- Private investigators, including investigators who traveled to Chicago, North Carolina, and many other places around the country;
- Photography experts, including the expert who testified that the photographs of O.J. Simpson wearing Bruno Magli shoes had been doctored;
- A forensic psychiatrist, in case O.J. decided to plead insanity. (He didn't.);
- A rotating team of court reporters to produce daily transcripts at trial so that the Simpson defense team could prepare as fully as possible for each day of trial;
- Jury specialists to advise regarding the types of people most likely to favor the defense, to provide mock juries on which the lawyers can test out their arguments, and to observe the jury at trial to gauge how it is reacting to the evidence.

How much did all of this cost? No one knows for certain, but estimates are in the $10 million range. Whatever it cost, it was exponentially more than indigent defendants get from the government, and far more than most criminal defendants can afford. And what did all of this money buy? According to Susan Estrich, a law professor at the University of Southern California, lavish defense expenses may be able to buy reasonable doubt by putting all of the prosecution's evidence under a microscope. In a case like the Simpson case that is based entirely on scientific and circumstantial evidence, with no eyewitnesses to the murder, no confession from the defendant, and no murder weapon to use as an exhibit, a huge defense budget can magnify "the usual foibles, errors, inadequacies and ineptness" of a criminal investigation.

NOTES AND QUESTIONS

1. ***"Equal Justice Under Law."*** Chiseled into the stone above the entrance to the United States Supreme Court are the words "Equal Justice Under Law." What does that phrase mean? Does it mean that everyone, rich or poor, is entitled to the same *quality of defense* in a criminal case? Or does it mean only that everyone is entitled to be tried in the *same courts* and under the *same laws*? What should the phrase mean in an ideal world?

2. *Limits on Defense Spending?* After reading about O.J. Simpson's lavish defense budget, would you favor a law limiting the amount of money criminal defendants could spend on their defense? (By the way, do you think limits on defense spending would be constitutional? If not, do you think the constitution should be amended?) Assuming limits on defense spending would be constitutional, how should the limits be set? Would the amount of the limit depend on the nature of the charges, on the maximum possible sentence, on the length of the trial, on the prosecution's budget for the case, or on other factors? (You'd allow defendants to spend more to defend against felony charges than misdemeanor charges, right?) Do you think these limits would work in practice?

3. *The Oklahoma City Bombing Trial Defense.* Not all court-appointed lawyers are poorly paid. Attorney Stephen Jones and his defense team reportedly spent about $10 million defending Timothy McVeigh against charges that he bombed the Oklahoma City federal building, killing 168 people. Mr. Jones personally spent thousands of hours on the case — so much time that he had to give up his private practice during the case. But the Oklahoma City bombing case was truly extraordinary — it involved the most deadly incident of terrorism by an American citizen in the history of the United States. Not many cases get that kind of attention. Should they? Should poor people in every case have access to the same level of funding as rich people? The same level of funding as Timothy McVeigh?

4. *Jury Consultants.* Some people were outraged that O.J. Simpson could afford such a deluxe defense, including jury consultants who could help the defendant pick a favorable jury. In Illinois, for example, a state legislator actually presented a bill to outlaw jury consulting. The theory was that jury consultants gave defendants an unfair advantage and enabled "guilty" defendants to get off. What do you think? Should defendants be permitted to hire people to advise them on how to pick the most favorable jury and how to persuade that jury to acquit?

5. *The Prosecution's Advantage.* Doesn't the prosecution usually have an enormous advantage? After all, the prosecution has all the resources of the state at its disposal-lawyers, investigators, support staff, experts, etc. — plus the ability to engage in undercover investigations (informants, wiretaps, etc.). Does this advantage make criminal trials unfair? Or does the defense overcome the prosecution's advantage in resources because the prosecution must prove its case beyond a reasonable doubt, which is a very high standard?

6. *Is Plea Bargaining Illegal?* Many defendants plead guilty to lesser charges as part of a plea bargain. Some of the plea bargains are with defendants who agree to testify for the prosecution in exchange for reduced charges or a more lenient sentencing recommendation from the prosecutor. Defense lawyers, of course, have nothing comparable to offer — they cannot offer co-defendants money to back up their own client's story, for example. In a remarkable case called *United States v. Singleton*, 144 F.3d 1343 (10th Cir. 1998), a panel of the Tenth Circuit held (over one dissent) that a prosecutor may not lawfully offer a criminal defendant lesser charges or a more lenient sentence in exchange for the defendant's agreement to turn state's evidence. Specifically, the court held that under 18 U.S.C. § 201(c)(2) — which prohibits any person from offering a witness "anything of value" in exchange for the witness's testimony — it is unlawful to induce a witness to testify for the state in exchange for lighter charges or the prosecution's recommendation of a lighter sentence. The court noted that § 201(c)(2) paralleled ABA Model Rule 3.4(b), which provides that a lawyer may not "offer an inducement to a witness that is prohibited by law."

Prosecutors across the country were astonished at the Tenth Circuit's ruling in *Singleton*. The July 20, 1998 issue of the National Law Journal ran a front-page story with a headline calling the decision "stunning," pointing out that the decision stripped prosecutors of powers they had long believed they had. Offering witnesses a good bargain in exchange for cooperation and testimony is standard procedure everywhere in America, at both state and federal levels. Nationally, prosecutors talked openly about asking Congress to negate the *Singleton* decision, and in Denver prosecutors announced plans to file a petition seeking a rehearing en banc.

But then something extraordinary happened. On July 10, 1998, before the prosecutors had even filed a petition for rehearing, the Tenth Circuit vacated the panel decision on its own motion and ordered a rehearing en banc. If you were on the Tenth Circuit and this issue came before your court as an issue of first impression, leaving you free to decide the case on policy grounds, how would you vote? For the sake of achieving equal justice under law through the adversary system, what are the arguments for and against allowing prosecutors to "buy" witness testimony by offering to reduce or drop charges or recommend a lighter sentence? And if prosecutors are allowed to buy cooperation by making plea deals, should defense lawyers be able to buy cooperation with cash or other promises to witnesses? For the Tenth Circuit's en banc opinion, see *United States v. Singleton*, 165 F.3d 1297 (10th Cir. 1999).

Chapter 15
CIVIL MATTERS AND THE ADVERSARY SYSTEM

We begin our examination of the adversary system in civil matters by looking at a fundamental question about confidentiality in the adversary system: When, if ever, must lawyers tell the other side about adverse evidence? In other words, when must lawyers reveal to adverse parties information that is harmful to their own clients?

A. DISCLOSURE OF ADVERSE EVIDENCE IN LITIGATION

We learned in the chapters on secrecy that mandatory disclosure rules are rare. A lawyer ordinarily is not required to reveal information that will help police officers solve crimes, for example. There is an exception for physical evidence, like guns and stolen goods — lawyers who possess and control physical evidence of a crime must turn it over to prosecutors. But apart from physical evidence, a lawyer is seldom required to reveal confidential information.

Permissive (discretionary) disclosure is more common. Under ABA Model Rule 1.6(a), you *may* disclose information with the client's express or implied consent, and under Rule 1.6(b) you *may* disclose information you reasonably believe necessary to prevent reasonably certain death or substantial bodily harm, for example, and you *may* disclose information in self-defense, or to collect a fee, or to seek advice from a lawyer in a different firm about compliance with the Rules of Professional Conduct, or to comply with law or a court order. But *mandatory* disclosures are rare. The ABA Model Rules of Professional Conduct mandate disclosure in only three situations:

- under Rule 3.3(a)(3), when the lawyer has offered false testimony and comes to know of its falsity, and the false testimony cannot be corrected without disclosure, or
- under Rule 3.3(b), when necessary to remedy criminal or fraudulent conduct relating to a proceeding in which the lawyer represents a client, or
- under Rule 4.1(b) when disclosure is necessary to avoid assisting a client's crime or fraud *and* Rule 1.6 does not prohibit the disclosure.

Some states mandate disclosure in other situations, particularly in situations where the client is about to kill or injure someone. However, the ABA ethics rules do not mandate disclosures except in the three situations just described.

A major premise of the ABA confidentiality rules (and of the confidentiality rules in the states) is that American justice is achieved through an adversary process. Thus, a lawyer's duty is to the client as an individual — not to society generally or to a specific client's adversaries. A lawyer has no obligation to help society at large or to help the other side — and has no right to do anything to harm the client absent a mandatory or permissive exception to the duty of confidentiality.

Is this the way things should be? Should the rules require a lawyer to disclose confidential information beyond the three narrow categories just detailed? If so, what? In this chapter, we will take a broad look at the adversary system in civil matters, which are usually not complicated by the Fifth Amendment right against self-incrimination and the Sixth Amendment's right to effective assistance of counsel.

Suppose the defendant knows of evidence, unknown to the plaintiff, without which the plaintiff cannot prove her case. Must the defendant disclose it? What should the defendant do? Here's how the New York County Bar viewed the situation many decades ago.

NEW YORK COUNTY LAWYER'S ASSOCIATION COMMITTEE ON PROFESSIONAL ETHICS

Opinion No. 309 (1933)

Question: In an action on behalf of an infant three years of age, for injuries sustained by falling off a porch owned by the defendant, due to the alleged negligence of the defendant, where there is no eyewitness known to the plaintiff's attorney, and thereafter when the case came to trial, the infant's case was dismissed on motion of the defendant's attorney on the ground that the infant plaintiff was unable to make out a sufficient case of circumstantial evidence. During the presentation of the plaintiff's case, said attorney for the defendant had an eyewitness to said accident actually present in court, and did not mention said fact, either to the plaintiff's attorney or to the Court, and kept the Court in ignorance of the fact that a person did exist who actually saw said accident, and was present in the court.

Was the failure of the defendant's attorney to disclose said information to the Court improper professional conduct?

AUTHORS' COMMENT:

Before you read the Committee's answer, what is your answer? And does your answer reflect what you think the rules of professional conduct *actually* require, or what you think the rules *ought* to require? (Is there a difference?)

Answer: In the opinion of the Committee the conduct of the defendant's attorney is not professionally improper. The fact of infancy does not call for a different reply.

NOTES AND QUESTIONS

1. ***Short Answer.*** That was a short answer. Do you agree with it? Would you qualify it in any way? For example, would you say that the lawyer's conduct was not professionally improper as long as the opposing side had a fair opportunity to discover the unknown witness on its own? Is it ever professionally improper for a lawyer not to help the other side by disclosing adverse evidence?

2. ***Three Choices:*** When you (as a lawyer) know of evidence in a civil case that would establish the claim or defense of the opposing party, what is your duty? Pick one of these three:

(a) You *must not disclose* the evidence to the adverse party or to the court.
(b) You *must disclose* the evidence to the adverse party or to the court.
(c) You *may disclose or not disclose*, as you see fit — you are free to choose either course of action.

Thus, whenever we write a rule about secrecy, we face three basic choices — the lawyer (a) must disclose, (b) must not disclose, or (c) can choose to disclose or not to disclose. Let's look at these questions from a variety of anecdotal and theoretical perspectives.

3. ***Williston's Way.*** In his autobiography, the great contracts scholar Samuel Williston describes an incident in which he was representing the defendant in a financial matter. The client's correspondence file contained a damaging fact that the plaintiff's lawyer had failed to bring out. The court decided the case in favor of Williston's client, "relying on a supposed fact which I knew to be unfounded. I had in front of me a letter that showed his error. Though I have no doubt of the propriety of my behavior in keeping silent, I was somewhat uncomfortable at the time." SAMUEL WILLISTON, LIFE AND LAW 271 (1940).

Did Williston do anything wrong?

4. ***Plaintiffs vs. Defendants.*** Does it make any difference if the shoe is on the other foot — if the plaintiff's lawyer knows of evidence that would entitle the defendant to win the case? In other words, does the duty to disclose depend on whether you represent a plaintiff or a defendant? (Later we'll look at the same question in a criminal case. For now, we're talking only about civil cases.) In C. Curtis, It's Your Law 17 (1954), the author argues that the plaintiff is in a different posture:

> If the ugly fact belongs to the plaintiff's case, it must go in with it; and if it is so ugly that it spoils the case, then either the plaintiff must withdraw his case or his lawyer must withdraw from it. . . .

Is this convincing? Why should a plaintiff be treated differently from a defendant? If the defendant pleads an affirmative defense and the defense case includes an "ugly fact," must that fact go in with the case about the defense? Is the rule that the party with the burden must produce the good, the bad, and the ugly? If so, why do we need cross-examination?

5. ***The Kutak Commission's View.*** The Kutak Commission's first public draft of the ABA Model Rules of Professional Conduct, issued in 1980, would have required a civil advocate (but not a criminal defense lawyer) to "disclose a fact known to the lawyer, even if the fact is adverse, when disclosure . . . is necessary to correct a manifest misapprehension resulting from a previous representation the lawyer has made to the tribunal." Discussion Draft Rule 3.1(d) (Jan. 30, 1980). A comment to this proposal stated that the rules of professional ethics in America "have not heretofore generally required an advocate to disclose facts that the tribunal plainly ought to know," but a change was justified because "the law of discovery now requires broad disclosure of relevant facts upon appropriate demand." Is the comment convincing? Should the ABA have adopted the Kutak Commission's draft?

The comment to Discussion Draft Rule 3.1 also stated: "the commission considered, but did not adopt, a provision requiring disclosure of facts known to a lawyer, which 'would have a substantial effect on the determination of a material issue.'" Would you have voted for or against that provision? How does the provision the Kutak Commission rejected differ from the draft of Rule 3.1(d) just quoted?

6. ***Federal Rules of Civil Procedure.*** In civil litigation, discovery devices such as interrogatories and depositions were developed to eliminate surprise at trial and to enable each party to evaluate the strengths and weaknesses of the opponent's case. But many people believe that lawyers (and their clients) abuse the discovery devices — that lawyers often withhold information (or object to requests for information) within the scope of legitimate requests, and serve discovery requests seeking mountains of information irrelevant to the litigation simply to cause delay, to increase the opponent's expenses, and to distract attention from the real issues in the case.

To ameliorate these abuses, in 1992 the Judicial Conference of the United States forwarded to the Supreme Court an amended version of Fed. R. Civ. P. 26(a)(1) that included automatic mandatory disclosure provisions. The amended rule was vehemently opposed by many trial lawyers, and the House of Representatives actually passed a bill that would have killed the amendment, but the Senate did not reject the proposal so the effort to kill the amendment failed. (Proposals to amend the Federal Rules of Civil Procedure automatically take effect unless *both* the House and Senate vote to oppose.) The amendment to Rule 26(a)(1) took effect on December 1, 1993, despite predictions that it would doom the adversary system.

The amended version of Rule 26(a)(1) requires that each party, without waiting for a request from the other side, disclose the names of witnesses and identify or produce documents relevant to all facts pleaded "with particularity." If you had been a member of Congress, would you have voted for automatic disclosure, or do you think it should be up to each side to ask the adversary for the information it wants? What are the advantages and disadvantages of automatic disclosure rules? Do they avoid surprise and unnecessary expense, or do they encourage lazy lawyering?

7. ***Disclosing Adverse Law.*** Go back to Professor Williston's case, where he had a document in his file that contradicted a mistaken factual argument by the plaintiff. Suppose the judge's determination in the case turns on a question of law rather than fact, and the adversary fails to cite a key case in its favor. Must Williston disclose this controlling case to the court? Should the rules draw a distinction between disclosure of adverse *facts* and disclosure of adverse *law*? Why or why not? For the ABA's answer, see MRPC 3.3(a)(3) and its comment.

B. FAIRNESS IN NEGOTIATIONS

Lawyers spend an enormous amount of their time negotiating, both in the context of resolving disputes (whether before or after suit is filed) and in the context of putting together deals (transactions). How does a lawyer's role as a negotiator differ from a lawyer's role as a courtroom advocate? Is a lawyer's role as negotiator when seeking to resolve a dispute different from the lawyer's role when seeking to put together a transaction?

In litigation, lawyers negotiate about discovery, scheduling, evidentiary issues, and settlement terms. Outside of litigation, lawyers negotiate real estate deals, contracts, tax reductions, business acquisitions, mergers, and other transactions. Clients usually have the final say over the terms of the ultimate bargain, but lawyers commonly dominate the negotiating process and have great influence over the client's decision to accept or reject any offer.

Generally, whether in litigation or in transactions, lawyers as negotiators are expected to get as much for their clients as possible. The ethics rules do not require that the results be objectively "fair." That wouldn't be a workable rule, because who would decide what was "fair"? Nor does any state require a litigation settlement to be "fair," or require that a deal to sell a house or draft an employment contract be "fair." (Settlements in class actions, actions involving minors, and other actions involving parties that need special protection are a different story, so court rules and statutes typically require that settlements of those actions be fair — but in most settlements, fairness is not a requirement and court approval of settlements is not required.)

Does the absence of a fairness requirement mean that there are no limits on negotiating tactics? Should there be limits? Even if a lawyer doesn't have to make a fair deal, does a lawyer have to ensure that a deal is not grossly unfair or unconscionable? After all, an unconscionable contract for the sale of goods would not be enforceable. Does a lawyer have a duty not to take too much advantage of suckers, softies, or stupid people?

Consider a practical question: Do you serve your clients well when you negotiate a lopsided deal? Think about your own experience. Have you ever negotiated a deal with a friend, parent, or employer that was so favorable to you that the other party felt cheated? What happened? If the other side feels cheated, does it want to stick to the deal — or look for ways to get out of it?

Suppose you negotiate such a good deal on a contract to supply your client with shirts that the shirt seller has only a razor-thin profit margin. Will the shirt supplier want to enter into another contract with your client, or would it prefer to find other buyers? Will the shirt supplier give the same service to your client to earn a few pennies per shirt as it will give to a customer who is paying top dollar? If something goes wrong, will the shirt maker want to preserve the contract, or escape from it? Will tough terms lead to a long-term relationship, or instead to the renegotiation or total breakdown of the contract as soon as the other side has the slightest excuse to claim that your client is in breach?

Similarly, in an employment setting, do you serve your client well when you negotiate excessively tough terms for hiring a new employee? Not if the employee tries to even things out by cutting corners, or keeps one eye open for a new job. Will an employee who is secretly looking for a new job work as hard as one who sees a long-term future with your client's company?

In a real estate setting, do you serve your client well if you don't level with the buyer about hidden flaws in the sale property? If these flaws later come to light, the buyer may try to rescind the contract or sue for fraud after the deal closes.

In short, you can negotiate a deal that is too good. The line may be deal-specific and hard to locate, but experience teaches that at some point, if you negotiate a deal that is too good, the deal won't last. And you don't serve a client well when you negotiate a contract that won't last. Negotiating a lopsided deal that is overwhelmingly favorable to your client may hurt the client more than it helps.

But this discussion only lightly touches the question we started with: Should the rules of ethics impose a *duty* to avoid lopsided or unconscionable deals? Do they impose such a duty now? After all, sometimes, your client may benefit if you press for every possible advantage in a deal, and grab for everything you can get. Can you do that? If the rules of professional conduct restrict your freedom to bargain, are the restrictions on the substance (outcome) of negotiations, or on procedure (bargaining techniques), or both?

Keep in mind the significant differences between litigation and transactions. If the parties to negotiations fail to arrive at an agreement, they simply walk away. If the negotiations succeed, the parties complete a transaction (like the sale of an apartment building), or enter into a long-term relationship (like an employment contract, or a supplier-retailer agreement). Since there is no court proceeding surrounding these negotiations, judicial approval is not required. If the parties reach an agreement, they implement it themselves. The courts do not enter into the picture unless the deal breaks down and leads to litigation.

In litigation, in contrast, the parties cannot easily walk away voluntarily. A plaintiff who walks away from a lawsuit must do so empty handed unless the defendant agrees to a settlement, and a defendant who walks away will be hit with a default judgment. Thus, parties to litigation are basically prisoners of the litigation, whereas parties negotiating a possible transaction are usually free to walk away and find other negotiating partners or alternative plans.

We now present two famous essays about negotiations outside the domain of litigation. The two essays present contradictory views about whether the results of negotiations must be fair. Is fairness a workable standard? If not, what would be a workable standard? Since there are no judges at a negotiation, who would enforce this standard — and how, and when? The following essays were published several decades ago, but they remain current because they address timeless issues.

ALVIN B. RUBIN, A CAUSERIE ON LAWYERS' ETHICS IN NEGOTIATION

35 La. L. Rev. 577, 589–90 (1975)*

The monopoly on the practice of law does not arise from the presumed advantages of an attorney's education or social status; it stems from the concept that, as professionals, lawyers serve society's interests by participating in the process of achieving the just termination of disputes. That an adversary system is the basic means to this end does not crown it with supreme value. It is a means, not end.

If he is a professional and not merely a hired, albeit skilled hand, the lawyer is not free to do anything his client might do in the same circumstances. The corollary of that proposition does set a minimum standard: the lawyer must be at least as candid and honest as his client would be required to be. The agent of the client, that is, his attorney-at-law, must not perpetrate the kind of fraud or deception that would vitiate a bargain if practiced by his principal. Beyond that, the profession should embrace an affirmative ethical standard for attorneys' professional relationships with courts, other

*

lawyers and the public: *The lawyer must act honestly and in good faith.* Another lawyer, or a layman, who deals with a lawyer should not need to exercise the same degree of caution that he would if trading for reputedly antique copper jugs in an oriental bazaar. It is inherent in the concept of an ethic, as a principle of good conduct, that it is morally binding on the conscience of the professional, and not merely a rule of the game adopted because other players observe (or fail to adopt) the same rule. Good conduct exacts more than mere convenience. It is not sufficient to call on personal self-interest; this is the standard created by the thesis that the same adversary met today may be faced again tomorrow, and one had best not prejudice that future engagement.

Patterson and Cheatham correctly assert that the basic standard for the negotiator is honesty. "In terms of the standards of the profession, honesty is candor. . . . " Candor is not inconsistent with striking a deal on terms favorable to the client, for it is known to all that, at least within limits, that is the purpose to be served. Substantial rules of law in some areas already exact of principals the duty to perform legal obligations honestly and in good faith. Equivalent standards should pervade the lawyer's professional environment.

The distinction between honesty and good faith need not be finely drawn here; all lawyers know that good faith requires conduct beyond simple honesty.

. . . .

Since bona fides and truthfulness do not inevitably lead to fairness in negotiations, an entirely truthful lawyer might be able to make an unconscionable deal when negotiating with a government agency, or a layman or another attorney who is representing his own client. Few lawyers would presently deny themselves and their clients the privilege of driving a hard bargain against any of these adversaries though the opponent's ability to negotiate effectively in his own interest may not be equal to that of the lawyer in question. The American Bar Association Committee on Ethics does not consider it improper for a lawyer to gain an unjust result in a tax controversy. Young lawyers, among the most idealistic in the profession, about to represent indigents, are advised that they be tough, especially against a patsy.

There is an occasional Micah crying in the wilderness:

> One should go into conference realizing that he is an instrument for the furtherance of justice and is under no obligation to aid his client in obtaining an unconscionable advantage. Of course, in the zone of doubt an attorney may and probably should get all possible for his client.

This raises the problem inevitable in an adversary profession if one opponent obeys a standard the other defies. As Countryman and Finman inquire,

> How is a lawyer who looks at himself as "an instrument for the furtherance of justice" likely to fare when pitted against an attorney willing to take whatever he can get and use any means he can get away with?

In criminal trial matters, *Brady v. Maryland* imposes constraints on the prosecutor as a matter of constitutional due process by requiring that he divulge evidence favorable to the accused. The only limitations in the Code of Professional Responsibility on sharp practice in plea bargaining are on the public prosecutor, who

> shall make timely disclosure to counsel for the defendant . . . of the existence of evidence, known to the prosecutor or other government lawyer, that tends to negate the guilt of the accused, mitigate the degree of the offense, or reduce the punishment.

It is obvious, as has already been pointed out, that this does not stem from an ethical standard for lawyers but on the duty of the government, a duty the government's lawyer performs as alter ego for his employer.

While it might strain present concepts of the role of the lawyer in an adversary system, surely the professional standards must ultimately impose upon him a duty not to accept an unconscionable deal. While some difficulty in line-drawing is inevitable when such a distinction is sought to be made, there must be a point at which the lawyer cannot ethically accept an arrangement that is completely unfair to the other side, be that opponent a patsy or a tax collector. So I posit a second precept: *The lawyer may not accept a result that is unconscionably unfair to the other party.*

A settlement that is unconscionable may result from a variety of circumstances. There may be a vast difference in the bargaining power of the principals so that, regardless of the adequacy of representation by counsel, one party may simply not be able to withstand the expense and bear the delay and uncertainty inherent in a protracted suit. There may be a vast difference in the bargaining skill of counsel so that one is able to manipulate the other virtually at will despite the fact that their framed certificates of admission to the bar contain the same words.

The unconscionable result in these circumstances is in part created by the relative power, knowledge and skill of the principals and their negotiators. While it is the unconscionable result that is to be avoided, the question of whether the result is indeed intolerable depends in part on examination of the relative status of the parties. The imposition of a duty to tell the truth and to bargain in good faith would reduce their relative inequality, and tend to produce negotiation results that are within relatively tolerable bounds.

But part of the test must be in result alone: whether the lesion is so unbearable that it represents a sacrifice of value that an ethical person cannot in conscience impose upon another. The civil law has long had a principle that a sale of land would be set aside if made for less than half its value, regardless of circumstance. This doctrine, called lesion beyond moiety, looks purely to result. If the professional ethic is *caveat negotiator*, then we could not tolerate such a burden. But there certainly comes a time when a deal is too good to be true, where what has been accomplished passes the line of simply-a-good-deal and becomes a cheat. . . .

It is to serve society's needs that professions are licensed and the unlicensed prohibited from performing professional functions. It is inherent in the concept of professionalism that the profession will regulate itself, adhering to an ethos that imposes standards higher than mere law observance. Client avarice and hostility neither control the lawyer's conscience nor measure his ethics. Surely if its practitioners are principled, a profession that dominates the legal process in our law-oriented society would not expect too much if it required its members to adhere to two simple principles when they negotiate as professionals: Negotiate honestly and in good faith; and do not take unfair advantage of another — regardless of his relative expertise or sophistication. This is inherent in the oath the ABA recommends be taken by all who are admitted to the bar: "I will employ for the purpose of maintaining the causes confided to me such means only as are consistent with truth and honor."

NOTES AND QUESTIONS

Is Rubin Right? Is Judge Rubin right? If you think he is right, how would you write a rule to carry out his ideas? If you think he is wrong, what are the counterarguments? Think about the counterarguments for a few minutes before you read the next piece, a widely read article attacking Judge Rubin's theories.

JAMES J. WHITE, MACHIAVELLI AND THE BAR: ETHICAL LIMITATIONS ON LYING IN NEGOTIATIONS

1980 AM. B. FOUND. RESEARCH J. 926–30*

The difficulty of proposing acceptable rules concerning truthfulness in negotiation is presented by several circumstances. First, negotiation is nonpublic behavior. If one negotiator lies to another, only by happenstance will the other discover the lie. If the settlement is concluded by negotiation, there will be no trial, no public testimony by conflicting witnesses, and thus no opportunity to examine the truthfulness of assertions made during the negotiation. Consequently, in negotiation, more than in other contexts, ethical norms can probably be violated with greater confidence that there will be no discovery and punishment. Whether one is likely to be caught for violating an ethical standard says nothing about the merit of the standard. However, if the low probability of punishment means that many lawyers will violate the standard, the standard becomes even more difficult for the honest lawyer to follow, for by doing so he may be forfeiting a significant advantage for his client to others who do not follow the rules.

The drafters [of the Model Rules] appreciated, but perhaps not fully, a second difficulty in drafting ethical norms for negotiators. That is the almost galactic scope of disputes that are subject to resolution by negotiation. One who conceives of negotiation as an alternative to a lawsuit has only scratched the surface. . . . Surely society would tolerate and indeed expect different forms of behavior on the one hand from one assigned to negotiate with terrorists and on the other from one who is negotiating with the citizens on behalf of a governmental agency. The difference between those two cases illustrates the less drastic distinctions that may be called for by differences between other negotiating situations. Performance that is standard in one negotiating arena may be gauche, conceivably unethical, in another. More than almost any other form of lawyer behavior, the process of negotiation is varied; it differs from place to place and from subject matter to subject matter. It calls, therefore, either for quite different rules in different contexts or for rules stated only at a very high level of generality.

A final complication in drafting rules about truthfulness arises out of the paradoxical nature of the negotiator's responsibility. On the one hand the negotiator must be fair and truthful; on the other he must mislead his opponent. Like the poker player, a negotiator hopes that his opponent will overestimate the value of his hand. Like the poker player, in a variety of ways he must facilitate his opponent's inaccurate assessment. The critical difference between those who are successful negotiators and those who are not lies in this capacity both to mislead and not to be misled. . . .

Of course there are limits on acceptable deceptive behavior in negotiation, but there is the paradox. How can one be "fair" but also mislead? Can we ask the negotiator to mislead, but fairly, like the soldier who must kill, but humanely? . . .

Pious and generalized assertions that the negotiator must be "honest" or that the lawyer must use "candor" are not helpful. They are at too high a level of generality, and they fail to appreciate the fact that truth and truthful behavior at one time in one set of circumstances with one set of negotiators may be untruthful in another circumstance with other negotiators. There is no general principle waiting somewhere to be discovered as Judge Alvin B. Rubin seems to suggest in his article on lawyer's ethics. Rather, mostly we are doing what he says we are not doing, namely, hunting for the rules of the game as the game is played in that particular circumstance.

The definition of truth is in part a function of the substance of the negotiation. Because of the policies that lie behind the securities and exchange laws and the demands that Congress has made that information be provided to those who buy and sell, one suspects that lawyers engaged in SEC work have a higher standard of truthfulness than do those whose agreements and negotiations will not affect public buying and selling of assets. Conversely, where the thing to be bought and sold is in fact a lawsuit in which two professional traders conclude the deal, truth means something else. Here truth and candor call for a smaller amount of disclosure, permit greater distortion, and allow the other professional to suffer from his own ignorance and sloth in a way that would not be acceptable in the SEC case. In his article Rubin recognizes that there are such different perceptions among members of the bar engaged in different kinds of practice, and he suggests that there should not be such differences. Why not? Why is it so clear that one's responsibility for truth ought not to be a function of the policy, the consequences and the skill and the expectations of the opponent? . . .

NOTES AND QUESTIONS

1. ***Which Side Are You On?*** Now that you have read Professor White's views, do you agree with Judge Rubin or with Professor White? Which arguments from each writer do you find most persuasive?

2. ***A Real Estate Deal.*** Suppose your client retains you to negotiate the purchase of a parcel of land on which stands a historic but run-down old mansion. Your client tells you that five years ago the owner, Grant, refused to sell to someone who planned to remodel the mansion and turn it into upscale condominiums. Your client also tells you that her own plan is to tear down the house and build a funeral parlor in its stead. Your client loves historic old houses, and lives in one herself, but she is not buying this one to live in — she's buying it to tear down so she can use the land to build her business. (Assume, for the sake of simplicity, that zoning is no problem because there are no historic preservation laws and no zoning restrictions on the property.)

You and your client both believe that Grant (the owner) would not sell to your client if Grant thought the house would be torn down and replaced by a funeral parlor, because Grant's friends and neighbors would not want a funeral home in their midst. Grant, himself, however, is moving to another state to be with his children. May you ethically do (or suggest your client do) any of the following things?

- May you talk about what a great house this is to live in, and how your client loves living in the historic mansion she owns now? (Literally, this is true. In fact, your client is actually looking for another old mansion to move to — but not this one.)
- May you orally agree to preserve the house, with the intention of breaching the agreement after the sale because, under the statute of frauds, oral understandings about the prospective use of real property are unenforceable in your state?
- May you agree in writing to preserve the house, with the intention of breaching the agreement after the sale because you think Grant will not be able to mount a lawsuit while living in another state, or cannot afford to hire a lawyer, or will not find out about the change until after the house is torn down, or (at worst) will be unable to prove significant damages even if he sues and wins?
- May you use a friend as a "straw man" to purchase the property from Grant, with the intention that the friend will transfer ownership to your client shortly after the sale closes. (If this is OK, can you ask the friend to tell Grant that she is looking forward to living in the old house? What if this is true, but the friend plans to live there only until your client lines up financing and investors for the funeral home? What if the friend plans to live in the house for two years while your client searches for other suitable properties?)

3. ***What if the Seller is a Bigot?*** Forget about the funeral home in the last example. Suppose instead your client is African-American, and you know that Grant is a bigot who will not sell to non-whites, even though such discrimination is illegal. Can you tell

Grant that the purchaser is white? Can you tell your client to give a white friend power of attorney to sign the closing documents on your client's behalf, so that Grant won't find out that your client is not white? Suppose during the sale negotiations, Grant's lawyer says, "You know that Grant will sell only to whites, don't you?" Can you just say, "Of course I know that," leaving Grant's lawyer with the impression that your client is white? In sum, is it OK to bend the rules to keep the other side from getting away with something odious or illegal?

4. ***Rule 4.1.*** How would the questions above be resolved by ABA Model Rule 4.1 and its Comment? If you don't find that rule to be much help, how would you rewrite it to make it more helpful in these situations?

Let's first clear up a related question: Are non-litigators held to higher standards than litigators in negotiations? Do "transactions" lawyers have a duty to be more fair than litigators? Some people think so, at least in certain settings. But one of the greatest living champions of the adversary system, Professor Monroe Freedman, does not see any difference. He thinks the distinction between litigators and office attorneys is "fallacious," and he argues that

> our legal system is basically an adversarial one, and every lawyer — whether drafting a contract, counseling in a business venture, writing a will, or performing any other service on behalf of a client — acts in such a way as to protect the client from being at a disadvantage in potential litigation. . . . [E]very lawyer is an advocate, irrespective of whether he or she ever enters a courtroom.

M. Freedman, Lawyers' Ethics in an Adversary System 20–24 (1975). You may not agree with Professor Freedman's assessment, but if you think the rules of negotiation should be different for different types of lawyers, you must be ready to explain why — and how — they should differ. To sharpen your thinking on this subject, we turn to the subject of settlement negotiations in litigation.

C. NEGOTIATION TO END LITIGATION

Let's leave the subject of negotiating real estate deals and move on to civil litigation. Should the ethical rules depend upon the context of the negotiations? If so, then the rules for negotiating litigation settlements should differ from the rules for negotiating transactions. In more sophisticated terms, should negotiations to resolve litigation (or potential litigation) be governed by different standards than negotiations aimed at creating legally enforceable rules for a new relationship between the parties (e.g., contracts, partnerships, employment agreements)? Is the distinction between settling disputes and developing deals an important factor in determining rules for negotiators? Think about that as you read the next several items.

Is there *any* situation in which you as a negotiator must help or warn the other side? What if your decision is a matter of life and death? What if you have information relating to the representation clearly protected by the confidentiality rules that could save the opposing party's life? To start the debate, here's an extreme litigation situation based on a dramatic life-or-death story arising out of a real case.

In *Spaulding v. Zimmerman*, 263 Minn. 346, 116 N.W. 2d 704 (1962), the plaintiff, a teenager, was injured in a severe auto accident. The defendant's lawyer, who had been retained by the defendant's insurance company, arranged for a doctor chosen by the defendant's insurance company to examine the plaintiff to assess his claimed injuries. The doctor discovered that the plaintiff had a "life-threatening aneurism" that might (or might not) have been caused by the accident. The plaintiff did not know about this potentially fatal condition because his personal physician and other doctors that he hired to assess his injuries failed to discover it.

Suppose you are the defendant's lawyer. If the plaintiff learns about this aneurism, you know that it will cause him to increase his settlement demand substantially. Before the plaintiff learns about the aneurism, however, the plaintiff makes a settlement demand. The demand is reasonable in light of what the plaintiff knows about the case, but it is far less than the plaintiff could obtain if he added the life-threatening aneurism to his list of injuries. As the defendant's lawyer, what should you do? Here are some options:

(a) reject the offer and keep litigating;
(b) disclose to the plaintiff that the insurance company's doctor found a life-threatening aneurism, then continue negotiating; or
(c) accept the plaintiff's offer without ever disclosing the aneurism; or
(d) accept the plaintiff's offer, finalize the settlement, and *then* disclose the aneurism; or
(e) do something else (which we leave to you to devise).

Which one would you choose? Why? Write your answer here:

Suppose the plaintiff's chances of survival depended on prompt diagnosis of the aneurism. Does your answer change? How and why? (Write a few words here.)

Suppose the diagnosis of a life-threatening condition is just a possibility or probability, rather than a certainty. For example, would your answer change if the examining doctor said, "the plaintiff *might* have a potentially fatal aneurism, but I'm not sure."

NOTES AND QUESTIONS

1. ***Morality vs. The Rules.*** Did you make your choice in *Spaulding v. Zimmerman* based on a determination that the rules of professional conduct require your result, or on moral grounds that supersede the ethical standards, or on some creative or technical analysis of the language of the confidentiality rules? Is there any legitimate way to interpret the rules that would allow you to disclose the aneurism without your client's consent? If not (i.e., if your client's consent is the only pathway to disclosure), are you obligated to press your client for consent to disclose the aneurism? (If the doctor's report goes directly to you and not to your client, do you even have to tell your client about the aneurism? Or can you settle the case and keep this terrible secret to yourself?)

ABA Model Rule 1.6(b)(1) was amended in 2002 to permit a lawyer to reveal confidential information to the extent the lawyer reasonably believes necessary to "prevent reasonably certain death or substantial bodily harm." Does the aneurism qualify? What if the doctor has told you that the chances of eventual death from the aneurism are "50/50." Is that "reasonably certain"?

Even if ABA Model Rule 1.6(b)(1) would permit disclosure, many states still have not adopted it. Assume that your state has not adopted it, that your state's rules would not allow disclosure without client consent, and that your client (the defendant) will not consent to disclosure. What is the strongest argument you can devise for disclosure on purely moral grounds? In other words, construct an argument that a lawyer *always* has an overriding duty, no matter what the rules say in any given situation, to "do the right thing." Make this argument even if you don't believe it. Write down a sentence or two describing your argument in the blank space here:

Now write down the counter-argument — the strongest argument you can make that a lawyer's personal morals *never* entitle the lawyer to disclose confidential information on purely moral grounds, no matter what the situation:

Finally, take the middle ground. Argue here that a lawyer *sometimes* has a moral right (duty?) to disclose confidential information even when disclosure clearly violates the rules of legal ethics — and provide some guidance (factors or considerations) about how a lawyer should choose whether or not to disclose when doing so would violate the ethics rules:

2. ***What's the Downside of not Disclosing?*** If the lawyer does not disclose the aneurism until after accepting the settlement, should the plaintiff be permitted to challenge the settlement on grounds of fraud by the defendant's lawyer?

If the defense lawyer does *not* disclose the aneurism and the plaintiff dies of the aneurism without ever learning about it, should the plaintiff's estate be permitted to sue the defense lawyer for not disclosing the aneurism? (The estate may sue the plaintiff's own doctor for malpractice, but that's a problem for medical ethics, not legal ethics.)

If the defense lawyer *does* tell the plaintiff about the aneurism and the case consequently settles for a much higher amount than the plaintiff had offered, can the defendant sue the defense lawyer for revealing confidential information? Can the defense lawyer be disciplined for revealing the confidential information without client consent?

3. ***Computational Errors.*** Now let's look at another situation. Here, the question isn't whether the lawyer should reveal information that may save a life, but whether the lawyer has a duty to correct the other side's mathematical or technical errors in a settlement agreement. If the other side's lawyer drafts a settlement agreement and makes a computational error favoring your client, do you have a duty to correct the error? Do you have to say, "Gee, there's a typo here — you gave my client $50,000 too much"? The ethics opinion that follows addresses this question. The opinion construes the old Canons, but the issue still arises under the rules in effect today.

ASSOCIATION OF THE BAR OF THE CITY OF NEW YORK, COMMITTEE ON PROFESSIONAL ETHICS

Opinion No. 477 (1939)*

Question. An attorney tried a matter before a quasi-judicial board. By the opinion which was handed down, some of the issues were decided in his favor and some against him. His adversary then served a computation, as permitted by the Rules, showing the amount he considered his client entitled to under the decision, and no objection having been taken thereto, judgment was entered in accordance with this computation as a matter of course.

The judgment is less than the adversary is entitled to under the decision, although not less than the attorney considers the adversary lawfully entitled to, regardless of the decision. The attorney is clear that his adversary has made a mistake in computation, not a mistake in construing the decision. The attorney believes that if he requests his client's permission to disclose the error, the client will refuse it.

The attorney inquires whether it is his duty to suggest the error to his adversary or to the Board and to consent on behalf of his client to modification of the judgment.

AUTHORS' COMMENT:

Before you read the Committee's answer, what is your answer? If you think it's OK to take advantage of the other side's error, why? If it's not OK to take advantage of the error, why not?

Answer. The situation here presented is not like that where a lawyer thinks his adversary is mistaken as to the proper legal remedy or in his view of the law or his construction of a court's decision. Where a lawyer knows his adversary has made a mistake about which there is no question, such as a typographical error or an error in computation, with the result that an erroneous judgment is entered, the Committee considers that as an officer of the Court, the lawyer is under a duty not to sit by and by his silence permit the Court to give a judgment which the lawyer knows is not in accordance with the Court's opinion. The Committee does not think that a lawyer is relieved of this duty by his belief that (apart from the decision) the result is not more favorable than his client is entitled to.

The Committee believes that the attorney should not suggest the error to the adversary or to the Court without first seeking the client's approval. Should the client disapprove, this Committee considers that the attorney should not consent on behalf of his client to the correction of the judgment. Is the attorney, however, under a duty to disclose the error contrary to the wishes of his client?

Canon 41 of the Canons of Professional Ethics of this Association reads:

> When a lawyer discovers that some fraud or deception has been practiced, which has unjustly imposed upon the court or a party, he should endeavor to rectify it; at first by advising his client, and if his client refuses to forego the advantage thus unjustly gained, he should promptly inform the injured person or his counsel, so that they may take appropriate steps.

It is believed that the foregoing applies although neither the lawyer nor his client is a party to the fraud or deception; hence, although there is no suggestion of fraud or deception in the present case, it would seem that by analogy this Canon may be taken as a guide where a lawyer has discovered a mistake which, if not disclosed, will result in

* Reprinted with permission of Columbia University Press and The Cromwell Foundation.

the Court taking action which is not in accordance with the Court's decision.

The attorney would be justified in asking to be relieved should his client refuse to approve his disclosing the error. The Committee does not feel that that course alone would satisfy the attorney's obligation. The Committee thinks that it would extend to disclosing the error even though that course met with the client's disapproval. An attorney "must obey his own conscience and not that of his client." (Canon 15)

The Committee does not think his disclosure under such circumstances is inconsistent with his obligation under Canon 37 to "preserve his client's confidence."

NOTES AND QUESTIONS

1. ***Do You Agree?*** Are you satisfied with the New York Committee's answer? If so, what arguments are most persuasive? If you don't agree, what are the best arguments against the Committee's answer?

2. ***Let Your Conscience be Your Guide?*** The Committee quotes Canon 15 to the effect that an attorney "must obey his own conscience and not that of his client." What does this mean? Is this true today? Does it mean that you have the authority — or the obligation — to disclose information to the other side whenever your conscience tells you to do so, even if your client objects? Wouldn't that be contrary to everything we've studied so far about the rules of secrecy and the theory of the adversary system?

If you think the attorney in the computational error situation has a duty to correct the error, how does the situation differ from the situation in New York County Lawyers' Opinion 309 (where the plaintiff's case was dismissed for lack of an eyewitness, but the defense attorney knew there was an eyewitness)?

If you think the attorney in the computational error situation does not have a duty to correct the error, then do you think an attorney has a duty to correct a client's perjury on the witness stand? (We'll get to that issue shortly.)

3. ***Personal Injury Litigation.*** Suppose that you and the defense lawyer are negotiating a personal injury settlement. Your key evidence is her doctor's honest opinion that the plaintiff's injuries make it impossible for her to return to work at her old job. About a week before you reached a settlement, the opposing lawyer asked whether your client's medical condition has improved, and whether she has seen any additional doctors. You truthfully answered "no." You soon agree on settlement terms.

Just before the settlement is to be signed, however, your client tells you that she has been treated by a new doctor whose medication has cured the problem. She is ready to return to her old job, which is still open. Must you tell the defense attorney about the cure? Does it matter whether you think your client and her doctor are overly optimistic and that the "cure" is unlikely to last? Would it matter if the defendant's lawyer last week had merely made a general inquiry as to "anything new," rather than asking specifically about medical developments? What if the defense attorney had not made any inquiry? Would you have a duty to disclose the new medical information even though the defense lawyer did not ask?

What if you found out about the supposed cure *after* the settlement was signed rather than before? (Your client was cured before the settlement, but you didn't find out until afterward.) Is there ever a duty to disclose an adverse fact after a case is settled? Should there be?

4. ***Correcting Erroneous Discovery Answers.*** In federal court litigation, Rule 26(e) of the Federal Rules of Civil Procedure requires you to correct erroneous interrogatory answers if you later learn that an answer was false when made. But the Federal Rules of Civil Procedure do not apply in negotiations to settle disputes *before* litigation is filed. In the pre-suit settlement context, should the rules of legal ethics require you to provide information to the other side in the same way that you must update and correct false interrogatory answers? Should there be a rule of legal ethics that you must

correct information you have supplied to the other side if you later learn that the information was false when it was communicated?

5. ***Other Kinds of Errors.*** How do the situations above compare to the kind of error described in the opinion that follows, where the bungling lawyer for one party had incorrectly reduced a commercial contract to writing, leaving out one of the key provisions on which the deal was based?

ABA STANDING COMMITTEE ON ETHICS AND PROFESSIONAL RESPONSIBILITY, INFORMAL OPINION 86-1518 (Feb. 9, 1986)*

A and B, with the assistance of their lawyers, have negotiated a commercial contract. After deliberation with counsel, A ultimately acquiesced in the final provision insisted upon by B, previously in dispute between the parties and without which B would have refused to come to overall agreement. However, A's lawyer discovered that the final draft of the contract typed in the office of B's lawyer did not contain the provision which had been in dispute. The Committee has been asked to give its opinion as to the ethical duty of A's lawyer in that circumstance.

The Committee considers this situation to involve merely a scrivener's error, not an intentional change in position by the other party. A meeting of the minds has already occurred. The Committee concludes that the error is appropriate for correction between the lawyers without client consultation.[1]

A's lawyer does not have a duty to advise A of the error pursuant to any obligation of communication under Rule 1.4 of the ABA Model Rules of Professional Conduct (1983). "The guiding principle is that the lawyer should fulfill reasonable client expectations for information consistent with the duty to act in the client's best interests and the client's overall requirements as to the character of representation." Comment to Rule 1.4. In this circumstance there is no "informed decision," in the language of Rule 1.4, that A needs to make; the decision on the contract has already been made by the client. Furthermore, the Comment to Rule 1.2 points out that the lawyer may decide the "technical" means to be employed to carry out the objective of the representation, without consultation with the client.

AUTHORS' COMMENT:

Do you agree that the client has already made the decision on the contract? Would the client tell the lawyer to keep silent if the client knew about the error? Should the client have the right to take advantage of the error? Before you read on, briefly write down your thoughts on whether or not the client has the right to take advantage of the error.

The client does not have a right to take unfair advantage of the error. The client's right pursuant to Rule 1.2 to expect committed and dedicated representation is not unlimited. Indeed, for A's lawyer to suggest that A has an opportunity to capitalize on the clerical error, unrecognized by B and B's lawyer, might raise a serious question of

[1] Assuming for purposes of discussion that the error is "information relating to [the] representation," under Rule 1.6 disclosure would be "impliedly authorized in order to carry out the representation." The Comment to Rule 1.6 points out that a lawyer has implied authority to make "a disclosure that facilitates a satisfactory conclusion" — in this case completing the commercial contract already agreed upon and left to the lawyers to memorialize. *We do not here reach the issue of the lawyer's duty if the client wishes to exploit the error.* [Emphasis added by authors.]

the violation of the duty of A's lawyer under Rule 1.2(d) not to counsel the client to engage in, or assist the client in, conduct the lawyer knows is fraudulent. In addition, Rule 4.1(b) admonishes the lawyer not knowingly to fail to disclose a material fact to a third person when disclosure is necessary to avoid assisting a fraudulent act by a client, and Rule 8.4(c) prohibits the lawyer from engaging in conduct involving dishonesty, fraud, deceit, or misrepresentation. . . .

NOTES AND QUESTIONS

1. ***Do You Agree?*** Do you like the ABA's opinion? What would you do in that situation?

2. ***What About Confidentiality?*** In a footnote, the ABA stated that "the omission of the provision from the document is a 'material fact' which under Rule 4.1(b) of the Model Rules of Professional Conduct must be disclosed to B's lawyer." Although relegated to a footnote, this is a very important conclusion. Is it correct? Doesn't Rule 4.1(b) remove the obligation to disclose a material fact to a third person if "disclosure is prohibited by Rule 1.6" (the confidentiality rule)? We can all agree that the omission of the provision is a "material fact," but can the Standing Committee say that this fact "must be disclosed" without analyzing Rule 1.6?

3. ***Incompetent Drafting.*** Suppose Lawyer B in ABA Op. 86-1518 had included the key provision, but had bungled the drafting so badly that the provision would not accomplish Lawyer B's purpose. (To use a simplistic example, suppose Lawyer B had insisted that Client A keep trucks out of Client B's parking lot, but Lawyer B then clumsily drafted the settlement to read, "A cannot park his *cars* in B's parking lot.") Would the reasoning of Opinion 86-1518 require disclosure or not? Where is the line between "merely a scrivener's error," on one hand, and "an intentional change in position by the other party," on the other hand? Is careless drafting a "scrivener's error" or an "intentional change"?

4. ***What if the Client Says No?*** The opinion dodges the most difficult issue. Footnote 1 says, "We do not here reach the issue of the lawyer's duty if the client wishes to exploit the error." What should the lawyer do if the client *does* wish to exploit the error? Suppose the client says, "Great! I never wanted that darned provision anyway, and now that incompetent lawyer has left it out. Let sleeping dogs lie. Don't say anything to the other side." Do you have to follow the client's instructions, or can you disclose?

5. ***The Rules the ABA Rejected.*** Consider some of the rules the ABA rejected in drafting the Model Rules of Professional Conduct. Rules 4.2 and 4.3 of the 1980, Discussion Draft of the Model Rules of Professional Conduct dealt with the role of the lawyer as negotiator. The adopted rules do not treat the lawyer-as-negotiator as a separate subject, although much of the substance of the earlier draft is included in the adopted rules. Several provisions of the original discussion draft relating to negotiation were omitted. Which ones would you have preferred to the rules as finally adopted?

Rule 4.2 Fairness to Other Participants

> (a) In conducting negotiations a lawyer shall be fair in dealing with other participants.

Rule 4.3 Illegal, Fraudulent or Unconscionable Transactions

> A lawyer shall not conclude an agreement, or assist a client in concluding an agreement, that the lawyer knows or reasonably should know is illegal, contains legally prohibited terms, would work a fraud or would be held to be unconscionable as a matter of law.

In place of the version of then-Rule 4.3 just quoted, the ABA adopted Rule 1.2(d), which provides, in part: "A lawyer shall not counsel a client to engage or assist a client in conduct that the lawyer knows is criminal or fraudulent. . . . " What are the arguments in favor of and against dropping the phrase "unconscionable as a matter of law" from Rule 1.2(d)?

6. ***Zero-Sum Games.*** One of the problems with the way we think about negotiation is that we perceive negotiation to be a zero-sum game, meaning that one side's gain necessarily leads to the other side's loss. Is that true? Or does a rising tide lift all boats, so to speak, so that a well thought-out resolution benefits all of the players? Can negotiation be something more than a tug-of-war where only one side can win, and where each advance by your side means a retreat by the other side? Are you uncomfortable about negotiating in the adversary system because you sense that each triumph for your client is a defeat for the opposing client? Would you feel better about negotiating if you thought you could help everyone — your client and the other parties — by doing a good job for your client? Maybe you can. Read the following article by Carrie Menkel-Meadow, a leading writer on the subject of negotiation.

CARRIE MENKEL-MEADOW, TOWARD ANOTHER VIEW OF LEGAL NEGOTIATION: THE STRUCTURE OF PROBLEM SOLVING

31 UCLA L. Rev. 754 (1984)*

The adversarial paradigm is based almost exclusively on the simple negotiation over what appears to be one issue, such as price in a buy-sell transaction, or money damages in a personal injury or breach of contract lawsuit. The common assumption in these cases is that the buyer wants the lowest price, the seller the highest; the plaintiff wants the money demanded in the complaint and the defendant wants to resist paying as much as possible. Each dollar to the plaintiff is a commensurate loss to the defendant; the same is true with the buyer and seller. Given this description of the paradigmatic negotiation, the negotiator's goal is simply to maximize gain by winning as much of the materiel of the negotiation as possible. Underlying this general assumption are really two assumptions: first, that there is only one issue, price; and second, that both parties desire equally and exclusively the thing by which that issue is measured, in most cases, money. . . .

While there may be some paradigmatic zero-sum games in legal negotiations, most are not zero-sum. For example, in a random search of 240 cases taken from 15 federal and state reporters most cases, in terms presented to the court, were not zero-sum disputes. Those that could be characterized as zero-sum were those which required a definitive ruling — evidentiary rulings in criminal cases, determinations that constitutional rights were infringed, or findings that contracts were applicable in particular situations. Most, however, presented multi-issue situations. Child custody can become joint custody, zoning cases permit variances, and bankruptcy can become financial reorganization. Not every legal dispute or transaction can be transformed into a nonzero-sum or cooperative game, but zero-sum games in legal negotiations may be more the exception than the rule. . . .

The assumption that only limited items are available in dispute resolution occurs because negotiation takes place in the shadow of the courts. Negotiators too often conclude that they are limited to what would be available if the court entered a judgment. To the extent that court resolution of problems results in awards of money damages and injunctions, negotiators are likely to limit their crafting of solutions to those remedies. To the extent that a court would not allow a particular remedy such as barter, exchange, apology, or retributory action, negotiators may reject or not even conceive of these solutions.

Similarly, because courts often declare one party a winner and the other a loser,

---

negotiators often conceive of themselves as winners and losers, and in court games, the result is usually "winner take all."

NOTES AND QUESTIONS

What is Creativity? Professor Menkel-Meadow concludes that problem-solving can be more effective for both sides than zero-sum negotiations over money — but problem-solving takes creativity. What is creativity? We can't explain that. How Picasso, Thomas Edison, and great lawyers get good ideas is a mystery. But you are more likely to be creative if you take a systematic approach to negotiations, constantly reviewing the needs and concerns of your client, the opposing side, and third parties affected by the suit, instead of fixating only on money. Keep asking questions like: "What does everyone want, and what does everyone need? What do we have that the other side needs? What do we need that the other side has? How do everyone's needs and wants fit together?" At the crossroads of the needs and wants is a creative settlement.

A systematic approach won't turn you into Picasso, but it might make you a pretty good paint-by-numbers artist. Read as much as you can about negotiation and problem-solving. You may be able to raise the quality of your service to your clients by reaching better settlements, and by reaching them more quickly. Stubbornly sticking to a zero-sum conception of negotiations often produces long drawn-out pitched battles, like World War I trench warfare, that last a long time and produce unsatisfactory results. As a bonus, taking a more human approach to negotiating may lower your anxiety level. As some great dealmakers have said, "If the deal's not good for my opponent, then it's not good for me." Your first duty is to your client, but you can't serve your client unless you understand what the other side needs and wants.

Chapter 16

THE NO-CONTACT RULE: COMMUNICATING WITH REPRESENTED PARTIES

We learned that a lawyer must zealously represent a client within the bounds of the law. This chapter concerns one of the most important boundaries set by the law — the so-called "no-contact rule." The no-contact rule provides, in essence, that a lawyer representing a client must not "communicate" about the subject of the representation with a person the lawyer "knows" to be represented by another lawyer in the matter, unless the lawyer either has (a) the consent of the other lawyer or (b) is authorized to communicate with the represented party by law or by a court order.

The no-contact rule applies to every task that a lawyer performs while representing a client. Three tasks that lawyers often perform are (1) investigating the facts during litigation, (2) negotiating settlements in litigation, and (3) negotiating contracts and other deals. Often, the person on the other side has a lawyer. This brings up the key question addressed in this chapter: When you represent a client, may you ethically communicate directly with other parties who have their own lawyers?

The answer to this question depends mainly on ABA Model Rule 4.2, which governs communications between lawyers and people who are represented by lawyers. To help answer the question, here is an outline on communicating with represented parties:

A. OUTLINE ON COMMUNICATING WITH REPRESENTED PARTIES

1. The Key Rule

The key rule regarding communications with represented persons is Rule 4.2, often called the "no-contact rule" or the "anti-contact rule." Many states have adopted ABA Model Rule 4.2. Massachusetts Rule 4.2, for example, provides as follows:

Rule 4.2. Communication with Person Represented by Counsel

> In representing a client, a lawyer shall not communicate about the subject of the representation with a person the lawyer knows to be represented by another lawyer in the matter, unless the lawyer has the consent of the other lawyer or is authorized to do so by law or a court order.

Rule 4.2 was amended slightly by the ABA in 2002, and was also slightly amended in 1995, but the rule has been essentially the same since 1983. Moreover, ABA Rule 4.2 is almost identical to DR 7-104(A)(1) of the old ABA Model Code of Professional Responsibility, so old authorities construing the no-contact rule continue to have considerable force. The no-contact rule has been adopted in every jurisdiction, usually with little variation. Accordingly, authorities from one jurisdiction are likely to be persuasive in another jurisdiction.

2. An Outline on Communicating with Represented Individuals

A. Individuals represented by counsel are off limits under Rule 4.2 whether they are adverse or not, unless:

    1. the individual's lawyer consents, or
    2. the communication is authorized by law or a court order.

B. A represented individual's *personal* consent is irrelevant under Rule 4.2 — only the individual's *lawyer* can consent to direct communication with another lawyer about the subject of the case.

C. A prosecutor is ordinarily authorized by law to communicate with represented parties *before indictment* (but not after indictment) as long as the prosecutor does not engage in egregious misconduct.

D. A private lawyer is ordinarily not authorized by law to communicate with a represented party to litigation except at a deposition (after giving notice to opposing counsel) or after obtaining a court order allowing the communication. Apart from depositions and communications expressly authorized by a court order, private lawyers are not authorized by law to communicate with represented parties.

3. Communicating with Represented Corporations

A. *Upjohn v. United States*, 449 U.S. 383 (1981), takes an expansive view of who is represented by counsel in the context of the corporation for purposes of the attorney-client privilege. *Upjohn* held that communications by and between corporate counsel and any employee are protected by the attorney-client privilege, if made (1) at the direction of corporate counsel, (2) concerning matters "within the scope of an employee's corporate duties," (3) for the purpose of obtaining confidential information or to secure legal advice, (4) under circumstances when such legal advice is considered confidential (and properly maintained as such). Does the Supreme Court's expansive interpretation of the attorney-client privilege apply in the context of the no-contact rule? Is every person who works for a corporation also considered a person "represented by counsel" for purposes of Rule 4.2 ? Jurisdictions are split on this question:

1. A few jurisdictions consider all *current* employees of a corporation to be off limits under the no-contact rule.
2. A few jurisdictions also consider some or all *former* employees of a corporation to be off limits under the no-contact rule.
3. But the overwhelming majority view regarding current employees is to consider only *some* of a corporation's current employees to be off limits. Other current employees are not protected by the no-contact rule and may be interviewed informally without the consent of the corporation's lawyer. In other words, courts have generally not applied *Upjohn* to the no-contact rule.
4. The majority view is also to allow communication with *all* of a corporation's former employees (except employees represented by their own counsel). The theory is that former employees are no longer automatically "represented" by the corporation's attorneys — they are considered "represented" only if they have hired their own counsel (or someone has hired counsel for them), or if they have affirmatively indicated that they want the corporation's counsel to represent them.

B. Current employees of corporations:

1. Management-level people — including all officers and directors of a corporation — are almost universally considered off limits under Rule 4.2.
2. Low-level employees are treated as persons "represented by counsel" under Rule 4.2 in some states but not in others. Courts are split on this question, but the strong trend is to limit the protection of Rule 4.2 to higher-level employees who have the authority to make decisions for or bind the corporation, and to other employees who are implementing the advice of counsel.

C. Former employees of corporations:

1. A few courts (a distinct minority) have held that the protections of Rule 4.2 extend even to a corporate party's former high-level employees, so that a lawyer may not communicate with a corporation's former high-level

employees without the consent of the corporation's lawyer.

2. But the strong trend is to let a lawyer interview all former employees who are not represented by counsel, if the lawyer abides by two restrictions:

   (1) The lawyer must not induce the former employee to divulge information subject to the corporation's attorney-client privilege, or even listen to such information if the former employee volunteers it, because the former employee has no right to waive the attorney-client privilege — only the corporation can waive the privilege; and

   (2) The lawyer must abide by the restrictions of Rule 4.3, which governs communications between lawyers and unrepresented parties. More specifically, Rule 4.3 requires three things:

      (i) The lawyer must make clear to an unrepresented former employee the nature of the lawyer's role in the representation, the identity of the lawyer's client, and the fact that the former employer is the adverse party.

      (ii) If the lawyer knows (or reasonably should know) that the unrepresented person "misunderstands the lawyer's role in the matter," the lawyer must make "reasonable efforts to correct the misunderstanding." See Rule 4.3.

      (iii) If the lawyer knows that the unrepresented person's interests conflict (or are reasonably likely to conflict) with the interests of the lawyer's client, then the lawyer must not give legal advice to the unrepresented person, except the advice to obtain counsel.

3. If a lawyer fails to abide by these restrictions when communicating with an unrepresented former employee (or any other unrepresented person), a court may prohibit further interviews of former employees and might even suppress any information obtained improperly during communications with former employees.

4. The basic lesson is, don't be greedy. If you try to get more information from a former employee than you are ethically entitled to, you may lose it all. The court may rule that all of the information you got from former employees is inadmissible.

4. Policies Behind the Rule

The basic policy behind the rule is to prevent the opposing attorney from undermining a represented party's attorney-client relationship or going behind the back of her attorney, effectively depriving her of counsel. To understand this policy, we need to think about why you might want to communicate with a represented adverse party if the rules did not prohibit you from doing so. Here are a few key reasons:

A. *Undermine the opposing lawyer.* You could undermine the opposing lawyer's control over her client by criticizing the lawyer, contradicting or questioning her version of the facts or the law, and generally driving a wedge between the opposing attorney and her client. This would make the opposing party's lawyer less effective, and might later lead the opposing party to accept a settlement offer even if his lawyer recommends rejection (or to reject an offer that the lawyer recommends).

B. *Obtain admissions and useful information.* You might obtain damaging admissions or helpful information or documents from the opposing party that you presumably would not have received if the opposing party's lawyer had been present. In particular, the opposing party might reveal information that is protected by the attorney-client privilege; without the advice of his own lawyer he either wouldn't know the privilege applies or wouldn't realize the dangers of waiving the privilege.

C. *Settle a case.* You might persuade the opponent to drop the case or settle it by selling the opposing party a settlement package. For example, if the opposing lawyer has been advising against settlement but the opposing client wants to settle, then communicating directly with the opposing party might lead to a settlement. Once the settlement is signed, it is likely to stay in place. (The opposing lawyer would have no standing to undo the settlement unless the client wanted to undo it, and even then it would be difficult to reverse.)

Since all of these objectives would effectively deprive the represented party of her chosen counsel or greatly diminish her counsel's value, the rules prohibit you from engaging in direct communications with represented parties absent authorization by law or court order or opposing counsel's consent. A solid attorney-client relationship is the foundation of the justice system, and the rules vigorously protect the attorney-client relationship against outside interference.

B. COMMUNICATING WITH A REPRESENTED ADVERSE PARTY

Communicating with represented parties is a difficult and complex subject. You have already read the basic rules in the outline above. Rule 4.2 prohibits you from communicating directly with a represented person about the subject matter of a representation unless the represented person's lawyer (*not* just the represented person) consents. There's an exception — if you are authorized by law or by a court order — but you are not likely to be authorized by law unless you work for the government and have some statutory authority to do so, or if you are deposing the adverse party upon notice to opposing counsel (in which case opposing counsel will be present), or if you obtain a court order to communicate directly with the represented party (which is rare).

Now let's read some examples of how the courts interpret and enforce Rule 4.2.

IN THE MATTER OF DISCIPLINARY PROCEEDINGS AGAINST BREY

490 N.W.2d 15 (1992)

PER CURIAM

. . . Attorney Brey was admitted to the practice of law in Wisconsin in 1984. Since 1985, he has served as district attorney for Taylor county. He has not previously been the subject of a disciplinary proceeding. . . .

In October, 1988, District Attorney Brey charged a man with seven counts of criminal conduct related to theft from vending machines, possession of an electric weapon and possession of marijuana and an amphetamine. When arrested, the defendant could not raise the court-ordered bail and remained in jail for several months awaiting trial. District Attorney Brey was aware that the defendant was represented by an attorney throughout the criminal proceeding.

On March 1, 1989, District Attorney Brey went to the jail and had the jailer take the defendant from his cell to the jail library. There, with no one else present, District Attorney Brey met and spoke with the defendant concerning the pending criminal action. In the course of that conversation, District Attorney Brey expressed his opinion on the defendant's attorney's handling of the case and made settlement offers to the defendant. Further, District Attorney Brey told the defendant that if the defendant told anyone of that meeting, District Attorney Brey would deny it had taken place. District Attorney Brey knew he did not have opposing counsel's permission to meet with the defendant nor had he ever discussed with defense counsel the need to meet with the defendant.

AUTHORS' COMMENT:

Does Rule 4.2 allow a D.A. to meet with a defendant represented by counsel? Why not? Why shouldn't Rule 4.2 allow a D.A. to meet with a defendant, even if the defendant has a lawyer, to try to reach a plea bargain?

Three weeks later, after the defendant told him of the meeting, the defendant's attorney moved the circuit court for an order barring District Attorney Brey from prosecuting the criminal action because of the meeting he had had with the defendant. Subsequently, in an application to the court for the appointment of a special prosecutor to pursue the criminal action, District Attorney Brey denied the allegation that he had met with the defendant.

During the course of the Board's investigation of the grievance filed by the defendant's attorney concerning this matter, District Attorney Brey three times provided responses to the Board between May and August of 1989 in which he denied having had contact with the defendant as alleged by his attorney. Two years later, at the meeting of the professional responsibility committee investigating this matter, District Attorney Brey admitted that he had in fact met with the defendant as had been alleged.

AUTHORS' COMMENT:

Lying to a disciplinary authority is about the dumbest thing you can do. If you ever have the misfortune to be investigated for a possible disciplinary violation, tell the truth and cooperate as fully as you can with the investigators. Even if you have done something wrong, disciplinary authorities will still look for what they call the "three C's" — cooperation, candor, and contrition.

[B]y meeting with the defendant and offering him a settlement of pending criminal charges without the defendant's lawyer being present and without his consent, when the district attorney knew the defendant was represented by counsel, District Attorney Brey violated [Rule] 4.2. Additionally, he knowingly made a false statement of fact to the court, in violation of [Rule] 3.3(a)(1), when he filed the application for appointment of special prosecutor in which he denied meeting with the defendant. Finally, by denying that meeting in his three letters to the Board, District Attorney Brey made a misrepresentation to the Board. . . .

We adopt the referee's findings of fact and conclusions of law. We do not, however, accept the referee's recommendation that Attorney Brey's misconduct be sanctioned by a public reprimand. The egregious nature of that misconduct requires more severe discipline.

District Attorney Brey used his prosecutorial power to approach a defendant in a setting underscoring that defendant's vulnerability and attempted to undermine the defendant's confidence in the legal representation he had received. . . .

The serious nature of Attorney Brey's misconduct as a prosecutor in this matter and the potential for harm to the defendant that it presented render a public reprimand insufficient . . . . More severe discipline is needed not only to impress upon Attorney Brey the need to scrupulously adhere to the rules of professional conduct in his position as prosecutor but also to deter him and others in similar positions from wielding their authority beyond the bounds of ethical conduct as prescribed by the court's rules.

NOTES AND QUESTIONS

1. ***What's the Big Deal?*** What's wrong with what Brey did? Why should Rule 4.2 prohibit it? Brey didn't threaten the defendant with harsher charges or a higher sentencing recommendation if the defendant refused to talk, and the defendant was apparently willing to talk with Brey. What's the problem?

2. ***Imagine a World Without the No-Contact Rule.*** Would it be better or worse to live in a world where the rules placed no restrictions of any kind on communications between a lawyer and a represented adversary? (You may think the answer is obvious, but remember you don't really understand why the rule is right until you can explain why the opposite rule would be wrong.)

C. THINGS THAT ARE *NOT* EXCEPTIONS TO RULE 4.2

Rule 4.2 is broad and tough. There are only two exceptions — you may communicate with a represented party only if you have the consent of opposing counsel or are "authorized to do so by law or a court order." Even these two exceptions are tricky. Let's take a closer look at some things that are *not* exceptions to the rule prohibiting communications with a person the lawyer knows to be represented by another lawyer in the matter.

"The opposing lawyer wouldn't communicate my settlement offers."

There is one common-sense and ostensibly fair reason why you might want to communicate directly with an opposing party: the opposing lawyer is not telling her client about reasonable offers of settlement. The opposing lawyer may be disorganized, or afraid to recommend settlement, or may not want to settle. This was part of the plot in the movie, *The Verdict.* Paul Newman received a very respectable settlement offer, but didn't tell his clients about it because he thought he could win big. (He did win big, but that kind of miracle usually happens only in the movies.)

The rules of professional conduct require you to pass along settlement offers to your client, though the obligation is implicit. Rule 1.4, entitled "Communicating with Client," provides that a lawyer shall "promptly inform the client of any decision or circumstance with respect to which the client's informed consent . . . is required by these Rules" — which would include a client's decision under Rule 1.2(a) "whether to settle a matter" and requires a lawyer to "keep the client reasonably informed about the status of the matter." Comment 2 to ABA Model Rule 1.4 expressly applies this rule to settlement offers, stating that a lawyer who receives a settlement offer from opposing counsel in a civil matter or a plea bargain offer in a criminal case "must promptly inform the client of its substance unless the client has previously indicated that the proposal will be unacceptable. . . . "

Some jurisdictions have put language similar to the commentary in the text of their rules. The District of Columbia, for example, borrows from the quoted comment to provide in its Rule 1.4(c): "A lawyer who receives an offer of settlement in a civil case or a proffered plea bargain in a criminal case shall inform the client promptly of the substance of the communication." Michigan's rules provide: "A lawyer shall notify the client promptly of all settlement offers, mediation evaluations, and proposed plea bargains." California provides: "A member of the State Bar shall promptly communicate to the member's client all amounts, terms and conditions of any written offer of settlement made by or on behalf of an opposing party."

But what if the opposing lawyer isn't playing by the rules? What if opposing counsel won't convey your settlement offers to her client? Should that entitle you to communicate directly with the opposing party about the settlement offer? Rule 4.2 does not make any exception in this situation. To make sure everyone understands this, the ABA Standing Committee on Ethics and Professional Responsibility issued Formal Opinion 92-362 (1992), which states:

> A party's lawyer who makes an offer of settlement to the lawyer for the opposing party may not under Model Rule 4.2 inquire of the offeree-party whether the offer has been communicated to the offeree, even if the offeror's lawyer entertains serious doubts that it has been so communicated.
>
> The Model Rules do not, however, forbid the offeror's lawyer, in fulfilling the lawyer's duty to counsel the client, to advise the offeror-client about the latter's ability to communicate on the matter directly with the offeree-party or about the lawyer's views as to the most efficacious method of doing so.

The ABA's view will probably be followed in most states, but not everyone agrees with it. The Roscoe Pound Foundation of the former Association of Trial Lawyers of America (ATLA, today called the American Association for Justice), a major national organization of attorneys for plaintiffs and criminal defendants, has proposed the following version of Rule 4.2:

> A lawyer shall not communicate regarding a legal matter with an adverse party who the lawyer knows is represented in that matter by an attorney, unless the lawyer has been authorized to do so by that party's attorney. *However, a lawyer may send a written offer of settlement directly to an adverse party, seven days or more after that party's attorney has received the same offer of settlement in writing.* [Emphasis added.]

Would that be an improvement over Rule 4.2? Would you go even further and *always* permit written offers of settlement be made directly to an opposing party as long as the opposing lawyer receives a copy of the offer at the same time?

"Everybody does it."

Another non-exception to Rule 4.2 is the "everybody does it" exception. In 1992, a Vermont lawyer named Vincent Illuzzi found out the hard way that violating the rule on communicating with represented parties doesn't become permissible just because it's a common practice. Mr. Illuzzi tried to settle cases by communicating directly with insurance adjusters even after he knew that the insurance companies were represented by lawyers. When he got caught, the Professional Conduct Board recommended a six-month suspension. Mr. Illuzzi argued that communicating with insurance adjusters was "accepted Vermont practice" and that "direct contact between plaintiffs' attorneys and insurance adjusters promotes judicial economy and the public interest." In *In re Illuzzi*, 616 A.2d 233 (Vt. 1992), the Vermont Supreme Court rejected both of these arguments, stating:

> Given the absence of ambiguity in the rule, we find irrelevant respondent's contention that it is the common and accepted practice for Vermont attorneys to have direct contact with insurance companies whose defense counsel have not consented to such contact. . . .
>
> [W]e need not assess the merits of respondent's argument that policy considerations favor such communication. One can fully adhere to the rule and yet receive the benefits of direct communication by contacting the insurance company's counsel and obtaining prior consent. If consent is not granted, the rule requires that all negotiation be conducted with defense counsel. . . .

If it is common practice for plaintiffs' attorneys to communicate directly with insurance adjusters, should we create a new exception to the rule? That is, should we amend Rule 4.2 to expressly allow lawyers to communicate with insurance adjusters, even over the objections of counsel for the insurance carrier?

"The opposing party came to me."

The reporters are filled with cases in which lawyers got in trouble for talking to opposing parties who sought out the lawyers. Is it OK to talk to an opposing party who calls you? No, it isn't. The dangers of talking directly with the opposing party are the same no matter who initiates the conversation.

We could easily argue in favor of an exception to Rule 4.2 if the opposing party initiates the communication. We could also deem it a temporary waiver of Rule 4.2 by the opposing party. After all, the opposing party could fire his attorney at any time. If the opposing party has the right to fire his lawyer and operate pro se for the entire case, why not allow the opposing party to fire his lawyer temporarily and operate pro se for an hour or two while he visits with you? This argument may be logical, but it does not reflect the law. The rules prohibit you from communicating with a represented opposing party even if the opposing party seeks you out and *wants* to talk to you. You have to take Rule 4.2 literally: you must not communicate with a represented opposing party unless you are authorized by law or a court order or have the consent of the opposing party's lawyer. Consent from the opposing party himself does not satisfy the no-contact rule.

"I was just investigating to see if I had a case."

Some lawyers think they have the right to communicate with represented opposing parties before filing suit. They don't. Rule 4.2 applies both before and after filing suit. You may be afraid that you will be sanctioned for filing a frivolous suit unless you can corroborate your client's story before filing suit, but that doesn't give you the right to violate the rules. The need to investigate before filing suit is not an exception to the no-contact rule.

D. THE "AUTHORIZED BY LAW" EXCEPTION

The only time you can communicate with a represented party without the lawyer's consent is when you are "authorized to do so by law or a court order." This exception mainly applies to private lawyers taking depositions in civil cases and to prosecutors or other government lawyers who have statutory authority to conduct undercover investigations.

Thorny problems arise when a prosecutor wants to communicate with a represented party during an undercover investigation. If Rule 4.2 is read too *broadly*, people engaged in crime can insulate themselves from undercover investigations just by hiring a lawyer. But if Rule 4.2 is read too *narrowly*, then government agents can communicate with represented parties at will, making the no-contact rules toothless. What is the proper balance? How should courts read Rule 4.2 in the context of criminal investigations? This question has caused deep divisions between prosecutors and defense attorneys. It is a very difficult question because the answer must not only analyze Rule 4.2 but must also balance legitimate law enforcement needs against the Sixth Amendment right to counsel and other constitutional rights. Because this is largely a question of constitutional law, we address it only briefly. The legendary Judge Irving Kaufman, then Chief Judge of the prestigious Second Circuit Court of Appeals, articulated the limits in a fascinating and still-influential opinion on the subject. (The opinion construes DR 7-104(A)(1) of the New York Code of Professional Responsibility, which for our purposes is substantially the same as Rule 4.2.)

UNITED STATES v. HAMMAD

858 F.2d 834 (2d Cir. 1988)

KAUFMAN, C.J.

[A federal grand jury was investigating an arson and Medicaid fraud. The main suspect had allegedly burned down his department store to destroy invoices that would have proved the Medicaid fraud. While the investigation was pending, before any indictments were handed down, the main suspect advised the U.S. Attorney's office that he was already represented by a lawyer. The prosecutor sent an informant named Goldstein to talk to the suspect, and the informant falsely told the suspect that he (the informant) had been served with a subpoena for documents related to the arson. The suspected arsonist said, "Let me see the subpoena." The federal prosecutor promptly went back to his office and prepared a phony subpoena, complete with the court's official stamp.]

[The informant then met with the arson suspect to show him the phony subpoena and get his reaction. The FBI audiotaped and videotaped the meeting. Predictably, the suspect thought the phony subpoena was real and suggested strategies for illegally avoiding compliance (such as destroying or hiding documents). The grand jury eventually saw and heard the tapes and indicted the suspect for mail fraud, arson, insurance fraud, and obstruction of justice.]

[The suspect moved to suppress the tapes and videotapes on grounds that "the prosecutor — through his 'alter ego' Goldstein — had violated ethical obligations by communicating directly with him after learning that he had retained counsel." The trial court (Judge Glasser) granted the motion and suppressed the tapes on grounds that the informant stood in the shoes of the prosecutor, and the prosecutor knew when he sent the informant that the suspect was already represented by counsel, so the prosecutor had violated DR 7-104. The Second Circuit's analysis was lengthy and complex. What follows is the heart of the court's opinion. Remember that DR 7-104 is essentially equivalent to Rule 4.2.]

The government contends that a broad reading of DR 7-104(A)(1) would impede legitimate investigatory practices. In particular, the government fears career criminals with permanent "house counsel" could immunize themselves from infiltration by informants. We share this concern and would not interpret the disciplinary rule as precluding undercover investigations. Our task, accordingly, is imposing adequate safeguards without crippling law enforcement.

The principal question presented to us herein is: to what extent does DR 7-104(A)(1) restrict the use of informants by government prosecutors prior to indictment, but after a suspect has retained counsel in connection with the subject matter of a criminal investigation? In an attempt to avoid hampering legitimate criminal investigations by government prosecutors, Judge Glasser resolved this dilemma by limiting the rule's applicability "to instances in which a suspect has retained counsel specifically for representation in conjunction with the criminal matter in which he is held suspect, and the government has knowledge of that fact." Thus, he reasoned, the rule exempts the vast majority of cases where suspects are unaware they are being investigated.

AUTHORS' COMMENT:

Under Judge Glasser's interpretation of the no-contact rule, a "career criminal" cannot insulate himself from undercover informants just by hiring a permanent "in-house" defense lawyer. The protections of the no-contact rule won't apply unless the defendant hires the lawyer for a specific investigation. Does Judge Glasser's reading of the rule satisfy you? It didn't satisfy the Second Circuit. Let's see why not.

While it may be true that this limitation will not unduly hamper the government's ability to conduct effective criminal investigations in a majority of instances, we nevertheless believe that it is unduly restrictive in that small but persistent number of cases where a career criminal has retained "house counsel" to represent him in connection with an ongoing fraud or criminal enterprise. . . . As we see it, under DR 7-104(A)(1), a prosecutor is "authorized by law" to employ legitimate investigative techniques in conducting or supervising criminal investigations, and the use of informants to gather evidence against a suspect will frequently fall within the ambit of such authorization.

Notwithstanding this holding, however, we recognize that in some instances a government prosecutor may overstep the already broad powers of his office, and in so doing, violate the ethical precepts of DR 7-104(A)(1). In the present case, the prosecutor issued a subpoena for the informant, not to secure his attendance before the grand jury, but to create a pretense that might help the informant elicit admissions from a represented suspect. Though we have no occasion to consider the use of this technique in relation to unrepresented suspects, we believe that use of the technique under the circumstances of this case contributed to the informant's becoming the alter ego of the prosecutor. Consequently, the informant was engaging in communications proscribed by DR 7-104(A)(1). . . .

Notwithstanding requests for a bright-line rule, we decline to list all possible situations that may violate DR 7-104(A)(1). This delineation is best accomplished by case-by-case adjudication, particularly when ethical standards are involved. As our holding above makes clear, however, the use of informants by government prosecutors in a pre-indictment, non-custodial situation, absent the type of egregious misconduct that occurred in this case, will generally fall within the "authorized by law" exception to DR 7-104(A)(1) and therefore will not be subject to sanctions.

On appeal, the government also claims that even if there was a violation of the disciplinary rule, exclusion is inappropriate to remedy an ethical breach. We have not heretofore decided whether suppression is warranted for a DR 7-104(A)(1). We now hold that . . . suppression may be ordered in the district court's discretion. . . .

NOTES AND QUESTIONS

1. ***"Egregious Misconduct."*** The *Hammad* test boils down to raw "ethics" in the colloquial sense. The main inquiry in deciding whether the no-contact rule has been violated will be whether the prosecutor has engaged in "egregious misconduct." Essentially the court is asking whether our sense of basic human decency tells us that the prosecutor's tactics were unfair or morally offensive.

2. ***Suppression as a Remedy.*** The *Hammad* court held that suppression could be ordered to remedy violations of the no-contact rule. Thus, prosecutors who violate the rule take a big risk, because they can lose the right to present crucial evidence, such as the incriminating audio and videotapes at issue in *Hammad*. Many courts have followed *Hammad's* lead by suppressing evidence obtained in violation of the no-contact rule.

E. A SPECIAL PROBLEM: COMMUNICATING WITH CORPORATE EMPLOYEES

So far, we've been dealing with communications between lawyers and represented individuals. Now we turn to a more difficult topic: communications between lawyers and employees of represented corporations. Are corporate employees considered as "parties" represented by counsel within the meaning of Rule 4.2? This question comes up whenever (a) a corporation is a named party to a suit, but (b) the corporation' s employees are not personally named as parties. (For example, if your client files suit against Apple Computer, then Apple's individual employees are not defendants in the suit unless you expressly name them as defendants.) The corporation itself is a "party," but even if you know that the corporation itself is represented by counsel, which individual officers, directors, employees, shareholders, or others are considered persons represented by that same counsel? When a lawyer represents a corporation, which individuals does that lawyer also automatically represent?

A corporation itself cannot talk; it is just a piece of paper — a certificate of incorporation. Who speaks for this piece of paper? Which human beings are "represented" by a lawyer when a corporation is a party? On the one hand, if *all* corporate employees are represented for Rule 4.2 purposes, then an opposing lawyer (or even a co-defendant's lawyer) cannot informally interview any corporate employee without the consent of the opposing lawyer. (Remember that under Rule 4.2 the consent has to come from the represented person's *lawyer*, not just from the party. Consent from the corporation's officers would therefore not be sufficient.) On the other hand, if *no* corporate employees are represented, then opposing lawyers can interview anyone at the corporation who will speak to them, and the corporation loses much of the protection of counsel. What is the right resting place in between these extremes?

The issue is clouded by two important sources. First, the *Upjohn* case (which we summarized in the outline at the start of this chapter) held that all corporate employees, from the custodian to the CEO, are "clients" for purposes of the attorney-client privilege. Should all "clients" for purposes of the attorney-client privilege also be deemed "represented" for purposes of Rule 4.2? If so, then all corporate employees are off limits for opposing counsel under Rule 4.2 because they are persons represented by counsel. If not, where do we draw the line?

Second, Rule 801(d)(2)(D) of the Federal Rules of Evidence, which concerns admissions by a party, says that the statement of a corporate agent within the scope of the agent's employment is not hearsay and is admissible in court as an "admission" by the party (i.e., the corporation) against its own interests. Thus, under Rule 801(d)(2)(D), an informal interview with a low-level corporate employee can produce an "admission" that can be used against the corporation in court. That makes it difficult for the corporation to control litigation, since hundreds of employees have the power to hurt the corporation by talking with opposing counsel. (However, keep in mind that MRCP 3.4(f) allows a corporation's lawyer to order the corporation's employees not to speak with opposing counsel.)

The courts and bar associations have not uniformly decided whether corporate employees are represented by counsel within the meaning of Rule 4.2 (and its Code predecessor DR 7-104). The following case, *Niesig v. Team I*, is a thoughtful case from New York's highest court, written by the woman who is now New York's Chief Judge. It has been highly influential and is still considered a leading case nationally.

NIESIG v. TEAM I

76 N.Y.2d 363, 558 N.E.2d 1030 (1990)

KAYE, J.

Plaintiff in this personal injury litigation, wishing to have his counsel privately interview a corporate defendant's employees who witnessed the accident, puts before us a question that has generated wide interest: are the employees of a corporate party also considered "parties" under Disciplinary Rule 7-104(A)(1) of the Code of Professional Responsibility, which [like Rule 4.2 of the Model Rules of Professional Conduct] prohibits a lawyer from communicating directly with a "party" known to have counsel in the matter? The trial court and the Appellate Division both answered that an employee of a counseled corporate party in litigation is by definition also a "party" within the rule, and prohibited the interviews. For reasons of policy, we disagree.

As alleged in the complaint, plaintiff was injured when he fell from scaffolding at a building construction site. At the time of the accident he was employed by DeTrae Enterprises, Inc.; defendant J.M. Frederick was the general contractor, and defendant

Team I the property owner. Plaintiff thereafter commenced a damages action against defendants. . . .

Plaintiff moved for permission to have his counsel conduct ex parte interviews of all DeTrae employees who were on the site at the time of the accident, arguing that these witnesses to the event were neither managerial nor controlling employees and could not therefore be considered "personal synonyms for DeTrae." . . .

The Appellate Division concluded . . . that current employees of a corporate defendant in litigation "are presumptively within the scope of the representation afforded by the attorneys who appeared in the litigation on behalf of that corporation." Citing *Upjohn Co. v. United States*, the court held that DeTrae's attorneys have an attorney-client relationship with every DeTrae employee connected with the subject of the litigation, and that the prohibition is necessitated by the practical difficulties of distinguishing between a corporation's control group and its other employees. The court further noted that the information sought from employee witnesses could instead be obtained through their depositions. . . .

DR 7-104(A)(1), which can be traced to the American Bar Association canons of 1908, fundamentally embodies principles of fairness. "The general thrust of the rule is to prevent situations in which a represented party may be taken advantage of by adverse counsel; the presence of the party's attorney theoretically neutralizes the contact." By preventing lawyers from deliberately dodging adversary counsel to reach — and exploit — the client alone, DR 7-104(A)(1) safeguards against clients making improvident settlements, ill-advised disclosures and unwarranted concessions.

There is little problem applying DR 7-104(A)(1) to individuals in civil cases. In that context, the meaning of "party" is ordinarily plain enough: it refers to the individuals, not to their agents and employees. The question, however, becomes more difficult when the parties are corporations — as evidenced by a wealth of commentary, and controversy, on the issue.

The difficulty is not in whether DR 7-104(A)(1) applies to corporations. It unquestionably covers corporate parties, who are as much served by the rule's fundamental principles of fairness as individual parties. But the rule does not define "party," and its reach in this context is unclear. In litigation only the entity, not its employee, is the actual named party; on the other hand, corporations act solely through natural persons, and unless some of their employees are also considered parties, they are effectively read out of the rule. The issue therefore distills to which corporate employees should be deemed parties for purposes of DR 7-104(A)(1), and that choice is one of policy. The broader the definition of "party" in the interests of fairness to the corporation, the greater the cost in terms of foreclosing vital informal access to facts.

The many courts, bar associations and commentators that have balanced the competing considerations have evolved various tests, each claiming some adherents, each with some imperfection. At one extreme is the blanket rule adopted by the Appellate Division and urged by defendants, and at the other is the "control group" test — both of which we reject. The first is too broad and the second too narrow.

Defendants' principal argument for the blanket rule correlating the corporate "party" and all of its employees — rests on *Upjohn v. United States*. As the Supreme Court recognized, a corporation's attorney-client privilege includes communications with low- and mid-level employees; defendants argue that the existence of an attorney-client privilege also signifies an attorney-client relationship for purposes of DR 7-104(A)(1).

Upjohn, however, addresses an entirely different subject, with policy objectives that have little relation to the question whether a corporate employee should be considered a "party" for purposes of the Disciplinary Rule. First, the privilege applies only to confidential communications with counsel, it does not immunize the underlying factual information — which is in issue here — from disclosure to an adversary. Second, the attorney-client privilege serves the societal objective of encouraging open communication between client and counsel, a benefit not present in denying informal access to factual information. Thus, a corporate employee who may be a "client" for purposes of the attorney-client privilege is not necessarily a "party" for purposes of DR 7-104(A)(1).

The single indisputable advantage of a blanket preclusion — as with every absolute rule — is that it is clear. No lawyer need ever risk disqualification or discipline because of uncertainty as to which employees are covered by the rule and which not. The problem, however, is that a ban of this nature exacts a high price in terms of other values, and is unnecessary to achieve the objectives of DR 7-104(A)(1).

Most significantly, the Appellate Division's blanket rule closes off avenues of informal discovery of information that may serve both the litigants and the entire justice system by uncovering relevant facts, thus promoting the expeditious resolution of disputes. Foreclosing all direct, informal interviews of employees of the corporate party unnecessarily sacrifices the long-recognized potential value of such sessions. "A lawyer talks to a witness to ascertain what, if any, information the witness may have relevant to his theory of the case, and to explore the witness' knowledge, memory and opinion — frequently in light of information counsel may have developed from other sources. This is part of an attorney's so-called work product." Costly formal depositions that may deter litigants with limited resources, or even somewhat less formal and costly interviews attended by adversary counsel, are no substitute for such off-the-record private efforts to learn and assemble, rather than perpetuate, information.

Nor, in our view, is it necessary to shield all employees from informal interviews in order to safeguard the corporation's interest. Informal encounters between a lawyer and an employee-witness are not — as a blanket ban assumes — invariably calculated to elicit unwitting admissions; they serve long-recognized values in the litigation process. Moreover, the corporate party has significant protection at hand. It has possession of its own information and unique access to its documents and employees; the corporation's lawyer thus has the earliest and best opportunity to gather the facts, to elicit information from its employees, and to counsel and prepare them so that they will not make the feared improvident disclosures that engendered the rule. . . .

AUTHORS' COMMENT:

What would be the practical effect of prohibiting lawyers from informally interviewing any employees of an opposing corporation? Would a blanket prohibition make litigation more expensive, because depositions cost much more than informal interviews? Would it increase the number of groundless suits, since lawyers would have trouble investigating the facts before filing suit? Would there be other adverse effects? Who would gain and who would lose if there were a blanket prohibition on talking to an opposing corporation's employees?

We are not persuaded, however, that the "control group" test — defining "party" to include only the most senior management exercising substantial control over the corporation — achieves that goal. Unquestionably, that narrow (though still uncertain) definition of corporate "party" better serves the policy of promoting open access to relevant information. But that test gives insufficient regard to the principles motivating DR 7-104(A)(1), and wholly overlooks the fact that corporate employees other than senior management also can bind the corporation. The "control group" test all but "nullifies the benefits of the disciplinary rule to corporations." Given the practical and theoretical problems posed by the "control group" test, it is hardly surprising that few courts or bar associations have ever embraced it.

By the same token, we find unsatisfactory several of the proposed intermediate tests, because they give too little guidance, or otherwise seem unworkable. In this category are the case-by-case balancing test, and a test that defines "party" to mean corporate employees only when they are interviewed about matters within the scope of their employment. The latter approach is based on Rule 801(d)(2)(D) of the Federal Rules of Evidence, a hearsay exception for statements concerning matters within the scope of employment. . . .

The test that best balances the competing interests, and incorporates the most desirable elements of the other approaches, is one that defines "party" to include corporate employees whose acts or omissions in the matter under inquiry are binding on the corporation (in effect, the corporation's "alter egos") or imputed to the corporation for purposes of its liability, or employees implementing the advice of counsel. All other employees may be interviewed informally.

Unlike a blanket ban or a "control group" test, this solution is specifically targeted at the problem addressed by DR 7-104(A)(1). The potential unfair advantage of extracting concessions and admissions from those who will bind the corporation is negated when employees with "speaking authority" for the corporation, and employees who are so closely identified with the interests of the corporate party as to be indistinguishable from it, are deemed "parties" for purposes of DR 7-104(A)(1). Concern for the protection of the attorney-client privilege prompts us also to include in the definition of "party" the corporate employees responsible for actually effectuating the advice of counsel in the matter.

In practical application, the test we adopt thus would prohibit direct communication by adversary counsel "with those officials, but only those, who have the legal power to bind the corporation in the matter or who are responsible for implementing the advice of the corporation's lawyer, or any member of the organization whose own interests are directly at stake in a representation." [C. Wolfram, Modern Legal Ethics § 11.6, at 613 (West 1985).] This test would permit direct access to all other employees, and specifically — as in the present case — it would clearly permit direct access to employees who were merely witnesses to an event for which the corporate employer is sued.

. . . .

. . . Defendants' assertions that ex parte interviews should not be permitted because of the dangers of overreaching, moreover, impel us to add the cautionary note that, while we have not been called upon to consider questions relating to the actual conduct of such interviews, it is of course assumed that attorneys would make their identity and interest known to interviewees and comport themselves ethically. . . .

AUTHORS' COMMENT:

Did the majority persuade you, or would you join the following concurring opinion by Justice Bellacosa? (There was no outright dissent.)

BELLACOSA, J., concurring.

I agree that the Appellate Division blanket test too broadly precluded ex parte interviews by defining the term "parties" as used in Disciplinary Rule 7-104(A)(1) to include all current employees of a corporate defendant. The Court instead adopts an "alter ego" definition which, as I see it, will function almost identically with the rejected test. Also, there is a sacrifice of an unnecessarily disproportionate amount of the truth-discovering desideratum of the litigation process. Lastly, there may be a circularity in the identification of and application to the "alter ego" test group, which could prolong pre-trial discovery and allow the shield of DR 7-104(A)(1) to be fashioned into a sword.

These concerns could be avoided by limiting "parties," for the purposes of this professional responsibility rule, only to those who are in the "control group" of the corporate defendant; that is, "only those among the most senior management who exercise substantial control over the corporation."

[T]he "control group" definition better balances the respective interests by allowing the maximum number of informal interviews among persons with potentially relevant information, while safeguarding the attorney protections afforded the men and women whose protection may well be of paramount concern — those at the corporate helm and the fictional entity itself, the corporation. Also, this approach is more consistent with the ordinary understanding and meaning of "party," and more reasonably fits the purpose for which the disciplinary rule exists; a professional responsibility purpose quite distinct from enactments in public law prescribing the rights and protections of parties to litigation.

Discovery of the truth and relevant proofs is the end to which litigation is the means. The fewer parties to whom counsel can informally turn in the quest for facts on behalf of a client's cause, the more cumbersome becomes the realization of this goal. . . .

NOTES AND QUESTIONS

Leading Case. The *Niesig* opinion has proved to be a leading case, widely followed in both state and federal courts. However, as the next case shows, the *Niesig* test has been refined to provide more specific guidance in the case of former corporate employees.

PATRIARCA v. CENTER FOR LIVING & WORKING, INC.

778 N.E.2d 877 (Mass. 2003)

SPINA, J.

A judge in the Superior Court issued a protective order on the basis of Mass. R. Prof. C. 4.2 barring counsel for the plaintiff, Ellen L. Patriarca, from any ex parte contact with former or future employees of the defendant, the Center for Living & Working, Inc. (center), on matters concerning their former employment or the pending litigation . . . [without] leave of court or of opposing counsel. . . . We granted the plaintiff's application for direct appellate review. Because the former employees in question are neither actually represented by the center, nor the type of employee covered by rule 4.2, as construed in *Messing, Rudavsky & Weliky, P.C. v. President & Fellows of Harvard College*, 436 Mass. 347, 764 N.E.2d 825 (2002) (*Messing*), the protective order must be vacated.

[T]he Superior Court . . . concluded that rule 4.2 may prohibit ex parte contact with former employees. He found that, in this case, the statements of former employees could be potentially admissible against the center, or that the former employees' acts or omissions could be imputed to the center. He issued an order barring Patriarca's counsel from "contacting any former employees of the defendant corporation on matters concerning their former employment and this litigation unless defense counsel is present or permission is granted from this court or from opposing counsel."

The defendants argue that rule 4.2 prevents ex parte contact with any former employee without first obtaining a ruling from the court in question or permission from the former employer's counsel. They claim that this degree of oversight is necessary because former employees may be able to divulge confidential or privileged information, and that a judge should be the gatekeeper by deciding in the first instance that the ban should be enforced to the extent to which a former employee's statements, made during the employment relationship and within the scope of employment, might be admissible in evidence in an action against the employer.

Patriarca argues that a blanket no-contact rule would provide institutional defendants with the power to control any information in the possession of anyone who ever worked at that institution. See *Messing, supra*, 436 Mass. at 358 ("Prohibiting contact with all employees of a represented organization restricts informal contacts far more than is necessary to [protect attorney-client privilege, or prevent clients from making ill advised statements without the counsel of their attorney]"); *Niesig v. Team I*, 76 N.Y.2d 363, 559 N.Y.S.2d 493, 558 N.E.2d 1030 (1990) (blanket ban rejected because it would exact high price and be unnecessary to achieve objectives of rule). She suggests that it is the rare case where a former employee would be in a position to make a statement that could bind the former employer and urges the court to place the burden of showing that a former employee might be in a position to make such admissions on the former employer. In the interest of promoting the search for the truth and furthering informal, efficient, and inexpensive information gathering at the discovery stage of a proceeding, she asks the court to allow broad access to former employees by opposing counsel, "subject to appropriate conditions."

AUTHORS' COMMENT:

If you were the judge, would you side with defendants or with the plaintiff? Why?

A threshold question is whether a particular employee is actually represented by corporate counsel. An organization may not assert a preemptive and exclusive representation by the organization's lawyer of all current (or former) employees as a means to invoke rule 4.2 and insulate them all from ex parte communication with the lawyers of potential adversary parties. . . . The American Bar Association Committee on Ethics and Professional Responsibility has stated that Model Rule 4.2, on which our rule 4.2 is based, "does not contemplate that a lawyer representing the entity can invoke the rule's prohibition to cover all employees of the entity, by asserting a blanket representation of all of them." ABA Formal Op. 95-396, § VI (1995). . . . See *Carter-Herman v. Philadelphia*, 897 F. Supp. 899, 903 (E.D. Pa. 1995) (rejecting "the notion that every city employee is automatically a represented party simply by virtue of his or her employment without any initiative on the part of the employee to obtain legal help from the City"); *Brown v. St. Joseph County*, 148 F.R.D. 246, 250 (N.D. Ind. 1993) ("no attorney has the right to appear as counsel for another without the latter's consent . . . and it follows that an attorney cannot properly hold himself out as representing a person who has not agreed to the representation") . . . . Thus, the center may not invoke rule 4.2 to claim that all current and former employees are represented, and therefore the protective order is overbroad. Any analysis must be employee specific. The center has made no factual showing that the former employees in question are actually represented by the center's (or their own personal) counsel.

We turn to the rule in the *Messing* case to determine whether the employees in question may be considered represented for purposes of rule 4.2. The purpose of rule 4.2 is to "protect the attorney-client relationship and prevent clients from making ill-advised statements without the counsel of their attorney." . . . However, we recognized that prohibiting ex parte contact with all employees of a represented organization went beyond the purpose of the rule, which was not to "protect a corporate party from the revelation of prejudicial facts." *Id.*, 436 Mass. 437, quoting *Dent v. Kaufman*, 185 W.Va. 171, 175, 406 S.E.2d 68 (1991). We sought a balance between the need to discover relevant facts and the competing need to protect the attorney-client relationship. *Id.*, 436 Mass. at 358–359. We construed rule 4.2 (and comment [4] thereto) to prohibit an attorney from having ex parte contact only with certain employees of an organization, namely, those "who exercise managerial responsibility in the matter, who are alleged to have committed the wrongful acts at issue in the litigation, or who have authority on behalf of the corporation to make decisions about the course of the litigation." . . . As construed, the rule allows "ex parte interviews without prior counsel's permission when an employee clearly falls outside of the rule's scope."

Patriarca was employed by the center as a registered nurse whose job responsibility was to manage the personal care attendant program, a program that provides persons who have permanent or chronic disabilities with assistance to allow them to live independently in their community instead of being institutionalized. . . . Two of the former employees with whom she made contact had been occupational therapists. A third was an assistant community department manager-supervisor and skills trainer. These three had worked closely with Patriarca and Bailey at the center. The fourth had been a business manager at the center and had witnessed the events which led to Patriarca's separation from the center.

These four former employees of the center do not come within any category of employee covered by rule 4.2. . . . None of them is alleged to have committed the wrongful acts at issue in the litigation. There is no evidence, under their job descriptions or otherwise, that any of them had authority on behalf of the corporation to make decisions about the course of the litigation. The question whether any of them exercised managerial responsibility in the matter, however, is less obvious.

We said in *Messing* that employees with managerial responsibility in the matter "include[d] only those employees who have supervisory authority over the events at issue in the litigation." *Id.*, 436 Mass. at 361. Patriarca alleges that Bailey pressured her to evaluate individuals who were not eligible for personal care services, to falsify documents to make it appear that certain individuals were eligible for personal care services, and finally to present false information to the Department of Medical Assistance by recommending more services for clients than was required. Her surviving claims against the center allege breach of contract and wrongful termination in violation of public policy. Thus, to find that the former employees in question exercised managerial responsibility in the matter, we must determine either that they were in a position to direct Bailey to conduct himself as alleged, or to cause the center to respond as alleged. The center makes no claim that the occupational therapists and the skills trainer had any such managerial responsibility.

The fourth employee, described by the center as "Director of PCA/Fiscal Intermediary Services and former Business Manager," was allegedly "a 'management' witness to the plaintiff's separation which ultimately led to this complaint," and "was a central part of [the center's] management team." Being a "witness" to the plaintiff's separation does not establish that the fourth employee was involved in supervising, planning, or directing the events and practices that led to this litigation. Based on the record before the motion judge, there is no basis to conclude that the fourth employee "exercised managerial responsibility in the matter" ([court's] emphasis added). *Id.*, 436 Mass. at 357.

Subject to the caveat just discussed, none of the four former employees in this case came within a protected category of employee identified by the *Messing* case while she was employed by the center. Thus, none would have been protected from ex parte contact while an active employee of the center. A change in status from current to former employee does not change the fact that each falls "outside of the rule's scope." *Messing, supra* at 359. They are not protected by rule 4.2 from ex parte contact by Patriarca's counsel. In making any ex parte contact with these former employees, Patriarca's counsel must, of course, be assiduous in meeting other ethical and professional standards found outside rule 4.2.

As to the ethical restrictions that direct an attorney's actions, see 1 G.C. Hazard & W.W. Hodes, The Law of Lawyering § 4.2:107, at 744.4 n.4 (Supp. 1998) ("interviewing lawyer must make his role clear, as rule 4.3 requires, and must neither ask for nor listen to statements that include privileged matter"); *Restatement (Third) of the Law Governing Lawyers* § 102 (2000) ("A lawyer communicating with a nonclient in a situation permitted under § 99 [of the Restatement] may not seek to obtain information that the lawyer reasonably should know the nonclient may not reveal without violating a duty of confidentiality to another imposed by law"); Mass. R. Prof. C. 4.4, 426 Mass. 1405 (1998) ("In representing a client, a lawyer shall not use means that have no substantial purpose other than to embarrass, delay, or burden a third person, or use methods of obtaining evidence that violate the legal rights of such a person"); Mass. R. Prof. C. 8.4 (a) ("It is professional misconduct for a lawyer to: (a) violate or attempt to violate the Rules of Professional Conduct, knowingly assist or induce another to do so, or do so through the acts of another").

The center argues that each of these four employees was subject to a written confidentiality agreement and that the kind of information that Patriarca's counsel would seek during ex parte interviews pertains to the practices of the center and is of the type covered by those confidentiality agreements. The text of the agreements, however, shows only that they are designed to protect the consumers' and employees' medical and personal information, having nothing to do with the interests that rule 4.2 was designed to protect. The confidentiality of this information is sufficiently protected if the names of any individual patients are not disclosed. See *Reproductive Servs., Inc. v. Walker*, 439 U.S. 1307, 99 S. Ct. 1, 58 L. Ed. 2d 16 (1978) (by deleting names of patients from medical records sought in discovery, patients' privacy would be adequately protected); *Williams v. Buffalo Gen. Hosp.*, 28 A.D.2d 777, 778, 280 N.Y.S.2d 699, 1967 N.Y. App. Div. LEXIS 3796 (N.Y. 1967) (claimant who wished to obtain medical records of patients on specific ward allowed to do so, without necessitating revelation of patients' names).

The question of the general applicability of rule 4.2 to former employees is one we need not address because, on the facts presented, the former employees in question would not have been protected, even while employed, from ex parte contact by rule 4.2. The majority of courts that have decided this issue have concluded that former employees, for the most part, do not fall within the constraints of rule 4.2. This is a question that invites input from the organized bar through the rule making process.

The protective order issued by the Superior Court is vacated. The case is remanded to the Superior Court for further proceedings consistent with this opinion.

So ordered.

NOTES AND QUESTIONS

1. ***Caution: Research Carefully.*** Although the *Patriarca* and *Niesig* opinions have been highly influential, not all courts agree with them. Interpretations of the no-contact rule remain a jurisdiction-by-jurisdiction matter. Because violations of Rule 4.2 are likely to be treated harshly, you should research the law in the jurisdiction where you are practicing or planning an interview before you interview any employees of an opposing corporation, partnership, association, or other entity that has counsel in a matter.

2. ***Co-Plaintiffs, Co-Defendants, and Non-Litigation Matters.*** Keep in mind that Rule 4.2 applies to co-defendants and co-plaintiffs, as well as to non-parties who have counsel in connection with any particular matter. It is not limited to opposing parties. Also, Rule 4.2 applies to all matters, whether or not they are in litigation. Thus, real estate deals, contract negotiations, and all other types of legal matters are subject to Rule 4.2.

3. ***Former Employees.*** As the *Niesig* opinion mentioned, courts are still struggling with whether a corporation's former employees are deemed represented by counsel under Rule 4.2 when the corporation is a party. Even courts in the same jurisdiction have sometimes been unable to reach agreement on this question. *Compare Public Serv. Elec. & Gas Co. v. Associated Elec. & Gas Ins. Servs.*, 745 F. Supp. 1037 (D.N.J. 1990) (all former employees are off limits to opposing counsel under Rule 4.2 and its Comment), *with Curley v. Cumberland Farms, Inc.*, 134 F.R.D. 77 (D.N.J. 1991) (former employees may be interviewed informally without violating Rule 4.2).

Chapter 17
THE CLIENT'S ROLE IN THE ADVERSARY SYSTEM

In our discussion of the adversary system, we have been concentrating on the lawyer's role. In this chapter, we consider the client's role in the adversary system. We know from our discussion of zealous advocacy that a lawyer should not intentionally fail or refuse to take legitimate steps that would advance a client's interests. As expressed in Canon 7 of the old ABA Model Rules of Professional Conduct, "A Lawyer Should Represent a Client Zealously Within the Bounds of the Law." As expressed in Comment 1 to ABA Model Rule 1.3, a lawyer should "take whatever lawful and ethical measures are required to vindicate a client's cause or endeavor." But that leads to the central question of this chapter: Who decides which lawful and ethical measures the lawyer will take — the lawyer, or the client? How do we allocate power between the lawyer and the client? Who controls the way a case is handled — you, or your client? We briefly examine these questions.

A. ALLOCATING POWER BETWEEN ATTORNEY AND CLIENT

Questions about allocation of power between lawyer and client are challenging because — with a few exceptions — the lines are fuzzy and imprecise. The ABA Model Rules deal with the question in Rule 1.2(a), which divides representation into two categories — "objectives" and "means." The client controls the objectives, but the lawyer (after consulting with the client) controls the means. More specifically, the lawyer must "abide by" the client's decisions about objectives, but need only "consult with" the client concerning the means by which the lawyer pursues the client's objectives.

These broad principles governing client control under Rule 1.2(a) are a lot like the famous *Erie* Doctrine that you learned about in Civil Procedure. The client controls the *substance* of the matter (the "objectives"), and you control the *procedure* (the "means"). But just as the dividing line between "substance" and "procedure" is often far from clear, so too the dividing line in Rule 1.2(a) between "objectives" and "means" is not always clear. The ABA has therefore carved out two specific categories of decisions that are reserved to a client:

- in a civil matter, a lawyer must abide by a client's decision whether to accept (or reject) an offer of *settlement;* and
- in a criminal case, a lawyer must abide by a client's decision as to:
    - whether to enter a *plea,*
    - whether to waive a *jury* trial, and
    - whether to *testify.*

In the next case, *Jones v. Barnes*, the Supreme Court struggles to answer questions about the allocation of power between lawyer and client. The client, a criminal defendant nicknamed "Froggy," was represented in his state appeal by an appointed lawyer named Melinger. Froggy instructed Melinger to raise a number of arguments, all of which were colorable (i.e., not frivolous), but Melinger raised only some of them, refusing to raise others. We can imagine the exchange that might have ensued between Melinger and his client Froggy when Melinger refused to take orders from Froggy about what arguments to raise on appeal:

Froggy: Hey, I am the client here. You have to follow my instructions! If the arguments I want you to make are not frivolous, you have to make them.

Melinger: Am I some sort of a puppet? Are you Geppetto? My job as your advocate is to take whatever ethical measures are required to maximize the chances that you will win. Raising every possible argument is a bad idea.

> Since I'm the one with the law degree, I'll decide which arguments to raise on appeal and which ones to leave on the cutting room floor.

Were Froggy's rights abridged by Melinger's refusal to make some of the nonfrivolous arguments Froggy told him to make? Should a lawyer be required to make whatever arguments the client instructs him to make, as long as the arguments are not frivolous? The Court splits over this issue.. Which side are you on?

JONES v. BARNES

463 U.S. 745 (1983)

MR. CHIEF JUSTICE BURGER delivered the opinion of the Court

[Barnes, nicknamed "Froggy," was convicted of robbery and assault in a New York state court. On appeal, Froggy sought a new trial. He asked his assigned counsel, Melinger, to raise various issues, but Melinger raised only three of those issues in his brief and oral argument. Melinger rejected the other issues because, in Melinger's view, they would not have aided Froggy in obtaining a new trial or were not based on evidence in the record — but Froggy raised them on his own by filing a pro se brief. The appellate court rejected all of the arguments and affirmed the conviction. Froggy then brought a federal habeas corpus action claiming that Melinger's failure to assert every nonfrivolous argument Froggy had requested violated his right to the effective assistance of counsel. The Second Circuit agreed, and stated a new *per se* rule that appointed counsel for an indigent criminal defendant must raise every nonfrivolous issue requested by the client. The Supreme Court granted certiorari.]

[B]y promulgating a *per se* rule that the client, not the professional advocate, must be allowed to decide what issues are to be pressed, the Court of Appeals seriously undermines the ability of counsel to present the client's case in accord with counsel's professional evaluation.

Experienced advocates since time beyond memory have emphasized the importance of winnowing out weaker arguments on appeal and focusing on one central issue if possible, or at most on a few key issues. Justice Jackson, after observing appellate advocates for many years, stated:

> One of the first tests of a discriminating advocate is to select the question, or questions, that he will present orally. Legal contentions, like the currency, depreciate through over-issue. The mind of an appellate judge is habitually receptive to the suggestion that a lower court committed an error. But receptiveness declines as the number of assigned errors increases. Multiplicity hints at lack of confidence in any one. . . . [E]xperience on the bench convinces me that multiplying assignments of error will dilute and weaken a good case and will not save a bad one.

Jackson, Advocacy Before the United States Supreme Court, 25 Temple L. Q. 115, 119 (1951).

Justice Jackson's observation echoes the advice of countless advocates before him and since. An authoritative work on appellate practice observes:

> Most cases present only one, two, or three significant questions. . . . Usually, . . . if you cannot win on a few major points, the others are not likely to help, and to attempt to deal with a great many in the limited number of pages allowed for briefs will mean that none may receive adequate attention. The effect of adding weak arguments will be to dilute the force of the stronger ones.

R. Stern, Appellate Practice in the United States 266 (1981).

AUTHORS' COMMENT:

This is good advice. A good appellate brief should focus on the key issues. But even though focusing on key issues is a good idea, that can't be the only concern. Our imagined brief exchange between Froggy and Melinger exposed a real tension between lawyer and client. Does the client have the constitutional right to force the lawyer to raise every colorable argument? Read on.

There can hardly be any question about the importance of having the appellate advocate examine the record with a view to selecting the most promising issues for review. This has assumed a greater importance in an era when oral argument is strictly limited in most courts — often to as little as 15 minutes — and when page limits on briefs are widely imposed. Even in a court that imposes no time or page limits, however, the new *per se* rule laid down by the Court of Appeals is contrary to all experience and logic. A brief that raises every colorable issue runs the risk of burying good arguments — those that, in the words of the great advocate John W. Davis, "go for the jugular," — in a verbal mound made up of strong and weak contentions.

For judges to second-guess reasonable professional judgments and impose on appointed counsel a duty to raise every "colorable" claim suggested by a client would disserve the very goal of vigorous and effective advocacy. . . . Nothing in the Constitution or our interpretation of that document requires such a standard. The judgment of the Court of Appeals is accordingly

Reversed.

Justice Brennan, with whom Justice Marshall joins, dissenting.

What is at issue here is the relationship between lawyer and client — who has ultimate authority to decide which nonfrivolous issues should be presented on appeal? I believe the right to "the assistance of counsel" carries with it a right, personal to the defendant, to make that decision, against the advice of counsel if he chooses.

[T]he Court argues that good appellate advocacy demands selectivity among arguments. That is certainly true — the Court's advice is good. It ought to be taken to heart by every lawyer called upon to argue an appeal in this or any other court, and by his client. It should take little or no persuasion to get a wise client to understand that, if staying out of prison is what he values most, he should encourage his lawyer to raise only his two or three best arguments on appeal, and he should defer to his lawyer's advice as to which are the best arguments. The Constitution, however, does not require clients to be wise, and other policies should be weighed in the balance as well.

It is no secret that indigent clients often mistrust the lawyers appointed to represent them. . . . There are many reasons for this, some perhaps unavoidable even under perfect conditions — differences in education, disposition, and socio-economic class — and some that should (but may not always) be zealously avoided. A lawyer and his client do not always have the same interests. Even with paying clients, a lawyer may have a strong interest in having judges and prosecutors think well of him, and, if he is working for a flat fee — a common arrangement for criminal defense attorneys — or if his fees for court appointments are lower than he would receive for other work, he has an obvious financial incentive to conclude cases on his criminal docket swiftly. Good lawyers undoubtedly recognize these temptations and resist them, and they endeavor to convince their clients that they will. It would be naive, however, to suggest that they always succeed in either task. A constitutional rule that encourages lawyers to disregard their clients' wishes without compelling need can only exacerbate the clients' suspicion of their lawyers. As in *Faretta*, to force a lawyer's *decisions* on a defendant "can only lead him to believe that the law conspires against him." In the end, what the Court hopes to gain in effectiveness of appellate representation by the rule it imposes today may well be lost to decreased effectiveness in other areas of representation.

Finally, today's ruling denigrates the values of individual autonomy and dignity central to many constitutional rights, especially those Fifth and Sixth Amendment rights that come into play in the criminal process. Certainly a person's life changes when he is charged with a crime and brought to trial. He must, if he harbors any hope of success, defend himself on terms — often technical and hard to understand — that are the State's, not his own. As a practical matter, the assistance of counsel is necessary to that defense. Yet, until his conviction becomes final and he has had an opportunity to appeal, any restrictions on individual autonomy and dignity should be limited to the minimum necessary to vindicate the State's interest in a speedy, effective prosecution. The role of the defense lawyer should be above all to function as the instrument and defender of the client's autonomy and dignity in all phases of the criminal process.

The Court subtly but unmistakably adopts a different conception of the defense lawyer's role — he need do nothing beyond what the State, not his client, considers most important. In many ways, having a lawyer becomes one of the many indignities visited upon someone who has the ill fortune to run afoul of the criminal justice system.

I cannot accept the notion that lawyers are one of the punishments a person receives merely for being accused of a crime. Clients, if they wish, are capable of making informed judgments about which issues to appeal, and when they exercise that prerogative their choices should be respected unless they would require lawyers to violate their consciences, the law, or their duties to the court.

NOTES AND QUESTIONS

1. ***Professionalism and Client Autonomy.*** In *Jones v. Barnes*, the Court's majority says that the role of the advocate "requires that he support his client's appeal to the best of his ability." This is similar to the Principle of Professionalism devised by Professor Murray Schwartz. That principle obligates a lawyer to "maximize the likelihood that the client will prevail in litigation."

Justice Brennan, in dissent, sees a different role for the appointed advocate. To Justice Brennan, "The role of the defense lawyer should be above all to function as the instrument and defender of the client's autonomy and dignity in all phases of the criminal process." Thus, the defense lawyer's role is to carry out the instructions of the client even if the defense lawyer disagrees with those instructions. The lawyer should advise the client about how to maximize the chances that the client will win, but if the client disagrees with the lawyer's advice, then Justice Brennan's defense lawyer must follow the client's orders.

Do you prefer Professor Schwartz's conception (maximizing the client's chance of victory), or Justice Brennan's conception (maximizing the client's dignity and autonomy)? Why? Are both approaches consistent with the concept of zealous advocacy within the bounds of law? If not, which one falls short?

2. ***Decisions Reserved to the Client.*** To summarize the structure of Rule 1.2(a), it divides control between a lawyer and client as follows:

- a lawyer shall *abide by* a client's decision concerning the *objectives* of representation;
- a lawyer shall *consult with* the client as to the *means* by which they are to be pursued;
- a lawyer shall *abide by* a client's decision whether to accept a *settlement* offer in a matter; and

- a lawyer shall *abide by* the client's decision, in criminal cases, as to: (1) whether to enter a *plea*, (2) whether to waive a *jury* trial, and (3) whether to *testify*.

3. ***Is Anything More Important than Winning?*** The Principle of Professionalism developed by Professor Schwartz says that the advocate's job is to maximize the chances that the client will prevail. Is this always true? Could a client ever have interests more important than winning?

Consider this situation: Unknown to you, Ned Varkin is a spy for the Taliban and has been trying to find out when NATO Forces plan to launch attacks against Taliban strongholds around Kandahar. One night, Varkin threw a rock through the window of an Air Force Major General outside Washington. Varkin was arrested and, although he never actually entered the home, he was charged with breaking and entering.

Varkin now hires you to defend him, but does not tell you that he is a Taliban spy. The prosecutor, figuring this is a two-bit attempted burglary, offers a plea bargain to a reduced charge of criminal trespass. The plea will entail only a short jail sentence, after which Varkin will be free. You review the evidence and think the government's case is weak because Varkin never got inside the home. You strongly advise Varkin to go to trial. Varkin, however, wants to take the plea so that the government will not investigate his case any further — he doesn't want anyone to find out that he's a Taliban spy, which you don't know about. Should Varkin's decision control even if he does not explain to you why he wants to take the plea?

4. ***The Court's Interests.*** Let's vary the Varkin question a bit. Suppose the same scenario, with the same plea bargain offer — but now you advise Varkin that going to trial is a terrible idea because he is sure to lose. Varkin replies that, as a Westerner, you couldn't possibly appreciate what was really at stake: "I may be a common criminal in your eyes, but there are many in my world who will view me as a hero for penetrating the American military machine on its home ground. I demand to go to trial." Does Varkin's decision control? Should we give a common criminal the right to take up the time of the judge, the prosecutor, the bailiff, and the jurors if you, the lawyer, consider the case a dead loser? Why does the Constitution protect the right of a defendant to go to trial when the client's only defense is to say, "Prove it!"? (See Rule 3.1, which provides that despite the broad ban on making frivolous claims or defenses, lawyers in a criminal case "may nevertheless so defend the proceeding as to require that every element of the case be established.")

5. ***The Lawyer's Interests.*** In both of the above scenarios about Varkin, the lawyer also has interests. If Varkin has a weak case, the lawyer may have an interest in accepting the plea to avoid losing at trial. (If you ever hear a lawyer say, "I've never lost a case," maybe it's because the lawyer settled every case that was not a sure winner.) Conversely, if Varkin has a strong case, some experienced lawyers may want to go to trial to chalk up another win, or to garner the publicity likely to be associated with defending a notorious client. Other experienced lawyers might not want to spend the time necessary to prepare for and conduct the trial, even in a strong case, if they could earn more money by working on their other cases. Some neophyte lawyers, in contrast, might be chafing at the bit to go to trial, even with a weak case, in order to gain experience. Other new lawyers might be afraid to go to trial even with a strong case for fear of screwing up and embarrassing themselves. Should any of these interests count for anything? Are they legitimate interests?

In our view, the lawyer's interests in fame and fortune should not count for anything. It would be a sad system if the lawyer's desire for money or publicity counted for more than the defendant's right to go to trial, or the defendant's right to plead guilty and avoid trial. An important part of professionalism — and an integral part of Professor Schwartz's Principle of Professionalism — is that a lawyer must submerge personal desires in favor of the client's desires. Theoretically, you have to forget about your own interests and think only about the client's interests. (We see this more graphically in our conflict of interest chapters. Rule 1.7(b) prohibits lawyers from accepting representations where their own interests may materially limit their ability to represent a client.)

If you agree that lawyers must put client interests ahead of their own, the challenge will be to act on that belief even after you have started practicing law, when putting the client's interests first will sometimes go against your own interests. The challenge then will be to recognize the influence that your own interests have upon your analysis, and to subordinate your interests to those of your client. It's not easy.

6. ***Does Lawyer Know Best?*** In *Jones v. Barnes*, Chief Justice Burger assumes that the lawyer knows best — not only about how many arguments to present, but also about which arguments to present. Do lawyers really know best? There are lots of smart lawyers with not-so-smart clients — but there are also plenty of smart clients with not-so-smart lawyers. Are stupid lawyers better advocates than smart clients? (Think about this question in connection with our materials on the unauthorized practice of law, discussing the laws in all 50 states that prohibit people without a law license from practicing law.)

7. ***Multiple Roles.*** Part of the confusion over the lawyer's role results because lawyers are often called upon to play multiple roles in the course of representing a client: confidante, cheerleader, intermediary with the opposition, and business advisor. Playing any one of these roles to the exclusion of the others will often make it more difficult to live up to the Principle of Professionalism. As Elihu Root famously put it: "About half the practice of a decent lawyer consists in telling would-be clients that they are damned fools and should stop."

8. ***Parallels to Medicine.*** Doctors also differ widely in their approaches to the professional relationship. Four basic models of the doctor-patient relationship are posited in MEDICAL ETHICS AND PROFESSIONALISM: A SYNOPSIS FOR STUDENTS, RESIDENTS, AND PRACTICING PHYSICIANS (2005):

Model No. 1: The high physician-control style. This model consists of an "active" doctor and an "inert" patient. The doctor virtually ignores the patient's views and tells the patient what to do, and the patient does it because the doctor is the boss.

Model No. 2: The biomedical style. This model involves a "guiding" doctor and a "cooperating" patient, but the focus of the doctor is mainly on the disease. The doctor elicits information from the patient about the specific symptoms that afflict the patient, and about the patient's feelings toward certain kinds of treatments, but the interaction is directed, purposeful, and designed to help the doctor make the final decision.

Model No. 3: The biopsychosocial style. This model, like the "biomedical" style, also consists of a "guiding" doctor and a "cooperating" patient in a relationship that is primarily focused on the disease, but the doctor also obtains psychological information in order to fully understand the patient's condition. The doctor elicits information from the patient as a means of acquiring the knowledge to pursue a course of treatment but understands that even the patient's feelings toward certain kinds of treatments are relevant to the patient's overall condition.

Model No. 4: The personal-focused style. This model consists of mutual participants in a cooperative relationship. The doctor is personable, friendly, and individually focused on the needs and desires of the patient, not the disease. In this model, the parties have relatively equal status, are equally dependent, and are engaged in activity satisfying to both parties.

Which model do you like best? Which model is likely to be most effective in maintaining the health of the patient? Think about the various doctors that you have visited over the years. Which doctors did you like best? Which doctors were most effective in keeping you healthy? Which of the four professional models did these doctors follow? Would the model that you like best in medicine also work best in law practice? Will your preferred model work best for all clients, or will the best model for law practice depend on the nature of the particular client and matter?

B. THE LAWYER'S INFORMAL CONTROL

Although Rule 1.2(a) gives clients the final say over various decisions (especially whether to settle a civil case and whether to accept a plea, demand a jury, and testify in a criminal case), the lawyer informally retains control over many of the client's decisions. Through the lawyer's ability to select and color the facts and legal arguments, and through the lawyer's persuasive skills and aura of authority, the lawyer can often persuade the client to render the decision the lawyer wants in an area over which the client has formal control under Rule 1.2(a).

Is it wrong for lawyers to influence or informally control their clients in areas where the professional rules reserve the final decision to the client? Suppose the client is about to make a bad decision — one that will be counterproductive in terms of the client's own stated goals. Is it ethical for the lawyer to persist in trying to talk the client out of making that bad decision? Is it ethical for the lawyer to exaggerate or to shade the law, or to color the facts, in an effort to persuade the client to change his mind?

Suppose for the sake of this discussion that it is not permissible for the lawyer to exaggerate or otherwise misrepresent in an effort to get the client to change his mind. Is it OK for a lawyer to play the role of an advocate in dealing with a client — not lying to the client, but using the advantage of the lawyer's education and experience to put the lawyer's views about the case in the best light? Or must lawyers always play it perfectly straight with clients?

NOTES AND QUESTIONS

1. ***Should Lawyers have a Veto?*** Even if the professional codes reserve certain decisions to clients, should lawyers have a veto over certain decisions? Consider Article I, Section 16 of the California Constitution: "A jury may be waived in a criminal case by the consent of both parties expressed in open court by the defendant *and the defendant's counsel.*" (Emphasis added.) In criminal cases, courts have interpreted this provision to require consent of both the defendant and the defendant's lawyer. Thus, a lawyer may veto the client's decision to waive a jury. Should lawyers have that veto right? Should lawyers also have veto power over the two other major client decisions, the right to plead guilty and the right to testify? And should lawyers in civil cases have veto power over a client's decision to accept or reject a settlement offer?

2. ***The Lawyer's Ultimate Veto: Withdrawal.*** Regardless of which decisions the rules formally allocate to the client, as a practical matter the lawyer often has the ultimate veto. If the court gives its permission, the lawyer can withdraw from representing the client, even if withdrawal will have a "material adverse effect" on the client. Under Rule 1.16(b), a lawyer may withdraw from representing a client if "(4) the client insists upon taking action that the lawyer considers repugnant or with which the lawyer has a fundamental disagreement" or "(7) other good cause for withdrawal exists." If the client's objective is to win the case (as it usually is), it is hard to characterize that objective as "repugnant or imprudent." But if the client repeatedly rejects the lawyer's advice so that there is a strain or even a breakdown in the lawyer-client relationship, the court may permit the lawyer to withdraw based on "other good cause." Should the client's rejection of the lawyer's advice qualify as "good cause" under Rule 1.16(b)(7) — even where the rules give the client the ultimate right to make the decision?

Suppose the client says, "I've decided to go to trial. I don't want to accept that plea bargain. The prosecutor's offer is no good." The lawyer says, "That's crazy! They'll convict you in ten minutes at trial. They have two eyewitnesses and your confession. If you don't take the plea bargain, I'll move to withdraw, and you can ask the court to appoint some other lawyer for you. Who knows what lawyer you'll end up with? You might get a real estate lawyer just admitted to the bar, or a former prosecutor who will sell you down the river!"

Notwithstanding the lawyer's warnings, the client insists on going to trial, so the lawyer moves to withdraw. The judge says, "Counsel, why are you moving to withdraw?"

The lawyer says, "Your Honor, the client won't take my advice. I've lost my effectiveness. There's been a breakdown in the attorney-client relationship. That's good cause for withdrawal under Rule 1.16."

If you were the judge, would you grant the motion based on the lawyer's representations, or deny the motion outright and force the lawyer to stay in the case, or ask further questions to obtain more information from the lawyer and client? If you aren't prepared to rule, what more do you need to know?

3. ***What if the Client doesn't Want a Defense?*** You have a duty to provide the best defense you can to your clients, even if you think they are flat-out guilty. Some clients, though, can make the task of providing the best defense nearly impossible. In *People v. McMillan*, 148 Misc. 2d 738, 1990 N.Y. Misc. LEXIS 539; 561 N.Y.S.2d 512, 1990 N.Y. Misc. LEXIS 539 (N.Y. Sup. Ct. 1990), for example, counsel was called upon to defend a client who had for three years kept nine of his children (ranging in age from infancy to fifteen years) literally imprisoned in a three-room apartment — never allowing them to leave the apartment, even for school or medical treatment — while frequently subjecting them to the worst kinds of atrocities: incest, assault, and other crimes. Defendant had also buried three of his other children, who were either stillborn or died as infants, in a park near the apartment house.

Although the evidence of McMillan's guilt was overwhelming and the only possible option to avoid extended incarceration was to plead not guilty by reason of insanity, McMillan repeatedly refused to allow counsel to enter such a plea and adamantly refused to cooperate in any psychiatric examination that might support such a defense. When the trial judge suggested that the defendant carefully listen to his lawyer, it was to no avail.

What should a lawyer do if the client doesn't want a defense? The court spoke to this question definitively:

> When a competent defendant — by his acts — has prevented the introduction of medical testimony on insanity and has specifically rejected the use of such a defense, that ends the question. To permit counsel — in front of the jury — to argue an insanity defense while his client verbally or otherwise opposes it would interfere with the defendant's due process rights and, to a lesser degree, the good order and the court's conduct of the trial. We all must be reminded from time to time, Judge, defense counsel, defendant and prosecutor, that we each have carefully delineated duties and rights and should not overreach.

4. ***The Best Justice System in the World?*** Because the judge, defense lawyer, defendant, and prosecutor each have carefully delineated duties and rights in our system of justice in the United States, we can legitimately claim that our system is the best system of justice in the world.

Of course, a claim of that magnitude cannot be proven empirically. But even so, it's hard to ignore the kind of unsolicited testimony offered by Zacarias Moussaoui, who pled guilty (against the advice of his lawyers) to conspiring to launch the September 11, 2001 terrorist attacks that killed nearly three thousand people. At the sentencing phase of Moussaoui's trial, prosecutors sought the death penalty, but the jury instead sentenced Moussaoui to life in prison without parole. An astonished Moussaoui then said: "I had thought I would be sentenced to death based on the emotions and anger toward me for the deaths on September 11, . . . But after reviewing the jury verdict and reading how the jurors set aside their emotions and disgust for me and focused on the law and the evidence . . . I now see that it is possible that I can receive a fair trial even with Americans as jurors."

5. ***Summing Up.*** We can sum up this chapter succinctly. You are bound by your oath and honor to use every legitimate weapon at your disposal on behalf of every client, even the "guilty." That's how lawyers who zealously represent the interests of their clients within the bounds of law make a difference. But no matter how smart you are, and no matter how unwise you think your client may be, the client ultimately decides the objectives of the representation, including whether to accept or reject a settlement offer in a civil case and whether the client will waive the right to a jury trial, enter a plea, or testify in a criminal case. The lawyer gets to make the ultimate decisions about "means," but only after consulting with the client so that the client has a meaningful chance to weigh in. That is how we allocate power between lawyer and client in our adversary system.

Chapter 18
THE PERPLEXING PROBLEM OF PERJURY

The adversary system has many aspects — keeping secrets, zealously representing your client by using every legitimate tactic to advance the client's interests, and not helping the other side unless the rules require you to do so or your client has given informed consent. All of these threads come together when we discuss the problem of perjury. How far can a lawyer go in letting a client or another witness stretch, ignore, or contradict the truth? Does the duty of candor to the court outweigh the duty of confidentiality to the client? Or does the duty of confidentiality to the client trump the duty of candor to the court? In this chapter we explore this tension.

A. WHAT IF YOUR CLIENT PLANS TO LIE — OR LIES — AT TRIAL?

One of the most difficult questions in law practice is: What if your client plans to lie — or does lie — at trial? What rules govern your conduct in that situation? What may you do, must you do, and what must you not do? In other words, what are your options and obligations?

Let's be more specific: May (or must) a lawyer *permit* a client to lie on the witness stand? Conversely, may (or must) a lawyer *prevent* a client from lying on the witness stand? And if a client does lie on the witness stand, what — if anything — must a lawyer do to rectify the situation?

These questions raise other questions. How does a lawyer know that a client is lying? What steps may or must a lawyer take to prevent the client from lying? And what if the client agrees to tell the truth but then surprises the lawyer by lying unexpectedly during trial?

The following opinion by the United States Supreme Court in *Nix v. Whiteside* wrestles with these and other questions. It is one of most important opinions the Supreme Court has ever issued on matters of legal ethics. But — as the concurring opinions make clear — the majority opinion leaves many questions unanswered, and may appear to answer questions that it lacks authority to answer. The case builds on everything we have said up to now about confidentiality, loyalty, and the adversary system. Read carefully.

B. *NIX v. WHITESIDE*

One of the most difficult questions in law practice is: What if your client plans to lie — or does lie — at trial? What rules govern your conduct in that situation? What may you do, what must you do, and what must you not do? In other words, what are your options and obligations?

Let's be more specific: May (or must) a lawyer *permit* a client to lie on the witness stand? Conversely, may (or must) a lawyer *prevent* a client from lying on the witness stand? And if a client does lie on the witness stand, what — if anything — must a lawyer do to rectify the situation?

These questions raise other questions. How does a lawyer know that a client is lying? What steps may or must a lawyer take to prevent the client from lying? And what if the client agrees to tell the truth but then surprises the lawyer by lying unexpectedly during trial?

The following opinion by the United States Supreme Court in *Nix v. Whiteside* wrestles with these and other questions. It is one of most important opinions the Supreme Court has ever issued on matters of legal ethics. But — as the concurring opinions make clear — the majority opinion leaves many questions unanswered, and may appear to answer questions that it lacks authority to answer. The case builds on everything we have said up to now about confidentiality, loyalty, and the adversary system. Read carefully.

NIX v. WHITESIDE

475 U.S. 157 (1986)

CHIEF JUSTICE BURGER delivered the opinion of the Court.

We granted certiorari to decide whether the Sixth Amendment right of a criminal defendant to assistance of counsel is violated when an attorney refuses to cooperate with the defendant in presenting perjured testimony at his trial.

A

Whiteside was convicted of second degree murder by a jury verdict which was affirmed by the Iowa courts. The killing took place on February 8, 1977 in Cedar Rapids, Iowa. Whiteside and two others went to one Calvin Love's apartment late that night, seeking marihuana. Love was in bed when Whiteside and his companions arrived; an argument between Whiteside and Love over the marihuana ensued. At one point, Love directed his girlfriend to get his "piece," and at another point got up, then returned to his bed. According to Whiteside's testimony, Love then started to reach under his pillow and moved toward Whiteside. Whiteside stabbed Love in the chest, inflicting a fatal wound.

Whiteside was charged with murder, and when counsel was appointed he objected to the lawyer initially appointed, claiming that he felt uncomfortable with a lawyer who had formerly been a prosecutor. Gary L. Robinson was then appointed and immediately began investigation. Whiteside gave him a statement that he had stabbed Love as the latter "was pulling a pistol from underneath the pillow on the bed." Upon questioning by Robinson, however, Whiteside indicated that he had not actually seen a gun, but that he was convinced that Love had a gun. No pistol was found on the premises; shortly after the police search following the stabbing, which had revealed no weapon, the victim's family had removed all of the victim's possessions from the apartment. Robinson interviewed Whiteside's companions who were present during the stabbing and none had seen a gun during the incident. Robinson advised Whiteside that the existence of a gun was not necessary to establish the claim of self defense, and that only a reasonable belief that the victim had a gun nearby was necessary even though no gun was actually present.

Until shortly before trial, Whiteside consistently stated to Robinson that he had not actually seen a gun, but that he was convinced that Love had a gun in his hand. About a week before trial, during preparation for direct examination, Whiteside for the first time told Robinson and his associate Donna Paulsen that he had seen something "metallic" in Love's hand. When asked about this, Whiteside responded [that] "in Howard Cook's case there was a gun. If I don't say I saw a gun I'm dead."

AUTHORS' COMMENT:

Your client has just indicated to you — for the first time — that he will say he "saw a gun." Put yourself in Gary Robinson's shoes and decide what you would do. Use the space below to write down two things you would tell your client at this point:

Robinson told Whiteside that such testimony would be perjury and repeated that it was not necessary to prove that a gun was available but only that Whiteside reasonably believed that he was in danger. On Whiteside's insisting that he would testify that he saw "something metallic" Robinson told him, according to Robinson's testimony,

> we could not allow him to [testify falsely] because that would be perjury, and as officers of the court we would be suborning perjury if we allowed him to do it; . . . I advised him that if he did do that it would be my duty to advise the Court of what he was doing and that I felt he was committing perjury; also, that I probably would be allowed to attempt to impeach that particular testimony.

Robinson also indicated he would seek to withdraw from the representation if Whiteside insisted on committing perjury.[2]

Whiteside testified in his own defense at trial and stated that he "knew" that Love had a gun and that he believed Love was reaching for a gun and he had acted swiftly in self defense. On cross examination, he admitted that he had not actually seen a gun in Love's hand. Robinson presented evidence that Love had been seen with a sawed-off shotgun on other occasions, that the police search of the apartment may have been careless, and that the victim's family had removed everything from the apartment shortly after the crime. Robinson presented this evidence to show a basis for Whiteside's asserted fear that Love had a gun.

The jury returned a verdict of second-degree murder and Whiteside moved for a new trial, claiming that he had been deprived of a fair trial by Robinson's admonitions not to state that he saw a gun or "something metallic." The trial court held a hearing, heard testimony by Whiteside and Robinson, and denied the motion. The trial court made specific findings that the facts were as related by Robinson.

The Supreme Court of Iowa affirmed respondent's conviction. That court held that the right to have counsel present all appropriate defenses does not extend to using perjury, and that an attorney's duty to a client does not extend to assisting a client in committing perjury. Relying on DR 7-102(A)(4) of the Iowa Code of Professional Responsibility for Lawyers, which expressly prohibits an attorney from using perjured testimony, and Iowa Code § 721.2, which criminalizes subornation of perjury, the Iowa

---

[2] Whiteside's version of the events at this pretrial meeting is considerably more cryptic:

> "Q. And as you went over the questions, did the two of you come into conflict with regard to whether or not there was a weapon?
>
> "A. I couldn't — I couldn't say a conflict. But I got the impression at one time that maybe if I didn't go along with — with what was happening, that it was no gun being involved, maybe that he will pull out of my trial."

court concluded that not only were Robinson's actions permissible, but were required. The court commended "both Mr. Robinson and Ms. Paulsen for the high ethical manner in which this matter was handled."

B

Whiteside then petitioned for a writ of habeas corpus in the United States District Court for the Southern District of Iowa. In that petition Whiteside alleged that he had been denied effective assistance of counsel and of his right to present a defense by Robinson's refusal to allow him to testify as he had proposed. The District Court denied the writ. Accepting the State trial court's factual finding that Whiteside's intended testimony would have been perjurious, it concluded that there could be no grounds for habeas relief since there is no constitutional right to present a perjured defense.

AUTHORS' COMMENT:

The factual finding that "Whiteside's intended testimony would have been perjurious" is crucial to the analysis of the client perjury problem. Note the difference between ABA Model Rule 3.3(a)(4) and ABA Model Rule 3.3(c), as they were in effect in 1986. Rule 3.3(a)(4) said that a lawyer shall not knowingly "offer evidence that the lawyer *knows* to be false." (Emphasis added.) Rule 3.3(c) said that a lawyer "may refuse to offer evidence that the lawyer *reasonably believes* is false." (Emphasis added.) Based on what you have read in the case so far, do you "know" that Whiteside's proposed testimony that he "saw a gun" would be false? Or do you "reasonably believe" that it would be false, or even merely *suspect* that it would be false? (Or do you think Whiteside is telling the truth?) How does the answer to this question affect your options and obligations?

The United States Court of Appeals for the Eighth Circuit reversed and directed that the writ of habeas corpus be granted. The Court of Appeals accepted the findings of the trial judge, affirmed by the Iowa Supreme Court, that trial counsel believed with good cause that Whiteside would testify falsely and acknowledged that under *Harris v. New York*, 401 U.S. 222 (1971), a criminal defendant's privilege to testify in his own behalf does not include a right to commit perjury. Nevertheless, the court reasoned that an intent to commit perjury, communicated to counsel, does not alter a defendant's right to effective assistance of counsel and that Robinson's admonition to Whiteside that he would inform the court of Whiteside's perjury constituted a threat to violate the attorney's duty to preserve client confidences. According to the Court of Appeals, this threatened violation of client confidences breached the standards of effective representation set down in *Strickland v. Washington*, 466 U.S. 668 (1984). The court also concluded that *Strickland*'s prejudice requirement was satisfied by an implication of prejudice from the conflict between Robinson's duty of loyalty to his client and his ethical duties.

II

B

In *Strickland v. Washington*, we held that to obtain relief by way of federal habeas corpus on a claim of a deprivation of effective assistance of counsel under the Sixth Amendment, the movant must establish both serious attorney error and prejudice. To show such error, it must be established that the assistance rendered by counsel was constitutionally deficient in that "counsel made errors so serious that counsel was not functioning as 'counsel' guaranteed the defendant by the Sixth Amendment." *Strickland*, 466 U.S., at 687, 104 S. Ct., at 2064. To show prejudice, it must be established that the claimed lapses in counsel's performance rendered the trial unfair so as to "undermine confidence in the outcome" of the trial.

In *Strickland*, we acknowledged that the Sixth Amendment does not require any particular response by counsel to a problem that may arise. Rather, the Sixth Amendment inquiry is into whether the attorney's conduct was "reasonably effective." To counteract the natural tendency to fault an unsuccessful defense, a court reviewing a claim of ineffective assistance must "indulge a strong presumption that counsel's conduct falls within the wide range of reasonable professional assistance." In giving shape to the perimeters of this range of reasonable professional assistance, *Strickland* mandates that "[p]revailing norms of practice as reflected in American Bar Association Standards and the like, . . . are guides to determining what is reasonable, but they are only guides."

AUTHORS' COMMENT:

"Prevailing norms of practice" include the ABA Model Rules of Professional Conduct and the Iowa Code of Professional Responsibility. The question the Court is answering now is what weight to give the "prevailing norms." Should violation of a rule of professional conduct automatically be considered *ineffective* assistance of counsel? Conversely, should adherence to a rule of professional conduct automatically be considered *effective* assistance of counsel? What do you think? Why? How does the Court decide this question? Read on.

Under the *Strickland* standard, breach of an ethical standard does not necessarily make out a denial of the Sixth Amendment guarantee of assistance of counsel. When examining attorney conduct, a court must be careful not to narrow the wide range of conduct acceptable under the Sixth Amendment so restrictively as to constitutionalize particular standards of professional conduct and thereby intrude into the State's proper authority to define and apply the standards of professional conduct applicable to those it admits to practice in its courts. In some future case challenging attorney conduct in the course of a state court trial, we may need to define with greater precision the weight to be given to recognized canons of ethics, the standards established by the State in statutes or professional codes, and the Sixth Amendment, in defining the proper scope and limits on that conduct. Here we need not face that question, since virtually all of the sources speak with one voice.

C

We turn next to the question presented: the definition of the range of "reasonable professional" responses to a criminal defendant client who informs counsel that he will perjure himself on the stand. We must determine whether, in this setting, Robinson's conduct fell within the wide range of professional responses to threatened client perjury acceptable under the Sixth Amendment.

In *Strickland*, we recognized counsel's duty of loyalty and his "overarching duty to advocate the defendant's cause." Plainly, that duty is limited to legitimate, lawful conduct compatible with the very nature of a trial as a search for truth. Although counsel must take all reasonable lawful means to attain the objectives of the client, counsel is precluded from taking steps or in any way assisting the client in presenting false evidence or otherwise violating the law.

Disciplinary Rule 7-102 of the Model Code of Professional Responsibility (1980), entitled "Representing a Client Within the Bounds of the Law," provides that

> (A) In his representation of a client, a lawyer shall not:
>
> (4) Knowingly use perjured testimony or false evidence.
>
> (7) Counsel or assist his client in conduct that the lawyer knows to be illegal or fraudulent.

This provision has been adopted by Iowa, and is binding on all lawyers who appear in its courts. The more recent Model Rules of Professional Conduct (1983) similarly admonish attorneys to obey all laws in the course of representing a client:

> *RULE 1.2 Scope of Representation*
>
> (d) A lawyer shall not counsel a client to engage, or assist a client, in conduct that the lawyer knows is criminal or fraudulent."

Both the Model Code of Professional Conduct and the Model Rules of Professional Conduct also adopt the specific exception from the attorney-client privilege for disclosure of perjury that his client intends to commit or has committed. DR 4-101(C)(3) (intention of client to commit a crime); Rule 3.3 (lawyer has duty to disclose falsity of evidence even if disclosure compromises client confidences). Indeed, both the Model Code and the Model Rules do not merely *authorize* disclosure by counsel of client perjury; they *require* such disclosure. See Rule 3.3(a)(4); DR 7-102(B)(1).

These standards confirm that the legal profession has accepted that an attorney's ethical duty to advance the interests of his client is limited by an equally solemn duty to comply with the law and standards of professional conduct; it specifically ensures that the client may not use false evidence. This special duty of an attorney to prevent and disclose frauds upon the court derives from the recognition that perjury is as much a crime as tampering with witnesses or jurors by way of promises and threats, and undermines the administration of justice.

The offense of perjury was a crime recognized at common law, and has been made a felony in most states by statute, including Iowa. An attorney who aids false testimony by questioning a witness when perjurious responses can be anticipated, risks prosecution for subornation of perjury under Iowa Code § 720.3 (1985).

It is universally agreed that at a minimum the attorney's first duty when confronted with a proposal for perjurious testimony is to attempt to dissuade the client from the unlawful course of conduct. Model Rules of Professional Conduct, Rule 3.3. A statement directly in point is found in the Commentary to the Model Rules of Professional Conduct under the heading "False Evidence":

> When false evidence is offered by the client, however, a conflict may arise between the lawyer's duty to keep the client's revelations confidential and the duty of candor to the court. Upon ascertaining that material evidence is false, the lawyer *should seek to persuade the client that the evidence should not be offered* or, if it has been offered, that its false character should immediately be disclosed.

The Commentary thus also suggests that an attorney's revelation of his client's perjury to the court is a professionally responsible and acceptable response to the conduct of a client who has actually given perjured testimony. Similarly, the Model Rules and the commentary, as well as the Code of Professional Responsibility adopted in Iowa expressly permit withdrawal from representation as an appropriate response of an attorney when the client threatens to commit perjury. Model Rules of Professional Conduct, Rule 1.16(a)(1), Rule 1.6, Comment (1983); Code of Professional Responsibility,

DR 2-110(B), (C) (1980). Withdrawal of counsel when this situation arises at trial gives rise to many difficult questions including possible mistrial and claims of double jeopardy.[6]

The essence of the brief *amicus* of the American Bar Association reviewing practices long accepted by ethical lawyers, is that under no circumstance may a lawyer either advocate or passively tolerate a client's giving false testimony. This, of course, is consistent with the governance of trial conduct in what we have long called "a search for truth." The suggestion sometimes made that "a lawyer must believe his client not judge him" in no sense means a lawyer can honorably be a party to or in any way give aid to presenting known perjury.

D

Considering Robinson's representation of respondent in light of these accepted norms of professional conduct, we discern no failure to adhere to reasonable professional standards that would in any sense make out a deprivation of the Sixth Amendment right to counsel. Whether Robinson's conduct is seen as a successful attempt to dissuade his client from committing the crime of perjury, or whether seen as a "threat" to withdraw from representation and disclose the illegal scheme, Robinson's representation of Whiteside falls well within accepted standards of professional conduct and the range of reasonable professional conduct acceptable under *Strickland*.

The Court of Appeals' holding that Robinson's "action deprived [Whiteside] of due process and effective assistance of counsel" is not supported by the record since Robinson's action, at most, deprived Whiteside of his contemplated perjury. Nothing counsel did in any way undermined Whiteside's claim that he believed the victim was reaching for a gun. Similarly, the record gives no support for holding that Robinson's action "also impermissibly compromised [Whiteside's] right to testify in his own defense by conditioning continued representation . . . and confidentiality upon [Whiteside's] *restricted* testimony." The record in fact shows the contrary: (a) that Whiteside did testify, and (b) he was "restricted" or restrained only from testifying falsely and was aided by Robinson in developing the basis for the fear that Love was reaching for a gun. Robinson divulged no client communications until he was compelled to do so in response to Whiteside's post-trial challenge to the quality of his performance. We see this as a case in which the attorney successfully dissuaded the client from committing the crime of perjury.

Whatever the scope of a constitutional right to testify, it is elementary that such a right does not extend to testifying *falsely*. In *Harris v. New York*, we assumed the right of an accused to testify "in his own defense, or to refuse to do so" and went on to hold

---

[6] In the evolution of the contemporary standards promulgated by the American Bar Association, an early draft reflects a compromise suggesting that when the disclosure of intended perjury is made during the course of trial, when withdrawal of counsel would raise difficult questions of a mistrial holding, counsel had the option to let the defendant take the stand but decline to affirmatively assist the presentation of perjury by traditional direct examination. Instead, counsel would stand mute while the defendant undertook to present the false version in narrative form in his own words unaided by any direct examination. This conduct was thought to be a signal at least to the presiding judge that the attorney considered the testimony to be false and was seeking to disassociate himself from that course. Additionally, counsel would not be permitted to discuss the known false testimony in closing arguments. See ABA Standards for Criminal Justice, 4-7.7 (2d ed. 1980). Most courts treating the subject rejected this approach and insisted on a more rigorous standard. The Eighth Circuit in this case and the Ninth Circuit have expressed approval of the "free narrative" standards. *Whiteside v. Scurr*, 744 F.2d 1323, 1331 (CA8 1984); *Lowery v. Cardwell*, 575 F.2d 727 (CA9 1978).

The Rule finally promulgated in the current Model Rules of Professional Conduct rejects any participation or passive role what[so]ever by counsel in allowing perjury to be presented without challenge.

> that privilege cannot be construed to include the right to commit perjury. Having voluntarily taken the stand, petitioner was under an obligation to speak truthfully.

Harris and other cases make it crystal clear that there is no right whatever — constitutional or otherwise — for a defendant to use false evidence.

The paucity of authority on the subject of any such "right" may be explained by the fact that such a notion has never been responsibly advanced; the right to counsel includes no right to have a lawyer who will cooperate with planned perjury. A lawyer who would so cooperate would be at risk of prosecution for suborning perjury, and disciplinary proceedings, including suspension or disbarment.

Robinson's admonitions to his client can in no sense be said to have forced respondent into an *impermissible* choice between his right to counsel and his right to testify as he proposed for there was no *permissible* choice to testify falsely. For defense counsel to take steps to persuade a criminal defendant to testify truthfully, or to withdraw, deprives the defendant of neither his right to counsel nor the right to testify truthfully. In *United States v. Havens* [1980], we made clear that "when defendants testify, they must testify truthfully or suffer the consequences." When an accused proposes to resort to perjury or to produce false evidence, one consequence is the risk of withdrawal of counsel.

On this record, the accused enjoyed continued representation within the bounds of reasonable professional conduct and did in fact exercise his right to testify; at most he was denied the right to have the assistance of counsel in the presentation of false testimony. Similarly, we can discern no breach of professional duty in Robinson's admonition to respondent that he would disclose respondent's perjury to the court. The crime of perjury in this setting is indistinguishable in substance from the crime of threatening or tampering with a witness or a juror. A defendant who informed his counsel that he was arranging to bribe or threaten witnesses or members of the jury would have no "right" to insist on counsel's assistance or silence. Counsel would not be limited to advising against that conduct. An attorney's duty of confidentiality, which totally covers the client's admission of guilt, does not extend to a client's announced plans to engage in future criminal conduct. In short, the responsibility of an ethical lawyer, as an officer of the court and a key component of a system of justice, dedicate d to a search for truth, is essentially the same whether the client announces an intention to bribe or threaten witnesses or jurors or to commit or procure perjury. No system of justice worthy of the name can tolerate a lesser standard.

The rule adopted by the Court of Appeals, which seemingly would require an attorney to remain silent while his client committed perjury, is wholly incompatible with the established standards of ethical conduct and the laws of Iowa and contrary to professional standards promulgated by that State. The position advocated by petitioner, on the contrary, is wholly consistent with the Iowa standards of professional conduct and law, with the overwhelming majority of courts, and with codes of professional ethics. Since there has been no breach of any recognized professional duty, it follows that there can be no deprivation of the right to assistance of counsel under the *Strickland* standard.

E

We hold that, as a matter of law, counsel's conduct complained of here cannot establish the prejudice required for relief under the second strand of the *Strickland* inquiry. Although a defendant need not establish that the attorney's deficient performance more likely than not altered the outcome in order to establish prejudice under *Strickland*, a defendant must show "that there is a reasonable probability that, but for counsel's unprofessional errors, the result of the proceeding would have been different." According to *Strickland*, "[a] reasonable probability is a probability sufficient to undermine confidence in the outcome." The *Strickland* Court noted that the "benchmark" of an ineffective assistance claim is the fairness of the adversary proceeding, and that in judging prejudice and the likelihood of a different outcome, "[a] defendant has no entitlement to the luck of a lawless decisionmaker."

Whether he was persuaded or compelled to desist from perjury, Whiteside has no valid claim that confidence in the result of his trial has been diminished by his desisting from the contemplated perjury. Even if we were to assume that the jury might have believed his perjury, it does not follow that Whiteside was prejudiced.

In his attempt to evade the prejudice requirement of *Strickland*, Whiteside relies on cases involving conflicting loyalties of counsel. In *Cuyler v. Sullivan*, 446 U.S. 335 (1980), we held that a defendant could obtain relief without pointing to a specific prejudicial default on the part of his counsel, provided it is established that the attorney was "actively represent[ing] conflicting interests."

Here, there was indeed a "conflict," but of a quite different kind; it was one imposed on the attorney by the client's proposal to commit the crime of fabricating testimony without which, as he put it, "I'm dead." This is not remotely the kind of conflict of interests dealt with in *Cuyler v. Sullivan*. Even in that case we did not suggest that all multiple representations necessarily resulted in an active conflict rendering the representation constitutionally infirm[ed]. If a "conflict" between a client's proposal and counsel's ethical obligation gives rise to a presumption that counsel's assistance was prejudicially ineffective, every guilty criminal's conviction would be suspect if the defendant had sought to obtain an acquittal by illegal means. Can anyone doubt what practices and problems would be spawned by such a rule and what volumes of litigation it would generate?

Whiteside's attorney treated Whiteside's proposed perjury in accord with professional standards, and since Whiteside's truthful testimony could not have prejudiced the result of his trial, the Court of Appeals was in error to direct the issuance of a writ of habeas corpus and must be reversed.

AUTHORS' COMMENT:

Would you join Chief Justice Burger's opinion, or would you concur or dissent? Before you read the three concurring opinions, ask yourself two questions: (1) Do you agree with the majority opinion's *result*? and (2) Do you agree with the *grounds* for reaching the majority's result?

JUSTICE BRENNAN, concurring in the judgment.

This Court has no constitutional authority to establish rules of ethical conduct for lawyers practicing in the state courts. Nor does the Court enjoy any statutory grant of jurisdiction over legal ethics.

Accordingly, it is not surprising that the Court emphasizes that it "must be careful not to narrow the wide range of professional conduct acceptable under the Sixth Amendment so restrictively as to constitutionalize particular standards of professional conduct and thereby intrude into the State's proper authority to define and apply the standards of professional conduct applicable to those it admits to practice in its courts." I read this as saying in another way that the Court *cannot* tell the states or the lawyers in the states how to behave in their courts, unless and until federal rights are violated.

Unfortunately, the Court seems unable to resist the temptation of sharing with the legal community its vision of ethical conduct. But let there be no mistake: the Court's essay regarding what constitutes the correct response to a criminal client's suggestion that he will perjure himself is pure discourse without force of law. As Justice Blackmun observes, *that* issue is a thorny one, but it is not an issue presented by this case. Lawyers, judges, bar associations, students and others should understand that the problem has not now been "decided."

I join Justice Blackmun's concurrence because I agree that respondent has failed to prove the kind of prejudice necessary to make out a claim under *Strickland v. Washington*, 466 U.S. 668 (1984).

JUSTICE BLACKMUN, with whom JUSTICE BRENNAN, JUSTICE MARSHALL, and JUSTICE STEVENS join, concurring in the judgment.

How a defense attorney ought to act when faced with a client who intends to commit perjury at trial has long been a controversial issue. But I do not believe that a federal habeas corpus case challenging a state criminal conviction is an appropriate vehicle for attempting to resolve this thorny problem. When a defendant argues that he was denied effective assistance of counsel because his lawyer dissuaded him from committing perjury, the only question properly presented to this Court is whether the lawyer's actions deprived the defendant of the fair trial which the Sixth Amendment is meant to guarantee. Since I believe that the respondent in this case suffered no injury justifying federal habeas relief, I concur in the Court's judgment.

This Court long ago noted: "All perjured relevant testimony is at war with justice, since it may produce a judgment not resting on truth. Therefore it cannot be denied that it tends to defeat the sole ultimate objective of a trial." *In re Michael*, 326 U.S. 224, 227 (1945). When the Court has been faced with a claim by a defendant concerning prosecutorial use of such evidence, it has "consistently held that a conviction obtained by the knowing use of perjured testimony is fundamentally unfair, and must be set aside if there is any reasonable likelihood that the false testimony could have affected the judgment of the jury" (footnote omitted). *United States v. Agurs*, 427 U.S. 97 (1976). Similarly, the Court has viewed a defendant's use of such testimony as so antithetical to our system of justice that it has permitted the prosecution to introduce otherwise inadmissible evidence to combat it. The proposition that presenting false evidence could contribute to (or that withholding such evidence could detract from) the reliability of a criminal trial is simply untenable.

It is no doubt true that juries sometimes have acquitted defendants who should have been convicted, and sometimes have based their decisions to acquit on the testimony of defendants who lied on the witness stand. It is also true that the Double Jeopardy Clause bars the reprosecution of such acquitted defendants, although on occasion they can be prosecuted for perjury. But the privilege every criminal defendant has to testify in his own defense "cannot be construed to include the right to commit perjury." *Harris v. New York*, 401 U.S., at 225.[5]

To the extent that Whiteside's claim rests on the assertion that he would have been acquitted had he been able to testify falsely, Whiteside claims a right the law simply does not recognize. "A defendant has no entitlement to the luck of a lawless decisionmaker, even if a lawless decision cannot be reviewed." *Strickland v. Washington*, 466 U.S., at 695. Since Whiteside was deprived of neither a fair trial nor any of the specific constitutional rights designed to guarantee a fair trial, he has suffered no prejudice.

[5] Whiteside was not deprived of the right to testify in his own defense, since no suggestion has been made that Whiteside's testimony was restricted in any way beyond the fact that he did not claim, falsely, to have seen a gun in Love's hand.

> **AUTHORS' COMMENT:**
>
> **You may have assumed that Whiteside would have been better off if his lawyer had allowed him to testify that he actually saw a gun. But Whiteside would have been better off only if the jury had believed the false testimony and found Whiteside not guilty. If the jury did *not* believe the false testimony, Whiteside might have ended up with worse problems than a conviction for second degree murder. Justice Blackmun now talks about those problems.**

[T]he lawyer's interest in not presenting perjured testimony was entirely consistent with Whiteside's best interest. If Whiteside had lied on the stand, he would have risked a future perjury prosecution. Moreover, his testimony would have been contradicted by the testimony of other eyewitnesses and by the fact that no gun was ever found. In light of that impeachment, the jury might have concluded that Whiteside lied as well about his lack of premeditation and thus might have convicted him of first-degree murder. And if the judge believed that Whiteside had lied, he could have taken Whiteside's perjury into account in setting the sentence.[6]

In the face of these dangers, an attorney could reasonably conclude that dissuading his client from committing perjury was in the client's best interest and comported with standards of professional responsibility.[7]

In short, Whiteside failed to show the kind of conflict that poses a danger to the values of zealous and loyal representation embodied in the Sixth Amendment. A presumption of prejudice is therefore unwarranted.

C

In light of respondent's failure to show any cognizable prejudice, I see no need to "grade counsel's performance." The only federal issue in this case is whether Robinson's behavior deprived Whiteside of the effective assistance of counsel; it is not whether Robinson's behavior conformed to any particular code of legal ethics.

Whether an attorney's response to what he sees as a client's plan to commit perjury violates a defendant's Sixth Amendment rights may depend on many factors: how certain the attorney is that the proposed testimony is false, the stage of the proceedings at which the attorney discovers the plan, or the ways in which the attorney may be able to dissuade his client, to name just three. The complex interaction of factors, which is likely to vary from case to case, makes inappropriate a blanket rule that defense attorneys must reveal, or threaten to reveal, a client's anticipated perjury to the court. Except in the rarest of cases, attorneys who adopt "the role of the judge or jury to determine the facts," *United States ex rel. Wilcox v. Johnson*, 555 F.2d 115, 122 (CA3 1977), pose a danger of depriving their clients of the zealous and loyal advocacy required by the Sixth Amendment.[8]

---

[6] In fact, the State apparently asked the trial court to impose a sentence of 75 years, but the judge sentenced Whiteside to 40 years' imprisonment instead.

[7] This is not to say that an attorney's ethical obligations will never conflict with a defendant's right to effective assistance. For example, an attorney who has previously represented one of the State's witnesses has a continuing obligation to that former client not to reveal confidential information received during the course of the prior representation. That continuing duty could conflict with his obligation to his present client, the defendant, to cross-examine the State's witnesses zealously.

[8] A comparison of this case with *Wilcox* is illustrative. Here, Robinson testified in detail to the factors that

I therefore am troubled by the Court's implicit adoption of a set of standards of professional responsibility for attorneys in state criminal proceedings. The States, of course, do have a compelling interest in the integrity of their criminal trials that can justify regulating the length to which an attorney may go in seeking his client's acquittal. But the American Bar Association's implicit suggestion in its brief *amicus curiae* that the Court find that the Association's Model Rules of Professional Conduct should govern an attorney's responsibilities is addressed to the wrong audience. It is for the States to decide how attorneys should conduct themselves in state criminal proceedings, and this Court's responsibility extends only to ensuring that the restrictions a State enacts do not infringe a defendant's federal constitutional rights. Thus, I would follow the suggestion made in the joint brief *amici curiae* filed by 37 States at the certiorari stage that we allow the States to maintain their "differing approaches" to a complex ethical question. The signal merit of asking first whether a defendant has shown any adverse prejudicial effect before inquiring into his attorney's performance is that it avoids unnecessary federal interference in a State's regulation of its bar. Because I conclude that the respondent in this case failed to show such an effect, I join the Court's judgment that he is not entitled to federal habeas relief.

JUSTICE STEVENS, concurring in the judgment.

Justice Holmes taught us that a word is but the skin of a living thought. A "fact" may also have a life of its own. From the perspective of an appellate judge, after a case has been tried and all the evidence has been sifted by another judge, a particular fact may be as clear and certain as a piece of crystal or a small diamond. A trial lawyer, however, must often deal with mixtures of sand and clay. Even a pebble that seems clear enough at first glance may take on a different hue in a handful of gravel.

As we view this case, it appears perfectly clear that respondent intended to commit perjury, that his lawyer knew it, and that the lawyer had a duty — both to the court and to his client, for perjurious testimony can ruin an otherwise meritorious case — to take extreme measures to prevent the perjury from occurring. The lawyer was successful and, from our unanimous and remote perspective, it is now pellucidly clear that the client suffered no "legally cognizable prejudice."

AUTHORS' COMMENT:

Concurring opinions are often most useful for understanding the limits of the majority opinion — for understanding what the case did *not* decide. The following paragraph is a classic example of this kind of concurrence, and is very helpful for understanding what *Nix v. Whiteside* left open for another day.

Nevertheless, beneath the surface of this case there are areas of uncertainty that cannot be resolved today. A lawyer's certainty that a change in his client's recollection is a harbinger of intended perjury — as well as judicial review of such certainty —

led him to conclude that respondent's assertion he had seen a gun was false. The Iowa Supreme Court found "good cause" and "strong support" for Robinson's conclusion. Moreover, Robinson gave credence to those parts of Whiteside's account which, although he found them implausible and unsubstantiated, were not clearly false. By contrast, in *Wilcox*, where defense counsel actually informed the judge that she believed her client intended to lie and where her threat to withdraw in the middle of the trial led the defendant not to take the stand at all, the Court of Appeals found "no evidence on the record of this case indicating that Mr. Wilcox intended to perjure himself," and characterized counsel's beliefs as "private conjectures about the guilt or innocence of [her] client."

should be tempered by the realization that, after reflection, the most honest witness may recall (or sincerely believe he recalls) details that he previously overlooked. Similarly, the post-trial review of a lawyer's pre-trial threat to expose perjury that had not yet been committed — and, indeed, may have been prevented by the threat — is by no means the same as review of the way in which such a threat may actually have been carried out. Thus, one can be convinced — as I am — that this lawyer's actions were a proper way to provide his client with effective representation without confronting the much more difficult questions of what a lawyer must, should, or may do after his client has given testimony that the lawyer does not believe. The answer to such questions may well be colored by the particular circumstances attending the actual event and its aftermath.

Because Justice Blackmun has preserved such questions for another day, and because I do not understand him to imply any adverse criticism of this lawyer's representation of his client, I join his opinion concurring in the judgment.

NOTES AND QUESTIONS

1. ***Which Opinion Would You Join?*** Would you join Chief Justice Burger's majority in *Nix*? Or would you sign on to one of the concurring opinions? Which one? Or would you concur on other grounds, or write your own dissent?

2. ***Isn't it the Jury's Job to Detect Perjury?*** Before we explore the rules regarding client perjury in detail, let's step back and address a fundamental question: Why *should* the lawyer keep the client or other witness from taking the witness stand when the lawyer believes or knows that the testimony will be false? Isn't the theory of the adversary system that each side presents its version of the story, and the jury (or the judge, in a bench trial) figures out who is lying and who is telling the truth? Isn't determining credibility ordinarily the jury's job, not the lawyer's job? If the jury is supposed to figure out who is lying, why should the rules prohibit a lawyer from putting a liar on the stand? We do not want lawyers advising or encouraging their clients to lie, of course, but if a client or other witness insists on testifying and wants to take a chance on lying, why should the lawyer have to be a policeman?

In the case of a witness who is not a client, the answer to this question is pretty simple. A lawyer does not owe a duty of loyalty to a witness who is not a client. But trials would quickly spin out of control if a lawyer could put on testimony considered helpful to a client without regard for whether the testimony was true or false. If parties could ethically put on false testimony, why not let lawyers hire actors and actresses to present whatever testimony would persuade the jury? Juries are pretty good lie detectors, but they are far from perfect, and a jury's mistake is hard to remedy because the Double Jeopardy Clause prevents the government from putting a person on trial for a second time if the person was acquitted at the first trial. Therefore, the rules quite sensibly prohibit a lawyer from calling a witness to the stand if the lawyer knows the witness will commit perjury.

However, in the case of a client, the answer is more complex. We should begin by distinguishing between civil matters and criminal matters. Neither plaintiffs nor defendants in civil cases have a constitutional right to testify, so an attorney who refuses to put a client on the witness stand in a civil case is not depriving the client of any constitutional right. Criminal defendants are different. In *Rock v. Arkansas*, 483 U.S. 44 (1987), the Supreme Court held that criminal defendants have a constitutional right (based on the Due Process Clause, the Fifth Amendment, and the Sixth Amendment) to testify in their own defense. If a lawyer mistakenly prevents a criminal defendant from testifying truthfully (because the lawyer is sure that the client is lying), then the lawyer is depriving the client of a sacred constitutional right. In that light, should a criminal defendant's constitutional right to testify outweigh the lawyer's obligation not to present false testimony? That is a difficult question, and one that we will continue to address.

3. *Levels of Certainty.* When analyzing a question about possible perjury, a key element in determining your options and obligations is your level of certainty. Rule 3.3 talks about two levels of certainty: (A) "knows" and (B) "reasonably believes." By implication, anything less than a reasonable belief forms a third category, which we can informally call (C) a "suspicion," "hunch," or "guess." (The rules do not give a name to this third category.) We will now explain how these three levels of certainty play a crucial role in determining your choices under Rule 3.3.

4. *How does Rule 3.3 Work Before the Testimony Has Been Offered?* Since *Nix v. Whiteside* was written in 1986, many states have amended their versions of Rule 3.3. We reprint the relevant portions of South Carolina Rule 3.3 below, clause by clause, with our commentary. (South Carolina has adopted ABA Model Rule 3.3 verbatim.) Does Rule 3.3 answer the questions posed in *Nix*? Does it agree with the results in *Nix*? Do you like Rule 3.3, or would you change it?

South Carolina Rule 3.3 Candor to the Tribunal

> (a) A lawyer shall not knowingly: . . .
>
> (3) offer evidence that the lawyer knows to be false. . . .

Thus, if a lawyer like Gary Robinson "knows" that his client or any other witness intends to testify falsely, the lawyer either must not put the witness on the stand, or must not ask questions that would elicit false answers. What does "knows" mean? The definition in South Carolina Rule 1.0 says:

> "Knowingly," known," or "knows" denotes actual knowledge of the fact in question. A person's knowledge may be inferred from the circumstances.[1]

Hmmm. That's a bit circular — "knows" means "actual knowledge" — but it is the only definition in the rules, and the Comment to the Terminology section does not discuss the definition of "knows." We think a more useful working definition is "beyond a reasonable doubt." If you have no reasonable doubts about a given fact, then you "know" that fact to be true.

Comment 8 to South Carolina Rule 3.3 sums up the mandate of Rule 3.3 this way:

> "The prohibition against offering false evidence only applies if the lawyer knows that the evidence is false. A lawyer's reasonable belief that evidence is false does not preclude its presentation to the trier of fact. A lawyer's knowledge that evidence is false, however, can be inferred from the circumstances. See Rule 1.0(g). Thus, although a lawyer should resolve doubts about the veracity of testimony or other evidence in favor of the client, the lawyer cannot ignore an obvious falsehood.[2]

In other words, if it is "obvious" to you that the testimony of a client or other witness would be false, you must not offer that testimony. But if you have reasonable doubts, you do not "know" the testimony is false.

Rule 3.3(a)(3) also discusses what to do when you have more than a mere suspicion or hunch, but something less than actual knowledge, that your client or other witness will testify falsely. In this situation, South Carolina Rule 3.3(a)(3) provides as follows:

> A lawyer may refuse to offer evidence, *other than the testimony of a defendant in a criminal matter*, that the lawyer reasonably believes is false. [Emphasis added.]

The quoted sentence of S.C. Rule 3.3(a)(3) distinguishes between (A) criminal defendants, and (B) all other people. The distinction is based on the United States

---

[1] South Carolina's definition of these terms is identical to the ABA definition, but the ABA definition is found in Rule 1.0(f) whereas South Carolina defines these terms in Rule 1.0(g).

[2] South Carolina's Comment 8 is identical to Comment 8 to ABA Model Rule 3.3, except that South Carolina refers to the definition in Rule 1.0(g) whereas the ABA refers to Rule 1.0(f), which is identical.

Constitution. As mentioned above, criminal defendants have a constitutional right to testify in their own defense, but clients in civil cases do not have a right to testify, and witnesses have no right to testify in civil or criminal cases. Thus, when we combine Rule 1.2(a) and Rule 3.3(a)(3), here is how things work:

- If a lawyer "knows" that a criminal defendant will testify falsely, the lawyer *must not* put on that evidence.
- If a lawyer "reasonably believes" that a criminal defendant will testify falsely (but the lawyer does not know), then the lawyer *must* put the client on the witness stand if the client, pursuant to Rule 1.2(a), makes the decision to testify.
- In a civil matter, if a lawyer "reasonably believes" that a client or any other witness will testify falsely, then the lawyer has discretion whether or not to call the person to the stand. In other words, a lawyer may ethically offer the testimony of a client or witness even though the lawyer has a reasonable basis for doubting the truth of the testimony. But in that situation the lawyer also has power to keep the witness off the stand and refuse to offer the testimony. However, Rule 1.2(a) requires a lawyer to "consult with the client" regarding the "means" by which the lawyer plans to achieve the "objectives" set by the client.
- If a lawyer in a civil matter merely suspects that a client or witness will testify falsely, then pursuant to Rule 1.2(a) the lawyer must consult with the client about whether to call the client or witness to testify, but again, the lawyer makes the final choice. As a technical matter, therefore, there is no difference between (A) a witness (including a client) who is telling the truth and (B) a witness the lawyer reasonably believes is lying. In either situation, the lawyer should consult with the client about whether to call the particular witness. Usually, a witness who is telling the truth will help the client's case, but a witness who is likely to lie may seriously harm the client's case.

To summarize, a criminal defendant always has the right to testify unless the lawyer knows that the testimony will be false. However, everyone else in the world (whether the client or merely a non-client witness) must defer to the lawyer's judgment regarding whether to call the witness to the stand at trial, unless the lawyer knows the witness will lie, in which case the lawyer must not call the witness.

Applying the "reasonably believes" clause of Rule 3.3(a)(3) to *Nix v. Whiteside*, Gary Robinson was required to put Whiteside on the stand (if Whiteside chose to testify) unless Robinson knew that Whiteside's plan to say "I saw a gun" was false. In other words, Robinson could ethically have allowed Whiteside to testify if he "reasonably believed" Whiteside would lie, but not if he knew he would lie. Allowing Whiteside to testify even though Robinson reasonably believed his testimony would be false is consistent with Rule 1.2(a), which provides that in a criminal case, a lawyer "shall abide by" the client's decision whether to testify. At the same time, prohibiting Whiteside from testifying if Robinson knew his testimony would be false is consistent with Rule 3.3(a)(3), which mandates that a lawyer shall not "offer evidence that the lawyer knows to be false."

5. ***How does Rule 3.3 Work After Testimony Has Been Offered?*** The prior note discussed how Rule 3.3(a)(3) works *before* a lawyer has offered testimony, which was essentially the situation addressed in *Nix v. Whiteside*. Justice Stevens noted in his concurring opinion in *Nix*, however, that the Court did not decide "the much more difficult questions of what a lawyer must, should, or may do *after* his client has given testimony that the lawyer does not believe." How does Rule 3.3(a)(3) work after the testimony has been offered?

Let's make this question more specific by imagining what could have happened in *Nix v. Whiteside*. Suppose that Whiteside, when cautioned by Robinson, had agreed to testify truthfully (*e.g.*, he promised to say, "I *thought* he had a gun but I didn't actually see one"). But suppose that when Whiteside got on the witness stand, he surprised Gary

Robinson by testifying falsely ("I saw a gun in Love's hand"). What then? That difficult problem is covered by the second sentence of South Carolina Rule 3.3(a)(3), which provides as follows:

> If a lawyer, the lawyer's client, or a witness called by the lawyer, has offered material evidence and the lawyer comes to know of its falsity, the lawyer shall take reasonable remedial measures, including, if necessary, disclosure to the tribunal. . . .[3]

Thus, the lawyer must take "reasonable remedial measures." We discuss some possible remedial measures below. If no other remedial measure will work, then the lawyer must disclose the perjury to the tribunal.

Rule 3.3(a)(3) thus would have required Robinson to take "reasonable remedial measures" to rectify the perjury, "including, if necessary, disclosure to the tribunal." But what about a lawyer's solemn duty of confidentiality under Rule 1.6? Do any of the exceptions in Rule 1.6 apply? As a quick review and as a way of locating authority to disclose a client's past perjury, we now review all the exceptions to the duty of confidentiality in Rule 1.6.

Starting with the two exceptions in Rule 1.6(a) — implied authority and client consent — certainly a lawyer would not be "impliedly authorized" to disclose Whiteside's perjury. A lawyer is impliedly authorized to disclose confidential information only when the disclosure would advance the client's interests, but disclosure here would torpedo Whiteside's case. We can also assume that Whiteside would not consent to disclosure of his perjury. (If he did consent, that would solve the problem — but if he were willing to consent to disclose that he lied, why did he lie in the first place?)

Moving to the exceptions in Rule 1.6(b), disclosure of past perjury would not fall within Rule 1.6(b)(1), which permits disclosure of confidential information only to prevent "reasonably certain death or substantial bodily harm."

Slightly more promising are Rules 1.6(b)(2) and (3). The South Carolina equivalents, Rules 1.6(b)(3) and (4), which use the ABA's language verbatim, provide as follows:

> (b) A lawyer may reveal information relating to the representation of a client to the extent the lawyer reasonably believes necessary: . . .
>
> (3) to *prevent* the client from committing a crime or fraud that is reasonably certain to result in substantial injury to the financial interests or property of another and in furtherance of which the client has used or is using the lawyer's services;
>
> (4) to *prevent, mitigate or rectify* substantial injury to the financial interests or property of another that is reasonably certain to result or has resulted from the client's commission of a crime or fraud in furtherance of which the client has used the lawyer's services; . . . [Emphasis added.]

If Whiteside went on trial today in South Carolina, would Rule 1.6(b)(2) or (3) permit Gary Robinson to disclose Whiteside's intention to commit perjury? Perjury is a "crime or fraud," and Whiteside "has used or is using the lawyer's services" to commit the crime or fraud (because only the lawyer can call a witness to the stand, unless the client fires the lawyer and proceeds pro se, which Whiteside did not do). But in a criminal case the perjury is not going to injure the "financial or property interests of another," so neither Rule 1.6(b)(2) nor Rule 1.6(b)(3) would permit disclosure of past perjury in a criminal case. Moreover, the perjury is already completed, so Rule 1.6(b)(2) is inapplicable — it applies only to "prevent" a client's crime, not to remedy a past crime. Rule 1.6(b)(3) might permit disclosure to "prevent, mitigate, or rectify" substantial financial harm from completed perjury in a *civil* case for damages (or even for injunctive relief), but that is not our scenario.

---

[3] The identical language appears in ABA Model Rule 3.3(a)(3).

The exception in Rule 1.6(b)(4), which permits disclosure "to secure legal advice about compliance with these rules," might seem promising at first blush, but that provision refers to obtaining legal advice from another lawyer, not from a judge. Judges provide legal rulings, not legal advice.

The exception in Rule 1.6(b)(5), which permits a lawyer to disclose confidential information in self-defense or to collect a fee, plainly does not apply here.

That leaves the exception in Rule 1.6(b)(6), which permits a lawyer to disclose confidential information to "comply with other law or a court order." This exception also does not apply to the client perjury situation. No substantive law requires a lawyer to disclose the fact that a client or other witness has committed perjury, and the court has not issued an order compelling disclosure because the court does not know you have anything to disclose.

In sum, no exception to Rule 1.6 would authorize disclosure of the confidential information that the client (or any other witness) has committed perjury during the litigation.

6. ***Rule 3.3(a)(3) and Rule 3.3(c) Trump Rule 1.6.*** No exception to Rule 1.6 applies, but no exception is needed because the plain language of Rule 3.3(a)(3) mandates the disclosure of past perjury if nothing else will remedy the problem. This plain reading of Rule 3.3(a)(3) is explicitly reinforced by South Carolina Rule 3.3(c), which states:

> (c) The duties stated in paragraphs (a) and (b) continue to the conclusion of the proceeding and apply even if compliance requires disclosure of information otherwise protected by Rule 1.6.[4]

Thus, we do not need an exception to Rule 1.6 to disclose past perjury, because Rules 3.3(a)(3) and (c) expressly trump the duty of confidentiality under Rule 1.6. The policy against perjured testimony and other false evidence is so strong that a lawyer not only may but *must* disclose the falsity to the court if no other action will remedy the problem. Indeed, Rule 3.3 is the *only* rule in the ABA Model Rules of Professional Conduct that expressly overrides the duty of confidentiality under Rule 1.6. (In some states, other rules also override the duty of confidentiality, but in the ABA Model Rules, only Rule 3.3 does so.)

In sum, without Rule 3.3(a)(3) and Rule 3.3(c), the duty of confidentiality would prohibit a lawyer from disclosing the fact that a client committed perjury or intended to commit perjury in a criminal case. With the combination of Rule 3.3(a)(3) and Rule 3.3(c), a lawyer is commanded to disclose a client's past perjury. The lawyer has no discretion. If no other remedial measures will cure the perjury, it will be "necessary" for the lawyer to disclose the perjury to the tribunal despite Rule 1.6.

7. ***Test Yourself.*** Here's a scenario that will help you test your knowledge of Rule 3.3. Suppose you represent a criminal defendant, Henry Bellwood, who is deciding, pursuant to Rule 1.2(a), whether to testify. You reasonably believe Bellwood's testimony will be false, but you are not sure. Under ABA Model Rule 1.4(a)(2), you are required to "reasonably consult with the client regarding the means by which the client's objectives are to be accomplished." What will you discuss with Mr. Bellwood when you consult with him about whether or not to testify?

Keep in mind the language in Rule 3.3(a)(3) providing that a lawyer who "comes to know" after the testimony that his client has lied on the stand must "take reasonable remedial measures, including, if necessary, disclosure to the tribunal." In light of that requirement, and in light of the considerations explained by Justice Blackmun in his concurring opinion in *Nix*, what would you include in your consultation with your client? And if the client decides, after the consultation, that he wants to testify, must you honor his request?

---

[4] South Carolina Rule 3.3(c) is identical to ABA Model Rule 3.3(c).

8. ***Rule 3.3(b) and Fraud Related to a Proceeding.*** So far we have concentrated mainly on Rule 3.3(a)(3), which covers only false evidence. Rule 3.3(b) is considerably broader. South Carolina Rule 3.3(b) provides as follows:

> A lawyer who represents a client in an adjudicative proceeding and who knows that a person intends to engage, is engaging or has engaged in criminal or fraudulent conduct related to the proceeding shall take reasonable remedial measures, including, if necessary, disclosure to the tribunal.[5]

Like Rule 3.3(a)(3), therefore, Rule 3.3(b) covers past, present, and future misconduct. And note that if you represent *any* client in a trial (or any other "adjudicative proceeding"), Rule 3.3(b) is triggered if any "person" — not just a client — plans, perpetrates, or has perpetrated a crime or fraud related to the proceeding. What might that encompass? Jury tampering, witness intimidation, and bribing a court official are three good examples.

Is Rule 3.3(b) broad enough to reach Charles Whiteside's intended perjury? At first blush it appears that way. Perjury is a crime, and — as the District Court in *Nix v. Whiteside* expressly found — Whiteside intended to commit perjury. If *Nix v. Whiteside* occurred today, Rule 3.3(b) would require Gary Robinson to take "reasonable remedial measures" to prevent Whiteside from committing perjury. Would those remedial measures include disclosure to the court that Whiteside intends to commit perjury? Only "if necessary" — and disclosure will not be "necessary" if other remedial measures could solve the problem. What other remedial measures might be effective here? Let's explore some possible "remedial measures" that a lawyer might take to thwart intended perjury.

9. ***Keeping the Client Off the Stand.*** The first and most effective remedial measure short of disclosure would be to keep Whiteside off the witness stand. If he doesn't testify at all, he cannot testify falsely. But keeping the client off the witness stand is a fairly drastic measure. Yet courts universally prohibit an attorney from assisting in presenting perjury, so putting on a client that the lawyer *knows* will commit perjury is not an option. Initially, therefore, the lawyer should try to talk the client out of committing perjury, using every persuasive device available.

If persuasion does not work — and let's assume it does not — then at that point the lawyer who knows the client will testify falsely can refuse to call the client to the stand. (If the lawyer did not know the testimony would be false, the client would have the absolute right to take the witness stand.) Does the lawyer have the right to keep the client off the stand if the lawyer knows the client will lie? Yes, in most jurisdictions. In *United States v. Curtis*, 742 F.2d 1070 (CA7 1984), for example, the Seventh Circuit upheld an attorney's refusal to call the defendant as a witness where the attorney believed that the defendant would commit perjury. But the attorney must be sure. In *United States ex rel. Wilcox v. Johnson*, 555 F.2d 115 (3d Cir. 1977), for example, the Third Circuit found a violation of the Sixth Amendment where the attorney could not state any basis for her belief that defendant's proposed alibi testimony was perjured.

10. ***Ask Only Questions That Will Not Elicit False Testimony.*** A related remedial measure would be to put Whiteside on the witness stand but not ask him any questions that elicit false testimony. In *Nix v. Whiteside*, for example, Gary Robinson could have put Whiteside on the stand but not ask any questions about what led to the murder, or what he saw right before he stabbed Calvin Love. That would avoid the perjury — but as a practical matter it is a terrible idea. The jury is sure to notice that Whiteside is not explaining the most crucial part of the case, and will sense that something is terribly wrong. In our view, a jury is like a series of computers strung together — a very powerful device that hears and analyzes everything that happens in the courtroom (and

---

[5] South Carolina has adopted ABA Model Rule 3.3(b) verbatim.

everything the jury expected to happen but didn't). Putting a criminal defendant on the witness stand but skipping over the key parts of the story is likely to do more harm than good.

11. *Move to Withdraw.* A third remedial measure, in theory, would be for the lawyer to move to withdraw from representing Whiteside. But would that *remedy* the intended perjury, or just pass the buck? Withdrawal would not remedy the perjury, and hence would not be a "reasonable remedial measure." Why not? First of all, permission of the tribunal is universally required before a lawyer may withdraw in a criminal case, and if the trial is scheduled to be held soon, the judge will rarely allow counsel to withdraw unless substitute counsel is ready, willing, and able to take over the case without delay. That doesn't typically happen when the client is indigent and the lawyer is appointed or is working pro bono. Most lawyers are not eager to take cases that pay little or nothing. Second, and more important, even if the court allowed the withdrawal, that would just pass the perjury problem along to the next lawyer — but this time Whiteside will be more careful to tell his lawyer from the outset that he "saw a gun." That way, his new lawyer would never "know" that he intended to commit perjury. But of course the judge knows that the lawyer's reason for moving to withdraw is to avoid assisting client perjury, so the judge will probably deny the motion because the judge realizes that withdrawal will not remedy the problem — and may even make it worse.

If a lawyer wants to withdraw to avoid sponsoring a client's intended perjury, the lawyer is wise to file the motion to withdraw well before trial. Once trial is imminent or underway — especially if the defendant has already testified (or has begun to testify) — a court is less likely to grant a motion to withdraw, because post-perjury withdrawal doesn't remedy anything.

A leading case on the damage that can be done by a motion to withdraw is *Lowery v. Cardwell*, 575 F.2d 727 (9th Cir. 1978) (cited in notes 1 and 6 of the majority opinion in *Nix*). In *Lowery*, a non-jury trial, the defendant was charged with first degree murder. Before trial, the defendant told her lawyer that she had been with the victim when he became violent, and that she had shot the victim in self-defense. The lawyer assumed that she planned to testify that way at trial. But on direct examination, the accused surprised her lawyer by testifying (totally at odds with her pretrial story to the lawyer) that she had neither been with the victim nor shot him. Immediately following the defendant's direct examination, defense counsel requested permission to withdraw. The lawyer's reason for wanting to withdraw — not communicated to the trial judge — was his belief that the defendant had committed perjury. When the court denied the lawyer's request for withdrawal, the lawyer asked the defendant no further questions, and in the closing argument did not refer to defendant's testimony that she had not shot the deceased. The defendant was convicted, and she appealed.

The Court of Appeals in *Lowery* reversed the conviction. The court held that the request for withdrawal by its very nature had signaled the judge that the defendant was lying, thus depriving the defendant of a fair trial and due process of law. One member of the appellate panel wrote separately to say that the withdrawal request had also deprived the defendant of effective assistance of counsel.

Does *Nix v. Whiteside* militate a different result? If a situation similar to the one in *Lowery v. Cardwell* arises again now, after *Nix v. Whiteside*, may the attorney move to withdraw? If so, what may the lawyer tell the court about the reason for moving to withdraw?

12. *The Narrative Method.* Yet another possible remedial measure is called the "narrative method." Once the client is on the stand, a lawyer using the narrative method asks only questions that will elicit testimony the lawyer believes to be true (or at least does not know to be false). When the lawyer gets to the crucial moment (for example, the part where Whiteside would say, "I saw a gun!"), the lawyer ceases to ask direct questions and simply says to the client, "Tell the jury what else happened." The defendant's lawyer does not ask any more questions, but simply stands to the side and allows the defendant ramble on in a pure narrative. The prosecutor then cross-examines as usual.

No doubt the jury thinks this narrative method is weird. The jury has seen the defense lawyer interrupt all of the other defense witnesses with lots of questions, but the same lawyer has allowed the defendant to ramble on about the most dramatic part of the story while the defense lawyer stood mute and aloof. Something strange is going on.

And it gets stranger still, because under the narrative method the defense lawyer is not permitted to use the false testimony during closing argument. In *Nix v. Whiteside*, how would this have sounded to the jury? It is a murder case. The defense theory is self-defense. Suppose Whiteside had said during his narrative, where false testimony is allowed: "He reached under his pillow and pulled out a gun. I stabbed him to keep him from shooting me. I did it purely in self defense." But in closing argument, the defense attorney does not mention this powerful, crucial testimony. The defense lawyer says nothing about a gun at all. The jury will almost certainly conclude that the defense lawyer does not believe the defendant's testimony. And if the defendant's own lawyer doesn't believe him, why should the jury believe him?

The narrative method is nicely capsulated in District of Columbia Rule 3.3(b), which provides as follows:

> When the witness who intends to give evidence that the lawyer knows to be false is the lawyer's client and is the accused in a criminal case, the lawyer shall first make a good-faith effort to dissuade the client from presenting the false evidence; if the lawyer is unable to dissuade the client, the lawyer shall seek leave of the tribunal to withdraw. If the lawyer is unable to dissuade the client or to withdraw without seriously harming the client, *the lawyer may put the client on the stand to testify in a narrative fashion, but the lawyer shall not examine the client in such manner as to elicit testimony which the lawyer knows to be false, and shall not argue the probative value of the client's testimony in closing argument.* [Emphasis added.]

Thus, the narrative method is a remedial measure of last resort, and the heart of the method is that (A) the lawyer does not ask specific questions that will draw out known false testimony, but rather asks only general questions at that point (e.g., "Tell the jury the rest of your story"), and (B) the lawyer does not argue to the jury that the false testimony is true or proves the defendant's innocence. These methods are "remedial" only in the sense that they distance the lawyer from the perjured testimony and t hey signal the jury, by waving brightly colored flags, that the jury should be extremely cautious in assessing the defendant's testimony.

Despite the drawbacks of the narrative method from the defendant's point of view, D.C. and a number of other jurisdictions allow a lawyer to use the narrative method. (Some jurisdictions permit it only with court permission, which means that the judge — who will later impose the sentence if the defendant is convicted — also knows the defendant is lying.)

The narrative method is a compromise. It does not actually remedy the perjury, but instead remedies the lawyer's involvement in presenting the perjury, and it gives the defendant an opportunity to testify that the defendant would not have if the lawyer refused to put him on the stand at all. In other words, the narrative avoids depriving the defendant of his constitutional right to testify truthfully. (Does a defendant also have a constitutional right for his lawyer to act normal during the direct examination? No court has yet said so.)

Is the narrative method a good compromise? If you were a judge in a jurisdiction that had not yet decided whether to permit the narrative method and a criminal defense lawyer asked for the court's permission to present the defendant's testimony in narrative fashion, would you allow it, or not?

13. *Present the Perjured Testimony Normally?* No U.S. jurisdiction currently allows a lawyer to present perjured testimony in the normal fashion (as opposed to the narrative method). Thus, presenting false testimony as if it were true would not only violate the Rules of Professional Conduct but would also violate criminal laws against suborning perjury. Nevertheless, presenting false testimony in the normal fashion is a theoretical option, so we will discuss it here.

When an attorney and client first meet, the attorney typically promises the client strict confidentiality and urges the client to tell the attorney "everything" (or words to that effect) so that the attorney can anticipate all of the evidence and arguments the other side will make and can provide the best possible representation to the client. Some attorneys add a warning that the lawyer's duty of confidentiality does not cover a client's intent to commit perjury, and if the lawyer later learns that the client has committed perjury, the lawyer will be obligated to breach confidentiality and tell the court.

If an attorney does give that warning, the client is probably smart enough not to tell the attorney the truth, the whole truth, and nothing but the truth. Therefore, if the client at some point says (for example), "I saw a gun," the attorney will not "know" that the client is lying and will have to put the client on the witness stand if the client wishes to testify. The lawyer may express doubt about the client's story, and may caution the client that the jury may not believe him, but unless the lawyer has solid evidence from other sources that the client is lying — which the lawyer often lacks — the lawyer will end up putting perjured testimony on the witness stand out of ignorance.

Unfortunately, suggesting to your client that he might be willing to commit perjury is a rather bad start to the attorney-client relationship — kind of like saying to your fiancé as part of a marriage proposal, "If you break off the engagement, I get the dog and I get the ring back." After all, warning about the negative side effects of perjury essentially suggests that the client may be a liar. Accordingly, many (probably most) criminal defense attorneys do not warn their clients about the adverse consequences that may result if the lawyer finds out the client intends to lie or has lied under oath. If an attorney does not warn the client about the consequences of perjury when describing the ethical duty of confidentiality, then the client is more likely to be upfront and candid with the lawyer, so the lawyer is more likely to learn the whole truth from the client and to find out early on if the client intends to commit perjury. But having failed to warn the client about perjury, the lawyer cannot keep the client off the witness stand without surprising the client, and cannot reveal actual perjury to the court without breaking the solemn pledge of confidentiality.

This creates a dilemma — or what the legendary Professor Monroe Freedman has called a "trilemma." (I am indebted to Professor Freedman for the ideas in this note.) A lawyer is supposed to do three things: (a) keep strict confidentiality, (b) learn all of the facts, and (c) be completely candid with the court.

A lawyer cannot always abide by all three duties. Honoring one breaches another. The trilemma is especially acute when the lawyer knows that his client intends to lie on the stand. A lawyer could prevent the problem from arising (i.e., avoid gaining knowledge that the client intends to lie) by deliberately violating the duty to learn all of the facts, practicing what is often called "selective ignorance" — but that would make it more difficult for the lawyer to defend the client effectively. A lawyer could violate the duty of confidentiality — but that would betray the client and break a solemn promise. Or a lawyer could violate the duty to be candid with the court by refusing to tell the court that the client is committing perjury — but that would morally taint the lawyer and risk erroneous decisions by a judge or jury if they fell for the perjury. All three options are bad, but the lawyer cannot fulfill all three duties. So, which duty should give way — strict confidentiality, learning the facts, or candor to the court?

If the lawyer has an absolute duty of confidentiality and the client knows it, then the lawyer will find out about the perjury before trial and will be in a position to counsel the client about the dangers of perjury, perhaps talking the client out of lying. The lawyer will tell the client that the jury is unlikely to believe perjured testimony, the prosecutor is likely to rip the testimony to shreds on cross-examination, the judge who sniffs out perjury is likely to give a longer sentence, and even if the client fools the judge and jury, the prosecutor may still bring perjury charges. (The Double Jeopardy Clause doesn't protect a criminal defendant against charges of perjury for lying at the criminal trial.) After hearing this sound advice, most clients will appreciate the huge risks and will abandon their plans to commit perjury. But not all clients will abandon their intention to commit perjury. If the lawyer does everything in the lawyer's power to talk the client out of committing perjury and the client still insists on testifying, should the lawyer have the right to put the client on the witness stand and let the jury do its job of determining credibility?

Many lawyers react negatively to that suggestion. They insist that a lawyer should not be an accomplice to perjury, should not facilitate perjury, should not aid and abet perjury. That is all well and good. Everybody agrees with that. Perjury is bad. But if a client believes that a lawyer's duty of confidentiality is not absolute, and if the client believes that the lawyer will betray the client if the lawyer disbelieves the client's story, then the client will not level with the lawyer and the lawyer will become the unwitting tool of perjury.

Professor Freedman has argued for many years that an absolute duty of confidentiality — and a duty to honor the client's decision to testify even if the lawyer *knows* the client will testify falsely — will ultimately result in less perjury in the system, not more. It will result in less perjury because the client, relying on the pledge of absolute confidentiality, will tell the lawyer the truth, giving the lawyer an opportunity to talk the client out of it. Most clients will listen and will not commit perjury. In the end, this will result in fewer instances of perjury than under the present system (the Rule 3.3 system), where the client is not fully candid with the lawyer (or the lawyer never probes for all the facts), so the lawyer does not "know" the client will commit perjury and therefore does not try vigorously to talk the client out of it.

Is Professor Freedman right? If a lawyer has sincerely tried every persuasive tool to talk a client out of committing perjury but the client still insists on taking the stand, should the lawyer be permitted to put the client on the stand, examine the client normally, and argue the truth of the client's testimony to the jury, without signaling to the judge or jury that the client is lying? Will that system result in more perjury in the long run, or less?

Chapter 19

CANDOR AND DECEPTION IN OFFERING TESTIMONY

In this chapter we examine some variations on candor and deception, and take a deeper look at the problem of preventing client perjury without trampling on a criminal defendant's constitutional rights. We also explore the problem of perjury in civil cases.

A. MAY YOU ETHICALLY MAKE THE FALSE LOOK TRUE?

Can you ever use false or erroneous testimony to prove your case? Is *Nix* limited to perjury or does it extend to other truth-obstructing tactics, such as aggressively cross-examining witnesses you believe to be telling the truth, or failing to correct errors in the prosecution's case if those errors are helpful to your client? On these questions, consider the Michigan ethics opinion that follows, a classic in the field.

STATE BAR OF MICHIGAN, INFORMAL ETHICS OPINION CI-1164 (1987)

Client is charged with armed robbery. He proposes to call some friends as witnesses at trial who will give truthful testimony that he was with them at the time of the crime. At the preliminary examination the victim had testified that the robbery occurred at the same hour and time to which the friends will testify. Client has confided to attorney that he robbed the victim; his theory on the time mix-up is that he stole the victim's watch and rendered him unconscious so that the victim's sense of time was incorrect when relating the circumstances of the robbery to the investigating detectives. Months later, at the preliminary examination, the victim relied on the detectives' notes to help him recall the time. Client and attorney have decided that client will not testify at trial. Would it be ethical for attorney to subpoena the friends to trial to testify that the client was with them at the alleged time of the crime?

DR 7-101 requires counsel to represent the client zealously. A defense attorney can present any evidence that is truthful; if the ethical rule were otherwise, it would mean that a defendant who confessed guilt to his counsel would never be able to have an active defense at trial.

The danger of an opposite approach is that sometimes innocent defendants "confess guilt" to their counsel or put forth a perceived "truthful" set of facts that do not pass independent scrutiny. Many crimes have degrees of guilt, as in homicide, where the "true facts" go to the accused's intent; something a jailed defendant may not be in a reflective mood to assess. Criminal defense counsel are not sent to the jail's interview room to be their client's one person jury and they certainly are not dispatched to court to be their client's hangman. Our society has made the decision to permit a person charged with crime to make full disclosure to his counsel without fear that, absent the threat of some future conduct (such as a threat to kill a witness), the lawyer will not disclose the information so provided.

The role of criminal defense counsel is to zealously defend the client within the boundaries of all legal and ethical rules. Therefore, if the information confidentially disclosed by the client were to prevent counsel from marshaling an otherwise proper defense, the client would, in effect, be penalized for making the disclosure. Such a policy, over a longer run, would tend to cause future defendants to fail to disclose everything to their lawyer; the result would be that they would receive an inadequate defense. Such an approach would be fundamentally inconsistent with the implicit representation made to defendants as a part of procedural due process that they may disclose everything to their lawyer without fear of adverse consequence.

It is the prosecution's responsibility to marshal relevant and accurate testimony of criminal conduct. It is not the obligation of defense counsel to correct inaccurate evidence introduced by the prosecution or to ignore truthful evidence that could exculpate his client. Although the tenor of this opinion may appear to risk an unfortunate result to society in the particular situation posed, such an attitude by defense counsel will serve in the long run to preserve the system of criminal justice envisioned by our constitution.

[I]t is perfectly proper to call to the witness stand those witnesses on behalf of the client who will present truthful testimony. The testimony of the friends will not spread any perjured testimony upon the record. Client indeed was with the witnesses at the hour to which they will testify. The victim's mistake concerning the precise time of the crime results in this windfall defense to the client.

In CI-394 (1979) this Committee reviewed a situation where there were tire marks at the scene of the crime. Defendant, after being charged with the crime, altered the tire treads on his car. An expert witness, retained by the defense, was misled when he examined the evidence of the tire tracks. We there opined that the defense attorney could not ethically present evidence through an expert witness when his opinion was based upon a set of circumstances where the client tampered with the evidence. To do so would perpetrate a fraud upon the court. The situation with the friends as alibi witnesses in the instant case does not involve tampering with evidence. One cannot suborn the truth.

AUTHORS' COMMENT:

The opinion has given the green light to the defendant's proposed alibi defense. But as Justice Blackmun pointed out in his concurrence in *Nix v. Whiteside*, a lawyer should not automatically assume that every available defense is in the client's best interests. The opinion reminds us that the proposed alibi defense may carry substantial downside risk. A lawyer cannot just be a cheerleader for the client; the lawyer has to be an objective, candid advisor as well as warn the client about risks. Always keep that in mind. It is better for a client to hear bad news from you and good news from the jury than good news from you and bad news from the jury.

It should be mentioned that it is appropriate for the attorney to discuss these concerns with his client. The attorney must guard against the natural human reaction in a desperate situation (eyewitness testimony to crime with mandatory prison sentence) to become so enamored of an unique defense opportunity that, in contemplating the small tree, he fails to see the forest. It is the convicted client who does the time, not the attorney. An alibi defense in the instant case may be foolish; the attorney has a responsibility to counsel his client accordingly. Defendants in serious criminal cases usually are willing to grasp at straws if their lawyer, by word or deed, suggests there is a chance at acquittal using such evidence. It may be in the best interest of the client not to present the alibi defense and, instead, negotiate for a guilty plea to a lesser offense. That evidence could ethically be presented does not mean that it should be. Obviously if the complaining witness gives positive identification of his assailant and if there is other inculpatory evidence, a jury may give very short shrift to the testimony, however true, of defendant's friends.

In the glare of the ethical question, counsel should not be blinded to the difficulty of his client's cause. All the evidence should be weighed and evaluated before deciding to go forward with an alibi defense. This thoughtful consideration of the client and his situation is the mark of a lawyer with high standards of integrity, appropriate discretion, and absolute honesty.

NOTES AND QUESTIONS

1. ***Truthfulness.*** To what extent does the Michigan State Bar Opinion rest on the "truthfulness" of the alibi testimony rather than on the state's burden of proof in criminal cases? Would the result be different if the lawyer suspected (but didn't know for sure) that the alibi evidence was false? What options would the lawyer have if he or she "reasonably believed" (but still did not "know") that the alibi defense was false?

2. ***Can You Threaten to Withdraw?*** After *Nix v. Whiteside*, could counsel in a case like the Michigan case threaten to withdraw to prevent the defendant from testifying — truthfully — that he was with his friends at the time in question? (Assume that's all the defendant planned to say.) Read MRPC 1.16 with this question in mind. On what basis could the lawyer threaten to withdraw? Would that basis make the withdrawal mandatory or permissive?

3. ***Making the False Look True.*** In *On Making the True Look False and the False Look True*, 41 Sw. L.J. 1135, 1146 (1988), Professor Murray Schwartz applies *Nix v. Whiteside* to the facts in Michigan Opinion CI-1164. He says:

> The defendant's lawyer could not, in the robbery hypothetical, exploit the victim's mistake as to time by arguing that it showed the defendant did not commit the robbery at all, for that would be a knowing false statement by the lawyer. The lawyer could argue only that the testimony of the victim and the friends (known to the lawyer to be truthful) showed that the prosecution had failed to carry its burden of showing that the defendant had committed the robbery. In short, untrue testimony should not be exploited for its probative value; it should be used only to show that the prosecution has failed to meet its burden of proof.

Do you agree? If you were on the jury, would you notice that the lawyer never said his client did not commit the robbery, but only that the prosecutor hasn't proved it beyond a reasonable doubt?

B. WHEN (AND WHAT) CAN YOU TELL THE COURT?

In *Nix v. Whiteside*, the lawyer for Whiteside never actually revealed to the court that his client intended to commit perjury. The lawyer merely *threatened* to disclose the client's perjurious intentions to the court, and that apparently convinced the client to tell the truth. What if things had gone further? What if the defendant's lawyer in *Nix* had been about to put his client on the witness stand when he first learned of the client's intention?

If a lawyer suspects, believes, or knows that a client intends to testify falsely at trial, what (if anything) should the lawyer tell the court? How sure must the lawyer be that the client will commit perjury at trial? This is a two-part inquiry: (a) Is the client's proposed testimony false? and (b) Will the client actually give the false testimony at trial (as opposed to telling the truth)? The following opinion in *United States v. Long*, issued by the same circuit that was reversed in *Nix*, helps to answer these questions. Are the steps set out in *Long* workable in practice?

UNITED STATES v. LONG

857 F.2d 436 (8th Cir. 1988)

HEANEY, CIRCUIT JUDGE.

Thaddeus Adonis Long and Edward Larry Jackson appeal from their convictions on a number of counts for their involvement in a check forging and bank fraud scheme. [The scheme involved cashing a United States treasury check for $434,188.80, payable to Land O'Frost, an Illinois company. The check was sent to Land O'Frost but ended up in the hands of Long. Jackson conspired with Long in a cloak-and-dagger scheme to cash the check, after which Long bought a Porsche for $28,000. Jackson's sentence was fifteen years.]

D. Ineffective Assistance of Counsel

Jackson contends his trial counsel was ineffective. To prevail on an ineffective assistance of counsel claim, a defendant must show that his or her attorney's performance "fell below an objective standard of reasonableness," *Strickland v. Washington*, 466 U.S. 668, 687–88 (1984), and that, but for this ineffective assistance, there is a reasonable probability that the outcome of the trial would have been different.

Finally, Jackson claims his attorney abandoned his role as Jackson's advocate and coerced Jackson not to testify. He allegedly did this by suggesting to the trial judge, out of the presence of the jury, that his client might perjure himself. This, according to Jackson, violated his sixth amendment right to effective assistance of counsel and his fifth amendment right to testify.

In *Nix v. Whiteside*, 475 U.S. 157 (1986), the Supreme Court addressed the troubling question of how an attorney should respond upon learning a client will commit perjury upon taking the stand. In that case, Emmanuel Whiteside was convicted of the murder of Calvin Love. At trial, Whiteside had claimed he stabbed Love in self-defense.

On collateral attack of that conviction, Whiteside alleged that his right to counsel and to testify had been violated because, although he took the stand, his attorney had coerced him not to testify that he had seen a gun in Love's hand before stabbing him. The trial court found that Whiteside would have perjured himself if he testified that he had seen the gun. It held that, because Whiteside's rights to effective assistance of counsel and to testify did not include the right to testify falsely, those rights were not violated. This Court reversed.

The Supreme Court overruled this Court. It held that when a defendant "announces" an intention to commit perjury, the defendant's rights to effective assistance of counsel and to testify are not violated if the attorney takes certain clear steps to prevent the presentation of that false testimony. Those steps include attempting to dissuade the client from testifying falsely, threatening to report the possibility of perjury to the trial court, and possibly testifying against the defendant should he be prosecuted for perjury. As the Court observed, neither right was violated, because the right to testify, assuming there is one,[4] does not "extend to testifying falsely," and because "the right to counsel includes no right to have a lawyer who will cooperate with planned perjury."

In the instant case, Jackson's lawyer asked to approach the bench after the government had presented its case. The lawyer told the trial judge that Jackson wanted to testify and that he was concerned about his testimony. The lawyer said he advised Jackson not to take the stand. The judge excused the jury and everyone else in the courtroom, except a United States Marshal, Jackson, and his lawyer. At that point, the lawyer said, "I'm not sure if it wouldn't be appropriate for me to move for a withdrawal from this case based upon what I think may be elicited on the stand. . . . I'm concerned about the testimony that may come out and I'm concerned about my obligation to the Court." The trial judge informed Jackson he had a right under the law to testify on his own behalf, which Jackson said he understood. The court also informed Jackson that his counsel was bound by his professional obligation not to place evidence before the court which he believed to be untrue. Jackson also said he understood this.

[4] The Supreme Court has since recognized explicitly the constitutional right to testify. *See Rock v. Arkansas*, 483 U.S. 44 (1987) (stating "it cannot be doubted that a defendant in a criminal case has the right to take the witness stand and to testify in his or her own defense").

The judge stated that Jackson could take the stand and give a narrative statement without questioning from his lawyer. The judge noted that if Jackson's attorney found "things which he believes to be not true . . . he may have other obligations at that point." The lawyer responded that he had again discussed the matter with Jackson and that Jackson had decided, on his own, not to testify. Upon questioning by the judge, Jackson again stated that he understood his right to testify and his attorney's obligations. Jackson thereupon informed the court that he did not wish to testify.

This case differs from *Whiteside* in three respects. Each difference raises important questions which can only be answered after an evidentiary hearing.

First, in *Whiteside*, a finding was made that Whiteside would have testified falsely had he given the testimony he initially wanted to give. Such a finding has not been made here. In terms of a possible violation of Jackson's rights, this is crucial. If, for example, Jackson's lawyer had no basis for believing Jackson would testify falsely and Jackson, in fact, wanted to testify truthfully, a violation of his rights would occur.

We do not know what measures Jackson's attorney took to determine whether Jackson would lie on the stand. He was required to take such measures as would give him "a firm factual basis" for believing Jackson would testify falsely. As we stated in our opinion in *Whiteside v. Scurr*, 744 F.2d at 1323, *rev'd on other grounds, sub nom. Nix v. Whiteside*, 475 U.S. at 157:

> Counsel must act if, but only if, he or she has "a firm factual basis" for believing that the defendant intends to testify falsely or has testified falsely. . . . It will be a rare case in which this factual requirement is met. Counsel must remember that they are not triers of fact, but advocates. In most cases a client's credibility will be a question for the jury.

The Supreme Court's majority opinion in *Whiteside* emphasizes the necessity of such caution on the part of defense counsel in determining whether a client has or will commit perjury. In discussing the attorney's duty to report possible client perjury, the majority states that it extends to "a client's *announced* plans to engage in future criminal conduct." (Emphasis added.) Thus, a clear expression of intent to commit perjury is required before an attorney can reveal client confidences.

AUTHORS' COMMENT:

What would be a "clear expression of intent to commit perjury"? Does the client have to say, "I'm going to lie"? Or is it enough for the client to insist that he will testify in a way that the lawyer knows to be false? Would the statement made by the defendant in *Nix v. Whiteside* ("I've got to say I saw a gun") be enough to meet the standards set out here in *Long*?

The concurring opinions in *Whiteside* support this interpretation. Justice Stevens advised circumspection: "A lawyer's certainty that a change in his client's recollection is a harbinger of intended perjury . . . should be tempered by the realization that, after reflection, the most honest witness may recall (or sincerely believe he recalls) details that he previously overlooked." And Justice Blackmun in his concurrence observed that "except in the rarest of cases, attorneys who adopt 'the role of the judge or jury to determine the facts' . . . pose a danger of depriving their clients of the zealous and loyal advocacy required by the Sixth Amendment."

Justices Blackmun and Stevens focus in their concurring opinions on the reasons the majority opinion carefully limits its holding to "announced plans" to commit perjury. The tensions between the rights of the accused and the obligations of her attorney are considerable in the context of potential client perjury. Justice Stevens points to the potential inaccuracy of a lawyer's perception. For many reasons, a lawyer's perception may be incorrect. Ideally, a client will tell her lawyer "everything." But "everything" may not be one consistent explanation of an event. Not only may a client overlook and later recall certain details, but she may also change intended testimony in an effort to be more truthful. Moreover, even a statement of an intention to lie on the stand does not necessarily mean the client will indeed lie once on the stand. Once a client hears the testimony of other witnesses, takes an oath, faces a judge and jury, and contemplates the prospect of cross-examination by opposing counsel, she may well change her mind and decide to testify truthfully.

As Justice Blackmun observes, an attorney who acts on a belief of possible client perjury takes on the role of the fact finder, a role which perverts the structure of our adversary system. A lawyer who judges a client's truthfulness does so without the many safeguards inherent in our adversary system. He likely makes his decision alone, without the assistance of fellow fact finders. He may consider too much evidence, including that which is untrustworthy. Moreover, a jury's determination on credibility is always tempered by the requirement of proof beyond a reasonable doubt. A lawyer, finding facts on his own, is not necessarily guided by such a high standard. Finally, by taking a position contrary to his client's interest, the lawyer may irrevocably destroy the trust the attorney-client relationship is designed to foster. That lack of trust cannot easily be confined to the area of intended perjury. It may well carry over into other aspects of the lawyer's representation, including areas where the client needs and deserves zealous and loyal representation. For these reasons and others, it is absolutely essential that a lawyer have a firm factual basis before adopting a belief of impending perjury.

The record before us does not disclose whether Jackson's lawyer had a firm factual basis for believing his client would testify falsely. This can only be adequately determined after an evidentiary hearing.

Second, in *Whiteside*, the defendant did testify and was " 'restricted' or restrained only from testifying falsely." Here, Jackson did not testify at all. It simply is impossible to determine from the record before us whether Jackson was "restrained" by his lawyer from giving truthful testimony. Again, this can only be determined after an evidentiary hearing.

Third, in *Whiteside*, the defense attorney did not reveal his belief about his client's anticipated testimony to the trial court. In contrast, the disclosure to the trial court here was quite explicit. The attorney said to the judge that he might have to withdraw because of what might be elicited on the stand.

Such a disclosure cannot be taken lightly. "Even in a jury trial, where the judge does not sit as the finder of fact, the judge will sentence the defendant, and such a disclosure creates significant risks of unfair prejudice' to the defendant."[6]

We note that, once the possibility of client perjury is disclosed to the trial court, the trial court should reduce the resulting prejudice. It should limit further disclosures of client confidences, inform the attorney of his other duties to his client, inform the defendant of her rights, and determine whether the defendant desires to waive any of those rights.

The trial judge here acted primarily with these concerns in mind. The judge discussed

[6] Before disclosing to the court a belief of impending client perjury, not only must a lawyer have a firm factual basis for the belief that his or her client will commit perjury, but the lawyer must also have attempted to dissuade the client from committing the perjury. *See Whiteside*, 475 U.S. at 169 ("It is universally agreed that, at a minimum, the attorney's first duty when confronted with a proposal for perjurious testimony is to attempt to dissuade the client from the unlawful course of conduct"). Such dissuasion is usually in the defendant's interest because, as Justice Stevens observes, "perjured testimony can ruin an otherwise meritorious case."

the conflict with only the attorney and his client present. He prevented further disclosures of client confidences. He advised Jackson of his right to testify and determined that Jackson understood his rights and his attorney's ethical obligation not to place false testimony before the court. He advised Jackson that if he took the stand, his lawyer would be required to refrain from questioning Jackson on issues which the lawyer believed Jackson would perjure himself and that Jackson would have to testify in narrative form.[7]

He then directly asked Jackson if he wished to testify. We add that a trial court should also impress upon defense counsel and the defendant that counsel must have a firm factual basis before further desisting in the presentation of the testimony in question.[8]

Under such a procedure, the chance for violations of the defendant's constitutional rights will be reduced, the revelation of further client confidences will be prevented, and the defendant can make a knowing waiver of her constitutional right to testify and to counsel. It will also be necessary to establish that the waiver was voluntary and that the defendant's rights were not violated prior to the waiver. Such inquiries, however, are best made at an evidentiary hearing.

Conclusion

The most weighty decision in a case of possible client perjury is made by the lawyer who decides to inform the court, and perhaps incidentally his adversary and the jury, of his client's possible perjury. This occurs when the lawyer makes a motion for withdrawal (usually for unstated reasons) or allows his client to testify in narrative form without questioning from counsel. Once this has been done, the die is cast. The prejudice will have occurred. At a minimum, the trial court will know of the defendant's potential perjury. For this reason, defense counsel must use extreme caution before revealing a belief of impending perjury. It is, as Justice Blackmun noted, "the rarest of cases" where an attorney should take such action.

Once the disclosure of the potential client perjury has occurred, the trial judge can limit the resulting prejudice by preventing further disclosures of client confidences, by informing the attorney of the obligation to his client, and by informing the client of her rights and determining whether she desires to waive any of them.

The determination whether the prejudice was undue must occur at an evidentiary hearing.[10]

NOTES AND QUESTIONS

1. ***Knowledge vs. Belief.*** Under *Long*, what should you do if you reasonably believe that your client will commit perjury, but you do not know for sure? Can you inform the court? Can you refuse to call your client as a witness? Can you have your client testify in a narrative? Can you suggest other options?

---

[7] When a lawyer is confronted during trial with the prospect of client perjury, allowing the defendant to testify in narrative form was recommended by the American Bar Association in its Standards for Criminal Justice, Proposed Standard 4-7.7 (2d ed. 1980). This Standard, however, has not been in force since 1979 when the American Bar Association House of Delegates failed to approve it. It has been criticized because it would indicate to the judge and sophisticated jurors that the lawyer does not believe his client, and because the lawyer would continue to play a passive role in the perjury. In this case, these concerns were largely removed because the judge had already been notified of the potential perjury and because the judge had instructed the attorney to proceed in this manner.

[8] We believe a trial court should also specifically inform a defendant of the possible consequences of false testimony: (1) the lawyer may reveal to the court what he believes to be false; (2) the lawyer may refrain from referring to the false testimony in final argument; and (3) the defendant may be prosecuted for perjury.

[10] Various methods have been suggested by commentators as an alternative to such a post hoc procedure.

2. ***Possible Solutions to the Attorney's Dilemma.*** What do you think of the two ideas in footnote 10 of *Long* — (1) "before allowing a defendant to give what a lawyer believes is perjurious testimony, a recess should be called, and a judge, other than the presiding judge, should hold a hearing and determine beyond a reasonable doubt that the defendant would commit perjury by testifying," and (2) "creating a board of attorneys to decide ethical issues"? Does a "mini-hearing" or an "ethics board" seem like a workable idea?

Extra credit: What could you do if your client intended to lie on the witness stand at the mini-hearing or before the ethics board? What other methods can you think of for deciding whether a client has committed (or plans to commit) perjury?

3. ***A "Miranda Warning" to Clients?*** When you discuss the attorney-client privilege and the ethical obligation of confidentiality with a client at the initial interview, must you warn the client about your disclosure obligations in the event the client intends to commit (or in fact commits) perjury? If so, what exactly should you say to your client?

C. PERJURY IN CIVIL CASES

Nix v. Whiteside and the cases and the ethics opinion we have read all concern criminal trials. Criminal trials present the most challenging situations because the rules of legal ethics must be read in harmony with the Sixth Amendment right to effective assistance of counsel and other constitutional rights. Perjury in criminal trials thus becomes a constitutional issue. Moreover, perjury in criminal cases usually occurs in open court, either during trial or at a hearing of some kind. There is little or no discovery in most criminal cases, and the defendant cannot be compelled to testify even if there is discovery, so perjury almost never occurs during a client's deposition in a criminal case.

Is anything different in civil litigation between private parties? After all, there is no right to effective assistance of counsel in civil cases, and the facts are generally developed through extensive discovery, including depositions under oath. Parties in civil litigation must submit to a deposition whether they want to or not. What may or must a lawyer in civil litigation do if the client lied during discovery?

In the next item, the ABA's Standing Committee on Ethics and Professional Responsibility explores that question. The opinion builds on Formal Op. 87-353 (1987), in which the Standing Committee considered the lawyer's obligations under ABA Model Rule 3.3 upon learning that a client intends to commit or has committed perjury in a criminal trial. In that opinion, the Standing Committee concluded that the lawyer's obligation to disclose client perjury to the tribunal pursuant to ABA Model Rule 3.3 superseded the lawyer's responsibility to keep client confidences under Rule 1.6. "It is now mandatory, under these Model Rule provisions," the Committee stated in Op. 87-353, "for a lawyer, who knows the client has committed perjury, to disclose this knowledge to the tribunal if the lawyer cannot persuade the client to rectify the perjury."

With that background, what do you think a lawyer should be required to do upon learning that a client has committed perjury at a civil deposition? (Rule 3.3 has been amended since 1993, and the paragraph numbers have changed. But the opinion's basic reasoning is still sound.)

For example, one suggests that before allowing a defendant to give what a lawyer believes is perjurious testimony, a recess should be called, and a judge, other than the presiding judge, should hold a hearing and determine beyond a reasonable doubt that the defendant would commit perjury by testifying. Another suggests creating a board of attorneys to decide ethical issues. Either of these procedures would assist attorneys in determining whether there is a firm factual basis for believing a client is about to commit perjury, although we do not say, at this point, that the Constitution necessarily requires their implementation.

ABA STANDING COMMITTEE ON ETHICS AND PROFESSIONAL RESPONSIBILITY, FORMAL OPINION 93-376 — THE LAWYER'S OBLIGATION WHERE A CLIENT LIES IN RESPONSE TO DISCOVERY REQUESTS (1993)*

A lawyer represents the agent for an insurance company in a contract action filed by an insured against both the company and the agent. The lawsuit was filed on a policy requiring proof of claim within 60 days of loss. The insured alleged that he had put such proof in the regular mail addressed to the agent on the 59th day, thereby providing timely notice under law and complying with the terms of the policy. Unfortunately, the insured did not obtain a mailing receipt or other evidence of posting. Subsequently, the insurance company refused to pay the claim on the ground that the required notice was never received.

Because the defendant agent would not be amenable to a trial subpoena, he was one of the first to be deposed after suit was filed. At the deposition, the plaintiff/insured hoped to prove timely mailing and receipt by the agent, while the defendants hoped to establish a basis for summary judgment in view of the lack of such timely mailing or receipt, as indicated by evidence offered by the agent in pretrial discovery. When asked at the deposition if he had received proof of claim by the 60th day, the agent replied that he had not, and produced a copy of his office mail log confirming this, which was marked as an exhibit in the deposition.

The deposition was transcribed according to local custom and the agent later stopped by the lawyer's office to review and sign it. The next day the lawyer sent a letter to plaintiff's counsel, pointing out plaintiff's serious problem of lack of proof of compliance with the policy requirement of timely notice, and enclosing a draft copy of a motion for summary judgment. She intended to file the motion as soon as she received notice from the court reporter that the deposition had been duly signed, sealed and filed with the court. Failing a favorable ruling on said motion (or reasonable settlement proposal by plaintiff), the lawyer planned to use the deposition at trial pursuant to Federal Rule of Evidence 804(b)(1).

Several days later, on a business trip, the lawyer ran into her client, the agent, at the airport. In the course of discussing the status of the case and the upcoming trial, the agent advised the lawyer that he had lied about not receiving insured's notice. In fact, it had arrived in his office on the 60th day and his secretary had entered its receipt in the office mail log with other incoming correspondence before placing the mail on his desk. The agent, however, had shredded the letter and altered the mail log to conceal the fact of receipt.

AUTHORS' COMMENT:

What now? What are you supposed to do when your client unequivocally admits that he shredded the key letter and altered the mail log? This admission is directly contrary to your client's deposition testimony, so you know the client has lied at the deposition. What are your responsibilities under the rules of legal ethics? Think about that for a few minutes and write down a brief plan in the space below before you read on.

In circumstances where a lawyer has offered perjured testimony or falsified evidence in an adjudicative proceeding, the Model Rules, like the predecessor Model Code of Professional Responsibility, adopt the view that remedial measures must be taken.

Although Rule 1.6 generally affords protection to client confidences, its confidentiality requirement is qualified by its own provisions, and by the effect of other Rules. Most notably in this context, the duty of confidentiality mandated by Rule 1.6 is explicitly superseded by the duty of disclosure in Rule 3.3. Thus, as was made clear in Formal Opinion No. 87-353, disclosure of a client's perjury is required by Rule 3.3 where a lawyer has offered material evidence to a tribunal and comes to know of its falsity, or when disclosure of a material fact is necessary to avoid assisting a criminal or fraudulent act by the client.

In the case at hand, there is no issue as to knowledge on the lawyer's part of the client's fraud; the client has made a direct admission to the lawyer after the fact. Similarly, there is no doubt that the perjury and other fraudulent acts of the client relate to a material fact, in that a necessary element of plaintiff's case is at issue. However, because the client's misrepresentations took place during pretrial discovery and none occurred in open court, the question arises whether the applicable rule of conduct is Rule 3.3 or Rule 4.1 ("Truthfulness in Statements to Others"). The issue is whether perjury or fraud in pretrial discovery should be regarded as a lack of candor toward the tribunal, governed by Rule 3.3, or untruthfulness toward the opposing party and counsel, as to which Rule 4.1 is the applicable provision. Unlike the duty of candor toward a "tribunal" in Rule 3.3, the duty of truthfulness toward "others" in Rule 4.1 does not expressly trump the duty to keep client confidences in Rule 1.6. If it is Rule 4.1 rather than Rule 3.3(a) that applies in this context, the prohibition on disclosure of client confidences in Rule 1.6 must be given full effect.

AUTHORS' COMMENT:

Do you understand this crucial difference? Rule 3.3(a)(3) applies when a lawyer "has offered material evidence and comes to know of its falsity," and it requires a lawyer to correct a client's false testimony "*even if* compliance requires disclosure of information otherwise protected by Rule 1.6." Rule 4.1(b), on the other hand, provides that a lawyer shall not knowingly "fail to disclose a material fact to a third person when disclosure is necessary to avoid assisting a criminal or fraudulent act by a client," and it applies "*unless* disclosure is prohibited by Rule 1.6." Which rule should apply when false testimony has been offered at a deposition but has not yet been used in negotiations or in court? Rule 3.3(a)(3), or Rule 4.1(b)? The Committee now addresses that key question.

It is clear that once the deposition is signed and filed and the motion for summary judgment submitted to the court, a fraud has been committed upon the tribunal which would trigger application of Rule 3.3(a). Indeed, we think that even before these documents are filed there is potential ongoing reliance upon their content which would be outcome-determinative, resulting in an inevitable deception of the other side and a subversion of the truth-finding process which the adversary system is designed to implement. Support for this view is found in case law holding that the duty of a lawyer under Rule 3.3(a)(2) to disclose material facts to the tribunal implies a duty to make such disclosure to opposing counsel in pretrial settlement negotiations. *See, e.g., Kath v. Western Media, Inc.*, 684 P.2d 98, 101 (Wyo. 1984) (letter contradicting testimony of a key witness should have been disclosed to opposing counsel in connection with settlement negotiations, under Rule 3.3 and DR 7-102(A)); *Virzi v. Grand Trunk Warehouse and Cold Storage Co.*, 571 F. Supp. 507, 509 (1983) (fact that client had died should have been disclosed to opposing counsel in pretrial settlement negotiations).

The Committee is therefore of the view that, in the pretrial situation described above, the lawyer's duty of candor toward the tribunal under Rule 3.3 qualifies her duty to keep client confidences under Rule 1.6. Continued participation by the lawyer in the matter without rectification or disclosure would assist the client in committing a crime or fraud in violation of Rule 3.3(a)(2).[5] Although the perjured deposition testimony and the altered mail log may not become evidence until they are offered in support of the motion for summary judgment or actually introduced at trial, their potential as evidence and their impact on the judicial process trigger the lawyer's duty to take reasonable remedial measures under Rule 3.3(a)(4).

It is important to note, however, that the Committee does not assert, nor should it be inferred from its analysis of Rule 3.3(a) in Opinion No. 87-353, that disclosure to the tribunal is the first and only appropriate remedial measure to be taken in situations arising under Rule 3.3(a)(4). As the Comment to Rule 3.3 makes clear, the duties of loyalty and confidentiality owed to her client require a lawyer to explore options short of outright disclosure in order to rectify the situation. Thus, the lawyer's first step should be to remonstrate with the client confidentially and urge him to rectify the situation. It may develop that, after consultation with the client, the lawyer will be in a position to accomplish rectification without divulging the client's wrongdoing or breaching the client's confidences, depending upon the rules of the jurisdiction and the nature of the false evidence. For example, incomplete or incorrect answers to deposition questions may be capable of being supplemented or amended in such a way as to correct the record, rectify the perjury, and ensure a fair result without outright disclosure to the tribunal. Although this approach would not appear to be feasible in the case at hand, it is nevertheless the type of reasonable remedial measure that should be explored initially by a lawyer when confronted by a situation in which she realizes that evidence she has offered or elicited in good faith is false.

In this case, if efforts to persuade the client to rectify fail, the lawyer must herself act to see that a fraud is not perpetrated on the tribunal. At a minimum she must withdraw from the representation, so as to avoid assisting the client's fraud in violation of Rules 3.3 and 1.2(d). See Rule 1.16(a)(1) (withdrawal mandatory where continued representation would result in a violation of rules of professional conduct). However, the Committee observed in Opinion No. 87-353, "withdrawal can rarely serve as a remedy for the client's perjury." While withdrawal may enable the lawyer to avoid knowing participation in the commission of perjury, Rule 3.3(a)(4) specifically requires the lawyer to do more than simply distance herself from the client's fraud when she has offered evidence that she learns was false; she must take "reasonable remedial measures" to alert the court to it. Moreover, under paragraph (b) of Rule 3.3, the lawyer's duties in this regard "continue to the conclusion of the proceeding," presumably even if the lawyer has withdrawn from the representation before this time.

It is possible that so-called "noisy withdrawal" procedures could be effective in the instant case, albeit in a way that is tantamount to disclosure. See ABA Formal Opinion No. 92-366 (August 8, 1992). Utilization of the withdrawal/disaffirmance approach suggested by Opinion No. 92-366 is appealing as a remedial measure because it is less intrusive on the confidential relationship between lawyer and client than outright disclosure to the tribunal under Rule 3.3(a). It may also have the advantage of directly and expeditiously rectifying the fraud in a way that does not compromise the tribunal and prevent the case from proceeding. On the other hand, "noisy withdrawal" may not be an entirely effective means of dealing with the type of client fraud likely to occur in the pretrial stages of a case. For instance, withdrawal would not be sufficient to correct

---

[5] The more general prohibition against assisting client fraud contained in Rule 1.2(d) would also be violated were the lawyer to continue to represent the client in the matter without taking steps to rectify the fraud, up to and including giving notice of withdrawal and disaffirmance of her work product. See ABA Formal Opinion No. 92-366 (August 8, 1992).

the fraud's impact on the case if the plaintiff decided to drop his or her lawsuit because of a perceived lack of proof prior to or notwithstanding the "noisy withdrawal." Also, a "noisy withdrawal" does not necessarily put either successor counsel or the opposing party on notice as to why the documents are being disaffirmed. Thus, notwithstanding withdrawal and disaffirmance, the fraud could continue to adversely affect the proceedings and ultimate disposition of the case. Direct disclosure under Rule 3.3, to the opposing party or if need be to the court, may prove to be the only reasonable remedial measure in the client fraud situations most likely to be encountered in pretrial proceedings.

NOTES AND QUESTIONS

1. ***Are You Satisfied?*** Are you happy with the ABA's answer in Formal Op. 93-376? If not, what bothers you? Should the lawyer have a greater or a lesser obligation of disclosure than the Standing Committee mandates in this opinion?

2. ***Limits of Withdrawal.*** Would the lawyer's withdrawal be deemed to remedy the perjury here? If so, why? If not, does Formal Op. 93-376 require the lawyer to do something more than withdraw? What does the lawyer have to do?

3. ***Noisy Withdrawal?*** Would a "noisy withdrawal" work? If so, and if the client refuses to correct the perjury voluntarily, is the lawyer *required* to make a noisy withdrawal? What would the lawyer say in the course of making a noisy withdrawal? In the space below, compose a short letter to opposing counsel making an appropriate noisy withdrawal in the situation outlined in Op. 93-376:

4. ***Can Witnesses in Civil Cases be Criminally Prosecuted for Perjury?*** After years of dull "green eyeshade" inquiries into the Whitewater real estate deals, Independent Counsel Kenneth Starr hit upon the Monica Lewinsky sex scandal. Mr. Starr's main focus was whether Monica Lewinsky and President Clinton had lied under oath in their testimony in the Paula Jones sexual harassment case. Critics of Mr. Starr immediately attacked him for investigating a crime that is seldom prosecuted. A few weeks after the scandal broke, however, noted ethics expert Stephen Gillers published an op-ed piece in *The New York Times* entitled *The Perjury Loophole*, which began like this:

> "Perjury in civil cases is virtually never prosecuted." Who said that? I did. And so did dozens of other purported experts when members of the news media asked us if Kenneth W. Starr, the independent counsel for Whitewater, would be looking into whether President Clinton and Monica S. Lewinsky lied under oath in the Paula Jones sexual harassment case. We were wrong.

Professor Gillers went on to cite several appellate cases affirming criminal convictions of witnesses who had lied under oath in civil cases, either in depositions or at trial. So, the answer to our question is that witnesses can be prosecuted for committing perjury at a deposition or at trial in a civil case. Of course, not every witness who is caught lying under oath in a civil case is prosecuted for perjury. What factors should influence a prosecutor in deciding whether or not to indict a lying witness for perjury?

Chapter 20
INTRODUCTION TO CONFLICTS OF INTEREST

To practicing lawyers, conflicts of interest are the single most common day-to-day issue of professional responsibility. Conflict issues are often difficult problems that require careful thought and detailed knowledge of the rules of professional conduct. Hundreds of judicial opinions each year address conflicts of interest, especially opinions ruling on motions to disqualify, disciplinary charges, and suits alleging legal malpractice and breach of fiduciary duty. And that's only the tip of the iceberg. Many conflicts in litigation are resolved informally, without a written opinion from the court. Many more conflicts of interest arise in non-litigation matters, such as estate planning, corporate work, partnership matters, and real estate deals. These non-litigation conflicts rarely reach court, so they rarely generate judicial opinions. And when lawyers turn down matters due to conflicts (or perceived conflicts), that is never reported in a case.

In short, conflicts of interest are a daily event in the lives of practicing lawyers, and lawyers worry about them a lot. Why are lawyers so worried about conflicts of interest? Maybe because of money. Conflicts of interest can cost a firm a lot of money in three ways:

1. *Erroneously accepting a matter can cost money.* A law firm that accepts a matter despite a conflict of interest may never get paid for its work. If a client discovers midway through a representation that its law firm has a conflict of interest, for example, the client may fire the law firm and refuse to pay any accrued bills. Worse, when a client fires a law firm on one matter, the client often fires the law firm on all of its matters (or at least won't give the firm any new matters), because once the law firm has breached its trust by dividing its loyalty, the client may never trust the law firm again. It's as if the law firm has had an affair, and the client wants a divorce. In the words of a song by Alabama:

> Well, I know a lady that's down on her love, 'cause I used to hold her and
> Have that special touch.
> But work took me a way from home late at nights, and
> I wasn't there when she turned out the lights.
> Then both of us got lonely and I gave into lust, and
> She just couldn't live with a man she couldn't trust.

Lady Down on Love (Ala. 1986). Once you lose a client's trust, it's hard for the client to continue living with you.

A client who leaves you may also eventually sue you. If the client is disappointed with the quality of your firm's representation, the client may sue your firm for legal malpractice or breach of fiduciary duty (sometimes both), pointing to the conflict of interest as the reason your firm didn't do a better job. "The firm wasn't looking out for *our* best interests," the client will say. "It was looking out for *another* client's best interests. It was trying to serve two masters, and we got the short end of the stick." You don't want to go there.

2. *Erroneously rejecting a matter costs money.* On the other hand, rejecting a matter that the firm could have accepted can also cost money. A law firm doesn't want to reject any matters on conflict of interest grounds if it doesn't have to. If the firm turns down a new case for an existing client, that client may feel a sense of betrayal. The client's first reaction may be, "But you're my lawyer! You've got to take my case." The law firm will then explain that the firm has a conflict of interest — e.g., "We can't represent you on this one because we are representing the other side in a different matter." Then comes the client's second reaction: "You work for that scoundrel? How can you represent someone like that!" This angry client, too, may feel a breach of trust and take some or all of its business out the door.

3. *Erroneously continuing a matter can cost money.* Even if you are perfectly justified in accepting a matter, you can lose money by continuing to work on the matter after a conflict arises. Not all conflicts are foreseeable at the inception of a representation. If a conflict arises during a representation, you have to deal with it properly. You may have to make additional disclosures to your clients, or you may have to withdraw from the matter (or withdraw from the conflicting matter, if that's an option). If you should get out but don't, it can cost you money just as if you had taken the case improperly in the first place. (Conversely, getting out if you don't have to will cost you as much money as rejecting a case unnecessarily in the first place.)

Thus, it can damage your pocketbook to accept or continue a case improperly, or to reject or withdraw from a case unnecessarily. If you don't know how to analyze conflicts of interest, sooner or later it's going to cost you money.

Of course, lawyers also worry that conflicts of interest will damage their reputations and ruin their client relations. A lawyer who is the target of a motion to disqualify is essentially being accused of being "unethical" — of falling below the minimum ethical level established by the ethics rules. We've talked to many lawyers who have been targets of motions to disqualify, and they generally agree that it's an unsettling feeling when a client or former client files a motion to disqualify or writes a letter accusing the lawyer of a conflict of interest. In addition, it's difficult or impossible to remain on good terms with a client who moves to disqualify you based on a conflict of interest.

Finally, lawyers are fearful of getting into disciplinary trouble for conflicts of interest. As a practical matter, though, money is a much greater concern than the threat of discipline. Courts, clients, and malpractice suits are all quite effective in policing conflicts of interest, so the disciplinary authorities concentrate their attention elsewhere. One exception is conflicts of interest that arise when lawyers enter into business deals with their clients. Disciplinary authorities police those conflicts carefully and mete out discipline harshly when they find a violation. We devote substantial attention to business transactions with clients in a later chapter.

As we've said before, attorney-client relationships rest on a dual foundation of secrecy and loyalty. You have read about secrecy, and have seen that keeping client information secret is essential if you want to earn the trust of your clients. Now we look at the other major element of that trust: loyalty. Loyalty means total devotion to the interests of a client. When you agree to serve a client, you also agree that you will not do anything to harm the client or to distract you or deflect you from pursuing the client's best interests as the client sees those interests. You agree to be loyal, as if this client were your only client.

This book shows you how to recognize, avoid, and cure conflicts of interest, so you won't take on or keep working on cases that you should reject, or reject cases that you should accept.

The main rules on conflicts of interest. In the ABA Model Rules of Professional Conduct, many separate rules govern conflicts of interest, especially Rules 1.7 through 1.13 and Rule 3.7.

In a nutshell, Rule 1.7 governs conflicts with current clients; Rule 1.9(a) and (b) govern conflicts with former clients; and Rule 1.10(a) says that conflicts under either Rule 1.7 or Rule 1.9 are imputed to all other lawyers in the firm, except "personal interest" conflicts that don't pose a "significant risk" to the conflicting client. With that simple framework in place, a more detailed outline on conflicts of interest will help you understand the larger context in which these rules operate.

A. AN OUTLINE ON CONFLICTS OF INTEREST

1. Concurrent vs. Successive Conflicts

A. There are two basic kinds of conflicts:

1. *Concurrent* conflicts (sometimes called "simultaneous" conflicts) are conflicts between a current client, on the one hand, and some other person or interest, on the other hand. Concurrent conflicts arise whenever a lawyer is unable (or might later become unable) to give 100% loyalty to a current client because of a competing loyalty to another current client, or because of loyalty to or personal interest in someone who is not a client, or to the lawyer's own personal, financial, political, or social interests. For example:

    a. *Conflict with another current client.* One current client may want to sue another current client, or buy real estate from another client, or form a partnership with another current client.
    b. *Conflict with a non-client.* A current client may want to sue or transact business with the lawyer's friend, relative, employer, or neighbor.
    c. *Conflict with the lawyer's own interests.* A client may want to get a zoning permit to build a noisy factory near where the lawyer lives, or a client may want to sue a company the lawyer owns, or sue the lawyer's political ally.

2. *Successive* conflicts (sometimes called "former client conflicts") are conflicts between a current client and a former client.

    a. For example, one of your current clients might be sued by one of your former clients, or a current client might want to negotiate a contract with your former client.
    b. A conflict with a former client might also arise if an opposing party put on one of your former clients as a witness and you had to cross-examine your former client.

B. *General rules on concurrent and successive conflicts.* Here are two general rules that will help you appreciate the great difference between concurrent conflicts and successive conflicts:

1. You may never ethically oppose one of your current clients without that client's consent. (Consent from the current client may not be sufficient, but it is always necessary.) In other words, your current clients always have a veto over being sued by you (or, more precisely, being sued by someone you represent) in any matter, related or unrelated to the work you are doing for the current client.
2. In stark contrast, you may ethically oppose a former client without that former client's consent *unless* the matter you are now working on is substantially related to a matter you previously worked on when you represented the former client. In other words, a former client never has a veto over being sued by someone you represent unless the current matter is substantially related to the former client's matter.

C. *When are two matters substantially related?* As a rough rule of thumb, two matters are substantially related when you would normally have been expected to learn confidential information about your former client in the course of that former representation that could be used against the former client on behalf of your new (current) client. In other words, if a lawyer would usually have learned confidential information in an earlier representation that could be turned against the former client in a pending representation, then the two matters are considered substantially related, and you cannot oppose your former client without the former client's informed consent (i.e., the former client has a veto).

D. *How do you tell the difference between a current client and a former client?* Since the consequences of labeling a person a current client rather than a former client are immense, how can we tell the difference? The basic rule is that a person is a current client if he *reasonably believes* he is a current client. There are two elements: the person has to *believe* he is a current client, and that belief has to be *reasonable*. If he doesn't believe he is a current client, or if he thinks he is a current client but that belief isn't reasonable, then he is not a current client. We look at the situation primarily from the client's perspective, not the lawyer's perspective. (There is a more detailed analysis of these issues in the chapter titled "Who Is a Client?").

2. Direct Adversity Conflicts vs. Materially Limiting Conflicts

ABA Model Rule 1.7 identifies two basic categories of concurrent conflicts, which we call "direct adversity" conflicts and "materially limiting" conflicts. Here is what those terms mean:

A. *Direct adversity conflicts.* Direct adversity conflicts arise when two of your current clients are directly opposing each other, either in a dispute or in a transaction, and you represent at least one of the two. For example, direct adversity arises if one of your current clients is suing another of your current clients, or if one client is a buyer in a real estate transaction and the other client is the seller in the same transaction. In other words, you have a direct adversity conflict when you represent the plaintiff in a suit against a defendant who is a client of yours in some other matter, or when you represent the defendant in a suit brought by a person who is a client of yours in some other matter, or when you represent the buyer in a transaction where the seller is a client of yours in the same matter or some other matter, or when you represent the borrower in a loan deal where the lender is a client of yours in the same matter or in some other matter. If you look across the table and see another current client of yours, you have a direct adversity client. But there are some differences between litigation and transactions.

1. *Litigation.* In litigation, a direct adversity conflict exists whenever two of your firm's clients are on opposite sides of the "v" in the case name. For example, suppose there is a lawsuit called *Powell v. Needham*, and both Powell and Needham are current clients of yours, and you are handling the litigation for one of them. (Not both. As you will soon see, you are never allowed to handle both sides of the same litigation. Rule 1.7(b)(3) establishes a *per se* rule against handling both sides of the same case. Thus, you cannot stand up in a courtroom and say, "Your Honor, I represent both the plaintiff and the defendant here." Even with the informed consent of both clients, the rules do not allow you to do that.)
2. *Transactions.* In transactions, you are directly adverse to a client whenever the person or entity sitting on the opposite side of the negotiating table is also a current client. (In relatively rare circumstances, such as a transaction in which both parties completely agree on all terms, you may ethically handle both sides of the same transaction, because Rule 1.7 contains no *per se* rule against representing both sides of a transaction. But remember that even in the situations in which you may represent both sides of the same transaction, you may do so only with the informed consent of both clients.)

B. *Materially limiting conflicts.* Materially limiting conflicts occur when a significant risk exists that your judgment on behalf of one client will be limited by competing loyalties to another current client, or to a third person (such as a friend, relative, or former client), or to your own personal or financial interests.

C. Thus, you have a "direct adversity" concurrent conflict whenever you represent one of your current clients directly against another current client, whether in litigation or in a transaction.

D. You have a "materially limiting" concurrent conflict whenever you perceive a "significant risk" that your ability to represent a client will be "materially limited" (i.e., hampered, impeded, diminished) by your responsibilities to one of four categories of people:

1. another current client;
2. a former client (which is a special type of third party);
3. any third party (including former clients and every other person or entity that is neither yourself (the first party) or a current client (the second party); and
4. your own personal interests, of whatever sort (whether business, social, romantic, political, economic, or otherwise).

E. If you have either a direct adversity conflict or a materially limiting conflict, then you may not accept or continue the representation unless you comply with all four criteria of Rule 1.7(b). Specifically:

1. Despite the conflict, you must "reasonably believe" that you will be able to provide "competent and diligent" representation to each client involved in the conflict;
2. The representation must not be prohibited by law;
3. If you are representing two or more parties in the same litigation, they may not be asserting any claims against each other (i.e., you may not handle both sides of the same litigation); and
4. Each client must give "informed consent" and must confirm that consent in writing.

F. You need *all* of the elements just listed, not just one element. If you are missing any of the mandatory elements in Rule 1.7(b), then you must either reject the representation (if you have not yet started representing the client) or seek to withdraw from representing at least one of the conflicting clients (if you are already in a conflict situation).

1. You must withdraw because Rule 1.16(a)(1) makes withdrawal mandatory if continued representation "will result in violation of the rules of professional conduct" — and if you cannot satisfy all four elements of Rule 1.7(b). In this situation you have an impermissible concurrent conflict and will violate Rule 1.7(b) unless you cure the conflict by withdrawing. Whether you must drop both clients or instead may continue representing one of the clients (and if you may continue representing one, which one) is a complicated issue that we will discuss later.
2. Although we are talking about meeting all four elements (i.e., all four subparagraphs) of Rule 1.7(b), the key elements of Rule 1.7(b) are (b)(1) (an objectively reasonable belief that you can represent each client competently and diligently in spite of the conflict) and (b)(4) (obtaining informed consent confirmed in writing from all clients that are affected by your conflict).
3. The elements in Rule 1.7(b)(2) (prohibited by law) seldom arise. But in some states, substantive laws beyond the ethics rules prohibit a lawyer from representing more than a single defendant in a capital case.

4. Likewise, the situation in Rule 1.7(b)(3) (handling opposing claims in the same case) rarely arises. Lawyers just don't do that because they intuitively know it's wrong or impossible to attack and defend a client in litigation at the same time.
5. In short, you can resolve most Rule 1.7(a) concurrent conflicts if an objectively reasonable lawyer would believe that the conflict won't prevent you from providing competent and diligent representation to each client affected by your conflict, *and* if each affected client consents (confirmed in writing) after being fully informed of the circumstances.

3. Actual vs. Potential Conflicts

There are two basic time frames for conflicts:

A. *Actual* conflicts are conflicts that already exist, even if nothing else happens. For example, if a lawyer discovers that she has filed suit against another one of her current clients, that presents an actual conflict. It is a conflict that exists right now, not one that might develop if various other events occur.
B. *Potential* conflicts are conflicts that might arise in the future, depending on some contingent event. For example, if a client asks you to investigate a potential suit that *might* require you to sue a former client, if the former client turns out to be involved in the underlying events, that presents a potential conflict.
    1. Keep in mind that the rules prohibit both actual and potential conflicts, but the dangers arising from actual conflicts are usually greater than the dangers from equivalent conflicts that are merely potential.
    2. For example, a lawsuit that actually names one of the lawyer's other clients as a defendant (thus creating an actual direct adversity conflict) is generally more dangerous than a lawsuit that eventually *might* name that same client as a defendant (a potential conflict) — but the potential conflict is nevertheless a conflict that must be measured against the rules.

4. Three Levels of Conflicts

There are three basic levels of conflicts:

A. *Immaterial* conflicts are conflicts so minor, trivial, or unlikely to arise that the rules do not regulate them. The lawyer need not disclose them to a client, or obtain the client's consent to them. For example, it is an immaterial conflict if a client wants to sue a large company in which the lawyer's wealthy second cousin owns only a few shares of stock.
B. *Consentable* conflicts (also called "waivable" conflicts) are conflicts serious enough to be regulated, but mild enough so that they can be cured or avoided if a client consents in writing after full disclosure of the situation. For example, it is typically a consentable conflict if a client wants to negotiate a mutually beneficial business deal with the lawyer's occasional golf partner, or with another current client of the lawyer.
C. *Non-consentable* conflicts (also called "non-waivable" conflicts) are conflicts so serious or so inherently dangerous that they cannot be cured or avoided even if a client consents in writing after full and complete disclosure. For example, it is a non-consentable conflict if one current client wants to mount a hostile takeover of another client's business, or if husband and wife want you to represent both of them in their contested divorce suit.

5. Personal vs. Vicarious Conflicts

There are two basic sources of conflicts:

A. *Personal* conflicts are conflicts that disqualify or restrict a lawyer because of something the lawyer has done personally (such as representing a client with adverse interests), or because the lawyer's own interests are at odds with the client's interests.

B. *Vicarious* (or "imputed") conflicts are conflicts in which the restrictions on a lawyer who *is* personally disqualified are imputed or attributed to another lawyer (usually in the same firm) who is *not* personally disqualified. In many states, when any *one* lawyer in a firm is disqualified personally, *all* other lawyers in the firm are disqualified vicariously.

    1. *Screens.* In some states, however, a law firm may avoid disqualification by building a "screen" or "wall" between the disqualified lawyer and the rest of the firm. There's a further discussion of screens in the chapter on imputed conflicts and firewalls.
    2. *Personal conflicts.* ABA Model Rule 1.10(a) has a special rule for personal conflicts of interest. Personal conflicts are not imputed from Lawyer A to the other lawyers in the firm if Lawyer A's disqualification "is based on a personal interest . . . and does not present a significant risk of materially limiting the representation of the client by the remaining lawyers in the firm."

6. Eight Events That Can Trigger Conflicts

Conflicts can arise from any of eight triggering events. In each of these triggering situations, lawyers and law firms should be alert for conflicts.

A. *New clients.* Whenever a firm takes on a new client, the firm must check to ensure that the new client is not the opponent in any existing matter in the firm. For example, a firm cannot take on a new client who is the defendant in an unrelated pending suit brought by one of the firm's existing clients unless the firm has informed consent of both the existing client *and* the new client.

B. *New matters.* Whenever a firm takes on a new matter for an existing client, the firm must check to ensure that the new matter does not create a conflict. For example, a firm may be able to prepare a new client's tax return or will without creating a conflict, but negotiating an acquisition or filing litigation for that same new client may create a conflict with the firm's other clients or former clients. Therefore, each new matter must be evaluated for conflicts on its own merits, even when the client with the new matter is an old client rather than a new client.

C. *New parties.* Even in existing matters, bringing in new parties may create conflicts, especially where the new parties are opponents in litigation.

D. *New issues.* Likewise, bringing up new issues in existing matters could create a conflict if the law firm takes a position on the new issue that directly conflicts with the position the firm is taking on the same issue for some other client in some other matter, *and* there is a significant risk that the lawyer's action on behalf of one client will materially limit the lawyer's effectiveness in representing the other client in a different legal matter. These are called "positional conflicts" or "issue conflicts." Comment 24 to ABA Model Rule 1.7 points to factors relevant to deciding when you need to discuss positional conflicts with clients.

E. *New attorneys.* Whenever a law firm hires a new attorney, the firm must make sure that the new attorney is not bringing conflicts to the firm. For example, a new attorney who formerly represented Acme Corporation at her old firm will create a conflict by joining a firm that is suing Acme Corporation. In other words, a lawyer drags around all of her former clients wherever she goes. (Once a former client, always a former client. You can turn a current client into a former client, but a former client always remains a former client.)

F. *New relationships.* Whenever a lawyer in a firm gets married, the firm must check to ensure that the lawyer is not opposing clients of his spouse or in-laws in any matter without the informed consent of the clients on both sides. (Similar conflicts can also arise if a lawyer's parent or child or close relative becomes a lawyer. The firm must check to ensure that the lawyer and his parent/child/relative are not opposing each other in any matter unless the client has given informed consent.)

G. *New witnesses.* Occasionally, a conflict can arise because a witness for the other side turns out to be a client or former client of the law firm that has to cross-examine that witness. For example, suppose a law firm currently represents Dr. Strangelove in a partnership law matter and simultaneously represents SARS Wars Consultants in a case alleging that SARS Wars negligently wrote ineffective instructions for a quarantine policy. If the plaintiff calls Dr. Strangelove as a fact witness or an expert witness, the firm representing Dr. Strangelove may have a conflict because it will have to cross-examine him when he takes the witness stand in the SARS case.

H. *Need for a lawyer's testimony.* This is a different type of conflict. Whenever a lawyer knows that she or another lawyer in her firm should be called or is likely to be called as a witness by any party, then the lawyer may not act as trial counsel except in certain circumstances. (This situation is covered under Rule 3.7, but that rule incorporates the standards of Rule 1.7 by cross-reference.)

7. Negative Consequences of Conflicts

Conflicts of interest can cause damage to the lawyer or law firm that violated the conflicts rules, to the disqualified lawyer's clients, and to the justice system.

A. *Harm to the disqualified lawyer or law firm.* This is a "3-D" problem:

   1. *Disqualification.* The lawyer causing the conflict is usually disqualified. Moreover, the entire firm may be disqualified through imputed or vicarious disqualification.
   2. *Discipline.* Lawyers who violate the conflict of interest rules may be subject to professional discipline.
   3. *Dollars.* Lawyers who are disciplined or disqualified usually lose fees and clients, and are often sued for legal malpractice because of the harm to the client caused by the conflicts violation.

B. *Harm to the disqualified lawyer's client.* Successful motions to disqualify opposing counsel also harm the client of the disqualified lawyer in three ways:

   1. The client is deprived of a lawyer who is familiar with the client and the case.
   2. The proceedings are delayed. Justice delayed may be justice denied, especially to a plaintiff who needs money, or to a defendant whose business or reputation is being damaged by the pendency of the suit.
   3. The client is forced to seek other counsel, and must pay the new lawyer to learn the basics of the case that the disqualified lawyer already knew. Since this is unfair to the client, some courts have forced the disqualified lawyer to refund some or all of the fees earned before the disqualification.

C. *Harm to the justice system.* Conflicts of interest harm the justice system by causing several types of delays:

   1. Delay while the lawyers bicker or litigate about the alleged conflicts.
   2. Delay while the client of the disqualified lawyer finds a new lawyer (if the court grants the motion to disqualify).

3. Delay while the new lawyer gets up to speed on the matter at hand.

8. When Are Conflicts of Interest Consentable?

Most conflicts with current clients are consentable, and virtually all conflicts with former clients are consentable. But some conflicts with current clients are non-consentable, meaning that client consent will not cure the conflict even if the client is willing to consent. This section of the outline will help you to distinguish consentable from non-consentable conflicts.

A. According to Rule 1.7, Comment 14, calling a conflict "non-consentable" means that "the lawyer involved cannot properly ask for such agreement or provide representation on the basis of the client's consent." Rule 1.7(b) identifies three categories of conflict that are always non-consentable (i.e., never consentable).

1. *Rule 1.7(b)(1):* The most common test for determining whether a conflict is consentable appears in Rule 1.7(b)(1): "the lawyer reasonably believes that the lawyer will be able to provide competent and diligent representation to *each* affected client." If the lawyer meets this test as to each client, the conflict is consentable. If not, this conflict is the first type of non-consentable conflict.
2. *A simple example.* Let's apply this test to a simple example. Suppose a new client named Kazzam Korp. wants to sue one of your longstanding major clients, Sony Corp., for breach of contract. Is the conflict consentable?

   a. The first key is whether you *believe* that you can competently and diligently represent the client now seeking representation (Kazzam) even though it is suing one of your current clients. If the answer to this question is no, then the conflict is non-consentable. But let's assume the answer is yes so we can go on to the next step.
   b. The second key question is whether your belief that you can competently and diligently represent the client is *reasonable*. In other words, would an objective, disinterested lawyer (i.e., a lawyer with no personal or financial stake in the matter) believe that you will be able to represent the other conflicting client competently and diligently despite your loyalty to your existing client, Sony? If the answer to this question is no, then the conflict is non-consentable. (You can see a pattern developing. A "no" answer to any of the key questions makes the conflict non-consentable. One strike and you're out.) But let's assume again that the answer is yes so we can continue the analysis.
   c. The third key is to ask the same questions regarding the *existing* client (Sony). In other words, you must ask the questions about competent and diligent representation from the perspective of "each" affected client, not just one client. This is a mental trick that takes some practice. In the Kazzam example, for instance, you have to think not only about whether your long and valued relationship with Sony will diminish your ability to do your best for Kazzam, but also whether filing suit against Sony will affect whatever legal work you are doing for Sony. Will you be able to accuse Sony executives of breaching a contract when you depose those executives in the Kazzam suit, and then meet with those same Sony executives in the afternoon to counsel them in an unrelated transaction? Will they trust you? Will you be loyal to them? To decide whether the conflict is consentable, you will have to answer those questions.

3. *Rule 1.7(b)(2):* A second type of conflict that is always non-consentable is a representation that is "prohibited by law." Such conflicts don't arise very often. Comment 16 to Rule 1.7 gives three examples of such conflicts.
   a. In some states "substantive law provides that the same lawyer may not represent more than one defendant in a capital case, even with the consent of the clients."
   b. Federal criminal statutes prohibit certain representations by a former government lawyer despite the informed consent of the former client.
   c. In addition, "decisional law in some states limits the ability of a governmental client, such as a municipality, to consent to a conflict of interest."
4. *Rule 1.7(b)(3):* A third type of non-consentable conflict occurs when the representation involves "the assertion of a claim by one client against another client represented by the lawyer in the same litigation or other proceeding before a tribunal." That is, you cannot handle both sides of the same litigation.
   a. For example, if you represent the plaintiff in a breach of contract suit, you may not also agree to represent the defendant in the same suit, even if both clients give their informed consent.
   b. Likewise, if you represent two co-defendants in an auto accident suit, you may not file a cross-claim on behalf of one co-defendant against the other co-defendant.
   c. Rule 1.7(b)(3) also prohibits two *different* lawyers from the same firm from representing parties on opposite sides of the "v." in the same litigation (whether plaintiff and defendant or defendant and third-party defendant). The imputation rule, Rule 1.10(a), imputes the non-consentable conflict to every other lawyer in your firm. Thus, if you cannot cure the conflict by obtaining client consent, then no other lawyer in your firm can cure the conflict by obtaining client consent.
      i. In other words, if you are representing a client in litigation, then no other lawyer in your firm may file a claim against your client or defend a claim by your client in that same litigation, even with informed consent from both clients.
      ii. Thus, if you represent Smith in *Smith v. Jones*, then your partner may not represent Jones in the same case. And if you represent Jones in *Smith v. Jones*, then your partner may not represent Smith.
      iii. The policy reason for making these conflicts non-consentable is that the public would lose faith in the legal system if it thought that lawyers from the same firm were on both sides of a given claim. Most people do not believe this would produce a fair result.

B. *Conflicts with former clients.* However, virtually all conflicts with former clients are consentable. Rule 1.9(a) provides only that you may not materially oppose a former client in a *substantially related matter* "unless the former client gives informed consent, confirmed in writing." The rule does not require that the former client's consent be objectively reasonable or rational — just that the consent be "informed." (Informed consent is sometimes referred to as consent given after "full disclosure," which was the language of the old ABA Model Code of Professional Responsibility.)

1. The reason for treating former clients differently is that you owe a much lower duty of loyalty to former clients than to present clients. You owe a high duty of loyalty to current clients, but almost no duty of loyalty to former clients.
2. Of course, you are free to show greater loyalty to your former clients than the rules require. As a courtesy, you can seek the consent of a former client even when consent is not needed (i.e., when your work for the new client is not "substantially related" to the work you did for the former client), or you can refuse to seek consent if you think a reasonable lawyer would advise the former client not to grant consent.
3. Remember, however, that Rule 1.7(a) requires you to ask whether there is a "significant risk" that your representation of your *current* client "will be materially limited by your responsibilities to another client, *a former client* or a third person" or by your own personal interests.

   a. Regarding the former client, usually the answer will be no. Since you no longer owe a duty of loyalty to your former client (except the duty not to use the former client's confidential information to its detriment), it will not ordinarily make much difference to you whether your opponent is a former client or a complete stranger.
   b. But if you do perceive a "significant risk" under Rule 1.7(a) because you are opposing a former client in a substantially related matter, then you may not seek your current client's consent to the representation unless you reasonably believe, per Rule 1.7(b)(1), that you will be able to provide diligent and competent representation to your current client even though the adversary is your former client. If you don't believe that, then the conflict is non-consentable.

C. If a conflict is consentable, then you may accept the representation provided the client gives informed consent and the consent is confirmed in writing. The next question, then, is what constitutes "informed consent"? What do you have to tell the client to obtain a valid consent?

9. Obtaining Consent to a Conflict

Unless a conflict is non-consentable, you may ethically accept or continue a representation despite the conflict if you obtain your client's "informed consent."

A. To obtain valid consent, you need to tell the client all information the client would find important in deciding whether or not to retain you (or continue to retain you) rather than getting another lawyer. As Comment 18 to Rule 1.7 explains: "Informed consent requires that each affected client be aware of the relevant circumstances and of the material and reasonably foreseeable ways that the conflict could have adverse effects on the interests of that client." The disclosures should ordinarily include your assessment of such things as:

   1. Any existing or potential conflicts with clients or others that might "materially limit" your zeal on behalf of the consenting client.
   2. The likelihood that the conflicts will grow so serious that they may require you to withdraw.
   3. The damage your client will suffer if you are required to withdraw.

B. Sometimes, when a conflict is between two current clients (Clients One and Two), you need to disclose to Client One some information relating to the representation of Client Two. However, because you have an ethical duty of confidentiality to Client Two under Rule 1.6, you cannot disclose Client Two's confidential information unless Client Two consents to the disclosures. (Disclosures for the purpose of obtaining a conflict waiver would not be "impliedly authorized.") If Client Two does not consent to the disclosures, then you cannot make the disclosures necessary to obtain Client One's informed consent, and you therefore cannot obtain a valid consent from Client One. The conflict is therefore non-consentable.

C. If a conflict arises under Rule 1.7(b) because of a significant risk that the new representation will be *materially limited* by your responsibilities to one or more *other current clients* (as opposed to former clients, third parties, or your own personal interests), then you must obtain informed consent from *every* client who may be adversely affected by the conflict. For example:

   a. Suppose two co-defendants want you to represent them in a civil negligence matter (like a case about an auto accident involving three cars — the plaintiff's car and the cars of the two co-defendants). Assuming you reasonably believe you can provide competent and diligent representation to both co-defendants, you must ask both clients for consent to the conflict. You must explain to each client such things as:

      i. The effect of the dual representation on any possible cross-claims they may have against each other. (You are prohibited from asserting cross-claims by one against the other because Rule 1.7(b)(3) absolutely prohibits you from asserting a claim against a party you represent in the same litigation, and consent cannot cure the conflict.)
      ii. What will happen if the conflict later becomes non-consentable. (You'll have to move to withdraw from representing both of them, so both clients will have to get a new attorney in the middle of the litigation.)
      iii. The effect on the attorney-client privilege if either one later blames the other. (Under the attorney-client privilege, neither client will be able to claim the privilege as to conversations with you if they get into a dispute with each other — so if each client eventually hires a new lawyer to file cross-claims blaming the other client for the accident, they will not be able to claim the attorney-client privilege for conversations they had with you while you represented both of them.)

D. Whatever disclosures need to be made, you should make the disclosures in writing. The rules do not require disclosure in writing — they require only that the *consent* be "confirmed" in writing. Therefore, you may ethically make the necessary disclosures orally rather than in writing. But written disclosure is far better for you and for the client.

   1. Written disclosure is better for the client because it is easier to understand, and allows the client to study the situation at leisure before deciding whether to consent to the conflict.
   2. Written disclosure is better for you as a lawyer because it makes a record of exactly what you told the client, thus minimizing the likelihood of later misunderstandings with the court or your client.

E. You are not required to obtain client consent to *immaterial conflict*. Immaterial conflicts are so remote or minor that they do not pose a "significant risk" that they will "materially limit" your representation of any client. In fact, since you don't need consent, you don't even have to *disclose* immaterial conflicts to a client. However, it often makes good business sense to disclose such conflicts and obtain the client's consent to them, because:

   1. The client, a court, or a disciplinary authority may later decide that the conflict is material and you therefore should have disclosed it and obtained your client's consent. Making disclosure and obtaining consent in conflicts

you consider immaterial will avoid making costly mistakes.

2. Honesty is the best policy. The more you tell the client about what you are doing, the more the client will trust you.
3. Clients are basically like travelers looking for a good place to stay. They want a place (a lawyer) they can trust. Your slogan regarding conflicts should therefore be the same as Holiday Inn's old slogan: "No surprises." Don't surprise your clients with conflicts. Tell them about all of your conflicts even if you don't have to, and tell them before the client learns about the conflict from someone else.

10. How Courts Decide Motions to Disqualify

How do courts decide whether to grant or deny motions to disqualify opposing counsel?

A. Courts nearly always start with the rules of legal ethics. The requirements of the rules of ethics vary from state to state, but most states model their rules of ethics quite closely on the ABA Model Rules. These rules have evolved in ways that generally codify case law on conflicts of interest.

B. Courts are not required to disqualify every lawyer who violates the conflict of interest rules, but courts do disqualify violators when "necessary to preserve the integrity of the adversary process." *Board of Education v. Nyquist*, 590 F.2d 1241 (2d Cir. 1979).

C. Courts are less likely to grant motions to disqualify that are raised long after a case begins, or that are raised as a tactic to pressure the other side into settlement. Nevertheless, courts enforce the rules of ethics unless the enforcement would cause unfair hardship to the disqualified lawyer's client or would damage the administration of justice (for example, by unduly delaying trial). Hardship to the disqualified lawyer (lost fees, embarrassment, etc.) is not considered.

11. Obstacles to Appealing Rulings on Motions To Disqualify

A Rulings on motions to disqualify opposing counsel are powerful weapons partly because they are very difficult to appeal. The United States Supreme Court decided three cases in the 1980s strictly limiting the right to appeal from rulings on motions to disqualify.

1. In *Firestone v. Risjord*, 449 U.S. 368 (1981), the Supreme Court held that an order *denying* a motion to disqualify in a civil case was not an appealable "final decision" under 28 U.S.C. § 1291.
2. In *Flanagan v. United States*, 465 U.S. 259 (1984), the Supreme Court held that an order *granting* a motion to disqualify opposing counsel in a *criminal* case was not an appealable final order and did not meet the conditions for an interlocutory appeal.
3. In *Richardson-Merrell, Inc. v. Koller*, 472 U.S. 424 (1985), the Supreme Court held that an order *granting* a motion to disqualify opposing counsel in a *civil* case likewise cannot be appealed until trial is over.

B. Together, these three decisions make it very difficult to appeal a trial court's rulings on motions to disqualify until the entire trial is over. This remains the law today.

C. Mandamus is still available to challenge an erroneous disqualification decision, but the standard for mandamus is high and petitions for mandamus are rarely granted.

B. A MEETING OF THE LAW FIRM'S CONFLICTS COMMITTEE

Let's get a short, practical inside view of the world of law firm conflicts. You are a partner at Woodson, Morgan & Kaplan. The firm has 36 lawyers, including nine lawyers in a branch office in Washington, D.C. The firm's practice is general and wide ranging, including litigation and transactions of many kinds.

You have recently been appointed to the firm's Conflicts Committee. The Conflicts Committee was established to help the firm comply with two rules. ABA Rule 5.1(a) provides that a partner in a law firm (and other lawyers with similar managerial authority) "shall make reasonable efforts to ensure that the firm has in effect measures giving reasonable assurance that all lawyers in the firm conform to the Rules of Professional Conduct." In addition, Comment 3 to Rule 1.7 states, in part: "To determine whether a conflict of interest exists, a lawyer should adopt reasonable procedures, appropriate for the size and type of firm and practice, to determine in both litigation and non-litigation matters the persons and issues involved. Ignorance caused by a failure to institute such procedures will not excuse a lawyer's violation of this Rule." (Citations omitted.) The Conflicts Committee's job is to help Woodson, Morgan & Kaplan decide whether the firm is complying with these conflict of interest rules.

The Committee has two other members, Alicia Rothschild (the Chair) and Lauren Melchrist. The Committee meets once a week, plus whenever an urgent situation arises. The Committee's decision on a conflict matter is final unless it is overruled by the firm's Executive Committee.

Today will be a typical meeting of the Committee. The Chair, Alicia, opens the meeting. "There are two matters on the agenda for today," she says. "The first is a possible suit against a current client. The second is a possible suit against a former client." For each matter we'll go through our usual four-part analysis:

- Is there an actual or potential conflict?
- If so, is it consentable?
- If consentable, what must we disclose to each affected client to obtain valid consent?
- As a business matter, do we want to seek consent (assuming the conflict is consentable), or should we turn the matter down for business reasons without troubling to seek consent?

1. *Suit Against a Current Client.*

Alicia begins: "The first item on our agenda is the possibility of a suit against a current client. A potential new client, Laser Industries, has asked us to bring suit against an important current client, Regal Menswear Co. Is this a conflict?"

"What's the rule?" you ask. This is always a good way to start a conversation about conflicts. Few other areas in legal ethics are governed as much by rules as conflicts of interest.

Lauren opens her book to Rule 1.7(a) and reads: "Rule 1.7(a) says that we have a conflict if either (1) 'the representation of one client will be directly adverse to another client;' or (2) there is a 'significant risk' that the representation of either the new client (Laser) or the current client (Regal Menswear) will be 'materially limited' by our responsibilities to 'another client, a former client or a third person or by a personal interest of the lawyer.' "

"Sounds like a problem here," says Alicia. "We would be directly opposing a current client (Regal Menswear), and Regal is an important client. We might feel limited in the methods we could use, or the claims we could bring. We might not want to accuse Regal of fraud, for example, and we might not want to give Regal's General Counsel a hard time in discovery because the General Counsel is the one who calls us with new matters."

"So we have a conflict," you say, "but can we take the case, despite the conflict, if we obtain our client's informed consent? Is this a consentable conflict, or not?"

"Well, let's look at the four categories of non-consentable conflicts," Lauren explains. "A conflict is non-consentable (meaning we can't even ask for consent, and can't rely on consent even if the client volunteers to consent) if any of the following situations exist: (A) we don't reasonably believe we can provide competent and diligent representation to one or more of the affected clients; (B) the conflict is prohibited by law; (C) we would be asserting a claim against another party that we represent in the same litigation; or (D) one or more of the affected clients will not allow us to make the disclosures we need to make to the other affected clients to obtain informed consent."

"We certainly don't fall into the 'same litigation' or 'prohibited by law' categories," Alicia says. "But do we reasonably believe we can do a good job for all clients here despite the risk of conflict? If so, we can get consent. If not, we can't ask — or if we do ask, and the client says 'yes,' that consent will be invalid, null and void, worthless."

"I think we can do a good job for Laser despite the theoretical worries about pulling our punches to spare Regal Menswear," Lauren says. "We mostly do transactions for Regal. We don't represent them in litigation."

"What difference does that make?" you ask. "We're still all one firm."

"Yes," says Alicia, "but if the same people who represent Regal Menswear in litigation were also handling Laser's suit against Regal, that would be more awkward. The same lawyers would be advocating for Regal one day and advocating against them the next day. It's hard to build up a client on Tuesday and then knock them down on Wednesday."

"Even if the matters are completely unrelated?" you ask.

"Yes, even if the matters are completely unrelated," says Lauren. "We can't sue a current client in any matter, related or unrelated, without that client's consent."

"Oh, that's the 'litigation' exception?" you ask.

"No, you're confusing this idea with Rule 1.7(b)(3), which basically says that you can never file a cross-claim, counterclaim, or any other type of claim against a party that you already represent *in that same litigation*. You can't be on both sides of the same litigation even if all clients give you the most informed consent in the history of the world. Representing both sides in the same litigation is non-consentable, period."

"Well," you ask, "do we represent Regal Menswear in this dispute already? I mean, did Regal contact us for advice on how to deal with a dispute with Laser, like ways of settling the dispute before Laser filed suit, or to ask us to negotiate a deal with Laser in hopes that Laser would not file suit?"

"Excellent question," Alicia says. "We checked, and we don't represent Regal in any matter having anything to do with this particular dispute."

"OK, so we can take it?" you ask.

"Maybe," Lauren says. "but we still have to make sure the conflict is consentable from Regal's perspective as well."

"Why wouldn't it be?" you ask. "You said we don't represent Regal in anything having anything to do with this dispute, and Regal is a huge company that isn't likely to be hurt by a single case against it."

"True," Lauren says, "but every concurrent conflict raises a loyalty question. Regal might be concerned that once we start opposing Regal in some litigation matters, we will change our attitude about the company and have trouble zealously representing Regal in other matters. Suppose we take the deposition of a Regal VP in the morning, really sticking his feet to the fire about trying to cover up some smoking gun documents, and then we have to meet with that same VP in the afternoon to counsel the company about revising its health insurance plan. That would be awkward, wouldn't it? The VP might feel he couldn't fully trust us anymore because we have been disloyal to Regal, and to him personally, by attacking him at the deposition. See the problem?"

"Yes, but I thought you said the matters were completely unrelated — that Laser's matter has nothing to do with the work we do for Regal."

"The *subject and facts* of the Laser suit are completely different from the subject and facts of the work we do for Regal," Alicia explains, "but the *people* are sometimes the same."

"So what's the bottom line?" you ask.

"The bottom line is that we don't think Laser's dispute will involve the same people at Regal or the same lawyers at our firm who work on Regal's matters," says Alicia. "We've looked into the facts far enough to figure that out. We, therefore, reasonably believe we can provide competent and diligent representation to Laser in its litigation, and to Regal in the unrelated matters we handle for it."

"OK, so far so good," says Lauren, "but what do we need to disclose to the clients to obtain consent?"

"We need to disclose all of the significant risks that lead us to believe there's a potential conflict," says Alicia. "And of course we need to start by explaining to Laser that Regal Menswear is a big client of ours, and by telling Regal that Laser plans to file suit against it."

"Will Laser let us tell Regal that Laser is planning to sue Regal?" you ask. "I mean, Laser doesn't want to lose the element of surprise."

"Right," says Lauren. "If Laser won't let us tell Regal about its plans to sue, then the conflict will be non-consentable, and it will be game over. But we anticipated that problem, so we told Laser we represent Regal and asked if we could reveal this. Laser said yes because it has already told Regal that it intends to sue if Regal won't make a fair settlement offer by next Tuesday, so the element of surprise is already gone."

"The bigger problem," adds Alicia, "is what we can tell Laser about Regal. We work on a lot of things for Regal that never become public — potential environmental hazards, questionable labor practices overseas, internal inquiries into possible securities fraud — and we certainly won't get Regal's consent to tell Laser about those projects. But Regal has agreed to let us list it as a client in Martindale-Hubbell, so that's well known. The question is whether Laser will be satisfied if we tell Laser that Regal is a big client in our non-litigation departments, without telling Laser any more."

"Will that be full disclosure?" you ask. "Do you have to tell Laser how much business we do with Regal — how much we bill each month on the average, or how many matters we are handling, etc.?"

"No," says Lauren, "informed consent doesn't require that level of detail. As long as Laser knows we do a lot of legal work for Regal, and are doing some work for Regal now, that satisfies Rule 1.7."

"I think we have to decide whether we want to take this matter for Laser if we can get consent, on the one hand, or turn it down for business reasons without even asking for consent, on the other hand," says Alicia. "I'm for taking it. Laser is a small company today, and this is a small matter, but small clients can grow into big clients. Taking on new matters for small clients is a good way to ensure the future of the firm."

"I agree," says Lauren. "I don't think this one small case will damage our relationship with Regal, and Laser will remember us for a long time because we'll be one of the first law firms Laser has ever hired. Not every law firm is willing to take a risk on a start-up company like Laser."

Alicia says she will arrange for the "responsible partner" for Regal to seek Regal's consent, and for the partner who was contacted by Laser to seek Laser's consent. " If both consent," Alicia says, "the lawyers who obtained oral consent will confirm the consent in writing by sending short letters briefly describing the conflict and noting the client's consent. Rule 1.7(b)(4) requires that consent be confirmed in writing, but we would do it even without the rule because we want a written record of the consent."

Alicia then moves on to the next item on the agenda.

2. *Suit Against a Former Client.*

"The next item on our agenda," says Alicia, "is a possible suit against a former client. Our current client, Walter Sklar, wants to file a fraud suit against the local Pontiac dealer, Jaeger Pontiac. We used to represent Jaeger Pontiac, but then Al Jaeger switched law firms. Now Mr. Sklar wants to sue Jaeger Pontiac for fraud, saying that Jaeger turned back the odometer on a dealer car to make it look like a brand new car."

"What's the rule?" you ask.

"Rule 1.9(a) says, basically, that you can't oppose a former client in a matter that is either the 'same' matter or a matter 'substantially related' to the former representation unless the former client consents."

"Well, that kills it," you say, "because this is a fraud suit, so we couldn't ask for consent anyway."

"No, that doesn't kill it," says Alicia. "When you're dealing with a *current* client, you normally can't ask for consent to a fraud suit because it will ruin your relationship with the current client. You can't accuse a current client of fraud in one matter ("You lied, didn't you, you two-faced phony!") and still do a good job for them in other matters, because the fraud allegations poison the attorney-client relationship. But when you're dealing with a *former* client, the nature of the suit doesn't matter. You don't owe them a duty of loyalty anymore, except for the duty not to abuse their confidential information, because you're not doing any more work for them. Accusing Jaeger Pontiac of fraud won't affect our other work for Jaeger because we're not doing any work for Jaeger now."

"All we owe Jaeger now is a duty of confidentiality, a duty not to use Jaeger's confidential information against them," says Lauren. "We owe them a duty of confidentiality because we promised right from the start, when we began representing Jaeger Pontiac, that we would keep all information relating to the representation strictly confidential. Under Rule 1.9(c), that duty continues to apply to former clients, except for information that has become 'generally known.' We can't go back on our promise of confidentiality just because Jaeger is no longer a client. Clients would hold back a lot of useful information if our promise of confidentiality expired when our representation ended."

"Yeah," says Alicia. "Imagine how clients would feel if we said to them, 'Tell us everything, and we'll keep it strictly confidential — unless you switch law firms, in which case we'll stab you in the back and use all of the information against you as soon as we get the chance.' So the rules don't allow us to breach confidentiality, even after our representation is over, unless the information has become generally known. Rule 1.9(c) specifically says that we can't use or reveal confidential information to harm a former client, and Rule 1.8(b) says just about the same thing."

"Okay," you say, "so let's get down to the main point: Are these two matters substantially related or not? What does 'substantially related' mean?"

"There are at least three different tests," says Alicia. "Under one test, which defines the words 'substantially related' very narrowly, the matters aren't substantially related unless the legal issues are identical. Under this test, very few cases are substantially related, and Rule 1.9(a) hardly has any teeth.

"Under the second test, two matters are substantially related if the earlier matter gave you 'insight' about how the client operates — things like how tough the person is in discovery disputes, how much money he has, or how he feels about getting involved in litigation, and how much he bluffs during settlement negotiations. Under this 'insight' test, almost everything is substantially related, and you can't sue a former client in a substantially related matter without consent. This gives former clients a veto over almost all later representations against them. Fortunately, very few courts use this test.

"Under the third test, two matters are substantially related if the information you would normally have been expected to acquire in one matter is *relevant* to material issues in the other matter. In other words, will the confidential information you probably acquired in the former matter be useful against the former client in the new matter? Can you turn the client's confidential information against them now in a way that would hurt them? This is the prevailing test, and it gives us quite a bit of leeway to oppose former clients while protecting former clients against abuse of their confidential information."

"So under the prevailing 'relevance' test," you ask, "are these matters substantially related or not?"

"That depends on what we did for Jaeger Pontiac before," Alicia says. "If all we did is franchise agreements, tax returns, and loan documents, then the matters probably are not substantially related. But if we defended fraud suits about odometers, or possibly if we *generally* defended Jaeger Pontiac against consumer fraud suits, then the matters are substantially related."

Alicia then asks what Lauren knows about our prior work for Jaeger Pontiac. "We mainly did contract things with General Motors and various loan agreements and disputes with GMAC and local banks. We did defend Jaeger in a fraud suit once when a customer claimed Jaeger didn't disclose all of the terms of the loan, but the case was decided on summary judgment in our favor because the documents made all of the proper disclosures and the customer didn't have any evidence to back up what he said."

"I don't think any of those things are substantially related," Alicia says, "so we can go ahead with this suit without getting consent from Jaeger Pontiac."

"That's right," says Lauren, "but I think we ought to notify Jaeger Pontiac before we sue, just as a courtesy. When we get ready to file, or when we get ready to write a letter, we just ought to call and alert Jaeger that we're going against Jaeger. And if Jaeger is already represented by his new law firm in this matter, then we can't communicate any further to Jaeger, because that would violate Rule 4.2's ban on direct communication with an opposing party represented by counsel."

"Won't notification just send up a red flag and cause Jaeger Pontiac to file a disqualification motion?" you ask.

"On the contrary," says Alicia. "Notifying Jaeger in advance might head off a disqualification motion. If Jaeger appreciates our courtesy, he might tell his lawyers not to run up a huge bill on a disqualification motion that he's likely to lose. And if Jaeger refers us to his lawyers, we will get a chance to argue that the matters are not substantially related *before* the lawyers dig in and file a written motion. People are usually more flexible before they commit to a position in writing. If Jaeger's lawyers make some good points we haven't thought about, we might change our mind before we file suit and get embarrassed by a strong motion to disqualify."

"Yeah, once people file a motion to disqualify and tell the court that you are engaging in unethical conduct," Lauren says, "it's hard for them to back down and say, 'Just kidding. Sorry for wasting everyone's time.' You definitely want to talk to the other side before they decide to file a motion to disqualify, because a lot of times you can talk them out of it. Conversely, if Jaeger convinces us that filing a fraud suit against it would violate Rule 1.9(a), then we would probably decide to withdraw rather than violate the ethics rules. No point in making headlines saying we are unethical and don't follow the rules."

"OK," says Alicia, "so we'll go ahead and take the case against Jaeger Pontiac, and we don't need consent, but tell the responsible partner to notify Jaeger of our intentions as soon as possible. If Jaeger is not represented by counsel yet, then we can talk to him about the suit and get his version of the facts before he retains counsel. Maybe we can even work out a settlement without firing a shot. And if Jaeger has already retained counsel, then he knows something is coming anyway, so we're not giving away any secrets if we tell him we're about to sue."

"That takes care of our Conflicts Committee meeting for today," says Alicia. "We'll meet again the same time next week."

C. ANOTHER MEETING OF THE CONFLICTS COMMITTEE

A week has gone by and it's time for the next meeting of the firm's Conflicts Committee. Below are the items on the agenda for this week's Committee meeting. Most of the matters raise questions about concurrent conflicts of interest, but a few raise conflicts of other kinds. As to each item on the agenda, be prepared to discuss three things:

1. Nature of the conflicts: What are the actual or potential conflicts? If the committee needs more information before making its decision, what specific information would you ask for?

2. Governing rules: What rules of professional conduct or other legal authorities govern the particular conflict?

3. Informed consent: If the conflict is consentable, what must the firm disclose to obtain informed consent to accept (or continue) the representation?

Items on the Conflict Committee's Agenda

A. A potential new client named Acme Widget Co. has asked our law firm to file suit against Ramrod Manufacturing Co., which is one of our firm's current clients. May we accept Acme's case?

B. A potential new client named Riffle Sheet Metal Corp. has asked us to negotiate a contract with Ramrod Manufacturing Co., which is still one of our firm's clients. May we accept Riffle's case?

C. A potential new client named Goggle Ltd. has been sued by our current client Ramrod Manufacturing Co. Goggle has asked us to represent it in defending against the suit. May we agree to defend Goggle?

D. A potential new client named Marcy Hamilton has received an offer to become Vice President for Import/Export at Ramrod Manufacturing Co. (still our firm's current client), and has asked our firm to negotiate the terms of her employment agreement with Ramrod. May we agree to negotiate against Ramrod on Ms. Hamilton's behalf?

E. Tulsa Rentals has gotten into a dispute with the Bel Aire Country Club over the condition of some tables and chairs that the club rented for a party last year. Tulsa Rentals says the club damaged the furniture. The club says that the furniture was already damaged when it was delivered, or was damaged by Tulsa Rentals in transport after the party. Both parties have asked us to represent them in resolving the dispute without litigation.

F. Our firm formerly handled a divorce for Walter Jenner, a wealthy man who owned several businesses and several homes. The divorce became a nasty fight about how to divide Jenner's property and businesses with his wife. In the end, Jenner kept several businesses and a home in Palm Beach. The divorce is over and we have not heard from Walter in about three years. Now, Roberta Mullins has asked our firm to negotiate a contract with Jenner to buy one of his companies. May we represent Ms. Mullins in negotiating the contract with Jenner?

G. One of the lawyer's in our firm's Trusts and Estates Department does estate planning for Dr. Sheila Birnsdorf, a surgeon at Barnes Hospital. A potential new client has asked us to file a medical malpractice suit against three defendants: Barnes Hospital, a surgeon at Barnes who operated on our potential new client, and a nurse who assisted with the operation. May we agree to represent the plaintiff?

H. We represent Olympia Malls in several shopping center ventures, helping Olympia in acquire land, obtain zoning variances, and draw up leases. Now Randy Arline has asked us to sue Town & Country Mall for negligently failing to clear ice from the parking lot, causing Arline to fall and break her arm. Town & Country Mall is a separate corporation but is wholly owned by Olympia Malls. May we sue Town & Country on Arline's behalf?

I. *Hiring a new associate.* The firm wants to make an offer to hire an experienced intellectual property lawyer named Andy Earlham, but first wants a report from our Conflicts Committee about whether hiring Earlham would create any conflicts. Earlham is currently a senior associate at Bryan, Armstrong & Mitchell, a large firm that represents (among many others) Control Data Corporation. Our firm is currently handling a suit *against* Control Data Corporation on behalf of a client named Video-Phone. Will our firm be creating a conflict by hiring Earlham?

J. *Representing a mother and an adopting couple.* A couple who wishes to adopt a child has asked our firm to give them legal advice and draw up the papers to bring about the adoption. The mother who wishes to place her child for adoption has also asked our firm to represent her. Can we represent both the birth mother and the adopting couple?

K. *Representing a business and its customer in writing a contract.* Our firm represents Envirotech, a company that manages the disposal of toxic waste. Envirotech has decided to acquire Lorac Trucking, a large trucking company, so that Envirotech will be able to cart away toxic waste without hiring an outside company. The executives of Envirotech and Lorac Trucking have jointly asked us to represent both Envirotech and Lorac Trucking in bringing about the acquisition.

L. Three years ago our firm was hired to defend Berkley Boats in a product liability suit after a sailboat manufactured by Berkley capsized and sank off Cape Cod. Two people drowned. Recently, a man and his young daughter drowned when a canoe built by Berkley was gashed by a rock and sank in some treacherous whitewater rapids on the Talem River in Oregon. The estates of the man and his daughter have asked our firm to bring a lawsuit against Berkley alleging negligent design and manufacture of the canoe. May we accept the engagement?

M. Our firm is especially well known for appellate litigation. In the past few years we have hired three former U.S. Supreme Court clerks who head up our Appellate Department. Two major companies in the public relations field recently squared off in a nasty lawsuit that just ended. Both companies have asked us to handle the appeal, and both seem willing to let our firm handle both sides (appellant and appellee) as long as we use different teams of lawyers for each client. May we do so?

Chapter 21
WHO IS A "CLIENT"?

Before we go any further in our study of conflicts, we need to ask a question you probably think doesn't need to be asked: Who is a "client"? In conflicts analysis, this is the single most important question. Everything we've said so far about conflicts of interest refers to duties to clients and former clients. If a person or entity isn't a current client and never was a client (or at least a prospective client), then you do not owe them a duty under the rules governing conflicts of interest. (You may owe duties to certain non-clients under other rules, such as ABA Model Rules 4.1, "Truthfulness in Statements to Others," and 4.4, "Respect for Rights of Third Persons," but you do not have duties to them under the conflict rules.) The rules of legal ethics reflect and embody fiduciary duties, but they do not create fiduciary duties to non-clients.

The question of who is a client is also vital in analyzing the attorney-client privilege and the duty of confidentiality. Rule 1.6 imposes a duty of confidentiality on a lawyer only if the person is a client, and Rule 1.9(c) imposes a duty of confidentiality only if a person is a former client. The attorney-client privilege applies only to communications between an attorney and client. Therefore, determining whether a person is a "client" is pivotal to determining whether a lawyer owes a duty of confidentiality to that person and to determining whether the attorney-client privilege applies to confidential communications with that person. In this chapter, however, we focus mainly on determining who is a current client or former client for purposes of the conflicts rules.

Deciding who is a client is a much harder question than it seems. We have to make two critical distinctions.

First, we must distinguish *clients* from *non-clients*. If a person is not a client, then that person has no rights under the conflict of interest rules.

Second, we must distinguish *current clients* from *former clients*. Current clients and former clients both have rights, but their rights are not equal. Lawyers owe much higher duties to current clients than to former clients.

This chapter covers these two issues — (1) How do we distinguish clients from non-clients? and (2) How do we distinguish current clients from former clients?

A. CLIENTS VS. NON-CLIENTS

Typically, a "client" is either (1) an individual who walks into your office and hires you to perform legal services, or (2) a corporation or other entity (e.g., a partnership or labor union) that acts through its agents to hire you to perform legal services. Because a corporation or other entity cannot speak for itself — an entity is just a piece of paper, like a certificate of incorporation or a partnership agreement — such "entity clients" must act through the individuals they employ. These individual constituents of the entity are the ones who have the power to engage you to represent the entity. In a corporation, commonly it is the General Counsel who is authorized to hire "outside counsel," but that authority may also (or instead) be vested in the Chairman of the Board, the Chief Executive Officer, the Chief Financial Officer, or others with high positions in the corporation.

In addition, courts have sometimes defined clients to include people that lawyers would not intuitively regard as clients. We like to call these people "phantom clients" because they are often almost invisible to routine conflicts checks. A prudent lawyer understands, however, that phantom clients can cause just as many conflict problems as ordinary, traditional clients. The main sources of such "phantom" clients are:

(1) trade association members,
(2) co-parties,

(3) potential clients (also called "prospective clients") who had consultation interviews with a firm, but who did not retain the firm (or are still deciding whether to do so),
(4) general partners (and, in some jurisdictions, limited partners) in partnerships,
(5) officers, employees, or shareholders in small corporations, and
(6) affiliates, divisions, parents, subsidiaries, and other companies in the same "corporate family" as companies for whom you have done legal work.

Lawyers used to not think much about phantom clients. A client was an individual that you met in person in your office to work through a legal problem, or someone you advised over the telephone or by letter. In those good old days, lawyers knew who their clients were (or at least thought they did). But a great deal changed in the mid-1970s when disqualification motions began to proliferate and courts became much more exacting about the meaning of the term "client."

The following case is the granddaddy of phantom client cases. It is a classic case whose often-cited analysis still rings true. It deals with a motion to disqualify a law firm for opposing a current client without consent — but the heart of the case is a battle over determining who the law firm's client is.

WESTINGHOUSE ELECTRIC CORP. v. KERR-McGEE CORP.

580 F.2d 1311 (7th Cir. 1978)

[Kirkland and Ellis ("Kirkland") was one of the largest law firms in Chicago and had a Washington, D.C. branch office as well. In 1975, in the wake of the Arab oil embargo of 1973–1974, Congress was considering bills to break up the oil companies, both vertically by separating their control over production, transportation, refining and marketing entities, and horizontally by prohibiting cross-ownership of alternative energy resources in addition to oil and gas. This proposed legislation threatened to force oil companies to divest themselves of millions of dollars of assets, including their massive uranium holdings. The sponsors of this legislation argued that oil companies were unlawfully restraining trade in the uranium industry. They were thus impeding the progress of nuclear power, which was considered necessary to free the United States of dependence on foreign oil. The American Petroleum Institute (the "API") hired Kirkland to persuade Congress that the oil companies were *not* monopolizing the uranium industry and that the uranium industry was highly competitive. Kirkland sent out confidential questionnaires to API members, including such giants as Gulf, Getty, and Kerr-McGee, and held confidential interviews with executives of major oil producers in API.]

[On October 15, 1976, Kirkland's Washington, D.C. office released a report arguing that the oil companies were competitive. On the same day, however, Kirkland's Chicago office filed a complaint on behalf of Westinghouse Electric Corporation ("Westinghouse") alleging that several API members, including many of those surveyed and interviewed by Kirkland during its API work, had engaged in an illegal conspiracy in restraint of trade in the uranium industry.]

[Soon after the complaint was filed, several defendants who were members of the API moved to disqualify Kirkland. The district court denied the motion to disqualify, primarily because (1) in the uranium survey, Kirkland had been representing the API, not its members, and (2) there was a "wall" between Kirkland's Chicago office and Kirkland's D.C. office, so even if the Chicago office was opposing a client of the D.C. office, the realities of modern law practice made disqualification an inappropriate remedy for a violation of the rules. By the time the Seventh Circuit wrote this opinion, Kirkland's representation of Westinghouse's uranium litigation had required the efforts of 8 to 14 of its attorneys and had generated some $2.5 million in legal fees.]

SPRECHER, J. delivered the opinion of the Court:

I

On February 25, 1976, Ritchie [of the API] wrote to Frederick M. Rowe, a partner in Kirkland's Washington office, retaining the firm to review the divestiture hearings and "prepare arguments for use in opposition to this type of legislation." On May 4, 1976, Ritchie added that the Kirkland firm's work for API "should include the preparation of possible testimony, analyzing the probable legal consequences and antitrust considerations of the proposed legislation" and "you should make an objective survey and study of the probable effects of the pending legislation, specifically including probable effects on oil companies that would have to divest assets." Ritchie noted that "[as] a part of this study, we will arrange for interviews by your firm with a cross-section of industry personnel." The May 4 letter to Rowe concluded with:

> Your firm will, of course, act as an independent expert counsel and hold any company information learned through these interviews in strict confidence, not to be disclosed to any other company, or even to API, except in aggregated or such other form as will preclude identifying the source company with its data.

On May 25, 1976, Ritchie sent to 59 API member companies a survey questionnaire seeking data to be used by Kirkland in connection with its engagement by API. In the introductory memorandum to the questionnaire, Ritchie advised the 59 companies that Kirkland had "ascertained that certain types of data pertinent to the pending anti-diversification legislation are not now publicly available" and the API "would appreciate your help in providing this information to Kirkland. . . . " The memorandum included the following:

> Kirkland, Ellis & Rowe is acting as an independent special counsel for API, and will hold any company information in strict confidence, *not to be disclosed to any other company, or even to API*, except in aggregated or such other form as will preclude identifying the source company with its data.

(Emphasis in original). The data sought was to assist Kirkland "in preparing positions, arguments and testimony in opposition to this type of legislative [divestiture]" and was not to be sent to API but rather to Kirkland.

AUTHORS' COMMENT:

Does the language of this letter remind you of the questionnaire sent to Upjohn's employees by Upjohn's general counsel? Recall that the questionnaire seeking information in *Upjohn* promised confidentiality and directed that all responses to the questionnaire be sent directly to the company's general counsel. Largely for that reason, the Supreme Court held that the communications in *Upjohn* were privileged. Keep the *Upjohn* case in mind whenever you read about corporations or other organizational parties.

Pursuant to the provision in Ritchie's May 4, 1976 letter to Rowe that interviews would be arranged with a cross-section of industry personnel, Nolan Clark, a Kirkland partner, interviewed representatives of eight oil companies between April 29 and June 15, 1976.

After going through several drafts, the final Kirkland report to API was released on October 15, 1976. The final report contains 230 pages of text and 82 pages of exhibits. References to uranium appear throughout the report and uranium is the primary subject of about 25 pages of text and 11 pages of exhibits. The report marshals a large number of facts and arguments to show that oil company diversification does not threaten overall energy competition. In particular the report asserts that the relatively high concentration ratios in the uranium industry can be expected to decline, that current increases in uranium prices are a result of increasing demand, that oil company entry into uranium production has stimulated competition and diminished concentration, that oil companies have no incentive to act in concert to restrict coal or uranium production and that the historical record refutes any charge that oil companies have restricted uranium output. The report concludes that "the energy industries, both individually and collectively, are competitive today and are likely to remain so."

As noted at the outset of this opinion, the API report was issued on the same day as the present antitrust suit was filed against several defendants, including Gulf, Kerr-McGee and Getty.

The district court . . . observed that "[perhaps] in recognition of the diametrically opposing theories of the API report and the Westinghouse complaint, Kirkland does not attempt to rebut the oil companies' charges that it has simultaneously taken inconsistent positions on competition in the uranium industry."

AUTHORS' COMMENT:

Is the district court saying that this is an "issue conflict"? Yes, but it's much more. In a classic "issue conflict" (also called a "positional conflict"), a law firm takes a position on behalf of one client that undermines a position simultaneously taken on behalf of another client in a matter whose parties are otherwise completely different and unrelated. Thus, the typical issue conflict poses no danger that the lawyers will use a client's confidential information against another client.

Here, however, the parties in the two matters are the same. Kirkland & Ellis is suing the oil companies on behalf of its client, Westinghouse, while simultaneously representing API — and the matters are related. Thus, there is a danger that Kirkland & Ellis will use confidential information supplied by the oil companies.

The question then becomes: Are the oil companies "clients" of Kirkland & Ellis? The district court addressed this question literally and answered no — the district court viewed Kirkland's client as the API, not the individual oil companies who belong to API. The Seventh Circuit is struggling to see whether the definition of a "client" should also include the companies that gave confidential information to Kirkland & Ellis, even though they had no formal retainer or attorney-client agreement with the firm.

II

The crux of the district court's determination was based upon its view that an "attorney-client relationship is one of agency to which the general rules of agency apply" and "arises *only* when the parties have given their consent, either express or implied, to its formation." (Emphasis supplied)

Of course in many respects and situations an attorney acts as a simple agent for the client, but the attorney is held to obligations to the client which go far beyond those of an agent and beyond the principles of agency, just as they transcend the legal bounds of an arms-length commercial transaction.

III

The client is no longer simply the person who walks into a law office. A lawyer employed by a corporation represents the entity but that principle does not of itself solve the potential conflicts existing between the entity and its individual participants.

Three district courts have held that each individual member of an *unincorporated* association is a client of the association's lawyer.

Here we are faced with neither an ordinary commercial corporation nor with an informal or unincorporated association, but instead with a nation-wide trade association with 350 corporate and 7,500 individual members and doing business as a non-profit corporation.

We need not make any generalized pronouncements of whether an attorney for such an organization represents every member because this case can and should be decided on a much more narrow ground.

There are several fairly common situations where, although there is no express attorney-client relationship, there exists nevertheless a fiduciary obligation or an implied professional relation:

(1) The fiduciary relationship existing between lawyer and client extends to preliminary consultation by a prospective client with a view to retention of the lawyer, although actual employment does not result.

(2) When information is exchanged between codefendants and their attorneys in a criminal case, an attorney who is the recipient of such information breaches his fiduciary duty if he later, in his representation of another client, is able to use this information to the detriment of one of the co-defendants, even though that co-defendant is not the one which he represented in the criminal case.

(3) When an insurer retains an attorney to investigate the circumstances of a claim and the insured, pursuant to a cooperation clause in the policy, cooperates with the attorney, the attorney may not thereafter represent a third party suing the insured nor indeed continue to represent the insurer once a conflict of interest surfaces.

In none of the above categories or situations did the disqualified or disadvantaged lawyer or law firm actually represent the "client" in the sense of a formal or even express attorney-client relation. In each of those categories either an implied relation was found or at least the lawyer was found to owe a fiduciary obligation to the laymen.

The professional relationship for purposes of the privilege for attorney-client communications "hinges upon the client's belief that he is consulting a lawyer in that capacity and his manifested intention to seek professional legal advice." The affidavits before the district court established that: the Washington counsel for Gulf "was given to believe that the Kirkland firm was representing both API and Gulf;" Kerr-McGee's vice president understood a Kirkland partner to explain that Kirkland was working on behalf of API and also its members such as Kerr-McGee; and Getty's vice president stated that in submitting data to Kirkland he "acted upon the belief and expectation that such submission was made in order to enable [Kirkland] to render legal service to Getty in furtherance of Getty's interests."

A fiduciary relationship may result because of the nature of the work performed and the circumstances under which confidential information is divulged.

AUTHORS' COMMENT:

The Seventh Circuit is satisfied that Kirkland was acting as a lawyer for (i.e., "represented") Gulf, Getty, and Kerr-McGee, and therefore ha d fiduciary duties to them. The question that remains is whether Kirkland should therefore be disqualified from prosecuting the antitrust suit against Gulf, Getty, and Kerr-McGee.

Kirkland argued that it should not be disqualified because it had set up a "Chinese Wall" between its Chicago office and its D.C. office. (A "Chinese Wall," also called a "screen," is an imaginary wall erected between lawyers working on conflicting matters.) The lawyers working on the Westinghouse antitrust suit were not supposed to discuss any aspect of their work with the lawyers working on the lobbying effort on behalf of the oil companies, and vice versa. Should this wall be enough to let Kirkland stay in the case? Circle one: Yes No.

[W]e do not recognize the wall theory as modifying the presumption that actual knowledge of one or more lawyers in a firm is imputed to each member of that firm. Here there exists a very reasonable possibility of improper professional conduct despite all efforts to segregate the two sizeable groups of lawyers. . . .

Gulf, Kerr-McGee and Getty each entertained a reasonable belief that it was submitting confidential information regarding its involvement in the uranium industry to a law firm which had solicited the information upon a representation that the firm was acting in the undivided interest of each company. . . . If Kirkland's size and multi-city status had any effect, it was in the direction of encouraging the oil companies to divulge confidential information. Whereas they might show reluctance to entrust their substantial assets and future fortunes to a sole practitioner or small law firm, Kirkland's substance and reputation would tend to comfort any apprehensions and open the lines of communication. In any event, there is no basis for creating separate disqualification rules for large firms even though the burden of complying with ethical considerations will naturally fall more heavily upon their shoulders.

NOTES AND QUESTIONS

1. ***The Client's Belief Is the Key.*** The *Westinghouse* court quotes Professor McCormick's famous evidence hornbook for the proposition that whether or not a person is a client "hinges upon the client's belief. . . . " A footnote contains the following quote from R. Wise, Legal Ethics 284 (1970), an old but respected book: "The deciding factor is what the prospective client thought when he made the disclosure, not what the lawyer thought."

Remember: What *you* think as a lawyer won't carry the day. The important factor in deciding who is a client is what your *client* thinks. If you think a person with whom you are dealing could have any room for doubt as to whether he is a client — especially if you think he is not a client — put the issue on the table and deal with it promptly and candidly. Remind the person, "I'm not your lawyer." Explain that you haven't accepted the case, or that you have finished the case and won't be doing any more work, or that you represent the organization rather than the individual. Then document the conversation with a letter to the would-be client, or at least to your file. If you give a person a good reason to think you are serving as his or her lawyer, the person may think just that — and when conflicts of interest arise, you'll have to pay the piper for allowing the ambiguity to survive. First thing to do, let's kill all the ambiguities. (Less commonly, lawyers sometimes do work for people they think are clients, but receive a rude awakening when the person says, "Hey, I never hired you to do that. I'm not paying your bill." Before you do work for a person, make sure the person is your client and wants you to do the work.)

2. *Mega-Firms.* The *Westinghouse* case illustrates the fundamental rule that you can't oppose a current client without the client's consent. The result for Kirkland & Ellis was that the firm was forced to give up a massive and highly lucrative antitrust case. Should this rule be applied so rigidly to large firms? Aren't large firms unusually vulnerable to disqualification because they represent so many different clients in so many different fields? Should there be an exception for lawyers who can show that they have been "toiling in the wilderness" — practicing in a part of the firm that is demonstrably remote from where the conflicting interests lie? Or is occasional disqualification just part of the price that firms pay for growing large?

3. *A Microsoft Scheme.* Here's a scenario: Suppose Microsoft wants to make sure that the best law firms in every major city in America are in its corner in every legal matter that comes up, whether it's real estate or litigation or contract negotiations. Phrased another way, Microsoft wants to make sure that no major law firm can oppose it, ever. How can Microsoft insure this?

Suppose Microsoft parcels out its work in each major city so that, say, three different firms in each city handle its real estate matters, five different firms handle its litigation matters, four firms take care of contract work, and so on. Maybe Microsoft would hire even more firms in the largest cities. (When your company has the lion's share of a multi-billion-dollar market, there's plenty of legal work to go around.)

Now suppose that one of Microsoft's competitors becomes unhappy about Microsoft's domination of the operating system market and wants to sue Microsoft for antitrust violations (such as monopolization, or contracts in restraint of trade). Or suppose a company wants to sue Microsoft for breach of a multi-million dollar contract. Who will ethically be able to take the suit? Who can oppose Microsoft? Can we rule out every major firm in America that currently represents Microsoft? By giving a steady stream of little projects to lots of different firms, has Microsoft bought itself insurance against being opposed by any of those firms? In short, will the scheme work? If so, is it fair? If not, should we change the rules so that it will work?

B. CURRENT CLIENTS VS. FORMER CLIENTS

Let's continue the Microsoft scenario so we can pose our second major inquiry: When does a current client become a former client? Microsoft may not have something for every firm to work on every day from now until eternity. Does Microsoft remain a current client during the lulls and lapses, or does Microsoft become a former client every time a project ends? Is Microsoft still a current client of a firm that has done work for Microsoft in the past but isn't handling anything at the moment? How do we tell the difference between a current client and a former client? These are hard questions. They are squarely faced in the next case, which also addresses the problem of mega-firm disqualification. Do you like the answers?

SWS FINANCIAL FUND A v. SALOMON BROTHERS INC.

790 F. Supp. 1392 (N.D. Ill. 1992)

BRIAN BARNETT DUFF, J.

On November 20, 1991, Hickey, represented by Schiff, Hardin and Waite, filed this suit against Salomon Brothers. Prompting this suit was a press release dated August 9, 1991, in which Salomon admitted to irregularities and rule violations in connection with its submitting bids at certain Treasury auctions. Sometime not long thereafter, plaintiffs sought Schiff's advice and took steps to present their claim to Salomon. Schiff has provided a substantial amount of legal services to various of the plaintiff entities since 1982.

Salomon Brothers' relationship with Schiff traces to October, 1989 when Marcy Engel, Vice-President and Counsel of Salomon Brothers, met Kenneth Rosenzweig, a Schiff partner, at a professional conference. Engel was impressed by Rosenzweig's work experience as a lawyer with the Commodity Futures Trading Commission (CFTC) and his knowledge of commodities law. Rosenzweig had worked for the CFTC for eight years prior to joining Schiff in 1987.

In May, 1990, Salomon authorized Engel to retain Mr. Rosenzweig to assist in putting together a compliance manual for Salomon's commodity futures trading operations. Rosenzweig worked on the project throughout 1990 and on November 20, 1990, he sent Salomon the final draft of Schiff's part of the compliance manual. During the course of the project, Rosenzweig met with a number of Salomon personnel and learned about the futures accounts of Salomon and Salomon's subsidiary, Plaza Clearing Corporation, and about the organization of Salomon's customer and proprietary futures business. According to Mr. Randall, Rosenzweig was also educated in detail about Salomon's management of customer order flow and its reaction to, or management decisions about, trading errors.

In a letter dated November 20, 1990 accompanying the work product on the compliance manual, Rosenzweig wrote:

> I have enclosed what I hope will be the final version (subject, as always, to legal and regulatory developments).

The November 20, 1990 letter, addressed to Terry Randall, concluded with Rosenzweig's stating that, "I have enjoyed working with you and Marcy [Engel] on this project . . . ."

AUTHORS' COMMENT:

After this letter, is Salomon still a client of Schiff, Hardin & Waite or not? The lawyer was asked to do one discrete project — develop a manual to show Salomon's employees how to comply with commodities futures trading regulations. The lawyer has sent Salomon what he considers a "final version" of the manual, "subject, as always, to legal and regulatory developments." Is the representation over? Is the lawyer (and his law firm) now free to oppose Salomon in litigation? Or is Salomon still a current client that cannot be sued without its consent? This is the question the court will now try to answer. What factors should the court consider?

Salomon states that as far as it was concerned the compliance manual project was never fully completed and is still ongoing. In either July or August, 1991, Randall requested that Mr. Rosenzweig provide Salomon with a computer diskette including all the material that Rosenzweig had prepared for the futures compliance manual. Rosenzweig sent the diskette to Mr. Randall along with a letter dated August 30, 1991, in which he stated, "Best of luck in (finally) completing this project!"

Apart from the compliance manual, Schiff undertook a number of other discrete research projects for Salomon, answering commodity law questions when they cropped up. For example, on May 17, 1990, Ms. Engel asked for advice relating to the use of U.S. Treasury securities in meeting the margin obligations for futures contracts. . . . Mr. Rosenzweig provided an answer in a telephone call to Ms. Engel on May 22, 1990.

It is not clear from the record what the other projects were, exactly when they were performed or what went into them. Ms. Engel refers to Schiff's having worked on "not fewer than six matters involving various compliance and regulatory issues."

Schiff most recently worked on a Salomon project on June 24–25, 1991. On June 24, Ms. Engel called Mr. Rosenzweig. During her telephone call, Engel posed a number of questions about the use of customer-owned Treasury securities in meeting futures contract margin requirements. Rosenzweig answered those questions in a letter to Engel dated June 25, 1991.

Since June 25, Schiff has not performed any legal work for Salomon. Nonetheless there has been a fair amount of contact between the two. In addition to the diskette request discussed above, Salomon personnel and Rosenzweig have corresponded on a number of matters. Tellingly, on August 13, 1991, Mr. Rosenzweig telephoned John Shinkle, then-General Counsel of Salomon, in order to receive his consent allowing Schiff to represent a commodity trading advisor in negotiations with Salomon. After Rosenzweig assured Shinkle that the matter was wholly unrelated to the work Schiff had done for Salomon in the past, Rosenzweig obtained Salomon's consent. Rosenzweig states in his affidavit that "in making that request, I was proceeding in the mistaken belief that Salomon's consent was required even though my last assignment from Salomon had been completed nearly two months earlier."

AUTHORS' COMMENT:

Why did Rosenzweig make this mistake? Did he forget that under Rule 1.9(a) he did not need consent to oppose a former client in a wholly unrelated matter (i.e., a matter not "substantially related")? Or did he think Salomon was still a current client in August of 1991, in which case he did need consent (because a lawyer always needs consent to act "directly adverse" to a current client). We'll never know, but at least you can avoid making the same mistake when you go into practice.

Rosenzweig has also sent two billings since June 25. The first of the two billings, sent on July 22, 1991, was accompanied by a letter from Mr. Rosenzweig to Ms. Engel in which he wrote:

> I appreciate the opportunity to provide legal services to you, as do others within our firm who participate in these matters. Please do not hesitate to contact me if you have any questions regarding the enclosed.

On September 13, 1991, Rosenzweig again sent Ms. Engel copies of previously submitted, unpaid bills for services rendered by Schiff in May and June, 1991. Rosenzweig's accompanying letter of September 13 lacked the hint of availability that was part of his July 22 letter.

AUTHORS' COMMENT:

What is the import of saying, "Please contact me if you have any questions regarding the enclosed"? Does that mean (1) we're still your lawyers, or (2) we've finished all of our work for you, but we'd like to start being your lawyers again? What does it mean that this "hint of availability" was not included in Rosenzweig's next letter? Are we just reading tea leaves here?

The last batch of correspondence between Rosenzweig and Salomon concerned a proposed rule change by the CFTC. During the course of a conference on commodities law held on October 16–18, 1991, Rosenzweig spoke with Engel and Randall about a proposed new rule submitted to the CFTC by the Chicago Mercantile Exchange. That rule was actively opposed by another client of Schiff's and Rosenzweig had prepared a comment letter on behalf of that other client. Mr. Rosenzweig attempted to enlist Salomon's support for the comment letter both at the conference and in two follow-up letters.

Rosenzweig enclosed with the first of the two letters, dated October 22, 1991, the comment letter sent to the CFTC on behalf of the other client, a copy of the proposed rule, and a description of what Schiff considered to be some of the practical effects of the rule. At the end of the letter, he wrote, "Please feel free to call me if you would like to discuss this further."

On December 17, 1991, Mr. Rosenzweig again encouraged Ms. Engel to send comments to the CFTC on behalf of Salomon Brothers. He again included the comment letter that Schiff had drafted for another client and again closed his letter stating, "Please feel free to call me if you have any questions or if you would like to discuss this further."

AUTHORS' COMMENT:

Does this episode prove anything? If Schiff was representing a client in drumming up support for a letter commenting on a proposed regulation, wouldn't its job have been to contact other players in the industry and persuade them to sign on? Suppose Schiff had sent a copy of the comment letter to Merrill Lynch, whom Schiff had never represented, and said, "Please call if you would like to discuss this further." Would that make Merrill Lynch a client? Does it make any difference that Schiff had represented Salomon in the past? If so, why?

Meanwhile, Schiff attorneys pursued their representation of Hickey, a representation directly adverse to Salomon Brothers. In fact, several meetings were held between the plaintiff, Schiff and Salomon Brothers legal personnel. On September 16, 1991, two months before the complaint was filed, plaintiffs' agent Robert Hickey and his attorney Roger Pascal of Schiff met with Salomon's newly appointed General Counsel, Robert Denham, and William McIntosh, Salomon's Director of New York Sales Management. Following that meeting, lawyers representing Salomon communicated with Schiff in efforts to reach a settlement or to find an alternative dispute resolution mechanism that would obviate the need for civil litigation. Schiff, however, apparently never informed Salomon during those communications that it had ever represented Salomon on any matter. For its part, Salomon's lawyers conducted negotiations with lawyers from Schiff unaware of, or at least without taking note of, Salomon's relationship with Schiff.

AUTHORS' COMMENT:

Does the client have any responsibility to check for conflicts? Salomon is negotiating lawyers from Schiff to avert a major lawsuit. Couldn't Salomon have said, "Hey, Schiff Hardin, how can you represent those guys against us? We're your client!" Did Salomon, by failing to say something like that, waive any rights Salomon may have had to disqualify Schiff Hardin? Should clients be jointly responsible with their lawyers to be on the lookout for conflicts, and to speak up when they perceive a conflict? (Unfortunately, the court isn't going to help us answer this question — Schiff Hardi n waived the argument by never raising it! But you should answer it. It's an important question.)

Schiff first informed a Salomon officer of the potential conflict in early December, 1991. Sometime in the first two weeks of December, Terry Randall called Mr. Rosenzweig. Randall states that he called in order to learn the status of the CFTC comment letter and to wish Rosenzweig a happy holiday. Then, Randall avers, "near the beginning of the call, Mr. Rosenzweig informed me that he could not discuss the comment letter . . . [and] that he could no longer advise Salomon due to a conflict." Rosenzweig remembers the call somewhat differently. According to Rosenzweig, Randall never mentioned the proposed CFTC rule change. Rosenzweig states that at the outset of the call, he informed Randall that if Randall was calling for substantive legal advice, he could not help because of a conflict. Rosenzweig averred, however, that he would have been willing to discuss the comment letter written on behalf of another client as any such discussion would have been in furtherance of representation of that other client and presumably would not have been time billed to Salomon. Rosenzweig asked whether Randall was aware that Schiff represented Hickey in the present lawsuit. Randall responded that he was aware of the suit but not of Schiff's involvement in it. Rosenzweig then stated that he had enjoyed working with Engel and Randall and hoped that he could resume doing work for Salomon once the Hickey lawsuit concluded. He also indicated that if Randall wished to continue the relationship, Salomon should discuss the matter internally.

AUTHORS' COMMENT:

If Rosenzweig hopes that he can "resume doing work for Salomon once the Hickey lawsuit concluded," does that create a conflict of interest? Do you think Rosenzweig will conduct the litigation against Salomon with less vigor because he hopes to attract the firm as a client again later? Or will he be as tough as possible, to impress Salomon with his no-holds-barred litigation skills?

According to Richard Scribner, Salomon's Director of Compliance, Mr. Randall promptly informed him that Schiff was involved in the Hickey suit against Salomon Brothers and that therefore Schiff could not advise Salomon in connection with the proposed new CFTC rule. Mr. Scribner states that he "was unaware of exactly what matters were involved in the Hickey suit, and [that he] simply did not focus on the conflict issue but put it temporarily out of [his] mind."

On January 3, 1992, Frederic Krieger, Salomon's newly appointed Vice-President and

Chief Compliance Counsel, made a social telephone call to Burton Rissman, a senior partner at Schiff. During the course of the social call, made to exchange New Year's greetings and to discuss Krieger's recent employment by Salomon, Krieger mentioned that he was aware that some Schiff attorneys were working on the commodities futures compliance manual. Mr. Rissman responded by reminding Krieger that Kenneth Rosenzweig was the attorney who had worked on the project and that Mr. Rosenzweig had completed his work on it. Krieger also states that Mr. Rissman told him that Schiff was unable to do further work for Salomon due to Schiff's representation of an unidentified party adverse to Salomon.

On January 7, 1992, Ms. Engel and Mr. Scribner called Andrew Klein, a partner at Schiff's Washington, D.C. office for the purpose of retaining his services on a matter unrelated to either the Hickey suit or the subject of Rosenzweig's work. Mr. Klein called Mr. Scribner on January 9, 1992 to inform him that there was a potential conflict of interest problem in light of Schiff's participation in the Hickey litigation. Klein asked Scribner whether Salomon would be amenable to a waiver and Scribner replied that a waiver was probable.

On January 9, 1992, both Mr. Krieger and Mr. Scribner spoke with Robert Denham, Salomon's General Counsel, about the conflict. According to Mr. Denham, he was unaware prior to January 9, 1992 that there was any connection between Schiff and Salomon Brothers outside of the Hickey lawsuit. The following day, January 10, 1992, Salomon notified Schiff and this court of the possibility of the present disqualification motion which was brought on January 30, 1992.

AUTHORS' COMMENT:

Now the court will systematically analyze the situation, starting with the first inquiry that we always have to make: Was Salomon a current ("present") client? If so, then Schiff can't oppose Salomon without consent even in unrelated matters. If not, then Schiff can oppose it without consent unless the new matter is "substantially related" to the old matters. Based on what you have heard so far, do you think Salomon was a current client of Schiff's when Schiff began opposing it?

Discussion

A. Salomon Was a Present Client

Salomon Brothers contends that Schiff's adverse representation of Hickey violated Rule 1.7 of the Rules of Professional Conduct for the Northern District of Illinois. Rule 1.7(a) regulates an attorney's ability to undertake representation adverse to a present client. It provides:

> A lawyer shall not represent a client if the representation of that client will be directly adverse to another client, unless:
>
> (1) the lawyer reasonably believes the representation will not adversely affect the relationship with the other client; and
>
> (2) each client consents after disclosure.

In the alternative, Salomon argues that even if its client relationship with Schiff had terminated, Schiff's participation in this lawsuit violates Rule 1.9. Rule 1.9(a) regulates an attorney's ability to undertake representation adverse to a former client. It provides:

> A lawyer who has formerly represented a client in a matter shall not thereafter represent another person in the same or a substantially related matter in which the person's interests are materially adverse to the interests of the former client unless the former client consents after disclosure.

This court concludes that Salomon Brothers was a *current* client of Schiff's at the time that Schiff undertook the adverse representation and that therefore Rule 1.7 applies. There is no question that Salomon Brothers was a client of Schiff's on June 25, 1991 — the last day on which Schiff performed billable work on Salomon's behalf. The question is whether their lawyer-client relationship ended somehow between then and the time that Schiff undertook its adverse representation. The comment to Rule 1.3 discusses the termination of a lawyer-client relationship. In pertinent part the comment states that:

> Unless the relationship is terminated as provided in Rule 1.16, a lawyer should carry through to conclusion all matters undertaken for a client. If a lawyer's employment is limited to a specific matter, the relationship terminates when the matter has been resolved. *If a lawyer has served a client over a substantial period in a variety of matters, the client may assume that the lawyer will continue to serve on a continuing basis unless the lawyer gives notice of withdrawal. Doubt about whether a client-lawyer relationship still exists should be clarified by the lawyer, preferably in writing, so that the client will not mistakenly suppose the lawyer is looking after the client's affairs when the lawyer has ceased to do so.* (Emphasis added [by the court].)

The undisputed facts demonstrate that Schiff served Salomon Brothers over a thirteen-month period, answering Salomon's commodity law questions as they arose. The comment makes clear that Salomon Brothers was entitled to "assume" that Schiff would continue to be its lawyer on a continuing basis and that Schiff had the responsibility for clearing up any doubt as to whether the client-lawyer relationship persisted. Consequently, this court finds that Salomon was a present client at the time Schiff began to represent Hickey against Salomon.

The case law also holds that, once established, a lawyer-client relationship does not terminate easily. Something inconsistent with the continuation of the relationship must transpire in order to end the relationship. Indeed, Schiff offered no case law supporting its position that its relationship with Salomon had come to an end. . . .

AUTHORS' COMMENT:

Now comes the kind of analysis you like to read. It explains the three basic ways that the attorney-client relationship can end. If you like reading black letter law, this Bud's for you.

Schiff cites *Artromick International, Inc. v. Drustar*, 134 F.R.D. 226 (S.D. Ohio 1991) . . . That court, however, ruled that the attorney-client relationship is terminated only by the occurrence of one of a small set of circumstances. First, the *Drustar* court stated that the relationship can be terminated by the express statement of either the attorney or the client. Second, acts inconsistent with the continuation of the relationship (e.g., the client's filing a grievance with the local bar association against the attorney) are a second means. In *Drustar*, the court ruled that the client was a former client because he had refused to pay the attorney's bill and had retained other lawyers to do legal work which that attorney had formerly performed. Third, even without overt statements or acts by either party, the relationship may lapse over time.

None of the three terminating events outlined in *Drustar* is present here. First, there was no express termination by either party. Moreover, an express termination made by Schiff would have been invalid if made for the purposes of dropping Salomon like a "hot potato" in order to obtain the more lucrative business Hickey could provide. See *Stratagem Development Corp. v. Heron International N.V.*, 756 F. Supp. 789 (S.D.N.Y. 1991).

Second, the parties' behavior was not inconsistent with the continuation of the relationship. Indeed, if anything, their behavior weighs very heavily in the direction of finding that the relationship was continuing. On August 13, about the time that Schiff began its work for Hickey against Salomon, Mr. Rosenzweig called Salomon's General Counsel to obtain consent for Schiff's representation of a commodity trading advisor in negotiations with Salomon. The other contacts between the firm and Salomon uniformly were conducted with the tone of a friendly, professional relationship, not at all inconsistent with the continuation of the lawyer-client relationship.

Third, it can not reasonably be stated that the relationship lapsed due to the passage of time. Within two months of finishing its last billable project on June 25, 1991, Schiff had begun its adverse representation. The complaint was filed November 20, less than six months later. By comparison, the lawyer in *Amalloy* began its adverse representation four years after last working for the client, yet the client was held to be a current client.

Thus, the court finds that Schiff's representation of Hickey in this suit violates Rule 1.7 of the Rules of Professional Conduct. . . .

AUTHORS' COMMENT:

Now that the court has found a violation of Rule 1.7, should the court disqualify Schiff? Why might the court not want to disqualify Schiff? If the court does not disqualify Schiff, will Schiff suffer any penalty at all for violating the rule against opposing a current client? Take a stab at these questions before you read on.

B. Disqualification Is Not the Appropriate Sanction

Salomon Brothers has assumed that disqualification automatically follows from a finding that a law firm has violated a conflict of interest rule. That assumption is not correct. . . . The reporter of the ABA Committee that drafted the Code of Professional Responsibility has stated that the Code, including the disciplinary rule governing conflicts of interest with current clients (DR 5-102), was aimed at discipline and was not meant as a guideline for disqualification.

"Although disqualification is ordinarily the result of a finding that a disciplinary rule prohibits an attorney's appearance in a case, disqualification is never automatic."

This court is unaware of any Seventh Circuit authority which requires disqualification upon a showing that a law firm has violated an ethical rule governing conflicts of interest. On the contrary, in *Freeman v. Chicago Musical Instrument Co.*, 689 F.2d 715 (7th Cir. 1982), a "former client" case, the court acknowledged that disqualification is a harsh sanction that should only be imposed where necessary. The Seventh Circuit wrote:

> Disqualification, as a prophylactic device for protecting the attorney-client relationship, is a drastic measure which courts should hesitate to impose except when absolutely necessary. A disqualification of counsel, while protecting the attorney-client relationship, also serves to destroy a relationship by depriving a party of representation of their own choosing.

Disqualification is one of three sanctions available to enforce the prophylactic conflicts rules. Disciplinary proceedings and civil remedies (i.e., malpractice suits and defenses for the non-payment of legal fees) can also be effective sanctions. In some ways, these other two sanctions are preferable to disqualification, because unlike disqualification, they impose costs only on the attorney who has violated the rules. To the extent that civil and disciplinary penalties accurately reflect the social cost of the risk posed by an attorney's misconduct, these sanctions alone could, in principle, provide sufficient deterrent. Disciplinary sanctions also can provide the necessary solemn denunciation of a violation of a lawyer's ethical duties.

Disqualification, by contrast, is a blunt device. The sanction of disqualification foists substantial costs upon innocent third parties. The innocent client (Hickey in this case) may suffer delay, inconvenience and expense and will be deprived of its choice of counsel. When disqualification is granted, sometimes the new attorney may find it difficult to master fully the subtle legal and factual nuances of a complex case (like this one), actually impairing the adversarial process.

Given the costs imposed by disqualification and the theoretical availability of alternative means of enforcement of the disciplinary code, a court should look to the purposes behind the rule violated in order to determine if disqualification is a desirable sanction. There are basically two purposes behind Rule 1.7. First it serves as a prophylactic to protect confidences that a client may have shared with his or her attorney. In that regard, Rule 1.9 shares the same concern as it prohibits an attorney from representing a client against a former client if the matter is "substantially related" to the matter(s) of the former client representation. The second purpose behind Rule 1.7 is to safeguard loyalty as a feature of the lawyer-client relationship. A client should not wake up one morning to discover that his lawyer, whom he had trusted to protect his legal affairs, has sued him — even if the suit is utterly unrelated to any of the work the lawyer had ever done for his client.

AUTHORS' COMMENT:

This sounds good. "A client should not wake up one morning to discover that his lawyer has sued him." There's only one thing wrong. A corporation doesn't "wake up" because it doesn't sleep. A corporation isn't a person, it's a thing. Should we worry about the feelings of a corporation the same way we worry about the feelings of a person? The court now talks about this.

The court must also inquire into whether Salomon's expectations of loyalty were so cavalierly trampled that disqualification is warranted as a sanction. In this case, Salomon's General Counsel, Robert Denham (appointed to his position on August 25, 1991) was completely unaware until January 9, 1992 that Schiff had ever provided any legal services to Salomon Brothers. This case is at the polar extreme from the case in which an individual has a personal relationship with a particular attorney who provides for all or substantially all of that client's legal needs. In such a case, were the attorney to "turn on" his client and sue him, disqualification would be appropriate. Materials filed under seal reflect that Salomon Brothers has engaged a number of other outside legal counsel, apart from Schiff, some of whom were retained to do financial futures work.

A court deciding a motion to disqualify in a case involving mega-firms (like Schiff) and mega-parties (like Salomon Brothers) should not be oblivious to "the way that attorneys and clients actually behave in the latter part of the twentieth century, and what they have come to expect from each other in terms of the continuation or termination of the relationship." As the *Drustar* court noted:

> The concepts of having a "personal attorney" or a "general corporate counsel" are much less meaningful today, especially among sophisticated users of legal services, than in the past. Clients may have numerous attorneys, all of whom have some implicit continuing loyalty obligations. Attorney specialization and marketing have contributed to this fractionalizing of a single client's business.

Were this court to rule that disqualification was mandated by Schiff's breach of Rule 1.7 in this case, the implications would be overwhelming. Clients of enormous size and wealth, and with a large demand for legal services, should not be encouraged to parcel their business among dozens of the best law firms as a means of purposefully creating the potential for conflicts. With simply a minor "investment" of some token business, such clients would in effect be buying an insurance policy against that law firm's adverse representation. Although lawyers should not be encouraged to sue their own clients (hence the sanctions discussed above), the law should not give large companies the incentive to manufacture the potential for conflicts by awarding disqualification automatically.

AUTHORS' COMMENT:

Does this mean you don't have to worry about getting disqualified even if you violate Rule 1.7? Nope — you still have to worry. The court now explains the limited scope of its opinion.

The foregoing discussion should not be misunderstood to mean that this court does not take very seriously a lawyer's ethical responsibilities to avoid conflicts of interest. Schiff should not have agreed to bring this suit against Salomon Brothers. Rule 1.7 prohibited it from doing so. The court, however, does not believe that the costly sanction of disqualification should be automatic for a breach of even so serious an obligation as that imposed by Rule 1.7. There is no danger in this case that Schiff's advocacy of Hickey will be less than fully zealous, the trial would not be tainted by Schiff's continued representation of Hickey, the subject of this litigation is not substantially related to the work Schiff has done for Salomon, and the disqualification would simply not be the appropriate remedy. The court's final concern is whether Schiff would fail adequately to carry out its commodities futures projects for Salomon Brothers. Salomon has not mentioned that this might be a possibility and the court sees no reason to fear that this might be a problem.

The court is cognizant that this decision may be viewed by some as a departure from the norm. Many courts, having determined that a conflict of interest exists, will automatically disqualify. The legal world is changing, however, and courts must be sensitive to the complexities and multiplicities of interests that come into play when enormous corporations and monster law firms interact in a dynamic legal economy. Accordingly, as discussed, this court does not believe that disqualification should be an automatic sanction and should not be imposed here.

Conclusion

Salomon Brothers' motion to disqualify Plaintiffs' attorney, the law firm of Schiff, Hardin and Waite, is denied.

NOTES AND QUESTIONS

1. ***Microsoft's Scheme Revisited.*** Based on the *Salomon Bros.* decision, it appears that Microsoft's scheme might well fail because the court would not automatically disqualify a law firm that was still representing Microsoft in another matter. But keep in mind that the *Salomon Bros.* court describes its own opinion as "a departure from the norm." The scheme might work in other courts. What could law firms do to protect themselves against giving up a big suit against Microsoft (or Salomon Bros.) in exchange for a small scrap of business from one of these giants? If you were on your firm's Executive Committee, what would you recommend?

One possibility would be for your firm to turn down small matters, even from big companies. But that's risky. After all, if you do a good job on a few small matters, maybe you'll start getting some big matters. One big client like Microsoft could make the firm's earnings skyrocket, not only from billings to Microsoft, but also because other companies might say, "Gee, if that firm is good enough for Microsoft, which can afford any law firm it wants, then we ought to use that firm, too."

Another possibility is to write termination letters every time the firm finishes a matter. These letters would say something like:

> Dear Mr. Gates:
>
> Enclosed is our final draft of the memorandum on FTC investigations that you asked us to prepare. Now that we have completed our work on this memorandum, we no longer have any active projects for Microsoft at our firm. We therefore no longer consider ourselves to be your lawyers (i.e., you are no longer a current client of our firm). If problems arise in the future, please contact us again and we will determine at that time whether we can renew our attorney-client relationship with your company. We would certainly like to represent your company again if we are ethically permitted to do so.

Does that sound good? It would make clear that the attorney-client relationship is over, but from a marketing point of view, isn't it a little odd? If you want to get more business from the client, wouldn't you be better off saying, "Please call us to discuss page 4 of the memorandum so that we can discuss strategy for responding to any future inquiries from the FTC." Or, "While working on this project, it occurred to us that your company should have a parallel memorandum concerning the Justice Department's investigative powers." If Microsoft doesn't want these extra services, it won't ask you to provide them. But if it does, you've got your nose a little further under the tent. And there's a lot of money in that tent.

Is there any way to phrase the termination letter to make it sound friendlier? What about saying something like this:

> Thank you for asking our firm to represent you and entrusting us with your legal matter. We have now completed all of the work you asked us to perform, and we do not plan to perform any additional work. Our attorney-client relationship is therefore at an end for now. However, if you have legal problems in the future, we would be delighted if you would call us again so that we can determine whether we will be able to renew our attorney-client relationship and represent you or advise you in the new matter.

A letter like that might ruffle some feathers because it makes clear that you no longer represent the client. But there is no way around the need for clearly stating your view that the representation has been concluded. Once you state that, the client cannot "reasonably believe" that you still represent it. Conversely, if you don't state that, you are open to future conflicts that can disqualify you from opposing the former client.

Most lawyers don't like to write clear termination letters. A bird in the hand is worth more than two in the bush. Salesmen say that the vast majority of their sales — around 80% — come from people who've bought from them before. It's much easier to make a sale to an existing customer or client than to make a sale to a first-time client. The same is true for law firms. Probably 80% of a firm's work is from regular clients, not brand new clients. It takes time to build up trust, and it takes time for a lawyer to learn a new client's business. Why not try selling your legal services to somebody who has already bought from you and trusts you, rather than expend time and energy attempting to attract a brand new client?

2. ***Prospective Clients.*** What if a person communicates with a law firm (whether by phone, in writing, or in-person) about the possibility of forming an attorney-client relationship, but the firm decides not to take the case (or the client decides not to retain the firm)? Is that person a former client, or not? May the same law firm later represent another client against the person who communicated with the firm but was never represented by the firm? That question has puzzled many lawyers and many courts. In 2002, the ABA adopted a special rule to govern this situation — see ABA Model Rule 1.18, entitled "Duties to Prospective Client." Since prospective clients who did not hire you are a species of former clients, we will study conflicts with prospective clients in the chapter on conflicts with former clients.

3. ***Legal Malpractice and Client Identity.*** The question of who is a client comes up not only in conflicts and confidentiality analysis but also in legal malpractice suits. The basic elements of a legal malpractice claim are (1) an attorney-client relationship existed, (2) substandard performance by the attorney, and (3) damages to the client arising out of the lawyer's substandard performance. If the plaintiff in a legal malpractice suit cannot establish that there was an attorney-client relationship, then the plaintiff cannot win the suit. The same analysis used to determine whether a person ever became a client for conflict of interest purposes also applies in legal malpractice suits, and in suits for breach of fiduciary duty.

A SCENARIO ON "WHO IS A CLIENT?"

Ariel Alpha is a business litigation lawyer and partner in the law firm of Alpha & Beta in the State of Dakota. The Alpha & Beta law firm was founded three years ago and operates from two offices, a headquarters building into which the firm moved just last month, located in Capital City, Dakota, and a second office located in Houston, Texas. Alpha finds the practice of contract litigation emotionally and economically rewarding, but the practice is not without its challenges.

In a recent conversation soon after you began practicing in Dakota, Ms., Alpha told you the following and asked whether you thought his law firm should be disqualified:

> "Last month my law firm signed-on a new client, Spamalot Filters, which offers e-mail spam filter services to businesses. Back in 2004, when spam wasn't nearly the problem it is today, Spamalot entered into a ten-year contract to filter e-mail for an online men's fashion company named E-Male. With the almost exponential growth of spamming, however, Spamalot determined that the E-Male account was taking up vastly more time than had been projected. Spamalot canceled the contract; E-Male countered with a suit for specific performance and damages; and that's when Spamalot hired us to defend them.
>
> "Upon investigating we learned that E-Male had been letting other companies route e-mail through its server (for a price, of course). The free-riders were basically stealing Spamalot's spam-filtering services — like people who tap into cable TV lines or video-tape movies in theatres and then sell those grainy rip-offs! So, since E-Male was at the center of this theft ring, we got aggressive.

Aggression is what Alpha & Beta is famous for. We not only filed affirmative defenses, but added a counterclaim on behalf of Spamalot, alleging fraud and breach of contract by E-Male and tortious interference with contract by several of the free-riders. Brilliant, huh?

"Now, E-Male has moved to disqualify our firm because a lawyer named Ava, who works in our Capital City office, previously worked at the law firm of Gamma & Delta, which is representing E-Male in the litigation against Spamalot.

"In addition — and E-Male's lawyers may not know this yet because we just realized it ourselves — last year a lawyer in our Houston office helped E-Male negotiate a long-term bank loan, and in March of this year a different attorney in the Houston office helped E-Male with the attempted acquisition of another online clothier for men, Y Jeans. E-Male's effort to acquire Y Jeans fell apart three months ago and E-Male hasn't contacted us since that deal failed."

Should Ariel's firm (Alpha & Beta) be disqualified from representing Spamalot against E-Male? Why or why not?

C. AMBIGUITY IN ENTITY REPRESENTATION

The following is a situation that can easily arise when a lawyer for an entity (corporation, partnership, etc.) investigates the facts in a suit against a corporation. Sometimes the lawyer for the corporation offers to also represent a corporate employee who was involved in the events giving rise to the suit, especially if the employee is named as a co-defendant. However, sometimes the lawyer represents only the corporation and lets the employee fend for himself, either because the common representation would present a risky (or non-consentable) conflict or because the employee is entitled to independent counsel. Often, if the corporation's lawyer spells out all aspects of the potential conflict to both the corporation and the individual employee, and the lawyer reasonably believes he can provide competent and diligent representation to both clients, the lawyer can obtain valid consent to jointly represent the corporation and the employee.

However sometimes the corporation's law firm forgets to make clear that it represents only the corporation and not the individual. If the individual gets the impression that the corporation's lawyers are also his own personal lawyers, the lawyers can get into a heap of trouble. In the following case, the lawyers who were investigating the facts of a tragic accident either did not make clear to a Coca-Cola truck driver that they represented only Coca-Cola, or else they forgot what they told the employee. The employee sued the lawyers for damages. In the following David-vs.-Goliath case, little David (the employee) won a round.

PEREZ v. KIRK & CARRIGAN

822 S.W.2d 261 (Tex. App. 1991)

J. Bonner Dorsey, J.

Ruben Perez appeals a summary judgment rendered against him on his causes of action against the law firm of Kirk & Carrigan . . . .

The present suit arises from a school bus accident on September 21, 1989, in Alton, Texas. Ruben Perez was employed by Valley Coca-Cola Bottling Company as a truck driver. On the morning of the accident, Perez attempted to stop his truck at a stop sign along his route, but the truck's brakes failed to stop the truck, which collided with the school bus. The loaded bus was knocked into a pond and 21 children died. Perez suffered injuries from the collision and was taken to a local hospital to be treated.

The day after the accident, Kirk & Carrigan, lawyers who had been hired to represent Valley Coca-Cola Bottling Company, visited Perez in the hospital for the purpose of taking his statement. Perez claims that the lawyers told him that they were his lawyers too and that anything he told them would be kept confidential.[1] With this understanding, Perez gave them a sworn statement concerning the accident.[2] However, after taking Perez' statement, Kirk & Carrigan had no further contact with him. Instead, Kirk & Carrigan made arrangements for criminal defense attorney Joseph Connors to represent Perez. . . .

AUTHORS' COMMENT:

There was nothing wrong with Coca-Cola sending attorneys to interview Perez. Nor was there anything wrong with the attorneys offering to represent Perez and promising to keep his information confidential (except that they apparently forgot to explain the potential conflict of interest — i.e., Coca-Cola might decide to blame Perez for the accident). But once the attorneys promised to keep everything Perez said confidential (see footnote 1 to the case), they couldn't later go back on that promise. In other words, the lawyers could not use Perez's confidential information against him. This case shows what can happen to lawyers who go back on their promise of confidentiality.

Some time after Connors began representing Perez, Kirk & Carrigan, without telling either Perez or Connors, turned Perez' statement over to the Hidalgo County District Attorney's Office. Kirk & Carrigan contend that Perez' statement was provided in a good faith attempt to fully comply with a request of the district attorney's office and under threat of subpoena if they did not voluntarily comply. Partly on the basis of this statement, the district attorney was able to obtain a grand jury indictment of Perez for involuntary manslaughter for his actions in connection with the accident.[3]

---

[1] The summary judgment affidavits offered by Perez show the following with regard to Kirk & Carrigan's representations to him at the time they took Perez' statement:

> *Ruben Perez* — "Kirk told me that they were lawyers hired by Valley Coca Cola, that they were my lawyers too, and that whatever I told them would be kept confidential. I trusted what these lawyers told me and I answered their questions."
>
> *Israel Perez (Ruben's father)* — "Before beginning the questions, Kirk told Ruben that they were his lawyers, that they were going to help him, and that what they, the lawyers, learned from Ruben would be kept a secret."
>
> . . . .

[2] Among other things, Perez generally stated that he had a previous accident while driving a Coke truck in 1987 for which he was given a citation, that he had a speeding violation in 1988, that he had not filled out a daily checklist to show that he had checked the brakes on the morning of the accident, that he had never before experienced problems with the brakes on his truck and that they were working just before the accident, that he tried to apply the brakes to stop the truck, but that the brakes for the trailer were not working at all to stop the truck . . . , that Perez did not have enough time to apply the emergency brakes, and that there was nothing the managers or supervisors at Valley Coca-Cola could have done to prevent the accident.

[3] By his summary judgment affidavit offered in support of Perez, Joseph Connors stated that, in his professional opinion as a board certified criminal law specialist, if he had known that the statement had been provided and had been able to have Perez explain his lack of training or knowledge about the brake system to the grand jury, Perez would not have been indicted for manslaughter. Ruben Perez also stated in his affidavit that Valley Coca-Cola Bottling Company had not given him any instruction in brake inspection, maintenance, or use in an emergency situation.

. . . Perez sued Kirk & Carrigan . . . for breach of fiduciary duty, negligent and intentional infliction of emotional distress, [and] violation of the Texas Deceptive Trade Practices-Consumer Protection Act . . . . Perez complained generally by his petition that Kirk & Carrigan had caused him to suffer public humiliation and emotional distress by turning over his supposedly confidential statement to the district attorney. . . .

By his sole point of error, Perez complains simply that the trial court erred in granting Kirk & Carrigan's motion for summary judgment. . . .

Breach of Fiduciary Duty

With regard to Perez' cause of action for breach of the fiduciary duty of good faith and fair dealing, Kirk and Carrigan contend that no attorney-client relationship existed and no fiduciary duty arose, because Perez never sought legal advice from them.

An agreement to form an attorney-client relationship may be implied from the conduct of the parties. Moreover, the relationship does not depend upon the payment of a fee, but may exist as a result of rendering services gratuitously.[4]

In the present case, viewing the summary judgment evidence in the light most favorable to Perez, Kirk & Carrigan told him that, in addition to representing Valley Coca Cola, they were also Perez' lawyers and that they were going to help him. Perez did not challenge this assertion, and he cooperated with the lawyers in giving his statement to them, even though he did not offer, nor was he asked, to pay the lawyers' fees. We hold that this was sufficient to imply the creation of an attorney-client relationship at the time Perez gave his statement to Kirk & Carrigan.

The existence of this relationship encouraged Perez to trust Kirk & Carrigan and gave rise to a corresponding duty on the part of the attorneys not to violate this position of trust. Accordingly, the relation between attorney and client is highly fiduciary in nature, and their dealings with each other are subject to the same scrutiny as a transaction between trustee and beneficiary. Specifically, the relationship between attorney and client has been described as one of uberrima fides, which means, "most abundant good faith," requiring absolute and perfect candor, openness and honesty, and the absence of any concealment or deception. In addition, because of the openness and candor within this relationship, certain communications between attorney and client are privileged from disclosure in either civil or criminal proceedings . . . .[5]

There is evidence that Kirk & Carrigan represented to Perez that his statement would be kept confidential. Later, however, without telling either Perez or his subsequently-retained criminal defense attorney, Kirk & Carrigan voluntarily disclosed Perez' statement to the district attorney. Perez asserts in the present suit that this course of conduct amounted, among other things, to a breach of fiduciary duty.

Kirk & Carrigan seek to avoid this claim of breach, on the ground that the attorney-client privilege did not apply to the present statement, because unnecessary third parties were present at the time it was given. However, whether or not the Rule 503 attorney-client privilege extended to Perez' statement, Kirk & Carrigan initially obtained the statement from Perez on the understanding that it would be kept confidential. Thus, regardless of whether from an evidentiary standpoint the privilege attached, Kirk & Carrigan breached their fiduciary duty to Perez either by wrongfully

[4] An attorney's fiduciary responsibilities may arise even during preliminary consultations regarding the attorney's possible retention if the attorney enters into discussion of the client's legal problems with a view toward undertaking representation.

[5] Disclosure of confidential communications by an attorney, whether privileged or not under the rules of evidence, is generally prohibited by the disciplinary rules governing attorneys' conduct in Texas. In addition, the general rule is that confidential information received during the course of any fiduciary relationship may not be used or disclosed to the detriment of the one from whom the information is obtained.

disclosing a privileged statement or by wrongfully representing that an unprivileged statement would be kept confidential. Either characterization shows a clear lack of honesty toward, and a deception of, Perez by his own attorneys regarding the degree of confidentiality with which they intended to treat the statement.

This type of deceitful and fraudulent conduct within the attorney-client relationship has been treated as a tortious breach of duty in other contexts.

Similarly, in the present case, the attorneys were at least under a fiduciary duty not to misrepresent to Perez that his conversations with them were confidential. Kirk & Carrigan should not now be able to assert the lack of attorney-client privilege . . . to excuse the harm caused by their own misrepresentation to Perez. We hold that it was error for the trial court to grant summary judgment on the ground that Kirk & Carrigan did not owe or breach a fiduciary duty to Perez.

In addition, however, even assuming a breach of fiduciary duty, Kirk & Carrigan also contend that summary judgment may be sustained on the ground that Perez could show no damages resulting from the breach. Kirk & Carrigan contend that their dissemination of Perez' statement could not have caused him any damages in the way of emotional distress, because the statement merely revealed Perez' own version of what happened. We do not agree. Mental anguish consists of the emotional response of the plaintiff caused by the tortfeasor's conduct. It includes, among other things, the mental sensation of pain resulting from public humiliation.

Regardless of the fact that Perez himself made the present statement, he did not necessarily intend it to be a public response as Kirk & Carrigan contend, but only a private and confidential discussion with his attorneys. Perez alleged that the publicity caused by his indictment, resulting from the revelation of the statement to the district attorney in breach of that confidentiality, caused him to suffer emotional distress and mental anguish. We hold that Perez has made a valid claim for such damages.

. . . .

In conclusion, for the reasons stated above, we sustain Perez' point of error. We *reverse* the summary judgment rendered against Perez and *remand* this case for trial.

NOTES AND QUESTIONS

1. ***Beware of Multiple Representation.*** The situation in *Perez* illustrates not just the problems of client identity but also the conflicts that often arise when a lawyer represents multiple clients in the same matter. When a lawyer represents both a corporation and an individual employee, the lawyer can more easily present a united defense ("The corporation didn't do anything wrong"), but the lawyer gives up the option of blaming the employee for the corporation's wrongdoing. After all, a lawyer cannot accuse his own client of misconduct, especially if the purpose is to advance the competing interests of another client (the corporation). When you read the chapter on conflicts with current clients, keep the *Perez* case in mind. It is a good example of what can go wrong.

2. ***Connection to Upjohn.*** Ordinarily, conversations between Perez and the lawyers representing Coca-Cola would have been protected as privileged under *Upjohn* and — as in *Upjohn* — the privilege would belong to the corporation to invoke or waive. Doesn't Coca-Cola have the right to waive the privilege? Usually, yes — and if the disclosures hurt a Coca-Cola employee like Perez, that would be the employee's tough luck. If the lawyers had the authority to make the disclosures, the only claim Perez could bring would be for libel or slander — and if the disclosures were truthful (as they were here), Coca-Cola would win.

Here, the lawyers allegedly told Perez that they were *his* lawyers, and would keep everything he said confidential. Once the lawyers told Perez they were acting as his own *personal* lawyers, they had an obligation to keep everything Perez said confidential, even though they had originally been retained by Coca-Cola and were being paid by Coca-Cola. (If the lawyers had carefully explained that they represented only Coca-Cola, or even Perez and Coca-Cola jointly, then they could ethically have disclosed the information to Coca-Cola. But the lawyers weren't careful, so they ended up as defendants.)

Chapter 22

CONFLICTS OF INTEREST WITH CURRENT CLIENTS

Of the various types of conflicts, concurrent conflicts arise most often. Concurrent conflicts arise in both litigation and transactional matters. (Transactions are deals like loans, real estate purchases, corporate acquisitions, contracts, or partnership formations — basically anything but litigation. This book will use the term "transactions" to cover all non-litigation matters, including "office practice" areas like wills, tax returns, and estate planning.) Concurrent conflicts can have serious consequences: disqualification, discipline, delay, and sometimes damages for malpractice — not to mention damage to the disqualified lawyer's reputation.

Moreover, if a concurrent conflict bars *any* lawyer in a firm from accepting a case, then the rule of "vicarious" or "imputed" disqualification embodied in ABA Model Rule 1.10(a) will disqualify *every* lawyer in the firm from undertaking the representation unless the conflict is a personal interest conflict that does not pose a significant risk of materially limiting the representation of the client by the non-conflicted lawyers at the firm. (Vicarious disqualification is the subject of an entire chapter later in this book.) Thus, it is crucial to identify concurrent conflicts, and then either avoid them or obtain client consent.

The following is a brief outline of the major kinds of concurrent conflicts and the method for analyzing them.

A. AN OUTLINE OF CONCURRENT CONFLICTS

1. Basics of Concurrent Conflicts

Definition: Concurrent conflicts arise in two situations: (1) whenever a lawyer directly opposes a current client ("direct adversity" conflicts), and (2) whenever a lawyer's loyalty to a current client is or may be materially compromised by a competing loyalty to any other *person* (whether a current client, former client, or some other third person), or by the lawyer's own *personal interests* (collectively "materially limiting" conflicts).

A. *Direct adversity conflicts.* Comment 6 to ABA Model Rule 1.7 explains: "Loyalty to a current client prohibits undertaking representation directly adverse to that client without that client's informed consent." The prohibition applies across the board, to all directly adverse representations, whether in litigation or in a transaction, and whether related or unrelated. The purpose of this broad prohibition is to avoid the feelings of betrayal and the damage to the attorney-client relationship that ordinarily follow when clients are attacked or directly opposed by their own lawyers.

B. *"Materially limiting" conflicts.* Comment 8 to ABA Model Rule 1.7 explains that loyalty is compromised and a conflict exists "if there is a significant risk that a lawyer's ability to consider, recommend or carry out an appropriate course of action for the client will be materially limited as a result of the lawyer's other responsibilities or interests." In other words, a lawyer has a concurrent conflict whenever the lawyer — consciously or unconsciously — may be tempted to give up any viable option that might advance a client's interest in order to serve or advance a competing interest. Conflicts in the "materially limiting" category arise far more often than "direct adversity" conflicts, and are much harder to identify than direct adversity conflicts.

C. A lawyer should not accept (or continue) any matter unless the lawyer is free, and is likely to remain free, to use every legitimate means to advance the client's interests, no matter who else might suffer. If other interests are competing for the lawyer's loyalty, then the lawyer cannot begin or continue representing the client unless the client gives "informed consent." (If a conflict is so serious that the lawyer cannot ask for or accept the client's consent, the concurrent conflict is called "nonconsentable" or "nonwaivable.")

D. *Kinds of competing interests.* What kinds of interests compete for a lawyer's loyalty? Here are four basic categories of competing interests:

   1. Another "client" (meaning another current client).
   2. A "former client" (a category of third person with special rights under the ethics rules).
   3. Some other "third person" (such as a friend, relative, or spouse) who is neither a client nor former client.
   4. The lawyer's own personal, financial, political, or social interests.

      a. Note that a lawyer's loyalty to a third person may overlap with a lawyer's personal interests.
      b. For example, if a client asks a lawyer to file suit against the lawyer's close friend, the lawyer's loyalty to the friend may make the lawyer litigate less aggressively against the friend. This may be characterized either as a conflict with a "third person" or as a conflict with the lawyer's own "personal interests."

2. Who is a "Client"?

As explained and explored at length in the previous chapter, the first step in determining whether a concurrent conflict exists is to determine whether at least one of the people to whom a lawyer owes loyalty is a current "client." To review briefly, the conflict of interest rules protect only clients and former clients. They do not protect those who never were clients. (Some rules of legal ethics do protect non-clients — see ABA Model Rules 3.4, 4.1, 4.2, 4.3, 4.4, all of which protect people who are not clients — but the conflict of interest rules are designed solely to protect clients and former clients.) Thus, the first question in any conflicts situation is whether the person is a "client."

A. *Basic rule.* The basic rule is that a person is a current client if he *reasonably believes* he is a current client. In other words, within the limits of objective reasonableness, we decide who is a client by looking at things from the client's perspective, not the lawyer's perspective. If a person believes that he is a current client of a firm, *and* if this belief is objectively reasonable, then we consider the person to be a client.

B. The world is divided into three kinds of people: (1) current clients, (2) former clients, and (3) "never-clients."

   1. *Current clients.* Current clients include everyone who has a reasonable belief that you are their lawyer — i.e., everyone who is reasonably relying on you to perform legal services. Clients may reasonably rely on you to perform legal services, and may thus consider themselves current clients, at any of four stages — (a) evaluation, (b) work, (c) follow-up, or (d) pattern of work:

      a. *Evaluation stage.* Suppose you interviewed a prospective client and promised to evaluate the client's matter, but have not yet finished your evaluation. Until you formally reject the matter (or the prospective client formally decides not to retain you), the prospective client is treated like a current client, and you owe the prospective client the same duties under the conflicts rules that you would owe to a client whose case you have already accepted.

i. The evaluation stage also triggers the duties of confidentiality and competence, and violations of these duties can subject you to suit for legal malpractice and/or breach of fiduciary duty, as well as to disciplinary action. You owe the same duties of confidentiality and competence to a client whose case you are evaluating as you do to a client whose case you have formally accepted.

ii. If you reject a case after evaluating it, the person whose case you rejected will be considered a former prospective client for purposes of the rules governing successive conflicts, including ABA Model Rule 1.18, which we will study later in the later chapter on successive conflicts.)

b. *Work stage.* Suppose a client has retained you to perform certain legal services or to accomplish a certain objective, and you are currently working on the matter. This means that you have not yet completed the work you agreed to perform. This is the obvious and classic "current client" situation.

i. This person is considered a current client until one of three things happens:

(1) you complete the services you promised to perform (or you accomplish the client's objective in some other manner), or

(2) you withdraw from the representation pursuant to ABA Model Rule 1.16, or

(3) the client fires you.

ii. The client is not required to know exactly what services you will be performing. For example, if the client says, "Obtain industrial zoning on this land so I can build a new factory," and you accept the representation, then the client can reasonably expect you to take every step needed to obtain industrial zoning, even if the client personally has no idea what those steps are. The client will remain a current client until you obtain the zoning or tell the client that you quit, or until the client fires you.

iii. Sometimes, however, the client will specify the exact services that you agree to perform — e.g., you agree to draft a will, or draft an employment contract, or file a tax return. The client will remain a current client until you have finished performing those discrete services. When those services are completed the attorney-client relationship ends, unless the client reasonably believes you will remain her attorney during a follow-up stage.

c. *Follow-up stage.* Completing the services your client asked you to perform does not always automatically end the attorney-client relationship. A "follow-up stage" begins when you complete the work that you agreed to perform (or accomplish the objective that you agreed to accomplish) but the client still reasonably expects you to perform additional follow-up services. The expectation of follow-up services is viewed from the client's perspective, not from your perspective. If the client *reasonably* expects future services in connection with the completed matter, that expectation maintains the client's status as a current client, even if the client did not communicate that expectation to you. For example:

i. You have settled a client's case for both money and injunctive relief, and the client reasonably expects you to monitor the opposing party's compliance with the settlement terms.
ii. You have closed a real estate deal in which your client has acquired some property, and the client reasonably expects you to give advice about environmental cleanup laws and zoning laws affecting the property.

d. *Pattern stage.* The pattern stage arises if the client has retained you to do legal work often enough to establish a pattern of an attorney-client relationship, entitling the client to say, "That's my lawyer" even when you are not currently doing any legal work or follow-up work for the client at that particular moment.

i. You may have completed every assignment the client has given you so far, but if the client has given you multiple assignments over a period of months or years, then the client may reasonably consider himself a current client until one of you formally ends the relationship.
ii. If you do not want to risk conflicts with a given client after you have finished your work for that client, you should write a termination letter. Lawyers generally do not like to write termination letters because lawyers like to keep as many clients as possible. But the more clients you keep, the more conflicts you will have.

2. *Former clients.* The former-client category includes anyone and everyone who was ever your client in the past, including both individuals and entities, whether you served them at your current law firm or at some former legal job. (If you worked on a client's matter as a law student, or anytime before you were admitted to the bar, you should research to see whether your jurisdiction treats those people as your former clients or not. At a minimum, most jurisdictions impose a duty of confidentiality toward those clients.) The rules governing successive conflicts are far more lenient than the rules governing concurrent conflicts, so former clients have less protection than current clients.
3. *Never-clients.* This category includes everyone who is not now and never was a client or prospective client — i.e., everyone who is neither a current client nor a former client. This category may seem obvious, but in a few situations people may think they are clients even though they are not, in which case a belief that they are current clients is not reasonable. For example:

a. *Organizations.* If you represent an organization, you do not automatically represent the corporation's officers, directors, or employees. As Rule 1.13(a) provides, "A lawyer employed or retained by an organization represents the organization acting through its duly authorized constituents." You may be permitted to represent both an organization and its officers, directors, or employees, but you do not automatically represent an organization's constituents just because the organization is your client.
b. *Parents and children.* If you represent a child, you do not automatically represent the parents. Thus, the parents are not your clients unless you expressly agree to represent them. Conversely, if you represent parents, you do not automatically represent the children.
c. *Third person paying a fee.* When someone other than your client is paying your legal fee (for example, when a corporation pays an

employee's legal fee, or a rich uncle pays a nephew's legal fee), the person paying the fee is not your client. That is why Rule 5.4(c) provides that a lawyer "shall not permit a person who recommends, employs, or pays the lawyer to render legal services for another to direct or regulate the lawyer's professional judgment in rendering such legal services."

C. *"Phantom" or "surprise" clients.* Usually, it is obvious whether a person is a current client, a former client, or a never-client. In some situations, however, the courts create "phantom" clients by implying an attorney-client relationship. These "implied" or "phantom" clients usually have the same status under the conflict of interest rules as ordinary clients. You should therefore be alert to the following categories of "phantom" current clients:

1. *Trade association members.* Trade associations (such as the National Association of Realtors or the American Petroleum Institute) are a dangerous and unexpected source of conflicts because courts may view a trade association's *members* as clients, even if you and your law firm believe you represent only the association itself and not the individual members.

   a. The key question is whether the trade association members supplied *confidential information,* such as their business plans for new product lines, to the association's law firm with the understanding that the lawyer would keep the information confidential.
   b. If so, then the members who supplied the confidential information are likely to be considered clients.

2. *Co-Parties.* Co-plaintiffs or co-defendants may be considered current clients if they give a lawyer confidential information as part of a common prosecution or defense. Even though the lawyer does not formally represent a co-party, courts may look upon the co-party as a client for purposes of the conflict of interest rules (though probably not for legal malpractice purposes, because the co-party has his own lawyer).
3. *Affiliates, Subsidiaries, Parents, Divisions.* Companies related to your clients may also be considered your clients. Whether a related company is considered a client or former client depends on how closely that company is related to the client for whom you have actually done work. There is no hard-and-fast rule to cover every situation, and the law varies from jurisdiction to jurisdiction.

   a. As a rule of thumb, if an entity has given you confidential information, either directly or through a related company, then you should treat the entity that gave you the information as your client.
   b. Likewise, if you have actually performed legal services for an entity, then you should treat that entity as your former client.

3. Conflicts Between Two Current Clients

Conflicts between two current clients can arise in five ways, ranked here roughly in order of decreasing seriousness:

A. *Representing opposing sides in same litigation.* Perhaps the most serious type of concurrent conflict is representing two different clients who directly oppose each other in the same litigation. Representing both sides in litigation is universally forbidden.

1. A lawyer or law firm can never handle both sides of the same lawsuit. Client consent is irrelevant and ineffective. This is a non-consentable conflict.

2. ABA Model Rule 1.7(b)(3) reflects this prohibition by adopting a per se rule against representing clients if the representation involves "the assertion of a claim by one client against another client represented by the lawyer *in the same litigation* or other proceeding before a tribunal." (Emphasis added.) The prohibition is a per se rule, meaning that client consent cannot, under Rule 1.7(b)(4), cure the problem.

B. *Representing opposing sides in a transaction.* In transactions, a lawyer usually may not represent both sides. For example, a lawyer may seldom represent both the buyer and seller, or the lender and borrower, or an acquired company and the acquiring company.

1. Rule 1.7(b) does not adopt a per se rule against representing both sides of a transaction. Rule 1.7(b)(3) applies only to "litigation." However, some state judicial decisions have adopted a per se rule against representing both sides of certain transactions, such as buyer and seller in a residential house closing. This is a jurisdiction-by-jurisdiction inquiry.
2. In theory, a lawyer could represent both sides of a transaction if the adverse parties have already agreed to all terms and simply need papers drawn up to formalize their agreement, but this situation is rare, and risky. If there are any material disputed terms in the transaction, the conflict may become non-consentable because Rule 1.7(b)(1) permits a lawyer to engage in a "concurrent conflict" only if the lawyer "reasonably believes that the lawyer will be able to provide competent and diligent representation to each affected client."

C. *Opposing a current client in unrelated litigation.* Opposing a client in litigation unrelated to the work you are doing is always a conflict and always requires client consent from the clients on both sides. As Comment 6 to Rule 1.7 says, "Absent consent, a lawyer may not act as an advocate in one matter against a person the lawyer represents in some other matter, even when the matters are wholly unrelated." In addition, because the lawyer's representation of the new client may be "materially limited" by duties to the current client, the lawyer will need informed consent from the new client as well. When one of your clients opposes another client, consent from one client will not be enough.

1. For example, suppose you represent Ben in a dispute with his medical insurance company, which refuses to pay for a medical procedure that the insurance company describes as experimental. A new client, Chris, has asked you to sue Ben for breach of a contract to buy Chris's home. (Ben backed out of the contract at the last minute to buy a different house.) The two matters are completely unrelated. Nevertheless, this situation presents both kinds of concurrent conflicts governed by Rule 1.7.

   a. From Ben's perspective, your representation of Chris creates a "direct adversity" conflict under Rule 1.7(a)(1). If you accept Chris's case, Ben will be directly opposed by his own lawyer (you), since you are still representing him against the medical insurance company. To Ben, this is a serious breach of loyalty — a betrayal. You have undoubtedly tried hard to get Ben to trust you in the medical insurance dispute, and now you are turning against him. Ben may decide to give informed consent to being directly opposed by you in Chris's case, but he also has the right to refuse consent. If he refuses consent, then you must not accept Chris's case against Ben. Chris will have to find another lawyer. (The other lawyer will have to be in a different law firm, because your "direct adversity" conflict will be imputed, under Rule 1.10(a), to every other lawyer in your firm.)

b. From Chris's perspective, your existing representation of Ben creates a "materially limiting" conflict under Rule 1.7(a)(2). Given your obligation of loyalty to Ben, Chris will perceive a "significant risk" that your representation of him against Ben in the house dispute will be "materially limited" by your responsibilities to Ben, who is "another client."

2. To generalize, under Rule 1.7(a)(1), a lawyer may *never* directly oppose another current client in any litigation matter unless the lawyer complies with all four subparagraphs of Rule 1.7(b), including informed consent from the client who is being directly opposed. Thus, a current client has an *absolute veto* against being opposed in any litigation matter — and this veto exists whether the new litigation is related or unrelated to the work the lawyer is doing for the current client.

3. To further generalize, under Rule 1.7(a)(2), a lawyer may never agree to represent a new client against an existing client unless the lawyer complies with all four subparagraphs of Rule 1.7(b), including informed consent from both of the opposing clients. Thus, a lawyer must always obtain consent from a new client before agreeing to oppose one of the lawyer's other current clients in litigation — and must also obtain consent from the client to be opposed. For example, if one of your current clients decides to sue another one of your current clients or defend against a suit brought by another one of your current clients, you may not accept the representation unless you obtain informed consent from the client who wants to sue or defend and from your other current client.

D. *Opposing a current client in an unrelated transaction.* It is always a conflict, though often a consentable one, to oppose a current client in a transaction unrelated to the work you are doing for the current client.

1. For example: suppose you do labor negotiations for a large corporation named Acme Smoked Fish Corp. You are approached by Superbowl Supply Company, which wants you to negotiate the terms of a contract to sell cafeteria supplies to Acme Corp. This kind of transaction is likewise prohibited unless *both* clients give their informed consent. Consent may be relatively easy to get because no litigation is involved and the parties may want to work together, but you still need consent from both clients. You cannot oppose Acme without its consent, even in friendly negotiations, and you need Superbowl's consent because your representation of Superbowl may be materially limited by your loyalty to Acme.

2. Your represent Woolsworthy, which is a competitor of J-Mart. The information you learn while representing Woolsworthy would be very helpful to J-Mart. (For example, you may know Woolsworthy's purchase costs, profit margin, marketing plans, or confidential research projects.) At least one court has held that this is a concurrent conflict if the danger of betrayal of Woolsworthy is "so great" that we should not trust a lawyer to represent its competitor absent Woolsworthy's informed consent. This is a distinct minority opinion. However, even if you are ethically permitted to represent both Woolsworthy and J-Mart, you may find that the clients are uncomfortable, and that as a business matter your firm should not represent both competitors.

3. However, representing two competing businesses at the same time — for example, simultaneously representing two different grocery chains in unrelated matters — may be an immaterial conflict. As Comment 6 to Rule 1.7 says, "simultaneous representation in unrelated matters of clients whose interests are only *economically* adverse, such as representation of competing economic enterprises in unrelated litigation, does not ordinarily constitute a conflict of interest and thus may not require consent of the

respective clients." For example, you could represent one grocery chain in a breach of contract suit against Heinz while representing another grocery chain in a tort claim brought by a customer who slipped and fell in a store (assuming these matters are unrelated) even though each chain may be better off economically (competitively) if the other chain loses its suit. The rules are not aimed at these purely economic conflicts.

E. *Multiple representation of allied parties.* It is always a conflict to represent more than one party in the same matter, even if the parties are allies. For example, it is always a conflict — though often a consentable one — to represent: (a) co-defendants in litigation (civil or criminal); (b) co-plaintiffs in litigation; (c) partners in a business or potential business; or (d) a corporation and its officers, directors, and employees in an investigation of the corporation's alleged wrongdoing.

1. The pre-2002 version of ABA Model Rule 1.7(b) provided that when a lawyer undertakes to represent multiple clients in a single matter, "the consultation shall include explanation of the implications of the common representation and the advantages and risks involved." The pre-2002 Comment to this language explained that in such multiple representations, an impermissible conflict could arise by reason of (a) substantial discrepancies in the parties' testimony, (b) incompatibility of the parties' legal positions, or (c) substantially different settlement possibilities for the different clients.
2. The current version of ABA Model Rule 1.7 no longer refers to multiple clients in the text, but the relevant part of Comment 18 notes that for a client's consent to be "informed," each client must be aware of "the relevant circumstances and of the material and reasonably foreseeable ways that the conflict could have adverse effects on the interests of that client." Specifically, a lawyer representing multiple clients in a single matter must explain "the implications of the common representation, including possible effects on loyalty, confidentiality and the attorney-client privilege and the advantages and risks involved."
3. In addition, Rule 1.7's Comment 29 (entitled "Special Considerations in Common Representation") expands on Comment 18 by urging lawyers representing multiple clients in the same matter to keep in mind that if the common representation fails due to an irreconcilable conflict, the failure can lead to "additional cost, embarrassment and recrimination. Ordinarily, the lawyer will be forced to withdraw from representing all of the clients if the common representation fails." In some situations, the risk of failure is so great that a lawyer may not even embark on the multiple representation. For example, "a lawyer cannot undertake common representation of clients where contentious litigation or negotiations between them are imminent or contemplated." Nor should a lawyer agree to represent multiple clients when it is unlikely that the lawyer can remain impartial between the clients. "Generally, if the relationship between the parties has already assumed antagonism, the possibility that the clients' interests can be adequately served by common representation is not very good."
4. *Advantages of multiple representation.* Despite the risks, multiple representation may have some distinct advantages.

    a. Multiple representation often saves on legal fees for clients in the short run, at least in hourly rate matters, because much of the factual and legal work for clients in the same matter will overlap. In economic terms, the "marginal cost" (the added cost) of doing the second client's work is much lower than the marginal cost of doing the first client's work.

b. The parties may also save time because scheduling meetings is easier when only one lawyer is involved rather than two (or three, or four).

c. If disputes begin to develop among clients in a transaction, a common lawyer may be able to help the parties work out their differences before problems erupt into litigation or ruin the deal.

5. *Disadvantages and risks of multiple representation.* At the same time, multiple representation has some risks and disadvantages.

   a. If a conflict develops, a common lawyer may subconsciously ignore the conflict, or even deliberately conceal it from the clients, so that the lawyer can continue the multiple representation.

   b. If a serious, insoluble conflict does surface — one that the lawyer cannot ignore, avoid, hide, or cure — then *all* parties may have to get new lawyers, resulting in additional time and expense. By saving time and money in the short run (paying only one lawyer's bill instead of two or more at the outset), the clients may end up wasting time and money in the long run (paying the first lawyer's bill plus a new lawyer's bill after the conflict becomes intolerable).

   c. If the common clients get into a dispute with each other, they will not be allowed to claim the attorney-client privilege for communications with the lawyer during the common representation. As indicated in Comment 30 to Rule 1.7, when a lawyer is considering representing more than one client in a single matter, a "particularly important factor" is the effect on the attorney-client privilege. The "prevailing rule" regarding the attorney-client privilege is that commonly represented clients cannot assert the privilege against each other. Hence, before agreeing to represent multiple clients, the lawyer should advise the clients that if they get into litigation with each other about the matter, the privilege will not protect either client's communications to the lawyer.

6. *Multiple representation in transactions.* Representing two or more people who have a common goal in a transaction (e.g., starting a new business) is ethically permitted under Rule 1.7 as long as the clients won't suffer too much if the proposed transaction falls apart. The "risk of adverse effect" has two components:

   a. What are the chances that the deal will fall apart? and

   b. If the deal does fall apart, what are the likely adverse consequences to the multiple clients? (Among other things, if the death of the deal leads the parties to litigate against each other, they will not have an attorney-client privilege for things they said to you as their common attorney while the deal was still pending, and all clients may have to get new lawyers.)

7. *Aggregate settlements.* A lawyer who represents two or more plaintiffs in the same matter may receive an "aggregate" settlement offer. For example, if a lawyer represents five pedestrians who were both hit by the defendant's runaway car, the defendant may offer an aggregate settlement of $50,000 for all five plaintiffs, leaving it to the lawyer and his clients to divide up the money as they see fit.

   a. Rule 1.8(g) permits a lawyer to accept such a settlement only if the clients give their informed consent in writing.

   b. Under Rule 1.8(g), the lawyer must disclose "the existence and nature of all the claims . . . involved and of the participation of each person in the settlement."

8. In sum, because of the high potential for conflicts, multiple representation in civil cases is risky, and should not be undertaken until the lawyer has assessed both the likelihood of a serious conflict and the consequences of such a conflict, and has made full and complete disclosure about the advantages and risks to all clients that the lawyer intends to represent.
9. *Multiple representation in criminal defense work.* Multiple representation in criminal matters is an even riskier proposition than multiple representation in civil matters. The ABA distinguishes sharply between civil and criminal matters. Comment 23 to Rule 1.7 says: "The potential for conflict of interest in representing multiple defendants in a criminal case is so grave that *ordinarily a lawyer should decline to represent more than one codefendant.*" [Emphasis added.]

F. *Indirect conflicts.* Potential conflicts arise when a lawyer represents different clients in different matters and one matter may adversely affect the other matter. For example:

1. Suppose your client American Boiler Co. asks you to help it obtain zoning for a factory next to property owned by Wharton Real Estate, a residential real estate developer that you represent in unrelated matters. It's clear that the value of Wharton's property would sharply decline if American Boiler obtains zoning for the factory. This is an indirect conflict — you are not directly opposing Wharton, but there is probably a "significant risk" that your zeal for American Boiler may be "materially limited" because you know that obtaining the zoning will seriously harm another client of yours (Wharton). However, the zoning request is not "directly adverse" to Wharton unless Wharton seeks to block American Boiler's zoning request.
2. Suppose your client QuickLube wants to acquire a Los Angeles company so that it can expand its oil change business into California. Meanwhile, your client JiffyLube (which is unaware of QuickLube's plans) also wants to enter the California market. This is probably an immaterial conflict that need not be disclosed, because California is a large enough market to support more than one oil change franchise. But if the two clients are competing to buy the same piece of land or to open stores in a shopping mall that allows only one oil change company, the conflict may develop into a direct adversity conflict.
3. There are thousands of possible examples of conflicts in this category. The common theme is that, although the clients are not directly attacking or opposing each other, one client either wants something that would (or could) harm the other client, or opposes something that would (or could) help the other client.

G. *Issue or "positional" conflicts.* It may or may not be a conflict to represent different parties in completely different matters if their legal positions are incompatible. Sometimes Client One wants to take a legal position in one matter that is the polar opposite of the position you plan to take for Client Two in some other matter. For example: suppose Client One, a plaintiff in a RICO action, wants to argue for a broad definition of "pattern," but Client Two, a defendant in a RICO action, wants to argue for a narrow definition of "pattern"; or suppose Client One, who wants to build a house near the ocean, wants to argue that zoning restrictions against building on the waterfront are unconstitutional, while Client Two, who already lives on the waterfront, wants to argue that such zoning restrictions are reasonable and constitutional.

1. Comment 24 to Rule 1.7 says that a lawyer ordinarily "may take inconsistent legal positions in different tribunals at different times on

behalf of different clients." Merely advocating a legal position for Client A that "might" create precedent harmful to Client B in an "unrelated matter" does not create a conflict. A conflict does exist, however, if there is "a significant risk that a lawyer's action on behalf of one client will create a precedent likely to seriously weaken the position taken on behalf of the other client."

2. Comment 24 to Rule 1.7 goes on to list the following "factors" that are relevant in determining whether you need to advise your clients about the risk of a positional conflict:

   a. Where are the cases pending?
   b. Is the issue substantive or procedural? (Substantive issues generally present more troubling conflicts.)
   c. What is the temporal relationship between the matters? (That is, which matter will lead to a judicial ruling or decision first? The second client is more likely to be hurt by the decision in the first matter than the first client is to be hurt by the decision in the second matter.)
   d. What is the significance of the issue to the immediate and long-term interests of the clients involved? (The more significant the issue, the more likely a conflict exists.)
   e. What were the clients' reasonable expectations in retaining the lawyer?

3. Comment 24 concludes by saying: "If there is a significant risk of material limitation, then absent informed consent of the affected clients, the lawyer must refuse one of the representations or withdraw from one or both matters."

4. Conflicts Between a Client and a Third Person

A. *Directly opposing a third party.* A conflict almost always arises when a lawyer is asked to oppose (or ought to oppose) a close friend, relative, spouse, powerful politician, or other person or entity important to the lawyer's personal or professional life. The conflict comes in two main varieties:

   1. A lawyer may be unwilling to oppose the person even though that person should be (or at least could be) a defendant in litigation. (These are situations in which an unconflicted lawyer would sue the person.)
   2. A lawyer may be willing to oppose the third person, but may be unable or unwilling to press the client's cause with maximum vigor against that person. (These are situations in which an unconflicted lawyer would represent her client with greater zeal.)

B. *Adversely affecting a third party.* A lawyer may also be reluctant to accept a matter knowing that a friend, relative, or other third person important to the lawyer may be adversely affected if the lawyer handles the matter successfully. For example:

   1. A lawyer may believe that adding First National Bank as a defendant in a loan fraud case will anger or implicate the lawyer's sister if she is an officer of the bank. The lawyer may therefore not want to sue the bank, or may not want to press the case too hard, or may not want to follow any investigative leads that suggest his sister's complicity in the fraud.
   2. A personal injury lawyer defending a client in an accident case may believe that the best defense is to blame one of the lawyer's good friends for causing the accident. The lawyer may therefore not assert this defense at all, or may not be motivated to assert it with zeal, or may recommend a settlement that goes very easy on his friend.

C. Conflicts with third persons often overlap conflicts with the lawyer's own interest. A lawyer's reluctance to press suit against his sister's company might be characterized either as a conflict with a third person or as a conflict with the lawyer's own social or financial interests. Therefore, conflicts with third persons are hard to separate from conflicts with a lawyer's own interests. But how we characterize the conflict makes no difference, because the rules and the result are the same in either case.

5. Conflicts with the Lawyer's Own Interests

A. ABA Model Rule 1.7(b) generally prohibits a lawyer from accepting a representation that actually or potentially conflicts with the lawyer's own interests. These conflicts come in hundreds of varieties. For example:

1. The lawyer knows that handling the matter competently will require a lot of travel and long hours in the near future, but the lawyer wants to stay home for a wedding and an uncle's 100th birthday party.
2. The lawyer knows that agreeing to defend a man accused of defrauding elderly people will make the lawyer unpopular, and perhaps subject the lawyer to threats or physical harm.
3. The lawyer is asked to bring suit against a small company in which the lawyer and her husband own a significant amount of stock.

B. *Business transactions with clients.* The lawyer's own financial interests are always implicated when the lawyer enters a business transaction with a current client. Business transactions between the lawyer and the client are governed not only by Rule 1.7(b), but also by Rule 1.8(a), which prohibits a lawyer from entering into any kind of business deal with a client (other than for legal fees) unless the lawyer satisfies three stringent and express conditions. As stated in Delaware Rule 1.8(a), those conditions are as follows:

1. "The transaction and terms on which the lawyer acquires the interest are fair and reasonable to the client and are fully disclosed and transmitted in writing in a manner that can be reasonably understood by the client";
2. "The client is advised in writing of the desirability of seeking and is given a reasonable opportunity to seek the advice of independent legal counsel on the transaction"; and
3. "The client gives informed consent, in a writing signed by the client, to the essential terms of the transaction and the lawyer's role in the transaction, including whether the lawyer is representing the client in the transaction."

C. Business deals between lawyers and clients are highly risky for lawyers — perhaps riskier than any other type of conflict.

1. Any failure to follow Rule 1.8(a) may result in a suit by the client against the lawyer for fraud, misrepresentation, and breach of fiduciary duties.
2. In many jurisdictions, business transactions between lawyers and clients are *presumptively fraudulent* or otherwise improper unless the lawyer proves to the contrary. The burden is on the lawyer to show that the transaction is fair and that the client was fully informed of all terms, in writing, before entering into the transaction.
3. Disciplinary cases against lawyers for violating the rules on business transactions with clients are legion, and the discipline imposed is typically harsh. Disbarments and lengthy suspensions are common penalties for those who transact business with clients without following the rules. (We have an entire separate chapter later on business transactions with clients.)

Now let's put the ideas of the outline to work. We'll start with a case about greed on the gridiron concerning the battle between the players and the owners in the National

Football League (the NFL) over the rights of players to have some say in whether they can be traded to a team they don't like. The dispute arose in the context of a class action. That's not a context you are likely to encounter often in your practice, but the *Lewis* case graphically illustrates concurrent conflicts in litigation.

In a class action, a small number of "named plaintiffs" (here, two football players) ask the court to "certify" them as adequate representatives for the large number of similarly situated people who will make up the "class" (here, another 250 NFL players). The lawyers for the proposed class representatives must also be adequate, which usually requires that the lawyers be free of conflicts (in addition to being competent, of course). In this case, the defendant, the NFL, opposes the certification of a class because the law firm representing the class (Weil, Gotshal & Manges, a major Wall Street firm) is simultaneously opposing some of the individual class members in another lawsuit. Can a law firm do that? Can lawyers represent a class in which some members are opponents of the law firm in other litigation?

LEWIS v. NATIONAL FOOTBALL LEAGUE

146 F.R.D. 5, 1992 U.S. Dist. LEXIS 16892 (D.D.C. Nov. 3, 1992)

LAMBERTH, J.

This matter comes before the court on Plaintiffs' Motion for Class Certification.

I. FACTS

This action is brought by two professional football players against the NFL and its twenty-eight member teams. The players purport to be representatives of a class of approximately 250 professional football players. . . . Plaintiffs seek a determination that the NFL's implementation of the first refusal/compensation system violates anti-trust laws and ask for trebled damages under those laws.

I. DISCUSSION

[The court found that the class and its representatives met the first three criteria for class certification. The court now addresses the fourth criterion, adequacy of representation. The court frequently refers to the "NFLPA," which is the National Football League Players Association, the NFL players union.]

c. Counsel's conflict of interest.

Finally, the NFL defendants note that counsel for the players in this case, the law firm of Weil, Gotshal & Manges, represents the NFLPA in other litigation [the *Golic* case] in which the NFLPA is suing football players, including approximately twenty members of the putative class, for breach of contract.[5] Weil, Gotshal also represents the named plaintiffs in this case and seeks to be counsel for the plaintiff class. Therefore, if the class is certified, Weil, Gotshal would both represent and be adverse to the approximately twenty defendants in the *Golic* case who are also class members here. Defendants argue that this conflict precludes a finding that class counsel are adequate, an implicit requirement of Rule 23(a)(4).

In reply, plaintiffs claim that defendants are attempting to "manipulate and distort the ethical rules." Although plaintiffs' argument is well-received, the dual representation is nonetheless a violation of relevant ethical principles.

Under D.C. Rule 1.7(b), absent full disclosure to and consent by the affected client (which plaintiffs have not demonstrated here),

[5] In that case, *NFLPA v. Golic*, C123-92 (N.J. Super.), the NFLPA alleges that several football players violated their licensing contracts with the NFLPA by signing licensing contracts with NFL Properties.

> A lawyer shall not represent a client with respect to a matter if:
>
> (1) a position to be taken by that client in that matter is adverse to a position taken or to be taken by another client in the same matter; [or]
>
> (2) such representation will be or is likely to be adversely affected by representation of another client.

D.C. Rule 1.7(b)(1)–(2). Both of these provisions are violated in this case.

AUTHORS' COMMENT:

Before you read the court's analysis of the conflict, try to solve it yourself. It's pretty easy. We're learning the fundamentals now, and if you think it through for a few minutes you should be able to analyze the conflict yourself.

First, Weil, Gotshal's position on behalf of NFLPA in *Golic* is directly adverse to the position of the players involved in both cases. Accordingly, as "it is much to be preferred that a representation that is likely to lead to a conflict should be avoided before the representation begins," (D.C. Rule 1.7, Comment P 16), Weil, Gotshal should not assume the representation for the plaintiff class. This is true "even though the lawyer does not represent the other client [here, the players] as to that position or even that matter [the breach of contract litigation]." D.C. Rule 1.7, Comment P 10.

Second, it is likely that Weil, Gotshal's representation of the NFLPA will adversely affect its representation of the player class. The court is deeply troubled by plaintiff counsel's suggestion that,

> to prevent any possible questions from being raised about the undivided loyalty of counsel, plaintiffs are willing to amend their class certification request to exclude those few NFL players whose contracts expired in 1989 and whom counsel understands have already been sued, or may be sued in the near future, by the NFLPA for breach of contract.

More troubling yet is the footnote comment that

> such an exclusion would hardly be an inequitable result given that these players have damaged the licensing system that funds this and other litigation challenging NFL player movement restraints by breaching their group licensing agreements with the NFLPA.

The court is concerned that plaintiffs' counsel could take this position yet still aver that there is no possible conflict of interest. Counsel have, quite simply, offered to betray almost ten percent of the plaintiff class. Such behavior clearly demonstrates that counsel's loyalty truly lies with the NFLPA, not with its members.

In addition, this loyalty likely will have a more specific adverse impact on the player class. In another NFL anti-trust trial before this court, *Brown v. Pro Football, Inc.*, information concerning non-football earnings was deemed relevant and allowed into evidence. Such confidential information, particularly information concerning licensing contracts, could be used to the players' detriment in the *Golic* breach of contract action (e.g., in the execution of judgments against players). The ethical rules are designed to protect clients from conflicts of interest of this type, and the court therefore finds that the representation is barred by Rule 1.7.

Plaintiffs' counsel attempt to save their representation by (1) questioning whether defendants may raise this issue, (2) noting that there is no argument in defendants' briefs that the NFLPA is not loyal to its players, (3) claiming that there is no question of disclosures of confidential information, and (4) offering to excise any tainted players. None of these arguments is helpful.

First, the court has an obligation under Fed. R. Civ. P. 23(a)(4) to ensure that the class is adequately represented, both by the named representatives and by the class counsel:

> If in maintaining the class action in [a case] the attorneys should be disqualified because of a conflict of interest, then certainly they are not "generally able to conduct the litigation" and there is inadequate representation of the class's interest.

In re Fine Paper Antitrust Litigation, 617 F.2d 22, 27 (3d Cir. 1980). As a result, any party, including the court sua sponte, may raise inadequacy of counsel issues. Second, it is Weil, Gotshal's loyalty in question, not the NFLPA's, and counsel's offer to abandon twenty class members is an explicit demonstration of a lack of the necessary loyalty. Third, the absence of confidential disclosures will not save a representation that is so conflicted on other terms. (Moreover, this ignores the potential, as discussed above, that confidential information could be used to the players' detriment.) Finally, the offer to exclude the twenty players has already been demonstrated to be damaging, not helpful, to counsel's position.

As the court finds that plaintiffs' counsel is inadequate, it cannot certify the class.

Under Local Rule 203(b), the court will allow plaintiffs leave to file an amended motion for class certification. In that motion, plaintiffs must demonstrate (1) that they have obtained new counsel to represent the class; or (2) that Weil, Gotshal & Manges have ceased their representation of the NFLPA in the *Golic* case and that they have cured all potential conflicts of interest. Such motion must be filed within thirty days of this date.

NOTES AND QUESTIONS

1. ***How Did This Happen?*** How did Weil, Gotshal get into this mess? Now it has to choose between getting new lawyers for the NFL players in the class action, or getting new lawyers for the NFLPA in the other litigation. Shouldn't the firm have realized before it took on the class action that it could not do both? (Maybe the named plaintiffs in the class action were informed of the potential conflict and consented to it. But what about the 20 players who are defendants in the NFLPA suit? Did they consent? Does Weil, Gotshal need their consent? If they did consent, would the judge have to approve of Weil, Gotshal as class counsel in the suit brought by the players?)

2. ***Hot Potatoes.*** Essentially, the court has ordered Weil, Gotshal to drop one of its cases like a hot potato. Not all courts would give the law firm the choice of which client to drop, but Weil, Gotshal has that choice here. How should it decide which case to drop? What if one client will have much more trouble finding a new lawyer than the other client? For example, what if Weil, Gotshal is one of only a few firms with special expertise in class actions, but many firms have the expertise to handle the NFLPA breach of contract case? Or what if the firm has spent 1,000 hours on the NFLPA case, which is almost over, but has spent only 40 hours on the class action, which has just started?

These "hot potato" issues have been arising with increasing frequency. Usually they arise when a law firm wants to withdraw from one matter like a hot potato in order to take on a more lucrative matter. Sometimes, like here, they arise because a law firm discovers an incurable conflict in the middle of two simultaneous representations.

3. ***Double Penalty?*** By the way, why shouldn't Weil, Gotshal have to drop *both* clients? If the law firm was negligent in taking on a new client that improperly conflicted with an existing client, why shouldn't it be punished by having to give up both

representations? Or would that really punish the clients as much as the law firm? (After all, the clients chose Weil, Gotshal, and presumably want the firm to continue representing them.)

4. ***Checking for Conflicts.*** To avoid getting booted out of cases, law firms should check very carefully for conflicts. How should they do this? What information should they get from new clients, and what should they do with it? Do they need to get information about potential conflicts when an existing client asks the law firm to take on a new matter? What about when the law firm hires a new lawyer? Yes, the firm has to check for conflicts in all of these situations.

Checking systematically for conflicts can be a daunting task, especially in large firms with branch offices all over the country (and sometimes all over the world). Large law firms typically hire special employees and set up custom-made software programs and massive databases to detect conflicts of interest. As you read through the many cases in these chapters on conflicts of interest, think about the kinds of information you would need to gather if you were in charge of monitoring conflicts of interest at your law firm.

5. ***Non-Consentable Conflicts.*** Ordinarily, when a law firm discovers a potential conflict, it can avoid disqualification and discipline by obtaining informed consent from *all* affected clients. (Remember, when you have a concurrent conflict between two clients, you have to get consent from all affected clients, not just one of them.) But some conflicts are non-consentable. In these situations, you are not allowed to ask for client consent, and if the client does consent, that consent is voidable. Cases about non-consentable conflicts are relatively rare, so we do not include any cases about them. We will instead spend our time on more common situations that often puzzle practicing lawyers.

6. ***Turning Down Cases to Avoid Conflicts.*** You may be tempted to take every case that comes along, figuring that more cases mean more money. But that isn't always so. If you get kicked out of a case, it will cost you money, and may cost you a client as well. (The client is typically upset that you didn't say anything about the potential conflict. The client has spent a lot of time and effort getting to know you and telling you confidential information about his problem, and now he has to start all over again with a new lawyer. Why didn't you tell him at the beginning so he could have hired a different lawyer in the first place?)

7. ***National Standards for Conflicts?*** You may recall that under the ABA Model Rules of Professional Conduct, you cannot oppose a *current* client in *any* matter, even if it is wholly unrelated, without the client's informed consent. But you can oppose a *former* client without consent as long as the new matter is not "substantially related" to the work you did for the former client. In Texas state courts there is no such distinction. Under Texas Rule of Professional Conduct 1.06 — which is unique in all the nation — you can oppose *anyone*, even a current client, as long as the new matter is not substantially related to the work you are doing for the current client.

Does that reasoning sound OK to you? It didn't go over well with the court in *In re Dresser Industries, Inc.*, 972 F.2d 540 (5th Cir. 1992). In that case, which continues to resonate today, the Fifth Circuit refused to apply Texas Rule 1.06 when Susman Godfrey, a well-known Houston law firm, filed a class action *against* Dresser Industries. Susman Godfrey had already *represented* Dresser in two unrelated pending suits. Thus, Susman Godfrey was suing its own client. The Fifth Circuit granted a writ of mandamus to disqualify Susman Godfrey from continuing the class action representation. The court held that *national* standards of legal ethics, not local ones, apply in ruling upon conflicts of interest. The court then stated:

> We turn, then, to the current national standards of legal ethics to first consider whether this dual representation amounts to impropriety. Neither the ABA Model Rules of Professional Conduct nor the Code of Professional Responsibility allows an attorney to bring a suit against a client without its

> consent. This position is also taken by the American Law Institute in its drafts of the Restatement of the Law Governing Lawyers.
>
> Unquestionably, the national standards of attorney conduct forbid a lawyer from bringing a suit against a current client without the consent of both clients. Susman's conduct violates all of these standards — unless excused or justified under exceptional circumstances not present here.
>
> Exceptional circumstances may sometimes mean that what is ordinarily a clear impropriety will not, always and inevitably, determine a conflicts case. . . . Susman, for example, might have been able to continue his dual representation if he could have shown some social interest to be served by his representation that would outweigh the public perception of his impropriety. Susman, however, can present no such reason. There is no suggestion that other lawyers could not ably perform his offices for the plaintiffs, nor is there any basis for a suggestion of any societal or professional interest to be served. This fact suggests a rule of thumb for use in future motions for disqualification based on concurrent representation: *However a lawyer's motives may be clothed, if the sole reason for suing his own client is the lawyer's self-interest, disqualification should be granted.* [Emphasis added.]

Even in Texas, therefore, lawyers cannot sue their own clients in federal court absent exceptional standards. What are exceptional circumstances? The *Dresser* court explained in a footnote that

> the Texas rules' allowance of some concurrent representation is based, in part, on a concern that concurrent representation may be necessary either to prevent a large company, such as Dresser, from monopolizing the lawyers of an area or to assure that certain classes of unpopular clients receive representation. Although we do not now reach the matter, our consideration of social benefit to offset the appearance of impropriety might allow such a representation if the balance clearly and unequivocally favored allowing such representation to further the ends of justice.

How would a large company such as Dresser go about "monopolizing the lawyers of an area"? If you can figure that out, you are starting to understand conflicts of interest at a tactical level — how litigants can use the conflicts rules to protect themselves and their clients (or to harm others).

8. ***The Price of Disqualification.*** When a law firm is disqualified for conflict of interest, it generally cannot recover any court-awarded fees for time spent after the conflict arose, and may even have to give back fees already earned. Under 11 U.S.C. §§ 327 and 328, which apply in bankruptcy cases, a conflict of interest by an attorney for a debtor can require disgorgement of fees. If there's anything worse than not getting paid for the work you've done, it's having to give back the money you were already paid for that work. (Even more frightening is that failing to disclose a conflict in a bankruptcy case may be a criminal offense, and at least one lawyer went to prison for failing to disclose a known conflict.)

B. THE FIRM'S CONFLICTS COMMITTEE MEETS AGAIN

It's time for another meeting of your firm's Conflicts Committee, of which you are still a member. Below are the items on the agenda for this week's Committee meeting. Most of the matters raise questions about concurrent conflicts of interest, but a few raise conflicts of other kinds. As to each item on the agenda, be prepared to discuss three things:

1. *Nature of the conflicts:* What are the actual or potential conflicts? (Since you do not have much information to go on, you will have to use your imagination to predict what kinds of conflicts will arise or could arise if the firm accepts the matter.)

2. *Governing rules:* What rules of professional conduct or other legal authorities govern the particular conflict?

3. *Decision or further questions:* Should the firm accept (or continue) the representation? This question breaks down into three subparts:

(a) If so, are there any conditions or prerequisites to accepting the matter? For example, must the client's consent be obtained? If so, what must be disclosed to the client to obtain a valid consent? Are there any limitations on the representation, such as parties the firm will not sue?

(b) If the firm cannot accept the matter, why not? Does some rule or other law prohibit you from accepting the matter, or is the firm rejecting the matter solely for policy reasons?

(c) If you cannot decide whether to accept the matter until you obtain further information, what additional information do you need?

Items on the Conflict Committee's Agenda

A. *Representing a young couple in estate planning.* The firm has been asked to draw up wills and give general estate planning advice to a young professional couple, Edith and Sidney Woodridge. They have a very strong and solid relationship with each other. So far, they have no children.

B. *Representing an older couple in estate planning.* The firm has been asked to undertake estate planning for a well-to-do couple, Judy and Murray Ulovsky. They have been married for 15 years, and have three children, ages 7, 12, and 21 — one by this marriage, one by adoption during this marriage, and one by the wife's previous marriage. The husband and wife were informally separated for a few months sixteen months ago, but they are now back together and say they are on excellent terms.

C. *Representing co-defendants in a contract suit.* A major shirt manufacturer has sued two of your clients, Carter Cotton Co. and Perry Ellis, for breach of contract. The shirt manufacturer alleges in the complaint that Carter breached its contract to supply pima cotton and that Perry Ellis breached its contract to timely design a line of pastel shirts. Carter and Perry Ellis have both asked you to defend them in the suit.

D. *Representing co-plaintiffs in an auto accident case.* A driver and passenger, Sarah and Michelle, were injured when a drunk driver ran into their car. The drunk driver who caused the accident has his own lawyer. Sarah and Michelle have come to the firm together to ask for representation.

E. *Representing business competitors.* The firm currently represents Capital Tool & Die Corp. in labor law matters. The firm has been asked to represent Argon Tool Co., a competitor, in Argon's upcoming negotiations with the union to which Argon's employees belong. The crucial issue will be wages.

F. *Forming a partnership.* Three people — Fred, Jean, and Terry — want to form a partnership to manufacture chocolate chip marshmallows. Fred is ready to invest $50,000 in cash. Jean will invest $10,000 and knows how to run the business. Terry has no money to invest but will become a full-time salesperson and manage the sales department. All three have asked you to help them form the partnership.

G. *Representing a company and its employees in litigation.* Karma Corp. has been sued by several shareholders in a securities fraud suit. The suit alleges that Karma Corp. leaked false information about a proposed merger, and doctored sales figures to make them look better. Only the corporation itself is named in the suit, but the plaintiffs will be deposing many of Karma's officers and employees. Karma has therefore asked that your firm represent both the corporation and its officers, directors, and employees.

H. *Representing parties with conflicting legal positions.* You represent Travelers Insurance, which insures many toxic waste sites. You also represent Magna Bank, which foreclosed on two toxic waste sites after the owners went bankrupt. In litigation pending in New Jersey, Travelers has argued that a bank that forecloses on a toxic waste site is liable for cleanup costs just as any other owner would be. Now, Magna Bank is involved in litigation in Ohio and wants your firm to argue that banks are not liable for cleanup costs at a toxic waste site after they acquire the site through foreclosure. Travelers is not involved in the Ohio litigation in any way, and Magna Bank is not involved in the New Jersey litigation in any way.

I. *Suing a relative's employer.* Ridley Norstrom has asked C. Duncan Alston, a partner at your firm, to file suit against Corn Poppers, Inc. for breach of contract. Your sister is Vice President of National Marketing for Corn Poppers and has worked for the company for five years. Would it change your analysis if your sister has worked there for only a few months in a low level job in the mail room? How about if the Corn Poppers employee is a good friend who has been your roommate since college graduation, rather than a relative?

J. *Representing multiple defendants in the same suit.* A dozen people got sick recently after eating a spinach salad at Leaves & Loaves, an upscale vegetarian restaurant. Several plaintiffs have sued both the restaurant and the company that supplied the spinach, Produce Supply Co. The restaurant and the produce supply company are on good terms and have asked our firm to defend them both in the litigation. May we do so?

K. *Settling a multi-party lawsuit.* Your firm filed suit last year on behalf of six homeowners against Helix Chemical Company, which had been polluting the ground water around Hempstead Lake Estates, where all six of your firm's clients live. Your firm did a great job and Helix recently offered to pay $600,000 plus your firm's attorney fees to settle the whole matter. Helix said your clients should decide how to divide up the money. What should your firm do?

L. *Negotiating against an old friend.* Mariah Karee has asked you to negotiate a new recording contract with her record company, Decca Audio. When you conduct your routine conflicts check, you learn that the main officer in charge of negotiating for her account will be Milt Potlich, an old college friend of yours. You are trying to develop your entertainment law practice, so you have invited Milt to several parties and dinners in the past couple of years, and he has invited you to some of his parties. The negotiations will usually be with Decca's lawyer rather than with Milt personally, but Milt will have a big hand in the negotiations, and he will look good if he can sign up Mariah again. Can you negotiate on Mariah's behalf?

M. *Representing multiple plaintiffs in the same suit.* A truck carrying noxious chemicals recently turned over on a street in a residential neighborhood in Mayberry. Twenty plaintiffs have asked our firm to represent them against Chemical Transport, the trucking company that was carrying the chemicals. Five are adults who were hospitalized with severe respiratory problems, resulting in hospital charges of over $50,000 each. Eight are children, in three different families, who were poisoned after ingesting contaminated soil from their front yards. Four potential plaintiffs had less than $1,500 each in property damage when their cars were damaged during the clean-up effort. Three other adults had no physical injuries, but lost two days of work as a result of the spill. May we agree to represent all twenty?

N. *Representing an actor and a film studio.* Another partner at your law firm represents Ynos Corp., a company which produces feature films. An actor has asked you to represent him in negotiations with several studios, including Ynos, in connection with the terms of his contracts for the next three films in which he will appear. May you accept the representation?

The following scenarios illustrate various provisions of ABA Model Rule 1.8, which addresses special types of conflicts that have historically posed problems. See if you can locate and apply the relevant provisions of Rule 1.8.

A. *Entering into a sexual relationship with a client.* While representing Global Refining, you do a lot of traveling in the U.S. and overseas. Usually, the trips concern ironing out problems with existing contracts or exploring potential new contracts. On many of these trips, Global sends the attractive Ingrid Manberg, its Vice-President for International Affairs (a rather unfortunate title, as it turns out). You typically stay in the same hotel (in separate rooms) and often have dinner together, sometimes with other parties to Global's contracts but often just the two of you. You generally discuss business over dinner, but sometimes after a couple of glasses of Chardonnay you have other thoughts. Would you be doing anything improper to start an intimate romance with Ms. Manberg?

B. *Financial assistance to clients.* You have two clients that are in dire financial straits. One of the clients is Georgine Croft, who was in a serious auto accident two years ago and has been unable to work since then. She gets some benefits, but not enough to pay her mortgage, feed her family, and pay for family health insurance. The auto accident was at least 90% the fault of the drunk driver who slammed into her, and you are virtually certain that she will win a verdict well over $300,000 at trial. Unfortunately, she cannot wait until trial, so she asks you to pay her mortgage between now and trial, and promises to pay you back out of the proceeds of her suit. May you ethically pay her mortgage?

A second client in financial trouble is Rodney Gabriel, a big-shot businessman around town with a secret but devastating gambling addition. You have been doing Rodney's estate planning for years, but he has not been able to pay your bills for several months and is at the end of his financial rope. Despite his fancy car and impressive house, Rodney is deeply in debt. He begs you to lend him enough money to pay off some of his loans, and he is willing to give you a second mortgage on his house (which has gone up sharply in value in recent years), to serve as security for your loan. May you ethically lend Rodney the money?

C. *Financial assistance to a former client.* You also have a former client who is in serious financial trouble. The former client is Lucille Shane, who was fired from her job as a receptionist more than two years ago and has been struggling to keep up her car payments. If she misses any more payments, the bank says it will repossess the car. You brought an employment discrimination case on Lucille's behalf, but it settled and is completely over, so she is a former client. (She agrees that she is a former client.) When she saw you yesterday at the grocery store, she took you aside and whispered, "I'm desperate. My brother-in-law is willing to lend me some money, but he insists on a guarantor. Can you please guarantee the loan? I promise I'll pay you back." May you ethically guarantee the loan?

D. *Gift horse.* Because of your expertise in estate planning, especially your encyclopedic knowledge of the gift tax, Mrs. Polk Wardwell, the main heiress of the Sulder real estate fortune, retained you several years ago to advise her about the most efficient means for transferring her wealth to her children and grandchildren while maintaining her own high standard of living. You spent many hours explaining complex trust documents to her, and she soon made you virtually a part of her family. You were often invited for Sunday dinner, and in the past few years you have even been an honored guest at her birthday parties (most recently her 95th, but she's still sharp as a tack). Yesterday, she came to your office to revise her will to cut out one of her grandchildren who insulted her in front of her family and friends. "I was going to give my prize thoroughbred Houdini to my grandchild," she said, "but now I want to give Houdini to you. Please make up a codicil recording that I leave Houdini to you when I die." May you accept this testamentary gift as long as you have one of your partners draft the codicil?

E. *Book and movie rights.* You are a celebrated criminal defense lawyer. Recently, you were asked to represent the infamous and feared BTP serial killer (we should say "alleged" serial killer, to be technically correct), who stalked victims in the Midwest for years but has finally been caught and indicted. You typically charge over $400 per hour to defend your clients, but BTP probably doesn't have enough money to buy even two hours of your time, much less pay for your legal services for an entire trial. He tried to get money from his family and friends, but they all turned him down. Now BTP has offered to give you book and movie rights to his entire story if you will represent him. The book and movie deals could be worth a lot more than the fees. May you accept BTP's offer?

Chapter 23

CONFLICTS OF INTEREST WITH FORMER CLIENTS

Our main focus up to now has been on concurrent conflicts — conflicts that threaten *current* clients. In this chapter we will look at successive conflicts, conflicts that threaten *former* clients.

There are vast differences between concurrent conflicts and successive conflicts, and these differences can have great practical impact on a law firm's profits. If you want to be fair to your clients and develop a successful (and profitable) law practice, you need to know how to distinguish a successive conflict from a concurrent conflict, and how the rules govern each type of conflict. Even more important to you at this stage of your career is understanding how to recognize successive conflicts when you change law firms.

This chapter begins with an outline of the differences between successive and concurrent conflicts, and then discusses three distinct issues, with an emphasis on what will happen if you change jobs from one law firm to another law firm — something most young lawyers do multiple times in their careers.

Issue # 1: The substantially related test. What is the meaning of the key term "substantially related" in ABA Model Rule 1.9? Everything depends on this term. If the matter you want to handle now and the matter you or your law firm handled before are not substantially related, then you don't have a conflict with a former client, and your former client has no right to veto your current representation.

Issue # 2: Acquiring information informally. When you work at a law firm, you learn information not only by working on client matters but also by talking with other lawyers around the office informally at lunch, in the halls, at the water cooler, and in other ways. If you acquire information about a client informally, may you later oppose that client? ABA Model Rule 1.9(b) says no.

Issue # 3: Prospective clients. Is a law firm disqualified by the former client conflict rules if the firm's only contact with the person was a preliminary interview or evaluation of the client's matter, and the person never actually hired the law firm to perform any work? ABA Model Rule 1.18 addresses this situation.

A. AN OUTLINE ON CONFLICTS WITH FORMER CLIENTS

1. Concurrent and Successive Conflicts Compared

Conflicts with former clients are governed by ABA Model Rule 1.9, which is far more lenient (i.e., less protective) than the general rule governing conflicts with current clients (Rule 1.7). To be specific, Rule 1.9 is more lenient in two main ways:

A. *Substantial relationship test.* Under Rule 1.7(a), a lawyer may not oppose a *current* client without that client's consent even in a matter *wholly unrelated* to the lawyer's other work for that client.

1. Under Rule 1.7, you must *always* obtain consent to oppose (be "directly adverse" to) a current client. You may *never* oppose a current client without that client's consent.
2. Under Rule 1.9(a), in contrast, you are not barred from opposing a *former* client unless the matter is *substantially related* to your earlier work (or your firm's earlier work) for the former client. You do not need the former client's consent unless the matter you are handling for your current client is substantially related to the matter you handled for your former client.

a. Thus, Rule 1.9 allows a former client to veto the new representation in a substantially related matter.
b. But in unrelated matters (or in matters that are barely related), consent is not required and the former client has no veto.

B. *Consent.* In conflicts with current clients, you may not even seek a client's consent if you cannot reasonably conclude that you "will be able to provide competent and diligent representation" to the client whose consent you are seeking. (See Rule 1.7, Comment 15.) Similarly, the pre-2002 version of the ABA Model Rules provided that you could not seek your client's consent if a reasonable lawyer would advise the client to refuse consent. (See pre-2002 Rule 1.7, Comment 5.) In conflicts with former clients, however, you can seek consent even if a reasonable lawyer would advise the former client not to consent. Rule 1.9 has no "reasonableness" test for obtaining consent from a former client. If a former client is willing to provide informed consent, then you are entitled to accept that consent even if you think the former client should not consent.

C. *Government agencies.* A special situation arises if your former client is a government agency. That situation is governed not by Rule 1.9 but instead by the unique provisions of ABA Model Rule 1.11 ("Special Conflicts of Interest for Former and Current Government Officers and Employees"). Conflicts for former and current government employees are too complex to cover in this outline.

2. Grounds for Personal Disqualification Under Rule 1.9

If you have moved from one law firm to another, then you need to worry about all of the clients that your former law firm represented, whether you personally represented those clients or not. If a matter that your current law firm is handling for a client is substantially related to a matter that your old (previous) law firm handled, then you may be personally disqualified from opposing your old firm's former client. This is true even if you never worked on the adverse client's matters at your old firm and are not working or planning to work on the substantially related matter at your new (current) firm. You may be personally disqualified for one of two reasons, either (A) you *personally* represented the former client at your current law firm or in any previous legal job, or (B) you did not personally represent the former client but, while at a previous legal job, you *acquired protected information* about the former client, in the same or a substantially related matter. The first situation is covered by Rule 1.9(a), and the second is covered by Rule 1.9(b).

A. *Rule 1.9(a):* You are disqualified from opposing any former client that you *personally* represented in the same or a "substantially related" matter while working at any previous law firm. In other words, every client whose matters you have personally worked on in the past is considered your former client, and you may not represent a person whose interests are "materially adverse" to your former client in a "substantially related" matter.

B. *Rule 1.9(b):* You are also disqualified if your previous *firm* represented a client that your current firm is now opposing in a substantially related matter <u>and</u> you *obtained confidential information* about the opposing client (your previous firm's client) while you were working at the previous firm. (If you have worked for more than one prior law firm, Rule 1.9(b) applies to clients of all of the firms where you have worked.)

C. *Informed consent.* A former client is always free to consent to a conflict whether it arises under Rule 1.9(a) or Rule 1.9(b). Specifically, both subparagraphs provide that the former client may waive the conflict by giving "informed consent, confirmed in writing." Thus, informed consent that is confirmed in writing will cure a Rule 1.9 conflict whether the former client is your own personal former client or is (or was) a client of your former firm.

1. The burden is on the lawyer or law firm to spot the former client conflict and to obtain the former client's informed consent. The burden is not on the former client to object.
2. If you or your firm fail to spot a Rule 1.9 conflict, or you spot it but fail to obtain the former client's consent, or the consent is not informed, or the informed consent is not confirmed in writing, then you are violating Rule 1.9.

3. The "Substantially Related" Test

The key to identifying conflicts with former clients is the "substantially related" test. However, there is no universal agreement on how to determine whether two matters are "substantially related."

A. The most common test is stated in Rule 1.9, Comment 3, which says that matters are "substantially related" for purposes of Rule 1.9 in two situations: (a) they "involve the same transaction or legal dispute" or (b) "there otherwise is a substantial risk that confidential factual information, as would normally have been obtained in the prior representation, would materially advance the client's position in the subsequent matter."

1. Comment 3 continues with two examples of substantially related matters:
    a. A lawyer who has represented a businessperson and learned extensive private financial information about that person may not then represent that person's spouse in seeking a divorce.
    b. Similarly, a lawyer who has previously represented a client in securing environmental permits to build a shopping center would be precluded from representing neighbors seeking to oppose rezoning of the property on the basis of environmental considerations. However, that lawyer would not be precluded, on the grounds of substantial relationship, from defending a tenant of the *completed* shopping center in resisting eviction for nonpayment of rent.
2. *Irrebuttable presumption under Rule 1.9(a) that you received confidential information.* If you *personally* represented the client in a substantially related matter, courts *presume* that you obtained confidential information relevant and material to the current matter. This presumption is generally irrebuttable.
    a. If you billed any time at all to a matter — no matter how little time and no matter what you did (reviewing documents, drafting pleadings, interviewing witnesses, performing due diligence, doing anything), most courts will say that you "represented" the client.
    b. Some courts have created an exception if a lawyer performed essentially pure legal research, and acquired no knowledge of the facts of the matter or the law firm's strategy in approaching the matter. In that limited situation, some courts will say that you did not "represent" the client. That is a rare situation, because most lawyers provide legal and factual context (or documents containing facts) when they give an assignment.

3. *Rebuttable presumption under Rule 1.9(b).* If your former *firm* (as opposed to you personally) represented the former client in a substantially related matter, courts generally presume that you acquired relevant confidential information. But this presumption is rebuttable.

   a. Courts give you an opportunity to rebut this presumption by showing that you did not have *access* to the former client's confidences.

   b. Rule 1.9, Comment 6, explains that access is a question of fact, and depends on all of the circumstances. For example:

      i. If you were formerly an *associate* at a *large firm* who never worked on the client's matters, never met with the former client, and *had access only to files you actually worked on* (as opposed to all of the firm's files), then you can probably rebut the presumption that you obtained confidential information about the previous matter.

      ii. At the other end of the spectrum, if you were formerly a *partner* at a *small firm,* and you regularly *reviewed files on all pending matters* or discussed them with your partners, you probably cannot rebut the presumption that you received confidences.

      iii. Each case is different, and the size and operating methods of the former firm are important. Mundane questions like "Who could get into the file room?" or "Did the lawyers typically discuss cases with each other at lunch?" or "Were the files locked up?" are highly relevant. Under Rule 1.9(b), confidential information that you received informally in the hallways is just as relevant as confidential information that a client gave you directly under Rule 1.9(a). Unless you can demonstrate that you did not have reasonable access to the former client's confidential information, then you will be disqualified under Rule 1.9(b) unless the former client gives informed consent, confirmed in writing.

4. *No revelations by former client.* When a former client moves to disqualify you or your law firm under Rule 1.9(a) or (b), the court does not require the former client to reveal what confidential information the former client conveyed to you, or what confidential information you obtained from the client or from documents or from other lawyers. Such a hearing would defeat the whole idea of protecting the former client's confidences. You cannot protect the former client's confidential information by revealing it. Rather, the court compares the former matter to the present matter and reaches a conclusion based on logic as to whether the two matters are substantially related. If so, and if you either personally represented the former client or had access to the former client's confidential information at a prior firm, then the court will presume that you received material confidential information whether or not you actually did.

   a. If former clients had to reveal what they told a former lawyer in order to disqualify the former lawyer, the information would no longer be confidential. The former client's effort to protect its confidential information by disqualifying its former lawyer (or a lawyer who was with a firm that represented it) would end up exposing the very confidential information the former client wants to protect, defeating the whole purpose of the motion to disqualify.

b. Therefore, courts look at the two matters in question (the present matter and the former matter). If the matters are "substantially related," we presume that the lawyer obtained confidential information in the former matter. To guard against the possibility that the lawyer with the information might be tempted to use it to help the current client (or might accidentally reveal the information), the rules disqualify the lawyer in the present matter unless the former client gives informed consent.

4. Imputed Disqualification and Conflict Checking Under Rule 1.9

ABA Model Rule 1.10(a) provides that "[w]hile lawyers are associated in a firm, none of them shall knowingly represent a client when any one of them practicing alone would be prohibited from doing so" by Rule 1.9. The odds are close to 100% that you will change jobs at least once during your legal career. (In fact, it is likely that you will do so a few times.) Every time you take a new job, Rule 1.10(a) will impute to your new law firm both (i) all of your conflicts under Rule 1.9(a) with your former clients, and (ii) all of your conflicts under Rule 1.9(b) with former clients of your old firms about whom you acquired confidential information. (Note that we said "old firms," plural. As you move through your legal career, you take all of your former clients with you forever. As we said earlier, "Once a former client, always a former client.") Accordingly, before your new law firm can hire you, it needs to check for conflicts of interest to see whether the law firm will be vicariously disqualified from any matters if it hires you. This section discusses how your new firm is likely to check for conflicts with your former clients. (Right now we're not discussing conflicts that arise because of your personal interests, such as family, friends, or financial interests.)

A. *Rule 1.9(a):* Checking for conflicts under Rule 1.9(a) is relatively easy. Let's say you are planning to leave your "old" firm (where you still work) and join a "new" firm (meaning new to you). Your new firm is likely to make you a conditional offer. "We'll hire you if your presence here won't create unacceptable conflicts."

1. Your "new" firm (the one you want to join) will typically show you a list of the new firm's currently active matters, and ask whether you, personally, represent or have represented the opposing parties in any of those matters (including at other law firms).

a. The clients you *currently* represent will become your *former* clients as soon as you move to your new firm, so they have to be included in the conflicts check.

b. The clients you represented in the past (those who are already former clients) will remain your former clients when you move to your new firm, so they also have to be included in the conflicts check.

c. The conflict check should encompass all types of matters, whether litigation, transactions, negotiations, drafting, or counseling. The same basic rules apply to conflicts with former clients in all types of matters. The rules on conflicts with former clients do not distinguish between litigation clients, transactional clients, and office practice clients.

2. If you currently represent or formerly represented adversaries of your new firm, then your new firm will ask whether any of the matters you are working on now or worked on in the past are the same as or substantially related to the matters your new firm is handling adverse to those clients.

a. In some situations, your confidentiality obligations under Rule 1.6 or Rule 1.9(c) will prohibit you from disclosing the nature of the matters you worked on or (more rarely) the identity of your old firm's clients. This may be the situation, for example, if you are representing a client in a transaction or business deal that has not yet been carried out (such as a planned merger or acquisition) or if you are helping a client in preparing a lawsuit that has not yet been filed (and the potential defendants do not yet know the suit is coming).
b. For example, suppose you are advising a client at your old firm about a possible divorce, but the client has not yet filed for divorce or notified her husband that she plans to file for divorce. Rule 1.6 prohibits you from telling your new firm about the nature of the matter or the identity of the client.
c. Similarly, if you are advising Smedley Corp. as an undisclosed principal in the acquisition of various parcels of real estate, or if you are advising Smedley Corp. in its plans to cease performance of a contract based on the other party's alleged breaches, you must not advise your new firm about the nature of that work unless you find an exception in Rule 1.6.
d. On the other hand, once litigation has been filed or a transaction or business deal has been carried out (or at least disclosed), Rule 1.6 and Rule 1.9(c) no longer prohibit you from disclosing that you are working on a particular matter, or previously worked on it.

3. If any matter that you are working on or previously worked on is substantially related to the matters your new firm is working on, then (with your permission) your new firm will tell your old firm that it has made you a conditional offer and needs consent from specific clients so that your new firm can ethically continue representing the new firm's clients who are adverse to your old firm's clients in the same or substantially related matters. (Your new firm should not contact the opposing party directly because of a rule called the "no-contact rule," ABA Model Rule 4.2. The rule prohibits a lawyer, in the course of a representation, from communicating with another represented party absent the consent of the lawyer for that party. We covered the no-contact rule in an earlier chapter.)
4. If the clients of your old firm consent, then your new firm needs to confirm this consent in writing.
5. If the clients of your old firm refuse to consent, then your new firm has three choices:

a. The firm may decide to hire you and withdraw (or seek consent to withdraw) from any conflicting matters that it is currently handling (or perhaps withdraw first and then hire you after the withdrawal is complete).
b. If the new firm can make a nonfrivolous argument that no conflict exists because the matters in question are not substantially related, the firm may decide to hire you and fight any motion to disqualify that your former clients (or your former firm's clients) may later file.
c. The firm may decide not to hire you at all because it is unwilling to withdraw or to risk disqualification. (It happens.)

B. *Rule 1.9(b):* Checking for conflicts under Rule 1.9(b) is extremely difficult (sometimes impossible), because now your new firm is checking your knowledge about clients you did *not* personally work on. The question is: even though you never did any legal work for a particular client at your old firm, did you nevertheless obtain confidential information about the client? (If so, it must be determined whether the confidential information that you have obtained is relevant and material to the matter adverse to the party in question.)

1. As under Rule 1.9(a), your new firm will ordinarily show you a comprehensive list of the firm's current adversaries.
   a. Under Rule 1.9(b), you have to try to remember whether you ever obtained any confidences about any of these clients informally (e.g., during lunch-table discussions, firm picnics, firm meetings, casual conversations with other lawyers, or in any other manner) while working at your old firm.
   b. You also have to inform your new firm whether you had access to all files at your old firm, or only to some of the files. If you are coming from a large firm, your new firm may want to know which lawyers you worked with, whether the firm was departmentalized, and other practical facts about how the firm operated.
2. This conflicts check is a delicate task because both you and your new firm must avoid discussing either the content of the confidential information or the details of the matters that your new firm is handling against the former client. Such a discussion would violate the former client's confidentiality, and immediately destroy any *firewall* (or ethical screen) the firm is trying to erect. (Firewalls, which keep information from moving from one lawyer in the firm to other lawyers in the firm, are discussed later in a separate chapter.)

That briefly sums up the major differences between concurrent conflicts and successive conflicts, the prevailing definition of substantially related, the concept of a former client, the idea of personal disqualification, and the methods a firm uses to determine whether any of its new lawyers are disqualified under Rule 1.9(a) or (b). Now we will examine these issues in more detail, beginning with a closer examination of the "substantially related" test. We then turn to a discussion of hot potato clients and the perils of preliminary interviews.

B. THE SUBSTANTIAL RELATIONSHIP TEST

When you want to oppose a former client, the $64,000 question is whether the present matter is substantially related to the matters you handled for your former client. The first question is whether the present and former matters are substantially related. If they are not, you have the green light to oppose your former client, without the former client's consent. In other words, if the present matter is not substantially related to the former matter, the former client has no say in the matter, and no veto.

Unfortunately, deciding whether two matters are "substantially related" is not always easy. One reason for the difficulty is that different courts have defined "substantial relationship" in different ways. In the next case, a New Jersey federal district court judge systematically reviews various tests and chooses the one he thinks is best. Would you choose the same test, or would you select one that is more liberal or more restrictive?

KASELAAN & D'ANGELO ASSOCIATES, INC. v. D'ANGELO

144 F.R.D. 235 (D.N.J. 1992)

SIMANDLE, J.

Presently before the court is the motion by plaintiffs, Kaselaan & D'Angelo Associates, Inc. and Hill International, Inc., to disqualify John J. Rosenberg, Esquire, and Varet, Marcus & Fink, P.C., as counsel for defendant William "Chip" D'Angelo.

Background

The present suit involves claims by plaintiffs, Kaselaan & D'Angelo, Inc. ("K&D") and Hill International, Inc. ("Hill International"), against defendant, William "Chip" D'Angelo ("D'Angelo").

On or about December 24, 1988, Hill International's predecessor, Hill Group, purchased all the issued and outstanding stock of K&D from defendant D'Angelo and his then partner, Valdur Kaselaan.

Pursuant to the agreement, D'Angelo was to remain an employee of K&D for the six-year period stated therein and to discharge his various obligations and responsibilities on behalf of K&D. As part of the agreement, defendant agreed to the following three limited restrictive covenants: (1) to refrain from soliciting or interfering with customers or clients of K&D, (2) to refrain from soliciting or interfering with employees of K&D, and (3) to refrain from misappropriating or disclosing confidential business information of K&D. Plaintiffs have now alleged that defendant has violated his covenants, engaged in unfair competition, engaged in tortious interference with business relations of clients and employees, misappropriated trade secrets and confidential information, and breached his duty of loyalty as an officer, director, and employee of K&D.

After suit was filed, defendant . . . retained as his counsel Varet, Marcus & Fink, P.C. ("Varet Marcus") . . . of which John J. Rosenberg, Esquire ("Mr. Rosenberg"), is a member. . . . [A]t the first day of defendant's deposition held on July 28, 1992, Mr. Rosenberg identified himself as lead counsel on the case. Once plaintiffs became aware of Mr. Rosenberg's prior representation of K&D, they filed the present disqualification motion because Mr. Rosenberg previously represented K&D as its lawyer.

Plaintiffs contend that Mr. Rosenberg began representing K&D on or about January 16, 1986, when he was an attorney with the firm of Friedman & Atherton, located in Boston, Massachusetts. According to plaintiffs, Mr. Rosenberg represented K&D in employment matters involving the following individuals: Paul Manna, James Dennison, Michael Collins, Michael Clarke, and William Eason. In response, defendant concedes that Mr. Rosenberg's prior representation of K&D is an "undisputed fact." He continued to represent K&D in such employment matters with present and former employees through at least March 29, 1990, which was 15 months after K&D bought out defendant D'Angelo. With this background in mind, this court will now consider the legal issues raised by this disqualification motion.

Discussion

Plaintiffs . . . allege that RPC 1.9(a)(1) mandates that this court disqualify Mr. Rosenberg because the present action is "substantially related" to matters which Mr. Rosenberg previously handled on behalf of plaintiff K&D.

A. Disqualification under RPC 1.9(a)(1)

RPC 1.9(a)(1) states the following:

> (a) A lawyer who has represented a client in a matter shall not thereafter:
>
> (1) represent another client in the same or a substantially related matter in which that client's interests are materially adverse to interests of the former client unless the former client consents after a full disclosure of the circumstances and consultation with the former client.

The current matter is not the "same" matter in which Mr. Rosenberg previously represented K&D. Plaintiffs argue, however, and defendant firmly disagrees, that the present matter is "substantially related" to matters which Mr. Rosenberg previously handled on behalf of K&D, thus requiring his immediate disqualification under RPC 1.9(a)(1). According to the New Jersey Supreme Court, a substantial relationship between matters will exist where the "adversity between the interests of the attorney's former and present clients has created a climate for the disclosure of relevant confidential information." *Reardon* [*v. Marlayne*, 83 N.J. 460, 474 (1980)]. . . . The purposes of RPC 1.9(a)(1) are threefold: protecting confidences, maintaining integrity, and preserving loyalty.

The basis for plaintiffs' assertion that a "substantial relationship" exists between the present matter and the previous matters which Mr. Rosenberg handled on behalf of K&D is that the subject matter of the present and former representations is the same. According to plaintiffs, Mr. Rosenberg actively represented K&D in connection with claims against former employees alleging misappropriation of trade secrets, tortious interference with customer relations, breach of duty of loyalty of an employee, and unfair competition. Plaintiffs specifically cite to the Paul Manna matter wherein they assert that Mr. Rosenberg engaged in six months of document drafting and settlement negotiations on behalf of K&D after Paul Manna had been terminated as an employee for reasons similar to the claims alleged in this action. Defendant, on the other hand, asserts that a "substantial relationship" exists only when the factual basis underlying the former representation applies to the subsequent representation. Thus, defendant asserts that the Paul Manna matter, for example, cannot justify disqualification because the circumstances of Manna's employment, his departure from K&D, or his subsequent suits are not at issue in the present litigation. In short, defendant asserts that plaintiffs have failed to show that the facts obtained from the prior representation would apply to the current representation. In light of this disagreement, an analysis of case law interpreting the meaning of "substantially related" is necessary.

In *Reardon*, defendant General Motors Corporation ("G.M.") sought to prevent plaintiff's attorney from representing plaintiff in a products liability suit alleging brake failure on the grounds that he had formerly represented G.M. in similar suits. In addressing the issue of "substantial relationship," the New Jersey Supreme Court recognized that "disqualification is mandated where the issues between the former and present suits are practically the same or where there is a 'patently clear' relationship between them." The court found that the substantial relationship test was "clearly satisfied" thus warranting disqualification since plaintiff's attorney had specifically represented G.M. on at least two occasions in suits involving alleged brake defects and failure. Thus, the "striking similarity" between plaintiff's case and the prior matters made "apparent both the legal and factual relationship of issues." As a result, plaintiff's counsel was disqualified from representing plaintiff against his former client.

Subsequent to *Reardon*, the Appellate Division had occasion to address the "substantial relationship" issue. In *Gray v. Commercial Union Ins. Co.*, 191 N.J. Super. 590 (App. Div. 1983), plaintiff brought suit against Commercial Union Insurance Company ("Commercial Union") alleging breach of his employment contract and Commercial Union moved to disqualify plaintiff's attorney. The pivotal issue was "under what circumstances a lawyer may represent a client whose interest is adverse to a party whom the lawyer represented in prior litigation." Plaintiff's attorney had represented Commercial Union's insureds in personal injury litigation for more than twenty years. The court found that a substantial relationship existed between the subject matter of the present employment contract action and the subject matter of the prior representat ion on behalf of Commercial Union defending tort cases despite the fact that the legal issues between the cases were not at all the same.

In reaching this result, the court reasoned that "the 'substantial relationship' standard should not be read in a mechanical or overly technical manner." Rather, the court looked to the dictates of *Reardon*, which held that a substantial relationship of issues is satisfied where the "adversity between the interests of the attorney's former and present clients has created a climate for disclosure of relevant confidential information." Recognizing that plaintiff's attorney's longstanding relationship with Commercial Union would necessarily have made him privy to confidential and proprietary information of Commercial Union, including its claims and litigation philosophy, its methods and procedures for defending claims and litigation, and its information regarding the administration of various business operations, the court held that plaintiff's attorney could use such information to the substantial disadvantage of his former client Commercial Union. Thus, a substantial relationship was established even though such general information may not have been specifically relevant to the merits of the employment contract dispute.

Finally, in *G.F. Industries v. American Brands*, 245 N.J. Super. 8 (App. Div. 1990), plaintiffs, G.F. Industries, Inc. and its recently acquired subsidiary, Sunshine Biscuits, Inc., sought to disqualify Chadbourne & Parke, the attorneys for defendant American Brands, Inc. Plaintiffs alleged that American Brands, the company from whom G.F. Industries purchased Sunshine, misrepresented the conditions of Sunshine's baking facilities and equipment at the time of the sale, specifically the ovens transferred with the sale. Plaintiffs argued that RPC 1.9(a)(1) mandated that Chadbourne be disqualified because Chadbourne had represented Sunshine and American Brands when American Brands owned Sunshine.

In upholding the trial court's decision to disqualify, the Appellate Division . . . found that Chadbourne represented Sunshine and American Brands in prior OSHA inspections of the same ovens and in the sale of Sunshine wherein the condition of the ovens was at issue. Thus, the Appellate Division affirmed the trial court's finding that Chadbourne's prior representation was substantially similar to the current representation which warranted disqualification under RPC 1.9(a)(1).

These three opinions represent the principal authorities in New Jersey interpreting the meaning of "substantially related" under RPC 1.9(a)(1). . . . [T]here are marked differences between the three decisions. *Reardon* stressed the similarity between the legal and factual issues involved in the present and prior representations. In that case both the present and prior representations involved product liability claims concerning defective automobile brakes which made the finding of a substantial relationship apparent.

G.F. Industries, on the other hand, emphasized that the same object, namely the Sunshine ovens, was the focus of the past and present representations even though the claims involving the ovens differed, those being an OSHA action, a sale of a subsidiary, and a misrepresentation claim.

Finally, *Gray* rejected an overly-technical reading of the term "substantially related" and apparently stressed that the longevity of the attorney's relationship with his former client warranted a finding of a "substantial relationship" since the attorney would necessarily have obtained confidential information that could be used to the former client's detriment. The court made this determination despite the dissimilarity of the legal issues at hand.

AUTHORS' COMMENT:

Which of the three tests just described do you favor? Should courts always use the same test, or does the appropriate test depend on the facts of the particular case? Which test would you apply to the case at bar? Would that test militate for disqualification, or against disqualification? Let's see which test the court chooses.

As is evident, the meaning of "substantially related" under RPC 1.9(a)(1) is broadly construed in New Jersey. Disqualification has been required where the legal and factual issues of the former and present representation are practically the same or clearly related, as in *Reardon*, or where there was a twenty-year relationship with the former client although involving dissimilar legal and factual issues, as in *Gray*, or where the former client's product or property was factually identical to the item at issue in the present suit although involving dissimilar legal issues, as in *G.F. Industries*.

[A] disqualification standard that equates "substantially related" to "factually identical" . . . is unnecessarily restrictive when compared to the plain language of RPC 1.9(a)(1) and New Jersey authorities.

Under the standard enunciated by the New Jersey Supreme Court in *Reardon*, and as adopted in RPC 1.9(a)(1), there is a substantial relationship between the present matter and the prior matters handled by Mr. Rosenberg on behalf of K&D since the adversity between the interests of K&D and D'Angelo has created a climate for the disclosure of relevant confidential information and the issues between the former and present matters are practically the same.

AUTHORS' COMMENT:

The two matters are substantially related, so Rosenberg is disqualified. But should Rosenberg's *entire firm* be disqualified? That's the next question.

C. Imputed Disqualification under RPC 1.10(a)

Having concluded that Mr. Rosenberg should be disqualified as defendant's attorney, this court also concludes that Varet Marcus should be disqualified under RPC 1.10(a), which reads as follows:

> When lawyers are associated in a firm, none of them shall knowingly represent a client when any one of them practicing alone would be prohibited from doing so by RPC 1.7 [or] RPC 1.9.

Since RPC 1.9(a)(1) and 1.9(a)(2) prohibit Mr. Rosenberg from representing the defendant in this litigation, his firm, Varet Marcus, is disqualified by imputation under RPC 1.10(a).

NOTES AND QUESTIONS

1. ***Do You Agree?*** Do you agree with the opinion in *Kaselaan*? Why or why not? If you were writing an appellate opinion reversing the lower court, what are the strongest arguments you could muster to justify reversal?

2. ***Not Just New Jersey.*** The *Kaselaan* case describes tests used far beyond New Jersey. Federal and state courts around the country have struggled over the meaning of "substantial relationship" since the phrase first came into the judicial vocabulary in the early 1950s. Not every state would define the three variations on the test in th e same way, but you can summon impressive precedent in favor of a more restrictive test or for a more liberal test. There is no universal agreement on the meaning of "substantial relationship."

3. ***Which Test is Best for Your Client?*** Which of the three tests set out in *Kaselaan* is best for your client? That depends on your client's situation. If you are moving to disqualify the opposing firm on grounds that it has a successive conflict, you want the broadest test possible; the one that will make as many cases as possible "substantially related." If you are defending against a motion to disqualify filed by the other side, on the other hand, then you want the narrowest possible test. The main reason for assigning the *Kaselaan* case is to drive home the point that the phrase "substantially

related" is flexible, and has been defined in a variety of ways. When you have a client, you have to search for the definition that best advances the interests of your client.

4. ***The Prohibition Against "Use" of Protected Information.*** ABA Model Rule 1.9(c) proscribes the "use" of protected information against a former client unless the information has become generally known. Where there is a risk that a lawyer will use information against a former client, the court can disqualify the lawyer. If the two matters are substantially related, then there is a much greater risk that the attorney will use information against the former client. Thus, the court can disqualify the lawyer under Rule 1.9(c) to guard against the attorney's improper use of confidential client information.

5. ***The Presumption of Shared Confidences.*** If two matters are substantially related, is the court required to assume that confidences will be shared within the firm? That is, must the court assume that a lawyer who formerly worked on a substantially related matter will now share relevant confidential information with lawyers working on the new case? In most states, the courts have said yes. But occasionally the courts have looked more carefully at the structure of the firm, the relationships among the lawyers, and the nature of the confidential information, and have allowed the firm to continue in a case as long as the firm adopted measures to prevent the disqualified lawyer from sharing protected information with the rest of the firm. Some state's ethics rules also formally adopt that position, permitting screens to overcome (or substitute for) a former client's objection to the present representation. What do you think?

6. ***The Burden of Proof.*** As in all other areas of law, the burden of proof is a crucial question on disqualification motions. Does the party moving for disqualification have the burden of proving that the lawyer should be disqualified, or does the lawyer opposing disqualification have the burden of proving that he should not be disqualified? Here is how one court saw the burden issue in the context of a motion to disqualify based on an initial consultation:

> When challenged, an attorney carries the burden to establish in a fact hearing that no confidential or privileged information was acquired in an initial consultation. If that burden is sustained, there is no conflict of interest in the attorney switching sides. If the burden is not sustained, a conflict exists and the attorney must step down.

How would an attorney meet this burden? How can an attorney prove what was *not* said? If the attorney says in a sworn affidavit, "I did not learn any confidential information in our initial consultation," is that enough? What if the client then comes back and says, "I told you several confidential things." Is that enough to disqualify the attorney, or does the client have to specify what those confidential things were? In baseball, the tie goes to the runner. In disqualification motions, what should happen in the case of a "tie" between the lawyer and the former client moving to disqualify the lawyer?

C. INFORMALLY ACQUIRED CONFIDENTIAL INFORMATION

As mentioned in the outline earlier in this chapter, Rule 1.9(b) will disqualify you from opposing a former client of your old law firm in a substantially related matter if you informally learned material confidential information about the former client in a substantially related matter, even though you yourself never did a lick of work or billed a single minute to that client's matters. This rule can trip you up when you change jobs because you often forget about information that you learned informally, and the person about whom you learned the information usually does not show up on your time records. The following opinion from the Kansas Supreme Court shows how this rule can play out when a young lawyer moves from one firm to another.

LANSING-DELAWARE WATER DISTRICT v. OAK LANE PARK, INC.

808 P.2d 1369 (Kan. 1991)

ALLEGRUCCI, J.

This is an interlocutory appeal . . . from an order entered by the district court disqualifying the law firm of Davis, Beall, McGuire & Thompson, Chartered, (Davis-Beall) from representing defendants in this matter. The disqualification occurred pursuant to Rule 1.10 of the Model Rules of Professional Conduct.

In August 1988, Gary A. Nelson began working as an associate attorney with the law firm of Chapman & Waters. Generally, every attorney at Chapman & Waters had access to and discussed all files of the firm. In July 1989, Douglas D. Sutherland joined Chapman & Waters as an associate. Sutherland and Nelson met while in law school and became friends. They socialized both before and after Sutherland joined Chapman & Waters.

The pending litigation was filed on August 15, 1989. Jeffrey L. Baxter, of Chapman & Waters, is lead counsel for plaintiff, while Sutherland is assisting. Nelson resigned his position at Chapman & Waters on February 18, 1990, and began working at Davis-Beall on February 24, 1990. Davis-Beall did not contact Chapman & Waters before offering Nelson the position. On March 12, 1990, Douglas G. Waters, a partner with Chapman & Waters, in a letter addressed to four members of the Davis-Beall firm, asked Davis-Beall to withdraw from this and three other cases because Nelson's employment created a real or potential conflict of interest. A letter dated March 21, 1990, from John F. Thompson of Davis-Beall informed Chapman & Waters that Davis-Beall would not withdraw from this or any other cases involving both firms. In his letter, Thompson identified six additional cases that involved both firms and informed Chapman & Waters that Nelson had been instructed to have no involvement with those cases and their files. Thompson stated that the files of all these cases "have been removed from the general filing area and Mr. Nelson has not had, nor will he have, access to such files." According to Thompson, Davis-Beall was confident that imposing the "Chinese Wall" "will result in no confidential information making its way to the members of the law firm of [Davis-Beall] via Mr. Nelson [and was] sufficient to protect all of the interests of all parties."

AUTHORS' COMMENT:

The Davis-Beall firm has set up a "firewall" to keep Nelson away from any files where Lansing (the party seeking the disqualification) is an opposing party. At least in theory, therefore, Nelson won't know what the issues ar e and won't be able to give the Davis-Beall lawyers any confidential information about Lansing that he picked up at his old job. If you represented Lansing and you received the letter from Davis-Beall telling you about the "Chinese Wall" around Nelson, how would you respond? Would you move to disqualify Davis-Beall, or would you try to work things out? How could you work things out? Why might you want to work things out?

On April 11, 1990, plaintiff filed a motion to disqualify the Davis-Beall firm because Nelson had acquired material and confidential information regarding this case while at Chapman & Waters. The district court held an evidentiary hearing on April 27, 1990, receiving only the testimony of Nelson, who testified that he did not recall providing any legal services for plaintiff while employed at Chapman & Waters. The only contact he recalled involving the case was a discussion with Sutherland about the mechanical aspects of how water could flow and a review of a map showing the area of Leavenworth County affected by the alleged water diversion where the defendants' trailer park was located. He admitted that, while at Chapman & Waters, cases were discussed by various members of the firm. He also indicated he was aware his wife, who is a public accountant, had reviewed and summarized aspects of the case for Chapman & Waters.

Sutherland testified that, during the six months that they worked together at the firm, he and Nelson had several specific conversations about this case, discussing it in detail at least five times. Sutherland recalled that they discussed damages calculations, burdens of proof, theories of conversion, and other theories. They reviewed several documents, including a diagram or map which depicted water flow in defendants' trailer park. Sutherland also recalled discussing with Nelson the possibility of employing Nelson's wife to provide damages calculations for this case. She did summarize information regarding plaintiff's accounts, and Sutherland recalled discussing the results with Nelson. Sutherland indicated that, while they were in the firm together, he regularly discussed his cases with Nelson. He considered the conversations privileged and material. Sutherland testified that, in the mornings, when he came to the office, he would discuss problems in his cases with Nelson because "he had always good, solid ideas on how to resolve some of the problems and he was a good one to bounce ideas off of."

The question which must be decided in this case is whether the law firm representing defendants must be disqualified because it employs an attorney who previously worked for the law firm that represents plaintiff.

For Rule 1.10 to apply, the attorney must acquire information protected by Rule 1.6 and 1.9(c).

Traditionally, under the Code of Professional Responsibility, an attorney's knowledge of his or her client's affairs was irrebuttably presumed to have been transmitted to other attorneys with the same law firm. But recently, courts allow the presumption to be rebutted by evidence that the attorney who was materially involved in the case did not share that information with his or her associates.

[T]he Comment to Rule 1.9 indicates that "where lawyers move from one firm to the other, courts must balance the previous client's right of confidentiality, the right of having a reasonable choice of legal counsel, and the right of lawyers to form new associations and take on new clients when leaving a previous association."

A court deciding a motion to disqualify counsel must balance several competing considerations, including the privacy of the attorney-client relationship, the prerogative of a party to choose counsel, and the hardships that disqualification imposes on the parties and the entire judicial process.

[T]he model rules do not disqualify an attorney merely because of that attorney's association with another attorney who represents a client. Instead, the model rules require the person to have acquired confidential and material information before that attorney is excluded. Once the lawyer is deemed to have acquired such information, however, the model rules bar representation by other members of the firm as well as by the "tainted" attorney. Rule 1.10.

We conclude that the findings by the district court are supported by substantial competent evidence and are sufficient to support disqualification of the Davis-Beall firm under Rule 1.10.

The second issue raised by Davis-Beall is whether a screening device should be allowed to protect a private law firm from the taint caused by a newly employed attorney who has a conflict of interest based upon the attorney's prior nongovernmental employment. Davis-Beall urges this court to allow an exception to the strict provisions of strict disqualification under Rule 1.10 if the law firm implements screening devices to prevent knowledge of the new attorney from tainting other members of the firm. This court rejected the availability of screening devices to cure the taint of the incoming attorney in *Parker*. There, we noted that the model rules "reject, for lawyers practicing in the private sector at least, any thought that the 'taint' of the incoming lawyer can be cured by screening him or her out of the affected client's matter, or by erecting a 'Chinese Wall' or by imposing a 'code of silence.' "

In drafting the model rules, the ABA considered adopting a provision that would not impute disqualification to private law firms hiring private attorneys if screening occurred. Proponents of this screening device pointed out that imposing a rule of vicarious disqualification arises from the assumption that attorneys will violate professional norms by disclosing former clients' confidences. Imposing vicarious disqualification penalizes clients and must make firms reluctant to hire attorneys collaterally from other firms. Yet the screening solution was rejected by the ABA and most courts addressing the issue. A few courts have attempted to use it in cases where disqualification would work a great hardship, and two states have incorporated it into their rules.

A client is entitled to have its confidences and secrets protected. The district court here found that Nelson had acquired information that was protected by Rule 1.6 and 1.9(c). Because Nelson acquired this information, he was disqualified and his disqualification was imputed to Davis-Beall pursuant to Rule 1.10(a). The model rule contains no provisions for use of screening devices in this situation. In fact, such a proposal was rejected at the time the model rules were adopted.

The judgment of the district court is affirmed.

NOTES AND QUESTIONS

Should Lawyers Change their Ways? Should Nelson have done anything different while he was at his old firm? When Sutherland wanted to talk about his case on behalf of Lansing, suppose Nelson had said, "Don't tell me anything about it. If you tell me anything confidential, I may end up getting disqualified a few years from now if I switch to a new firm and the new firm is opposing your client in this matter or in a substantially related matter — and my new firm will get disqualified with me, because a firewall can't cure the taint." Wouldn't that sound ridiculous? And would it be any fun to work in a place where no one would talk to you about a case because they feared disqualification someday, somehow, somewhere down the road? (We will discuss firewalls in greater detail in a later chapter.)

D. PERILS OF PRELIMINARY INTERVIEWS

As an outline in an earlier chapter mentioned, "phantom" former clients can result from preliminary interviews. These "preliminary interview clients" — now typically called "prospective clients" — usually cause problems when they become former clients rather than when they are current clients, because they are current clients only for the short time during the interview, investigation, and evaluation stages of your wo rk on their problem, while your firm and the prospective client are considering whether to enter into an attorney-client relationship. That "prospective client" period may last anywhere from a few minutes (as in a short phone call in which you turn down the matter) to a few weeks or even months (as might happen if your firm needs expert medical evaluations of the client before deciding whether to accept the case, or if the client takes a long time to make up his mind about hiring you).

If your firm and the prospective client decide to enter into an attorney-client relationship, then the former client issues do not arise until that relationship is over. But if your firm rejects the prospective client, or if the prospective client rejects your firm, then we have a special species of former-client problem. That is, a former client problem arises if (a) the law firm tells the prospective client, "We're not going to handle your problem," or (b) the prospective client says, "We're not going to use your law firm," or (c) the prospective client never calls back to follow up.

Forever afterwards, the people who divulged confidential information in a preliminary interview are former clients, and cannot be opposed in substantially related matters without their consent, unless the firm has taken explicit measures to guard against phantom clients. (These methods are detailed below.)

The problem is a frequent one, but until 2002 the ABA Model Rules of Professional Conduct did not expressly address it. In 2002, however, the ABA added a new Rule 1.18, entitled "Duties to Prospective Client," that addresses the prospective client problem in detail. Many states have adopted rules based on ABA Model Rule 1.18. For example, Pennsylvania Rule 1.18 provides as follows:

Rule 1.18 Duties to Prospective Client

(a) A person who discusses with a lawyer the possibility of forming a client-lawyer relationship with respect to a matter is a prospective client.

(b) Even when no client-lawyer relationship ensues, a lawyer who has had discussions with a prospective client shall not use or reveal information learned in the consultation, except as Rule 1.9 would permit with respect to information of a former client.

(c) A lawyer subject to paragraph (b) shall not represent a client with interests materially adverse to those of a prospective client in the same or a substantially related matter if the lawyer received information from the prospective client that could be significantly harmful to that person in the matter, except as provided in paragraph (d). If a lawyer is disqualified from representation under this paragraph, no lawyer in a firm with which that lawyer is associated may knowingly undertake or continue representation in such a matter, except as provided in paragraph (d).

(d) When a lawyer has received disqualifying information as defined in paragraph (c), representation is permissible if:

(1) both the affected client and the prospective client have given informed consent, or;

(2) all of the following apply:

(i) the disqualified lawyer took reasonable measures to avoid exposure to more disqualifying information than was reasonably necessary to determine whether to represent the prospective client;

(ii) the disqualified lawyer is screened from any participation in the matter and is apportioned no part of the fee therefrom; and

(iii) written notice is promptly given to the prospective client.[1]

NOTES AND QUESTIONS

1. ***An Illustrative Case.*** A good illustration of a phantom preliminary interview client can be found in an environmental cleanup case, *Bridge Products, Inc. v. Quantum Chemical Corp.*, 1990 U.S. Dist. LEXIS 5019 (N.D. Ill. April 27, 1990). Bridge Products held a so-called "beauty contest" to choose a law firm to handle an important environmental case. During the beauty contest, Bridge interviewed five firms, including the large Chicago firm of Sidley & Austin (now Sidley Austin Brown & Wood), to decide which firm to retain. Bridge decided not to retain Sidley & Austin. However, one of Bridge's *opponents* in the same suit later did hire Sidley & Austin.

---

[1] Subparagraphs (a), (b), and (c) of Pennsylvania Rule 1.18 are identical to ABA Model Rule 1.18(a)–(c). However, Pennsylvania has slightly reorganized Rule 1.18(d). The reorganization does not change the meaning at all, but we think Pennsylvania Rule 1.18(d) is easier to understand than ABA Model Rule 1.18(d). Can you see the differences?

(Environmental cleanup suits often have dozens of parties, and relatively few firms handle environmental cleanup suits, so it's not unusual for more than one party in a suit to contact the same firm.)

As soon as Sidley & Austin appeared on behalf of Bridge's opponent, Bridge moved to disqualify Sidley & Austin. The court granted the motion. It found that there had been an "implied" attorney-client relationship between Bridge and Sidley & Austin, because Bridge had divulged confidential information to Sidley & Austin with the reasonable belief that Sidley & Austin was acting as its attorney at the time of the interview and would maintain its confidences. In particular, Bridge had discussed its desire to settle the case, and suggested some strategies for settling it. Bridge may have been confused about whether it could expect confidentiality, but the court said the law firm — not the client — would have to pay the price for this confusion. The court "rejected the concept of a Chinese Wall where the infected attorney is not an associate who has come from another firm or government service, but is simply another lawyer within the firm in question." Thus, because of a brief preliminary interview that did not result in any legal work (or any fees) for the firm, Sidley & Austin was disqualified from participating in a large and lucrative environmental suit.

2. ***Exceptions.*** Preliminary interviews are not always enough to turn a non-client into a client. In *Hughes v. Paine, Webber, Jackson and Curtis, Inc.*, 565 F. Supp. 663 (N.D. Ill. 1983), for example, the court held that a preliminary interview was not enough to disqualify a firm where the party moving for disqualification knew that the firm already represented its opponent in other litigation. Was the court in *Hughes* correct? Or should an interview with a potential client force a law firm to withdraw from a matter the firm was already handling before the interview, even if the firm has declined the new matter? (Would that make it too easy for people to set up opposing law firms for disqualification?)

3. ***Guarding Against Implied Clients.*** Are there things lawyers can do during preliminary interviews to guard against creating implied clients? In *Bridge Products, Inc. v. Quantum Chemical Corp., supra*, the court suggested three steps a firm can take to avoid disqualification due to a preliminary interview:

- *Notice.* The firm can give the prospective client notice that the interview is "purely preliminary," and that confidences should not be disclosed and may not be protected.

- *Advance conflict waiver.* The firm can have the prospective client sign a "conflicts waiver" stating that any disclosures might later be used against the person (thus making the prospective client "wary of making indiscriminate disclosures").

- *No fee.* The firm should not bill the prospective client for the preliminary interview.

In Comments 3 and 4 to Rule 1.18, the ABA suggests some other ideas for avoiding disqualification by a former prospective client. For example, to avoid acquiring disqualifying information from a prospective client, "a lawyer considering whether or not to undertake a new matter should limit the initial interview to only such information as reasonably appears necessary for that purpose." If the information necessary to make the decision indicates that a conflict of interest or other reason for non-representation exists, the lawyer should either inform the prospective client or decline the representation. Also, a lawyer "may condition conversations with a prospective client on the person's informed consent that no information disclosed during the consultation will prohibit the lawyer from representing a different client in the matter." In addition, the lawyer may seek the prospective client's express agreement that the lawyer may later use the prospective client's confidential information on behalf of other clients.

Do you think these steps are realistic? Suppose you start an interview with a new client by saying, "Before we start, I just want you to know that this is a purely preliminary interview, and you shouldn't tell me anything confidential, because we may have a conflict of interest, and if we do have a conflict, we're going to stick with our current client, and anything you say here may be used against you. Now go ahead and tell me about your legal problem." Do you think the potential client will open up, or clam up?

E. A DISQUALIFICATION SCHEME

If every preliminary interview automatically resulted in "former client" status, a party opposing a law firm could easily hatch a scheme to disqualify the firm. Here's how the scheme would work:

Suppose Plaintiff Crabb & Sons has sued Defendant Rogers Plumbing for breach of contract. (Rogers Plumbing failed to complete a job in a new office building on time. Rogers blames its pipe distributor for late deliveries, but has not sued the pipe distributor yet.) Plaintiff is represented by the Jones Night law firm, and Rogers is very impressed with Jones Night's work. Rogers attorney predicts that if the suit keeps up the way it's going, Jones Night is going to win. "How can I get rid of Jones Night?" the Defendant thinks to himself. How about moving to disqualify? Sounds good, but so far Jones Night hasn't done anything to warrant disqualification.

Then the light goes on in Defendant's brain. "I know! I've got a surefire plan!" says Defendant. "I'll send my Senior Vice President to interview at the Jones Night firm on an urgent basis about some of our other legal problems, like our dispute with our pipe distributor. We've suffered damages because of several late deliveries, including the late delivery of the pipes needed to complete the job at issue in the pending suit against Jones Night. My VP will say he wants to negotiate a new contract with a supplier (which is technically true). He won't tell Jones Night that this problem is substantially related to the current suit against us by Crabb & Sons. Jones Night has so many lawyers that the lawyer who interviews my VP won't even know we're one of the firm's adversaries in a related suit. During the interview, my VP will give Jones Night some confidential information, and that will 'poison' the whole firm. By the time the firm completes its check for conflicts of interest in our new case, it will be too late for the firm to avoid disqualification in the pending case. We'll move to disqualify the whole Jones Night firm on grounds that we are a 'former client' in a 'substantially related' matter. When Jones Night gets disqualified, Crabb & Sons will have to spend a lot of money and suffer a long delay finding new counsel and getting them up to speed. The Crabbs will end up begging us to settle and end the litigation. What a great plan!"

Clever, but is it clever enough to fool a court? Suppose the scheming Defendant carries out his plan and interviews at the Jones Night firm. The Jones Night lawyer conducting the interview does not take any precautions to guard against receiving confidential information and does not undertake a conflicts check until after the interview is over. Suppose you are the judge assigned to write the opinion deciding the motion to disqualify, and your ambivalent law clerk hands you the following two draft opinions for your consideration. The drafts reach opposite results. Which one will you choose? Will you add or delete anything from either opinion?

CRABB & SONS v. ROGERS PLUMBING

Draft Opinion # 1 for the Court's Consideration

ANDERSON, J.

. . . When the Rogers Plumbing Vice-President was interviewed by Jones Night for over an hour, Rogers Plumbing immediately became a "client" of Jones Night. It makes no difference that Jones Night later discovered a conflict and could not accept Rogers Plumbing as a client. Rogers was nevertheless a client until Jones Night formally rejected the matter. (Nor would it have mattered if Rogers had decided after the interview, for whatever reason, not to retain Jones Night. A preliminary interview elevates a person to "client" status no matter who makes the ultimate decision not to go forward.)

We accept at face value the claim of Rogers Plumbing that it imparted confidential information to Jones Night during the interview. We cannot test that claim without finding out exactly what was said during the interview, and that would force Rogers to waive confidentiality and the attorney-client privilege. Obviously, we should not force Rogers to waive confidentiality and the attorney-client privilege in order to enforce its right to confidentiality as a former client. *See* Rule 1.9(c) (protecting confidences of former clients).

Once Rogers became a client of Jones Night, that firm was prohibited from opposing Rogers in any matter that was "substantially related" to the subject of the preliminary interview unless Rogers gives its informed consent. *See* Rule 1.9(a). The matters in question are substantially related because they arose out of the same transaction. Here, Rogers did not consent, and indeed is moving to disqualify.

Jones Night argues that disqualification is unwarranted here because Rogers is a small company and must have known that Jones Night was already opposing it in a closely related matter. See *Hughes*. We consider that irrelevant. Comment 1 to Rule 1.7 says that law firms should adopt "reasonable procedures appropriate for the size and type of firm and practice" to detect conflicts of interests. The burden must be on the law firm, not the client, to know and enforce the conflict of interest rules.

If "reasonable procedures" had been in place at Jones Night, the preliminary interview in question here would never have taken place. The firm would have identified Rogers Plumbing as an opposing party, and would not have interviewed Rogers in connection with any matter. (Rule 1.7 prohibits law firms from opposing current clients in any matter, related or unrelated, so Jones Night would not have been able to represent Rogers in any matter as long as Jones Night continued to oppose Rogers in the Crabb & Sons suit.) Next time, Jones Night will not rush into a preliminary interview with a prospective client until the firm has had time to conduct a thorough conflicts check.

Moreover, even without undertaking a conflicts check, Jones Night could have avoided disqualification by advising the prospective client that the firm had not yet completed a conflicts check, and that the prospective client should not impart any confidential information to the lawyer until the conflicts check was completed.

We refuse to consider a prospective client's "motive" in requesting an interview with a law firm. Questions of motive are always fact intensive and generally require live testimony. If we accepted Jones Night's arguments, we would need to permit Jone s Night to cross-examine officers from Rogers Plumbing to determine whether its motive was to disqualify Jones Night. If that were allowed, every motion to disqualify opposing counsel under Rule 1.9 would become a mini-trial, robbing the court's time and robbing Rule 1.9 of its clearly stated meaning. If the rules become blurry and motions to disqualify become expensive and time-consuming, few former clients will bother to bring them. This would undermine trust between attorneys and clients, and in the long run would undermine confidence in the adversary system.

The problem here, pure and simple, was greed. Jones Night was so eager to get a new client that it rushed headlong into an interview without checking for conflicts or warning the potential client that the firm might later find a conflict and reject the case. If law firms were not in such a hurry to make money, they would take time to check for conflicts before interviewing any new client. Law firms that skip that step do so at their own peril.

The Jones Night firm is disqualified, and Crabb & Sons is given 30 days to obtain substitute counsel. Jones Night is prohibited from billing Crabb & Sons for any time expended on this matter after the date on which it interviewed Rogers Plumbing. If

Jones Night has already billed Crabb & Sons for any time spent after interviewing Rogers Plumbing, the firm is ordered to refund any amounts already paid on account. Finally, Jones Night is ordered to pay the reasonable expenses, including attorney fees, that Rogers Plumbing incurred in moving to disqualify Jones Night.

CRABB & SONS v. ROGERS PLUMBING

Draft Opinion # 2 for the Court's Consideration

ANDERSON, J.

If the facts alleged by Jones Night are true, Rogers Plumbing devised a clever scheme to disqualify Jones Night because Jones Night was representing Rogers' adversary effectively. If we allow Jones Night to succeed, lawyers will be unable to serve potential clients quickly and will be unable to serve some existing clients at all.

More than greed is to blame here. Lawyers try to serve clients quickly. If a potential client requests an immediate appointment, the client and the system of justice are served if the lawyer agrees to see the potential client as soon as possible. The sooner the lawyer sees the potential client, the sooner the lawyer can provide legal advice. If the prospective client's situation is deteriorating, the lawyer can advise how to minimize the damage. If there is no cause of action, the lawyer can advise against litigation, thus saving court time. If there is a cause of action, the lawyer can begin investigating the facts while memories are still fresh and documents are still available.

No inquiry into the former client's "motive" is needed. The only question is whether the former client knew, before the interview, that the firm represented an adversary in litigation. The answer is either yes or no. Clients are not charged with knowing the conflict of interest rules, but even unsophisticated laymen are likely to sense a conflict of interest in hiring a law firm that already opposes them in a related matter. The problem is made worse by the fact that Rogers Plumbing was already represented by counsel here. If Rogers had a question about conflicts of interest, it could have consulted with its own counsel — or any other lawyer besides Jones Night — before interviewing at Jones Night.

The idea that a person automatically becomes a "client" at a preliminary interview is a relatively recent idea. The main purpose of expanding the definition of "client" to cover preliminary interviews is to ensure that law firms do not cynically turn against those who accept the law firm's invitation to trust the firm at the initial interview. Another purpose is to ensure that lawyers are liable for malpractice if they fall below the standard of care required in dealing with potential clients. Neither purpose will be frustrated if Jones Night is allowed to remain in this suit.

As for the question of trust, we need disqualify only the lawyer who actually conducted the preliminary interview with Rogers Plumbing, as well as any other lawyers at Jones Night who discussed the case or worked on it with that lawyer. This is a small circle — perhaps as few as one lawyer — and can easily be sealed off with a "Chinese Wall" so that Rogers Plumbing's confidential information will not reach the rest of the firm. (The well-known *Westinghouse* opinion does not apply here; there the firm was actively representing both sides in an antitrust dispute.)

As for the question of malpractice, it is unrelated to the disqualification motion. If Jones Night gave Rogers Plumbing bad advice during the preliminary interview, and if Rogers Plumbing suffered damages as a result, then Rogers can sue Jones Night for malpractice. But the fact that a law firm is potentially liable for bad advice given to a prospective client does not require disqualifying the law firm as long as confidences are protected.

The rules of ethics were not meant to be used by lawyers or clients for unethical purposes. The drafters of the rules never intended that unscrupulous people would be able to use the conflict of interest rules to deprive opponents of their chosen counsel. As long as Jones Night implements measures to protect the secrets (if any) that were imparted to Jones Night at the initial interview with Rogers Plumbing, the motion to disqualify is DENIED.

F. CAN YOU DROP A CLIENT LIKE A "HOT POTATO"?

You now know that current clients have much greater protection than former clients. You know that your law firm may never directly oppose one of your firm's current clients without that client's consent, even if the directly adverse matter is totally unrelated to the matters you are handling for the current client. But you also know that if the current client could be transformed into a former client, then you would be free to oppose the former client in any matter as long as it was not "substantially related" to the matters you handled for that client during the attorney-client relationship. Former clients don't have a veto except in substantially related matters. Can you exploit that difference to your advantage by "firing" a current client in the middle of a representation, dropping the client like a proverbial "hot potato"?

Let's make the question more concrete. Suppose you come to the unhappy conclusion that one of your current clients is causing you a conflict of interest that will keep you from taking on a new and more profitable case. To pick an extreme example, suppose you are doing California commercial real estate matters for a current client named RealCal Corp. and a new client, Tiffany Boxster, wants to sue RealCal Corp. (your current client) because one of RealCal's client's corporate trucks crashed into her car. Under Rule 1.7(a)(1), you may not accept the truck crash matter unless you obtain RealCal's informed consent. As long as RealCal remains a current client, you cannot oppose RealCal in any matter, even if the new matter is totally unrelated, unless you obtain RealCal's informed consent, confirmed in writing. But if RealCal were only a former client, then you could oppose RealCal in any matter without its consent as long as the new matter is not substantially related to the work you formerly did for RealCal. Can you fire RealCal (i.e., withdraw from handling all of RealCal's matters), thus transforming RealCal from a current client to a former client? Can you turn a current client into a former client by saying, "We're no longer your lawyers — get yourself a new lawyer"? In short, can you drop the problem client like a hot potato? Let's look at this in some depth, because it provides a good review of everything we've learned so far about conflicts.

When taking on a new client that would cause a conflict, the firm can't keep both clients without consent. If the old client won't consent, then the firm must make a hard choice: it has to choose between the old client and the new client. This often reduces to a bottom-line choice. If the new client is likely to generate higher fees in the long run, the firm may try to "fire" its old client to make way for the new one. Can the firm ethically do this?

The answer usually turns on whether we analyze the conflict under the "current client" rule (Rule 1.7) or the "former client" rule (Rule 1.9). If we use the "former client" rule, then the firm can oppose its "former" client (the "fired" client) as long as the new matter is not "substantially related" to the matter the firm was handling for the fired client. But if we use the "current client" rule — if we don't allow a firm to convert a current client into a former client by "firing" the client — then the firm cannot oppose the fired client, even if the new matter is totally unrelated to any matter the firm ever handled for the fired client.

The firm may want to convert the current client to a former client with the wave of a wand ("Hocus, pocus! We quit! Now you're a former client"). If it can't do this, then the firm must reject the new client. But even after the firm rejects the new client, the old client (the client the firm tried to fire) may not give any new business to your firm. (By analogy, if you try to fire one of your employees but for some reason the employee challenges the firing and ends up staying, do you think that almost-fired employee is going to work with you in the future if he can avoid it?) That leaves the law firm in the worst of all possible worlds — the firm didn't take on the new client because of a conflict with the old client, but now the old client is giving all of its new business (and maybe even transferring its current business) to another law firm. Instead of having two clients, the firm has no clients.

So far, the court cases and ethics opinions on the question of firing a client are mixed. Whether a law firm may "fire" a client, and thus transform the client from a current client into a former one, depends on two main factors: (1) What led to the conflict? and (2) When and how did the law firm drop the client causing the conflict? Those are questions of fact. As the next case shows, courts will analyze these questions with great care when a former client moves to disqualify a law firm that used to represent it. The case is especially poignant because it involves a conflict that arose when a dispute erupted between two existing clients. Does the case reach the right decision? What does the case teach you about the right way to "fire" a client that is causing a conflict of interest?

STRATAGEM DEVELOPMENT CORP. v. HERON INTERNATIONAL N.V.

756 F. Supp. 789 (S.D.N.Y. 1991)

KRAM, DISTRICT JUDGE

Defendants in this case, involving claims of breach of a real estate joint venture agreement, have moved for disqualification of Epstein, Becker & Green ("Epstein Becker" or the "Firm") as plaintiff's counsel, because of alleged dual representation. Epstein Becker has taken certain steps to withdraw as counsel in other legal matters in which it represented a subsidiary of the defendants in this case; but there remains a question about the effectiveness of the Firm's withdrawal as counsel in the other matters.

Background

The Parties

[Before this dispute, Epstein Becker represented Stratagem Development Company concerning a joint venture with a company called Heron International. The goal of the joint venture was to put up a new office building in Manhattan to be called Heron Tower II. Stratagem's job was to buy the land, and Heron's job was to arrange for construction.]

[At the same time that Epstein Becker represented Stratagem in the Heron Tower II venture, the Firm also represented one of Heron's wholly-owned subsidiaries, Fidelity Service Corporation (FSC), in some labor disputes known as the "Bevona" matters. (For conflicts of interest purposes, representing a company's wholly-owned subsidiary is equivalent to representing the company itself.) The Bevona matters had nothing to do with the Heron Tower venture, but a problem arose when Stratagem's agreement with Heron broke down.]

The Present Action

On November 10, 1989, Jerrold F. Goldberg, a member of Epstein Becker, wrote to Kathleen Panciera, an officer of Heron, to review the status of the Bevona matters.

On June 27, 1990, Heron terminated the agreement between it and Stratagem relating to Heron Tower II.

Just over two weeks later, Goldberg again wrote to Panciera. After listing the active matters in which his firm represents FSC "and other Heron Entities," he stated:

> In light of the recent unfortunate developments between Heron and Stratagem Development Corp., of which I am sure you are aware, we must raise the question of our continued representation of Fidelity Services Corporation in connection with this labor matter.

Kenneth J. Kelly, Esq., of Epstein Becker, followed up with a letter, dated August 3, 1990, to Ms. Panciera. The letter pointedly stated:

> We will soon commence an action against Heron Properties and Heron International. Unless we hear otherwise from you, we plan to resign as Heron's counsel in the federal action and arbitration [FSC's Bevona matters] on the day we file Stratagem's complaint.

AUTHORS' COMMENT:

How important is timing? If the Epstein firm had withdrawn from representing FSC (i.e., Heron) immediately when it learned of the impending conflict with Stratagem, do you think the court would have denied the motion to disqualify? Would FSC then have been a "former" rather than a "current" client when the Epstein firm began representing Stratagem against Heron? If so, the firm could have kept Stratagem as a client in this matter.

On August 8, 1990, Peter Kompaniez, the CEO of FSC, wrote back, expressing "surprise[] at your statement that your firm 'will soon commence an action against Heron Properties and Heron International.' " He stated that it would be a violation of various provisions of New York's Code of Professional Responsibility for Kelly's firm to sue Heron.

Another Epstein Becker lawyer, Samuel Goldman, replied on August 14, 1990, as follows:

> From the tone and tenor of your letter, it is apparent that you would feel uncomfortable if we were to continue to represent Fidelity Service Corp. in the captioned litigation. Accordingly, we hereby notify you that we are withdrawing as counsel to Fidelity in this lawsuit.
>
> As you are aware, we have represented Stratagem Development Corp. in all of its dealings with Heron since the inception of the relationship between these two companies. There is no conflict in our continued representation of Stratagem.

The parties' attorneys exchanged two further letters in subsequent weeks; by September 4, 1990, Michael Delikat, Esq., of the law firm of Baer Marks & Upham ("Baer Marks") had contacted Epstein Becker to advise that it would take over the representation of FSC in the Bevona matters. During that conversation, as related in a confirming letter from Mr. Delikat to Mr. Goldberg, Mr. Delikat indicated that he would "prepare a formal substitution and forward same to you under separate cover. In the meantime, I would appreciate receiving a copy of the entire file at your earliest convenience."

The contemplated exchange of files and substitution forms did not take place at that time.[6] Less than a month later, on October 2, 1990, Epstein Becker filed the complaint in this action.

---

[6] The parties engage in a great deal of finger-pointing on this subject: Delikat, on behalf of FSC, states that he never sent the form because Epstein Becker did not forward the files as promised; Epstein Becker in turn accuses FSC of directing Baer Marks not to send the form in order to better situate Heron to prevail in

Defendants point out that coincidentally, also on October 2, 1990, Mr. Goldberg wrote to Stanley Bass, Staff Counsel of the United States Court of Appeals for the Second Circuit to attend to some ministerial matters in the Bevona actions. In that letter, he identified Epstein Becker as the attorneys for Fidelity Service Corp. By way of explanation, Mr. Goldberg now submits that he was left no alternative but to describe himself as FSC's counsel because of Baer Marks' failure to forward the signed substitution form.

On October 9, 1990, Heron's counsel in the instant action wrote to this Court, indicating its intention to file the present motion; that same day, Epstein Becker sent the files in the Bevona matter to Baer Marks. Two days later, Mr. Goldberg forwarded to Baer Marks a substitution of counsel form. The substitution form has not yet been filed.

AUTHORS' COMMENT:

Note that the facts that the court relies on come almost entirely from letters or affidavits written by the lawyers. This is typical in disqualification motions. Therefore, when the red flag goes up on a possible conflict of interest with a current client, you should write memos to your files explaining exactly how you perceive the situation and how you justify your position under the ethics rules. Failure to do so suggests that you did not have reasonable justification for violating the rules, or never gave the conflict questions thought. You may also want to write letters to your clients and to opposing counsel explaining your position. When you write these letters and memos, be objective and not emotional. The letters may later come to light, and judges will scrutinize them as carefully as they would scrutinize a brief on the merits.

Discussion

There are two different standards by which courts evaluate disqualification motions because of alleged dual representation; which standard to apply depends on whether the representation of the two clients is simultaneous or successive. When the firm concurrently represents both parties, Courts are to apply a *per se* prohibition; but if the case involves former clients of the firm, the Court will inquire into whether there is a "substantial relationship" between the two matters.

Defendants in the present case argue that Epstein Becker did not effectively withdraw from its representation of FSC in the Bevona matters until at least October 9, when it finally sent the files to Baer Marks, and perhaps later, because the substitution form has not been filed to this day. They therefore advocate the application of the *per se* rule. Equally predictably, plaintiffs argue for application of the "substantial relationship" test, stating that FSC "has not been Epstein Becker's client since September 4, 1990," approximately one month before the instant complaint was filed.

As the Second Circuit has explained, in order to justify application of the more lenient "substantial relationship" test, the firm in question must show that "the representation of a former client has been terminated and the parameters of such relationship have been fixed." In the present case, the parties vigorously dispute the question of precisely when, if ever, Epstein Becker effectively withdrew from representing FSC. However,

the instant motion. The Court notes that the letter does not indicate that Delikat's sending of the form was contingent upon receipt of the files.

Epstein Becker does concede that it represented FSC as late as September 4, 1990. Accordingly, the record is undisputed that the Firm was clearly contemplating, if not actively planning, litigation against its client's parent corporation as early as July 13, 1990. The Court must therefore conclude that the Firm was still in FSC's employ when it investigated and was drafting the complaint against FSC's parent company. Because Epstein Becker had not clearly terminated its representation of FSC and fixed the parameters of its representation of FSC by the time preparations for the instant litigation were begun, Epstein Becker is *per se* ineligible to represent Stratagem in this matter.

As is evident from this series of letters, Epstein Becker was not able to obtain the requisite consent from its client FSC before undertaking representation adverse to FSC's parent company. Absent such prior consent, a firm is to remain with the client in the already-existing litigation and seek new counsel to represent the other, not vice-versa.

Epstein Becker points out that Samuel Goldman has been Stratagem's real estate lawyer since 1983. It thereby attempts to refute Heron's theory that Epstein Becker dropped FSC "like a hot potato" in order to represent a more favored client.

Epstein Becker's obligations to Stratagem do not trump those it owes to FSC, even if they pre-dated them. Once Epstein Becker undertook to represent FSC, it assumed the full panoply of duties that a law firm owes to its client. Epstein Becker may not undertake to represent two potentially adverse clients and then, when the potential conflict becomes actuality, pick and choose between them. Nor may it seek consent for dual representation and, when such is not forthcoming, jettison the uncooperative client. Under these circumstances, Epstein Becker has no choice but to withdraw from representing either client in this case.

Conclusion

For the reasons stated above, defendants' motion for disqualification of plaintiff's counsel is GRANTED.

NOTES AND QUESTIONS

1. ***"A Bird in the Hand. . . . "*** Should Epstein Becker have paid more attention to the old maxim that "a bird in the hand is worth two in the bush"? Instead of being hyper-aggressive and trying to keep both clients, the firm could have gracefully bowed out of the labor matter for FSC and helped it to find other counsel. If Epstein Becker and FSC had parted on friendly terms, the firm probably would not have ended up being chastised publicly in the opinion for acting unethically.

2. ***Clients have Feelings.*** Heron is undoubtedly angry at Epstein Becker. When Epstein Becker fired Heron as a client, Heron had to find a new law firm — and then Heron had to resort to this nasty litigation to disqualify Epstein Becker from opposing it. Do you think Heron will ever take its legal business back to Epstein Becker? Not likely. But if Epstein Becker had instead withdrawn from FSC's labor matter on cordial terms as soon as the conflict arose, maybe Epstein Becker could have helped FSC find a lawyer who would not try to lure FSC as a client in other maters, and FSC might have come back to the Epstein firm as a client once the conflicting matter was resolved. In addition, FSC probably would not have moved to disqualify Epstein Becker in the first place.

3. ***Stealing Clients.*** When the court disqualified Epstein Becker, the firm may also have lost Stratagem as a client for more than just this one case. Stratagem had to find a new law firm to litigate the dispute with Heron. The new law firm may try to "steal" all of Stratagem's business from Epstein Becker. Lawyers do not "own" clients — a client may discharge a lawyer for any reason or no reason at all — but Epstein Becker could reasonably expect that any newly introduced firm might try to "steal" Stratagem,

urging Strategem to use the new firm not just for the Heron Tower matter, but for *all* of Stratagem's future legal needs. Worse, the new firm may also try to convince Stratagem to transfer all other *pending* legal matters from Epstein Becker to the new firm. Or, the new firm may try to hire the Epstein Becker partner who did Stratagem's legal work for many years as a way of persuading Strategem to stick with the new firm. If any of these things happen, Epstein Becker is going to lose a lot of business that it could have kept by avoiding the conflict of interest.

4. ***Good Ethics is Good Business.*** Here's the point: Good ethics isn't just nice; it's also good business. In trying to hang on to two clients in a conflict situation, Epstein Becker may well have wound up losing both clients permanently.

5. ***Why is this Happening so Often?*** The "hot potato" problem presented in *Stratagem* is popping up more and more often, for four reasons. First, law firms continue to merge, split, "downsize," and hire laterals. All of this movement of lawyers brings together clients who may have conflicts. Second, clients are also more prone than ever to move from one firm to another, creating new conflicts. Third, lawyers (and clients) seem increasingly eager to file motions to disqualify, and increasingly reluctant to consent to conflicts. Fourth, and perhaps most important here, we live in a litigious era where people are more likely than in the past to get into disputes — and the more disputes, the more conflicts there are.

Chapter 24
IMPUTED CONFLICTS AND FIREWALLS

We have spent considerable time in earlier chapters talking about situations in which a lawyer *personally* faces disqualification due to a conflict of interest. We now ask whether the personal disqualification of *one* lawyer in a law firm requires the disqualification of *all* the lawyers in the firm. If one lawyer in the firm is *personally* disqualified, is every other lawyer in the firm *vicariously* disqualified? In other words, is the first lawyer's conflict "imputed" to the rest of the firm? Is the conflict *contagious*, so to speak? Will everyone in the firm "catch" the disqualification if one lawyer in the firm is "infected" with a disqualifying conflict?

Before we explore the approaches taken by the ABA and various states, let's set out a problem that presents a number of issues regarding imputed conflicts:

Problem: Revolvers and Laterals

Consider a law firm with four partners — John, Paul, George, and Ringo — who have a general civil litigation practice. The firm has no associates. (Not very realistic, but it simplifies the problem a lot, so be glad.) Before opening their civil practice, the four partners had different legal backgrounds.

- *John* was a lawyer at the United States Department of Justice, where he worked on an antitrust action against the toy industry for price fixing and deceptive trade practices.
- *Paul* was in private practice at a law firm that represented Rugerasers, Inc., a company that manufactures erasers that have tiny pictures of Rugrats on them. ("Rugrats" was a popular children's TV series from 1991–2004.)
- *George* was a prominent commercial arbitrator, and later a federal judge.
- *Ringo* was a lawyer at the Consumer Protection Division of the Federal Trade Commission, where he shared an office with an attorney who was conducting an investigation of the toy industry and its safety warnings for children, especially those toys used by children under the age of three. Raymond did not work on the toy industry investigation (or any other phase of the case), but he frequently heard his office-mate talking about it. As far as Raymond remembers, the FTC decided not to take action because there were not enough complaints about particular toys to justify rulemaking or other proceedings.

This week, distraught parents (Mr. and Mrs. Aggrieved) came in and asked the firm to sue Rugerasers in a tort suit because their child was seriously injured when she swallowed the tiny erasers. (The tiny erasers are easily confused with Rugrats vitamins, which are a bestselling children's vitamin that TV commercials say are "great for you.") The request that the firm file suit poses three questions:

(1) Is any individual lawyer in the firm disqualified from handling the suit against Rugerasers?

(2) If any individual partner is disqualified, may that partner overcome the disqualification by obtaining consent from someone? (If so, whose consent?)

(3) If the firm cannot obtain consent (or does not wish to seek consent), may the firm nevertheless take the case without consent if it builds a firewall?

Think about these questions as you read the materials in this chapter.

A. THE ABA'S CURRENT APPROACH TO IMPUTED DISQUALIFICATION

"Imputed" disqualification refers to disqualification of all lawyers in a firm based on the personal disqualification of another lawyer (or lawyers) at the firm. The ABA's approach to imputed disqualification depends on the nature of the conflict in question.

Five rules govern the imputation of conflicts: Rule 1.8(k), Rule 1.10(a), Rule 1.11(b)–(c), Rule 1.12, and Rule 1.18(d). We will now discuss each of those rules. We begin with Pennsylvania Rule 1.8(k):

Rule 1.8(k) Conflict of Interest: Current Clients: Specific Rules

> (k) While lawyers are associated in a firm, a prohibition in the foregoing paragraphs (a) through (i) that applies to any one of them shall apply to all of them.

Rule 1.8(k) says that if any lawyer in the firm has a conflict under Rules 1.8(a)–(i), then every lawyer in the firm suffers from the same conflict. To understand Rule 1.8(k), we need to study the other ten paragraphs of Rule 1.8. (It might help you to think of paragraphs (a) through (j) as "The Ten Commandments," since there are ten of them, but unlike the other Ten Commandments, which are half "Thou shalt not" and half "Thou shall," all of the commandments in Rule 1.8 are of the "Thou shalt not" variety). Paragraphs (a) through (j) of Rule 1.8 prohibit a wide range of conflicts with current clients, either absolutely or unless certain conditions are met, including:

(a) business transactions with clients

(b) using confidential information to the client's disadvantage

(c) accepting gifts or testamentary bequests from clients

(d) selling literary or media rights to the client's story

(e) giving financial assistance to the client (except advancing litigation expenses)

(f) accepting legal fees from a third party

(g) negotiating aggregate settlements for multiple clients

(h) limiting future legal malpractice liability or settling actual or potential malpractice claims

(i) acquiring a proprietary interest in a client's cause of action

(j) engaging in sexual relations with a client

Under Rule 1.8(k), all of the prohibitions in Rule 1.8 apply to all lawyers in a firm *except* the prohibition on sexual relations with a client. In other words, if Rule 1.8 prohibits *any* lawyer in the firm from engaging in certain conduct, then Rule 1.8(k) prohibits *every* lawyer in the firm from engaging in that conduct, except sex with clients.

Just to get the sex question out of the way, sex with clients is considered a personal thing. A lawyer who *personally* represents a client must not have sex with that client unless the lawyer and client had a "consensual sexual relationship" before the representation began. However, Rule 1.8(j) does not prohibit *other* lawyers in the firm (i.e., all of the lawyers who do not personally represent that client) from engaging in sexual relations with the firm's client during the representation. This is a compromise between those who argued that the ABA should not regulate sexual relations between consenting adults, even when the consenting adults are lawyer and client, and those who argued that the ABA should flatly prohibit sexual relations between lawyers and clients (unless they had engaged in sex before the representation began).

Keep in mind that other rules might still prohibit one lawyer in a firm from representing a client who is having sexual relations with another lawyer in the firm. For example, if Arthur is representing Barbara Anne in her divorce and learns that his law partner Carl is in an intimate romantic relationship with Barbara Anne, Arthur might find it difficult to defend Barbara Anne (e.g., to refute her husband's allegations of adultery). In terms of Rule 1.7, which states the general rule on conflicts of interest, Arthur might face a "significant risk" that his representation of Barbara Anne in her divorce will be "materially limited" by Arthur's "personal interest" in not embarrassing his partner, Carl. (Arthur might be reluctant to take Carl's deposition as part of the investigation in the divorce case, for example, especially if Carl is a more powerful partner in the firm than Arthur.) In those circumstances, Arthur would have a concurrent conflict under Rule 1.7(a)(2) and would be disqualified from representing Barbara Anne unless he met all of the conditions in Rule 1.7(b) (including Barbara Anne's informed consent). But the disqualification would be based on an independent analysis under Rule 1.7, not on imputation of the prohibition in Rule 1.8(j), because the prohibition on sexual relations with a client is not imputed to any lawyer who does not personally represent the client in question.

Regarding the rest of the prohibitions in Rule 1.8, Comment 20 to Rule 1.8 gives the following example: "one lawyer in a firm may not enter into a business transaction with a client of another member of the firm without complying with paragraph (a) even if the first lawyer is not personally involved in the representation of the client."

Finally, note that a number of the prohibitions in Rule 1.8 cannot be cured by client consent. Specifically, client consent does not overcome any of these prohibitions:

- the prohibition in Rule 1.8(c) against soliciting a substantial gift or preparing an instrument giving the lawyer a substantial gift;
- the prohibition in Rule 1.8(d) against negotiating literary or media rights;
- the prohibition in Rule 1.8(e) against financial assistance to a client; or
- the prohibition in Rule 1.8(i) against acquiring a proprietary interest in the client's cause of action.

Therefore, a law firm may not evade or overcome those prohibitions by obtaining client consent, even to involvement by another lawyer in the firm not working on the matter in question. The whole point of Rule 1.8(k) is to impute conflicts to every lawyer in the firm whenever any one lawyer in the firm would be disqualified under Rules 1.8(a)–(i). If consent would not cure the individual disqualification, it cannot cure the imputed disqualification either.

Now let's move on to the general imputation rule regarding all other concurrent and successive conflicts. To lay the foundation, let's take a minute to briefly review the rules governing concurrent and successive conflicts.

Rule 1.7 provides that a lawyer shall not represent a client if the representation involves a "concurrent conflict of interest," which is defined as either:

- representing one current client against another current client, or
- taking a "significant risk" that your representation of one client will be "materially limited" by your responsibilities to:
    - another client,
    - a former client,
    - a third person, or
    - your own personal interests.

Rule 1.9(a) provides that a lawyer who has personally represented a client in the past must not later oppose the former client in a "substantially related" matter (or the same matter) unless the former client gives informed consent, confirmed in writing.

Rule 1.9(b) provides that a lawyer who has not personally represented a client in the past but who worked at a firm that did represent that client must not later oppose that client in a "substantially related" matter (or the same matter) if the lawyer acquired confidential information about the firm's client related to the firm's representation.

With that background, we can better understand ABA Model Rule 1.10(a), which has also been widely adopted by many states. For example, Colorado Rule 1.10(a) provides as follows:

Rule 1.10 Imputation of Conflicts of Interest: General Rule

> (a) While lawyers are associated in a firm, none of them shall knowingly represent a client when any one of them practicing alone would be prohibited from doing so by Rule 1.7 or Rule 1.9, unless the prohibition is based on a

> personal interest of the prohibited lawyer and does not present a significant risk of materially limiting the representation of the client by the remaining lawyers in the firm.[1]

In other words, if Rule 1.7 or Rule 1.9 prohibit *any* lawyer in the firm from representing a certain client, then Rule 1.10(a) generally prohibits *every* lawyer in the firm from representing that client. (We call this the *Three Musketeers Rule*. "One for all and all for one." If *anyone* in the firm is disqualified due to a conflict of interest, *everyone* in the firm is disqualified, unless it's a personal conflict that isn't likely to affect representation by other parties.) But there's an exception for personal interest conflicts. A disqualification arising under Rule 1.7 is not imputed to other lawyers in the firm if:

- the disqualifying conflict is based on the disqualified lawyer's *personal* interests (as opposed to the interests of another current client, former client, or third person), and
- the disqualified lawyer's personal interest conflict does not pose a "significant risk" that the remaining lawyers in the firm will be materially limited if they undertake or continue the representation in question.

Thus, if *any* lawyer in a firm has a "concurrent conflict" with another client or a former client or a third party, then *every* lawyer in the firm is disqualified by that conflict. But if a lawyer in the firm has a conflict arising only out of the lawyer's personal interests (e.g., friends, relatives, money, or politics), then the conflict is *not* imputed to any other lawyer at the firm *unless* it presents a "significant risk" of "materially limiting" the representation of the client by the other lawyers in the firm. It might present a significant risk, for example, if the lawyer with the personal conflict is a powerful lawyer in the firm, especially if the personally conflicted lawyer is also supervising the work of the lawyers handling the matter.

Rule 1.10(a) is also qualified by paragraphs (b), (c), and (d) of Rule 1.10. Paragraph (b) explains what happens when a lawyer who was personally disqualified leaves the firm. The general theory underlying imputed conflicts is that if one lawyer in the firm has confidential information about a former client, then every lawyer in the firm might have the same information. Thus, if any lawyer is disqualified because the lawyer gained (or probably gained) confidential information about another client or former client, the entire firm is tainted by an imputed conflict of interest. But does the firm remain tainted forever, even after the personally disqualified lawyer is gone? Or (instead) does the imputed conflict disappear once the source of the imputed conflict (the personally disqualified lawyer) leaves the firm? The ABA position is that the imputed conflict goes away when the personally disqualified lawyer goes away, provided no other lawyer in the firm has confidential information that could be used against the former client. Following the ABA Model verbatim, Colorado Rule 1.10(b) provides as follows:

> (b) When a lawyer has terminated an association with a firm, the firm is not prohibited from thereafter representing a person with interests materially adverse to those of a client represented by the formerly associated lawyer and not currently represented by the firm, unless:
>
> > (1) the matter is the same or substantially related to that in which the formerly associated lawyer represented the client; and(2) any lawyer remaining in the firm has information protected by Rules 1.6 and 1.9(c) that is material to the matter.

Let's put Rule 1.10(a) and Rule 1.10(b) together. Suppose your law firm laterally hires a lawyer named Dave Barry from another law firm, and suppose that Dave is personally disqualified from opposing one of his former clients (call it Winchester Corporation) in any matter substantially related to the matters he (or his firm) previously handled. Under Rule 1.10(a), Dave's disqualification is imputed to every lawyer in your law firm

---

[1] Colorado Rule 1.10(a) is identical to ABA Model Rule 1.10(a).

as long as Dave remains disqualified. However, under Rule 1.10(b) the disqualification evaporates — disappears — vanishes — when Dave leaves the firm *unless* other lawyers in the firm still have confidential information that is material to a substantially related matter. If they do have such information, the imputed disqualification lives on until all of the lawyers with material confidential information have left the firm (which may never happen).

But so far something is missing from Rule 1.10. What about client consent? May your firm escape from an imputed disqualification by getting consent from the client or former client that is causing the conflict? Yes. Colorado Rule 1.10(c) (again adhering to the ABA Model) provides as follows:

> (c) A disqualification prescribed by this rule may be waived by the affected client under the conditions stated in Rule 1.7.

What does Rule 1.10(c) mean? In particular, what are "the conditions stated in Rule 1.7"? Comment 6 to Colorado Rule 1.10 explains the Rule as follows:

> [6] Rule 1.10(c) removes imputation with the informed consent of the affected client or former client under the conditions stated in Rule 1.7. The conditions stated in Rule 1.7 require the lawyer to determine that the representation is not prohibited by Rule 1.7(b) and that each affected client or former client has given informed consent to the representation, confirmed in writing. In some cases, the risk may be so severe that the conflict may not be cured by client consent. . . .[2]

Thus, the law firm will need a current client's consent if any lawyer in the firm has a conflict between: (i) a current client and another current client; (ii) a current client and a third party; (iii) a current client and a former client; or (iv) a current client and the lawyer's own personal interests where the personal interest conflict poses a significant risk of materially limiting the representation by other lawyers in the firm. In addition, that consent must adhere to the standards in Rule 1.7(b), which in Colorado include the following (with emphasis added):

(1) "The lawyer ***reasonably*** believes that the lawyer will be able to provide competent and diligent representation to each affected client;"
(2) "the representation is not prohibited by law;"
(3) the lawyer (or different lawyers from the same law firm) won't be handling both sides of the same litigation; and
(4) "***each*** affected client gives informed consent" and this consent is "confirmed in writing."[3]

Unless *all* of these conditions can be met, the lawyer will be unable to obtain valid client consent, and therefore must not even try to obtain consent. In other words, the conflict is non-consentable. If a conflict is non-consentable under Rule 1.7(b), then it is also non-consentable under Rule 1.10(c), and there is no way to escape from the underlying conflict or from its imputation to the other lawyers in the firm.

Finally, Rule 1.10(d) includes a kind of disclaimer: the rule does not apply to conflicts of interest that arise when lawyers move from the private sector to the government or vice-versa. Tracking the ABA's language verbatim, Colorado Rule 1.10(d) provides as follows:

> (d) The disqualification of lawyers associated in a firm with former or current government lawyers is governed by Rule 1.11.

---

[2] The quoted portion of Colorado's Comment 6 tracks the ABA Comment exactly, but at the end of Comment 6 Colorado adds the following helpful language: "For a discussion of the effectiveness of client waivers of conflicts that might arise in the future, see Rule 1.7, Comment [22]. For a definition of informed consent, see Rule 1.0(e)."

[3] The Colorado language in quotation marks is identical to the equivalent provisions in ABA Model Rule 1.7(b).

In other words, when discussing a current or former government lawyer (and the "Revolver" problem at the beginning of this chapter involves several of them), then the imputation of conflicts is not governed by Rule 1.10 at all. Instead, Rule 1.10(d) provides that imputation of current or former government lawyers is governed by Rule 1.11. That is the perfect segué to Rule 1.11, which is the third of the ABA Model Rules that govern imputed conflicts of interest.

Rule 1.11, which has been adopted by many states but with some variations, begins by stating the basic disqualification of former government lawyers. South Carolina Rule 1.11(a), which is identical to ABA Model Rule 1.11(a), provides as follows:

Rule 1.11 Special Conflicts of Interest for Former and Current Government Officers and Employees

> (a) Except as law may otherwise expressly permit, a lawyer who has formerly served as a public officer or employee of the government:
>
> (1) is subject to Rule 1.9(c); and
>
> (2) shall not otherwise represent a client in connection with a matter in which the lawyer participated personally and substantially as a public officer or employee, unless the appropriate government agency gives its informed consent, confirmed in writing, to the representation.

Rule 1.11(a) thus sets out the circumstances under which a former government officer or employee is *personally* disqualified from working on a matter at a private firm. (Note that the rule just quoted applies to any lawyer who served in the government, whether he or she was working as a lawyer or in any other capacity. For example, an Assistant Secretary of State is not acting as a lawyer but may participate in many matters that have legal overtones, and may thus be closely connected to legal work being performed at private law firms.)

The key question for this chapter is: When are a former government lawyer's personal conflicts imputed to the rest of the lawyers in the firm? The answer is radically different from the answer we would reach if we followed Rule 1.10(a). The imputed disqualification rule for former government officers or employees is stated in South Carolina Rule 1.11(b), which (like its ABA equivalent) provides as follows:

> (b) When a lawyer is disqualified from representation under paragraph (a), no lawyer in a firm with which that lawyer is associated may knowingly undertake or continue representation in such a matter unless:
>
> (1) the disqualified lawyer is timely *screened* from any participation in the matter and is apportioned no part of the fee therefrom; and
>
> (2) written notice is promptly given to the appropriate government agency to enable it to ascertain compliance with the provisions of this rule.

The term "screened," which appears in Rule 1.11(b)(2), is defined in South Carolina Rule 1.0(*l*) as follows:

> (*l*) "Screened" denotes the isolation of a lawyer from any participation in a matter through the timely imposition of procedures within a firm that are reasonably adequate under the circumstances to protect information that the isolated lawyer is obligated to protect under these Rules or other law.[4]

Comment 9 to South Carolina Rule 1.0 elaborates on the purpose and implementation of a screen as follows:

> [9] The purpose of screening is to assure the affected parties that confidential information known by the personally disqualified lawyer remains protected. The personally disqualified lawyer should acknowledge the obligation not to communicate with any of the other lawyers in the firm with respect to the matter.

---

[4] South Carolina Rule 1.0(*l*) is identical to ABA Model Rule 1.0(k).

> Similarly, other lawyers in the firm who are working on the matter should be informed that the screening is in place and that they may not communicate with the personally disqualified lawyer with respect to the matter. Additional screening measures that are appropriate for the particular matter will depend on the circumstances. . . .[5]

To "implement, reinforce and remind all affected lawyers" about the screen, South Carolina Comment 9 continues by suggesting that the following procedures "may be appropriate":

- "a written undertaking by the screened lawyer to avoid any communication with other firm personnel and any contact with any firm files or other materials relating to the matter"
- "written notice and instructions to all other firm personnel forbidding any communication with the screened lawyer relating to the matter"
- "denial of access by the screened lawyer to firm files or other materials relating to the matter" and
- "periodic reminders of the screen to the screened lawyer and all other firm personnel."

South Carolina Comment 10 (which is the same as Comment 10 to ABA Model Rule 1.0) reminds law firms that to be effective, screening measures must be implemented "as soon as practical after a lawyer or law firm knows or reasonably should know that there is a need for screening." Ideally, that means the screen should be in place when the former government lawyer arrives at her first day of work at the firm. If a conflict is discovered after the former government lawyer has arrived — for example, if the firm wants to take on a new matter that presents a conflict — then the firm should implement the screen within a matter of hours or days after learning of the conflict, not weeks or months.

Rule 1.11(c) covers a different type of conflict — a conflict arising from a former government lawyer's possession of what is called "confidential government information" (to be defined soon) — and it too permits screening. Because the rule consists of one long paragraph, we break it down into its component parts, as if it were several separate paragraphs. South Carolina Rule 1.11(c), based verbatim on the ABA Model, begins with a broad prohibition:

> (c) Except as law may otherwise expressly permit, a lawyer having information that the lawyer knows is *confidential government information* about a person acquired when the lawyer was a public officer or employee, may not represent a private client whose interest are adverse to that person in a matter in which the information could be used to the material disadvantage of that person.

Again borrowing from the ABA Model, South Carolina Rule 1.11(c) continues with a definition of the term "confidential government information," which is the trigger for applying the rule:

> As used in this Rule, the term "confidential government information" means information that has been obtained under governmental authority and which, at the time this Rule is applied, the government is prohibited by law from disclosing to the public or has a legal privilege not to disclose and which is not otherwise available to the public. . . .

In other words, information qualifies as "confidential government information" if it meets three criteria:

- The information was "obtained under governmental authority," such as a

---

[5] The quoted language from South Carolina's Comment was adopted verbatim from the equivalent ABA Comment.

subpoena or civil investigative demand issued by a government agency, *and*,

- at the time Rule 1.11(c) is applied, *either*:
  - the government is prohibited by law from disclosing to the public, or
  - the government has a legal privilege not to disclose the information

— *and* —

- The information is not otherwise available to the public.

If a lawyer in a firm has "confidential government information," may other lawyers in the firm handle the case? As under Rule 1.11(b), the answer is "yes" provided the firm takes certain steps, including screening the lawyer who has the confidential government information. South Carolina drives home this point by ending Rule 1.11(c) with this sentence:

> A firm with which that lawyer [the one having "confidential government information"] is associated may undertake or continue representation in the matter only if the disqualified lawyer is *timely screened* from any participation in the matter and is apportioned no part of the fee therefrom.[6]

Thus, as long as your firm (i) promptly builds an effective screen and (ii) does not give the disqualified lawyer any share in the fee, then other lawyers at the firm may ethically handle the matter even though the former government lawyer has confidential government information.

Rule 1.11 ends with two more paragraphs. A long paragraph (d) governs lawyers who move from government service to private practice or other nongovernmental employment. We skip it because it's not relevant to imputed disqualification. A short paragraph (e) defines the term "matter" as used in Rule 1.11, and we quote South Carolina Rule 1.11(e) here for the sake of completeness:

> (e) As used in this Rule, the term "matter" includes:
>
> (1) any judicial or other proceeding, application, request for a ruling or other determination, contract, claim, controversy, investigation, charge, accusation, arrest or other particular matter involving a specific party or parties; and
>
> (2) any other matter covered by the conflict of interest rules of the appropriate government agency.[7]

The key to the definition is that a thing isn't a "matter" for purposes of Rule 1.11 unless it involved a "particular matter involving a specific party or parties." Rulemaking, for example, isn't a "matter" under the definition in ABA Model Rule 1.11(e) because rules are for everyone and they don't involve a "specific party." (Some jurisdictions reject that narrow definition and expressly include rulemaking as part of the definition of "matter.")

A fourth ABA Model Rule governing imputed conflicts is Rule 1.12, which treats former judges and their law clerks, as well as other neutrals, like former government lawyers. The basic prohibition of Rule 1.12, as stated in the Colorado Rules of Professional Conduct, provides:

> *Rule 1.12 Former Judge, Arbitrator, Mediator or Other Third-Party Neutral*
>
> (a) . . . [A] lawyer shall not represent anyone in connection with a matter in which the lawyer participated personally and substantially as a judge or other adjudicative officer, or law clerk to such a person or as an arbitrator, mediator or other third-party neutral, unless all parties to the proceeding give informed consent, confirmed in writing.[8]

---

[6] The quoted South Carolina language is based verbatim on the closing sentence of ABA Model Rule 1.11(c).

[7] South Carolina's version is taken verbatim from ABA Model Rule 1.11(e).

[8] Colorado Rule 1.12(a) is based verbatim on ABA Model Rule 1.12(a).

Thus, a judicial law clerk who participates "personally and substantially" in a case pending before the court and then moves to any other legal job — whether in private practice, in government, at an in-house legal department, etc. — may not later represent *any* party in that matter absent informed consent from *all* parties to the proceeding. Under Rule 1.12(c), however, the conflict is not imputed to the remaining lawyers in the disqualified former law clerk's firm if they are screened on the same basis as former government lawyers. Pennsylvania Rule 1.12(c), which is identical to ABA Model Rule 1.12(c), provides as follows:

> (c) If a lawyer is disqualified by paragraph (a), no lawyer in a firm with which that lawyer is associated may knowingly undertake or continue representation in the matter unless:
>
> (1) the disqualified lawyer is timely screened from any participation in the matter and is apportioned no part of the fee therefrom; and
>
> (2) written notice is promptly given to the parties and any appropriate tribunal to enable them to ascertain compliance with the provisions of this rule.

Does this language sound familiar? It should. Compare Rule 1.11(b), which is almost identical. That makes sense, because judges and their law clerks are essentially a special species of government lawyer.

There's an exception for "partisan" arbitrators (which refers to arbitrators selected by one of the parties essentially as its advocate within the arbitration panel of three or more arbitrators). Rule 1.12(d) provides that "[a]n arbitrator selected as a partisan of a party in a multimember arbitration panel is not prohibited from subsequently representing that party." That makes sense because a partisan arbitrator was never supposed to be neutral in the first place.

The final ABA Model Rule that governs imputed conflicts is Rule 1.18, relating to prospective clients, defined in Rule 1.18(a) as a "person who discusses with a lawyer the possibility of forming a client-lawyer relationship with respect to a matter. . . . " As we saw in the chapter on conflicts with former clients, the basic prohibition in Rule 1.18 is described in Pennsylvania Rule 1.18(b) and (c), as follows:

Rule 1.18 Duties to Prospective Client

> (b) Even when no client-lawyer relationship ensues, a lawyer who has had discussions with a prospective client shall not use or reveal information learned in the consultation, except as Rule 1.9 would permit with respect to information of a former client.
>
> (c) A lawyer subject to paragraph (b) shall not represent a client with interests materially adverse to those of a prospective client in the same or a substantially related matter if the lawyer received information from the prospective client that could be significantly harmful to that person in the matter, except as provided in paragraph (d).

Pennsylvania Rule 1.18(c) then continues with standard imputation language — the same language seen in other rules — and ends with the following sentence:

> If a lawyer is disqualified from representation under this paragraph, no lawyer in a firm with which that lawyer is associated may knowingly undertake or continue representation in such a matter, except as provided in paragraph (d).

What is "provided in paragraph (d)"? Most of Rule 1.18(d) concerns screens. The following is Colorado Rule 1.18(d)(2), which (like its ABA counterpart) sets forth the screening provision that combines the unique with the familiar:

> (d) When the lawyer has received disqualifying information as defined in paragraph (c), representation is permissible if: . . .

(2) the lawyer who received the information took reasonable measures to avoid exposure to more disqualifying information than was reasonably necessary to determine whether to represent the prospective client; and

(i) the disqualified lawyer is timely screened from any participation in the matter and is apportioned no part of the fee therefrom; and

(ii) written notice is promptly given to the prospective client.[9]

Thus, the rules governing conflicts with prospective clients are more like the rules governing former government lawyers than the rules governing lawyers who move laterally from one private firm to another. A former prospective client may waive a Rule 1.18 conflict, but if the former prospective client does not waive the conflict, Rule 1.18(d) permits the imputed conflicts to be cured by screening, just as Rule 1.11 permits a former government lawyer's imputed conflicts to be cured by screening — whereas, in contrast, Rule 1.10 does not permit imputed conflicts arising from a private-to-private firm lateral lawyer's former clients to be cured by screening.

That sums up the ABA's five current rules governing imputed conflicts of interest. However, the ABA's current approach is only one of many possible approaches to imputed conflicts. We now turn to some of those other approaches.

B. OTHER APPROACHES TO IMPUTED CONFLICTS OF INTEREST

In this section we discuss the ABA's pre-2002 approach to imputed conflicts, the Restatement's approach, and the approach of some states to imputed conflicts.

1. The ABA's Pre-2002 Approach to Imputed Conflicts

In the past, the ABA itself took a somewhat different approach to imputed conflicts from its current approach. Before 2002, ABA Model Rule 1.10(a) provided that while lawyers are associated in a firm, "none of them shall knowingly represent a client when any one of them practicing alone would be prohibited from doing so by Rules 1.7, 1.8(c), 1.9, or 2.2."

(Rule 2.2, which addressed a lawyer's role as an "intermediary" between two disputing clients, was deleted in 2002.) Thus, before 2002, Rule 1.10(a) automatically imputed *every* conflict based on a lawyer's personal interests. If *any* lawyer in a firm had a conflict arising from a personal interest, old ABA Rule 1.10(a) disqualified the lawyer's *entire firm* unless the former client consented after consultation, even if there was no "significant risk" that the underlying personal interest conflict wouldn't have any effect on a representation by the other lawyers in the firm. The premise of old Rule 1.10(a) was that only total disqualification of an entire firm could cure a client's anxiety that the conflict materially limiting the personally disqualified lawyer would also materially limit the zeal of the other lawyers at the firm. Screening under Rule 1.11 could cure conflicts involving former government lawyers (just as it still does), but screening could not cure conflicts arising from a lawyer's personal interests.

Moreover, the pre-2002 version of Rule 1.10 did not impute any of the conflicts arising under Rule 1.8 except the prohibition in Rule 1.8(c) on preparing a legal instrument (such as a will or codicil) giving the lawyer a "substantial gift." The remaining conflicts arising under Rule 1.8 were not imputed at all because the ABA had not yet adopted Rule 1.8(k). Since the adoption of Rule 1.8(k), *all* of the conflicts arising under Rule 1.8 except sexual relations with a client have been imputed to *every* lawyer in a firm. When Rule 1.8 prohibits one lawyer in a firm from engaging in certain conduct (other than sex with a client), then Rule 1.8(k) prohibits all lawyers in the firm from engaging in that same conduct.

---

[9] Colorado Rule 1.18(d) was adopted verbatim from ABA Model Rule 1.18(d).

The old ABA approach to conflicts arising under Rule 1.9 was the same as it is under the "new" (post-2002) ABA approach, so all conflicts arising under Rule 1.9 were imputed to all of the other lawyers in the firm unless the former client gave informed consent. Thus, all conflicts with a lawyer's own former clients, and all conflicts with clients of a former firm about whom the lawyer acquired material confidential information, were imputed to all lawyers at the firm. If the former client refused consent, the imputed conflicts could not be cured by screening. That remains the ABA's approach today.

2. The Restatement Approach to Imputed Conflicts

The Restatement of the Law Governing Lawyers, and the ethics rules of many states, permit law firms to avoid imputed disqualification by screening the personally disqualified lawyer. Restatement § 123, for example, generally imputes conflicts of interest to all lawyers in a firm, but Restatement § 124 permits the firm to overcome imputed conflicts with former clients by providing that a former client conflict does not affect an "affiliated lawyer" when there is "no substantial risk that confidential information of the former client will be used with material adverse effect on the former client" because:

> (a) any confidential client information communicated to the personally prohibited lawyer is unlikely to be significant in the subsequent matter;
>
> (b) the personally prohibited lawyer is subject to screening measures adequate to eliminate participation by that lawyer in the representation; and
>
> (c) timely and adequate notice of the screening has been provided to all affected clients.

Under Restatement § 124, therefore, screening will not cure an imputation problem if the former client *did* communicate confidential information to the personally disqualified lawyer that is likely to be "significant" in the matter adverse to the former client. But otherwise, timely and effective screening and notice will cure conflicts with former clients (i.e., conflicts arising under ABA Model Rule 1.9). Do you like that approach?

3. The Pro-Screening Approach Taken by Some States

A handful of states go even further than the Restatement by permitting screening to cure imputed conflicts with former clients no matter how significant the confidential information possessed by the personally disqualified lawyer. For example, Illinois Rule 1.10(b) provides:

> (b) When a lawyer becomes associated with a firm, the firm may not represent a person in a matter that the firm knows or reasonably should know is the same or substantially related to a matter in which the newly associated lawyer, or a firm with which that lawyer was associated, had previously represented a client whose interests are materially adverse to that person unless:
>
> > (1) the newly associated lawyer has no information protected by Rules 1.6 or 1.9 that is material to the matter; or
> >
> > (2) the newly associated lawyer is screened from any participation in the matter.

The Illinois rule on imputation of conflicts with former private clients thus differs from both the ABA's approach (which says screens cannot automatically cure any imputed conflicts with former clients) and the Restatement's approach (which says screens can cure some but not all imputed conflicts with former clients). In sum, the approaches we set out above describe a "always-sometimes-never" spectrum:

- Under the Illinois approach, screens can *always* overcome imputed conflicts with former clients.

- Under the Restatement's approach, screens can *sometimes* overcome imputed conflicts with former clients absent the former client's consent.
- Under the ABA approach, screens can *never* overcome imputed conflicts with former clients absent the former client's consent.

Which approach do you favor?

C. APPLYING VARIOUS APPROACHES TO CONFLICTS WITH FORMER CLIENTS

Now we're going to apply various approaches to conflicts with former clients so that you can decide which one you think makes the most sense.

The ABA's strict approach probably makes sense when the former client in question was at one time represented by the *same firm* that now seeks to oppose it in a "substantially related" matter. For example, a law firm that once represented Computer Consultants Corp. ("CCC") in drafting an employment contract with its President will not be permitted to turn around and represent the President in a suit *against* CCC for a breach of contract if the suit arises out of that very same contract, unless CCC consents. If CCC will not consent, courts taking the ABA's approach will disqualify the entire firm to prohibit the firm from betraying the former client by "changing sides" — from opposing a client that the firm used to represent. It looks unseemly for a law firm to stab a former client in the back. This is a problem of loyalty.

But when a lawyer changes law firms (rather than the law firm changing sides), the situation looks different. The "old" law firm is still representing the client, so it is not changing sides. The lateral lawyer (i.e., the "moving" lawyer, the one changing jobs) will be screened and will have nothing to do with the matter adverse to his former client (or his firm's former client), so he isn't changing sides, either. Where's the loyalty problem? Many would say there is no loyalty problem in that situation. Does it make sense to impute conflicts from the lateral lawyer even if his new firm erects effective and timely screens? That's the question we now address.

Let's first define what we mean by a timely and effective screen, or "firewall." A "firewall" is a metaphorical "wall of separation" between a lawyer who has a conflict and the rest of the firm. (As we noted at the outset, a "firewall" is variously referred to as a "Chinese Wall," a "screen," an "ethical wall," a "cone of silence," or a "zone of silence." Historically, when the legal profession used the phrase Chinese Wall, it was because the phrase called up the image of the Great Wall of China, probably the most famous wall in history, which was built to be impenetrable and worked well for thousands of years.) Such firewalls usually have four components:

1. *Restrictions on the disqualified lawyer.* The lawyer who is personally disqualified must not discuss the case with any other lawyers in the firm (whether or not they are working on the case) or with officers or agents of the conflicted client or clients. The personally disqualified lawyer must be completely isolated from the substantially related matter — the disqualified lawyer must be isolated from all contact with the current client and the witnesses and lawyers involved in the case.
2. *Restrictions on other lawyers.* The other lawyers in the firm must not discuss the case with the lawyer who is personally disqualified, and must be careful not to discuss the case where the disqualified lawyer might overhear the conversation. If the disqualified lawyer inadvertently begins talking about the former client, the other lawyers in the firm must tell him to stop.
3. *Implementation measures.* The law firm must take concrete measures to implement the wall by ensuring that all lawyers in the firm understand and abide by the restrictions. For example:

- The firm should circulate a memorandum to all attorneys in the firm advising them not to discuss the present or former case with the disqualified attorney.
- The firm should make the files of the "conflict" matter inaccessible to the disqualified attorney, either by putting them in a special place (preferably under lock and key) or by making them subject to a sign-out system.

4. *Timing.* If at all possible, all of these steps should be taken before the conflict ripens, or at least immediately upon learning of the conflict. If the firm waits until an opponent files a motion to disqualify, it is usually too late to set up a firewall.

Remember that neither the ABA Model Rules nor any state's rules permit a law firm to use a firewall to overcome a *current* client's objections (and hence escape disqualification). In other words, if a *current* client moves to disqualify a firm, and if the court agrees that a disqualifying conflict exists, then a firewall ordinarily cannot prevent disqualification. (We won't say never, because courts rule on motions to disqualify on a case-by-case basis and may sometimes decide that delay or other factors militate against disqualification even if the rules have been violated.) The utility of screens, where they are effective at all, is generally limited to curing imputed conflicts with former clients.

With these basic concepts in mind, let's study some concrete situations, starting with a story by Lawrence Fox, a partner at the Philadelphia-based firm of Drinker, Biddle & Reath LLP and a former Chair of both the ABA Section of Litigation and the ABA Standing Committee on Ethics and Professional Responsibility (which writes ABA ethics opinions).

LAWRENCE J. FOX, MY LAWYER SWITCHED SIDES; DON'T WORRY, THERE'S A SCREEN*

The litigation department breakfasts always seemed to be scheduled for the wrong day of the week. Just when the key deposition loomed with its 10:00 A.M. start, the chairman insisted everyone meet at 7:30 in the tired windowless conference room on 13, the one with the boring duck prints that were always askew. Obligations and self-interest overcame the need for last-minute deposition preparations. After all, associate reviews were just around the corner. She wondered, as she raced to be on time, why she had ever bothered to switch firms. It was true: they weren't all identical; they were just the same. They made you feel the same — tired and overworked — and the paycheck was delivered with the same heavy resentment. They made you feel the same anxiety that you would not meet the firm's billable hour "targets," the euphemism employed by the chair of each firm to describe her 2,200 hour quota. She had to find a better way, she thought, as she slumped resignedly into the well-worn conference room chair. How many hours had she spent in this room? In these meetings? Being bored?

Barely listening, she maintained her studied attentive pose, one she had mastered to get her through those interminable depositions. She would follow her usual rule: make an attempt at one cogent remark, but otherwise remain silent. Talking at meetings like this could only hurt her chances for partnership (as if she cared), and no one ever made partner because of her "performance" at departmental meetings. Wait, look alert, pick your moment, and then get out as soon as possible.

The conversation turned to privileged documents: something about whether you could withhold internal corporate memos in document discovery on the grounds of privilege when they were addressed to multiple executives as well as in-house general counsel. Her mind wandered back to the practice of one of her clients at the old firm. Suddenly sensing this anecdotal tidbit as "her" moment, she shared with the assembled group, "When I was at Bryans & Putnam, one of our clients, City Trust Company, had a bright line rule: so long as the document had counsel's name or initials on

---

it . . . anywhere — as writer, addressee, copied in or later sent the document — they deemed it privileged. It made it real easy to decide which documents to withhold."

Several minutes later, as the discussion rejected her formulation as far too broad, even unprofessional, it suddenly occurred to her. Of course! The firm had litigation against City Trust Company, she was "screened" from that litigation (she had prepared some early interrogatories for City Trust) and she had suddenly revealed a City Trust confidence to everyone. Panic replaced boredom; nausea gripped her. What should she do? What would her firm colleagues do? Was her career going up in smoke before her eyes? She had broken her trust; she hadn't intended to, she hadn't been thinking. It was just a passing remark. She rose shakily, mumbled an apology and hurried to the ladies' room.

Her mind raced back to her first thoughts about leaving her old firm. The headhunter had called and indicated how easy it was to place a young associate practicing in Pennsylvania, one of the few states that provided for screening of private lawyers when they switched firms. It made looking for a job so much simpler. She did not have to worry about whether the possible new employers had cases against her old clients. If the headhunter found a firm that liked her, she could just accept the job without worrying about potential conflicts. If any were discovered, the Pennsylvania rules would simply require that she be screened from those matters.

She felt comfortable with that arrangement. She knew how she viewed client confidences — she would never share them. In fact, it gave her great pride to think of herself as a lawyer of integrity, one who could be trusted with confidential information. Indeed it was one of things that drove her husband crazy — the way she always knew the best secrets weeks before he would hear about it at a cocktail party or read about it in the newspaper. She even felt flattered when, after the two matters from which she had to be screened were identified, the chairman of her new firm's professional responsibility committee said to her that the firm was not going to take any elaborate measures to screen her because the firm had a long tradition of placing substantial trust in their associates.

But now! What could she do? Maybe she shouldn't do anything. If she talked to anyone at her new firm that would just emphasize the importance of her disclosure. Would her new firm then have to resign from handling the City Trust matters? One of them involved Pegasus Construction Company, her new firm's largest litigation client. And did she have to tell City Trust? Or anyone at Bryans & Putnam? So many questions! No one to turn to. She was spinning with concerns. It was too much to handle. She would leave early — it would be her first pre-8:00 P.M. departure in weeks — and maybe she could persuade her husband that dinner at that new Thai restaurant on South Street would be in order . . . she needed a chance to clear her head, to regroup.

The next day dawned early and bright — the kind of day that gave June such a good reputation. The dinner had been close to perfect, perhaps a tad too much wine. And while she hated to admit it, it may have been the wine that permitted her to see the situation clearly.

There was no doubting her mistake; she shouldn't have blurted out those remarks at the meeting the day before, but it was only after the dinner that she recalled how upset she had been originally when she learned that City Trust took this position on the privilege. She recalled with clarity how it had offended her at the time, how surprised she was that the partners at old Bryans & Putnam had so blithely accepted the client's notion of privilege. So was there really anything wrong with what she had said? If City Trust's position were defensible . . . maybe she had an obligation to tell someone, maybe her new firm would be obliged to resign. But since it was her view that City Trust was wrong, there really was no harm. If her colleagues who worked on City Trust matters at her new firm used her information to press a little harder for documents that City Trust withheld on the ground of privilege, it would be for the courts to decide who was right. And it wasn't like she had shared confidential facts about the case.

As she contemplated all of this, she couldn't really tell whether it was the weather, the Cabernet Sauvignon, or the chicken satay that had induced this new sense of calm; the problems of yesterday had been put to rest and, particularly pleasing, she had handled the entire matter herself. Off she went to work with a new lightness in her step, not unlike the way she felt the day she learned she had passed the bar exam. Maybe she would go for partner after all.

NOTES AND QUESTIONS

1. ***Are you Skeptical about Firewalls?*** After reading Fox's story, are you skeptical that firewalls can work at a law firm? Those who oppose rules allowing firewalls to overcome a former client's objections argue that the key issue isn't whether we trust lawyers, but whether we really believe we can control human nature. Was there any evidence of bad faith when the lawyer in "Don't Worry" revealed the confidential information about City Trust's "bright line" rule on identifying privileged documents? Of course not. It was just old fashioned human error.

2. ***What are the Costs of Ignoring Firewalls?*** Even if you are skeptical about whether firewalls can really seal off confidences and secrets, you need to balance your skepticism against the costs of *not* allowing firewalls to cure conflicts of interest when lawyers switch from one private firm to another. What are those costs?

The main cost is a severe restriction in mobility for lawyers who want to move from one firm to another. The mirror image of that cost is that when lawyers do move laterally from one firm to another, the new firm may be disqualified because of a successive conflict. Disqualification, in turn, has several costs: (a) it deprives the new firm's client of its chosen counsel; (b) it deprives the new firm of revenue; and (c) it causes delay while the substitute firm (the one that takes over for the disqualified firm) learns about the matter. Are these costs heavy enough, or frequent enough, to outweigh the concerns of former clients that their confidential information will be accidentally or intentionally revealed?

3. ***The Adverse Impact on your Career.*** The screening issue matters to you personally. Whether law firms can escape vicarious disqualification by building a "screen" or "firewall" around lateral hires who are personally disqualified from opposing their former clients (or clients of their former firms about whom they learned material confidential information) will have a big impact on your career, especially on your ability to change jobs. If a former client will not consent to a conflict, should the law firm nevertheless be permitted to go ahead without consent if it instructs all lawyers in the firm not to talk to the disqualified lawyers (and vice-versa) about the substantially related matters, and makes the paper and electronic files inaccessible to the disqualified lawyers? In Illinois — as we will see in the *Cromley* case below — the screen will overcome the former client's objections to the conflict. That will make it relatively easy for you to move from one law firm to another in Illinois, because any former client conflicts that you bring to your new firm can be cured by building a screen. Your new firm won't have to choose between hiring you and continuing an important representation.

But in a state that has adopted a strict rule like ABA Rule 1.10(a) (i.e., a rule that says screens can never negate conflicts without client consent), you will find it much harder to move from one firm to another. If screens don't work, the lawyers at a firm that hires you will be concerned that somewhere down the road they will be forced to drop or decline a lucrative client because you acquired confidential information about the opposing party at your previous job. That confidential information about an opposing party is the ethical equivalent of the Bubonic Plague. It will make you *persona non grata* at many firms, because they will not want to risk disqualification.

You might think the hiring firm could just ask you who you have confidential information about when it considers hiring you. But as a practical matter, it is extremely hard to check on this. The firm cannot ask, "Who were your clients?" or "What matters did you work on?" Instead, because ABA Rule 1.9(b) also applies to clients you never worked for but acquired material confidential information about, the hiring firm has to say, "Tell us the names of every client that you ever learned anything about at your old job, whether you learned it by working on the case, talking to other lawyers at lunch, or overhearing a conversation in an elevator." That isn't an easy question to answer, because you don't carry a list like that around in your head. You can't possibly remember everything you know (or knew but forgot). You probably won't think of it until a client or your new firm gets into litigation with, say, Acme Corporation, and one of the lawyers at the firm asks to you, "Do you know anything about our opponent Acme?" You may not have thought about Acme when you were hired, but this question may ring a bell. Now you may say, "Oh, yeah, Acme. I did pick up some confidential information about Acme, now that you mention it. One morning over coffee, another associate talked to me about a case she was handling for Acme." By that point it's too late. If ABA Rule 1.10(a) is applied literally, your *entire firm* is disqualified on the basis of your confidential knowledge. (Remember the disqualification of the Davis-Beall firm in *Lansing-Delaware Water District v. Oak Lane Park, Inc.*, in our chapter on conflicts with former clients, because associate Gary Nelson had talked informally to another associate over coffee early one morning? Nelson had never billed a minute to the case in question, but that casual conversation with a friend at the firm disqualified Nelson personally and his entire new law firm by imputation, because Kansas did not allow screens to overcome conflicts with former clients.)

Even if you could make a list of all the clients you learned about at your former firm, it might not do any good. The hiring firm can't see into the future, and it doesn't know who all of its future opponents will be. To pick up on the Acme example, suppose that when you were hired by the new firm you said, "I know quite a bit about Acme Corporation. I worked on a matter for them." Your new firm may say, "Don't worry. We don't have any matters against Acme, and we don't expect to get any."

But a year later — under Murphy's law, anything that can go wrong will go wrong — a big client of your new firm wants to sue Acme. "We have a major antitrust claim against Acme," the CEO of your firm's best client will tell a senior partner, "and we'd like your firm to handle it. We don't care what it costs." This case could generate mega-bucks in fees. But upon circulating the routine conflicts memo, the senior partner learns that you worked on a matter for Acme while you were at your old firm, and the new suit against Acme is closely related to the work you did for Acme at your old firm. What now? Can your firm handle the case against Acme?

If ABA Rule 1.10(a) is applied literally, your new firm will have to decline the matter based on your knowledge. The rainmakers at your new firm will be mad as hell, probably at you, even though the conflict isn't your fault. After all, you told them about Acme when you joined the firm, and they said "No problem." If it's a big case, they might even *fire* you to clear the decks to sue Acme. (Remember that ABA Rule 1.10(b) allows a firm to cure a conflict by terminating the infected lawyer, as long as the infected lawyer hasn't spread the confidential information to any lawyer who remains at the firm.) Is that fair? Should you get fired because the ABA favors a rigid rule on vicarious disqualification?

Wait — it gets worse. The problem can arise even if your firm was already handling the case when you got there. Here the scenario is a little different. The hiring firm says, "We've got some litigation against Acme. Do you know any confidential information about Acme?" You say, "No, I don't. I never represented Acme or worked on any of Acme's matters, and I never learned anything about Acme at my old firm, even at lunch or in the coffee room." But a few weeks or months later, after you are hired and are beginning to settle in, your old firm moves to disqualify your new firm. The motion is supported by an affidavit from a lawyer in the old firm who says he talked with you about the Acme case over lunch a few times. That's bad news for you and your new firm. If ignorance is no defense, forgetfulness is even less of a defense. Even if you don't remember what you learned in these alleged lunches, you "acquired information protected by Rules 1.6 and 1.9(c)" while you were at your old firm.

What happens now? Can your new firm keep on handling the Acme case if it immediately builds a firewall to keep you away from that case? If not — if firewalls aren't enough to avoid disqualification — then the firm has to tell its client, "Sorry. We've got to quit handling your case against Acme because we hired a new associate who talked to another lawyer about Acme over lunch a few times at his old job." The client will be furious. "What the hell are you talking about?" the gruff CEO will say. "Why didn't you tell us this in the beginning, so we could have chosen another firm in the first place? Our people have spent hundreds of hours with you telling you the facts and searching for documents and information and going over strategy. Now we'll have to duplicate a lot of that with our new lawyers. And how do we know you won't get disqualified from other matters you're handling for us, if you can't even check an easy conflict like this?"

Kiss that client goodbye. Losing the client in one matter may mean losing the client in all matters — forever. The law firm that takes over the case after your firm is disqualified may want to keep the client, including all of its new matters that arise in the future.

The firm that's hiring you obviously doesn't want to get into this pickle, so if firewalls won't work, then the firm may just cut down on its lateral hiring — meaning it will cut down on your opportunity to move from one job to another. (Once again, your new firm may be able to escape the conflict by utilizing ABA Rule 1.10(b), the provision that lets termination cure a former client conflict — but that provision won't help you, because you'll be the one that gets fired.) How do you like that strict approach to imputed conflicts?

In the chapter on conflicts with former clients, we read the opinion in *Lansing-Delaware Water District v. Oak Lane Park, Inc.*, 808 P.2d 1369 (Kan. 1991), the case in which associate Gary Nelson moved from the law firm of Chapman & Waters to the law firm of Davis–Beall, and caused the entire Davis–Beall firm to be disqualified. Because Nelson had informally discussed this case with another Chapman & Waters associate, Douglas Sutherland, when he was still working there, the trial court found that Nelson was personally disqualified under Rule 1.9(b). The entire Davis–Beall firm was therefore vicariously disqualified under Rule 1.10(a). The court also held that a "screen" or "Chinese Wall" could not cure the conflict and overcome the former client's objections. The court said:

> In drafting the model rules, the ABA considered adopting a provision that would not impute disqualification to private law firms hiring private attorneys if screening occurred. Proponents of this screening device pointed out that imposing a rule of vicarious disqualification arises from the assumption that attorneys will violate professional norms by disclosing former clients' confidences. Imposing vicarious disqualification penalizes clients and must make firms reluctant to hire attorneys collaterally from other firms. Yet the screening solution was rejected by the ABA and most courts addressing the issue. A few courts have attempted to use it in cases where disqualification would work a great hardship, and two states have incorporated it into their rules.
>
> A client is entitled to have its confidences and secrets protected. The district court here found that Nelson had acquired information that was protected by MRPC 1.6 and 1.9(c). Because Nelson acquired this information, he was disqualified and his disqualification was imputed to Davis-Beall pursuant to MRPC 1.10(a). The model rule contains no provisions for use of screening

devices in this situation. In fact, such a proposal was rejected at the time the model rules were adopted.

If you were on your state bar's Ethics Committee, would you recommend a strict rule or a liberal rule on vicarious disqualification? That is, would you permit screening to overcome a former client's objections and cure a conflict with a former client arising out of a lateral's move to a new job?

4. ***Dangers of Firewalls.*** Attorneys are not likely to change the way they talk informally about their cases. They will always talk about their cases, and that's good. Two heads are better than one, so the client gets better service without getting a bigger bill. (The custom is that attorneys don't charge for these informal talks — or at least the attorney who isn't formally working on the case doesn't charge for the time. Not everyone follows this custom, but it is prevalent.) Consequently, attorneys who move from one firm to another are always going to bring with them some confidential information about matters they did not work on. Because they gained this information casually and informally, they have no formal records of their work or their knowledge, making it hard for them to remember, and hard for the other side to prove.

The rules must address this migration of confidential information — nobody wants to let attorneys use confidential information against their former clients, or against clients of their former firms. But firewalls may not be the solution, because they pose certain dangers. What are the dangers of allowing firms to use firewalls as a defense to disqualification? Why might the walls break down or leak?

Whatever the dangers of firewalls, some courts allow them. Why? Are the reasons convincing? Here's a case that approved a Chinese Wall. Do you like the result?

CROMLEY v. BOARD OF EDUCATION

17 F.3d 1059 (7th Cir.1994)

RIPPLE, J.

Marcella Ann Cromley, a high school teacher, brought an action under 42 U.S.C. § 1983. She claimed that she had been denied various administrative positions because she had exercised her right to free speech as guaranteed by the First Amendment and made applicable to the states by the Fourteenth Amendment. The district court granted summary judgment to the defendants, Board of Education of Lockport Township High School District 205. . . . It also denied Ms. Cromley's motion to disqualify defendants' attorneys. . . .

I

BACKGROUND

A. The First Amendment Retaliation Claim

Ms. Cromley has been a high school reading instructor in the Lockport Township High School District 205 since 1974. She had served as the Chair of the Reading Department and "Chapter I Coordinator" from 1978 to 1987. In December 1986, two students complained to her of sexual misconduct by a male teacher in her department, Donald Meints. After Ms. Cromley informed her supervisor, principal Richard Dittle, he undertook an investigation. Interviews with the students and with Meints established that the allegations were basically true. The principal and other administrators decided that Meints should be reprimanded and warned. Although a written summary of the reprimand was placed in the District office file, no report was included in Meints' personnel file or sent to the Illinois Department of Children and Family Services ("DCFS").

However, on February 12, 1987, Ms. Cromley reported the incident to DCFS. Moreover, on March 4, 1987, Ms. Cromley, as Reading Department Chair, gave Meints a harsh written evaluation, in which she noted the students' allegations. Meints, in turn, sent an angry rebuttal to the plaintiff, principal, and union representative. On March 27, 1987, school officials notified Ms. Cromley that the Reading Department was being merged with the English Department and would be chaired by a teacher from the English Department. Ms. Cromley's later applications to serve as Chapter I Coordinator, Associate English Department Chair, and English Department Chair were denied. Until 1987 she had been praised and reappointed each year as Chair of the Reading Department; however, her principal's 1986–87 evaluation of her work reported personnel problems in the department and concerns over her effectiveness in the department. There was evidence, as well, of friction between Ms. Cromley and both the principal and the superintendent. In light of these clashes, the principal and assistant superintendent agreed that they could not recommend either Ms. Cromley or Mr. Meints for leadership positions.

Ms. Cromley filed suit on November 12, 1987 under 42 U.S.C. § 1983, against the Board of Education, the named administrators, and Donald Meints. The complaint alleged that the defendants had retaliated against her because she had complained to DCFS about the sexual misconduct of Meints, a complaint which she asserted was protected speech.

On November 8, 1989, after two years of pretrial litigation, Ms. Cromley's attorney, Larry Weiner, accepted a partnership in the law firm of Scariano, Kula, Ellch & Himes, Chtd., which was representing the defendants. The district court granted Mr. Weiner's oral motion to withdraw as Ms. Cromley's attorney on November 29, 1989, and, on December 15, 1989, Mr. Weiner formally became a partner. Ms. Cromley moved for the disqualification of the Scariano firm from representation of the defendants.

B. District Court Decisions

By Order of March 19, 1990, the district court denied Ms. Cromley's motion to disqualify defendants' attorneys on the ground that the "barriers erected between the attorney and his new law firm with respect to this case are sufficient to rebut the presumption of shared confidences."

II

Analysis

. . . The approach taken by this circuit for determining whether an attorney should be disqualified is a three-step analysis.

> First, we must determine whether a substantial relationship exists between the subject matter of the prior and present representations. If we conclude a substantial relationship does exist, we must next ascertain whether the presumption of shared confidences with respect to the prior representation has been rebutted. If we conclude this presumption has not been rebutted, we must then determine whether the presumption of shared confidences has been rebutted with respect to the present representation. Failure to rebut this presumption would also make the disqualification proper.

Schiessle v. Stephens, 717 F.2d 417, 420 (7th Cir. 1983).

AUTHORS' COMMENT:

The *Schiessle* case is well known and often cited for the proposition that firewalls should be allowed to cure conflicts with a lateral's former clients (or with the clients of the laterals old firm). It remains a leading case in the Seventh Circuit. However, most other circuits do not follow it. Should they? Should law firms routinely be allowed to oppose a former client in a substantially related matter even when a screened-off partner in the firm has gained crucial confidential information from a former client that could hurt the former client in the present matter?

The "substantial relationship" test is easily met in this case. It is undisputed that the subject matter under scrutiny both before and after Mr. Weiner changed law firms was the litigation brought by Ms. Cromley against the School Board. The only change made was attorney Weiner's shift from the firm of Schwartz & Freeman, the firm representing Ms. Cromley, to that of Scariano, Kula, Ellch & Himes, the firm representing the School Board. Because Mr. Weiner's representation of Ms. Cromley before he moved to the Scariano firm is substantially related to his new firm's relationship to the School Board, a "presumption of shared confidences" arises:

> Implicit in a finding of substantial relationship is a presumption that particular individuals in a law firm freely share their client's confidences with one another. . . . However . . . the presumption that an attorney has knowledge of the confidences and secrets of his firm's clients is rebuttable.

As a first step in deciding whether that presumption has been rebutted, "we must determine whether the attorney whose change of employment created the disqualification issue was actually privy to any confidential information his prior law firm received from the party now seeking disqualification of his present firm."[3] The rebuttal can be established either by proof that "the attorney in question had no knowledge of the information, confidences and/or secrets related by the client in the prior representation," or by proof that screening procedures were timely employed in the new law firm to prevent the disclosure of information and secrets. Uncontroverted affidavits are sufficient rebuttal evidence.

Because Mr. Weiner, Ms. Cromley's attorney for two years, clearly had confidential information from his client when he moved to the firm representing the defendant School Board, we must focus on whether the Scariano law firm that Mr. Weiner later joined has demonstrated that it had established an effective screening procedure to block the disclosure of Ms. Cromley's confidences within the "new" firm.

> The presumption of shared confidences could be rebutted by demonstrating that "specific institutional mechanisms" (e.g., "firewalls") had been implemented to effectively insulate against any flow of confidential information from the "infected" attorney to any other member of his present firm.

[3] In *Analytica, Inc. v. NPD Research Inc.*, 708 F.2d 1263 (7th Cir. 1983), this court held that the presumption of shared confidences was irrebuttable when an entire law firm changed sides. We acknowledged in *Analytica*, however, that a lawyer who changes jobs and moves to a firm retained by an adversary "can avoid disqualification by showing that effective measures were taken to prevent confidences from being received by whichever lawyers in the new firm are handling the new matter." In the case now before us, one attorney changed employment from the firm representing the plaintiff to a firm representing the defendants. This circumstance falls within the exception recognized in *Analytica*; therefore our analysis does not conflict with that decision.

. . . The types of institutional mechanisms that have been determined to protect successfully the confidentiality of the attorney-client relationship include: (1) instructions, given to all members of the new firm, of the attorney's recusal and of the ban on exchange of information; (2) prohibited access to the files and other information on the case; (3) locked case files with keys distributed to a select few; (4) secret codes necessary to access pertinent information on electronic hardware; and (5) prohibited sharing in the fees derived from such litigation. Moreover, the screening devices must be employed "as soon as the 'disqualifying event occurred.' "

Other factors have been considered helpful in determining whether adequate protection of the former client's confidences has been achieved: the size of the law firm, its structural divisions, the "screened" attorney's position in the firm, the likelihood of contact between the "screened" attorney and one representing another party, and the fact that a law firm's and lawyer's most valuable asset is "their reputations for honesty and integrity, along with competence." In addition, the attorneys in question must have affirmed these screening devices under oath. The district court must find that the internal safeguards applied indeed did shield effectively the "tainted attorney."

AUTHORS' COMMENT:

Do these protections strike you as sufficient to guard against the misuse of the former client's confidences? If so, how are these protections to be enforced? If not, what additional protections do you think are needed?

In this case, the defendants have rebutted the presumption of shared confidences by describing the timely establishment of a screening process. When Mr. Weiner joined the firm he was denied access to the relevant files, which were located in a different office, under the control of David Kula, the partner handling the case. Mr. Weiner and all employees of the firm were admonished not to discuss any aspect of the case, and all were subject to discipline. In addition, Mr. Weiner was not allowed to share in the fees derived from this case. The defendants also submitted the affidavit of David Kula, the attorney representing them. In that sworn statement Mr. Kula stated that, as soon as he was informed that his law firm was discussing with Mr. Weiner the possibility of Mr. Weiner's joining the law firm, he and Mr. Weiner "agreed that absolutely nothing of a substantive nature regarding the instant lawsuit would occur" until decisions were made and the clients were made aware of them. The affidavit describes the procedures that were put in effect from December 15, 1989, the date that Mr. Weiner joined the firm. Mr. Weiner's new office was in Scariano's downtown Chicago building, and Mr. Kula's office was located in the firm's Chicago Heights office; each came to the other office only for specific business. Mr. Kula maintained the files for this case in his private office. When it implemented specific screening procedures, the firm required all members and employees of the firm to read and sign the memorandum describing the internal rules. Mr. Kula affirmed that "all of the admonitions of the screening memo have been adhered to by all attorneys and all support staff employed by this firm." We conclude, as did the district court, that the Scariano law firm successfully rebutted the presumption of shared confidences by proving that the screening procedures were timely employed and fully implemented.

AUTHORS' COMMENT:

Now are you satisfied? Has the new firm done enough to protect Mr. Weiner's former client in this case? Even if it has, will the public in general be satisfied? Will clients put full faith and trust in their lawyers if they know that a lawyer can jump to the other side at any time? Is the possibility of public mistrust a reason to adopt a per se rule that would disqualify the firm of a turncoat lawyer no matter what kind of wall it sets up? Reflect on that question for a minute before you read on.

Nevertheless, Ms. Cromley contends that a per se rule of disqualification is needed in this case: This court should require the withdrawal both of her former attorney and of the Scariano law firm he joined while representing her. Even if "specific institutional mechanisms" are in place, she insists, they cannot go far enough "to maintain public confidence in the legal profession."

We cannot agree with this contention. In the first place, the presumption of shared confidences has been found to be irrebuttable only when an entire law firm changes sides, see *Analytica*, and not when one attorney changes sides. Moreover, in *Freeman*, this court recognized that, although the court's duty is "to safeguard the sacrosanct privacy of the attorney-client relationship," it must also be recognized that "disqualification, as a prophylactic device for protecting the attorney-client relationship, is a drastic measure which courts should hesitate to impose except when absolutely necessary." Thus, in deciding the appropriate safeguards necessary in the case of attorney disqualification, we must balance the respective interests of the parties and the public. We hold that the measures employed by the Scariano law firm sufficiently screened Ms. Cromley's former counsel from the School Board's present counsel.

Taking another approach, Ms. Cromley also suggests that Mr. Weiner has not avoided "even the appearance of professional impropriety," in contravention of Canons 4 and 9 of the American Bar Association's Code of Professional Responsibility. We are constrained to disagree; we believe that the carefully constructed safeguards do indeed avoid the appearance of impropriety:

> The test has been described by this circuit as embodying the substance of Canon 4 of the A.B.A. Code of Professional Responsibility, which protects the confidences of a client against disclosure and possible use against him, and of Canon 9, which provides that an attorney must avoid even the appearance of impropriety. Thus, the question before a district court considering a motion for disqualification is "whether it could reasonably be said that during the former representation the attorney might have acquired information related to the subject matter of the subsequent representation."

Accordingly, our analysis under the three-prong "substantial relationship" test, which has led us to the conclusion that disqualification is not required, likewise causes us to conclude that attorney Weiner has not breached the Code of Professional Ethics in his representation of Ms. Cromley.

The district court, following the three-step test for disqualification of attorneys, found that the barriers erected between the attorney and his new firm were appropriate. The record is devoid of any evidence that Mr. Weiner actually divulged client confidences. Therefore, we conclude that the district court did not err in determining that Scariano's screening process was sufficient to prevent disqualification. . . . *Affirmed.*

NOTES AND QUESTIONS

1. ***Do You Agree?*** The *Cromley* opinion is highly controversial. Do you agree with the *Cromley* opinion? Why or why not? Why do you think most courts have rejected the approach taken in *Cromley*?

2. ***The Restatement Approach.*** As we mentioned earlier, the Restatement has lined up in between *Cromley* and the ABA's anti-screen position. Section 124(2) of the Restatement allows firewalls to overcome an imputed disqualification when there is "no substantial risk" that confidential information of the former client will be used with material adverse effect on the former client because (a) whatever confidential client information was acquired by the personally prohibited lawyer "is unlikely to be significant in the subsequent matter"; (b) the personally disqualified lawyer "is subject to screening measures adequate to eliminate participation by that lawyer in the representation"; and (c) the law firm, the client, or someone else has given "timely and adequate notice of the screening . . . to all affected clients." Do you favor the Restatement approach? How does it differ from ABA Rule 1.10(a) and the Seventh Circuit's rule in *Cromley*? Which rule is better? (Better for whom — clients or lawyers?)

3. ***Former Government Lawyers.*** As you recall, ABA Model Rule 1.11 allows firewalls when a lawyer moves from the government to private practice. Why the difference? Why don't the Model Rules allow firewalls when an attorney moves from one private firm to another, as in *Cromley*?

4. ***Does Size Matter?*** Suppose the firm that attorney Weiner joined in *Cromley* was just a two-lawyer firm. Could a screen be effective there? How about a three-lawyer firm? After all, the lawyers in a very small firm usually see each other nearly every day, and have to work together to manage the firm and supervise the employees. If you don't think a screen would work at a two-lawyer or three-lawyer firm, how about at a five-lawyer firm, or a twenty-five lawyer firm, or a fifty-five lawyer firm? Is there a certain size below which a screen can't possibly work often enough to be trusted? In other words, should screens be per se ineffective in firms smaller than a certain number of lawyers? (Should screens be per se effective if a firm is larger than a certain number of lawyers?)

5. ***Is it a Question of Trust — or a Question of Perception?*** Doesn't the ABA trust lawyers to keep secrets? If you move from your old firm to a new firm, and you have a lot of valuable information about an opponent of your firm, will you keep it secret? After all, disclosing the information could subject you to serious sanctions for violating ABA Rule 1.6, including suspension or disbarment — after which it would be difficult to find a new job even if you were eventually readmitted. Besides, you value your integrity. You want your clients to trust you, and you want your new colleagues to respect you. But how would the public perceive the situation? If you changed law firms while loaded with sensitive confidential information, imagine the possible newspaper headlines and the juicy story the reporters could write, such as:

IS LAW FIRM BUYING FOE'S SECRETS?

> Magnus & Helm, one of the city's largest law firms, today hired a new lawyer who has spent the past several years working on the Acme side of the hard-fought *Davis v. Acme* litigation. Although Magnus & Helm denies that it will obtain any confidential information from the new lawyer, several prominent lawyers have expressed concern that confidential information inevitably leaks, even if accidentally, when a lawyer moves to a new firm.

What would the public's perception be? Would the public be right? Will secrets inevitably slip out? Or can lawyers be trusted to keep secrets even when it would be to their economic advantage to share the secrets with their new colleagues?

6. ***A Green-Horn Story.*** What if a partner puts a lot of pressure on you? You're out on the tenth green, just you and the partner handling the Acme litigation, Bob Higgins. No one else is within earshot. Suddenly, Bob cocks his gray head and says to you, "You know, you could really help me out just by telling me a couple of things about Acme. They are things we'll probably find out in discovery anyway, sooner or later, but you could save me a lot of headaches, and save our client a lot of money, if you just tell us what you know about Acme's pricing policies from 1990 to 1993."

You're coming up for partner soon, and you know that Bob really wants the information or he wouldn't put you in this awkward position — and take the risk that you'll report him to the firm's Ethics Committee (or to the bar). If you say, "Sorry, that's confidential," how will he react? How will his friends react? What should you do? Mull it over.

7. ***A Sample Firewall Memorandum.*** Whether your firm uses a firewall to comply with ABA Rule 1.11, or to comply with the rules in a jurisdiction that allows screens, or to help your firm get a former client's consent to a conflict in a state that does not recognize screens, the most important component of a proper firewall is a memorandum formally establishing the screen and notifying the lawyers and staff in the firm about the guidelines. Here is a sample memorandum:

M E M O R A N D U M

TO: All Lawyers and Staff

Melissa Magruder has joined our firm as of today. To abide by the conflict of interest rules, we have screened Ms. Magruder off from all involvement in *Acme v. National Sulfur*, because she formerly represented National Sulfur in a matter that may be related. Therefore, all attorneys and staff must follow these rules:

1. No one is to talk with Magruder about anything relating to *Acme v. National Sulfur.*

2. No one may ask Magruder about her prior representation of National Sulfur, or about any information she may have gained during that representation.

3. Magruder may not have access to the paper or electronic files of *Acme v. National Sulfur.* The paper files will be kept in a separate location under the control of the partner in charge of the case, not in the central file room. They must be signed out each time they are used so that we can, if necessary, present a court with evidence that Magruder has not seen them. The electronic files must be protected by a password not known to or communicated to Magruder.

Breaches of these rules could potentially result in our disqualification from representing Acme in the *National Sulfur* case. That would embarrass the firm and cause inconvenience and expense to our client Acme. It would also cause us to lose substantial fees in this matter (and perhaps to lose other future business from Acme). We trust all personnel will faithfully abide by these rules. If you have any questions, contact the undersigned immediately.

It takes only a few minutes to write a memo like this, but these few minutes can save you and your firm many hours of trouble, and perhaps many hours of work that goes uncompensated due to a conflict of interest. When it comes to firewalls, an ounce of prevention is truly worth a pound of cure.

8. ***Don't Delay in Setting Up a Screen.*** Some states (like Illinois) expressly allow firewalls as a cure for conflicts with former clients in substantially related matters. (That

was the main point of the *Crowley* case.) If a wall is properly set up, then the firm can oppose its former client (or the former client of a lateral hire) even over the former client's objection. But even in the states that allow firewalls as a substitute for client consent, the walls must be set up promptly, using written procedures issued to every attorney in the firm. What happens if that isn't done? Would a court disqualify an entire firm from handling a huge case just because of a technical violation of the screening rules, even if there's no evidence that the lateral hire leaked any of his former client's confidences to his new firm? You bet it would — as Chicago's Winston & Strawn found out in *SK Handtool Corp. v. Dresser Industries, Inc.*, 619 N.E.2d 1282 (Ill. App. Ct. 1993).

In *SK Handtool Corp.*, Winston & Strawn hired a lawyer named Durschlag who had represented SK Handtool and its owners for several years while he was at Chicago's largest firm, Sidley & Austin. In fact, SK was Durschlag's best client when he was at Sidley & Austin. Durschlag had helped SK sell its business to Dresser Industries, and then had monitored the litigation that Sidley & Austin was handling for SK when the deal went sour.

Guess who was handling Dresser's side of the litigation against SK Handtools? Yes, Winston & Strawn. As soon as Durschlag moved to Winston & Strawn, a partner at Sidley & Austin called Winston & Strawn to demand that Winston & Strawn withdraw from representing Dresser against SK. Winston & Strawn brazenly refused — and didn't even set up a firewall around Durschlag until four weeks later, when Sidley & Austin filed a motion to disqualify Winston & Strawn. The court granted the motion to disqualify, and the appellate court affirmed.

The *SK Handtool* opinion noted that Winston & Strawn had worked about *10,000 hours* on the case before it was disqualified. How long is 10,000 hours? Suppose the average lawyer at a large Chicago firm racks up 2,000 hours of billable hours per year. Then five lawyers would need to spend half their time on the case for two full years to run up 10,000 hours. What would that cost the client? Suppose the average lawyer on the case charges $350 per hour. Then 10,000 hours would cost the client $3.5 million. That's a good case for any size firm. Too bad Winston & Strawn lost it for failing to set up a proper firewall right away. Meanwhile, the *SK Handtool* case got the following press on an old feature of LEXIS called "Hotlaw," which commented on hot new cases:

> A law firm may be disqualified from representing its clients where a lawyer newly hired by the firm had worked in the past for the client's adversary even though most of the firm's work for the client was done prior to the new hire's joining the firm. According to Stephen Gillers, NYU Law School legal ethics specialist, some firms "avoid any taint by not hiring laterally or only on rare occasions." Additionally he stated, in New York, law firms are required to wait until a lawsuit is resolved before bringing on a new lawyer with a potential conflict.

What do you think of the comment that some firms avoid conflict problems by refusing to hire laterally, or doing so rarely? Is that good for you or not? Maybe it's good in the short run, because jobs that could be filled by laterals will be filled instead by new lawyers. However, if a large firm wants to establish or rapidly expand a new department, it may need to hire laterally. If the firm wants to establish an environmental law department, for example, it can't wait for all of the associates to mature into partners who are able to attract business and handle sophisticated client matters. Like a baseball team, the firm has to hire a star free agent. But the star can't handle the new department all alone — the star needs help, in the form of new associates. One of those new associates could be you. So lateral moves sometimes expand the total job market.

In the long run, the reluctance to hire laterals will make it harder for you to move from one firm to another. If you practice law for forty years, you may want to change jobs quite a few times. If laterals are not welcome at most firms, it will be hard to move.

You may have to move to a different geographic area to avoid a conflict. And your old firm doesn't have to keep you on until you find a new job — so if it's hard to find a new job, you may just be out of a job.

9. ***Does a Strict Rule Help Clients?*** A strict rule on conflicts of interest is supposed to help clients by ensuring that their confidences will not be used against them by an attorney who moves to an opposing firm. But what about the effect of a strict rule on current clients? Suppose the state adopts a rule that a law firm can't hire a new lawyer until a case raising a conflict is resolved. That may be good for the client of the firm that the lateral lawyer is leaving, but what about clients of the firm that will be hiring this same lateral? Can you imagine the conversation between two partners in the hiring firm? It might go like this:

> MANAGING PARTNER: How's the Cowznofski case coming along — the one against Northwest Airlines? Is it almost settled?
>
> LITIGATION PARTNER: No, there are plenty of billable hours left in the Cowznofski file. We still have twenty or thirty witnesses left to depose, and some motions to compel Northwest to turn over some "smoking gun" documents. It's a nasty case. It could go on for another year.
>
> MANAGING PARTNER: We can't wait that long. We want to beef up our Bankruptcy Department — that's where all the action is now — and the woman we want to hire to head up the Bankruptcy Department represents Northwest in all of its bankruptcy work. That's a big account, and she's a real star. It's Wanda Gordon, of Hill, Dale, and Valli. She's a big name, with a big book of business, and her move to our firm would be a good fit.
>
> LITIGATION PARTNER: I can try to hurry the Cowznofski case along, but if we settle now, we'll be giving up the advantage of some important discovery coming up.
>
> MANAGING PARTNER: See what you can do to bluff your way into a good settlement. If we wait much longer, our star bankruptcy lawyer may not be available — and we need her, soon. Our firm is already in trouble. Our real estate business and our antitrust work is way down. It's headed south like a busload of retirees going to Florida. It would take the legal equivalent of *Jurassic Park* to bring back real estate and antitrust work. If we don't find a new source of billings soon, we'll have to lay off some of the associates, and cut way back on our new hiring. That won't be good for your litigation clients, either. The best hope for the firm is to bank on bankruptcy. See what you can do to settle that Cowznofski case soon, so we can clear the way to go north by Northwest, financially speaking.

Is this conversation realistic? We hope not, but who knows? It's hard to believe that law firms, especially large ones that are in trouble, don't at least *think* about things like this when it comes to conflicts in lateral hiring. So who wins with a strict rule? Does Northwest Airlines, which might get better service at the new firm than at the old one? Does Cowznofski, whose case will be rushed to settlement to make way for its opponent's lawyer? Does a strict rule help Wanda Gordon, the star who can't move yet because of the conflict rules? Does a strict rule help you? What's the point of a strict rule against lateral hires if it doesn't help anyone? OK, maybe it helps clients who don't move when their lawyers move. Is that enough to justify a strict rule?

10. ***Problem: Revolvers and Laterals.*** Let's return to the problem at the beginning of this chapter and address it in light of the various approaches we have discussed to conflicts that arise when lawyers switch from one private firm to another or from public service to a private firm. Based on the current ABA Model Rules of Professional Conduct, answer the questions posed at the outset:

(1) Is any individual lawyer in the firm disqualified from handling the suit against Rugerasers?

(2) If any individual partner is disqualified, may that partner overcome the disqualification by obtaining consent from someone? (If so, whose consent?)

(3) If the firm cannot obtain consent (or does not wish to seek consent), may the firm nevertheless take the case without consent if it builds an ethics wall (a.k.a., a "Chinese Wall")?

Once you have answered those questions, compare your answer to the answer you will get if you apply the ABA's former rules, the Restatement, and the Illinois approach. Which approach is closest to the approach you would take with respect to each lawyer (John, Paul, George, and Ringo) if you could write the rules yourself?

Chapter 25
BUSINESS TRANSACTION WITH CLIENTS

You can make lots of money practicing law. But there is one tree in the Garden of Eden from which you should not eat: business deals with your clients. Business deals with clients are technically a subset of concurrent conflicts, but they are so fraught with risk that we're giving them their own separate chapter.

Business transactions with clients are governed by Rule 1.8(a). If you are very, very careful to follow every nuance of Rule 1.8(a) to the letter, you may ethically enter into a business deal with a client. The rules of legal ethics allow it. But be careful. Next to stealing from your clients, one of the quickest ways to get into trouble is to enter into business deals with your clients. The best advice, in our view, is: *Don't do it.* Don't enter into business deals with your clients. The risk is nearly always much greater than the reward.

At first, you may think you're doing the client a favor by entering into the deal. Maybe the client needs a loan, and says to you, "Please lend me the money. I've been turned down at a lot of banks." Or maybe your client is starting up a business and is looking for investors. The client says to you, "I need funding, and there's no one I'd rather give this opportunity to than you, my lawyer. Get in on the ground floor. This could be your chance to make some serious money."

Yes, it could be your chance to do your client a favor or to make some serious money, but it could also be your chance to get suspended or disbarred. Sooner or later, many deals with clients go sour. If a deal crashes and burns, the client is likely to be bitter about the business failure and hounded day and night by creditors. The client, now desperate, may lash out like a wounded bear at everyone that comes near, including you. When you try to collect your loan as a creditor or assert your rights as a shareholder, your former client and friend may become irrational and resist your efforts. When you persist in trying to protect your own financial interests, your former client may complain to the bar association about you, alleging that you took advantage of her trust or somehow violated Rule 1.8(a) when you first entered into the deal.

If a client complains that you cheated her in a business transaction during the attorney-client relationship, your number may be up. The courts and disciplinary authorities have been extremely protective of clients in these situations because lawyers are generally in a vastly superior bargaining position whenever entering into transactions with clients. Lawyers tend to have a better understanding of the terms, the drafting choices, the risks, the remedies, and every other aspect of business transactions. Unless you have precisely followed every letter of the rules on business deals with clients, you will be headed for almost certain discipline — and harsh discipline at that.

A. THE RULES ON BUSINESS TRANSACTIONS WITH CLIENTS

What are the rules that you must follow? Delaware Rule 1.8(a) lays down the law as it stands in many jurisdictions:

> (a) A lawyer shall not enter into a business transaction with a client or knowingly acquire an ownership, possessory, security or other pecuniary interest adverse to a client unless:
>
> (1) the transaction and terms on which the lawyer acquires the interest are fair and reasonable to the client and are fully disclosed and transmitted in writing to the client in a manner which can be reasonably understood by the client;

(2) the client is advised in writing of the desirability of seeking and is given a reasonable opportunity to seek the advice of independent counsel in the transaction; and

(3) the client gives informed consent, in a writing signed by the client, to the essential terms of the transaction and the lawyer's role in the transaction, including whether the lawyer is representing the client in the transaction.[1]

Thus, if you want to enter into a business deal with a client, or if you want to "acquire an ownership, possessory, security or other pecuniary interest adverse to a client," you must adhere to five requirements:

1. The deal, including all of its terms, must be fair and reasonable to the client.
2. You must fully disclose the terms of the deal *in writing* — and not in legal mumbo-jumbo, but in words that the client can understand (meaning that *your* client can understand them, not some hypothetical "average" client).
3. You must urge the client *in writing* to seek an independent lawyer to counsel him about the deal.
4. You must give the client a reasonable amount of time to find and consult with independent counsel.
5. You must obtain the client's informed consent *in a writing* that (a) spells out the main terms of the deal, (b) states whether or not you are representing the client in the deal, and (c) is signed by the client.

Unless you follow all five of these separate requirements precisely, a grievance by a dissatisfied client will very likely lead to suspension, disbarment, or other professional discipline. The disciplinary authorities don't fool around on complaints under Rule 1.8(a).

When does Rule 1.8(a) apply? It applies to every business transaction between you and one of your clients (other than "a standard commercial transaction . . . for products or services that the client generally markets to others," see Rule 1.8, Comment 1, such as buying a product from a client's store or getting your teeth checked out by a client who is a dentist). For example, Rule 1.8(a) applies when you:

- lend money to a client
- borrow money from a client
- buy a car or a house or any other substantial goods or services from a client (again, other than a standard commercial transaction)
- sell anything substantial to a client
- invest in a client's business venture
- accept an investment from a client in a company in which you own a substantial interest

Thus, you cannot lend, borrow, buy, sell, invest, or accept investments if a client is on the other end of the transaction unless you comply *to the letter* with Rule 1.8(a).

B. WHAT IF YOU DON'T FOLLOW THE RULES?

What if you don't follow Rule 1.8(a) exactly? You are asking for trouble. But what if your client is not hurt? What if you enter into a business transaction with a client and the client comes out whole, or maybe even makes a little money? Are you OK? Do courts follow a "no harm, no foul" rule? No, they don't. You must follow the letter of the law on business transactions with clients. If you fail to fully disclose the exact terms of the transaction, or if the terms are not fair and reasonable to the client, or if you do not put those terms in plain English that your client could readily understand, or if you fail to reduce the terms to writing, or if you forget to tell your client that she ought to consult with independent counsel, or if you do not give your client a reasonable opportunity to get an independent lawyer's advice, or if you fail to get the client's signature on a

[1] Delaware Rule 1.8(a) is identical to ABA Model Rule 1.8(a).

document that states the main terms of the transaction and tells the client whether you are or are not representing her — in other words, if you fail to touch even one of the bases set out by Rule 1.8(a), then you are in trouble. You are subject to discipline for failing to adhere to the rules even if your client doesn't lose one red cent.

What if the transaction is outside the scope of your work for the client, and you're not giving the client any legal advice about the transaction? For example, suppose you come across a terrific opportunity for investment — one so good that you personally plan to invest as much as you can spare. This is really a great opportunity, so you want to share it with your friends, including some of your clients. Is that covered by the rules of professional conduct? Yes, it is. The rules don't care a whit whether you are working on the deal for your client, or whether the deal is totally independent of your work for the client. The trigger is whether the deal is with a client, period. If it is, you have to follow the rules with exactitude.

What does that mean? How much do you have to disclose about your investment opportunity to satisfy Rule 1.8(a)? Is it enough to say (truthfully, of course), "This is a great investment. I'm sinking a lot of my free cash into it myself?" Is it enough to be honest and act in completely good faith? The next case will help you answer these questions, and it will drive home the enormous scope of your liability when you start lending to, borrowing from, or investing together with your clients. The case was decided under DR 5-104, which was the ABA Model Code's predecessor to ABA Model Rule 1.8(a), but the concepts remain the same.

IN THE MATTER OF BREEN

830 P.2d 462 (Ariz. 1992)

Claborne, J.

The State Bar of Arizona charged Dennis M. Breen, III, Respondent, with several violations of the Arizona Code of Professional Responsibility.

A formal complaint was filed against Respondent, and a hearing was held before State Bar Local Hearing Committee 5-D ("Committee"). The Committee concluded that Respondent violated several ethical rules by repeatedly engaging in activities which resulted in obvious existing and potential conflicts of interest. The Committee recommended that Respondent be suspended from the practice of law for two years and that, as a condition of reinstatement, he be required to pass the State Bar exam on the subject of ethics and successfully complete either twelve hours of continuing legal education in the field of ethics or a course in ethics at an accredited law school. Respondent objected to the Committee's Findings of Fact, Conclusions of Law, and Recommendations. Those objections were heard by the Disciplinary Commission ("Commission") which voted to affirm and adopt the Committee's determination. Respondent appeals from the Commission report.

AUTHORS' COMMENT:

The Committee recommends that Breen be suspended for two years and not allowed back into the legal profession until he passes the ethics part of the bar exam again and takes ethics CLE courses or the ethics course at a law school. We don't suppose you want to take this course over again after you finish law school — but if you enter into a business deal with a client without following the rules, you might have to.

Facts

Respondent was admitted to the Arizona bar in 1978. Before admission to the Arizona bar, the Respondent was licensed to practice law in New York State. He worked in New York in an investor capacity. The facts in this matter arise from Respondent's representation of a husband and wife ("the clients") from 1979 to 1982. In 1985, the clients successfully prosecuted a malpractice action against Respondent in the Pima County Superior Court and were awarded a judgment against Respondent for approximately $90,000.

Respondent's violations arise out of seven different matters, each of which was considered in detail by the Committee and Commission. Since the ethical violations in some of the matters are the same, we elect not to outline each matter, but discuss three which we find representative.

[W]hile acting as an investment broker, Respondent urged the clients to invest in two oil ventures, Pioneer Oil and Viola Oil. Respondent received a commission on all investments he raised in the form of credits toward his own investment, a fact known to the clients. However, in connection with the investments, Respondent never obtained competitive bids on the drilling contracts nor did he conduct independent investigations of geology reports from the drillers. The ventures were managed by persons with no experience in the oil business, a fact known to Respondent. None of the drilling produced any oil. The Committee found that although acting as a businessman rather than an attorney in this matter, Respondent was to be held to the same standard of ethics and competence in any transaction with a client as if he were actually acting as an attorney. The Committee then found that Respondent failed to act as a reasonable attorney in exercising his professional judgment for the protection of his clients, a violation of DR 5-104. The Commission affirmed this decision.

Discussion

1. The Violations

Although Respondent's clients knew he was receiving commissions on their oil investments, he did not act as a prudent businessman. There was never a competitive bid on the oil drilling contracts, the people managing the properties had no experience in the oil business, and there was never a real investigation concerning the geology of the area where the wells were to be drilled. A drilling that produced oil would actually have been a surprise. We have often said a lawyer's intent of acting with improper motives is not material to the application of DR 5-104. What is important is that clients are entitled to depend on the fairness of their lawyers and know they have some reasonable amount of protection. Certainly, competitive bidding, selecting people who have experience in the oil business, and investigating the structure and composition of the drilling area are basic to oil development. Respondent urged his clients to enter into two oil ventures which had not followed these basic oil business practices, while obtaining a personal advantage by way of the commissions paid on these investments.

It cannot be said that these investments were not questionable. They were. Respondent could not have known whether the oil ventures were good or bad since he made no rudimentary investigation. When a lawyer has this lack of information and fails to disclose it to his client, he can do substantial harm to his client. Full disclosure to a client under DR 5-104(A) requires that the attorney give the client specific advice about the need to seek independent counsel and explain to the client in detail all risks associated with the business transaction. . . . [C]lients, sophisticated or not, rely upon the judgment of their lawyers even though the particular transaction may involve no legal advice. Here, Respondent received a commission for obtaining his clients as investors in an oil venture. Even though Respondent completely disclosed the commission, the fact remains that his clients had or should have had a reasonable belief in their lawyer's judgment. It is our belief that even though there was a full disclosure by Respondent, the fiduciary relationship between lawyer and client still existed. The facts support the perception that the clients believed they were dealing with "a person whose advice and counsel should be given weight and respect, rather than as one whose words must be taken with that grain of salt that the law expects from people dealing with those who are not fiduciaries."

AUTHORS' COMMENT:

If business transactions with clients are so fraught with danger, why don't we just ban them altogether? Why don't the rules say, "A lawyer shall not enter into a business transaction with a client," period? The court now tries to answer this question.

We have said that the better rule may be to completely prohibit lawyer-client business dealings. Yet, the practical difficulties with such an absolute bar . . . prevent[] its enactment. As a general rule, and to minimize ethical problems, no lawyer should allow a client to invest or otherwise participate in the lawyer's business ventures unless the client obtains independent legal advice. Nothing else will protect our profession's integrity and the public interest.

Therefore, we do not now impose an absolute bar on this type of transaction. We wish, however, to emphasize that when a lawyer receives a personal benefit apart from the client's fee from a transaction in which he represents a client, the lawyer's ethical obligation is not always fulfilled by merely disclosing the existence of the personal stake, explaining the potential consequences, and obtaining the client's consent. There is an inherent potential for a conflict of interest in such situations, and the lawyer must always ensure that his or her personal interest does not interfere with the unfettered exercise of professional judgment the client is entitled to expect under the circumstances. The best way to achieve this, of course, is to see that the client has independent advice.

With the gradual disappearance of rural America and the advancing complexities of modern life, the reason for continuation of less than a complete prohibition of lawyer-client business dealings may also be disappearing.

We feel the Committee and Commission findings are reasonable, that they are justified by the entire record, and we therefore adopt all of them.

2. The Sanctions

Still, we must decide whether to impose the Commission's recommended sanctions. Although Respondent disputes some of the facts found by the Committee and the Commission, the record supports the findings made.

We begin with the reason for attorney discipline. The purpose of discipline is not to punish the offender, but to protect the public and deter other attorneys from the same kind of conduct. In deciding the type of sanction, if any, that should be imposed, we consider a number of factors. These factors include the duty violated, the mental state of the lawyer, the potential or actual injury caused by the misconduct, and the existence of aggravating or mitigating factors.

We agree with the Committee and Commission and impose a two-year suspension with the requirement that reinstatement will be conditional upon passing the Arizona Bar ethics exam and successfully completing either twelve hours of continuing legal education in the field of ethics or a course in ethics at an accredited college of law.

AUTHORS' COMMENT:

That seems like a pretty tough penalty — but wait until you read the dissent!

CORCORAN, J., dissenting.

I respectfully dissent.

I believe that Respondent's egregious misconduct requires disbarment. I agree with the hearing committee of the State Bar which concluded:

> We believe that Respondent failed to rise even to the level of ethics required of the average business man, and we believe that, as an attorney, Respondent should have adhered to a higher standard of ethics than that expected of a member of the general public.

Respondent should be disbarred.

NOTES AND QUESTIONS

1. ***Hard Test.*** The *Breen* court is typical of court decisions on business deals with clients. Courts have little tolerance for bad business deals between clients and lawyers, and the test is stacked heavily against the lawyers. As the *Breen* court said in a footnote: "Courts and legal scholars seem to believe that the fiduciary relationship of lawyer and client requires a test that is demanding of the lawyer and tolerant and forgiving of the client." That's a test you don't want to take.

2. ***How Did Anyone Find Out?*** How did the disciplinary committee find out about Breen? Because his clients sued him for legal malpractice, and won a $90,000 judgment against him. The evidence against Breen was so strong that the trial judge (as well as one of the clients) filed a complaint with the State Bar. The Bar then investigated and found a pattern of bad transactions with clients. You just read the ultimate result.

3. ***A More Conventional Situation.*** The *Breen* opinion is significant both because it shows how far courts will go to penalize business transactions with clients and because it offers a thoughtful discussion of the policy behind the rules allowing business transactions with clients. We want to give you a more conventional example of a business deal with a client as well. Here it is, short and sweet. The lesson is simple: Don't borrow money from your clients. Go to a bank. You may pay more in interest, but at least you won't get suspended from the practice of law.

THE FLORIDA BAR v. BLACK

602 So. 2d 1298 (Fla. 1992)

MCDONALD, J.

. . . [Attorney Martin L. Black] borrowed funds from a client, left the client completely unsecured in the transaction, failed to advise the client of his right to separate representation, promised to pay the client a usurious rate of interest, never informed the client of the illegality of the transaction, and used the client in an effort to obtain a personal loan. Ultimately, the client was repaid and suffered no loss, but, while these transactions were occurring, the client suffered exposure to potential damage.

The referee, in aggravation, found that Black had a selfish motive, his client was vulnerable, and Black had substantial experience in the law and should have known better. In mitigation the referee noted that Black had no prior disciplinary record, made a timely good faith effort to make restitution or to rectify the consequences of his misconduct, was remorseful, made a full and free disclosure to the bar and cooperated in these proceedings, and had no intent to deprive his client of property or to deceive him. The referee's factual findings are supported by the record, and we approve them.

Lawyers must be extremely careful in their personal dealings with clients. Lawyers act in a special fiduciary capacity with their clients and must avoid using that relationship for personal gain. This case is one where a lawyer in difficult personal circumstances seized upon a chance for an emergency loan when he was unable to obtain funds elsewhere. He took advantage of an unsophisticated client, and a clear violation exists. On the other hand, the extensive mitigation as found by the referee militates against a severe punishment.

[W]e suspend Martin L. Black from the practice of law for sixty days. The sixty-day suspension will begin thirty days from the date this opinion is filed, thereby giving Black time to close out his practice according to the Rules Regulating The Florida Bar and protect his clients' interests. He shall accept no new business from the date this opinion is filed. Following the suspension, Black will be on probation for two years during which time his files are subject to inspection at any time by The Florida Bar. As a further condition of probation, he must take and successfully pass the ethics portion of The Florida Bar Examination within that two-year period.

NOTES AND QUESTIONS

1. ***Brother, Can You Spare Me a Dime?*** When lawyers have serious money problems, they tend to do things they wouldn't normally do — often things that violate the rules. Attorney Black borrowed money from a client when he got into an "emergency." Unfortunately, he picked the wrong way out of his troubles.

Money doesn't come easy, even to lawyers. Sometimes you may need to borrow. But don't be shortsighted. If you get into money trouble, don't borrow from a client; get help. See a financial counselor, or one of your law partners, or someone who can help you through the tough times. Borrow money on your credit cards, or from a finance company, or from any legitimate source. But don't borrow money from a client. If you try to take the short way out, you may get suspended. Then you'll have *real* money problems.

Likewise, if your client gets into serious money problems, don't lend your client money. Lending to a client can get you into just as much trouble as borrowing from a client. Instead, find someone who can help the client develop a long-term solution to the money problems. Loyalty to a client doesn't require you to become a banker.

2. ***Can You Resist Temptation?*** You can resist temptation if you want to. A little practice resisting temptation may help. Here's a role-play on business transactions with clients.

A Scenario on Business Deals with Clients

Dunwood Abercrombie and Mrs. Edith Buxton are wealthy clients of Loeber & Harrington, a small but well regarded real estate law firm. Mr. Abercrombie and Mrs. Buxton operate as partners in real estate syndications, and are highly leveraged (i.e., they operate using a lot of borrowed money). They are on their way to see their lawyers to discuss the tax consequences of purchasing a condominium for investment purposes. Just before they left for the attorney's office, the bank called and told them that they were being refused the $500,000 mortgage they had applied for because credit records demonstrate that they are too heavily leveraged (they owe too much already) and have missed payments in the past on two other properties.

On the way to the lawyers' office Mrs. Buxton developed the idea that maybe the lawyers at Loeber & Harrington would welcome the opportunity to join them in the condominium investment because the lawyers are doing well and might be looking for a good investment. The proposed investment involves purchase of a three-story condominium for $3,575,000 for use as a rental property.

When Mr. Abercrombie and Mrs. Buxton suggest that the lawyers go in with them to buy the condominium, how should the lawyers at Loeber & Harrington respond? (By the way, in case it matters to you, Mr. Abercrombie and Mrs. Buxton are very good clients of the firm — they have paid about $2,500,000 in legal fees over the last few years.)

If the lawyers want to go forward with the condominium investment, what do the Rules of Professional Conduct require? What should or must the lawyers tell the clients? What are the actual or potential conflicts? Can the clients waive any potential conflicts? Should there be a per se rule prohibiting such business arrangements between lawyers and clients? Should the lawyers enter into this deal? What can go wrong?

C. THE FIRM'S CONFLICTS COMMITTEE MEETS AGAIN

You are still a member of your firm's Conflicts Committee and it is time for another meeting. Below are the items on the agenda for this week's Committee meeting. As to each item on the agenda, be prepared to discuss three things:

1. *Nature of the conflicts:* What are the actual or potential conflicts?

2. *Governing rules:* What rules of professional conduct or other legal authorities govern the particular conflict?

3. *Decision or further questions:* Should the firm accept (or continue) the representation? This question breaks down into three subparts:

> (a) If so, are there any conditions or prerequisites to accepting the matter? For example, must the client's consent be obtained? If so, what must be disclosed to the client to obtain a valid consent? Are there any limitations on the representation, such as parties the firm will not sue?
>
> (b) If the firm cannot accept the matter, why not? Does some rule or other law prohibit you from accepting the matter, or is the firm rejecting the matter solely for policy reasons?
>
> (c) If you cannot decide whether to accept the matter until you obtain further information, what additional information do you need?

Items on the Conflict Committee's Agenda

A. *Investing in a client's business.* Several of your college classmates have asked you to provide legal assistance to help them organize a small business. They cannot afford to pay you, so they have offered instead to give you a share of the venture's profits, and to enter into a three-year retainer agreement in which the company will guarantee you a minimum annual fee of $30,000 for legal services. They also ask you if you or your law partners would like to invest in the business so you can be "in on the ground floor." Is the suggested arrangement permitted? If so, under what conditions?

B. *Borrowing money from a client.* C. Duncan Alston, a partner at your firm, represents a wealthy client named Danforth Kensington. Alston recently suffered some serious losses trading collateralized debt obligations (CDOs) and gold futures, and he needs money. Your firm's law practice is booming, but many of the cases are on contingent fee and Alston won't have the money for awhile. Mr. Kensington has offered to lend Alston $20,000 to tide him over for the next six months. Alston has agreed to pay above-market rates for the loan and to have your firm do the paperwork so there won't be any attorney fees for Kensington. Can Alston go ahead?

C. *Lending money to a client.* Your firm represents a wonderful business woman named Zoe Braid. She had a lot of money at one time and was in a lucrative position at

Signa Insurance, but the company squeezed her out and she's fallen on hard times. Your firm sued Signa on Ms. Braid's behalf for breach of contract and age and sex discrimination, and Cigna's attorney has virtually caved in. Your firm is negotiating a settlement, and the main sticking point now is damages. Your firm's accounting expert is studying the problem, and you expect that the case will settle in the $500,000 range — but not for at least three or four months. Ms. Braid, though, can't wait. She has just come across an outstanding business opportunity, and she needs money quickly to make the investment. She has asked to borrow $200,000 from your firm immediately, at fair market rates, no more than what a bank would charge. She will pay you back as soon as her case settles. OK?

Chapter 26

INTRODUCTION TO LEGAL FEES: LEGAL SERVICES FOR CLIENTS WHO CAN PAY

In this chapter, we introduce a fundamental tension that lies at the heart of the legal profession: is the practice of law a *profession* or a *business*? This is essentially a debate about one thing: money. How do lawyers make money, who pays the money, and how do lawyers give it back? Writ large, the debate over whether the practice of law is a business or a profession reflects the constant struggle between the ideal that lawyers have a duty to serve the public and the reality that in order to serve the public, lawyers have to make a living.

Since the mid-1980s, much of this business vs. profession debate has played out in the form of a high-minded discussion about lawyer professionalism and the need for the legal profession to recommit itself to the solid, inspiring values that supposedly defined the legal profession of a bygone era. In the following provocative remarks, however, Professor Monroe Freedman of Hofstra University School of Law challenged the notion that lawyers once adhered to higher standards of professionalism than they do today. In *The Lawyer as a Professional: The Golden Age of Law that Never Was*, Professor Freedman said:

> [N]o one has managed to provide a date for the golden age of professionalism. All we know is when it wasn't. It wasn't in 1605, when, in *King Lear*, Shakespeare expressed the quintessence of "nothing" as "the breath of an unfee'd lawyer." And it wasn't in 1645, when Virginia enacted legislation expelling "all mercenary lawyers" on the ground that "many troublesome suits are multiplied by the unskillfulness and covetousness of attorneys, who have more intended their own profit and their inordinate lucre than the good and benefit of their clients." Nor was the golden age in 1853, when Charles Dickens wrote in *Bleak House* that "the one great principle of English law is to make business for itself." Neither was it in 1887, when a Georgia bar report complained of a "growing tendency to regard [the legal profession] as a trade, . . . a career for money-making — for accumulating wealth." And surely the golden age of professionalism was not in 1904. That was the year that future Secretary of State Elihu Root, delivering a Yale Law School graduation address, told his audience that the truly successful lawyer could aspire to "some prize of business life" even, maybe, the presidency of a corporation. Only a year later, Louis Brandeis, then a prominent Boston attorney, was complaining in an article that lawyers had "become largely a part of the business world." And a year after that, legal scholar Roscoe Pound bemoaned in an essay that the legal profession was devolving into a trade. In fact, the latter half of the 20th century came early that year, because Pound also found it necessary to denounce "exaggerated contentious[ness]" in litigation. The golden age had still not begun in 1934. . . . Associate Justice Harlan Stone observed in an address at the University of Michigan Law School, "The successful lawyer of our day more often than not is the . . . general manager of a new type of factory, whose legal product is increasingly the result of mass production methods."[1]

This chapter introduces the roots of the business/profession debate and asks you to explore your own feelings about the proper role of the financial and business aspects of the legal profession. In this chapter, we consider the problems with various types of fee

---

[1] Reprinted from the TEXAS LAWYER, January 7, 1991, by the Texas Center for Law and Professionalism, *available at* http://www.txethics.org/resources_lawyerprofessional.asp?view=2Freedman (last visited Nov. 5, 2008).

arrangements. In the next chapter, we consider how the legal profession can serve people who cannot afford to pay legal fees under any arrangement.

A. THE FIVE BASIC TYPES OF LEGAL FEES: FLAT, HOURLY, CONTINGENT, VALUE, AND HYBRID

Before we get into the complexities of legal fees, let's briefly describe and discuss the five basic types of legal fees: flat, hourly, contingent, value, and hybrid.

Flat fees. A flat fee is a fee that a lawyer will charge to complete a given service whether it takes a long time or a short time. It is simultaneously a minimum fee and a maximum fee. Like minimum fees, flat fees are still permissible in every jurisdiction. Of course, like all fees, flat fees must be reasonable and must be at least partially refundable. If the lawyer does not finish the job, the lawyer must refund a fair portion of the flat fee.

Why do lawyers charge flat fees? First, it saves them a lot of administrative time. It takes time to keep track of time — to record the time, transfer the time to a bill, review the bill for errors and fairness, and perhaps explain the bill to the client. ("Why did it take four hours to go to the county courthouse?" the client may want to know.) Flat fees make it unnecessary to record or explain time.

Second, low flat fees attract clients. Clients compare flat fees for the same services. A client who sees advertisements saying that one lawyer charges $500 for a name change and another lawyer charges only $300 for a name change is likely to go with the less expensive lawyer. This may not be a wise choice because the lower priced lawyer may take longer or be more likely to bungle the job, but many clients are willing to take that risk. If enough clients opt for the lower flat fee, the low-fee lawyer will have a "volume" practice, doing the same basic tasks over and over. If those tasks can be routinized, they can be done in a fraction of the time (and thus a fraction of the cost) it would take a general practitioner to do the same work. A volume practice works on the same principle as Henry Ford's Model T assembly line — doing the same tasks over and over leads to efficiencies of scale.

If the client terminates a flat fee lawyer before the job is done, however, figuring out how much of a flat fee to refund can be tricky. Suppose a lawyer agrees to do a residential house closing for a flat fee of $1,000, up front. After the lawyer has gathered some documents and prepared some of the necessary papers, the client learns that the house is infested with termites and she informs the lawyer that she will not be going through with the closing. How much is the lawyer required to refund?

The usual way is to figure out what percentage of the work the lawyer has already done and refund the unperformed percentage times $1,000. Thus, if the lawyer has done 60% of the work, the lawyer would refund $400 (representing the 40% of the work that has not yet been done). But there's a problem. How does the lawyer calculate what percentage of the work has been done? Doing the legal work for a house closing is not like downloading software from the Internet — there's no blue bar telling the lawyer what percentage of the work has been done. The lawyer simply has to make a good faith estimate.

Another way to calculate the refund is for the lawyer to charge by the hour for the work already done, refunding the remainder. Suppose the lawyer charges $250 per hour and does 3 hours of work before the client calls off the deal. The lawyer would then refund $250. But if the lawyer wants to use this method, then the engagement letter or retainer agreement should state explicitly that the lawyer's rate for this work is $250 per hour, and if the client terminates the lawyer before the work is complete then the lawyer will charge for all completed work (up to the amount of the flat fee) at the lawyer's hourly rate. This may be a fair and objective way to calculate the refund, but it requires the lawyer to keep track of time spent, thus taking away one of the main advantages for the lawyer of charging flat fees in the first place.

Contingent fees. A lawyer charging a contingent fee does not charge any fee unless the client obtains some monetary recovery. If there is a recovery, the lawyer takes a fee (and the costs and expenses of litigation) out of the recovery. If there is no fee, the lawyer usually absorbs the costs and expenses of litigation out of his own pocket. Thus, lawyers have a high incentive to obtain some recovery on behalf of their clients, because if they don't obtain any recovery, they don't earn any fee.

Despite the advantages of contingent fees, many people believe that contingent fees should be prohibited or strongly regulated. For example, some critics say that: (1) contingent fees encourage "nuisance" suits that clog the courts and impose unfair burdens on blameless defendants and their insurance companies; (2) contingent fees make it more profitable for plaintiffs' lawyers to accept inadequate settlements that provide some fees rather than to go to trial and risk no fee; and (3) contingent fees unjustly enrich lawyers who charge substantial contingent fees (typically one-third or more) even for cases in which liability is clear and some monetary recovery is virtually certain. Most countries in the world prohibit contingent fees. Should the legislatures or the legal profession ban contingent fees, or at least control them beyond the limited controls in effect now? (We cover the problems of contingent fees in more detail in a separate chapter.)

At a minimum, should lawyers be required to offer their clients a choice between an hourly rate and a contingent fee? The ABA Standing Committee on Ethics and Professional Responsibility has said so. In Informal Opinion 86-1521 (1986), the Standing Committee stated:

> [W]hen there is any doubt whether a contingent fee is consistent with the client's best interest, which can normally be determined only in light of all the facts and circumstances after consultation with the client, the lawyer must offer the client the opportunity to engage counsel on a reasonable fixed fee basis before entering into a contingent fee arrangement.

Do you agree? What kind of client might prefer an hourly rate to a contingent fee, and why? What kind of client would prefer a contingent fee to an hourly rate?

Hourly rate fees. In an hourly fee arrangement, you charge for each hour you work, so your economic incentive is primarily to work as many hours as possible on a given matter. If you are a partner, the more hours you work, the more money you will earn. If you are an associate, you will often be pressured to work a certain number of billable hours per year. The more hours you bill, the more money you will make for the firm and the more impressed the partners will be. In either case, time is money. The more time, the more money. Results don't matter in hourly rate matters (at least in the short run). You get paid win or lose. You bill for your time, not for the results. Thus, an hourly rate environment may distort a lawyer's judgment and skew client relations.

Surprisingly, most lawyers did not begin charging by the hour until the 1950s, when clients began demanding that lawyers bill on the same basis as nearly all other professionals. Other professionals (except doctors) billed by the hour, which seemed logical and fair. Clients paid only for the legal work that was actually done. A lawyer who needed more hours to complete a task was paid more, and a lawyer who needed fewer hours to complete a task was paid less. But, as might have been predicted by the law of unintended consequences, hourly rates spawned a variety of problems. Here are examples of some of the problems associated with hourly rate billing:

Inefficient work. When lawyers work on an hourly rate, working inefficiently is profitable. Why use someone else's model pleadings if you can bill a different client to start over from scratch on a similar project? The longer it takes you to do something — the less efficiently you work — the more you can bill.

Overkill. Overkill is also profitable. Why do a quick-and-dirty, $5,000 job, on a legal problem if the client can afford to pay $10,000? The extra $5,000 in research may have very little benefit to your client — some lawyers say that you find out 90% of what you need to know in the first 10% of your legal research — but doing the "deluxe" job has a lot of benefit to your law firm because more hours mean more revenue, and more "profits per partner," which is a key statistic that many lawyers hone in on when deciding on career moves (such as merging with another firm, moving to a different firm, or staying with the current firm).

Unnecessary projects. Talking the client into letting you do new work is also a money maker. When a regulatory agency proposes a new rule, for example, it pays to convince your client to retain you to draft up some comments on the proposed rule. If the new rule is adopted, it pays to convince your client that you should analyze the new rule for its possible impact on your client's business. Of course, it may turn out that the proposed or final rule will have very little impact on your client — but even if the rule would have little impact on your client's fortunes, billing for the time it takes you to comment and interpret a rule can have a big impact on your own fortune.

Lack of mentoring. Mentoring was for generations a vital way of transmitting the values and skills of experienced lawyers to inexperienced lawyers. But lawyers who bill by the hour are reluctant to spend time intensively mentoring younger attorneys, because clients do not want to pay for on-the-job training, especially when competitive forces have pushed up hourly rates in order to pay the high salaries commanded by young lawyers.

Decreased pro bono work. The more law firms charge by the hour, the more acutely they seem to feel the loss of revenue that results when lawyers in the firm perform pro bono work.

Decreased associate satisfaction. When law firms bill by the hour, law firm revenue is directly proportional to the number of hours billed. The higher the billable hours, the higher the law firm revenue. This correlation has led to enormous pressure on associates to bill more hours. The more hours associates bill, the unhappier they seem to become.

In short, when the client is paying for time instead of for results, the lawyer has an incentive to work inefficiently, to do more work than the client needs, to convince the client to buy legal services that the client could do without, to spend less time mentoring young lawyers, and to spend less time on pro bono work — and young lawyers caught up in the billable hours tournament grow increasingly unhappy at work.

Of course, hourly rate economics at law firms is not all one-sided. They come with some built-in controls. For example:

Clients can fire expensive lawyers. A client has the right to fire a lawyer any time for any reason. If a lawyer is sending bills that are too high, the client can fire the lawyer in the middle of the matter and get a new lawyer who charges less.

Clients can find another lawyer for future matters. If you bill an hourly client too much (in total), the client may go elsewhere for legal services next time, or may not pay your firm's full bill. If the client is a corporation or a wealthy individual who is likely to have many legal needs over time, charging too much will kill the goose that can lay golden eggs.

Clients appreciate value. If you do a good job for a client without overkill (meaning without racking up a huge bill), your client will benefit financially and may have more money to spend on legal fees in the long run.

Good work generates referrals. If you deliver legal work at a good value (meaning you complete hourly rate tasks reasonably quickly and deliver a reasonable bill), your clients may recommend you to others.

Reasonable rates help clients grow. If your client is a small business, good legal work at reasonable rates can help the client grow, and a growing client always has new and more complex legal problems.

Corporations can shift more legal work to you. If your client is a large business, it can usually shift some legal tasks from its in-house lawyers to your firm or from other outside law firms to your law firm. The lower your bills, the more likely the client is to shift the business to you.

Value billing. As its name implies, value billing charges a client based on the value of the work to the client rather than simply the effort and skill expended by the lawyer. Value billing comes in three basic forms: (a) the lawyer and client negotiate the value of a project at the beginning of a matter (meaning that value billing is just a form of flat fee); (b) the lawyer and client negotiate the value of a project at the end of the matter (sometimes with a formula in place in case the lawyer and client cannot reach agreement); and (c) the lawyer unilaterally determines the value at the end of the matter.

Before lawyers began charging by the hour, they typically charged based on the value of the work to the client. Typically, the lawyer alone calculated the value at the end of the matter, taking into account factors such as the results obtained, the importance of the work to the client, the lawyer's level of expertise, and the amount of effort it took to do the work. Clients liked value billing because they did not pay a lot for services that turned out to be worth little. Lawyers thus had an incentive to deliver value.

Today, clients seldom trust lawyers enough to say, "When you finish your work on the matter, just charge me what you think the work is worth." That is too open-ended. On the other hand, lawyers seldom trust clients enough to let clients decide what the work is worth after the lawyer has already done it. Therefore, lawyers and clients using value billing are more likely to negotiate the fair value of a lawyer's work either before or after the work is done.

Hybrid fees. Hybrid fees combine two or more of the four types of billing arrangements just described — flat, hourly, contingent, and value. Here are some examples:

Contingent hourly fees. A lawyer might charge a client a contingent hourly rate, to be paid only if the client wins, and to be paid without reference to the amount of recovery. Typically, a lawyer's contingent hourly rate is higher than the lawyer's regular (non-contingent) hourly rate. If the client recovers a sum of money, the client would pay the lawyer $300 per hour, up to the amount of the client's recovery (unless the lawyer and client set a lower maximum fee). To illustrate, if the lawyer usually charges clients $200 per hour win or lose, the lawyer might charge a client a contingent hourly rate of $300 per hour to prosecute the client's lawsuit, with a maximum fee of $30,000. Let's look at some possible results under this arrangement.

If the lawyer spends 50 hours on the case and settles for $60,000, then the lawyer will take a fee of $15,000 (= $300 × 50), which is less than a standard one-third contingent fee. But if the lawyer spends 100 hours on the case and recovers the same $60,000, then the lawyer will take a fee of $30,000 (= $300 × 100), which is considerably more than a standard one-third contingent fee. If the lawyer spends 100 hours and recovers only $40,000, the lawyer will still take a fee of $30,000, which would amount to a contingent fee of 75%. And if the lawyer spends 100 hours and recovers only $20,000, then the client will still have to pay the $30,000 maximum fee, meaning that the client will have to give the entire $20,000 recovery to the lawyer and will still owe the lawyer $10,000 out of the client's own pocket. For that reason, the lawyer and client might agree that the maximum fee will be no more than the client recovers. And of course if the recovery is zero (i.e., the defense wins a complete victory), then the client will not have to pay the lawyer any fee at all.

Sliding scale contingent hourly rates. A variation on the basic contingent hourly fee would be a sliding scale contingent hourly fee — the greater the client's recovery, the greater the hourly rate. For example, if the client won (or settled for) only $100,000, then the contingent hourly rate might be $100 per hour. If the recovery is $200,000, then the fee is $200 per hour. If the recovery is $400,000, then the fee will be $400 per hour — and so on. As in the basic contingent hourly arrangement, the lawyer might charge a minimum fee, win or lose, no matter how few hours the lawyer put in before the matter ended, and the lawyer might set a maximum fee no matter how many hours the lawyer put in.

In yet another variation on the sliding scale contingent hourly fee, in Note, *An Alternative to the Contingent Fee*, 1984 UTAH L. REV. 485, the authors suggest that lawyers charge a low hourly rate if the client loses (or wins less than a specified amount), but a much higher hourly rate if the client wins or settles for more than a specified amount. For example, a client might agree to pay a lawyer $100 per hour win or lose if the client recovers less than $50,000, but agree to pay the lawyer $300 per hour if the client recovers more than $50,000. (Some adjustments need to be made at the $50,000 borderline — otherwise, a client who recovers $50,001 will pay three times as much as a client who recovers $49,999.)

Complex contingent fee formulas. More complex formulas are also possible, and some commentators have suggested them. For example, in Clermont & Currivan, *Improving on the Contingent Fee*, 63 CORNELL L. REV. 530 (1978), the authors propose a contingent fee formula that would combine both the lawyer's time charge for the hours devoted to the case and a percentage of the amount by which the gross recovery exceeds that time charge. For example, suppose the lawyer spent 100 hours at $100 per hour (for a total hourly charge of $10,000) and won $50,000, then the lawyer would earn a percentage of the $40,000 difference between the recovery amount and the hourly charge. This formula encourages lawyers to work harder and smarter without working longer, i.e., to put in only those hours that boost the ultimate recovery. The hourly rate gives the lawyer an incentive to put in enough time to achieve a decent settlement (rather than recommending that the client settle the case quickly on terms unfavorable to the client), but the contingent portion gives the lawyer a stake in the outcome. Do you like this formula? Is it good for clients? Is it good for lawyers?

Under all of these variations on hybrid fees, the key question is: who benefits — lawyers, clients, or both?

Challenge round. Here is a challenge for you: design an ideal legal fee system. You may combine features of hourly rates, contingent fees, flat fees, value billing, and whatever other billing methods occur to you. Then explain how your ideal fee system solves the problems addressed in this chapter. In other words, design a fee system that (a) is affordable for all clients who have a serious need for legal help and (b) gives both lawyers and clients the right incentives.

B. HOW MUCH IS TOO MUCH?

Are lawyers too expensive? Most clients think so. So do people who would like to be clients but can't afford a lawyer (or think they can't afford a lawyer). This section focuses on possible ways to control the cost of legal services.

What does it mean to say that lawyers are too expensive? For example, does it mean that some people who need legal services cannot afford them? Does it mean that lawyers are unfairly using their monopoly power (i.e., only lawyers may legally practice law) to charge excessive fees to those who can afford them? Does it mean that lawyers are taking advantage of ignorant or uneducated clients by charging more than their legal services are worth?

These are complex questions. In a market economy, we generally assume that prices reflect value. People may be disappointed or angry or frustrated that lawyers charge a lot, but does that mean that lawyers charge too much? To make headway, we need to narrow the inquiry. Three central questions are:

1. Should we limit how much lawyers may charge? If so, what should the limit be?
2. Who should set that limit — the profession, the legislature, or the courts?
3. Apart from limits, what can be done to reduce legal fees?

To address these questions, we quickly look at these issues from the perspective of four different (and somewhat artificial) economic groups: (1) poor people; (2) the middle class; (3) wealthy individuals; and (4) businesses.

Poor people. Some people cannot afford enough food and shelter, much less lawyers. Yet poor people also have legal needs. Poor people get injured on the job, have auto accidents, get evicted, lose government benefits, and get fired. What can we do to make legal services available to people who cannot afford them unless they are free or almost free?

The middle class. Middle class individuals really get squeezed when it comes to legal services. They are too well off to qualify for free government-sponsored legal services, but too poor to afford quality legal services, especially for preventive purposes, such as making a will or drafting an employment contract. The tax laws also make things hard for such individuals. Businesses can deduct legal fees on their tax returns as business expenses, but individuals cannot deduct legal fees for personal matters. Thus, legal fees for such things as drafting a will, litigating a divorce, or reviewing a contract to buy a house are not tax deductible.

Businesses also can (to some extent) pass the cost of legal services along to customers, whereas individuals cannot. Individuals who want to sue someone can typically pay plaintiffs' lawyers (such as personal injury lawyers) on a contingent fee basis, which does not require any money up front, but contingent fees are not available to defend against litigation or to pay for non-litigation matters work (such as real estate deals, wills, and contracts).

Should the legal profession take steps to help middle class individuals afford lawyers? Or should we leave the fate of the middle class to the marketplace, hoping that the vast middle class market will spur lawyers to find innovative ways to serve the middle class at lower prices?

Wealthy individuals. Wealthy individuals usually can afford legal services. For the wealthy, legal services are often an investment. Estate planning and tax advice typically save much more in the long run than they cost. (That's the idea, anyway.) We are not going to spend much time talking about controls on legal fees for wealthy individuals. The wealthy usually have a lot of choices when they shop for lawyers and can look out for themselves.

Businesses. Corporations and other profit-making businesses can generally afford basic legal services. Moreover, legal fees for business purposes are tax deductible (like other business expenses), and businesses can to some extent pass legal fees on to their customers in the form of higher prices. Also, most businesses protect themselves by purchasing insurance policies that pay legal fees when the business is sued. Therefore, high legal fees are not nearly as serious a problem for most businesses as they are for individuals.

But are legal fees so high that they push companies into bankruptcy, or keep them from growing, especially during a weak economy? Even during a strong economy, when businesses try to pass legal fees on to customers by raising prices, aren't all of us burdened to some degree by high legal fees? Is this a problem that the legal profession should address?

We begin by addressing the limits of attorney fees. How much is too much? When we write a rule to control legal fees, what should the rule say about the upper limits a lawyer can charge? Or should lawyers be permitted to charge whatever the traffic will bear?

The current rule, Rule 1.5(a), provides only the most general guidance. It commands only that a lawyer's fee shall not be "unreasonable." That's pretty vague. What's "unreasonable"?

Rule 1.5(a) tries to put some meat on the bones by listing a series of "factors to be considered in determining the reasonableness of a fee" — things such as:

- the time and labor required
- the novelty and difficulty of the questions involved
- the skill needed to perform the services properly
- the fee customarily charged in the same locality for similar services
- the amount involved and the results obtained
- the experience, reputation, and ability of the lawyer performing the services
- whether the fee is fixed or contingent

Do these factors provide enough guidance? Suppose you are charging an hourly rate. Are you allowed to charge more than your regular hourly rate if the questions are "novel" and "difficult"? If the questions are novel and difficult, won't you have to spend more time on the case? Likewise, are you entitled to charge an above-normal hourly rate if the matter will require an enormous amount of skill? Isn't your level of skill built into your hourly rate? After all, Rule 1.5(b) expressly lists "the experience, reputation, and ability of the lawyer" as a factor in considering rates.

Should we make the rule more specific? Should we put some real teeth in the rules governing fees? How about these ideas for teeth:

Maximum hourly rate? Should we set a maximum hourly rate for lawyers? The maximum rate could be based on years of experience — the longer a lawyer has practiced law, the more the lawyer can charge. (For example, we could say that 2008 graduates cannot charge over $100 per hour, but 1980 graduates can charge up to $250 per hour.) Each state — maybe even each city or county — would be allowed to vary these maximums, so lawyers in New York, New York (it's a wonderful town) would be allowed to charge more than lawyers in Rocky Mount, North Carolina or Wichita, Kansas.

If you like that idea, think about this: If AT&T wants to pay its lawyers $450 per hour, why should we stop them? Why should we protect a big corporation from excessive legal fees? Maybe we should only protect individuals and small businesses from excessive fees. But even if you could decide who to protect, how would you decide the proper maximum hourly rate?

We now look at the idea of protecting individuals from excessive fees. Suppose J.P. Morgan is the best trust and estates lawyer in town. He's smart as a whip (he was on the Yale Law Journal), he limits his practice to trusts and estates, he frequently attends CLE programs in his field, and he diligently reads new cases, law reviews, bar journal articles, etc. (Of course, Morgan doesn't bill clients for any of this educational time — he considers it a cost of doing business that is reflected in his impressive hourly rate.) Morgan also has a posh brownstone office on the Upper West Side, furnished with real antiques. His clients like this elegant ambience because it makes them feel at home, even though the high rent adds many dollars to Morgan's rate.

Because of Morgan's expertise, he can save wealthy clients a zillion dollars on their estate taxes (sometimes two zillion). A wealthy client named Rockefeller has heard about Morgan's expertise and agrees to pay Morgan's ginormous fee ($1,000 per hour) to review his taxes and plan his estate. Should we prevent Rockefeller from paying Morgan what Morgan wants to charge? After all, Rockefeller can go to a different lawyer if he doesn't think Morgan is worth the cost. And Morgan can stop studying so much (and can move to a cheaper office furnished by OfficeMax) if he isn't allowed to charge enough to support his style of practice. Should we limit what an outstanding lawyer can charge a wealthy and sophisticated client?

If your answer is no — if you think we should let Morgan charge Rockefeller as much as he wants — then should Morgan be allowed to charge *everyone* the same sky-high rate? Suppose Rockefeller has a high-living friend named Sam Sherwood who appears to be very wealthy but really isn't. Sherwood drives a Lexus with gold trim, takes expensive vacations in Hawaii and Morocco, and belongs to the prestigious (and pretentious) Swainwood Country Club, but Sherwood hasn't saved any money for his retirement or for his kids' college education. Sherwood also has huge credit card debts at 14.9% APR. The main reason Sherwood wants to retain Morgan is so people will *think* he is wealthy. (Sherwood imagines people saying, "Sherwood goes to Morgan for his estate planning work. He must be *very* wealthy to afford those high fees!") Should Morgan be permitted to charge Sherwood as much as he charged Rockefeller?

If you think Morgan is required to charge a lower rate to Sherwood than to Rockefeller, are you suggesting a system where lawyers have to check (or even audit!) the tax returns or net worth statements of every potential client to decide on the proper hourly rate? Will the guideline for fees be, a la Marx, "From each according to his ability"?

To phrase the question in the abstract, should the reasonableness of a fee depend on the financial situation of the *client* or on the skill and expertise of the *lawyer*? Or does it depend on other factors, such as the actual value of the work to the particular client, or the level of difficulty of the particular service the lawyer performs in a given case, or the presence of competition within a given specialty? (Those sound like some of the factors in Rule 1.5, but many lawyers have a standard hourly rate for every client, except in pro bono matters.)

Now let's turn the question around for a minute. Suppose Laurel N. Hardy is a trusts and estates lawyer who graduated near the bottom of his class at Paducah School of Law and Cosmetology but recently inherited enough money to finance a fancy uptown brownstone office that is furnished even more elegantly than Morgan's office. To prove that the market values his talents, Hardy decides to set his hourly rate at the same level as Morgan's. Is this unethical? Can Hardy be disciplined for charging as much as Morgan even though he doesn't have the "experience, reputation, and ability" of Morgan?

If clients are willing to pay Hardy what he charges, how can we say it's unreasonable? If clients aren't willing to pay Hardy what he charges, he won't have any clients — he'll just sit in front of his computer screen playing Solitaire or surfing the Internet. And if Hardy does better in practice than he did in law school, maybe he'll do work that's just as good as J.P. Morgan's. So why should the rules of legal ethics worry about a lawyer's hourly rate?

Let's get to something more dramatic than estate planning. What if the client is desperate? For example, suppose the client's husband has kidnapped their child and the client is willing to pay anything to get the child back — anything! The lawyer says, "I'll get the child back, but I charge $1,000 per hour for that kind of work." Is that unethical? Does it depend whether the lawyer's "regular" hourly rate for other matters is only (*only?*) $500 per hour? Can a lawyer have one rate for difficult, nasty matters like child kidnapping cases, and a much lower rate for routine matters like UCC filings?

So far, our theoretical methods for controlling hourly rates don't seem to have much practical value. We now discuss another possible way of limiting fees: maximum total fees.

Maximum total fees? Suppose we put an overall cap on how much a lawyer can charge for a given task, no matter how many hours it takes or who performs the services. For example, suppose we say, "No lawyer can charge more than $500 for an uncontested divorce. Any lawyer who charges more than $500 for an uncontested divorce can be disciplined for ripping people off." There would be specified maximums for other services as well. Would that work? Lawyers advertise prices for uncontested divorces in the newspaper every day. (Homework assignment: Look in the classified section of your daily newspaper for lawyer ads. If you're a couch potato, look in the *TV Guide*. Do lawyers advertise fees? How much do they charge for various legal services?) Potential clients can compare prices for uncontested divorces the same way they compare prices for DVD players or life insurance. Do you think the legislature should make it a crime for a store to charge "too much" for an iPod? If not, why should it be an ethics violation for a lawyer to charge too much for an uncontested divorce? (Maybe it should, but *why*?)

If you are persuaded that specific maximum amounts are not a feasible way to control legal fees, where do you draw the line? How do you give meaning to Rule 1.5(a)'s mandate that a lawyer's fee "shall be reasonable"? Would you favor doing away with that rule and letting the marketplace determine fees? Or is there some role for the rules of legal ethics in setting legal fees?

C. IMPROPER TERMS IN FEE AGREEMENTS: NON-REFUNDABLE FEES

Maybe the problem with Rule 1.5(a) is that the rule is concerned with the *amount* of a legal fee rather than with the *terms* of the fee. Rule 1.5 does not explain what terms would be prohibited. Here is a case that does. *Cooperman* concerns fee agreements providing that the initial retainer is "non-refundable" even if a client fires the attorney before the attorney finishes the work. Should lawyers be permitted to charge non-refundable fees?

IN THE MATTER OF COOPERMAN

83 N.Y.2d 465 (1994)

BELLACOSA, J.

The issue in this appeal is whether the appellant attorney violated the Code of Professional Responsibility by repeatedly using special nonrefundable retainer fee agreements with his clients. Essentially, such arrangements are marked by the payment of a nonrefundable fee for specific services, in advance and irrespective of whether any professional services are actually rendered. . . .

. . . The first five charges derive from a written fee agreement to represent an individual in a criminal matter. It states: "My minimum fee for appearing for you in this matter is Fifteen Thousand ($15,000) Dollars. This fee is not refundable for any reason whatsoever once I file a notice of appearance on your behalf." One month after the agreement, the lawyer was discharged by the client and refused to refund any portion of the fee. The Grievance Committee sent Cooperman a Letter of Caution relating to this matter. He rejected the admonition, claiming the fee was nonrefundable. The Letter of Caution was the second such letter admonishing him not to accept the kind of fee arrangements at issue here.

Charges 6 through 10 refer to a written retainer agreement in connection with a probate proceeding. It states in pertinent part: "For the MINIMAL FEE and NON-REFUNDABLE amount of Five Thousand ($5,000) Dollars, I will act as your counsel." The agreement further provided: "This is the minimum fee no matter how much or how little work I do in this investigatory stage . . . and will remain the minimum fee and not refundable even if you decide prior to my completion of the investigation that you wish to discontinue the use of my services for any reason whatsoever." The client discharged Cooperman, who refused to provide the client with an itemized bill of services rendered or refund any portion of the fee, citing the unconditional nonrefundable fee agreement.

The last five charges relate to a fee agreement involving another criminal matter. It provides: "The Minimum Fee for Mr. Cooperman's representation . . . to any extent whatsoever is Ten Thousand ($10,000) Dollars. . . . The above amount is the MINIMUM FEE no matter how few court appearances are made. . . . The minimum fee will remain the same even if Mr. Cooperman is discharged." Two days after execution of the fee agreement, the client discharged Cooperman and demanded a refund. As with the other clients, he demurred.

AUTHORS' COMMENT:

Unlike the two fee agreements above, the fee agreement here does not use the word "non-refundable." Instead, the agreement uses the term "minimum." Should this make a difference? Let's look at two examples:

First, suppose that before Cooperman ever goes to court or does any work, the client fires him. Can the client get back any portion of the $10,000 "minimum fee"? If not, what's the difference between a "minimum fee" and a non-refundable fee?

Second, assume instead that Mr. Cooperman is a fabulous lawyer and, without ever going to court, he convinces the prosecutor to offer a terrific plea bargain that is much better than the client had expected. If Cooperman did only a few hours of work but finished the job he was hired to do, can the client get back any part of the $10,000 minimum fee? If not, is the fee agreement ethical? If you think it's not ethical, is there ever a time when a lawyer can charge and collect a minimum fee? The court doesn't comment on this until the very end of the case. What is your opinion?

. . . The particular analysis begins with a reflection on the nature of the attorney-client relationship. Sir Francis Bacon observed, "The greatest trust between [people] is this trust of giving counsel." This unique fiduciary reliance, stemming from people hiring attorneys to exercise professional judgment on a client's behalf — "giving counsel" — is imbued with ultimate trust and confidence. The attorney's obligations, therefore, transcend those prevailing in the commercial market place. The duty to deal fairly, honestly and with undivided loyalty superimposes onto the attorney-client relationship a set of special and unique duties, including maintaining confidentiality, avoiding conflicts of interest, operating competently, safeguarding client property and honoring the clients' interests over the lawyer's. To the public and clients, few features could be more paramount than the fee — the costs of legal services. The Code of Professional Conduct and Responsibility reflects this central ingredient by specifically mandating, without exception, that an attorney "shall not enter into an agreement for, charge or collect an illegal or excessive fee" (DR 2-106[A]), and upon withdrawal from employment "shall refund promptly any part of a fee paid in advance that has not been earned" (DR 2-110[A][3]). Accordingly, attorney-client fee agreements are a matter of special concern to the courts and are enforceable and affected by lofty principles different from those applicable to commonplace commercial contracts.

Because the attorney-client relationship is recognized as so special and so sensitive in our society, its effectiveness, actually and perceptually, may be irreparably impaired by conduct which undermines the confidence of the particular client or the public in general. In recognition of this indispensable desideratum and as a precaution against the corrosive potentiality from failing to foster trust, public policy recognizes a client's right to terminate the attorney-client relationship at any time with or without cause (DR 2-110[b][4]). This principle was effectively enunciated in Martin v. Camp (219 NY, supra): "The contract under which an attorney is employed by a client has peculiar and distinctive features . . . [thus] notwithstanding the fact that the employment of an attorney by a client is governed by the contract which the parties make . . . the client with or without cause may terminate the contract at any time."

AUTHORS' COMMENT:

The client's right to fire an attorney at any time for any reason is the central legal principle underlying the court's reasoning here. Every state recognizes that right. But if the client fires the attorney, does the attorney have any right to compensation? The court now discusses that angle.

The unqualified right to terminate the attorney-client relationship at any time has been assiduously protected by the courts. An attorney, however, is not left without recourse for unfair terminations lacking cause. If a client exercises the right to discharge an attorney after some services are performed but prior to the completion of the services for which the fee was agreed upon, the discharged attorney is entitled to recover compensation from the client measured by the fair and reasonable value of the completed services. We have recognized that permitting a discharged attorney "to recover the reasonable value of services rendered in quantum meruit, a principle inherently designed to prevent unjust enrichment, strikes the delicate balance between the need to deter clients from taking undue advantage of attorneys, on the one hand, and the public policy favoring the right of a client to terminate the attorney-client relationship without inhibition on the other."

Correspondingly and by cogent logic and extension of the governing precepts, we hold that the use of a special nonrefundable retainer fee agreement clashes with public policy because it inappropriately compromises the right to sever the fiduciary services relationship with the lawyer. Special nonrefundable retainer fee agreements diminish the core of the fiduciary relationship by substantially altering and economically chilling the client's unbridled prerogative to walk away from the lawyer. To answer that the client can technically still terminate misses the reality of the economic coercion that pervades such matters. If special nonrefundable retainers are allowed to flourish, clients would be relegated to hostage status in an unwanted fiduciary relationship — an utter anomaly. Such circumstance would impose a penalty on a client for daring to invoke a hollow right to discharge. . . . Cooperman even acknowledges that the essential purpose of the nonrefundable retainer was to prevent clients from firing the lawyer, a purpose which, as demonstrated, directly contravenes the Code and this State's settled public policy in this regard.

Nevertheless, Cooperman contends that special nonrefundable retainer fee agreements should not be treated as per se violations unless they are pegged to a "clearly excessive" fee. The argument is unavailing. . . . Cooperman's claim, in any event, reflects a misconception of the nature of the legal profession by turning on its head the axiom that the legal profession "is a learned profession, not a mere money-getting trade" (ABA Formal Opinion No. 250).

DR 2-110(A)–(B) of the Code of Professional Responsibility [which is comparable to Rule 1.16(d) and (b)] adds further instruction to our analysis and disposition:

Withdrawal from Employment.

(A) *In general.* . . .

(3) A lawyer who withdraws from employment shall refund promptly any part of a fee paid in advance that has not been earned.

(B) *Mandatory withdrawal.* A lawyer representing a client before a tribunal, with its permission if required by its rules, shall withdraw from employment, and a lawyer representing a client in other matters shall withdraw from employment, if:. . . .

(4) The lawyer is discharged by [the] client.

We believe that if an attorney is prohibited from keeping any part of a pre-paid fee that has not been earned because of discharge by the client, it is reasonable to conclude also that an attorney may not negotiate and keep fees such as those at issue here. . . .

Since we decide the precise issue in this case in a disciplinary context only, we imply no views with respect to the wider array of factors by which attorneys and clients may have fee dispute controversies resolved. Traditional criteria, including the factor of the actual amount of services rendered, will continue to govern those situations (see, DR 2-106[B]). Thus, while the special nonrefundable retainer agreement will be unenforceable and may subject an attorney to professional discipline, quantum meruit payment for services actually rendered will still be available and appropriate.

. . . The conduct of attorneys is not measured by how close to the edge of thin ice they skate. The measure of an attorney's conduct is not how much clarity can be squeezed out of the strict letter of the law, but how much honor can be poured into the generous spirit of lawyer-client relationships. The "punctilio of an honor most high" (*Meinhard v Salmon*, 249 NY, supra, at 464) must be the prevailing standard. . . .

[W]e intend no effect or disturbance with respect to other types of appropriate and ethical fee agreements. Minimum fee arrangements and general retainers that provide for fees, not laden with the nonrefundability impediment irrespective of any services, will continue to be valid and not subject in and of themselves to professional discipline.

Order affirmed, with costs.

NOTES AND QUESTIONS

1. ***Tough Discipline.*** The *Cooperman* case has lessons not only about legal fees but also about professional discipline. What discipline do you think Cooperman got? He was suspended from the practice of law for *two years!* That's a harsh sanction. Why was it so harsh? Because Cooperman had been warned before about his fee practices — not once, but twice. In 1985, the Grievance Committee gave Cooperman a Letter of Caution warning him "not to accept non-refundable retainers." A year later, Cooperman nevertheless entered into another "non-refundable fee" retainer agreement. When he refused to refund fees to a client who fired him, he was again issued a Letter of Caution. He revised his retainer agreement slightly by using the term "minimum fee" instead of "nonrefundable fee," but it still allowed him to keep unearned fees if the client fired him. Lesson: A word to the wise should be sufficient. If the disciplinary authorities ever warn you that a practice is unethical, stop it right away. Don't keep skating on thin ice.

2. ***Majority Rule.*** The *Cooperman* case is in accord with the law in most jurisdictions. Most states prohibit non-refundable fees. *Cooperman* was decided under DR 2-110(A)(2) of the New York Code of Professional Responsibility, but it is consistent with Rule 1.16(d), which provides that upon withdrawal one of a lawyer's obligations is "refunding any advance payment of fee or expense that has not been earned or incurred." And withdrawal occurs whether the client fires the lawyer or the lawyer resigns for mandatory or permissive reasons. The key holding of *Cooperman* is that a lawyer who stops working before completing the work the lawyer was engaged to perform must refund any part of the fee that was not earned. A lawyer cannot keep legal fees for legal work that was never performed.

3. ***"Minimum Fees" are Different.*** The last paragraph of the *Cooperman* opinion confused a lot of people by implying that "minimum fees" are still ethical as long as they are not "laden with the nonrefundability impediment." What does that mean? The Court of Appeals didn't explain minimum fees, but the intermediate appellate opinion in *Cooperman* (which was affirmed) did. The intermediate appellate court said:

> The notion of a so-called "minimum fee" as a forecast of the lowest amount that a lawyer will charge . . . as the fee for carrying a contemplated legal task through to completion, is a useful one. It enables a client to know, in advance , the minimum amount he or she can expect to pay to attempt to achieve the desired result through the use of the lawyer's services, and enables the client to compare the fees of other lawyers for the same services.

For example, suppose a potential client talks to a lawyer about forming a new corporation. The lawyer says, "I charge $200 per hour. My minimum fee for an incorporation is $2,000 and I demand that up front." The lawyer does not quote a maximum fee or an estimated fee for this particular project. What does the $2,000 "minimum fee" mean? It means that if the lawyer completes all necessary work, the lawyer is entitled to the minimum fee no matter how little time the lawyer spent. It is like a flat fee, except that if the lawyer spends *more* time on the project than expected, then the client has to pay for all of the time at the lawyer's regular hourly rate. Thus, if the lawyer spends 5 hours, the fee will be $2,000. If the lawyer spends 8 hours, the fee will be $2,000. If the lawyer spends 15 hours, the fee will be $3,000 (= $200 × 15).

Why should minimum fees be permitted if non-refundable fees are prohibited? Because minimum fees contain two types of useful information. First, they help clients decide whether it's worth it to go forward with a project at all. If the $2,000 minimum fee is too steep, a client might decide to abandon the idea of incorporating and make do with a partnership or some other form of business ownership. Second, minimum fees help clients decide between one lawyer and another. For example, suppose the client now goes to another lawyer whose minimum fee for the same service is only $1,200. If the client thinks the second lawyer is competent to handle the project, then the client may decide to use the second lawyer. If the project can be completed quickly, the client can save $800 by choosing the lawyer whose minimum fee is only $1,200. (If the project turns out to be complex, then both lawyers will exceed the minimum fee and it's not clear which lawyer will cost less in the end.) Thus, a minimum fee helps the client choose between two lawyers, and helps a client decide whether or not to go forward with a project.

Minimum fees must be at least partially refundable. If the lawyer does not finish the job, the lawyer must refund the unearned portion of any fee that was paid in advance. Here, if the lawyer works for 5 hours at $200 per hour and the client then decides (for whatever reason) to terminate the lawyer or not to go through with the incorporation, the lawyer must refund the unearned portion of the fee (here $600).

Do you agree that minimum fees should be permitted but non-refundable fees should be prohibited? Are you confident that you can tell the difference between a "non-refundable" fee and a "minimum" fee? In a few words, how do you explain the difference?

D. MAKING LEGAL FEES MORE AFFORDABLE FOR THE MIDDLE CLASS

How can we make legal services more affordable for the middle class? This is a tough problem because we live in a free market economy where price controls are generally disfavored and seldom imposed. Thus, legal fees are basically governed by the law of supply and demand. The two main ways of bringing down costs in a free market economy are to decrease demand or increase supply.

Decreasing the demand for lawyers. Decreasing demand is hard because the forces that drive demand are largely beyond the control of the legal profession. People get into disputes; they get sued; they get injured; they want a will; they need an employment contract; they want to get out of a bad contract. People need lawyers for all sorts of reasons. The more laws, the more deals, and the more litigation, the greater the demand for legal services. The legal profession can't do much about this. Of course, encouraging people to take preventive measures to avoid legal problems and disputes in the first place is probably the best way to reduce demand for legal services, but those solutions are largely beyond the scope of this book. We prefer to focus on the supply side, where the legal profession has more ability to control the course of events.

Increasing the supply of lawyers. Many people think there are already too many lawyers in America, but that's a subjective judgment. The fact is that if there were more lawyers, then the cost of legal services for the middle class would be almost certainly decrease (or at least rise less rapidly). The greater the supply of lawyers, the more price competition there will be among lawyers, and the lower prices will be compared to what they would be with a smaller supply of lawyers. How can the legal profession help increase the supply of lawyers for the middle class? Here are some possibilities:

Educate more lawyers. The most obvious way to increase supply is to educate more lawyers. How could we educate more lawyers? Here are some ideas:

Increase funding to law schools. The government could increase funding to law schools, and increase the funds available for student loans (or reduce interest rates on student loans), so that more law students could pay full tuition. That would enable law schools to expand by hiring more professors and accepting more students. (The same result could be accomplished by raising more money from alumni and other non-government sources, but law schools already seem to be trying very hard to raise more money.)

Shorten law school. If we shortened law school to only two years, law schools would produce 50% more lawyers. If there were 300 students in a class, for example, then over a six-year period the law school would graduate 900 students (that's three full classes finishing two years) instead of only 600 lawyers (two full classes finishing three years). Moreover, these two-year lawyers wouldn't be as deeply in debt upon graduation (assuming tuition held steady), so lawyers could lower their fees and still afford to pay back their loans.

A related idea is to offer either a two-year program or a three-year program in law school, but those who graduated in two years could obtain only limited law licenses. For example, the state could say that lawyers with a two-year diploma could not appear in court until they completed a third year of law school or obtained a certain amount of experience in practice.

Is it a good idea to graduate more lawyers? That may depend on who you are. If you are already in law school, or already in practice, you probably don't want more competition. It's hard enough to scrape by already. But if you were in high school and couldn't get into law school unless law schools expanded, or couldn't afford law school unless it was shortened to two years, you might think increasing the number of lawyers was a great idea.

What if you were a client (or a prospective client)? Would more lawyers and more competition help you or hurt you? On one hand, accepting more applicants to law school, or shortening law school to two years, might drive quality down. On the other hand, more competition might drive quality up as lawyers strive harder and harder to please clients and distinguish themselves from other lawyers. Which result do you think is more likely?

Expand roles for non-lawyers. If we don't want to graduate more lawyers, maybe we need to give up some of our monopoly to non-lawyers. The courts or the legislature could decide that non-lawyers could perform some kinds of services now reserved for lawyers. (A few states have already done this.) The legal profession could also be less aggressive in enforcing the laws against unauthorized practice. How do you like that approach for increasing the supply of legal services to the middle class?

Chapter 27
LEGAL SERVICES FOR CLIENTS WHO CANNOT PAY

In the previous chapter, we discussed the five main types of fee agreements: flat, hourly, contingent, value, and hybrid. But some people cannot afford to pay legal fees out of their own pockets under any type of fee arrangement. This chapter looks at how our system of justice delivers legal services to those who cannot pay at all. The chapter covers three main topics: (1) government provision of legal services; (2) fee shifting statutes; and (3) pro bono work.

The system in which individual clients pay for their own legal fees is consistent with America's ethos of rugged individualism and free market economy, but it is insufficient to meet the need or desire for legal services among America's needy. Some have described the United States as a country that is "over-lawyered and underserved," noting that we have more *licensed* lawyers per person than any other country. Yet, the legal needs of the poor remain largely unmet. Even in the face of claims that the United States has too many lawyers, few would deny that when it comes to meeting the legal needs of the poor, there are too few. Periodical studies, such as the 2002 report issued by ABA Consortium on the Delivery of Legal Services, regularly conclude that only 10% to 20% of the non-criminal legal needs of the poor are being met. (Criminal needs are generally met because cases like *Gideon v. Wainwright* and *Argersinger v. Hamlin* require the state to supply a criminal defense lawyer for a person facing incarceration who is too poor to afford a lawyer.)

The evidence is overwhelming that poor people cannot find lawyers to serve many of their most pressing needs — needs involving basic elements of life such as housing, divorce, and government benefits. The poor simply cannot afford to pay even relatively inexpensive lawyers. Should society just let the poor fend for themselves when it comes to legal assistance? Or should we find a way to provide lawyers for the poor? If so, how? And what about the middle class, who are as a practical matter almost as unable to afford legal fees? What should we do for them?

A. PROVIDING LEGAL SERVICES FOR THOSE IN NEED

How do poor people get lawyers? We live in a highly-bureaucratic, highly-regulated state where the ability of each individual to organize and advocate for himself is not simply expected, but prized. For such a system to work, we must generally assume that people with legal problems can find a lawyer to ascertain and enforce their rights. This is especially true with public benefits. Just as the rich need tax lawyers to make sure they don't pay more than they are required to pay *to* the government, the poor need lawyers to make sure they don't receive less than they are entitled to *from* the government. But if people are too poor to afford a lawyer, what can they do?

Turn the question around. Does society have an obligation to provide lawyers for those who are too poor to afford lawyers? If so, how should society provide legal services to poor people? We begin by listing some options about how to serve the poor:

a. *Lawyers generally.* We could ask all lawyers to provide *pro bono* services to the poor. (*Pro bono* work could be either voluntary or mandatory. We'll debate that later in the chapter.)
b. *Lawyers employed by the government.* One way to give the poor legal services is for the government to pay the salaries of lawyers for the poor. This is routinely done now through Legal Services Corporation. Since the late 1970s, Congress has generally appropriated in the range of $300 million to $400 million per year (about $1.00 to $1.50 per year per American) to pay lawyers in offices all over the country to represent poor people. If this isn't enough money to hire lawyers to serve the poor, how should we raise the rest of the necessary money? For example, should we (i) raise federal or state taxes and earmark them for legal

services, (ii) transfer existing federal or state budget dollars from other programs to legal services programs, (iii) rely on private donations for the extra money, or (iv) do something else? (By the way, as of 2007, all but six states allocate at least some state funds to civil legal aid.)

c. *Contracts with private law firms.* Instead of hiring full-time lawyers, the government could contract with private law firms to provide a certain quantity of legal services (e.g., a certain number of hours, or a certain number of cases) to poor people at little or no charge.

d. *Lawyers employed by non-profit organizations.* Non-profit organizations, funded by private contributions, can hire lawyers to provide legal services for the poor. (Non-profit organizations can also recruit volunteer lawyers to serve the poor, but that goes into the category of *pro bono* work. Here, we're talking about paid staff attorneys, not volunteers.)

e. *Judicaid.* Another idea is to set up a system for legal services parallel to Medicaid. Under Medicaid, a poor person can go to any doctor who accepts Medicaid, and the government will pay the doctor's fees, up to certain limits. (The doctors agree to charge only what Medicaid pays.) Under a parallel program for legal services, often called Judicaid, poor people could go to any lawyer who agreed to participate in the program, and the government would pay the lawyer's fees. These programs are still relatively rare in America and have not been established at the national level. (In fact, they are so rare that when we put "judicaid" into the Google search box, the result said, "Did you mean to search for: *Medicaid*?")

f. *"Legal fee stamps."* Legal fee stamps (which don't actually exist) would be like food stamps — they could be used to pay for legal services from any lawyer who agreed to accept them, but they could not be used to pay for anything other than legal fees (just as food stamps cannot be used to buy anything but food).

g. *Public interest law firms.* The IRS has a special set of regulations to govern "public interest law firms," known as PILF's. These are private law firms that agree to accept a high percentage of their cases without regard to the fee or a possibility of a fee. That enables poor people to hire these law firms. PILF's are basically a hybrid between non-profit groups and profit-making private firms. They are usually organized as non-profit 501(c)(3) corporations (the main classification for tax-exempt organizations), and if they meet the strict IRS criteria for PILF's then they are not taxed on all or part of their income. In effect, the government subsidizes these PILF's by not charging them taxes. (A helpful description of many different public interest law firms is available at www.marquette.edu — search the site for "public interest law firms.")

h. *Law school clinics.* Law school clinics are similar to public interest law firms, but they are typically funded by your tuition dollars (and sometimes by government grants) rather than by direct private contributions (though some law school clinics do conduct their own fundraising campaigns).

i. *Court appointed lawyers.* Another possible solution would be to give courts authority to appoint lawyers for poor people in civil matters, just as courts already have the authority to appoint lawyers for defendants in criminal matters. When a poor person arrives in court without a lawyer to litigate a divorce, an eviction, or a child custody dispute, for example, the court could appoint a lawyer to handle the case, at government expense.

j. *The English Rule.* Under the so-called English Rule, the loser pays the winner's attorney fees. (This is a vast oversimplification of the rules actually in force in England, but it captures the basic idea.) If America adopted the English Rule, then a poor person who brought a successful case could require the losing defendant to pay the plaintiff's legal fees, and a poor person who prevailed after being unjustly sued could require the plaintiff to pay the defense lawyer's legal fees.

k. *Non-lawyers under attorney supervision.* We could train non-lawyers to serve the poor in specialized matters. This would greatly lower the cost of providing these services. (Laws prohibiting the unauthorized practice of law, which are on the books in every state, currently make it illegal for non-lawyers to provide legal services except under the supervision of a lawyer — but requiring lawyer supervision adds substantially to the cost of using nonlawyers.)

Which of these options do you think would be likely to work best? Should society focus on implementing and strengthening one or two of these options, or should society use them all depending on geographic location and other circumstances?

B. FEE-SHIFTING STATUTES

Lawyers for poor people are in short supply all around, but the shortage of lawyers is especially acute in civil rights cases, such as police brutality cases, prisoners' rights suits, housing discrimination cases, and employment discrimination suits. Commentators estimate that only 1% of all lawyers handle civil rights cases. Look in the Yellow Pages — you'll see that only a handful of lawyers claim to practice civil rights or employment discrimination law. Plaintiffs seeking to bring civil rights cases usually have a hard time finding a lawyer who is even willing to listen to their story in an initial interview, much less represent them in lengthy and complex litigation.

Why are there so few civil rights lawyers? One reason is that civil rights cases are very hard to win. Police brutality, for example, is notoriously difficult to prove because most people still trust the word of a police officer over the word of someone who was allegedly breaking the law. Employment discrimination is also difficult to prove. The employer nearly always argues that the plaintiff's job performance was inadequate, and that the person hired in the plaintiff's place had a superior record. Prisoners' rights suits are probably the most difficult of all. Could a lawyer find a less attractive plaintiff? The plaintiff may have been convicted of rape or murder or other terrible crimes, and is now in court complaining that the cells are too crowded or the medical care is inadequate or the policies on censoring mail are too strict. Few lawyers can build an economically viable law practice representing convicted criminals on these claims.

To make matters worse, civil rights suits typically pit a poor, powerless person against an opponent with far greater resources and staying power — either the government or an employer. Any lawyer who files a civil rights suit must be prepared to litigate for a long time before seeing any fees.

But civil rights cases need to be litigated. Civil rights cases protect us against the abuses of corporations and government entities. They also enforce the rights of all people, no matter how low their station in life, to be free of discrimination. Unless individual plaintiffs can find lawyers to enforce their civil rights, the civil rights laws of this country — all the product of long social and political struggles — may prove hollow.

How can we attract more lawyers to handle civil rights cases? How can we compensate lawyers enough to make it worthwhile for them to represent plaintiffs in civil rights cases?

Hourly rates obviously won't work because most civil rights plaintiffs don't have enough money to pay the fees. Contingent fees usually won't work well either, because juries are often reluctant to award large damages against the government (since government money comes from taxpayers, including the jurors themselves) or against government employees (like police officers), who are not well paid and who risk their lives every day to serve the public. Moreover, civil rights cases often seek mainly declaratory or injunctive relief rather than damages. A lawyer can't take a contingent fee out of an injunction — there's no pile of money out of which the lawyer can scoop a fee.

Non-profit groups recruit volunteers to handle some civil rights cases, but volunteers are often hard to find. One of the authors (Simon) was on the Legal Steering Committee of the ACLU Chapter in St. Louis for six years in the 1980s and 1990s, and it was often hard to find a lawyer willing to handle civil rights suits that the Committee thought had substantial merit. Most lawyers do not have the experience or the time to handle civil rights cases, even if they are willing to take on the government.

Some non-profit groups have raised enough money to afford staff attorneys, but staff attorneys have many duties besides bringing lawsuits. Staff attorneys are also charged with training volunteer attorneys, giving speeches, designing educational programs for the public, writing op-ed columns, and monitoring government policies, for example. They don't have time to get involved in constant litigation, so even non-profit organizations that have staff attorneys are forced to turn away many potential cases.

What is left? Is there any way to attract attorneys to take civil rights cases? Yes, there is. The way is fee-shifting statutes — federal or state statutes providing that when a plaintiff prevails in a civil rights case, the court can order the defendant to pay the plaintiff's attorney fees. Let's take a closer look.

Fee-shifting now applies in suits brought under every major anti-discrimination law (such as Title VII, the Age Discrimination in Employment Act, the Americans with Disabilities Act, and the Fair Housing Act), as well as in broader categories of civil rights cases.

The fee-shifting statutes are generally "one-way" statutes — only a prevailing *plaintiff* can ordinarily win attorney fees. A prevailing defendant cannot win fees unless the plaintiff's suit was frivolous, groundless, or unreasonable, or unless the plaintiff continued to litigate after it clearly became so. One-way shifting is a compromise between the traditional American Rule (under which each side pays its own fees no matter who wins) and the so-called English Rule (under which the loser pays the winner's fees). If the plaintiff wins or obtains some significant relief by way of settlement, the defendant must pay the plaintiff's fee, but if the defendant wins, the plaintiff does not have to pay the defendant's fee. (What would happen if two-way fee shifting were automatic for both sides? How many plaintiffs would want to sue their employers or their landlords knowing they would have to pay the defendant's attorney fees if they lost?)

One federal statute with particularly wide-ranging effects is the Civil Rights Attorneys' Fees Award Act of 1976, 42 U.S.C. § 1988, which provides that in civil rights suits brought under a number of specified statutes, "the court, in its discretion, may allow the prevailing party, other than the United States, a reasonable attorney's fee as part of the costs." This statute, often referred to simply as "§ 1988," provides attorney fees to the prevailing party in all kinds of civil rights cases alleging abuses of power by the government.

Although the language of § 1988 gives a court discretion to award the prevailing party a reasonable attorney's fee (or not), in practice the award of fees is almost automatic. If you represent a plaintiff who wins a civil rights suit, you are ordinarily entitled to your regular hourly rate multiplied by the reasonable number of hours you worked on the case. This is called the "lodestar." It's like a contingent hourly rate — if you win, you get paid by the hour (plus your reasonable litigation expenses), but if you lose, you don't get paid at all.

The next case shows how this formula works. The plaintiffs were Chicano citizens who lived in Riverside, California. One night, without a warrant and for no apparent reason, the police broke up the plaintiffs' party with a tear gas raid. The Chicanos found two lawyers, both of them recent law graduates, who sued the City of Riverside and the police. The lawyers litigated the case for over five years, together spending just under 2,000 hours on the case. They eventually won $33,000 in damages for their clients and $245,000 in fees for themselves — more than seven times the amount of the jury's verdict. Is this reasonable? See what the Supreme Court says. Would you line up with the majority, or with the dissent?

CITY OF RIVERSIDE v. RIVERA

477 U.S. 561 (1986)

JUSTICE BRENNAN announced the judgment of the Court and delivered an opinion in which JUSTICE MARSHALL, JUSTICE BLACKMUN, and JUSTICE STEVENS join.

The issue presented in this case is whether an award of attorney's fees under 42 U.S.C. § 1988 is *per se* "unreasonable" within the meaning of the statute if it exceeds the amount of damages recovered by the plaintiff in the underlying civil rights action.

I

Respondents, eight Chicano individuals, attended a party on the evening of August 1, 1975, at the Riverside, California, home of respondents Santos and Jennie Rivera. A large number of unidentified police officers, acting without a warrant, broke up the party using tear gas and, as found by the District Court, "unnecessary physical force." Many of the guests, including four of the respondents, were arrested. The District Court later found that "[t]he party was not creating a disturbance in the community at the time of the break-in." Criminal charges against the arrestees were ultimately dismissed for lack of probable cause.

[In 1976, respondents sued the City of Riverside, its chief of police, and 30 individual police officers for violating their constitutional rights and numerous state laws. The complaint sought damages and declaratory and injunctive relief. In 1977, 23 of the individual police officers moved for summary judgment: the District Court granted summary judgment in favor of 17 of the 30 named police officers. The case against the remaining defendants went to trial in 1980. The jury returned a total of 37 individual verdicts in favor of the respondents and against the city and five individual officers, finding 11 violations of federal constitutional rights, four instances of false arrest and imprisonment, and 22 instances of negligence.] Respondents were awarded $33,350 in compensatory and punitive damages: $13,300 for their federal claims, and $20,050 for their state-law claims.[1]

Respondents also sought attorney's fees and costs under § 1988. They requested compensation for 1,946.75 hours expended by their two attorneys at a rate of $125 per hour, and for 84.5 hours expended by law clerks at a rate of $25.00 per hour, a total of $245,456.25. The District Court found both the hours and rates reasonable, and awarded respondents $245,456.25 in attorney's fees. . . .

III

Petitioners, joined by the Solicitor General as *amicus curiae*, maintain that *Hensley*'s lodestar approach is inappropriate in civil rights cases where a plaintiff recovers only monetary damages. In these cases, so the argument goes, use of the lodestar may result in fees that exceed the amount of damages recovered and that are therefore unreasonable. Likening such cases to private tort actions, petitioners and the

---

[1] Counsel for respondents explained to the District Court that respondents had not pursued their request for injunctive relief because "the bottom line of what we would ask for is that the police officers obey the law. And that is virtually always denied by a court because a court properly, I think, says that for the future we will assume that all police officers will abide by the law, including the Constitution." The District Court's response to this explanation is significant:

> "[I]f you [respondents] had asked for [injunctive relief] against some of the officers I think I would have granted it. . . . I would agree with you that there is a problem about telling the officers that they have to obey the law. But if you want to know what the Court thought about some of the behavior, it was — it would have warranted an injunction."

Solicitor General submit that attorney's fees in such cases should be proportionate to the amount of damages a plaintiff recovers. Specifically, they suggest that fee awards in damages cases should be modeled upon the contingent fee arrangements commonly used in personal injury litigation. In this case, assuming a 33% contingency rate, this would entitle respondents to recover approximately $11,000 in attorney's fees.

The amount of damages a plaintiff recovers is certainly relevant to the amount of attorney's fees to be awarded under § 1988. It is, however, only one of many factors that a court should consider in calculating an award of attorney's fees. We reject the proposition that fee awards under § 1988 should necessarily be proportionate to the amount of damages a civil rights plaintiff actually recovers.

AUTHORS' COMMENT:

Why should the government pay the victor in a civil rights suit like this? The plaintiffs were damaged and brought suit to recover damages. If this were an ordinary tort suit like an auto accident, the fee would come out of the plaintiffs' damages. Why should the rule be any different just because this suit is brought to redress a civil rights violation rather than an ordinary tort? Justice Brennan will now answer that question.

A

As an initial matter, we reject the notion that a civil rights action for damages constitutes nothing more than a private tort suit benefiting only the individual plaintiffs whose rights were violated. Unlike most private tort litigants, a civil rights plaintiff seeks to vindicate important civil and constitutional rights that cannot be valued solely in monetary terms. And, Congress has determined that "the public as a whole has an interest in the vindication of the rights conferred by the statutes enumerated in § 1988, over and above the value of a civil rights remedy to a particular plaintiff. . . . " Regardless of the form of relief he actually obtains, a successful civil rights plaintiff often secures important social benefits that are not reflected in nominal or relatively small damages awards. In this case, for example, the District Court found that many of petitioners' unlawful acts were "motivated by a general hostility to the Chicano community," and that this litigation therefore served the public interest:

> The institutional behavior involved here . . . had to be stopped and . . . nothing short of having a lawsuit like this would have stopped it. . . . [T]he improper motivation which appeared as a result of all of this seemed to me to have pervaded a very broad segment of police officers in the department.

In addition, the damages a plaintiff recovers contributes significantly to the deterrence of civil rights violations in the future. This deterrent effect is particularly evident in the area of individual police misconduct, where injunctive relief generally is unavailable.

Congress expressly recognized that a plaintiff who obtains relief in a civil rights lawsuit "'does so not for himself alone but also as a "private attorney general," vindicating a policy that Congress considered of the highest importance'. . . . If the citizen does not have the resources, his day in court is denied him; the congression al policy which he seeks to assert and vindicate goes unvindicated; and the entire Nation, not just the individual citizen, suffers." 122 Cong. Rec. 33313 (1976) (remarks of Sen. Tunney).

Because damages awards do not reflect fully the public benefit advanced by civil rights litigation, Congress did not intend for fees in civil rights cases, unlike most private law cases, to depend on obtaining substantial monetary relief. Rather, Congress made clear that it "intended that the amount of fees awarded under [§ 1988] be governed by the same standards which prevail in other types of equally complex Federal litigation, such as antitrust cases and *not be reduced because the rights involved may be nonpecuniary in nature.*" Senate Report (emphasis added). "[C]ounsel for prevailing parties should be paid, as is traditional with attorneys compensated by a fee-paying client, '*for all time reasonably expended on a matter.*'" *Id.* . . . Thus, Congress recognized that reasonable attorney's fees under § 1988 are not conditioned upon and need not be proportionate to an award of money damages. The lower courts have generally eschewed such a requirement.

B

A rule that limits attorney's fees in civil rights cases to a proportion of the damages awarded would seriously undermine Congress' purpose in enacting § 1988. Congress enacted § 1988 specifically because it found that the private market for legal services failed to provide many victims of civil rights violations with effective access to the judicial process. These victims ordinarily cannot afford to purchase legal services at the rates set by the private market. . . . Moreover, the contingent fee arrangements that make legal services available to many victims of personal injuries would often not encourage lawyers to accept civil rights cases, which frequently involve substantial expenditures of time and effort but produce only small monetary recoveries. . . .

A rule of proportionality would make it difficult, if not impossible, for individuals with meritorious civil rights claims but relatively small potential damages to obtain redress from the courts. This is totally inconsistent with the Congress' purpose in enacting § 1988. Congress recognized that private-sector fee arrangements were inadequate to ensure sufficiently vigorous enforcement of civil rights. In order to ensure that lawyers would be willing to represent persons with legitimate civil rights grievances, Congress determined that it would be necessary to compensate lawyers for all time reasonably expended on a case.

This case illustrates why the enforcement of civil rights laws cannot be entrusted to private-sector fee arrangements. The District Court observed that "[g]iven the nature of this lawsuit and the type of defense presented, many attorneys in the community would have been reluctant to institute and to continue to prosecute this action." The court concluded, moreover, that "[c]ounsel for plaintiffs achieved excellent results for their clients, and their accomplishment in this case was outstanding. The amount of time expended by counsel in conducting this litigation was reasonable and reflected sound legal judgment under the circumstances." Nevertheless, petitioners suggest that respondents' counsel should be compensated for only a small fraction of the actual time spent litigating the case. In light of the difficult nature of the issues presented by this lawsuit and the low pecuniary value of many of the rights respondents sought to vindicate, it is highly unlikely that the prospect of a fee equal to a fraction of the damages respondents might recover would have been sufficient to attract competent counsel.[10]

Moreover, since counsel might not have found it economically feasible to expend the amount of time respondents' counsel found necessary to litigate the case properly, it is even less likely that counsel would have achieved the excellent results that respondents'

---

[10] The [Solicitor General] suggests that "[t]he prospect of recovering $11,000 for representing [respondents] in a damages suit (assuming a contingency rate of 33%) is likely to attract a substantial number of attorneys." However, the District Court found that the 1,946.75 hours respondents' counsel spent litigating the case was reasonable and that "[t]here was not any possible way that you could have avoided putting in that amount of time. . . . " We reject the Solicitor General's suggestion that the prospect of working nearly 2,000 hours at a rate of $5.65 an hour, to be paid more than ten years after the work began, is "likely to attract a substantial number of attorneys."

counsel obtained here. Thus, had respondents had to rely on private-sector fee arrangements, they might well have been unable to obtain redress for their grievances. It is precisely for this reason that Congress enacted § 1988. . . .

IV

. . . In the absence of any indication that Congress intended to adopt a strict rule that attorney's fees under § 1988 be proportionate to damages recovered, we decline to adopt such a rule ourselves.

JUSTICE POWELL, concurring in the judgment.

. . . Petitioners argue for a rule of proportionality between the fee awarded and the damages recovered in a civil rights case. Neither the decisions of this Court nor the legislative history of § 1988 support such a "rule." The facts and circumstances of litigation are infinitely variable. Under *Hensley*, of course, "the most critical factor [in the final determination of fee awards] is the degree of success obtained." Where recovery of private damages is the purpose of a civil rights litigation, a district court, in fixing fees, is obligated to give primary consideration to the amount of damages awarded as compared to the amount sought. In some civil rights cases, however, the court may consider the vindication of constitutional rights in addition to the amount of damages recovered. In this case, for example, the District Court made an explicit finding that the "public interest" had been served by the jury's verdict that the warrantless entry was lawless and unconstitutional. . . .

AUTHORS' COMMENT:

Now we're going to hear from the dissenters. What arguments do you expect them to make? This was a close case — a 5-4 majority, and one of the majority votes was Justice Powell's narrow concurrence — so the dissenters were trying to make the strongest possible arguments in hopes of shifting a vote. Are you persuaded by what they say?

CHIEF JUSTICE BURGER, dissenting.

I join Justice Rehnquist's dissenting opinion. I write only to add that it would be difficult to find a better example of legal nonsense than the fixing of attorney's fees by a judge at $245,456.25 for the recovery of $33,350 damages.

The two attorneys receiving this nearly quarter-million-dollar fee graduated from law school in 1973 and 1974; they brought this action in 1975, which resulted in the $33,350 jury award in 1980. Their total professional experience when this litigation began consisted of Gerald Lopez' 1-year service as a law clerk to a judge and Roy Cazares' two years' experience as a trial attorney in the Defenders' Program of San Diego County. For their services the District Court found that an hourly rate of $125 per hour was reasonable.

Can anyone doubt that no private party would ever have dreamed of paying these two novice attorneys $125 per hour in 1975, which, considering inflation, would represent perhaps something more nearly a $250 per hour rate today? . . .

Justice Rehnquist, with whom The Chief Justice, Justice White, and Justice O'Connor join, dissenting. . . .

The analysis of whether the extraordinary number of hours put in by respondents' attorneys in this case was "reasonable" must be made in light of both the traditional billing practices in the profession, and the fundamental principle that the award of a "reasonable" attorney's fee under § 1988 means a fee that would have been deemed reasonable if billed to affluent plaintiffs by their own attorneys. This latter principle was stressed . . . by this Court in *Hensley*:

> Counsel for the prevailing party should make a good-faith effort to exclude from a fee request hours that are excessive, redundant, or otherwise unnecessary, just as a lawyer in private practice ethically is obligated to exclude such hours from his fee submission. 'In the private sector, "billing judgment" is an important component in fee setting. It is no less important here. Hours that are not properly billed to one's *client* also are not properly billed to one's *adversary* pursuant to statutory authority.' (emphasis in original).
>
> [T]he District Court's fee award of $245,456.25, based on a prevailing hourly rate of $125 multiplied by the number of hours which respondents' attorneys claim to have spent on the case, is not a "reasonable" attorney's fee under § 1988.

Suppose that A offers to sell Blackacre to B for $10,000. It is commonly known and accepted that Blackacre has a fair market value of $10,000. B consults an attorney and requests a determination whether A can convey good title to Blackacre. The attorney writes an elaborate memorandum concluding that A's title to Blackacre is defective, and submits a bill to B for $25,000. B refuses to pay the bill, the attorney sues, and the parties stipulate that the attorney spent 200 hours researching the title issue because of an extraordinarily complex legal and factual situation, and that the prevailing rate at which the attorney billed, which was also a "reasonable" rate, was $125. Does anyone seriously think that a court should award the attorney the full $25,000 which he claims? Surely a court would start from the proposition that, unless special arrangements were made between the client and the attorney, a "reasonable" attorney's fee for researching the title to a piece of property worth $10,000 could not exceed the value of the property. Otherwise the client would have been far better off never going to an attorney in the first place, and simply giving A $10,000 for a worthless deed. The client thereby would have saved himself $15,000.

Obviously the billing situation in a typical litigated case is more complex than in this bedrock example of a defective title claim, but some of the same principles are surely applicable. If A has a claim for contract damages in the amount of $10,000 against B, and retains an attorney to prosecute the claim, it would be both extraordinary and unjustifiable, in the absence of any special arrangement, for the attorney to put in 200 hours on the case and send the client a bill for $25,000. Such a bill would be "unreasonable," regardless of whether A obtained a judgment against B for $10,000 or obtained a take-nothing judgment. And in such a case, where the prospective recovery is limited, it is exactly this "billing judgment" which enables the parties to achieve a settlement; any competent attorney, whether prosecuting or defending a contract action for $10,000, would realize that the case simply cannot justify a fee in excess of the potential recovery on the part of either the plaintiff's or the defendant's attorney. All of these examples illuminate the point made in *Hensley* that "the important factor" in determining a "reasonable" fee is the "results obtained." The very "reasonablene ss" of the hours expended on a case by a plaintiff's attorney necessarily will depend, to a large extent, on the amount that may reasonably be expected to be recovered if the plaintiff prevails. . . .

The plurality, explains the position advanced by petitioner and the Solicitor General concerning fee awards in a case such as this, and then goes on to "reject the proposition that fee awards under § 1988 should necessarily be proportionate to the amount of damages a civil rights plaintiff actually recovers." I agree with the plurality that the importation of the contingent-fee model to govern fee awards under § 1988 is not warranted by the terms and legislative history of the statute. But I do not agree with the plurality if it means to reject the kind of "proportionality" that I have previously described. Nearly 2,000 attorney-hours spent on a case in which the total recovery was only $33,000, in which only $13,300 of that amount was recovered for the federal claims, and in which the District Court expressed the view that, in such cases, juries typically were reluctant to award substantial damages against police officers, is simply not a "reasonable" expenditure of time.

NOTES AND QUESTIONS

1. ***How Much are Civil Rights Worth?*** Justice Rehnquist was no doubt right that a client buying a parcel of real estate worth only $10,000 would not pay a lawyer $25,000 to determine whether the seller had good title to the land. But *Rivera* is not about land, it is about civil rights and equal justice under law. How much is that worth? Did the majority in *Rivera* correctly award $245,000 in fees to the plaintiffs' lawyers, or should the court have awarded less? If less, how much, and on what basis?

2. ***Fee Waiver Demands.*** Because statutory attorney fees can be very large (as *Rivera* vividly illustrates), defendants are always looking for ways to reduce fee awards. Some defendants will therefore condition settlement on the plaintiff's waiver of fees. For example, a defendant may offer to pay the plaintiff personally a fair settlement if the plaintiff will waive all statutory attorney fees. (The plaintiff has the right to waive fees because the fee-shifting statutes award fees to the prevailing *party*, not to the prevailing party's attorney.)

In *Evans v. Jeff. D.*, 475 U.S. 717 (1986), decided right after *Rivera*, the Supreme Court upheld the practice of asking a civil rights plaintiff to waive fees as a condition of settlement. The case was a class action brought by a Legal Services attorney seeking better conditions for children in an Idaho mental institution. On the eve of trial, the State of Idaho offered to give the plaintiffs virtually all of the relief they were seeking — but only if their attorney, Johnson, agreed to waive all of his fees. Johnson agreed, but when the parties appeared in court to get formal approval of the class action settlement (because class actions cannot be settled without court approval), Johnson complained to the court, which then struck down the fee waiver demand but approved the rest of the settlement. The defendant appealed and the issue eventually made it to the Supreme Court.

In the Supreme Court, Johnson argued that the offer put him in an ethical bind because he faced a conflict between accepting the settlement offer (which was plainly in his clients' best interest, since they could not have won any greater relief at trial) and insisting on his fees (which was in the best interests of Legal Services Corporation, which would keep any fees based on Johnson's work). Justice Stevens rejected Johnson's argument with the following reasoning:

> Although respondents contend that Johnson, as counsel for the class, was faced with an "ethical dilemma" when petitioners offered him relief greater than that which he could reasonably have expected to obtain for his clients at trial (if only he would stipulate to a waiver of the statutory fee award), and although we recognize Johnson's conflicting interests between pursuing relief for the class and a fee for the Idaho Legal Aid Society, we do not believe that the "dilemma" was an "ethical" one in the sense that Johnson had to choose between conflicting duties under the prevailing norms of professional conduct. Plainly, Johnson had no *ethical* obligation to seek a statutory fee award. His ethical duty was to serve his clients loyally and competently.

If fee waiver demands are permissible, will some lawyers refuse to accept future civil rights cases? Justice Brennan, joined by Justice Marshall and Justice Blackmun, thought so. They wrote:

> The cumulative effect this practice will have on the civil rights bar is evident. It does not denigrate the high ideals that motivate many civil rights practitioners to recognize that lawyers are in the business of practicing law, and that, like other business people, they are and must be concerned with earning a living. The conclusion that permitting fee waivers will seriously impair the ability of civil rights plaintiffs to obtain legal assistance is embarrassingly obvious.
>
> Because making it more difficult for civil rights plaintiffs to obtain legal assistance is precisely the opposite of what Congress sought to achieve by enacting the Fees Act, fee waivers should be prohibited. . . .

3. ***Fee Negotiations in Personal Injury Cases.*** We now move outside the civil rights context. Suppose the client is not a civil rights client but rather a routine personal injury client on a contingent fee. Does the lawyer have to advise the client that the client can net more money if the attorney waives part of the contingent fee? Must the attorney say, "You want $75,000 but the defense is offering only $100,000 and I get a third of that so you're left with only $66,667 under the current offer. I'll tell you what. I'll waive part of my fee, and I'll take only 25% of the damages instead of 33%, so you'll be left with the $75,000 you want. I can't ethically stand in the way of a good settlement just to protect my fee"? Does the attorney in a personal injury case have to say that? Where does it end? Suppose the defendant offers only $75,000 instead of $100,000. Does the plaintiff's attorney have to waive his entire fee if the client is willing to settle for $75,000? If that's not the rule, should it be? Should an attorney ever be allowed to let his interest in a fee stand in the way of a good settlement?

To change the perspective, can the client insist that the attorney reduce his fee to achieve a settlement? Apparently not. In *Hagans, Brown & Gibbs v. First Nat'l Bank*, 783 P.2d 1164 (Alaska 1989), the Alaska Supreme Court held that if a client refuses to settle solely to exert leverage against the attorney to reduce the attorney's fee, the client may be liable for breaching the implied contractual duty of good faith and fair dealing. Apparently what's good for the goose is not good for the gander; under *Evans*, the *defendant* can condition settlement on a total waiver of the plaintiff's attorney's fees, but under *Hagans* the *plaintiff* can get sued for conditioning settlement on even a partial waiver of the plaintiff's attorney's fees.

C. PRO BONO WORK

Another possible solution to the problem of providing legal services to clients who cannot pay is for lawyers themselves to provide the necessary services at no, or reduced, charge. Indeed, lawyers are expected to do just that. As Rule 6.1 says: "Every lawyer has a professional responsibility to provide legal services to those unable to pay."

The expectation that lawyers will render legal service for the public good free of charge, however, conflicts with "the real-life fact that lawyers earn their livelihood at the bar." *Bates v. State Bar of Arizona*, 433 US. 350, 368, (1977). Efforts to realize both objectives — providing pro bono services and making a decent (or better) living — have been the source of longstanding tensions for lawyers, personally, professionally, and socially. In large part, the source of the tension is the lack of agreement about the nature of *pro bono publico* service. All agree that pro bono roughly translates from Latin as "for the public good," but much else is uncertain. What qualifies as the "public good"? Must the entire public benefit from pro bono efforts, or substantially all, or at least a significant portion? Is pro bono work a positive requirement imposed by law, a moral admonition imposed by one's conscience (peers, the court, or society), or merely an expectation? Perhaps the answer to these questions depends on the cause being advocated by the person asking the questions.

The notion that lawyers may be pressed into service for the benefit of the public is a venerable one, tracing its origins to at least the 14th Century. Historians have not yet determined whether pro bono service seven centuries ago was against the will of the lawyer or whether it was compensated in any way, but what survives historically to this day is that lawyers are seen as a uniquely available resource that can be called upon to help the public. Until the 1980s, pro bono service was voluntary in every jurisdiction. Courts had power to appoint lawyers to serve as counsel in particular cases (mostly criminal cases), but the bar did not require lawyers to provide pro bono service, in the sense of uncompensated work that might potentially interfere with their capacity to earn their livelihood. Accordingly, lawyers who did not provide pro bono service were not in any way punished. Rather, the bar strongly encouraged lawyers to perform pro bono service, especially for the poor, who would otherwise go without counsel. The bar established referral services and other programs to help poor people find lawyers willing to handle their cases for little or no fee, but the bar did not compel lawyers to perform pro bono service, or even to report whether they were or were not performing such services.

For some, however, merely encouraging lawyers to serve the poor was not enough. These lawyers began to increase the amount of pro bono work lawyers were performing. What drove these pro bono enthusiasts forward? Perhaps they were motivated by a desire to see others experience what they themselves had experienced; or by a desire to counter criticisms that the legal profession was selfish and self-interested; or by a sense of shame that they themselves had done so little; or by a recognition that increasingly anti-tax and anti-spend political leaders were not likely to address crying social needs of the country. Whatever the inspiration, a handful of local bars began to require lawyers to perform pro bono service. Some jurisdictions required lawyers to perform a certain number of hours of legal work for the poor; others required lawyers to handle one or two cases a year for the poor (for example, one divorce case per year); while other jurisdictions required lawyers annually to perform any kind of pro bono service, whether for the poor or otherwise. However, these mandatory programs did not spread to other jurisdictions, so in almost every jurisdiction pro bono work remains voluntary.

Voluntary (as opposed to mandatory) pro bono work probably provides enough lawyers to perform certain kinds of tasks. Lots of lawyers serve on bar association committees or on the boards of major civic organizations. That kind of pro bono work, however, carries some inherent benefits. In bar association work, for example, lawyers meet other lawyers, which often generates referrals for paying business. Also, bar association work is socially comfortable — lawyers like to be around other lawyers because they feel at ease with them. Similarly, assisting major non-profit organizations, such as symphonies and art museums, provides opportunities for lawyers to rub elbows with the rich and powerful donors and political figures who often serve on boards of such prominent organizations. The "free" time committed to these organizations, therefore, is a form of investment — an effort that lawyers hope will in time pay off (literally) directly or indirectly. It is, in effect, a highly effective form of advertising.

Legal services for the poor, however, are a different story. In this area, many observers believe that there is a crisis. Moreover, as our discussion elsewhere suggested, the legal needs of the poor are increasing rapidly while the pool of volunteer pro bono attorneys remains about the same. Some might, nevertheless, argue that it is contrary to the American way to order people to serve others without pay. Still others are calling for mandatory pro bono programs. And, although some proponents are willing to move slowly (while the bar and the courts give lawyers a chance to increase pro bono efforts voluntarily), others favor moving ahead rapidly and aggressively.

No state yet requires lawyers to perform pro bono work, but a few jurisdictions require lawyers to report how much pro bono work they do, and various other jurisdictions ask lawyers to report, when paying their annual (or bi-annual) bar dues, how much pro bono work they have done. Florida's Rule 4-6.1, adopted in 1993, was one of the first rules in the country requiring lawyers to report their pro bono hours. Here are the most pertinent parts of the rule:

Florida Rule 4-6.1 Pro Bono Public Service

(a) *Professional Responsibility.* Each member of The Florida Bar in good standing, as part of that member's professional responsibility, should (1) render pro bono legal services to the poor and (2) participate, to the extent possible, in other pro bono service activities that directly relate to the legal needs of the poor. . . .

(b) *Discharge of the Professional Responsibility to Provide Pro Bono Legal Service to the Poor.* The professional responsibility to provide pro bono legal services as established under this rule is aspirational rather than mandatory in nature. The failure to fulfill one's professional responsibility under this rule will not subject a lawyer to discipline. The professional responsibility to provide pro bono legal service to the poor may be discharged by:

(1) annually providing at least 20 hours of pro bono legal service to the poor; or

(2) making an annual contribution of at least $350 to a legal aid organization.

(c) *Collective Discharge of the Professional Responsibility to Provide Pro Bono Legal Service to the Poor.* Each member of the bar should strive to individually satisfy the member's professional responsibility to provide pro bono legal service to the poor. Collective satisfaction of this professional responsibility is permitted by law firms only under a collective satisfaction plan that has been filed previously with the circuit pro bono committee and only when providing pro bono legal service to the poor:

(1) in a major case or matter involving a substantial expenditure of time and resources; or

(2) through a full-time community or public service staff; or

(3) in any other manner that has been approved by the circuit pro bono committee in the circuit in which the firm practices.

(d) *Reporting Requirement.* Each member of the bar shall annually report whether the member has satisfied the member's professional responsibility to provide pro bono legal services to the poor. Each member shall report this information through a simplified reporting form that is made a part of the member's annual dues statement. The form will contain the following categories from which each member will be allowed to choose in reporting whether the member has provided pro bono legal services to the poor:

(1) I have personally provided ___ hours of pro bono legal services;

(2) I have provided pro bono legal services collectively by: (indicate type of case and manner in which service was provided);

(3) I have contributed $___ to: (indicate organization to which funds were provided);

(4) I have provided legal services to the poor in the following special manner: (indicate manner in which services were provided); or

(5) I have been unable to provide pro bono legal services to the poor this year; or

(6) I am deferred from the provision of pro bono legal services to the poor because I am: (indicate whether lawyer is: a member of the judiciary or judicial staff; a government lawyer prohibited by statute, rule, or regulation from providing services; retired, or inactive).

The failure to report this information shall constitute a disciplinary offense under these rules.

(e) *Credit Toward Professional Responsibility in Future Years.* In the event that more than 20 hours of pro bono legal service to the poor are provided and reported in any 1 year, the hours in excess of 20 hours may be carried forward and reported as such for up to 2 succeeding years for the purpose of determining whether a lawyer has fulfilled the professional responsibility to provide pro bono legal service to the poor in those succeeding years.

(f) *Out-of-State Members of the Bar.* Out-of-state members of the bar may fulfill their professional responsibility in the states in which they practice or reside.

In adopting the rule, the Florida Supreme Court touched on many issues central to the pro bono debate. The court's opinion follows. Although the opinion is more than fifteen years old, it still rings true, and still expresses a relatively progressive view on pro bono issues.

AMENDMENTS TO RULES REGULATING THE FLORIDA BAR

630 So. 2d 501 (Fla. 1993)

OVERTON, J.

This cause is before the Court to review proposed pro bono rules prepared by The Florida Bar/Florida Bar Foundation Joint Commission on the Delivery of Legal Services to the Indigent in Florida. These proposed rules were prepared solely to address the legal needs of the poor in Florida pursuant to this Court's direction. . . .

In adopting these rules, we emphasize that they are aspirational rather than mandatory. The rules establish specific goals to assist each lawyer in Florida in fulfilling the commitment a lawyer makes upon taking the oath to become an officer of the court: "I will never reject from any consideration personal to myself the cause of the defenseless or oppressed." Although all licensed lawyers in Florida take this oath, some respondents still argue that this Court has no authority to establish pro bono guidelines. Moreover, they claim that the rules are mandatory rather than aspirational and amount to nothing more than a social program for the general welfare of the public. On the other hand, some respondents assert that the proposed rules do not go far enough, arguing that the rules should be mandatory rather than aspirational and claiming that the implementation of mandatory pro bono is the only way to ensure that legal services will be provided to the poor.

. . . [T]his Court, as the administrative head of the judicial branch, has the responsibility to ensure that access to the courts is provided for all segments of our society. Given the number of reports presented to this Court that document the legal needs of the poor, we find it necessary to implement the attached rules. Justice is not truly justice if only the rich can afford counsel and gain access to the courts. Consequently, these rules are being implemented in the hopes that they will act as a motivating force for the provision of legal services to the poor by the members of this state's legal profession.

We realize, however, that the rules we adopt in today's opinion will not be the prime motivating force in making the legal system work through the provision of pro bono services — only lawyers themselves can do that. Nevertheless, . . . we hope that the lawyers of this state, as officers of our courts, will recognize the clear legal needs of the indigent in this state and will act to provide the necessary services. We do not believe that mandatory pro bono is necessary to fulfill that goal. As such, the rules are aspirational rather than mandatory, and the failure to meet the aspirational standards set forth in the rules will not constitute an offense subject to discipline.

On the other hand, we do expect members of the Bar, through the simplified report form that will be made a part of the annual dues statement, to report how they have assisted in addressing the legal needs of the poor. We believe that accurate reporting is essential for evaluating this program and for determining what services are being provided under the program. This, in turn, will allow us to determine the areas in which the legal needs of the poor are or are not being met. Because we find that reporting is essential, failure to report will constitute an offense subject to discipline.

Further, we do not believe that the hourly pro bono service recommendation in the rules constitutes an unreachable aspiration for a lawyer in today's society. The rules recommend a minimum of twenty hours service per year for each member of the Bar. The American Bar Association, at its February 1993 meeting, adopted a suggested standard of fifty hours service per year. A.B.A. Model Rules of Professional Conduct Rule 6.1 (1993) ("A lawyer should aspire to render at least (50) hours of pro bono publico legal services per year.") The American Bar Association's suggested service standard is significantly greater than the twenty-hour goal we adopt through this opinion. We note that some law firms today set a goal for their partners and associates of 1800 to 2100 billable hours per year. By those standards, the suggested goal of twenty hours per year in these rules is minimal.

AUTHORS' COMMENT:

Do you agree with Florida's goal of twenty hours per year? If not, would you set the goal at more than twenty hours a year or less than twenty hours a year? Why?

While we approve the substance of the proposed rules, we find that certain modifications are necessary to address a number of issues raised in this proceeding. . . .

Definition of "Legal Services to the Poor"

The entire focus of this action has been to address the legal needs of the poor. That objective is distinguishable from other types of uncompensated public service activities of the legal profession. Clearly, this Court has the constitutional responsibility to ensure access to the justice system. Although other public service by the legal profession is important, no authority exists for this Court to address, through the Rules Regulating The Florida Bar, uncompensated public service activities not directly related to services for the courts and the legal needs of the poor. As such, we find that the proposed rules should be modified to eliminate any reference to services not related to the legal needs of the poor. Additionally, we find that the rules should clearly indicate that their purpose is to establish aspirational goals and to motivate the legal profession to provide necessary legal services to the poor. . . . It is also our intention that the definition include legal services not only to indigent individuals but also to the "working poor." The rules have been modified accordingly. . . .

Collective Discharge of a Lawyer's Pro Bono Responsibility

The proposed rules significantly restrict the collective discharge of a lawyer's responsibility to provide legal services to the poor but does allow such collective discharge in very limited circumstances. As we read the rule, it encourages lawyers to personally provide this service so that each lawyer may experience this responsibility firsthand and, consequently, better understand the needs that must be served. Nevertheless, the rules recognize that some types of cases, such as death penalty representations, must be given collective credit in view of the substantial time, effort, and expense that is usually involved. To not allow such collective credit would actually act as a deterrent to obtaining counsel in such cases where legal representation is essential. As such, we approve the collective-discharge provisions as written. We also believe that approval of the collective discharge provisions should encourage large law offices to fund full-time public service staffs. This, in turn, will assist in making available an increased amount of public pro bono legal services, particularly in cases that require substantial time and support commitments.

AUTHORS' COMMENT:

Do you support or oppose the option allowing lawyers to fulfill their pro bono responsibilities by having other lawyers in their firm perform the work? For example, if one lawyer in a ten-lawyer firm performs 200 hours of pro bono work by working on a big case for a year, should that fulfill the annual 20-hour pro bono obligation of all ten lawyers in the firm? Why or why not?

Reporting Requirements

As previously indicated, in order to evaluate the effectiveness of pro bono services, a simplified reporting scheme is necessary. Some responses we have received argue that a reporting requirement makes this program mandatory rather than aspirational. We reject that contention. Granted, some peer pressure may exist as a result of the reporting requirement. However, given that the reporting requirement is the only true way to evaluate how the legal needs of the poor are being met, we find that the merits of the reporting requirement greatly outweigh any perceived pressure to participate. Indeed, if peer pressure motivates lawyers to participate, we find that such pressure may be beneficial in this instance.

. . . .

Out-of-State Members

A significant number of lawyers licensed to practice law in Florida reside and practice outside of this state. Even so, we find that they should not be excluded from their responsibility to provide legal services to the poor. We hold, however, that such services or, alternatively, financial contributions may be made in the states in which they practice or reside. The proposed rules have been modified accordingly.

. . . .

. . . For the reasons expressed, we approve the rules as modified in the attached appendix, and we direct that they shall become effective October 1, 1993.

It is so ordered.

BARKETT, CHIEF JUSTICE, specially concurring.

As expressed in the majority opinion and in this Court's prior opinions, I certainly agree that lawyers have a responsibility to help assure meaningful access to the courts for all of our citizens. I also have noted previously that pro bono work enables lawyers to understand the problems besetting the vast majority of our citizens in a way that simply reading about them does not. It is only when the more influential members of our society truly understand the legal problems of most Floridians that meaningful solutions will be sought and found to assure access to the courts, without which there never will be equal justice.

Accordingly, I agree with much of the majority's opinion. I write separately, however, to make some additional observations about some of the provisions in the new rules.

First, like some other members of the Court, I am troubled by the $350 buy-out provision. I am not comfortable with providing such an easy incentive to avoid the more significant, necessary, and direct help that is essential if the impact is to be real. Moreover, there is an inherent inequity when those who cannot afford to pay are asked to provide twenty hours of work, and those with money can "buy out" for the value of a few hours. . . .

AUTHORS' COMMENT:

Are you troubled by the $350 "buy-out provision," which says that lawyers don't personally have to perform legal services if they donate $350 to an organization that provides legal services to the poor? Why do you support or oppose the buy-out provisions?

Finally, we cannot forget that access to the courts is, in the final analysis, the responsibility of the State. No amount of pro bono service by lawyers will ever meet the existing need. I must confess to the nagging worry that a recognition of lawyers' pro bono responsibilities may obfuscate the fact that our democracy and system of justice is predicated on the ability of all citizens to access the courts. . . . [B]asic legal aid must be viewed as every citizen's right and not as an act of charity. At the very least, lawyers must bring the overwhelming need for legal services to the attention of legislative bodies and do everything possible to see that the need is met.

McDonald, J., specially concurring

. . . Everyone concerned is endeavoring to constitutionally make available legal services to all in need of them. The proposed rule changes, recognizing that the responsibility for this task rests on society generally, describe what a minimal contribution by attorneys is appropriate to be consistent with their ethical obligations. As an aspirational guideline, I have no quarrel with the exception that the paltry contribution of $350 should substitute for twenty hours of work. This alternative should be at least $1,000, which would relate to $50 per hour, a figure few lawyers accept as an hourly rate today. While I prefer no amendment, the ones approved by the majority are not unreasonable if we insist on this course.

AUTHORS' COMMENT:

Do you agree with Justice McDonald that the $350 "buy-out" amount is "paltry" and should be much higher? Whether you think the amount should be higher or lower than $350, do you think the amount of the buy-out should be tied to a lawyer's hourly rate, to a lawyer's annual income, to a lawyer's net worth, or to some other measure? Assuming the rule contains a buy-out provision (even if you disagree with the concept), how would you decide on the amount of the buy-out provision?

Kogan, J. concurring in part, dissenting in part.

I continue to adhere to my earlier views regarding the pro bono obligations of Florida attorneys. With regard to the present case, I concur in the majority opinion with the exception of the $350.00 "buy-out" provision. I find it ethically repugnant to suggest that an obligation inhering in each attorney personally can be discharged merely by a contribution of money. Under this provision, financially able attorneys can buy their way clear of the aspirational duty to help the poor, while less financially able attorneys who take their ethical obligations seriously will be constrained to donate services. Both should be treated equally.

NOTES AND QUESTIONS

1. ***Did Mandatory Reporting Make a Difference in Florida?*** How did Florida's experiment with mandatory reporting of pro bono hours work out? Apparently it was a great success. A 1999 Florida Bar Journal article entitled "*Florida Lawyers Set Record in Donating Services and Money to Poor*" described the impact of the new rule:

> More than 20,000 Florida attorneys provided free legal services to the poor and contributed more than $1.4 million to legal aid organizations, according to a recent report by The Florida Bar's Standing Committee on Pro Bono Services.
>
> Since the inception of the Supreme Court's voluntary pro bono plan almost five years ago, the number of hours provided to assist the poor in legal has increased 50 percent and the contributions have increased 63 percent, reported this week by the committee to the Bar's Board of Governors. The information was obtained from the mandatory disclosure regarding activity contained on lawyers' annual Florida Bar fee statements.
>
> Bar members are asked to volunteer at least 20 hours of pro bono service or give a $350 contribution to a legal aid organization.
>
> "The participation of Florida lawyers shows beyond question that our lawyers are committed to helping others, irrespective of their client's ability to pay a fee," said Bar president Edward R. Blumberg of Miami. "I know of no profession that makes this kind of commitment to giving something back to the community and to society." . . .
>
> During 1996–97, Florida lawyers reported 842,304 hours of pro bono work and more than $1.4 million in direct legal aid funding. Using 1994–1995 as the program's base year, the number of hours increased from 561,352 and the contributions from $876,837.
>
> The report said, at a median billable rate of $150 per hour, more than $120 million worth of time was donated to the poor. The figure exceeds the $27 million in funding provided to Florida legal aid offices by the federal Legal Services Corporation and The Florida Bar Foundation.
>
> "Florida lawyers have willingly embraced their professional obligation to provide legal services to those who otherwise would be unable to afford them," said Cynthia A. Everett, chair of the standing committee. "Despite the negative perception of lawyers sometimes portrayed in the media, the report shows that lawyers are hardworking, generous and dedicated to providing access to the courts for all segments of society."
>
> Here are some typical scenarios:
>
> - A volunteer attorney helped a 90-year-old invalid woman recover the money she gave a roofing company to repair her roof. The roofing company made poor and faulty repairs.
> - A mentally disabled client was tricked into signing for a mortgage on her house. Once the client cashed the $35,000 check, the client's caseworker took the money and disappeared. The house went into foreclosure. The pro bono attorney successfully set aside the court's default judgment and saved the client's home.

- A female victim of domestic violence sought refuge at a local abuse shelter. With the assistance of a volunteer attorney, she obtained a preliminary injunction against her husband. After a hearing, the couple reached a settlement that divided a joint savings account containing the proceeds of the husband's workers' compensation claim.

Those are just a few of the documented instances of how volunteer attorneys made a difference in an impoverished segment of society. Although voluntary pro bono plan's growth is positive, Bar leaders continue to search for ways to provide greater legal assistance in areas of family, juvenile, consumer finance and housing law.

2. ***Are Other Professions as Generous?*** In the article just quoted, the Florida Bar President says that no other profession "makes this kind of commitment to giving something back to the community"? Is that true? Do you have any experience working in another profession, or do you have friends or relatives who work in other professions? Do these other professions have pro bono requirements or aspirational rules?

3. ***Should your State Adopt a Pro Bono Rule Like Florida's?*** Now that you've read all the reasons underlying Florida's pro bono rule and seen the statistics showing how the rule is working in Florida, are you in favor of adopting a similar (or identical) rule in your state? Or would you prefer a rule like ABA Model Rule 6.1? How does ABA Model Rule 6.1 differ from Florida's Rule 4-6.1?

4. ***Mandatory Record Keeping?*** As an alternative to mandatory reporting, would you favor mandatory record keeping of pro bono hours? Lawyers would have to keep track of their pro bono hours the same way they have to keep track of their lawyer trust accounts. Failure to keep the required pro bono records would be a disciplinary offense, just as failure to keep trust account records is a disciplinary offense. Would mandatory record keeping, without mandatory reporting, be an effective way of encouraging pro bono work? Would you give the state the power to conduct random audits of lawyers' pro bono records?

5. ***Should Pro Bono Work be Mandatory?*** Below are two opposing arguments on mandatory pro bono work. Which side do you take? Or do your views differ from both arguments?

In favor of mandatory pro bono

We have been trying to get lawyers to do more pro bono work on a volunteer basis for decades, and the voluntary approach doesn't work. It doesn't work because the law is an intensely competitive field, with far more lawyers than society needs (at least for paying clients!). The sole practitioners are struggling to survive in the profession, and the big firm lawyers are struggling to make partner or to get a bigger share of the partnership pie. And once somebody makes it big, it seems a lot easier to write a check to a public interest group than to serve a client directly. So instead of getting the best lawyers, poor people get the most idealistic lawyers, or the publicity hounds, or the lawyers who can't attract enough paying clients.

The only way to end this cycle is to institute mandatory pro bono programs. And there are a lot of good reasons for doing that. First, mandatory pro bono programs are in the bar's self-interest. If lawyers don't find a way to provide services for poor people, then the government will make them provide services for poor people. I'm sure lawyers think they can do a better job devising a mandatory pro bono program than the government can.

Second, lawyers who do pro bono work invariably say it is one of the most satisfying experiences of their professional lives. Lawyers in America are so caught up in the quest for money, money, money that they forget the ideal of client service — the ideal of helping people make better lives for themselves. When lawyers help poor people fight off an unfair eviction, or obtain food stamps, or defend a client against a lawsuit by a sleazy door-to-door salesman, they regain the ideal of lawyers as public servants. Pro bono work is like exercise — people don't want to do it, but they feel much better afterwards.

Third, voluntary programs are unfair because 20% of the lawyers end up doing 90% of the work. Why should all of the work fall on such a small group? The only way to distribute the work load equally is through a mandatory program.

The complaints about mandatory pro bono are bogus. The one about not doing a good job unless you want to do something is ridiculous. Private lawyers all have plenty of clients they hate, but they work hard for those clients, and they claim to do a good job. As for the argument that we don't require lawyers to give to charity, that's just dead wrong. Lawyers do have to give to charity; it's called taxes. Those who are fortunate enough to take from society in the form of good jobs, property, and successful investments have to give back to society in the form of taxes to help poor people. The same principle should apply to pro bono. Lawyers have a state-conferred monopoly on a highly lucrative profession — a profession that thrives on complex laws and procedures. Lawyers have a responsibility to pay a "tax of time" to help poor people navigate through the maze of these complex laws and procedures. And as for training lawyers, matching them with clients, and recognizing their efforts, just make pro bono mandatory and watch what happens. Lawyers will demand these things, and the bar will respond. It's like the Legal Profession course. Before it was required, only a few professors wrote textbooks in the area. After it was required, the textbooks appeared by the dozen. Once mandatory pro bono programs are adopted, the services lawyers need to implement the program successfully will crop up automatically just by operation of the free market.

If you do not agree with the argument, where does the argument go wrong? Do you agree instead with the following argument?

Against mandatory pro bono

The best way to increase pro bono work is for the organized bar to improve volunteer programs. Specifically, the bar needs to do three things.

First, the bar needs to increase training so that more lawyers know how to provide the kinds of services people really need — unusual areas of the law like consumer credit, landlord-tenant, welfare payments, and subsidized housing. Very few lawyers know anything about these areas, and they are hard areas to learn because they depend on complex federal statutes, regulations, and administrative procedures. Lawyers who spend most of their time on areas such as wills, personal injury, or divorce matters don't have time to learn these areas on their own, and don't want to take cases in these areas until they learn them.

Second, the bar needs to match up lawyers with people who need the kinds of services the lawyers provide. A lawyer isn't going to spend three months learning about Social Security benefits if potential clients aren't even going to know he works in that area. Before a lawyer will invest the time to learn a new field, the bar has to guarantee that it will send him some pre-screened clients in the area — clients who have real problems that need the services of a lawyer with specialized training. Pro bono lawyers aren't going to spend their money advertising to get non-paying clients, and they don't want to spend their time screening potential clients who don't have real problems, or whose problems are in some other area of the law.

Third, the bar needs to recognize the efforts of people who devote a lot of time to pro bono work. Let's face it: there's a lot more incentive to do good if you have a chance of getting some business out of it in the long run. The business won't come from the pro bono clients, but it will come from the publicity about who is doing good — from things like awards dinners where pro bono lawyers get their pictures in the paper shaking hands with the Mayor or the bar association president. Those pictures generate paying business.

If the bar would do these three things, then no one would be talking about mandatory pro bono programs any more than we talk about requiring lawyers to give to charity.

The people who favor mandatory pro bono don't understand human nature. The most powerful force in the world is money. That's what built America. And as a group, lawyers respond more to economic incentives than others. That's why they went into law in the first place. (Some people went into law to do good, but they are already doing more than their share of pro bono work — a mandatory program wouldn't affect them.) If you can find a way to make pro bono efforts pay off at the bottom line, then lawyers will do it voluntarily and do it well. If you make it mandatory, people are going to resent it, and neither the clients nor the lawyers will get the full potential benefit. Besides, unless people want to do pro bono work, they aren't going to do a good job.

If you don't agree with this argument, what's wrong with it? Where's the flaw? Was the first argument right?

6. *What is the Ideal Pro Bono Rule?* Now that you have heard many different arguments on the pro bono question, check the boxes you agree with in the following chart to express your ideas about the ideal pro bono rule — the one you would adopt if you were the King of America and could make the law by decree:

THE IDEAL PRO BONO RULE

FEATURE	*YES*	*NO*
Mandatory?		
Target number of pro bono hours? (If yes, how many? State a number.)	If yes, how many hours?	
Emphasis on service to the poor? Give a number of hours, a percentage of time, or an adjective like "majority" or "substantial."	If yes, how is the emphasis measured?	
Reporting requirement?		
Collective responsibility for law firms (as opposed to individual responsibility for each lawyer)?		
"Buy-out" feature (allowing lawyers to pay money instead of performing pro bono services)?	If yes, how is the buy-out measured?	
Carry-over feature (allowing lawyers to apply this year's excess hours to next year's requirements)?		
Financial penalties for failing to meet the requirements?	If yes, how is the penalty measured?	
Professional discipline (censure, suspension, or disbarment) for failing to meet any of the pro bono rule requirements?		
Are non-resident lawyers obligated to abide by the pro bono rule in state (as opposed to doing pro bono work in their home state)?		

Feel free to add other features that we did not address in our chart.

Chapter 28
CONTINGENT FEES: PROMISE AND PROBLEMS

In an earlier chapter we introduced contingent fees. In this chapter, we focus on contingent fees in greater depth, raising both the enormous promise and the many problems associated with contingent fees. We single out contingent fees because historically contingent fees have been the most controversial and the most regulated type of fee arrangement. (As already mentioned, most countries in the world ban contingent fees — though England very recently lifted the ban and now allows them.) Why does America permit lawyers to charge contingent fees? What problems do they cause? Should contingent fees be permitted in criminal cases? What would happen if contingent fees were prohibited?

A. THE PROMISE OF CONTINGENT FEES

Chiseled into the marble above the entrance to the United States Supreme Court are the words, "Equal justice for all." Equal justice for all is a bedrock American value. Contingent fees embody that value and reflect the belief that a person may not be able to obtain equal justice if they are not first able to obtain a lawyer. Contingent fees may help people to obtain lawyers. The promise of contingent fees is access to a lawyer, and thus access to the courts and our magnificent system of justice.

Many scholars and court opinions have articulated the reasons for allowing contingent fees. A concise statement of the policies behind contingent fees is found in *Arnold v. The Northern Trust Co.*, 506 N.E.2d 1279 (1987), a case challenging the enforcement of a contingent fee agreement against a minor:

> Significant considerations of public policy underlie the enforcement of reasonable contingent-fee agreements. "Contingent fee contracts are the basic means by which much litigation in tort is conducted in this State." Such agreements are the "poor man's key to the courthouse door": they enable persons who cannot afford to retain an attorney on an hourly or fixed-fee basis to pursue their claims with competent counsel. Contingent fees are thus rooted in our commitment to equal justice for both those of moderate means and the wealthy.
>
> These considerations do not evaporate simply because the party in need of legal assistance is a minor. To the contrary, the court's duty to protect minors is consistent with the policy of promoting access to the courts through reasonable contingent-fee agreements. A court can do nothing for a minor not before it, and injured minors are as likely as adults to require the key to the courthouse which contingent-fee contracts provide. If contingent-fee contracts were uniformly unavailable in cases involving minors and attorneys could only receive fees on a quantum meruit basis, the likely result would be to deprive many minors of quality legal representation.

The same could be said of contingent fees for all people, not just minors. Courts cannot protect or enforce the rights of people not before them, and if contingent fees were prohibited — if all attorneys were required to charge an hourly or flat rate (i.e., *quantum meruit*) — many people would not be able to find a lawyer. Why do we say this? Here's our logic:

1. Many people don't have the money to pay a lawyer unless they obtain a substantial amount of damages.
2. Virtually every case entails one or more risks, for example:
   (a) *Losing.* The client may lose, either at trial or on appeal. A lawyer who has a "portfolio" of cases can afford to lose some cases (and therefore not get paid), just as an investor with a portfolio of stocks can afford for some

stocks to go down as long as other stocks go up. An investor who owns 50 stocks doesn't need every stock to be a winner if the gains on the winners outweigh the losses on the losers over the long run. But an individual client (such as a personal injury client) cannot take the risk of paying an attorney by the hour and then losing, because the client doesn't have a portfolio of cases — the client has one case.

(b) *Winning only a little.* The client may prevail but may win very little. The client may win so little (or be forced to settle for so little) that the client can't afford to pay the attorney's fee.

(c) *Remittitur.* The client may win, but win too much, leading the judge to order a remittitur (reduction) on grounds that the verdict was excessive.

(d) *Nonpayment.* The client might win but the defendant may refuse to pay, or be unable to pay, the judgment.

(e) *Reversal.* The client might win a substantial judgment but the judgment may be reversed on appeal.

With this background on risk in place, we will explore some interesting features of contingent fees and the alternatives to contingent fees.

Lawyers and the Risk of Losing. Lawyers are willing to take the risks just outlined in contingent fee cases because (as mentioned) lawyers have a portfolio of cases, not just one case. Some cases will be worth a lot and some will be worth little or nothing, but over the long run the lawyer can make a living by collecting a contingent fee on all of the winners (those that settle for a decent amount and those that generate sizeable jury verdicts) despite collecting no fee on the losers. In other words, the winners subsidize the losers. But that is not true of clients — especially personal injury clients and wrongful death clients — who typically have just one case to win or lose. The fact that plaintiffs have just one case whereas plaintiffs' lawyers have a portfolio of cases creates some problems we discuss below.

The Dual Function of Contingent Fees. Contingent fees serve two complementary functions.

First, contingent fees insure that lawyers will get a fee in all successful cases, whether or not the client can afford to pay a fee (giving lawyers a substantial upside).

Second, contingent fees protect clients against having to pay legal fees if they lose (protecting clients against a substantial downside). Said another way, contingent fees make it economically feasible for lawyers to *accept* some cases they might lose (because the winning cases effectively subsidize the fees in the losing cases) and make it economically feasible for clients to *bring* some cases they might lose (because clients do not pay anything unless they win).

Does this dual function encourage weak suits that should not be brought? Would banning contingent fees discourage strong suits that would not be brought if the plaintiff faced ruinous fees in the event of a defense verdict? In other words, do contingent fees strike the right balance between opening the courthouse to meritorious suits while closing it to suits that lack merit?

Contingent Fees in Large vs. Small Cases — Do the Math. Contingent fees provide substantial economic benefits to plaintiffs with relatively small cases. Suppose a lawyer agrees to represent a personal injury plaintiff on a 1/3 contingent fee. The lawyer spends 50 hours and wins only $12,000 at trial. The lawyer takes her 1/3 fee, which comes to $4,000. For the lawyer, that comes to an effective rate of $80 per hour for the 50 hours. The client takes home $8,000. (Let's forget about expenses for the moment.)

Compare that to the situation in which the lawyer does not offer a contingent fee (nothing compels a lawyer to do so) and instead agrees to represent the plaintiff for $100 per hour. Suppose the lawyer spends the same 50 hours on the case. That adds up to a $5,000 fee, leaving the client only $7,000 ($12,000 − 5,000 = 7,000).

As the lawyer spends more hours on the case at an hourly rate, the less the client keeps. If the lawyer spends 120 hours on the case, for example, then the lawyer takes all $12,000 and the client wins nothing. If the lawyer spends more than 120 hours on the case, the client will actually *owe* the lawyer money. Thus, a client who sues for damages and pays a lawyer by the hour risks losing even if he wins! He can end up worse off than if he had never sued, even in a case with some merit.

In large cases, in contrast, the plaintiff is usually better off with an hourly rate. Suppose the plaintiff was catastrophically injured and obtains a judgment or settlement of $3,000,000. If the plaintiff has hired the lawyer on a 1/3 contingent fee, the lawyer will earn a fee of $1,000,000 and the client will take home $2,000,000. If plaintiff had instead hired the lawyer on an hourly rate, at $100 per hour, then the client will pay a lower fee as long as the lawyer spends less than 10,000 hours on the case. (Check it out: $100/hour × 10,000 hours = $1,000,000.)

Of course, no lawyer spends 10,000 hours on a personal injury case. Maybe an antitrust case would take that much time, spread over many years and many lawyers in a large firm. But even a huge personal injury case would more likely take the lawyer in the realm of 1,000 hours (just to get the right order of magnitude). A plaintiff could buy 1,000 hours of a lawyer's time for only $100,000 — so if the plaintiff won the same $3,000,000, the plaintiff would take home $2,900,000. That's an extra $900,000 for the plaintiff compared to a 1/3 contingent fee. That's not chickenfeed.

Here's another example, using somewhat more modest numbers. Suppose a client is likely to recover about $60,000. Under a 1/3 contingent fee, the lawyer will earn a fee of $20,000. The lawyer would have to work 200 hours to run up a $20,000 fee at an hourly rate of $100 ($200 × 100 = $20,000). If the lawyer can competently litigate the case in less than 200 hours, the client would seem to be better off paying $100 an hour rather than paying a 1/3 contingent fee.

In sum, when damages are relatively low, the client is usually better off with a contingent fee, because a lawyer's hourly rate fee might eat up all of the plaintiff's winnings. A contingent fee arrangement at least guarantees that the client won't end up owing the lawyer any money. If a client is not well off financially, a guarantee that the client can't lose money on the case may be very important. However, if the damages are high (i.e., if the client expects to recover a substantial amount of money), the client is often better off paying an hourly fee.

B. SOME PROBLEMS WITH CONTINGENT FEES

Contingent fees may be the key to the courthouse door for many clients, but many problems can arise in contingent fee arrangements. Let's build all of the problems around one medical malpractice example. Suppose your client has an operation and something goes wrong, so she ends up with her right arm paralyzed. The doctors apologize, but your client wants to sue. You take the case on a 1/3 contingent fee. Eventually the other side makes a settlement offer. By elaborating on this example with several variations, we'll illustrate the main criticisms of contingent fee arrangements:

Do Contingent Fees Cause Frivolous Suits? Some people say that contingent fees generate lots of frivolous lawsuits. The argument is that since clients don't have to make any investment to bring a suit (because the lawyer is advancing the costs and not charging anything for the legal work unless the client obtains some money), and since the lawyer bears all the risk, clients will press even the silliest claims. The client's theory in bringing a frivolous claim (also called a "nuisance suit") is that the defendant (or at least the defendant's insurance company) will pay less to settle with the plaintiff early in the suit than it would pay the lawyers to litigate the suit to judgment. Thus, the defendant in a nuisance suit is better off paying a quick settlement to the plaintiff than paying legal fees to the lawyers to litigate the case. In our medical malpractice example, for instance, maybe the client was explicitly warned that her operation carried a serious risk of paralysis, and maybe the doctors didn't do anything wrong during the operation.

If the case goes to trial, the legal fees will be a fortune. Because bringing suit is cost-free for the client, the client can exploit this situation by suing for the nuisance value. If the client had to pay her lawyer by the hour, the defendant could call the plaintiff's bluff by continuing to litigate until the plaintiff could not afford to keep litigating any longer.

The argument that contingent fees lead to frivolous cases has some merit, but there is a strong counterargument. Good contingent fee lawyers screen their cases carefully, because they don't make any money on losers. Medical malpractice cases are especially tough, so the main plaintiffs' malpractice firms typically screen out 90% to 95% of all cases, accepting only a handful. Do hourly rate lawyers screen out as many cases? No, they don't. Why would they? Hourly rate lawyers make money whether the client wins or loses.

There are some contingent fee lawyers who make money by bringing lots of nuisance suits, but there are not many. And there are probably just as many hourly rate lawyers who bring nuisance suits. The contingent fee isn't to blame for frivolous suits.

In short, contingent fees make it easier for clients to bring frivolous suits, but they also give lawyers the incentive to screen out frivolous cases. There's just not enough money to be made by filing nuisance suits, because if they don't settle right away, the ruse doesn't work and the lawyer probably ends up dropping the suit, settling for a small amount after a lot of work, or going to trial and losing. None of those are good ways to make money.

What Happens When Clients Won't Settle? Another problem with contingent fees arises when the client is dead set against settlement. Sometimes, you want to settle a case and your client doesn't. For example, suppose you've spent about 100 hours on your medical malpractice case and the case is almost ready for trial. The defendant then offers $300,000 in settlement. You would keep one-third, which would make your fee $100,000. That comes to $1,000 per hour. Not bad! Then you'll go on to the next case, and if you can keep doing this — if you keep getting similar clients and settling their cases for similar amounts (some more, some less, of course) — then your overall income will be $1,000 per hour, which comes to . . . let's see . . . 50 weeks times 40 hours per week times 1,000 per hour . . . that's $2,000,000 per year. Wow! Personal injury is an attractive field.

Since settle-and-run is your business model, you want to grab that $300,000 settlement offer in your med-mal case. After all, a bird in the hand is worth two in the bush. If you don't grab the settlement, two bad things could happen. One, is that you could go to trial and lose. Sorry, Charlie, no fee. Or, you could go to trial and win, but your effective hourly rate would be lower than $1,000 per hour — possibly much lower.

Let's illustrate. Suppose you were to reject the $300,000 settlement offer, go to trial and win $600,000. That's twice the settlement offer and will give you twice the fee. (Your fee will now be $200,000.) Is that good? It depends (a) how long it took you to do it, and (b) what you could have done with the time instead. (Economists call the second factor "opportunity cost," the cost of pursuing one opportunity instead of another. Right now, you are incurring a substantial short-run opportunity cost by attending law school, since you could otherwise get a full-time job, but it's worth it because you will one day profit from your investment and end up ahead of the game. Your higher income after law school will more than make up for your lost income — your opportunity cost — during law school.)

Let's estimate it will take you an extra 200 hours to get this case ready for trial and conduct the trial. You will have spent 200 hours earning an additional $100,000 in fees, which comes to only $500 per hour for the extra work. That's nothing to sneeze at, but it's only half the $1,000 per hour that you would earn if your client accepts the pending $300,000 settlement offer. Maybe you could have done better by settling this case and devoting your time to another case until it generated a high settlement offer. Maybe you had another case like the first one and could have earned $1,000 per hour by litigating zealously and forcing the defendant to settle for a decent amount. Your own financial interest is therefore to settle the medical malpractice case now so you can concentrate your effort on the second case, or on a new case.

But there's one hitch. You can't settle without the client's authority. Rule 1.2(a) says: "A lawyer shall abide by a client's decision whether to accept an offer of settlement of a matter." And your client doesn't want to settle. Your client wants to go to trial. Why? Every client has different reasons for wanting to go to trial. Maybe your client is the martyr type who wants the world to know what happened to him. ("I don't even care if I lose," your client says, "as long as we go to trial so I can tell everyone what that evil doctor did.") Or maybe your client is the Las Vegas type who wants to go for the big bucks. ("I know I could lose," your client says, "but if I settle I'll never know if I could have won a million. I've got to go for it! Hey, you never know!") Or maybe your client is the vengeful sort. ("I'm not letting that slimy snake out of this so easy. I want him to suffer through a trial so I can see him squirm on the witness stand.") Whatever the reason, your client doesn't want to settle.

If things ended there, we wouldn't be criticizing the contingent fee. You would remain loyal to your client and do your level best to go to trial and win. But lots of lawyers don't do that. Instead, they pressure the client to settle. This is fine if the settlement is really in the best interest of the client. But sometimes, the offer is not in the client's best interest and the lawyer's main reason for wanting to accept it is to guarantee a fee. In that case, the lawyer may start making things up to persuade the client to settle. The lawyer might say, "things really look pretty bad. Their expert is one of the leading neurologists in the country and he'll make our expert look like an amateur at trial. If I were you, I'd settle while you have the chance." If the client still won't settle, the lawyer may drag his feet and practically abandon the case, hoping that sooner or later the defendant will make another settlement offer and next time the client will take it. The idea for the disloyal lawyer is to minimize the amount of additional time spent on the case. Either way, the client suffers so that the lawyer can profit. The danger wouldn't be there with an hourly fee, since the lawyer would earn the same hourly fee by continuing the case. Hourly rate lawyers always make more money by going to trial than by settling because the meter keeps running.

What Happens When Clients Won't go to Trial? While some clients won't settle, the opposite problem also occurs — some clients refuse to go to trial, even when the defendant refuses to settle on reasonable terms. Sometimes a lawyer is eager to go to trial but the client wants to settle. The usual situation is that the lawyer sees a chance to strike it rich with a huge verdict, but the client would rather be safe than sorry, or the client needs some money right away to pay the rent and stave off the bill collectors, or the client is just more realistic than the lawyer about the likely outcome, and feels that the settlement offer is fair. If the lawyer pressures the client to go to trial in these situations, the benefit of the contingent fee option is perverted. Rather than shifting risk from the client to the lawyer, the contingent fee in this situation shifts the risk from the lawyer to the client.

Ordinarily, the client benefits by giving the lawyer a piece of the action in the form of a share in the outcome. The client also benefits by shifting the risk to the lawyer, who has a portfolio of cases to work on and can afford to invest his time in the litigation on a contingent basis, not charging the client anything in the event of a loss. But now those advantages get turned on their head. Because the lawyer has a stake in the outcome, the lawyer has a strong incentive to go to trial if he thinks he can make more money (maybe a lot more money) by doing that. And because the lawyer has a portfolio of cases (unlike the client, who has all of his eggs in one basket), the lawyer is willing to gamble by going to trial. If the lawyer talks the client out of a fair settlement in a try for a larger fee, then the fee arrangement may be to blame.

But this criticism may also prove too much. Hourly rate lawyers often have at least as great an incentive to pressure clients to go to trial, since continuing litigation always results in more money for hourly rate lawyers. Beyond that, the publicity incentive is equally strong for hourly rate lawyers.

Perhaps the criticisms of lawyers on contingent fees stem from the fact that contingent fee lawyers tend to represent individuals who are relatively unsophisticated, rather than businesses and wealthy individuals who are relatively sophisticated. Contingent fee lawyers can therefore influence their clients more than hourly rate lawyers can. But that is not a criticism of contingent fees; it is a criticism of plaintiffs' lawyers. Prohibiting or restricting contingent fees would not be likely to change this situation.

Are Contingent Fees Too Large? The last major criticism of contingent fees is that they are too large. This criticism has three branches: (A) contingent fees often don't carry any risk (or at least not enough risk to justify the typical 1/3 contingent fee); (B) contingent fees result in outrageously high effective hourly rates; and (C) contingent fees yield excessively high dollar amounts in terms of absolute dollars. Let's analyze each of these three criticisms.

> A. *Should contingent fees reflect risk?* Many plaintiffs' lawyers charge the same percentage (typically 1/3) for every case, including "sure thing" cases where there really is no contingency (i.e., no risk of losing). For example, lawyers sometimes charge a contingent fee for collecting death benefits from an insurance company, or for negotiating a settlement of a rear-end collision where the plaintiff was standing still at a stop light when hit. These cases are "no-brainers." The liability of the defendant is not really in question. The only issues are the amount of damages and the amount of time the insurance company can stall (and earn interest) before it has to pay the policy proceeds.
>
> Courts nevertheless typically honor these standard contingent fee agreements (in the rare cases when they are challenged), and ethics committees have seldom considered them unreasonable. But some commentators have argued that the percentage of a contingent fee ought to be related to an objective evaluation of the risk of losing. Should attorneys charge higher contingent fees for riskier cases, and lower contingent fees for cases where liability is pretty certain? Would the market force plaintiffs' attorneys to lower their standard percentage fee on low-risk cases, or would it just encourage plaintiffs' attorneys to raise their standard percentage fee on high-risk cases?
>
> B. *Do contingent fees result in outrageous effective hourly rates?* Critics also charge that when contingent cases settle early, the effective hourly rate is way out of proportion to the lawyer's skill or effort in the case. For example, if a case settles for $90,000 after a lawyer has put in only 10 hours of work, the standard 1/3 contingent fee is $30,000 and the hourly rate amounts to $3,000. Not only is that far beyond what hourly rate lawyers of similar skill and experience typically charge, but the lawyer may be selling out the client by agreeing to a settlement so early in the case. Where there's smoke, there's fire, and if the other side is willing to make a substantial offer at the very outset of a case, then the other side must know something the plaintiff's lawyer doesn't know about the weakness of the defendant's case. If the lawyer were charging by the hour, the lawyer might reject the initial offer and continue discovery to find out why the other side is ready to make an offer so early in the case.
>
> C. *Do contingent fees yield excessive dollar amounts?* Critics also argue that in cases of serious injury, a standard 1/3 contingent fee agreement gives lawyers far too large a fee. For example, in a medical malpractice case where the plaintiff wins a $3,000,000 judgment at trial, the lawyer wins a fee of $1 million. Critics consider that too large for five reasons:

1) The lure of such huge fees causes lawyers to file too many medical malpractice suits.

2) Juries, who know that plaintiffs' lawyers are on contingency, sometimes add the fee onto the judgment so the plaintiff gets all the money she deserves (i.e., be made whole, even after paying the lawyer). In our $3 million medical malpractice example, the jury might have assessed the plaintiff's real damages at $2 million but awarded $3 million so that the plaintiff would be able to keep $2 million (her real damages) after paying the 1/3 contingent fee. (You can never prove that the jury did this.) These inflated jury verdicts contravene the traditional "American Rule" that parties pay their own legal fees, and they drive up the costs of medical malpractice insurance and cause doctors to practice medicine far more defensively (e.g., ordering tests and procedures they otherwise would not order), thus sharply increasing the cost of medical care with relatively little added benefit for the patient.
3) The money really ought to go to the victim, not to the lawyer. In our example, the victim gets $2 million and the lawyer gets $1 million. Shouldn't the victim get $2.5 million and the lawyer only $500,000, or something more equitable?
4) Even in difficult cases where a huge judgment results from the lawyer's skill and diligence, a gigantic fee is still out of proportion to the lawyer's skill and efforts. In our example, if the lawyer worked 1,000 hours to achieve the $3 million judgment (and the corresponding $1 million fee), the lawyer would be earning $1,000 per hour ($1,000 × 1,000 hours = $1,000,000). Even very good lawyers are seldom worth that, the argument goes. Even at the most elite Wall Street firms in New York, it is rare that any lawyer charges $1,000 per hour.
5) Huge contingent fees are not necessary to attract lawyers to handle plaintiffs' cases. In our example, lawyers would be attracted to take the case even if the maximum fee were "only" $500,000, or even $300,000, rather than $1 million.

C. SHOULD CONTINGENT FEES BE ALLOWED IN CRIMINAL CASES?

Every jurisdiction in the United States prohibits contingent fees in criminal cases. Rule 1.5(d) provides that a lawyer "shall not enter into an arrangement for, charge, or collect . . . (2) a contingent fee for representing a defendant in a criminal case." Why this prohibition? What is wrong with contingent fees in criminal cases? Three reasons are typically advanced for prohibiting contingent fees in criminal cases:

1. *Preventing exploitation.* The prohibition prevents defense attorneys from taking advantage of criminal defendants, who may be willing to pay excessive fees to stay out of prison.
2. *Removing temptation to use illegal litigation methods.* The prohibition on contingent fees in criminal cases removes the temptation for criminal defense attorneys to falsify evidence, use perjured testimony, and use other improper methods to obtain an acquittal. (This rationale seems to assume that obtaining a "not guilty" verdict is necessary to earn a contingent fee.)
3. *Removing incentive to recommend rejection of plea bargains.* The prohibition removes the incentive for a defense lawyer to recommend that the defendant go to trial instead of accepting a plea agreement. If contingent fees were allowed — and if the contingent fee were an "all-or-nothing" arrangement (big fee for acquittal, no fee for any type of conviction), defense lawyers would have a strong economic incentive to convince their clients to turn down plea bargains and go to trial, since a guilty plea would deprive the lawyers of their fees.

Do these arguments persuade you? If contingent fee agreements in criminal cases won't cause the problems that the critics claim they will, why should we prohibit them? And isn't it possible that clients would actually benefit from contingent fee agreements? The only people who could sign contingent fee arrangements are people who have enough money to pay their defense lawyers in cash if they win. If these people pay for their defense by the hour or on a flat rate (as they must under current rules) and they get convicted and go to prison, they not only lose the money they paid for defense fees, but also the opportunity to earn money while in prison. Why should we prohibit these people from making contingent fee arrangements? Wouldn't contingent fee arrangements operate like a kind of insurance policy for these defendants, leaving their families money to live on if the defendant is convicted and sent to prison (in which case the defendant would pay no fee)?

Of course, indigent defendants would be unlikely to use contingent fee arrangements in criminal cases, because indigents get free counsel at the state's expense. (That's the consequence of *Gideon v. Wainwright* and its progeny.) A few lawyers might accept a contingent fee payable out of an indigent's future wages, but that would be highly speculative because most poor people can't turn things around very quickly. Most lawyers wouldn't have any interest representing indigent defendants on contingent fees. But is that a reason to deny contingent fee agreements to those who *can* afford to hire counsel?

What other advantages and disadvantages can you think of from permitting contingent fees in criminal defense? Do the advantages outweigh the dangers? If the advantages outweigh the dangers, what are the political forces within the bar that continue to prevent contingent fees in criminal cases? Are the courts worried that criminal defendants would actually get better representation under a contingent fee system than under the current flat rate or hourly rate system, and that more defendants would therefore be acquitted, or would negotiate more favorable plea bargains than under the present system?

D. PAYING A CLIENT'S LIVING EXPENSES

One of the rationales for allowing contingent fees is that they help redress the imbalance of power and resources between poor or middle class plaintiffs (who typically cannot afford to pay legal fees unless they obtain a recovery) and cash-rich corporate defendants (who can afford to pay legal fees for months or years). But redressing the balance regarding the payment of fees does not redress the imbalance in resources to survive. Many plaintiffs, especially those who are out of work due to injury or employment discrimination, soon run out of savings (if they had any) to pay for food, rent, utilities, transportation, and other necessities of everyday life. May a lawyer advance living expenses to a client during the litigation?

In most jurisdictions, the answer is no. A typical version of Rule 1.8(e) provides as follows:

> A lawyer shall not provide financial assistance to a client in connection with pending or contemplated litigation, except that:
>
> (1) a lawyer may advance court costs and expenses of litigation, the repayment of which may be contingent on the outcome of the matter; and
>
> (2) a lawyer representing an indigent client may pay court costs and expenses of litigation on behalf of the client.

Thus, Rule 1.8(e)(1) allows a lawyer to "advance court costs and expenses of litigation," which include such things as filing fees, deposition costs, travel expenses, witness fees, expert witnesses, and medical exams for purposes of proving damages, and to seek repayment only if the client wins or settles, just as the lawyer receives a legal fee only if the client wins or settles. (In the case of an "indigent" client, the lawyer may actually "pay" the court costs and litigation expenses, without ever seeking repayment.) However, if the client cannot afford to continue the litigation because the client needs money immediately, the client is out of luck. If the client needs money for food, or for medical care (for which the client has no insurance), or to avoid losing her home to foreclosure, the client in most jurisdictions is out of luck. Under Rule 1.8(e), the lawyer can neither lend the client the money nor guarantee repayment to a bank or other lender.

Why not? What are the states afraid of? Are states afraid that plaintiffs' lawyers would abuse the power to advance living expenses? How? Or are the states afraid that plaintiffs themselves will gain more staying power and thus be able to litigate more effectively against big corporations and insurance companies?

The District of Columbia's Break with Tradition. In 1991, the District of Columbia broke with tradition by adopting a new rule of legal ethics, Rule 1.8(d), that permits a lawyer to pay or otherwise provide "financial assistance which is *reasonably* necessary to permit the client to institute or maintain the litigation or administrative proceeding." The official Comment to D.C. Rule 1.8(d) explains the reasons for the new rule as follows:

> [U]nder Rule 1.8(d), a lawyer may pay medical or living expenses of a client to the extent necessary to permit the client to continue the litigation. The payment of these additional expenses is limited to those strictly necessary to sustain the client during the litigation, such as medical expenses and minimum living expenses. The purpose of permitting such payments is to avoid situations in which a client is compelled by exigent financial circumstances to settle a claim on unfavorable terms in order to receive the immediate proceeds of settlement. This provision does not permit lawyers to "bid" for clients by offering financial payments beyond those minimum payments necessary to sustain the client until the litigation is completed. . . .

Since then, a few other jurisdictions (including Louisiana, Mississippi, and Montana) have amended their rules to permit lawyers to provide modest financial assistance to their clients. Do you prefer the minority rule that permits a lawyer to advance limited financial assistance to a litigation client, or do you prefer the majority rule that prohibits any financial assistance to a client beyond the costs and expenses of litigation?

E. WHAT IF CONTINGENT FEES WERE PROHIBITED?

Contingent fees make lawyers available to those who cannot afford lawyers unless they win or settle for a significant sum of money. If percentage contingent fees were prohibited in the United States (as they are prohibited in most countries), what would happen? Most likely, many lawyers would stop representing injured people unless those people could afford to pay by the hour. Most injured clients cannot afford to pay by the hour, win or lose, and most lawyers won't take the risk of working for relatively poor clients for a possible fee if they have opportunities to work for wealthier clients for a definite fee. Since most personal injury and wrongful death clients cannot afford to pay a lawyer by the hour unless and until they win their cases, the supply of lawyers for personal injury and wrongful death clients might dry up if contingent fees were banned.

An optimist might hope that lawyers in all kinds of practice (not just personal injury lawyers) would respond to a ban on percentage contingent fees by lowering their hourly rates so that more people could afford lawyers. We think that would be unlikely to happen. A typical hourly rate for a lawyer is roughly $275. This varies geographically, of course, just as rent and home prices and taxes vary geographically, but $275 is a useful ballpark figure. Most people can't afford anywhere near $275 an hour for all of the hours it typically takes a lawyer to litigate a case from beginning to end (or even from beginning to middle). Lawyers would have to cut their rates in half, or more, to bring legal fees within the range the public could afford. That's not going to happen.

If contingent fees were banned, hourly rate lawyers (like commercial litigators) who want to move into the personal injury field would probably try to get around the ban on contingent fees by *billing* clients for hourly rate fees during the action but not *collecting* the fees until the client won or settled the case. If the client won, the lawyer would take the full amount of the overdue fee (probably with interest) out of the proceeds of the action. If the client lost, the lawyer would not make any effort to collect from indigent clients because you can't get blood out of a turnip, and would seldom sue even those clients who could afford to pay part of the bill. We doubt that disciplinary authorities would file charges against lawyers for failing to sue clients for past due fees, especially where clients were judgment proof or would lose their houses and cars if the lawyer prevailed in a suit for fees.

But if hourly rate lawyers began charging what amounted to contingent hourly fees, then hourly rates would be likely to rise across the board. Lawyers could not keep charging the same hourly rates if only some clients paid the bills (which is inherent in a contingent fee system), and as in the current percentage contingent fee system, the winners in a contingent hourly rate system would have to subsidize the losers. Since lawyers do not know at the outset which cases are winners and which are losers, the lawyers would raise their hourly rates to all clients to account for the statistical likelihood that some clients would lose their cases and be unable to pay the accumulated bills at the end of the case.

Chapter 29

HOW DO LAWYERS GET CLIENTS?

If you join a private firm after you graduate from law school, how will you get clients? In larger firms, lawyers are colloquially divided into "finders" (who find new clients), "minders" (who supervise and synthesize the legal work for those clients), and "grinders" (who put their noses to the grindstone as the minders direct). How do "finders" attract business? And what will you eventually need to do to bring in clients of your own? What does it take to be a rainmaker?

Lawyers in private practice have three main ways of attracting clients: (1) recommendations by word of mouth; (2) court appointments; (3) advertising and solicitation. This chapter focuses on advertising and solicitation. ("Advertising" refers to communications directed to the public at large, whereas "solicitation" refers to publicity aimed at particular people known to need particular legal services — e.g., people facing foreclosure, people who have been arrested for DWI, or people who have just been in an auto accident.)

The rules regarding advertising and solicitation are complicated and have a long and winding history.

A. A BRIEF HISTORY OF LAWYER ADVERTISING: 1800 TO 1977

In Modern Legal Ethics 776 (1986), Professor Charles Wolfram summarized the early history of lawyer advertising this way:

> . . . Traces of lawyer advertising have been found as early as 1802, when a lawyer published a "card" in a Tennessee newspaper. Similar advertisements appeared regularly until well after the Civil War, although it began to decrease in many areas as it acquired the "stigma of vulgarity." Victorian snobbery denigrating any calling that besmirched itself by taking on the trappings of a "trade" led the socially ambitious elements of the organized bar to oppose lawyer advertising. Virtue was to be its own display, and the young lawyer of pluck, competence, and trustworthiness would soon gain a substantial client following through a deserved good reputation. . . .

In 1908, however, newspaper advertising (the only form of advertising then used) disappeared because the ABA adopted the Canons of Professional Ethics (forerunner to the Code of Professional Responsibility and the Model Rules of Professional Conduct). Canon 27 began as follows: "It is unprofessional to solicit professional employment by circulars, advertisements, through touters or by personal communications or interviews not warranted by personal relations. . . . " Within a few years, the states universally embraced Canon 27. By the Roaring Twenties, not a single jurisdiction allowed lawyers to advertise. The Canons held sway, with various minor changes, for more than sixty years.

In 1970, the ABA replaced the old Canons of Professional Ethics with a new Code of Professional Responsibility. The Code of Professional Responsibility continued the sweeping ban on lawyer advertising. DR 2-101(A) and (B) of the ABA Code of Professional Responsibility, which were adopted in essentially every state, provided as follows:

> (A) A lawyer shall not prepare, cause to be prepared, use, or participate in the use of any form of public communication that contains professionally self-laudatory statements calculated to attract lay clients . . . .
>
> (B) A lawyer shall not publicize himself, or his partner, or associate, or any other lawyer affiliated with him or his firm, as a lawyer through newspaper or magazine advertisements, radio or television announcements, display advertise-

> ments in the city or telephone directories or other means of commercial publicity, nor shall he authorize or permit others to do so in his behalf.

The theory behind the ban was explained in Ethical Consideration (EC) 2-9, which provided as follows:

> The traditional ban against advertising by lawyers . . . is rooted in the public interest. Competitive advertising would encourage extravagant, artful, self-laudatory brashness in seeking business and thus could mislead the layman. Furthermore, it would inevitably produce unrealistic expectations in particular cases and bring about distrust of the law and lawyers. Thus, public confidence in our legal system would be impaired by such advertisements of professional services. . . . History has demonstrated that public confidence in the legal system is best preserved by strict, self-imposed controls over, rather than by unlimited, advertising.

EC 2-10 recognized "the value of giving assistance in the selection process through forms of advertising that furnish identification of a lawyer," and therefore permitted a lawyer to be identified as a lawyer in the "classified section of the telephone directory," in an "office building directory," and on a "letterhead and professional card." All other forms of advertising were flatly prohibited, regardless of content. But these blanket restrictions on lawyer advertising soon began to fall by the wayside. Today, every jurisdiction allows lawyers to advertise. How did we get from a strict and universal ban on lawyer advertising to an era in which lawyers everywhere advertise in every type of media? That's a great story, and is our next topic.

NOTES AND QUESTIONS

1. ***How Would You Find a Lawyer?*** In a world without lawyer advertising, how would you find a lawyer? Suppose you were injured in an accident, or wanted to get divorced, or needed to write a will. Since you are a law student, you might ask a professor to recommend a lawyer, or you might have a relative or friend (or friend of the family) who is a lawyer. But if you were not a law student and had no friends or relatives who are lawyers, how would you find a lawyer who knew how to handle your matter?

2. ***The Price Is Right?*** As a matter of economics, how does a prohibition on advertising any given product or service affect prices? Does a total ban on advertising drive prices up or down? Explain why.

3. ***Advertising Prices.*** Should lawyers be permitted to advertise their prices for relatively routine services, like drafting a simple will, handling a residential house closing, or filing an individual bankruptcy? What are some advantages to allowing such advertising? What are some problems that might arise if lawyers are allowed to advertise prices for particular services?

4. ***Free Advice.*** Suppose a lawyer would like to run a newspaper ad saying, "If you were injured by Vioxx, do not assume that it is too late to file a lawsuit. In some states, the statute of limitations does not begin to run until you discover that you have been harmed by a defective drug." Or, "If creditors are hounding you day and night, you may be able to stop them completely by filing for personal bankruptcy." Do letters like this help or harm the people who receive them?

5. ***Targeted Communications.*** By checking public court records, a lawyer has learned the names of people (total strangers) whose homes are being foreclosed upon. Should the lawyer be permitted to write an unsolicited letter to these people saying, "Please call me. By using our nation's bankruptcy laws, I may be able to stop the foreclosure." Or should a lawyer be allowed to write a letter to people arrested for DWI saying, "Police records indicate that you were recently charged with driving while intoxicated. You should not try to defend yourself but should hire a lawyer to represent you. I have experience defending DWI cases."

6. ***"You Have My Sympathy . . . and Here's My Phone Number."*** Should a law firm be permitted to write to relatives of people killed in a train crash to say, "We are truly sorry about your loss. Please accept our sympathy. If you believe that your loved one's death was the fault of the railroad company, please contact us to discuss your legal rights."? Should a lawyer be allowed to place an advertisement in the newspaper saying the same thing?

7. ***In-Person Solicitation.*** Should a lawyer be permitted to approach an injured person face to face to ask if the person needs a lawyer? Should the answer depend on whether the injured person is still in the hospital, or still bedridden, or is illiterate? What are some of the dangers of in-person solicitation that might not be present in newspaper or TV ads?

B. THE SUPREME COURT'S ODYSSEY THROUGH LAWYER ADVERTISING

The revolution in lawyer advertising was not made in Congress or in the state legislatures. Nor was it made in the American Bar Association, or in the state bar associations, or in the state supreme courts; it was made in the United States Supreme Court. The journey has not always been easy for the Court — there have been dissenters in almost every case about legal advertising — but the direction has been sure and steady. Starting in 1977, usually over stiff opposition from the organized bar, the Court has consistently expanded the rights of lawyers to advertise truthful and non-misleading information in print and, by implication, in the broadcast media. We trace the Court's odyssey from 1977 to today.

1. The Revolution of 1977: Lawyers Win the Right to Advertise Prices

The first step in lawyer advertising was *Bates v. State Bar of Arizona*, 433 U.S. 350 (1977). Two law partners, Bates and O'Steen, wanted to operate a "legal clinic" that would charge relatively low fixed fees for routine legal services, such as uncontested divorce, an adoption, a personal bankruptcy, or a name change. To make it possible to charge low fixed fees, they needed a volume practice so that they could standardize the forms and procedures for handling certain types of cases, thus reducing the time needed to handle each matter. To generate a large number of clients, Bates and O'Steen ran the following simple newspaper advertisement:

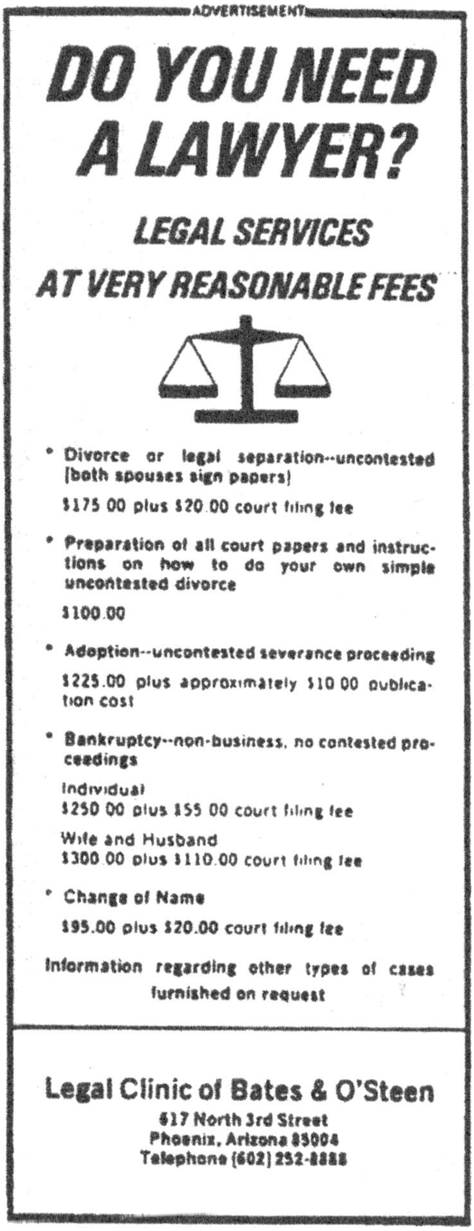

This advertisement would attract little attention today, but in 1976 Arizona (and every other jurisdiction in the United States) strictly prohibited lawyers from advertising in newspapers. Arizona therefore disciplined Bates and O'Steen, suspending them from law practice for one week each. Bates and O'Steen appealed all the way to the United States Supreme Court, arguing that lawyers have a First Amendment right to advertise their fees and services.

The organized bar fought hard to maintain blanket restrictions on lawyer advertising. The following are excerpts from the Supreme Court's majority opinion, written by Justice Blackmun, and from the partially dissenting opinion by Justice Powell. (The separate opinions of Chief Justice Burger and Justice Rehnquist are omitted.)

BATES v. STATE BAR OF ARIZONA

433 U.S. 350 (1977)

Mr. Justice Blackmun delivered the opinion of the Court.

. . . The heart of the dispute before us today is whether lawyers also may constitutionally advertise the prices at which certain routine services will be performed. Numerous justifications are proffered for the restriction of such price advertising. We consider each in turn:

1. *The Adverse Effect on Professionalism.* Appellee [the State Bar of Arizona] places particular emphasis on the adverse effects that it feels price advertising will have on the legal profession. The key to professionalism, it is argued, is the sense of pride that involvement in the discipline generates. It is claimed that price advertising will bring about commercialization, which will undermine the attorney's sense of dignity and self-worth. The hustle of the marketplace will adversely affect the profession's service orientation, and irreparably damage the delicate balance between the lawyer's need to earn and his obligation selflessly to serve. Advertising is also said to erode the client's trust in his attorney: Once the client perceives that the lawyer is motivated by profit, his confidence that the attorney is acting out of a commitment to the client's welfare is jeopardized. And advertising is said to tarnish the dignified public image of the profession.

We recognize, of course, and commend the spirit of public service with which the profession of law is practiced and to which it is dedicated. The present Members of this Court, licensed attorneys all, could not feel otherwise. And we would have reason to pause if we felt that our decision today would undercut that spirit. But we find the postulated connection between advertising and the erosion of true professionalism to be severely strained. At its core, the argument presumes that attorneys must conceal from themselves and from their clients the real-life fact that lawyers earn their livelihood at the bar. We suspect that few attorneys engage in such self-deception.[19] And rare is the client, moreover, even one of the modest means, who enlists the aid of an attorney with the expectation that his services will be rendered free of charge. In fact, the American Bar Association advises that an attorney should reach "a clear agreement with his client as to the basis of the fee charges to be made," and that this is to be done "(a)s soon as feasible after a lawyer has been employed." EC 2-19. If the commercial basis of the relationship is to be promptly disclosed on ethical grounds, once the client is in the office, it seems inconsistent to condemn the candid revelation of the same information before he arrives at that office.

Moreover, the assertion that advertising will diminish the attorney's reputation in the community is open to question. Bankers and engineers advertise, and yet these professions are not regarded as undignified. In fact, it has been suggested that the failure of lawyers to advertise creates public disillusionment with the profession. The absence of advertising may be seen to reflect the profession's failure to reach out and serve the community: Studies reveal that many persons do not obtain counsel even when they perceive a need because of the feared price of services or because of an inability to locate a competent attorney. Indeed, cynicism with regard to the profession may be created by the fact that it long has publicly eschewed advertising, while condoning the actions of the attorney who structures his social or civic associations so as to provide contacts with potential clients.

Indeed, it appears that even the medical profession now views the alleged adverse effect of advertising in a somewhat different light from the appellee. A Statement of the

---

[19] Counsel for the appellee at oral argument readily stated: "We all know that law offices are big businesses, that they may have billion-dollar or million-dollar clients, they're run with computers, and all the rest. And so the argument may be made that to term them noncommercial is sanctimonious humbug."

Judicial Council of the American Medical Association provides in part:

> *Advertising* The Principles (of Medical Ethics) do not proscribe advertising; they proscribe the solicitation of patients. . . . The public is entitled to know the names of physicians, the type of their practices, the location of their offices, their office hours, and other useful information that will enable people to make a more informed choice of physician. . . .

It appears that the ban on advertising originated as a rule of etiquette and not as a rule of ethics. Early lawyers in Great Britain viewed the law as a form of public service, rather than as a means of earning a living, and they looked down on 'trade' as unseemly. Eventually, the attitude toward advertising fostered by this view evolved into an aspect of the ethics of the profession. But habit and tradition are not in themselves an adequate answer to a constitutional challenge. In this day, we do not belittle the person who earns his living by the strength of his arm or the force of his mind. Since the belief that lawyers are somehow "above" trade has become an anachronism, the historical foundation for the advertising restraint has crumbled.

2. *The Inherently Misleading Nature of Attorney Advertising.* It is argued that advertising of legal services inevitably will be misleading (a) because such services are so individualized with regard to content and quality as to prevent informed comparison on the basis of an advertisement, (b) because the consumer of legal services is unable to determine in advance just what services he needs, and (c) because advertising by attorneys will highlight irrelevant factors and fail to show the relevant factor of skill.

We are not persuaded that restrained professional advertising by lawyers inevitably will be misleading. Although many services performed by attorneys are indeed unique, it is doubtful that any attorney would or could advertise fixed prices for services of that type. The only services that lend themselves to advertising are the routine ones: the uncontested divorce, the simple adoption, the uncontested personal bankruptcy, the change of name, and the like the very services advertised by appellants. Although the precise service demanded in each task may vary slightly, and although legal services are not fungible, these facts do not make advertising misleading so long as the attorney does the necessary work at the advertised price.[27] The argument that legal services are so unique that fixed rates cannot meaningfully be established is refuted by the record in this case: The appellee, State Bar itself sponsors a Legal Services Program in which the participating attorneys agree to perform services like those advertised by the appellants at standardized rates. Indeed, until the decision of this Court in *Goldfarb v. Virginia State Bar*, 421 U.S. 773 (1975), the Maricopa County Bar Association apparently had a schedule of suggested minimum fees for standard legal tasks. We thus find of little force the assertion that advertising is misleading because of an inherent lack of standardization in legal services.

The second component of the argument that advertising ignores the diagnostic role fares little better. It is unlikely that many people go to an attorney merely to ascertain if they have a clean bill of legal health. Rather, attorneys are likely to be employed to perform specific tasks. Although the client may not know the detail involved in performing the task, he no doubt is able to identify the service he desires at the level of generality to which advertising lends itself. . . .

The third component is not without merit: Advertising does not provide a complete foundation on which to select an attorney. But it seems peculiar to deny the consumer, on the ground that the information is incomplete, at least some of the relevant information needed to reach an informed decision. The alternative the prohibition of

[27] One commentator has observed: "(A) moment's reflection reveals that the same argument can be made for barbers; rarely are two haircuts identical, but that does not mean that barbers cannot quote a standard price. Lawyers perform countless relatively standardized services which vary somewhat in complexity but not so much as to make each job utterly unique."

advertising serves only to restrict the information that flows to consumers. Moreover, the argument assumes that the public is not sophisticated enough to realize the limitations of advertising, and that the public is better kept in ignorance than trusted with correct but incomplete information. We suspect the argument rests on an underestimation of the public. In any event, we view as dubious any justification that is based on the benefits of public ignorance. Although, of course, the bar retains the power to correct omissions that have the effect of presenting an inaccurate picture, the preferred remedy is more disclosure, rather than less. If the naivete of the public will cause advertising by attorneys to be misleading, then it is the bar's role to assure that the populace is sufficiently informed as to enable it to place advertising in its proper perspective.

3. *The Adverse Effect on the Administration of Justice.* Advertising is said to have the undesirable effect of stirring up litigation. The judicial machinery is designed to serve those who feel sufficiently aggrieved to bring forward their claims. Advertising, it is argued, serves to encourage the assertion of legal rights in the courts, thereby undesirably unsettling societal repose. There is even a suggestion of barratry.

But advertising by attorneys is not an unmitigated source of harm to the administration of justice. It may offer great benefits. Although advertising might increase the use of the judicial machinery, we cannot accept the notion that it is always better for a person to suffer a wrong silently than to redress it by legal action. As the bar acknowledges, "the middle 70% of our population is not being reached or served adequately by the legal profession."[33] Among the reasons for this underutilization is fear of the cost, and an inability to locate a suitable lawyer. Advertising can help to solve this acknowledged problem: Advertising is the traditional mechanism in a free-market economy for a supplier to inform a potential purchaser of the availability and terms of exchange. The disciplinary rule at issue likely has served to burden access to legal services, particularly for the not-quite-poor and the unknowledgeable. A rule allowing restrained advertising would be in accord with the bar's obligation to "facilitate the process of intelligent selection of lawyers, and to assist in making legal services fully available." ABA Code of Professional Responsibility EC 2-1 (1976).

4. *The Undesirable Economic Effects of Advertising.* It is claimed that advertising will increase the overhead costs of the profession, and that these costs then will be passed along to consumers in the form of increased fees. Moreover, it is claimed that the additional cost of practice will create a substantial entry barrier, deterring or preventing young attorneys from penetrating the market and entrenching the position of the bar's established members.

These two arguments seem dubious at best. Neither distinguishes lawyers from others, and neither appears relevant to the First Amendment. The ban on advertising serves to increase the difficulty of discovering the lowest cost seller of acceptable ability. As a result, to this extent attorneys are isolated from competition, and the incentive to price competitively is reduced. Although it is true that the effect of advertising on the price of services has not been demonstrated, there is revealing evidence with regard to products; where consumers have the benefit of price advertising, retail prices often are dramatically lower than they would be without advertising. It is entirely possible that advertising will serve to reduce, not advance, the cost of legal services to the consumer.[35]

The entry-barrier argument is equally unpersuasive. In the absence of advertising, an attorney must rely on his contacts with the community to generate a flow of business. In

---

[33] The ABA survey . . . indicates that 35.8% of the adult population has never visited an attorney and another 27.9% has visited an attorney only once.

[35] . . . Even if advertising causes fees to drop, it is by no means clear that a loss of income to lawyers will result. The increased volume of business generated by advertising might more than compensate for the reduced profit per case.

view of the time necessary to develop such contacts, the ban in fact serves to perpetuate the market position of established attorneys. Consideration of entry-barrier problems would urge that advertising be allowed so as to aid the new competitor in penetrating the market.

5. *The Adverse Effect of Advertising on the Quality of Service.* It is argued that the attorney may advertise a given "package" of service at a set price, and will be inclined to provide, by indiscriminate use, the standard package regardless of whether it fits the client's needs.

Restraints on advertising, however, are an ineffective way of deterring shoddy work. An attorney who is inclined to cut quality will do so regardless of the rule on advertising. And the advertisement of a standardized fee does not necessarily mean that the services offered are undesirably standardized. Indeed, the assertion that an attorney who advertises a standard fee will cut quality is substantially undermined by the fixed-fee schedule of appellee's own prepaid Legal Services Program. Even if advertising leads to the creation of "legal clinics" like that of appellants' clinics that emphasize standardized procedures for routine problems it is possible that such clinics will improve service by reducing the likelihood of error.

6. *The Difficulties of Enforcement.* Finally, it is argued that the wholesale restriction is justified by the problems of enforcement if any other course is taken. Because the public lacks sophistication in legal matters, it may be particularly susceptible to misleading or deceptive advertising by lawyers. After-the-fact action by the consumer lured by such advertising may not provide a realistic restraint because of the inability of the layman to assess whether the service he has received meets professional standards. Thus, the vigilance of a regulatory agency will be required. But because of the numerous purveyors of services, the overseeing of advertising will be burdensome.

It is at least somewhat incongruous for the opponents of advertising to extol the virtues and altruism of the legal profession at one point, and, at another, to assert that its members will seize the opportunity to mislead and distort. We suspect that, with advertising, most lawyers will behave as they always have: They will abide by their solemn oaths to uphold the integrity and honor of their profession and of the legal system. For every attorney who overreaches through advertising, there will be thousands of others who will be candid and honest and straightforward. And, of course, it will be in the latter's interest, as in other cases of misconduct at the bar, to assist in weeding out those few who abuse their trust.

In sum, we are not persuaded that any of the proffered justifications rise to the level of an acceptable reason for the suppression of all advertising by attorneys.

MR. JUSTICE POWELL, with whom MR. JUSTICE STEWART joins, concurring in part and dissenting in part.

. . . [W]ithin undefined limits today's decision will effect profound changes in the practice of law, viewed for centuries as a learned profession. The supervisory power of the courts over members of the bar, as officers of the courts, and the authority of the respective States to oversee the regulation of the profession have been weakened. Although the Court's opinion professes to be framed narrowly, and its reach is subject to future clarification, the holding is explicit and expansive with respect to the advertising of undefined 'routine legal services.' In my view, this result is neither required by the First Amendment, nor in the public interest. . . .

Even the briefest reflection on the tasks for which lawyers are trained and the variation among the services they perform should caution against facile assumptions that legal services can be classified into the routine and the unique. In most situations it is impossible both for the client and the lawyer to identify with reasonable accuracy in advance the nature and scope of problems that may be encountered even when handling a matter that at the outset seems routine. Neither quantitative nor qualitative measurement of the service actually needed is likely to be feasible in advance. . . .

Even if one were to accept the view that some legal services are sufficiently routine to minimize the possibility of deception, there nonetheless remains a serious enforcement problem. . . .

I am apprehensive, despite the Court's expressed intent to proceed cautiously, that today's holding will be viewed by tens of thousands of lawyers as an invitation — by the public-spirited and the selfish lawyers alike — to engage in competitive advertising on an escalating basis. Some lawyers may gain temporary advantages; others will suffer from the economic power of stronger lawyers, or by the subtle deceit of less scrupulous lawyers. Some members of the public may benefit marginally, but the risk is that many others will be victimized by simplistic price advertising of professional services "almost infinite in variety and nature . . . ." Until today, in the long history of the legal profession, it was not thought that this risk of public deception was required by the marginal First Amendment interests asserted by the Court.

2. The Dividing Line: In-Person Solicitation Can Be Prohibited

The year after *Bates*, the Supreme Court drew a bright line that has remained ever since. In *Ohralik v. Ohio State Bar Association*, 436 U.S. 447 (1978), the Court upheld a state's disciplinary action against a lawyer who solicited cases in person from two teenage girls who had been injured in an auto accident. The Court rejected the lawyer's argument that in-person solicitation was entitled to just as much First Amendment protection as newspaper advertisements. The Court held that states may impose a blanket prohibition against in-person solicitation as a "prophylactic measure" because in-person solicitation is likely to be overbearing, and there will be no independent witnesses to prove what the lawyer actually said. However, the Court did *not* hold that in-person solicitation is improper or unconstitutional. The Court simply held that in-person solicitation was not protected by the First Amendment.

The next five advertising cases decided by the Supreme Court have a common theme: with respect to written advertising (such as letters, newspapers, and other written media), the state may not impose an outright ban on information that is not misleading. In other words, lawyers may communicate virtually anything in writing as long as it is not false or misleading.

3. Lawyers for Non-Profit Groups May Solicit Cases by Mail

The next case after *Bates* to approve written solicitation was a relatively easy one because it involved solicitation by a lawyer for a non-profit organization, the ACLU. In *In re Primus*, 436 U.S. 412 (1978) (decided the same day as *Ohralik*), the Court held that a lawyer for a public interest organization has the First Amendment right to solicit cases by letter, as long as the lawyer will not personally profit from the solicitation. (Left open was the question whether non-profit public interest lawyers could solicit cases in person.)

4. Petty State Restrictions Are Unanimously Struck Down

The next advertising case was *In re R.M.J.*, 455 U.S. 191 (1982). In *R.M.J.*, the Court unanimously reversed discipline against a lawyer from St. Louis who had violated several of Missouri's highly restrictive rules on legal advertising. In the wake of *Bates*, Missouri had replaced its blanket ban on advertising with rules that specified the kinds of information an attorney could advertise, including the precise fields of law an attorney could mention in advertisements (e.g., "Tort Law" and "Property Law"). R.M.J. violated these rules by advertising that he handled "Personal Injury" and "Real Estate" (which were not approved terms), as well as "Zoning" and "Contrac ts" (which were not covered by any terms on the approved list). He also stated that he was licensed in both Illinois and Missouri — a helpful fact for people who lived on one side of the Mississippi River and worked on the other. Finally, he sent announcements about his practice to lawyers and others that he did not know.

The Missouri Bar Administration sought disbarment; the Missouri Supreme Court issued a private reprimand; but the United States Supreme Court unanimously reversed, holding that a state could not blanketly prohibit lawyers from advertising truthful information that was neither actually nor inherently misleading. That remains the basic standard today.

5. Illustrations and Truthful Legal Advice Win Approval

The next advertising case decided by the Supreme Court was *Zauderer v. Office of Disciplinary Counsel of Ohio*, 471 U.S. 626 (1985). Zauderer ran a "targeted" newspaper advertisement seeking legal business from women who had suffered infertility or other injuries from an intrauterine contraceptive device known as the Dalkon Shield. The Dalkon Shield had been taken off the market as unsafe in 1974. Within 10 years about 10,000 women sued the manufacturer, but thousands more who had been harmed by the Dalkon Shield had not yet sued. To solicit these suits, Zauderer ran an advertisement in 36 Ohio newspapers that began with a drawing of the Dalkon Shield and said:

> **DID YOU USE THIS IUD?**
>
> The Dalkon Shield Interuterine [*sic*] Device is alleged to have caused serious pelvic infections resulting in hospitalizations, tubal damage, infertility, and hysterectomies. It is also alleged to have caused unplanned pregnancies ending in abortions, miscarriages, septic abortions, tubal or ectopic pregnancies, and full-term deliveries. If you or a friend have had a similar experience *do not assume it is too late to take legal action against the Shield's manufacturer*. Our law firm is presently representing women on such cases. The cases are handled on a contingent fee basis of the amount recovered. If there is no recovery, no legal fees are owed by our clients. [Emphasis added.]

Zauderer "received over 200 inquiries regarding the advertisement, and he initiated lawsuits on behalf of 106 of the women who contacted him as a result of the advertisement." Ohio disciplined Zauderer for the ad, but the Supreme Court for the most part reversed. The state "stipulated that the information and advice regarding Dalkon Shield litigation was not false, fraudulent, misleading or deceptive and that the drawing was an accurate representation of the Dalkon Shield." The issue, therefore, was whether the state could prohibit accurate, nonmisleading, "targeted" newspaper ads. The Court said:

> . . . The advertisement's information and advice concerning the Dalkon Shield was, as the Office of Disciplinary Counsel stipulated, neither false nor deceptive: in fact, it was entirely accurate. The advertisement did not promise readers that lawsuits alleging injuries caused by the Dalkon Shield would be successful, nor did it suggest that appellant had any special expertise in handling such lawsuits other than his employment in other such litigation. Rather, the advertisement reported the indisputable fact that the Dalkon Shield had spawned an impressive number of lawsuits and advised readers that appellant was currently handling such lawsuits and was willing to represent other women asserting similar claims. In addition, the advertisement advised women that they should not assume that their claims were time-barred — advice that seems completely unobjectionable in light of the trend in many States toward a "discovery rule" for determining when a cause of action for latent injury or disease accrues. The State's power to prohibit advertising that is "inherently misleading," thus cannot justify Ohio's decision to discipline appellant for running advertising geared to persons with a specific legal problem.

Since the ad was not false or misleading, the state had to establish a "substantial governmental interest" for prohibiting the ad. Ohio argued that prohibiting targeted newspaper ads served the same interests as banning in-person solicitation, but the Supreme Court disagreed:

> Our decision in *Ohralik* was largely grounded on the substantial differences between face-to-face solicitation and the advertising we had held permissible in *Bates*. In-person solicitation by a lawyer, we concluded, was a practice rife with possibilities for overreaching, invasion of privacy, the exercise of undue influence, and outright fraud. In addition, we noted that in-person solicitation presents unique regulatory difficulties because it is "not visible or otherwise open to public scrutiny." These unique features of in-person solicitation by lawyers, we held, justified a prophylactic rule prohibiting lawyers from engaging in such solicitation for pecuniary gain, but we were careful to point out that "in-person solicitation of professional employment by a lawyer does not stand on a par with truthful advertising about the availability and terms of routine legal services."

These concerns did not apply to Zauderer's ad, because a written advertisement does not invade anyone's privacy. More importantly, print advertising "poses much less risk of overreaching or undue influence" than in-person solicitation because written advertisements "lack the coercive force of the personal presence of a trained advocate." Nor does a printed advertisement "involve pressure on the potential client for an immediate yes-or-no answer to the offer of representation."

Ohio also argued that targeted ads would "stir up litigation," but in an important passage the Court rejected this argument as well:

> . . . [I]t is important to think about what it might mean to say that the State has an interest in preventing lawyers from stirring up litigation. It is possible to describe litigation itself as an evil that the State is entitled to combat: after all, litigation consumes vast quantities of social resources to produce little of tangible value but much discord and unpleasantness. . . .
>
> But we cannot endorse the proposition that a lawsuit, as such, is an evil. Over the course of centuries, our society has settled upon civil litigation as a means for redressing grievances, resolving disputes, and vindicating rights when other means fail. There is no cause for consternation when a person who believes in good faith and on the basis of accurate information regarding his legal rights that he has suffered a legally cognizable injury turns to the courts for a remedy: "we cannot accept the notion that it is always better for a person to suffer a wrong silently than to redress it by legal action." *Bates.* That our citizens have access to their civil courts is not an evil to be regretted; rather, it is an attribute of our system of justice in which we ought to take pride. The State is not entitled to interfere with that access by denying its citizens accurate information about their legal rights. . . .

Ohio next tried to justify its prohibition against legal advice in lawyer advertising (i.e., "do not assume it is too late to take legal action"). Ohio called this a "prophylactic rule" needed to ensure that attorneys did not give false or misleading advice in an effort to secure legal business. A total ban on legal advice was therefore necessary, the state argued, because the state would face an enormous problem in distinguishing false legal advice from true legal advice. The Supreme Court disagreed. The statements in Zauderer's ad were "easily verifiable and completely accurate," and distinguishing deceptive from nondeceptive advice in legal advertising was no harder than distinguishing the true from the false in any other field. (The Court also noted that the new ABA Model Rules of Professional Conduct permitted all advertising that was not "false or misleading," implying that the ABA did not think this task would be too hard for the states.)

The Court then explained the philosophy behind its advertising decisions:

> Our recent decisions involving commercial speech have been grounded in the faith that the free flow of commercial information is valuable enough to justify imposing on would-be regulators the costs of distinguishing the truthful from the false, the helpful from the misleading, and the harmless from the harmful. The value of the information presented in appellant's advertising is no less than that contained in other forms of advertising — indeed, insofar as appellant's advertising tended to acquaint persons with their legal rights who might otherwise be shut off from effective access to the legal system, it was undoubtedly more valuable than many other forms of advertising. . . . An attorney may not be disciplined for soliciting legal business through printed advertising containing truthful and nondeceptive information and advice regarding the legal rights of potential clients.

Finally, the Court struck down Ohio's ban on illustrations. If accurate illustrations could be prohibited in legal advertising on grounds that illustrations were potentially misleading, then illustrations could be prohibited in all advertisements. As to Ohio's argument that illustrations robbed advertising of "dignity," the Court said it was not sure that "dignity" was a sufficiently substantial state interest to justify a total ban on illustrations.

Justice O'Connor, then-Chief Justice Burger, and Justice Rehnquist concurred in part and dissented in part. They objected mainly to the use of legal advice to lure clients. In their view, "the use of unsolicited legal advice to entice clients poses enough of a risk of overreaching and undue influence to warrant Ohio's rule. . . . "

6. Targeted Mail: Like In-Person Solicitation or Like a Newspaper Ad?

Zauderer and *Ohralik* set the stage for the Court's next advertising case, *Shapero v. Kentucky State Bar*, 486 U.S. 466 (1988). *Zauderer* involved targeted newspaper advertisements. *Shapero* involved targeted mail. Shapero, a Kentucky attorney, wanted to mail letters "to potential clients who have had a foreclosure suit filed against them." (He could easily get lists of foreclosure defendants from public court records.) Shapero's proposed letter to these foreclosure defendants said:

> It has come to my attention that your home is being foreclosed on. If this is true, you may be about to lose your home. Federal law may allow you to keep your home by *ORDERING* your creditors to *STOP* and give you more time to pay them.
>
> You may call my office anytime from 8:30 a.m. to 5:00 p.m. for *FREE* information on how you can keep your home.
>
> Call *NOW*, don't wait. It may surprise you what I may be able to do for you. Just call and tell me that you got this letter. Remember it is *FREE*, there is *NO* charge for calling.

The Kentucky Attorneys Advertising Commission did not find the letter to be false or misleading in any way, but it refused to approve the letter because it violated Kentucky's version of ABA Model Rule 7.3, which prohibited mail to people known to need specific legal services. The Kentucky Supreme Court affirmed, and the United States Supreme Court granted certiorari.

The main question facing the Supreme Court was whether Shapero's targeted letter was more like the in-person solicitation condemned in *Ohralik*, or more like the targeted newspaper advertisement protected in *Zauderer*. The Court analyzed this question as follows:

> In *Zauderer* . . . [w]e distinguished written advertisements containing such information or advice from in-person solicitation by lawyers for profit, which we held in *Ohralik* a State may categorically ban. The "unique features of in-person

solicitation by lawyers [that] justified a prophylactic rule prohibiting lawyers from engaging in such solicitation for pecuniary gain," we observed, are "not present" in the context of written advertisements.

Our lawyer advertising cases have never distinguished among various modes of written advertising to the general public. . . . Thus, Ohio could no more prevent Zauderer from mass-mailing to a general population his offer to represent women injured by the Dalkon Shield than it could prohibit his publication of the advertisement in local newspapers. Similarly, if petitioner's letter is neither false nor deceptive, Kentucky could not constitutionally prohibit him from sending at large an identical letter opening with the query, "Is your home being foreclosed on?," rather than his observation to the targeted individuals that "It has come to my attention that your home is being foreclosed on." . . .

The court below . . . concluded that the State's blanket ban on all targeted, direct-mail solicitation was permissible because of the "serious potential for abuse inherent in direct solicitation by lawyers of potential clients known to need specific legal services." By analogy to *Ohralik*, the court observed:

> Such solicitation subjects the prospective client to pressure from a trained lawyer in a direct personal way. It is entirely possible that the potential client may feel overwhelmed by the basic situation which caused the need for the specific legal services and may have seriously impaired capacity for good judgment, sound reason and a natural protective self-interest. Such a condition is full of the possibility of undue influence, overreaching and intimidation.

[R]espondent's facile suggestion that this case is merely "*Ohralik* in writing" misses the mark. In assessing the potential for overreaching and undue influence, the mode of communication makes all the difference. Our decision in *Ohralik* that a State could categorically ban all in-person solicitation turned on two factors. First was our characterization of face-to-face solicitation as "a practice rife with possibilities for overreaching, invasion of privacy, the exercise of undue influence, and outright fraud." Second, "unique . . . difficulties," would frustrate any attempt at state regulation of in-person solicitation short of an absolute ban because such solicitation is "not visible or otherwise open to public scrutiny." Targeted, direct-mail solicitation is distinguishable from the in-person solicitation in each respect.

Like print advertising, petitioner's letter — and targeted, direct-mail solicitation generally — "poses much less risk of overreaching or undue influence" than does in-person solicitation. Neither mode of written communication involves "the coercive force of the personal presence of a trained advocate" or the "pressure on the potential client for an immediate yes-or-no answer to the offer of representation." Unlike the potential client with a badgering advocate breathing down his neck, the recipient of a letter and the "reader of an advertisement . . . can 'effectively avoid further bombardment of [his] sensibilities simply by averting [his] eyes,'" *Ohralik*. A letter, like a printed advertisement (but unlike a lawyer), can readily be put in a drawer to be considered later, ignored, or discarded. In short, both types of written solicitation "[convey] information about legal services [by means] that [are] more conducive to reflection and the exercise of choice on the part of the consumer than is personal solicitation by an attorney." Nor does a targeted letter invade the recipient's privacy any more than does a substantively identical letter mailed at large. . . .

[A] truthful and nondeceptive letter, no matter how big its type and how much it speculates can never "[shout] at the recipient" or "[grasp] him by the lapels," as can a lawyer engaging in face-to-face solicitation. The letter simply

> presents no comparable risk of overreaching. And so long as the First Amendment protects the right to solicit legal business, the State may claim no substantial interest in restricting truthful and nondeceptive lawyer solicitations to those least likely to be read by the recipient. . . .

The Supreme Court therefore reversed and remanded. But Justice O'Connor filed a bitter dissent, joined by Justice Scalia and then-Chief Justice Burger (who once said publicly that a person should "never, never, never hire a lawyer who advertises"). Justice O'Connor said:

> . . . I agree with the Court that the reasoning in *Zauderer* supports the conclusion reached today. That decision, however, was itself the culmination of a line of cases built on defective premises and flawed reasoning. As today's decision illustrates, the Court has been unable or unwilling to restrain the logic of the underlying analysis within reasonable bounds. The resulting interference with important and valid public policies is so destructive that I believe the analytical framework itself should now be reexamined.

She was especially troubled by the legal advice that Shapero gave. She said: "The advice contained in unsolicited 'free samples' is likely to be colored by the lawyer's own interest in drumming up business, a result that is sure to undermine the professional standards that States have a substantial interest in maintaining." She also believed that "a personalized letter is somewhat more likely 'to overpower the will and judgment of laypeople who have not sought [the lawyer's] advice.' "

Her arguments did not prevail, however, and targeted mailing is now an accepted and frequent form of lawyer advertising all over the country. Courts and state bars are still struggling to decide whether lawyers should be prohibited from targeting letters to personal injury victims for a certain period of time after the injury — various states have suggested anywhere between 15 days and 45 days — and we will address the question of timing after we conclude the history of the Supreme Court's cases on lawyer advertising. But basic protection for targeted mail now appears to be solidly in place.

7. Claims of Specialization Get Limited Protection

The next case in the Court's line of advertising cases is *Peel v. Attorney Registration and Disciplinary Commission of Illinois*, 496 U.S. 91 (1990). Illinois had disciplined Peel for putting the following statement on his letterhead:

Certified Civil Trial Specialist

By the National Board of Trial Advocacy

Licensed: Illinois, Missouri, Arizona

The statement was truthful; Peel had passed all of the tests to become "certified" by the National Board of Trial Advocacy (the NBTA). Moreover, the certifying organization — the NBTA — was legitimate and well respected, not some "fly-by-night" diploma mill. To obtain NBTA certification as a trial specialist, a lawyer had to conduct at least 45 trials, including 15 jury trials. The lawyer also had to be endorsed by six other prominent lawyers, and had to pass both a rigorous written examination and an all-day oral examination.

Could it be that the reason the Illinois Supreme Court objected was that it failed to grasp "the distinction between statements of opinion or quality and statements of objective facts that may support an inference of quality"?

The U.S. Supreme Court ultimately read it that way. In the plurality opinion by Justice Stevens, the Court held that the statement was truthful (and in that sense not misleading). Accordingly, the Court found no state interest to outweigh the First Amendment right to advertise truthfully. However, to avoid confusion about Illinois' concerns, the Court said the state could require a disclaimer, explaining that the State of Illinois designated individuals as "certified" or "specialist" only with respect to lawyers in three fields: patent, trademark and admiralty.

8. Truthful Information Gets Another Endorsement

The next Supreme Court lawyer advertising case was *Ibanez v. Florida Department of Business and Professional Regulation*, 512 U.S. 136 (1994). Silvia Ibanez, a licensed Florida lawyer, was also a Certified Public Accountant (CPA) licensed by Respondent Florida Board of Accountancy (an official state agency), and she was a "Certified Financial Planner" (CFP), a designation authorized by the Certified Financial Planner Board of Standards (a private organization). Ms. Ibanez referred to her credentials as a CPA and CFP next to her name in her yellow pages listing, on her business card, and on her letterhead. The Florida Board of Accountancy reprimanded her, accusing her of "false, deceptive, and misleading" advertising. The Board argued that the designation "CFP" "inherently misleads the public into believing that state approval and recognition exists," as with the CPA designation. A Florida court upheld the discipline but the United States Supreme Court reversed, stating:

> The State's burden is not slight; the "free flow of commercial information is valuable enough to justify imposing on would-be regulators the costs of distinguishing the truthful from the false, the helpful from the misleading, and the harmless from the harmful." "Mere speculation or conjecture" will not suffice; rather the State "must demonstrate that the harms it recites are real and that its restriction will in fact alleviate them to a material degree." *Zauderer*. . . .

The only dissenters in *Ibanez* were Justice O'Connor and Chief Justice Rehnquist. They agreed that Ms. Ibanez had the right to use the term "CPA," but dissented on grounds that the term "CFP" was potentially misleading because it would lead a reasonable consumer to conclude that the two "certifications" were conferred by the same entity — the State of Florida.

9. Targeted Mail Revisited: Solicitation After an Accident

In 1995, the Supreme Court decided a case with the strange name of *Florida Bar v. Went For It, Inc.*, 515 U.S. 618 (1995). The case revolved around two Florida rules of professional conduct restricting a lawyer's right to send targeted mail to accident victims or their families within thirty days after an accident or disaster. Specifically, Florida's Rule 4.7-4(b)(1) provided:

> A lawyer shall not send, or knowingly permit to be sent, . . . a written communication to a prospective client for the purpose of obtaining professional employment if:
>
> (A) the written communication concerns an action for personal injury or wrongful death or otherwise relates to an accident or disaster involving the person to whom the communication is addressed or a relative of that person, unless the accident or disaster occurred more than 30 days prior to the mailing of the communication.

A companion rule, Florida's Rule 4-7.8(a), provided:

> A lawyer shall not accept referrals from a lawyer referral service unless the service: (1) engages in no communication with the public and in no direct contact with prospective clients in a manner that would violate the Rules of Professional Conduct if the communication or contact were made by the lawyer.

"Together," the Supreme Court said, "these rules create a brief 30-day blackout period after an accident during which lawyers may not, directly or indirectly, single out accident victims or their relatives in order to solicit their business."

Stuart McHenry, a Florida personal injury lawyer who owned a lawyer referral service called "Went For It, Inc.," challenged the blackout rules. He alleged that he routinely sent targeted solicitations to accident victims or their survivors within 30 days after accidents and that he wished to continue doing so in the future. Similarly, Went For It, Inc. represented that it wished to contact accident victims or their survivors within 30 days of accidents and to refer potential clients to participating Florida lawyers. The federal district court, citing *Bates* and other Supreme Court advertising cases, held that 30-day blackout period violated the First Amendment. The Eleventh Circuit affirmed. The Supreme Court, in a tense 5-4 decision, reversed, holding that Florida's rules were constitutionally valid. The Supreme Court began by noting that the standard of review in lawyer advertising cases (and commercial speech cases generally) was not strict scrutiny but rather "intermediate" scrutiny, under which the government may regulate commercial speech that is not misleading if the government satisfies a three-pronged test: "[F]irst, the government must assert a substantial interest in support of its regulation; second, the government must demonstrate that the restriction on commercial speech directly and materially advances that interest; and third, the regulation must be 'narrowly drawn.'" With that framework in place, the Supreme Court turned to Florida's asserted interest:

> The Florida Bar asserts that it has a substantial interest in protecting the privacy and tranquility of personal injury victims and their loved ones against intrusive, unsolicited contact by lawyers. This interest obviously factors into the Bar's paramount (and repeatedly professed) objective of curbing activities that "negatively affect the administration of justice." Because direct mail solicitations in the wake of accidents are perceived by the public as intrusive, the Bar argues, the reputation of the legal profession in the eyes of Floridians has suffered commensurately. The regulation, then, is an effort to protect the flagging reputations of Florida lawyers by preventing them from engaging in conduct that, the Bar maintains, "'is universally regarded as deplorable and beneath common decency because of its intrusion upon the special vulnerability and private grief of victims or their families.'"

The majority had "little trouble crediting the Bar's interest as substantial." To meet the second prong of intermediate scrutiny, the Florida Bar submitted a 106-page summary of its 2-year study of lawyer advertising and solicitation. The summary contained statistical and anecdotal data "supporting the Bar's contentions that the Florida public views direct-mail solicitations in the immediate wake of accidents as an intrusion on privacy that reflects poorly upon the profession." As described by the majority opinion:

> The anecdotal record mustered by the Bar is noteworthy for its breadth and detail. With titles like "Scavenger Lawyers" and "Solicitors Out of Bounds" newspaper editorial pages in Florida have burgeoned with criticism of Florida lawyers who send targeted direct mail to victims shortly after accidents. The study summary also includes page upon page of excerpts from complaints of direct-mail recipients. For example, a Florida citizen described how he was "'appalled and angered by the brazen attempt'" of a law firm to solicit him by letter shortly after he was injured and his fiancee was killed in an auto accident. Another found it "'despicable and inexcusable'" that a Pensacola lawyer wrote to his mother three days after his father's funeral. Another described how she was "'astounded'" and then "'very angry'" when she received a solicitation following a minor accident. Still another described as "'beyond comprehension'" a letter his nephew's family received the day of the nephew's funeral. One citizen wrote, "'I consider the unsolicited contact from you after my child's accident to be of the rankest form of ambulance chasing and in incredibly poor taste. . . . I cannot begin to express with my limited vocabulary the utter contempt in which I hold you and your kind.'"

Against this background, the Court held that the 30-day blackout period was "reasonably well-tailored to its stated objective of eliminating targeted mailings whose type and timing are a source of distress to Floridians, distress that has caused many of them to lose respect for the legal profession," thus satisfying the third prong of the intermediate scrutiny test. The Court therefore upheld Florida's rule.

The four dissenters — Justices Kennedy, Stevens, Souter, and Ginsburg — believed that Florida's rule failed all three prongs of the intermediate scrutiny test and flew in the face of strong precedents such as *Shapero v. Kentucky Bar Association,* which had given broad protection to targeted mail ten years earlier. Justice Kennedy's dissenting opinion stated:

> Attorneys who communicate their willingness to assist potential clients are engaged in speech protected by the First and Fourteenth Amendments. That principle has been understood since *Bates v. State Bar of Arizona,* 433 U. S. 350 (1977). The Court today undercuts this guarantee in an important class of cases and unsettles leading First Amendment precedents, at the expense of those victims most in need of legal assistance. . . .
>
> [W]hen an accident results in death or injury, it is often urgent at once to investigate the occurrence, identify witnesses, and preserve evidence. Vital interests in speech and expression are, therefore, at stake when by law an attorney cannot direct a letter to the victim or the family explaining this simple fact and offering competent legal assistance. Meanwhile, represented and better informed parties, or parties who have been solicited in ways more sophisticated and indirect, may be at work. Indeed, these parties, either themselves or by their attorneys, investigators, and adjusters, are free to contact the unrepresented persons to gather evidence or offer settlement. This scheme makes little sense. . . .
>
> . . . The very fact that some 280,000 direct mail solicitations are sent to accident victims and their survivors in Florida each year is some indication of the efficacy of this device. Nothing in the Court's opinion demonstrates that these efforts do not serve some beneficial role. A solicitation letter is not a contract. Nothing in the record shows that these communications do not at the least serve the purpose of informing the prospective client that he or she has a number of different attorneys from whom to choose, so that the decision to select counsel, after an interview with one or more interested attorneys, can be deliberate and informed. And if these communications reveal the social costs of the tort system as a whole, then efforts can be directed to reforming the operation of that system, not to suppressing information about how the system works. The Court's approach, however, does not seem to be the proper way to begin elevating the honor of the profession.

NOTES AND QUESTIONS

1. ***Two Points of Universal Agreement.*** Based on the Supreme Court's long line of cases about lawyer advertising, two points are abundantly clear. First, lawyers have no First Amendment right to use advertisements that are false or misleading. Second, lawyers have no right to engage in in-person solicitation or live telephone solicitation. Accordingly, every jurisdiction prohibits false and misleading advertising and almost every jurisdiction prohibits in-person solicitation. All other restrictions on lawyer advertising must be tested to determine whether they violate a lawyer's First Amendment right to engage in truthful, non-misleading advertising.

2. ***The First Amendment Test.*** The Supreme Court's test for First Amendment issues involving lawyer advertising (and other forms of commercial speech) is as follows:

- First, "the government must assert a substantial interest in support of its regulation";
- Second, "the government must demonstrate that the restriction on commercial speech directly and materially advances that interest"; and
- Third, "the regulation must be 'narrowly drawn.' "

The remaining notes occasionally ask you to apply that First Amendment test to various types of regulations.

3. ***Model Rule 7.1.*** The starting point of every First Amendment analysis of the content of a lawyer advertisement is to determine whether the ad is false or misleading. In other words, your main task is to determine whether a given advertisement complies with a rule such as South Carolina's Rule 7.1, which provides, in part:

Rule 7.1 *Communications Concerning a Lawyer's Services*

> A lawyer shall not make false, misleading, deceptive, or unfair communications about the lawyer or the lawyer's services. A communication violates this rule if it:
>
> (a) contains a material misrepresentation of fact or law, or omits a fact necessary to make the statement considered as a whole not materially misleading

4. ***Targeted Mail.*** As you read in the summary of *Zauderer*, the Supreme Court held that lawyers have a First Amendment right to place targeted advertisements in newspapers seeking clients who have been harmed by particular products or particular events (such as a train crash or apartment fire). In *Shapero*, the Supreme Court went a step further by holding that lawyers have the First Amendment right to send letters to people known to need legal services of a particular type (such as bankruptcy or criminal defense). Targeted ads and letters must not be false or misleading. But targeted mail presents at least three important issues: (1) blackout periods; (2) targeted emails; and (3) targets in chat rooms. We will now address these issues in turn.

5. ***Blackout Periods.*** In *Went-for-It*, the Supreme Court held that Florida did not violate the First Amendment by imposing a 30-day "blackout" period on targeted mail solicitations to accident victims and their survivors. Some jurisdictions (most recently New York) have followed Florida's lead. Others (like California) have considered and rejected blackout periods after accidents. Who has the better of the argument in the debate below:

In favor of a 30-day blackout period	*Against a 30-day blackout period*
The legal profession is a noble and dignified profession at the heart of the rule of law and our system of justice. But the influence of lawyers in contemporary American society is at risk because lawyers have an image problem. Since the Supreme Court held in *Bates* that lawyers have the First Amendment right to advertise, many members of the public see lawyers as money-hungry vultures without feelings and eager to profit from the pain of others. We should not make the problem worse by allowing lawyers to send targeted letters the instant an injury occurs. When a widow is in mourning after the sudden death of her husband, that is no time to send her a letter offering to represent her against those allegedly responsible for her husband's death. When parents are in shock over the death of a child in a school bus accident, it is a crass intrusion on their privacy to send a letter advising them to hire the lawyer who sent the letter. When a community is grieving after a refinery explosion, only a person obsessed with money and devoid of manners would write a letter suggesting that the victims assuage their grief by filing a lawsuit.	If everyone knew their legal rights and knew competent lawyers who handle injury cases, targeted mail would be unnecessary. But many people do not know their legal rights, and many people either do not know any lawyers or do not know which lawyers handle injury cases. Since most lawyers cannot afford to advertise on TV or radio, targeted mail increases the chance that a person in need of a lawyer will actually see the lawyer's advertisement soon after an accident.

In favor of a 30-day blackout period	*Against a 30-day blackout period*
Although only a small percentage of lawyers have the audacity and poor taste to contact injured people or the grieving loved ones of those killed in accidents, all lawyers suffer from the negative image of lawyers and the hostile attitude against lawyers caused by such greedy and insensitive tactics. Even if lawyers have the First Amendment right to contact accident victims and their loved ones by mail, people deserve at least 30 days to grieve and reflect before being bombarded with offensive and intrusive letters inciting litigation.	Seeing the lawyer's advertisement shortly after an accident is often crucial to preserving an accident victim's legal rights, for three reasons. First, some claims (e.g., no-fault claims in N.Y.) must be filed within 30 days. If a lawyer must wait 30 days to send a targeted letter, the victim's claim may be lost. Second, accident victims unrepresented by counsel may settle their cases quickly for inadequate sums. Insurance companies are not bound by any blackout period, so they may freely contact an accident victim immediately after an accident to offer a settlement. To an average person, a settlement offer of thousands of dollars may seem like a huge amount of money, but to a lawyer experienced in evaluating cases, such an offer may be far too low. Finally, if an accident victim does not retain counsel soon after an accident, crucial evidence may be lost and witnesses may disappear or forget what they saw.

In favor of a 30-day blackout period	*Against a 30-day blackout period*
In this age where lawyers have many ways to advertise their services other than sending targeted letters, and where potential clients can find injury lawyers in the Yellow Pages, on TV, and on the Internet, a 30-day cooling off period is good for clients and good for the society as a whole.	Concerns about the "image" of the legal profession are expressed mainly by defense lawyers who hope their careless clients will not be sued, and by well-known plaintiffs' lawyers who, as celebrities, are hardly the kind of lawyers who need help to become known to clients. The poor and the middle class in this country consider lawyers to be their champions — their only hope for getting the compensation they deserve from powerful but negligent corporations. Targeted mail helps these people find lawyers who are not afraid to stand up to power. Anyone who doesn't want a targeted letter can just throw it away. The rest of us should have the right to receive targeted letters ASAP.

6. *Targeted Email?* Should the rules permit lawyers to send targeted emails to people known to need particular types of legal services? For example, should a lawyer be allowed to send an email to a person who has just won the lottery saying, "Now that you have much greater financial resources, you should have a written will, or should revise any will you have now." Or should a lawyer be allowed to send an email to a person who just got a ticket for reckless driving saying, "If you are looking for a lawyer who has represented thousands of people in traffic courts throughout our region, call me."

7. *Chat Rooms.* If targeted email is permitted, how about chat rooms? Suppose there is a web site called www.bad-drugs.org in which people complain and exchange information about the harmful effects of Vioxx (or Ritalin or Fen-Phen or some other drug). Should a lawyer be permitted to post a message in that chat room saying, "I am a lawyer who has experience representing victims of bad drugs. If you would like to discuss your legal rights and remedies, call me at 1-800-BAD-DRUG." If you think that is too aggressive, may the lawyer lurk until someone complains about a specific problem, then post a message saying, "I am a lawyer. I might be able to help you. If you would like me to contact you confidentially, please email me your phone number." If that's too aggressive for your taste, should a lawyer be permitted to troll chat rooms looking for people who post messages asking if anyone knows a lawyer who handles bad drug cases? What are the arguments for and against each of these scenarios?

8. ***"Call us at 1-800-PIT-BULL."*** Does Rule 7.1 permit a law firm to use the telephone number "1-800-PIT-BULL"? If not, why not? How about 1-800-BULL-DOG? Do you see any difference between the two phone numbers? How about the following phone numbers:

1-800-LAWYERS

1-800-INJURED

1-800-HELP

1-800-WIN-SUIT

1-800-VICTORY

9. ***Are Canines Ok?*** Could a law firm use a bulldog as the law firm's symbol? For example, could a law firm show a picture of a bulldog on its web site and say: "Our bulldog represents qualities that are important to clients: loyalty, dependability, tenacity and vigilance"? Check out www.wcsr.com, the web site of Womble Carlyle, a prominent law firm based in Winston-Salem, North Carolina. The firm has a "mascot" named Winston, and says that ads featuring Winston "have turned on such characteristics as persistence, loyalty, dependability and vigilance — all very desirable traits in a champion bulldog . . . or lawyer." The "biography" of Winston continues:

Over time, Winston has become so associated with the Firm that he's evolved into our "brand." People frequently tell us that whenever they see a bulldog, they think of Womble Carlyle, or conversely, when they hear or see our name, they visualize our bulldog ads. Since it's pretty tough to differentiate law firms, we're very proud of what our prized mascot has accomplished. So, thanks, Winston; and thanks to all of you for your interest in how he came to be.

10. ***Monikers.*** May a lawyer or law firm use a moniker or nickname like "Hank 'The Hammer,' " "The Heavy Hitters," or "The Dream Team"? Should lawyers be permitted to use names like that as a web site address?

11. ***"Contract Killers."*** Should the lawyer advertising rules permit the following targeted letter and letterhead?

Rodriguez & Baylock

Contract Killers

Dear Company President:

We read in today's newspaper that your company is in a contract dispute with a vendor. Perhaps you entered into a contract a few months or years ago that seemed favorable at the time but has since turned out to be an unfortunate agreement that is costing your company money.

Our law firm has substantial experience in contract disputes. Sometimes we can renegotiate contracts to make the terms more favorable to our clients. Other times, we can find creative defenses to suits against our clients for breach of contract.

If your company would like to renegotiate a bad contract or wants to mount a vigorous and aggressive defense against a suit for breach of contract, please call us. We may be the law firm for you.

Sincerely,

Reuben Rodriguez

Attorney at Law

C. ARE SOME LAWYERS "SUPER LAWYERS" OR THE "BEST LAWYERS IN AMERICA"?

Some companies rate lawyers and publish the ratings. The oldest and best known of these rating services is Martindale-Hubbell, whose highest rating is "AV." In many states, special magazines or magazine sections identify some lawyers as "Super Lawyers." Other lawyers are listed in a book called "Best Lawyers in America." Should lawyers be permitted to cooperate with Martindale-Hubbell, Super Lawyers, or Best Lawyers publications? The New Jersey Supreme Court's Committee on Attorney Advertising (which is appointed by the New Jersey Supreme Court) addressed this issue in July 2006. Did the Committee get it right?

OPINION 39

Advertisements Touting Designation as "Super Lawyer" or "Best Lawyer in America"
N.J. Committee on Attorney Advertising (July 2006)

The Committee has received complaints and inquiries relating to New Jersey lawyers advertising themselves or their colleagues as "Super Lawyers" and/or "Best Lawyers in America." The issue is whether advertisements in any medium of distribution publicizing certain New Jersey lawyers as "Super Lawyers" or "Best Lawyers in America" violate the prohibition against advertisements that are comparative in nature, *RPC* 7.1(a)(3), or that are likely to create an unjustified expectation about results, *RPC* 7.1(a)(2). It is the Committee's position that this type of advertisement is prohibited by the *Rules of Professional Conduct.*

This new form of comparative advertising first appeared in an advertising insert to a 2005 *New Jersey Monthly* magazine and subsequent stand-alone magazine, both devoted primarily to advertisements by law firms promoting their designation as "Super Lawyers." A 2006 *New Jersey Monthly* "Super Lawyers" magazine and subsequent stand-alone magazine have now been published.

The advertisements appearing in both magazines were solicited as paid-for advertising, with the size of the advertisements dependent on the price paid. The primary focus of those advertisements was to congratulate the chosen lawyers for their designation as "Super Lawyers."

The "Super Lawyer" designations have spawned a new surge of attorney marketing in the form of advertisements placed in New Jersey lawyer-directed papers, in local newspapers and by distribution to the public through attorney mailers, flyers, brochures, telephone book listings, and on websites, all of which tout the "Super Lawyer" label and congratulate or promote the so-called "Super" lawyers.

The Committee has also received inquiries concerning the propriety of the advertising and promotion of a New Jersey attorney's status as a "Best Lawyer in America." There are some differences between the "Super Lawyer" and "Best Lawyer" descriptions. First, the "Best Lawyer" methodology of selection is based solely on peer review interviews with a premium placed on those who have been selected as a "Best Lawyer" in previous years.[1] Second, the "Best Lawyer" selection is not focused upon

---

[1] The methodology used by the media corporation to award the "Super Lawyer" designation is unclear. Although the designations are purportedly based in part on a poll of practicing New Jersey attorneys and

encouraging lawyers to advertise in an advertising supplement and appears to market its "Best Lawyer" compendium primarily to other lawyers. However, "Best Lawyer" seems to be trending towards a "Super Lawyer" business plan with similar advertising supplements in other jurisdictions, but not yet in New Jersey.

This Committee has not previously addressed this issue. The Advisory Committee on Professional Ethics, however, has addressed the propriety of attorney advertising through *Who's Who in New Jersey*. ACPE Opinion 311, 98 *N.J.L.J.* 633 (July 24, 1975). That Committee concluded that an attorney may be listed in a directory which is used primarily for reference purposes but warned that attorneys must be wary of directories whose primary purpose is publicizing the listings and must also be careful of using self-laudatory statements in those listings. The Committee recognizes that this Opinion was issued prior to significant law changes in the field of attorney advertising but finds that some of the underlying concerns noted in the Opinion remain viable today.

Advertising which promotes a designation such as "Super Lawyer" or "Best Lawyer in America" does not comply with *RPC* 7.1(a)(3). *RPC* 7.1(a)(3) states that a communication is misleading if it "compares the lawyer's service with other lawyers' services." Use of superlative designations by lawyers is inherently comparative and, thus, not within the approved ambit of New Jersey's *Rules of Professional Conduct*. Such titles or descriptions, based on an assessment by the attorney or other members of the bar, or devised by persons or organizations outside the bar, lack both court approval and objective verification of the lawyer's ability. These self-aggrandizing titles have the potential to lead an unwary consumer to believe that the lawyers so described are, by virtue of this manufactured title, superior to their colleagues who practice in the same areas of law.

Similarly, this type of advertising does not comply with *RPC* 7.1(a)(2). *RPC* 7.1(a)(2) states that a communication is misleading if it "is likely to create an unjustified expectation about results the lawyer can achieve. . . . " When a potential client reads such advertising and considers hiring a "super" attorney, or the "best" attorney, the superlative designation induces the client to feel that the results that can be achieved by this attorney are likely to surpass those that can be achieved by a mere "ordinary" attorney. This simplistic use of a media-generated sound bite title clearly has the capacity to materially mislead the public.

Moreover, the Committee notes that the entire insert to the *New Jersey Monthly* "Super Lawyers" publication, including biographical sketches and even the listing of attorneys, is marked by the magazine as an advertisement. For this reason, and also because of the proximity of attorney advertisements to magazine text on individual "Super Lawyers," any advertisements placed in the "Super Lawyers" magazine insert or stand-alone version are prohibited, even when such advertisements do not include the words "Super Lawyer." It is inevitable that a member of the public, reading an article about a certain attorney who has been designated by the magazine as a "Super Lawyer," will note a nearby advertisement congratulating that lawyer (though not using the prohibited words "Super Lawyer"), and will attribute the marketing designation to the subject of the advertisement. Hence, the placement of an attorney advertisement in the magazine insert serves the same purpose as the use of the superlative, inherently comparative, marketing title. Therefore, the Committee has decided that attorney advertisements, even those advertisements that do not repeat the moniker of "Super Lawyer," appearing in the "Super Lawyer" magazine insert, are prohibited.

---

input from non-attorneys, then weighted in accordance with a non-disclosed system established by the publishers, Law & Politics and/or its sister corporation Key Professional Media, they do not make available the specific methodology for objective review or analysis. A careful review of the selective aspects of the promotional methodology, however, underscores the arbitrary selection and ranking process used by the publisher, and provides no empirical or legally sanctioned support for the results.

Further, it may be that biographical sketches appearing in the "Super Lawyers" insert to the *New Jersey Monthly* magazine are paid for by the subject attorneys or written in whole or in part by the attorneys. If this is so, then the "article" is misleading as it appears to be journalistic material but is, in fact, mere self-promotion. Accordingly, to the extent biographical sketches or other "articles" in the "Super Lawyers" insert are paid for by the subject attorneys or written in whole or in part by the attorneys, such "articles" must bear the word "advertisement" in large print at the top.

Lastly, the Committee has reviewed the survey sent to New Jersey lawyers that supports the selection of attorneys for the "Super Lawyer" designation. It is the Committee's position that participation in a survey of this type, where an attorney knows or reasonably should know that the survey would lead to a descriptive label that is inherently comparative such as "Super Lawyer" or "Best Lawyer," is inappropriate.

The survey results for "Super Lawyer" designation are not intended to cater to other attorneys but, rather, are designed for mass consumption. In contrast, other ratings organizations such as Martindale-Hubbell, which rates attorneys AV, BV or CV, are directed toward other attorneys. Martindale notes that not all attorneys or firms are rated and that most attorneys as they become more experienced move from a CV towards an AV rating. These ratings are familiar to other lawyers and likely have minimal recognition to the public.

Accordingly, advertisements describing attorneys as "Super Lawyers," "Best Lawyers in America," or similar comparative titles, violate the prohibition against advertisements that are inherently comparative in nature, *RPC* 7.1(a)(3), or that are likely to create an unjustified expectation about results, *RPC* 7.1(a)(2).

NOTES AND QUESTIONS

1. ***Do You Agree?*** Are you persuaded by the Advertising Committee's analysis? If so, are you persuaded because of New Jersey's particular rules, or do you think every jurisdiction should reach the same result based on the prohibition against false or misleading advertising by lawyers?

2. ***Check Out the Web Sites.*** Check out the web sites of Martindale-Hubbell, Super Lawyers, and Best Lawyers at www.martindale.com, www.superlawyers.com, and www.bestlawyers.com. What rating system does each company use? (Click around to find out as much as you can.) Does your view about the correctness of N.J. Opinion 39 depend on whether the rating systems used by Super Lawyers and Best Lawyers are "scientific" or "accurate"? Or would you prohibit lawyers from describing themselves as "Super" or "Best" no matter how the ratings are compiled?

3. ***Stay Tuned.*** The defendants (the publishers of Super Lawyers and Best Lawyers) appealed the Advertising Committee's decision in Opinion 39, and the appeal is still pending. Moreover, shortly after Opinion 39 was issued, the New Jersey Supreme Court granted a stay of enforcement of the opinion. Briefing has been completed, but the final decision has not been handed down.

Chapter 30
HOW DO LAWYERS GET IN TROUBLE?

As a lawyer, you live in a glass house. Like Caesar's wife, you must be above reproach. You can get into trouble with the bar not only for your conduct as a lawyer, but also for your conduct outside the practice of law, including your personal life. In this chapter, we first look at the ways lawyers get into trouble as lawyers, and then at how lawyers get into trouble for activities outside the practice of law.

A. MISCONDUCT IN THE PRACTICE OF LAW

The annual report of the Illinois Attorney Registration and Disciplinary Commission (ARDC) to the state's Supreme Court includes a section discussing the various ways that lawyers get into trouble in their law practices. In 2006, the ARDC docketed 5,801 investigations of over 4,000 lawyers licensed in Illinois. As you can see from the following excerpt from the report, more than 68% of the grievances (complaints) in Illinois in 2006 (a total of 3,979) involved allegations that the lawyer either (a) neglected legal work, or (b) failed to communicate with the client. Does this surprise you? Aren't both of these failings easy for a lawyer to cure?

The information presented here about the leading causes of disciplinary complaints against lawyers licensed in Illinois depicts a pattern that we believe is typical of many, if not most, other jurisdictions. We know that a lot of students don't like sorting through statistics, but these charts and numbers are worth the effort. You can learn a lot by looking at a careful analysis of how lawyers get into trouble.

2006 ANNUAL REPORT OF THE ARDC ILLINOIS SUPREME COURT

April 27, 2007

II. Report on Disciplinary Matters and Non-Disciplinary Action Affecting Attorney Status

A. Investigations

Charts 2 and 3 report the classification of investigations docketed in 2006, based on an initial assessment of the nature of the misconduct alleged, if any, and the type of legal context in which the facts apparently arose. Chart 2 reflects that the most frequent areas of a grievance are neglect of the client's cause, failure to communicate with the client, fraudulent or deceptive activity and excessive fees.

Chart 2: Classification of Charges Docketed in 2006 by Violation Alleged

Type of Misconduct	*Number**
Neglect	2,596
Failing to communicate with client, including failing to communicate the basis of a fee	1,383
Fraudulent or deceptive activity, including lying to clients, knowing use of false evidence or making misrepresentation to a tribunal or non-client	921
Excessive or improper fees, including failing to refund unearned fees	827

* Totals exceed the number of charges docketed in 2006 because in many charges more than one type of misconduct is alleged.

Type of Misconduct		*Number**
Improper trial conduct, including using means to embarrass, delay or burden another or suppressing evidence where there is a duty to reveal		368
Improper management of client or third party funds, including commingling, conversion, failing to promptly pay litigation costs or client creditors or issuing NSF checks		361
Filing frivolous or non-meritorious claims or pleadings		309
Conduct prejudicial to the administration of justice, including conduct which is the subject of a contempt finding or court sanction		304
Conflict of Interest:		273
Rule 1.7: concurrent conflicts	176	
Rule 1.9: successive conflicts	51	
Rule 1.8(a)–(e): (i): self-dealing conflicts	37	
Rule 1.8(f)–(h): improper agreement to limit liability/avoid disciplinary action	7	
Rule 1.8(i): improper acquisition of interest in client matter	1	
Rule 1.12: former judge or arbitrator	1	
Failing to properly withdraw from representation, including failing to return client files or documents		164
Criminal activity, including criminal convictions, counseling illegal conduct or public corruption		164
Failing to provide competent representation		132
Not abiding by a client's decision concerning the representation or taking unauthorized action on the client's behalf		130
Improper commercial speech, including inappropriate written or oral solicitation		111
Practicing in a jurisdiction where not authorized		91
Improper communications with a party known to be represented by counsel or unrepresented party		66
Prosecutorial misconduct		51
Failing to preserve client confidences or secrets		47
Threatening criminal prosecution or disciplinary proceedings to gain advantage in a civil matter		31
Failing to supervise subordinates		28
Aiding a nonlawyer in the unauthorized practice of law		25
Practicing after failing to register		22
Improper division of legal fees with another lawyer		15
Failing to maintain an appropriate attorney-client relationship with disabled client		11
Improper *ex parte* communication with judge		11
Improper division of legal fees/partnership with nonlawyer		10
Sexual harrassment/abuse or violation of law prohibiting discrimination		9
Failing to comply with Rule 764		8
Failing to report misconduct of another lawyer or judge		8
Incapacity due to chemical addiction or mental condition		7
Improper employment where lawyer may become a witness		6
Improper extrajudicial statement		6

Type of Misconduct	*Number**
False statements in a bar admission or disciplinary matter	5
Assisting a judge in conduct that violates the judicial code	3
Failing to pay tax obligation in bad faith	3
Bad faith avoidance of a student loan	2
Failing to report lawyer's discipline in another jurisdiction	2
Investigation of bar applicant	2
Judicial candidate's violation of Judicial Code	2
False statements about judge, jud. candidate or public official	1
Failing to reveal client confidences necessary to prevent death/serious bodily harm	1
No misconduct alleged	301

Consistent with the experience in Illinois in prior years, the areas of law practice which were most likely to lead to a grievance alleging attorney misconduct were criminal law, domestic relations, tort, and real estate, as shown in Chart 3.

Chart 3: Classification of Charges Docketed in 2006 by Area of Law

Area of Law	*Number**
Criminal/Quasi-Criminal	1,184
Domestic Relations	900
Tort (Personal Injury/Property Damage)	706
Real Estate/Landlord-Tenant	561
Probate	328
Labor Relations/Workers' Comp	259
Bankruptcy	217
Contract	200
Debt Collection	161
Criminal Conduct/Conviction	145
Civil Rights	143
Immigration	141
Corporate Matters	93
Local Government Problems	46
Tax	29
Patent and Trademark	17
Social Security	10
Adoption	9
Mental Health	7
Other	204
Undeterminable	172

* Totals exceed the number of charges docketed in 2006 because in many charges more than one area of law is involved.

NOTES AND QUESTIONS

1. ***Are You Surprised?*** Are you surprised at the practice areas in which the most lawyers are the target of grievances? Are you surprised at the practice areas in which the fewest lawyers draw grievances? What do you think explains the difference between areas of practice in which many lawyers are the targets of complaints and those where few lawyers are targeted?

2. ***Would Standardized Operating Practices Help?*** How many of the items on the ARDC charts fall within areas where lawyers could establish standard operating routines? How many could be organized in such a way that the tasks being performed would be easily visible to at least one other person in the office? How many of the operations could be organized in such a way that final responsibility for satisfactory completion could be assigned to a single person (or at the very least a small group of persons)? How many of the operations could be organized in a way that allowed (or, perhaps, even required) a second person to review the operation from start to finish?

3. ***An Ounce of Prevention?*** Should disciplinary counsel in all states — and ethics professors — focus on preventing misconduct rather than on reading, understanding, and adhering to ethics rules? If you think so, how would you focus on preventing misconduct?

4. ***Bad Habits Die Hard.*** In many ways, lawyers are just law students who have gotten older. If you have bad habits and routines now, as a lawyer you are likely to have to have bad habits and routines — unless, that is, you change your habits and routines before you graduate. As you think about the ARDC's list and how you, your course in legal ethics, and the legal profession as a whole ought to respond to it, ask yourself whether we are creating working environments in which lawyers will act ethically (even when they may not want to do so). Consider that question, too, as you review the circumstances and rules that apply to other instances of misconduct. Lawyers do too many different things wrong for us to provide an exhaustive examination of the rules and circumstances, but the nature of the problem is illustrated below in the context of a particular kind of misbehavior, sexual misconduct with clients.

B. SEXUAL MISCONDUCT WITH CLIENTS

This book focuses on professional conduct, not morality. We are teachers, not preachers. But professional conduct and morality do sometimes intersect or overlap. Certain types of behavior by lawyers are just beyond the moral limits of what the profession will tolerate. Sexual misconduct by lawyers raises many of those issues. We deal with it here for three reasons.

First, there is a growing awareness that sexual misconduct between "professionals" and their clients is a serious problem in our society, and the legal profession is not excluded from the list of miscreant professions. As shocking — even disgusting — and sometimes illegal as the news reports about the sexual abuses of school teachers (elementary and secondary), college and university professors, clergymen, doctors, dentists, and politicians, they are not important to a legal ethics course simply because they reflect breaches of social norms. Rather, they are of relevance here because they challenge us to ask whether those calling themselves professionals bear a separate and unique responsibility — a responsibility that is beyond that of the general society — for their conduct with respect to their clients.

Second, given the length of time that the issue has been around — sex with clients has sometimes been called the bar's "dirty little secret" — it is fair to ask why until relatively recently the ethical rules governing lawyers did not explicitly address the issue. Indeed, not until the early 1990s did the subject reach the agendas of most lawyer regulatory forums. In one state after another, lawyers and legislators began looking seriously at the problem of sex with clients, but for a long time the ABA and several other jurisdictions took the traditional view outlined below by Virginia's State Bar Counsel:

> The fact that Virginia does not have a rule explicitly barring sexual relations between attorneys and clients does not mean that the bar cannot prosecute a lawyer for sexually exploiting an attorney-client relationship. The pertinent RPCs are 1.7(b) and 8.4(b). 1.7(b) provides that a lawyer shall not represent a client if the lawyer's own interests may materially limit the representation of the client. 8.4(b) states that it is professional misconduct for a lawyer to commit a criminal or deliberately wrongful act that reflects adversely on the lawyer's honesty, trustworthiness or fitness as a lawyer.

Barbara Ann Williams, *Inside the Office of Bar Counsel: "Sex, Lies and Bar Complaints"*, VIRGINIA LAWYER REGISTER, Nov. 2001, at 1, *available at,* http://www.vsb.org/publications/valawyer/nov01/barcounsel.pdf (last last visited Nov. 5, 2008).

Third, we again ask the implicit operational question with which we began this chapter: Are there ways of structuring the practice of law that can advance the goal of delivering legal services to clients in a professional and ethical manner? The first case provides a graphic picture of the problem and a good review of the law in the area of sexual relations between lawyers and clients.

STATE OF OKLAHOMA EX REL. OKLAHOMA BAR ASSOCIATION v. SOPHER

1993 Okla. LEXIS 63; 1993 OK 55

ALMA WILSON, J.

The Bar Association filed a complaint against the respondent alleging that he had engaged in unprofessional conduct. The respondent and counsel for the Oklahoma Bar Association appeared before a trial panel of the Professional Responsibility Commission and agreed to findings of fact, conclusions of law, and a recommendation for discipline. The trial panel adopted the stipulations and the recommendation for discipline that the respondent be publicly reprimanded.

The parties agreed that the respondent violated the mandatory provisions of Rule 8.4(d) of the Oklahoma Rules of Professional Conduct. That rule provides in pertinent part that "It is professional misconduct for a lawyer to . . . (d) engage in conduct that is prejudicial to the administration of justice. . . . " The respondent agrees that his conduct, which resulted in a bar complaint, is a violation of that rule.

The facts are taken from the stipulations submitted by the parties and adopted by the trial panel. A woman who had previously been employed as a secretary for the respondent came to his office to discuss two legal matters. One matter involved a charge against her in Oklahoma City Municipal Court for committing a lewd act while she was employed as an exotic dancer at an Oklahoma City bar. In the other matter, the woman related that her boyfriend, while exercising visitation with their son, had taken him to live in California. The respondent agreed to represent the woman on both matters for a retainer of $700.00. The woman paid the respondent all that she had with her, $30.00. She agreed to pay the balance at a later date.

As she got up to leave, the respondent came around his desk, put his arm around her and hooked his finger in the top of her blouse. He then pulled her blouse out, looked down it and commented, "Don't expose yourself." The woman's mother had accompanied her to the respondent's office and had been waiting in the reception area. When the daughter left the respondent's office, he motioned the mother to come into his office. Without knowing what had just occurred, she went in while the daughter waited in the reception area. The respondent did the same thing to the mother that he did to the daughter. He looked down the mother's blouse and said, "How's it going down there?" She then left the respondent's office.

As the mother and daughter were on the elevator in the office building, they learned that each had been subjected to the same offensive conduct by the respondent. They then drove to the office of another lawyer whom the mother knew. That lawyer telephoned the respondent, who agreed to return the $30.00 that the daughter had paid him.

According to the stipulated facts, the respondent would testify that at the time of the incident he believed his conduct would not be offensive due to his previous acquaintance with the mother and the jocular nature of their relationship, which was one that had sometimes involved the sharing of off-color humor. The Bar Association maintains that the conduct was patently offensive and not excused by any prior relationship.

AUTHORS' COMMENT:

Was the conduct offensive? Should the lawyer be disciplined? If so, what should the discipline be? If not, why not?

The respondent admits and acknowledges that, in hindsight, his conduct was inappropriate and that the mother and daughter were genuinely offended by it. The parties agree that whatever the nature of the respondent's previous relationship with the mother and daughter, his conduct was neither justified nor appropriate in an attorney-client setting. Counsel for the Bar Association commented during the hearing that the respondent had cooperated with the investigation and that his cooperation should be considered in mitigation of his behavior. . . .

The matter before us is one of first impression in this state. Although we find no cases with identical facts, we do find lawyer disciplinary cases from other jurisdictions involving unwelcome and uninvited sexual advances between lawyers and their clients. The discipline administered has ranged from public reprimand to disbarment, based on the severity of the actions or multiple unprofessional acts by the attorney involved. The more severe cases involve criminal charges as well.

The Supreme Court of Indiana publicly reprimanded a lawyer who grabbed his client, kissed her and raised her blouse. *In the Matter of Darrell Adams*, 428 N.E.2d 786 (Ind. 1981). That court found that the lawyer's actions constituted illegal conduct involving moral turpitude and adversely reflected on his fitness to practice law. The Indiana Disciplinary Commission and Adams tendered an agreement for a public reprimand as the sanction for Adams' professional misconduct. The court commented:

> Realizing that the publication of this opinion will have a detrimental effect on the Respondent's legal practice, we find the proposed discipline appropriate under the facts of the present case. It should be obvious that Respondent sought to exploit the attorney-client relationship for his personal physical pleasure. Conduct of this ilk is particularly repugnant while the client is dependent upon the attorney for guidance and assistance.

In *Committee on Professional Ethics v. Durham*, 279 N.W.2d 280 (Iowa 1979), a female attorney was disciplined for sexual contact between her and a male client who was an inmate in a penitentiary. The Supreme Court of Iowa found that the attorney had engaged in kissing and embracing during the visits in question, as well as occasional caressing or fondling. The conduct was observed and reported by the officials of the penitentiary. The court explained that the attorney's conduct was not reprehensible per se, but she was publicly reprimanded because she had entered the institution in the capacity as lawyer for the inmate, and that the conduct reflected adversely on her fitness to practice law. The court observed:

> Sexual contact with a client in a professional context is not activity which a reasonable member of the bar would suppose to be allowed by the [Iowa Code of Professional Responsibility for Lawyers]. Such conduct is well outside that which could be termed temperate and dignified and would amount to professional impropriety, both in terms of the dictionary definitions and general understanding of the words used.

In *People v. Zeilinger*, 814 P.2d 808 (Colo. 1991), an attorney received a public reprimand for engaging in sexual relations with a woman whom he was representing in a dissolution of marriage action. The dissolution involved custody of minor children and property settlement. The Supreme Court of Colorado found that the actions of the attorney reflected on his fitness to practice law, and involved a conflict of interest. The court commented:

> Aside from the consequences on the respondent's own life and professional practice, engaging in a sexual relationship with a client undergoing a divorce may destroy chances of a reconciliation, and blind the attorney to the proper exercise of independent judgment. There is also a significant danger that when the division of property or the custody of minor children is contested, the attorney may himself become the focus of the dissolution or custody proceedings, be called as a witness, and thereby inflict great harm on the client.

The Supreme Court of Missouri suspended an attorney for six months where he made uninvited sexual advances toward an incarcerated female client, and for making additional sexual advances, including brushing his hand across her breasts, after she had been released from custody. These actions also resulted in his being criminally charged with sexual abuse, third degree. *In re Littleton*, 719 S.W.2d 772 (Mo. 1986). . . . That court observed:

> Respondent and [client] entered into a professional relationship. [Client] had a right to expect that respondent would conduct himself in that relationship in a manner consistent with the honorable tradition of the legal professional — a tradition founded on service, integrity, vigorous commitment to the client's best interests, and an allegiance to the rule of law. Instead of remaining true to that tradition, however, respondent chose to exploit it, seeking to turn the professional relationship into a personal one. . . .

Because the attorney had also accepted $1,000.00 from third parties as bond money and failed to return it to them, the court determined that suspension was the appropriate discipline.

Taking advantage of the attorney-client relationship by making sexual advances accompanied by offensive touching is professional misconduct and will result in disciplinary action against the attorney when the matter is brought to the attention of this Court. Clients are in a vulnerable position. Exploiting the client for gratification of the attorney will not be tolerated by this Court. . . .

We reprimand the respondent John P. Sopher and admonish him that such uninvited sexual advances are unprofessional conduct not to be condoned by this Court. We order that the respondent bear the costs of this proceeding in the amount of $300.25.

Respondent Publicly Reprimanded.

AUTHORS' COMMENT:

Is a public reprimand a severe enough sanction for what attorney Sopher did? Or is it too severe? Check out the dissent.

OPALA, J. dissenting.

This tempest-in-a-teapot factual backdrop makes this case unfit as a vehicle for today's message of warning that (a) yesteryear's sexual law-office games will no longer be tolerated and (b) the Bar's disciplinary cognizance may indeed focus on a male lawyer's display of excessive macho in the context of an attorney-client relationship. I would resist the temptation by administering a private reprimand and deferring the court's sweeping pronouncement on a new, more sensitive, "gender-inoffensive" professional etiquette to be followed by the practicing bar.

NOTES AND QUESTIONS

1. ***Tempest in a Teapot?*** The dissent calls the conduct in the *Sopher* case "a-tempest-in-a-teapot." Was it? Does it matter to you whether the lawyer in question has done this kind of thing before? Does it matter whether sexual misconduct toward clients is a serious problem in the profession, as opposed to a rare event?

2. ***The Appropriate Discipline.*** The majority in *Sopher* issued a public reprimand. The dissent would have issued a private reprimand. (In a private reprimand, the name of the lawyer would not appear in the opinion, or the opinion would not be published.) Some of the cases discussed in the opinion issued suspensions or disbarments. If you had been on the Oklahoma Supreme Court for the *Sopher* opinion, what discipline would you have recommended?

C. CRIMINAL PROSECUTIONS OF DISHONEST LAWYERS

So far we have looked at cases in which lawyers have been disciplined by the bar. But in recent years, professional discipline has not been the only problem confronting errant lawyers. Increasingly — perhaps reflecting a growing populist sentiment — prosecutors have resorted to criminal prosecution of dishonest lawyers. We won't dwell on this because, even with the increases, the statistical probability that any lawyer will become the target of a criminal prosecution (not to mention a criminal conviction) remains low. The vast majority of lawyers, like the vast majority of most licensed professionals, are not criminals. But we include the next case about a crooked lawyer because it is important to emphasize the critical distinction between disciplinary sanctions and criminal punishment.

Disciplinary sanctions are imposed pursuant to the judiciary branch's administrative oversight of the legal profession. Protecting the public, judicial administration, and the legal profession is its limited purpose. By contrast, enforcement of the criminal laws is an executive branch function, intended to vindicate the general society's interest in the enforcement of laws prohibiting conduct that threatens public safety and welfare. Therefore, for law students, as future lawyers, the important thing to understand is that lawyer regulation is a complex, multilayered, and overlapping process that is influenced, both, by principles of comity and public opinion.

The lead defendant in the case that follows was Morris Eisen, a well-known and highly successful personal injury lawyer who was the lead trial attorney in his own firm. He was talented and probably could have done very well without committing fraud. But greed (or something) drove him to cheat in at least eighteen personal injury cases. He and several of his partners and investigators were convicted under the powerful RICO statute for a pattern of racketeering activity involving fraud — and even the legendary Alan Dershowitz, who argued Eisen's appeal, couldn't get the conviction reversed.

UNITED STATES v. EISEN

974 F.2d 246 (2d Cir. 1992)

JON O. NEWMAN, J.

Morris J. Eisen, P.C. ("the Eisen firm") was a large Manhattan law firm that specialized in bringing personal injury suits on behalf of plaintiffs. The defendants, seven of the Eisen firm's attorneys, investigators, and office personnel, were tried jointly on two counts of conducting and conspiring to conduct the affairs of the Eisen firm through a pattern of racketeering activity, in violation of 18 U.S.C. §§ 1962(c), (d) (1988). The indictment alleged, as the underlying acts of racketeering, that each of the defendants committed, among other crimes, numerous acts of mail fraud, in violation of 18 U.S.C. § 1341, and bribery of witnesses. . . .

AUTHORS' COMMENT:

Did you see or read *The Firm*? Tom Cruise (Mitchell McDeere) got the members of his firm on mail fraud. It's a powerful weapon, and now it's being turned against lawyers. Did you think *The Firm* was just fiction?

The evidence at trial established that the defendants conducted the affairs of the Eisen law firm through a pattern of mail fraud and witness bribery by pursuing counterfeit claims and using false witnesses in personal injury trials, and that the Eisen firm earned millions in contingency fees from personal injury suits involving fraud or bribery. The methods by which the frauds were accomplished included pressuring accident witnesses to testify falsely, paying individuals to testify falsely that they had witnessed accidents, paying unfavorable witnesses not to testify, and creating false photographs, documents, and physical evidence of accidents for use before and during trial. The Government's proof included the testimony of numerous Eisen firm attorneys and employees as well as Eisen firm clients, defense attorneys, and witnesses involved in the fraudulent personal injury suits. Transcripts, correspondence, and trial exhibits from the fraudulent personal injury suits were also introduced.

. . . .

NOTES AND QUESTIONS

1. ***Tricks of the Trade.*** The lawyers in *Eisen* had a big bag of tricks. Take potholes, a typical cause of personal injuries in New York City. The Eisen firm made phony yardsticks to measure potholes in city streets, then photographed the phony yardsticks lying across the pothole to "prove" that it was twice as wide as it really was. Sometimes, the lawyers or investigators dug up a pothole to make it bigger — or photographed a big pothole on another street, and bribed the photographer to testify that he took the photo at the site of the accident. Pretty clever — but not clever enough. The lawyers can think about what went wrong while they sit in federal prison for a few years.

2. ***What Happened to Confidentiality?*** Some of the witnesses against Eisen and the other defendants were lawyers in Eisen's firm. How could they testify about their cases? What rule allowed them to do it? There are several possible ways. Maybe the clients consented. Or maybe the communications were never protected by the attorney-client privilege in the first place because of the crime-fraud exception.

Wouldn't the information still be protected by ABA Model Rule 1.6? No, because the lawyers here were testifying in court, under compulsion, pursuant to court order. (The defendants didn't testify because they had a Fifth Amendment privilege not to testify against themselves, but their partners and associates could be called to testify against them, and compelled to testify under penalty of contempt.)

D. MISCONDUCT OUTSIDE THE PRACTICE OF LAW

In the early 1990s, Robert Fulghum wrote a book called ALL I NEEDED TO KNOW I LEARNED IN KINDERGARTEN. You may feel the same way about this course. We realize that, so we've generally focused on facets of law practice that you did not learn in kindergarten. We have talked much more about conflicts and confidentiality than about honesty and integrity. But we have at least to warn you that you can get in trouble not only for what you do *in* your law practice but also for what you do *outside* of your law practice. If we didn't, there would be a big hole in this book. Therefore, we're now going to discuss honesty and integrity outside the practice of law — in your social life, political life, and sex life.

You already know that the kinds of misconduct we are about to discuss are wrong. We're not teaching you right from wrong. But we want to make sure you realize the drastic consequences misconduct can have on a lawyer's career even though the misconduct takes place outside the law office and does not directly involve any clients.

1. Illegal Conduct

Under the old Code of Professional Responsibility, which was in effect in most states from about 1970 until around 1985, a lawyer could be disbarred or otherwise disciplined for engaging in "illegal conduct involving *moral turpitude*." Today, most states have eliminated moral turpitude as a criterion. Instead, Rule 8.4(b) makes it professional misconduct for a lawyer to "commit a criminal act that reflects adversely on the lawyer's honesty, trustworthiness or fitness as a lawyer in other respects." However, many courts and judges continue to think in terms of moral turpitude in deciding whether a lawyer's misconduct merits discipline.

The next case was decided under California's old Code of Professional Responsibility, which used "moral turpitude" as a litmus test. The case is a little piece of history. The lawyer charged with wrongdoing, Donald Segretti, was a bit player in the Watergate scandal that ultimately led to Richard Nixon's resignation as President. This case revolves not around Watergate but rather around Segretti's pranks in various political contests. For us, though, the question is whether Segretti's conduct would, today, warrant discipline under Rule 8.4(b). That is, does the conduct described in the case adversely reflect on Segretti's "honesty, trustworthiness or fitness as a lawyer in other respects"? What do you think?

SEGRETTI v. STATE BAR

15 Cal. 3d 878, 126 Cal. Rptr. 793, 544 P.2d 929 (1976)

THE COURT.

. . . Segretti, a 34-year-old attorney, was admitted to practice in 1967. In L.A. 30423 he was charged in a notice to show cause with, among other things, committing specified acts involving moral turpitude in connection with the 1972 campaign of Richard Nixon for reelection as President of the United States.

L.A. 30424 involves Segretti's conviction on two counts of violating 18 United States Code section 612 (publication or distribution of political statements)[1] and one count of violating 18 United States Code section 371 (conspiracy) by conspiring to violate section

[1] Section 612 provides: "Whoever willfully . . . causes to be published or distributed . . . any . . . statement relating to . . . any person who has publicly declared his intention to seek the office of President . . . of the United States . . . in a primary . . . election . . . which does not contain the names of the persons,

612. In 1973, he pleaded guilty to the offenses and was sentenced to consecutive one-year prison terms, but execution of all except six months of the sentence was suspended, and he was placed on probation for three years. No appeal was filed from the judgment. After our receipt of the record of conviction, we referred the matter to the State Bar for a hearing and report as to whether the facts and circumstances surrounding the offenses involved moral turpitude or other misconduct warranting discipline and, if so found, for a recommendation as to discipline.

The State Bar consolidated the two proceedings for hearing. The board determined that the facts and circumstances surrounding Segretti's conviction and apparently acts alleged in the notice to show cause and found to be true involved moral turpitude or other misconduct warranting discipline. The board recommended that discipline be imposed, but was unable to agree on the extent of the discipline.[2]

In May 1967, a few months after his admission to practice, Segretti was inducted into the Army. He served in the Judge Advocate General's Corps for over four years, including a year in Vietnam, and was honorably discharged in September 1971.

During the summer of 1971 Dwight Chapin and Gordon Strachan, who were members of President Nixon's staff and friends of Segretti, offered employment to Segretti after his Army discharge in connection with President Nixon's campaign for reelection. Chapin told Segretti that his duties would consist of pulling pranks on Democratic presidential aspirants and that the purpose of the activities was to foster a split among such aspirants so that it would be less likely that the party would unite behind the one finally receiving the nomination. Chapin also told Segretti that he should use a fictitious name when carrying out his duties in order to insulate himself from association with President Nixon's office in the event the activities came to public light. Segretti accepted the employment for a number of reasons, including his favoring President Nixon's policy regarding ending the war in Vietnam. Segretti believed at that time that the mischievous acts he was to perform were in the nature of college pranks.

Later that summer, at the suggestion of Strachan or Chapin, Segretti met with Herbert Kalmbach, counsel to President Nixon, and Kalmbach and Segretti agreed that Segretti would work for a yearly salary of $16,000 plus expenses. Segretti, thereafter in 1971 and 1972, received a total of about $45,000, including salary and expenses. At the time of his employment, he felt privileged to be employed by persons connected with the White House.

AUTHORS' COMMENT:

Segretti was hired by the President's lawyer! Did Kalmbach know what Segretti was being hired to do? If he did, should Kalmbach himself be disciplined? If Kalmbach didn't know what Segretti was being hired to do, was Kalmbach incompetent, in violation of MRPC 1.1?

After his discharge from the Army, Segretti recruited others to assist him in his new

---

associations, committees, or corporations responsible for the publication or distribution of the same . . . shall be" punished in a specified manner. . . .

[2] Five board members recommended five years suspension, stay of execution of such suspension, and probation for that period on conditions including three years suspension. One board member voted against the recommendation on the ground that two rather than three years suspension should be imposed as a condition of probation. Four board members believed Segretti should be disbarred.

The local committee recommended five years suspension, with two years thereof suspended upon conditions relating to Segretti's passing a legal ethics course and being employed as a law clerk.

employment. He never received a clear outline of what he was to do, and he and his associates "thought up over a beer or two" a number of the acts they committed.

For several months, commencing about December 1971, Segretti and others conspired to violate section 612 and committed overt acts in furtherance of the conspiracy. Also during the period from about December 1971 to June 1972, Segretti committed the two section 612 violations and engaged in other misconduct. The most serious acts committed by him were:

Preparation and Distribution of Letters, Allegedly Written by Citizens for Muskie Committee, Falsely Accusing Senators Hubert Humphrey and Henry Jackson of Sexual Improprieties

Segretti, without authorization of the Citizens for Muskie Committee, wrote and caused to be distributed on the letterhead of that committee a letter accusing Senators Humphrey and Jackson of sexual improprieties. The accusations were false, as Segretti then knew. Senators Humphrey, Jackson, and Muskie were all candidates for the Democratic nomination for president.

Segretti testified that, when he wrote the letter, it was not his desire to have anyone believe the contents thereof and that instead he wanted to create confusion among the candidates. Upon later reexamination of the letter, he found it difficult to reconcile his expressed intent with the letter's contents.

The letter was Segretti's own idea. When he sent a copy to Chapin and told him it cost $20 to have the letter distributed, Chapin said that for the $20 Segretti received up to $20,000 free publicity. One of the section 612 violations and the conspiracy conviction involved this letter.

Preparation and Distribution of News Release on Senator Humphrey's Stationery, Without His Consent, Containing False Allegations Regarding Mental Illness of Representative Shirley Chisholm

Segretti wrote and caused to be distributed on Senator Humphrey's stationery, without his consent, a news release alleging that Representative Chisholm once had been committed to a mental institution and was still under psychiatric care. The allegations were false, as Segretti then knew. Representative Chisholm was also a Democratic candidate.

According to Segretti, he did not intend anyone to believe the allegations but wanted people to believe that the news release was distributed by Senator Humphrey. After Segretti sent Chapin a copy of the release, Chapin told Segretti that he laughed on reading it.

Letters Written on Stationery of Senator Eugene McCarthy, Without His Consent, Asking that McCarthy and Chisholm Delegates Switch Their Votes to Senator Humphrey

In his efforts to cause dissension among the Democratic candidates, Segretti had printed on the letterhead of Senator McCarthy, another Democratic presidential candidate, without his consent, letters suggesting that McCarthy and Chisholm delegates switch their votes to Humphrey. The letters purported to be signed by a worker in the McCarthy campaign. Segretti admitted that the signature was a forgery, but did not indicate who signed the letter. He had a number of the letters distributed to certain McCarthy and Chisholm delegates. Some of the letters he mailed without postage so that they would be returned to the McCarthy headquarters and persons there would be aware of the letters.

Article in Los Angeles Newspaper Reproducing Bogus Letters

Segretti caused to be prepared and inserted in the May 26, 1972, Los Angeles Free Press a full-page display, the heading of which read, "Is Mayor Yorty Involved in a Plot to Sabotage McGovern." The article contained the bogus switch vote letters hereinabove described and a letter on Mayor Yorty's campaign stationery falsely accusing Yorty of responsibility for the switch vote letters. The letter containing the false accusation was purportedly written by a disgusted Yorty supporter but was, in fact, Segretti's handiwork.

False Notices Regarding Free Lunch and Drinks at Certain Headquarters of Senators Humphrey and Muskie

Segretti caused notices to be released to the effect that free lunches and drinks would be distributed at certain headquarters of Senators Humphrey and Muskie at specified times. The notices were false and were intended by Segretti to cause confusion in the campaigns of those candidates.

Other Bogus Campaign Material

Segretti had printed and distributed other bogus campaign material. For example, he had printed and distributed (1) bumper stickers reading, "Humphrey; he started the war; don't give him another chance. Democrats for Peace Candidate" and (2) posters reading, "Help Muskie — Support Busing More Children Now. Mothers Backing Muskie Committee." No such organizations existed, as Segretti then knew.

Miscellaneous

Segretti and an associate, ostensibly acting for Muskie organizers, ordered liquor and other items for the campaign workers. They also invited foreign guests to a Muskie fund-raising dinner, provided for their delivery to the dinner by limousine, and hired a magician to entertain. The purpose of their actions was to cause confusion at the Muskie dinner.

Segretti collaborated with an associate regarding placing of stink bombs at a Muskie picnic and at Muskie headquarters. Segretti was later told that a stink bomb had been placed in Muskie's headquarters, but did not know who placed it there. . . .

AUTHORS' COMMENT:

Did the acts described so far involve "moral turpitude"? Or were they just innocent pranks? Is a person who carried out these pranks fit to practice law? What factors are most important to you? How do you define conduct that falls below the minimum that you expect and demand of a lawyer? Come to your own conclusion before you read the court's analysis.

Claim That Segretti's Acts Did Not Involve Moral Turpitude

There is no merit to a contention by Segretti that his acts did not involve moral turpitude. As above appears, he repeatedly committed acts of deceit designed to subvert the free electoral process. Even if credence were given to his dubious claim that he did not intend the recipients to believe the allegations of some of the material in question, he admittedly intended the recipients to be deceived as to the source of the material. A member of the bar should not under any circumstances attempt to deceive another. . . . "An attorney's practice of deceit involves moral turpitude." . . .

Discipline

Segretti, as we have seen, engaged in gross misconduct over a period of several months.

There are, however, a number of mitigating circumstances. Segretti has no prior disciplinary record. . . . During the period of over four years he was in the Judge Advocate General's Corps he displayed honesty and trustworthiness and performed his legal duties in an outstanding manner. . . . He was only 30 years old at the time of the misconduct . . . and thought he was acting under "the umbrella of the White House." It is important to note that the misconduct was not committed in his capacity as an attorney. . . . After he committed the improper acts, he recognized their wrongfulness, expressed regret, and cooperated with the investigating agencies. . . . He has already " 'suffered the ignominy of a criminal conviction, [and] has served time in a [federal] penal institution. . . . ' " He voluntarily abstained from the practice of law during the instant proceedings . . . , and although he has been a member of the State Bar for some eight years, he has not yet practiced as an attorney except for the period he was in the Judge Advocate General's Corps.

. . . .

For these reasons, it is ordered that Segretti be suspended from the practice of law for five years; that execution of such suspension be stayed; and that he be placed on probation for that period upon condition that he shall be suspended from the practice of law for the first two years thereof. . . . [W]e further order as a condition of probation that prior to the end of Segretti's period of actual suspension he passes the Professional Responsibility Examination. This order is effective 30 days after filing of this opinion.

NOTES AND QUESTIONS

1. ***Conduct Outside the Practice of Law.*** Should lawyers ever be disciplined for misdeeds that they commit outside the scope of professional employment? Why or why not? To focus specifically on Segretti, keep in mind that no client was hurt by his conduct, and no judicial proceeding was tainted. Nor did Segretti use his legal skills or invoke his status as an attorney in committing any of his dirty tricks. Why should a lawyer be suspended from law practice when his misconduct was separate and independent of his role as a lawyer? *See also In Re Lamberis*, 443 N.E.2d 549, 551 (1982), involving an attorney who submitted work plagiarized from two publications to Northwestern University in satisfaction of requirements for his masters degree in law. "This court has often disciplined attorneys for conduct arising outside the practice of law." The court concluded: "[W]e believe that the respondent's conduct warrants discipline. In imposing discipline in this case we do not intend to imply that attorneys must conform to conventional notions of morality in all questions of conscience and personal life." But just why is it that attorneys should not have to conform to conventional notions of morality in all questions of conscience and personal life?

2. ***Watergate and the Law School Curriculum.*** Did you know that the ABA did not require law students to take a course on professional responsibility until after Watergate? The Watergate scandal caught dozens of lawyers engaging in wrongdoing, including President Nixon and his Attorney General, John Mitchell. Lawyers sank to a new low in the public eye, and the ABA concluded that every law school needed to provide students with systematic instruction in legal ethics. Was this a good idea? Will this course help you avoid temptation after you become a lawyer?

3. ***Tax Law Violations.*** To narrow the question about offenses independent of the practice of law, let's look at tax law violations. Suppose a lawyer is convicted of willfully failing to file a tax return. Should the lawyer be suspended or disbarred? Do tax crimes reflect adversely on a lawyer's "honesty, trustworthiness or fitness as a lawyer in other respects"? Here's what the California Supreme Court had to say on this subject in *In re Rohan*, 21 Cal. 3d 195, 145 Cal. Rptr. 855, 578 P.2d 102 (1978):

> An attorney as an officer of the court and counselor at law occupies a unique position in society. His refusal to obey the law, and the bar's failure to discipline him for such refusal, will not only demean the integrity of the profession but will encourage disrespect for and further violations of the law. This is particularly true in the case of revenue law violations by an attorney. "'Governments cannot operate effectively unless their revenue laws are obeyed. Such a violation of the tax laws by an attorney is a matter of serious concern because he necessarily must advise clients with respect to their obedience of such laws. Furthermore, the legal profession is one which is peculiarly charged with the administration of our laws and therefore it is incumbent upon lawyers to set an example for

> others in observing the law. The intentional failure to file income tax returns evinces an attitude on the part of the attorney of placing himself above the law.' "

Do you agree with this reasoning? What about traffic offenses? Tax violations don't directly endanger life, but speeding and reckless driving do. And what about drug offenses? Suppose an attorney is found in possession of three joints of marijuana. Should that attorney be disciplined? Why or why not? What if the attorney used marijuana or LSD as a law student, but did not disclose this on the bar application? Should that attorney be disciplined? Why or why not? If so, should the bar refuse to license law graduates who used marijuana or other drugs during law school, even if they did not become addicted? What about alcoholics? Are alcoholics a greater risk or embarrassment to the legal profession than occasional marijuana users?

4. ***"He's Suffered Enough Already."*** Of course, we agree that lawyers should be punished for engaging in illegal conduct. But punishment is not the issue. The issue is, why should a lawyer be suspended or disbarred *on top of* criminal sanctions if the lawyer had an unblemished record as a lawyer? Does the conviction reveal a character flaw? Does the Bar not wish to be associated with felons? Does the public demand revocation of the license to practice? Is the Bar protecting the public from dangerous people? Is the Bar concerned about appearances? (In case you're wondering, the authors believe that lawyers should be disciplined in addition to criminal penalties. The point of these questions is to get you to articulate the reason for the parallel penalties in a way that satisfies you.)

5. ***Would Segretti be Disciplined Today?*** As noted in the introduction to this chapter, the rules in force in most jurisdictions today no longer use the phrase "moral turpitude." In place of that phrase, Missouri's Rule 8.4(b) is typical, defining "misconduct" as any criminal act — whether a felony or a misdemeanor — that "reflects adversely on the lawyer's honesty, trustworthiness or fitness as a lawyer in other respects." Did Segretti's conduct meet that standard?

2. Sexual Misconduct Outside of Law Practice

Should sexual misconduct between lawyers and people other than clients be grounds for discipline as a lawyer? If so, how severe should the penalties be?

We raise these questions because of the growing awareness of the effects of interpersonal conflicts, especially violence against women (wife battering, date rape, rape by strangers, etc.). Because, unfortunately, lawyers are not above committing acts of violence against their significant others — usually wives and girlfriends — male lawyers, in particular, are seen by some as in need of stern reminders that their law license may be at stake if they abuse women. The next two cases provide these warnings, and raise broader questions about the qualities that make a person fit or unfit to practice law.

THE PEOPLE OF THE STATE OF COLORADO v. WALLACE

837 P.2d 1223 (Colo. 1992)

PER CURIAM.

An inquiry panel of the Supreme Court Grievance Committee approved a *stipulation, agreement, and conditional admission of misconduct* [italics added] entered into between the respondent and the assistant disciplinary counsel, and recommended that the respondent be suspended from the practice of law for three months. . . .

I.

The respondent was admitted to the bar of this court on October 25, 1989, is registered as an attorney upon this court's official records, and is subject to the jurisdiction of this court. The respondent stipulated to the following facts:

a. On January 8, 1991, respondent assaulted his girlfriend, Beth Ann Fair, causing her severe bodily injury, including cartilage torn from her sternum.

b. As a result of the January 8, 1991 incident, respondent entered a plea of guilty to assault, in violation of Section 6-4-10 of the City Code of the City of Littleton.

c. Respondent was sentenced to 180 days in jail, 165 of which were suspended. Respondent served 10 days of the remaining 15 days; five days were suspended for good behavior.

d. In November, 1990, respondent struck Ms. Fair in the head, causing severe damage to her nose, eye socket, and sinuses, resulting in at least one surgical procedure. No criminal charges were brought against respondent as a result of that incident.

e. Respondent has assaulted Beth Ann Fair on more than one occasion, and both parties have caused or attempted to cause physical injury to each other.

f. The assaults perpetrated by respondent on Ms. Fair usually involved the use of alcohol by one or both persons.

g. Since his arrest in January, respondent has participated in AMEND (Abusive Men Exploring New Directions), a treatment program for batterers, and is successfully pursuing treatment with that organization.

h. Respondent is also actively participating in Alcoholics Anonymous, including starting a new AA Chapter in southwest Denver.

i. Respondent has paid and asserts that he will continue to pay any and all medical bills associated with injuries received by Ms. Fair.

j. There have been no further incidents between Ms. Fair and respondent since January 1991, and respondent has continued to maintain regular visitation with their two children, as well as to make regular child support payments.

k. Respondent self-reported the conviction through his counsel to the Office of Disciplinary Counsel on March 21, 1991. The respondent admitted that his conduct violated DR 1-102(A)(6) (a lawyer shall not engage in conduct that adversely reflects on the lawyer's fitness to practice law), and C.R.C.P. 241.6(5) (any act or omission violating the criminal laws of a state or of the United States constitutes grounds for lawyer discipline).

AUTHORS' COMMENT:

As you see, Mr. Wallace's violent episodes did not involve injury or threat to a client in any way. The entire story concerns his relationship with his girlfriend. Should Mr. Wallace's conduct disqualify him from practicing law? Why or why not?

II.

In the stipulation, the respondent agreed to the imposition of a sanction in the range from a private censure to a three-month suspension from the practice of law. The inquiry panel approved the stipulation and unanimously recommended that the respondent be suspended for three months. The respondent argued before the inquiry panel and before this court that a private censure was appropriate.

In support of a private sanction, the respondent points out that he has no prior disciplinary record, that he was not motivated by dishonesty or selfishness, and that his alcoholism led to the misconduct. In addition, the respondent contends that his payment of Fair's medical bills demonstrates a good faith effort to rectify the consequences of his misconduct; that he reported the assault conviction to the Office of Disciplinary Counsel and has cooperated with the disciplinary authorities; that he is inexperienced in the practice of law; and that he has demonstrated good character or reputation. Finally, the respondent asserts that his "effort and progress in rehabilitation since the time of the misconduct is particularly noteworthy;" and that he is sincerely remorseful.

We do not minimize the importance of the steps toward rehabilitation that the respondent has already taken, nor are we unmindful of the consequences flowing from a suspension as opposed to private discipline. Our primary duty in attorney discipline cases, however, is to protect the public from unfit practitioners, and the respondent's multiple acts of violence are indicative of a "dangerous volatility which might well prejudice his ability to effectively represent his clients' interests given the pressures associated with the practice of law."

A private censure, because it does not inform the public about a lawyer's misconduct, "should be used only when the lawyer is negligent, when the ethical violation results in little or no injury to a client, the public, the legal system, or the profession, and when there is little or no likelihood of repetition."

The respondent's rehabilitation may well reduce the chances that such an incident of violence will be repeated. However, as in *People v. Senn*, 824 P.2d 822 (Colo. 1992), the respondent's conduct went beyond mere negligence. The intoxicated attorney-respondent in Senn argued with his wife and discharged a pistol while aiming it at a point several feet above her head. We publicly censured the respondent in Senn.

Unlike the respondent in Senn, however, this respondent's conduct not only posed a significant danger of serious injury, but actually caused serious injury and caused it on more than one occasion. We conclude, as did the inquiry panel, that the seriousness of the respondent's misconduct warrants at least a short period of suspension. . . .

NOTES AND QUESTIONS

1. ***Does the Public Need to Know?*** The court says that, because a "private censure" — also known as an "admonition" or "private admonition" — does not inform the public about a lawyer's misconduct, it should only be used when the lawyer is negligent; when the ethical violation results in little or no injury to a client, the public, the legal system, or the profession; and when there is little or no likelihood of repetition. Putting aside, for the moment, the facts of *Colorado v. Wallace*, is it ever appropriate for a court to impose a private sanction after formal charges have been filed? Is it ever appropriate for a court to impose a private sanction in a matter involving serious misconduct? The ABA Model Rules for Lawyer Disciplinary Enforcement (2002), largely do away with private sanctions — see Rule 10, ("Sanctions").

2. ***Do Lawyers Live in Glass Houses?*** Still, the larger question remains: As a lawyer should you expect to live in a glass house, where your life is under constant scrutiny? Is it fair that with one false move you could lose your license, even for conduct outside your law practice? Should it be that way? Should violence in romantic relationships be a violation of the Rules of Professional Conduct? Why or why not?

3. ***Should Lawyers in Public Service be Held to Even Higher Standards?*** Prosecutors are public servants. Like police officers, prosecutors are responsible for enforcing the law. If they break the law, should they be held to even higher standards than other lawyers? Do you agree with the result in the next case?

IN THE MATTER OF MAX K. WALKER, JR.

597 N.E.2d 1271 (Ind. 1992)

PER CURIAM.

The Respondent, Max K. Walker Jr., was charged in a disciplinary complaint with violations of Rules 8.4(a), 8.4(b), 8.4(c), and 8.4(d) of the Rules of Professional Conduct for Attorneys at Law. . . .

The unchallenged findings establish that Respondent represented the grievant in her dissolution of marriage action which was concluded in December, 1982. Shortly thereafter, they developed a personal relationship which lasted until 1987 when it began to deteriorate.

On March 5, 1987, Respondent visited the grievant's home after having consumed several alcoholic beverages. They discussed their deteriorating relationship, which discussion evolved into an argument. The grievant asked Respondent to leave her house and walked into her bedroom, expecting him to leave. Instead, Respondent followed her into the bedroom. In the course of the ensuing argument, the grievant suggested that the Respondent should "go (and have sex)" with a woman with whom he had cocktails with earlier. Respondent then straddled the grievant, slapped her several times, and hit her in the face with a closed fist cutting her lip. As Respondent was leaving the residence, he forcibly took the telephone from and pushed the grievant's nine-year old daughter. The incident was reported to the police but the incident report was lost and was not introduced in evidence.

At the time of the incident, Respondent was Chief Deputy Prosecuting Attorney for Elkhart County. The prosecutor, who was also Respondent's law partner, advised the grievant that she had a right to a special prosecutor. She declined but requested that Respondent receive counseling, pay her medical bills, pay for her daughter's counseling and have no further contact with her. All of these requests were met. The incident was reported in the local press and Respondent received considerable publicity.

AUTHORS' COMMENT:

If this were a private lawsuit, it would apparently have been settled on the terms just described — the victim made several demands, and Mr. Walker met all of them. But this is not just a private case, because the respondent holds a public office. Should that make a difference? What is the public interest here?

Respondent urges this Court to conclude that no professional misconduct occurred. His argument is that the physical altercation was the culmination of a private, adult relationship, and that the battery "arose instantaneously" after provocation.

The circumstances presented by the findings reveal an act of domestic violence. This admittedly criminal conduct is not and did not remain a private matter. We are not persuaded by the claim of provocation, nor are we comforted by the fact that the grievant's daughter, also a victim of Respondent's conduct, recovered after some counseling sessions. Respondent's position as deputy prosecutor requires even stricter scrutiny of this conduct. Respondent's duty to conform his behavior to the law does not arise solely out of his status as an attorney. As an officer charged with the administration of the law, Respondent's behavior has the capacity to bolster or damage public esteem for the system. Were those whose job it is to enforce the law break it instead, the public rightfully questions whether the system itself is worthy of respect. The damage this incident has undoubtedly brought to the public's esteem will be addressed only if Respondent is held accountable. We conclude that, as a prosecuting attorney, Respondent engaged in conduct prejudicial to the administration of justice in violation of Rule 8.4(d).

Also, Respondent's conduct reflects upon his fitness as a lawyer and constitutes a violation of Rule 8.4(b). Not every violation of the penal code reflects upon an attorney's suitability as a practitioner. The issue is whether there exists a nexus between the misconduct and the Respondent's duties to his clients, the courts, or the legal system. Another important assessment is the impact of the conduct on the public's perception of Respondent's fitness as a lawyer. As a part-time prosecutor, Respondent inevitably encounters domestic assaults, and this incident calls into question his ability to zealously prosecute or to effectively work with the victims of such crimes. As a part-time practitioner, Respondent's effectiveness with his own clients or with adversaries in situations involving issues of domestic violence is compromised by his own contribution to this escalating societal problem. In both his capacities, we believe the perception of his fitness is tainted.

. . . .

In light of the foregoing, we find that the appropriate sanction is a suspension from the practice of law, and that Respondent's reinstatement should be automatic. It is, therefore, ordered that Max K. Walker, Jr. is suspended from the practice for a sixty-day period. . . .

NOTES AND QUESTIONS

1. ***Is the Sanction Harsh Enough?*** Walker was suspended for only sixty days. In the case before, Wallace was suspended for only three months. Is a suspension of two or three months enough? Too much? Just right? What factors are you considering? Should there be a minimum suspension for sexual violence? Why or why not? If so, what should the minimum suspension be? Should it matter whether the lawyer has already spent time in jail before the disciplinary hearing?

2. ***Money Crimes.*** Which should be sanctioned more heavily — crimes of violence against women, or crimes involving money, such as stealing, or tampering with a jury to win a civil case, or making up evidence to enhance damages? Does it matter whether the money crimes are committed in the practice of law rather than outside it? Does it matter whether the misconduct jeopardizes public confidence in the entire justice system or in the legal profession as a whole?

3. ***The Ultimate Question.*** The ultimate question is: What kinds of misconduct outside the practice of law should disciplinary counsel pursue and seek to sanction most severely? One response is to consider the theoretical framework that is generally applicable under the ABA Standards for Imposing Lawyer Sanctions (1986). *The Standards for Imposing Lawyer Sanctions* apply an approach developed by the Joint Committee on Professional Sanctions (which consisted of members of the ABA's: Standing Committee on Professional Discipline, Judicial Administration Division, and Joint Committee on Professional Discipline). In pertinent part, that framework requires a court to answer four questions:

1) What ethical duty did the lawyer violate? (A duty to a client, the public, the legal system, or the profession?)
2) What was the lawyer's mental state? (Did the lawyer act intentionally, knowingly, or negligently?)
3) What was the extent of the actual or potential injury caused by the lawyer's misconduct? (Was there a serious or potentially serious injury?) and
4) Are there any aggravating or mitigating circumstances?

Are these the right questions to ask? How do they apply to the various rules violations you have read about in this book?

Chapter 31
ARE YOU YOUR BROTHER'S KEEPER?

Are you your brother's (or sister's) keeper? When you hear about other lawyers doing something wrong, or other lawyers ask you or order you to do something that violates the rules, what are you supposed to do? Consider these examples:

- What if you hear that another lawyer is stealing money from the estate of an elderly widow?
- What if a partner in your firm asks you to alter accounting records to cover up a client's fraud, or asks you to introduce into evidence some records you know the client has altered?
- What if you have a clear conflict of interest in a case, but a partner orders you to work on the case and not to disclose the conflict to the client?
- What if you hear that another lawyer is neglecting cases because of an alcohol or drug problem?
- What if you are a partner and learn that one of your partners or associates is paying kickbacks to an insurance adjuster to get higher settlements?

These scenarios raise three questions that we address in this chapter:

- *Whistleblowing.* Are you allowed — or even required — to inform the disciplinary authorities about the unethical conduct?
- *Unethical orders.* May you follow orders that you know or believe to be unethical, even if you will be fired if you disobey?
- *Vicarious liability for violations.* Can you be held personally accountable for unethical conduct by your partners or associates even if you are not involved?

A. THE OBLIGATION TO REPORT ANOTHER LAWYER

In the examples we just gave, your obligation to report depends on how certain you are that what you heard is true. That is, Rule 8.3(a) imposes a duty to inform on other lawyers in some, but not all, circumstances. As South Carolina's Rule 8.3(a) says (with emphasis added):

> A lawyer who knows that another lawyer has committed a violation of the rules of professional conduct that raises a substantial question as to that lawyer's honesty, trustworthiness or fitness as a lawyer in other respects *shall inform* the appropriate professional authority.

The rule appears to say more than it does, because most such rules contain a broad exception. Rule 8.3(c) says that Rule 8.3(a) "does not require disclosure of information otherwise protected by Rule 1.6. . . . " When would information be protected by Rule 1.6? There are three situations.

First, Rule 1.6 would apply if a lawyer learns about another lawyer's misconduct in the course of representing that lawyer regarding alleged or possible misconduct. Thus, if a lawyer comes to you for legal advice about how to respond to charges that the lawyer used client trust funds for personal expenses, and the lawyer admits to you that he stole money from client accounts, you are not required to reveal the information. South Carolina's Comment 5 to Rule 8.3 reflects this exception: "The duty to report professional misconduct does not apply to a lawyer retained to represent a lawyer whose professional conduct is in question." This exception is not surprising. Lawyers who are accused of professional misconduct (or who want advice about whether they have violated the rules) have the right to counsel. As in any other attorney-client relationship, the right to counsel and the lawyer's duty of confidentiality would be undermined if the information communicated to counsel were not protected by Rule 1.6.

Second, Rule 1.6 applies if you learn about another lawyer's misconduct while representing the lawyer in a matter relating to the misconduct. For example, suppose you represent a lawyer who is selling some real estate. During the transaction, before it closes, you find out that the lawyer has forged the deed to the property. Because the misconduct relates to your representation of the lawyer, the information about the misconduct falls within the definition of "confidential information" in Rule 1.6. Whether you may disclose the information therefore depends on whether one of the exceptions in Rule 1.6 applies. If an exception applies, then you must disclose the lawyer's misconduct. If an exception does not apply, then you must not disclose the lawyer's misconduct because Rule 1.6 trumps Rule 8.3(a).

Third, Rule 1.6 applies if you learned of another lawyer's misconduct while representing a client other than that lawyer. For example, suppose you represent a bank in a loan default case. The bank claims that the borrower committed fraud on the application. At the borrower's deposition, the borrower claims that her former attorney advised her to lie about certain information on the loan application. Advising a client to lie on a loan application violates Rule 1.2(d), which prohibits a lawyer from counseling or assisting a client in committing fraud. Do you have to report the violation? No. The information relates to your representation of your client in the loan default case, so it is protected by Rule 1.6. Could you report the information if you want to? Only if you obtain consent from your client (in this case, the bank). This is the thrust of South Carolina's Comment 3 to Rule 8.3:

> A report about misconduct is not required where it would involve violation of Rule 1.6. However, a lawyer should encourage a client to consent to disclosure where prosecution would not substantially prejudice the client's interests.

Are you required to seek the client's consent to disclosure? No. You "should" — at least if consent won't "substantially prejudice" your client — but nothing in the rule says that you must seek consent. (You can't disclose without consent, but you don't have to seek consent if you don't want to disclose.) When would disclosure of another lawyer's misconduct "substantially prejudice the client's interests"? It's hard to generalize about that one, but let's think about some examples.

Suppose you represent a woman injured in an auto accident. She authorizes you to settle if the other side pays her $10,000. You communicate this demand to the lawyer for the insured (the defendant), and the defendant's lawyer surprises you by saying, "How about if we pay you $25,000 instead of $10,000?" That knocks your socks off — it's the first time a defendant has ever offered more than you have demanded. But there's a catch. Out of your fee, which will now be about $5,000, the defendant's lawyer says you'll have to "donate" a couple thousand dollars to the defense lawyer to make up for the hourly fees he will lose by settling so quickly. When you look shocked, the defense lawyer says, "C'mon, this is how it's done here. Everybody comes out ahead. Your client will get a lot more money, I'll get more fees than I would under my firm's partnership agreement, you'll more than double your own fee, and the insurance company will come out the same — they'll just pay more money to your client instead of paying us more legal fees for a long, drawn-out court battle. OK? Deal?"

You know that the kickback scheme is illegal — it's a fraud on both the insurance company and on the defense lawyer's firm. (If the case went on and the hourly rate legal fees went to his law firm, the fees would have to be divided among all the partners in the firm.) Do you have to report the scheme?

Let's see. The settlement negotiations are clearly "relating to the representation" of your client, and so they are protected by Rule 1.6. Should you seek your client's consent to disclose? The problem is, if you disclose the scheme to the disciplinary authorities, it may delay the suit for a long time — the insurance company may hire a different lawyer, who will need to spend time learning about the case, and will be super-stingy with the insurance company's settlement money just to prove how tough he is (and to prove he's not part of the same pay-off scheme). The delay would prejudice your client. On the other hand, you obviously cannot participate in the illegal scheme, so your client will probably never get $25,000. What should you do about reporting?

Let's look at a different angle. Suppose you are working in a law firm and one of the other lawyers in your firm is doing something seriously unethical. You talk to the partners at the firm and tell them what's going on. The partners agree that the other lawyer's conduct is a problem, but they won't do anything about it. What now? Have you done your job by reporting the other lawyer to your superiors, or do you have to go further? Do you have to report your fellow lawyer directly to the disciplinary authorities?

New York's highest court answered the second question in a context that may be very important to you. Wieder, an associate at a law firm, believed another associate at the firm was acting unethically while representing Wieder in a condominium purchase, and Wieder reported the situation to the partners. The partners refused to do anything about the situation, so Wieder did what he believed the rules required him to do and reported the situation to the disciplinary authorities. After awhile he withdrew his complaint out of fear his firm would fire him, but then the situation with the unethical associate got worse and he cajoled the law firm into reporting the misconduct. Soon afterwards, Wieder was fired. The law firm said it had the right to fire him, but Wieder said it was against public policy to fire him for complying with his obligation to report a violation of the disciplinary rules. Who was right? The New York Court of Appeals now tackles that question.

WIEDER v. SKALA

80 N.Y.2d 628, 609 N.E.2d 105, 1992 N.Y. LEXIS 4240 (1992)

HANCOCK, J.

Plaintiff, a member of the bar, has sued his former employer, a law firm. He claims he was wrongfully discharged as an associate because of his insistence that the firm comply with the governing disciplinary rules by reporting professional misconduct allegedly committed by another associate. The question presented is whether plaintiff has stated a claim for relief either for breach of contract or for the tort of wrongful discharge in violation of this State's public policy. The lower courts have dismissed both causes of action on motion as legally insufficient under CPLR 3211(a)(7) on the strength of New York's employment-at-will doctrine. For reasons which follow, we modify the order and reinstate plaintiff's cause of action for breach of contract.

I.

[P]laintiff alleges that he was a commercial litigation attorney associated with defendant law firm from June 16, 1986 until March 18, 1988. In early 1987, plaintiff requested that the law firm represent him in the purchase of a condominium apartment. The firm agreed and assigned a fellow associate (L.L.) "to do 'everything that needs to be done.' " For several months, L.L. neglected plaintiff's real estate transaction and, to conceal his neglect, made several "false and fraudulent material misrepresentations." In September 1987, when plaintiff learned of L.L.'s neglect and false statements, he advised two of the firm's senior partners. They conceded that the firm was aware "that [L.L.] was a pathological liar and that [L.L.] had previously lied to [members of the firm] regarding the status of other pending legal matters." When plaintiff confronted L.L., he acknowledged that he had lied about the real estate transaction and later admitted in writing that he had committed "several acts of legal malpractice and fraud and deceit upon plaintiff and several other clients of the firm."

The complaint further alleges that, after plaintiff asked the firm partners to report L.L.'s misconduct to the Appellate Division Disciplinary Committee as required under DR 1-103(A) of the Code of Professional Responsibility,[1] they declined to act. Later, in

[1] DR 1-103(A) provides:

an effort to dissuade plaintiff from making the report himself, the partners told him that they would reimburse his losses. Plaintiff nonetheless met with the Committee "to discuss the entire matter," but he withdrew his complaint "because the firm had indicated that it would fire plaintiff if he reported [L.L.'s] misconduct." Ultimately, as a result of plaintiff's insistence, in December 1987 the firm made a report concerning L.L.'s "numerous misrepresentations and [acts of] malpractice against clients of the firm and acts of forgery of checks drawn on the firm's account." Thereafter, two partners "continuously berated plaintiff for having caused them to report [the] misconduct." The firm nevertheless continued to employ plaintiff "because he was in charge of handling the most important litigation in the firm." Plaintiff was fired in March 1988, a few days after he filed motion papers in that important case.

Plaintiff claims in his lawsuit that defendants wrongfully discharged him as a result of his insistence that L.L.'s misconduct be reported as required by DR 1-103(A). In the fourth cause of action, he alleges that the firm's termination constituted a breach of the employment relationship. In the fifth cause of action, he claims that his discharge was in violation of public policy and constituted a tort for which he seeks compensatory and punitive damages. . . . .

II

We discuss first whether, notwithstanding our firmly established employment at will doctrine, plaintiff has stated a legal claim for breach of contract in the fourth cause of action. The answer requires a review of the three cases in which that doctrine is fully explained.

The employment at will doctrine is a judicially created common-law rule "that where an employment is for an indefinite term, it is presumed to be a hiring at will which may be freely terminated by either party at any time for any reason or even for no reason" (*Murphy v. American Home Prod.*, 58 NY2d 293, 300–301). In *Murphy*, this Court dismissed the claim of an employee who alleged he had been discharged in bad faith in retaliation for his disclosure of accounting improprieties. In so doing, we expressly declined to follow other jurisdictions in adopting the tort-based abusive discharge cause of action for imposing "liability on employers where employees have been discharged for disclosing illegal activities on the part of their employers," being of the view "that such a significant change in our law is best left to the Legislature."

AUTHORS' COMMENT:

The law in most states is similar to the law in New York as stated in the *Murphy* case. An employee who is hired without a promise that the employment will last for a certain length of time is an employee "at will," and can be fired at any time for any reason not against public policy. The main question in this case is whether it is against public policy for a law firm to fire a lawyer for reporting (or insisting that the firm report) a disciplinary violation by another lawyer.

With respect to the contract cause of action asserted in Murphy, the Court held that

A lawyer possessing knowledge, not protected as a confidence or secret, of a violation of DR 1-103 that raises a substantial question as to another lawyer's honesty, trustworthiness or fitness in other respects as a lawyer shall report such knowledge to a tribunal or other authority empowered to investigate or act upon such violation.

plaintiff had not shown evidence of any express agreement limiting the employer's unfettered right to fire the employee. . . .

In contrast, plaintiff's performance of professional services for the firm's clients as a duly admitted member of the bar was at the very core and, indeed, the only purpose of his association with defendants. Associates are, to be sure, employees of the firm, but they remain independent officers of the court responsible in a broader public sense for their professional obligations. Practically speaking, plaintiff's duties and responsibilities as a lawyer and as an associate of the firm were so closely linked as to be incapable of separation. It is in this distinctive relationship between a law firm and a lawyer hired as an associate that plaintiff finds the implied-in-law obligation on which he founds his claim.

We agree with plaintiff that in any hiring of an attorney as an associate to practice law with a firm there is implied an understanding so fundamental to the relationship and essential to its purpose as to require no expression: that both the associate and the firm in conducting the practice will do so in accordance with the ethical standards of the profession. Erecting or countenancing disincentives to compliance with the applicable rules of professional conduct, plaintiff contends, would subvert the central professional purpose of his relationship with the firm — the lawful and ethical practice of law.

The particular rule of professional conduct implicated here (DR 1-103[A]), it must be noted, is critical to the unique function of self-regulation belonging to the legal profession. Although the bar admission requirements provide some safeguards against the enrollment of unethical applicants, the Legislature has delegated the responsibility for maintaining the standards of ethics and competence to the Departments of the Appellate Division. . . . DR 1-103(A) places upon each lawyer and judge the duty to report to the Disciplinary Committee of the Appellate Division any potential violations of the Disciplinary Rules that raise a "substanstial question as to another lawyer's honesty, trustworthiness, or fitness in other respects." Indeed, one commentator has that noted, "the reporting requirement is nothing less than essential to the survival of the profession."

AUTHORS' COMMENT:

DR 1-103(A) as just quoted is virtually identical to Rule 8.3(a). Note that it does not require you to report every disciplinary violation you hear about, but only those violations of which you have "knowledge" and that raise a "substantial question as to another lawyer's honesty, trustworthiness, or fitness in other respects." You can assume that lying raises such a question.

Moreover, as plaintiff points out, failure to comply with the reporting requirement may result in suspension or disbarment. Thus, by insisting that plaintiff disregards DR 1-103(A), defendants were not only making it impossible for plaintiff to fulfill his professional obligations but placing him in the position of having to choose between continued employment and his own potential suspension and disbarment. We agree with plaintiff that these unique characteristics of the legal profession in respect to this core Disciplinary Rule make the relationship of an associate to a law firm employer intrinsically different from that of the financial managers to the corporate employers in *Murphy* and *Sabetay*. The critical question is whether this distinction calls for a different rule regarding the implied obligation of good faith and fair dealing from that applied in *Murphy* and *Sabetay*. We believe that it does in this case, but we, by no means, suggest that each provision of the Code of Professional Responsibility should be deemed incorporated as an implied in law term in every contractual relationship between or among lawyers.

It is the law that in "every contract there is an implied undertaking on the part of each party that he will not intentionally and purposely do anything to prevent the other party from carrying out the agreement on his part." The idea is simply that when A and B agree that B will do something, it is understood that A will not prevent B from doing it. The concept is rooted in notions of common sense and fairness. "What courts are doing [when an omitted term is implied]," Professor Corbin explains, " . . . is but a recognition that the parties occasionally have understandings or expectations that were so fundamental that they did not need to negotiate about those expectations."

Just such fundamental understanding, though unexpressed, was inherent in the relationship between plaintiff and defendant law firm. Defendants, a firm of lawyers, hired plaintiff to practice law and this objective was the only basis for the employment relationship. Intrinsic to this relationship, of course, was the unstated but essential compact that in conducting the firm's legal practice both plaintiff and the firm would do so in compliance with the prevailing rules of conduct and ethical standards of the profession. Insisting that as an associate in their employ plaintiff must act unethically and in violation of one of the primary professional rules amounted to nothing less than a frustration of the only legitimate purpose of the employment relationship. . . .

Accordingly, the judgment appealed from and the order of the Appellate Division brought up for review should be modified, with costs to plaintiff, by denying defendant's motion to dismiss the fourth cause of action and, as so modified, affirmed.

NOTES AND QUESTIONS

1. ***Does the Size of the Fraud Matter?*** Apparently the size of the transaction is not an important factor in deciding whether a lawyer has an obligation to report misconduct. The *Murphy* case, which figures so prominently in the *Wieder* decision, involved "at least $50 million in illegal account manipulations of secret pension reserves which improperly inflated the company's growth in income." Wieder's personal real estate transaction was much smaller.

2. ***Must You Report a Failure to Report?*** Suppose you and another associate at your firm learn that another lawyer at your firm, Terry Cornwall, is violating the disciplinary rules in a way that raises a substantial question as to Cornwall's honesty, trustworthiness, or fitness to practice law in other respects. Under Rule 8.3(a), both you and your friend are therefore obligated to report Cornwall's violation to the authorities. What if you report it but your friend doesn't? Does your friend's failure to report Cornwall's violation run afoul of Rule 8.3(a)? Yes, but is it an offense that must be reported? In other words, does your friend's failure to report a disciplinary offense raise a substantial question as to his honesty, trustworthiness, or fitness to practice law in other respects?

3. ***What Part of "Report" Don't You Understand?*** *Wieder* makes clear that substantial (although not absolute) protections exist for those who report. What is, perhaps, not so clear is whether the courts have left any room for lawyers *not* to report in extraordinary circumstances. The next case, an emotionally charged case from Louisiana, is one court's effort to provide some guidance.

IN RE RIEHLMANN

891 So. 2d 1239 (La. 2005)

Respondent Michael G. Riehlmann, an attorney licensed to practice law in Louisiana, is a criminal defense attorney . . . formerly employed as an Assistant District Attorney in the Orleans Parish District Attorney's Office. One evening in April 1994, respondent met his close friend and law school classmate, Gerry Deegan, at a bar near the Orleans Parish Criminal District Court. Like respondent, Mr. Deegan had been a prosecutor in the Orleans Parish District Attorney's Office before he "switched sides" in 1987. During their conversation in the bar, Mr. Deegan told respondent that he had that day learned he was dying of colon cancer. In the same conversation, Mr. Deegan confided to respondent that he had suppressed exculpatory blood evidence in a criminal case he prosecuted while at the District Attorney's Office. Respondent recalls that he was "surprised" and "shocked" by his friend's revelation, and that he urged Mr. Deegan to "remedy" the situation. It is undisputed that respondent did not report Mr. Deegan's disclosure to anyone at the time it was made. Mr. Deegan died in July 1994, having done nothing to "remedy" the situation. . . .

Nearly five years after Mr. Deegan's death, one of the defendants whom he had prosecuted in a 1985 armed robbery case was set to be executed by lethal injection on May 20, 1999. In April 1999, the lawyers for the defendant, John Thompson, discovered a crime lab report which contained the results of tests performed on a piece of pants leg and a tennis shoe that were stained with the perpetrator's blood during a scuffle with the victim of the robbery attempt. The crime lab report concluded that the robber had Type "B" blood. Because Mr. Thompson has Type "O" blood, the crime lab report proved he could not have committed the robbery; nevertheless, neither the crime lab report nor the blood-stained physical evidence had been disclosed to Mr. Thompson's defense counsel prior to or during trial. Respondent claims that when he heard about the inquiry of Mr. Thompson's lawyers, he immediately realized that this was the case to which Mr. Deegan had referred in their April 1994 conversation in the bar. On April 27, 1999, respondent executed an affidavit for Mr. Thompson in which he attested that during the 1994 conversation, "the late Gerry Deegan said to me that he had intentionally suppressed blood evidence in the armed robbery trial of John Thompson that in some way exculpated the defendant."

In May 1999, respondent reported Mr. Deegan's misconduct to the ODC. In June 1999, respondent testified in a hearing on a motion for new trial in Mr. Thompson's armed robbery case. During the hearing, respondent testified that Mr. Deegan had told him that he "suppressed exculpatory [blood] evidence that . . . that seemed to have excluded Mr. Thompson as the perpetrator of an armed robbery." Respondent also admitted that he "should have reported" Mr. Deegan's misconduct, and that while he ultimately did so, "I should have reported it sooner, I guess."

AUTHORS' COMMENT:

Mr. Deegan, the subject of Riehlmann's report, is dead, and Riehlmann guesses he "should have reported it sooner." Better late than never? Did Riehlmann have acceptable reasons for his delay in reporting Deegan's misconduct? The court now addresses these questions.

On September 30, 1999, respondent gave a sworn statement to the ODC in which he was asked why he did not report Mr. Deegan's disclosure to anyone at the time it was made. Respondent replied: I think that under ordinary circumstances, I would have. I really honestly think I'm a very good person. And I think I do the right thing whenever I'm given the opportunity to choose. This was unquestionably the most difficult time of my life. Gerry, who was like a brother to me, was dying. And that was, to say distracting would be quite an understatement. I'd also left my wife just a few months before, with three kids, and was under the care of a psychiatrist, taking antidepressants. My youngest son was then about two and had just recently undergone open-heart surgery. I had a lot on my plate at the time. A great deal of it of my own making; there's no question about it. But, nonetheless, I was very, very distracted, and I simply did not give it the important consideration that it deserved. But it was a very trying time for me. And that's the only explanation I have, because, otherwise, I would have reported it immediately had I been in a better frame of mind.

Disciplinary Proceedings

Formal Charges

On January 4, 2001, the ODC filed one count of formal charges against respondent alleging that his failure to report his unprivileged knowledge of Mr. Deegan's prosecutorial misconduct violated Rules 8.3(a) (reporting professional misconduct) . . . and 8.4(d) (engaging in conduct prejudicial to the administration of justice) of the Rules of Professional Conduct. . . . .

[R]espondent answered . . . that Rule 8.3(a) "merely requires that an attorney possessing unprivileged knowledge of a violation of this Code shall report such knowledge to the authority empowered to investigate such acts. It is undisputed that respondent did report his knowledge of Deegan's statements to Thompson's attorneys, with the clear understanding that this information would be reported to the District Attorney and the Court, undeniably authorities empowered to investigate Deegan's conduct."

Formal Hearing

When this matter proceeded to a formal hearing before the committee, respondent testified that his best recollection of his conversation with Mr. Deegan in 1994 "is that he told me that he did not turn over evidence to his opponents that might have exculpated the defendant." Nevertheless, when asked whether he recognized during the barroom conversation that Mr. Deegan had violated his ethical duties, respondent replied, "Well, certainly." Respondent admitted that he gave the conversation no further thought after he left the bar because he was "distracted" by his own personal problems.

Hearing Committee Recommendation

In its report filed with the disciplinary board, the hearing committee concluded that respondent did not violate Rule 8.3(a), but that he should be publicly reprimanded for his violation of Rule 8.4(d). Considering the evidence presented at the hearing, the committee made a factual finding that during the 1994 barroom conversation, Mr. Deegan explained to respondent that he did not turn over evidence in a case that might have exculpated a defendant, but "equivocated on whether the evidence proved the innocence of a defendant." Moreover, the committee found . . . no clear and convincing evidence that Mr. Deegan identified John Thompson by name in the disclosure to respondent in 1994. The committee believed respondent's testimony that he did not draw a connection between Mr. Deegan's 1994 statements and the Thompson case until 1999, when he heard about the inquiry of Mr. Thompson's lawyers.

Based on its factual findings, the committee found that respondent did not violate Rule 8.3(a) because he did not have "knowledge of a violation" that obligated him to report . . . Deegan to the ODC or to any other authority. The committee pointed out that it believed respondent's testimony that Mr. Deegan made equivocal statements in 1994 that did not rise to the level of a "confession" that Deegan had actually suppressed the crime lab report nine years earlier. The committee found Mr. Deegan qualified his statement that the evidence "might" have exculpated the defendant, and furthermore, agreed that if the evidence did not tend to negate the defendant's guilt, Mr. Deegan would have had no obligation to turn over that evidence under . . . *Brady v. Maryland*, 373 U.S. 83 (1963). . . . [C]onsequently, the committee determined that respondent would have had no violation to report. The committee found Mr. Deegan's statements at most suggested a potential violation of the ethical rules, but the committee declined to construe Rule 8.3(a) to require a lawyer to report a potential violation of an ethical rule by another lawyer.

Although the committee did not find that respondent violated Rule 8.3(a), the committee found he violated Rule 8.4(d), which imposes a "broader obligation to ensure that justice is fairly administered," by his "complete inaction after the barroom disclosure." The committee found respondent's conversation with Mr. Deegan "was of sufficient importance that not pursuing Deegan for a disclosure or to rectify the situation, failing to investigate further, and ultimately not taking any affirmative action for five years constituted conduct that hindered the administration of justice." . . .[1] In light of the mitigating factors present, and finding that a suspension would serve no useful purpose in this case, the committee recommended the imposition of a public reprimand. Both respondent and the ODC filed objections to the hearing committee's recommendation.

AUTHORS' COMMENT:

Disciplinary proceedings typically progress in stages. The Hearing Committee's finding that Riehlmann did not violate Rule 8.3(a) and its recommendation of a public reprimand (a very mild sanction, much less severe than suspension or disbarment) will now be reviewed by Louisiana's Disciplinary Board, an intermediate review body, before going up to the Louisiana Supreme Court. Do you think the Hearing Committee reached the right result? Make up your own mind before you read the Disciplinary Board's analysis.

The Disciplinary Board Recommendation

The disciplinary board adopted the hearing committee's factual findings but rejected its application of Rule 8.3(a) of the Rules of Professional Conduct. The board determined that a finding of a violation of Rule 8.3(a) requires clear and convincing evidence that an attorney (1) possessed unprivileged knowledge of an ethical violation and (2) failed to report such knowledge to a tribunal or other authority empowered to investigate or act upon such violation. Concerning the knowledge requirement, the board considered various legal authorities interpreting both Louisiana Rule 8.3(a) and Model Rule 8.3(a), and determined that a lawyer's duty to report professional misconduct is triggered when, under the circumstances, a reasonable lawyer would have "a firm opinion that the conduct in question more likely than not occurred." The board explained that the requisite knowledge under Rule 8.3(a) is "more than a mere suspicion, but less than absolute or moral certainty."

Employing this analysis, the board concluded the committee erred in its finding that respondent had no duty to report because Mr. Deegan's statements were equivocal. The board found respondent must have understood from his 1994 conversation with Mr. Deegan that Mr. Deegan had suppressed Brady evidence. . . .

The board then turned to a discussion of whether respondent's failure to report Mr. Deegan's misconduct for more than five years after learning of it constituted a failure to report under Rule 8.3(a). The board acknowledged that Rule 8.3(a) does not provide any specific time limit or period within which the misconduct must be reported.

[1] [Editor's Note: The committee weighed aggravating and mitigating factors relative to Deegan's conduct: The committee determined the baseline sanction for such conduct by respondent is a reprimand. As aggravating factors, the committee recognized respondent's experience in the practice of law (admitted 1983) and the vulnerability of the victim, Mr. Thompson. In mitigation, the committee acknowledged the absence of a prior disciplinary record, absence of a dishonest or selfish motive, personal or emotional problems (including the terminal colon cancer of his best friend, Mr. Deegan; marital problems; and the health problems both he and his son were experiencing), timely good faith effort to rectify the consequences of Mr. Deegan's misconduct, full and free disclosure to the disciplinary board and a cooperative attitude toward the proceeding, character and reputation, and remorse.]

Nevertheless, the board reasoned that Rule 8.3(a) serves no useful purpose unless it is read to require reporting to an appropriate authority within a reasonable time under the circumstances. Therefore, absent special circumstances, the board determined that a lawyer must report his knowledge of misconduct "promptly." Applying these principles to the instant case, the board determined respondent's disclosure in 1999 of misconduct he discovered in 1994 was not timely and did not satisfy the requirements of Rule 8.3(a). The board also found that respondent's conduct violated Rule 8.4(d) because his inactivity following Mr. Deegan's disclosure was prejudicial to the administration of justice.

The board found respondent knowingly violated a duty owed to the profession, and that his actions resulted in both actual and potential injury to Mr. Thompson. The board noted that if respondent had taken further action in 1994, when Mr. Deegan made his confession, Mr. Thompson's innocence in connection with the armed robbery charge may have been established sooner. The board also observed that negative publicity attached to respondent's actions, thereby causing harm to the legal profession. The board determined the baseline sanction for respondent's conduct is a suspension from the practice of law. . . .

In light of the significant mitigating factors in this matter, the board recommended that respondent be suspended from the practice of law for six months. One board member dissented and would recommend a suspension of at least one year and one day.

AUTHORS' COMMENT:

Has the Disciplinary Board analyzed Rule 8.3(a) correctly? In deciding whether you agree or disagree with the Disciplinary Board's analysis of Rule 8.3(a), which facts do you consider most important?

DISCUSSION

. . . The American legal profession has long recognized the necessity of reporting lawyers' ethical misconduct. When the American Bar Association adopted its first code of ethics in 1908, Canon 29 of the Canons of Professional Ethics, entitled "Upholding the Honor of the Profession," encouraged lawyers to "expose without fear or favor before the proper tribunals corrupt or dishonest conduct in the profession, . . . "Charles W. Wolfram, Modern Legal Ethics 683 n. 16 (1986). More than sixty years later, the ABA enacted Disciplinary Rule 1-103(A) of the Model Code of Professional Responsibility, the predecessor of the current Rule 8.3(a) of the Model Rules of Professional Conduct. [T]he duty to report is not merely an aspiration but is mandatory, the violation of which subjects the lawyer to discipline. . . .

[T]here are several differences between the Model Rule and the Louisiana Rule that was in effect in 2001, at the time the formal charges were filed in this case. Most significantly, Model Rule 8.3 requires a lawyer to report the misconduct of another lawyer only when the conduct in question "raises a substantial question" as to that lawyer's fitness to practice. Louisiana's version of Rule 8.3 imposed a substantially more expansive reporting requirement, in that our rule required a lawyer to report all unprivileged knowledge of any ethical violation by a lawyer, whether the violation was, in the reporting lawyer's view, flagrant and substantial or minor and technical. A task force of the Louisiana State Bar Association concluded that it was inappropriate to put a lawyer "in the position of making a subjective judgment" regarding the significance of a violation, and felt it was preferable instead "to put the burden on every lawyer to report all violations, regardless of their nature or kind, whether or not they raised a substantial question as to honesty, trustworthiness, or fitness." . . .

We now turn to a more in depth examination of the reporting requirement in Louisiana. At the time the formal charges were filed in this case, Louisiana Rule 8.3(a) provided:

> A lawyer possessing unprivileged knowledge of a violation of this code shall report such knowledge to a tribunal or other authority empowered to investigate or act upon such violation.

Thus, the rule has three distinct requirements: (1) the lawyer must possess unprivileged knowledge of a violation of the Rules of Professional Conduct; (2) the lawyer must report that knowledge; and (3) the report must be made to a tribunal or other authority empowered to investigate or act on the violation. We will discuss each requirement in turn.

Knowledge

[A]bsolute certainty of ethical misconduct is not required before the reporting requirement is triggered. The lawyer is not required to conduct an investigation and make a definitive decision that a violation has occurred before reporting; that responsibility belongs to the disciplinary system and this court. On the other hand, knowledge requires more than a mere suspicion of ethical misconduct. We hold that a lawyer will be found to have knowledge of reportable misconduct, and thus reporting is required, where the supporting evidence is such that a reasonable lawyer under the circumstances would form a firm belief that the conduct in question had more likely than not occurred. As such, knowledge is measured by an objective standard that is not tied to the subjective belief of the lawyer in question.

When to Report

Once the lawyer decides that a reportable offense has likely occurred, reporting should be made promptly. The need for prompt reporting flows from the need to safeguard the public and the profession against future wrongdoing by the offending lawyer. This purpose is not served unless Rule 8.3(a) is read to require timely reporting under the circumstances presented.

Appropriate Authority

Louisiana Rule 8.3(a) requires that the report be made to "a tribunal or other authority empowered to investigate or act upon such violation." . . . [A]s the comments to Model Rule 8.3(a) explain, the report generally should be made to the bar disciplinary authority. . . . .

DETERMINATION OF RESPONDENT'S MISCONDUCT AND APPROPRIATE DISCIPLINE

Applying the principles set forth above to the conduct of respondent in the instant case, we find the ODC proved by clear and convincing evidence that respondent violated Rule 8.3(a). First, we find that respondent should have known that a reportable event occurred at the time of his 1994 barroom conversation with Mr. Deegan. [R]espondent's conversation with Mr. Deegan at that time gave him sufficient information that a reasonable lawyer under the circumstances would have formed a firm opinion that the conduct in question more likely than not occurred. Regardless of the actual words Mr. Deegan said that night, and whether they were or were not "equivocal," respondent understood from the conversation that Mr. Deegan had done something wrong. . . . It simply defies logic that respondent would now argue that he could not be sure that Mr. Deegan actually withheld *Brady* evidence because his statements were vague and non-specific.

We also find that respondent failed to promptly report Mr. Deegan's misconduct to the disciplinary authorities. As respondent himself acknowledged, he should have reported Mr. Deegan's statements sooner than he did. There was no reason for respondent to have waited five years to tell the ODC about what his friend had done.

. . . In Louisiana, only this court possesses the authority to define and regulate the practice of law, including the discipline of attorneys. In turn, we have delegated to disciplinary counsel the authority to investigate and prosecute claims of attorney misconduct. Furthermore, while a trial court bears an independent responsibility to report attorney misconduct to the ODC, only this court may discipline an attorney found guilty of unethical behavior. Therefore, respondent is incorrect in arguing that he discharged his reporting duty under Rule 8.3(a) by reporting Mr. Deegan's misconduct to Mr. Thompson's attorneys, the District Attorney, and/or the Criminal District Court. It is undisputed that respondent did not repo[6]rt to the appropriate entity, the ODC, until 1999. That report came too late to be construed as "prompt."

Having found professional misconduct, we now turn to a discussion of an appropriate sanction. In considering that issue, we are mindful that the purpose of disciplinary proceedings is not primarily to punish the lawyer, but rather to maintain the appropriate standards of professional conduct, to preserve the integrity of the legal profession, and to deter other lawyers from engaging in violations of the standards of the profession. . . . Respondent's actions violated the general duty imposed upon attorneys to maintain and preserve the integrity of the bar. While . . . an attorney's failure to comply with the reporting requirement is a "serious offense," in the instant case, we find that respondent's conduct was merely negligent.

[R]espondent's failure to report Mr. Deegan's bad acts necessitates that some sanction be imposed. Respondent's knowledge of Mr. Deegan's conduct was sufficient to impose on him an obligation to promptly report Mr. Deegan to the ODC. Having failed in that obligation, respondent is himself subject to punishment. Under all of the circumstances presented, we conclude that a public reprimand is the appropriate sanction.

NOTES AND QUESTIONS

1. ***No Excuses?*** The *Riehlmann* court's analysis grapples with gut-wrenching circumstances. Riehlmann had to cope with his best friend's terminal cancer, his own marital separation, his two-year-old child's open-heart surgery, and his own depression and psychiatric care. The court, nevertheless, held that Riehlmann's failure to file a prompt report about Deegan with the bar disciplinary authorities violated Rule 8.3(a). After *Riehlmann*, will any circumstances excuse a lawyer from promptly reporting another lawyer's serious ethical misconduct?

2. ***What Raises a "Substantial Question"?*** In *Riehlmann*, Deegan's misconduct was pretty egregious — deliberately withholding powerful *Brady* material from the defense in a murder case. No doubt that raised a "substantial question" as to Deegan's "honesty" or "trustworthiness." Many times, however, the seriousness of the misconduct will not be so clear. Perhaps this Comment to Massachusetts Rule 8.3 will be helpful:

> [3] While a measure of judgment is required in complying with the provisions of the Rule, a lawyer must report misconduct that, if proven and without regard to mitigation, would likely result in an order of suspension or disbarment, including misconduct that would constitute a "serious crime." . . . [A] serious crime is "any felony, and . . . any lesser crime a necessary element of which . . . includes interference with the administration of justice, false swearing, misrepresentation, fraud, willful failure to file income tax returns, deceit, bribery, extortion, misappropriation, theft, or an attempt or a conspiracy, or solicitation of another, to commit [such a crime]." In addition to conviction of a felony, misappropriation of client funds or perjury before a tribunal are common examples of reportable conduct. . . .

---

[6] Although our primary focus is on Rule 8.3(a), we also note that respondent's conduct violated Rule 8.4(d).

3. ***How Prompt is "Promptly"?*** How soon do you have to report to meet the *Riehlmann* court's requirement that you report another lawyer's misconduct "promptly"? The Comment to Massachusetts Rule 8.3 is again helpful:

> [3A] In most situations, a lawyer may defer making a report under this Rule until the matter has been concluded, but the report should be made as soon as practicable thereafter. An immediate report is ethically compelled, however, when a client or third person will likely be injured by a delay in reporting, such as where the lawyer has knowledge that another lawyer has embezzled client or fiduciary funds and delay may impair the ability to recover the funds.

Do you think the jurisdiction in which you plan to practice should follow this comment?

B. DO YOU EVER HAVE TO REPORT YOUR BOSS?

Do you ever have to turn in your boss? Suppose a partner in your firm tells you to do something you believe or know violates the rules of professional conduct. What are your obligations? Are you excused if you are "just following orders" from a partner or other senior lawyer? Let's explore this question.

Suppose a partner asks you to draft and file a complaint against one of your firm's former clients, and you protest that you need client consent because the matter is substantially related (in fact, almost identical) to a matter you worked on for the former client. (You know it's substantially related, because you worked on the earlier matter.) The partner shrugs off your protest, saying, "Look, your job is to do the research and file the papers we tell you to file. I'll take care of the ethical aspects of the practice — and I'm telling you there's nothing unethical about filing this suit. So just do it!"

You dutifully draft and file the complaint, signing it as counsel of record. The next day, the former client's lawyer files a grievance with the disciplinary authorities — not against the partner, but against you! Have you done anything wrong? Can you say that you were just following orders?

No, you can't. If you know you are doing something wrong, you must not do it — and if you know your boss is ordering you to do something wrong, you probably have to report your boss unless the information is protected by Rule 1.6. The "just following orders" part of the question is controlled by Rule 5.2, "*Responsibilities of a Subordinate Lawyer,*" which says:

> (a) A lawyer is bound by the Rules of Professional Conduct notwithstanding that the lawyer acted at the direction of another person.
>
> (b) A subordinate lawyer does not violate the Rules of Professional Conduct if that lawyer acts in accordance with a supervisory lawyer's reasonable resolution of an arguable question of professional duty.

A paragraph of the Comment neatly explains the relationship between these two subdivisions:

> When lawyers in a supervisor-subordinate relationship encounter a matter involving professional judgment as to ethical duty, the supervisor may assume responsibility for making the judgment. Otherwise a consistent course of action or position could not be taken. If the question can reasonably be answered only one way, the duty of both lawyers is clear and they are equally responsible for fulfilling it. However, if the question is reasonably arguable, someone has to decide upon the course of action. That authority ordinarily reposes in the supervisor, and a subordinate may be guided accordingly. For example, if a question arises whether the interests of two clients conflict under Rule 1.7, the supervisor's reasonable resolution of the question should protect the subordinate professionally if the resolution is subsequently challenged.

Would you turn in your boss for violating the rule against suing former clients in substantially related matters without obtaining consent? (Do you have to report it? Does blatant disregard for Rule 1.9 raise a substantial question as to your boss's honesty, trustworthiness, or fitness to practice law in other respects?)

Let's put *Wieder* and Rule 5.2 together. Suppose a partner tells you to do something blatantly unethical — e.g., the partner tells you to sue a former client in a substantially related matter without first seeking consent (as above), or barks at you: "Sign this affidavit. It's false, but you have to sign it because otherwise the judge will dismiss our case!" You refuse, but the partner orders you to do it, and in a moment of fear and dread you sign the false affidavit. After a few sleepless nights, you realize that the partner's use of the false affidavit raises a substantial question as to his honesty and trustworthiness. You are, therefore, required to report the partner to the disciplinary authorities, and you do so. Can you be fired for making the report? *Wieder* says no.

This should give you some courage to report serious violations even by the people you work for. If the question is "reasonably arguable," you're protected because your superior's call — even if it turns out to be wrong — immunizes you. If it is not a reasonably arguable call, you are still protected if you refuse to engage in the unethical conduct and, if necessary, report your boss to the disciplinary authorities. By acting ethically it's heads you win; tails you win. So, there is no need to shirk your responsibility. If what the rule requires of you is clear, you cannot defend by saying, "I was only following orders," because (as *Wieder* shows) you cannot get fired for doing the right thing. Moreover, protecting the public, the courts, and the profession — not to mention your own interests and the firm's best interests — require you to follow the rules. Follow the rules and report serious violations. Reporting your boss is not exactly the yellow brick road to a successful career, but it beats getting suspended or disbarred for ignoring a superior's serious ethical violations or following orders to help commit them.

C. VICARIOUS LIABILITY: RESPONSIBILITY FOR YOUR PARTNERS AND ASSOCIATES

Are you your brother's keeper? The materials we just read — about Rule 8.3(a) — suggest that to some extent you are. You have to report another lawyer's serious violations of the rules of professional conduct not only because those rules ultimately protect that lawyer, but because they protect the interests of all other lawyers as well. Look at it this way: As lawyers, we are largely and uniquely self-governing. We are self-governing in the sense that the judges of the highest courts in each jurisdiction — nearly all lawyers — write and enforce the rules that regulate the legal profession as a whole and subject individual lawyers to professional discipline. The commentary to Rule 1 of the ABA Model Rules for Lawyer Disciplinary Enforcement makes clear that the right to exercise such discipline should be directly and exclusively controlled by the highest court in the jurisdiction. Furthermore, Rule 2's commentary places the model in context:

> With more than 700,000 lawyers licensed to practice in the United States, the highest courts of the states cannot handle discipline and disability matters directly by themselves. The [Lawyer Disciplinary] agency assists the court in the exercise of its inherent power to supervise the bar, inquiring into all matters assigned to its jurisdiction by the court's rules of disciplinary enforcement. The agency performs prosecutorial and adjudicative functions, and reports its findings and recommendations to the court."

If you are a partner, or if you supervise other lawyers in the firm, you also have additional obligations because Rule 5.1 makes you responsible for the conduct of other lawyers in your firm under certain circumstances. Here is what Missouri's Rule 5.1 says:

> *Rule 5.1. Responsibilities of a Partner or Supervisory Lawyer*
>
> (a) A partner in a law firm, and a lawyer who individually or together with other lawyers possesses comparable managerial authority in a law firm, shall

make reasonable efforts to ensure that the firm has in effect measures giving reasonable assurance that all lawyers in the firm conform to the Rules of Professional Conduct.

(b) A lawyer having direct supervisory authority over another lawyer shall make reasonable efforts to ensure that the other lawyer conforms to the rules of professional conduct.

(c) A lawyer shall be responsible for another lawyer's violation of the rules of professional conduct if:

(1) the lawyer orders or, with knowledge of the specific conduct, ratifies the conduct involved; or

(2) the lawyer is a partner or has comparable managerial authority in the law firm in which the other lawyer practices, or has direct supervisory authority over the other lawyer, and knows of the conduct at a time when its consequences can be avoided or mitigated but fails to take reasonable remedial action.

(Rule 5.3 imposes almost precisely parallel responsibilities regarding non-lawyers that work in your firm.) What does Rule 5.1 mean? How does it play out in practice? Let's look at a case about some lawyers who learned the meaning of Rule 5.1 the hard way — by getting in trouble.

WHELAN'S CASE

1992 N.H. LEXIS 196 (N.H. Dec. 31, 1992)

THAYER, J.

. . . Daniel G. Smith . . . handled all of Mrs. DesRosiers' financial affairs, including balancing her checkbook, and drafted her original will in 1984, a revision in 1986, and a codicil in 1987.

At the time of the events underlying this action, Mrs. DesRosiers was over ninety years old and in poor health. The respondent and his wife, Heide, had lived on Greensborough Road, next door to Mrs. DesRosiers, since 1974. Heide Whelan visited her almost daily and provided emotional support and physical care. When Mrs. Whelan was unable to visit Mrs. DesRosiers, the respondent would do so. In 1983, the respondent was admitted to the New Hampshire bar and became a partner with Smith and Clauson in 1985, practicing under the name of Clauson, Smith & Whelan.

In 1987, Mrs. DesRosiers asked the respondent to draft a codicil to her will because she wanted to leave her real estate to the respondent and his wife. The respondent informed Mrs. DesRosiers that it would be improper for him to draft such a codicil and that she should see her own attorney, Daniel Smith, the respondent's partner. Attorney Smith drafted the codicil in which Mrs. DesRosiers left her house and property on Greensborough Road to the respondent and his wife. The codicil provided that "Heide has done innumerable kindnesses for me and has cared for me when I have needed care." Mrs. DesRosiers died in 1989.

This court has held that by drafting the 1987 codicil benefiting his partner, Attorney Smith violated Rule 1.8(c), prohibiting a lawyer from preparing an instrument giving the lawyer or the lawyer's spouse any substantial gift from a client, and Rule 1.10(a), providing that while lawyers are associated in a firm, none of them shall knowingly represent a client when any one of them practicing alone would be prohibited from doing so. In *the Matter of Daniel G. Smith, Esq.*, (1991).

The committee requested that the respondent be suspended from the practice of law for violating the Rules cited above, and Rules 5.1(c)(2) and 8.4(a), which provide, respectively, that a lawyer shall be responsible for another lawyer's violation if the lawyer is a partner in the law firm in which the other practices, and that it is professional misconduct for a lawyer to knowingly assist or induce another to violate or attempt to violate the Rules of Professional Conduct, or to do so through the acts of another. . . .

The respondent contends that he did not violate any Rule and has maintained the position that mere knowledge that a course of conduct has taken place is not enough to support a finding that an attorney violated the Rules; rather, the attorney must know that the course of conduct is prohibited by the Rules.

AUTHORS' COMMENT:

Would you accept the respondent's defense? He knew what his partner was doing, but didn't know it was against a rule of professional conduct. Does he have to know all of the rules to comply with his obligations under Rule 5.1? Read on.

The respondent's defense is basically one of ignorance of the Rules of Professional Conduct, which is no defense. We hold that lawyers, upon admission to the bar, are deemed to know the Rules of Professional Conduct. "Attorneys in this State have the obligation to act at all times in conformity with the standards imposed upon members of the bar as conditions for the right to practice law."

We conclude that as a member of the New Hampshire bar, the respondent is charged with knowledge of the Rules of Professional Conduct; therefore, he violated Rules 5.1(c)(2) and 8.4(a). It was incumbent upon the respondent and Attorney Smith to obtain an informed waiver of the conflict of interest from Mrs. DesRosiers in order to have one partner draft a codicil benefiting another partner. In the alternative, the attorneys should have declined to prepare the codicil and suggested to Mrs. DesRosiers that she engage other counsel. . . .

NOTES AND QUESTIONS

1. ***What Is the Right Penalty?*** What penalty should attorney Whelan get for failing to supervise his partner properly? Attorney Smith (Whelan's partner) was publicly censured (a minor sanction) for engaging in the underlying misconduct, but New Hampshire's disciplinary authorities sought to suspend Whelan from the practice of law (a much stiffer sanction) for his supervisory failure. Why should the person who merely suggested the wrongful conduct get a stiffer sanction than the person who actually committed the misconduct? The answer is that Whelan personally received a monetary benefit by letting Smith draft the improper codicil, whereas Smith himself did not. The New Hampshire Supreme Court didn't agree with the committee, and imposed the sanction of public censure — meaning it published this case, so that you and other members of the public could read it.

2. ***What Should Whelan and Smith Have Done?*** If the rules in 1991 had been identical to today's rules (and they were in fact almost identical), what could Whelan and Smith have done to avoid getting into trouble here? First of all, as soon as a law firm client suggested making a gift to a lawyer in the firm, Whelan should have consulted the rules — including Rule 1.8(c), which prohibits a lawyer from preparing on behalf of a client (other than a relative) any instrument (such as a will or codicil) leaving a "substantial gift" (such as cash or real estate) to the lawyer, and Rule 1.8(k), which imputes that conflict (and most other Rule 1.8 conflicts) to every other lawyer associated with the firm. (Note that neither subparagraph permits a lawyer to escape by obtaining client consent.) Based on those two rules, Whelan should have referred Mrs. DesRosiers to a lawyer in a different law firm so that she could get independent

advice on her plan to leave her real estate to Whelan. And if Whelan somehow didn't come across Rules 1.8(c) and 1.8(k), then Smith should have declined the representation and referred Mrs. DesRosiers to a lawyer in another firm. Those simple steps would have saved both lawyers a lot of embarrassment, anxiety, and loss of reputation.

3. ***What Must Partners Do?*** Rule 5.1(a) requires partners in a firm "make reasonable efforts to ensure that the firm has in effect measures giving reasonable assurance that all lawyers in the firm conform to the Rules of Professional Conduct." What efforts would be "reasonable"? Should a firm have to hold training programs on legal ethics? Give everyone in the firm a copy of the Rules of Professional Conduct? Make sure everyone reads the rules? Give a test on the rules? Pay for lawyers to attend CLE programs on legal ethics? The courts and disciplinary authorities have not given definitive answers to any of these questions yet, and the Comment to Rule 5.1 doesn't help much. What do you think?

4. ***Is Rule 5.1 Tough Enough — or Too Tough?*** Does Rule 5.1 go far enough in requiring law firms to ensure that all lawyers in the firm follow the Rules? The rule could be a lot tougher. For example, shouldn't Rule 5.1(b) require a supervisory lawyer to *search out* ethical problems likely to arise in a particular case and to ensure that the subordinate lawyer knows how to handle these problems? Shouldn't Rule 5.1(c) make supervisory lawyers responsible for a subordinate lawyer's misconduct if the supervisor "should have known" of the subordinate's violation, even if the supervisory lawyer did not actually know? On the other hand, maybe Rule 5.1 is too tough. Since all lawyers are members of the bar and are personally responsible to abide by the Rules of Professional Conduct, why should a supervisory lawyer be responsible for another lawyer's violations of the Rules unless, as envisioned by Rule 5.1(c)(1), the supervisory lawyer ordered or knowingly ratified the specific conduct in question? Isn't that rule alone enough?

Chapter 32

LEGAL MALPRACTICE AND OTHER SUITS AGAINST LAWYERS

A. INTRODUCTION

In 1960, lawyers in America could not buy malpractice insurance. Why? Because no one sold it. No one sold it because no one needed it. Suits for legal malpractice were extremely rare. No doubt lawyers committed malpractice then, just as they do now, but remember, the transition-decade of the 1950s, which gave birth to the 1960s, was much different than today. It was a world marked by an optimistic sense of upward mobility and an almost universally shared sense of — and ambition towards becoming — what it meant to be a "normal" American. The Greatest Generation had won the war, American cultural and economic values were dominant at home and abroad, and any threat to the country's continued stability and prosperity could easily be attributed to our Cold War enemies.

Characterizing that different era, David Brooks, the much lauded in-house conservative columnist for the *New York Times*, observed in a June 16, 2005 column that the essence of the 1950s was that it was middlebrow — blessed with an earnestness of purpose that saw identification with cultural and intellectual elites as the means to elevate even those who could not envision that they would actually ever attend an opera or sit down in their living rooms to discuss the Enlightenment with Will and Catherine Durant. The passing of the '50s, then, was not simply a giving way to technological, scientific, social change; it was, as Brooks describes it, equally due to an intellectual assault against "the earnest and optimistic middle-class arrivistes who were tromping over everything and dumbing down their [the intellectual's] turf." It was a time of social forces whose time had come and would not be denied: new household appliances, pent-up economic demand, and an increased sense of egalitarianism — indeed, entitlement — brought on in no small part by the expanded roles and experience of sacrifice of a post-war generation that was experiencing disillusionment about the Korean War and which, not so insignificantly, included significant numbers of women, blacks, and other minorities.

Is there any wonder (or the least bit of surprise or regret) that the nation's growing disinclination to defer to the infallibility of authority figures — to reject the '50s reluctance to attack society's leaders "because it's just not done. . . . " or "It would be so . . . *impolite*!" — were part of what was swept away in the social revolution of the '60s? Without middlebrow pretenses as a prop, though, popular culture (including the ways in which individuals saw themselves in relation to such centers of authority as universities, religious hierarchies, and the legal system) also had to change. Says Brooks, "It was no longer character-oriented" it became "personality-oriented." But that was not the worst of it. If the elites had no greater claim to standing than any other loyal, hardworking American, there was nothing to be lost by challenging them.

And challenge them they did. In the late 1960s, society began challenging authority in new ways. The Vietnam protests; the riots in Detroit, Watts, Newark, and other cities; Eugene McCarthy's and Robert Kennedy's challenge to Lyndon Johnson for the White House; and the whole hippie culture (summarized by Dr. Timothy Leary as "Turn on, tune in, drop out") permanently transformed American society. For the professions, too, the era of deference ended. No longer did the public — the clients and patients, for example — assume that their doctor or lawyer was right about everything . . . or anything.

In the 1970s, many of the men and women who marched to protest against the Vietnam War began to march off to law school. When these rebels got out of law school, the old country club era of the legal profession was gone. No longer was the law a homogenous all-male, all-white profession. No longer did lawyers constantly defer to each other out of courtesy.

All of this new boldness was fueled, of course, by the leading lawyer TV show of the 1970s, the Watergate hearings. These hearings featured attorney-President Richard Nixon as the accused, and many of his lawyer-henchmen (including Donald Segretti) as accusers or co-conspirators. Some lawyers were heroes — Harvard-educated Sam Ervin, with his folksy drawl, and his fellow southerner Howard Baker were two of the good guys — but in the end lawyers got a serious black eye. After Watergate, the public's image of lawyers took a nosedive. Maybe that's why the nation did not elect another lawyer as President from 1972 (Nixon's second election) to 1992, when the election of Bill Clinton ushered in a new saga.

The point is that along with the lack of public trust that the post-war decades brought us came a new willingness to challenge lawyers. There was also a general breakdown in civility throughout society, including the legal profession. Not only were clients willing to stand up and accuse their lawyers of malpractice, but other lawyers were willing to represent these clients against their colleagues at the bar.

The shared legacy of the '60s is, thus, our recognized loss of what up to that time was assumed to be a common reference and shared sense of social standards, predicated upon an unquestioned deference to authority. Whether that break with the past has been worth it remains, and is likely to remain for some time, a topic of social-political debate. But it might be said, as did the noted Judge Richard Posner in weighing the pluses and minuses in a related context: "Popular culture has always offended the fastidious. That of the 1950s was not as raunchy as today's, but today's popular culture does not ridicule obese people, ethnic minorities, stammerers and effeminate men, as the popular culture of the 1950s did, so it may be doubted whether there has actually been a net decline in the moral tone of popular culture."

What we can share now, as an historical legacy, is that by the 1970s, suits for legal malpractice began to proliferate. In the 1980s, they exploded. In the 1990s, they leveled off somewhat but continued at a high rate. Lawyers, like doctors, architects, truck drivers, and a long list of other malfeasors are no longer safe from charges of malpractice; the duty to take care is a duty imposed on all of us. As important, though, is that we understand and appreciate that, as a society, the individuals we charge with assuring that the duties that private citizens (including lawyers) owe to each other, are carried out are *the lawyers*.

It is also worth keeping in perspective that not everyone won their legal malpractice lawsuit. Legal malpractice cases are often hard to prove. Not only must the plaintiff prove that the lawyer mishandled the underlying case — no easy task in itself — but the plaintiff must also prove that if the defendant lawyer had not breached a duty in handling the case, then the plaintiff would have won the underlying cause of action. This is what is called a "trial-within-a-trial." It means that the plaintiff in a legal malpractice action has to put on the case he would originally have put on if his lawyer had handled the case correctly in the first place, and convince the jury, both, (1) that the case that should have been presented was a winner, and (2) that the reason the case wasn't a winner is that the lawyer fell below the community standard of care (i.e., the degree of skill used by most lawyers in the community) in handling the case. In addition, though, as with every suit for negligence or breach of contract, the plaintiff has to prove damages — and in some jurisdictions that means proving that the judgment that the plaintiff should have obtained would have been collectible (i.e., the defendant had money or insurance to pay the judgment).

B. THE ELEMENTS OF A LEGAL MALPRACTICE CLAIM

Legal malpractice claims are by far the most common claims against lawyers, so we'll now look at the elements of legal malpractice in more detail. Legal malpractice standards have developed under the common law rather than by statute, so you can't just look up the elements in a statute book. Moreover, as with most torts and breach of contract claims, legal malpractice is a matter of state rather than federal law. Consequently, the law is a product of the fifty states and the District of Columbia. Many common threads run through this jurisprdence, but there are also many quirks and idiosyncracies. (By the way, it's not entirely clear whether a legal malpractice suit is a tort or a breach of contract — most courts characterize it as a tort, but some still characterize it as a breach of contract. As a practical matter, it doesn't usually make much difference. In this book, though, we refer to legal malpractice as a tort, which is the prevailing view.)

The ABA Model Rules of Professional Conduct make no effort to define legal malpractice. On the contrary, paragraph 20 of the Scope section of the ABA Model Rules says: "Violation of a rule should not itself give rise to a cause of action against a lawyer nor should it create any presumption in such a case that a legal duty has been breached. . . . The Rules are designed to provide guidance to lawyers and to provide a structure for regulating conduct through disciplinary agencies. They are not designed to be a basis for civil liability." Nevertheless, paragraph 20 continues, "since the Rules do establish standards of conduct by lawyers, a lawyer's violation of a Rule may be evidence of breach of the applicable standard of conduct."

Fortunately, the *Restatement of the Law Governing Lawyers*, published in 2000 by the American Law Institute, contains an entire chapter entitled "Lawyer Civil Liability." Other chapters define the attorney-client relationship. We introduce the subject of legal malpractice (and other suits against lawyers) by looking at the sections of the *Restatement* that deal with the attorney-client relationship and lawyer liability. Keep in mind, of course, that the Restatement is just that — a restatement. Like all Restatements, it has persuasive force but not the force of law.

A lawyer's general duties to clients are set forth in § 16 of the Restatement. Section 16 provides:

§ 16. Lawyer's Duties to Client in General

> To the extent consistent with the lawyer's other legal duties and subject to the other provisions of this Restatement, a lawyer must, in matters within the scope of the representation:
>
> (1) proceed in a manner reasonably calculated to advance a client's lawful objectives, as defined by the client after consultation;
>
> (2) act with reasonable competence and diligence;
>
> (3) comply with obligations concerning the client's confidences and property, avoid impermissible conflicting interests, deal honestly with the client, and not employ advantages arising from the client-lawyer relationship in a manner adverse to the client; and
>
> (4) Fulfill any valid contractual obligations to the client.

Thus, the Restatement places special emphasis on confidentiality, conflicts of interest, honesty, and loyalty — the same things we have emphasized in this book.

The basic elements of legal malpractice are set out as follows:

§ 48. Professional Negligence — Elements and Defenses Generally

> [A] lawyer is civilly liable for professional negligence to a person to whom the lawyer *owes a duty of care* . . . if the lawyer *fails to exercise care* . . . and if

> *that failure is a legal cause of injury* . . . unless the lawyer has a defense. . . .

(We've deleted the cross-references to other Restatement sections, which make the language confusing and hard to read.) Thus, the elements of legal malpractice are familiar to you from your first year Torts course:

- a duty of care
- a failure to exercise care
- an injury caused by the failure to exercise care

Of course, the highest duty of care is to a client (as opposed to a non-client). The Restatement phrases the duty to a client as follows:

> *§ 50. Duty of Care to Client*
>
> [A] lawyer owes a client the duty to exercise care . . . in pursuing the client's lawful objectives in matters covered by the representation.

Simple. A lawyer owes a client a duty of care.

Next, the Restatement addresses the element that is common (and crucial) to every tort you have studied: the standard of care. What is the standard of care for lawyers? Here's how the Restatement phrases it:

> *§ 52. The Standard of Care*
>
> (1) [A] lawyer who owes a duty of care must exercise the competence and diligence normally exercised by lawyers in similar circumstances.
>
> (2) Proof of a violation of a rule or statute regulating the conduct of lawyers:
>
> (a) does not give rise to an implied cause of action for professional negligence or breach of fiduciary duty;
>
> (b) does not preclude other proof concerning the duty of care in Subsection (1) or the fiduciary duty; and
>
> (c) may be considered by a trier of fact as an aid in understanding and applying the standard of Subsection (1) . . . to the extent that (i) the rule or statute was designed for the protection of persons in the position of the claimant and (ii) proof of the content and construction of such a rule or statute is relevant to the claimant's claim.

Abstractly stated, then, the standard of care for lawyers is ten words: "competence and diligence normally exercised by lawyers in similar circumstances." How does a dissatisfied client prove that the lawyer failed to exercise the competence and diligence normally exercised by lawyers in similar circumstances?

One way to show a breach of the standard of care is to present expert testimony explaining what competent and diligent lawyers normally do in similar situations. In some jurisdictions, presenting expert testimony about the standard of care is required unless the alleged error is so obvious (like missing a statute of limitations or failing to file an answer to a complaint) that even a lay jury can see the problem. For example, in *Hatfeld v. Herz*, 109 F. Supp. 2d 174 (S.D.N.Y. 2000), the court said (quoting a series of New York cases):

> The courts generally require malpractice plaintiffs to "proffer expert opinion evidence on the duty of care to meet their burden of proof in opposition to a properly supported summary judgment motion." "However, the requirement that plaintiff come forward with expert evidence on the professional's duty of care may be dispensed with where 'ordinary experience of the fact finder provides sufficient basis for judging the adequacy of the professional service.' " ("Unless a juror's ordinary experience provides sufficient basis to assess the adequacy of the professional service, or the attorney's conduct falls below any standard of due care, expert testimony is necessary to establish that the attorney acted negligently.")

Another way to show a breach of the standard of care is to demonstrate that the lawyer violated a relevant legal ethics rule that was "intended for the protection of persons in the position of the claimant." Often, this proof is made by calling an expert witness on legal ethics, who will talk about the rules and how the defendant lawyer violated them. (We will see more about the importance of the ethics rules in the *Mirabito* case below.)

The next element of legal malpractice is the old *Palsgraf* element: proximate cause. Restatement § 53 says:

§ 53. Causation and Damages

> A lawyer is liable . . . only if the lawyer's breach of a duty of care or breach of fiduciary duty was a legal cause of injury, as determined under the generally applicable principles of causation and damages.

Thus, there are no special rules for determining causation in legal malpractice cases. The inquiry will follow "generally applicable principles of causation and damages," as in any other kind of tort case. (So, be glad you remember *Palsgraf*!)

When we come to the matter of affirmative defenses, however, consider the following special principles, which do apply:

§ 54. Defenses; Prospective Liability Waiver; Settlement with a Client

> (1) Except as otherwise provided in this Section, liability . . . is subject to the defenses available under generally applicable principles of law governing respectively actions for professional negligence and breach of fiduciary duty. A lawyer is not liable . . . for any action or inaction the lawyer reasonably believed to be required by law, including a professional rule.
>
> (2) An agreement prospectively limiting a lawyer's liability to a client for malpractice is unenforceable.
>
> (3) The client or former client may rescind an agreement settling a claim by the client or former client against the person's lawyer if:
>
> > (a) the client or former client was subjected to improper pressure by the lawyer in reaching the settlement; or
> >
> > (b) (i) the client or former client was not independently represented in negotiating the settlement, and (ii) the settlement was not fair and reasonable to the client or former client.
>
> (4) . . . .

Thus, § 54 starts by explaining that a lawyer's liability for malpractice or breach of fiduciary duties is ordinarily governed by the same "generally applicable principles" that apply to nonlawyers, but a lawyer is not liable if the lawyer "reasonably believed" he or she was following a "professional rule" (*e.g.*, an ethics rule) or other law. In other words, a lawyer may defend against a suit for malpractice or breach of a fiduciary duty by saying, "I had to handle the matter that way because the rules required me to do it." But § 54(2) and (3) also explains that lawyers — unlike nonlawyers — may *not* escape liability either through (a) an *advance* agreement limiting the lawyer's liability for malpractice or breach of fiduciary duty, under any circumstances, or (b) a settlement of the claims *unless* (i) the lawyer didn't exert improper pressure, *and* (ii) the client had a separate lawyer regarding the settlement, *and* (iii) the settlement was "fair and reasonable."

For good measure, subparagraph (4) adds that a lawyer is subject to discipline for making an advance agreement limiting malpractice liability unless the client has a lawyer, and is subject to discipline for settling an existing legal malpractice claim unless the lawyer told the client in writing that the client ought to have an independent lawyer regarding the settlement. Thus, § 54(4) almost exactly tracks ABA Rule 1.8(h), which states:

> A lawyer shall not make an agreement prospectively limiting the lawyer's liability to a client for malpractice unless permitted by law and the client is independently represented in making the agreement, or settle a claim for such liability with an unrepresented client or former client without first advising that person in writing that independent representation is appropriate in connection therewith.

Under ABA Model Code DR 6-102(A), agreements seeking to prohibit a client from taking action to sue for future malpractice claims were covered, but nothing in the Code precluded settlements with a client who had already sued or otherwise asserted a claim against you for malpractice. New York and other Code-based states filled this void by adding language similar to the second half of Rule 1.8(h), starting with "or settle a claim for such liability. . . . "

In a nutshell, lawyers have the same defenses as other professionals, *plus* the defense that the lawyer reasonably believed that the rules of legal ethics compelled the lawyer's behavior, but *minus* two defenses: 1) that the client agreed not to sue the lawyer for malpractice, and 2) that the client settled a claim that had already accrued. But the absence of that second defense can be overcome by three showings: (a) that the client had a separate lawyer, (b) that the settlement was fair and reasonable, and (c) that the lawyer didn't exert improper pressure on the client to settle.

With defenses out of the way, let's return to the subject of liability.

C. OTHER COMMON CLAIMS AGAINST LAWYERS

Legal malpractice is the most common, and thus the most familiar source of lawyer liability, but it's far from the only one. Now we'll look at some others.

The other main bases for liability are: (1) breach of fiduciary duty, (2) breach of contract, (3) liability to third parties (i.e., someone other than the client), and (4) vicarious liability. Here is how the Restatement deals with each of these.

1. Breach of Fiduciary Duty

Nearly every legal malpractice suit brought today is paired with a claim for breach of fiduciary duty. The elements of that duty as stated in § 16(3) of the Restatement (reprinted earlier in this chapter), require a lawyer to:

- comply with obligations concerning the client's confidences;
- comply with obligations concerning the client's property;
- avoid impermissible conflicting interests;
- deal honestly with the client; and
- not employ advantages arising from the client-lawyer relationship in a manner adverse to the client.

Restatement § 49 sets forth the elements of a breach of fiduciary duty in terms that basically parallel the requirements of § 48 for legal malpractice:

§ 49 Breach of Fiduciary Duty — Generally

> In addition to other possible bases of civil liability . . . a lawyer is civilly liable to a client if the lawyer breaches a fiduciary duty to the client set forth in § 16(3) and if that failure is a legal cause of injury . . . unless the lawyer has a defense. . . .

Putting §§ 16(3) and 49 together, a lawyer breaches a fiduciary duty if the lawyer fails to safeguard a client's confidences, mishandles the client's property, engages in impermissible conflicts, is dishonest with the client, or uses the attorney-client relationship to take advantage of the client. The lawyer is liable for the breach of fiduciary duty if it injures the client, unless the lawyer successfully invokes one of the defenses that would defeat a legal malpractice claim.

2. Breach of Contract

The Restatement has very little new to say about breach of contract. Section 55 says:

§ 55 Civil Remedies of a Client Other Than for Malpractice

> (1) A lawyer is subject to liability to a client for injury caused by breach of contract in the circumstances and to the extent provided by contract law.
>
> (2) A client is entitled to restitutionary, injunctive, or declaratory remedies against a lawyer in the circumstances and to the extent provided by generally applicable law governing such remedies.

Thus, when a client sues a lawyer for breach of contract, the lawyer faces the same liability and the same remedies as would anybody else in the same situation — damages, restitution, specific performance, etc.

3. Liability to Third Parties

Clients aren't the only ones who sue lawyers. Third parties (i.e., nonclients) can also sue lawyers for alleged wrongs arising out of the lawyer's representation of a client. (Obviously lawyers can be sued for things not related to representing clients, just like all other citizens can be sued, but that's a separate issue. We're talking now about suits by nonclients related to the representation of clients.)

Lawyer liability to nonclients presents a dilemma for the adversary system. The problem is closely related to the concept of conflicts of interest. In theory, a lawyer is supposed to serve each client with 100% devotion. Concerns about others — i.e., concerns about third parties — are not supposed to play any role in the lawyer's duties to clients. A lawyer obviously cannot ethically commit *fraud* against adversaries or other third parties, but fraud is the water's edge — a lawyer may ethically go right up to the edge of the water in the service of a client. Likewise, a lawyer may *advise* a client to take into account the welfare of third parties, and, if necessary, seek to withdraw from representing a client who refuses to take into account such advice. But as long as a lawyer continues to represent a client, the lawyer must use all legitimate means to advance the client's objectives.

But what if the client's objectives are bound up with the fortunes of third parties? What if the client wants to sell a stock, or acquire a company, and the third party is willing to do the deal only if the lawyer gives an opinion that the deal is legal and valid? If the lawyer gives such an opinion negligently (e.g., without doing enough legal research, or without asking the client any questions), can the third party sue the lawyer? If so, then the lawyer has to worry not only about the interests of her client but also the interests of the third party, which may lead to divided loyalty. But if not, then lawyers have enormous leeway to allow third parties to be disadvantaged.

Or what if a wealthy client wants to create a trust for her youngest child so that the child can afford college even if the client dies while the child is young? If the lawyer creates the trust in a way that doesn't work (e.g., a way that violates the state's trust law, or that violates the famous Rule Against Perpetuities), may the child later sue the lawyer? We face the same dilemma. If the lawyer has to worry about the child's interests in addition to the client's interests, will the divided loyalty impair the lawyer's ability to serve the client?

Or what if the client is the guardian for a minor child, and the client's obligation is to look out for the best interests of the child? Does that mean that the lawyer also has to look out for the best interests of the child? Is the real client the guardian, or the child? If we say (as the law in many states does say) that the client is the guardian rather than the child, may the child sue the lawyer if the lawyer assists the guardian in an action that goes against the best interests of the child? Here, again, we worry that the lawyer's fear of being sued by the child will impair the lawyer's duties to the guardian.

The Restatement is sensitive to the unique problems presented by holding a lawyer liable to third parties. The Restatement therefore has special sections setting forth the duty of care to nonclients, and another section setting forth defenses and exceptions a lawyer can invoke when sued by a nonclient. The duty of care to nonclients is stated in § 51:

§ 51 Duty of Care to Certain Nonclients

> For purposes of liability . . . a lawyer owes a duty to use care . . . :
>
> (2) to a nonclient when and to the extent that:
>
> (a) the lawyer or (with the lawyer's acquiescence) the lawyer's client invites the nonclient to rely on the lawyer's opinion or provision of other legal services, and the nonclient so relies; and
>
> (b) the nonclient is not, under applicable tort law, too remote from the lawyer to be entitled to protection;
>
> (3) to a nonclient when and to the extent that:
>
> (a) the lawyer knows that a client intends as one of the primary objectives of the representation that the lawyer's services benefit the nonclient;
>
> (b) such a duty would not significantly impair the lawyer's performance of obligations to the client; and
>
> (c) the absence of such a duty would make enforcement of those obligations to the client unlikely; and
>
> (4) to a nonclient when and to the extent that:
>
> (a) the lawyer's client is a trustee, guardian, executor, or fiduciary acting primarily to perform similar functions for the nonclient;
>
> (b) the lawyer knows that appropriate action by the lawyer is necessary with respect to a matter within the scope of the representation to prevent or rectify the breach of a fiduciary duty owed by the client to the nonclients, where (i) the breach is a crime or fraud or (ii) the lawyer has assisted or is assisting the breach;
>
> (c) the nonclient is not reasonably able to protect its rights; and
>
> (d) such a duty would not significantly impair the lawyer's performance of obligations to the client.

Thus, there are three situations in which the Restatement recognizes duties to nonclients (and liability when failing to meet those duties injures the nonclient, unless the lawyer has a valid defense):

- ***Reliance — subparagraph (2):*** When a nonclient accepts the lawyer's invitation to rely on the lawyer's opinion or services, and the nonclient is not (*Palsgraf* again) "too remote" to deserve protection, then the lawyer may be liable to the third party.
- ***Intention to benefit — subparagraph (3):*** When the client tells the lawyer that the client's purpose is to confer a benefit on a third party, and it's likely that the only person who could enforce the client's intention is the third-party beneficiary, then the lawyer may be liable to the third party.
- ***Representing a trustee, guardian, executor, or other fiduciary — subparagraph (4):*** When the lawyer represents a trustee, guardian, executor, or some other fiduciary, and the lawyer fails to stop or remedy a criminal or fraudulent breach of fiduciary duty, or the lawyer assists any breach of fiduciary duty, then the lawyer may be liable to the nonclient.

Because lawyer liability to nonclients is at odds with the usual operation of the adversary system and the lawyer's duty of total loyalty to a client, the Restatement also sets up some special defenses and exceptions for lawyers who are sued by a nonclient. Section 57 provides:

§ 57 Nonclient Claims — Certain Defenses and Exceptions to Liability

(1) In addition to other absolute or conditional privileges, a lawyer is absolutely privileged to publish matter concerning a nonclient if:

(a) the publication occurs in communications preliminary to a reasonable anticipated proceeding before a tribunal or in the instituion or during the course and as part of such a proceeding;

(b) the lawyer participates as counsel in that proceeding; and

(c) the matter is published to a person who may be involved in the proceeding, and the publication has some relation to the proceeding.

(2) A lawyer representing a client in a civil proceeding or procuring the institution of criminal proceedings by a client is not liable to a nonclient for wrongful use of civil proceedings or for malicious prosecution if the lawyer has probable cause for acting, or if the lawyer acts primarily to help the client obtain a proper adjudication of the client's claim in that proceeding.

(3) A lawyer who advises or assists a client to make or break a contract, to enter or dissolve a legal relationship, or to enter or not enter a contractual relation, is not liable to a nonclient for interference with contract or with prospective contractual relations or with a legal relationship, if the lawyer acts to advance the client's objectives without using wrongful means.

In other words, § 57 sets up defenses to three special types of claims:

- ***Libel or slander — subparagraph (1):*** If a lawyer represents a client in anticipated or pending litigation, and the lawyer tells someone involved in the litigation information about a nonclient that is related to the litigation, the lawyer is not liable to the nonclient for defamation.
- ***Malicious prosecution — subparagraph (2):*** A lawyer who files a civil suit against a nonclient on a client's behalf, or who urges prosecutors to file criminal charges against a nonclient, is not liable to the nonclient if the lawyer has probable cause to do so or lawfully does so to advance the client's legal claim.
- ***Special contractual claims — subparagraph (3):*** A lawyer who represents or advises a client in making, breaking, or deciding not to enter into a contract, and who is motivated by a desire to lawfully advance the client's objectives, is not liable to any nonclient who is hurt by the client's actions or decisions.

Now that you've had a basic tour of the law of legal malpractice and the law governing other types of claims against lawyers, let's look in more depth at some important issues, starting with the standard of care.

D. THE STANDARD OF CARE

Perhaps the most important question in a legal malpractice case is: What is the standard of care? How about the Rules of Professional Conduct, which govern all lawyers and which state the minimum that the state requires of lawyers to avoid discipline? Good thought — and (as we have seen) the Restatement endorses this idea in § 52(2)(c), which provides that a judge or jury seeking to understand and apply the standard of care in a legal malpractice case may consider proof that the defendant lawyer violated a relevant rule of professional conduct (or any other relevant rule or statute regulating the conduct of lawyers) if "the rule or statute was designed for the protection of persons in the position of the claimant . . . " Thus, the plaintiff in a legal malpractice case may introduce proof of the content and construction of rules — including the Rules of Professional Conduct — that were "intended for the protection of persons in the position of the claimant."

The Preamble to the ABA Model Rules of Professional Conduct agrees that the rules of legal ethics are relevant in determining the standard for professional liability. It states:

> [20] Violation of a Rule should not itself give rise to a cause of action against the lawyer nor should it create any presumption that a legal duty has been breached. The Rules are designed to provide guidance to lawyers and to provide a structure for regulating conduct through disciplinary agencies. They are not designed to be a basis for civil liability. . . . *Nevertheless, since the Rules do establish standards of conduct by lawyers, a lawyer's violation of a Rule may be evidence of breach of the applicable standards of conduct.* [Emphasis added.]

The ABA added the italicized sentence in 2002. It thus moved beyond the old ABA Model Code of Professional Responsibility, which had stated simply: "The Code . . . does [not] undertake to define standards for civil liability of lawyers for professional conduct."

How do courts weigh the rules of professional conduct in determining the community standard for lawyer behavior? We have chosen the following well reasoned case from California to explain the uneasy relationship between the Rules of Professional Conduct and the standard of care for legal malpractice purposes.

MIRABITO v. LICCARDO

4 Cal. App. 4th 41; 5 Cal. Rptr. 2d 571 (Cal. App. 1992)

PETERSON, J.

. . . Edmond Mirabito (hereafter Edmond) operated a shoe shop in San Francisco for over 41 years. An astute investor, Edmond placed the proceeds of his endeavors into a number of successful investments, including income property in San Francisco, raw land in Santa Rosa, and various stocks.

Leonard J. Liccardo (hereafter Leonard) was Edmond's second cousin. Edmond had known Leonard since he was born and had helped him through law school. Edmond attended Leonard's moot court hearings and was proud of his accomplishments. After Leonard completed law school, Edmond employed him as his attorney on numerous occasions, having him draft leases and prepare legal documents.

By 1983, Edmond was ready to retire so he went to Leonard for an estate plan. After viewing a list of Edmond's assets, Leonard commented that Edmond had "done very well." He then tried to interest Edmond in a variety of high technology investments. Edmond was not interested but Leonard persisted, indicating that if Edmond would loan $100,000 for a particular investment Leonard would personally guarantee it. Based on this assurance, Edmond agreed and made a $100,000 loan in September 1983.

Over the following 16 months, Leonard persuaded Edmond to invest over $1.5 million in various enterprises, personally guaranteeing that the money would be returned. In large part, Edmond raised the money by mortgaging his various properties. Even though Leonard was acting as Edmond's attorney at the time, he never advised Edmond to seek independent counsel.

AUTHORS' COMMENT:

Quick: Did Leonard have to advise Edmond to seek independent counsel? Not exactly — but under the Model Rules he did have to give Edmond a "reasonable opportunity" to get the advice of an independent lawyer. Don't be deceived by this difference. If you want to stay out of trouble when you get mixed up with your clients' money, tell your clients to get their own lawyer. And be sure to disclose to your client, and to your client's lawyer, in writing, all of the relevant facts and circumstances. (For example, Leonard should have said, "I'm guaranteeing your $700,000 investment — on top of all the other investments you've made — but you should know that I filed for personal bankruptcy last year.") Finally, you will want to bear in mind th at, by design, Model Rule 1.8, "Conflict of Interest: Current Clients: Specific Rules," discourages transactions with clients in a not so subtle way: It requires that the client be "advised in writing of the desirability of seeking . . . independent legal counsel. . . . " Better yet, don't enter into business transactions with clients. It's the easiest way to get into disciplinary trouble, and you're likely to get sued for malpractice on top of it.

In late 1984, Leonard persuaded Edmond to invest over $700,000 in a movie venture, again personally guaranteeing that the money would be repaid. Leonard never told Edmond he was personally involved in the movie venture and never advised him to seek independent counsel. In addition, Leonard never mentioned that he had filed for personal bankruptcy earlier that year.

The various investments in which Edmond had placed his money were a failure. Leonard was unable to make good on his guarantees; thus, Edmond lost his property in Santa Rosa to a bank foreclosure. In all, Edmond lost nearly $4 million as the result of his investments with Leonard.

[Edmond sued Leonard for fraud, alleging that Leonard breached his fiduciary duties. When Edmond died his widow carried on the suit on behalf of the estate.] After a 13-day trial, the jury rendered its verdict in favor of Edmond and against the estate, awarding Edmond damages of $2,510,000. . . .

II. Discussion

A. Rules of Professional Conduct

Appellant's first claim of error relates to the use of the Rules of Professional Conduct of the State Bar at trial. In order to understand this argument, some background is necessary.

. . . In connection with the fraud claims, Edmond alleged that Leonard had breached his fiduciary duties. This allegation was premised on the attorney/client relationship which existed between Edmond and Leonard. Edmond maintained that, pursuant to former rule 5–101 of the Rules of Professional Conduct of the State Bar (hereafter rules), Leonard had a duty to fully disclose the circumstances surrounding the various investments in which he had placed his money, and should have offered him the opportunity to obtain independent counsel prior to investing.[1]

---

[1] Former rule 5-101 provided, "A member of the State Bar shall not enter into a business transaction with a client or knowingly acquire an ownership, possessory, security, or other pecuniary interest adverse to a client

On the first day of trial, appellant moved in limine to bar the introduction of evidence concerning the rules. Essentially, appellant argued the rules only establish disciplinary standards by which attorneys' conduct is measured and are not intended to provide for civil liability. The trial court was unpersuaded and allowed Edmond to present testimony from several attorneys, including one who specialized in professional ethics, who stated that prior to entering into a business transaction with a client an attorney is required to fully disclose the circumstances surrounding the proposed investment, and to offer the client the opportunity to seek independent counsel. Subsequently, the trial court approved several jury instructions which were patterned after the rules and permitted them to be read to the jury.

On appeal, appellant . . . maintains the trial court should not have allowed testimony or permitted jury instructions concerning the rules because those rules do not establish an attorney's civil liability. . . .

Since Edmond's fraud claims were based, in part, upon Leonard's alleged breach of his fiduciary duties, it was incumbent upon Edmond to establish what "duties" Leonard was alleged to have breached. It is well established that an attorney's duties to his client are governed by the rules. Those rules, together with statutes and general principles relating to other fiduciary relationships, all help define the duty component of the fiduciary duty which an attorney owes to his client. . . .

In the present case . . . the rules could be used to help prove whether Leonard had breached his fiduciary duties to Edmond as was alleged in the cross-complaint. The court did not err in permitting testimony regarding those rules or by instructing the jury with them. . . .

The judgment is *affirmed*.

NOTES AND QUESTIONS

1. ***Fiduciary Duties.*** As we saw in the materials on conflicts of interest, fiduciary duties are part and parcel of the practice of law. The attorney-client relationship is a fiduciary relationship, and an attorney thus owes fiduciary duties to clients. What are those duties? They are many, but the principal ones are the ones we have been studying:

- *Loyalty.* You have a duty to avoid conflicts of interest, and to put the client's interest first and foremost.
- *Competence.* You have a duty to serve the client skillfully. If you hold yourself out as a specialist, then you have a duty to exhibit an even higher level of skill than a generalist.
- *Diligence.* You have a duty to attend to the client's affairs in a timely manner, moving them along at a reasonable pace so that the client does not lose anything significant through delay.
- *Disclosure.* You have a duty to tell the client all of the facts that the client might find useful in making decisions about the representation.
- *Confidentiality.* You have a duty to keep information relating to the representation secret unless disclosure to third parties is authorized by the rules — and the duty not to use any of the client's information for your own advantage unless the client gives informed consent.

---

unless (1) the transaction and terms in which the member of the State Bar acquires the interest are fair and reasonable to the client and are fully disclosed and transmitted in writing to the client in a manner and terms which should have reasonably been understood by the client, (2) the client is given a reasonable opportunity to seek the advice of independent counsel of the client's choice on the transaction, and (3) the client consents in writing thereto." . . . [Note: This rule served as the model for Rule 1.8(a) of the ABA Model Rules of Professional Conduct. It is almost identical to MRPC 1.8(a). — Eds.]

Those are the basic fiduciary duties, and all of them find parallels in the Rules of Professional Conduct. If you are accused of breaching fiduciary duties, the plaintiff will certainly try to present evidence that you violated the Rules of Professional Conduct. In most courts, the judge will allow this, just as in the *Mirabito* case.

2. ***Malpractice and Legal Fees.*** How do suits for legal malpractice and breach of fiduciary duty get started? Surely you remember the best all-purpose guess in a capitalist system — money. Many malpractice suits get started as arguments over legal fees. The client thinks the bill is too high and won't pay. The lawyer gets angry and sues the client. But in about 95% of all suits against clients for legal fees, the client counterclaims for legal malpractice. The counterclaim is simple: "I don't owe the money because the attorney screwed up — and, in fact, the attorney screwed up so badly that the attorney owes *me* money."

How can you avoid getting into these scrapes with your clients? First of all, communicate with your client. Let your client know what you are doing, not just when you win a motion (or lose one), but when you write a letter, file a motion, or interview a witness. Clients don't know how much work we do to earn a living. We have to tell them. The easiest way to tell them is to send copies of everything we write. Many attorneys do this by sending copies with a simple note saying "FYI" ("For Your Information") or with a short cover letter briefly explaining the item. If your clients see that you are busy and are constantly working and moving their cases forward, they will be less likely to challenge the fee when the bill arrives. And keep in mind that communicating with a client isn't just good business, it's ethically required. See ABA Rule 1.4 ("Communication").

When you *do* get into a fee dispute with a client — and you will sometimes, because some people don't like to pay their bills, and sometimes your bills may be too high — take advantage of fee arbitration programs set up by state and local bars. In the *Davis* case, which we just read, the court dropped a footnote at the end: "We would like this case to serve as a reminder that arbitration is offered through the State Bar to resolve fee disputes between lawyers and clients." In Pennsylvania, the leading malpractice insurers give a healthy discount on legal malpractice insurance to law firms that pledge to use the state bar's fee arbitration program before suing clients for past due fees. These fee arbitration programs work because they are generally fair to both sides.

3. ***What's the Policy?*** Why shouldn't breach of a rule of professional conduct automatically create a cause of action for legal malpractice? The theory is that the purpose of the rules is different from the purpose of the tort of legal malpractice. The rules are preventive — they are designed to keep attorneys away from troublesome situations. The disciplinary authorities can go after an attorney for violating a rule even if the attorney repairs the harm to the client before the disciplinary proceedings begin, and even if the client didn't suffer any harm in the first place. But a client cannot successfully sue an attorney for legal malpractice unless the client suffers damages. As in all torts, damages is an element of the claim. No damages, no tort. No harm, no foul.

Let's say it a different way. The civil liability system (legal malpractice) is designed to make the client whole. It is a compensatory system, designed not to punish the attorney (though it does that, too) but rather to compensate the client. The disciplinary system, on the other hand, does nothing for the client, but rather is designed to remove the maladroit attorney from the practice of law. Discipline is a form of quality control for the profession, not compensation for the client.

4. ***Why Are Lawyers Different?*** When it comes to policing competence, what's the difference between lawyers and, say, doctors or electricians or plumbers? Is it any harder to assure that lawyers provide competent services than it is to assure that other professionals perform competently?

The following excerpt addresses this issue. The question was whether the statute of limitations for legal malpractice should begin to run at the time of the breach (i.e., when the lawyer screwed up), or when the client found out (or should have found out) that the lawyer screwed up. The California Supreme Court decided that the statute of limitations in a legal malpractice action does not begin to run until the facts upon which the action is based are, or should have been, discovered. This gives the client a better chance to succeed in a legal malpractice action, since it lengthens the statute of limitations. Are you convinced by the court's reasoning, which is based largely on "the special nature of the relationship between the professional man and his client"?

NEEL v. MAGANA

6 Cal. 3d 176, 98 Cal. Rptr. 837, 491 P.2d 421 (1971)

. . . In the first place, the special obligation of the professional is exemplified by his duty not merely to perform his work with ordinary care but to use the skill, prudence, and diligence commonly exercised by practitioners of his profession. If he further specializes within the profession, he must meet the standards of knowledge and skill of such specialists.

Corollary to this expertise is the inability of the layman to detect its misapplication; the client may not recognize the negligence of the professional when he sees it. He cannot be expected to know the relative medical merits of alternative anesthetics nor the various legal exceptions to the hearsay rule. If he must ascertain malpractice at the moment of its incidence, the client must hire a second professional to observe the work of the first, an expensive and impractical duplication, clearly destructive of the confidential relationship between the practitioner and his client.

In the second place, not only may the client fail to recognize negligence when he sees it, but often he will lack any opportunity to see it. The doctor operates on an unconscious patient; although the attorney, the accountant, and the stockbroker serves the conscious client, much of their work must be performed out of the client's view. In the legal field, the injury may lie concealed within the obtuse terminology of a will or contract; in the medical field the injury may lie hidden within the patient's body; in the accounting field, the injury may lie buried in the figures of the ledger.

Finally, the dealings between practitioner and client frame a fiduciary relationship. The duty of a fiduciary embraces the obligation to render a full and fair disclosure to the beneficiary of all facts which materially affect his rights and interests. . . .

Thus the fact that a client lacks awareness of a practitioner's malpractice implies, in many cases, a second breach of duty by the fiduciary, namely, a failure to disclose material facts to his client. Postponement of accrual of the cause of action until the client discovers, or should discover, the material facts in issue vindicates the fiduciary duty of full disclosure; it prevents the fiduciary from obtaining immunity for an initial breach of duty by a subsequent breach of the obligation of disclosure.

NOTES AND QUESTIONS

"For a Limited Time Only . . . " Suppose your client advises you that she can afford only $1,000 for your services and your normal fee is $100 per hour. May you provide in your retainer agreement that you will work for 10 hours and then stop? ABA Rule 1.5(a)(5) says that "the time limitations imposed by the client or by the circumstances" are a factor to be considered in determining the fee. On the other hand, you have to provide "competent representation," and the Comment to ABA Rule 1.1 expressly states that competent handling of a particular matter "includes inquiry into and analysis of the factual and legal elements of the problem" and "adequate preparation." Can you agree to work only a limited number of hours even if you won't be able to make an adequate inquiry and won't be able to complete "adequate" preparation?

Role-Play Instruction: Legal Malpractice

Student #1 is a client. Student #2 is her lawyer. Student #1 is divorcing her husband. In this brief session, Student #2 will review with Student #1 the settlement he has just accomplished for his client. Student #1 will be receiving spousal support of $1,000 a month until she finds a job and $1,000 a month in child support from her former husband, a doctor. The house will be held jointly until the oldest child reaches 15 (three years from now) and then will be sold and the proceeds evenly divided between spouses. Student #2 thinks this is a very good settlement and has already signed the agreement on behalf of his client.

Student #1 should ask Student #2 about a recent newspaper article she read which said something about a spouse's right to get some portion of a doctor's income where the spouse supported the doctor through medical school. (There have been numerous cases like this in recent years in community property states like California and in equitable distribution jurisdictions like New York.) Student #2 (who seems not to be familiar with these cases) should say that he doesn't think the case applies here because Student #1 wasn't her husband's sole support when he was in medical school.

Immediately after this session Student #1 will consult with Student #3 to see if she has a malpractice claim against Student #2. Student #3 should be prepared to analyze the malpractice claim. The class will then discuss whether Student #1 has a malpractice claim against Student #2 and if so, what she can recover.

E. MALPRACTICE AND INEFFECTIVE ASSISTANCE IN CRIMINAL CASES

Malpractice also occurs in criminal cases, where it is usually examined in the context of post-conviction remedy petitions. In that context, the malpractice goes under the rubric of "ineffective assistance of counsel" and the remedy is a new trial. Although occasionally a criminal defendant who has been wrongly convicted can bring a traditional malpractice case against his lawyer and win money damages, in this section we will focus primarily on ineffective assistance claims.

1. Claims of Ineffective Assistance of Counsel

Ineffective assistance of counsel is essentially the constitutional equivalent of legal malpractice. The Sixth Amendment guarantees every criminal defendant the right to "assistance of counsel" at trial, which has long been interpreted to mean "effective" assistance of counsel. If a court finds that a defendant has not received effective assistance of counsel and has therefore suffered prejudice, the defendant may be entitled to a new trial.

Ineffective assistance of counsel claims typically arise when a person who has been convicted of a crime decides to blame the lawyer for the conviction. (Only those who are convicted allege ineffective assistance — you can't sue your lawyer for malpractice if you win.) The usual starting point is with the filing of a habeas corpus petition (or the state law equivalent) alleging that a lawyer mishandled a defense. The lawyer is not technically a defendant, but the lawyer's reputation is on the line. (Would you want everyone to read a court opinion saying you screwed up a case?) The defendant can't go free even if he proves ineffective assistance, but he can get a new trial. (If the malpractice occurs at the plea bargaining stage, should the defendant get a second bite at a plea bargain? That's an open question. What do you say?)

The standard for deciding ineffective assistance claims was definitively set forth in *Strickland v. Washington*, 466 U.S. 668 (1984). To get a new trial, the defendant must prove two things:

(1) the lawyer's conduct fell below the range of professionally acceptable conduct, and

(2) the client suffered prejudice in the sense that the verdict was probably affected by the lawyer's incompetence.

If the defendant proves that the lawyer mishandled the case but fails to prove prejudice, then the defendant does not get a new trial. That would be like proving malpractice but not proving damages in a civil case — it would just be an academic exercise affording consolation but no remedy to the unfortunate client.

If, on the other hand, the defendant succeeds on a petition alleging ineffective assistance of counsel, he is normally entitled to a new trial. That is not the remedy when a plaintiff succeeds in a civil malpractice suit. Should it be? Why or why not? If not, what should be the remedy when a plaintiff wins a civil malpractice suit?

The two-pronged *Strickland* test for proving ineffective assistance of counsel is hard to meet, but it can be done. Nearly always, the lawyer's sin is the sin of *omission* — something the lawyer failed to do, rather than something the lawyer did but did incorrectly. For example, a lawyer may be ineffective if he fails to call a certain witness, fails to raise a certain defense, or fails to investigate certain leads.

We'll now read a recent example of judicial thinking on ineffective assistance of counsel. The case concerns an allegation of ineffective assistance at the plea bargaining stage. Here, instead of a new trial, the defendant wants the right to accept a plea bargain he rejected before he went to trial.

The opinion revolves largely around the Federal Sentencing Guidelines, which took effect during the late 1980's. At the time of the opinion, the Supreme Court's seminal decision in *United States v. Booker*, 543 U.S. 220 (2005), making the Federal Sentencing Guidelines advisory rather than mandatory had yet to be decided. However, the underlying rationale of the Guidelines were not in dispute. They operated much like points on a driver's license — the more crimes you commit, and the more severe the crimes, the heavier the likely sentence. If you commit enough crimes, you are a "career offender" and the recommended sentence will be sharply increased. Suppose, though, that your lawyer doesn't explain this calculus to you, so you reject a plea bargain under which you would have served only 5 years. You then go to trial and get convicted. Based on your previous record, the court pronounces you a "career offender" and gives you 21 years. You could have accepted a deal for only 5 years! You got an *extra 16 years in prison* because you had an incompetent lawyer! Can you successfully claim ineffective assistance of counsel and get another chance to accept the plea bargain? That's what the next case is about.

UNITED STATES v. DAY

969 F.2d 39 (3d Cir. 1992)

BECKER, J.

William Day . . . seeks to have his conviction and sentence set aside. Day's primary claim is that his trial counsel afforded him ineffective assistance of counsel regarding a plea offer by giving him substandard advice about his sentence exposure under the Sentencing Guidelines. More specifically, Day alleges that his counsel failed to explain his possible career offender status and told him that the maximum prison sentence that he could receive if he stood trial was eleven years, when in fact he is serving nearly twenty-two years and could have received a far greater sentence. Day contends that this deficient advice led him to decline a plea offer that would have resulted in a five-year sentence. He now seeks to plead guilty pursuant to the alleged plea bargain and to have that five-year sentence imposed instead of his current sentence. . . .

We hold that Day's petition raises a facially valid claim of ineffective assistance of counsel during plea bargaining. We have previously held that constitutionally significant prejudice can inhere from ineffective assistance at that stage, and Day's petition alleges both clearly deficient performance by counsel and sufficient prejudice.

The district court therefore erred in not conducting a hearing on that claim, unless it can conclude on remand that there is no "reasonable probability" that it would have approved the alleged plea agreement. . . . [2]

I. Procedural History

A jury convicted Day along with five codefendants of possession with intent to distribute and conspiracy to distribute a large quantity of cocaine. . . . Day's Presentence Investigation Report calculated his offense level as 28 (a base level of 26, plus 2 because a handgun was present) and his criminal history category as IV (he had 8 points). Those scores would have created a sentence range of 110 to 137 months (9 years, 2 months to 11 years, 5 months). Because Day had two previous convictions for violent felonies, however, the probation officer noted that Day might be considered a career offender under U.S.S.G. § 4B1.1, under which his offense level would be elevated to 34 (the statutory maximum for the offense was more than 25 years) and his criminal history category to VI. The district court concluded that Day was a career offender and sentenced him to 262 months (21 years, 10 months) in prison, at the bottom of the applicable range of 262 to 327 months. On direct appeal, we summarily affirmed. . . .

II. Discussion. . . .

B. Ineffective Assistance of Counsel Regarding Sentence Exposure and Plea Bargaining

The principles governing ineffective assistance of counsel claims are familiar, and we need not belabor them here. A defendant has a Sixth Amendment right not just to counsel, but to "reasonably effective assistance" of counsel. To gain relief for a violation of this right, a defendant must show both unprofessional conduct and, in most cases, prejudice as a result. More precisely, the claimant must show that (1) his or her attorney's performance was, under all the circumstances, unreasonable under prevailing professional norms, and unless prejudice is presumed, that (2) there is a "reasonable probability that, but for counsel's unprofessional errors, the result would have been different." "A reasonable probability is a probability sufficient to undermine confidence in the outcome."

1. Day's Allegations

Day's petition alleges that his trial counsel failed to explain that Day might be classified as a career offender and be subject to enhanced penalties under the Sentencing Guidelines. Day claims that had he been told of his true sentence exposure, he would have accepted the government's plea bargain offer and received a five-year sentence instead of the approximately twenty-two-year sentence that he now faces. . . .

2. Deficient Performance of Counsel

We believe that Day's petition states a claim for substandard performance of counsel under the first prong of *Strickland v. Washington*, 466 U.S. 668 (1984). *United States ex rel. Caruso v. Zelinsky*, 689 F.2d 435 (3d Cir. 1982), is particularly instructive. Caruso alleged that the county prosecutor had offered his trial counsel a plea bargain whereby in exchange for a guilty plea on one murder charge, all other charges would be dropped. Caruso claimed that his counsel never communicated the offer to him, and that, as a result, he stood trial and received a mandatory life sentence instead of the lesser sentence that he would have received under the plea bargain. We held that the plea bargain stage was a critical stage at which the right to effective assistance of

---

[2] Additionally, Day claimed that his appellate counsel was ineffective for failing to raise his trial counsel's ineffective assistance on appeal.

counsel attaches, and we concluded that Caruso's allegations stated a Sixth Amendment claim.

Although in this case Day concedes that he was notified of the terms of the plea bargain, he alleges that the advice that he received was so incorrect and so insufficient that it undermined his ability to make an intelligent decision about whether to accept the offer. That, we hold, also states a Sixth Amendment claim.

We cannot state precisely what standard defense counsel must meet when advising their clients about the desirability of a plea bargain and, concomitantly, about sentence exposure. Because the Sentencing Guidelines have become a critical, and in many cases, dominant facet of federal criminal proceedings, we can say, however, that familiarity with the structure and basic content of the Guidelines (including the definition and implications of career offender status) has become a necessity for counsel who seek to give effective representation.

We do not suggest that, to comply with the Sixth Amendment, counsel must give each defendant anything approaching a detailed exegesis of the myriad arguably relevant nuances of the Guidelines. Nevertheless, a defendant has the right to make a reasonably informed decision whether to accept a plea offer. See *Hill v. Lockhart*, 474 U.S. 52, 56–57 (1985) (voluntariness of guilty plea depends on adequacy of counsel's advice); *Von Moltke v. Gillies*, 332 U.S. 708, 721 (1948) ("Prior to trial an accused is entitled to rely upon his counsel to make an independent examination of the facts, circumstances, pleadings and laws involved and then to offer his informed opinion as to what plea should be entered.").

Knowledge of the comparative sentence exposure between standing trial and accepting a plea offer will often be crucial to the decision whether to plead guilty. See, for example, *Williams v. State*, 326 Md. 367, 605 A.2d 103 (1992) (counsel's conduct was constitutionally deficient in failing to advise petitioner of mandatory 25-year sentence upon conviction at trial when offer to plead guilty to lesser offense involved exposure only to 10-year sentence); *Commonwealth v. Napper*, 254 Pa. Super. 54, 385 A.2d 521 (1978) (counsel ineffective in giving no advice about desirability of plea offer with three-year maximum sentence when trial risked ten to forty years and defendant's chances of acquittal were slim).

Therefore, we conclude that if Day is correct that he was seriously misled about his sentence exposure when the likelihood of his conviction was overwhelming, he received ineffective assistance of counsel. On appeal, the government suggests that Day is a classic second-guesser of a strategy (namely, standing trial) that was sound at the time but looks mistaken in retrospect. That may be, but in the absence of a record we simply cannot tell. Further proceedings are necessary to determine whether the [attorneys'] performance was in fact deficient.

3. Prejudice

Even if Day received substandard assistance from counsel, to justify relief he must prove sufficient prejudice. The district court ruled that Day could not have suffered prejudice because a defendant can suffer no prejudice by standing a fair trial. That view has some force. We squarely rejected it, however, in Caruso, where we wrote:

> The State argues that because Caruso received a fair trial he is not entitled to a habeas remedy even if he could prove ineffective assistance of counsel in the manner alleged. This argument is untenable on the plea bargaining issue. Failure by defense counsel to communicate a plea offer to defendant deprives defendant of the opportunity to present a plea bargain for the consideration of the state judge and, on acceptance by the state judge, to enter a guilty plea in exchange for a lesser sentence. A subsequent fair trial does not remedy this deprivation.

Other circuits have reached similar conclusions.

In short, we and most other courts have concluded that the Sixth Amendment right to effective assistance of counsel guarantees more than the Fifth Amendment right to a fair trial. Because we conclude that prejudice is theoretically possible, the question becomes whether Day alleges sufficient prejudice in fact, which requires consideration of whether Day would have accepted the alleged plea offer and whether the district court would have approved it.

The government mocks Day's contention that although he did not plead guilty when he believed that his sentence exposure was approximately eleven years, he would have pleaded guilty had he known that he would receive a sentence of almost twenty-two years. We do not find the contention so implausible that it was properly dismissed without a hearing. Day was fortunate to be sentenced at the low end of the Guideline range for career offenders, so, if his claim is true, he risked far more than an extra ten years and five months in jail. But even using the lower figure, we do not find it at all implausible that a young man would think twice before risking over 3800 extra days in jail just to gain the chance of acquittal of a crime that he knew that he had committed.

The district court's opinion instead emphasized how difficult it will be to determine whether Day would have pleaded guilty had he received better advice from counsel. In its view,

> [T]here is no reliable way for the court to reconstruct what would have happened had defendant more fully contemplated the plea option. He may have pled guilty and he still may not have. There is no reliable way for the court to hypothesize as to what sentence would have been imposed had defendant pled guilty. He may have testified or he may not have. He may have testified truthfully or he may not have. He may have provided "substantial" assistance to the government or he may not have. . . .

. . . We must therefore vacate this portion of the district court's judgment and remand this issue for further proceedings. The district judge should allow Day's retained counsel to amend his petition to clarify his allegations. Unless the district judge can then conclude that there is no "reasonable probability" that he would have approved the alleged plea agreement, he should order the government to answer the amended petition and hold an evidentiary hearing. . . .

NOTES AND QUESTIONS

1. ***What Remedy?*** If you were the district court handling the *Day* case on remand, what remedy would you devise?

2. ***Deliberate Ineffective Assistance?*** The district court in *Day* worried that criminal defense lawyers would deliberately be ineffective at the plea bargain stage so that their clients, if convicted, could have a second bite at the plea bargain apple. Do you think this will happen? Why or why not? What would be the risks of deliberately being ineffective? The Third Circuit's opinion in *Day* addressed this fear in a lengthy footnote that included the following paragraph:

> Most defense lawyers, like most lawyers in other branches of the profession, serve their clients and the judicial system with integrity. Deliberate ineffective assistance of counsel is not only unethical, but usually bad strategy as well. For these reasons, and because incompetent lawyers risk disciplinary action, malpractice suits, and consequent loss of business, we refuse to presume that ineffective assistance of counsel is deliberate. Moreover, to the extent that petitioners and their trial counsel may jointly fabricate these claims later on, the district courts will have ample opportunity to judge credibility at evidentiary hearings.

2. Traditional Legal Malpractice Claims

A successful claim of ineffective assistance of counsel entitles a defendant to a new trial, but does not entitle the defendant to any damages. Only a suit for legal malpractice can result in damages. Can a defendant sue a lawyer for legal malpractice in criminal defense? If so, should the defendant have to prove that the judge or jury in the underlying criminal case would more likely than not have found him not guilty if the lawyer had handled the defense effectively? Should the defendant have to prove that he was actually innocent? And if the defendant languishes in prison for years before a more competent lawyer recognizes the legal malpractice, or before a court overturns the conviction, what about the statute of limitations? Should it run, or be tolled, during the quest for post-conviction relief? Here is a case from the Iowa Supreme Court that grapples with these issues — and reminds us that conflicts of interest often spur suits for legal malpractice.

TROBAUGH v. SONDAG

668 N.W.2d 577 (Iowa 2003)

CADY, JUSTICE. . . .

I. BACKGROUND FACTS AND PROCEEDINGS

In January 1989, Charles A. Trobaugh (Trobaugh) was charged in Pottawattamie County with assault with intent to inflict serious injury, assault with a dangerous weapon, and possession of a firearm by a felon. Assistant County Attorney Patrick A. Sondag (Sondag) signed the initial complaints filed against Trobaugh. Subsequent to signing the complaints, Sondag took a position as an Assistant Public Defender in the same county. He then became Trobaugh's defense attorney in the same case in which he had signed the initial complaints. Whether Sondag informed Trobaugh of his prior employment as a county attorney and his role in initiating Trobaugh's prosecution remains at the core of this controversy. Nevertheless, Trobaugh eventually accepted a plea agreement and pled guilty to the charges of displaying a dangerous weapon and possession of a firearm by a felon. He was then incarcerated for eleven months.

Six years later, Trobaugh again faced criminal charges, this time for a federal drug offense for which he was later convicted. Apparently because his 1989 conviction resulted in an enhancement of his federal sentence, Trobaugh began to reexamine the circumstances of his prior state court conviction. In June 1997, his new attorney discovered that Sondag had both signed the initial complaint against Trobaugh in 1989 and represented him in his defense against the same charges.

Trobaugh immediately raised Sondag's potential conflict of interest as a ground for relief in a pending postconviction action. This action was dismissed as time barred. A second postconviction relief action followed but was later withdrawn. He then filed a federal court action against Sondag and others alleging, among other things, conspiracy to bring about his 1989 conviction. This claim was dismissed on a motion for summary judgment. Finally, in June 2000, Trobaugh filed a third application for postconviction relief. This application was successful and he was granted a new trial in November 2000. On remand, he pled guilty to the charge of possession of a firearm by a felon while his other two related Pottawattamie County charges were dismissed.

In late November 2000, Trobaugh filed a claim for monetary damages with the State Appeal Board pursuant to the Iowa Tort Claims Act, alleging the representation by Sondag, a state employee, was tainted by legal malpractice. Shortly after the board denied his claim in April 2001, Trobaugh filed a civil claim in the district court. Sondag moved to dismiss the claim on a number of grounds, two of which he renews on appeal: (1) Trobaugh's tort claim is barred by the two-year statute of limitations . . . and (2) his claim is the functional equivalent of claims barred by the Tort Claims Act. The district court granted Sondag's motion to dismiss, concluding Trobaugh's claims were untimely because they had accrued in June 1997 when he first discovered the potential conflict of interest. Trobaugh appeals from the court's grant of Sondag's motion. . . .

III. Relief After Conviction and the Discovery Rule

The resolution of this appeal requires us to focus on the point in time at which Trobaugh's claim of legal malpractice was or should have been "discovered." . . . "[A] cause of action based on negligence does not accrue until a plaintiff discovers the injury or by the exercise of reasonable diligence should have discovered it." . . .

Ultimately, our resolution hinges on whether a claim for legal malpractice in the criminal case context can be discovered prior to the plaintiff receiving relief from the conviction that allegedly resulted from negligent representation. This issue has arisen in similar forms in a number of cases in other jurisdictions. Not surprisingly, the courts facing this issue have produced a divergence of opinion on the proper approach to take.

Many courts have concluded that some form of relief from a conviction is necessary before a criminal defendant can successfully bring a civil lawsuit for legal malpractice against a former attorney. In fact, some of these courts go so far as to require a criminal defendant to prove his innocence in the course of his civil case before being allowed to recover. Under this required-relief approach, a civil claim for legal malpractice is typically considered discovered and begins to accrue at the time relief from a conviction is granted. A court taking this approach to the issue generally grounds its conclusions on one of a number of policy-based considerations, including:

> equitable principles against shifting responsibility for the consequences of the criminal's action; the paradoxical difficulties of awarding damages to a guilty person; theoretical and practical difficulties of proving causation; the potential undermining of the postconviction process if a legal malpractice action overrules the judgments entered in the postconviction proceedings; preserving judicial economy by avoiding relitigation of settled matters; creation of a bright line rule determining when the statute of limitations runs on the malpractice action; availability of alternative postconviction remedies; and the chilling effect on thorough defense lawyering.

Of course, a number of courts have concluded that a defendant need not achieve relief from a conviction before bringing a claim for legal malpractice. The upshot of this no-relief-required approach is that a claim for legal malpractice is found to accrue before relief from a conviction is achieved, often upon the discovery of the facts related to the attorney's negligent conduct. Some proponents of this approach assert that requiring relief from a conviction forces a court to entertain an untenable legal fiction:

> "[P]ersons convicted of a crime will be astonished to learn that, even if their lawyers' negligence resulted in their being wrongly convicted and imprisoned, they were not harmed when they were wrongly convicted and imprisoned but, rather, that they are harmed only if and when they are exonerated."

Other courts have concluded that the no-relief-required approach is simply the most effective choice because it permits respect for the policies behind statutes of limitations while also preserving the role of remedies allowing relief from a conviction, particularly as a consideration for a legal malpractice claim.

AUTHOR'S COMMENT:

Of the approaches just described, which one do you like the best? Which one is fairest to lawyers, clients, courts, and society? In particular, would you require a criminal defendant to obtain relief from a criminal conviction before he is permitted to sue his former criminal defense attorney for legal malpractice?

Upon considering all of the issues presented and the wealth of commentary on this issue by other courts, we conclude that the approach that requires a defendant to achieve relief from a conviction before advancing a legal malpractice action against his former attorney is superior in this particular area of the law. In reaching this conclusion, we are persuaded by the extensive, well-reasoned policy arguments underlying the relief-required approach. Most importantly, we believe this approach best preserves key principles of judicial economy and comity, including the avoidance of multiple proceedings related to the same factual and procedural issues, respect for other statutorily created processes such as postconviction relief, and the prevention of potentially wasteful practices such as requiring a plaintiff to file a legal malpractice claim which may never come to fruition due to one of a number of factors.

We thus also conclude that a claim for legal malpractice in the criminal case context is not discovered and does not accrue until relief from a conviction is achieved. Admittedly, this conclusion may pose difficulties for parties in that claims may rest uncontested for numerous years before accruing in the aftermath of successful relief from a conviction. Nevertheless, the very nature of many actions for relief from a conviction requires the consideration of late-discovered grounds for such relief. Despite the potential age of such claims, actions for relief are a functioning part of the criminal system, and we believe related actions may similarly operate in the civil context. In addition, the previously mentioned principles of economy and comity, as well as the advantage of having a clear demarcation of the point in time when the claim accrues, outweigh the potential hazards of arguably stale claims.

Ultimately, the application of our conclusions on these issues to Trobaugh's claim leads us to conclude that his claim accrued upon the district court's granting of his third postconviction relief petition on November 9, 2000. For this reason, both his State Appeal Board and civil filings were timely. . . .

Reversed and Remanded.

NOTES AND QUESTIONS

1. Strong Trend. The *Trobaugh* case follows the strong trend to bar a convicted defendant from prevailing against a criminal defense lawyer for legal malpractice unless and until the conviction is overturned on appeal. Why is that? Do you agree that a criminal defendant should not be permitted to sue for legal malpractice unless the conviction is wiped out? Should we make it hard or easy for a criminal defendant to sue a lawyer for legal malpractice?

2. A "Two Track" Procedure? The *Trobaugh* court notes that some courts have imposed a "two track" procedure for legal malpractice claims arising in the criminal context. These courts require a plaintiff to file both (a) an action for relief from a conviction and (b) a civil lawsuit in a timely fashion. (If necessary, the aggrieved plaintiff asks the civil court to exercise its equitable powers to stay the civil action while the action for relief from the conviction proceeds.) Other courts have observed that achieving relief from a conviction should simply be a factor analyzing causation and damages for legal malpractice purposes. The *Trobaugh* court recognized that these approaches "present certain advantages," but rejected them as "inefficient methods for allowing the pursuit of a malpractice claim, especially in light of the conclusiveness of our chosen method requiring relief from a conviction before the advancement of the civil claim." Would you favor the two track procedure, requiring the plaintiff to file both a civil action and an action for relief from the conviction in order to preserve the right to pursue the civil action?

Chapter 33
IMPROVING LEGAL EDUCATION

A. INTRODUCTION

We know that you complain about law school. What generation of law students hasn't complained about law school? This chapter offers yet another opportunity to vent — and to talk in an organized fashion about something that greatly affects you. This is not, though, a general gripe session. It is a serious attempt to harness the power of students to generate ideas for making American legal education better. The authors of this book are law professors, and have not been law students for many years. If we really want to improve legal education, we need your help.

To get you in the right frame of mind, imagine the following situation:

Your law school's old dean recently retired in frustration and exhaustion. The law school promptly embarked on a search for a dynamic, creative person. The school realized that the old image of a dean was outmoded. In the old days, up through the mid-1980s, law school deans were chosen mainly for their scholarly achievement. But hiring a person mainly for their achievements as a scholar won't work in the world today. Things are too tough, too competitive. The dean's job isn't what it used to be. In the old days, a dean set the academic tone for a school. He (it was almost always a "he" until the mid-1980s) played a major role in the hiring process, encouraged scholarship by tenured professors, and decided whether the scholarship of junior professors met the school's standards for promotion and tenure.

Today, the job is different. A dean has to be a spokesperson, cheerleader, budget officer, fundraiser, politician, and recruiter as much as a scholar. Applications to law schools are down, costs are up, the job market is rough, and competition for students is increasing. The dean has to be someone with a vision of how to improve the law school, raise substantial funds, attract quality students, persuade alumni to hire the school's graduates, and govern the law school, which means giving an increasingly active role to student organizations.

The Dean Search Committee considered dozens of candidates. After rejecting lots of *Harvard Law Review* types who had published numerous obscure law review articles, the law school interviewed you. You had a lot of ideas about legal education, and valuable firsthand experience as a student. In an unconventional move that made headlines throughout the world of legal education, the Dean Search Committee unanimously voted to recommend you as the next dean. In announcing your appointment, the Chair of the Dean Search Committee said, "Our new dean knows what students want, and knows what needs to be done to improve this law school and put it on the map." Nice intro, Dean. Congratulations!

Now it's time for you to stop talking the talk and start walking the walk. It's time to put your ideas into action. (By the way, I hope that you have a knack for fundraising; you'll need it. The University is engaged in a belt-tightening round of budget cuts, so you won't be able to look to the University for increased funds. You're going to have to do it all on your own, either by generating more revenue and contributions or by spending less.)

Your school's strongest attribute is the fervent loyalty of its alumni. More than half the lawyers in the state are your graduates. Although only a low percentage have ever given to the law school (and an even lower percentage are annual givers), there is no doubt that the hearts of alumni everywhere forever skip a beat at the sight of your law school's colors. Many of the lawyers at the major law firms, many judges, and many influential businesspeople in your geographic area are your alums, as are many high-profile lawyers, corporate heads, and national politicians around the country. If you can inspire them to give, they have the money to give.

Oh, by the way, there are a few insider details you'll want to become more familiar with now that you are Dean. Your school is under pressure from its accrediting and membership bodies (including the ABA) to address its historic lack of student and faculty diversity. Faculty scholarship is in the "minimally adequate" range. The oldest professors tend to revise well-worn casebooks or treatise chapters. The middle-aged professors write law review and bar journal articles of slight quality and little relevance. Only the untenured and recently tenured professors are producing exciting law review scholarship and nationally-respected blogs.

There's a related problem here, too. Faculty governance is weak. Committees, in effect, work for the law school's heavily white-male Executive Committee; the progressive professors in the clinical program are significantly marginalized; the law school has no international programs and no academic institutes; and the faculty has not received a formal budget report in over a decade, nor seriously undertaken strategic planning in years.

Still, that is not the worst of it. The single biggest threat facing you is that the accrediting body has threatened to begin the process of de-accrediting the law school if it does not build a new law school building. If assurances are not forthcoming, the next step will be to require that you and the University President appear before the accreditation review committee. The committee believes that the present dark, crowded, asbestos-laden, technology-bare building is an impediment to the education process. Fortunately (or unfortunately) the University and law school agree with this assessment. In fact, the law school has been working on the project for five years, during which time it has raised 25% of the originally projected cost. Regrettably, due to a variety of delays (including the new dean search) and due to inflation in the construction and labor markets, the projected costs for the new building have increased 125%. (In other words, despite raising significant sums over the past five years, you have to raise more money now to finish the building than when the fundraising started.) Moreover, the campaign effort prior to your arrival can best be described as anemic. The law school has yet to establish a statewide building campaign committee, undertake a campaign feasibility study, create a major gifts officer position, secure a lead-gift from a major contributor; or establish a communications operation to communicate regularly with alumni, friends, opinion-makers and law school/University constituents.

You start tomorrow, though, and we are pulling for you. Good luck. It's a tough job, but you took the job because you wanted a challenge. And it's not going to get any easier! The politicians and well-connected alums have had a long history of expecting "friends to be treated as friends," and they are not shy about telling you so. You have a lot of work to do and a lot of constituencies to please!

B. THE MACCRATE REPORT

Before you spend your first day behind the dean's desk, you will want to study a bit more about legal education. A quick primer is available in the form of the 338 pages of the *MacCrate Report* (plus 75 pages of appendices), but since you won't have time to read it before you begin your stint as dean, we'll help you test some of its key assumptions: (1) that students "lack an adequate understanding of the requirements for competent practice, the process by which a new member of the profession prepares for practice and attains competence, and the role that law schools play in that process" and (2) that an appreciation of the relevant skills and values, "can serve as an aid to law students in preparing for practice."

In your new job, as a new kind of dean, your focus is primarily the vibrancy and standing of your law school. We have little doubt, therefore, that you will want students to play an active role in setting the psychological and social tone of the law school with respect to such factors as the curriculum, co-curricular programs, and alumni relations. We also have little doubt that you will not want to abdicate your ultimate responsibility to run the law school to outsiders or even to inside partisans. You want students to join in a cooperative leadership role, not just follow, but you also understand that such an outcome requires that you know what you want to achieve through your law school's course of study, and why.

That's the easy part, though; it only requires that you know you. But even with self-understanding, you will have to make some assumptions about those with whom you work. For example, just as the MacCrate Report suggested would be a good thing, your instincts will be to assume that the entire law school community is committed to the important values that can be inferred from such standards as the ABA Model Rules of Professional Conduct (as interpreted through the various state standards): *Providing Competent Representation; Pursuing Justice, Fairness, and Morality; Improving the Legal Profession; Improving Oneself as a Lawyer.* Moreover, you will also want to assume that there is general agreement about the need to graduate students who, — to the highest degree achievable through legal education — have mastered and are committed to such MacCrate-type goals as:

- continuing competence in one's field of practice;
- promoting and assuring Justice, Fairness and Morality;
- ensuring access to legal services;
- improving legal institutions;
- participating in improving the legal profession;
- training and preparing new lawyers;
- fighting bias and invidious discrimination; and
- pursuing self-actualization.

It is in light of the above goals and values, therefore, that we ask you to consider the following overview. In other words, as Dean, you are now ready to test your assumptions against at least one version of the many possible realities you will have to face as the educational leader of the law school community. Read on.

C. YET ANOTHER LOOK AT THE LEGAL CONTINUUM

Periodically over the past quarter century, legal education has convulsed with one study after another addressing a supposed gap between the nation's largely academically oriented law schools and the practicing bar's more rudimentary needs for lawyers who are well-trained in the basics of delivering what clients *think* they are paying for: advocacy, drafting, negotiating, and client counseling. The 1983 Cramton Report[1]; the views summarized by the McKay Task Force (1991);[2] and the 1992 publication of the ABA's highly publicized *MacCrate Report*, can each be best understood as reflecting such historical episodes. And the cycle continues. Most recently the debate between the guild and the academy — a figurative effort to define legal education as taking place on a continuum with the law schools and the law firms as the end-points — is reflected in the reports of the Carnegie Foundation for the Advancement of Teaching, *Educating Lawyers: Preparation for the Profession of Law*[3] (2007) and the Clinical Legal Education Association's recently published *Best Practices for Legal Education*[4] (2007).

Indeed, a flare-up concerning the 2007 rewrite of Standard 302[5] warrants note almost entirely because of the behind the scenes uproar it created among the nation's law school deans. The amendments were intended to make more explicit the requirements for law

---

[1] Final Report of the Task Force on Professional Competence (1983).

[2] Appendix C, *Report of the Subcommittee on Hearings and Conferences of the Task Force on Law Schools and the Profession: Narrowing The Gap*, Robert B. McKay, Chair to July 1990 [Deceased], Cory M. Amron, Joseph D. Harbaugh and Harold L. Rock (October 1991).

[3] By William M. Sullivan, Anne Colby, Judith Welch Wegner, Lloyd Bond, Lee S. Shulman.

[4] Roy Stuckey and Others.

[5] Section of Legal Education and Admissions to the Bar, American Bar Association, Standards for Approval of Law Schools and Interpretations, Standard 302 (1998).

school accreditation under the Council of the Section of Legal Education and Admissions to the Bar's Standards for the Approval of Law Schools. Even after the comment period, however, the proposal was combustible enough to generate fear that the deans might take the unprecedented step of expressing their concerns through a formal statement expressing no-confidence in the approval process. They were incensed that the Council had provided for insufficient discussion of a provision backed by clinicians, which the deans believed would require more law school resources to be devoted to practical skills training. The objection was not to skills training per se, but to the concern that guild-like work rules were being insinuated into the accreditation process on behalf of clinicians — not of students — and others such as legal writing instructors and a narrow group of law firm interest. In the end, the deans were mollified, but not before characterizing the amendment as yet another instance of the organized bar acting like an old fashion trade association — this time in flagrant disregard of the deans' own obligations to speak for the broad interest of their law schools.

This is not to say that all law schools (or even a majority of them) omit, diminish, or are deficient in their attention to the critical functions of legal education. Nor do the facts suggest that most law firms believe that they are at risk of being unable to hire sufficient lawyers to provide (and bill for) what are euphemistically called *routine legal services.* To the contrary, notwithstanding loud claims by many outside the legal academy (and some within) that law professors are generally disdainful and dismissive of practitioners — and especially contemptuous of the idea that their students should become "mere practitioners" — the literature actually suggests that most on both sides of the debate would concede that it is not about whether any good is being done; it is about whether legal education can do better.

Ironically, too, what appears to many to be academic elitism may, instead, actually be a product of status- and profit-seeking competition within the practicing bar, itself. This would explain why the law firms most often portrayed as aligned with the law schools in pursuit of what critics see as the ideal of *the last great liberal education* tend to fall into three groups. In the first are the large and mega law firms, many of which provide their own training for new associates. In the second fall those firms that are corporate-oriented or self-described as "full-service." They do not accept the idea that there is a specific practice for which lawyers can be *trained* and they are critical of the bar for being traditional, hide-bound, and increasingly unwilling to compete like (and in cooperation with) other deliverers of professional services, such as doctors, accountants and engineers. And finally there is the third group of perennial mavericks: those firms describing themselves as legal boutiques — meaning that by their very nature they view themselves as practicing at the fast-paced frontiers of the law where the *routine* in any respect is viewed skeptically.

What binds the three groups in their opposition to those who would give higher priority to bridge the gap-type programs is not a lesser commitment to the goal of lawyer competence or the role of legal education in achieving it, but a fundamental difference of perspective about how that objective can best be achieved. Instead of viewing themselves and law schools as engaged in training students for what is sometimes derisively dismissed as *the trade of lawyering,* their message is that law schools are doing precisely what is (and has always been) needed of them: graduating increasingly well-educated students capable of assuming the responsibilities of a lawyer no-matter the ever-changing environment in which they must operate. For a substantial number, if not the vast majority of law firms, then, law schools and law firms are precisely in sync with respect to the desired balance that should exist. Although continually in need of recalibration, the academics and their allies within the legal profession agree that what graduating students should know and what law firms, themselves, should endeavor to teach their new associates ought strategically to be left only broadly defined.

But even if a truce can be hammered out between sides in the general war, there is still ample opportunity for the law schools' culture conflict to erupt in skirmishes between its most passionate partisans. Currently there are 200 ABA-accredited law schools and numerous state-accredited ones.[6] The battles on these varied fronts is a different, although related, battle to the one raging nationally — different, that is, from the fight about whether legal education's overarching purpose should be to provide a broad learning experience that equips students to teach themselves or an experience in which students are taught what they need to know about how to apply specific critical skills to the real-life problems of representing clients. Even if it is conceded that neither summary-profile does justice to the complexity of the other side's position, the caricatured descriptions of the sides in the big war makes clear that there is one point about which even the local partisans are in agreement: The larger, theoretical issues aside, there is a need — perhaps, simply because the opportunities appear so readily at hand — to make more efficient use educationally of some ubiquitous, but currently unused forums in which law students might be educated. Part-time employment situations, summer clerkships, externship placements and putting practitioners in the classrooms offer opportunities to advance legal education regardless of which side of the goals debate one comes down.

Part-time Employment

For instance, part-time student employment, where students work as clerks for law firms, government agencies, or the judiciary, have only barely begun to be officially incorporated into law school curriculums. To advance beyond currently accepted teaching activities such as classroom discussions of students' workplace diaries, however, will require that law schools embrace more fundamental change.

Chief among those changes will have to be a new consensus about how and where students learn best. Presently, for example, law schools do not schedule classes to accommodate the work-schedules that law firms set. Far from being accommodating, law school accreditation standards require reasonable measures to assure that students are not substantially employed — meaning more than about 10 hours per week for full-time students. This is one reason why mandated and bar exam related courses are commonly scheduled to assure that students are engaged in formal classroom study, rather than devoting hours to their employers. But at an even more fundamental level, law schools would need to accept that time taken away from the tightly structured, systematized presentations and reviews of materials in classrooms could more usefully be committed to non-professional instructors whose primary commitments are, first, to their clients, second to their firms, and only at some tertiary level to legal education.

Summer Employment

Similar concerns arise with respect to efforts to make summer employment part of the formal educational process. Proponents point out, for example, that in Commonwealth countries satisfactory completion of an apprenticeship program has long been a requirement for licensing. As the closest thing that we have in the United States to such a non-law school, experienced-based instruction, proponents urge that the hours spent by students in summer clerkships under the tutelage of practicing lawyers should be seen as adding reality and depth to the educational process. Such work allows students to experience situations, clients, and lawyers in ways that their casebooks can only describe.

---

[6] "As of June 2008, a total of 200 institutions . . . [were] approved by the American Bar Association: 199 confer the first degree in law (the J.D. degree); the other ABA approved school is the U.S. Army Judge Advocate General's School, which offers an officer's resident graduate course, a specialized program beyond the first degree in law. Eleven of the 200 law schools are provisionally approved." http://www.abanet.org/legaled/approvedlawschools/approved.html. [This site was last visited on, Nov. 5, 2008.]

That added benefit is, no doubt, why roughly a half-dozen jurisdictions continue the practice of allowing candidates to qualify to sit for the bar exam by serving apprenticeships, rather than graduating from law school. Under Vermont's Law Office Study Program, for example, what is required is that bar applicants complete three-fourths of their undergraduate degree requirements; complete twenty-five hours annually of in-service training under a licensed attorney (who is required to file detailed progress reports every six months with the state board of bar examiners); and pass Vermont's bar exam.

Externships

With respect to the third of the proposed experienced-based learning environments, externships, the chief difficulty in incorporating them into the formal curriculum largely mirrors the objections raised with respect to part-time and summer employment programs. In a phrase, "lack of supervision" captures it. For one thing, the quality of the employment experience is so apt to vary that law faculty have been loathe to attach substantial pedagogical value to it. Not only, as has been mentioned, are such real-world interactions conducted primarily for the client's sake (and not for purposes of advancing student learning), but the amount of faculty supervision required to coordinate and adequately monitor the workplace so that quality learning opportunities can be exploited is daunting. Even to enroll a small portion of the students in a typical law school in such a program would require enormous resources.

It is also difficult to forget the history of abuses that have occurred in the name of mandated work experiences. That history poses an immediate concern whether the suggested program involves part-time employment, summer employment, externships, or apprenticeships. In the 1980's, before an accreditation crack-down ended widespread abuses, several schools sought to develop reputations for innovativeness by virtually farming out their students to private practitioners, government law offices, and nonprofit organizations. The pitch was that everybody benefited because it meant additional free personnel for the law firms, a hoped-for inside track to a job for law students, and billable credit-hours for the law schools. The reality, however, was something the accreditors saw as potentially far less positive: poorly trained and exploited students; ill-served clients; students distracted from the classroom by the lure of real-world practice that might lead to a job; and the erosion of the law schools' standards and standing within and without the legal academy.

Optimism about efforts to promote student employment situations as the *new classrooms* has also been dimmed by another consideration: recognition that all of the experiential learning situations are subject to inherent conflicts of interest. First, there is the inherent pressure on both law schools and employers to keep overhead cost as low as possible. The more work employers can extract from students, the better off the employers are. Similarly, the more students the law school can place, the greater the tuition revenues. Second, there are the problems inherent in turning over the keys to the profession, as it were, to someone (or a group of some ones) who is an economic competitor. Unless someone other than the law firm employers are empowered to make and evaluate the placements, the need for strict oversight will be considerable. When a work experience is a requirement for graduation, it not only represents an enormous transfer of academic authority to nonacademic personnel, but also provides those who are currently lawyers significant sway over who can become a lawyer.

Nor is the situation improved much by having the placement experience come after graduation. Although such a delay lessens the bar's influence over who can graduate, it increases lawyers' ability to influence who will be admitted to practice. One needs only to recall the country's history with apprenticeship programs during the 1940s and '50s to recognize the dangers. Significant numbers of women and racial minorities found their entry to the legal profession blocked — not for lack of talent but for lack of the profession's interest in mentoring those with differences. Notwithstanding the progress that has been made over the last eighty years, therefore, it is worth considering whether women and minorities are confident enough with their status in the legal profession that they wish willingly to place their career prospects in the hands of their predominantly male, white, economic competitors.

Practitioners in the Classroom

There is, however, a fourth potential strategy for increasing skills training for law students. That proposal is to increase the number and frequency of lawyers serving as adjunct and visiting professors and professors practicing law. There are several anticipated benefits flowing in each direction. From the practitioners' side, we might expect practicing lawyers to devote more time to their teaching, perhaps even taking on responsibilities such as committee service, in an effort to truly integrate themselves into the life of the law school. We could also expect greater commitments of time by adjunct faculty members for such activities as office hours, attending (and speaking at) faculty colloquiums, and simply joining other faculty members for lunch or a cup of coffee in the lounge. Reciprocally, we can envision that faculty members might take up employment as lawyers with large and small law firms, in institutional and public service roles, and on behalf of government. Such placements would provide law professors the opportunity to immerse themselves in the details of practice, while simultaneously refreshing their lawyering skills and having the opportunity to assess the most current of issues facing the practice. Still, more than anything specific that might be envisioned from what we might call cross-professionalization, the real benefit is likely to be an increased respect and understanding of academics in practice and lawyers in academia.

Although the chief problems described above with respect to the potential for conflicts of interest are also associated with cross-professionalization efforts, the hope is that the increased exposure of lawyers and law professors will also carry with it sufficiently high visibility that participants will have little choice but to act cooperatively and competently. Should that hope prove overly optimistic, we will be faced with the same problems of lawyers attempting to balance their need, first, to serve their clients; second to sustain an income; and only thirdly to educate the next generation of lawyers. Ironically, too, in the cross-professionalization context, the protections of the ivory tower will no longer be available to lawyers turned practioners. Law professors engaged in the practice of law will soon find that their obligations, too, are conflicted. The same duty to put the needs of the client (and perhaps even income) ahead of the obligations of teaching, scholarship and service will apply.

Still we can take comfort in the knowledge that although the exploration for alternative means of advancing legal education remains fraught with controversy, there seems little likelihood of alternatives that do not involve compromises emerging. Either the legal profession, as a whole, will embrace the idea of working together to resolve problems or we can brace ourselves for yet another study addressing a supposed gap between the nation's largely academically oriented law schools and the practicing bar.

NOTES AND QUESTIONS

1. ***What Are Your Priorities?*** You've just read some other people's ideas about how legal education ought to be changed. Do you now have a focus for what needs to be done? What do you plan to do first to improve legal education? In particular, would you add more practice-oriented courses? If so, how would you staff them — more full-time, tenured or tenure-track professors, or practitioners serving as adjunct professors, or non-tenure track jobs for clinicians and other "skills" teachers, or in some other way?

2. ***Where's the Money?*** Does your school have the money to implement your ideas? If not, where should the school get the money? Cut existing programs or salaries? Raise tuition? Tap new fundraising sources?

3. ***U.S. News & World Report.*** As Dean, how much importance do you attach to the annual rankings in U.S. News & World Report? The MacCrate Report was written before U.S. News & World Report began their efforts to provide an annual quality

ranking of U. S. law schools. Although both the ABA Council on Legal Education and Admission to the Bar and the Association of American Law Schools continue to disparage such efforts as empirically unsound, factually misleading, incomplete, and self-serving, the annual rankings have grown in importance. They are an important contributor to the cash-flow of its publisher; a decision-making tool for student-applicants; and a propaganda source for university and college presidents, rival law schools, and the law school's fidgety alumni, friends and supporters.

The situation surrounding the U.S. News rankings has deteriorated precipitously. Hardly a year goes by without another revelation about how some law school has "gamed" the law school rankings process in order to achieve the appearance of higher quality (meaning a higher U.S. News ranking). For example, law schools have reportedly used the following strategies (tricks? schemes?) to improve their rankings in U.S. News:

- Undertaking massive publicity campaigns, complete with Hollywood-style swag books, glossy brochures, magazines and calendars, either as a year-round campaign or as an Oscar-style initiative, strategically launched to reach likely voters just before their ballots are due to be returned to U.S. News;
- Acquiescing in efforts by alumni in nearby major law firms to use law firm resources secretly to conduct a publicity campaign in the law school's name;
- Sending letters of rejection to the most highly credentialed students the school could identify — even absent any realistic chance that the students might actually desire to attend the law school — in order to increase the selectivity of the school's admission profile;
- "Buying" highly credentialed applicants by awarding full and full-plus scholarships for those who agree to attend the school;
- Declining to report graduation-day employment figures for graduating seniors in order to force U.S. News to substitute a statistical average that is higher than the school could actually have reported;
- Initiating a summer admissions program so that otherwise modestly credentialed students can be admitted during a semester other than the fall semester, when they would drag-down the profile of the admitted class (U.S. News counts only the students admitted for the fall semester);
- Artificially limiting the number of qualified-but-modestly-credentialed applicants the law school admits in order not to lower the admission profile;
- Declining to admit applicants, but advising them that if they enroll at another law school then they will be approved for transfer after their first year (U.S. News does not count transfer students in a law school's first year admission profile);
- Improving the faculty/student ratio by limiting faculty leaves to the spring semester so that a larger number of faculty can be counted as teaching during the fall semester, when U.S. News calculates the student/faculty ratio;
- Adding legal writing instructors (or other faculty members with less than full faculty status) to the faculty rolls in order to increase the faculty/student ratio;
- Monetizing the value of Lexis and Westlaw (and other vendors), then allocating the value across the student body as a law school contribution towards financial aid;
- Redesignating faculty who are engaged in administrative work as non-administrative full-time faculty members who merely "advise" the school's administrative staff about law school administration (thus increasing the number of full-time faculty and improving the faculty/student ratio);
- Counting emeritus faculty, visiting faculty, and faculty members on leave as part of the faculty head-count (again, to improve the faculty/student ratio); and
- Recalculating the university's overhead contribution to the law school (e.g., lights, heat, security, shuttle transportation, university-allocated student

> scholarships) in order to increase the average financial support that the law school provides to each student.

Are any of these practices acceptable, moral, or ethical? Are any unacceptable, immoral, or unethical? Can law schools that engage in such practices credibly claim to be committed to promoting ethics and professionalism? Is this the classic problem of "who will watch the watchman"? If so, who will?

The MacCrate Report assumed that ethics and professionalism are transmitted when professors inculcate skills and values in students. Professor Powell disagrees. He sees professional growth as a natural product of continuously evolving interactions of people and technology over time. Thus, as the profession grows more diverse (by, for example, gender, race, wealth, and class) and new technologies are introduced (e.g., Google, iPod, the Internet, Wi-Fi, and Smartboards), new possibilities for thinking and acting present themselves. The process is open-ended, evolutionary, and continuous, as new and old members of the profession are constantly challenged by previously unimagined circumstances and possibilities. For the sake of survival, relevancy, and primacy, each segment of the profession borrows and adapts what is worthwhile, integrating what is useful and discarding the rest (e.g., an outmoded rule, process, or style).

As Frans Johansson observed in THE MEDICI EFFECT: BREAKTHROUGH INSIGHTS AT THE INTERSECTION OF IDEAS, CONCEPTS & CULTURES, 23–24 (2004) with respect to one powerful diversity factor, *immigration*:

> This force [immigration] will lead to a plethora of cultural intersections and a host of groundbreaking ideas for those bold enough to explore them. Cross-cultural ideas will be more easily introduced to a more diverse audience. . . . [As] when the Latin American artist Shakira . . . shot to the top of the charts. . . . [with] . . . songs [that] combined Arabic and Latin sounds . . . .

If we view the transmittal of professional skills and values as a process by which the old inculcate the young, don't we risk missing the intersections? Are we putting law schools in the proverbial predicament of old military generals, who are always fighting the last war?

Enough emphasis on values? Assuming that, as the new Dean, you are comfortable about what skills and values are needed for future lawyers, the question remains whether your law school places enough emphasis on values as opposed to skills? Is law school even the right place to inculcate values? If not, where is the right place?

NOTES AND QUESTIONS

1. ***How Valuable Are Skills Courses?*** Does your school offer enough skills courses (e.g., live-client clinics, pre-trial practice, trial techniques, appellate advocacy, interviewing and counseling, negotiation and alternative dispute resolution, and business planning and drafting)? Have you taken advantage of whatever offerings exist? If so, were they worth your time? If you have not taken skills courses, why not?

2. ***What About Your Law School?*** Has your law school embarked on any programs to improve the educational value of part-time legal work? If not, should it?

3. ***What Will Work?*** Of the ideas you have just read, which ones do you think will work? Which ones won't?

4. ***What Can You Afford?*** Some of the ideas above sound expensive. Others don't. What can you afford to implement?

5. ***What Are the Law School's Options?*** If you can't afford to implement some of the ideas that you want to implement, where will you get the money? Remember the three basic choices: (1) cut existing programs or salaries, (2) raise tuition, or (3) raise more

money. Of course, you can use these methods in combination. Which methods do you intend to use if you need more money?

6. ***Another Option?*** Thus far, we have focused on what a law school can do to enhance and expand the educational experience. Consider, though, whether law firms themselves might do more. The MacCrate Report, published in 1992, is now more than fifteen years old. From its publication to the present, however, few law firms of any kind (whether large, medium, small, or solo) have declared that experience-based learning is such a high priority that the firm will no longer even interview a law graduate who has not taken a clinical course or participated in an employment program supervised by the law school. If a significant number of law firms in your area made such a declaration, what would be the effect? Has the legal profession tried to have it both ways or is there some other reason that law firms have resisted putting pressure on law students to take courses that are more practice oriented?

7. ***Has the Continuum Broken Down?*** During the 1970s, law firms — including even some small law firms — hired new graduates at the beginning of their careers with the expectation that the graduates would not do much work at the firm during the summer after graduation but would instead devote the majority of their time to studying for the bar. What is the current expectation? Has the profession experienced a paradigm shift, as a result of which the legal profession now views law schools as having the responsibility to deliver finished lawyers — turn-key style — to law firms in exchange for the payment of high starting salaries? Is this a fair trade-off? But if the big firms justify shifting the education obligation on the basis of their high salaries, how does that explain the conduct of small firm and solo practitioners, who seem to have the same expectations but do not pay high salaries?

8. ***Has the Profession Lost Its Way?*** On the basis of what you have read in this chapter, is the legal profession experiencing a decline in professionalism or merely a change of behavior over time as it deals with new interactions of peoples and technologies?

Chapter 34

WHO ARE THE LAWYERS?

"Who are the lawyers?" To ask this question is to ask many different questions at once. How many lawyers are there in America? Where do they work? How many work for private firms, how many for government, how many for corporations, how many for public interest organizations? Of the lawyers in private practice, how many lawyers are solo practitioners? How many work for small firms, medium firms, or large firms? This is a broad and complex topic. We discuss it only briefly.

"Who are the lawyers?" is also a question about diversity. How many lawyers are male, and how many are female? How many lawyers are African-American or Hispanic, or Asian or some other minority? These are narrower questions, and they are the questions on which we will focus in this book.

A. THE GROWTH OF THE LEGAL PROFESSION

The phenomenal growth in the number of lawyers since World War II has been accompanied by an unprecedented increase in demand for legal work, both from business clients and on behalf of previously unrepresented individuals. One result has been that by 1990 the profession had become a $91 billion-a-year service industry, employing more than 940,000 people, and surpassing the medical profession in the number of licensed professionals, with one lawyer for every 320 persons in the United States.

In 1992 the Council of the ABA Section of Legal Education and Admissions to the Bar — the entity that oversees accreditation of law schools — published the Report of the Task Force on Law Schools and the Profession: Narrowing the Gap (*The MacCrate Report*). The report offered a list of recommendations for improving legal education and, as the most prominent of several reports issued between 1992 and 2007, continues to serve as an important historical reference about the transformation of the legal profession that began some half-century ago, following the end of the Korean War — a period that we will simply refer to as the modern era. As Abe Krash, an attorney whose practice spanned 50 years of that period, noted in *The Changing Legal Profession*, a chronicle for the DC Bar's *For Lawyers* column (*available at*, http://www.dcbar.org/for_lawyers/resources/publications/washington_lawyer/january_2008/changes.cfm (last visited, March 8, 2008)) the modern era represents some sharp changes from most students grandfather's generation:

> [A] present-day young attorney, viewing a practice in 1950, would be struck, among other things, by the much smaller size of law firms, the almost complete absence of women and minority lawyers, and the lack of computers and other sophisticated communication devices.

The most striking changes affecting the practice of law might, thus, be summarized in five words: size, gender, color, concentration, and technology. The last of these hardly needs explanation; technology — cell phones, e-mails, the Internet, notebook computers, video conferencing, and more — has changed the speed at which law is practiced as well as the depth and precision associated with the variety of communications related to the practice of law. The other considerations, however, also define what it means to be a lawyer in the 21st Century. To speak of size, for instance, is to appreciate that every lawyer is one of about a million other individuals. It is a large number, but more importantly, it represents a huge force engaged in a common calling. What's more, the profession it represents continues to grow in size and impact. Today there are not only more lawyers, but larger law firms, more paralegals, investigators, forensic experts, technicians, and support staff; more office space devoted to lawyering; more law schools; more law students; and, yes, more money (estimated at over a $100 billion-a-year) devoted to the delivery of legal services.

But mission and aspirations aside, it is the kinds of people who make up today's legal profession who are the most dramatic aspect of the change. The legal profession is long past the time when the county docket call was as much about gathering the old boys' club as it was about judicial administration, but the effects still linger. In part, today we measure ourselves as a profession in relation to how unthinkable it would be for any responsible voice to echo the views of Justice Bradley's concurrence in *Bradwell v. Illinois*, 16 Wall. (83 U. S.) 130, 140–141 (1873), holding that it was not a denial of Equal Protection for Illinois to refuse to license a woman to practice law, because:

> [T]he right of females to pursue any lawful employment for a livelihood assumes that it is one of the privileges and immunities of women as citizens to engage in any and every profession, occupation, or employment in civil life. It certainly cannot be affirmed, as an historical fact, that this has ever been established as one of the fundamental privileges and immunities of the sex. On the contrary, the civil law, as well as nature herself, has always recognized a wide difference in the respective spheres and destinies of man and woman. Man is, or should be, woman's protector and defender. The natural and proper timidity and delicacy which belongs to the female sex evidently unfits it for many of the occupations of civil life.

To our credit, we count the number of women in the legal profession today at about a third of the nation's lawyers, although it continues to be the case that a much smaller percentage of them (roughly 18% nationwide) are partners at major law firms. Still, the long-term trend looks good; about one-half of the nation's law school students are women, as are about half of the newly-hired lawyers each year.

The color of the profession has also changed. African Americans, who total about 50,000 (or 5%), still make up the largest number of people of color, but the numbers of Hispanic/Latino lawyers has grown to about 30,000 (or 3%) and those who are Asian Americans — the fastest growing racial demographic — constitute about 29,000.

Almost as significant as the changes in the demographics of the profession, though, has been a continuing evolution in what lawyers do. In 1975, when Professors John P. Heinz and Edward O. Laumann published CHICAGO LAWYERS: THE SOCIAL STRUCTURE OF THE BAR (Russell Sage Foundation, 1982), they reported that Chicago lawyers were primarily engaged with the problems of people. However, their follow-up study twenty years later, URBAN LAWYERS: THE NEW SOCIAL STRUCTURE OF THE BAR (University of Chicago Press, 2005), noted a dramatic shift: "[B]y the mid-1990s the corporate area of practice had become more than twice as big as the personal and small business sector of Chicago lawyers."

NOTES AND QUESTIONS

Has the Legal Profession Grown Too Fast? Is this even a meaningful question (or simply a political or economic gibe)? We have just considered some of the ramifications of the growth of the legal profession as a consequence of rapid acceleration beginning in the mid-1960's. It certainly makes the case for asking, "Is this a good thing?" But in a free, democratic society such as ours — where individual freedom and the free market are sacrosanct and virtually synonymous, shouldn't we ask a broader question: For whom is it a good thing that there has been a significant growth in the number of lawyers?

B. LET'S TAKE A SECOND LOOK!

We have elsewhere referenced The MacCrate Report (1992), but without placing it in the historical context that gave rise to it — a period when many conservative political and economic voices looked with alarm at a transformation that was taking place in terms of the United State's demographics, economy, and international standing. These were turbulent times which saw the break-up of the Soviet Union (1991), the collapse of apartheid in South Africa (1994), and most significantly for lawyers, the transformation of the U.S. economy in terms of debt — moving from the status of creditor to debtor nation in 1985 — and globalization (with the signing of NAFTA (1992) and the WTO (1995). It was a time when even many thoughtful voices foresaw an end to "The American Century." The future was thought to belong to the rising new "Seven Tiger" economies of Asia, led by the supposedly leaner and meaner economic mavens of "Japan Inc.," which had boomed during much of the 1980s. And, regrettably, it was also a time when the search for explanations for the dramatic turn of economic events in the U.S. often led to facile answers targeting the legal profession. Indeed, you may be aware of some of the wildest claims. In case you aren't — since we were not, ourselves, immune from such excesses — we have saved a few comments from our earlier edition:

1. The Japanese, who *license* many more engineers than lawyers[1], have a saying: "Lawyers only know how to carve up a pie, but engineers know how to make the pie grow larger."
2. Our society would be better off if fewer people would go into law and more people would go into other, more useful professions.
3. Not enough lawyers serve the poor and the middle class.
4. The number of law students enrolled in J.D. programs has increased every year since 1985. (Applications peaked at 99,300 in 1991, but enrollment has continued to increase.) In 1993–1994, according to the ABA, there were 43,644 first year students and 127,802 law students in J.D. programs in accredited law schools. Dean Robert Clark of Harvard Law School predicts that at current growth rates, in thirty years "there will be more lawyers than people."

The point is not that the Jeremiads of the '90s were completely wrong, but that the world looks a lot different decades later. We now know, for instance, that when the Berlin Wall fell on November 9, 1989, symbolizing the end of Eastern European Communist rule, the call that went out from Russia and most of the rest of the former Eastern Bloc for U.S. assistance was both surprising and reaffirming. The assistance requested was hardly for our engineers — or even our doctors, scientists, or teachers. Confronted with the challenge of operating in a global economy, the emerging capitalist recognized the need to establish new economic and political regimes. And what they wanted as much as American capital was American-style lawyering — especially transaction and criminal defense lawyers. You know, the folks who don't make anything.

The world did not turn to Japan for innovative economic or social leadership. Having exploited its two-track lawyer system for several decades — a system in the European mode that educates thousands of students in the law, as undergraduates, but then limits those able to gain licensure to a ratio involving the number of judges and prosecutors — what was once touted as "Japan Inc." now shows signs of envying the American Model that was so recently caricatured. Kana Inagaki's August 22, 2006 report for the Associated Press, "Major Legal Reforms Expected to Bring Wave of New Lawyers in Japan," suggests that the Japanese — seemingly admitting to the realities of being a post-industrial, communications-age, advanced capitalist democracy operating in a global economy — have recently slated a major overhaul of the Japanese legal system. By 2018 they will, among other things, vastly increase the number of lawyers, judges and prosecutors; create more civil and criminal law specialists; and add to the already growing number of more than 72 American-style, graduate-level, law schools, many of which come complete with Socratic-style teaching.

As if by Adam Smith's invisible hand, today it is the United States economy that benefits from increasing numbers of lawyers choosing to practice outside the civil/

---

[1] Note the qualified language we have used here: "license" as opposed to "produce." Because law is an undergraduate degree in much of the world, speaking of a country's production of lawyers may understate the fact that on a per capita basis the country may be producing more persons who are trained in the law than does the United States. This is a point we elaborate upon in the principle text.

criminal justice system. Along with the growth of in-house counsel positions, the profession has also seen the growth of the non-lawyer-lawyer (including the multidisciplinary practice lawyer).

Perhaps even more pertinent to the changed circumstances in which we view lawyers today are factors related to the information and technology revolution that was well underway by the mid-90s. Even if the longest period of economic expansion in the history of the nation cannot be seen as reflecting, at least in part, the role that lawyers play in our economy, the one thing that is sure is that changes in technology now allow lawyers to do more, faster, cheaper and more expertly than at any time in history. So, consider the following suggestion that, like the nose-counting critics arguing two decades ago that there were too many lawyers, the MacCrate Report also missed the point in failing to see the longer-term issues confronting the profession and the nation.

BURNELE VENABLE POWELL,* SOMEWHERE FARTHER DOWN THE LINE: MACCRATE ON MULTICULTURALISM AND THE INFORMATION AGE

69 WASH. L. REV. 637 (1994)[2]

III. AN OVERVIEW OF THE PROFESSION — GAPS AND ALL. WHOSE CONTINUUM? WHOSE VALUES? WHOSE SKILLS?

. . . The inherent limits of . . . MacCrate's diorama of the profession are best illustrated by the Report's treatment of the professional emergence of two groups: women and minorities. MacCrate notes, for example, that the most significant change during the 1970s and 1980s was, perhaps, the growth in the number of women choosing the law as a career. This change came first in the law schools and then throughout the legal profession. Women students in ABA-approved law schools, for example, increased from approximately 4 percent in the mid-1960s to more than 40 percent in the 1990s. This change apart, the pace at which women have entered the profession is dramatically at odds with the rate at which women have assumed power positions. Considerations such as age and tenure have continued to limit access by women to positions of power.

Although MacCrate correctly noted that the legal profession is moving in the direction of gender equality, its discussion of the emergence of women in the profession does not profess to go beyond demographic concerns. In an overview that is remarkable only for its almost militant insistence on simply running the numbers, MacCrate's concerns are with asking whether women are present, rather than why; how many, rather than to what effect; and under what conditions, rather than with what potential. Because these concerns are essentially queries about status, the profession that MacCrate models is, not surprisingly, one in which the concerns of women lawyers are personal and intra-professional (e.g., pregnancy, rape, sexual harassment in the workplace, judicial treatment of domestic violence, sexual relations between attorneys and clients, gender stereotyping and biases within the practice, courts, and the profession).

Missing from MacCrate is the wider discussion of the *diversity duality*: what the gender diversification of the profession in combination with enhanced communications (and the access to ideas that it represents) is likely to mean to the profession's ability to deliver services to clients. It is essential that there be a historical record of the status of women within the profession, but the reality remains that most women are not members of the profession. Furthermore, of those who are, any optimistic view must assume that few entered the profession to focus on their own status. The drive to make gender irrelevant in its invidious applications to the practice of law is first, and

* Professor Powell was then-Professor of Law, University of North Carolina.

[2] Footnotes have been omitted.

foremost, a drive to transform the lives and vindicate the interests of clients, no matter the client's gender.

Similarly, in discussing the formal opening of the legal profession to lawyers from racial, ethnic, religious and cultural minorities, MacCrate's approach is chronological, demographic, and descriptive. It takes note, for example, that black lawyers were formally excluded from the legal profession until 1943, and that it was not until 1950 that the first African-American lawyer was knowingly admitted to the ABA. Relying on an analysis by the National Bar Association Magazine of the status of African-American lawyers, MacCrate noted that 80 percent of all black lawyers were in 10 states, and have a practice profile which is "at marked variance with the distribution of majority lawyers."

MacCrate's focus, however, is again on status concerns such as the statistics of minorities within the profession as it looks to "the advances of the past two decades and . . . [the] promise for the future." The report concludes that a "promising beginning" has been made, but "[T]he goal of equal opportunity within the profession is still a long way from realization." As with its treatment of the significance of gender diversification, however, MacCrate's overview presents the issue of racial diversification from the least interesting perspective. Rather than discuss how, if at all, the entry of African-Americans into the profession is likely to affect the delivery of legal services, the application of legal principles, or public acceptance of the rule of law, MacCrate is satisfied simply to note the presence of African-American lawyers.

Thus, in laying the foundation for its discussion of the important skills and values requisite for the education of lawyers, MacCrate's concern with the legal profession's demographic changes reflects its desire to establish the diversity of the profession only as a predicate for its argument that the unitary concept of being a lawyer is in jeopardy. The need to view skills and values as a part of a professional crusade to overcome differences, however, rests on an assumption that is unstated and unexamined: that we can know in any meaningful sense whose values and what skills the future will demand.

NOTES AND QUESTIONS

1. ***Do Lawyers (and Law Students) Have a Special Obligation to Join in This Debate?*** Is it clear who has the upper hand in the debate about the future of the legal profession? What is your sense of where the legal profession is — where it's going — today? How have you come to have those views? What is your reason for being in law school? Why do you think most of your classmates are in law school? Why do you think most lawyers practice law? Compare your answers to these questions with the answers of your classmates.

2. ***How Many Lawyers Are There, Anyway?*** By the way, just how many lawyers are there? The ABA has counted them. There were over 1.1 million lawyers actively practicing in the United States as of 2008 (*viz.*, individuals who were both *educated* in the law and *licensed*) — more than in any other country in the world. Moreover, this count focuses only on the gross numbers and does not take into account *non-lawyer-lawyers*, or even dares to think about more sophisticated measures, such as lawyers as a function of the size of the economy in which they practice. But consider the following discussion.

MARC GALANTER*, "NEWS FROM NOWHERE: THE DEBASED DEBATE ON CIVIL JUSTICE"**

71 DENV. U.L. REV. 77-114 (1993)

Public discussion of our civil justice system resounds with a litany of quarter-truths: America is the most litigious society in the course of all human history; Americans sue at the drop of a hat; the courts are brimming over with frivolous lawsuits; courts are a first rather than a last resort; runaway juries make capricious awards to undeserving claimants; immense punitive damage awards are routine; litigation is undermining our ability to compete economically. Each of these is false, but in a complicated way; so let me address this structure of myth, starting with some of the more specific assertions and moving on to the sweeping generalities.

I. Too Many Lawyers?

The first example is the assertion that the United States is home to seventy percent of the world's lawyers. Dropped casually by Vice President Quayle in his August 1991 speech to the American Bar Association (ABA), it was parroted by President Bush, Cabinet members, members of Congress and media experts, and became a familiar factoid in the rhetoric of the 1992 campaign.

This is certainly an alarming figure. It suggests a monstrous deviation from the rest of the world and insinuates that lawyers are a kind of cancerous excrescence on American society. As someone who has studied lawyers comparatively, I wondered how this percentage was determined. Looking at the supporting Council on Competitiveness documents, I could find no sign of anything that could be called a calculation. The seventy percent figure seems to be a retread of an item that surfaced a decade ago, having no apparent terrestrial origin, that the United States had two-thirds of the world's lawyers. The two-thirds item was retailed by Chief Justice Burger as part of his indictment of litigious America. It was subsequently used by Justice O'Connor and others, and became part of the speeches of Governor Lamm of Colorado about America's descent to doom. After the round-up to seventy percent in 1991, the two-thirds figure dropped out of use, apart from a reappearance in the Republican Platform.

Counting lawyers cross-nationally is a daunting undertaking, plagued by poor data and a bushel of apples and oranges problems. However these are resolved, it is clear that the seventy percent figure is very far from the mark. An informed guess would be something less than half of that. Counting conservatively, American lawyers make up less than a third and probably somewhere in the range of one-quarter of the world's lawyers, using that term to refer to all those in jobs that American lawyers do (including judges, prosecutors, government lawyers and in-house corporate lawyers).

Is that too many? It is roughly the United States's proportion of the world's gross national product (GNP) and less than our percentage of the world's expenditures on scientific research and development. America is a highly legalized society that relies on law and courts to do many things that other industrial democracies do differently. For a long time the United States has supported far higher numbers of lawyers per capita than nations with comparable economies. There is no reason to think American lawyers are less efficient than their counterparts elsewhere, although it appears they are called upon to do more than lawyers elsewhere. This is perhaps due to the dispersal of wealth, the fragmentation of authority, the absence of traditional elites or other reasons. In the past generation the number of lawyers increased dramatically from 285,933 in 1960 to 655,191 in 1985 — an increase of 129%. But this recent growth is not a distinctly

---

* Evjue-Bascom Professor of Law and South Asian Studies, Director of the Institute for Legal Studies, University of Wisconsin — Madison

** Copyright 1993, Marc Galanter. The Martin P. Miller Centennial Lecture, delivered at the University of Denver College of Law, October 2, 1992.

American phenomenon. The number of lawyers has been increasing everywhere — in many places at a faster rate than in the United States. For example, in the same period the number of lawyers increased by 147% in England and by 253% in Canada, while the number of private practitioners in Germany increased by 156%.

What is striking about the seventy percent figure is not that the estimate was so overblown, but that those who peddled it had reason to know it was a tall tale and that neither Vice-President Quayle nor anyone else who thought it was a relevant fact deemed it important to make an informed, rather than a wild, guess.

However, the United States' lawyer totals compare with those of others, we do have more lawyers and many lament this condition. The President's Council on Competitiveness deplored the "baleful effects" of having too many lawyers. The principal intellectual foundation for the view that lawyers hurt the economy is the work of University of Texas finance professor Stephen Magee. Magee has tried to show that the countries with the highest lawyer populations suffer from impaired economic growth. Magee's conclusion is wrong. His first version was shown to be false and his latest version is no stronger. The best research on the topic reaches entirely different conclusions.

In Magee's first take on this issue, he claimed that all lawyers are economically destructive. Apart from being silly on its face, that conclusion resulted from an empirical analysis containing major methodological errors. His analysis compared the lawyer populations and economic growth rates of 34 countries, and concluded that the more lawyers a country has, the lower is its rate of growth. That analysis is shot through with problems. First, Magee relied on poor lawyer data — his lawyer figures for several countries were substantially incorrect. Second, he employed a peculiar research design that used lawyer data in 1983 to predict economic growth from 1960 to 1985 — even though his own figures showed that the number of lawyers in 1983 bore little relation to the number in 1960. Third, Magee's research did not take into account ("control for") any other known influences on economic growth, including such powerful influences as a country's level of political instability. Finally, the conclusion resulted in large part from the coincidence of low economic growth rates and high lawyer populations in two "outliers" (Argentina and Nepal), whose legal systems and economies bear little relation to our own.

After critics pointed out those failings, Magee refurbished his research, and now claims that only lawyers above a certain optimal number hurt an economy. Stated that simply, the view has an intuitive plausibility: surely if all Americans were lawyers and did nothing else, our economy would have problems. Magee's leap to the conclusion that there are, in fact, too many lawyers in the United States is a different matter.

. . . .

Careful analyses of the effect of lawyers on the economy find no support for the Magee hypothesis; indeed, they find that lawyers have no significant effect at all on overall economic growth. The Magee analysis rests on many of the familiar but unproven contentions about the civil justice system. He assumes that the presence of "excess" lawyers is evidenced by the presence of "predatory" litigation, as distinguished from justified or beneficial litigation. But he provides no evidence of the frequency of bad litigation independent of the conclusion that there are too many lawyers.

II. The Cost of the Legal System

Another count in the indictment of the civil justice system is its excessive cost. Vice-President Quayle reported that "the legal system . . . now costs Americans an estimated $ 300 billion a year. . . . " This figure seems to derive from the Agenda for Civil Justice Reform of the President's Council on Competitiveness, which starts its accounting of litigation costs by stating:

> A recent article in *Forbes* estimates that individuals, business and governments spend more than $ 80 billion a year on direct litigation costs and higher insurance premiums and a total of up to $ 300 billion indirectly, including the cost of efforts to avoid liability.

Forbes didn't actually conduct any analysis of its own: the authors of a story on plaintiffs' lawyers cited publicist Peter Huber who, they recounted:

> focused attention on the total "tort tax" on the economy. Huber estimates that individuals, businesses and governments pay at least $ 80 billion a year directly, in such ways as litigation costs and higher insurance premiums, and a total of $ 300 billion indirectly, counting the cost of efforts to avoid liability.

Huber proffered these figures in his 1988 book in the course of equating tort liability with a tax [that] directly costs American individuals, businesses, municipalities and other government bodies at least $ 80 billion a year, a figure that equals the total profits of the country's top 200 corporations. But many of the tax's costs are indirect and unmeasurable. . . . The extent of these indirect costs can only be guessed at. . . .

Huber does not report any investigation or analysis of his own. Instead, he cites two sources. For the eighty billion direct cost figure he gives a citation to Chief Executive [M]agazine that turns out to be a round table discussion among executives. In the course of that discussion, Robert Malott, chairman and CEO of FMC, and a prominent Republican fundraiser and the Business Roundtable's "point man on product liability," devoted a single sentence to the magnitude of liability costs:

> It's estimated that insurance liability costs industry about $ 80 billion a year, roughly the equivalent of the profitability of the top 200 corporations in the U.S. The number of liability lawsuits has risen over 10 years by 600 percent.

. . . .

For the move from eighty to three hundred billion, Huber multiplies eighty billion by three and half — and rounds up. The three and half multiplier is taken from an editorial in the Journal of the American Medical Association that refers to a study of practice changes attributed to malpractice by physicians surveyed in 1984. Thus Huber's "estimate" consists of multiplying the undocumented surmise of Mr. Malott by the ratio of physician-reported changes to malpractice insurance premiums. There is no discussion of the representativeness of this species of liability, of this segment of time, or of the suitability of this measure.

Even though Malott . . . appears to have addressed the costs of product liability, Huber adopted his figure as an estimate of the direct cost of all tort litigation. When the estimate, if that is the term, was adopted by the *Forbes* writers it was as the cost of all torts. The Council on Competitiveness and Vice-President Quayle, who purported to address the entire civil justice system, present these borrowed figures as the cost of all civil litigation to the United States economy.

. . . .

Quite apart from their origin in conjecture and the vacillation about just what is being measured, most "cost of litigation" figures have two deeper and more significant flaws. First, they conflate costs and transfers. A significant portion of the wealth that flows through the litigation system is compensation delivered to creditors and wronged parties to which they are entitled under the going rules. This half (or more) of the supposed cost is a cost to defendants, but it is not a cost of the system or a cost to the country, for the wealth is not lost but only transferred to different hands. That it costs so much to effectuate these rightful transfers is a scandal — but controlling these transaction costs should not be confounded with reducing the rights of claimants. Second, they talk about costs in isolation from benefits. Our accounts should reflect not only the costs but the benefits of enforcing such transfers, which afford vindication, induce investments in safety, and deter undesirable behavior. For instance, the sums transferred by successful patent infringement litigation are not only not lost, but maintain the credibility of the patent system which in turn creates powerful incentives. To put forward estimates of gross costs — even ones that are not make-believe — as a guide to policy displays indifference to the vital functions that the law performs. America's institutions of remedy and accountability and the lawyers that staff them are portrayed as burdensome afflictions. They are viewed as costs and thus as deadweight losses.

. . . .

III. The Competitiveness Charge

Many nasty effects have been attributed to lawyers and litigation. Earlier critiques of the civil justice system focused on the erosion of community, the decline of self-reliance, the atrophy of informal self-regulatory mechanisms, and the fostering of a corrosive adversary culture. In the latest round, these have been eclipsed by concern that the civil justice system is undermining the country's economic performance. . . . Escalating product liability litigation is blamed for undermining competitiveness by raising costs, diverting investment, and discouraging innovation. That product liability litigation is increasing inexorably, driven by the greed of entrepreneurial lawyers, the wrongheadedness of activist judges, and the rising litigiousness of ordinary Americans is a key count in the indictment of America's civil justice system.

. . . .

Is it legitimate to "put aside" asbestos cases? Asbestos litigation is a painful problem that displays much of the worst about our system of litigation — high costs, repetitive litigation, severe delays, and inconsistent awards. Asbestos litigation presents a problem of assuring justice to victims (and to their injurers). It also presents a problem of congestion in many courts. But each of these — the justice problem and the congestion problem — is quite distinct from the supposed problem of excessive product liability litigation debilitating the American economy.

. . . .

Eventually, there will be no more asbestos cases, as the pool of victims is depleted. This is due first to the deadly effects of asbestos, and secondly to the powerful preventive effects produced by the asbestos litigation. No one can say that we cannot have another such epidemic about another product. But if we did it too would be distinct from the pattern of ordinary product liability litigation. It would have no effect on the fortunes of the companies that make the tens of thousands of other products.

If we turn to those other companies, it would appear that they have experienced a significant decrease in their exposure to product liability cases. It is possible, of course, that product liability claims increased . . . even while case filings decreased — because more claims are paid without the filing of a lawsuit or because larger numbers of claims are combined into single filings. But those who point to the burden of product liability law have provided no evidence that either of these eventualities has occurred. It might be objected that our figures are only for filing in federal courts. It is well known that the vast majority of civil cases are brought in state courts. The federal court data is not necessarily representative of trends in the state courts, where the great bulk of cases are brought.

No one knows the total amount of product liability litigation in the state courts. Only a handful of states count these cases separately on a regular basis. There is some scattered evidence, however, from which we can derive a rough sense of the presence of product liability claims in the state courts. We do know that product liability is much less prominent in state court dockets than in the federal courts. Several studies suggest that product liability cases make up only two or three percent of the tort cases in state courts. For example, a National Center for State Courts study found that in one month in 1988 product liability made up 2.1% of tort filings in twenty-four large urban trial courts. That year product liability cases were thirty-six percent of tort filings in the federal courts.

We can infer that a sizable portion of product liability litigation takes place in the federal courts. The prominence of federal courts in the world of product liability is shown by a General Accounting Office study that examined product liability litigation for the years 1983 through 1985 in five states. It found that forty-six percent of the cases tried to verdict were tried in the federal courts. It appears that federal courts are the site of one third or more of all product liability litigation. Since the federal cases on the whole involve higher stakes, it is probable that most of the money that is awarded in product liability cases is awarded in the federal courts.

It is possible that while federal filings have been going down, state filings have increased. Again, the available information is extremely sketchy. The best account of the relation between federal and state filing rates was an earlier study by the General Accounting Office, comparing data on two products and on two states, concluding that "state court filings matched federal court filings in the direction of change" and that there was "a trend toward filing in federal courts." I know of no reason to believe that these observations are atypical or that this pattern has changed and that filings in state courts are now moving in the opposite direction from those in federal courts.

Two sets of figures compiled by the National Center of State Courts confirm this impression. The first are figures for product liability filings in courts in five states for varying periods since 1985 that reveal no general upward trend or downward trend in state filings. The second set of figures traces separately the number of automobile torts and non-automobile torts filed in the courts of seven states from 1985 to 1990. Again, the number of non-automobile torts, which includes all product liability cases, is essentially flat, while the number of automobile torts increased over this period. Although the evidence is fragmentary, it provides no support for the view that there has been a significant increase in product liability filings in state courts.

In the federal courts, which have been the heartland of product liability litigation, there has been a significant decline in filings relevant to the vast majority of companies. There is no evidence from which to conclude that there has been an offsetting increase in product liability claims in state courts. The decline in product liability filings fits together with a number of other things that suggest that the world of product liability claims is contracting rather than growing. First, Professors Henderson and Eisenberg found that after the early 1980s plaintiffs were less successful at trial and defendants secured favorable opinions from courts in an increasing portion of cases. Second, Professors Rustad and Koenig, tracing the number of punitive damage awards in product liability cases in both state and federal courts, discovered that there were many fewer punitive awards in product cases than is often assumed. . . .

Third, there are not only fewer awards and fewer lawsuits; there are fewer claims. . . .

These studies depict a sustained contraction of product liability exposure rather than the runaway expansion that alarms adherents of the jaundiced view of civil justice. Apart from calling into question the supposed mounting litigiousness of the American people, this contraction should induce skepticism about the asserted role of product liability litigation in undermining the competitiveness of American business.

. . . .

IV. The Missing Knowledge Base

In the end the competitiveness argument only restates the question of the performance of the United States liability system — a question about the net cost of the system and its benefits and about the costs and benefits of the realistic alternatives. We are in the dark — not because there are a few missing items of information, but because we do not have the needed knowledge base. The most basic data about our civil justice system are not collected systematically and cumulatively. That baseless fictions about the number of lawyers, cursory surmises about the costs of the civil justice system, unfounded notions about product liability litigation and fables about damaged competitiveness continue to be taken seriously testifies both to the paucity of information and to a widespread disinclination to employ the information we do have.

Why do we tolerate a knowledge base about the legal system that is so thin and spotty? Compared to the economy or health care or education, research about legal processes, especially civil, is ludicrously thin; so thin that it is perfectly routine for far-reaching policy proposals to be advanced on the basis of tendentious macro-anecdotes and voodoo numbers. The fund of basic information that we take for granted in discussions of the economy, health care or education simply does not exist. To maintain credibility in public debate about education or health or defense, participants have to critically take account of a shared fund of information. Players in the legal policy arena, however, can with impunity disregard reliable information, make up dubious facts and repeat discredited fables. Anything goes, it seems.

The derelict state of the discourse about legal policy is surprising because lawyers, in their role as adversaries, are dogged in challenging and dissecting evidence. But adversarial contention is not the same as delighting in employment of the most severe critical standards. And acuteness in dealing with evidence and inference in specific cases does not necessarily carry over to analysis of large social aggregates. For example, a careful study showed that South Carolina lawyers were not much better than the state's doctors in estimating the number, size, and patterns of jury verdicts in that state.

But what about our vast archipelago of law schools, whose professors and students fill hundreds of journals with the products of legal scholarship? This great flood of scholarship does not provide an adequate knowledge base, because, basically, it is not interested in the working of the legal system. Speaking of the "extraordinary imbalance in academic legal research," Judge Posner noted:

> An attitude of complete neglect to what is after all the great story of American law in the modern era, and that is the extraordinary growth in the size of the profession since 1960 accompanied by an extraordinary increase in the volume of litigation and other legal activities. We do not have in the academy a significant, cogent body of thinking about why this had occurred and what the consequences are.

We think of the contemporary legal academy as the inheritor of the legal realist concern for the law in action, but the incorporation of legal realist insights has been selective: legal scholarship fervently embraced the critical deconstruction of texts, but remained diffident toward the investigative, empirical side of the realist legacy.

Abetted by the bar, law schools have largely defaulted on their responsibility to contribute to knowledge about the working of the legal process. It is as if we had a medical establishment consisting entirely of practicing physicians and theoretical biologists, with no research institutions like the National Institutes of Health and no public health monitoring facilities like the Centers for Disease Control!

. . . .

Notwithstanding the deficiencies of our legal system, it is worth recalling that one realm in which the United States has remained the leading exporter is what we may call the technology of doing law — constitutionalism, judicial enforcement of rights, the organization of law firms, alternative dispute resolution and public interest law. For all their admitted flaws, American institutions provide influential models for the governance of business relations, the processing of disputes, and the protection of citizens.

The legal system that we inhabit is expanding rapidly and is being reshaped by both new technologies within, and the demands of a changing world without. The legal system is one of the mechanisms by which society monitors and regulates the world of incessant change. The efficacy of the legal response depends not only on the quality of our knowledge about the world, but on our understanding of the legal system as well. The absence of an adequate knowledge base not only impairs the optimal use of the legal system, but also makes the legal profession vulnerable to attack.

The hostility toward lawyers so much in evidence today has much deeper sources than the deficiencies of our knowledge base. It is deeply rooted in society's fundamental ambivalence about law and is accentuated by the discomforts of the increasing legalization of society. Our system of civil justice is beset by many problems, particularly problems of securing justice cheaply and expeditiously for all Americans. But we should be mindful of the accomplishments as well as the discomforts. Increasingly, ordinary people can use this system to hold to account society's managers and authorities. It is this "litigation up" that fuels the sense of outrage of so many well-placed critics by challenging the leeways and immunities enjoyed by those in charge.

NOTES AND QUESTIONS

1. ***More on the "Too Many Lawyers," Contention.*** For similar material on this point, see Ray August, *Mythical Kingdom of Lawyers: America Doesn't Have 70 Percent of the Earth's Lawyers*, A.B.A. J., Sept. 1992, at 72–74 (suggesting a different ranking for the world's most lawyer-populated country).

2. ***Has the Quality of This Debate Improved Over the Years?*** Professor Galanter offered his critique more than a decade ago. That history invites inquiry into whether the nature or quality of the above-described debate continues. When you were last gathered in an environment where informal discussion could be carried, did disclosure that you were studying to become a lawyer trigger a response that the country is already being over-lawyered; or that lawyers have left the country hamstrung by people who contribute nothing to the country's economic well-being by their jackal-like dividing of ravished carcasses; or that lawyers promote needless, but self-serving, litigation? Or, perhaps, you hear a different line of attack? What did you say in response?

Chapter 35
THE DIVERSITY OF THE LEGAL PROFESSION

Like women, minorities (*viz.*, primarily people of color) were basically shut out of the legal profession until recent decades. This was a loss to the legal profession, to the clients that minority lawyers might have served, and ultimately to us as a nation (socially and economically), to the extent that we underperformed for lack of unutilized capacities. This chapter tells the encouraging story of recent progress in achieving diversity in the legal profession, then looks at some special challenges faced by lawyers of color and women — indeed by discriminated groups of all types, including individuals whose sexual orientation[1], physical capacities, or religious preferences do not predominate in our society.

A. INCREASED DIVERSITY IN THE LEGAL PROFESSION

The number of people of color in the legal profession — most notably African-Americans, Latinos, Native Americans, and Asians — has been increasing since the early 1970s, though not as rapidly as the increase in the number of women, the other large cohort against which the profession has traditionally discriminated. Understanding of the rate and scope of that progress requires understanding, first, that the pattern of discrimination that we are focused on is not simply a problem of the legal profession; historically it has been the pattern of the general society. Thus, women and people of color have faced (and continue to face) substantial obstacles to achieving success in the high-prestige sectors of professional and business life because that is the basis on which we choose to organize ourselves as a society. The question for this chapter, however, is not why this has occurred, but how, if at all, the legal profession (and particularly law firms, large and small) might respond. We begin, therefore, with a base-line assessment of the progress of minority attorneys in recent decades.

Elsewhere we have noted that the MacCrate Report ("Legal Education and Professional Development — An Educational Continuum," 23–27 (ABA 1992)) provides helpful historical material regarding many of the issues that transformed the legal profession in the post-Korean War era. It was during that period, especially during the 1970s and '80s, that the demographics of the legal profession began to change. Consider *MacCrate's dates* for what they suggest about, both, what the legal profession has accomplished and how much has yet to be done.

1. In 1869, Howard University Law School was federally charted as a law school;
2. Over the next 78 years, Between 1939 and 1947, two other law schools, North Carolina Central University Law School (1939) and Texas Southern University Law School (1947) were established;
3. In 1943 the American Bar Association lifted its formal ban on the membership of African Americans;
4. In 1950 the first African American lawyer was knowingly admitted to the ABA;
5. In 1964, the Association of American Law Schools, for the first time, reported no denials of admissions because of an applicant's race (and 433 African Americans attending predominantly white law schools);
6. In the 1991–92 academic term, the number of black law students in accredited

[1] Although no full treatment is undertaken here, we share the view that the status of gay, lesbian and transgendered individuals is an emerging concern for the legal profession. They have increased in both numbers and acceptance, as statistically indicated by the growing numbers of gay and lesbian lawyers that the National Association of Law Placement, which keeps track of numbers regarding minorities in the legal profession, has published about gay and lesbian lawyers. For an account of how that came about and statistics for New York law firms, see Edward Adams, *Firms Report Totals of Gay Attorneys, Lobbying by Activists Prompts Data Collection*, N.Y.L.J., July 7, 1997.

law schools numbered 8,149 (6.3%), while total minority enrollment (of which African Americans constituted 42%) was also up, primarily as a result of increases in Asian and Hispanic students.

Consider, additionally, the point made in a previous chapter:

7. "African Americans . . . total about 50,000 (or 5%) . . . of [lawyers] . . . Hispanic/Latino lawyers . . . about 30,000 (or 3%) and those who are Asian Americans . . . about 29,000."

NOTES AND QUESTIONS

1. ***Does Any of This Trouble You?*** As you read the above dates and statistics, did it occur to you that the years identified as the pivotal period during which changes were occurring in the legal profession very likely describe the era when most of the lawyers you know (perhaps even your parents and relatives) would have been in law school? If your response is that neither your parents nor anyone you know in that generation went to law school, that doesn't end the inquiry. Think about your law school's most recent retirees; they would also fit the timeline. The question that underlies all these situations would be the same: Is one generation (roughly 35 years) enough time to have resolved the issues of exclusion and separation to which the legal profession committed itself even before 1869? Should the legal profession as a whole be encouraging more people of color, more women, or more white males — that is to say, people of talent, regardless of race or gender — to enter the legal profession? How about to enter certain branches of the legal profession, such as government, in-house counsel, private law firms, or the criminal justice system? Why? How?

2. ***Is Diversity Good?*** Is diversity good for the legal profession? Does diversity benefit clients, the public, or law firms?

3. ***Futures Projection.*** Suppose for the moment that you either answered the last four questions negatively or that you are genuinely agnostic about the answers; you simply do not know what the answers are. Now consider the likely impact of a "futures" projection made by President George W. Bush's then — Chair of the U.S. Equal Employment Opportunity Commission (EEOC), Cari M. Dominguez in *Views from the EEOC — Evolving Trends in the 21st Century Workplace* (From the September/October 2003 issue of DIVERSITY & THE BAR, *available at*, http://www.mcca.com/index.cfm?fuseaction=page.viewpage&pageid=999 (last visited August 20, 2008).) Dominguez foresees three "Megatrends" — *Dramatic Demographic Shifts* in the workplace (equaling more women; more racial, ethnic, and linguistic groups; and younger workers); *Increased Application of Technology to Recruiting* (including e-recruiting throughout cyberspace); and *Globalization of the Work* ("allowing workers to apply for jobs, interview and even work for companies while living oceans away"). As she sees it, therefore, "The challenge of every employer is to stay in step with these continual workplace changes, to be vigilant and identify potential discrimination issues before they develop, and, through a concerted effort, to look for the "cure" to discrimination, rather than always having to treat its symptoms."

4. ***What Do You Think?*** Are the questions implicitly raised by Dominquez of relevance? (Do we have any choice whether to become a more diverse profession? What are the consequences of not becoming more diverse? Are there benefits from diversity for clients, the public, or law firms?)

5. ***How Can We Increase Diversity?*** If diversity in the legal profession is beneficial to society, how can we increase diversity? Does the legal profession have an obligation to encourage more people of color to become lawyers, and to help them advance in the profession? To be more concrete:

- What effort is your law school making to recruit more people of color?
- What effort is your law school making to help foster an environment where minorities can succeed as students?

- What effort is your law school making to help people of color find part-time or summer work at law firms during law school?
- What effort is your law school making to help people of color find jobs after law school?
- What efforts are law firms making to recruit people of color?

6. ***Recruitment.*** Are law schools and law firms doing enough to recruit people of color, to help them succeed in law school or on the job? If not, what more could be done? Who should do it? Does the following discussion provide any insights into what can be done?

PAUL FREEMAN, GAINING AND RETAINING DIVERSITY: HOW WELL DO LAW FIRMS KEEP THEIR PROMISE OF A DIVERSE ENVIRONMENT?*

When Stephen Graham graduated from Yale Law School, his career options were more limited than those of most of his classmates. Graham is an African-American, and in 1976 a diverse workforce was not a priority for law firms. In fact, some firms refused to hire any minority lawyer, even one with a Yale pedigree. Despite this bias, Graham became the first African-American lawyer and then partner at Perkins Coie. Now a partner at Orrick, Herrington & Sutcliffe, he heads that firm's Seattle office.

Today, of course, many firms, particularly larger ones, are trying to become more diverse, racially and otherwise. They have diversity policies and committees and training, and they've taken steps to boost the number of minority lawyers. Those efforts have succeeded, but only to an extent. Recruiting — and retaining — minority lawyers is a Sisyphean task, and a truly diverse lawyer workforce remains an elusive goal.

The drive for diversity has been sparked by several developments. One is a steady flow of studies and surveys, like a 2001 survey conducted by the Glass Ceiling Task Force, a group of lawyers from bar associations and other organizations in Washington State. This survey determined that while 11 percent of Washington associates are minorities, just 3 percent are equity partners. It also found underrepresentation of minorities in firm governance and in the highest quartile of firm compensation.

Also driving the quest for diversity is monetary pressure. Many corporate clients monitor their law firms' diversity efforts and insist that minority and women attorneys from the firms be assigned to their matters. "It's become an imperative with many, many corporations that the law firms they use must have diversity, and that is a motivator for a lot of firms," says Sheryl Willert, the first African-American partner at Seattle's Williams, Kastner & Gibbs and for six years that firm's managing director.

Recruiting lawyers of color isn't easy, partly because qualified candidates are in short supply. At the law school level, where many firms focus their diversity efforts, "minorities form a small part of the applicant pool. Then if you think of the portion of that pool attracted to Seattle, you have an even smaller number," says Graham.

For this reason, firms like Seattle's Perkins Coie and Orrick find it easier to recruit minorities for their summer associate programs from first-year law school classes. "There are fewer firms going after first-year students," says Graham, who notes that of the three summer associates arriving soon at his office, all from the first-year class, one is nonwhite, an East Asian student.

When a law firm has few or no minority lawyers, minority law students and lawyers are reluctant to join it. "If you're in an office where there are no other African-American lawyers, do you want to be the first and for a while the only one?" asks Mark Hutcheson, chairman of Seattle's Davis Wright Tremaine. Though Willert advanced

---

* Copyright © 2005 Key Professional Media Inc. *available at* http://www.wsba.org/lawpoliticsgainingandretainingdiversity.pdf.

despite being the first African-American at Williams, Kastner & Gibbs, she agrees with that assessment. "People of color are prone not to go into places where they'll be the only ones, where they're expected to change and conform to norms as opposed to people understanding their culture."

When Davis Wright associate Andrew Mar was a law student considering post-graduation employment options, it was important to him as an Asian-American that Davis Wright has Asian-American partners. "With firms that didn't have minority partners," he asked himself, "was it possible for me to become a partner? Davis Wright, having some, answered that question."

To attract minority law students, some firms have set up special fellowships. Seattle's Perkins Coie pioneered this strategy in Washington, awarding its first fellowship more than a decade ago. The fellowships typically provide a summer associate position for a first-year minority law student along with several thousand dollars toward the student's second-year tuition.

According to Leif Ormseth, a shareholder at the Seattle office of Heller Ehrman White & McAuliffe, which just launched a fellowship program for that office, a key objective is to give the firm more visibility among minority law students. "It's the first year of the program, and we received a remarkable number of interesting applications," he says.

Another firm with a fellowship program is Davis Wright, which casts a wide net when recruiting from law schools. "We target schools where we think there will be a bigger pool of minority candidates, like Howard University Law School, in Washington, D.C.," says Hutcheson.

Williams Kastner & Gibbs doesn't do such targeted recruiting, but the firm has hired a number of minority summer associates through the annual Northwest Minority Job Fair, in which law firm representatives gather to interview first-year minority law students for summer clerkships. "We've found the program to be very beneficial to students who have participated," says Willert.

Though efforts to attract minority lawyers occur primarily at the law school level, some firms aim for diversity at the lateral level, too. Like many law firms, Davis Wright now hires more lawyers laterally than from law schools. Says Hutcheson, "We're trying to get the word out to practice group chairs and partners in charge of offices that if they're looking to add expertise laterally, they should keep in mind lawyers of color."

Seattle's Graham & Dunn, which hires only laterals, has told its Seattle headhunter to actively seek out qualified minority candidates. This strategy has helped boost the percentage of lawyers of color at the firm to a respectable 15 percent. "It's hard to overstate the importance of the aggressive headhunter approach," says hiring committee chair Mark Finkelstein.

Hiring minority lawyers has a domino effect. "Once you become successful [in hiring minorities] — provided you can retain them — people of color look at your firm and conclude it's a place where they can feel comfortable," says Finkelstein.

But retaining minority lawyers is even harder than recruiting them. Consider David Reed's experience. A past president of the Loren Miller Bar Association and now an in-house lawyer in the Seattle office of Atlanta-based AFC Enterprises Inc., Reed spent a year at Davis Wright. When he arrived, he was one of four African-American lawyers there. By the time he left a year later, the other three African-American lawyers had already departed. "That was part of why I left," says Reed.

Why such a struggle to retain minority lawyers? One reason is that qualified minority lawyers, like their qualified nonminority peers, are constantly wooed by prospective employers, including corporations able to offer stock options. "Our clients and other employers of lawyers want to cherry-pick our people, including people who are diverse," says Davis Wright's Hutcheson. Ormseth points out that a highly competent minority lawyer recently exited Heller Ehrman to teach at a leading law school.

The most difficult group for firms to retain is minority women lawyers. According to the American Bar Association, about 12.1 percent of this group leave their firms within the first year of practice, more than 85 percent by the seventh year. By the eighth year, the attrition rate is nearly 100 percent. "Women minority lawyers have a double bias against them, because of their gender and their ethnicity or race," says Nashra Rahman, a lawyer and Bangladesh native who serves as facilitator for the King County Bar Association Committee on Gender Equality in the Legal Profession.

People who have studied the retention problem or experienced it firsthand identify mentoring as a solution. Rahman points out that minority lawyers often are the first in their families to go into law and don't understand how law firms work. "Becoming a partner is more than doing good work; you have to understand the system. In addition, minorities face negative stereotypes about their abilities and feel they have to work twice as hard in order to prove themselves." Mentoring, she says, helps compensate for these disadvantages.

Graham wouldn't have succeeded at Perkins Coie, he says, without the mentoring he received from former Perkins partner Tom Alberg, ironically a white man. "He took me under his wing. Nobody, minority or otherwise, will survive without a mentor." According to Mar, Davis Wright's mentoring program, which pairs each novice lawyer with two senior lawyers, "helps me understand the nature of the firm and what it takes to succeed."

Kim Tran, a mid-level associate at Seattle's Stafford Frey Cooper, where 15 percent of the lawyers are minorities, says the mentoring program is one reason her firm does a good job retaining minority attorneys. The firm also encourages minority lawyers to become active in their communities; Tran, for example, is a director of the Asian Bar Association of Washington. Time spent on such activities counts as billable time. "That shows more than lip service [to diversity]," she says.

In Reed's view, a number of firms — he mentions Perkins, Davis Wright and Seattle's Foster Pepper & Shefelman — are doing a credible job of addressing the diversity issue. He's optimistic about the future of diversity. "What I see out there is some light at the end of the tunnel."

Graham is less sanguine. He compares mentoring programs to "arranged marriages — some work, some don't." Mentoring succeeds, he believes, only when a real bond is forged between mentor and minority lawyer. That's more likely to happen, he says, when they have similar backgrounds; it's less likely when a nonminority mentors a minority. "What's important is to match up people with mentors who understand the unique obstacles minorities face."

What's more, Graham asserts, when diversity is measured by the number of minority partners, the drive for diversity is stalled. "If you look at the number of minority partners, the number is stuck among all minorities at about 3 percent."

He thinks he knows why. To succeed in a law practice, a lawyer must be able to generate business, and that requires a network of contacts. White males can capitalize on that famed old boy network, says Graham. "There's no comparable network to help women and minorities build practices. So these groups start their careers a step or two behind in that regard."

As a result, Graham says, many minority lawyers reach a point in their careers when they're expected to generate business but can't do this as well as their majority peers. "Ultimately they're asked to leave because by objective measure they're not making the same contribution [or they leave on their own] because practice is just not fun."

The key to true diversity, he says, is awareness. "There must be greater awareness that diversity is woefully lacking plus acknowledgment that bias still exists in our society." Law firms then must take steps to counter this bias, he says. And minorities must continue battling for equality and not give up. "They need patience, perseverance and perspective."

B. WOMEN IN THE LEGAL PROFESSION

In the 1960s fewer than five percent of the students at most law schools were women. These days, more than fifty percent of law students in the United States are women, and about thirty percent of all lawyers are women. So, after all these years, how is it that only about fifteen percent of federal judges and law firm partners are women, only about ten percent of law school deans and general counsels are women and only about five percent of managing partners of large firms are women? An overview of some of the barriers women have experienced in reaching the highest levels of the legal profession is provided in the following article by Professor Deborah L. Rhode.

DEBORAH L. RHODE, GENDER AND THE PROFESSION: THE NO PROBLEM PROBLEM

30 Hofstra L. Rev. 1001(2002)*

II. Gender Stereotypes

Gender stereotypes influence behavior at both conscious and unconscious levels and work against women's advancement in several respects. First, and most fundamentally, characteristics traditionally associated with women are at odds with those traditionally associated with professional success, such as assertiveness, competitiveness, and business judgment. Some lawyers and clients still assume that women lack the aptitude for complex financial transactions or the combativeness for high-stakes litigation. Yet professional women also tend to be rated lower when they adopt "masculine," authoritative styles, particularly when the evaluators are men. Female lawyers routinely face some variation of this double standard and double bind. They risk appearing too "soft" or too "strident," too "aggressive" or not "aggressive" enough. And what is assertive in a man often seems abrasive in a woman.

A related obstacle is that women often do not receive the same presumption of competence as men. In large national surveys, between half and three-quarters of female attorneys believe that they are held to higher standards than their male counterparts or have to work harder for the same results. Even in experimental situations where male and female performance is objectively equal, women are judged more critically and their competence is rated lower.

The problem is particularly great when evaluators have little accountability and those evaluated are women of color or other identifiable minorities. These women find that their mistakes are more readily noticed and their achievements are more often attributed to luck or affirmative action. About two-thirds of black lawyers, compared with only about ten percent of white lawyers, believe that minority women are treated less fairly than white women in hiring and promotion. Most disabled and openly lesbian lawyers similarly report adverse effects on employment opportunities.

The force of traditional stereotypes is compounded by the subjectivity of performance evaluations and by other biases in decision-making processes. People are more likely to notice and recall information that confirms prior assumptions than information that contradicts them. Attorneys who assume that women with children are less committed or that women of color are less qualified will recall their errors more readily than their insights. They will note the times mothers leave early, not the times they stay late. A related problem is that people share what psychologists label a "just world" bias. They want to believe that, in the absence of special treatment, individuals generally get what they deserve and deserve what they get. So if women are

---

underrepresented in positions of greatest prominence, the most psychologically convenient explanation is that they lack the necessary qualifications or commitment.

These assumptions can then become self-fulfilling prophecies. Expectations affect evaluations, which then affect outcomes that reinforce initial expectations. Senior attorneys are less likely to support women who appear unlikely to succeed. Women who are not supported are more likely to leave. Their disproportionate attrition then perpetuates the assumptions that perpetuate the problem. All of these obstacles are greater for women of color, who have the lowest law firm retention rate of any group, and who are still frequently mistaken for clerical or support personnel.

The problem is compounded by the disincentives to raise it. Women who express concerns often hear that they are "humorless," or "overreacting," or exercising "bad judgment." The tendency in many workplaces is to shoot the messenger, which obviously gets in the way of important messages being heard.

III. Mentoring and Support Networks

A second, equally persistent and pervasive problem is the lack of access to informal networks of mentoring, contacts, and client development. Many men who endorse equal opportunity in principle fall short in practice; they end up supporting those who seem most similar in backgrounds, experiences, and values. Some male attorneys report reluctance to mentor or to be seen alone with female colleagues because of concerns of sexual harassment or "how it might be perceived." Others enjoy the bonding that occurs in all-male events. Even women who make real sacrifices to get a foot in the door find that a foot is all they get in. Working mothers short on time, interest, or innate ability have nonetheless learned to play golf, which makes it all the more aggravating when they still aren't invited to play.

It is, of course, not only men who fail to mentor their women colleagues. Even women leaders who are sensitive to gender-related problems are sometimes reluctant to become actively involved in the solution, particularly in workplaces where they risk being perceived as "whiners," or as biased in favor of other women. Despite these risks, many senior women do what they can but are too overcommitted to provide adequate mentoring for all the junior colleagues who need assistance. And female attorneys at all levels who have substantial family commitments also have difficulty making time for the informal social activities that generate collegial support and client contacts.

The result is that many female lawyers remain out of the loop of career development. They are not given enough challenging, high visibility assignments, nor are they included in social events that yield professional opportunities. Problems of exclusion are greatest for those who appear "different" on other grounds as well as gender, such as race, ethnicity, disability, or sexual orientation. As one anonymous participant in a Los Angeles bar survey described his firm's attitude toward gay and lesbian attorneys: "Don't have any, don't want any."

IV. Workplace Structures

A final obstacle involves workplace structures that fail to accommodate personal needs and commitments, particularly family responsibilities. The good news is that the profession has woken up to the fact that this is a problem. The bad news is that we are still so far from a solution. Less than a fifth of surveyed lawyers are well satisfied by the balance between their personal and professional lives.

The most obvious ongoing failure is inhumane hours and a resistance to reduced or flexible schedules. . . . The problem is reinforced by the increasing pace and competition of legal life. Technological innovations have created expectations of instant responsiveness and total availability, while increasing billable hour quotas have pushed working hours to new and often excessive limits. Lawyers remain perpetually on call — tethered to the workplace through cell phones, emails, faxes, and beepers. "Face time" is taken as a proxy for commitment, ambition, and reliability under pressure. The result is a "rat race equilibrium" in which most lawyers feel that they would be better off with shorter or more flexible schedules, but find themselves within institutional structures that offer no such alternatives.

Even in workplaces that in theory offer these options, a wide gap persists between formal policies and actual practices. Although over 90% of surveyed law firms report policies permitting part-time schedules, only about 3% of lawyers actually use them. Most women surveyed believe, with good reason, that any reduction in hours or availability will carry a permanent price.

The result is yet another double standard and another double bind. Working mothers are held to higher standards than working fathers and are often criticized for being insufficiently committed, either as parents or professionals. Those who seem willing to sacrifice family needs to workplace demands appear lacking as mothers. Those who want extended leaves or reduced schedules appear lacking as lawyers. These mixed messages leave many women with the uncomfortable sense that whatever they are doing, they should be doing something else. All the coping strategies are problematic. A woman lawyer is hammered in a custody battle for reading briefs during a piano recital; a lawyer who misses recitals is told by her daughter that what she really wanted for Christmas was "more time with mommy"; a senior partner complains that when he needed affidavits for an unexpected motion, mommy was at a recital. Too many women are in no-win situations. Assumptions about the inadequate commitment of working mothers can influence performance evaluations, promotion decisions, and opportunities for the mentoring relationships and challenging assignments that are prerequisites for advancement.

The problem is compounded by the sweatshop schedules that are increasingly common, particularly in major law firms. Hourly requirements have increased dramatically over the last two decades, and what has not changed is the number of hours in the day. Few supervisors are as blunt as the partner who informed one junior colleague that "law is 'no place for a woman with a child.' " But that same message is sent by resistance to "special" treatment for working mothers. Moreover, women who do not have partners or children often have difficulty finding time for relationships that might lead to them. Particularly in large firms, unmarried associates report finding it " 'difficult to have a cat, much less a family.' " As one lawyer responded to a bar survey on quality of life: " 'This is not a life.' "

Although the absence of family-friendly policies is not just a "women's issue," the price is paid disproportionately by women. Despite a significant increase in men's assumption of domestic work over the last two decades, women in two-career couples continue to shoulder the major burden. Part of the reason is that workplaces that only grudgingly accommodate mothers are even less receptive to fathers. Only about ten to fifteen percent of surveyed law firms and Fortune 1000 companies offer the same paid parental leave to men and women. Only about ten percent of male professionals take significant leaves, and few feel free to ask for more than a few weeks. As a male lawyer explained to the Boston Bar Association work/family task force, it may be " 'okay [for men] to say that [they] would like to spend more time with the kids, but it's not okay to do it, except once in a while.' " In short, men cannot readily get on the "mommy track." Women cannot readily get off it.

* * *

. . . A wide array of research indicates that making initiatives like alternative or reduced work schedules available in practice not just in principle can help increase productivity and reduce attrition, recruitment, and stress-related costs. Bleary, burned out lawyers are not providing efficient services. Other research makes equally plain that lawyers, like most other individuals, tend to overvalue income as a source of satisfaction. Most people believe that twenty-five percent more income would significantly improve their lives. But particularly at lawyers' salary levels, it rarely does so. It just ratchets expectations and desires up to a new level. Balanced lives offering time for family, friends, and pro bono commitment are far more likely to yield fulfillment than the additional financial benefits available from sweatshop hours. Yet this is not always apparent to entering attorneys, who after years of genteel poverty, find spiraling salaries overwhelmingly appealing. Studies of workplace satisfaction could be a sobering reminder of the hidden price of current priorities.

NOTES AND QUESTIONS

1. ***Changing Cultures.*** What can a junior lawyer do to change the cognitive processes of supervisors and the culture of their workplace? In addition to noting how many women hold positions of power within the workplace (and how recently they have attained those positions) how much accurate information can a law student obtain regarding these issues during the interviewing process?

2. ***What Happens in a Worst Case Scenario?*** Many lawyers, for a variety of reasons, would simply find a job with a new employer when the workplace becomes unacceptable. But some lawyers have sued their former legal employer. A recent article by Joan C. Williams and others discusses such lawsuits: Joan C. Williams, Stephanie Bornstein, Diana Reddy & Betsy A. Williams, *Law Firms as Defendants: Family Responsibilities Discrimination in Legal Workplaces*, 34 Pepperdine L. Rev. 393 (2007). Among the reasons identified for why lawyers sue are:

- Poor reviews and lesser assignments after announcing a pregnancy
- Lesser chance to advance as a mother, especially to partner
- Stigma and retaliation after taking a leave
- Stigma and marginalization while on a reduced or part-time schedule
- Hostile work environment including harassment related to caregiving responsibilities.

In addition, Williams and her co-authors identified an emerging area of litigation termed *family responsibilities discrimination*, which they define as "discrimination against workers based on their family caregiving responsibilities for children, elderly parents, or ill spouses and partners." Such discrimination includes "not only pregnancy discrimination and the 'maternal wall' that blocks women's advancement when they become mothers, but also discrimination against men who seek to take on a larger family caregiving role for young children, elderly parents or ill spouses than traditional gender stereotypes of men envision. When an employer treats an employee based on stereotypes that reflect how the employer believes the employee will or should behave because of his or her family caregiving responsibilities (rather than based on the employee's individual interests or performance), the employer has engaged in family responsibilities discrimination. Examples include (1) assigning a mother to less important "mommy track" work based on the assumption that she will be less committed to work or (2) retaliating against a male employee who takes time off to care for his elderly parent or ill wife when time off is otherwise liberally available.

3. ***But, Our Law Firm Has a Part-Time Policy.*** Many legal workplaces have adopted an official policy permitting lawyers to work part-time work or other flexible working arrangements. But, only a tiny fraction of the eligible lawyers use those policies — about four percent or so. Many lawyers are afraid that seeking alternative working arrangements, even for a limited period of time, will jeopardize their career success.

C. WHY DO WE DIVERSIFY?

It is repeatedly asked of proponents for vigorous diversity initiatives: What is the objective of your efforts? This is more than simply a question about whether there should be diversity; it is also an inquiry about who is intended to benefit from it.

Accordingly, the question is, in part, intended to explore whether diversity is thought to meet a societal need or the needs of some favored community — whether the intent is to equip a racially, ethnically, or gender-specific group for their personal benefit, or instead to marshal the strengths of such groups for what would otherwise be a societal mission. For example, does the need to pursue diversity arise because there are many talented women and people of color who otherwise will not join large firms, or will not enter law practice altogether? Is it because poor African-Americans and Hispanics cannot rise out of poverty and powerlessness unless they have role models and social leaders? Is it because minority clients want minority lawyers, or because minority lawyers can identify with the needs and experiences of minority clients? (*See, e.g.*, Nina Burleigh, *Women in Law: Black Women Lawyers Coping with Dual Discrimination*, 74 A.B.A.J. 64 (1988), and Linda Davila, *The Underrepresentation of Hispanic Attorneys in Corporate Law Firms*, 39 STANFORD L. REV. 1403 (1987), with respect to women and Hispanics.)

The three megatrends that Chair Dominguez identifies — Demographics, Technology and Globalization — appear, for her, to answer the question of why the legal profession should strive for increased diversity: One either aligns with the megatrends or as a consequence is buried, tsunami style, by them. Judge Cardiss Collins and superlawyer (and Presidential confidant) Vernon Jordan, however, have staked out conflicting positions with respect to another suggested answer. For Judge Collins it is, at least in part, a matter involving the need for the African-American community to develop expertise and power. Or as he put it in *The Role of the Black Attorney in the 1980's: A Challenge to Become Specialists, Associates, and Renovators*, 7 BLACK L.J. 54 (1978):

> After black lawyers effectively grasp the concepts of specialization and association, they must deal with the concept of renovation. They must renovate their entire perception of roles in the black community. For too many years, too many black lawyers have allowed themselves to become hired hands of the establishment, while leaving unaddressed issues which are crucial to the viability of blacks in the area of business. Black lawyers must strive to build confidence within the community. They must throw away the perception of Perry Mason and gain management techniques so they can emerge from the pits of pecuniary oppression and join the system before it breaks down.

Jordan, however, takes another view. As if indirectly responding to Judge Collins, in *Black Lawyers Cannot Be Relegated to a Professional Ghetto*, 7 BARRISTER NO. 2, at 46 (1980), Jordan warns:

> While there is a pressing need for minority leaders to serve the minority community, it is as important for minority lawyers to become fully integrated into all aspects of the profession. Black lawyers cannot be relegated to a professional ghetto narrowly defined by the residential ghetto's legal services needs.
>
> Rather, minorities must have access to the same positions of power and prestige as their white counterparts. The continuing absence of black partners and associates in major law firms is a disgrace to the profession. The growing responsibilities and rewards of corporate legal employment have to include minority lawyers as well.

What other reasons might the legal profession have for wanting to create a structure and an atmosphere in which women and people of color can reach their fullest potential?

NOTES AND QUESTIONS

1. ***Is a Synthesis Possible?*** Can the views of Dominguez, Collins, and Jordan be reconciled?

2. ***Is This a "Martin Niemoeller Moment"?*** Does the issue that Dominguez, Collins and Jordan are wrestling with have relevance to you? Is that the case if you are a white male or female?

3. ***Does the Legal Profession Have an Obligation?*** Does the legal profession have an obligation to recruit people of color and women and help them reach their potential as lawyers? (We're talking about *all* minorities — gay men, lesbians, people with disabilities, foreign-born people, religious people of color, etc.) If so, where does this obligation come from? That is, why should the legal profession help women and people of color?

4. ***How Can We Help?*** How can law firms help women and minorities achieve their potential? This is a hard question for law students to answer because they are usually not familiar with the practical problems of managing a law firm work force, and are often unfamiliar with the problems faced by women and minority lawyers. It may help, therefore, to think about the problem at a law school level. What is your law school doing to address the problems of women and people of color? What do you think these problems are? Has your law school (or any student organization) made any systematic effort to find out what changes could be made to address these problems? Are there effective channels of communication for women and people of color who have complaints about law school? Who speaks for people of color? Has the curriculum and the placement apparatus responded to any concerns voiced by women and people of color? What more could you and your law school be doing to help women and people of color get the maximum out of law school?

5. ***Hey, What About White Males?*** Some of the concerns that trouble African-American and Hispanic lawyers (and to some extent female lawyers) may also trouble white males. Perhaps a relevant metaphor is the one that Professor Loni Guineaur of Harvard Law School, has particularly championed: the canary in the mine. Are you familiar with the metaphor — specifically how it has been used to explain the beneficial externalities that have been associated, for example, with enactment of the Americans with Disabilities Act? Think about the effects of creating ramp-way access to curbsides and entrance/exit-ways. Think also about kitchen designs with lower table and counter-tops, flat-levered faucet handles, and large-numbered clocks and dials. Despite in many instances having been initiated in response to the needs of the physically handicapped, today both the fully able and the less-able see the benefits of what was once an unconventional design. Could it be that, like the canary in the mineshaft, people of color and women are sounding the alarm about the need for fundamental reforms to address situations that are holding the entire legal profession back? Could the call for diversity be a call for fundamental changes in the practices of the legal profession, which will eventually be seen as benefiting both people of color and non-minorities alike?

D. ASIAN-AMERICAN LAWYERS

An unanticipated, but to many a welcomed, development in recent years has been the rapid increase in the number of Asian-American lawyers. Today, Asian-Americans are the largest single minority group in the country's major law firms. How and why did this happen? The following article chronicles the recent attraction of law to Asian-Americans and the acceptance of Asian-American lawyers by large law firms.

CHRIS KLEIN, ASIAN-AMERICANS FIND PLACE IN THE PROFESSION: PACIFIC RIM AND TECH BOOMS CREATE MAJOR FIRMS' BIGGEST MINORITY

THE NATIONAL LAW JOURNAL, February 17, 1997*

AT A PARTY in Boston in the early 1970s, Cedric C. Chao mentioned he was considering law school. Six old family friends — "uncles," he calls them — cornered him and gave him an earful. "They told me what a big mistake it would be," recalls Mr. Chao. His uncles described the legal profession as an old boys' network in which it would be impossible for a person of Chinese origin to rise in the ranks.

" 'If you stick to medicine or science,' " they told me, " 'it will be harder to hold you down because your ability will show through.' "

Such warnings didn't deter him. Mr. Chao earned a J.D. from Stanford Law School in 1977, and, after clerking for a federal judge and serving as an assistant U.S. attorney in San Francisco, he joined that city's Morrison & Foerster L.L.P. in 1981. He made partner in 1983, uncles and old boys notwithstanding.

He's currently one of three leaders of the firm's international practice group. In fact, he's one of the pioneers of a burgeoning migration.

The number of Asian-Americans in the legal profession and at large firms has exploded in recent years to the point, some say, that Asian-American lawyers are in a position to accomplish what Mr. Chao's uncles said was impossible — creating their own mutual-aid network.

"We're reaching a critical mass," says Paul W. Lee, chair of the corporate department at Boston's white-shoe, 314-lawyer Goodwin, Procter & Hoar L.L.P. "We're reaching leadership positions, which gives us the chance to mentor younger lawyers coming in so they don't have to fight as much."

Critical Mass

According to the 1996 NLJ survey of women and minorities in the profession, in 1996 there were 1,750 Asians at the 250 largest firms in the country, the largest minority group in the profession. In the past five years, the combined number of Asian and Native American lawyers rose 63 percent, to a total of 1,808 — more than 20 percentage points greater than the overall minority growth rate in the profession over the same span. [NLJ, 4-29-96.]

If indeed an Asian-American presence at law firms is at a critical mass, lawyers attribute the change to three different booms — Pacific Rim business, high technology and Asian immigration. All put lawyers with pan-Asian cultural fluency in a particularly advantageous position in the 1980s, along with lawyers with science expertise, says Paul H. Chan, president of the National Asian Pacific American Bar Association, or NAPABA, and administrative counsel to Colorado's attorney general.

Some call such lawyers "refugee engineers" — Asian-Americans with scientific backgrounds or degrees who have abandoned the laboratory for law offices.

Refugee Engineers

"There are opportunities for careers in law and technology that would be attractive to Asians who initially sought careers in engineering or the sciences," says Charlene S. Shimada (who goes by the nickname Chuck), 43, managing partner of the San Francisco headquarters of McCutchen, Doyle, Brown & Enersen L.L.P. Ms. Shimada is one of 34 Asian-American attorneys at the firm, three of whom are partners. Nine blacks and five Hispanics round out the minority legal staff. She adds there are job options today "that didn't even exist when I was making career decisions."

Ivan K. Fong, a partner at D.C.'s Covington & Burling, has a master's in chemical engineering from the Massachusetts Institute of Technology. As a student, he also liked to write, and worked for the school paper. He decided to take the Law School Admissions Test "on a lark," he recalls; he did well enough to get into Stanford Law School. Yet even now, at an inside-the-Beltway law firm, Mr. Fong has chosen not to forsake chemistry.

Mr. Fong, one of two Asian-Americans at the firm (the other is an associate), adds that he has tried to tailor his practice so that a lot of it involves technology issues, such as environmental risk assessment, IP litigation and pharmaceutical and medical-device regulatory matters. "I enjoy problem-solving in science and in law," he says.

In many ways, the silicolonization of global markets — which has resulted in an explosion in intellectual property work over the past decade — has worked to the advantage of lawyers with technological knowledge. The refugee engineers, it turns out, are in high demand these days.

Pacific Rim

If technology law and IP are hot, Pacific Rim business is aflame. As firms strive for lucrative joint venture and project finance work, they're seeking lawyers who can offer the best of both worlds: fluency in Asian business culture and American legal practice. This has, to some extent, given Asian-American attorneys new clout in the profession, legal observers say.

AUTHORS' COMMENT:

This article was written before the Asian economic crisis hit in mid-1997. That crisis slowed or reversed growth in the Pacific Rim, especially in Indonesia, Malaysia, Korea, and Thailand. Many major Asian projects, both public and private, were scaled-back, postponed, or canceled. Nevertheless, the long-run outlook for Asian economies, including China, remained bright, with the U.N. Economic and Social Commission for Asia and the Pacific projecting in 2004 that "Fueled by continued brisk growth in China, Asia Pacific economies are expected to grow by a combined 6.2 percent this year." (*See UN: China To Grow By 8.4 Percent*, Footwear News, April 26, 2004 (Fairchild Publications, Inc.)

They're certainly a force at San Francisco's Graham & James L.L.P., where 24 of 55 Asian-American attorneys are partners — by far the most of any NLJ 250 firm. Charles D. Paturick, the firm's managing partner, says Graham & James actively seeks Asian-American attorneys because of its practice's "concentration" in Pacific Rim business.

That helps explain why Graham & James has more attorneys of Asian extraction than any other U.S. firm but one — New York's Davis Polk & Wardwell, which has 73, though only four are partners.

Something To Offer

The booming markets of Asia may have helped catapult Wilson Chu into the partnership ranks at Dallas' Haynes and Boone L.L.P., after moving up Main Street from Vial, Hamilton, Koch & Knox in the early 1990s. In addition to Mr. Chu, Haynes and Boone has seven Asian-American associates.

Mr. Chu says that as one of many senior associates specializing in corporate law, he felt the need to separate himself from the pack.

"I said to myself, 'How am I going to make myself different from everyone else?' There are about a gazillion corporate lawyers," he relates. "But I have something different." That something is a Chinese background, an understanding of the culture and command of the Cantonese language.

"There is a bond" between Asian-American lawyers and their Asian clients and contacts across the ocean, says Mr. Chao of Morrison & Foerster, which has 52 Asian-American lawyers — seven are partners — 19 Hispanics and 18 blacks.

Mr. Chao does a significant amount of Pacific Rim work — sometimes on matters involving Asian companies that have set up subsidiaries in the United States. He says the Asian business culture has its own flavor.

For example, he explains, it's gauche to solicit business on first meeting; sometimes it takes several encounters before the parties get down to brass tacks.

"At some point you can drop a hint," says Mr. Chao, but, he adds, you have to know the proper moment.

* * *

Old Stereotypes

* * *

Mr. Lee adds that the Pacific Rim boom has helped perpetuate a related stereotype: "Lots of firms assume that just because you're Asian-American you want to work for Asian clients. What we want is the opportunity to do serious work," no matter what the practice area.

But Mr. Chu, of Haynes and Boone, who is chair of the NAPABA partners' forum, has a more positive take on the issue. To him, "the pigeonholing doesn't seem unwelcome," he says. "I like being an international lawyer. I'm absolutely proud of my position, being in charge of the Asia Pacific practice. I'm sure the IP guys feel the same way" about their practice, he adds. Yet Mr. Chu and other Asian-Americans lawyers worry that despite the significant gains they've made, there's still a glass ceiling, "that it's easy for us to get into law firms but difficult to make partner."

Statistics bear them out. Although Asian-Americans are numerically better represented at top law firms than any other minority group, their presence in partnership ranks is not correspondingly large. According to the NLJ's most recent survey of women and minorities in the profession, of all Asian-Americans in the top 250 U.S. firms, 14.3 percent are partners, compared with 21.5 percent of African-Americans, 24.8 percent of Hispanics and 44.9 percent of whites.

Numbers, Age, Stereotypes

Demographics explain some of the disparity, says Prof. Wallace D. Loh, former dean of the University of Washington School of Law and now the chancellor of the University of Colorado. He contends that most attorneys of Asian extraction are simply younger than black and Hispanic lawyers. Professor Loh says the Immigration Reform Act of 1964, which allowed more immigrants to enter the United States from Asian and Third World countries, resulted in a "demographic bulge" of Asians in the late 1960s. People born during the following years, along with children of the Vietnamese who came to this country after the fall of Saigon in 1975, are now appearing in law schools and at law firms.

Still, age accounts for only part of the partnership equation, attorneys say. While naturalized Asians and Asian-Americans may have the advantage in dealing with clients of common background overseas, they may be at a disadvantage in approaching the typical big-firm client. "It is the case that increasingly one's ability to attract business is a criterion" for making partner at a big firm, says Ms. Shimada of McCutchen Doyle. "Often for women and people of color, that's an area where they've had to struggle."

The struggle appears to be getting slightly easier as a class of Asian owners of large, mainstream businesses emerges in the United States, particularly on the West Coast. Mr. Chao says his ethnic background has worked to his advantage in garnering new business for his firm. "There's a large Asian-American entrepreneurial community" in California, he says. "Naturally [these entrepreneurs] are drawn to Asian-American professionals to serve them."

By contrast, in Texas, where the Asian population is much smaller, Mr. Chu says the question is, "Do you know how to operate in a white-male-dominated business? Do you know how to relate to these guys?" He does, he says, because he grew up playing tennis with them in Dallas.

Indeed, the gender of the attorneys who wield most of the power in the profession gives Asian-American men an advantage Asian-American women might not have. The latter face a double whammy, Ms. Shimada says: racial bias and gender bias. That makes it especially hard for them to develop mentor relationships.

One professor who has been tracking the progress of women and minorities in the profession — and who asked for anonymity — agrees with this view, but goes one step further.

Asian Women

"My theory is that Asian men are now treated like white men, but Asian women still suffer from double discrimination," the professor posits. "Even in California, Asian women are still categorized as meek, mild, soft, passive." While it's true that there are significantly fewer Asian-American female partners than male partners, legal observers cautiously predict that progress may be in the offing. Partners of real power have emerged as role models, if not mentors.

Among them are Ms. Shimada, who handles complex commercial litigation; Sylvia Fung Chin, a partner who works on international corporate and securities matters at New York's White & Case; and Alice Young, a partner and chair of the Asia Pacific practice at New York's Kaye, Scholer, Fierman, Hays & Handler L.L.P.

Race Matters

But for Ms. Shimada and many of her Asian-American counterparts, male and female, the desire to strike big-firm gold was not a motivation for entering the profession. As it was for many Asian-Americans who came out of law school in the 1970s, the law's main draw for her was that it could be "a vehicle for social change."

Many in the first wave of Asian lawyers focused on civil rights law, Mr. Tang of Preston Gates & Ellis says. Nowadays, minority attorneys fret that firms are hiring Asian-Americans in large part to fill an unspoken minority quota, and in the process making it harder for blacks and Hispanics. Wendell Holland, a former partner in the Philadelphia office of Pittsburgh's Reed Smith Shaw & McClay and now vice president at Voorhees, N.J.-based American Water Works Co., says he's not surprised when law firms play a numbers game. "Law firms might not just pad their numbers, but show a set of statistics" that they think the world will approve of because the total number of minorities is reasonable, says Mr. Holland, who is black.

Firms may have internal reasons as well for favoring Asians. Coming of age during the civil rights era made Asian-American lawyers particularly sensitive to the impression that they're a "model minority," as Dale Minami, name partner at San Francisco's

Minami, Lew & Tamaki, put it. He worries about the quick rise of Asian-Americans at big firms compared with the slow progress made by African-Americans and Hispanics in terms of sheer numbers.

"The danger is that Asian-Americans are used as a buffer because we're perceived as being acceptable," says Mr. Minami, whose firm represents a number of Asian-American celebrities, including figure skater Kristi Yamaguchi.

Mr. Paturick of Graham & James does not refer to such tendencies as being responsible for the abundance of Asians at his firm and the scarcity of blacks, but rather to the location and nature of the firm's business. "If we were a firm sitting in Kansas City or Chicago or New York doing standard U.S. domestic work, I assume we'd have a typical cross-section on racial lines."

Bias probably has helped shape the profession's racial profile, says Prof. Martha C. West, of the University of California at Davis School of Law, who keeps tabs on employment discrimination issues in the business world and in the academy.

Most Asian-American lawyers would agree, but that hasn't discouraged or deterred them. Professor Loh of the University of Colorado says: "Once you start having large numbers of [Asian-Americans] in law schools you begin to see them in firms. And now we see them in public office." Gary Locke, an attorney, was elected governor of Washington this year. He is the first Chinese-American governor in U.S. history, and the first Asian-American governor of a mainland U.S. state.

NOTES AND QUESTIONS

1. ***Is It Just About the Money?*** Do you think that the fortunes of Asian-American lawyers should be tied to the economic health of the Asia-Pacific Rim economies?

2. ***What is the Capitalist Message?*** Is the legal profession caught in a chicken-and egg-dilemma, unable to advance people of color and women until an economic target that can be exploited has first been identified? To what extent is the bedrock principle of capitalist economics relevant here: "One creates wealth by identifying under-valued resources and moving them to their highest and best use"?

3. ***What is the Moral Message?*** Is it immoral to view other lawyers as means (*viz.*, factors of production) rather than ends — fellow human beings with the same desire to fulfill themselves as you or me?

4. ***For Whom Does the Bell Toll?*** Here's your last assignment: Re-read the preceding article, "Asian-Americans Find Place in the Profession: Pacific Rim and Tech Booms Create Major Firms' Biggest Minority," a couple of times. However, on this time through:

a. assume that the item of commerce is oil, water, or gold, which has fostered a large newly emerging middle-class in Africa;

b. substitute for each of the Asians identified a new name by adding the suffix "-son" to their surname and the designation "African-American" whenever Asian is mentioned or Hispanic whenever black or an African-American is mentioned; and

c. try it a third time substituting names ending in the suffix "-dez" and the designation "Hispanic."

Do these last two readings describe an inchoate future that is currently emerging? Does that future have to include today's stereotypes, assumptions, and limiting expectations?

E. GAY AND LESBIAN LAWYERS

Another minority group that has increased in both numbers and acceptance is gay and lesbian lawyers. One sign of the growing numbers of gay and lesbian lawyers is that the National Association of Law Placement, which keeps track of numbers regarding other minorities, recently began publishing statistics about gay and lesbian lawyers. The following story explains how that came about and includes some statistics for New York law firms.

EDWARD ADAMS, FIRMS REPORT TOTALS OF GAY ATTORNEYS, LOBBYING BY ACTIVISTS PROMPTS DATA COLLECTION

NEW YORK LAW JOURNAL, July 7, 1997*

AFTER A YEAR of being lobbied by activists, most of New York's largest law firms are reporting the numbers of openly gay and lesbian attorneys in their ranks. But some experts question the accuracy of the figures.

Eighteen of the city's 25 largest firms, seven more than last year, are reporting the number of openly gay and lesbian attorneys employed. The data is included on their National Association for Law Placement forms, which are filed with area law schools before the fall recruiting season. NALP first requested the information on gays in 1996.

The percentage of openly gay and lesbian attorneys ranges from a high of 5.2 percent at Milbank, Tweed, Hadley & McCloy to a low of 0.3 percent at Coudert Brothers.

But NALP executive director Paula A. Patton said she would not base any conclusions on those figures, since some firms are estimating the number of openly gay and lesbian lawyers they employ, rather than surveying attorneys.

When the 1996 forms were released, several members of the Lesbians & Gay Men in the Profession Committee of the Association of the Bar of the City of New York concluded their own firms were undercounting gay and lesbian lawyers, said chair Rosalyn H. Richter, who is deputy administrative judge for the Bronx Criminal Court.

The committee is urging firms to circulate the NALP form to all attorneys so lawyers can report their own demographic characteristics, Judge Richter said. In addition to sexual orientation, the form requests information about gender, race and physical disabilities.

Alternatively, the committee recommends firms send a memorandum or E-mail to all lawyers, asking those who wish to be counted to identify themselves to the recruiting director, Judge Richter said.

The committee is "vehemently opposed to leaving [the form] blank or putting zero," she said. Six of the 25 largest firms did not answer the question this year.

Privacy Concerns

In January, the committee convened a training session that attracted recruiting directors from a dozen firms, and sent a follow-up letter on June 25 to New York legal employers with more than 100 attorneys.

"The biggest concern we heard from the firms was, 'We don't want to invade people's privacy,' " Judge Richter said. "But if someone is openly gay and self-identifying [to the firm], then they are waiving the privacy concern," she noted.

But even asking the question troubles some firms. "Among the most wrenching decisions [gays and lesbians] have to make in their lives is how open they want to be about the very private matter of their sexual preference," said Debevoise & Plimpton hiring partner John S. Kiernan.

Asking lawyers whether they want to identify themselves as gay or lesbian "puts a degree of personal pressure on them that" some lawyers may object to, he said.

AUTHORS' COMMENT:

Do you agree that asking lawyers whether they want to identify themselves as gay or lesbian "puts a degree of personal pressure on them"? Why or why not? How is gathering statistics about gay and lesbian lawyers different from gathering statistics about black lawyers or Asian-American lawyers or Hispanic lawyers? Do you have a solution to the privacy problem?

Rather than decline to answer, the firm reports 10-plus openly gay and lesbian lawyers, based on information from a group of gay and lesbian associates who volunteered to speak with law students interviewing with the firm.

The sensitive nature of sexual orientation was why Skadden, Arps, Slate, Meagher & Flom did not include the data in 1996, according to hiring partner Wallace L. Schwartz. "The first year, we were concerned about not offending anybody" by asking about sexual orientation, he said.

Skadden Comfortable

But once the question was being asked by NALP, "gay people were coming forward to volunteer to be counted," said Mr. Schwartz. "Based on that, we felt comfortable that we weren't doing anything that would cause a concern." Skadden has 11 openly gay and lesbian attorneys, or about 2 percent of its 585-attorney New York office.

To gauge the reliability of the information reported by the firms, next year's NALP form will require firms to say whether the demographic data is the firm's "best estimate" or came from lawyers "self-identifying" their demographic characteristics, said NALP's Ms. Patton.

That change drew praise from Joseph P. Barri, who heads Boston's Partners Group, which includes 25 gay and lesbian law firm partners and corporate general counsel.

"If a firm is unwilling to let its people self-identify, it may very well have an agenda that's not coincidental with the truth, and that's very important information to convey to the law students," said Mr. Barri.

At least until next year's forms are released, Ms. Patton said, "the burden is still on the student to ask [firms] more questions" about what the data really means.

NOTES AND QUESTIONS

1. ***Why Does NALP Collect This Data?*** Why does the National Association of Law Placement collect data on the number of gays and lesbians (or any other minority group) in law firms? As a law student, do you find the information valuable? As a lawyer, would you want to respond to a questionnaire asking whether you were gay or lesbian?

2. ***What About Where You Work?*** What is the environment like for gays and lesbians where you work? What is the firm's attitude toward openly gay and lesbian lawyers? Do any gay or lesbian lawyers have significant power within the firm? Have you personally witnessed or heard about incidents of discrimination against gays and lesbians at the firms where you have worked? If so, what were they? Are the firms where you have worked making any effort to combat discrimination against gays and lesbians? What measures could you recommend?

F. WORK / LIFE BALANCE

In addition to being a professional, every lawyer is also a human being. Perhaps it is stating the obvious, but there is a limit to the number of hours of work a human being can realistically perform year in and year out. In many practice settings, particularly large law firms, attorneys are routinely expected to work more than 60 hours a week. In the 1960's, billing about 1300 hours per year was considered a regular schedule for an attorney. These days, a number of firms require their attorneys to meet annual billable hour quotas of 2100 hours or even 2400 hours every year. As you can anticipate, this creates some challenges for those lawyers determined to maintain physical health and some semblance of a personal life. These pressures are experienced by almost all practicing attorneys, whatever their backgrounds. Hoping to assist lawyers seeking to move their workplace cultures toward more humane standards, in 2001 the ABA Commission on Women issued a manual setting out a model alternative work schedule and a model family leave and medical policy. The following excerpt describes some of the problems lawyers often experience in current legal practice settings.

ABA COMMISSION ON WOMEN, BALANCED LIVES: CHANGING THE CULTURE OF LEGAL PRACTICE

(2001)*

Particularly in large firms, where grueling schedules are most common, some women find it "difficult to have a cat, much less a family." A lawyer who billed 2200 hours in the year she was on maternity leave summarized the experience: "truth be told, that's no way to have a child."

The hardships associated with extended hours are often exacerbated by unpredictable and uncontrollable timing. Part of the problem is inherent in legal practice. Especially in some fields, lawyers are routinely held hostage to schedules not of their own making. Court-imposed deadlines, client demands, and sudden market or legal developments can create unpredictable hours. New technologies impose expectations of immediate responses. In the view of many supervising attorneys, extended and unexpected schedules are part of life in the law. [Those who] want to be "players" . . . should be willing to play by the existing rules. Those rules allocate pay, promotions, and sometimes even official 'client first' awards for lawyers willing to put their personal lives on perpetual hold. From this perspective, the choice resembles one that leading litigators are famous for putting to associates in high stakes cases, "Would you rather sleep or win?"

But such cases are not the mainstay of legal practice. Nor are all problems of oppressive schedules an inevitable byproduct of effective client representation. As noted earlier, while some peak demands are an inherent feature of practice, others are attributable to inadequate concern about the quality of life available for subordinates. Surveys of junior attorneys recount in depressing detail the unnecessary all night shifts, interrupted vacations, and frayed relationships that result from inadequate or insensitive planning by supervisors. Not all personal sacrifices are worth the price. One recent winner of a "client first" by a Portland firm was a woman who canceled her trip to her first family reunion in 20 years. In recounting the story to an ABA Journal reporter, an associate put the relevant question, "Why are we rewarding this?"

Other problems in workplace policies involve the inadequacy of family-related benefits. . . . Many lawyers lack access to quality services, such as onsite childcare centers, emergency back-up care arrangements, and referrals for eldercare, before and after-school programs, and parental support groups. Inadequate access to such assistance can adversely affect job performance, morale and retention. . . .

The gap between what many lawyers need and what many legal employers provide is partly attributable to gaps across generations and gender. Most of those holding managerial positions are men who grew up in an era in which they were not expected to assume time-consuming family responsibilities. Few of these lawyers have had significant experience with the conflicts facing primary caretakers. Some of these men question whether mothers experiencing such conflicts can or should hold demanding legal positions, although rarely is anyone as candid as the partner who informed a colleague that "law is no place for a woman with a child." A more commonly expressed view is that the younger generation's expectations of balanced lives are unrealistic and unreasonable. Lawyers often believe that if they managed without special accommodation or family-related needs, so can others. Recurrent refrains in management circles are: "I had to give up a lot. You [should] too." "I had a family. I didn't get time off. Why should you?" "It worked for me [to use full-time infant care] so it should work for you." Some lawyers who built their careers at substantial personal expense find it hard to empathize with younger colleagues who seem oblivious to those tradeoffs and who demand options that prior generations never had.

By contrast, these younger lawyers often see no reason to replicate the sacrifices of their predecessors. Other businesses and professions are attempting to accommodate balanced lives. Why can't law? In recent surveys, most men as well as women indicate a willingness to take lower salaries in exchange for more time with their families.

NOTES AND QUESTIONS

1. ***What About Sequencing a Career?*** Does it make sense to think of a series of five-year plans when looking at a career in the law? Perhaps putting in an overwhelming number of hours during the early years is needed so that a young lawyer can accumulate the expertise needed to develop good judgment. Then, after earning respect and mastering a particular field, the lawyer can include activities in addition to practicing law. Or, following the path taken by D.C. Circuit Court of Appeals Judge Patricia Wald, some new graduates might be able to step back into a more demanding legal career after a few years of focusing on responsibilities in their personal lives.

2. ***Connection Between Stress, Depression and Substance Abuse?*** Studies of practicing lawyers have found that attorneys are more likely to struggle with substance abuse and depression than are members of the general public. Maintaining at least a few close friendships and sustaining activities outside the practice of law can be helpful in dealing with such problems before they become entrenched. What are you doing now, while you are in law school, to maintain some balance in your life?

Chapter 36

FIGHTING DISCRIMINATION IN THE LEGAL PROFESSION: HOW SHOULD THE LEGAL PROFESSION FIGHT DISCRIMINATION?

We have spent some time reading about the progress and problems of women and people of color in the legal profession. These readings suggest that women and people of color still face discrimination within the profession. Dozens of studies by state bars and other organizations have documented the varieties of discrimination in great detail.

A. OPTIONS FOR ELIMINATING DISCRIMINATION

What should the legal profession do to eliminate discrimination against women and people of color? A number of options readily spring to mind:

- Encourage more lawyers to accept discrimination cases against lawyers and law firms that invidiously discriminate.
- Encourage lawyers to report judges who make inappropriate remarks about women and people of color, especially in court.
- Encourage corporate clients to consider a wide range of lawyers when staffing their legal matters.
- Spend more money out of bar association budgets to educate lawyers and law firms about the value of diversity and the ways to help women and people of color reach full potential as lawyers.
- Adopt ethics rules making it a violation to discriminate invidiously against women and people of color.

We address only the last idea in this section — an anti-discrimination rule. We focus on this question, in part, out of recognition that a generational split may exist within the legal profession about the appropriate strategy for eliminating invidious discrimination within the legal profession. Beginning in 1994 (followed by further attempts in 1995 and 1998[1]), competing proposals outlawing bias and prejudice were placed on the debate-agenda on the ABA's House of Delegates, but were subsequently withdrawn. Essentially two competing "anti-discrimination" proposals, each in the form of a proposed amendment to ABA Model Rule 8.4, subparagraph (g), have been th e focus. Although parliamentary efforts to craft a compromise, to substitute motions, or to reduce

---

[1] In 1998 competing proposals condemning bias and prejudice were on the ABA's agenda but were withdrawn on the eve of the House of Delegates meeting. A proposed amendment to Rule 8.4, sponsored by the ABA's Criminal Justice Section, would have made it professional misconduct to:

(1) commit, in the course of representing a client, any verbal or physical discriminatory act, on account of race, ethnicity, or gender, if intended to abuse litigants, jurors, witnesses, court personnel, opposing counsel or other lawyers, or to gain a tactical advantage; or

(2) engage, in the course of representing a client, in any continuing course of verbal or physical discriminatory conduct, on account of race, ethnicity or gender, in dealings with litigants, jurors, witnesses, court personnel, opposing counsel or other lawyers, if such conduct constitutes harassment.

A competing proposal, sponsored by the ABA's Standing Committee on Ethics and Professional Responsibility, would have left the text of Rule 8.4 alone but would have added the following new paragraph to the comment:

> A lawyer who, in the course of representing a client, knowingly manifests by words or conduct, bias or prejudice based on race, sex, religion, national origin, disability, age, sexual orientation or socioeconomic status, violates paragraph (d) [of Rule 8.4] when such actions are prejudicial to the administration of justice. Legitimate advocacy respecting the foregoing factors does not violate paragraph (d).

initiatives to mere hortatory language have served to dampen this debate, resolving the matter has not proved easy. Still, nothing has equaled the drama of the 1994 debate, when at the last minute competing proposals were withdrawn after the sponsors announced their intentions to bring a joint proposal to the ABA's next meeting (i.e., the February 1995 Mid-Year Meeting).

Although the two proposals primarily differed in their scope, what was most significant about them was that the one that called most aggressively for reform was offered by the ABA Young Lawyers Division, where membership is limited to lawyers 35 years of age and younger. More specifically, the Young Lawyers' proposal provided that it would be professional misconduct for a lawyer to:

> (g) commit a discriminatory act prohibited by law or to harass a person on the basis of sex, race, age, creed, religion, color, national origin, disability, sexual orientation or marital status, where the act of discrimination or harassment is committed in connection with a lawyer's professional activities.

The Report in support of the Young Lawyers Division's proposal explained as follows:

> The amendment is designed to regulate conduct in all manifestations of a lawyer's professional activities, and thereby avoid the inexplicable nuances of a rule which would allow reprehensible behavior to go unchecked merely because it is calculatedly inflicted outside the courtroom or after a case is concluded. Encompassing the all too common courtroom antics, the proposed rule will reach also to each situation where a lawyer is engaged in endeavors associated with professional activities.
>
> The proposed amendment will apply to professional activities regardless of whether the lawyer is representing a client. Implicit therein is the notion that the administration of justice must be protected from offensive conduct committed by officers of the court in all instances where a lawyer is called upon by virtue of the distinction of being a member of our profession. To do otherwise makes a mockery of the concept of fair and impartial administration of justice for all, and enhances the perception that lawyers are somehow outside or above the law. To do otherwise fuels the notion that honoring the spirit of the law is less important than knowing how to violate a law or rule in a manner where one will not be caught, or in which the offensive activity will fall between the cracks. The victim is left shaken and helpless, without recourse and questioning how our system of justice knowingly permits such shameless behavior to go unpunished.
>
> The proposal must regulate a lawyer's conduct both inside and outside the courtroom because all lawyers represent the judicial system each time they act within their professional capacity. A public perception of fairness and equality within the judicial system is essential to maintaining the integrity of the system. The proposed resolution is not unlike existing model rules that prohibit lawyers from "engaging in conduct that is prejudicial to the administration of justice," and these rules might serve as a guide to its application.[2]

In an effort to preempt the Young Lawyers Division, a narrower proposal was submitted by the ABA Standing Committee on Ethics and Professional Responsibility. Although it too called for prohibiting invidious discrimination by lawyers, it sought to limit the circumstances when the prohibition would apply, by providing that it would be professional misconduct for a lawyer to:

> (g) knowingly manifest by words or conduct, in the course of representing a client, bias or prejudice based upon race, sex, religion, national origin, disability, age, sexual orientation or socio-economic status. This paragraph does not apply

[2] Committee Reports do not represent official policy of the ABA. They are for information only, and the opinions are those of the authors of the report.

to a lawyer's confidential communications to a client or preclude legitimate advocacy with respect to the foregoing factors.

Accordingly, the Report in support of the Standing Committee's 1994 proposal explained, in pertinent part:

> The Committee's proposed amendment has three essential aspects. The first is its limitation to situations in which the lawyer is representing a client in a legal matter. The Committee considers that lawyer words or conduct occurring in the context of any type of legal practice should reflect respect both for the rule of law and for the sense of professionalism that distinguishes those dedicated to the practice of law. The amendment will serve this purpose.
>
> The second aspect is the Rule's identification of particular types of bias or prejudice that are to be prohibited. These forms of bias or prejudice have been included because they refer to factors that are generally viewed as deserving special protection from discrimination. The proposed amendment establishes a standard of conduct broader than that mandated by statutory enactments; this standard enables the profession to set an example of fairness and impartiality that is at the core of its commitment to the public interest. In furtherance of its intention not to develop the amendment as corollary to statutory law, the Committee chose to employ the concept of "bias or prejudice" rather than the more narrowly and legally determined concept of "discrimination."
>
> The third aspect of the rule comprises its exceptions. In order to avoid inquiry into a lawyer's confidential communications to a client, the rule exempts those communications from its ambit. The rule, as well, does not preclude legitimate advocacy by the lawyer with respect to the specified factors. An example of this would be when the national origin of a party is a factor in selecting a jury for a particular case. The Committee did not, however, intend by use of the word advocacy to limit the applicability of the exception to lawyer conduct in formal proceedings; the exception is intended to apply with equal force to the lawyer's counseling function.

NOTES AND QUESTIONS

1. ***Competing Approaches:*** Which of the two competing proposals do you favor? If you were drafting a model rule for the ABA, what would your rule say?

   a. More specifically: Should bias and discrimination by a lawyer violate the rules of professional conduct?
   b. If a lawyer discriminates against another lawyer or an employee or any other person, or if the lawyer does or says derogatory things based on a person's race, religion, sex, etc., should the lawyer be subject to professional discipline?
   c. The last is a complex question, primarily asking:

      - Would an anti-discrimination rule add anything to existing laws that already prohibit discrimination?
      - What categories should be covered by an anti-discrimination rule? Sex, race, religion, disability, and national origin are obvious choices, but what about sexual orientation, age, marital status, and family responsibility?
      - What should the rule cover? Should it cover only employment discrimination by lawyers, or should it also cover conduct demonstrating bias and prejudice in litigation and in other facets of law practice? Should the rule extend to discriminatory acts outside of law practice, or should it govern only conduct in a lawyer's professional capacity?

2. ***Update on the ABA's Efforts to Fight Discrimination.*** Despite their efforts after the ABA's 1994 Annual Meeting, the Young Lawyers Division and the Standing Committee on Ethics and Professional Responsibility were unable to agree on a single proposal to attack discrimination. The Young Lawyers Division tried to win favor for its

own proposal, but it could not muster enough support to pass an amendment to the rules. The Young Lawyers Division therefore withdrew its proposal to amend Rule 8.4 and instead sponsored the following resolution, which was adopted by the ABA House of Delegates:

> RESOLVED, That the American Bar Association:
>
> (a) condemns the manifestation by lawyers in the course of their professional activities, by words or conduct, of bias or prejudice against clients, opposing parties and their counsel, other litigants, witnesses, judges and court personnel, jurors and others, based upon race, sex, religion, national origin, disability, age, sexual orientation or socio-economic status, unless such words or conduct are otherwise permissible as legitimate advocacy on behalf of a client or a cause;
>
> (b) opposes unlawful discrimination by lawyers in the management or operation of a law practice in hiring, promoting, discharging or otherwise determining the conditions of employment, or accepting or terminating representation of a client;
>
> (c) condemns any conduct by lawyers that would threaten, harass, intimidate or denigrate any other person on the basis of the aforementioned categories and characteristics;
>
> (d) discourages members from belonging to any organization that practices invidious discrimination on the basis of the aforementioned categories and characteristics;
>
> (e) encourages affirmative steps such as continuing education, studies, and conferences to discourage the speech and conduct described above.

After these proposals were withdrawn, the sponsors issued a joint statement expressing hope that more time and additional comments would permit the Criminal Justice Section and the Standing Committee to develop one proposal with broad support.

3. ***Activity in the States.*** In the states, critics of the ABA often accuse it of being too far ahead of their jurisdictions. The usual pattern is for the ABA to appoint a blue-ribbon commission comprised of some of the most knowledgeable and high-profile lawyers from throughout the nation. After the commission has investigated, drafted proposed recommendations, and held public hearings on the issue, they prepare a final report with recommendations. When a consensus seems possible, the commission drafts a resolution asking the ABA House of Delegates to declare the positions of the report as the association's policy, for example, as an amendment to the ABA Model Rules. If adopted by the House of Delegates as ABA policy, the ABA thereafter works with the respective state jurisdictions through various constituency groups and legal bodies to win adoption of the new policy or rule in the jurisdiction (*e.g.*, the Conference of Chief Justices, state bar associations, the Association of Corporate Counsel, the American Association for Justice, and the Chamber of Commerce). In turn, at the initiative of the state's highest court or the state's bar association, each jurisdiction will establish its own blue-ribbon commission, complete with reports, recommendations, and resolutions, urging adoption of the new rule.

Interestingly enough, in the area of bias and discrimination, the states have been much more assertive than the ABA. Neither the Rules of Professional Conduct nor the Code of Professional Responsibility contains specific provisions about bias or discrimination. The ABA has chosen, instead, to rely upon the hortatory language of the Preamble to the Model Rules and the prohibition of lawyer misconduct stated in Model Rule 8.4. The Preamble, which the Model Rules describe as providing "general orientation," simply suggests that a lawyer, as a citizen, "should conform to the requirements of the law . . . in professional service to clients and in . . . business and personal affairs."

The more specific, ethically binding, provision is, thus, the kind of rule found at Missouri's Rule 8.4, which makes it professional misconduct for a lawyer to:

(b) commit a criminal act that reflects adversely on the lawyer's honesty, trustworthiness or fitness as a lawyer in other respects;
(c) engage in conduct involving dishonesty, fraud, deceit or misrepresentation; [or]
(d) engage in conduct that is prejudicial to the administration of justice . . .

But the rules of many states address bias and discrimination much more specifically than the Missouri-ABA approach. Here are some examples:

California: California adopted a rule which provides, in part:

(B) In the management or operation of a law practice, a member shall not unlawfully discriminate or knowingly permit unlawful discrimination on the basis of race, national origin, sex, sexual orientation, religion, age or disability in:

(1) hiring, promoting, discharging or otherwise determining the conditions of employment of any person; or
(2) accepting or terminating representation of any client.

(C) No disciplinary investigation or proceeding may be initiated by the State Bar against a member under this rule unless and until a tribunal of competent jurisdiction, other than a disciplinary tribunal, shall have first adjudicated a complaint of alleged discrimination and found that unlawful conduct occurred. . . .

Idaho: Idaho amended its Rule 4.4(a) to prohibit "conduct intended to appeal to or engender bias against a person on account of that person's gender, race, religion, national origin, or sexual preference . . . ."

Illinois: Illinois Rule 8.4(a)(5) was amended to prohibit "adverse discriminatory treatment of litigants, jurors, witnesses, lawyers, and others, based on race, sex, religion, or national origin."

New Mexico: New Mexico added a Rule of Professional Conduct 16-300, which provides:

> In the course of any judicial or quasi-judicial proceeding before a tribunal, a lawyer shall refrain from intentionally manifesting, by words or conduct, bias or prejudice based on race, gender, religion, national origin, disability, age, or sexual orientation against the judge, court personnel, parties, witnesses, counsel or others. This rule does not preclude legitimate advocacy when race, gender, religion, national origin, disability, age or sexual orientation is material to the issues in the proceeding.
>
> The official State Bar Commentary to New Mexico Rule 16-300 explains that the phrase "judicial or quasi-judicial proceeding" covers all courts, government agencies, boards, commissions, or departments, and "also encompasses arbitration or mediation proceedings, whether or not court ordered."

Texas: Members of the Texas State Bar voted narrowly to approve a bar-sponsored proposal to prohibit discrimination in connection with an adjudicatory proceeding.

Washington, D.C.: Washington, D.C. adopted the following rule:

> A lawyer shall not discriminate against any individual in conditions of employment because of the individual's race, color, religion, national origin, sex, age, marital status, sexual orientation, family responsibility or physical handicap.
>
> Do you favor any of these anti-discrimination rules? Why or why not? If you were drafting a model rule to add to the ABA Model Rules of Professional Conduct, what would your rule say? Based on the selection of state rules above and on your own ideas, draft a model rule to govern bias and discrimination by lawyers.

Existing federal laws, as well as the laws of many states, already prohibit employment discrimination on the basis of age, race, sex, disability (also called "physical handicap"), religion, color, and national origin. What does a rule of professional conduct accomplish that existing employment discrimination laws do not? A rule accomplishes at least three new things.

First, a rule can expand the groups of people that are protected. For example, unlike the federal statute, the D.C. rule prohibits discrimination on the basis of marital status, sexual orientation, and family responsibility.

Second, a rule can reach small employers who are not covered by existing laws. For economic and political reasons, most federal and state discrimination laws reach only those employers who employ more than a certain number of people. (Title VII, for example, does not reach employers with fewer than 15 employees.) But in the rules of professional conduct, what difference should size make? Is it any less odious for a sole practitioner to turn down a job applicant because she's Mexican or Jewish or African-American than it is for a large firm to do so?

Third, and most important, a lawyer who violates a rule of professional conduct can be suspended or disbarred from the practice of law. Even if a court found that a lawyer had violated existing laws prohibiting employment discrimination, the court could not interfere with the lawyer's right to practice law. Only a disciplinary authority can do that. But under the current rules of professional conduct in most states, employment discrimination by itself is not an offense.

The D.C. rule quoted above accomplishes all three of these objectives. It protects new groups, reaches all lawyers, and adds the remedies of suspension and disbarment for violation. But is this enough? Shouldn't a rule of professional conduct go beyond employment discrimination?

4. ***What is the Best Way to Accomplish the Goal?*** Should Model Rule 8.4 be amended specifically to fight discrimination in the legal profession? Of the following choices, which would you support?

(a) adding a new subparagraph to Rule 8.4? or

(b) leaving the text of Rule 8.4 unchanged but add language to the Comment condemning discrimination? or

(c) leaving Rule 8.4 and its comment alone but implement the 1995 resolution condemning bias and prejudice? or

(d) none of the above.

Why?

B. EMPOWERING MINORITY PARTNERS WITHIN A LAW FIRM

Another option for promoting diversity within the legal profession was mentioned earlier in this chapter: encourage corporate clients to consider a wide range of lawyers when staffing their legal matters. What are the pressures and considerations within law firms and corporate legal departments that influence these decisions? Those of you who have experience in the business world are probably aware of the power of organizational culture. The following article, written by Philip L. Harris, a partner at Jenner & Block, a large law firm in Chicago, was originally published in the CHICAGO DAILY LAW BULLETIN. It discusses the dynamics of staffing legal matters in a large law firm with a corporate practice and gives Harris' views on the impediments to diversifying law firms and the most promising strategies for change.

PHILIP L. HARRIS, A CANDID DISCUSSION: ENHANCING THE STATUS OF BLACK PARTNERS

30 CHICAGO DAILY LAW BULLETIN (July 1, 2007)[*]

Most of us understand that disturbing attitudes about race and equality continue to plague our profession. . . . According to the Chicago Lawyer's annual surveys, in 1992 only 0.9 percent of partners in large firms were black. In the 2007 survey, that number had risen to only 1.8 percent. . . . The disturbing attitudes and behavior that we see in our law firms are exacerbated by the discomfort that we feel when discussing race. Instead of talking about the underlying problem, we talk about the "business case for diversity" and make sanitized arguments like "our goal to increase or maintain profitability dictates that we change." Many attorneys in my presence — both black and white — have expressed deep frustration over the nature of discussions about race in law firms. Too often the dialogue is constrained by what some observers imprecisely call "political correctness." The problem is . . . a refusal by most members of the legal community to recognize that our practices, language, and institutional structures maintain and perpetuate racial boundaries. . . . . [W]e have not come to terms with what racial equality means in terms of our attitudes and beliefs about intellect. . . . Our goal should be to win what I like to call the "merit race": one where the finish line is the general acceptance among leaders in large firms of the proposition that all of us have an equal capacity to achieve intellectual excellence in complex endeavors. . . . [O]ur professional culture has deeply embedded attitudes and behaviors that impede our progress.

Leaders can remove barriers

Effective leaders in law firms, like their counterparts in the larger society, play a critical role in the development of beliefs and attitudes. They can encourage the adoption of policies that are likely to change behavior in the short term. My life experience has convinced me that many people do not have fixed opinions on racial equality. . . . Nearly all black attorneys at large firms have been the only black person in the room — many times. How many among the white leadership have had a comparable experience? Why does that matter? How many influential white attorneys grew up without encountering black youths as peers? . . . How many have referred to "qualified minorities" but not "qualified whites" when discussing recruitment, or have heard such references and not even noticed?

Our principal goal should be to raise expectations by eliminating the pernicious view that diversity results in lower quality. One colleague uses the phrase "presumption of incompetence" to explain the hurdle that black attorneys must overcome every time they take on a new assignment or engagement. Leaders in firms and corporate law departments can raise expectations by treating black partners as men and women capable of playing lead roles as working or service attorneys in major engagements, or who can retool and develop new skills when necessary to support the bottom line in the same way that white partners often do. If there is one thing that I can say unequivocally about large firms it is this: partners almost always will follow their leaders and clients because they fear the consequences of not doing so. . . .

Recruitment, mentoring and retention

Attitudes about race, in my experience, make efforts to recruit, mentor, and retain black partners ineffective. I frequently have heard white attorneys give seemingly race-neutral explanations for the relative absence of black partners in their law firms. The explanations given in the early 1990s are similar to the ones I hear today in the legal community. These include:

> "Black partners prefer careers in government."
>
> "Black partners prefer to practice on the East Coast, particularly in New York City and Washington, D.C."
>
> "Black partners feel a stronger need to give back to their communities, so they prefer to work in the nonprofit world."
>
> "Black graduates of elite law schools are much more likely to teach than to join a private law firm."

I am not convinced that black attorneys are less likely than white attorneys to want to work in large law firms, where they can generate substantial income and demonstrate excellence in the context of high-profile cases and transactions. Certainly, one should never draw such a conclusion without asking the black attorneys themselves. The real problem is not that blacks have a disdain for making a lot of money as partners at large law firms. Rather, it is that too often senior colleagues unwittingly convey a belief that black partners do not possess an equal capacity for intellectual excellence. The absence of effective mentoring reinforces that problem. Because blacks often conclude that the only way they will survive as partners is by generating business as "rainmakers," they fail to become integrated within the culture of the firms in the way that "service partners" do.

Recruiting

Large law firms do not measure the ability of a young attorney to function at a high level in the firm based on law school grades and class rank alone. They seek to hire law school graduates and lateral attorneys with the skills, values, and personalities that make them a good fit for the firm — and thus more likely to stay with the firm for their entire careers. It is ironic, then, that when it comes to the recruitment of blacks, firms often struggle with the concept of choosing a candidate based on factors other than grades and class rank. That irony becomes more intense when large firms focus their recruiting on a relatively limited selection of law schools. In his book detailing the experience of a black attorney at one large law firm in Chicago (The Good Black, Dutton 1999), Paul M. Barrett observes that it is "not an unusual opinion among white lawyers" that "there are lots of minorities, African-Americans in particular, who are running around with Harvard and Yale degrees and who are not qualified in any sense."

Many partners at large law firms believe that blacks are hired based on "affirmative action principles," meaning that, even if they went to Harvard and Yale, they are thought to possess a lower level of intellect than their white classmates. If we are presumed to be less qualified, then we are much less likely to be given the plum assignments within the firm, or to attain partnership based on the development of a reputation for excellence. For that reason, many of us choose to focus on business development — a path to partnership at large firms that most white partners do not take.

Mentoring

Few would dispute the value of good mentoring in large law firms. I have heard many firm leaders, and consultants to them, say that lawyers who succeed in large firms do so in large part because they had good mentors. Working in a large firm is not easy, and every associate and young partner needs an effective mentor who is able to find them good assignments, to introduce them to clients, and to be their cheerleader throughout the workplace (including after they make a mistake).

What is seldom acknowledged is that young black partners, particularly those who are recruited laterally, would benefit immensely from having mentors who are key leaders in the firm. Today, those mentors almost always will be white men. I had mentors — mostly white men and women — who were invested in my success. When I made a mistake, they protected me as necessary and told me what to do the next time around. My mentors gave me good work, spent hours of billable and nonbillable time instructing me on how to improve my writing and oral advocacy skills, and introduced me to clients. When they introduced me to clients or, for that matter, to other attorneys in the firm, they talked as if I were one of the best associates in the firm. In the process, they boosted my self-confidence and raised my profile in the eyes of other partners. That is the essence of good mentoring and, without it, I would have abandoned the idea of practicing at a large law firm long ago.

Interestingly, though, as I moved into the partnership ranks, it became clear to me that I was expected to mentor every young black attorney who joined the firm — often regardless of whether we even practiced in the same area. . . . . Within a law firm, mentors should be chosen based on their ability to guide a younger attorney successfully through a practice area. The mentor and mentee ideally should be in the same practice area and the mentor should become an advocate for the mentee. Particularly with respect to black attorneys, the mentor's most important role, in addition to providing professional advice, is to talk to other partners about the mentee's excellence.

Retention: An overview

Most partners at large law firms generally fall into one of two categories: those who have business (here I will call them "rainmakers"), and those who do not ("service" partners). A rainmaker is a partner who originates business that in many cases is portable, meaning that it will go with the partner if he leaves for another firm. Partners who are rainmakers often are compensated at high levels to discourage them from leaving the firm. A service partner, in contrast, is an attorney who reaches that status through her recognition as a highly skilled practitioner or "working attorney." The service partner in some cases has expertise in a relatively esoteric practice area and is deemed to be valuable to the partnership for that reason. In other instances, the service partner is more of a generalist who is deemed to possess skills that are transferable to virtually any issue in her practice area. Thus, it is not unusual to see a service partner "retool" whenever it is necessary to protect her status as a partner. This means that a litigation service partner may spend several years defending an antitrust case, and then move with equal credibility to the defense of a toxic tort case after the antitrust case settles.

Every large law firm needs both rainmakers and service partners. My argument here also has nothing to do with the relative job security of rainmaker versus service partners. . . . Rainmakers become vulnerable when they lose their business, and service partners become vulnerable when the firm believes that they are fungible assets. Black partners at large law firms almost always are or are expected to be rainmakers. Some might see that as evidence that the few blacks who become partners at these law firms enjoy an exalted status. But, in my experience, what it really demonstrates is that the service route to partnership is not available to blacks because, from the day they are hired, they operate under a presumption of incompetence. . . .

Retention of the service partner

As a general rule, it is easier for law firms to retain service partners than partners who make rain. Indeed, partners with business frequently receive calls from legal recruiters who provide plenty of financial incentive for them to consider moving business to another law firm. Service partners, however, either do not generate their own work or do not have a portable business relationship. They are dependent upon other partners for their work and, as a result, rely on their skill and expertise to maintain their status.

Many large firms have two types of partners: non-equity and equity partners. The former are compensated on a salaried basis and usually at lower levels than equity partners, who are paid through a distribution of the firm's profits at the end of each fiscal year. Critical to the discussion here is an understanding of an undeniable fact: every large firm has a significant percentage of service partners who attain equity status without generating any business, and who are very highly compensated. Most large firms have billable hours guidelines for all partners. They are unlikely to relax those guidelines for service partners because those partners pose little threat to the firm's profitability if they leave. Thus, the service partner must meet these guidelines year after year. Often, the service partner is given the responsibility of a lieutenant in the army: she picks her troops, determines what levels are necessary, and prepares them for battle — all with the explicit support of a senior partner who generally is an important rainmaker.

The rainmakers with power in a firm protect the service partner at compensation time. They are able to do this because, in many large firms, partner compensation is determined largely by subjective or non-formulaic perceptions of value. I have heard key rainmakers say, for example, that certain service partners are "indispensable to my practice." At the best firms, service attorneys are known for their high skill level. They are considered to be, in a word, smart. They also appear to epitomize the culture of the firm. They show up at the right parties and celebrations, are on speaking terms with the key partners in the firm, serve on teams that market to new and existing clients for business, and have a way of ending up on the big cases and deals. Hence, success as a service partner requires intellect, a reputation for intellect (not always the same thing), and effective networking. . . . Unfortunately, perceptions of intellectual inferiority enter here.

I was once asked, as part of a diversity initiative, to interview a senior partner at the firm who had millions of dollars of business. Like many of his peers, he relied on a small network of service partners to staff his cases. During the interview, I expressed my opinion that the firm would make instant progress on the diversity front if he picked a "lieutenant" who was black — excluding myself from consideration, of course, so as to avoid a possible conflict of interest. He said that he thought that was a good idea and would be happy to do so, as long as the candidate was "qualified." I do not know whether he posed the same question about potential white lieutenants, but my experience leads me to doubt it. This senior partner missed out on a tremendous opportunity to move the firm forward in the area of racial equality.

Even though they do not have portable business relationships, service partners often are asked to participate in firm marketing activities. Almost without exception, the role of the service partner in the prospective engagement is identified before the business pitch is made. I have heard many black attorneys ponder why they are asked to be the face of the firm in marketing materials or presentations, but not asked to help service the client when the work comes in the door. Often, the answer given is that the black attorney lacks the requisite experience and, by reasonable inference, does not have the ability to retool quickly in a way that would allow him or her to play a meaningful role. That way of thinking perpetuates the absence of change.

When black attorneys at large firms become highly paid equity partners who fall into this service partner category in the same proportion as their white counterparts, then the merit race will have been won. These smart attorneys will have attained the even more important status of attorneys who are thought to be smart. Very few black attorneys enjoy this status today in large law firms, particularly in the practice areas that most partners believe require high intellect. The relative absence of black service partners working in the corporate and complex commercial litigation practice areas at large law firms is impossible to ignore. More commonly, blacks are asked to or expected to or choose to be rainmakers. Because there is an element of free will to this, it should be acknowledged that many black equity partners feel better off being rainmakers because they do not believe that they ever would be highly compensated as a service partner.

Retention of the rainmaker partner

Blacks who reach equity partner status almost always attain that status because they have significant portable business relationships. However, black attorneys tend to make rain differently from the most successful white partners I know. White partners who are major business originators often reach that status based on their reputations as working attorneys. That is, they are thought to have reached the top of the profession in terms of the skill set that they possess, and as a result large companies seek them out to represent the companies in major or "bet-the-company" cases and transactions.

Black rainmakers, in contrast, frequently are asked or expected to sell other partners in their firms. Indeed, I challenge partners who are reading this article to identify more than a handful of black equity partners who have become rainmakers by selling their skills as a principal lead attorney on a major engagement. . . . The principal advantage to being a rainmaker is that you do not have to ask other partners for work — something that I have heard many black partners say, for a variety of reasons, they do not like to do. I have been told on more than one occasion, when I asked others for work, that a case was not the "right" one for me, but that I would be kept in mind for future assignments. I also have been asked to become involved in a matter that was deemed to be right for me — either because the presiding judge was black, the jury pool included significant minority representation, or the client was black. This raises a much larger question that I cannot answer: namely, do these same people believe a case is not a good fit for me or other black partners when the judge is white, the jury pool non-diverse, or the client is thought to prefer a white attorney?

Interaction with in-house counsel

In-house counsel at corporations wield incredible power over law firms. The corporate client is the lifeblood of the large law firm; without that client's business, the large law firm cannot generate acceptable revenue levels. In the area of diversity, that powerful role became apparent in 1999, when a prominent leader in a corporate law department encouraged his peers to flex their muscles and end or limit relationships with firms lacking a "meaningful interest" in being diverse. However, most attorneys would agree that few law firms have been fired for failing to employ black partners as lead attorneys on major engagements. Indeed, over the last 15 years, profits per partner have risen dramatically at some of the most non-diverse law firms in the country. Thus, there has been little empirical evidence to support the argument that large firms need to be diverse in order to sustain acceptable levels of profitability.

In-house counsel face a variety of pressures that discourage them from requiring diversity when it comes to lead roles on major legal engagements. Publicly, many recommend that minority partners focus on relationship-building activities that will help them generate business over the long term. They are right, of course, but there are many white partners in large firms who quickly are asked to play lead roles in major engagements without ever having engaged in relationship building activities.

Privately, some in-house counsel acknowledge their concern that if they lose a big case or a deal falls apart, then their own job security could be at risk. If they lose with the most "qualified" and experienced outside counsel, then they are less likely to be criticized than if they had retained supposedly more risky minority counsel. Large law firms know this, and many of the leaders at law firms thus staff cases as if there were an exception to the business case for diversity in major engagements. If corporate clients do not actually pull business when this happens, a vicious cycle takes place that works as follows: The corporation says that it wants its law firms to be diverse. The law firms hire diverse associates and publicly announce their support for diversity initiatives. The law firms, which are increasing billing rates to increase profits per partner, market aggressively to secure major engagements. The partners who serve as principals on these engagements are the ones with the highest billing rates. They are almost always white. In some cases, they will staff those cases with minority associates, but the lead roles will be played by white partners who are said to possess the requisite "experience." The cycle will become entrenched when the black partner is assured of never being given the opportunity to obtain the requisite experience as a principal attorney on a major engagement. It takes an ardent proponent of diversity to give an exceptional black partner the opportunity to serve as the company's first black lead attorney in a major engagement. In these circumstances, the in-house attorney effectively is saying to his or her corporation: I am comfortable with the selection of this counsel and am prepared to support my decision to the general counsel, chief executive officer or board of directors regardless of the outcome. Unfortunately, this rarely happens.

Some in-house counsel have encouraged law firms to enter into alliances with minority-owned firms for purposes of joint representation in major cases or transactions. These alliances may serve a useful purpose in engagements that require depth and knowledge that the minority-owned law firm might not possess. However, to the extent that the minority-owned law firm always remains second-chair, there is a risk that views about the inferior skill level of the minority attorneys will be perpetuated. Similarly, if minority partners in large firms are never given the opportunity to migrate from smaller to larger engagements for a client, then they will be typecast as people who are "not qualified" to serve as the lead attorney in a major engagement. The reality is that these problems will go away when the corporations that pay millions of dollars in fees to large law firms demand that black partners play lead roles in major cases and transactions. That will cause dramatic change in large firms in the short term. . . .

NOTES AND QUESTIONS

1. ***Pressure from Corporate Clients.*** In recent years some corporations have advised law firms seeking to represent them as outside counsel that they should not expect to receive appointments if their firms do not reflect significant racial and gender diversity. Is this an appropriate stance by corporate America? If the law firm about which you are most familiar was given such a reminder, how do you believe they would act? Are law firms simply incapable of reforming themselves without such outside pressure?

2. ***Navigating Politics in Big Firm Practice.*** What strategies for navigating the world of big firm corporate practice have you seen successful lawyers use? Is there a point at which a lawyer needs to reassess how much he or she is willing to give up in order to continue on the equity partnership track?

3. ***Relevance of Diversity Issues in Other Practice Settings.*** How applicable are the issues Mr. Harris addresses to the world of prosecutors, in-house counsel, or lawyers working at smaller law firms? Can you think of additional strategies for empowering all lawyers and including their varying perspectives in the legal work that is being conducted?

TABLE OF CASES

[References are to pages]

[References are to pages]

[References are to pages]

INDEX

[References are to pages.]

A

B

[References are to pages.]

[References are to pages.]

[References are to pages.]

G

H

I

L

M

N

P

[References are to pages.]